D0138432

MANAGEMENT CONTROL SYSTEMS

TENTH EDITION 2000

MANAGEMENT CONTROL SYSTEMS

Robert N. Anthony
Ross Graham Walker
Professor of Management Control, Emeritus
Graduate School of Business Administration
Harvard University

Vijay Govindarajan
Earl C. Daum
1924 Professor of International Business
Director, William F. Achtmeyer Center for Global Leadership
The Amos Tuck School of Business Administration
Dartmouth College

Boston   Burr Ridge, IL   Dubuque, IA   Madison, WI
New York   San Francisco   St. Louis
Bangkok   Bogotá   Caracas   Lisbon   London   Madrid   Mexico City
Milan   New Delhi   Seoul   Singapore   Sydney   Taipei   Toronto

McGraw-Hill Higher Education

A Division of The **McGraw-Hill** Companies

 This book is printed on acid-free paper.

1 2 3 4 5 6 7 8 9 0 DOC/DOC 0 9 8 7 6 5 4 3 2 1 0

ISBN 0-07-231635-7

Vice president/Editor-in-chief: *Michael W. Junior*
Sponsoring editor: *Stewart Mattson*
Editorial assistant: *Erin Cibula*
Marketing manager/Marketing coordinator: *Richard Kolasa / Melissa Larmon*
Project manager: *Laura Griffin*
Production supervisor: *Rose Hepburn*
Freelance design coordinator: *Laurie J. Entringer*
Supplement coordinator: *Mark Sienicki*
New media: *Ed Przyzycki*
Compositor: *Shepherd Incorporated*
Typeface: *10 / 12 Century Schoolbook*
Printer: *R. R. Donnelley & Sons Company*

Library of Congress Cataloging-in-Publication Data

Anthony, Robert Newton (date)
    Management control systems/Robert N. Anthony, Vijay Govindarajan.—10th ed.
      p. cm.
    Includes bibliographical references and indexes.
    ISBN 0-07-231635-7
    1. Industrial management. 2. Industrial management—Case studies. 3. Cost control. I.
Govindarajan, Vijay.

  HD31 .A589 2000
  658.15—dc21   00-027292

www.mhhe.com

To our wives: Katherine and Kirthi
—Bob and VG

With special appreciation to my parents, Padma and Vijayaraghavan, and to my daughters, Tarunya and Tapasya
—VG

ABOUT THE AUTHORS

Robert N. Anthony is the Ross Graham Walker Professor Emeritus of Management Control at Harvard Business School. Harvard has been his home base, except between 1940 and 1946 when he was in the Navy Supply Corps, and between 1965 and 1968 when he was Assistant Secretary of Defense, Controller.

Professor Anthony is the author or coauthor of 27 books; they have been translated into 14 languages. He has been an Irwin author since 1956 and consulting editor of Irwin's Robert N. Anthony/Willard J. Graham series in Accounting. His *Essentials of Accounting* (Addison-Wesley), now in its seventh edition, is a widely used programmed text.

Professor Anthony has been a director of Carborundum Company and Warnaco, Inc., both Fortune 500 companies, and for 30 years has been a trustee of Colby College, including five years as chairman of the board. He has been a consultant to many companies and government agencies, including General Motors Corporation, American Telephone & Telegraph Company, Eastman Kodak Company, the General Accounting Office, and the Cost Accounting Standards Board. He has also participated in

short educational programs in North America, South America, Europe, Australia, and Asia.

Among Professor Anthony's awards are honorary MA and LHD degrees from Colby College, election to the Accounting Hall of Fame, the Distinguished Accounting Educator Award from the American Accounting Association, the Accounting Educator of the Year Award from Beta Alpha Psi, the Meritorious Service Award from the Executive Office of the President, the Distinguished Public Service Medal of the Department of Defense, Comptroller General's Award of the U.S. General Accounting Office, and Distinguished Service Award of the Harvard Business School Association.

Vijay Govindarajan is the Earl C. Daum 1924 Professor of International Business at the Amos Tuck School of Business Administration at Dartmouth College. At Tuck, he is the Faculty Director for the Global Leadership 2020 Program. His major research interests are in the areas of global strategy, industry transformation, and strategy execution. Professional credits include: Outstanding Faculty, named by *Business Week* in its *Guide to Best B-Schools;* Top Ten Business School Professor in Corporate Executive Education, named by *Business Week;* and Outstanding Teacher of the Year, voted by MBA students.

Prior to joining the faculty at Tuck, Professor Govindarajan was on the faculties of The Ohio State University, Harvard Business School, and the Indian Institute of Management (Ahmedabad, India). He has also served as a visiting professor at INSEAD (Fontainebleau, France), the International University of Japan (Urasa, Japan), and Helsinki School of Economics (Helsinki, Finland).

Professor Govindarajan was ranked by *Management International Review* as one of the Top 20 North American Superstars for research in strategy and organization. One of his papers was recognized as "one of the ten most-often cited articles" in the entire 40-year history of the prestigious *Academy of Management Journal*. Professor Govindarajan has also received numerous other scholarly awards, including the 1991 Glueck Best Research Paper Award in Business Policy and Strategy from the Academy of Management and the 1995

Notable Contribution to Management Accounting Literature Award from the Management Accounting Section of the American Accounting Association.

More than 50 articles by Professor Govindarajan have appeared as book chapters and in journals such as *Academy of Management Journal; Academy of Management Review; Strategic Management Journal; Accounting, Organizations and Society; Decision Sciences; Journal of Business Strategy; Business Horizons;* and *Sloan Management Review*. His co-authored books include *Management Control Systems* (McGraw-Hill, 2001), *Strategic Cost Management* (The Free Press, 1993), and *World Wise: Building the Global Corporation of Tomorrow* (to be published).

Professor Govindarajan has served as a consultant to various corporations, including Abbott Labs, AT&T, Champion, Kodak, B. F. Goodrich, GTE, Hewlett-Packard, IBM, JP Morgan, Motorola, Thomson Corp., PriceWaterhouseCoopers, StoraEnso, and Weyerhaeuser.

He has been a keynote speaker at the *Business Week* CEO Forum, the *Economist Intelligence Unit* Conference, and the Human Resource Planning Society National Meeting. He has been extensively written about or quoted in the popular press. During January-February 1998, the global business daily *The Financial Times* published four of Dr. Govindarajan's co-authored papers in a series on "Mastering Global Business."

Professor Govindarajan received his doctorate from the Harvard Business School and was awarded the Robert Bowne Prize for the best thesis proposal. He also received his MBA with distinction from the Harvard Business School, where he was included in the Dean's Honor List. Prior to this, Professor Govindarajan received his Chartered Accountancy degree in India. He was awarded the President's Gold Medal for his outstanding performance in obtaining the first rank.

TABLE OF CONTENTS

Foreword   xv
Preface   xix
An Overview

**1   The Nature of Management
     Control Systems   1**

Basic Concepts   1
Boundaries of Management Control   5
Road Map for the Reader   15
Summary   18
Case 1–1: Nucor Corporation (A)   20
Case 1–2: Motorola, Inc.   30
Case 1–3: Stewart Box Company   39
Case 1–4: Xerox Corporation (A)   46

PART I

**THE MANAGEMENT CONTROL
ENVIRONMENT**

2   Behavior in Organizations   55

Goals   55
Goal Congruence   59
Informal Factors That Influence
     Goal Congruence   59
The Formal Control System   63
Types of Organizations   65

Functions of the Controller   71
Summary   74
Case 2–1: Nucor Corporation (B)   76
Case 2–2: General Motors
     Corporation   78
Case 2–3: Rendell Company   84
Case 2–4: Digital Equipment
     Corporation   93
Case 2–5: National Tractor
     and Equipment Company   100

**3   Responsibility Centers: Revenue
     and Expense Centers   108**

Responsibility Centers   108
Revenue Centers   112
Expense Centers   114
Administrative and Support Centers   119
Research and Development Centers   120
Marketing Centers   124
Summary   125
Case 3–1: Vershire Company   127
Case 3–2: New Jersey Insurance
     Company   133
Case 3–3: NYPRO, Inc.   140
Case 3–4: Whiz Calculator Company   150
Case 3–5: Westport Electric
     Corporation   155
Case 3–6: Grand Jean Company   160

4   Profit Centers   164

General Considerations   164
Business Units as Profit Centers   169
Other Profit Centers   171
Measuring Profitability   174
Summary   179
Case 4–1: Profit Center Problems   180
Case 4–2: North Country Auto, Inc.   181
Case 4–3: Boise Cascade Corporation   188
Case 4–4: Abrams Company   197

5   Transfer Pricing   201

Objectives of Transfer Prices   201
Transfer Pricing Methods   202
Pricing Corporate Services   211
Administration of Transfer Prices   214
Summary   217
Appendix Some Theoretical
     Considerations   218
Case 5–1: Transfer Pricing Problems   221
Case 5–2: Birch Paper Company   226
Case 5–3: General Appliance
     Corporation   228
Case 5–4: Strider Chemical
     Company   237
Case 5–5: Medoc Company   240

**6   Measuring and Controlling
     Assets Employed   243**

Structure of the Analysis   243
Measuring Assets Employed   246
EVA versus ROI   258
Additional Considerations in Evaluating
     Managers   263
Evaluating the Economic Performance
     of the Entity   264
Summary   265
Case 6–1: Investment Center Problems
     (A)   267

Case 6–2: Investment Center
     Problems (B)   271
Case 6–3: Quality Metal Service
     Center   275
Case 6–4: Aloha Products   283
Case 6–5: Industrial Products
     Corporation   288
Case 6–6: Marden Company   295
Case 6–7: Lemfert Company   296

PART II

THE MANAGEMENT CONTROL PROCESS

7   Strategic Planning   300

Nature of Strategic Planning   300
Analyzing Proposed New Programs   307
Analyzing Ongoing Programs   310
Strategic Planning Process   314
Summary   318
Appendix Merck's Research Planning
     Model   319
Case 7–1: Allied Office Products   322
Case 7–2: Copley Manufacturing
     Company   329
Case 7–3: DairyPak   335
Case 7–4: Emerson Electric
     Company   346

8   Budget Preparation   360

Nature of a Budget   360
Other Budgets   366
Budget Preparation Process   368
Behavioral Aspects   372
Quantitative Techniques   375
Summary   376
Case 8–1: Sound Dynamics, Inc.   378
Case 8–2: Boston Creamery, Inc.   390
Case 8–3: Riverview   401

9 Analyzing Financial Performance Reports 408

Calculating Variances 408
Variations in Practice 417
Limitations of Variance Analysis 422
Summary 423
Case 9–1: Variance Analysis Problems 425
Case 9–2: Solartronics, Inc. 427
Case 9–3: Galvor Company 429

10 Performance Measurement 441

Performance Measurement Systems 441
Interactive Control 453
Summary 458
Appendix Dell Computer Corporation and Sears 458
Case 10–1: Analog Devices, Inc. 463
Case 10–2: CUP Corporation 477
Case 10–3: Enager Industries, Inc. 484
Case 10–4: Warren Insurance Company 488
Case 10–5: General Electric Company 498

11 Management Compensation 505

Research Findings on Organizational Incentives 505
Characteristics of Incentive Compensation Plans 506
Incentives for Corporate Officers 512
Incentives for Business Unit Managers 513
Agency Theory 522
Summary 527
Case 11–1: Lincoln Electric Company (A) 529
Case 11–2: Worthington Industries 544
Case 11–3: Anita's Apparel 548
Case 11–4: Wayside Inns, Inc. 554

PART III

VARIATIONS IN MANAGEMENT CONTROL

12 Controls for Differentiated Strategies 564

Corporate Strategy 564
Business Unit Strategy 570
Top Management Style 580
Summary 582
Case 12–1: Pelican Instruments, Inc. 584
Case 12–2: PC&D, Inc. 586
Case 12–3: 3M Corporation 598
Case 12–4: Texas Instruments and Hewlett-Packard 601
Case 12–5: Texas Instruments 605

13 Service Organizations 620

Service Organizations in General 620
Professional Service Organizations 622
Financial Service Organizations 627
Health Care Organizations 630
Nonprofit Organizations 633
Summary 636
Case 13–1: O'Reilley Associates 638
Case 13–2: Williamson and Oliver 642
Case 13–3: Harlan Foundation 651
Case 13–4: Piedmont University 654
Case 13–5: Chemical Bank 657
Case 13–6: Metropolitan Bank 670
Case 13–7: Citibank Indonesia 678

14 Multinational Organizations 686

Cultural Differences 686
Transfer Pricing 688
Exchange Rates 694
Summary 705
Appendix SFAS No. 52 Foreign Currency Translation 705

Case 14–1: AB Thorsten   708
Case 14–2: Lincoln Electric
     Company (B)   715
Case 14–3: Nestlé S.A.   720
Case 14–4: Xerox Corporation (B)   728

15   Management Control of Projects   732

Nature of Projects   732
The Control Environment   735
Project Planning   739

Project Execution   743
Project Evaluation   749
Summary   753
Case 15–1: Northeast Research
     Laboratory   755
Case 15–2: Modern Aircraft
     Company   763

Company Index   765

Topical Index   770

FOREWORD

The first edition of this book was published 35 years ago. The publisher has asked me to comment on changes that have been made in it.

The first edition, written with my colleagues John Dearden and Dick Vancil, consisted of short readings, rather than coherent text material. It had 42 cases, compared with 68 in the tenth edition.

Nevertheless, our approach to the subject was similar to the approach we use now. We focus on management control systems, which are systems intended to help implement strategies. Management control is the middle one of three types of planning and control processes. It is bounded on one side by strategy formulation, which is essentially unsystematic, and on the other side by task control, which can be highly structured. The focus is on management, and the criteria for judging management actions are efficiency and effectiveness. This was the first text with such a focus.

The first edition described what are still the most important ideas: responsibility accounting, expense centers, profit centers, investment centers, transfer pricing, key variables, discretionary expenses, and budgets. We had some material on behavioral considerations, but

nowhere near the emphasis that we now give to this subject. We had scarcely anything about differences in management control systems associated with different types of companies (e.g., focus on product differentiation contrasted with a focus on low costs; single business, related businesses, and conglomerates; multinational companies; service companies; financial institutions; nonprofit organizations; governments). Banks and other financial institutions have made tremendous progress in their management control systems in the last 30 years; so have hospitals. By contrast, governments, especially the federal government, have a long way to go. We did not even mention executive compensation as a motivating device, nor the management control of projects. We did not discuss goal congruence as such. In recent editions there is much material on these important topics.

The most important change in substance has been the emphasis on what we now call *strategic planning,* which is chronologically the first step in the management control process. In the first edition, there was a short reading and one case on this topic, reflecting the fact that few companies had formal strategic planning systems. Beginning in the 1970s, more companies began to use this process, then called *programming* or *long-range planning*. The first attempts were generally unsuccessful. Cases in editions published in the 1970s and early 1980s described these efforts; in general they involved too much paperwork and not enough rigorous thinking about the future. Currently, the process is working well in many companies.

The next most important changes were associated with the development of computers. In the first edition, we had two cases in which the issue was whether the company should acquire a computer. The facts in one of these are interesting: the proposed UNIVAC equipment required 1,400 square feet of space, including air conditioning of 60 tons and 75 KVA of current (compared with 3 square feet, no air conditioning, and trivial power requirements for today's desk-top computers); 23 instructions (compared with an unlimited number in desk-top computers today); memory of 10,000 characters (compared with more than 2 billion). The price of the UNIVAC was $488,000 (compared with about $2,000 for an excellent desk-top system). Our first edition had two readings that warned against going overboard on computers: "Can Management Information Be Automated?" and "Seven Deadly Dangers in EDP."

We did not foresee the implications of the electronic interchange of information within a company and among companies. Magnetic character recognition was used for checks, a tiny forerunner of the widespread use of bar codes. We did not even imagine that prices of security transactions originating in stock exchanges throughout the world would be available to users everywhere in decision-assisting form in a matter of seconds, and that in some cases they would automatically trigger buy or sell decisions. There were no computer-controlled machines.

Use of the Internet and of intranets within a company is only about 10 years old. Operating data, budget formulations, and reports of actual performance can now be transmitted rapidly and at low cost. Information can be compared with that of other companies.

New, useful techniques and ideas have been developed: satisfactory profits, computer models for companies and specific problems, expert systems, net present value, risk/reward trade-offs, benefit/cost analysis, learning curves, decision trees, sensitivity analysis, linear programming, even nonlinear programming.

But we also described several techniques that at one time were hot topics but that now have disappeared. Human resource accounting—treating employees as assets in the accounts—was much talked about in the 1970s, but was rarely practiced and is now scarcely even mentioned. Many books have been written about zero-based budgeting, a technique now generally believed to be impractical. Similarly for PERT cost and statistically significant analysis of variances.

We also use new terms found in the literature and in practice for old ideas: business units for certain types of profit centers; activity-based costing for job-order costing; cost drivers for bases of allocation; total quality management and value chain analysis for any organized effort to improve operations; "empowerment" for delegating authority.

There have been two other coauthors. Norton Bedford made significant contributions to concepts. Vijay Govindarajan brings a deep understanding of the relationship between strategy formulation and management control, based on his own practical experience and outstanding research.

Inferences

Many educators and critics of education maintain that the knowledge that students learn in a business school will be obsolete within a few years. The above review suggests that such a conclusion is overly pessimistic. The management control framework that students learned decades ago is still generally valid today. "Life-long learning" is important, but it consists of fitting detailed improvements into the overall framework, which is a lot easier than learning a subject from scratch. Admittedly, a new framework will be developed some day; we developed ours in the 1950s. Faculty must be aware of this possibility, and adopt it if it comes, but until then they need not worry that the framework they now teach will shortly be irrelevant.

Thus, two implications for the future emerge from this review. First, technology will lead to improvements in the effectiveness and efficiency of the management control function in ways not now foreseen. But, second, although the ideas will be articulated more clearly, the framework is unlikely to change; it is grounded on human nature.

Robert N. Anthony
April 2000

PREFACE

The Tenth Edition of *Management Control Systems* provides concepts, text, and cases for a course in management control systems. The book is designed to allow students to gain knowledge, insights, and analytical skills related to how a firm's managers go about designing, implementing, and using planning and control systems to implement a firm's strategies. It does not deal extensively with topics such as cost accounting and budgeting procedures, which are discussed in separate accounting courses. The book gives roughly equal emphasis to (1) the techniques of the management control process (e.g., transfer pricing, budget preparation, management compensation), and (2) the behavioral considerations involved in the use of these techniques (e.g., motivation, goal congruence, relative roles of superiors and subordinates).

The book is organized into three main parts. Chapter 1 introduces the overall conceptual framework for the book. Part I (Chapters 2 to 6) describes the environment in which management control takes place (responsibility centers). Part II (Chapters 7 to 11) describes the sequential steps in the typical management control process (strategic planning, budget preparation, operations, analysis of operations). Part III (Chapters 12 to 15) describes variations in management control systems (controls for differentiated strategies, service organizations, multinational organizations, and project control).

Changes to Text Material

While retaining the strengths of the ninth edition, we have made a number of changes in both text and case material that we hope will increase their usefulness. In undertaking this revision, we surveyed users of the ninth edition. This revision has benefited from their constructive comments and suggestions.

Several improvements have been made to assist student learning. These include: expanded chapter introductions, more diagrams and exhibits, real-world examples, consistent terminology, expanded chapter summaries, and an up-to-date reference list in each chapter. In particular, we have made the following changes to the text:

- The text has been organized into 15 chapters (as compared to 18 chapters in the ninth edition). The restructuring and condensing of the text have made it more concise.

- More prominence and coverage are given to three concepts: economic value added, balanced scorecard, and interactive control.
- More materials have been added in several chapters on computers and the Internet, and how information technology impacts management control.
- In Chapter 2, we have added more materials on human behavior in organizations, an understanding of which is critical for management control.
- In Chapter 6, we have expanded the coverage on economic value added.
- Chapter 10, "Performance Measurement," involved a major rewrite. We have given more coverage to blending financial and nonfinancial measures in performance reports.
- We have given more importance and coverage to aligning controls to strategy in Chapter 12.
- In Chapter 13, we have added control problems in financial service organizations.
- Chapter 14, "Multinational Organizations," gives more coverage to cross-cultural issues in control within multinationals.

We are confident that you will find the text material in this tenth edition well organized, concisely written, laden with current examples, and consistent with the current theory and practice of management control.

Changes in Cases
A key strength of this book is the collection of cases that emphasize actual practice. The cases come from Harvard Business School, the Tuck School at Dartmouth, and from a number of other schools, both in the United States and abroad. The cases not only require the student to analyze situations, but also give the student a feel for what actually happens in companies, a feeling that cannot be conveyed adequately in the theoretical text. In this sense, the cases can be viewed as extended examples of practice.

The cases are not necessarily intended to illustrate either correct or incorrect handling of management problems. As in most cases of this type, there are no right answers. The educational value of the cases comes from the practice the student receives in analyzing management control problems and in discussing and defending his or her analysis before the class.

We have retained those cases that users have found most helpful in accomplishing the objective of their course. Of the 68 cases in this edition, 48 are retained from the ninth edition. We have 20 (30 percent) new cases in this edition.

The following cases are either revised or new to the tenth edition:

Case 1–1	Nucor Corporation (A)
Case 2–1	Nucor Corporation (B)
Case 2–4	Digital Equipment Corporation
Case 2–5	National Tractor and Equipment Company
Case 3–1	Vershire Company (a rewrite of T&J's)
Case 3–3	NYPRO, Inc.
Case 4–3	Boise Cascade Corporation
Case 6–3	Quality Metal Service Center
Case 6–4	Aloha Products (a rewrite of Pasy Company)
Case 7–2	Allied Stationery Products
Case 7–3	Dairy Pak
Case 10–1	Analog Devices
Case 10–2	CUP Corporation
Case 11–2	Worthington Industries
Case 12–1	Pelican Instruments
Case 12–2	PC&D
Case 12–3	3M Corporation

Case 13–1   O'Reilley Company (a rewrite of Cookie, Inc.)

Case 14–1   AB Thorsten

Case 14–2   Lincoln Electric Company (B)

We are confident that instructors will find that this case collection does an excellent job of meeting classroom needs for several reasons:

- Many cases are based on major corporations such as General Electric, Champion International, Xerox, ITT, Skandia, 3M, Texas Instruments, Hewlett-Packard, General Motors, Nestlé, Motorola, Lincoln Electric, Nucor, Citibank, Chemical Bank, Nordstrom, and Emerson Electric.

- The collection offers a rich diversity of domestic, foreign, and international companies.

- The cases expose students to varied contexts: small organizations, large organizations, manufacturing organizations, service organizations, and nonprofit organizations.

- The collection presents contemporary, interesting situations that students will recognize, enjoy, and learn from.

- We have given significant attention to case length. A major effort has been made to ensure that a majority of the cases are short. We still include a few medium to long cases, "two-day" cases, and "two-part" cases.

- The case collection is flexible in terms of course sequencing, and the cases are comfortably teachable.

Target Audience
This book is intended for any of the following uses:

- A one-semester or one-quarter course for *graduate* students who have had a course in management accounting and who wish

to study management control in greater depth.

- A one-semester or one-quarter course for *undergraduate* juniors or seniors who have already had one or two courses in management accounting.

- *Executive development* programs.

- A *handbook* for general managers, management consultants, computer-based systems designers, and controllers—those who are involved in or are affected by the management control process.

Acknowledgments
We have benefited from the help of many people in the evolution of this book over ten editions. Students, adopters, colleagues, and reviewers have generously supplied an untold number of insightful comments, helpful suggestions, and contributions that have progressively enhanced this book.

The course from which the material in this book was drawn was originally developed at the Harvard Business School by the late Ross G. Walker. We wish to acknowledge his pioneering work in the development of both the concepts underlying the courses and the methods of teaching these concepts. We thank the following members and former members of the Harvard Business School faculty who have contributed much to the development of this book: Francis J. Aguilar, Robert H. Caplan, Charles J. Christenson, Robin Cooper, Russell H. Hassler, Regina E. Herzlinger, Julie H. Hertenstein, Robert A. Howell, Gerard G. Johnson, Robert S. Kaplan, Warren F. McFarlan, Kenneth Merchant, Krishna G. Palepu, John K. Shank, Robert Simons, Richard F. Vancil, and John R. Yeager.

In addition, we wish to acknowledge the assistance provided by Robert H. Deming, James S. Hekiman, John Maureil, Chei-Min Paik, and Jack L. Treynor. We also wish to thank the users who responded to our survey.

Specific comments on the ninth edition were provided by Jay Barnes, Boston; Tarakorn Chairatsamekul, Thailand; William Manders, the Netherlands; T. C. V. Narasimha Rao, India; G. Sethu, India; Dr. Ken Harling, Ontario; Xiao Feng Li, NC; R. C. Sekhar, India; Morgan Ivor; and Thomas Vigetorp. Many thanks to these users of the book.

Joseph Fisher, Indiana University, contributed the material on agency theory included in Chapter 11. Anant K. Sundaram, The Amos Tuck School of Business Administration, Dartmouth College, contributed the material on exchange rates and performance evaluation included in Chapter 14. Our sincere thanks to Joe Fisher and Anant Sundaram for their fine contributions.

We owe many thanks to Anita Warren, who skillfully edited the text.

The selection of cases is always vital to a successful management control systems course. In this context, our sincere appreciation goes to the supervisors and authors who are responsible for case development. Each has been recognized in the citations to the cases. We are particularly indebted to the companies whose cooperation made the cases possible.

Permission requests to use Harvard copyrighted cases should be directed to the Permissions Manager, Harvard Business School Publishing Division, Boston, MA 02163. Requests to reproduce cases copyrighted by Osceola Institute should be directed to Professor Vijay Govindarajan.

The organization and development of the vast amounts of material necessary to complete this project was no small task. A special note of thanks to Ms. Joyce Kenison, secretary to Professor Govindarajan, who professionally managed thousands of pages of original text and revisions with secretarial and computer skills that were invaluable. We also thank Stewart Mattson, Laura Griffin, and Erin Cibula at our publisher, McGraw-Hill Higher Education, for their help and commitment to our project.

In writing this text, we hope that you will share our enthusiasm both for the rich subject of management control and for the learning approach that we have taken. As always we value your recommendations and thoughts about the book. Your comments regarding coverage and content will be most welcome, as will your calling our attention to specific errors. Please contact: Vijay Govindarajan, Earl C. Daum 1924 Professor of International Business, The Amos Tuck School of Business Administration, Dartmouth College, Hanover, NH 03755; Phone (603) 646-2156; Fax (603) 646-1308; E-mail VG@dartmouth.edu.

Robert N. Anthony
Vijay Govindarajan

March 2000
Hanover, NH

1

THE NATURE OF MANAGEMENT CONTROL SYSTEMS

We begin this chapter by defining the three terms in the book's title: control, management, and systems. In the second section of the chapter, we distinguish the management control function, which is our focus, from two other functions that also involve planning and control: strategy formulation and task control. The third section of this chapter contains a road map providing an overview of the whole book and a brief description of the contents of each chapter.

Basic Concepts

Control

Press the accelerator, and your car goes faster. Rotate the steering wheel, and it changes direction. Press the brake pedal, and the car slows or stops. With these devices, you *control* speed and direction; if any of them is inoperative, the car does not do what you want it to. In other words, it is out of control.

An organization must also be controlled; that is, devices must be in place to ensure that its strategic intentions are achieved. But controlling an organization is much more complicated than controlling a car. We will begin by describing the control process in simpler systems.

Elements of a Control System. Every control system has at least four elements:

1. A *detector* or sensor—a device that measures what is actually happening in the process being controlled.
2. An *assessor*—a device that determines the significance of what is actually happening by comparing it with some standard or expectation of what *should* happen.

2

EXHIBIT 1–1

*Elements of the
control process*

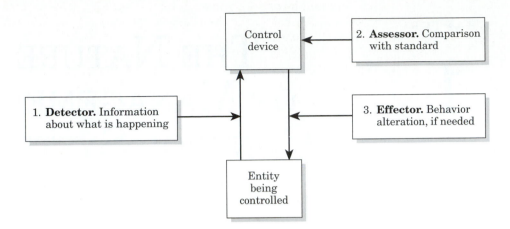

3. An *effector*—a device (often called "feedback") that alters behavior if the assessor indicates the need to do so.
4. A *communications network*—devices that transmit information between the detector and the assessor and between the assessor and the effector.

These four basic elements of any control system are diagrammed in Exhibit 1–1. We shall describe their functioning in three examples of increasing complexity: the thermostat, which regulates room temperature; the biological process that regulates body temperature; and the driver of an automobile, who regulates the direction and speed of the vehicle.

Thermostat. The components of the thermostat are: (1) a thermometer (the detector), which measures the current temperature of a room; (2) an assessor, which compares the current temperature with the accepted standard for what the temperature should be; (3) an effector, which prompts a furnace to emit heat (if the actual temperature is lower than the standard) or activates an air conditioner (if the actual temperature is higher than the standard) and which also shuts off these appliances when the temperature reaches the standard level; and (4) a communications network, which transmits information from the thermometer to the assessor and from the assessor to the heating or cooling element.

Body Temperature. Most mammals are born with a built-in standard of desirable body temperature; in humans that standard is 98.6° F. The elements of the control mechanism by which the body strives to maintain that standard are: (1) the sensory nerves (detectors) scattered throughout the body; (2) the hypothalamus center in the brain (assessor), which compares information received from detectors with the 98.6° F standard; (3) the muscles and organs (effectors) that reduce the temperature when it exceeds the standard (via panting and sweating, and opening the skin pores) and raise the temperature when it falls below the standard (via shivering and closing the skin pores); and (4) the overall communications system of nerves.

This biological control system is homeostatic—that is, self-regulating. If the system is functioning properly, it automatically corrects for deviations from the standard without requiring conscious effort.

The body temperature control system is more complex than the thermostat, with body sensors scattered throughout the body and hypothalamus directing actions that involve a variety of muscles and organs. It is also more mysterious; scientists know *what* the hypothalamus does but not *how* it does it.

Automobile Driver.   Assume you are driving on a highway where the legal (i.e., standard) speed is 65 mph. Your control system acts as follows: (1) your eyes (sensors) measure actual speed by observing the speedometer; (2) your brain (assessor) compares actual speed with desired speed, and, upon detecting a deviation from the standard, (3) directs your foot (effector) to ease up or press down on the accelerator; and (4) as in body temperature regulation, your nerves form the communication system that transmits information from eyes to brain and brain to foot.

But just as body temperature regulation is more complicated than the thermostat, so the regulation of a car is more complicated than the regulation of body temperature. This is because there can be no certainty as to what action the brain will direct after receiving and evaluating information from the detector. For example, once they determine that the car's actual speed exceeds 65 mph, some drivers, wanting to stay within the legal limit, will ease up on the accelerator, while others, for any number of reasons, will not. In this system, control is not automatic; one would have to know something about the personality and circumstances of the driver to predict what the actual speed of the automobile would be at the end point of the process.

Management

An organization consists of a group of people who work together to achieve certain common *goals* (in a business organization a major goal is to earn a satisfactory profit). Organizations are led by a hierarchy of managers, with the chief executive officer (CEO) at the top, and the managers of business units, departments, sections, and other subunits ranked below him or her in the organizational chart. The complexity of the organization determines the number of layers in the hierarchy. All managers other than the CEO are both superiors and subordinates; they supervise the people in their own units, and they are supervised by the managers to whom they report.

The CEO (or, in some organizations, a team of senior managers) decides on the overall *strategies* that will enable the organization to meet its goals. Subject to the approval of the CEO, the various business unit managers formulate additional strategies that will enable their respective units to further these goals. *The management control process is the process by which managers at all levels ensure that the people they supervise implement their intended strategies.*

Contrast with Simpler Control Processes. The control process used by managers contains the same elements as those in the simpler control systems described above: detectors, assessors, effectors, and a communications system. Detectors report what is happening throughout the organization; assessors compare this information with the desired state; effectors take corrective action once a significant difference between the actual state and the desired state has been perceived, and the communications system tells managers what is happening and how that compares to the desired state.

There are, however, significant differences between the management control process and the simpler processes described earlier:

1. Unlike in the thermostat or body temperature systems, *the standard is not preset.* Rather, it is a result of a conscious planning process. In this process, management decides what the organization should be doing, and part of the control process is a comparison of actual accomplishments with these plans. Thus, the control process in an organization involves planning. In many situations, planning and control can be viewed as two separate activities. Management control, however, involves both planning and control.

2. Like controlling an automobile (but unlike regulating room or body temperature), *management control is not automatic.* Some detectors in an organization may be mechanical, but the manager often detects important information with her own eyes, ears, and other senses. Although she may have routine ways of comparing certain reports of what is happening with standards of what should be happening, the manager must personally perform the assessor function, deciding for herself whether the difference between actual and standard performance is significant enough to warrant action, and, if so, what action to take. Then, since actions intended to alter an organization's behavior involve human beings, the manager must interact with at least one other person to effect change.

3. Unlike controlling an automobile, a function performed by a single individual, *management control requires coordination among individuals.* An organization consists of many separate parts, and management control must ensure that each part works in harmony with the others, a need that exists only minimally in the case of the various organs that control body temperature and not at all in the case of the thermostat.

4. *The connection from perceiving the need for action to determining the action required to obtain the desired result may not be clear.* A manager acting as assessor may decide that "costs are too high" but see no easy or automatic action guaranteed to bring costs down to what the standard says they should be. The term *black box* describes an operation whose exact nature cannot be observed. Unlike the thermostat or the automobile driver, a management control system is a black box. We cannot know what action a given

manager will take when a significant difference between actual and expected performance, nor what (she assesses if any) action others will take in response to the manager's signal. By contrast, we know exactly when the thermostat will signal the need for action and what that action will be; and, in the case of the automobile driver, the assessor phase may involve judgment, but the action itself is mechanical once the decision to act has been made.

5. *Much management control is self-control;* that is, control is maintained not by an external regulating device like the thermostat, but by managers who are using their own judgment rather than following instructions from a superior. Drivers who obey the 65 mph speed limit do so not because a sign commands it, but because they have consciously decided that it is in their best interest to obey the law.

Systems

A system is a prescribed and usually repetitious way of carrying out an activity or a set of activities. Systems are characterized by a more or less rhythmic, coordinated, and recurring series of steps intended to accomplish a specified purpose. The thermostat and the body temperature control processes described above are examples of systems. Management control systems, as we have seen, are far more complex and judgmental.

Many management actions are unsystematic. Managers regularly encounter situations for which the rules are not well defined and thus must use their best judgment in deciding what actions to take. The effectiveness of their actions is determined by their skill in dealing with people, not by a rule specific to the system (though the system may suggest the general nature of the appropriate response). *If all systems ensured the correct action for all situations, there would be no need for human managers.*

In this book, we focus primarily on the systematic, i.e., formal, aspects of the management control function. One can describe in considerable depth the various steps in the formal system, the information that is collected and used in each step and the principles that govern the system's operation as a whole. But it is very difficult, except in general terms, to describe the appropriate actions for managers encountering situations not contemplated in the formal system. These depend, among other factors, on the skills and personalities of the people involved, their relationships with one another, and the environment within which a particular problem arises. It is important to recognize, however, that these informal processes are strongly affected by the way the organization's formal control systems are designed and operated.

Boundaries of Management Control

In this section, we define management control and distinguish it from two other systems—or activities—that also require both planning and control: strategy formulation and task control. Serious mistakes can be made if principles and generalizations specific to one system are applied in another.

EXHIBIT 1–2

General relationships among planning and control functions

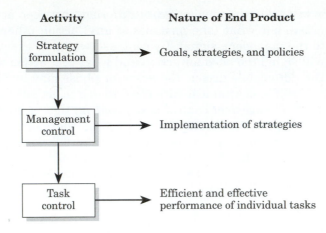

Activity	Nature of End Product
Strategy formulation	Goals, strategies, and policies
Management control	Implementation of strategies
Task control	Efficient and effective performance of individual tasks

As you will see, management control fits between strategy formulation and task control in several respects. Strategy formulation is the least systematic of the three; task control is the most systematic; and management control lies in between. Strategy formulation focuses on the long run, task control focuses on short-run activities, and management control is in between. Strategy formulation uses rough approximations of the future, task control uses current accurate data, and management control is in between. Each activity involves both planning and control; but the emphasis varies with the type of activity. The planning process is much more important in strategy formulation, the control process is much more important in task control, and planning and control are of approximately equal importance in management control.

The relationships of these systems of activities to one another are indicated in Exhibit 1–2. In the following sections we define management control, strategy formulation, and task control in greater detail and further describe the differences between them.

Management Control

Management control is the process by which managers influence other members of the organization to implement the organization's strategies. Several aspects of this process are amplified below.

Management Control Activities. Management control involves a variety of activities, including:

- *Planning* what the organization should do.
- *Coordinating* the activities of several parts of the organization.
- *Communicating* information.
- *Evaluating* information.

- *Deciding* what, if any, action should be taken.
- *Influencing* people to change their behavior.

Management control does not necessarily require that all actions correspond to a previously determined plan, such as a budget. Such plans are based on circumstances believed to exist at the time they were formulated. If these circumstances have changed at the time of implementation, the actions dictated by the plan may no longer be appropriate. While a thermostat responds to the actual temperature in a room, management control involves anticipating future conditions in order to ensure that the organization's objectives are attained. If a manager discovers a better approach—one more likely than the predetermined plan to achieve the organization's goals—the management control system should not obstruct its implementation. In other words, *conforming to a budget is not necessarily good, and departure from a budget is not necessarily bad.*

Goal Congruence.   Although systematic, the management control process is by no means mechanical; rather, it involves interactions among individuals, which cannot be described in mechanical ways. Managers have personal as well as organizational goals. The central control problem is to induce them to act in pursuit of their personal goals in ways that will help attain the organization's goals as well. *Goal congruence* means that, insofar as is feasible, the goals of an organization's individual members should be consistent with the goals of the organization itself. The management control system should be designed and operated with the principle of goal congruence in mind.

Tool for Implementing Strategy.   Management control systems help managers move an organization toward its strategic objectives. Thus, *management control focuses primarily on strategy execution.*

> **Example.**   As of 1999, Wal-Mart with sales revenues of over $140 billion was the largest retailer in the world, thanks to its winning strategy of selling branded products at low cost. The company's management control system was directed toward the efficient management of store operations, which in turn conferred a cost advantage companywide. Data from over 3,500 individual stores on items such as sales, expenses, and profit and loss were collected, analyzed, and transmitted electronically on a real-time basis, rapidly revealing how a particular region, district, store, department within a store, or item within a department was performing. This information enabled the company to reduce the likelihood of stockouts and the need for markdowns on slow-moving stock, and to maximize inventory turnover. The data from "outstanding" performers among the 3,500 stores were used to improve operations in "problem" stores. Further, the company was able to reduce pilferage-related losses, a major concern, by instituting a policy of sharing 50 percent of the savings from decreased pilferage in a particular store, as compared to the industry standard, among that store's employees.[1]

---

[1]"Wal-Mart Inc.," a case and an analysis of the case prepared by Rob Lynch, 1996; updated 1999.

8

EXHIBIT 1–3

*Framework
for strategy
implementation*

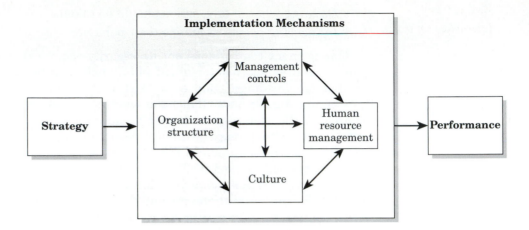

Management controls are only one of the tools managers use in implementing desired strategies. As indicated in Exhibit 1–3, strategies are also implemented through the organization's structure, its management of human resources, and its particular culture.

Organizational structure specifies the roles, reporting relationships, and division of responsibilities that shape decision-making within an organization. *Human resource management* is the selection, training, evaluation, promotion, and termination of employees so as to develop the knowledge and skills required to execute organizational strategy. *Culture* refers to the set of common beliefs, attitudes, and norms that explicitly or implicitly guide managerial actions.

Financial and Nonfinancial Emphasis. *Management control systems encompass both financial and nonfinancial performance measures.* The financial dimension focuses on the monetary "bottom line"—net income, return on equity, etc.; but virtually all organizational subunits have nonfinancial objectives—product quality, market share, customer satisfaction, on-time delivery, and employee morale.

Aid in Developing New Strategies. As discussed earlier, the primary role of management control is to ensure the execution of chosen strategies. In industries that are subject to rapid environmental changes, however, management control information, especially of a nonfinancial nature, can also provide the basis for considering new strategies. This function, illustrated in Exhibit 1–4, is referred to as *interactive control.*[2] Interactive control calls management's attention to developments—both negative (e.g., loss of market share; customer complaints) and positive (e.g., the opening up of a new

---

[2]Robert Simons, "Control in an Age of Empowerment," *Harvard Business Review,* March–April 1995, pp. 80–88.

Exhibit 1–4

Interactive control

market as a result of the elimination of certain government regulations)—that indicate the need for new strategic initiatives. Interactive controls are an integral part of the management control system.

Strategy Formulation

Strategy formulation is the process of deciding on the goals of the organization and the strategies for attaining these goals. In this book, we use the word *goals* to describe the broad overall aims of an organization, and the term *objectives* to describe specific steps to accomplish the goals within a given time frame.

Goals are *timeless;* they exist until they are changed, and they are changed only rarely. For many businesses, earning a satisfactory return on investment is an important goal; for others, attaining a large market share is equally important. Nonprofit organizations also have goals; in general, they seek to provide the maximum services possible with available funding. In the strategy formulation process, the goals of the organization are usually taken as a given, although on occasion strategic thinking can focus on the goals themselves.

Strategies are big plans, important plans. They state in a general way the direction in which senior management wants the organization to move. A decision by an automobile manufacturer to produce and sell an electric automobile would be a strategic decision.

The need for formulating strategies usually arises in response to a perceived threat (e.g., market inroads by competitors, a shift in consumer tastes, or new government regulations) or opportunity (e.g., technological innovations, new perceptions of customer behavior, or the development of new applications for existing products). A new CEO, especially one brought in from the outside, usually perceives both threats and opportunities differently from how his or her predecessor did. Thus, changes in strategies often occur when a new CEO takes over.

> **Examples.**   Louis V. Gerstner became the CEO of IBM in 1993. In the course of the next six years, he transformed the company from a mainframe computer manufacturer to a leader in networking systems, computer services, and e-business solutions.

Michael C. Armstrong took over the helm of AT&T in the mid-90s. By 1999 the company had undergone a major strategic overhaul, changing from a long-distance telephone operator to the nation's largest cable provider through the acquisition of companies such as TCI Communications for $50 billion and MediaOne for $60 billion.[3]

Other examples of companies at which new CEOs have made a huge difference include Michael Eisner at Disney, Ray Gilmartin at Merck, and John Reed at Citicorp.

Strategies to address a threat or opportunity can arise from anywhere in an organization and at any time. New ideas do not emanate solely from the research and development team or the headquarters staff. Virtually anyone might come up with a "bright idea," which, after analysis and discussion, can form the basis for a new strategy. *Complete responsibility for strategy formulation should never be assigned to a particular person or organizational unit.* Providing a means of bringing worthwhile ideas directly to the attention of senior management without allowing them to be blocked at lower levels is important.

Distinctions between Strategy Formulation and Management Control. *Strategy formulation is the process of deciding on new strategies; management control is the process of implementing those strategies.* From the standpoint of systems design, the most important distinction between strategy formulation and management control is that strategy formulation is essentially unsystematic. Threats, opportunities, and new ideas do not occur at regular intervals; thus, strategic decisions may be made at any time.

Furthermore, the analysis of a proposed strategy varies with the nature of the strategy. Strategic analysis involves much judgment, and the numbers used in the process are usually rough estimates. By contrast, the management control process involves a series of steps that occur in a predictable sequence according to a more-or-less fixed timetable, and with reliable estimates.

Analysis of a proposed strategy usually involves relatively few people—the sponsor of the idea, headquarters staff, and senior management. By contrast, the management control process involves managers and their staffs at all levels in the organization.

Task Control

Task control is the process of assuring that specified tasks are carried out effectively and efficiently.

Task control is *transaction-oriented*—that is, it involves the performance of individual tasks according to rules established in the management control process. Task contol often consists of seeing that these rules are followed; a function that in some cases does not even require the presence of human

---

[3]"Ma Bell Restored," *The Economist,* December 11, 1999, p. 54.

beings. Numerically controlled machine tools, process control computers, and robots are mechanical task control devices. Their function involves humans only when the latter prove less expensive or more reliable; this is likely to happen only if unusual events occur so frequently that programming a computer with rules for dealing with these events is not worthwhile.

Many task control activities are scientific; that is, the optimal decision or the appropriate action for bringing an out-of-control condition back to the desired state is predictable within acceptable limits. For instance, the rules for economic order quantity determine the amount and timing of purchase orders. Task control is the focus of many management science and operations research techniques.

Most of the information in an organization is task control information: the number of items ordered by customers, the pounds of material and units of components used in the manufacture of products, the number of hours employees work, and the amount of cash disbursed. Many of an organization's central activities—including procurement, scheduling, order entry, logistics, quality control, and cash management—are task control systems. Some of them, though mechanical, can be extremely complicated.

> **Examples.**   An entire steel mill may be controlled by electronic devices, with each piece of equipment instructed by a computer to carry out prescribed tasks. The computer senses the environment (e.g., the temperature of a steel ingot). If its findings indicate a departure from the desired state, it either initiates corrective action or, if it lacks the capacity to do so on its own, conveys the need for correction to a computer that controls all the computers in one section of the mill. This computer in turn may refer the problem to a coordinating computer for the mill as a whole. The Manufacturing Resource Planning (MRP II) system used to control manufacturing operations in many companies requires millions of lines of computer instructions. The gear-switching mechanisms used to connect two parties in a telephone conversation cost billions of dollars. And systems for program trading and other types of decisions made by traders in the financial markets involve complicated decision rules and minute-by-minute information about the prices of hundreds of financial instruments.

As the above examples suggest, certain activities that were once performed by managers are now automated and have thus become task control activities. This shift from management control to task control frees some of the manager's time for other management activities (unless it eliminates the manager's position).

Distinctions between Task Control and Management Control.   The most important distinction between task control and management control is that many task control systems are scientific, whereas management control can never be reduced to a science. By definition, management control involves the behavior of managers, and this cannot be expressed by equations. Serious errors may be made when principles developed by management scientists for task control situations are applied to management control situations. In

EXHIBIT 1–5   Examples of Decisions in Planning and Control Functions

Strategy Formulation	Management Control	Task Control
Acquire an unrelated business	Introduce new product or brand within product line	Coordinate order entry
Enter a new business	Expand a plant	Schedule production
Add direct mail selling	Determine advertising budget	Book TV commercials
Change debt/equity ratio	Issue new debt	Manage cash flows
Adopt affirmative action policy	Implement minority recruitment program	Maintain personnel records
Devise inventory speculation policy	Decide inventory levels	Reorder an item
Decide magnitude and direction of research	Control of research organization	Run individual research project

management control, managers interact with other managers; in task control, either human beings are not involved at all (as in some automated production processes), or the interaction is between a manager and a nonmanager.

In management control the focus is on organizational units; in task control the focus is on specific tasks performed by these organizational units (e.g., manufacturing Job No. 59268, or ordering 100 units of Part No. 3642).

Management control is concerned with the broadly defined activities of managers deciding what is to be done within the general constraints of strategies. Task control relates to specified tasks, most of which require little or no judgment to perform.

Exhibit 1–5 identifies differences among management control, task control, and strategy formulation by giving examples of each.

Impact of the Internet on Management Control

The information revolution started with the invention of the telephone by Alexander Graham Bell in the late 19th century. For consumers, the telephone provided a significant benefit—convenience. People no longer had to visit a store to get information about a product, determine its availability, or place an order. The pace of the information revolution accelerated with the invention of computers, gaining tremendous momentum in the 1990s with the advent of the Internet.

The Internet provides major benefits that the telephone does not:[4]

- *Instant access.* On the Web, huge amounts of data can be sent to anyone, anywhere in the world in a matter of seconds.

---

[4]Bruce Judson, *Hyper Wars* (New York: Scribner, 1999).

- *Multi-targeted communication.* The Internet has a vastly expanded one-to-many reach; one Web entry can reach millions of people.
- *Costless communication.* A business that uses telephone operators to interface with customers must pay for telephone personnel salaries, toll-free ("800") calls, and the bricks and mortar to support the customer service function. Communication with customers via the Internet avoids all these costs.
- *Ability to display images.* Unlike the telephone, the Web enables consumers to see the products being offered for sale.
- *Shifting power and control to the individual.* Perhaps the most dramatic benefit of the Web is that the individual is "virtually king." Consumers are in control and can use the Web 24 hours a day at their own convenience without being interrupted or unduly influenced by sales representatives or telemarketers.

With these advantages the Internet has dramatically changed the rules of the game in the business-to-individual consumer sector.

Example.   Prior to 1995, most books were purchased in bookstores or from printed catalogs. In July 1995, Amazon.com began offering books for sale on its Web site. In 1999, over 10 million customers bought $1.4 billion worth of books and CDs from Amazon.com via the Internet. The virtual store format of Amazon.com provides several advantages: better convenience (24-hour, 7 days a week shopping); better selection (Amazon.com offered 4.7 million titles versus 200,000 books in the biggest bricks-and-mortar Barnes & Noble retail outlet); better price (resulting from lower investments in inventory and fixed assets; in 1999, Barnes & Noble had $3 billion in assets and generated $3 billion in sales whereas Amazon.com had *negative* $50 million in assets and generated $1.4 billion in sales revenues); and better customer service (personalized recommendations based on purchase patterns of customers). In November 1999, four years after it started, the market capitalization of Amazon.com was $25 billion—a value higher than the combined market value of two established national chains, Barnes & Noble and Borders.[5]

The Internet has also radically changed business-to-business commerce.

Examples.   In November 1999, Ford announced the creation of AutoXchange, a giant online market that would transfer Ford's $80 billion annual purchases of components and materials from more than 30,000 suppliers to the Web. Ford expected three significant benefits as a result. First, 20 percent cost savings were expected from efficiencies in procurement and reductions in inventory. Second, because of tighter supply chain integration, cycle times in developing new products were expected to be reduced. Finally, by reinventing the supply chain, Ford expected to custom-build automobiles and deliver them to customers within a few days.[6]

---

[5]"Amazon's Delta," *The Economist,* November 20, 1999, p. 78.
[6]"Riding the Storm," *The Economist,* November 6, 1999, pp. 63–64.

Similarly, companies have used the Internet to reconfigure their relationships with corporate customers. Take the case of Cisco Systems, the Silicon Valley company, which supplied hardware—routers, servers, switches, etc.—that was at the heart of communication networks. In 1999, 80 percent of sales revenues of Cisco came from unassisted transactions from its Web site. To quote Bruce Judson: "Cisco's Web site allows customers to configure products with complex features, with its "intelligent configurator" software rejecting orders where specific components would be incompatible with other parts. Inaccuracies on orders processed through the Internet have actually dropped from more than 25 percent before this automated system existed to less than one-tenth of a percent now. Annual savings from Cisco's site, which reflect the other administrative efficiencies in addition to the elimination of order errors, are estimated at over $250 million a year, and the absence of errors has also allowed Cisco to improve delivery time by three days. For Cisco, the Internet has meant faster service, quicker production cycles, and savings."[7]

The impact of the Internet on the world of business has been monumental. What, then, has been the Internet's impact on management controls within an organization? Management control systems involve information, and organizations require an infrastructure to process that information. The Internet provides that infrastructure, making the processing of information easier and faster, with fewer errors. On the Web, a manager can collect huge amounts of data, store that data, analyze it in different forms, and send it to anyone in the organization. Managers can also use this information to customize and personalize their reports.

The Internet facilitates coordination and control through the efficient and effective processing of information; but *the Internet cannot substitute for the fundamental processes that are involved in management control.* This is because implementing strategies through management controls is essentially a social process and, thus, cannot be fully automated. The availability of electronic access to data bases contributes little to the judgment calls required to design and operate an optimal control system. Such judgments involve:

1. Understanding the relative importance of the various, and sometimes competing, goals that drive individuals to act, e.g., personal achievement versus collective achievement, value creation for customers and shareholders rather than for oneself, etc.
2. Aligning various individual goals with those of the organization.
3. Developing specific objectives by which business units, functional areas, and individual departments will be judged.
4. Communicating strategy and specific performance objectives throughout the organization.
5. Determining the key variables to be measured in assessing an individual's contribution to strategic goals.

---

[7]Judson, *Hyper Wars,* p. 93.

6. Evaluating actual performance relative to the standard and making inferences as to how well the manager has performed.
7. Conducting productive performance review meetings.
8. Designing the right reward structure.
9. Influencing individuals to change their behavior.

In sum, although the Internet has vastly improved information processing, the fundamental elements of management control—what information to collect and how to use it—are essentially behavioral in nature and thus not amenable to a formula approach.

Road Map for the Reader

This book is organized into three parts, each of which is described briefly below.

The Management Control Environment (Part I)

In Chapter 2, we describe some of the characteristics of organizations that affect the management control process, focusing primarily on the behavior of individuals within an organization.

In Chapters 3, 4, 5, and 6 we define and describe several different types of responsibility centers, and discuss the considerations involved in assigning *financial* responsibility to various organizational subunits. (The incorporation of nonfinancial measures into management control systems is discussed in Part II of the book, primarily in Chapter 10.)

Chapter 3 introduces the basic concept of responsibility centers. *A responsibility center is an organization unit headed by a manager who is responsible for its activities.* Each responsibility center has inputs and outputs. Inputs are the resources that the responsibility center uses in doing whatever it does. Outputs are the results of the center's work. Technically, these outputs are products, but they are not necessarily products sold to outside customers. Services rendered by one responsibility center to another are also products. Responsibility centers can be classified according to the degree to which their inputs and outputs can be measured in monetary terms.

Chapter 3 describes expense centers and revenue centers. *In an expense center, inputs are measured as monetary costs; but outputs are either not measured at all, or measured in quantitative, nonmonetary terms.* In an expense center the manager is responsible primarily for expense control. There are two types of expense centers. In an *engineered* expense center, actual costs are compared with standard costs to determine how efficiently the center has operated. In a *discretionary* expense center, there is no way to determine reliable standard costs, and expenses vary at the discretion of the manager and his or her superiors. The efficiency of a discretionary expense center cannot be measured.

In a revenue center, revenues are measured in monetary terms, but expenses are not matched with these revenues. Branch sales offices are often revenue centers. A comparison of budgeted and actual revenues indicates the effectiveness of the revenue center.

Chapter 4 deals with *profit centers, in which both revenues and the expenses associated with generating these revenues are measured; the difference between them is profit.* Actual profit compared with budgeted profit is a measure of the manager's efficiency.

If a profit center provides outputs to other responsibility centers, or if it receives inputs from other responsibility centers, prices must be established for these outputs and inputs. These prices are called *transfer prices,* as distinguished from market prices, that is, those charged to outside customers. Developing transfer prices in a way that facilitates management control is discussed in Chapter 5.

In Chapter 6, we discuss *investment centers, in which both profit and the investment (i.e., the assets) used in carrying out that center's responsibility are measured.* The return on investment is the broadest measure of the manager's efficiency and effectiveness.

The Management Control Process (Part II)

Much of the management control process involves informal interactions between one manager and another or between a manager and his or her subordinates. Informal communications occur by means of memoranda, meetings, conversations, and even by facial expressions. Recently the term *management by walking around* has come to signify the importance of this information. The informal interactions take place within a formal planning and control system. Such a system includes the following activities: (1) strategic planning, (2) budget preparation, (3) execution, and (4) evaluation of performance. Each activity leads to the next, in a regular cycle. Collectively, they constitute a closed loop.

In Chapter 7, we discuss *strategic planning, which is the process of deciding on the major programs that the organization will undertake to implement its strategies and the approximate amount of resources that will be devoted to each.* The output of the process results in a document called the *strategic plan* (or, in some companies, the *long-range plan*). Strategic plans cover a period that extends over several years (typically three or five). In a profit-oriented company each principal product or product line is a *program.* In a nonprofit organization the principal services that the organization provides are its programs.

Strategic planning is the first step in the management control cycle. In a company that uses a calendar year, the planning usually takes place in the spring or summer of the year that precedes the budget year. At that time decisions are made that take account of any changes in strategies that have occurred since the last strategic plan was developed.

Budget preparation is discussed in Chapter 8. *An operating budget is the organization's plan for a specified time period, usually a year.* The budget represents a fine-tuning of the strategic plan, incorporating the most current information. In the budget, revenues and expenses are rearranged from programs to responsibility centers; thus, the budget shows the expenses that each manager is expected to incur. The process of preparing the budget is essentially one of negotiation between the managers of each responsibility center and their superiors. The end product of these negotiations is an agreed-upon statement of the anticipated expenses for the coming year (if the responsibility center is an expense center), or the planned profit or expected return on investment (if the responsibility center is a profit center or an investment center).

In Chapters 9, 10, and 11 we discuss performance measurement, performance evaluation, and management compensation.

During the year, managers execute the program or part of a program for which they are responsible and also report on what has happened in the course of fulfilling that responsibility. Ideally, reports are structured so that they provide information about both programs and responsibility centers. Reports on responsibility centers may show budgeted and actual information, financial and nonfinancial performance measures, and internal and external information. These reports keep managers at higher levels informed about the status of the various programs in their charge and also help to ensure that the work of the various responsibility centers is coordinated.

The managers' reports also are used as a basis for control. *The process of evaluation is a comparison of actual expenses and those that should have been incurred under the circumstances.* If the circumstances assumed in the budget process are unchanged, the comparison is between budgeted and actual amounts. If circumstances have changed, these changes are taken into account. Ultimately, the analysis leads to praise or constructive criticism of the responsibility center managers.

Chapter 9 deals with the analysis and evaluation of financial performance measures.

Chapter 10 expands the focus of performance evaluation to discuss the incorporation of nonfinancial measures and to consider the design of a *balanced scorecard,* incorporating both financial and nonfinancial measures. This chapter also contains a discussion of *interactive controls*—the use of management control information (especially the nonfinancial variety) in developing new strategies.

Chapter 11 describes the considerations involved in designing management incentive compensation plans.

Variations in Management Control (Part III)

The chapters in Part II describe the typical management control process. In Part III we describe several variations from this pattern: differentiated controls for differentiated strategies (Chapter 12); service organizations (Chapter 13); and multinational organizations (Chapter 14).

The final chapter (Chapter 15) describes the management control of projects. This differs somewhat from the management control of ongoing operations, which has been our focus up to this point.

Summary

A system is a prescribed way of carrying out any activity or set of activities. The system used by management to control the activities of an organization is called the management control system. Management control is the process by which managers influence other members of the organization to implement the organization's strategies. Management control is facilitated by a formal system that includes a recurring cycle of activities.

Management control is one of three planning and control functions that are present in almost every organization. The other two are: strategy formulation, the largely unsystematic process of identifying threats and opportunities and deciding on new strategies in response; and task control, the process of assuring that specified tasks are carried out effectively and efficiently.

The book is divided into three parts. Part I discusses the control environment in an organization. Control is exercised by managers who supervise responsibility centers. Part II describes the management control process, which consists of a set of regularly recurring activities: strategic planning, budget preparation, execution, and performance evaluation. Part III describes control systems that depart from the typical pattern.

Suggested Additional Readings

Anthony, Robert N. *The Management Control Function.* Boston: Harvard Business School Press, 1989.

Clinton, B. D., and K. Hsu. "Linking Manufacturing Control to Management Control." *Management Accounting,* September 1997, pp. 18–24.

Collins, Jim. "Turning Goals into Results." *Harvard Business Review,* July–August 1999, pp. 70–84.

Dent, Jeremy F. "Global Competition: Challenges for Management Accounting and Control." *Management Accounting Research* 7, no. 2 (June 1996), pp. 247–69.

Drake, A. R., S. Haka, and S. P. Ravenscroff. "Cost System and Incentive Structure Effects on Innovation, Efficiency, and Profitability in Teams." *The Accounting Review* 74, no. 3 (July 1999), pp. 323–45.

Evans, P., and T. S. Wurster. *Blown to Bits: How the New Economics of Information Transforms Strategy.* Boston: Harvard Business School Press, 1999.

Evans, P., and T. S. Wurster. "Get Real about Virtual Commerce." *Harvard Business Review,* November–December 1999, pp. 84–98.

Govindarajan, Vijay. "A Contingency Approach to Strategy Implementation at the Business Unit Level: Integrating Administrative Mechanisms with Strategy." *Academy of Management Journal* 31, no. 4 (1988), pp. 828–53.

Govindarajan, Vijay, and Joseph Fisher. "Impact of Output versus Behavior Controls and Resource Sharing on Performance: Strategy as a Mediating Variable." *Academy of Management Journal,* June 1990, pp. 259–85.

Kaplan, Robert, and David Norton. *Balanced Scorecard.* Boston: Harvard Business School Press, 1996.

Maciariello, J. A., and C. J. Kirby. *Management Control Systems.* Englewood Cliffs, NJ: Prentice-Hall, 1994.

Otley, David. "Management Control in Contemporary Organizations: Towards a Wider Framework." *Management Accounting Research* 5, no. 4 (September–December 1994), pp. 289–99.

Shank, John K., and Vijay Govindarajan. *Strategic Cost Management.* New York: Free Press, 1993.

Simons, Robert. *Levers of Control.* Boston: Harvard Business School Press, 1995.

Walther, Thomas, Henry Johansson, John Dunleavy, and Elizabeth Hjelm. *Reinventing the CFO.* New York: McGraw-Hill, 1997.

CASE 1–1
NUCOR CORPORATION (A)

We are a cyclical business. . . . Basically when you are at the peak of the cycle—times are good, interest rates are low, people are building—our margins increase. When we go to the trough, of course, the margins are squeezed. But over the last 25 years Nucor has never had a losing quarter. Not only a losing quarter, we have never had a losing month or a losing week.[1]

John D. Correnti, President and CEO, Nucor

In 1998 Nucor was a Fortune 500 company with 6,900 employees and sales of $4.3 billion in steel and steel-related products. Its chairman, F. Kenneth Iverson, had headed the company for more than 30 years. During his tenure, the steel industry faced a number of problems, including foreign competition, strained labor relations, and slowed demand for steel (related in part to the substitution of alternative materials). Despite these industry challenges, Nucor's sales during Iverson's tenure grew at an annual compound rate of about 17 percent per annum. Selected comparative financial data are shown in Exhibit 1. In different years, both Iverson and Nucor CEO John Correnti were named Steelmaker of the Year by *New Steel* magazine.

History

Nucor traced its origins to auto manufacturer Ransom E. Olds, who founded Oldsmobile and, later, Reo Motor Cars. Through a series of transactions, the company Olds founded eventually became the Nuclear Corporation of America, a company involved in the nuclear instrument and electronics business in the 1950s and early 1960s.

The firm suffered several money-losing years and in 1965, facing bankruptcy, installed 39-year-old Ken Iverson as president.

Iverson has a bachelor's degree in aeronautical engineering from Cornell and a master's degree in mechanical engineering from Purdue. He began his professional career as a research physicist and held several technical and management positions in the metals industry. He joined Nuclear Corporation of America as a vice president in 1962 and was appointed president three years later.

Iverson focused the failing company on two businesses: making steel from recycled scrap metal and fabricating steel joists for use in nonresidential construction. In 1972 the firm changed its name to Nucor Corporation. By 1998 it had become America's second-largest steel maker.

Operations

Nucor located its diverse facilities in rural areas across the United States, establishing strong ties to its local communities and its work force. As a leading employer with the ability to pay top wages, it attracted hard-working, dedicated employees. These factors also allowed Nucor to select from among competing locales, siting its operations in states with tax structures that encouraged business growth and regulatory policies that favored the company's commitment to remaining union-free. By 1998 Nucor and its subsidiaries consisted of nine businesses, with 25 plants. These businesses included the following:

This case was prepared by Vijay Govindarajan. The cooperation and help provided by F. Kenneth Iverson, chairman, Nucor Corporation, in preparing this case study is greatly appreciated. Copyright © V. Govindarajan.

[1]Richard Franklin, "An Interview with John D. Correnti, President and CEO, Nucor Corporation," *The Wall Street Corporate Reporter,* September 9–15, 1996, pp. 19–20.

EXHIBIT 1   Selected Financial Data 1993–1997

	Sales 1997 ($ in billons)	Return on Equity (5-year average) % 1993–1997	Debt/Capital % 1997	5-Year Sales Growth % 1993–97	Profit Margin % 1997
Nucor	$4.1	18%	7%	23%	8%
Texas Industries* (parent of Chaparral Steel)	1.0	12	22	12	8
National Steel[†]	3.1	7	27	6	7
USX-US Steel[†]	6.8	10	21	7	6
Bethlehem Steel[†]	4.7	Deficit	28	3	Deficit
LTV[†]	4.3	11	18	3	1
Northwestern Steel*	0.6	2	71	7	Deficit
Industry Median	$1.9	10%	30%	8%	3%

*Mini-mill.

[†]Integrated steel producer.

Source: *Forbes,* January 12, 1998, pp. 196–97.

Nucor Steel
Products: steel sheet, bars, angles, light structural carbon and alloy steels
Plants: Darlington, S.C.; Norfolk, Nebr.; Jewett, Tex.; Plymouth, Utah; Crawfordsville, Ind.;   Hickman, Ark.; Mt. Pleasant, S.C.

Nucor-Yamato Steel Company
Products: wide-flange steel beams, pilings, heavy structural steel products
Plant: Blytheville, Ark.

Vulcraft
Products: steel joists, joist girders and steel deck for building construction
Plants: Florence, S.C.; Norfolk, Nebr.; Fort Payne, Ala.; Grapeland, Tex.; Saint Joe, Ind.; Brigham City, Utah

Nucor Cold Finish
Products: cold-finished steel products for shafting, precision machined parts
Plants: Norfolk, Nebr.; Darlington, S.C.; Brigham City, Utah

Nucor Fastener
Products: standard steel hexhead cap screws, hex bolts, socket head cap screws
Plants: Saint Joe, Ind.; Conway, Ark.

Nucor Bearing Products, Inc.
Products: unground and semi-ground automotive steel bearings, machined steel parts
Plant: Wilson, N.C.

Nucor Building Systems
Products: metal buildings, metal building components
Plants: Waterloo, Ind.; Swansea, S.C.

Nucor Grinding Balls
Products: steel grinding balls used by the mining industry to process ores
Plant: Brigham City, Utah

Nucor Wire
Products: stainless steel wire
Plant: Lancaster, S.C.

Strategy

Nucor's strategy focused on two major competencies: building steel manufacturing facilities economically and operating them productively. The company's hallmarks were continuous innovation, modern equipment, individualized customer service, and a commitment to producing high-quality steel and steel products at competitive prices. Nucor was the first in its industry to adopt a number of new products and innovative processes, including thin-slab cast steel, iron carbide, and the direct casting of stainless wire.

In 1998 Nucor produced a greater variety of steel products than did any other steel company in the United States—both low-end (non-flat) steel, such as reinforcing bar, and high-end (flat) steel, including motor lamination steel used in dishwashers, washers, and dryers, as well as stainless steel used in automotive catalytic converters and exhaust systems.

Nucor's major customer segments were the construction industry (60 percent), the automotive and appliance industries (15 percent), and the oil and gas industries (15 percent), with the remaining 10 percent divided among miscellaneous users. All the company's low-end steel products (50 percent of its total output) were distributed through steel service centers. Its high-end products (the other 50 percent) were sold directly to original equipment manufacturers (OEMs), fabricators, or end-use customers.

Nucor's ratio of debt to total capital was not allowed to exceed 30 percent. In 1997 that ratio was 7 percent. The company did not believe in acquisitions or mergers, choosing instead to commit to internally generated growth. It had no plans to diversify beyond steel and steel-related products.

Organization Structure

Compared to the typical Fortune 500 company with 10 or more management layers, Nucor's structure was decentralized, with only the four management layers, illustrated below:

Chairman / Vice Chairman / President
Vice President / Plant General Manager
Department Manager
Supervisor

"We have a very flat organization structure," said president and CEO John Correnti. "The standard joke in the company is if you are a janitor and you get five promotions, you have Correnti's job. If you take a typical organization chart, it is the typical pyramid. You take our company, you turn the pyramid upside down; 6,800 people do not work for me, I work for 6,800 people."[2]

In 1998 Nucor's board of directors had only six members: the current chairman, president, and chief financial officer, and three retired Nucor executives. Only 22 employees (including clerical staff) worked at the corporate head office, which was located in an unassuming office building across the street from a shopping mall. All other employees worked in one of the company's 25 plants, each of which employed, on average, between 250 and 300 people.

The general manager at each plant was granted considerable autonomy, essentially operating the facility as an independent business. Each plant could source its inputs either from another Nucor plant or from the outside market. With the day-to-day decisions being made on site and the lines of communication to employees kept open and informal, problems could be solved quickly without having to wait for decisions from headquarters. "We are honest-to-God autonomous," said the general manager of one plant. "That means that we duplicate efforts made in other parts of Nucor. The company might develop the same computer program six times. But the advantages of local

[2]Ibid., p. 20.

autonomy are so great, we think it is worth it."[3] One such advantage, noted Iverson, was greater operating efficiency. "None of our divisions are in the same town as our Charlotte, North Carolina, headquarters," he said. "If any of them were, us headquarters types would always be over there making suggestions and wasting their time with our opinions. A general manager running a division in Charlotte would feel like he was living with his mother-in-law."[4]

Other remarks by Iverson provided insight into the company's tolerance for experimentation and willingness to take risks: "We try to impress on our employees that we are not King Solomon. We use an expression that I really like: 'Good managers make bad decisions.' We believe that if you take an average person and put him in a management position, he'll make 50 percent good decisions and 50 percent bad decisions. A good manager makes 60 percent good decisions. That means 40 percent of those decisions could have been better. We continually tell our employees that it is their responsibility to the company to let the managers know when they make those 40 percent decisions that could have been better. . . . The only other point I'd like to make about decision making is, don't keep making the same bad decisions."[5]

In a 1998 interview, Iverson said that "management can't be effective without taking some amount of risk. A group of us were just recently thinking about the pluses and minuses of sinking millions of dollars into a new process for pickling steel, removing all the rust before finishing it. Right now, that's done by using acid.

But maybe it can be done better, faster, cheaper electrolytically. . . . I can't stand it when there are not strange ideas (like this one) floating around the company."[6]

Human Resource Policies

Nucor was very selective in recruiting employees and was able to choose from a large applicant pool. Noted Iverson, "Darlington [S.C.] needed eight people, and we put a little ad in the county weekly newspaper that said, 'Nucor Steel will take some applications on Saturday morning at 8:30 for new employees.' When we went out there for the interviewing, there were 1,200 people lined up in that plant. We couldn't even get into the plant to get to the personnel department. . . . Finally, we called the state police and said, "You've got to do something. We've got a traffic jam out here.' And the cop on duty said, 'We can't do it, because we've got three people out there applying for jobs ourselves!' "[7]

Employee relations at Nucor were based on four principles:

1. Management is obligated to manage Nucor in such a way that employees will have the opportunity to earn according to their productivity.
2. Employees should feel confident that if they do their jobs properly, they will have a job tomorrow.
3. Employees have the right to be treated fairly.
4. Employees must have an avenue of appeal when they believe they are being treated unfairly.

As part of its commitment to fairness, Nucor had a grievance procedure that allowed any

---

[3]Ken Iverson, *Plain Talk* (New York: John Wiley & Sons, 1998), p. 27.
[4]Ibid., p. 37.
[5]F. Kenneth Iverson, "Effective Leadership: The Key Is Simplicity," in Y. K. Shetty and V. M. Buchler, eds., *The Quest for Competitiveness* (New York: Quorum Books, 1991), p. 287. Quoted in Pankaj Ghemawat and Henrions J. Stander, "Nucor at Crossroads," Harvard Business School Case, 1984, pp. 8–9.

[6]"The Art of Keeping Management Simple," interview with Ken Iverson, *Harvard Management Update,* May 1998, p. 7.
[7]Ibid., p. 42.

employee to ask for a review of a grievance if he or she felt the supervisor had not provided a fair hearing. The grievance could move up to the general manager level and, if the employee was still not satisfied, could be submitted to headquarters management for final appeal.

General managers were required to hold annual dinners with every employee, meeting with groups of 25 to 100 at a time. These meetings gave employees a chance to discuss problems relating to scheduling, equipment, organization, and production. The ground rules were simple: All comments were to be business related and not involve personalities, and all criticism was to be taken under advisement by management for decisive action. Like traditional New England town meetings, the format was free and open. Topics varied widely from year to year, and sometimes the sessions lasted well beyond midnight.

Another key aspect of Nucor's relationship with its workers was its commitment not to lay off or furlough employees in periods when business was down. Instead of reducing the work force during recessionary periods (as was the usual industry practice), Nucor would reduce the work week. A former employee of an integrated steel company said, "At Nucor, the cold-mill manager says that almost all of the improvements have come from operators and operating supervisors. At my former plant, operators are reluctant to suggest improvements for fear of reducing or eliminating another worker's job."[8]

Nucor's labor force was not unionized. An employee at Nucor Steel in Hickman, Arkansas, presented the majority view: "Why is Nucor nonunion? I see two main reasons. First, it's just not needed. Nucor takes very good care of its employees. Its pay and benefits package is top-notch. No one has been capriciously fired. There are no layoffs. Nucor listens to its employees

through monthly crew meetings, annual dinners, and employee surveys. We just don't need union mediators. . . . The second reason is that we all work together. We don't need divisiveness. We don't need adversaries. We can talk among ourselves and work out our own problems."[9] Iverson noted the effectiveness of this approach: "People like to work here. For example, the last time we had a union organizer in Darlington, we had to send management out to protect the union guy passing out the pamphlets."[10]

Compensation

Nucor provided employees with a performance-related compensation system. All employees were covered under one of four compensation plans, each featuring incentives for meeting specific goals and targets.

1. Production Incentive Plan. This covered most Nucor workers. Under this plan, employees directly involved in manufacturing were paid weekly bonuses based on actual output in relation to anticipated production tonnages produced. The bonuses were paid only for work that met quality standards and were pegged to work group, rather than individual output. (Each work group contained 25 to 40 workers.) The formulas for determining bonuses were nondiscretionary. Once the standard output was determined, it was not revised unless there was a significant change in the way a production process was performed due to a source other than the workers in the bonus group. Bonuses were tied to attendance and tardiness standards. If one worker's tardiness or attendance problems caused the group to miss its weekly output target, every member of the group was denied a bonus for that week. "This bonus system is very tough," said Iverson. "If

[8]Anthony Edwards, "How Efficient Are Our Work Practices?" *New Steel,* July 1996. p. 31.

[9]Claude Riggin, "Freedom and a Hell of a Lot More at Nucor," Newsfront column, *New Steel,* July 1996.
[10]"Steel Man Ken Iverson," *Inc,* April 1986, pp. 41–42.

you are late, even only five minutes, you lose your bonus for the day. If you are thirty minutes late or you are absent for sickness or anything else, you lose your bonus for the week. Now, we have four forgiveness days per year when you might need to close on a house or your wife is having a baby, but only four."[11]

Maintenance personnel were assigned to each shift, and they participated in the bonus along with the other members operating on that shift; no bonus was paid if equipment was not operating. Production supervisors were also a part of the bonus group and received the same bonus as the employees they supervised. The weekly output by, and bonus for, each work group were displayed at the front entrance to the factory. While there were no upper caps, the production incentive bonus, in general, averaged 80 to 150 percent of the base wage.

Iverson gave an example of how this plan worked: "In the steel mills, there are nine bonus groups: three in melting and casting, three in rolling, and three in finishing and shipping. Take melting and coating, for example. We start with a base of 12 tons of good billets per hour: Above that, the people in the group get a 4 percent bonus for every ton per hour. So if they have a week in which they run, say, 32 tons per hour—and that would be low—that's an 80 percent bonus. Take the regular pay, the overtime pay, everything, multiply it by an additional 80 percent—and we give them that check along with their regular check the next week."[12]

2. Department Manager Incentive Plan. Nucor's department managers oversaw the production supervisors and, in turn, reported directly to the general manager of their plant. They earned an annual incentive bonus based on the performance of the entire plant to which they belonged. The targeted performance criterion here was return on assets. Every plant operated as a stand-alone business unit. All the

plants had the same performance target: a return of 25 percent or better on the assets employed within that plant. In recent years, bonuses averaged 82 percent of base salary.

3. Non-Production and Non-Department Manager Incentive Plan. All employees not on the Production Incentive Plan or the Department Manager Incentive Plan—including accountants, engineers, secretaries, clerks, and receptionists—received a bonus based primarily on each plant's return on assets. It could total over 25 percent of an employee's base salary. Every month each plant received a chart showing its return on assets on a year-to-date basis. This chart was posted in the employee cafeteria or break area together with another chart that showed the bonus payout; this kept employees appraised of their expected bonus levels throughout the year.

4. Senior Officers Incentive Plan. The designation "senior officers" included all corporate executives and plant general managers. Nucor senior officers did not have employment contracts, nor did they participate in any profit sharing, pension, or retirement plans. Their base salaries were lower than those received by executives in comparable companies. Senior officers had only one incentive compensation system, based on Nucor's return on stockholders' equity above certain minimum earnings. A portion of pretax earnings was placed into a pool that was divided among the officers. If Nucor did well, the officers' bonuses, in the form of stock (about 60 percent) and cash (about 40 percent), could amount to several times their base salaries. If Nucor did poorly, an officer's compensation was only base salary and, therefore, significantly below the average pay for this level of responsibility. As with all Nucor incentive compensation bonus plans, there were no discretionary bonuses.

During a slack period in the 1980s, Iverson was named the Fortune 500 CEO with the

---

[11]Ibid., pp. 44–45.
[12]Ibid.

lowest compensation. He saw this as an honor. "When I walked through a plant during that period of time when we had to cut back to a four-day work week, or even three-and-a-half days, I never heard an employee who complained," he said. "His pay may have been cut 25 percent, but he knew that his department head was cut even more and that the officers were cut, percentagewise, even more than that. I call it our 'share-the-pain' program. . . . Management should take the biggest drop in pay because they have the most responsibility."[13]

Information Systems

Every week each plant sent data to headquarters on the following six operations-related variables: bids, orders, production, backlog, inventory, and shipments. Taken together, these numbers provided a snapshot of the plant's basic operations. The figures for all 25 plants were pulled together onto one 8.5″ * 11″ sheet of paper. Each plant also submitted a second weekly report comparing the numbers on the six variables for the current week with those for the previous week, and the numbers for the most recent 13-week period with those for the corresponding period in the previous year. This second group of data from all 25 plants was compiled in a four-page report. Thus, all weekly data for the 25 plants were pulled together onto just five sheets of paper for corporate review.

Each plant also submitted a monthly report comparing actual to budgeted figures for sales revenue, costs, contribution, and return on assets employed.

Iverson made the following observations regarding the design of Nucor's information systems: "We don't look over the shoulders of our general managers and we don't ask them to submit voluminous reports explaining their actions. But that doesn't mean we are not paying attention. Delegation without information is

suicide. . . . In short, while we work hard to get the information we need, we've worked just as hard to keep our reports streamlined and ourselves free of 'information overload.' A lot of managers seem to miss the link between information overload and their compulsion to overcontrol their operations. But the connection is really obvious. Too much information puts you in the same position as too little information—you don't know what's going on. And when you don't know what's going on, it is hard to stay out of your people's hair. It's hard to tell them 'trust your instincts,' and really mean it."[14]

All the plant general managers met as a group with headquarters management three times a year—in February, May, and November—to review each plant's performance and to plan for the months and years ahead. In addition, detailed performance data on each plant were distributed to all plant managers on a regular basis. Plant general managers and machine operators also commonly visited each other's mills.

Benefits

Nucor took an egalitarian approach toward employee benefits. Senior executives did not enjoy such traditional perquisites as company cars, corporate jets, executive dining rooms, or executive parking places. "Our corporate dining room is the deli across the street," remarked Iverson.[15] All employees traveled in economy class. Certain benefits, such as Nucor's profit-sharing and scholarship programs, its employee stock purchase plan, and its service awards, were not available to Nucor's officers. All employees had the same holidays, vacation schedules, and insurance programs, and all, including the CEO, wore the same green hard hats. (In a typical manufacturing company, people wore different colored hats in accordance with status or seniority, and the CEO's often was gold-plated!)

---

[13]Ibid., p. 44.

[14]Iverson, *Plain Talk,* pp. 37–39.
[15]Ibid., p. 59.

Every Nucor annual report contained the names of every employee listed alphabetically on the front cover.

The company maintained a profit-sharing plan for employees below the officer level, contributing a minimum of 10 percent of Nucor's pretax earnings each year. Of this amount, approximately 15 to 20 percent was paid out to employees in March of the following year as cash profit sharing. The remainder was placed in trust and allocated to employees based on their earnings as a percentage of the total earnings paid throughout Nucor. The employees themselves made no contributions to this plan. They became fully vested after seven full years of service and received payment when they retired or terminated employment with Nucor. In the 1990s, several employees had more than $300,000 in the trust.

Nucor had a monthly stock purchase plan featuring a 10 percent Nucor matching contribution, and a 401(k) retirement savings plan that included a matching contribution of 5 to 25 percent of the employee's contribution based on Nucor's return on shareholders' equity. Additionally, employees received five shares of Nucor common stock for each five years of continuous service as well as standard medical, dental, disability, and life insurance coverage and standard vacation and holiday packages.

Nucor's benefit program also attested to the company's commitment to education. On-the-job training was a matter of policy, with employees being taught to perform multiple functions. The Nucor Scholarship Fund provided awards of up to $2,200 a year for up to four years to employees' children who pursued higher education or vocational training past high school. In 1996 the plan covered more than 600 students attending some 200 different learning institutions. According to Correnti, these scholarships cost Nucor about $1.3 million a year but created a priceless reservoir of good will. "This gets Nucor around the dinner table at night," he said. "It creates loyalty among our employees. . . . Our turnover is so miniscule we do not even measure it."[16]

Nucor encouraged employees to recruit their friends and relatives to work for the company. As an industry observer remarked, "In fact, for existing employees, Nucor often means *N*ephews, *U*ncles, *C*ousins, and *O*ther *R*elatives."[17]

Technology

Nucor did not have a formal R&D department, a corporate engineering group, or a chief technology officer. Instead, it relied on equipment suppliers and other companies to do the R&D, and they adopted the technological advancements they developed—whether in steel or iron making, or in fabrication. Teams composed of managers, engineers, and machine operators decided what technology to adopt.

Integrated steel companies produced steel from iron ore using blast furnaces. Nucor successfully adopted the "mini-mill" concept—first developed in Europe and Japan—in the plant it built in Darlington, South Carolina, in 1969. Unlike integrated steel companies, mini-mills did not start with iron ore; instead, they converted scrap steel into finished steel using small-scale electric furnaces. Nucor purchased its scrap requirements from third-party agents at open market prices. For the non-flat, commodity segment of the steel industry (reinforcing bar for construction and rods for pipe, rail, and screws), mini-mills had a cost advantage over integrated steel producers, eventually driving the latter out of the low end of the steel industry.

Until the mid-1980s, however, mini-mills could not produce the flat steel products required by automotive and appliance customers, and this high-end market was monopolized by the

---

[16]Franklin, "An Interview with John D. Correnti." 1996, p. 19.

[17]Joseph A. Maciariello, *Lasting Value* (New York: John Wiley & Sons, 2000), pp. 140–41.

integrated steel producers. Then, in 1987, Nucor made history by building the first mini-mill that could make flat steel (in Crawfordsville, Indiana), thus gaining entry into the premium segment of the steel industry.

At its Crawfordsville facility, Nucor gambled on the thin-slab casting technology developed by SMS Schloemann-Siemag, a West German company. Staff engineers from more than 100 steel companies visited SMS to explore this technology, which had been demonstrated in a small pilot but not yet proven commercially. But Nucor adopted the process first, obtaining the rights from SMS by signing a nonexclusive contract with an additional technology flowback clause. Nucor's investment in the Crawfordsville plant represented approximately five times the company's 1987 net earnings and virtually equaled the stockholders' total equity in the company that year!

By 1997 Nucor had built two more mini-mills (in Hickman, Arkansas, and Charleston, South Carolina), both using the thin-slab casting process to produce flat-rolled sheet steel. The first competitive facility to make thin-slab-cast flat-rolled steel did not appear until 1995—eight years after Nucor's pioneering effort.

In 1987 Nucor's pursuit of technical excellence had led to the establishment of Nucor-Yamato Steel Company, a facility jointly owned by Nucor and Yamato Kogyo of Japan, which operated a structural steel mill in the United States that used its own continuous-casting technology.

Several years later, Nucor became concerned that mini-mill start-ups by several other companies would significantly increase the price of scrap steel or even cause scrap to become wholly unavailable. To guard against that possibility, the company established a plant in Trinidad, West Indies, in 1994. This plant successfully adopted a commercially unproven technology to make iron carbide, a substitute for scrap steel, which it supplied to the flat-rolled plant in Crawfordsville. However, in 1998 Nucor concluded that the iron carbide supplied by the Trinidad facility was uneconomical and closed the facility.

In addition to developing new plants, Nucor was committed to continuously modernizing its existing ones. Its philosophy was to build or rebuild at least one mill every year, in the latter case rebuilding entirely rather than just "put(ting) new pipes in parts of the old mill." In building new plants or rebuilding existing plants, the company did not rely on outside contractors, but instead handed the responsibility for design and construction management to a small group of engineers selected from existing Nucor facilities. For example, when it decided to add a second rolling mill at Nucor-Yamato in Blytheville, Arkansas, it assigned the meltshop supervisor in the first mill to coordinate the design and construction of the meltshop in the second mill. As Greg Mathis, this meltshop supervisor, observed, "They put it all on my shoulders—the planning, the engineering, the contracting, the budgets. . . . I mean, we are talking about an investment of millions of dollars and I was accountable for all of it. It worked out fine . . . because my team and I knew what not to do from our experience running the meltshop on the first line."[18]

Further, the actual construction of the plant was done by workers from the local area, who were aware that they would subsequently be recruited to operate the mills as well.

Iverson explained the rationale behind this approach to technology management: "We accept that roughly half of our investments in new ideas and new technologies will yield no usable results. . . . Every Nucor plant has its little storehouse of equipment that was bought, tried, and discarded. The knowledge we gather from our so-called 'failures' may lead us to spectacular success. . . . We let employees invest in technology. People in the mills identify and select most of the technology. Technology is advancing too quickly on too many fronts. No small group of executives can possibly keep fully informed."[19]

In 1991 President Bush awarded Iverson the National Medal of Technology, America's highest award for technological achievement.

Future

For Iverson, the national medal was not a culmination but a signpost along the way. "Our biggest challenge (in the future) is to continue to grow the company at 15–20 percent per year, and to keep earnings parallel with this growth," he said. "Business is like a flower: You either grow or die."[20]

Questions

1. Why has Nucor performed so well?
   a. Is Nucor's industry the answer?
   b. Is it the "mini-mill" effect?
   c. Is it market power (scale economies)?
   d. Is it a distribution channel advantage?
   e. Is it a raw material advantage?
   f. Is it a technology advantage?
   g. Is it a location advantage?
   h. Is it the result of an entrenched brand name?
   i. Is it Nucor's choice of a unique strategy?
   j. Is it Nucor's ability to execute its strategy?

2. What are the most important aspects of Nucor's overall approach to organization and control that help explain why this company is so successful? How well do Nucor's organization and control mechanisms fit the company's strategic requirements?

3. A crucial element of Nucor's success is its ability to mobilize two types of knowledge: plant construction and start-up know-how; and manufacturing process know-how. What mechanisms does Nucor employ to manage knowledge effectively?
   a. What mechanisms help the company accumulate these two types of knowledge in individual plants?
   b. What mechanisms exist within the company to facilitate sharing this knowledge among its 25 plants?
   c. How does Nucor transfer knowledge to a greenfield, start-up operation?

4. Nucor repeatedly has demonstrated the ability to be a successful first mover in the adoption of new technology. How does the company's approach to organization and control contribute to this first-mover advantage?

5. Would you like to work for Nucor?

6. Why have competitors not been able to imitate Nucor's performance so far?

---

[19]Ibid., pp. 5, 96, 150.
[20]"The Art of Keeping Management Simple," Interview with Ken Iverson.

CASE 1–2
MOTOROLA INC.

The controller of Motorola's newly formed Application Specific Integrated Circuit (ASIC) Division sensed that he and his staff could play a significant part in determining the success of what promised to be an important new business. Not only was his division competing in a new and dynamic market with unique requirements but it also was radically changing the way in which it delivered its product. These circumstances led the controller to reassess the most basic issues involved in designing a management control system: What should be measured? How should it be measured? Who should measure it? and, For whom should it be measured?

The Company

Founded in 1928, Motorola soon became widely known for its radios and other consumer electrical and electronic products. By the 1960s, it sold semiconductor products, communications equipment, and components to consumers, industrial companies, and the military throughout the world.

Headquartered in Schaumberg, Illinois, in 1984, Motorola achieved over $5.5 billion in sales, employed over 99,000 people, and spent $411 million in research and development. It was one of the few American companies that marketed a wide range of electronic products, from highly sophisticated integrated circuits to consumer electronic products.

Organization

The company was organized along product and technology lines. Each business unit was

structured as a sector, group, or division, depending on size.

The Semiconductor Products Sector (SPS) was headquartered in Phoenix, Arizona; sales in 1984 were over $2.2 billion, which was 39 percent of Motorola's net sales. The sector sold its products worldwide to original equipment manufacturers through its own sales force. Semiconductor products were subject to rapid changes in technology. Accordingly, SPS maintained an extensive research and development program in advanced semiconductor technology.

Formation of the ASIC Division

In the early 1980s, the Semiconductor Products Sector produced a large line of both discrete semiconductor components and integrated circuits. Integrated circuits (ICs) can be thought of (at least functionally) as miniature circuit boards. For example, the designer of a video cassette recorder could replace a 12″ * 12″ circuit board and all its individual components with a single 1″ * 1″ integrated circuit on a silicon chip, saving space and reducing power consumption. By 1985, worldwide sales of integrated circuits reached $20.2 billion.

Among integrated circuit manufacturers, Motorola was widely known for its design and process expertise, and it became a leader in the increasingly popular semicustom integrated circuits.

Semicustom integrated circuits are designed using predetermined functional blocks. In the early 1980s, Motorola produced a version of semicustom ICs called "gate arrays." Each "gate" on a gate array was a transistor that performed a single operation. These were interconnected to produce the desired set of functions. One chip could contain a thousand or more gates. Each was designed to meet the require-

This case was prepared and copyrighted by Joseph Fisher and Steven Knight, The Amos Tuck School of Business Administration, Dartmouth College.

ments of a specific customer. Gate array customizations were relatively cheap and quick to manufacture, and they were designed by computer-aided design systems. By 1984, the market for gate arrays had grown to $455 million. Sales in 1985 were expected to be $740 million, and the market was estimated to reach $1.4 billion in sales annually by 1990. The high-performance gate array market totaled $90 million in 1984. Forecasts stated that the market should grow to $600 million by 1990.

Motorola manufactured high-performance gate arrays using two different semiconductor technologies: (1) bipolar and (2) complementary metal-oxide semiconductor (CMOS). Bipolar technology provided increased speeds at which the circuit could perform but at the cost of increased power consumption (and increased difficulty in meeting cooling requirements) when compared to CMOS technology. For this reason, the demand for CMOS gate arrays was expected to grow more rapidly than that for bipolar gate arrays. In 1984, CMOS captured 40 percent of the market. This was expected to increase to 70 percent.

Bipolar gate arrays were produced in Phoenix by the Logic Division of the SPS. Under the Logic Division, Motorola's bipolar gate array business grew rapidly. Motorola achieved a dominant share of this market and became the acknowledged technological leader.

CMOS gate arrays were produced in Austin, Texas, by the Microprocessor Products Group. Since Motorola focused on maintaining its position in the microprocessor market, the CMOS gate arrays did not receive adequate attention in this group. As a result, Motorola had only a small share of the CMOS gate arrays market and faced stiff competition from such companies as LSI, Hitachi, Toshiba, Fujitsu, and NEC.

To exploit fully the growing demand for semicustom integrated circuits, Motorola organized the Application Specific Integrated Circuit (ASIC) Division as part of the Semiconductor Products Sector in 1984. In 1985, the ASIC Division occupied Motorola's Chandler facility, the newest of the company's five Phoenix-area locations. Typically, Motorola worked closely with a customer to design the semicustom integrated circuit. However, several designs were considered standard designs and were kept in stock.

Organization of ASIC Division

The division was organized along functional lines (see Exhibit 1).

EXHIBIT 1

Organization of ASIC division

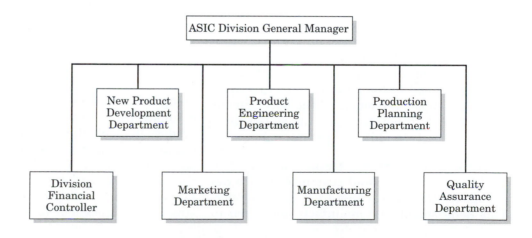

Product Engineering Department. Product engineering interacted with the customer and assumed the role of a troubleshooter in dealing with customer complaints. It was responsible for the technical aspects of ongoing product manufacturing. Engineers were assigned to one or more products and served the customers for these products. If a customer had a complaint about an integrated circuit, product engineering responded to the request. Therefore, product engineering was the technical interface between the company and customer for existing products.

Product engineers designed the manufacturing process for existing products, and they typically were responsible for customer-driven capital expenditures. If a customer wanted or required an additional manufacturing process that required a capital expenditure, the process engineering department made a feasibility study. This study divided costs between nonrecurring engineering expenses (NRE) and the per unit cost of production after the initial NRE. In addition, an estimate of revenues was made to estimate product profitability. This report was examined by the marketing department to ensure that the assumptions and estimates made by the product engineers were reasonable.

Part of the start-up cost of a new product was the nonrecurring engineering cost (NRE). This cost included design and software development cost but typically did not include investment in process technologies, unless a very specialized piece of equipment was a unique requirement of the product's manufacture. The NRE was billed to the customer in two stages: 30 percent upon agreement of the development contract and 70 percent upon the shipment of the first prototype-units.

Production Planning Department. The production planning and customer service department scheduled orders from the customer. This department told manufacturing when to start production and when the product run should be finished. Since Motorola did not have a computerized production planning system, this work was done with only standard microcomputer software, such as spreadsheets. Orders had to be tracked manually through the factory floor. When the product was shipped, the department billed the client and reported this information to the financial controller.

Marketing Department. The marketing department was responsible for identifying initial prospects and making sales to them. In addition, the department had certain responsibilities for product pricing and accurate forecasting of market demands.

Once a prospect was identified, the marketing department acted as a liaison to ensure that the requirements of the product were accurately communicated from the prospect to the new products development group. The new products development group then estimated a manufacturing cost, and the marketing department calculated a price, using a target margin of around 60 percent above manufacturing cost. This price was adjusted to take into account the competitive conditions of the market. The marketing department also forecasted the sales volume for the product for the next five years.

New Product Development Department. The new product development group was responsible for the translation of customer product specifications into manufacturable designs and for the production of prototypes. As mentioned above, this group provided an estimate of the manufacturing cost to the marketing group. After the design was completed, the cost estimate was refined; it was included in the product implementation plan, along with yield requirements. Before the product design could be released to the manufacturing department, the product was produced in the development fabrication area with production tooling. At this stage the process had to meet minimum yield specifications. This yield was not the yield estimated in calculating the long-run manufacturing cost of the product, but simply a yield that would be satisfactory as production moved rapidly down a learning curve. The learning curve was estimated to be about 70 percent for most products in the ASIC Division. A 70 percent learning curve implies that unit costs for total production volume will decrease by 30 percent every time the cumulative production volume doubles.

Each month the new products development group provided the financial controller department an updated forecast of future capital expense requirements; this was used in capital planning by the finance department.

Quality Assurance Department.   Quality assurance (QA) was responsible for the outgoing quality of the product. After many of the processes on the manufacturing floor, QA inspectors sampled the product for quality. These tests included electrical and visual/mechanical tests. The electrical tests were straightforward (i.e., if the product failed to conduct properly, the product was rejected). The visual/mechanical tests were more subjective. Defects in this area could be misprinting, illegible printing, discolored components, or bent lead wires. Many of these did not affect the viability of the circuit but only its visual appearance. Quality assurance people knew that the Japanese were very sensitive to visual quality and that the product had to be visually perfect if Motorola was to be competitive in the Japanese market. One of the major responsibilities of QA was to convey to manufacturing what constituted a rejection of the product. One manager in QA said that the group should assume the role of a pseudo customer.

QA attempted to take a noncombative role with the other departments; it preferred to function in a preventive role. QA had trainers who discussed with manufacturing operators what constituted a rejection. This program had

two benefits: (1) operators became aware that they needed to produce to a certain quality level; and (2) if the product was below acceptable quality at any stage in production, it would be rejected immediately by the operator, thus saving further manufacturing costs. Recently, a procedure was instituted that, if a product was rejected, the whole line stopped until QA and the production floor could determine the cause(s).

Manufacturing Department.   The manufacturing department consisted of hourly workers, supervisors, and a manufacturing engineering staff. The hourly workers were directly involved in operating production machinery and inspecting work-in-process. Manufacturing engineering was charged with sustaining the production processes and methods used in the assembly and test operations. The group's focus was on the manufacturing process, rather than on specific products.

ASIC Market

The managers of the new division realized that the semicustom integrated circuit business had different requirements for success than the commodity-type business from which it grew.

In the semicustom gate arrays market, the customer created a unique design from the "building blocks" provided by Motorola designers. This involvement by the customer in the middle of the development cycle was different from that in the other semiconductor products offered by Motorola. Motorola provided design services to the customer and managed a relatively involved customer relationship. Thus, Motorola's organization focused on its customers, rather than on its products.

The customers of the ASIC division were typically computer manufacturers, such as DEC, Apple Computer, Unisys, Cray, and Prime Computer. These customers competed in markets characterized by rapidly changing technology and rapid introduction of new products. Shortening the product delivery time was a primary concern for them. High quality, quick development time, and the ability to achieve volume production rapidly were paramount in capturing the business of these customers. Compared with these factors, price was of secondary importance.

Some customers, such as Hewlett-Packard, were developing just-in-time (JIT) manufacturing systems and stated their needs for timely deliveries and high-quality incoming components.

Motorola Manufacturing and Accounting Systems

Prior to moving, the ASIC Division was part of another corporate sector. Bipolar production, prior to moving, used Motorola's existing manufacturing and accounting systems. In the plant, machines and workers were organized along functional lines. Each machine was controlled as part of a functional group, and was in close physical proximity with other machines that performed a similar function. This functional design resulted in large physical movements of product over relatively large distances on the factory floor. Each manufactured part had a designated routing through the factory.

In this factory design, there were 29 cost centers, whose inventory was valued at standard cost. The inventory was grouped by stage of completion for costing purposes. The routing of the product through the factory typically included the following steps: (1) piece parts, where the various raw materials were purchased and prepared; (2) wafer fabrication, where the silicon wafers containing the logic arrays were produced; (3) die, where the wafers were tested and cut into individual circuits or chips and mounted to the substrate of the package (permanent chip enclosure); (4) assembly, where lead wires were attached to the chip and the packaging completed; (5) test, where the packaged chip was tested according to customer

specifications; and (6) finished goods, where the finished products were packaged for shipping.

This system required extensive recordkeeping. An entry was made every time the product was moved from one cost center to another. A frequent physical audit of inventories was required to track and verify product amounts.

Material, labor, and overhead standards were updated twice a year. Nevertheless, the standards were often obsolete, because of the dynamic environment and the steep learning curves. Overhead was allocated to the product based on direct labor. Direct labor was meticulously tracked in order to cost labor to the product and to provide allocation of overhead to the product. The manufacturing manager estimated that between 8 percent and 12 percent of an employee's productive time was spent in recordkeeping.

Direct labor was paid an hourly wage and a bonus. The bonus was largely determined by comparison of actual direct labor hours to standard labor hours for each employee.

The functional design of the factory caused difficulty in placing responsibility for an individual product. Expediters in the production planning department performed a crucial task in making sure important products were being completed in a timely fashion. Even so, the plant was plagued with slow throughput times. Management felt that turn-around time on the integrated circuits was too slow, compared with competing Japanese firms.

The functional design also resulted in large inventories and large batch sizes. The large batch size resulted in work-in-process (WIP) inventories between functional stations and resulted in large finished goods inventories that were effectively produced but perhaps unwanted by the customer.

Many people felt that, rather than helping managers cope with the complexity of the manufacturing system, the accounting system was actually exacerbating the problem. The division controller noted, "The first important realization of the accounting department is that we were sometimes a barrier to progress. The accounting systems resulted in overall dysfunctional activities and impeded movement to new manufacturing techniques."

The standard cost system was cumbersome and not well understood by factory employees. Factory employees had difficulty in tying a variance to a specific problem. Because a variance did not highlight the actual problem, an appropriate solution to a variance was difficult to determine. The typical factory worker thought the variance report was irrelevant and, therefore, ignored it.

The timeliness of reports was also a problem. Standard costs were generated monthly. The lack of daily or weekly feedback made it difficult to pinpoint the cause of an unfavorable variance. The monthly variance was an accumulation of many favorable and unfavorable activities, which variance analysis did not specifically identify. Moreover, the variance reports were not timely. The books were closed on the seventh working day after the end of the month. An additional seven working days were required to generate actual costs and the variance report. By the time the reports were received in the factory floor, the manufacturing department was halfway through another accounting period.

Because of the dynamic environment facing a chip manufacturer, the determination of standards was very difficult. New chip designs were constantly flowing through the factory, and the steep learning curve contributed to the rapid obsolescence of standards. The standards were generally perceived as being out of date.

Since the variances were affected by volume, in many cases the way to decrease an individual variance was to keep the employees and machines fully used and produce large lot sizes. This had the undesired result of building up WIP inventory between the work stations and production of products that were not immediately required by a customer. At the same time, products required by a customer might not be produced. This resulted in a buildup of finished goods inventory and out-of-stock orders simultaneously.

In the new plant, there was a dramatic increase in overhead costs and a corresponding decrease in direct labor costs. The allocation of overhead by direct labor no longer seemed relevant.

Opportunities for Change

The manager of the newly formed ASIC Division realized that the opening of a new production facility in Chandler represented an opportunity to introduce substantial changes in the division's manufacturing operations. Accordingly, the new plant's floor layout was designed to be particularly suited to the JIT philosophy and to the specific processes of the plant. One manager at the Chandler site expressed the opinion that reorganizing an existing functional facility to accomplish a JIT plant would have been far more difficult.

The factory was organized around nine cells: (1) assembly preparation; (2) 72-pin assembly; (3) 149-pin assembly; (4) other assembly; (5) sealing, mechanical testing, and marking; (6) heat sink; (7) burn-in; (8) production testing and packing; and (9) warehousing and shipping. (Exhibit 2 is a diagram of the plant layout.) Not all products went through all cells—for example, not all chips required heat sinks. However, all of the chips produced at the Chandler plant were processed in most of the cells.

Products moved from cell to cell in the order shown in Exhibit 2. The wafers (each consisting of a number of chips) were placed in a die cage when they arrived at the plant. From the die cage, the wafers were taken to the die prep cell, where the gate arrays on wafers that had not been tested at the wafer fabrication facility were checked with a probe to determine which arrays were good. Arrays that did not pass inspection were marked, and, when the wafer was cut into individual chips, the marked arrays were thrown away.

EXHIBIT 2

Layout of Chandler plant

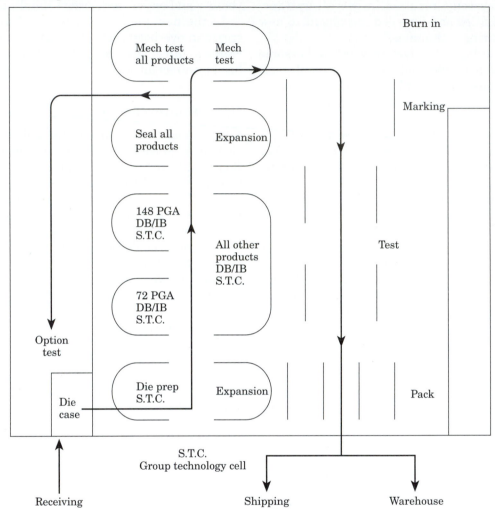

Next, the chips were taken to one of the three assembly cells (72-pin, 149-pin, other), depending on the product family and number of connections that needed to be made to the chip. In the assembly cells, the electrical connections to the chip were made. In the sealing, mechanical testing, and marking cell, the chips were sealed in a protective package, tested, and marked for identification. In this cell, some low-volume chips were diverted from the normal product flow into a special option line. This line was for very-low-volume ICs, which were usually built for customers who used them for prototypes and testing. The focus of this option line was fast turnaround time; for new ICs, a dozen or so units could be shipped within three weeks from the time the design was accepted. Higher-volume ICs were routed through the remaining

Exhibit 3

Layout of assembly cell

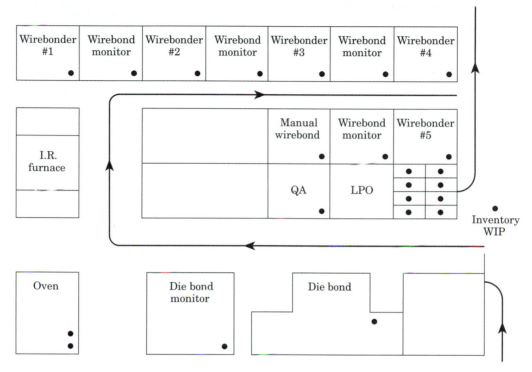

cells. As noted, not all ICs were sent to the heat sink and burn-in cells, but all went through the testing, warehousing, and shipping cells.

Most of the processes were machine-paced, and most of the machinery was complex and expensive. This was particularly true of the assembly and test cells. For example, automated test machines at the end of the option line cost over $2 million each.

Each of the cells was run by a production team, which was supervised by a team leader. Work flow was controlled through a pull system, with designated areas where limited inventory was allowed between work stations. (A pull manufacturing system is characterized by triggering production when inventory is removed from finished goods stock.) If the storage area before a work station was full, the preced-

ing station had to remain idle. One of the assembly cells is diagrammed in Exhibit 3. In this cell, chips were attached to the bottom portion of the permanent enclosure (package) in the die bond station, and they moved through the cell as shown by the arrows; the final operation performed in the cell was attaching lead wires in the wirebond stations. The cell was so designed that the product moved in one direction along a U-shaped path.

The Role of the Management Control System

The controller of the ASIC Division was acutely aware of the tendency of outdated and cumbersome control systems to hinder progress in manufacturing operations. He felt strongly that his office should not merely stand aside but should take a positive position in promoting the changes throughout the division. However, he wondered what kind of managerial control system would complement and even guide the progressive changes taking place in the division's operations.

Questions

1. What are the key success factors for Motorola's ASIC Division?
2. Does a traditional standard cost system address these key success factors?
3. What are good measures of these key success factors?
4. How would you control the plant using these measures and the current structure of the plant?

CASE 1-3
STEWART BOX COMPANY

Stewart Box Company was a well-established manufacturer of paperboard cartons and boxes, which were sold primarily as packages for consumer products. The cartons were manufactured in the company's carton factory. The raw material for the carton factory was paperboard, which was manufactured in the company's paperboard mill adjacent to the carton factory. The plant complex also included a 60,000–square foot warehouse where finished orders were stored pending delivery. The company had approximately 425 employees in 1993. Robert Stewart, the president, was also a large stockholder.

The company marketed its products within a radius of about 500 miles from its factory, which was located in a fairly small town. It had sales engineers, who were compensated on the basis of a nominal salary, plus commission. In the marketing organization were six other persons, including three who prepared price quotations for prospective customers according to specifications obtained from the customers. The company had an excellent reputation for product quality and customer service.

The paperboard and carton industry was characterized by strong competition because of the potential overcapacity that existed in most plants. Because of this overcapacity, competition for large orders was particularly keen, and price cutting was common. Stewart met this competition by designing special boxes to customer specifications, by actively catering to its customers' wishes, and by strict adherence to promised delivery dates.

The production process required that the paperboard mill operate continuously on three

shifts for maximum efficiency, but the carton factory operated an average of only one and one-half shifts per day.

A partial organization chart is shown as Exhibit 1. The paperboard mill and the carton factory were profit centers. In the carton factory were 10 production departments, each consisting of a printing press or a group of similar presses and associated equipment, and each headed by a foreman. There were five service departments, which performed functions such as ink manufacture, quality control, and warehouse storage; each was headed by a supervisor. Each of these 15 departments was an expense center. The 10 production departments were production cost centers, and the 5 service departments were service cost centers.

Accounting System

The company had a job-cost accounting system, using standard costs. The board mill was a single cost center, operating a single paperboard manufacturing machine. A rate per machine-hour was established annually, which combined direct labor and manufacturing overhead costs. Manufactured paperboard was charged to the carton factory at a transfer price that included standard cost plus a standard return on the assets employed in the board mill. The profit component of this charge was subtracted from the inventory amounts as shown on the financial statements (because generally accepted accounting principles do not permit a profit allowance to be included in inventory).

In the carton factory, each order was a job. The job was costed at the standard cost of the materials used on the job, a standard rate per press hour for the time that the job used on presses, and a standard rate per direct labor-hour for other operations. These rates included

This case was prepared by Robert N. Anthony and revised by Vijay Govindarajan. Copyright by the President and Fellows of Harvard College.

EXHIBIT 1

Organization chart

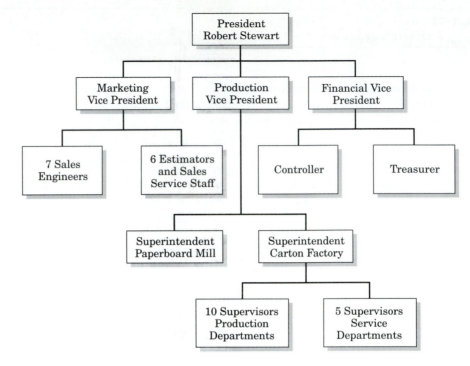

both labor and factory overhead costs and were estimated annually. The system also collected actual labor and overhead costs for each responsibility center.

Strategic Planning

The company had a five-year plan, which it revised annually. The management team (president, vice presidents, and superintendents) spent a total of about two days each summer discussing and agreeing on this revision. In 1993, for example, the sales estimates for 1994–98 indicated that the capacity of the warehouse would become inadequate by 1995. This led to an investigation of alternative warehousing arrangements and a decision to build a larger warehouse and to tear down the existing one. The capital required for this warehouse was significant, and it was decided to borrow part of the cost and to finance the remainder from funds generated by operations.

As an aid in deciding on proposed capital acquisitions, the company calculated the net present value and a profitability index whenever the available information was sufficiently reliable to warrant a formal analysis. About 85 percent of the proposals in terms of numbers, but less than 50 percent in terms of dollar magnitude, were in this category. Exhibit 2 is an example of the numerical part of such an analysis. (The accompanying explanation is omitted.) It is for the replacement of a printing press which was so old and worn that maintenance and operating costs were high. The decision was made to acquire this press in 1993, and the $32,000 cost was included in the capital budget for 1994.

Over a period of about five years the company conducted a review of each facet of its operations. For production operations, it usually hired a consulting firm expert in carton manufacturing methods to conduct this review. For marketing and general administrative func-

EXHIBIT 2   Analysis of Proposed Printing Press

	Tax Calculation	Present Value Calculation
Annual cash inflows:		
Saving in maintenance costs		$ 3,200
Saving in direct labor costs		9,920
Saving in power		1,600
Saving in supplies		800
Annual pretax cash inflow	$15,520	15,520
Less: Depreciation* 32,000 ÷ 10	3,200	
Additional taxable income	12,320	
Additional income tax 34% * 12,320		4,189
Annual aftertax cash inflow		8,131
Present value of cash inflows ($A_{10/10}$ = 6.145)		49,961
Investment in press installed		32,000
Net present value		$ 17,961
Profitability index $49,961/$32,000		1.56

*For simplicity in this illustration, straight-line depreciation is used. The company actually used sum-of-the-years'-digits depreciation for income tax purposes.

tions, it used the management services division of the firm of certified public accountants that audited its financial statements.

Budget Preparation

The controller was responsible for the mechanics of the annual budgeting process. He saw to it that the sales staff prepared sales estimates. These were discussed at length in a meeting attended by Mr. Stewart, the marketing vice president, and the controller. After final sales estimates were agreed upon, the controller communicated these estimates to heads of responsibility centers as a basis for their budget preparation.

Some budget items were stated as a fixed amount per month, others were stated as variable amounts per unit of output, and still others were stated as a fixed amount per month plus a variable amount per unit of output. For the production departments, output was measured in terms of machine-hours or direct labor-hours; and for the service departments, it was measured in terms of an appropriate measure of activity, such as pounds of ink manufactured.

Each responsibility center head discussed his proposed budget first with the controller (who had had long experience in the industry and hence could point out discrepancies or soft spots), and in the case of the carton factory, with its superintendent. Mr. Stewart then discussed the proposed budgets for the board mill and the carton factory with the superintendents of these profit centers. He discussed the marketing budget with the marketing vice president. From these discussions, an approved budget emerged. It consisted of a master budget showing planned revenues and expenses at the estimated sales volume, a variable budget for each responsibility center showing the fixed amount per month and the variable rate per unit of output for each significant item of expense, a purchasing budget, and a cash budget. Standard unit costs and overhead rates were revised if necessary so that they were consistent with the approved budget.

Product Pricing

Pricing was a crucial element in the company's marketing tactics. Prices were prepared by the company's estimators for each bid or order on the basis of sales specifications and the appropriate standard cost elements as shown in tables the company had developed for this purpose. To the calculated amount of total factory costs, there were added allowances for selling and administrative expenses, sales commissions, cash discounts, and a profit margin. These allowances were expressed as percentages, and were based on the budget. A sample price estimate is reproduced as Exhibit 3.[1] The price calculated in the estimate was often adjusted for quotation purposes. It might be lowered to meet competitive conditions, or it might be increased because the design work on the order was judged to be particularly good, or for other reasons. In Exhibit 3, the calculated selling price came to $45.00 per thousand boxes, but the actual quotation was increased to $49.00.

Estimators of several companies met regularly under the auspices of a trade association to price sample boxes according to their own formulas. Based on these meetings, Mr. Stewart concluded that, while most of his competitors were shaving prices below formula, Stewart's quoted prices were higher than the calculated estimate about 65 percent of the time and lower 15 percent of the time. "It all depends on the competition and on your assessment of the whole situation," he once said.

On some occasions, the company departed from its normal pricing practices. This usually happened when orders for cartons were not in sufficient volume to keep the board mill working at capacity. On these occasions the company took orders for paperboard at prices below full cost in order to keep the board mill busy. Such contribution pricing was not used often, however.

Reports

Each month an income statement was prepared (Exhibit 4). It was constructed to focus on the performance of the two profit centers. Also, a spending report was prepared for each of the 15

expense centers in the carton factory. An example is given in Exhibit 5.

In addition, Mr. Stewart received a variety of other reports on a regular basis. The *internally generated* reports were as follows:

1. Balance sheet, monthly.
2. Selling, general and administrative statement, monthly.
3. Overdue accounts receivable, monthly.
4. Overdue shipments, monthly.
5. Inventory size, monthly.
6. Raw materials shrinkage report, monthly.
7. Cash and securities listing, monthly.
8. Actual sales, weekly, with a monthly comparison of actual and budgeted sales.
9. Carton factory production, monthly. This included operating hours statistics and efficiency percentages.
10. Outstanding orders (backlog), weekly.
11. Machine production report, daily.
12. Quality control report, monthly.

Mr. Stewart examined the reports illustrated in Exhibits 4 and 5 carefully. If there were important departures from plan, he discussed them with the manager responsible. Other reports were prepared primarily for the use of some other executive, and Mr. Stewart received only an information copy. He might or might not glance at these reports in a given month, but he was certain to do so if he suspected that trouble might be brewing in the area covered by the report.

Mr. Stewart also paid close attention to several *external* reports he received regularly from the industry trade association. They showed current economic trends, the probable effects of these trends on different segments of the paperboard carton industry, and sales orders, actual sales, production volume, and other related statistics for all members of the association.

---

[1]Many of the abbreviations and terms in this form are peculiar to the company. The purpose of Exhibit 3 is only to illustrate the form used in preparing a price estimate. An understanding of its details is not necessary.

EXHIBIT 3 Price Estimate

Preparatory Cost	Production	Rate	Unit	Material Cost		Mfg. Cost	
	per hours						
	F. or E.						
Original Plates	F. or E.						
Electros 9 3/4 * 9 1/4		30.30	28	848	40		
Wood				25	58		
Rule				54	54		
Composing							
Die Making	③	7.76	41.8			324	37
Make-Ready-Ptg.	2X	20.48	30.0			614	40
Make-Ready-C. & C.	11.55	18.00	15.8			284	40
Total Preparatory Cost				928	52	1223	17
Quantity Cost							
Board 65,005 (3 3/4)	171.00 + 25			8892	69		
Board				40	00		
Ink				177	60		
Ink				526	32		
Cases Corrugated	700	.48	1429	685	92		
Cellulose Material							
Board, Storage & Handling		2.99				97	25
Cutting Stock							
Printing		36.32	66				
Cut and Cease						1300	94
Stripping	.933 – 4	.285 +	120			626	56
Cellulose							
Auto Gluing		.899	.466 +	17	98	763	58
Hand Gluing							
Wrapping or Packing		10.405				148	69
Inspection							
Total Quantity Cost				10,322	53	2,937	02
Total Preparatory Cost				928	52	1,223	17
Total Cost to Make				11,251	05	4,160	19
Selling & Administration		45 + 8	(% + $)			1,880	09
Material Forward						11,251	05
Shipping 56 +		11.60 +	260,287			352	86
Freight and Cartage		.64				385	84
Total Cost						18,030	03
Profit		20%				3,606	00
Total Selling Price						21,636	03
Finished Stock Price							
Commission & Discount		4%				865	44
Total Selling Price						22,501	48
Selling Price per M-Calculated						45	00
Selling Price per M-Quoted						49	00

EXHIBIT 4 Stewart Box Company
Income Statement ($000 omitted)

	December 1993		12 Months 1993	
	Actual	*Variance**	*Actual*	*Variance**
Board Mill				
External sales	$ 83	$ 19	$ 550	$ 61
Transfers to carton factory	269	26	3,152	208
Total revenues	352	45	3,702	269
Cost of goods sold	270	(26)	2,929	(247)
Gross margin	82	19	773	22
Volume variance		24		54
Other variances		(21)		(22)
Selling and administrative expenses	48	(6)	598	(10)
Board mill profit	34	16	175	44
Carton Factory				
Sales	1066	35	12,749	397
Standard cost of goods sold	787	(29)	9,063	(208)
Gross margin	279	6	3,686	189
Manufacturing variances		26		64
Selling expenses	80	(8)	883	(19)
Administrative expenses	19	2	229	11
Carton factory profit	180	26	2,574	245
Company				
Total factory and mill profits	214	42	2,749	289
Corporate expenses	83	3	731	29
Nonoperating income (loss)	(6)		(19)	3
Income before income tax	125	45	1,999	321
Income tax	43	(14)	(680)	(104)
	82	31	1,319	217

*( ) = unfavorable.

EXHIBIT 5 Spending Report, Department 14 (two-color Miehle printing presses)

	December 1993		12 Months 1993	
	Actual	*Variance**	*Actual*	*Variance**
Labor—pressmen	$ 9,416	$ (171)	$129,691	$(1,035)
Labor—helpers	3,318	(74)	46,365	(376)
Press supplies	597	192	5,246	234
Repairs	2,355	(966)	13,699	192
Power	774	106	10,190	515
Other controllable overhead	387	83	5,510	738
Total controllable costs	16,847	(830)	210,701	268
Departmental fixed cost	3,882	—	46,579	—
Allocated costs	5,363	—	64,358	—
Total costs	$26,092	—	$321,638	—
Volume variance		(544)		1,619
Total variance		($1,374)		$ 1,887

*( ) = unfavorable.

Questions

1. The following questions relate to Exhibit 4 and the December 1993 amounts:
   a. A transfer price was used in connection with two items. What are these two items?
   b. Assuming that inventory levels did not vary in December, what was the actual cost of goods manufactured in the carton factory?
   c. Why is the assumption in question *b* necessary to answer that question?
   d. What is the budgeted amount of corporate expenses?
   e. In December was activity in the board mill above or below the standard volume?
2. The following questions relate to Exhibit 5 and the December amounts:
   a. What was the actual cost of labor—pressmen?
   b. What was the budgeted amount of total controllable cost?
   c. What amount of total controllable cost was applied to products?
   d. Why do no amounts appear in the spending variance column for departmental fixed costs and allocated costs?
3. As his assistant, write a memorandum calling Mr. Stewart's attention to matters you think he should note when he reads Exhibit 4.
4. Do the same with Exhibit 5.
5. What do you regard as the particularly strong points of the system described in this case? What are its weak points? Can you suggest ways of overcoming these weaknesses?

Case 1–4
Xerox Corporation (A)

Al Senter, after 25 years with Xerox, reached the top of his profession in 1990—Vice President of Finance. A director said, "In many ways Al is the product of the Xerox society, self-confident and outspoken. He is vocal about the proactive role the Xerox financial people must play to make the new company culture work. Al firmly believes in the active participation of the business controllers in decision making." Al remembered the analytical era of the 1970s where accuracy and rigid systems were more important than listening to the customer. The controllers were the numbers people, and there was never enough data or analysis. During this era some good people left the company, and Xerox faced new competitors in the battle for market share. The company, however, changed with the quality cultural revolution of the 1980s. One never satisfied to harvest history, Al had a new agenda which continues and enhances the work started during the previous decade. According to Al,

> The control function must add value to the products by working with line management. We need to actively participate with management in making better decisions. The only way we can do this is to have open communication, top-flight and well-trained people, and to be on the cutting edge of information technology. Finance has to partner with marketing and technology and make clear the value we add. If we can't add value, then we don't belong at Xerox. Our financial team is pretty darn good. We trust each other, and the FEC (Financial Executive Council) is highly respected throughout the company. I keep looking at world-class financial organizations for ideas, and the more I look, the more I

appreciate what we have at Xerox. We know, of course, that there are areas where we can improve, and we are addressing them.

Company Background

Xerox, the document company, was a multinational corporation serving the global document-processing and financial services markets. They developed, manufactured, and marketed copiers and duplicators, facsimile products, scanners, workstations, computer software, supplies, and other related equipment in over 130 countries. Their financial services operations included insurance, equipment financing, investments, and investment banking. This case focuses on the document-processing activities of the company.

Xerox was one of the outstanding business success stories in the world. From 1946 to 1973, their annual sales growth exceeded 25 percent, while the annual growth of earnings exceeded 35 percent. This amazing record was due to the dominant position Xerox created in the plain paper copier business. In 1959 the company introduced the revolutionary 914 plain paper copier. This generation of equipment motivated the explosion in the copying business from 20 million copies made annually in 1957 to 9.5 billion copies made annually in 1965.[1] In 1990, the world copy business was over 900 billion copies.

The original patent for the plain paper copier expired in 1970, sending an invitation to potential competitors. In the next decade US firms (IBM and Kodak) and Japanese firms (Canon, Minolta, and others) entered the large and small copy machine industry. Exhibit 1 pro-

---

This case was prepared by Lawrence P. Carr, Associate Professor at Babson College. Copyright © by Lawrence Carr.

[1]These data and other pertinent information are contained in the story of the Xerox revitalization. See Gary Jacobson and John Hillkirk, *Xerox: American Samurai* (New York: Macmillan, 1986).

EXHIBIT 1   **Financial Highlights of Xerox Corporation**
(dollars in millions, except per share and employee data)

	1991	1990	1989	1980	1970	1960
Revenue						
Document Processing	13,819	13,583	12,431	8,037	1,690	40
Total Xerox	17,830	17,973	17,229	8,037	1,690	40
Net income						
Document Processing	537	549	488	553	192	3
Total Xerox	454	243	704	565	192	3
Financial position (Total Xerox)						
Current assets	21,766	20,178	18,253	3,515	842	15
Total assets	31,658	31,635	30,088	7,514	1,929	56
Long-term debt	6,247	7,149	7,511	898	382	5
Shareholders' equity	5,140	5,051	5,035	3,630	918	29
Net income per common share	$3.86	$1.66	$6.41	$6.69	$2.33	$0.13
Dividend per common share	$3.00	$3.00	$3.00	$2.80	$0.65	$0.05
Employees at year-end (Document Processing)	100,900	99,000	99,000	117,247	59,267	2,973

vides the Xerox corporate financial highlights for the past three decades.

During this rapid growth period, Xerox built its worldwide business network. Joe Wilson, the legendary chairman and creator of the name Xerox, decided to grow the company as rapidly as possible.[2] The company sought foreign partners who offered immediate entry into overseas markets. The swift growth, proprietary technology and sales methods (leasing contracts rather than equipment sales) required local people familiar with the culture and market. In 1956 Xerox entered into a 50/50 joint venture with the Rank Organization PLC, forming Rank Xerox Limited. This gave Xerox market access to Europe, Africa, and the Middle East. In 1962 Xerox formed a partnership with Fuji Photo Film Company in Japan to create Fuji Xerox. This gave Xerox access to Japan and Asia. At the same time, separate arrangements were made with the South and Central American countries. Their ownership structure varied based on the country and the local partner.

In the early 70s, Xerox was more concerned with a US government antitrust suit than with the market entry of domestic and foreign competition. Only at the end of the decade did they recognize the serious competitive problem. The growth, income, and balance sheet strength of Xerox were impressive, attracting more investors who were pleased with the financial performance. Xerox operating managers, however, began to feel the competitive pressure. Between 1970 and 1980, Xerox's market share, as measured by US copier revenues, fell from 96 percent to 45 percent. The Japanese attacked the low and medium range of the copier market, while the domestic competitors made inroads in the high-end equipment market. To further frustrate Xerox management, the Japanese firms were selling their equipment at Xerox's manufacturing cost.

David Kearns became chairman in 1982, and was well aware of the significant market share

---

[2]Jacobson and Hillkirk, *Xerox,* p. 63.

EXHIBIT 2   Excerpts from the Xerox Training Literature

The Xerox Quality Strategy— "Leadership through Quality"

- The fundamental principle of this quality strategy is meeting customer requirements.
- The definition of quality is meeting the customer's requirements all of the time.
- The program started with a vision at the top. Senior management drives the program. However, employee involvement is absolutely key. It is the people who do the work, and they know how to do it best. Training and sharing of information are critical to the LTQ implementation.
- Quality is a strategic tool used to improve competitiveness and organizational effectiveness. The focus is on the processes as well as products.
- Quality is a long-term process requiring continuous improvement and management patience.
- Three major components of LTQ are:

1. Employee Involvement (EI): Problem-solving process using quality circles, people empowerment, Ishikawa's fish bone chart, and other tools to understand cause and effect of problems.
2. Competitive Benchmarking: Establish standards for comparing internal performance.

Implement the best practices learned to improve performance.

3. The Quality Improvement Process: Review and continually improve all internal processes by following a process which focuses on meeting customer requirements.

- Leadership through quality is a fully integrated business process.

Competitive Benchmarking

- The continuous process of measuring Xerox's products, services, and business practices against the toughest competitors or those companies renowned as the leaders.
- The goal is superiority in all areas—quality, product reliability, and cost.
- Benchmarking is a learning experience where the best practices are observed and measured to create targets for future achievement.
- It is part of the total quality leadership program requiring employee involvement and is linked to each operating unit's business plan and strategy.
- It requires the integration of competitive information, practices, and performance into decisionmaking and communication functions at all levels of the business.

---

losses. The competition was formidable since they were financially strong, technologically advanced, and enjoyed excellent customer relations. Xerox developed a corporate revitalization plan called "Leadership through Quality." It was built upon the early work in competitive benchmarking and employee involvement. Exhibit 2 outlines the central features of these programs, which served as the cornerstone of the new Xerox culture. In addition, Xerox senior managers started to improve the cumbersome management process. The corporate reporting and planning process was very long and

bureaucratic, with more detail than most managers could absorb. Even worse, the reporting formats were not even consistent between divisions. Xerox improved its management information system and standardized reporting formats to address many of these problems.

Kearns passed the leadership of Xerox to Paul Allaire in 1991, having achieved a company turnaround in the 80s. His strategy changed the culture of Xerox and gave it the competitive muscle to regain market share and make improvements in the company operations. The 1990 annual report reflects some of their success.

Document Processing achieved the following demonstrable results:

- Customer satisfaction levels increased in every market served by the company.
- Revenues rose by 9 percent to a record $13.6 billion.
- Profits increased by 23 percent to $599 million.
- Return on assets improved by over 2 points to 14.6 percent.
- $1.1 billion in cash was generated.[3]

Organization

The emphasis was on 9 business divisions, supported by 3 geographic customer operations divisions. These 12 units were organized under three operation families. The primary focus for the management of Xerox was the business management level, which promoted more effective linkages between markets and technologies. These divisions had end-to-end responsibility for satisfying the customer. They were ". . . responsible for Xerox offerings—research and technology, development, manufacturing, marketing, sales, service, administration all work together seamlessly to 'put it together' better and faster for the customers . . ."[4]

The Finance and Control Function

The central focal point for the finance function at Xerox was the Financial Executive Council (FEC). The membership consisted of the senior Corporate Finance staff and the chief financial officers from the major Xerox operating organizations. The FEC evolved in the 1980s in response to the senior financial managers' goal of further improving the finance operations and obtaining a greater involvement by the Finance executives. According to Al, ". . . they felt financial managers (controllers) could contribute in the formulation of management decisions at the operating units. The move was basically from an accounting policy group to a group which added more value to the management process. In the spirit of Leadership through Quality, the financial practices required streamlining and major revision. The FEC set the course for becoming a world-class financial operation based on their benchmark studies."

Note, the FEC evolved in parallel with the start of the LTQ and Benchmarking activities. The new Xerox LTQ culture demanded an involved and proactive finance group. The key to the value added concept was in helping line managers make more enlightened business decisions. In addition, the FEC was the central developer of the company's financial human resource talent. Executive management recognized the strength and talent of the FEC and regularly used them as a sounding board for policy and strategic considerations.

The FEC actively promoted the building of trust in the Xerox finance community. They typically met once a quarter for 2 days and discussed a wide range of financial and business matters with a structured but informal atmosphere. Many of the members had been on the FEC for 10 years. They knew one another very well, and freely expressed their ideas and opinions. This group engineered the finance and accounting changes in Xerox as the organization and business practices changed drastically in the 1980s. Raghunandan Sachdev ("Sach"), corporate controller and one of the FEC founding members, made the following comment, "It is not clear how the FEC evolved, but Finance needed to stop second-guessing line managers. We had a choice either to become glorified auditors or to get involved in decisions early and become part of the management process. We knew we could add value to the process and provide managers with valuable analysis and advice. Today the general managers listen to their finance people, use them as sounding boards and have a very close working relationship."

---

[3]*Xerox 1990,* Annual Report.
[4]*Xerox 2000: Putting It Together,* a company document describing the organizational changes made in 1992.

Financial Organization. The 12 business unit controllers in the document processing organization reported directly (solid line) to the general manager of their respective business unit. They had a dotted line relationship to corporate finance for their fiduciary roles, financial reporting, and professional development. The document processing financial organization of Xerox was a modified matrix, multinational organization with the business unit controller having both solid and dotted line reporting responsibility. The Business divisions, with responsibility for product development and manufacturing, managed their business throughout the world. The Customer Operations divisions were organized geographically and managed customer relationships. The management control system concentrated on the responsibility and performance of the 12 business divisions.

There were numerous subunits, such as manufacturing facilities, distribution and service centers, and sales offices, within each business division. Each business unit had its own organization whereby the subunit controller reported directly to his or her general manager and dotted line to the division controller. The following summarizes the global document processing operational organization.

Business Divisions. As outlined above, the Business divisions were responsible for the overall management of their product business areas worldwide.

US Customer Operations. US Customer Operations provided sales, service, and customer administration support to the United States as contracted with the Business divisions. They purchased document processing and related equipment from the 9 business divisions.

Rank Xerox Limited. They were a 51/49 percent joint venture with the Rank organization when Xerox acquired the majority share in 1969 and operated the company. Rank Xerox marketed and serviced document processing and related equipment in Europe, Africa, and parts of Asia for the Business divisions. The Rank Xerox legal entity also contained manufacturing facilities in Europe. For example, in Holland, they had an extensive sales organization as well as a major production facility that supplied equipment for many other countries including the United States. In this case, the Venray plant results legally were consolidated with the Rank Xerox results. For performance purposes, the plant provided product to the Business division. Thus, the plant controller was at the intersection of the performance organization matrix. He reported dotted line to the Rank Xerox CFO and solid line to the plant general manager. The plant general manager reported directly to the Office Document Products Business Division CEO with a dotted line to the Rank Xerox Business Division CEO.

Americas Customer Operations. This group marketed and serviced document processing products for the Business divisions in Canada, South and Central America, China, and Hong Kong. Some of the South and Central American operations were joint ventures with local companies. In these instances Xerox maintained a majority share and management responsibility.

Fuji Xerox. This was a 50/50 joint venture with Fuji Film Corporation of Japan. They developed, manufactured, marketed, and serviced Fuji Xerox document processing products in Japan and other territories in the Pacific Rim. They functioned as an independent Japanese corporation, buying and selling to other Xerox divisions.

Development & Manufacturing. In 1992 the functions of this organization (to develop and manufacture Xerox document processing products, including copiers, duplicators, electronic printers, facsimiles products, scanners, computer software, and supplies) were integrated into the 9 business divisions wherever possible. A core Corporate Strategic Services organization provided contracted support to the divisions. In general, if the development or manufacturing facility produced at least 90 percent of their output for a specific business, they were placed in that business group. If these facilities supported multiple business groups, they were placed in the Corporate Strategic Services group.

For external financial reporting purposes, Xerox followed the legal organizational structure. For example, Fuji Xerox was an affiliated company, and Xerox only reported the results of the equity investment in Fuji Xerox. In the Venray example above, they consolidated the factory results with the Rank Xerox results. Xerox incorporated the Rank Xerox (a majority-owned subsidiary) results with the total company through consolidation. For performance measurement, Venray results were reported through their Business divisions. The operational management accounting reports, or performance reporting, focused on Business division results. Management wanted to match accountability and responsibility by operating unit within a business area. Both the financial and management control reporting systems functioned in parallel. A former foreign business unit controller said, "We have to focus on our key objectives and deliver the planned results. This requires we manage our local environment, which may not cooperate with the original plan."

Management Control.   The measurement system began with the planning process. Each operating unit within a Business division or Customer Operations division developed its annual and long-range plans. These plans were consolidated into the Business and Customer Operations division plans. This was a common business practice, with reviews and feedback sessions as the planning process cycled through the organization. The overriding principle was that the division general managers were responsible for managing and controlling their environments to deliver the committed results.

With Leadership through Quality (which included competitive benchmarking), manage-ment utilized operational measures, such as market share, customer satisfaction, and various quality statistics, as a major part of their measurement scheme. These data augmented the traditional financial-based performance measures, such as return on investment. Competitive benchmarking provided standards of world class performance, and managers were expected to improve, over time, to these levels. Operating units set targets (number of machine installs per machine type, number of customers per territory, on-time delivery rates, service response time levels, customer satisfaction ratings, etc.) for achievement. John McGinty, vice president of control, explains, "We learned that activities of a business cause the numbers to happen. Also, we need to get a better notion of time and be able to put an equivalent dollar on time. These quality-related concepts help provide the control framework process of predictive deliverables."

Measurements were a combination of financial and operational targets. Return on assets and a set of operational statistics, based on the critical success factors of the business unit, were the measures. Each operating unit had a set of custom-designed targets. Management linked growth and profit measures to the unit's business economy with operational measures linked to world-class benchmarking performance.

Reporting.   Until 1987 the monthly reporting process included a complete financial package. Reports were due on a very tight time schedule, with full reporting to be complete on the fourth work day. Operating activity statistics, added to the schedule in 1987, were readily available at month's end and did not have to wait for the accounting close. The FEC discussed the time and costs versus the information value of global monthly financial results. They determined that monthly financial results in full detail from all the units were not necessary. Units now reported specific, but limited, data (consisting of sales, profits, and key operational statistics) on a monthly basis. For corporate reporting, only a quarterly full financial close of the books was necessary. The value of information had not changed, but there was a significant reduction in the number of indirect people involved in the process. The individual operations continued to produce the data needed to manage their respective business, but with a decrease in corporate reporting requirements.

An informal reporting system had also evolved. Open and honest communication reinforced the controller's dotted line connection to corporate. For example, Sach talked to all of his dotted line associates at least once a week to understand the direction their businesses were taking in the current quarter and the full year. These talks were informative and centered around problems and business risks. The FEC maintained a standard of "no surprises" and promoted trust among the controllers. The unit controllers knew both the financial and operational matters of their business unit. This was the result of the partnering with line management. The informal network was not a hammer but rather an open discussion of issues. Naturally the informal channel of reporting complemented the formal channel.

Questions

1. Outline the management control system at Xerox. What are the key elements that make the system work?
2. What recent trends at Xerox do you see influencing the management control process?
3. In your opinion, how important are organizational culture and individual personalities in the Xerox control process?

THE MANAGEMENT CONTROL ENVIRONMENT

In Chapter 1 we defined management control as the process by which managers influence other members of the organization to implement the organization's strategies. This process relates to two different types of activities: ongoing operations; and discrete projects. In Part I and Part II we discuss the management control of ongoing operations. The management control of discrete projects (e.g., research and development projects, construction projects, the production of a motion picture) is described in Chapter 15.

In Chapter 2 we discuss the broad area of behavior in organizations: goal congruence, the multiple stakeholder approach, formal and informal management systems, organization structure, and the controller function.

In the next four chapters, we discuss responsibility centers, which are the organization units that are central to the management control process. A *responsibility center* is an organization unit headed by a manager who is responsible for its activities.

In Chapter 3, we discuss the characteristics of a responsibility center. All responsibility centers produce outputs (i.e., they do something), and all have inputs (i.e., they use resources). They fall into four categories, based on the measurements used to report the inputs and outputs of their operations. These categories are: (1) revenue centers, (2) expense centers, (3) profit centers, and (4) investment centers.

In *revenue centers,* which are typically found in a company's marketing operation, the management control system measures output in monetary terms. Revenue centers are discussed in Chapter 3.

In *expense centers* the opposite is the case; the system measures input (i.e., costs) in monetary terms. Expense centers are also discussed in Chapter 3.

In *profit centers* the system tracks both inputs and outputs in monetary terms; inputs consist of expenses, and outputs consist of revenues. Profit is the difference between them. Profit centers are discussed in Chapter 4.

Many profit centers transfer products (both goods and services) to other profit centers within the company. The value of these transferred products is called a *transfer price*. Chapter 5 describes how this value is determined and other aspects of transfer pricing.

In *investment centers* the control system applies monetary measures to both inputs and outputs and to the investment used within the responsibility center itself. We discuss investment centers in Chapter 6 and describe some of the organizational considerations involved in deciding whether a responsibility center should, or should not, be treated as an investment center.

Chapters 3 through 6 describe the considerations involved in assigning *financial responsibility* to responsibility centers. The choice of a financial metric depends on the behavior expected from subordinates relative to the organization's strategies. The managers of cost centers emphasize cost control; the managers of revenue centers focus on generating revenues; the managers of profit centers direct their actions toward improving profits; and the managers of investment centers look to enhancing profits in relation to the assets employed. In Chapter 10 we will describe the *balanced scorecard,* which blends financial measures with nonfinancial measures, as a tool for strategy execution.

BEHAVIOR IN ORGANIZATIONS

Management control systems influence human behavior. *Good* management control systems influence behavior in a goal congruent manner; that is, they ensure that individual actions taken to achieve personal goals also help to achieve the organization's goals.

We begin this chapter by describing some typical organizational goals. We then expand the concept of goal congruence, describing how it is affected both by informal actions and by formal systems. The formal systems can be divided into two categories: "rules," broadly defined; and systematic methods for planning and for maintaining control.

Different structures are used to implement strategies in various types of organizations; an effective management control system should be designed to fit the particular structure.

In the final section of the chapter, we describe the role of the controller—the person responsible for the design and operation of the management control system.

Goals

Although we often refer to the goals of a corporation, a corporation does not have goals; it is an artificial being with no mind or decision-making ability of its own. Corporate goals are determined by the chief executive officer (CEO) of the corporation, with the advice of other members of senior management; and they are usually ratified by the board of directors. In many corporations, the goals originally set by the founder persist for generations. Examples are Henry Ford, Ford Motor Company; Alfred P. Sloan, General Motors Corporation; Walt Disney, Walt Disney Company; George Eastman, Eastman Kodak; and Sam Walton, Wal-Mart.

Profitability

In a business, profitability is usually the most important goal. Profitability is expressed, in the broadest and most conceptually sound sense, by an equation that is the product of two ratios:

$$\frac{\text{Revenues} - \text{Expenses}}{\text{Revenues}} * \frac{\text{Revenues}}{\text{Investment}} = \text{Return on investment}$$

An example is:

$$\frac{\$10,000 - \$9,500}{\$10,000} * \frac{\$10,000}{\$4,000} = 12.5\%$$

The first ratio in this equation is the *profit margin percentage:*

$$(\$10,000 - \$9,500) / \$10,000 = 5\%$$

The second ratio is the *investment turnover:*

$$\$10,000 / \$4,000 = 2.5 \text{ times}$$

The product of these two ratios is the *return on investment:* 5% * 2.5 times = 12.5%. Return on investment can be found by simply dividing profit (i.e., revenues minus expenses) by investment; but this method does not draw attention to the two principal components: profit margin and investment turnover.

In the basic form of this equation, "investment" refers to the shareholders' investment, which consists of proceeds from the issuance of stock, plus retained earnings. One of management's responsibilities is to arrive at the right balance between the two main sources of financing: debt and equity. The shareholders' investment (i.e., equity) is the amount of financing that was not obtained by debt, that is, by borrowing. For many purposes, the source of financing is not relevant; "investment" thus means the total of debt capital and equity capital.

"Profitability" refers to profits in the long run, rather than in the current quarter or year. Many current expenditures (e.g., amounts spent on advertising or research and development) reduce current profits but increase profits over time.

Some CEOs stress only part of the profitability equation. Jack Welch, CEO of General Electric Company, explicitly focused on revenue; he stated that General Electric should not be in any business in which its sales revenues were not the largest or the second largest of any company in that business. This does not imply that Welch neglected the other components of the equation; rather it suggests that in his mind there was a close correlation between market share and return on investment.

Other CEOs, however, emphasize revenues for a different reason: because for them company size is a goal. Such a priority can lead to problems. If expenses are too high, the profit margin will not give shareholders a good return on their investment. Even if the profit margin is satisfactory, the organization may still not earn a good return if the investment is too large.

Some CEOs focus on profit either as a monetary amount or as a percentage of revenue. This focus does not recognize the simple fact that if additional profits are obtained by a greater-than-proportional increase in investment, each dollar of investment has earned less.

Maximizing Shareholder Value

In the 1980s and 1990s the term "shareholder value" appeared frequently in the business literature. This concept is that the appropriate goal of a for-profit corporation is to maximize shareholder value. Although the meaning of this term was not always clear, it probably refers to the market price of the corporation's stock. We believe, however, that achieving *satisfactory profit* is a better way of stating a corporation's goal, for two reasons.[1]

First, "maximizing" implies that there is a way of finding the maximum amount that a company can earn. This is not the case. In deciding between two courses of action, management usually selects the one it believes will increase profitability the most. But management rarely, if ever, identifies all the possible alternatives and their respective effects on profitability. Furthermore, profit maximization requires that marginal costs and a demand curve be calculated, and managers usually do not know what these are. If maximization were the goal, managers would spend every working hour (and many sleepless nights) thinking about endless alternatives for increasing profitability; life is generally considered to be too short to warrant such an effort.

Second, although optimizing shareholder value may be a major goal, it is by no means the only goal for most organizations. Certainly a business that does not earn a profit at least equal to its cost of capital is not doing its job; unless it does so, it cannot discharge any other responsibilities. But economic performance is *not* the *sole* responsibility of a business, nor is shareholder value. Most managers want to behave ethically, and most feel an obligation to other stakeholders in the organization in addition to shareholders.

> **Example.**   Henry Ford's operating philosophy was *satisfactory profit,* not *maximum profit.* He wrote, "And let me say right here that I do not believe that we should make such an awful profit on our cars. A reasonable profit is right, but not too much. So it has been my policy to force the price of the car down as fast as production would permit, and give the benefits to the users and laborers—with resulting surprisingly enormous benefits to ourselves.[2]

---

[1] In 1957 Herbert Simon coined the term *satisficing* to describe the appropriate goal, a concept that was an important basis for his award of the Nobel Prize for economics. Although later than his original paper on this topic, a convenient source for his analysis is Herbert A. Simon, *The New Science of Management Decision* (Englewood Cliffs, NJ: Prentice Hall, 1977).

[2] Henry Ford, *My Life and Work* (Garden City, NY: Doubleday, Page & Co., 1922), p. 162.

By rejecting the maximization concept, we do not mean to question the validity of certain obvious principles. A course of action that decreases expenses without affecting another element, such as market share, is sound. So is a course of action that increases expenses with a greater-than-proportional increase in revenues, such as expanding the advertising budget. So, too, are actions that increase profit with a less than proportional increase in shareholder investment (or, of course, with no such increase at all), such as purchasing a cost-saving machine. These principles assume, in all cases, that the course of action is ethical and consistent with the corporation's other goals.

Risk

An organization's pursuit of profitability is affected by management's willingness to take risks. The degree of risk-taking varies with the personalities of individual managers. Nevertheless, there is always an upper limit; some organizations explicitly state that management's primary responsibility is to preserve the company's assets, with profitability considered a secondary goal. The Asian financial crisis during 1996–1998 is traceable, in large part, to the fact that banks in Asia's emerging markets made what appeared to be highly profitable loans without paying adequate attention to the level of risk involved.

Multiple Stakeholder Approach

Organizations participate in three markets: the capital market, the product market, and the factor market. A firm raises funds in the *capital market,* and the public stockholders are therefore an important constituency. The firm sells its goods and services in the *product market,* and customers form a key constituency. It competes for resources such as human capital and raw materials in the *factor market,* and the prime constituencies are the company's employees and suppliers and the various communities in which the resources and the company's operations are located.

The firm has a responsibility to all these *multiple stakeholders*—shareholders, customers, employees, suppliers, and communities. Ideally, its management control system should identify the goals for each of these groups and develop scorecards to track performance.

> **Examples.**   In 1996, the Acer Group, headquartered in Taiwan, was one of the largest computer companies in the world, with annual sales in excess of $7 billion. The company subscribed to the multiple stakeholder approach and managed its internal operations to satisfy the needs of several constituencies. To quote Stan Shih, the founder and chairman: "The customer is no. 1, the employee is no. 2, the shareholder is no. 3. I keep this message consistent with all my colleagues. I even consider that the company's banks, suppliers and others we do business with are our stakeholders; even society is a stakeholder. I do my best to run the company that way."[3]

---

[3]"The 'Fast Food' Computer Company: An Interview with Stan Shih," *Strategy & Business,* Fourth Quarter 1996, pp. 52–56.

Lincoln Electric Company is well known for its philosophy that employee satisfaction was more important than shareholder value. James Lincoln wrote: "The last group to be considered is the stockholders who own stock because they think it will be more profitable than investing more in any other way. The absentee stockholder is not of any value to the customer or to the worker, since he has no knowledge of nor interest in the company other than greater dividends and an advance in the price of his stock."[4] Donald F. Hastings, Chairman and Chief Executive Officer, emphasized that this was still the company's philosophy in 1996.[5]

Goal Congruence

Senior management wants the organization to attain the organization's goals. But the individual members of the organization have their own personal goals, and they are not necessarily consistent with those of the organization. The central purpose of a management control system, then, is to ensure (insofar as is feasible) a high level of what is called "goal congruence." *In a goal congruent process, the actions people are led to take in accordance with their perceived self-interest are also in the best interest of the organization.*

Obviously, in our imperfect world, perfect congruence between individual goals and organizational goals does not exist—if for no other reason than that individual participants usually want as much compensation as they can get while the organization maintains that salaries can go only so high without adversely affecting profits.

An adequate control system will at least not encourage individuals to act *against* the best interests of the organization. For example, if the system emphasizes cost reduction and a manager responds by reducing costs at the expense of adequate quality or reduces costs in his or her own unit by imposing a more-than-offsetting increase on another unit, the manager has been motivated, but in the wrong direction.

In evaluating any management control practice, the two most important questions to ask are:

1. What actions does it motivate people to take in their own self-interest?
2. Are these actions in the best interest of the organization?

Informal Factors That Influence Goal Congruence

Both formal systems and informal processes influence human behavior in organizations; consequently, they affect the degree to which goal congruence can be achieved. This book is primarily concerned with formal control systems—strategic plans, budgets, and reports. But it is important for the designers of formal systems to take into account the informal processes, such as work ethic, management style, and culture, because in order to implement

---

[4]James Lincoln, *A New Approach to Industrial Economics* (New York: Devin-Adair Company, 1961), pp. 38–39.

[5]Quoted in J. A. Maciariello, *Lasting Value* (New York: Wiley, 1999), pp. 121–26.

organization strategies effectively the formal mechanisms must be consistent with the informal ones. Therefore, before discussing the formal system, we will describe the informal forces, both internal and external, that play a key role in achieving goal congruence.

External Factors

External factors are norms of desirable behavior that exist in the society of which the organization is a part. These norms include a set of attitudes, often collectively referred to as the *work ethic,* which is manifested in employees' loyalty to the organization, their diligence, their spirit, and their pride in doing a good job (rather than just putting in time). Some of these attitudes are local—that is, specific to the city or region in which the organization does its work. In encouraging companies to locate in their city or state, chambers of commerce and other promotional organizations often claim that their locality has a loyal, diligent work force. Other attitudes and norms are industry-specific. The railroad industry, for example, has norms different from those of the airline industry. Still others are national; some countries, such as Japan and Singapore, have a reputation for excellent work ethics.

> **Example.**   Silicon Valley—a stretch of northern California about 30 miles long and 10 miles wide—is one of the major sources of new business creation and wealth in the American economy. Silicon Valley attracts people with certain common characteristics: an entrepreneurial spirit, a zest for hard work, high ambition, and a preference for informal work settings.

Internal Factors

Culture.   The most important internal factor is the organization's own culture—the common beliefs, shared values, norms of behavior, and assumptions that are implicitly accepted and explicitly manifested throughout the organization. Cultural norms are extremely important since they explain why two organizations, with identical formal management control systems, may vary in terms of actual control.

> **Example.**   Johnson & Johnson (J&J) has a strong corporate culture, as exemplified by the company's credo (see Box 2–1). One cannot fully understand the effect of J&J's formal control systems without considering the influence of their credo on the behavior of its employees. This was demonstrated during the Tylenol crisis in 1982. After taking poisoned Tylenol capsules, seven people died. J&J withdrew *all* Tylenol capsules from the US market, even though all the poisoned capsules were sold in Chicago, the tampering occurred outside J&J premises, and the individual responsible was not a J&J employee. The company also undertook a massive publicity campaign to inform health professionals and the public of the steps it was taking to prevent such tampering in the future. Altogether, J&J spent over $100 million in response to the Tylenol crisis. Company employees maintain that their actions during the crisis stemmed from their strong belief in the company's

Box 2–1

OUR CREDO

Johnson & Johnson

We believe our first responsibility is to the doctors, nurses and patients,
to mothers and all others who use our products and services.
In meeting their needs everything we do must be of high quality.
We must constantly strive to reduce our costs
in order to maintain reasonable prices.
Customers' orders must be serviced promptly and accurately.
Our suppliers and distributors must have an opportunity
to make a fair profit.

We are responsible to our employees,
the men and women who work with us throughout the world.
Everyone must be considered as an individual.
We must respect their dignity and recognize their merit.
They must have a sense of security in their jobs.
Compensation must be fair and adequate,
and working conditions clean, orderly and safe.
Employees must feel free to make suggestions and complaints.
There must be equal opportunity for employment, development
and advancement for those qualified.
We must provide competent management,
and their actions must be just and ethical.

We are responsible to the communities in which we live and work
and the world community as well.
We must be good citizens—support good works and charities
and bear our fair share of taxes.
We must encourage civic improvements and better health and education.
We must maintain in good order
the property we are privileged to use,
protecting the environment and natural resources.

Our final responsibility is to our stockholders.
Business must make a sound profit.
We must experiment with new ideas.
Research must be carried on, innovative programs developed
and mistakes paid for.
New equipment must be purchased, new facilities provided
and new products launched.
Reserves must be created to provide for adverse times.
When we operate according to these principles,
the stockholders should realize a fair return.

Source: "Johnson & Johnson (A)," case prepared by Francis J. Aguilar, Harvard Business School, case 384-053.

credo, which underscores the responsibility of the company to the public regardless of any potentially negative impact on short-term profits.[6]

A company's culture usually exists unchanged for many years. Certain practices become rituals, carried on almost automatically because "this is the way things are done here." Others are taboo ("we just don't do that here"), although no one may remember why. Organizational culture is also influenced strongly by the personality and policies of the CEO, and by those of lower-level managers with respect to the areas they control. If the organization is unionized, the rules and norms accepted by the union also have a major influence on the organization's culture. Attempts to change practices almost always meet with resistance, and the larger and more mature the organization, the greater the resistance is.

Management Style.   The internal factor that probably has the strongest impact on management control is management style. Usually, subordinates' attitudes reflect what they perceive their superiors' attitudes to be, and their superiors' attitudes ultimately stem from the CEO. (This is another way of saying, "an institution is the lengthened shadow of a man.")[7]

Managers come in all shapes and sizes. Some are charismatic and outgoing; others are less ebullient. Some spend much time looking and talking to people ("management by walking around"); others rely more heavily on written reports.

> **Example.**   When Reginald Jones was appointed CEO of General Electric in the early 1970s, the company was a large, multi-industry company that performed fairly well in a number of mature markets. But the company did have its problems: a price-fixing scandal that sent several executives to jail, coupled with GE's sound defeat in, and subsequent retreat from, the mainframe computer business. Jones's management style was well suited to bringing more discipline to the company. Jones was formal, dignified, refined, bright, and both willing and able to delegate enormous amounts of authority. He instituted formal strategy planning and built up one of the first strategic planning units in a major corporation.[8]
>
> When Jones retired in 1980, the GE Board deliberately selected Jack Welch, a man with a very different management style, to succeed him. Welch was outspoken, impatient, informal, an entrepreneur. These qualities were well suited to the growth era of the 80s and the 90s. Actions taken by Welch between 1981 and 1999—mega-acquisitions, a shift from manufacturing to services, rapid globalization into Europe and Asia, the implementation of concepts such as workout and six sigma quality, integration of the Internet into all of GE's businesses—put General Electric on a solid growth trajectory.[9] During that period, GE's sales

---

[6]"Johnson & Johnson (A)," case prepared by Professor Francis J. Aguilar, Harvard Business School, case 384-053.

[7]Ralph Waldo Emerson, *Self-Reliance* (1841).

[8]Robert E. Lamb, "CEOs for This Season," *Across the Board,* April 1987, pp. 34–41.

[9]Thomas A. Stewart, "See Jack Run Europe," *Fortune,* September 27, 1999, pp. 124–36.

increased four-fold, from $27 billion in 1981 to $101 billion in 1998, and profits increased six-fold, from $1.6 billion in 1981 to $9.2 billion in 1998. GE's stock price rose by 3,100 percent from $4.20 in March 1981 to $133.75 by November 1999—triple the S&P 500's increase during the same period.

The Informal Organization.   The lines on an organization chart depict the formal relationships—that is, the official authority and responsibilities—of each manager. The chart may show, for example, that the production manager of Division A reports to the general manager of Division A. But in the course of fulfilling his or her responsibilities, the production manager of Division A actually communicates with many other people in the organization as well with other managers, support units, the headquarters staff, and people who are simply friends and acquaintances. In extreme situations, the production manager, with all these other communication sources available, may not pay adequate attention to messages received from the general manager; this is especially likely to occur when the production manager is evaluated on production efficiency rather than on overall performance. The realities of the management control process cannot be understood without recognizing the importance of the relationships that constitute the informal organization.

Perception and Communication.   In working toward the goals of the organization, operating managers must know what these goals are and what actions they are supposed to take in order to achieve them. They receive this information through various channels, both formal (e.g., budgets and other official documents) and informal (e.g., conversations). Despite this range of channels, it is not always clear what senior management wants done. An organization is a complicated entity, and the actions that should be taken by any one part to further the common goals cannot be stated with absolute clarity even in the best of circumstances.

Moreover, the messages received from different sources may conflict with one another, or be subject to differing interpretations. For example, the budget mechanism may convey the impression that managers are supposed to aim for the highest profits possible in a given year, whereas senior management does not actually want them to skimp on maintenance or employee training since such actions, although increasing current profits, might reduce future profitability. The information operating managers receive as to what they are supposed to do is vastly less clear than the information the furnace receives from the thermostat in the simple system described in Chapter 1.

The Formal Control System

The informal factors discussed above have a major influence on the effectiveness of an organization's management control. The other major influence is the formal systems. These systems can be classified into two types: (1) the management control system itself, which is the central subject of this book; and (2) rules, which are described in this section.

Rules

We use the word *rules* as shorthand for all types of formal instructions and controls, including: standing instructions, job descriptions, standard operating procedures, manuals, and ethical guidelines. Rules range from the most trivial (e.g., paper clips will be issued only on the basis of a signed requisition) to the most important (e.g., capital expenditures of over $5 million must be approved by the board of directors).[10] Unlike the directives implicit in budget numbers, which may change from month to month, most rules are in force indefinitely; that is, they exist until they are modified, which happens infrequently.

Some rules are guides; that is, organization members are permitted, and indeed expected, to depart from them, either under specified circumstances or when their own best judgment indicates that a departure would be in the best interests of the organization. For example, even though a rule specifies the criteria for extending credit to customers, the credit manager may approve credit for a customer who does not currently meet these criteria, but who has been valuable to the company in the past and is likely to become so again. Such departures may require the approval of higher authority, however.

Some rules are positive requirements that certain actions be taken (e.g., fire drills at prescribed intervals). Others are prohibitions against unethical, illegal, or other undesirable actions. Finally, there are rules that should never be broken under any circumstances: a rule prohibiting the payment of bribes, for example, or a rule that airline pilots must never take off without permission from the air traffic controller.

Some specific types of rules are listed below.

Physical Controls.   Security guards, locked storerooms, vaults, computer passwords, television surveillance, and other physical controls may be part of the control structure.

Manuals.   Much judgment is involved in deciding which rules should be written into a manual, which should be considered to be guidelines rather than fiats, how much discretion should be allowed, and a host of other considerations. Manuals in bureaucratic organizations are more detailed than are those in other organizations; large organizations have more manuals and rules than small ones; centralized organizations have more than decentralized ones; and organizations with geographically dispersed units performing similar functions (such as fast-food restaurant chains) have more than do single-site organizations.

With the passage of time, some rules become outdated. Manuals and other sets of rules should therefore be reexamined periodically to ensure that they are still consistent with the wishes of current senior management.

---

[10]For a thorough treatment of this topic, see Kenneth A. Merchant, *Control in Business Organizations* (Marshfield, MA: Pitman, 1985).

Under the pressure of day-to-day activities, this need is often overlooked; in this case, the manuals are likely to include rules for situations that no longer exist and practices that are obsolete. Permitting such rules to remain undercuts the perceived validity of the manual as a whole.

System Safeguards.   Various safeguards are built into the information processing system to ensure that the information flowing through the system is accurate, and to prevent (or at least minimize) fraud of every sort. These include: cross-checking totals with details; requiring signatures and other evidence that a transaction has been authorized; separating duties; counting cash and other portable assets frequently; and a number of other procedures described in texts on auditing. They also include checks of the system performed by internal and external auditors.

Task Control Systems.   In Chapter 1 we defined task control as the process of assuring that specific tasks are carried out efficiently and effectively. Many of these tasks are controlled by rules. If a task is automated, the automated system itself provides the control. Task control systems are beyond the scope of this book.

Formal Control Process

Exhibit 2–1 is a sketch of the formal management control process (including aspects of it we will discuss, by chapter number). A strategic plan implements the organization's goals and strategies. All available information is used in making this plan. The strategic plan is converted to an annual budget that focuses on the planned revenues and expenses for individual responsibility centers. Responsibility centers are also guided by rules and other formal information. They carry out the operations assigned to them, and their outcomes are measured and reported. Actual results are compared with those in the budget to determine whether performance was satisfactory. If it was, the responsibility center receives feedback in the form of praise or other reward. If it was not, the feedback leads to corrective action in the responsibility center and possible revision of the plan. The sketch in Exhibit 2–1 is valid only as a generalization. As we shall show in later chapters, the formal control process in practice is far less straightforward than this sketch indicates.

Types of Organizations

A firm's strategy has a major influence on its structure.[11] The type of structure, in turn, influences the design of the organization's management control systems. Although organizations come in all sizes and shapes, their structures can be grouped into three general categories:

---

[11]Alfred D. Chandler, Jr., *Strategy and Structure* (Cambridge, MA: MIT Press, 1962).

EXHIBIT 2–1

*The formal
control process*

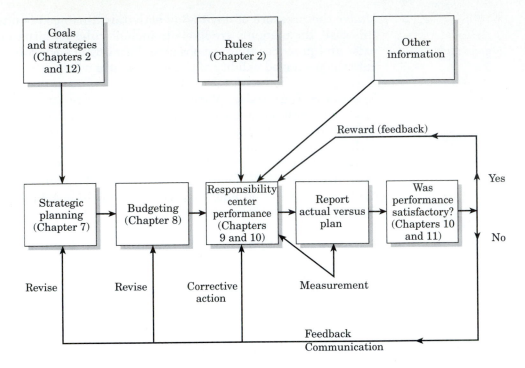

1. A functional structure, in which each manager is responsible for a specified function such as production or marketing.
2. A business unit structure, in which business unit managers are responsible for most of the activities of their particular unit, and the business unit functions as a semi-independent part of the company.
3. A matrix structure, in which functional units have dual responsibilities.

Abbreviated organization charts for each type are shown in Exhibit 2–2. The discussion here is limited to functional and business unit organizations; matrix organizations are discussed in Chapter 15.

Functional Organizations

The rationale for the functional form of organization involves the notion of a manager who brings specialized knowledge to bear on decisions related to a specific function, as contrasted with the general-purpose manager who lacks that specialized knowledge. A skilled marketing manager and a skilled production manager are likely to make better decisions in their respective fields than would a manager responsible for both functions. Moreover, the skilled specialist should be able to supervise workers in the same function better than the generalist would, just as skilled higher-level managers should be able to provide better supervision of lower-level managers in the same or similar function. Thus, *an important advantage of a functional structure is efficiency.*

Exhibit 2–2

Types of organizations

A. Functional Organization

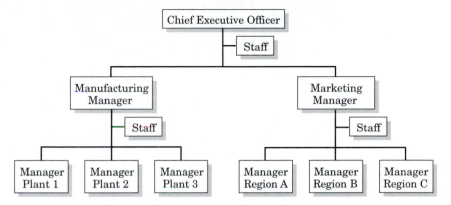

B. Business Unit Organization

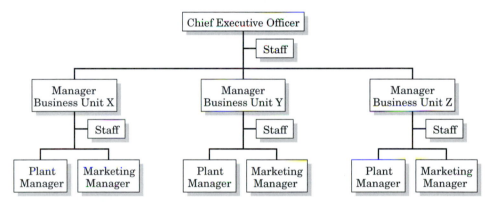

C. Matrix Organization

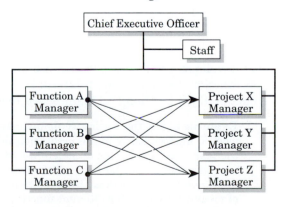

There are several disadvantages to a functional structure. First, in a functional organization there is no unambiguous way of determining the effectiveness of the separate functional managers (e.g., the managers of marketing and of production) because each function contributes jointly to the organization's final output. Therefore, there is no way of measuring what fraction of profit was contributed by each. Similarly at lower levels in the organization there is no way of determining how much of the profit was earned respectively by the several production departments, the product engineering department, and the sales office.

Second, if the organization consists of managers in one function who report to higher-level managers in the same function, who, in turn, report to still higher-level managers in that function, then a dispute between managers of different functions can be resolved only at the top, even though it may have originated at a much lower organizational level. For example, the marketing department may want to satisfy a customer's need for a certain quantity of product even if it requires overtime work by the manufacturing department—the cost of which the manufacturing department may be unwilling to incur. Theoretically, such a dispute would have to be settled at headquarters, even though it may involve just a single branch sales office and one small department of a single manufacturing plant. Taking the issue up through several levels in the organization and then communicating the decision down to the level where it originated can be time consuming and frustrating.

Third, functional structures are inadequate for a firm with diversified products and markets.

Example. In 1999, Deere & Co. was organized into four business units: Agricultural Equipment (tractors, combines, harvesters, etc., targeted at farmers); Construction Equipment (bulldozers, backhoes, excavators, etc., targeted at building contractors); Consumer Equipment (lawnmowers, snowblowers, etc., targeted at individual homes); and Credit (a unit that provided financing for equipment purchase). Given the diversity of products and customer segments that the company served, Deere & Co. could not adopt a functional structure.

Finally, functional organizations tend to create "silos" for each function, thereby preventing cross-functional coordination in areas such as new product development. This problem can be mitigated by supplementing the vertical functional structure with lateral cross-functional processes such as cross-functional job rotation and team-based rewards.

Examples. At the Boeing company, there was a time when design engineers worked independently of the production and operations people who actually built the plane. "Here it is," the designers would say. "Now, go build it." As a result, Boeing's production people were given overly costly, hard-to-build designs. Boeing broke down these functional hierarchies by creating "design-build teams," composed of members from all the different functions (the 777 project used these design-build teams exclusively). Under this "teaming" approach, production employees talked directly with engineering, resulting in an innovative and efficiently built product that rapidly became the industry standard.[12]

Glaxo Wellcome, the world's largest seller of pharmaceuticals, felt that its scientists were lacking in business sense. As a result, it changed from a functional hierarchical structure to a structure of "therapeutic strategy teams" consisting of both scientists and business managers, in an effort to bring the two sides of its operation closer together.[13]

Business Units

The business unit form of organization is designed to solve problems inherent in the functional structure. *A business unit, also called a division, is responsible for all the functions involved in producing and marketing a specified product line.* Business unit managers act almost as if their units were separate companies. They are responsible for planning and coordinating the work of the separate functions—ensuring, for example, that the plans of the marketing department are consistent with production capabilities—and for resolving the disputes that arise between these functions. Their performance is measured by the profitability of the business unit. This is a valid criterion because profit reflects the activities of both marketing and production.

> **Example.**   Nabisco's business units used different distribution systems for different products. For example, its biscuit unit used its own trucks and salespeople to deliver directly to retailers' shelves—a costly approach, but one that management believed was justified in terms of improved customer relations and closer control over store inventory and sales.[14]

Although business unit managers exercise broad authority over their units, headquarters reserves certain key prerogatives. At a minimum, headquarters is responsible for obtaining funds for the company as a whole, and for allocating these funds to the various business units in accordance with its determination as to best use. Headquarters also approves budgets and judges the performance of business unit managers, sets their compensation, and, if the situation warrants, removes them. Finally, headquarters establishes the "charter" of each business unit—that is, the product lines it is permitted to make and sell and/or the geographical territory in which it can operate, and, occasionally, the customers to which it may sell.

Headquarters also establishes companywide policies, which, depending on the wishes of the CEO, may be few and general, or may be codified in several thick volumes of manuals. Headquarters staff offices may assist the business units in production and marketing activities and in specialized areas such as

---

[12]Seth Lubove, "Destroying the Old Hierarchies," *Forbes,* June 3, 1996, pp. 62–71.

[13]Richard Evans, "A Giant Battles Its Drug Dependency," *Fortune,* August 5, 1996, pp. 88–92.

[14]Lori Bongiorno, "It's Put Up or Shut Up Time," *Business Week,* July 8, 1996, pp. 100–101.

human resources, legal affairs, public relations, and controller and treasury matters. These headquarters functions are crucial; without them, the business units would be better off as separate companies.

An advantage of the business unit form of organization is that it provides a training ground in general management. The business unit manager should demonstrate the same entrepreneurial spirit that characterizes the CEO of an independent company.

Another advantage of this type of structure is that because the business unit is closer to the market for its products than headquarters is, its manager may make sounder production and marketing decisions than headquarters might, and the unit as a whole can react to new threats or opportunities more quickly.

Offsetting these advantages is the possibility that each business unit staff may duplicate some work that in a functional organization is done at headquarters. The business unit manager is presumably a generalist, but his or her subordinates are functional specialists, and they must deal with many of the same problems addressed by specialists both at headquarters and in other business units as well. In some cases, the layers of business unit staff may cost more than the value gained by divisionalization. Moreover, skilled specialists in certain functions are in short supply, and individual business units may be unable to attract qualified people. These problems could be mitigated by supplementing the business unit organization with certain centralized functional expertise.

> **Example.**   At Boeing's commercial aircraft group, the design and manufacture of planes was divided into product lines with narrow bodies (the 737 and the 757) and wide bodies (the 747, the 767, and the 777). However, the fabrication of major structural components required very large and expensive computer-controlled machine tools that were deemed too expensive to duplicate in each product line. Instead, a central fabrication unit was created and all manufacturing activities requiring scale and skill were placed within it and shared across product lines. This structure was a hybrid of products and functions.[15]

Another disadvantage of the business unit form is that the disputes between functional specialists in a functional organization may be replaced by disputes between business units in a business unit organization. These may involve one business unit infringing upon the charter of another. There may also be disputes between business unit personnel and headquarters staff.

Implications for System Design

If ease of control were the only criterion, companies would be organized into business units whenever feasible. This is because in a business unit organization, each unit manager is held responsible for the profitability of the unit's

---

[15]Jay Galbraith, *Designing Organizations* (San Francisco: Jossey-Bass, 1995), p. 29.

product line, and presumably plans, coordinates, and controls the elements affecting that profitability. Control is not the only criterion, however. A functional organization may be more efficient because larger functional units provide the benefits of economies of scale. Also, a business unit organization requires a somewhat broader type of manager than the specialist who manages a specific function, and competent general managers of this type may be difficult to find.

Because of the apparently clear-cut nature of profit responsibility in a business unit organization, designers of management control systems sometimes recommend such an organization without giving appropriate weight to the other considerations involved. This is a mistake; the systems designer must always fit the system to the organization rather than the other way around. In other words, although the control implications of various organization structures should be reviewed with senior management, *once management has decided that a given structure is best, all things considered, then the system designer must take that structure as given.* Enthusiasts for one control technique or another may overlook this essential point.

The point also is important in other contexts. For example, many advertising agencies follow the practice of shifting account supervisors from one account to another at fairly frequent intervals to gain a fresh take on promoting the clients' products. This practice increases the difficulty of measuring the performance of an account supervisor because the fruits of an advertising campaign may take a long time to ripen. Nevertheless, the systems designer should not insist that the rotation policy be abandoned simply to make performance measurement easier. The system does not exist to serve the system designer; rather, the reverse is true.

Functions of the Controller

We shall refer to the person who is responsible for designing and operating the management control system as the controller. Actually, in many organizations, the title of this person is chief financial officer (CFO).[16]

The controller usually performs the following functions:

- Designing and operating information and control systems.
- Preparing financial statements and financial reports (including tax returns) for shareholders and other external parties.

---

[16]The chief financial officer typically is responsible both for the controllership function (as described here) and also for the treasury function. The title came into common use in the 1970s. At that time, its professional association, the Controllers Institute, became the Financial Executives Institute. The controller and the treasurer report to the chief financial officer. Because we do not discuss the treasurer's function, we use the narrower term, *controller*.

The spelling "comptroller" is also used. This spelling originated with an error made in the 18th century in translating from French to English, but the erroneous spelling has become embedded in dozens of federal and state statutes and in the bylaws of many companies and still persists. "Comptroller" is pronounced the same as "controller".

- Preparing and analyzing performance reports, interpreting these reports for managers, and analyzing program and budget proposals from various segments of the company and consolidating them into an overall annual budget.
- Supervising internal audit and accounting control procedures to ensure the validity of information, establishing adequate safeguards against theft and fraud, and performing operational audits.
- Developing personnel in the controller organization and participating in the education of management personnel in matters relating to the controller function.

Prior to the advent of computers, the controller (or CFO) was usually responsible for *processing* the information required by the management control system. Currently, companies typically have a chief information officer (CIO) who carries out this responsibility. In some companies, the CIO reports to the chief financial officer; in others, the CIO reports directly to senior management.

Relation to Line Organization

The controllership function is a staff function. Although the controller is usually responsible for the design and operation of the systems which collect and report information, the *use* of this information is the responsibility of line management. The controller may be responsible for developing and analyzing control measurements and for recommending actions to management. Other possible charges may include monitoring adherence to the spending limitations laid down by the chief executive, controlling the integrity of the accounting system, and safeguarding company assets from theft and fraud.

As stated above, however, the controller does not make or enforce management decisions. The responsibility for actually exercising control runs from the CEO down through the line organization.

The controller does make some decisions, however—primarily those that implement policies decided on by line management. For example, a member of the controller organization often decides on the propriety of expenses listed on a travel voucher since most line managers prefer not to get involved in discussions about the cost of meals or why the traveler felt it necessary to fly first class rather than economy class.

Controllers also play an important role in the preparation of strategic plans and budgets. And they are often asked to scrutinize performance reports to ensure accuracy, and to call line managers' attention to items deserving further inquiry. In this capacity, controllers are acting somewhat like line managers themselves. The difference is that the their decisions can be overruled by the line manager to whom the subordinate manager is responsible.

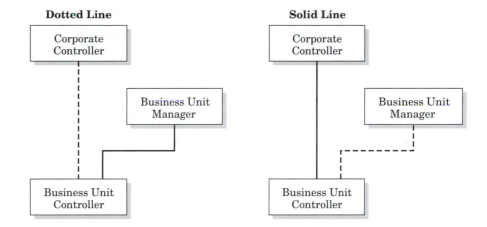

EXHIBIT 2–3

Alternative controller relationships

The Business Unit Controller

Business unit controllers inevitably have divided loyalty. On the one hand, they owe some allegiance to the corporate controller, who is presumably responsible for the overall operation of the control system. On the other hand, they also owe allegiance to the managers of their own units, for whom they provide staff assistance. Two possible types of relationships are diagrammed in Exhibit 2–3.

In some companies, the business unit controller reports to the business unit manager, and has what is called a *dotted line* relationship with the corporate controller. Here, the business unit general manager is the controller's immediate boss, and has ultimate authority in the hiring, training, transferal, compensation, promotion, and firing of controllers within that business unit. These decisions are rarely made, however, without input from the corporate controller.

> **Example.**   General Electric Company used this approach. To quote Bernard Doyle of General Electric: "Our controllership structure is based on a strong functional reporting line. The business unit controllers report directly to the general managers of their business units, but they have a functional or 'dotted line' responsibility to the chief financial officer of the company. The glue that holds it together is that the people in those business unit functional jobs can be appointed only from a slate of candidates the corporate chief financial officer first approves, and he has the unqualified right to remove these people. But, as importantly, these people are the chief financial officers of their business units. They are team players."[17]

----

[17]Jonathan B. Schiff, "Interview with Bernard Doyle of General Electric," *Controllers Quarterly* 6, no. 3 (1990), pp. 2–5.

In other companies, business unit controllers report directly to the corporate controller—that is, the corporate controller is their boss, as indicated by a *solid line* on the organization chart. ITT used this approach.[18]

There are problems with each of these relationships. If the business unit controller works primarily for the business unit manager, there is the possibility that he or she will not provide completely objective reports on business unit budgets and business unit performance to senior management. On the other hand, if the business unit controller works primarily for the corporate controller, the business unit manager may treat him or her as a "spy from the front office," rather than as a trusted aide.

Regardless of the reporting relationships, it is expected that the controller will not condone or participate in the transmission of misleading information or in the concealment of unfavorable information. The overall ethical responsibilities inherent in the position do not countenance such practices.

> **Example.**   In a talk to new business unit controllers, Helmut Maucher, the CEO of Nestlé, the world's largest food company, said: "As controller, you report to the business unit manager. The business unit manager has complete responsibility for the unit. However, in rare cases something may happen that means your loyalty to the unit manager is finished and your loyalty to the company takes over. I want a clear line of command, but everything has it limits; and, in that case, you cannot excuse yourself. I want your loyalty in general to be to the business unit manager; but, if he has five girlfriends and drinks too much, you must tell us at headquarters. This is your higher priority of loyalty."

Summary

Every organization has one or more goals. Profitability is an important goal, but a firm should also adopt goals vis-à-vis multiple stakeholders, including employees, suppliers, customers, and the community.

Senior management obviously wants the organization to attain its goals, but individual members of the organization have personal goals as well, and these are not in all respects consistent with the organization's goals. The central purpose of the management control system is to assure goal congruence; that is, the system should be designed in such a way that the actions it leads people to take in their perceived self-interest are also in the best interest of the organization.

Informal factors have a major influence on goal congruence. The most important of these factors is an organization's culture. Every management control system must recognize that an informal organization exists alongside the formal one and take this into account in the system design. Management style also has a major influence on control. But even in the best of cases, both

---

[18]Vijay Sathe, *Controllership in Divisionalized Firms: Structure, Evaluation, and Development* (New York: American Management Association, 1978), pp. 20–21.

communication and the individual interpretation of information are bound to be imperfect.

In addition to the informal factors, the control process is also affected by the rules, guidelines, and procedures that make up the formal control system.

Companies can choose from three basic organization structures: functional, business unit, and matrix. The specific choice of organizational structure influences the design of the management control system.

The controller is responsible for the design and operation of the control system; but, as a staff officer, he or she does not make management decisions. In companies organized into business units, the appropriate relationship between the business unit controller and the corporate controller is always subject to debate.

Suggested Additional Readings

Collins, James C., and Jerry I. Porras. "Building Your Company's Vision." *Harvard Business Review,* September–October 1996, pp. 65–77.

Galbraith, Jay R. *Designing Organizations.* San Francisco: Jossey-Bass, 1995.

Govindarajan, Vijay, and Anil K. Gupta. "Linking Control Systems to Business Unit Strategy: Impact on Performance." *Accounting Organizations and Society* X, no. 4 (1985), pp. 51–66.

Govindarajan, Vijay, and Joseph G. San Miguel. "Contingent Relationship between the Controller and Internal Audit Functions in Large Organizations." *Accounting Organizations and Society* IX, no. 2 (1984), pp. 179–88.

Gupta, Anil K., and Vijay Govindarajan. "Business Unit Strategy, Managerial Characteristics, and Business Unit Effectiveness at Strategy Implementation." *Academy of Management Journal* 27, no. 1 (1984), pp. 25–41.

Hamel, Gary. "Bringing Silicon Valley Inside." *Harvard Business Review,* September–October 1999, pp. 70–86.

Kanter, Rosabeth Moss, Barry A. Stein, and Jack Todd. *The Challenge of Organizational Change.* New York: Free Press, 1992.

Keating, Patrick J., and Stephen P. Jablonsky. *Changing Roles of Financial Management.* New York: Financial Executives Research Foundation, 1990.

Maciariello, J. A. *Lasting Value.* New York: Wiley, 1999.

March, James G., and Herbert A. Simon. *Organizations.* New York: John Wiley & Sons, 1993.

Pfeffer, J. *The Human Equation: Building Profits by Putting People First.* Boston: Harvard Business School Press, 1998.

Prahalad, C. K., and Gary Hamel. *Competing for the Future.* New York: Free Press, 1995.

CASE 2–1
NUCOR CORPORATION (B)

In January 1999, in a boardroom coup, Ken Iverson, chairman of Nucor, was forced into retirement. In June 1999, his successor, John Correnti, was voted out of power. The board appointed 68-year-old David Aycock chairman, chief executive, and president of Nucor. Aycock had joined Nucor in 1954, became a director in 1971, and president in 1984; he retired in 1991. He stayed on Nucor's board after 1991 as the second-largest individual shareholder.

The main bone of contention was the long-term strategic direction of the company. The board wanted a fundamental shift in Nucor's strategy which Iverson and Correnti resisted. Several industry and other trends led the board to reconsider strategy. First, overall steel demand in the United States was growing at less than 1.5 percent annually. Second, market share that Nucor could take away from integrated steel companies and other mini-mills was limited. Third, many companies had replicated the mini-mill idea. Finally, low-cost steel imports had made major inroads in the United States by 1999. In this context, the board asked, How could Nucor sustain its historically high growth rates? The board contemplated several strategic and organizational changes that would have been heresy under Iverson and Correnti: pursuing acquisitions, expanding into global markets, building blast furnaces, diversifying into non-steel areas, adding new organizational layers, and changing the composition of the board.

Aycock was convinced that Nucor had to break from the past to meet the company's aggressive growth goals. "How can we step up to the next level?" he asked. "Foreign and domestic rivals have been turning up the heat. We have plucked all the ripe, low-hanging grapes.

Nucor needs new moves."[1] In a symbolic gesture, the framed *New Steel* magazine covers featuring Iverson and Correnti as Steelmakers of the Year were removed from the head office.

Under Iverson, the company did not believe in acquisitions; he was committed to building new plants from scratch. Aycock, however, advocated acquisitions, "Every company hits a plateau. You just can't go out and build new plants to grow," he said. With steel prices down in 1999, he believed firms could be acquired at bargain prices and was looking at several companies, including Gallatin Steel in Kentucky.

Iverson kept Nucor a domestic company, partly because he was concerned about exporting the company's unique culture to foreign locations. In contrast, Aycock expressed the following perspective on global expansion: "Steel is not just a local market anymore, and our product must be global." According to Aycock, Nucor's future growth hinged on its ability to enter South America and Asia using local partners.

Iverson pioneered the mini-mill concept. Aycock wanted to build blast furnaces, the hallmark of integrated steel producers, noting, "Blast furnaces can deal with a weakness that could become critical as the firm grows. Unlike integrated firms, which use pig iron produced by blast furnaces, mini-mills rely on scrap metal. A blast furnace can diminish the firm's reliance on the notoriously fickle scrap market.

---

[1] All the quotations in this case are drawn from the following sources: "Steel: Growing Pains," *The Economist,* November 16, 1999, p. 68; "New Boss at Charlotte, N.C.-based Steelmaker Looks to Acquisitions," *The Charlotte Observer,* June 11, 1999; "Nucor: Meltdown in the Corner Office," *Business Week,* June 21, 1999, p. 37; and "Basis for Executive Shakeup at Nucor Disputed," *The Charlotte Observer,* June 27, 1999.

This case was prepared and copyrighted by Vijay Govindarajan.

It is a terrible misconception that integrated firms have to stay 'integrated' and mini-mills must stay 'mini.'"

Iverson's policy was to be a single industry player, concentrating on steel and steel-related products. Aycock insisted that Nucor consider diversifying beyond steel. "It's ridiculous to think we can keep growing this company just in steel and steel products," he said. "The firm's base can be expanded beyond steel to other manufacturing areas where the Nucor model will work." John Tumazos, a longtime steel analyst with Sanford C. Bernstein, remarked, "Nucor would likely look at manufacturing setups similar to Nucor's joist business—nonunion shops with a team production concept or a product adaptable to Nucor's team system. I expect they will be in manufactured products that are philosophically like a joist line, where you are paying a bunch of guys based on the unit output of the team and they are pulling together like a crew."

Iverson took pride in overseeing the operations of about 25 plants with lean corporate staff. Aycock emphasized the need to add more management layers. As he explained, "When Nucor was a niche player, Iverson's intuitive style served it well. But with revenues now ex-ceeding $4 billion—and the company on track to become the largest steelmaker in output—it was time for more long-term planning. Our size means the boss simply can't know everything that goes on. Each top executive must have no more than seven plant managers reporting to him. This will mean better oversight and monitoring of costs. It may also provide a broader base of talent to succeed me." In November 1999, the company added two executive vice presidents between Aycock and the plant managers.

The composition of the board also changed. Iverson's board consisted of current and former Nucor employees. Aycock recruited outside the company; by November 1999, outside directors made up two-thirds of Nucor's board.

Questions

1. Do you agree that Nucor must undergo a deep change to survive and prosper in the 21st century? How do you evaluate the specific shifts in strategy?

2. Can Nucor preserve its unique culture and control systems under its new strategic direction?

3. Would you like to work for Nucor under David Aycock?

CASE 2–2
GENERAL MOTORS CORPORATION

In an article in the *NACA Bulletin,* January 1, 1927, Albert Bradley described the pricing policy of General Motors Corporation. At that time, Mr. Bradley was general assistant treasurer; subsequently, he became vice president, executive vice president, and chairman of the board. The following description consists principally of excerpts from Mr. Bradley's article.

General Policy

Return on investment is the basis of the General Motors policy in regard to the pricing of product. The fundamental consideration is the average return over a protracted period of time, not the specific rate of return over any particular year or short period of time. The long-term rate of return on investment represents the official viewpoint as to the highest average rate of return that can be expected consistent with a healthy growth of the business, and may be referred to as the economic return attainable. The adjudged necessary rate of return on capital will vary as between separate lines of industry as a result of differences in their economic situations; and within each industry there will be important differences in return on capital, resulting primarily from the relatively greater efficiency of certain producers.

The fundamental policy in regard to pricing product and expansion of the business also necessitates an official viewpoint as to the normal average rate of plant operation. This relationship between assumed normal average rate of operation and practical annual capacity is known as standard volume.

The fundamental price policy is completely expressed in the conception of standard volume and economic return attainable. For example, if

it is the accepted policy that standard volume represents 80 percent of practical annual capacity, and that an average of 20 percent per annum must be earned on the operating capital, it becomes possible to determine the standard price of a product—that is, that price which with plants operating at 80 percent of capacity will produce an annual return of 20 percent of the investment.

Standard Volume

Costs of production and distribution per unit of product vary with fluctuation in volume, because of the fixed or nonvariable nature of some of the expense items. Productive materials and productive labor may be considered costs that are 100 percent variable, since within reasonable limits the aggregate varies directly with volume, and the cost per unit of product, therefore, remains uniform.

Among the items classified as manufacturing expense or burden there exist varying degrees of fluctuation with volume, owing to their greater or lesser degree of variability. Among the absolutely fixed items are such expenses as depreciation and taxes, which may be referred to as 100 percent fixed since within the limits of plant capacity the aggregate will not change, but the amount per unit of product will vary in inverse ratio to the input.

Another group of items may be classified as 100 percent variable, such as inspection and material handling; the amount per unit of product is unaffected by volume. Between the classes of 100 percent fixed and 100 percent variable is a large group of expense items that are partially variable, such as light, heat, power, and salaries.

In General Motors Corporation, standard burden rates are developed for each burden center, so that there will be included in costs a reasonable average allowance for manufacturing expense. In order to establish this rate, it is first necessary to obtain an expression of the estimated normal average rate of plant operation.

Rate of plant operation is affected by such factors as general business conditions, extent of seasonal fluctuation in sales likely within years of large volume, policy with respect to seasonal accumulation of finished and/or semifinished product for the purpose of leveling the production curve, necessity or desirability of maintaining excess plant capacity for emergency use, and many others. Each of these factors should be carefully considered by a manufacturer in the determination of size of a new plant to be constructed, and before making additions to existing plants, in order that there may be a logical relationship between assumed normal average rate of plant operation and practical annual capacity. The percentage accepted by General Motors Corporation as its policy in regard to the relationship between assumed normal rate of plant operation and practical annual capacity is referred to as standard volume.

The degree of variability of manufacturing expense having been determined, the established total expense at the standard volume rate of operations can be estimated. A *standard burden rate* is then developed, which represents the proper absorption of burden in costs at standard volume. In periods of low volume, the unabsorbed manufacturing expense is charged directly against profits as unabsorbed burden, while, in periods of high volume, the overabsorbed manufacturing expense is credited to profits, as overabsorbed burden.

Return on Investment

Factory costs and commercial expenses for the most part represent outlays by the manufacturer during the accounting period. An exception is depreciation of capital assets, which have a greater length of life than the accounting period. To allow for this element of cost,

there is included an allowance for depreciation in the burden rates used in compiling costs. Before an enterprise can be considered successful and worthy of continuation or expansion, however, still another element of cost must be reckoned with. This is the cost of capital, including an allowance for profit.

Thus, the calculation of standard prices of products necessitates the establishment of standards of capital requirement, as well as expense factors, representative of the normal average operating condition. The standard for capital employed in fixed assets is expressed as a percentage of factory cost, and the standards for working capital are expressed in part as a percentage of sales, and in part as a percentage of factory cost.

The calculation of the standard allowance for fixed investment is illustrated by the example in Exhibit 1.

The amount tied up in working capital items should be directly proportional to the volume of business. For example, raw materials on hand should be in direct proportion to the manufacturing requirements—so many days' supply of this material, so many days' supply of that material, and so on—depending on the condition

Exhibit 1   Allowance for Fixed Investment

Investment in plant and other fixed assets	$15,000,000
Practical annual capacity	50,000 units
Standard volume, percent of practical annual capacity	80%
Standard volume equivalent (50,000 * 80%)	40,000 units
Factory cost per unit at standard volume	1,000
Annual factory cost of production at standard volume (40,000 * $1,000)	$40,000,000
Standard factor for fixed investment (ratio of investment to annual factory cost of production; $15,000,000 ÷ $40,000,000)	0.375

Exhibit 2   Illustration of Method of Determination of Standard Price

	In Relation to	Turnover per Year	Ratio to Sales Annual Basis	Ratio to Factory Cost Annual Basis
Cash	Sales	20 times	0.050	—
Drafts and accounts receivable	Sales	10 times	0.100	—
Raw material and work-in-process	Factory cost	6 times	—	0.16 ⅔
Finished product	Factory cost	12 times	—	0.08 ⅓
Gross working capital			0.150	0.250
Fixed investment				0.375
Total investment				0.625
Economic return attainable, 20%			—	—
With the investment ratio multiplied by this, the necessary net profit margin is arrived at			0.030	0.125
Standard allowance for commercial expenses, 7%			0.070	—
Gross margin over factory cost			0.100	0.125

$$\text{Selling price, as a ratio to factory cost} \ = \ \frac{1+b}{1-a} = \frac{1+0.125}{1-0.100} = 1.250$$

$$\text{If standard cost} \ = \ \$1,000$$

$$\text{Then standard price} \ = \ \$1,000 * 1.250 = \$1,250$$

and location of sources of supply, transportation conditions, etc. Work-in-process should be in direct proportion to the requirements of finished production, since it is dependent on the length of time required for the material to pass from the raw to the finished state, and the amount of labor and other charges to be absorbed in the process. Finished product should be in direct proportion to sales requirements. Accounts receivable should be in direct proportion to sales, being dependent on terms of payment and efficiency of collections.

The Standard Price

These elements are combined to construct the standard price as shown in Exhibit 2. Note that the economic return attainable (20 percent in the

illustration) and the standard volume (80 percent as shown in Exhibit 1) are long-run figures and are rarely changed;[1] the other elements of the price are based on current estimates.

Differences among Products

Responsibility for investment must be considered in calculating the standard price of each product as well as in calculating the overall price for all products, since products with identical accounting costs may be responsible for in-

---

[1]A Brookings Institution survey reported that the principal pricing goal of General Motors Corporation in the 1950s was 20 percent of investment after taxes. See Robert F. Lanzilloti, "Pricing Objectives in Large Companies," *American Economic Review,* December 1958.

EXHIBIT 3   Variances in Standard Price, Due to Variances in Rate of Capital Turnover

	Product A		Product B		Total Product (A plus B)	
	Ratio to Sales Annual Basis	Ratio to Factory Cost Annual Basis	Ratio to Sales Annual Basis	Ratio to Factory Cost Annual Basis	Ratio to Sales Annual Basis	Ratio to Factory Cost Annual Basis
Gross working capital	0.150	0.250	0.150	0.250	0.150	0.250
Fixed investment	—	0.500	—	0.250	—	0.375
Total investment	0.150	0.750	0.150	0.500	0.150	0.625
Economic return attainable 20%	—	—		—	—	—
With the investment ratio ratio multiplied by this, the necessary net profit margin is arrived at	0.030	0.150				
Standard allowance for commercial expenses, 7%			0.030	0.100	0.030	0.125
	0.070	—	0.070	—	0.070	—
Gross margin over factory cost	0.100	0.150	0.100	0.100	0.100	0.125
	a	b	a	b	a	b
Selling price, as a ratio to factory cost $= \dfrac{1+b}{1-a}$	$\dfrac{1.0+0.150}{1.0-0.100}=1.278$		$\dfrac{1.0+0.100}{1.0-0.100}=1.222$		$\dfrac{1.0+0.125}{1.0-0.100}=1.250$	
If standard cost equals	$1,000		$1,000		$1,000	
Then standard price equals	$1,278		$1,222		$1,250	

vestments that vary greatly. In Exhibit 2, a uniform standard selling price of $1,250 was determined. Let us now suppose that this organization makes and sells two products, A and B, with equal manufacturing costs of $1,000 per unit and equal working capital requirements, and that 20,000 units of each product are produced. However, an analysis of fixed investment indicates that $10 million is applicable to product A, while only $5 million of fixed investment is applicable to product B. Each product must earn 20 percent on its investment in order to satisfy the standard condition. Exhibit 3 illustrates the determination of the standard price for product A and product B.

From this analysis of investment, it becomes apparent that product A, which has the heavier fixed investment, should sell for $1,278, while product B should sell for only $1,222, in order to produce a return of 20 percent on the investment. Were both products sold for the composite average standard price of $1,250, then product A would not be bearing its share of the investment burden, while product B would be correspondingly overpriced.

Differences in working capital requirements as between different products may also be important due to differences in manufacturing methods, sales terms, merchandising policies, etc. The inventory turnover rate of one line of products sold by a division of General Motors Corporation may be 6 times a year, while inventory applicable to another line of products is turned over 30 times a year. In the second case, the inventory investment required per dollar cost of sales is only one fifth of that required in the case of the product with the slower turnover. Just as there are differences in capital requirements as between different classes of product, so may the standard requirements for the same class of product require modification from time to time due to permanent changes in manufacturing processes, in location of sources of supply, more efficient scheduling and handling of materials, etc.

The importance of this improvement to the buyer of General Motors products may be appreciated from the following example. The total inventory investment for the 12 months ended September 30, 1926, would have averaged $182,490,000 if the turnover rate of 1923 (the best performance prior to 1925) had not been bettered, or an excess of $74,367,000 over the actual average investment. In other words, General Motors would have been compelled to charge $14,873,000 more for its product during this 12-month period than was actually charged if prices had been established to yield, say, 20 percent on the operating capital required.

Conclusion

The analysis as to the degree of variability of manufacturing and commercial expenses with increases or decreases in volume of output, and the establishment of "standards" for the various investment items, makes it possible not only to develop "Standard Prices," but also to forecast, with much greater accuracy than otherwise would be possible, the capital requirements, profits, and return on capital at the different rates of operation, which may result from seasonal conditions or from changes in the general business situation. Moreover, whenever it is necessary to calculate in advance the final effect on net profits of proposed increases or decreases in price, with their resulting changes in volume of output, consideration of the real economics of the situation is facilitated by the availability of reliable basic data.

It should be emphasized that the basic pricing policy stated in terms of the economic return attainable is a policy, and it does not absolutely dictate the specific price. At times, the actual price may be above, and at other times below, the standard price. The standard price calculation not only affords a means of interpreting actual or proposed prices in relation to the established policy, but at the same time affords a practical demonstration as to whether the policy itself is sound. If the prevailing price of product is found to be at variance with the standard price other than to the extent due to temporary causes, it follows that prices should be adjusted; or else, in the event of conditions being such that prices cannot be brought into line with the standard price, the conclusion is necessarily drawn that the terms of the expressed policy must be modified.[2]

Questions

1. An article in *The Wall Street Journal,* December 10, 1957, gave estimates of cost figures in "an imaginary, car-making division in the Ford–Chevrolet–Plymouth field." Most of the data given as part of this question are derived from that article. Using these data, compute the standard price. Working capital ratios are not given; assume that they are the same as those in Exhibit 2.

---

[2]This paragraph is taken from an article by Donaldson Brown, then vice president, finance, General Motors Corporation, in *Management and Administration,* March 1924.

Investment in plant and other fixed assets	$600,000,000
Required return on investment	30% before income taxes
Practical annual capacity	1,250,000
Standard volume—assume	80%
Factory cost per unit:	
Outside purchases of parts	$ 500*
Parts manufactured inside	$ 600*
Assembly labor	75
Burden	125
Total	$1,300

*Each of these items includes $50 of labor costs.

"Commercial cost," corresponding to the 7 percent in Exhibit 2, is added as a dollar amount, and includes the following:

Inbound and outbound freight	$ 85
Tooling and engineering	50
Sales and advertising	50
Administrative and miscellaneous	50
Warranty (repairs within guarantee)	15
Total	$250

Therefore, the 7 percent commercial allowance in Exhibit 2 should be eliminated, and in its place $250 should be added to the price as computed from the formula.

2. What would happen to profits and return on investment before taxes in a year in which volume was only 60 percent of capacity? What would happen in a year in which volume was 100 percent of capacity? Assume that nonvariable costs included in the $1,550 unit cost above are $350 million (i.e., variable costs are $1,500 − $350 = $1,200). In both situations, assume that cars were sold at the standard price established in question 1, since the standard price is not changed to reflect annual changes in volume.

3. In the 1975 model year, General Motors gave cash rebates of as high as $300 per car off the list price. In 1972 and 1973 prices had been restricted by price control legislation, which required that selling prices could be increased only if costs had increased. Selling prices thereafter were not controlled, although there was always the possibility that price controls could be reimposed. In 1975, demand for automobiles was sharply lower than in 1974, partly because of a general recession and partly because of concerns about high gasoline prices. Does the cash rebate indicate that General Motors adopted a new pricing policy in 1975, or is it consistent with the policy described in the case?

4. Was this policy good for General Motors? Was it good for America?

CASE 2–3
RENDELL COMPANY

Fred Bevins, controller of the Rendell Company, was concerned about the organizational status of his divisional controllers. In 1985 and for many years previously, the divisional controllers reported to the general managers of their divisions. Although Mr. Bevins knew this to be the general practice in many other divisionally organized companies, he was not entirely satisfied with it. His interest in making a change was stimulated by a description of organizational responsibilities given him by the controller of the Martex Corporation.

The Rendell Company had seven operating divisions: the smallest had $50 million in annual sales and the largest over $500 million. Each division was responsible for both the manufacturing and the marketing of a distinct product line. Some parts and components were transferred between divisions, but the volume of such interdivisional business was not large.

The company had been in business and profitable for over 50 years. In the late 1970s, although it continued to make profits, its rate of growth slowed considerably. James Hodgkin, later the president, was hired in 1980 by the directors because of their concern about this situation. His first position was controller. He became executive vice president in 1983 and president in 1984. Mr. Bevins joined the company as assistant controller in 1981, when he was 33 years old. He became controller in 1983.

In 1980, the corporate control organization was primarily responsible for (1) financial accounting, (2) internal auditing, and (3) analysis of capital budgeting requests. A budgetary control system was in existence, but the reports prepared under this system were submitted to the top management group directly by the operating divisions, with little analysis by the corporate control organization.

Mr. Hodgkin, as controller, thought it essential that the corporate control organization play a more active role in the process of establishing budgets and analyzing performance. He personally took an active role in reviewing budgets and studying divisional performance reports and hired several young analysts to assist him. Mr. Bevins continued to move in the same direction after his promotion to controller. By 1985 the corporate organization was beginning to be well enough staffed so that it could, and did, give careful attention to the information submitted by the divisions.

Divisional controllers reported directly to the divisional general managers, but the corporate controller always was consulted prior to the appointment of a new division controller, and he also was consulted in connection with salary increases for divisional controllers. The corporate controller specified the accounting system to which the divisions were expected to conform and the general procedures they were to follow in connection with budgeting and reporting performance. It was clearly understood, however, that budgets and performance reports coming from a division were the responsibility of that division's general manager, with the divisional controller acting as his staff assistant in the preparation of these documents. For example, the divisional general manager personally discussed his budget with top management prior to its approval, and although the divisional controller usually was present at these meetings to give information on technical points, his role was strictly that of a staff man.

Most of the divisional controllers had worked for Rendell for 10 years or more. Usually they

This case was prepared by Robert N. Anthony, Harvard Business School. Copyright © by the President and Fellows of Harvard College Harvard Business School case 109-033.

worked up through various positions in the controller organization, either at headquarters, in their division, or both. Two of the divisional controllers were in their early 30s, however, and had only a few years' experience in the headquarters controller organization before being made, first, divisional assistant controller and then divisional controller.

Mr. Bevins foresaw increasing difficulties with this relationship as the corporation introduced more modern control techniques. For one thing, he thought the existing relationship between himself and the divisional controllers was not so close that he could urge the development and use of new techniques as rapidly as he wished. More important, he thought that he was not getting adequate information about what was actually happening in the divisions. The divisional controller's primary loyalty was to his division manager, and it was unreasonable to expect that he would give Mr. Bevins frank, unbiased reports. For example, Mr. Bevins was quite sure that some fat was hidden in the divisional expense budgets and that the divisional controllers had a pretty good idea where it was. In short, he thought he would get a much better idea of what was going on in the divisions if reports on divisional activities came directly from controllers working for him, rather than for the divisional manager.

Mr. Bevins, was, therefore, especially interested in the controller organization at the Martex Company as he learned about it from E. F. Ingraham, the Martex controller, when he visited that company.

Until his visit to Martex, Mr. Bevins had not discussed the organization problem with anyone. Shortly thereafter, he gave William Harrigan, his assistant controller, a memorandum describing his visit (see the appendix to this case) and asked for Mr. Harrigan's reaction. Mr. Harrigan had been with Rendell for 25 years and had been a divisional controller before going to headquarters in 1982. Mr. Bevins respected his knowledge of the company and his opinion on organizational matters. Mr. Harrigan was accustomed to speaking frankly with Mr. Bevins. The gist of his comments follows:

I don't think the Martex plan would work with us; in fact, I am not even sure it works at Martex in the way suggested by the job descriptions and organization charts.

Before coming to headquarters, I had five years' experience as a divisional controller. When I took the job, I was told by the corporate controller and by my general manager that my function was to help the general manager every way I could. This is the way I operated. My people got together a lot of the information that was helpful in preparing the divisional budget, but the final product represented the thinking and decisions of my general manager, and he was the person who sold it to top management. I always went with him to the budget meetings, and he often asked me to explain some of the figures. When the monthly reports were prepared, I usually went over them, looking for danger signals, and then took them in to the general manager. He might agree with me, or he might spot other things that needed looking into. In either case, he usually was the one to put the heat on the operating organization, not me.

We did have some problems. The worst, and this happened several times a year, was when someone from the corporate controller's office would telephone and ask questions such as, "Do you think your division could get along all right if we cut $X out of the advertising budget?" Or, "Do you really believe that the cost savings estimate on this equipment is realistic?" Usually, I was in complete agreement with the data in question and defended them as best I could. Once in a while, however, I might privately disagree with the "official" figures, but I tried not to say so.

Questions of this sort really should be asked of the general manager, not of me. I realize that the head office people probably didn't think the question was important enough to warrant bothering the general manager, and in many cases, they were right. The line is a fine one.

The business of the division controller's being an "unbiased source of information" sounds fine when you word it that way, but another way to say it is that he is a front office spy, and that doesn't sound so good. It would indeed make our life easier if we could count on the divisional controllers to give us the real lowdown on what is going on. But if this is to be their position, then we can't expect that the general manager will continue to treat his controller as a trusted assistant. Either the general manager will find somebody else to take over this work unofficially, or it won't get done.

I think we are better off the way we are. Sure, the budgets will have some fat in them, and not all the bad situations will be highlighted in the operating reports, and this makes our job more difficult. But I'd rather have this than the alternative. If we used the Martex method (or, rather, what they claim is their method), we can be sure that the divisional controller will no longer be a member of the management team. They'll isolate him as much as they can, and the control function in the division will suffer.

Questions

1. What is the organizational philosophy of Martex with respect to the controller function? What do you think of it? Should Rendell adopt this philosophy?

2. To whom should the divisional controllers report in the Rendell Company? Why?

3. What should be the relationship between the corporate controller and the divisional controllers? What steps would you take to establish this relationship on a sound footing?

4. Would you recommend any major changes in the basic responsibilities of either the corporate controller or the divisional controller?

Appendix
Notes on Martex Controller Organization

Mr. Ingraham, the corporate controller, reports directly to the president and has reporting to him all division controllers and other accounting, data processing, and analysis groups. The Martex Company's descriptions of responsibility and organization charts are included herein (Exhibits 1, 2, 3, and 4) and indicate the structure and function of the organization.

The controller's organization is charged with the responsibility of establishing cost and profit standards in the corporation and of taking appropriate action to see that these standards are attained. It reviews all research projects and assigns names and numbers to them in order to coordinate research activities in the various divisions and their central research. The organization also handles all matters involving cost and profit estimates.

The present size of divisional controllers' staffs ranges from 3 to 22. Division controllers are not involved in preparing division profit and loss statements; these are prepared by a separate group for all divisions and the corporation.

Line-Staff Relationships

A division manager has no staff of his own, not even a personal assistant. He receives staff assistance from two sources.

First, he has some people assigned to him from the general staff—typically, a controller, an engineer, and a purchasing agent.

All division management and all the corporate staff are located in the corporate headquarters building. However, the assigned staff are located physically with their staff colleagues; for example, a divisional controller and his assistants are located in the controller's section of the building, not near his divisional manager's office.

Second, the division can call on the central staff to the extent that the manager wishes. The divisions are charged for these services on the basis of service rendered. The central staff units are listed in the General Staff Services box of Exhibit 2.

Division Manager-Controller Relationships

The success of the Martex controller organization and its relations with divisional managers appears to be largely the result of managers and controllers having grown up with the arrangement and accepting it long before they arrived at their managerial positions.

Some additional factors that appear to contribute to their successful relationship are the following:

1. A uniform and centralized accounting system.
2. Predetermined financial objectives for each division.
   a. Growth in dollar sales.
   b. A specified rate of profit as a percent of sales.
3. Profit sharing by managers and controllers.

Accounting System

The controller's division has complete control of the accounting system. It determines how and what accounts will be kept. The controller's division has developed an accounting system that is the same for all divisions. Mr. Ingraham pointed out that no division had a system perfectly tailored to its needs, but he believed that the disadvantages to the divisions were more than offset by having a system uniform over all divisions and understood by all concerned. Mr. Ingraham indicated it was likely that, if Martex divisions were free to establish their own accounting systems, every division would have a different one within two years, and interpretation by corporate management would be difficult, if possible at all.

The accounting system appears to provide a common basis for all divisional financial reports and analyses, and it aids in maintaining the bond of confidence between division managers and controllers.

Division Objectives

The corporation has established two financial objectives for each division. These are (a) growth in dollar sales, (b) a specified rate of profit as a percent of sales.

These objectives are determined in advance by recommendations of the controller's division with the advice and counsel of divisional managers. The objectives are long range in nature; the target profit rate has been changed only three times since 1965.

The particular percentage of sales selected as the target profit rate is based on several factors, among which are (1) the patentability of products, (2) a desired rate of return on investment, (3) the industry's margin of profit, and (4) the industry's rate of return on investment. These factors and others determine the profit rate finally selected.

Within limits, attainment of these financial objectives represents the primary task required of division general managers by corporate management.

Profit Sharing

Divisional managers receive about 75 percent of their total compensation from profit sharing and stock options. Divisional controllers receive about 25 percent of their compensation from profit sharing—half from a share in divisional profits and the other half from corporate profits.

Division Managers' View of the System

Mr. Ingraham indicated that divisional managers like to have divisional controllers report to the corporate controller because (1) it gives them an unbiased partner armed with relevant information, (2) the controller is in a better position to do the analysis needed for decision making, and (3) when cost reports are issued there is little or no argument about them among affected parties.

EXHIBIT 1   Position Descriptions from the Martex Management Guidebook

Controller

The trend of modern business management is to change the basic concept of the controller's position from that of an administrative function concerned largely with accounting detail to that of an important position in management as it relates to the control of costs and the profitable operation of the business as a whole.

The more our business becomes diversified with operations scattered throughout the United States, the greater is the need for an officer to whom the president delegates authority with respect to those factors affecting costs and profits in the same manner as he may delegate authority to others in strong staff positions.

In our vertical type of organization there is a great need for an appointed officer whose responsibility it is to establish budgetary standards of operations and objective percent of profit on sales targets for each of the operating divisions and domestic subsidiaries. He shall also establish budgetary standards of operation for staff functions in line with divisional and overall company profit objectives. When the standard of operations or profit target is not attained, the controller has the right and the responsibility within his delegated authority to question the failure and recommend changes to accomplish the desired result.

The controller shall work with the various divisions of the company through divisional controllers assigned to each major operating division and staff function. It is not intended that the controller take the initiative away from the division managers, since the responsibility for efficient operations and profits is assumed by the managers. However, the controller and his staff should have the right and the responsibility to expect certain operating results from the division head; and when a difference of opinion occurs as to the reasonableness of the demand for results, the matter should then be referred by either party to the president.

Along with the foregoing, the following responsibilities are an essential part of the position and apply to the corporation and its subsidiaries:

1. The installation and supervision of all accounting records.
2. The preparation, supervision, and interpretation of all divisional and product profit and loss statements, operating statements, and cost reports, including reports of costs and production, research, distribution, and administration.
3. The supervision of taking and costing of all physical inventories.

4. The preparation and interpretation of all operating statistics and reports, including interpretation of charts and graphs, for use by management committees and the board of directors.
5. The preparation, as budget director, in conjunction with staff officers and heads of divisions and subsidiaries, of an annual budget covering all operations for submission to the president prior to the beginning of the fiscal year.
6. The initiation, preparation, and issuance of standard practice regulations and the coordination of systems, including clerical and office methods relating to all operating accounting procedures.
7. Membership of the controller or his designated representative in all division and subsidiary management committees.

He shall be responsible for the selection, training, development and promotion of qualified personnel for his organization and their compensation within established company policy. He shall submit to the president an organization plan for accomplishing desired objectives.

The controller may delegate to members of his organization certain of his responsibilities, but in so doing he does not relinquish his overall responsibility or accountability for results.

Treasurer and Assistant Treasurers

Subject to the rules and regulations of the Finance Committee, the treasurer is the chief financial officer and generally his functions include control of corporate funds and attending to the financial affairs of the corporation and its domestic and foreign subsidiaries wherever located. More specifically the duties and responsibilities are as follows:

Banking.   He shall have custody of and be responsible for all money and securities and shall deposit in the name of the corporation in such depositories as are approved by the president all funds coming into his possession for the company account.

Credits and collections.   He shall have supervision over all cashiers, cash receipts, and collection records and accounts receivable ledgers. He shall initiate and approve all credit policies and procedures.

Disbursements.   He shall authorize disbursements of any kind by signature on checks. This includes direct su-

EXHIBIT 1   (*continued*)

pervision over accounts payable and payroll departments and indirect supervision over all receiving departments for the purpose of checking on the accuracy of invoices presented for payment. He shall maintain adequate records of authorized appropriations and also determine that all financial transactions covered by minutes of management and executive committees and the board of directors are properly executed and recorded.

General financial reports.   He shall prepare and supervise all general accounting records. He shall prepare and interpret all general financial statements, including the preparation of the quarterly and annual reports for mailing to stockholders. This also includes the preparation and approval of the regulations on standard practices required to assure compliance with orders or regulations issued by duly constituted governmental agencies and stock exchanges.

He shall supervise the continuous audit (including internal controls) of all accounts and records and shall supervise the audit and procedures of Certified Public Accountants.

Taxes.   He shall supervise the preparation and filing of all tax returns and shall have supervision of all matters relating to taxes and shall refer to the general counsel all such matters requiring interpretation of tax laws and regulations.

Insurance property records.   He shall supervise the purchase and placing of insurance of any kind including the insurance required in connection with employee benefits. He shall be responsible for recommending adequate coverage for all ascertainable risks and shall maintain such records as to avoid any possibility that various hazards are not being properly insured. He shall maintain adequate property records and valuations for insurance and other purposes and, if necessary, employ appraisal experts to assist in determining such valuations and records.

Loans.   He shall approve all loans and advances made to employees within limits prescribed by the Executive Committee.

Investments.   As funds are available beyond normal requirements, he shall recommend suitable investments to the Finance Committees. He shall have custody of securities so acquired and shall use the safekeeping facilities of the banks for that purpose. As securities are added or removed from such vaults or facilities, he shall be accompanied by an authorized officer of the corporation.

Office management.   He shall be responsible for the coordination of all office management functions throughout the company and its domestic subsidiaries.

Financial planning.   He shall initiate and prepare current and long-range cash forecasts, particularly as such forecasts are needed for financing programs to meet anticipated cash requirements for future growth and expansion. He shall arrange to meet sinking fund requirements for all outstanding debenture bonds and preferred stock and shall anticipate such requirements whenever possible.

He shall have such other powers and shall perform such other duties as may be assigned to him by the board of directors and the president.

The treasurer shall be responsible for the selection, training, development, and promotion of qualified personnel for his organization and their compensation within established company policy. It is expected that since he will have to delegate many of the duties and responsibilities enumerated above, he shall confer with and submit to the president an organization plan and chart.

The treasurer may delegate to members of his organization certain of his responsibilities together with appropriate authority for fulfillment; however, in so doing he does not relinquish his overall responsibility or accountability for results.

The treasurer is a member of the Finance, Retirement, and Inventory Review Committees.

EXHIBIT 2

Martex organization chart, Division A, January 1, 1985

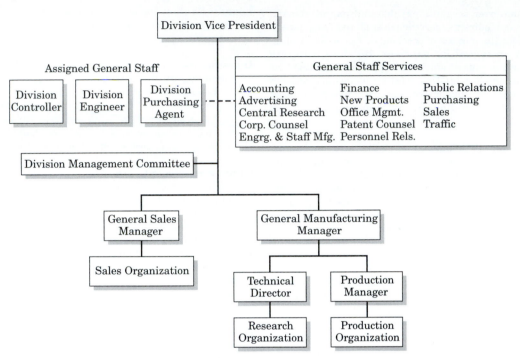

Note: Various levels on the chart do not necessarily indicate relative importance of positions.

EXHIBIT 3

Organization chart of Martex controller's division, January 1, 1985

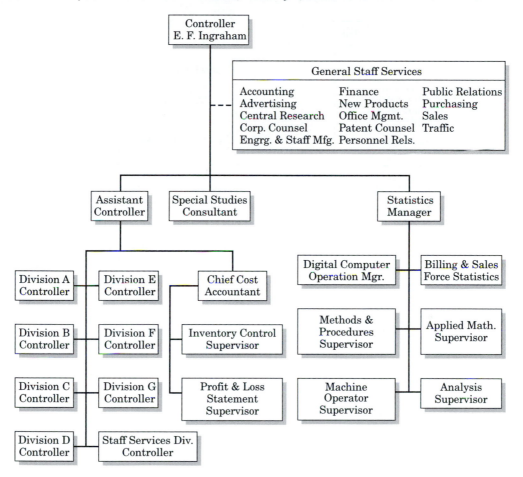

EXHIBIT 4

Organization chart of Martex treasurer's division, January 1, 1985

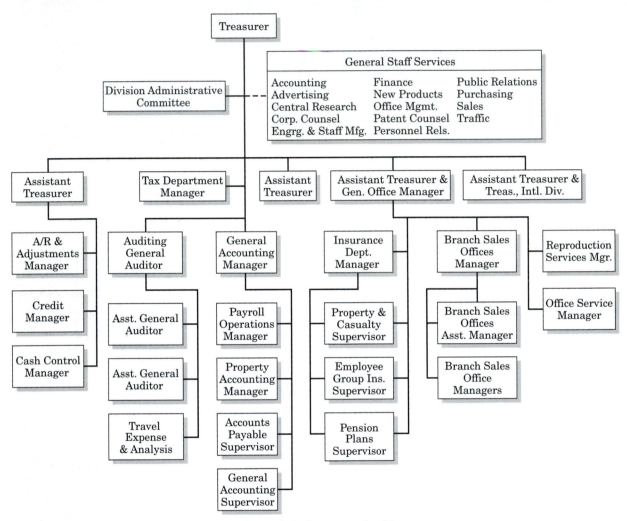

Note: Various levels on the chart do not necessarily indicate relative importance of positions.

Case 2–4
Digital Equipment Corporation

"We have to do something that will really make a difference. Our managers need to develop a sense of business management and accountability across the entire organization. It seems that only the division's senior managers are held accountable. We need to change our behavior and culture. We are no longer a cost center! The new product line structure gives us the opportunity to finally become profitable. Corporate will not tolerate our losses and cash drain for much longer." John Gavin, the Digital Semiconductor (DS) group controller, was expressing his sense of urgency at his weekly staff meeting.

Digital Semiconductor was a business unit of Digital Equipment Corporation. This particular meeting focused on finding ways the finance department could add value and better support the division. There had been numerous changes over the past five years in the DS business strategy, operational process, organizational structure, and business financial measurements. All of these changes required the finance staff to provide more meaningful data and help the line managers make more informed decisions. John was growing impatient and wanted to drive the changes at DS more quickly. He believed finance could drive the business practice changes to make DS more competitive as a stand-alone business.

When DS became a formal business unit, profit and cash flow, not cost and spending, became key elements of performance. DS had successfully, albeit painfully, transformed itself from a large R&D and manufacturing cost center to a profit center. It established internal transfer prices, initiated a new externally focused sales and marketing department, shed underutilized manufacturing facilities, con-

structed a merchant-size leading-edge manufacturing facility, and was currently in the process of finding another semiconductor company to share manufacturing capacity. Despite these positive changes the division was still operating at a loss; however, John believed DS was poised for needed growth.

At his staff meeting, John wanted to know what his staff thought it would take to change the still existing "spend and technology" mentality. He was looking for ways to stimulate the division to drive for growth and eventual profitability. He believed the product line organization was a major step to this goal.

History

The semiconductor division grew as part of Digital Equipment Corporation's (DEC's) rapid expansion in the 1970s. DEC and other computer companies felt that they needed to control and direct the technology of the key component suppliers for their computers. The speed, power, and size of the semiconductor chips were critical to the computer's capability. Management felt this direct relationship could not be left to a third party supplier. The computer chip technology was essential and DEC built its capability in this area. Located in eastern Massachusetts, the company had ready access to the necessary engineering, development, and manufacturing resources.

FABs (semiconductor manufacturing facilities) were built and development capabilities expanded as DS served as a key captive supplier to Digital. They were treated as a cost center with a very generous budget. Investment and spending at DS were tied to Corporate returns on overall computer investments. DS did not need to justify successful returns on these investments based on their individual revenues

This case was prepared by Professor Lawrence P. Carr, Babson College. Copyright © by Lawrence P. Carr.

EXHIBIT 1   Digital Key Financial Data

DIGITAL EQUIPMENT CORPORATION
Financial Summary
($ millions)

	1996	1995	1994	1993	1992	1991	1990	1989	1988
Sales	$14,563	$13,813	$13,451	$14,373	$13,931	$13,911	$12,943	$12,742	$11,475
Net income	($112)	$122	($2,156)	($251)	($2,796)	($617)	$74	$1,073	$1,306
Cash	$2,039	$1,602	$1,181	$1,634	$1,337	$1,924	$2,009	$1,655	$2,164
Employeee Summary[1]									
Regular[2]			77,800	89,900	107,900	115,100	116,900	118,400	113,900
Other		5,000	4,300	5,900	5,900	7,100	7,400	7,600	
Total	59,100	61,700	82,800	94,200	113,800	121,000	124,000	125,800	121,500

1. Note that the 1994 Annual Report distinguished employees as "Regular" and "Other," offering no supporting explanation. All annual reports prior to 1994 combined the two categories.
2. Not broken out in 1995 or 1996.

and shipment volumes. Their charter was to push the technology envelope and provide leading-edge products for the very successful VAX computer line and other equipment of Digital. DS expanded production to meet the ever increasing demand of Digital. DS product development worked very closely with the VAX computer designers to ensure Digital's market leadership through microchip technology. The philosophy and core of the strategy was to spend what was necessary to maintain the technological leadership in computer chips. Digital was financially very successful, achieving record profits and sales (1988 sales $11,475 million, profit $1,741 million). Exhibit 1 provides a summary of key financial historical data. In this environment, investment and spending at DS were not the prime concerns for Digital management.

This successful arrangement began to unravel as Digital faced massive losses in 1990 through 1994. There were two restructuring charges of over $2.5 billion and the founder and chairman, Ken Olsen, left the company. The computer industry was shifting to services, PCs, networks, and work stations and away from the central computer concept. Digital began the painful process of downsizing and refocusing its strategy.

Just prior to these changes DS received approval and embarked on a major defining development project—the Alpha Chip. This chip would be the fastest, most powerful on the market. The Alpha technology was based on a 64-bit, RISC architecture. The industry, led by Intel, used a 32-bit, CISC architecture. Alpha computers would outperform any available competitor. There was a 15-year financial projection with capital spending in the first 5 years of over $1 billion to support this strategy.

In 1997 Digital returned to profitability. One of the driving forces was the reorganization of Digital into business units and product lines. DS became a separate business unit and is now in the process of establishing product lines within the division. With this new organizational arrangement, they had the ability and motivation to sell their chips in the open market to customers other than Digital. At the same time, the other Digital divisions were not dependent upon or required to obtain their chip needs from DS. They could go to outside suppliers. The President of Digital, Bob Palmer, former head of DS, wanted each business unit to stand on its own economic performance.

Digital Semiconductor

The corporate changes were embraced by senior management and the DS financial staff. Now, basic questions about the cost benefit relationship of budget and capital spending could be asked. These relationships, however, were not fully understood by the large technical professional population at DS. This talented group was striving to stay on the cutting edge of new technology and felt this battle was the key to DS and Digital's future success. It was a major cultural change for chip designers to consider costs along with pushing the envelope of science. The Vice President of Engineering made the following comment:

"In the past we made individual product investment decisions at the top with second-hand data and no real market contact. The marketing and engineering efforts were disconnected. Product and process program tracking was done within the functional stove pipes. We lacked metrics to monitor projects and had no idea how to achieve ROI."

With the ability to go outside Digital for orders, DS had to build a new sales and marketing team to develop the external market business. Furthermore, it had to find better ways to serve the other Digital business units. In the new product line organization, other Digital units filled their computer chip needs from both DS and outside suppliers.

Semiconductor Manufacturing

Semiconductor devices were made from silicon which was material refined from quartz. Silicon was melted and grown into long crystals. The purified silicon was sliced into wafers on which integrated circuits were patterned. Circuitry was patterned on the wafers in multiple layers so that a wafer contained a set of dies or computer chips. The next step was the probe, where each integrated circuit was tested. The non-functioning dies were marked and removed. Each of the dies was diced from the wafer using a diamond saw. The good dies were placed in a ceramic package and wire connectors were attached. Once the device was completely packaged it was tested to ensure electrical specifications were met. Exhibit 2 shows the process and cost accumulation.

It was important to note that the cost structure went from a cost per wafer to a cost per die during the probe process. Yield was very critical to the cost of the process. The denser and more powerful the chip the less the die yielded. It was not uncommon to have less than 50 percent yield of good die. Yield was based on a number of factors including design, manufacturing learning curve, and the quality of the process.

Product Lines

After several years operating as a profit center end building the new business skills for technical managers, the DS management committee came to the conclusion that the product line concept made sense for their division. The new VP of marketing favored product lines as the potential sales channels were different for separate families of chip products. There was a single sales force representing all of the products, but it was clear that market segments based on product characteristics were forming. Product development was clustered around families of technologies and also favored the product line concept.

The complexity of manufacturing was different for each product family and the central production was able to easily shift between families

EXHIBIT 2   Semiconductor Manufacturing Process and Cost

Semiconductor Manufacturing Process

	Silicon Wafers Fabrication	→	Probe	→	Assembly	→	Test
	• Repeat process for layers • Insulate (oxide) • Coated • Masked, UV light • Strip		• Test die • Market rejects		• Cut die • Good die to package • Seal		• Test

Semiconductor Manufacturing Cost

Wafer cost	+ Fact OH + Direct L&M	+ Fact OH + Direct L&M	+ Fact OH + Direct L&M	
Cost wafer	Cost wafer	Cost wafer	Cost die	Cost die
			Cost die	

Die yield per wafer is the key factor in the cost per die.

---

of products. Product and process development were working together to support both manufacturing and development. The implementation of an ABC cost and management system made a strong impact at the division. It permitted a much better understanding of the cost structure of the products. John Gavin and his staff developed reports that created a better understanding of the cost drivers at the manufacturing level. The management group, however, had little experience in reporting monthly and quarterly financial results and at analyzing cash flow.

Division financial reports were complex and not yet at a product line level. The corporatewide cost containment program required very close scrutiny of expenses. The DS financial reports were dissected to determine the needed corrective action to get the division back on their 15-year financial plan. Cost containment was made more complex as many managers were often seeing the DS financial reports for the first time. The managers needed a better understanding of finance practices and the financial managers needed to work more closely with the line managers. John saw this as an opportunity for his department to add real value to the process.

Dividing the DS division into product lines was a natural evolution. Bob Palmer credited much of Digital's successful turnaround to the product line organization. He put profit and loss responsibility into the product line managers' hands and measured their performance. All the divisions were encouraged to follow this model. The DS division managers struggled with the product line organization until the operations committee (DSMC) was formed. These key functional and operations managers drove the evolution of the product line concept. Many of them, seeking a practical implementation plan, became product line leaders to start the process. They felt this was the best way to achieve the overall DS strategy:

Be a profitable semiconductor business while supporting the strategic needs of Digital and our external customers through leadership semiconductor products that provide time-to-market advantages in performance, functionality and cost.

Keep Digital Semiconductor on the competitive technology road map.

Make Alpha an industry standard by supporting Digital and gaining additional Alpha customers.

DS was divided into six product lines representing their major microprocessor and peripheral product families. The plan was to develop separate product line financial reports and measure the product line managers against their profit and cash flow targets. Ed Caldwell, VP and General Manager of DS, said: "The plan is to manage DS revenue and investment as a portfolio of products. We will set individual revenue and investment targets for each product line to meet the division's total targets. Budgets, forecasts, and measures of DS performance will be by product line."

A product line was defined as the integration of the activities of marketing, product development, and product engineering to manage a set of common products to achieve ROI. They viewed the product line in a holistic context where the product line management would define revenue opportunities, make investment trade-offs, manage products through their life cycle, manage controllable costs, and set prices. The VP of Engineering said, "We will measure their results and dispense rewards. The product line managers will be autonomous and accountable."

This undertaking required communication clarity. It was radically different from the existing culture. Exhibit 3 is the memo for the DS management committee outlining the structure of the product line organization.

Implementation

The DS finance staff was given the task of designing and implementing a reporting system based on the new product line organization. A team was immediately formed to split the income statement by product line. The revenue, booking, and direct expenses were easy to identify by product line. The real problem was unraveling the central administrative costs and the shared production costs. The team dreaded the problem of allocating such a large percentage of the product line expenses. On the administrative side product lines wanted to know what they were getting for the expense. DS management decided to charge the product lines only for the direct administrative support expenses. In essence, it created a sev-

enth product line which had no revenue but all of the central administrative costs such as Finance, HR, Division staff, SAP, and interest expenses.

The manufacturing side of the expenses was much more complicated. As outlined in Exhibit 2 the cost of an individual chip was dependent on the die yield from the wafer and the die yield after assembly and test. In simple terms, yield in semiconductor manufacturing was a function of the complexity of the chip and the experience of the manufacturing facility. In other words, a simple chip made on a regular basis would have much higher yields (>50%). A very complex chip made for the first time would normally experience very low yields (<3%). At DS the product lines ranged in complexity of product and frequency of production. The central issue was, Did the transfer pricing system outlined in the memo sufficiently cover this problem? Gavin further wondered how to charge FAB underutilization. While he wanted to develop balance sheets and statements of cash flow for each product line, he knew with central manufacturing and central services this was out of the question, for now.

The finance implementation team worked closely with the product line managers, keeping them well informed as they developed the profit and loss statements and the rules of reporting. They restated the past year in product line terms and used this as the basis of budgeting for the new business year. As the new year progressed, the dialogue and financial understanding at each monthly business review meeting improved. Finance made adjustments and clarifications to the reporting rules as the year progressed. The emphasis was on understanding the real product line performance and avoiding the application of new rules to enhance reported results.

Questions

1. As a potential product line manager at DS, what is your reaction to the memo in Exhibit 3?

EXHIBIT 3   **Digital Semiconductor Memo**

TO: **DS Extended Staff**
FROM: **DS Management Committee**
SUBJ: **Changing the way we measure and manage DS financial performance**

As we continue the migration towards a formalized product line structure and an integrated manufacturing structure for Digital Semiconductor, we will be implementing this year a new financial measurement and reporting system. The purpose of this memo is to summarize the new system and describe its current status and ongoing implementation plan, and, most importantly, serve as a reference document for you to use to inform the people in your organization.

Each product line will be measured as a full profit/loss center with specific and individualized goals for profit contribution. Some product lines will carry a larger requirement to generate cash to help fund the investments necessary in new product development. All revenues, engineering and marketing spending, product-specific manufacturing, and sales spending will be measured and reported by product line. In addition, each product line will be charged a competitive manufacturing product cost for each of its products. We will utilize the existing manufacturing cost model supported by product engineering with the following standard costs for yielded full lots at standard cycle times:

Mfg. process 1	$1,500/wafer
Mfg. process 2	$500/wafer
Mfg. process 3	$1,600/wafer
Mfg. process 4	$2,000/wafer

Non-standard lots for product development and characterization
(i.e. split lots, non-full lots) will be charged a 50% premium
(e.g. cost 1.5X). Hot lots will be charged a 100% premium
(e.g. cost 2X)

These competitive manufacturing process costs were set top-down and reflect competitive costs that we have benchmarked with appropriate companies in the industry, as well as through data from Sematech participants. The goal for FY97 is to set wafer standards bottoms-up by calculating for each process flow the aggregated activity-based costs of executing each fabrication step, assuming best-in-class cost-of-ownership/cost-of-operation for each piece of equipment and best-in-class line yield. Given that wafer cost standards will be kept competitive, the onus is now on the product lines to manage die size and continuously improve individual product yield to achieve best-in-class gross margins. Product lines will also be held accountable for assessing predictable demand planning for their wafer capacity needs.

Under this new system, the fabs and post-fab operations (probe/assembly/test) will be run as cost centers, and measured on their ability to achieve these competitive activity-based cost standards. Process development costs, certain other base technology costs, and general sales and administrative costs will be carried at the DS level. To ensure overall DS profitability, profit targets for the product lines will be set to cover these aggregate, unallocated DS costs. Accounting for under-utilization and mix variances is still to be determined.

It will take us until December 1st to restate our FY96 financial goals under this new context (the bottom line DS revenue/profit/cash flow goals will NOT change), and until Q3 to design, implement, and debug a new financial measurement and reporting system to allow us to automatically track our progress against our restated plan. Mary Hall is leading the effort to implement the product line measurement and reporting system; Bill Nordengren is leading the effort to implement the manufacturing measurement and reporting system, including the variance "buckets" to be held at the DS level. We already have working a reasonably accurate weekly reporting process (billings/bookings/backlog) on a product line basis, and are in the process of tying the monthly corporate expense reporting systems into an automated system that parses it by product line. We have yet to start the work on measuring and reporting product line cost-of-goods sold. In the meantime, we will use manual methods to track performance against our restated product line and manufacturing goals.

If you have any questions, please send a note asking for clarification, or talk to any one of the members of the DS Management Committee. We also ask you to be proactive in communicating this new financial architecture to all of your folks so that they better understand how we intend to manage ourselves, and become more effectively engaged in helping DS achieve its profitability goals.

2. Given the organizational architecture of the product lines, how should the manufacturing facility (FAB) be treated?

3. What are the critical tasks of finance to support this new organization? As John Gavin, what is your biggest concern?

4. Is the product line concept appropriate for DS? What are the positive and negative aspects of the product line structure, considering the (1) measurements, (2) transfer pricing, and (3) organizational structure?

5. Will the product line concept change the behavior of the division? Is there anything else DS can do to change the culture?

6. What other management control recommendations would you make to DS management given their drive to profitability?

Case 2–5
National Tractor and Equipment Company

National Tractor and Equipment Company, Inc., was a manufacturer of a number of products, including a wide line of farm tractors. Tractors were divided into several fairly well-defined types, according to their capacity, and National manufactured tractors of each type. This case deals with one of these types, here referred to as a type X.

Fixed costs represented a relatively large share of total costs at National, and, therefore, achieving a strong sales position was an important means of reducing unit costs and improving profits. Consequently, a major objective of the company was to be the sales leader in each of the several types. If National was not the leader during a particular year, its goal was to surpass whoever was the leader. If National was the leader, its goal was to maintain the size of its lead.

The company had experienced a rather erratic showing in sales of the type X tractors over the previous several years. Though National had been the sales leader in four of the previous six years (1970–75) its lead in 1973 and 1974 had been slim, and in 1975 its chief competitor took over first place. Meanwhile, profits of this division of its business had fluctuated widely. Accordingly, early in 1976, the controller's department made a sales analysis of the type X tractor division.

William Lawrence, who was given the job of making the analysis, decided to use the approach the controller had used for other analyses. Usually these analyses started with a comparison of actual costs or actual profit with some benchmark, such as the budget or the fig-

ures for some prior year when performance was satisfactory. The analyst then sought to isolate and quantify the various causes of the difference between actual and the standard applied in that particular case.

In the case of tractors, since management's objective was to surpass the sales leader, unit sales of the leading competitor—here called "competitor A"—seemed to be the most logical standard. Competitor A had sold 13,449 type X tractors in 1975, compared with 10,356 for National—a deficiency of 3,093. (A copy of Mr. Lawrence's analysis as presented to management appears as an appendix to this case.)

Mr. Lawrence began his analysis by looking at the profits and return on assets of the type X tractor division (see Appendix Exhibit 1). Both had improved significantly over the 1973 and 1974 levels. However, in 1975 National dropped from the first-place sales position it had held during 1973 and 1974 and this was of grave concern to management. Furthermore, its market share had decreased from 25.0 percent to 23.5 percent (see Appendix Exhibit 2). Both of its major competitors had increased their market shares, and competitor A had outsold National for the first time in five years.

Mr. Lawrence next prepared the sales portion of the table that appears as Exhibit 3 in the appendix. This exhibit compares sales of type X tractors by National and competitor A for the preceding three years, 1973–1975. The major task, then—and this was the crux of the analysis—was to identify and analyze those factors that accounted for the volume difference in each of the three years.

After he had completed this initial analysis, Mr. Lawrence, representing the controller's department, met with representatives of the sales department and the product development de-

This case was prepared by J. S. Hekimian under the supervision of R. N. Anthony, Harvard Business School. Copyright © by the President and Fellows of Harvard College. Harvard Business School case 161-010.

partment. Together, they discussed the various factors that might have accounted for the volume differences in each of the three years under review. Using their collective judgments and estimates, they broke down the volume difference into as many specific factors as they could agree on. All the remaining factors, they decided, must have accounted for the remaining difference, although they could not agree on the proportions, so they gave the total under other factors.

The first matter that Mr. Lawrence called to the attention of this group was that a major fire in one of competitor A's plants in the latter part of 1974 had severely limited production. He had compiled monthly production estimates for competitor A for 1974 and two prior years. He then had gathered estimates of industry sales during those years and developed certain relationships that seemed to him to hold among estimated monthly sales, actual monthly sales, and actual monthly production for 1972 and 1973 by competitor A. When he applied these relationships to 1974, it seemed evident to him that competitor A had produced significantly fewer type X tractors than it normally would have during the months when its plant was shut down.

Mr. Lawrence then had looked at sales patterns during 1972 and 1973 so that he could make an estimate of how much this lost production had resulted in a shifting of demand from 1974 to 1975; he tried to estimate how many competitor A customers for type X tractors delayed purchase of a new type X tractor from 1974 to 1975 because of the fire. In addition to research with the data available in his office, Mr. Lawrence traveled around the country and talked to distributors and dealers. He became convinced that a large number of potential purchasers of tractors annually had deferred their purchases of new type X tractors. Some of competitor A's dealers had had no type X tractors in stock in the latter part of 1974 because of the fire and others had had only a limited supply.

On the basis of Mr. Lawrence's analysis and the collective judgments of the other members, the group agreed that the fire caused a shift of 1,500 of competitor A's tractor sales from 1974 to 1975. This shift was recorded as a minus factor in 1975 and a plus factor in 1974.

Sales of type X tractors to government agencies was another factor studied by this group. Since government sales figures were published, the group ascertained that National outsold competitor A by 138 units. Government sales depended almost entirely on price; therefore, this was the type of business a tractor manufacturer could "buy" depending on how badly he wanted it.

Mr. Lawrence had done a considerable amount of research into the advantage that competitor A enjoyed because of its larger owner body.[1] National's owner body had always been smaller than competitor A's, but National had made sizable gains since 1967. There was a tendency for the owner of a tractor to buy the same make when he purchased a new tractor; thus, competitor A enjoyed an advantage. Mr. Lawrence wanted to know *how much* this advantage was. An annual survey made by the trade association of the industry indicated the behavior of a representative sample of buyers of new type X tractors. This survey indicated that owners of competitor A's tractors were more loyal than were National tractor owners (see Table 1). Using these survey results, Mr. Lawrence was able to calculate the advantage to competitor A of its larger owner body. Although only the calculations for 1975 are shown, he applied the same methodology to 1973 and 1974. Members of the group were impressed with this analysis and agreed to accept Mr. Lawrence's figures—a net advantage of 700 units for competitor A in 1975.

The next factor he analyzed was product differences. National did not have so varied a product line as did competitor A. Because of this, National dealers were at a competitive

---

[1]Owner body is the number of tractors in the hands of owners.

disadvantage for certain models of type X tractors. The group was able to agree on the approximate extent of this disadvantage.

The last main heading for variances listed in Exhibit 3 was other factors, which the group thought accounted for the remaining difference between National's sales and competitor A's sales. Mr. Lawrence had prepared a thorough analysis of these factors, too. For example, he had heard that competitor A built a more efficient and more durable type X tractor. He tried to quantify the effect of these variables by use of the data shown in Tables 3 and 4. He also requisitioned five National type X tractors and five competitor A type X tractors, and arranged to have these tractors tested at National's experimental farm to determine their operating characteristics, including power, performance, durability, reliability, and economy. Mr. Lawrence himself actually drove some of these

tractors. He also inspected each tractor and its performance at the end of the testing period.

The group could not agree, however, on the quantitative effect on sales volume of these factors or of the remaining factors listed under other. Therefore, they were represented by one figure. The total variance of all the factors affecting market penetration, of course, equaled the difference in sales between National and competitor A.

Questions

1. Are analyses of this type within the proper scope of a controller's function?
2. Can you suggest a better way of making the analysis?
3. What action, if any, should be taken on the basis of this study?

APPENDIX
AN ANALYSIS OF TYPE X TRACTORS*

Profits, Assets, and After-Tax Returns

Exhibit 1 depicts National's profits, assets, and return on assets for the years 1970–75. Profits have ranged from a high of $2.7 million in 1972 to a loss of $200,000 in 1974 and a profit of $2.5 million in 1975. Return on assets employed in 1975 was 20.5 percent after taxes.

Market Penetration versus Competition

Exhibit 2 shows National's penetration of the domestic market for type X tractors for 1970–75, compared with its two major competitors.

National's penetration rose from 24.3 percent in 1970 to a peak of 35.5 percent in 1971. In 1975, National's penetration was 23.5 percent. Competitor A's penetration, which was 27.9 percent in 1970, fell to a

low of 21.8 percent in 1971 and then increased to 30.5 percent in 1975. In four out of the last six years, National outsold competitor A in the type X tractor market. Competitor B's penetration moved from 27.4 percent in 1970 to 23.0 percent in 1971 but declined to 9.9 percent in 1973, rising to 21.2 percent in 1975.

Exhibit 3 sets forth those factors that accounted for differences in market penetration between National and competitor A—its chief competitor in the type X tractor market. The upper portion of the exhibit compares National's and competitor A's sales during the years 1973–75. The lower portion of the table shows the various factors that account for the differences between National's and competitor A's share of the market in each of these years. National's volume was 10,611 units in 1973, compared to competitor A's 10,246. In 1975, National's volume was 10,356 units, representing a market penetration of 23.5 percent, compared with A's volume of 13,449 units and 30.5 percent of the market. In 1975, National was outsold by 3,093 units.

---

*Prepared by the controller's department.

EXHIBIT 1

Profits, assets, and after-tax returns

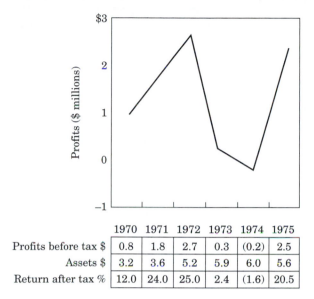

	1970	1971	1972	1973	1974	1975
Profits before tax $	0.8	1.8	2.7	0.3	(0.2)	2.5
Assets $	3.2	3.6	5.2	5.9	6.0	5.6
Return after tax %	12.0	24.0	25.0	2.4	(1.6)	20.5

Turning to the specific factors that account for this volume difference, we have estimated that the effect of a major fire at one of competitor A's plants in the last half of 1974, which halted production for nearly five months, resulted in a deferral of demand for 1,500 of its type X tractors from 1974 to 1975. This estimate is based on our knowledge of competitor A's output in 1974, compared with other years, and represents our best estimate on what sales might have been without the fire. In 1975, these 1,500 units represented 3.4 percent of market penetration. In 1975, National sold 138 more units to government agencies, equivalent to 0.3 percent of market penetration. We shall examine the effect on our market penetration of differences in the size of our respective owner bodies in subsequent tables.

The product differences result from gaps in our product line that prevent National from entering certain segments of the type X tractor market, thereby providing competitor A with a clear product advantage. For example, competitor A offers a larger variety of attachments and related equipment, which increase the number of different jobs its tractor can perform. We have estimated, for each year, the net market advantage accruing to competitor A because of its broader product line.

EXHIBIT 2

Market penetration versus competition

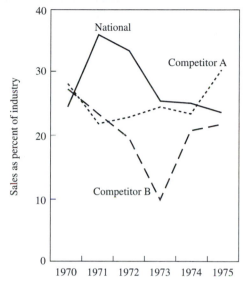

Industry penetration						
National %	24.3	35.5	33.0	25.5	25.0	23.5
Competitor A	27.9	21.8	22.8	24.5	23.1	30.5
Competitor B	27.4	23.0	19.6	9.9	20.7	21.2

Volume (000 tractors)						
National	10.9	12.8	15.6	10.6	8.4	10.4
Competitor A	12.5	7.9	10.8	10.2	7.8	13.4
Competitor B	12.3	8.3	9.3	4.1	7.0	9.3
Other	9.2	7.1	11.6	16.7	10.5	11.0
Industry total	44.9	36.1	47.3	41.6	33.7	44.1

Other factors, whose effects cannot be measured quantitatively, are summarized at the bottom of Exhibit 3, including customer attitudes toward National with respect to operating cost, durability, quality, and similar factors. In 1975, these other factors, in total, represented a net advantage to National of 955 units, or 2.2 percent of market penetration.

Basis for Estimated Advantage to Competitor A of Owner Body

Exhibit 4 shows the estimated number of National and competitor A type X tractors in operation for the years 1967–75.

EXHIBIT 3   Sales of Type X Tractors and Factors Affecting Market Penetration (National versus Competitor A, 1973 to 1975)

	Jan.–Dec. 1973		Jan.–Dec. 1974		Jan.–Dec. 1975	
	Units	*Percent of Market**	*Units*	*Percent of Market**	*Units*	*Percent of Market**
Sales:						
National	10,611	25.5%	8,431	25.0%	10,356	23.5%
Competitor A	10,246	24.5	7,828	23.1	13,449	30.5
National over/(under) A	365	1.0%	603	1.9%	(3,093)	(7.0%)
Factors affecting market penetration:						
Effect of major fire at one of competitor A's plants	—	—	1,500	4.5	(1,500)	(3.4)
Sales to government agencies	(3)	—	321	1.0	138	0.3
Competitor A's advantage in size of owner body	(850)	(2.0)	(660)	(1.9)	(700)	(1.6)
Product differences	(269)	(0.6)	(1,071)	(3.2)	(1,986)	(4.5)
Other factors:						
Customer attitudes toward National						
Operating cost						
Durability and quality						
National's price position	1,487	3.6	513	1.5	955	2.2
National's distribution system						
Sales administration						
Other factors						
Total variance	365	1.0%	603	1.9%	(3,093)	(7.0%)

*These percentages were calculated from the rounded numbers given on the preceding page; if calculated from the exact number of units, they would be somewhat different.

In 1967, it is estimated that competitor A had approximately 88,000 type X tractors in operation, while National had approximately 27,000 units in use. By 1975, National units in operation had more than quadrupled to a level of approximately 127,000 units. Competitor A units, on the other hand, had increased by almost 100 percent to a level of 158,000 units. During this period, National units as a percent of competitor A increased from 31 percent in 1967 to 80 percent in 1975. At the same time, our variance, in terms of units, decreased from 60,700 in 1967 to 31,200 in 1975.

Because of the importance of owner loyalty, competitor A's advantage in owner body represents an automatic advantage in market penetration, as indicated in the succeeding pages.

1975 Type X Replacement Patterns

Table 1 indicates the relative loyalty in 1975 of National and competitor A type X tractor owners. In this sample, 48 percent of the National owners who replaced a tractor bought a new National, 27 percent bought an A model, and 25 percent bought some other type X tractor. In contrast, 73 percent of A owners bought a new A, 14 percent bought some type X tractor other than National, and 13 percent

EXHIBIT 4

Units in operation

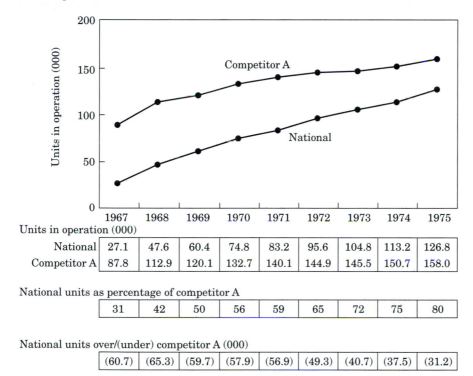

Units in operation (000)	1967	1968	1969	1970	1971	1972	1973	1974	1975
National	27.1	47.6	60.4	74.8	83.2	95.6	104.8	113.2	126.8
Competitor A	87.8	112.9	120.1	132.7	140.1	144.9	145.5	150.7	158.0

National units as percentage of competitor A

31	42	50	56	59	65	72	75	80

National units over/(under) competitor A (000)

(60.7)	(65.3)	(59.7)	(57.9)	(56.9)	(49.3)	(40.7)	(37.5)	(31.2)

of A owners purchased a National tractor when they reentered the market.

Effect on Differences in Owner Body on 1975 Tractor Purchases

In Table 2, we have calculated the effect of owner bodies on type X tractor purchases in 1975. We have used actual figures for the size of National and competitor A owner bodies but have assumed that all other factors, including owner loyalty rates, are equal. In this calculation, we have applied National loyalty to both National and competitor A owner bodies. Based on these premises, one would expect National to have a deficiency in market penetration relative to competitor A of 1.6 percent solely as a result of the differences in the size of the two owner bodies,

with National market penetration at 27.9 percent and competitor A penetration at 29.5 percent.

Type X Tractor Warranty Expenses[1]

Some indication of National's type X tractor quality and durability problem is found in the level of our warranty expense as shown in Table 3. From 1970 to 1973, our warranty expense on the average type X

---

[1]Warranty expense is the amount spent by National for replacements and repairs to tractors in use for which it had accepted responsibility. The company kept detailed records of such costs, broken down not only in the main classifications indicated in Table 4 but also for individual parts within each classification.

tractor increased from \$21.48 to \$55.06, an increase of \$33.58 per unit. Since 1973 warranty costs have declined to \$31.38, a reduction of \$23.68. Expense on all components, with the exception of the hydraulic system, has increased over 1970 levels. It seems clear that warranty costs of over \$31 per unit are too high and represent an unsatisfactory level of quality as far as the user is concerned.

National N-50 Type X Tractor—Warranty and Design[2] Cost

Table 4 indicates changes in warranty expense and design costs per unit on the N-50 tractor in the 1973, 1974, and 1975 models. In total, during this period,

warranty expense has been reduced approximately \$33, while design costs have increased \$36. Engine warranty expense on this model had declined \$40 per unit, while design costs have increased \$24. In the case of the transmission, warranty expense has increased \$3.30 per unit, despite an increase of \$1.77 pet unit in design costs.

---

[2]Design cost refers to the costs of the tractor itself. These costs are a function of the way in which the tractor is designed. For example, the total standard costs of the 1973 model was \$9.78 more than the total standard cost of the 1972 model; the designers had devised a more expensive tractor in 1973. In making the comparisons, wage rates and material costs are held constant.

TABLE 1*

	Make Purchased			
Make Replaced	*National*	*A*	*Other*	*Total*
National	48%	27%	25%	100%
Competitor A	13	73	14	100
Other	17	20	63	100

*Source: Replacement analysis published annually by trade association.

TABLE 2

	Make Purchased (thousands of units)			
Make Replaced	*National*	*A*	*Other*	*Total Purchased*
National	5.0	2.8	2.6	10.4
Competitor A	3.6	6.4	3.4	13.4
Other	3.7	3.8	12.8	20.3
Total	12.3	13.0	18.8	44.1
Penetration	27.9%	29.5%	42.6%	100.0%
National (under) competitor A:				
Percentage points (1.6)				
Units (0.7)				

TABLE 3   Warranty Expense

	Model Year						1975 (Over)/ Under 1970	
	1970	*1971*	*1972*	*1973*	*1974*	*1975*	*Per Unit*	*Percent*
Engine	$11.30	$ 7.56	$28.05	$28.40	$22.58	$12.76	$(1.46)	(13%)
Transmission	3.70	3.09	3.90	6.60	6.00	7.19	(3.49)	(94)
Hydraulic system	.80	.46	.74	5.21	1.35	.57	.23	29
Electrical	.65	1.14	1.93	3.88	4.40	3.27	(2.62)	(403)
Other	5.03	4.20	5.20	10.97	8.90	7.59	(2.56)	(51)
Total	21.48	16.45	39.82	55.06	43.23	31.38	(9.90)	(46%)

TABLE 4   Changes by Year

	1973 (Over)/Under 1972 Warranty Design		1974 (Over)/Under 1973 Warranty Design		1975 (Over)/Under 1974 Warranty Design		1975 (Over)/Under 1972 Warranty Design	
Engine	$ 9.80	$(3.74)	$24.00	$(12.99)	$ 6.48	$ (7.62)	$40.28	$(24.35)
Transmission	(2.69)	(1.31)	0.59	—	(1.20)	(0.46)	(3.30)	(1.77)
Hydraulic system	(4.48)	(8.90)	3.87	0.94	0.77	(2.97)	0.16	(10.93)
Electrical	(1.93)	—	(.53)	(1.09)	1.13	0.32	(1.33)	(0.77)
Other	(5.70)	4.17	2.00	(.50)	1.33	(1.73)	(2.37)	1.94
Total	(5.00)	(9.78)	29.93	(13.64)	8.51	(12.46)	33.44	(35.88)

RESPONSIBILITY CENTERS: REVENUE AND EXPENSE CENTERS

3

Management control focuses on the behavior of managers in responsibility centers. Responsibility centers are discussed in Chapters 3 through 6. In these chapters we review the considerations involved in assigning *financial responsibility* (in terms of costs, revenues, profit, and assets) to organization subunits.

We begin Chapter 3 by describing the nature of responsibility centers in general and the criteria of efficiency and effectiveness that are relevant in measuring the performance of their managers. We then define two different types of responsibility centers: revenue centers (described briefly) and expense centers (discussed at length). Expense centers can be divided into two categories: engineered expense centers and discretionary expense centers. We consider three of the most common types of discretionary expense centers: administrative and support centers, research and development (R&D) centers, and marketing centers.

In Part II of the book, we discuss how to supplement financial controls with nonfinancial performance measures.

Responsibility Centers

A responsibility center is an organization unit that is headed by a manager who is responsible for its activities. In a sense, a company is a collection of responsibility centers, each of which is represented by a box on the organization chart. These responsibility centers form a hierarchy. At the lowest level are the centers for sections, work shifts, and other small organization units. Departments or business units comprising several of these smaller units are higher in the hierarchy. From the standpoint of senior management and the board of directors, the entire company is a responsibility center, though the term is usually used to refer to units *within* the company.

EXHIBIT 3–1

*Responsibility
center*

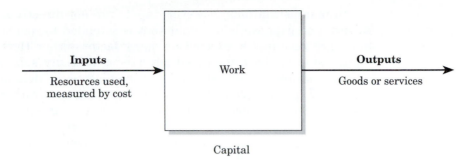

Nature of Responsibility Centers

A responsibility center exists to accomplish one or more purposes, termed its *objectives*. The company as a whole has goals, and senior management decides on a set of strategies to accomplish these goals. The objectives of the company's various responsibility centers are to help implement these strategies. Because every organization is the sum of its responsibility centers, if each responsibility center meets its objectives, the goals of the organization will have been achieved.

Exhibit 3–1 illustrates the core operation of every responsibility center. Responsibility centers receive inputs, in the form of materials, labor, and services. Using working capital (e.g., inventory, receivables), equipment, and other assets, the responsibility center performs its particular function, with the ultimate objective of transforming its inputs into outputs; either tangible (i.e., goods) or intangible (i.e., services). In a production plant, the outputs are goods. In staff units, such as human resources, transportation, engineering, accounting, and administration, the outputs are services.

The products (i.e., goods and services) produced by a responsibility center may be furnished either to another responsibility center, where they are inputs, or to the outside marketplace, where they are outputs of the organization as a whole. *Revenues* are the amounts earned from providing these outputs.

Relation between Inputs and Outputs

Management is responsible for ensuring the optimum relationship between inputs and outputs. In some centers, the relationship is causal and direct, as in a production department, for example, where the inputs of raw material become a physical part of the finished goods. Here, control focuses on using the minimum input necessary to produce the required output according to the correct specifications and quality standards, at the time requested, and in the quantities desired.

In many situations, however, inputs are not directly related to outputs. Advertising expense is an input that is intended to increase sales revenue; but since revenue is affected by many factors other than advertising, the relationship between increased advertising and any subsequent increase in revenue is rarely demonstrable, and management's decision to increase advertising expenditures is typically based on judgment rather than data. In research and development, the relationship between inputs and outputs is even more ambiguous; the value of today's R&D effort may not be known for several years, and the optimum amount that a given company should spend for R&D is indeterminable.

Measuring Inputs and Outputs

Much of the input that responsibility centers use can be stated as physical measurements—hours of labor, quarts of oil, reams of paper, and kilowatt-hours of electricity. In a management control system these quantitative amounts are translated into monetary terms; money is a common denominator that allows the value of several different resources to be combined or compared. The monetary value of a given input is ordinarily calculated by multiplying a physical quantity by a price per unit (e.g., hours of labor times a rate per hour). The resulting monetary sum is called "cost"; this is the way a responsibility center's input is commonly expressed. *Cost is a monetary measure of the amount of resources used by a responsibility center.*

Note that inputs are *resources used* by the responsibility center. Patients in a hospital or students in a school are not inputs. Rather, inputs are the resources that the hospital or school uses to accomplish the objective of treating the patients or educating the students.

It is much easier to measure the cost of inputs than to calculate the value of outputs. For example, annual revenue may be an important measure of a profit-oriented organization's output, but that figure will not express all that the organization did during that year. Inputs such as R&D activity, human resources training, and advertising and sales promotion may not affect output of the year in which they occur. Nor is it possible to measure accurately the value of the work done by a public relations department, a quality control department, or a legal staff. In nonprofit organizations, there may be no quantitative measure of output whatsoever; a college can easily measure the number of students graduated, but not how much education each of them acquired. Many organizations do not even attempt to measure the outputs of such responsibility centers. Others use an approximation, or *surrogate numbers,* while acknowledging its limitations.

Efficiency and Effectiveness

The concepts of input, output, and cost can be used to explain the meaning of *efficiency* and *effectiveness,* which are the two criteria by which the performance of a responsibility center is judged. These terms are almost always used in a comparative, rather than an absolute, sense. We do not ordinarily say that Responsibility Center A is 80 percent efficient; instead, we say that it is more (or less) efficient than its competitors, more (or less) efficient now than it was in the past, more (or less) efficient compared to its budget, or more (or less) efficient than Responsibility Center B.

Efficiency is the ratio of outputs to inputs, or the amount of output per unit of input. Responsibility Center A is more efficient than Responsibility Center B if it (1) uses fewer resources than Responsibility Center B but produces the same output, or (2) uses the same amount of resources but produces a greater output.

Note that the first criterion does not require that output be quantified; it is only necessary to judge that the outputs of the two units are approximately the same; if so, assuming both centers are performing their jobs in a satisfactory manner and the respective jobs are of comparable magnitude, the unit with the lower inputs (i.e., lower costs) is the more efficient. In the second criterion, however, where the input is the same but the output differs, some quantitative measure of output is required; this is a more difficult calculation.

In many responsibility centers, efficiency is measured by comparing actual costs with some standard of what those costs should have been at the measured output. Though this method can be somewhat useful, it has two major flaws: (1) recorded costs are not precise measures of the resources actually consumed; and (2) the standard is merely an approximation of what ideally should have happened under the prevailing circumstances.

In contrast to efficiency, which is determined by the relationship between input and output, *effectiveness is determined by the relationship between a responsibility center's output and its objectives.* The more this output contributes to the objectives, the more effective the unit. Since both objectives and outputs are difficult to quantify, effectiveness tends to be expressed in subjective, nonanalytical terms, e.g., "College A is doing a first-rate job, but College B has slipped somewhat in recent years."

Efficiency and effectiveness are not mutually exclusive; every responsibility center ought to be both efficient and effective—in which case, the organization ought to be meeting its goals in an optimum manner. A responsibility center, which carries out its charge with the lowest possible consumption of resources, may be efficient, but if its output fails to contribute adequately to the attainment of the organizations' goals, it is not effective. If a credit department handles the paperwork connected with delinquent accounts at a low cost per unit, it is efficient; but if, at the same time, it is unsuccessful in making collections (or needlessly antagonizes customers in the process), it is ineffective.

In summary, a responsibility center is efficient if it does things right, and it is effective if it does the right things.

The Role of Profit.   A major objective of any profit-oriented organization is to earn a satisfactory profit. Thus, profit is an important measure of effectiveness. Furthermore, since profit is the difference between revenue (a measure of output) and expense (a measure of input), it is also a measure of efficiency. *Thus, profit measures both effectiveness and efficiency.* When such an overall measure exists, it is unnecessary to determine the relative importance of effectiveness versus efficiency. When such a measure does not exist, however, it is feasible and useful to classify performance measures as relating either to effectiveness or to efficiency. But this kind of situation has the problem of balancing two types of measurements. How, for example, does one compare the profligate perfectionist, who may be effective but not efficient, with the frugal manager, who uses less input but produces less than the optimum output?

Types of Responsibility Centers

There are four types of responsibility centers, classified according to the nature of the monetary inputs and/or outputs that are measured for control purposes: revenue centers, expense centers, profit centers, and investment centers. Their respective characteristics are shown in Exhibit 3–2. In revenue centers, output is measured in monetary terms; in expense centers, inputs are so measured; in profit centers, both revenues (output) and expenses (input) are measured; and in investment centers, the relationship between profit and investment is measured.

Each type of responsibility center requires a different planning and control system. In the remainder of this chapter we briefly review the planning and control techniques used in revenue centers, and then move on to a more extensive discussion of the techniques used in expense centers. Profit centers are discussed in Chapter 4 and investment centers in Chapter 6.

Revenue Centers

In a revenue center, output (i.e., revenue) is measured in monetary terms, but no formal attempt is made to relate input (i.e., expense or cost) to output. (If expense was matched with revenue, the unit would be a profit center.) Typically revenue centers are marketing/sales units that do not have authority to set selling prices and are not charged for the cost of the goods they market. Actual sales or orders booked are measured against budgets or quotas, and the manager is held accountable for the expenses incurred directly within the unit; but the primary measurement is revenue.

> **Example.**   In 1999, two companies, Servico and Impac Hotel Group, merged to create Lodgian, Inc., one of the largest owners and operators of hotels in the United States. Lodgian reorganized itself into six regions, each with a Regional Vice President, a Regional Operations Manager, and a Regional Director of Sales & Marketing. The sales and marketing functions were constituted as revenue centers, with the goal to significantly improve market share.[1]

---

[1]"Lodgian Merger Integration Proceeding on Schedule," *PR Newswire,* January 25, 1999.

EXHIBIT 3–2

Types of responsibility centers

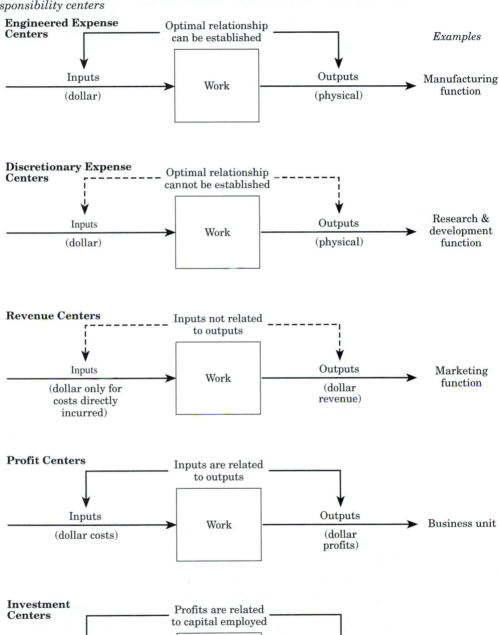

We do not cover revenue centers, though we do discuss the management of revenue in the section on profit centers (Chapter 4).

Expense Centers

Expense centers are responsibility centers whose inputs are measured in monetary terms, but whose outputs are not. There are two general types of expense centers: engineered and discretionary. These labels relate to two types of cost. *Engineered costs* are those for which the "right" or "proper" amount can be estimated with reasonable reliability—for example, a factory's costs for direct labor, direct material, components, supplies, and utilities. *Discretionary costs* (also called *managed costs*) are those for which no such engineered estimate is feasible. In discretionary expense centers, the costs incurred depend on management's judgment as to the appropriate amount under the circumstances.

Engineered Expense Centers

Engineered expense centers have the following characteristics:

- Their input can be measured in monetary terms.
- Their output can be measured in physical terms.
- The optimum dollar amount of input required to produce one unit of output can be determined.

Engineered expense centers are usually found in manufacturing operations. Warehousing, distribution, trucking, and similar units within the marketing organization may also be engineered expense centers, as may certain responsibility centers within administrative and support departments, for instance, accounts receivable, accounts payable, and payroll sections in the controller department; personnel records and the cafeteria in the human resources department; shareholder records in the corporate secretary department; and the company motor pool. Such units perform repetitive tasks for which standard costs can be developed. These engineered expense centers are usually located within departments that are discretionary expense centers.

In an engineered expense center, output multiplied by the standard cost of each unit produced measures what the finished product *should* have cost. The difference between the theoretical and the actual cost represents the efficiency of the expense center being measured.

We emphasize that engineered expense centers have other important tasks not measured by cost alone; their supervisors are responsible for the quality of the products and the volume of production as well as for efficiency. Therefore, the type and level of production are prescribed, and specific quality standards are set, so that manufacturing costs are not minimized at the expense of quality. Moreover, managers of engineered expense centers may be responsible for activities such as training and employee development that are not related to current production; their performance reviews should include an appraisal of how well they carry out these responsibilities.

There are few, if any, responsibility centers in which all cost items are engineered. Even in highly automated production departments, the use of indirect labor and various services can vary with management's discretion. Thus, the term *engineered expense center* refers to responsibility centers in which engineered costs predominate, but it does not imply that valid engineered estimates can be made for each and every cost item.

Discretionary Expense Centers

Discretionary expense centers include administrative and support units (e.g., accounting, legal, industrial relations, public relations, human resources), research and development operations, and most marketing activities. The output of these centers cannot be measured in monetary terms.

The term "discretionary" does *not* imply that management's judgment as to optimum cost is capricious or haphazard. Rather it reflects management's decisions regarding certain policies: whether to match or exceed the marketing efforts of competitors; the level of service the company should provide to its customers; and the appropriate amounts to spend for R&D, financial planning, public relations, and a host of other activities.

One company may have a small headquarters staff, while another company of similar size and in the same industry may have a staff 10 times as large. The senior managers of each company may each be convinced that their respective decisions on staff size are correct, but there is no objective way to judge which (if either) is right; both decisions may be equally good under the circumstances, with the differences in size reflecting other underlying differences in the two companies.

Furthermore, management's view as to the proper level of discretionary costs is always subject to change—especially when new management takes over.

Examples.   Percy Barnevik, CEO of Asea Brown Boveri, was known for slashing corporate staff after completing major acquisitions. For instance, the staff in his US subsidiary, Combustion Engineering, was reduced from 600 people to 100 over a two-year period, and the staff in his German subsidiary was reduced from 1,600 people to 100 in three years.[2]

In the first six months after joining IBM as its chief executive officer in 1993, Louis V. Gerstner formed 12 task forces to study growth opportunities, installed a new senior management committee structure, changed the process of evaluating new technology, created a new 11-member executive committee and a 34-member management council, brought in a new chief financial officer and a new senior vice president for human resources and administration, ordered 35,000 layoffs and a $1.75 billion cut in overhead expenses, and changed the basis for management compensation.[3]

---

[2]William Taylor, "The Logic of Global Business: An Interview with ABB's Percy Barnevik," *Harvard Business Review,* March–April 1991, p. 99.

[3]*Business Week,* October 4, 1993, p. 89.

In a discretionary expense center, the difference between budget and actual expense is *not* a measure of efficiency. Rather, it is simply the difference between the budgeted input and the actual input, and does not incorporate the value of the output. If actual expenses do not exceed the budget amount, the manager has "lived within the budget"; but since, by definition, the budget does not purport to predict the optimum amount of spending, living within the budget does not necessarily indicate efficient performance.

In the following section, we discuss management control systems for discretionary expense centers in general. We then discuss the special considerations involved in designing systems for three of the most common types of discretionary expense centers: administrative and support centers, R&D centers, and marketing centers.

General Control Characteristics

Budget Preparation.   Management makes budgetary decisions for discretionary expense centers that differ from those for engineered expense centers. For the latter, it decides whether the proposed operating budget represents the unit cost of performing its task efficiently. Its volume is not a major concern; this is largely determined by the actions of other responsibility centers—for instance, the marketing department's ability to generate sales. By contrast, management formulates the budget for a discretionary expense center by determining the magnitude of the job that needs to be done.

The work done by discretionary expense centers falls into two general categories: continuing and special. *Continuing* work is done consistently from year to year, such as the preparation of financial statements by the controller's office. *Special* work is a "one-shot" project—for example, developing and installing a profit-budgeting system in a newly acquired division.

A technique often used in preparing a discretionary expense center's budget is *management by objectives, a formal process in which a budgetee proposes to accomplish specific jobs and suggests the measurement to be used in performance evaluation.*

The planning function for discretionary expense centers is usually carried out in one of two ways: incremental budgeting or zero-base review.

Incremental Budgeting.   In this model, the discretionary expense center's current level of expenses is taken as a starting point. This amount is adjusted for inflation, anticipated changes in the workload of continuing job, special job, and—if the data are readily available—the cost of comparable jobs in similar units.

Incremental budgeting has two drawbacks. First, the discretionary expense center's current level of expenditure is accepted and not reexamined during the budget preparation process. Second, managers of these centers typically want to increase the level of services, and thus tend to request additional resources, which—if they make a sufficiently strong case—are usually provided. This tendency is expressed in *Parkinson's Second Law:* Overhead costs tend to increase, period. There is ample evidence that not all of this upward creep is necessary; when a company faces a crisis or when a new management takes over, overhead costs are sometimes drastically reduced without any adverse consequences.

Despite these limitations, most budgeting in discretionary expense centers is incremental. Time does not permit more thorough analysis.

Zero-Base Review.   An alternative budgeting approach is to make a thorough analysis of each discretionary expense center on a rolling schedule, so that all are reviewed at least once every five years or so. Such an analysis is often called a zero-base review.[4]

In contrast with incremental budgeting, this intensive review attempts to ascertain, *de novo,* that is, from scratch, the resources actually required to carry out each activity within the expense center. This analysis establishes another new base, at which point the annual budget review simply attempts to keep costs reasonably in line with this base until the next review takes place, five years down the line. It is expected that expenses will creep up gradually during the interval, and this is tolerated.

Certain basic questions are often raised in the course of this analysis: (1) Should the function under review be performed at all? Does it add value from the standpoint of end use customers? (2) What should the quality level be? Are we doing too much? (3) Should the function be performed in this way? (4) How much should it cost?

Information from other sources, including similar units within the company, trade associations and other outside organizations, and companies in other industries with superior performance (i.e., via *benchmarking*) is often useful for comparison purposes. Such comparisons may raise the interesting question: If Company X can get the job done for Y dollars, why can't we?

It is important to note, however, that achieving comparability is a difficult matter, as is determining a "correct" relationship between cost and output in a discretionary cost situation—not to mention the problems inherent in adopting an outside average as the standard.

Zero-base reviews are time-consuming, and they are likely to be traumatic for the managers whose operations are being reviewed (this is one reason for scheduling such reviews so infrequently). Also, managers will not only do their best to justify their current level of spending, but may also attempt to thwart the entire effort, regarding the zero-base review as something to be

---

[4]A zero-base review is to be distinguished from a zero-base budget (ZBB). Zero-base budgeting has been advocated in the literature, was tried in some government agencies and companies in the 1970s, and now has been abandoned. The procedure took more time than was available during the budget preparation process.

put off indefinitely in favor of "more pressing business." If all else fails, they will sometimes cast sufficient doubt on the inquiry's findings as to render them inconclusive, with the result that the status quo prevails.

In the later 1980s and the 1990s, many companies conducted zero-base reviews, usually as a reaction to a downturn in profitability. These efforts were often called *downsizing,* or, euphemistically, *rightsizing* or *restructuring,* or *process reengineering.*

> **Example.**   Aetna, a large insurance company, began a restructuring program in 1990. It reorganized its three divisions into 15 profit centers and reduced work force by more than 10 percent, resulting in savings of $156 million.[5]

Cost Variability.   Unlike costs in engineered expense centers, which are strongly affected by short-run volume changes, costs in discretionary expense centers are comparatively insulated from such short-term fluctuations. This difference stems from the fact that in preparing the budgets for discretionary expense centers, management tends to approve changes that correspond to anticipated changes in sales volume—e.g., allowing for additional personnel when volume is expected to increase, and for layoffs or attrition when volume is expected to decrease. Since personnel and personnel-related costs are by far the largest expense items in most discretionary expense centers, the annual budgets for these centers therefore tend to be a constant percentage of budgeted sales volume.

Furthermore, once managers of discretionary expense centers hire additional personnel or plan for attrition in accordance with the approved budget, it is uneconomical for them to adjust the work force for short-run fluctuations; hiring and training personnel for short-run needs is expensive, and temporary layoffs hurt morale.

Type of Financial Control.   Financial control in a discretionary expense center is quite different from that in an engineered expense center. In the latter, the objective is to become cost competitive by setting a standard and measuring actual costs against this standard. By contrast, the main purpose of a discretionary expense budget is to control costs by allowing the manager to participate *in the planning,* sharing in the discussion of what tasks should be undertaken, and what level of effort is appropriate for each. Thus, in a discretionary expense center, financial control is primarily exercised at the planning stage *before* the costs are incurred.

Measurement of Performance.   The primary job of a discretionary expense center's manager is to obtain the desired output. Spending an amount that is "on budget" to do this is considered satisfactory; spending more than that is cause for concern; and spending less may indicate that the planned

---

[5]*Financial World,* November 24, 1992, pp. 22–23.

work is not being done. In discretionary centers, as opposed to engineered expense centers, the financial performance report is not a means of evaluating the efficiency of the manager.

If these two types of responsibility centers are not carefully distinguished, management may erroneously treat a discretionary expense center's performance report as an indication of the unit's efficiency, thus motivating those making spending decisions to expend less than the budgeted amount, which, in turn, will lower output. For this reason, it is unwise to reward executives who spend less than the budgeted amount.

Control over spending can be exercised by requiring the superior's approval before the budget is overrun. Sometimes, a certain percentage of overrun (say, 5 percent) is permitted without additional approval.

It is important to note that the preceding paragraphs are solely related to financial control. *Total control* over discretionary expense centers is achieved primarily through nonfinancial performance measures. For example, the best indication of the quality of service for some discretionary expense centers may be the opinion of their users.

Administrative and Support Centers

Administrative centers include senior corporate management and business unit management, along with the managers of supporting staff units. *Support centers* are units that provide services to other responsibility centers.

Control Problems

The control of administrative expense is especially difficult because of (1) the problems inherent in measuring output, and (2) the frequent lack of congruence between the goals of departmental staff and of the company as a whole.

Difficulty in Measuring Output.   Some staff activities, such as payroll accounting, are so routinized that their units are, in fact, engineered expense centers. In other activities, however, the principal output is advice and service—functions that are virtually impossible to quantify, much less evaluate. Since output cannot be measured, it is not possible to set cost standards against which to measure financial performance. Thus, a budget variance cannot be interpreted as representing either efficient or inefficient performance. If the finance staff were to be given an allowance to "develop an activity-based management system," for example, a comparison of actual cost to budgeted cost would not indicate whether or not the assignment had been carried out effectively, regardless of the expense involved.

Lack of Goal Congruence.   Typically, managers of administrative staff offices strive for functional excellence. Superficially, this desire would seem to be congruent with company goals; but, in fact, much depends on how one defines excellence. Though a staff office may want to develop the "ideal" system, program, or function, the ideal may be too costly relative to the additional profits that perfection may generate. The "perfect" legal staff, for example, will not approve any contract that contains even the slightest flaw; but the cost of maintaining a staff large enough to guarantee this level of assurance may outweigh the potential loss from minor flaws. At worst, a striving for "excellence" can lead to "empire building" or to "safeguarding one's position" without regard to the welfare of the company.

The severity of these two problems—the difficulty of measuring output and the lack of goal congruence—is directly related to the size and prosperity of the company. In small and medium-sized businesses, senior management is in close personal contact with staff units and can determine from personal observation what they are doing and whether a unit is worth its cost. And in businesses with low earnings, regardless of size, discretionary expenses are often kept under tight control. In a large business, however, senior management cannot possibly know about, much less evaluate, all staff activities; and if that company is also a profitable one, there is temptation to approve staff requests for constantly increasing budgets.

Support centers often charge other responsibility centers for the services that they provide. For example, the management information services department may charge others for computer services. These responsibility centers are profit centers and are discussed in Chapter 4.

Budget Preparation

The proposed budget for an administrative or support center usually consists of a list of expense items, with the proposed budget being compared with the current year's actual expenses. Some companies request a more elaborate presentation, which may include some or all of the following components:

- A section covering the basic costs of the center—including the costs of "being in business" plus the costs of all intrinsically necessary activities for which no general management decisions are required.
- A section covering the discretionary activities of the center, including a description of the objectives and the estimated costs of each.
- A section fully explaining all proposed increases in the budget other than those related to inflation.

These additional sections are clearly worthwhile only if the budget is large and/or management wishes to determine the proper extent of the center's activities. In other situations, the amount of detail depends on the importance of the expenses and the desires of management.

Research and Development Centers

Control Problems

The control of research and development centers presents its own characteristic difficulties, in particular, difficulty in relating results to inputs; and lack of goal congruence.

Difficulty in Relating Results to Inputs.   The results of research and development activities are difficult to measure quantitatively. In contrast to administrative activities, R&D usually has at least a semitangible output in the form of patents, new products, or new processes; but the relationship of output to input is difficult to appraise on an annual basis because the completed "product" of an R&D group may involve several years of effort. Thus, inputs as stated in an annual budget may be unrelated to outputs. Furthermore, even when such a relationship can be established, it may not be possible to reliably estimate the value of the output. And even when such an evaluation can be made, the technical nature of the R&D function may defeat management's attempt to measure efficiency. A brilliant effort may come up against an insuperable obstacle, whereas a mediocre effort may, by luck, result in a bonanza.

Lack of Goal Congruence.   The goal congruence problem in R&D centers is similar to that in administrative centers. The research manager typically wants to build the best research organization money can buy, even though that may be more expensive than the company can afford. A further problem is that research people often do not have sufficient knowledge of (or interest in) the business to determine the optimum direction of the research efforts.

The R&D Continuum

The activities conducted by R&D organizations lie along a continuum, with basic research at one extreme and product testing at the other. Basic research has two characteristics: (1) it is unplanned, with management at best specifying the general area to be explored; and (2) there is often a significant time lapse between the initiation of research and the introduction of a successful new product.

> **Example.**   In the biotechnology field nearly 26 years elapsed from the time Watson and Crick defined the structure of the DNA molecule, in 1958, until the first product resulting from that work was launched. And it took nearly 24 years (from 1936 to 1960) for basic research efforts to culminate in the successful introduction of a copy machine by Xerox Corporation.

Since financial control systems have little value in managing basic research activities, alternative procedures are often employed. In some companies, basic research is included as a lump sum in the research program and its budget. In others, no specific allowance is made for basic research as such, but there is an understanding that scientists and engineers can devote part of their time (perhaps 15 percent, or one day a week) to exploring in whatever direction they find most interesting, subject only to the informal agreement of their supervisor.

> **Examples.**   The discovery of "warm" superconductivity in 1986, one of the most important breakthroughs of the decade, was made by two scientists at the IBM research laboratory in Zurich, who were working "on their own time." IBM senior

management in Armonk, New York, did not even know that such research was under way.

Scientists at 3M Corporation were allowed, indeed expected, to spend up to 15 percent of their working time toward projects of their own choosing and for which prior approval from superiors was not required.[6]

For projects involving product testing, however, it *is* possible to estimate the time and financial requirements—perhaps not as precisely as for production activities, but with sufficient accuracy to permit a reasonably valid comparison of actual and budget amounts.

As a project moves along the continuum—from basic research, to applied research, to development, to production engineering, to testing—the amount spent per year tends to increase substantially. Thus, if it appears that a project will ultimately turn out to be unprofitable (as is the case for 90 percent of projects, by some estimates), it should be terminated as soon as possible. It is difficult to make such decisions in the early stages, however, since project sponsors usually describe the work-in-progress in the most favorable light. In some cases failure is not discernible until after the product reaches the market.

> **Example.**   After 10 years of research and development and many tens of millions of dollars of expense, Polaroid Corporation introduced its instant movie camera, Polavision, with great fanfare at its shareholder meeting in 1977. "A new art has been born," said Dr. Edwin Land, Polaroid's chairman at the time. But home video cameras quickly came to dominate the market, and by 1981 Polavision was gone, without ever having made a profit.

R&D Program

There is no scientific way of determining the optimum size of an R&D budget. Many companies simply use a percentage of average revenues as a base (preferring an average to a percentage of specific revenues in a given year because the size of an R&D operation ought not to be affected by short-term revenue swings). The specific percentage applied is determined in part by a comparison with competitors' R&D expenditures and in part by the company's own spending history. Depending on circumstances, other factors may also come into play: For example, senior management may authorize a large and rapid increase in the budget if it appears that there has been (or is about to be) a significant breakthrough.

The R&D program consists of a list of programs plus a blanket allowance for unplanned work (as mentioned earlier); it is usually reviewed annually by senior management. This review is often conducted by a research committee consisting of the CEO, the research director, and the production and marketing managers (the latter are included because they will use the output of

---

[6]Ronald A. Mitsch, "Three Roads to Innovation," *Journal of Business Strategy,* September–October 1990, pp. 18–21.

those research projects that turn out to be successful). This committee makes broad decisions as to which projects to undertake, which to expand, which to cut back on, and which to discontinue. These decisions, of course, are highly subjective, but they are within the established policy limits on total research spending. Thus, the research program is determined not by calculating the total amount of approved projects, but rather by dividing the "research pie" into what seem to be the most worthwhile slices.

Annual Budgets

If a company has decided on a long-range R&D program and has implemented this program with a system of project approval, the preparation of the annual R&D budget is a fairly simple matter, involving mainly the "calendarization" of the expected expenses for the budget period. If the budget is in line with the strategic plan (as it should be), approval is routine—it primarily serves to assist in cash and personnel planning. Preparation of the budget allows management to take another look at the R&D program with this question in mind: "In view of what we now know, is this the best way to use our resources next year?" The annual budget process also ensures that actual costs will not exceed budgeted amounts without management's knowledge. Significant variances from the budget should be approved by management before they are incurred.

Measurement of Performance

At regular intervals, usually monthly or quarterly, most companies compare actual expenses with budgeted expenses for all responsibility centers and ongoing projects. These comparisons are summarized for managers at progressively higher levels to assist the managers of responsibility centers in planning their expenses and to assure their superiors that those expenses are remaining at approved levels.

In many companies, management receives two types of financial reports on R&D activities. The first type compares the latest forecast of total cost with the approved amount for each active project. It is prepared periodically for the executives who control research spending, to help them determine whether changes should be made in the list of approved projects. The second type of financial report consists of a comparison between budgeted expenses and actual expenses in each responsibility center. Its main purpose is to help research executives anticipate expenses and make sure that expense commitments are being met. Neither type of financial report informs management as to the effectiveness of the research effort. Such information is formally provided by progress reports, which form a partial basis for management's judgments about the effectiveness of a given project. It is important to note, however, that management's primary tool in evaluating effectiveness is face-to-face discussion.

Marketing Centers

In many companies, two very different types of activities are grouped under the heading of marketing, with different controls being appropriate for each. One group of activities relates to the filling of orders. These are referred to as *order filling* or *logistics* activities; and, by definition, take place *after* an order has been received. The other group of activities relates to efforts to obtain orders, and, obviously, take place *before* an order has been received. These are the true marketing activities, and are sometimes labeled as such; they may also be called *order-getting* activities.

Logistics Activities

Logistics activities are those involved in moving goods from the company to its customers and collecting the amounts due from customers in return. These activities include transportation to distribution centers, warehousing, shipping and delivery, billing and the related credit function, and the collection of accounts receivable. The responsibility centers that perform these functions are fundamentally similar to the expense centers in manufacturing plants. Many are engineered expense centers that can be controlled through imposing standard costs and adjusting budgets to reflect these costs at different levels of volume.

In most companies, the "paperwork" involved in filling orders and collecting receivables is now accomplished quickly and at low cost by using the Internet.

Marketing Activities

Marketing activities are those undertaken to obtain orders for company products. These activities include test marketing; the establishment, training, and supervision of the sales force; advertising; and sales promotion—all of which have characteristics that present management control problems.

While it is possible to measure a marketing organization's output, evaluating the effectiveness of the marketing effort is much more difficult. This is because changes in factors beyond the marketing department's control (e.g., economic conditions or the actions of competitors) may invalidate the assumptions on which the sales budgets were based.

In any case, meeting the budgetary commitment for marketing expenses is not a major criterion in the evaluation process, because the impact of sales volume on profits tends to overshadow cost performance. If a marketing group sells twice as much as its quota, it is unlikely that management will be concerned that it exceeded its budgeted cost by 10 percent to bring in those sales. The sales target, not the expense target, is the critical factor.

The control techniques applicable to logistics activities are generally not applicable to order-getting activities. Failure to appreciate this fact can lead to incorrect decisions. For example, there is often a reasonably good correlation between sales volume and the level of sales promotion and advertising expense. This could be taken to mean that sales expenses vary as a result of sales volume, but such a conclusion would be erroneous. Flexible budgets that adjust to changes in sales volume cannot be used to control selling expenses incurred *before* the sale took place. Neither should advertising or sales promotion expense budgets be adjusted to accommodate short-run changes in sales volume. As indicated above, many companies budget marketing expenses as a percentage of budgeted sales, but they do so not because sales volume causes marketing expense, but rather on the belief that the higher the sales volume, the more the company can afford to spend on advertising.

In summary, there are three types of activities within a marketing organization, and, consequently, three types of activity measures. First, there is the order-filling or logistics activity, many of whose costs are engineered expenses. Second, there is the generation of revenue, which is usually evaluated by comparing actual revenue and physical quantities sold with budgeted revenue and budgeted units, respectively. Third, there are order-getting costs, which are discretionary because no one knows what the optimum amounts should be. Consequently, the measurement of efficiency and effectiveness for these costs is highly subjective.

Summary

A responsibility center is an organization unit that is headed by a manager who is responsible for its activities. In this chapter, we described two types of responsibility centers: revenue centers and expense centers. Performance in these centers is judged by the criteria of efficiency and effectiveness. In revenue centers, revenues are measured and controlled separately from expenses.

There are two broad types of expense centers: engineered and discretionary. In engineered expense centers, it is possible to estimate the "right" amount of costs that should be incurred to produce a given level of output. In discretionary expense centers, on the other hand, budgets describe the amounts that can be spent, but it is not possible to determine with exactitude the optimum levels of these expenses. Therefore, financial controls are not intended to measure efficiency or effectiveness.

The principal types of discretionary expense centers are administrative and support centers, R&D centers, and marketing centers. Control is extremely difficult in R&D units, somewhat difficult in true marketing units (as contrasted with logistic units), and less difficult in administrative and support units—but still more problematic than in manufacturing units.

Suggested Additional Readings

Hammer, Michael E., and Steven A. Stanton. "How Process Enterprises Really Work." *Harvard Business Review,* November–December 1999, pp. 99–107.

Horngren, Charles T., George Foster, and Srikank Datar. *Cost Accounting: A Managerial Emphasis.* Englewood Cliffs, NJ: Prentice Hall, 2000.

Institute of Management Accounting. *Statements on Management Accounting. Statement 4B,* "Cost Management for Logistics"; *Statement 4P,* "Effective Benchmarking"; *Statement 4V,* "Allocation of Service and Administrative Costs"; *Statement 4F,* "Allocation of Information Systems Costs"; *Statement 4I,* "Cost Management for Freight Transportation"; and Statement 4K, "Cost Management for Warehousing." 1995.

Koning, John W. *The Manager Looks at Research Scientists.* Madison, WI: Science Tech Publishers, 1988.

Kotler, Philip. *Marketing Management: Analysis, Planning, and Control.* Englewood Cliffs, NJ: Prentice Hall, 2000.

CASE 3–1
VERSHIRE COMPANY

In 1996 Vershire Company was a diversified packaging company with several major divisions, including the Aluminum Can division—one of the largest manufacturers of aluminum beverage cans in the United States. Exhibit 1 shows the organization chart for the Aluminum Can division. Reporting to the divisional general manager were two line managers, vice presidents in charge of manufacturing and marketing. These vice presidents headed all of the division's activities in their respective functional areas.

The Aluminum Can division's growth in sales slightly outpaced sales growth in the industry at large. The division had plants scattered throughout the United States. Each plant served customers in its own geographic region, often producing several different sizes of cans for a range of customers that included both large and small breweries and soft drink bottlers. Most of these customers had between two and four suppliers and spread purchases among

them. If the division failed to meet the customer's cost and quality specifications or its standards for delivery and customer service, the customer would turn to another supplier. All aluminum can producers employed essentially the same technology, and the division's product quality was equal to that of its competitors.

Industry Background[1]

Traditionally, containers were made from one of several materials: aluminum, steel, glass, fiber-foil (paper and metal composite), or plastic. The metal container industry consisted of the hundred-plus firms that produced aluminum and tin-plated steel cans. Aluminum cans were used for packaging beverages (beer and soft drinks), while tin-plated steel cans were used primarily for food packaging, paints, and aerosols. In 1970, steel cans accounted for 88 percent of the metal can production, but by the 1990s aluminum had come to dominate the

---

This case was adapted by Anil R. Chitkara (T'94) under the supervision of Professors Vijay Govindarajan and Robert N. Anthony. The case is based (with permission) on an earlier case prepared by Professor David Hawkins.

[1]The industry background is based on a similar description in the Crown Cork and Seal Company case, prepared by Professor Hamermesh, Harvard Business School.

EXHIBIT 1

Aluminum can division

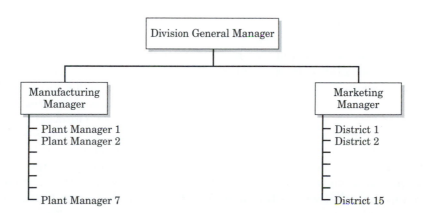

industry. In 1996, aluminum cans accounted for over 75 percent of metal can production. The soft drink bottlers who purchased the containers were primarily small independent franchisees of Coca-Cola and Pepsi Cola, which represented their independent bottlers in negotiating terms with the container companies.

Five beverage container manufacturers accounted for 88 percent of the market. The minimum efficient scale for a container plant was five lines and it cost $20 million in equipment per line. Raw materials typically accounted for 64 percent of the production cost. Other costs included labor (15 percent), marketing and general administration (9 percent), transportation (8 percent), depreciation (2 percent), and research and development (2 percent).

For beverage processors, the cost of the can usually exceeded the cost of the contents, with the container accounting for approximately 40 percent of the total manufacturing cost. Most beverage processors maintained two or more suppliers; and some processors integrated backward, manufacturing cans themselves. One large beverage company produced one-third of its own container requirements and ranked as one of the top five beverage container producers in the industry.

Prior to the early 1970s, cans were produced by rolling a sheet of steel, soldering and cutting it to size, and attaching both the top and the bottom. In 1972 the industry was revolutionized when aluminum producers perfected a two-piece process in which a flat sheet of metal was pushed into a deep cup and a top was attached. By 1996 the manufacturing process had become even more efficient, producing over 2,000 cans per minute.

In addition to production efficiency, aluminum had other advantages over steel: It was easier to shape; it reduced the problems of flavoring; it permitted more attractive packaging because it was easier to lithograph; and it reduced transportation costs because of its lighter weight. Additionally, aluminum was a more attractive recycling material, with a ton of scrap aluminum having almost three times the value of a ton of scrap steel. Four global companies supplied aluminum to can producers: Alcoa, Alcan, Reynolds, and Kaiser. Two of these companies, Alcoa and Reynolds, also manufactured aluminum containers.

Budgetary Control System

Divisions of Vershire Company were structured to encompass broad product categories. Divisional general managers were given full control of their businesses with two exceptions: the raising of capital and labor relations, which were both centralized at head office. The budget was used as the primary tool to direct each division's efforts towards common corporate objectives.

Sales Budget

In May, each divisional general manager submitted a preliminary report to corporate management summarizing the outlook for sales, income, and capital requirements for the next budget year, and evaluating the trends anticipated in each category over the subsequent two years. These reports were not detailed and were usually fairly easy to pull together since each division was already required to predict market conditions in the current year and to anticipate capital expenditures five years out as part of the strategic planning process.

Once the divisional general managers had submitted these preliminary reports, the central market research staff at corporate headquarters began to develop a more formal market assessment, examining the forthcoming budget year in detail and the following two years in more general terms. A sales forecast was then prepared for each division; and these forecasts were combined to create a forecast for the entire company.

In developing division forecasts, the research staff considered several topics, including general economic conditions and their impact on customers, and market share for different products by geographic area. Fundamental assumptions were made as to price, new products, changes in particular accounts, new plants, inventory carry-overs, forward buying, packaging trends, industry growth trends, weather conditions, and alternative packaging. Each product line, regardless of size, was reviewed in the same manner.

These forecasts were prepared at the head office in order to ensure that basic assumptions were uniform and that overall corporate sales forecasts were both reasonable and achievable. The completed forecasts were forwarded to their respective divisions for review, criticism, and fine-tuning.

The divisional general managers then compiled their own sales forecasts from the bottom up, asking each district sales manager to estimate sales for the coming budget year. The district managers could request help from the head office or the divisional staff but in the end assumed full responsibility for the forecasts they submitted.

All district sales forecasts were consolidated at the division level for review by the vice president for marketing, but no changes were made in a district's forecast unless the district manager agreed. Likewise, once the budget had been approved, any changes had to be approved by all those responsible for that budget.

This process was then repeated at the corporate level. When all the responsible parties were satisfied with the sales budget, the figures became fixed objectives, with each district being held responsible for its own portion. The entire review and approval process had four objectives:

1. To assess each division's competitive position and formulate courses of action to improve upon it.
2. To evaluate actions taken to increase market share or to respond to competitors' activities.
3. To consider undertaking capital expenditures or plant alterations to improve existing products or introduce new products.
4. To develop plans to improve cost efficiency, product quality, delivery methods, and service.

Manufacturing Budget

After final approval at the divisional and corporate levels, the overall sales budget was translated into a sales budget for each plant, broken down according to the plants from which the finished goods would be shipped. At the plant level, the sales budget was then categorized according to price, volume, and end use.

Once the sales numbers were estimated, each plant budgeted gross profit, fixed expenses, and pretax income. Profit was calculated as the sales budget less budgeted variable costs (including direct material, direct labor, and variable manufacturing overhead—each valued at a standard rate) and the fixed overhead budget. *The plant manager was held responsible for this budgeted profit number even if actual sales fell below the projected level.*

Cost standards and cost reduction targets were developed by the plant's industrial engineering department, which also determined budget performance standards for each department, operation, and cost center within the plant—including such items as budgeted cost reductions, allowances for unfavorable variances from standards, and fixed costs such as maintenance labor.

Before plant budgets were submitted, controller staff from the head office visited each plant. These visits were extremely important because they provided an opportunity for plant managers to explain their situation and allowed controllers to familiarize themselves with the reasoning behind the managers' numbers so that they could better explain them when they were presented to corporate management. The controllers also used these visits to provide guidance as to whether the budgeted profits were in line with corporate goals, and to reinforce the notion that headquarters was in touch with the plant.

Each visit usually lasted about half a day. Most of the time was devoted to reviewing the budget with the plant manager and any supervisors the managers wished to include in the meetings; but time was also allocated for a plant walk-through so controllers could see for themselves how (and what) the employees were doing.

On or before September 1, plant budgets were submitted to the division head office, where they were consolidated and presented to the divisional general managers for review. If the budgets were not quite in line with management's expectations, plant managers were asked to look for additional savings. When the divisional general manager was satisfied with the budget, the budget was sent to the Chief Executive Officer (CEO), who either approved it or asked for certain modifications. The final consolidated budget was submitted for approval at the Board of Directors meeting in December.

Once a budget had been approved, it was difficult to change. Any problems that arose between sales and production at a given plant were extracted to be solved by people in the field. If a customer called with a rush order that would disrupt production, for example, production could recommend various courses of action but it was the sales manager's responsibility to get the product to the customer. If the sales manager determined that it was essential to ship the product right away, that would be done. The customer was always the primary concern.

Performance Measurement and Evaluation

On the second business day after the close of each month, every plant faxed certain critical operating variances which were combined into a "variance analysis sheet." A compilation of all variance sheets was distributed the following morning to interested management. Plant managers were not supposed to wait until these

monthly statements were prepared to identify unfavorable variances; rather, they were expected to be aware of them (and to take corrective action) on a daily basis.

Four business days after the close of every month, each plant submitted a report showing budgeted and actual results. Once these reports were received, corporate management reviewed the variances for those items where figures exceeded budgetary amounts, thus requiring plant managers to explain only the areas in which budgeted targets had not been met. The focus was on net sales, including price and mix changes, gross margin, and standard manufacturing costs.

The budgeted and actual information submitted is summarized in Exhibit 2. Supplemental information was provided by supporting documents (see Exhibit 3). Both reports were consolidated for each division and for the entire company, and distributed the next day.

The fixed costs were examined to see if the plants had carried out their various programs, if the programs had met budgeted costs, and if the results were in line with expectations.

Management Incentives

The sales department had sole responsibility for the price, sales mix, and delivery schedules. The plant manager had responsibility for plant operations and plant profits.

Plant managers were motivated to meet their profit goals in a number of ways. First, only capable managers were promoted, with profit performance being a main factor in determining capability. Second, plant managers' compensation packages were tied to achieving profit budgets. Third, each month a chart was compiled showing manufacturing efficiency[2] by plant and division. These comparative efficiency charts were

[2]Manufacturing efficiency =
$$\frac{\text{Total actual variable manufacturing costs}}{\text{Total standard variable manufacturing costs}} * 100$$

EXHIBIT 2   Performance Evaluation Report for a Plant for the Month of November*

| | Month | | |
Items	Actual $	Variance $	Year-to-Date Variances $
Total Sales			
Variances due to			
Sales price			
Sales mix			
Sales volume			
Total Variable Cost of Sales			
Variances due to			
Material			
Labor			
Variable overhead			
Total Fixed Manufacturing Cost			
Variances in fixed cost			
Net Profit			
Capital Employed			
Return on Capital Employed			

*Numbers in this exhibit have been omitted.

EXHIBIT 3   Supplemental Reports

Individual Plant Level Reports

Report	Content
Analysis of sales by customer groups	Detailed analysis of sales volume, sales dollars, profit dollars, and profit margin by end user customers (e.g., beer companies, aerosol companies, soft drinks companies)
Analysis of sales	More detailed backup analysis to Exhibit 2 regarding variances due to sales price, sales mix, and sales volume
Analysis of costs	More detailed backup analysis to Exhibit 2 regarding variances due to variable costs and fixed costs of manufacturing

Division Level Reports

Report	Content
Comparative analysis of profit performance	Comparison of sales and profits across plants
Comparative analysis of manufacturing efficiency	Comparison of efficiencies in variable and fixed costs across plants

highly publicized by most plant managers despite the inherent unfairness in comparing plants that produced different products requiring different setup times, etc. Some plants ran internal competitions between production lines and departments to reduce certain cost items, rewarding department heads and foremen for their accomplishments.

Questions

1. Outline the strengths and weaknesses of Vershire Company's planning and control system.

2. Trace the profit budgeting process at Vershire, starting in May and ending with the Board of Directors' meeting in December. Be prepared to describe the activities that took place at each step of the process and present the rationale for each.

3. Should the plant managers be held responsible for profits? Why? Why not?

4. How do you assess the performance evaluation system contained in Exhibits 2 and 3?

5. On balance, would you redesign the management control structure at Vershire Company? If so, how and why?

CASE 3–2
NEW JERSEY INSURANCE COMPANY

On July 16, 1987, John W. Montgomery, a member of the budget committee of the New Jersey Insurance Company, was reading over the current budget report for the law division in preparation for a conference scheduled for the next day with the head of that division. He held such conferences quarterly with each division head. Mr. Montgomery's practice was to think out in advance the questions he wished to ask and the points he thought he should make about each division's performance.

The law division of the New Jersey Insurance Company (NJIC) was responsible for all legal matters relating to the company's operations. Among other things, it advised company management on current and prospective developments in tax and other legislation and on recent court decisions affecting the company. It represented the company in litigation, counseled the departments concerned on the legal implications of policies, such as employee benefit plans, and it examined all major contracts to which the company was a party. It also rendered various legal services with respect to the company's proposed and existing investments.

As shown in Exhibit 1, the head of the law division, William Somersby, reported directly to top management. This relationship ensured that Mr. Somersby would be free to comment on the legal implications of management decisions, much the same as would an outside counsel. The law division was divided into five sections. This case is concerned with only two of these sections, the individual loan section and the corporate loan section. It does not attempt to describe completely the work of these two sections or the professional service rendered by the lawyers.

Individual Loan Section

The individual loan section was responsible for the legal processing of loans made to individuals and secured by mortgages on real property. The loan instruments were submitted by independent companies situated throughout the country. The company made no loans directly to individual borrowers, although at one time it had made direct loans in the New Jersey area. Most common among the loans submitted by the independent companies were FHA, VA, and conventional loans on homes. These loans usually were made directly by banks or similar financial institutions organized for the purpose. They would batch together a number of loans and sell them to NJIC in a package. The insurance company purchased many thousands of such loans each year.

The investment division of the company was responsible for establishing the terms of these loans, including their amount, interest rate, and maturity. An independent company would submit to the investment division an offer to sell a mortgage loan. It was the function of this division to determine whether or not the property to be mortgaged and the mortgagor were acceptable to NJIC for a mortgage loan. After the proposed loan was approved and its terms worked out, the investment division would forward to the law division the note, mortgage, and related papers which it received from the seller.

The major function of the individual loan section was to perform the legal work necessary on all new loans purchased and on all existing

This case was prepared by J. S. Hekimian under the supervision of Robert N. Anthony, Harvard Business School. Copyright by the President and Fellows of Harvard College. Harvard Business School case 106-049.

Exhibit 1

Partial organization chart

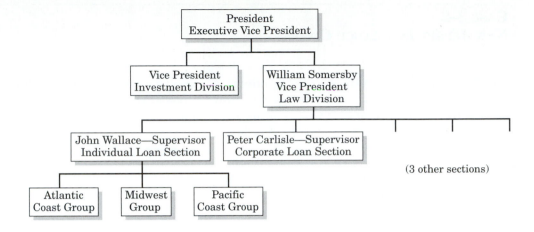

loans. Among other things, it had to check all the loan instruments to make sure they did, in fact, protect the interests of NJIC as required by law and by the investment division. Organizationally, the section was divided into three groups, each headed by an attorney and each responsible for a geographical section of the country—Atlantic Coast, Midwest, and Pacific Coast. In addition to the three attorneys, there was one who helped out in busy spots and took over a group in case of sickness or vacation and another who was in a training status.

Other than these five attorneys and a supporting secretarial staff, the section was comprised of 26 so-called mortgage examiners. These were persons who had had no formal legal training, but who had been selected carefully and trained by the company to check and approve certain of the loan transactions that came into the section. Because of the repetitive nature of the routine loan transactions, management believed that properly selected and trained individuals could, under the supervision of lawyers, perform this task, which at one time had been performed only by lawyers. Problem cases were referred by the mortgage examiners to the attorneys. John Wallace, head of the individual loan section, estimated that initially it took about three months to train a person to do this type of

work. It then took about a year and a half of on-the-job training and experience before the examiner achieved a satisfactory rate of output and two to three years before the average examiner reached optimum performance.

Since the work performed by the mortgage examiners was repetitive, management felt that it could exercise considerable control over a substantial part of this section. Based on a time study, a work standard of 12 loan transactions per examiner per day had been established some years previously, and this standard later was raised to 15. Records were maintained within the section of the number of loan transactions received each day, the number processed by each examiner, and the backlog.

In evaluating the work of individual examiners, some judgment had to be exercised in applying this standard. For example, in the Atlantic Coast group, an examiner sometimes received a batch of loan transactions in which the mortgaged properties were in a single, large housing subdivision. The legal issues in these transactions tended to be the same. In other parts of the country, however, loans tended to come from scattered localities and, thus, would be quite different from one another in many respects. A supervisor, therefore, in applying the standard would have to be familiar with the type of work an examiner was doing.

Budget Process

Although considerable control could be achieved over the output of individual examiners, control over the entire section was a more difficult problem. Each September, the budget committee of the company issued a memorandum to all division heads, asking them to prepare a budget for the operation of their division during the following year.

The basic intent of the budget process was to get division heads to plan and report in advance the scope of their operations for the following year. Usually, the budgets were prepared by anticipating first the changes in activity levels from the current year and then the cost implications of these changes. Management checked each individual budget for reasonableness, and also checked the total expected cost and revenue to ensure that the overall anticipated profit was satisfactory. The budget was viewed as a device for informing management of the plans a division head had for the coming year so that management could appraise these plans in relation to what other divisional heads had planned and in relation to company policy. The budget was also considered to be a measure of a division head's ability to plan the division's operations and then to operate in accordance with that plan.

On receipt of the budget committee's memorandum in September, division heads began forecasting operations within their divisions for the following year. First, each section head made plans for the section. For example, the individual loan section obtained an estimate of the amount of money that the investment division would have available for individual loans in the following year. Based partially on this estimate and partially on its estimated needs for other activities, the individual loan section developed a budget. This estimate, along with the estimated budgets for the other sections of the law division, was reviewed by Mr. Somersby. The law division then sent its budget to the budget committee for review. Usually, the law division's figures were accepted. Each quarter during the year, actual performance to date was compared with budgeted performance. Heads of divisions were required to explain large deviations from projected estimates.

Although management within the law division could, in theory, vary the size of the staff in the individual loan section, in fact, there was great reluctance to increase or decrease the work force unless a definite trend in volume was apparent. One reason for this was company policy. The company felt a great responsibility toward its employees, and as a matter of policy, would lay off or discharge employees only for serious offenses. This same policy made management reluctant to hire new employees unless there was assurance that the need for them was permanent. Therefore, the law division tended to maintain a staff sufficient to handle a minimum work load, and it supplemented this with overtime.

Another reason for the tendency to maintain a level work force of mortgage examiners was the cost of selecting and training them. Management went to great pains to select outstanding clerks for these jobs. This was followed by a thorough course of study and on-the-job training. Because of this large investment, management wanted to be sure that anyone trained for this job would be needed permanently in the section.

Management within the individual loan section, in attempting to achieve control over the section as a whole and yet in keeping with company policy, had devised several controls. Occasionally, when the work load lessened, supervisors would call the investment division to see if they could get some work that, although perhaps not quite ready to be sent over as a complete batch, could, nevertheless, be sent in parts. Also, since in periods when loan applications were low, foreclosures tended to increase, the mortgage examiners were trained to handle some aspects of foreclosures, and this provided a degree of dovetailing in the work flow. Other than these measures, however, the division preferred to rely on overtime work. The use of outside law firms was out of the question for this type of work because of the far greater cost, even in comparison with overtime wages.

Corporate Loan Section

The corporate loan section was a much different kind of operation. A corporate loan, generally for a much larger amount than an individual loan, was made directly by NJIC to a borrower, such as an industrial or commercial enterprise or a public utility. The loan might be either secured or unsecured. An important advantage to the borrower of this type of loan, compared with a loan evidenced by a bond issue sold to the general public, was that the borrower was not required to furnish a formal prospectus or to file a registration statement with the SEC.

In this type of loan, financial determinations, such as the amount of the loan, interest rate, timing of repayments, restrictive covenants, and so forth were made by the investment division, as was the case with individual loans, but by a different section in that division. Because of the size and complexity of corporate loans, the corporate loan section worked closely with the investment division people, who made these financial determinations. This involved sitting in on the negotiations and rendering advice on all the terms of the transaction. It was the responsibility of the corporate loan section to ensure that the final loan instruments protected the interests of NJIC in the manner intended by the financial people.

On this type of loan, for various reasons, the corporate loan section almost without exception retained well-known outside counsel. One important reason was that an opinion from such an independent law firm contributed to the marketability of the investment in the event of a sale at a later date. Further, in many of these transactions, a number of other investors were involved, and NJIC's law division could not appropriately represent these other investors. If NJIC was the leading investor, it did, however, select the outside counsel to be retained. In addition, it was not possible, without greatly increasing the size of the present staff, for company attorneys to handle all the legal work connected with this type of loan, especially at the time of peak loads. Under this system, any one lawyer had a large number of loan negotiations in process at all times with various outside counsel, and this was beneficial both to the individual and to the company in providing lawyers with a broad base of experience in a variety of situations. The background and experience of company attorneys assured the company of consistency of policy in the negotiation of direct placements.

A substantial part of the work in corporate loans consisted of drafting legal documents. The extent to which company attorneys relied on outside counsel to perform parts of this work depended on the complexity of the transaction (company attorneys tended to do more of the work on more complex transactions) and on how busy company attorneys were. In general, company attorneys handled, as a minimum, enough of the work to be thoroughly familiar with all aspects of the transaction. In many cases, they prepared the first drafts of all legal papers. But in the event that first drafts were left to outside counsel, company attorneys reviewed the work and redrafted it as necessary.

Borrowers were required to pay all expenses incurred in employing outside counsel. However, NJIC made clear to both prospective borrowers and to outside counsel that the counsel were representing NJIC and that their loyalty belonged to NJIC, much the same as for a company attorney. Even though the borrower paid the fee for outside counsel, the head of the corporate loan section, Peter Carlisle, checked closely on the fees charged by outside counsel. Over the years, a thorough tabulation of fees charged for different types of legal work throughout the country had been built up. Mr. Carlisle, simply by referring to this tabulation, could readily determine whether a particular fee was apparently out of line. If there was any substantial deviation, he looked into the case more closely to determine if there was some reasonable explanation; if not, he discussed the matter with the outside counsel and adjusted the fee. Over the years, NJIC had established excellent working relationships with many law firms throughout the country.

The control procedure in this section was substantially different from that in the individual loan section. At the initiation of each transaction, Mr. Carlisle was consulted by the attorney to whom it was referred. Reassignments to equalize the work load of the various attorneys were made as necessary. A degree of control also was achieved through weekly staff conferences with Mr. Carlisle. At this conference, lawyers raised individual problems they had encountered. In addition to keeping Mr. Carlisle informed in detail on what was going on, the conference provided an opportunity for each staff member to draw on the experience of other lawyers, and it served as a vehicle for developing a consistent policy on various matters. Also, the discussion of current negotiations made it more likely that, in case of illness, another lawyer would be prepared to take over the work.

Another control device was the current work assignment report, which each attorney in the section submitted to Mr. Carlisle. Because corporate loan transactions took varying amounts of time to complete, ranging from several weeks to many months, it was found that daily and, in some cases, weekly reports were not feasible. Accordingly, each attorney submitted a report when his work situation suggested to him that a new one was desirable. Each report covered all the time elapsed since the preceding report.

At the top of this report the lawyer briefly indicated his current work status, such as "fully occupied" or "available." Although a detailed format was not prescribed, in general the report described briefly how the lawyer's present jobs were going, what kinds of problems were involved, and what he had completed since his previous report. These reports, in addition to supplementing Mr. Carlisle's knowledge of what was being done in this section, helped tell who was available for more work.

The amount of time a lawyer had to spend on a particular job was not predictable. Major variables were the number and complexity of restrictive covenants in an unsecured note, for example, and the terms and provisions of the security instruments in a secured transaction. The number and complexity of the various covenants in these security instruments did not necessarily vary with the size of the loan, but depended, rather, on the nature, size, and credit standing of the corporate borrower. Many times, a relatively small loan was more complicated than a larger one.

Also, even though the details of a loan had been worked out initially to the satisfaction of the borrower and NJIC, and even though the loan had been in effect for a considerable time, borrowers frequently came back to NJIC to ask for waivers or modifications—that is, they requested changes in the restrictive covenants, the terms, or other conditions or agreements. Such events increased the difficulty of planning in advance how a lawyer was to spend his time.

Unusually heavy work loads in the section were met not only by overtime but also by increasing to the extent feasible the amount of work given to outside counsel. Within limitations, the lawyer responsible for a particular job generally decided how much work would be assigned to outside counsel.

Although the corporate loan section followed the same budget procedure as the individual loan section, one of the variable factors—that is, the extent to which work was delegated to outside counsel—did not affect the budget, since the borrower paid for these services.

Budget Reports

Mr. Montgomery was thoroughly familiar with the background information given above as he began his review of the law division's budget performance for the first half of 1987. The report he had before him consisted of a summary page for the law division (Exhibit 2) and a page for each of the five sections, two of which are shown in Exhibits 3 and 4. The budget figures on the report were one-half the budgets for the year.

Questions

1. In what ways does Mr. Somersby control the operation of the sections of his division? In what ways does top management control the operation of the law division?

2. What possibilities for improving control, if any, do you think should be explored?

3. As Mr. Montgomery, what comments would you make and what questions would you ask Mr. Somersby about the performance of the two sections of the law division for the first six months of 1987?

Exhibit 2   Budget Report, Law Division—First Six Months, 1987

Sections	Budget	Actual	Over Budget	Under Budget
Individual loans	$1,330,893	$1,385,154	$54,261	
Corporate loans	$1,176,302	$1,130,073		$46,229
(Three other sections omitted)	—	—	—	—
Total	$5,082,448	$5,107,822	$25,374	
Number of full-time employees	166	160		6

Exhibit 3   Budget Report, Individual Loan Section—First Six Months, 1987

Costs	Budget	Actual	Over Budget	Under Budget
Employee costs:				
Salaries, full time	$ 924,092	$ 932,201	$ 8,109	
Salaries, part time	—	—	—	
Salaries, overtime	4,500	33,610	29,110	
Borrowed labor	—	5,905	5,905	
Employee lunches	17,055	19,180	2,125	
Insurance retirement, SS, etc.	206,024	208,051	2,027	
Total	1,151,671	1,198,947	47,276	
Direct service costs (Photography, reproduction, etc.):	10,219	12,459	2,240	
Other costs:				
Rent	100,230	100,230		
Office supplies	2,267	3,067	800	
Equipment depreciation and maintenance	11,940	11,940		
Printed forms	3,842	5,367	1,525	
Travel	2,835	3,155	320	
Telephone	7,577	8,690	1,113	
Postage	3,057	3,227	170	
Prorated company services	36,810	37,405	595	
Professional dues	50	100	50	
Miscellaneous	395	567	172	
Total	169,003	173,748	4,745	
Grand total	$1,330,893	$1,385,154	$54,261	
Number of full-time employees	46	46		

EXHIBIT 4   Budget Report, Corporate Loan Section—First Six Months, 1987

Costs	*Budget*	*Actual*	*Over Budget*	*Under Budget*
Employee costs:				
Salaries, full time	$ 838,720	$ 807,488		$31,232
Salaries, part time	3,000	—		3,000
Salaries, overtime	3,000	—		3,000
Employee lunches	10,325	9,355		970
Insurance retirement, SS, etc.	219,681	211,872		7,809
Total	1,074,726	1,028,715		46,011
Direct service costs (Photography, reproduction, etc.):	4,367	3,720		647
Other costs:				
Rent	61,953	61,953		
Office supplies	1,850	2,955	1,105	
Equipment depreciation and maintenance	7,740	7,740		
Printed forms	445	915	470	
Travel	1,930	1,880		50
Telephone	2,275	2,835	560	
Postage	420	390		30
Prorated company services	20,213	18,357		1,856
Professional dues	200	200		
Miscellaneous	183	413	230	
Total	$97,209	$97,638	$ 429	
Grand total	$1,176,302	$1,130,073		$46,229
Number of full-time employees	26	24		2

CASE 3–3
NYPRO, INC.

NYPRO's corporate controller, Ted Lapres, was having serious concerns about his company's internal reporting system. While there was certainly a wealth of reported information available, Ted was worried that the rapid growth in information technology was making NYPRO's internal reporting system obsolete. He suspected they might even measure the wrong things. The heart of NYPRO's performance reporting system was the daily P&L (profit and loss) report. Gordon Lankton, the President, had introduced the daily P&L over 30 years before. He still personally reviewed the numbers with each of the 23 plant general managers every day. Ted, however, never had great enthusiasm for the daily P&L. "This is Gordon's report, and all the general managers know it. I occasionally review these numbers but realize that analysis and written feedback is part of Gordon's daily ritual. I use a variety of other means to stay in contact with the widely dispersed operating companies."

NYPRO was a large custom injection molding company with sales of over $200 million in 1995. During the past 20 years it had grown from a single plant in central Massachusetts to 18 production facilities located throughout the world. In the last 5 years it had doubled sales. The company was privately held with over 2,000 employees. Currently, it was pursuing the Baldrige Quality Award and had an excellent reputation as a sensitive and caring employer.

The published NYPRO mission was quite clear. "To be the best in the world in precision plastics injection molding . . . creating value for our customers, employees and communities." Its strategy was to partner with major precision plastic users in the medical and computer/communication industries. It offered modern, clean-room, high-quality, globally available plastic parts. NYPRO customers included Johnson & Johnson, Verbatim, 3M, H-P, Abbott Labs, and Gillette.

History and Strategy

In the early 1970s NYPRO was one of over 2,000 injection molders; it had sales around $4 million per year. Competition, based mainly on price, was fierce. Gordon, driven by an entrepreneurial spirit and a global vision, purchased the company. He quickly changed many of the operating procedures and led the effort to develop a new strategy. He was convinced NYPRO could break out of the pack. Key elements of the strategy included the following:

- Develop the capability to make unique plastic pieces of high quality.
- Develop the molding process for large-scale operations.
- Build a worldwide network of custom rejection molding operations.
- Partner and joint venture with employees and other companies.
- Develop clean-room manufacturing capability.

The company concentrated on selling to Fortune 100 companies with unique plastic molding requirements. This focus differentiated them from the competition comprised mainly of local small molding shops who considered the plastic molding process an art form. NYPRO maintained consistently high quality standards and production flexibility to meet specific customer requirements. An old-timer liked to recount how Gordon walked away from a large-volume order for a commodity product because it was not unique. Sales grew to $10 million in 1975, $45 million in 1980, $50 million in 1985, and $200 million in 1994. Sales were doubling in size every five years.

The NYPRO headquarters and several production facilities were housed in a large sprawling former carpet mill in Clinton, Massachusetts. The company renovated the building to provide for manufacturing, engineering, and administrative support facilities. The new main plastic injection molding operation consisted of approximately 20 machines in a two-level clean-room environment. This part of the Clinton operation had been replicated in 18 locations throughout the US and the world as the company expanded. New stand-alone facilities were located near major customers in order to be a better supply partner. The Clinton molding operation served as the model and benchmark for these remote stand-alone injection molding facilities.

Organization

The company had a flat decentralized organization with a lean headquarters staff. Each molding facility was a profit center with a responsible general manager and controller. Treasury and accounting were coordinated by headquarters. The corporate sales team sold on a worldwide basis using, as appropriate, the geographically dispersed sales force. Randy Barko, the VP of Sales, explained:

> We concentrate on the major global companies and this requires a sophisticated and unique set of selling skills. We can control and coordinate the negotiation and bid process at headquarters. The local sales force works with us on the local level and also generates business from other companies in the geographical region. As a matter of fact, when you plot our locations you will see they are all close to one of our major customers. We can negotiate globally and deliver locally.

NYPRO was divided into 23 profit centers. Each profit center and general manager was judged based on their stand-alone performance.

The various operational controllers reported directly to the profit center general manager and indirectly for professional and coordination purposes to the corporate controller, Ted Lapres. The general managers were given the authority to run their businesses and take the necessary actions to meet their goals. NYPRO fostered promotion from within and placed a high premium on proactive entrepreneurial management. Exhibit 1 outlines the organization. The central sales and marketing group produced about 80 percent of the sales with the remaining 20 percent generated by local sales efforts.

Another interesting characteristic of the organization was the fact that each profit center was its own legal entity with an internal Board of Directors. Corporate officers, managers, and other senior profit center managers served on the profit center boards. Ted served on five boards, about the average for a senior corporate manager. Some managers, however, served on as many as seven boards. Each profit center held on-site quarterly board meetings where the financial, operational, and other business issues were discussed. Ted said:

> This makes for high travel expenses and more time out of the office than I would like. Once I get to the profit center however, I benefit from the direct talks and the free flow of information. It is difficult when you are traveling to Asia and Europe on a regular basis, but I really get to know what is going on by walking around and talking to the people. If we have a profit center with problems and I am not on the board, I get one of the corporate board members to act as my representative as they check into specific problems.

At NYPRO's current size, the organizational structure appeared to operate well. There were strains, but incremental additions were smoothly assimilated into the company structure.

The Process

The injection molding process involved feeding raw plastic material into the barrel of a molding machine. The small beads of plastic material were melted upon entering the machines

EXHIBIT 1
NYPRO Inc., Clinton, Massachussetts, as of May 1994

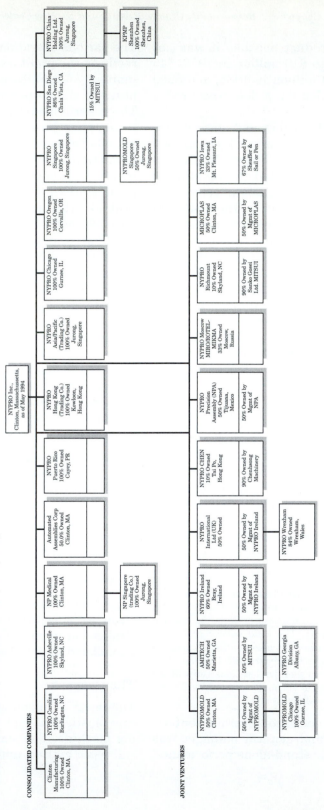

CONSOLIDATED COMPANIES

JOINT VENTURES

and then mixed with various plastic resins and injected into the mold. Once properly cured (hardened and cooled), the new plastic part was ejected from the mold and the process was repeated. This sequence was called a cycle.

The type of plastic, mold cycle, and the tolerances of the part depended on customer specifications. Each part required a specific set of tools (molds). The molding machines were set up to run a specific job or part. NYPRO had automatic plastic material feed systems located on the floor below the machine level. Normally, 20 molding machines were set in a clean-room environment for production. The completed parts were removed from the mold by robot, and placed on a conveyer system for assembly, packaging, and shipment. The process was designed to run 7 days a week, 24 hours a day. In the ideal world, run time was interrupted only for setup and scheduled maintenance. The injection molding machinery was key to continuous process and keeping within customer specifications. NYPRO partnered with its machine supplier and used state-of-the-art equipment.

The complexity of any manufacturing job at NYPRO depended on the number of cavities that a specific mold required. A complex mold may have tight dimensional tolerance and a series of cavities to be filled with each injection. More material was required to fill all the cavities and the cavities closer to the machine's injection nozzle might cure and receive more material before the cavities at the far end of the mold were filled. The number of cavities could vary from one to 400. NYPRO managers knew a job with a large number of cavities could drive the manufacturing yield numbers way down.

Pricing

The corporate sales and marketing group was responsible for all customer pricing. They used a cost-based pricing model, adding the material cost, machine rate (including facility overhead), times the cycle time. They then added a 25 per-cent margin for sales, general administration, and profit to arrive at a price quote. Machine rates, at budgeted capacity, were set each year and served as the basis for the price quotes. They then adjusted the formula based on the volume of the job and the projected available capacity. The local sales force worked with corporate sales to service the large national accounts and, at the same time, develop local customers.

Corporate "sold" the jobs to the various production facilities (profit centers) using a cost-based transfer pricing system. The production facility received an agreed-upon profit above the calculated cost of the job, while any remainder stayed with corporate to help cover corporate expenses. Facility preference was given to the operation closest to the customer.

The Daily P&L Report

This report served as the primary control data report for NYPRO. By 11:00 AM each day, each facility reported the key data for the previous three shifts. Exhibit 2 shows the format of this one-page comprehensive report and Exhibit 3 provides amplifying information. The report had been computerized in the early 1970s, and it was developed into a daily profit and loss statement 15 years later. This served as the scorecard for corporate management to judge the performance of each production facility and for the general managers to evaluate their operations. The NYPRO guide-line stated:

> No company can go forward without profits—profits are needed to buy new equipment, to provide employees with more benefits, and to expand the business. Profits are the scorecard of most business—and they are NYPRO's scorecard.
>
> At NYPRO, the molding machines are the profit center. In the hotel business, it's the hotel room—in the restaurant business, it's the table—in the retail store, it's the shelf space—and in the airline business, it's the seat. . . . Our machines are our hotel rooms. We need to keep them all occupied all of the time. We need to get the best price (value added in terms of dollar per hour) based on providing the best service. We need to improve the standards and improve productivity (yield).

EXHIBIT 2   NYPRO Comprehensive Daily P&L Report

GM-PRD05 RUN 9/20/88 PYROTHERM THURSDAY VALUE ADDED REPORT FROM 9/15/88 TO 9/15/88 PAGE 1
AT 11:34:47

VALUE ADDED IS SALES VALUE MINUS MATERIAL COST, DIRECT LABOR COST, INSERT COST, ASSEMBLY COST, PACKAGING COST.

STANDARD VALUE ADDED IS BASED ON RUNNING 100% YIELD FOR 82% OF AVAILABLE HOURS.

PROFIT EQUALS ACTUAL VALUE ADDED INCOME MINUS STANDARD VALUE ADDED COST.

* = W. I. P PRODUCTION

1	2	3	4	5	6	7	8
		CUST		HOURS	UTIL	STANDARD	ACTUAL
MA	SM	NAME	PART DESCRIPTION	RUN	%	CYCLE	PIECES
01	CV	ABBOTT	STRAIGHT RIB DOUBLE	24.0	100	11.5	36,754
02	BC	DURACE	VENT INSULATOR	23.0	96	10.2	75,972
03	CV	BAXTER	Y-CONNECTOR	22.0	92	23.0	56,000
04	*RB	N.P. I	CHECK VALVE CAP CLEA	23.0	96	9.5	132,000
05	LS	KOEHLE	FILLER WINDOW	20.0	83	30.0	4,500
05	LS	KOEHLE	CELL COVER	20.0	83	30.0	2,250
05	WP	MILLIP	LIFEGARD TOP CAP BLU	4.0	100	24.3	864
06	DP	HEWLET	C-DOME #01295-40030	24.0	100	60.0	6,912
07	*RB	N.P. I	CHECK VALVE HSG-WHIT	24.0	100	8.5	156,000
08	KS	KORES	PAWL, PSA MULTISTRIK	20.0	83	14.0	5,134
09	KS	MINN	DOOR LOCK SLIDER	23.0	96	10.0	59,500
10	LS	OSLO C	11-4W9 N.O./N.O HOU	14.0	58	15.0	8,964
11	WP	ASTRA	NEEDLE SHEATH TOP	17.0	94	16.2	72,000
11	WP	ASTRA	NEEDLE CAP BTM	5.0	83	24.0	20,000
12	CV	BAXTER	PLASTIC PIVOT P-173	24.0	100	12.8	28,482
13	BC	PILOT	PEN TAIL PLUG BLACK	22.0	92	10.9	238,300
14	WP	BASSIC	BOTTON SEAL-REV B	16.0	94	9.2	28,500
14	WP	BASSIC	TOP SEAL RW14035-RE	6.0	86	24.5	3,747
19	RB	N.P. I	NP CHECK VALVE CAP 4	12.0	50	11.5	12,000

TOTAL	AVAILABLE HOURS	364.0	VALUE ADDED STD	13,320	
	HOURS RUN	323.0	VALUE ADDED ACT	14,076	68.4 %
	UTILIZATION	.89	LABOR	1,877	9.1 %
	AVERAGE YIELD	100 %	MATERIAL COST	4,399	21.4 %
	EARNED HOURS	341.7	INSERT COST		%
	% ATTAINMENT	94 %	ASSEMBLY COST		%
			PACKAGING COST	227	1.1 %

TOTAL SALES VALUE	PYROTHERM	20,580	100 %

TOTALS

		TOTAL SALES VALUE	20,580	
		*W.I.P SALES VALUE	2,475	
		ASSEMBLY COST		
AVAILABLE HOURS	364.0	SALES VALUE PRODUCTION	20,500	100.0 %
HOURS RUN	323.0	EST. COST OF REJECTS	617	3.0 %
UTILIZATION	.89	MATERIAL COST	4,399	21.4 %
AVERAGE YIELD	100 %	EST. MATERIAL LOSS (26.0%)	264	1.3 %
EARNED HOURS	341.7	INSERT COST		%
% ATTAINMENT	94 %	PACKAGING COST	227	1.1 %
		DIRECT LABOR	1,877	9.1 %
		OTHER MANUFACTURING COST	7,600	36.9 %
		TOTAL MFG COST	14,984	72.8 %
		GROSS MARGIN	5,596	27.2 %
		EST. S & A COST	3,500	17.0 %
		EST. PROFIT FOR TODAY	2,096	10.2 %

144

EXHIBIT 2 Continued

9	10	11	12	13	14	15	16
YLD	OPERS	MATERIAL		VALUE ADDED	STANDARD GROSS	DOLLARS/HRS	
%	7.00/HR	COST	%	ACT	MARGIN %	STD	ACT
122	.7	3	0	980	41	32	41
117	.7	149	19	534	7	19	23
101	.7	159	14	866	43	39	39
95	.7	233	21	599	22	28	26
94	.7	167	13	975	69	52	49
94	.7	274	27	648	52	35	32
73	1.3	242	50	198	44	72	50
120	1.2	435	20	1,574	40	53	66
96	.7	311	22	949	41	41	40
100	.7	74	12	443	17	22	22
90	.7	283	23	818	35	40	36
67	.7	146	13	865	62	95	62
119	.8	916	43	1,092	50	53	64
83	.7	197	44	226	51	55	45
106	1.2	414	29	814	20	32	34
68	.7	156	16	689	43	48	31
114	.7	149	9	1,513	65	82	95
106	.7	69	18	279	41	44	47
80	.7	23	23	15	115-	3	1

AVERAGE $ PER HR
STD   ACTUAL

44.62   (40.85)

TOTAL OPERATORS REQUIRED (THEORETICAL)   33.5

+ – AVERAGE $ PER HOUR – +
STD   ACTUAL   BE A 89%

44.62   40.85   34.29

TOTAL OPERATORS REQUIRED (THEORETICAL)   33.5
TOTAL OPERATORS (ACTUAL)   15
DIRECT LABOR UTILIZATION   223%

Exhibit 3 is an explanation of the data in the daily P&L. The bottom of the report summarizes the results of the machines in each of the production facilities. This was the daily report card for each of the facilities. Gordon said:

> If you drop in 50 new jobs with new molds you see an operation's performance deteriorate very quickly. The daily report will show the job value add well below our target of $1,000 per day and the job yield data should also correlate. This tells me there is a problem at the facility. Something I would see if I could walk around the facility every day the way I did when we were only in Clinton. Hopefully, the daily report helps the local managers gauge the profitability of their jobs. Job complexity and yields are key to making money in this business. We have to bid the job correctly if we want to be profitable.

Other Reports

While the daily P&L served as the cornerstone report for the profit centers, there were other key weekly and monthly reports. The weekly report, Exhibit 4, focused on the key operational data (safely, quality, employees, productivity, and on-time shipments) and the summary financial information (sales and profits). The monthly reports were primarily financial and contained an analysis of the profit and loss statement, including a detailed assessment of cost and a comparison to budget and forecast. Ted liked to use a comparison of plant contribution as a comparative measure of performance (Exhibit 5).

> This puts each plant on equal footing and I can see how the manager controls the manufacturing and administrative expenses given the level of sales. The system allows me to look at plants as well as job contribution margins. The percentage contribution is a good common yard stick.

The primary operational measure was the monthly Benchmarking Report. This was a newly developed report done in chart form comparing all of the facilities. Exhibit 6 shows the Machine Utilization benchmark. Other benchmarks included: Accident Incidence Rate, Yield, Raw Material On Hand, On Time Ship-

EXHIBIT 3   Detail on NYPRO Daily P&L Report

Column	Description
1	The molding machine number in the production facility
2	The sales account manager
3	The name of the customer
4	The specific part run
5	Hours the machine is running producing acceptable parts
6	Machine utilization: hours run producing parts, available 24 hours
7	Is the best cycle time in seconds ever achieved?
8	The number of actual acceptable parts produced
9	Actual pieces (col. 8), standard pieces [machine hours (col. 5) * standard cycle time (col. 7)]
10	Number of operators assigned to each machine
11	New material cost at standard based on produced part weight
12	The material cost as a percentage of the total selling price of the part
13	Sales values—material cost, direct labor cost, interest cost, assembly cost, packaging cost
14	The gross product (Sales – Cost of goods sold) for each job
15	The standard dollars per hour = value added per machine hour that could be achieved if the job ran at 100% yield based on 82% of available hours
16	Actual dollars per hour: The machine hour rate that was actually achieved; or the actual number of dollars per hour to cover overhead based on actual pieces produced.

ments, Gross Reject Percent, Headcount Per Machine Utilized, Customer Return Incidents, Value Added/Employee/Week, Material Percent of Sales, Pretax Return on Assets, and Total Payroll Percent of Sales. Each plant general manager strove to be "Best in NYPRO Class." The reports in Exhibits 4, 5, and 6 were circulated monthly for each profit center and served as the basis of the monthly performance review.

Exhibit 4   Weekly Report

NYPRO CLINTON   WEEK #   39/95

1. SAFETY			
Accidents This Week	0		
Description, Date, Cause			
Accidents Year To Date	2		

2. QUALITY	THIS WEEK	LAST WEEK	YEAR TO DATE
Customer Returns % SVP	0.00%	0.37%	0.27%
Final Rejects % SVP	0.57%	0.19%	0.39%
In-Process Rejects % SVP	2.01%	2.21%	1.23%
TOTAL (GROSS) REJECTS	2.58%	2.77%	1.89%
Customer Return Details Description, Value, Cause			

3. PRETAX PROFITS	THIS WEEK	MO. TO DATE	YEAR TO DATE
Estimated	189	1,258	6,979
Budget	225	1,126	6,720
Variance	(36)	131	259

4. SALES	THIS WEEK	MO. TO DATE	YEAR TO DATE
Actual	1,290	7,548	55,340
Budget	1,477	7,387	53,824
Variance	(187)	161	1,517

5. EMPLOYEES			
Headcount (Equivalent)	589	583	567
Sales Per Person/Week	2.190	2.590	2.504
Turnover (Persons)	2	10	63

6. PRODUCTIVITY			
Utilization (# Machines: 91)	78%	79%	71%
Yield	84%	84%	87%
Effectiveness	65%	67%	62%

7. ON-TIME SHIPMENTS	94%	90%	83%

SIGNIFICANT
EVENTS/COMMENTS:

Controller: Date
President: Date

EXHIBIT 5   Comparison of Plant Contribution FY 1995 (11 Months)

	Plant 1	Plant 2	Plant 3	Plant 4	Plant 5	Plant 6	Plant 7	Plant 8
Sales (SVP)	54,892	28,140	13,584	11,447	7,618	7,268	9,177	5,568
Material	11,932	11,245	6,529	4,815	3,755	2,500	3,494	586
Direct labor	7,265	1,229	1,182	1,100	800	802	854	500
Indirect labor	7,014	3,415	1,498	1,379	710	915	1,118	242
Payroll benefits	7,211	2,208	1,010	836	491	417	477	255
Total	21,490	6,852	3,690	3,315	2,001	2,134	2,449	997
Supplies and services	5,058	3,132	914	998	625	1,048	1,333	368
Depreciation	2,647	1,787	584	447	563	556	533	215
Cost of goods sold	41,127	23,016	11,717	9,575	6,944	6,238	7,809	2,166
Gross margin	13,765	5,124	1,867	1,872	674	1,030	1,368	3,402
%	25.08%	18.21%	13.74%	16.35%	8.85%	14.17%	14.91%	61.10%
Selling expense	322	336	67					
Admin expense	891	1,259	613	722	313	406	569	449
Interest expense	2,445	(115)	277	54	321	306	224	138
Other	2,884	1,141	(64)	(17)	—	(32)	4	481
Pretax	7,223	2,503	974	1,113	40	350	571	2,334
Pretax %	13.16%	8.89%	7.17%	9.72%	0.53%	4.82%	6.22%	41.92%
Add								
Margin revenue			1,592	492	1,349	599	1,286	
Interest income	2,445		201	18	71	206	144	137
Management fees								
Corporate charges	2,992	1,364						672
Other						185		
Adjusted contribution	12,660	3,867	2,767	1,623	1,460	1,340	2,001	3,143
%	23.06%	13.74%	20.37%	14.18%	19.17%	18.44%	21.80%	56.45%
Adjusted %	23.06%	13.74%	18.23%	13.59%	16.28%	17.03%	19.13%	56.46%

Incentives

NYPRO had a quarterly profit-sharing plan for all employees: It was based on the gross margin percent compared to the standard cost. The incentive funds were pooled for each facility and distributed based on salary level. Normally, the quarterly bonus was 50 hours of salary (approximately 7 percent). Corporate employee bonuses were based on a weighted average of all the production facilities. Sales personnel received an incentive based on the level of sales. Corporate management bonuses were based on the profit percent and the profit improvement. Senior managers and various other employees also shared in a stock bonus program based on the value of the company as compared to book value.

The Dilemma

Ted knew that without reasonable coordination and control the success of NYPRO could

EXHIBIT 6

Machine utilization

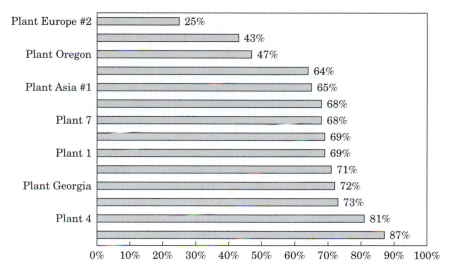

Machine Utilization Benchmarking

unravel very quickly. Yet, at the same time, the company culture would not permit a growth in the bureaucracy. Gordon's belief in independence, entrepreneurship, quality, and value were well instilled throughout the decentralized organization. Doubling sales every five years required significant capital expenditures. The strategy of seeking a few large customers put pressure on pricing and added the risk of sales dependency on a few. Ted said:

> We will soon be a $500 million operation. Can we just keep adding incrementally to our reporting and control system? I am troubled by the amount of detail in the reports. Perhaps we should focus on the end results to manage the business. How much detail can one digest? Should we go to a regional organization and add another layer of management? Right now, I am concerned whether we accurately capture the profitability of our jobs. Do we really know our costs? Are we leaving money on the table? We use a cost buildup to determine a customer's price. On some of the complex jobs we underestimated the complexity and the yield. We are targeting

the large global corporations. A pricing mistake can be disastrous.

Was the controllers' organization doing all the things possible to ensure the stability and sustained growth of NYPRO?

Questions

1. Do you think the daily P&L should be continued? Was it based on good cost accounting data and principles?

2. What other measures would you recommend? Should they replace the daily P&L, or should they be additional?

3. Do you see any opportunity to employ an ABC–type cost system?

4. Given the daily and monthly reports, was this enough control to manage this growth company? Did they need more balance in their reporting system?

CASE 3–4
WHIZ CALCULATOR COMPANY

In August Bernard Riesman was elected president of the Whiz Calculator Company. Riesman had been with the company for five years, and for the preceding two years had been vice president of manufacturing. Shortly after taking over his new position, Riesman held a series of conferences with the controller to discuss budgetary control. The new president thought that the existing method of planning and controlling selling costs was unsatisfactory, and he requested the controller to devise a system that would provide better control over these costs.

Whiz Calculator manufactured a complete line of electronic calculators, which it sold through branch offices to wholesalers and retailers, as well as directly to government and industrial users. Most of the products carried the Whiz brand name, which was nationally advertised. The company was one of the largest in the industry.

Under the procedure then being used, selling expenses were budgeted on a "fixed" or "appropriation" basis. Each October, the accounting department sent to branch managers and to other managers in charge of selling departments a detailed record of the actual expenses of their departments for the preceding year and for the current year-to-date. Guided by this record, by estimates of the succeeding year's sales, and by their own judgment, these department heads drew up and submitted estimates of the expenses of their departments for the succeeding year. The estimates made by the branch managers were then sent to the sales manager, who was in charge of all branch sales. He determined whether or not they were rea-

sonable and cleared up any questionable items by correspondence. Upon approval by the sales manager, the estimates of branch expenses were submitted to the manager of marketing, Paula Melmed, who was in charge of all selling, promotional, and warehousing activities.

Melmed discussed these figures and the expense estimates furnished by the other department heads with the managers concerned, and after differences were reconciled, she combined the estimates of all the selling departments into a selling expense budget. This budget was submitted to the budget committee for final approval. For control purposes, the annual budget was divided into 12 equal amounts, and actual expenses were compared each month with the budgeted figures. Exhibit 1 shows the form in which these monthly comparisons were made.

Riesman believed that there were two important weaknesses in this method of setting the selling expense budget. First, it was impossible for anyone to ascertain with any feeling of certainty the reasonableness of the estimates made by the various department heads. Clearly, the expenses of the preceding year did not constitute adequate standards against which these expense estimates could be judged since selling conditions were never the same in two different years. One obvious cause of variation in selling expenses was the variation in the "job to be done," as defined in the sales budget.

Second, selling conditions often changed substantially after the budget was adopted, but there was no provision for making the proper corresponding changes in the selling expense budget. Neither was there a logical basis for relating selling expenses to the actual sales volume obtained or to any other measure of sales effort. Riesman believed that it was reasonable to expect that sales expenses would increase,

---

This case was prepared by Professor Robert N. Anthony and James Reece. Copyright by the President and Fellows of Harvard College. Harvard Business School case 174-051.

EXHIBIT 1   Budget Report Currently Used

Branch Sales and Expense Performance
Branch A

Month: October   Mgr: N.L. Darden

	This Month				
	Budget[†]	Actual	Over*/Under	Percent of Sales	Over*/Under Year-to-Date
Net sales	310,000	261,000	49,000	—	70,040*
Manager's salary	2,500	2,500	—	0.96	—
Office salaries	1,450	1,432	18	0.55	1,517
Sales force compensation	15,500	13,050	2,450	5.00	3,502*
Travel expense	3,420	3,127	293	1.20	1,012*
Stationery, office supplies	1,042	890	152	0.34	360
Postage	230	262	32*	0.10	21
Light and heat	134	87	47	0.03	128
Subscriptions and dues	150	112	38	0.04	26
Donations	125	—	125	0.00	130
Advertising expense (local) ...	2,900	2,700	200	1.03	1,800*
Social security taxes	1,303	1,138	165	0.44	133*
Rental	975	975	—	0.37	—
Depreciation	762	762	—	0.29	—
Other branch expense	2,551	2,426	125	0.93	247*
Total	33,042	29,461	3,581	11.29	4,512*

[†]One-twelfth of annual budget.
*Unfavorable.

though not proportionately, if actual sales volume were greater than the forecasted volume; but that, with the existing method of control, it was impossible to determine how large the increase in expenses should be.

As a means of overcoming these weaknesses, the president suggested the possibility of setting selling cost budget standards on a fixed and variable basis, a method similar to the techniques used in the control of manufacturing expenses. The controller agreed that this approach seemed to offer the most feasible solution, and he, therefore, undertook a study of selling expenses to devise a method of setting reasonable standards. Over a period of several years, the accounting department had made many analyses of selling costs, the results of which had been used for allocating costs to products, customers, and territories and in assisting in the solution of certain special problems, such as determining how large an individual order had to be in order to be profitable. Many of the data accumulated for these purposes were helpful in the controller's current study.

The controller was convinced that the fixed portion of selling expenses—the portion independent of any fluctuation in sales volume—could be established by determining the amount of expenses that had to be incurred at the minimum sales volume at which the company was likely to operate. He, therefore, asked Paula Melmed to suggest a minimum volume figure and the amount of expenses that would have to be incurred at this volume. A staff assistant studied the company's sales records over several business cycles, the long-term outlook for sales, and sales trends of other companies in the industry. From the report prepared by this assistant, Melmed concluded that sales volume would not drop below 65 percent of current factory capacity.

Melmed then attempted to determine the selling expenses that would be incurred at the minimum volume. With the help of her assistant, she worked out a hypothetical selling organization that, in her opinion, would be required to sell merchandise equivalent to 65 percent of factory capacity, complete as to the number of persons needed to staff each branch office and the other selling departments, including the advertising, merchandising, and sales administration departments. Using current salary and commission figures, the assistant calculated the amount required to pay salaries for such an organization. Melmed also estimated the other expenses, such as advertising, branch office upkeep, supplies, and travel, that would be incurred by each branch and staff department at the minimum sales volume.

The controller decided that the variable portion of the selling expense standard should be expressed as a certain amount per sales dollar. He realized that the use of the sales dollar as a measuring stick had certain disadvantages in that it would not reflect such important influences on costs as order size, selling difficulty of certain territories, changes in buyer psychology, and so on. The sales dollar, however, was the measuring stick most convenient to use, the only figure readily available from the records then being kept, and also a figure that everyone concerned thoroughly understood. The controller believed that a budget that varied with sales would certainly be better than a budget that did not vary at all. He planned to devise a more accurate measure of causes of variation in selling expenses after he had an opportunity to study the nature of these factors over a long period of time.

As a basis for setting the variable expense standards, using linear regression, the controller determined a series of equations that correlated actual annual expenditures for the principal groups of expense items for several preceding years with sales volume. Using these equations, which showed to what extent these items had fluctuated with sales volume in the past, and modifying them in accordance with his own judgment as to future conditions, the controller determined a rate of variation (i.e., slope) for the variable portion of each item of selling expense. The controller thought that after the new system had been tested in practice, it would be possible to refine these rates, perhaps by the use of a technique analogous to the time-study technique that was employed to determine certain expense standards in the factory.

At this point the controller had both a rate of variation and one point (i.e., at 65 percent capacity) on a selling expense graph for each expense item. He, therefore, was able to determine a final equation for each item. Graphically, this was equivalent to drawing a line through the known point with the slope represented by the rate of variation. The height of this line at zero volume represented the fixed portion of the selling expense formula. Exhibit 2 illustrates the procedure, although the actual computations were mathematical rather than graphic.

The selling expense budget for the coming year was determined by adding the new standards for the various fixed components and the indicated flexible allowances for the year's estimated sales volume. This budget was submitted to the budget committee, which studied the fixed amounts and the variable rates underlying the final figures, making only minor changes before passing final approval.

The controller planned to issue reports each month showing actual expense for each department compared with budgeted expenses. The variable portion of the budget allowances would be adjusted to correspond to the actual volume of sales obtained during the month. Exhibit 3

EXHIBIT 2

Budget for "other branch expense," Branch A

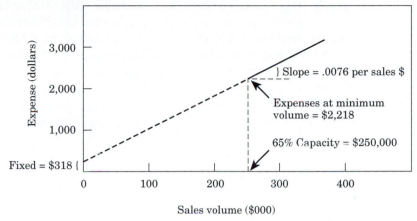

EXHIBIT 3   Budget Report Proposed by Controller

Expense Budget Report

Branch: A
Manager: N.L. Darden
Month: October

	Budget Factors		This Month		Year-to-Date	
	Fixed	*Variable*	*Flexible Budget*	*Actual*	*Over*/ Under*	*Over*/ Under*
Net Sales			261,000	261,000		
Manager's salary	2,500	—	2,500	2,500	—	†
Office salaries	139	0.0041	1,209	1,432	223*	
Sales force compensation	—	0.0500	13,050	13,050	—	
Travel expense	568	0.0087	2,839	3,127	288*	
Stationery, office supplies	282	0.0026	961	890	71	
Postage	47	0.0006	204	262	58*	
Light and heat	134	—	134	87	47	
Subscriptions and dues	10	0.0005	141	112	29	
Donations	20	0.0003	98	—	98	
Advertising expense (local)	35	0.0100	2,645	2,700	55*	
Social security taxes	177	0.0036	1,117	1,138	21*	
Rental	975	—	975	975	—	
Depreciation	762	—	762	762	—	
Other branch expense	318	0.0076	2,302	2,426	124*	
Total	5,967	0.0880	28,937	29,461	524*	

†The controller had not recalculated budgets for previous months, and figures were therefore not available for this column.
*Unfavorable.

shows the budget report that he planned to send to branch managers.

One sales executive privately belittled the controller's proposal. "Anyone in the selling game knows that sometimes customers fall all over each other in their hurry to buy, and other times, no matter what we do, they won't even nibble. It's a waste of time to make fancy formulas for selling cost budgets under conditions like that."

Questions

1. From the information given in Exhibits 1 and 3, determine insofar as you can whether each item of expense is (*a*) variable with sales volume, (*b*) partly variable with sales volume, (*c*) variable with some other factors, or (*d*) not related to output volume at all.

2. What bearing do your conclusions in question 1 have on the type of budgeting system that is most appropriate?

3. Should the proposed sales expense budgeting system be adopted? Why or why not?

4. What other suggestions do you have regarding the sales expense reporting system for Whiz Calculator?

CASE 3–5
WESTPORT ELECTRIC CORPORATION

On a day in the late autumn of 1987, Peter Ensign, the controller of Westport Electric, Michael Kelly, the manager of the budgeting department (reporting to Ensign), and James King, the supervisor of the administrative staff budget section (reporting to Kelly) were discussing a problem raised by King. In reviewing the proposed 1988 budgets of the various administrative staff offices, King was disturbed by the increases in expenditures that were being proposed. He believed that, in particular, the proposed increases in two offices were not justified. King's main concern, however, was with the entire process of reviewing and approving the administrative staff budgets. The purpose of the meeting was to discuss what should be done about the two budgets in question and to consider what revisions should be made in the approval procedure of administrative staff budgets.

Organization of Westport

Westport Electric is one of the giant US corporations that manufactures and sells electric and electronic products. Sales in 1983 were in excess of $9 billion, and profits after taxes were over $750 million. The operating activities of the corporation are divided into four groups, each headed by a group vice president. These groups are: the Electrical Generating and Transmission Group, the Home Appliance Group, the Military and Space Group, and the Electronics Group. Each of these groups is comprised of a number of relatively independent divisions, each headed by a divisional manager. The division is the basic operating unit of the corporation, and each is a profit center. The divisional manager is responsible for earning an adequate profit on his investment. There are 25 divisions in the corporation.

At the corporate level there is a research and development staff and six administrative staff offices, each headed by a vice president, as follows: finance, industrial relations, legal, marketing, manufacturing, and public relations. The responsibilities of the administrative staff offices, although they vary depending upon their nature, can be divided into the following categories.

1. *Top management advice.* Each of the staff offices is responsible for providing advice to the top management of the corporation in the area of its specialty. Also, all of the staff vice presidents are members of the Policy Committee, the top decision-making body of the corporation.

2. *Advice to operating divisions and other staff offices.* Each staff office gives advice to operating divisions and, in some instances, to other staff offices. (An example of the latter is the advice the legal staff might give to the finance staff with respect to a contract.) In theory, at least, the operating divisions can accept or reject the advice, as they see fit. In most cases, there is no formal requirement that the operating divisions even seek advice from the central staff. In fact, however, the advice of the staff office usually carries considerable weight and divisional managers rarely ignore it.

3. *Coordination among the divisions.* The staff offices have the responsibility for coordinating their areas of activities among the divisions. The extent of this coordination varies considerably, depending upon the nature of the activity. For example the finance staff has the greatest amount of this coordination to do, because it is necessary to establish and maintain a consistent accounting and budgetary control system. On the other hand, the legal and public

This case was prepared by John Dearden. Copyright by Osceola Institute.

EXHIBIT 1

Organizational chart—
January 1, 1988

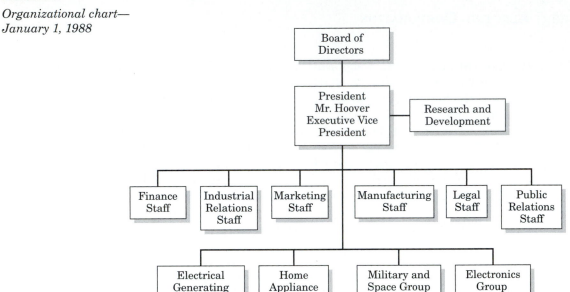

relations staffs have no direct representation in the activities of the division.

Exhibit 1 is an organizational chart of the Westport Electric Corporation.

The Budgeting Organization

Exhibit 2 provides a partial organization chart of the finance staff. As you can see from the chart, Ensign, the controller, reports to the finance vice president. Reporting to him is Kelly, who is in charge of the budgeting department. Reporting to Kelly is King, who is in charge of the administrative staff budget section.

Approval Procedure

Information Submitted.   In the early autumn of each year, the budgeting department is-

sues instructions and timetables for the preparation, submission, and approval of the budgets for the coming year. Since we are concerned in this case with the administrative staff budgets, we will limit our description to the nature of the information submitted by each administrative staff office.

Each staff office completes the following schedule.

Budget by Expense Classification.   This schedule shows the proposed budget, last year's budget, and the current year's expected actual costs, by expense classification (professional salaries, clerical salaries, supplies, consulting services, utilities, and so forth). The purpose of this schedule is to compare the new budget with the current year's budget and the current year's expected actual costs by expense categories.

EXHIBIT 2

*Finance staff—
January 1988*

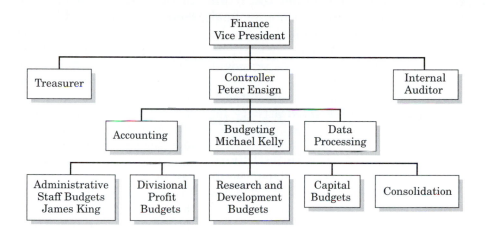

Budget by Activity. This schedule shows the same information as the previous schedule except that the information is classified by organizational component. The purpose of this schedule is to show which activities are being increased, which decreased, and which new activities are being proposed.

Explanation of Changes. This schedule is really a letter that accompanies the budget proposal and explains the reasons for the proposed budget. Explanations are divided into the following categories: economic changes (i.e., changes in the general level of wages and materials); increases or decreases in existing activities; new activities added and old activities dropped.

These reports are submitted by each administrative staff office to the budgeting department two weeks before the office is to present its proposed budget.

Presentation of Budget Proposal. Each administrative staff office budget was approved by the president and the executive vice president in a budget review meeting. The finance vice president sat in on all the budget presenta-

tions, but had no official power to approve or disapprove.

On the day scheduled for presentation, the vice president of the administrative staff office whose budget was to be approved would make a presentation to the president and executive vice president. The presentation would be based on the budget schedules previously submitted, but the explanations justifying the proposals might go into much greater detail. For example, last year the marketing vice president used three-dimensional color slides to describe a new activity that he was proposing to organize.

Attending these meetings were the president, the executive vice president, the administrative staff office vice president and his principal executives, the financial vice president, the controller, the budgeting manager, and the particular budget supervisor involved.

Typically, a budget meeting would proceed as follows: The presentation would be made by the administrative staff vice president. During the presentation, questions would be raised by the president and the executive vice president. These would be answered by the administrative staff vice president or one of his executives. At the end of the presentation, the president and executive vice president would decide whether to approve the budget or whether to curtail some of the proposed activities. Before the final decision, the finance vice president would be asked to comment. In almost every case, he would agree with the decision of the president and executive vice president.

Once approved, the budget became authorization to undertake the budgeted activity for the coming year.

Function of the Budgeting Department. The functions of the budgeting department with respect to administrative staff budgets has been to prescribe the schedules to be submitted and timetable for their submission and to "keep the presentations honest." In fulfilling the last function, the budgeting department analyzed the proposed budgets and made sure that the facts were correctly stated. For instance, they checked to make sure that the increases due to economic changes were accurate; or if some present activity were to be dropped, they made sure that the cost of this activity was shown as a reduction so that the cost savings could not be used to hide an increase in another activity. The details of the presentation were worked out beforehand between James King and the administrative assistant to the administrative staff vice president involved. When the presentation was made, the budgeting department would be asked to concur with the financial information being presented. The budgeting department, however, took no position on the appropriateness of the proposed budget or the efficiency of the activity. It was this situation that bothered James King.

Budget Evaluation

This was James King's second year as supervisor of the administrative staff budget section. Prior to that, he had been the budget manager in the Electric Stove Division. At the divisional level, the budget analysts exercised considerable influence over the level of efficiency represented in the operating budgets. For example, in the Electric Stove Division, the divisional controller attended every divisional budget meeting and argued long and hard for rejecting any budget that he believed was not sufficiently "tight." Because he had had a considerable amount of experience in the operations of that division, he was usually successful. King found it hard to reconcile the attitude of the finance vice president (who never seemed to raise any objections to the proposed budgets) with his former boss, the controller of the Electric Stove Division. Consequently, he asked to meet with Ensign and Kelly to see if something could be done to improve the evaluation techniques for administrative staff budgets. Below is an edited version of the meeting between Ensign, Kelly, and King on this problem.

King: All we do about these budgets is to make sure that the accounting figures are correct. We don't do anything about the efficiency represented by the figures, and I know for a fact that it is lousy in at least two cases, and I have my suspicion about some of the others.

Kelly: Tell Peter about Legal.

King: Earlier this year, you remember, we hired a consultant to work with our Data Processing Group. We gave the contract to the legal staff to look over, and it took them three months before they approved it. They had all kinds of nitpicking changes that didn't amount to a hill of beans, but which took up everybody's time.

Shortly after the contract was approved, I had a college friend visiting who's a lawyer in one of the biggest New York firms. We discussed the matter, and he looked over the original contract and the revised one and was astounded at the time that it had taken to get it approved. He said that a simple contract like that would be handled in a day or two by an outside lawyer. Since then, I find that everyone in the organization seems to feel the same way about Legal. They take forever to do a five-minute job, and they never stick their necks out in the slightest.

To add insult to injury, this year the legal staff is asking for a 30 percent increase in their budget to take care of the added cost resulting from the expansion of their work load. The trouble is that, unless we do something, they will get this increase.

Ensign: If everyone feels that the Legal staff is so inefficient, why should Mr. Hoover [the president] approve their budget?

King: I think that Mr. Hoover has neither the time nor the knowledge to evaluate the Legal staff. Any time Mr. Hoover asks for anything from them, he gets superdeluxe treatment. Since none of us are lawyers we have a hard time proving inefficiency, but we know it is there.

Ensign: What is the other budget that you think is out of line?

King: Industrial Relations—especially management training: We are spending more money on senseless training than you can shake a stick at. It's not only costing us money, but it is wasting management's time. For instance, last month we all had to take a course in quality control. It was the most simple-minded course I have ever seen. They gave us a test at the end to see how much progress we made. I gave a copy of the test to my secretary, and she got a 100 percent, without taking the course, or really even knowing what quality control is. Out in the division, the training was even worse. At one time they had a slide film that was supposed to teach us economics in three lessons! The film consisted of "Doc Dollar" explaining to "Jim Foreman" about money markets, capitalism, and so forth. We all felt that it was an insult to our intelligence. In their new budget, Industrial Relations is proposing to increase training by nearly 50 percent, and because the general profit picture is so good, it will probably be approved.

Ensign: If the training program is so bad, why don't we hear more complaints?

King: I will have to admit that I feel more strongly than most of the other people. A lot of managers and supervisors just go along with these programs because to be against management training is like being against motherhood. Also, the personnel evaluation forms that Industrial Relations prescribes have a section on the performance of the individual in these courses. I guess people are afraid to rebel against them because it might hurt their chances of promotion. The point is, at best, they are not worth the money that they cost. No one seems to get much out of them as far as I can see, so we certainly don't want to *increase* the training budget.

The conversation continued for some time. Although he did not express it in exactly these terms, King's other concern was a lack of goal congruence between the activities of the administrative staff office and the earnings for the corporation. It seemed to him that each administrative staff officer, at best, wanted to have the "best" operation in the country and, at worst, was simply interested in building an empire. Even the best operation, however, might cost much more than it was worth in terms of increasing profits. He was also concerned about the ability of the president and the executive vice president to evaluate the efficiency and the effectiveness of the staff offices, or even to decide whether additional activities were really worthwhile. King, therefore, believed it was necessary for someone to evaluate the budget proposals critically, as they did at the divisional level.

The meeting closed with Ensign asking Kelly and King to prepare a proposal that would solve the issue raised in the meeting.

Question

What should Westport Electric do about the evaluation problem raised in the case?

CASE 3–6
GRAND JEAN COMPANY

The Grand Jean Company was founded in the mid-19th century. The firm survived lean years and the 1929 depression largely as the result of the market durability of its dominant product—blue denim jeans. Grand Jean had been a market leader with "wash-and-wear," bell-bottom and flare jeans, and modern casual pants. By 1989 it was one of the world's largest clothing manufacturers. It offered a wide variety of dress and fashion jeans for both men and boys and a complete line of pants for women. It enjoyed a reputation for reasonably priced, quality pants. The company sold 40 million pairs of pants last year.

Production

In each of the last 30 years, Grand Jean sold virtually all its production and often had to begin to ration its pants to buyers as early as four months prior to the close of the production year. The company owned 25 manufacturing plants. The plants' capacity varied, but the average output was about 20,000 pairs of pants per week. With the exception of two or three plants that usually produced only blue denim jeans, the plants produced various types of pants. The firm augmented its own production capacity by contracting with independent manufacturers. Currently, there were 20 such contractors making all lines of Grand Jean's pants (including blue denim jeans). Last year contractors produced one-third of the total pants sold by Grand Jean.

Tom Wicks, vice president for production operations (see organization chart in Exhibit 1),

commented on the firm's use of outside contractors: "The majority of these contractors have been with us for five years or more. Several of them have served Grand Jean efficiently and reliably for over 30 years. In our eagerness to get the pants made, we understandably link with some independents who don't know what they are doing and are forced to go out of business after a year or so because their costs are too high. Usually we can tell from an independent's experience and per unit contract price whether or not he's going to survive.

"Contract agreements are made by me and my staff. The ceiling or maximum price we are willing to pay for each type of pants is very well established by now. If a contractor impresses us as being both reliable and capable of making quality pants, we will pay him that ceiling. If we aren't sure, we might bid a little below that ceiling for the first year or two, until the contractor proves himself."

Due to intense domestic and foreign competition, the failure rate in the garment industry was quite high. Hence, new entrepreneurs often stepped in and assumed control of existing facilities.

The Control System

Mr. Wicks continued: "We treat our 25 plants as expense centers. Operations at each plant have been examined thoroughly by industrial and cost engineers. You know, time-and-motion studies and all. I'm quite proud of the standard times and costs we have in place. We have even developed learning curves that tell us how long it will take production of a given type of pants to reach the standard hours allowed per pair after initial start-up or a product switch-over. We know the rate at which total production time per pair reaches standard for every basic

---

Adapted (with permission) by Professor Joseph G. San Miguel from a case prepared by Professor Charles T. Horngren, *Cost Accounting,* fifth edition, Prentice-Hall, Inc. Copyright by Charles T. Horngren and Joseph G. San Miguel.

Exhibit 1

*Grand Jean
Company organization
chart*

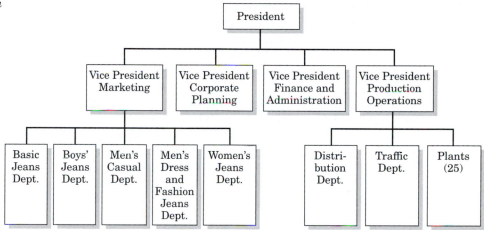

style of pants we make. We use this information for budgeting a plant's cost. The marketing staff estimates the quantity of pants of each type it wants produced each year. That information is used to divide total production among the plants. If possible, we like to put one plant to work for a whole year on one type of pants. That saves start-up and changeover costs. Since we can sell all we make, we try to keep our plants at peak efficiency. Unfortunately, the marketing folks always manage to complicate production schedules with a lot of midyear changes in pant needs, so this objective is difficult to meet.

"The plant budgeting begins with me and my staff determining what a plant's quota (in pairs of pants) for each month should be for one year ahead of time. We look at the plant's past performance and add a little to this because we expect people to improve around here. These yearly budgets are updated at the end of each month in light of the previous month's production. If a plant manager beats this budget figure, we feel he has done a good job. If he cannot meet the quota, his people have not been working at what the engineers feel is a very reason-

able level of speed and efficiency. Or possibly absenteeism or worker turnover, big problems in our plants, have been excessively high. When the quota has not been reached, we want to know why and want the problem corrected as quickly as we can.

"Given the number of pants that a plant actually produces in a month, we can determine the number of standard labor hours allowed for that month. We compare this figure against the actual labor hours to determine how a plant manager performed as an expense center. I phone every plant manager each month to give prompt feedback on either satisfactory or unsatisfactory performance.

"We also look for other things in evaluating a plant manager. Have his community relations been good? Are his employees happy? The owners of this company are very concerned about these factors."

An annual bonus constituted the core of Grand Jean's reward system. Mr. Wicks and his two chief assistants rated each plant manager's performance on a 1-to-5 scale, where 5 was the highest rate. At year-end, Grand Jean's top management determined a bonus base by evaluating the firm's overall performance and profits for the year. The bonus base had been as high as $10,000. The performance rating for each member of Grand Jean's management cadre was multiplied by this bonus base to determine a given manager's bonus. For example, a manager with a 3-point rating would receive a $30,000 bonus.

Grand Jean's management group included many finance and marketing specialists. The casewriter noted that these personnel, who were located at corporate headquarters, were consistently awarded higher ratings by their supervisors than were plant managers. This difference consistently approached a full point.

The five marketing departments listed in Exhibit 1 under the vice president of marketing are treated as revenue centers. Marketing forecasts are used to set sales unit and sales dollar targets. The performance of marketing department managers is measured on the basis of meeting these targets. To meet changing consumer demand, frequent changes in product mix were necessary. The sales force sells all types of jeans within an assigned territory. Their compensation consists of salary plus 8 percent sales commissions. Commissions represent roughly half the average salesperson's compensation. The customers are retail stores and clothing distributors. For marketing department performance assessment, the sales of each line of pants are assigned to the respective marketing department (i.e., basic jeans, etc.). Marketing department managers participated in the company's bonus system.

Evaluation of the System

Mia Packard, a recent business school graduate, gave the casewriter her opinions regarding Grand Jean's production operations and its management control procedures: "Mr. Wicks is one of the nicest executives I've ever met, and a very intelligent businessman. But I really don't approve of the system he uses to evaluate his plant managers. On a recent plant visit as part of my company orientation program, I accidentally discovered that the plant manager was 'hoarding' some of the pants produced over quota. He does this in good months to protect himself against future production deficiencies. That plant manager was really upset that I stumbled onto his pant storehouse. He insisted that other managers did the same thing and begged me not to tell Mr. Wicks. This is odd behavior for a company that usually has to turn away orders near the end of the year! I suspect that most plant managers aren't really pushing for maximum production. If they do increase output, their quotas are going to go up, and yet they won't receive any immediate monetary rewards to compensate for the increase in their responsibilities or requirements. If I were a plant manager, I wouldn't want my production exceeding quota until the end of the year.

"Also, Mr. Wicks worked his way up the ranks of the company. He was a very good plant manager himself and feels that everyone should run a plant the way he did. For example, in Mr. Wicks's plant there were 11 workers for every supervisor or member of the office and administrative staff. Since then, Mr. Wicks has elevated this supervision ratio of 11:1 to some sort of sacred index of leadership efficiency. All plant managers aim for it and, as a result, usually understaff their offices. Because of this, we can't get timely and accurate reports from plants. There simply aren't enough people in the offices out there to generate the information we desperately need when we need it!

"Another thing! Some of the plants have been built within the last five years and have much newer equipment. Yet there is no difference between the standard hours determined in these plants and the older ones. The older sewing machines break down more often, require more maintenance, and probably aren't as easy to work with."

Questions

1. How would you describe the goal(s) of the company as a whole? Is this, or are these, the same as the goal(s) of the company's marketing organization and the company's 25 managers of manufacturing plants? Explain.

2. Evaluate the current management planning and control system for the manufacturing plants and the marketing departments. What are the strengths and weaknesses?

3. One plant manager recommended that plants be operated as profit centers because it would overcome some of the problems discovered by Mia Packard and the casewriter. This plant manager commented, "[My] competitor is the nearby independent manufacturer that makes the same pants for Grand Jean as my plant makes. And this outsider might also make pants for Grand Jean's competitors. Because of the competitive market, only the best managed plants survive in this business. Therefore, like the outside company's manager I should have bottom line responsibility and be rewarded accordingly." Do you agree or disagree with the profit center concept for Grand Jean's 25 manufacturing plants? How would this approach affect the plant managers' decisions, performance, etc.?

4. If Grand Jean's manufacturing plants were treated as profit centers, three alternatives were suggested for recording revenues for each plant:
   a. Use the selling price recorded by Grand Jean's sales personnel for pants sold to retailers and distributors.
   b. Use full standard manufacturing cost per unit plus a "fair" fixed percentage markup for gross profit.
   c. Use the average contract price Grand Jean paid outside companies for making similar pant types.

   Evaluate these three alternatives. Which one would you recommend? Why is your selection the best one?

PROFIT CENTERS

When a responsibility center's financial performance is measured in terms of profit (that is, by the difference between the revenues and expenses), the center is called a *profit center*. Profit is a particularly useful performance measure since it allows senior management to use one comprehensive indicator rather than several (some of which may be pointing in different directions). In the first part of this chapter, we discuss the considerations involved in deciding whether to establish a profit center in the first place. We then focus on organizing business units as profit centers, with a reminder that the terms *business units* and *profit centers* are *not synonymous*. Next, we describe how production and marketing functions can be constituted as profit centers. In the remainder of the chapter, we discuss alternative ways to measure a profit center's *profitability*.

General Considerations

A *functional organization* is one in which each principal manufacturing or marketing function is performed by a separate organization unit. When such an organization is converted to one in which each major unit is responsible for both the manufacture and the marketing, the process is termed *divisionalization*. As a rule, companies create business units because they have decided to delegate more authority to operating managers. Although the degree of delegation may differ from company to company, complete authority for generating profits is never delegated to a single segment of the business.

Conditions for Delegating Profit Responsibility

Many management decisions involve proposals to increase expenses with the expectation of an even greater increase in sales revenue. Such decisions are said to involve expense/revenue trade-offs. Additional advertising expense is an example. Before it is safe to delegate such a trade-off decision to a lower-level manager, two conditions should exist.

1. The manager should have access to the *relevant information* needed for making such a decision.
2. There should be some way to measure the effectiveness of the trade-offs the manager has made.

A major step in creating profit centers is to determine the lowest point in an organization where these two conditions prevail.

All responsibility centers fit into a continuum ranging from those that clearly should be profit centers to those that clearly should not. Management must decide whether the advantages of giving profit responsibility offset the disadvantages, which are discussed below. As with all management control system design choices, there is no clear line of demarcation.

Prevalence of Profit Centers

Although E. I. du Pont de Nemours & Company and General Motors Corporation divisionalized in the early 1920s,[1] most companies in the United States remained functionally organized until after the end of World War II. Since that time many major U.S. corporations have divisionalized and have decentralized profit responsibility at the business unit level. Alfred P. Sloan (General Motors) and Ralph J. Cordiner (General Electric) have documented the philosophy of divisionalization and profit decentralization.[2]

A survey by Govindarajan, conducted in 1994, shows the extent to which Fortune 1,000 companies in the United States had incorporated the profit center concept. Of the 638 usable responses, 93 percent were from companies that included two or more profit centers (Exhibit 4–1).[3] The survey results from other countries also indicate a heavy reliance on the profit center concept.

> **Examples.** Chemical Bank adopted the profit center concept and instituted profitability measurements for management control, prompting the bank to drop some unprofitable programs, such as the "Student-Plus" account (an effort to attract student accounts by offering lower rates on the particular products and services students used; it was a good idea, but the accounts lost money).
>
> The profit center approach also helped Chemical to measure branch profitability more accurately. Historically, if a customer had an account at one branch, that

---

[1]See Alfred D. Chandler, Jr., *Strategy and Structure* (Cambridge, MA: MIT Press, 1962), chapters 2 and 3.

[2]Alfred P. Sloan, Jr., *My Years with General Motors* (Garden City, NY: Doubleday, 1964); Ralph J. Cordiner, *New Frontiers for Professional Managers* (New York: McGraw-Hill, 1956).

[3]Vijay Govindarajan, "Profit Center Measurement: An Empirical Survey," The Amos Tuck School of Business Administration, Dartmouth College, 1994.

EXHIBIT 4–1   Use of Profit Centers

	United States[a]	Holland[b]	India[c]
Number of questionnaires sent	1,000	N/A	N/A
Number of responses	666	N/A	N/A
Response rate	67%	N/A	N/A
Number of usable responses	638	72	105
Companies with two or more profit centers	93%	89%	68%

---

[a]Vijay Govindarajan, "Profit Center Measurement: An Empirical Survey," The Amos Tuck School of Business Administration, Dartmouth College, 1994.

[b]Elbert De With, "Performance Measurement and Evaluation in Dutch Companies," Paper presented at the 19th Annual Congress of the European Accounting Association, Bergen, 1966.

[c]V. Govindarajan and B. Ramamurthy, "Transfer Pricing Policies in Indian Companies: A Survey," *The Chartered Accountant* XXXII, no. 5 (November 1983), pp. 296–301.

branch got credit for all the customer's business even when the customer used ATMs or services at other branches. The new system allowed the bank to know which customers were using which branches and/or ATMs. And it helped the individual branches to identify small target markets, prompting Chemical to add an "ethnic market segment" to its system to better serve New York's Asian, African-American, and Hispanic communities.[4]

Novell's chairman and president Robert Frankenberg used the profit center approach to identify and eliminate several unprofitable businesses such as AppWare and Processor Independent Netware.[5]

Financial control systems have come under considerable criticism over the past 20 years. Nevertheless, corporations have not abandoned these systems but continue to use them as tools to implement strategies. At the same time, they are aware of their shortcomings, and, as we discuss in Chapters 10 and 11, many of them have begun to employ a *scorecard* with a mix of financial and nonfinancial performance measures.

In this and the next two chapters, we examine the considerations involved in appropriately assigning *financial responsibility* to organizational subunits.

Advantages of Profit Centers

Establishing organization units as profit centers provides the following advantages:

- The *quality* of decisions may improve because they are being made by managers closest to the point of decision.

---

[4]Robert A. Bennett, "Taking the Measure of Bank Profits," *US Banker* 104, no. 4 (April 1996), pp. 36–42.

[5]Doyle, T. C., "Novell to Focus on Profit Centers," *Computer Reseller News,* September 5, 1994, p. 202.

- The *speed* of operating decisions may be increased since they do not have to be referred to corporate headquarters.

- Headquarters management, *relieved of day-to-day decision-making,* can concentrate on broader issues.

- Managers, subject to fewer corporate restraints, are freer to use their imagination *and initiative.*

- Because profit centers are similar to independent companies, they provide an excellent *training ground* for general management. Their managers gain experience in managing all functional areas, and upper management gains the opportunity to evaluate their potential for higher-level jobs.

- *Profit consciousness* is enhanced since managers who are responsible for profits will constantly seek ways to increase them. (A manager responsible for marketing activities, for example, will tend to authorize promotion expenditures that increase sales, whereas a manager responsible for profits will be motivated to make promotion expenditures that increase profits.)

- Profit centers provide top management with ready-made information on the *profitability of the company's individual components.*

- Because their output is so readily measured, profit centers are particularly responsive to pressures to improve *their competitive performance.*

Examples.   ABB (Asea Brown Boveri), a European multinational in the business of power generation, transmission, and distribution, was organized into 4,500 small profit centers—each with profit and loss responsibility and meaningful autonomy. Percy Barnevik, ABB's CEO explained why: "We are fervent believers in decentralization. When we structure local operations, we always push to create separate legal entities. Separate companies allow you to create real balance sheets with real responsibility for cash flow and dividends. With real balance sheets, managers inherit results from year to year through changes in equity. Separate companies also create more effective tools to recruit and motivate managers. People can aspire to meaningful career ladders in companies small enough to understand and to be committed to."[6]

Many Japanese companies use profit centers. The Kyocera Corporation, a technology company, divided itself into 800 small companies (nicknamed *amoebas*), which were expected to trade both internally and externally. Higashimaru Shoyu, a soy sauce maker, turned each stage in the production process into a separate profit center, instructing these separate units to buy and sell to one another.[7] Matsushita, a consumer electronics giant, operated its divisions as profit centers and focused managers' attention on two numbers—profit margin and the "bottom line." The consumer electronics industry was characterized by two factors: product life cycles tended to be short; and profit margins were higher in the initial stages of

---

[6]William Taylor, "The Logic of Global Business: An Interview with ABB's Percy Barnevik," *Harvard Business Review,* March–April 1991, p. 99.

[7]"In Faint Praise of the Blue Suit," *The Economist,* January 13, 1996. pp. 59–60.

the product life cycle than in the later stages. The focus on "profit margins" motivated managers to introduce new products, and the focus on the "bottom line" motivated managers to extract the maximum profits from current products.[8]

Difficulties with Profit Centers

However, the creation of profit centers may cause difficulties:

- Decentralized decision-making will force top management to rely more on management control reports than on personal knowledge of an operation, entailing some *loss of control.*

- If headquarters management is more capable or better informed than the average profit center manager, the *quality* of decisions made at the unit level may be *reduced.*

- *Friction* may increase because of arguments over the appropriate transfer price, the assignment of common costs, and the credit for revenues that were formerly generated jointly by two or more business units working together.

- Organization units that once cooperated as functional units may now be in *competition* with one another. An increase in profits for one manager may mean a decrease for another. In such situations, a manager may fail to refer sales leads to another business unit better qualified to pursue them; may hoard personnel or equipment that, from the overall company standpoint, would be better off used in another unit; or may make production decisions that have undesirable cost consequences for other units.

- Divisionalization may impose *additional costs* because of the additional management, staff personnel, and record keeping required, and may lead to task redundancies at each profit center.

- Competent *general managers* may not exist in a functional organization because there may not have been sufficient opportunities for them to develop general management competence.

- There may be too much emphasis on *short-run profitability* at the expense of long-run profitability. In the desire to report high current profits, the profit center manager may skimp on R&D, training programs, or maintenance. This tendency is especially prevalent when the turnover of profit center managers is relatively high. In these circumstances, managers may have good reason to believe that their actions may not affect profitability until after they have moved to other jobs.

- There is no completely satisfactory system for ensuring that optimizing the profits of each individual profit center will *optimize the profits of the company as a whole.*

---

[8]James Brian Quinn, "Matsushita," Tuck School, Darmouth College, 1994.

Business Units as Profit Centers

Most business units are created as profit centers since managers in charge of such units typically control product development, manufacturing, and marketing resources. These managers are in a position to influence revenues and costs and as such can be held accountable for the "bottom line." However, as pointed out in the next section, a business unit manager's authority may be constrained in various ways, which ought to be reflected in a profit center's design and operation.

Constraints on Business Unit Authority

To realize fully the benefits of the profit center concept, the business unit manager would have to be as autonomous as the president of an independent company. As a practical matter, however, such autonomy is not feasible. If a company were divided into completely independent units, the organization would lose the advantages of size and synergy. Furthermore, in delegating to business unit management all the authority that the board of directors has given to the CEO, senior management would be abdicating its own responsibility. Consequently, business unit structures represent trade-offs between business unit autonomy and corporate constraints. The effectiveness of a business unit organization is largely dependent on how well these trade-offs are made.

Constraints from Other Business Units.   One of the main problems occurs when business units must deal with one another. It is useful to think of managing a profit center in terms of control over three types of decisions: (1) the product decision (what goods or services to make and sell); (2) the marketing decision (how, where, and for how much are these goods or services to be sold?); and (3) the procurement or sourcing decision (how to obtain or manufacture the goods or services). If a business unit manager controls all three activities, there is usually no difficulty in assigning profit responsibility and measuring performance. In general, the greater the degree of integration within a company, the more difficult it becomes to assign responsibility to a single profit center for all three activities in a given product line; that is, if the production, procurement, and marketing decisions for a single product line are split among two or more business units, separating the contribution of each business unit to the overall success of the product line may be difficult.

Constraints from Corporate Management.   The constraints imposed by corporate management can be grouped into three types: (1) those resulting from strategic considerations; (2) those resulting because uniformity is required; and (3) those resulting from the economies of centralization.

Most companies retain certain decisions, especially financial decisions, at the corporate level, at least for domestic activities. Consequently, one of the major constraints on business units results from corporate control over new investments. Business units must compete with one another for a share of the available funds. Thus, a business unit could find its expansion plans thwarted because another unit has convinced senior management that it has a more attractive program. Corporate management also imposes other constraints. Each business unit has a "charter" that specifies the marketing and/or production activities that it is permitted to undertake, and it must refrain from operating beyond its charter, even though it sees profit opportunities in doing so. Also, the maintenance of the proper corporate image may require constraints on the quality of products or on public relations activities.

> **Example.**   In the mid-90s, Kinko's Inc., the largest 24-hour photocopying chain in the United States, centralized many of its operations. The company originally developed as a partnership, with each partner owning and operating Kinko's stores in different territories, and each unit within the company was responsible for its own purchasing and much of its own financing. When Kinko's centralized financing in 1996, it saw interest expenses drop from $50 million to $30 million. It anticipated similar savings from implementing a more efficient purchasing system.[9]

Companies impose some constraints on business units because of the necessity for uniformity. One constraint is that business units must conform to corporate accounting and management control systems. This constraint is especially troublesome for units that have been acquired from another company and that have been accustomed to using different systems.

> **Example.**   In 1989 Schering-Plough Corporation finally completed a seven-year effort to install a companywide accounting and control system. One major reason the process took so long was the difficulty of persuading the company's business units to adopt the corporate-specified system. In contrast, General Electric Corporation required that only a small amount of numerical information be submitted to headquarters according to a specified format; and Nestlé Company allowed business units to report to headquarters in English, French, German, or Spanish, since most senior managers were multilingual.

Corporate headquarters may also impose uniform pay and other personnel policies, as well as uniform policies on ethics, vendor selection, computers and communication equipment, and even the design of the business unit's letterhead.

In general, corporate constraints do not cause severe problems in a decentralized structure as long as they are dealt with explicitly; business unit management should understand the necessity for most constraints and should accept them with good grace. The major problems seem to revolve around corporate service activities. Often business units believe (sometimes rightly) that they can obtain such services at less expense from an outside source.

---

[9]Nanette Byrnes, "Kinko's Goes Corporate," *Business Week,* August 19, 1996, p. 58–59.

**Other
Profit
Centers**

Examples of profit centers, other than business units, are described below.

Functional Units

Multibusiness companies are typically divided into business units, each of which is treated as an independent profit-generating unit. The subunits within these business units, however, may be functionally organized. It is sometimes desirable to constitute one or more of the functional units—e.g., marketing, manufacturing, and service operations—as profit centers. There is no guiding principle declaring that certain types of units are inherently profit centers and others are not. Management's decision as to whether a given unit should be a profit center is based on the amount of *influence* (even if not total control) the unit's manager exercises over the activities that affect the bottom line.

Marketing.   A marketing activity can be turned into a profit center by charging it with the cost of the products sold. This transfer price provides the marketing manager with the relevant information to make the optimum revenue/cost trade-offs; and the standard practice of measuring a profit center's manager by the center's profitability provides a check on how well these trade-offs have been made. The transfer price charged to the profit center should be based on the standard cost, rather than the actual cost, of the products being sold. Using a standard cost base separates the marketing cost performance from that of the manufacturing cost performance, which is affected by changes in the levels of efficiency that are beyond the control of the marketing manager.

When should a marketing activity be given profit responsibility? When the marketing manager is in the best position to make the principal cost/revenue trade-offs. This often occurs where different conditions exist in different geographical areas—for example, a *foreign marketing activity*. In such an activity, it may be difficult to control centrally such decisions as how to market a product; how to set the price; how much to spend on sales promotion, when to spend it, and on which media; how to train salespeople or dealers; where and when to establish new dealers.[10]

Manufacturing.   The manufacturing activity is usually an expense center, with the management being judged on performance versus standard costs and overhead budgets. This measure can cause problems, however, since it does not necessarily indicate how well the manager is performing all aspects of his job. For example:

---

[10]In a 1989 survey of members of the Controllers Council of the Institute of Management Accountants, 70 percent of the respondents treated marketing activities as revenue centers, rather than as profit centers (*Controllers Update,* February 1990, p. 1).

- A manager may skimp on quality control, shipping products of inferior quality in order to obtain standard cost credit.
- A manager may be reluctant to interrupt production schedules in order to produce a rush order to accommodate a customer.
- A manager who is measured against standards may lack the incentive to manufacture products that are difficult to produce—or to improve the standards themselves.

Therefore, where if performance of the manufacturing process is measured against standard costs, it is advisable to make a separate evaluation of such activities as quality control, production scheduling, and make-or-buy decisions.

One way to measure the activity of a manufacturing organization in its entirety is to turn it into a profit center and give it credit for the selling price of the products minus estimated marketing expenses. Such an arrangement is far from perfect, partly because many of the factors that influence the volume and mix of sales are beyond the manufacturing manager's control. However, it seems to work better in some cases than the alternative of holding the manufacturing operation responsible only for costs.

Some authors maintain that manufacturing units should not be made into profit centers unless they sell a large portion of their output to outside customers; they regard units that sell primarily to other business units as *pseudo* profit centers on the grounds that the revenues assigned to them for sales to other units within the company are artificial. Some companies, nevertheless, do create profit centers for such units. They believe that, if properly designed, the system can create almost the same incentives as those provided by sales to outside customers.

Service and Support Units.   Units for maintenance, information technology, transportation, engineering, consulting, customer service, and similar support activities can all be made into profit centers. These may operate out of headquarters and service corporate divisions, or they may fulfill similar functions within business units. They charge customers for services rendered, with the financial objective of generating enough business so that their revenues equal their expenses. The prevalence of such practices is shown in Exhibit 4–2. (The firms that charge "based on usage" probably treat these units as profit centers.) Usually, the units receiving these services have the option of procuring them from an outside vendor instead, provided the vendor can offer services of equal quality at a lower price.

> **Examples.**   In order to lower costs, Singapore Airlines created profit centers such as Singapore Airlines Engineering Company and Singapore Airport Terminal Services (which had three profit centers of its own: airport services, catering, and security). These units were designed so that Singapore Airlines could obtain the same services from outside vendors instead if it wished to do so.[11]

---

[11]Joan Feldman, "Divide and Prosper," *Air Transport World,* May 1995, pp. 39–45.

EXHIBIT 4–2   Prevalence of Charging for Administrative Services

	Method of Determining Charge (by percent)			
Administrative Service Category	*Percent of Firms That Charge**	*Usage (actual or estimated)*	*Prorated*	*Other*
1. Finance and accounting	73%	35%	54%	11%
2. Legal	70	35	55	10
3. Electronic data processing	87	63	29	8
4. General marketing services	73	35	56	9
5. Advertising	72	50	41	9
6. Market research services	70	36	54	10
7. Public relations	63	24	62	14
8. Industrial relations	70	32	56	12
9. Personnel	70	35	53	12
10. Real estate	62	37	53	10
11. Operations research department	60	47	42	11
12. Purchasing department	51	40	51	9
13. Top corporate management overhead	63	13	72	15
14. Corporate planning department	61	20	66	14

*The total for the denominator includes only respondents who answered "yes" or "no" and excludes missing values and respondents who answered "not applicable."

Source: Richard F. Vancil, *Decentralization: Management Ambiguity by Design* (Burr Ridge, IL: Dow Jones-Irwin, 1979), p. 251.

Swissair converted its Engineering and Maintenance Division (EMD) from a cost center into a profit center to gain greater control over EMD's cost structure and also to make EMD both more responsive to the needs of its internal customers and more competitive for its external customers. In short, Swissair wanted EMD to be an independent, entrepreneurial operation making profits for the company.[12]

When service units are organized as profit centers, their managers are motivated to control costs in order to prevent customers from going elsewhere, while managers of the receiving units are motivated to make decisions about whether using the service is worth the price.

Example.   AT&T's central information resource function, Information Management Services, operated as a profit center for the company. In 1992 it had revenues of $2 billion and 7,000 professional employees.[13]

---

[12]Perry Flint, "Cost Center to Profit Center," *Air Transport World* 32, no. 3 (March 1995), p. 20.

[13]"Double Duty CEO," *Financial Executive,* July–August 1992, pp. 15–16.

Other Organizations

A company with branch operations that are responsible for marketing the company's products in a particular geographical area is often a natural for a profit center. Even though the branch managers have no manufacturing or procurement responsibilities, profitability is often the best single measure of their performance. Furthermore, the profit measurement is an excellent motivating device. Thus, the individual stores of most retail chains, the individual restaurants in fast-food chains, and the individual hotels in hotel chains are profit centers.

Measuring Profitability

There are two types of profitability measurements used in evaluating a profit center, just as there are in evaluating an organization as a whole. First, there is the measure of *management performance,* which focuses on how well the manager is doing. This measure is used for planning, coordinating, and controlling the profit center's day-to-day activities and as a device for providing the proper motivation for its manager. Second, there is the measure of *economic performance,* which focuses on how well the profit center is doing as an economic entity. The messages conveyed by these two measures may be quite different from each other. For example, the management performance report for a branch store may show that the store's manager is doing an excellent job under the circumstances; while the economic performance report may indicate that because of economic and competitive conditions in its area the store is a losing proposition and should be closed.

The necessary information for both purposes usually cannot be obtained from a single set of data. Since the management report is used frequently, while the economic report is prepared only on those occasions when economic decisions must be made, considerations relating to management performance measurement have first priority in systems design—that is, the system should be designed to measure management performance routinely, with economic information being derived from these performance reports as well as from other sources.

Types of Profitability Measures

A profit center's economic performance is always measured by net income (that is, the income remaining after all costs, including a fair share of the corporate overhead, have been allocated to the profit center). The performance of the profit center manager, however, may be evaluated by five different measures of profitability: (1) contribution margin, (2) direct profit, (3) controllable profit, (4) income before income taxes, or (5) net income. The nature of these measures is indicated by the income statement example in Exhibit 4–3. Their relative popularity is summarized in Exhibit 4–4. Each is discussed below.

EXHIBIT 4–3   Example of a Profit Center Income Statement

		Profitability Measure
Revenue	$ 1,000	
Cost of sales	600	
Variable expenses	180	
Contribution margin	220	**(1)**
Fixed expenses incurred in the profit center	90	
Direct profit	130	**(2)**
Controllable corporate charges	10	
Controllable profit	120	**(3)**
Other corporate allocations	20	
Income before taxes	100	**(4)**
Taxes	40	
Net income	$ 60	**(5)**

EXHIBIT 4–4   Percentages of Companies Using Different Methods of Measuring Profit

Types of Expenses Charged to the Profit Center	*United States[a]*	*Holland[b]*	*India[c]*
Depreciation charge	98%	96%	98%
Fixed expense incurred in the profit center	99	N/A	N/A
Corporate general and administrative expenses allocated to the profit center	64	44	N/A
Income tax expense	40	22	10

[a]Percentage based on the 593 companies (93%) who reported two or more profit centers in the survey. Govindarajan, "Profit Center Measurement," p. 1.
[b]Elbert De With, "Performance Measurement and Evaluation in Dutch Companies," Paper presented at the 19th Annual Congress of the European Accounting Association, Bergen 1996.
[c]Govindarajan and Ramamurthy, "Transfer Pricing Policies in Indian Companies: A Survey," pp. 296–301.

(1) Contribution Margin.   Contribution margin reflects the spread between revenue and variable expenses. The principal argument in favor of using it to measure the performance of profit center managers is that since fixed expenses are beyond their control, managers should focus their attention on maximizing contribution. The problem with this argument is that its premises are inaccurate; in fact, almost all fixed expenses are at least partially controllable by the manager, and some are entirely controllable. As discussed in Chapter 3, many expense items are discretionary; that is, they can be changed at the discretion of the profit center manager. Presumably, senior management wants the profit center to keep these discretionary expenses in line with amounts agreed on in the budget formulation process. A focus on the contribution margin tends to direct attention away from this responsibility. Further, even if an expense, such as administrative salaries, cannot be changed in the short run, the profit center manager is still responsible for controlling employees' efficiency and productivity.

(2) Direct Profit.   This measure reflects a profit center's contribution to the general overhead and profit of the corporation. It incorporates all expenses either incurred by or directly traceable to the profit center, regardless of whether or not these items are within the profit center manager's control. Expenses incurred at headquarters, however, are not included in this calculation.

A weakness of the direct profit measure is that it does not recognize the motivational benefit of charging headquarters costs.

> **Example.**   Knight-Ridder, the second-largest newspaper publisher in the United States, measured each of its newspapers based on direct profit. The publisher set specific targets for direct profit at each of its newspapers. For 1996 the *Miami Herald* had a target of 18 percent and the *Philadelphia Inquirer* and the *Philadelphia Daily* (which were operated as one unit) had a target of 12 percent.[14]

(3) Controllable Profit.   Headquarters expenses can be divided into two categories: controllable and noncontrollable. The former category includes expenses that are controllable, at least to a degree, by the business unit manager—information technology services, for example. If these costs are included in the measurement system, profit will be what remains after the deduction of all expenses that may be *influenced* by the profit center manager. A major disadvantage of this measure is that because it excludes noncontrollable headquarters expenses it cannot be directly compared with either published data or trade association data reporting the profits of other companies in the industry.

(4) Income before Taxes.   In this measure, all corporate overhead is allocated to profit centers based on the relative amount of expense each profit center incurs. There are two arguments against such allocations. First, since the costs incurred by corporate staff departments such as finance, accounting, and human resource management are not controllable by profit center managers, these managers should not be held accountable for them. Second, it may be difficult to allocate corporate staff services in a manner that would properly reflect the amount of costs incurred by each profit center.

There are, however, three arguments in favor of incorporating a portion of corporate overhead into the profit centers' performance reports. First, corporate service units have a tendency to increase their power base and to enhance their own excellence without regard to its effect on the company as a whole. Allocating corporate overhead costs to profit centers increases the like-

---

[14]Kambiz Foroohar, "Chip Off the Old Block," *Forbes,* June 17, 1996, pp. 48–49.

lihood that profit center managers will question these costs, thus serving to keep head office spending in check. (Some companies have actually been known to sell their corporate jets because of complaints from profit center managers about the cost of these expensive items.) Second, the performance of each profit center will become more realistic and more readily comparable to the performance of competitors who pay for similar services. Finally, when managers know that their respective centers will not show a profit unless all costs, including the allocated share of corporate overhead, are recovered, they are motivated to make optimum long-term marketing decisions as to pricing, product mix, etc., that will ultimately benefit (and even ensure the viability of) the company as a whole.

If profit centers are to be charged for a portion of corporate overhead, this item should be calculated on the basis of budgeted, rather than actual, costs, in which case the "budget" and "actual" columns in the profit center's performance report will show identical amounts for this particular item. This ensures that profit center managers will not complain about either the arbitrariness of the allocation or their lack of control over these costs, since their performance reports will show no variance in the overhead allocation. Instead, such variances would appear in the reports of the responsibility center that actually incurred these costs.

(5) Net Income.   Here, companies measure the performance of domestic profit centers according to the bottom line, the amount of net income after income tax. There are two principal arguments against using this measure: (1) aftertax income is often a constant percentage of the pretax income, in which case there would be no advantage in incorporating income taxes; and (2) since many of the decisions that affect income taxes are made at headquarters, it is not appropriate to judge profit center managers on the consequences of these decisions.

There are situations, however, in which the effective income tax rate does vary among profit centers. For example, foreign subsidiaries or business units with foreign operations may have different effective income tax rates. In other cases, profit centers may influence income taxes through their installment credit policies, their decisions on acquiring or disposing of equipment, and their use of other generally accepted accounting procedures to distinguish gross from taxable income. In these situations, it may be desirable to allocate income tax expenses to profit centers, not only to measure their economic profitability but also to motivate managers to minimize tax liability.

Revenues.   Choosing the appropriate revenue recognition method is important. Should revenues be recorded when an order is made, when an order is shipped, or when cash is received?

In addition to that decision, there are other issues relating to common revenues that may require consideration. In some situations two or more profit centers may participate in a successful sales effort; ideally, each center should be given appropriate credit for its part in the transaction. For example, a salesperson from Business Unit A may be the main company contact with a certain customer, but the orders the customer places with that salesperson may be for products carried by Business Unit B. The Unit A salesperson would not be likely to pursue such orders if all resulting revenues were credited to Unit B. Similarly, a bank customer with an account in Branch C may prefer to do some business with Branch D, perhaps because it is more conveniently located. Branch D may not be eager to service this customer if all the revenue so generated is credited to Branch C.

Many companies do not devote a great deal of attention to solving these common revenue problems. They take the position that the identification of precise responsibility for revenue generation is too complicated to be practical, and that sales personnel must recognize they are working not only for their own profit center but also for the overall good of the company. Other companies attempt to untangle the responsibility for common sales by crediting the business unit that takes an order for a product handled by another unit with the equivalent of a brokerage commission or a finder's fee (or, as in the case of a bank, by granting explicit credit to the branch that performs a service even though the account of the customer being served is maintained at another branch).

Management Considerations.   Each type of profitability measure described in Exhibit 4–3 is used by some companies. Most companies in the United States include some, if not all, of the costs discussed earlier in evaluating the business manager, whether or not they are under his or her control. For example, many U.S. multinational corporations measure the performance of managers of foreign subsidiaries in dollars. Performance, thus, is affected by fluctuations in the value of the dollar relative to the host currency—a matter wholly beyond the individual manager's control.

Most of the confusion in measuring the performance of profit center managers results from failing to separate the measurement of the manager from the economic measurement of the profit center. If one considers the measurement of the manager alone, the solution often becomes evident: *Managers should be measured against those items they can influence, even if they do not have total control over those items.* In the typical company, these items probably include all expenses incurred directly in the profit center. Managers should be measured on an aftertax basis only if they can influence the amount of tax their unit pays; and items that they clearly cannot influence, such as currency fluctuation, should be eliminated.

Following these guidelines, however, does not solve all the problems. Degrees of influence vary; and there are always items over which a manager may exercise some influence but little real control. Thus variance analysis is always important in evaluating management performance. But even the best variance analysis system will still require the exercise of judgment; and one way to make this judgment more reliable is to eliminate all items over which the manager has no influence (or report them in such a way that variances do not develop).

Summary

A profit center is an organization unit in which both revenues and expenses are measured in monetary terms. In setting up a profit center a company devolves decision-making power to those lower levels that possess relevant information for making expense/revenue trade-offs. This move can increase the speed of decision-making, improve the quality of decisions, focus greater attention on profitability, and provide a broader measure of management performance, among other advantages.

Constraints on a profit center's autonomy may be imposed by other business units and by corporate management. These constraints need to be recognized explicitly in the operation of profit centers.

Under appropriate circumstances, even the production or marketing function can be constituted as a profit center, although considerable judgment is required to accomplish this successfully.

Measuring *profit* in a profit center involves judgments regarding how revenues and expenses should be measured also. In terms of revenues, choice of a revenue recognition method is important. In terms of expenses, measurement can range from variable costs incurred in the profit center to fully allocated corporate overhead, including income taxes. Judgments regarding the measurement of revenues and costs should be guided not just by technical accounting considerations, but more importantly by behavioral considerations. The key is to include those expenses and revenues in profit center managers' reports that the managers can *influence,* even if they cannot totally control them.

Suggested Additional Readings

Alter, Allan E. "The Profit Center Paradox." *Computerworld* 29, no. 17 (April 1995), pp. 101–5.

Chow, C. W., Y. Kato, and K. A. Merchant. "The Use of Organizational Controls and Their Effects on Data Manipulation and Management Myopia: A Japan vs. U.S. Comparison." *Accounting Organizations and Society,* 1996, pp. 175–92.

Dearden, John. "Measuring Profit Center Managers." *Harvard Business Review,* September–October 1987, pp. 84–88.

Govindarajan, Vijay. "Decentralization, Strategy, and Effectiveness of Strategic Business Units in Multi-Business Organizations." *Academy of Management Review* 11, no. 4 (1986), pp. 844–56.

Maciariello, J. A., and C. J. Kirby. *Management Control Systems.* Englewood Cliffs, NJ: Prentice Hall, 1994.

Vancil, Richard F. *Decentralization: Management Ambiguity by Design.* Burr Ridge, IL: Dow Jones-Irwin, 1979.

Walsh, Francis J. *Measuring Business-Unit Performance.* Research Bulletin no. 206. New York: The Conference Board, 1987.

CASE 4–1
PROFIT CENTER PROBLEMS

1. AMAX Automobiles

AMAX Automobiles was a car company with three product lines. Line A was aimed at the luxury segment, line B at the upscale segment, and line C at the mass market segment. Each of the three product lines was sold under a different brand name and used different distribution systems. Lines A, B, and C were currently produced and marketed by Divisions A, B, and C, respectively.

Some components were common to the three divisions. Some of these common components were sourced externally while others were manufactured inside the company. Also, there existed considerable scope for technology and know-how transfer across divisions. Specifically, product innovations seemed to originate in Division A and then migrate to Divisions B and C. However, process innovations seemed to originate in Division C and then migrate to Divisions A and B.

Question

How should AMAX be organized and controlled?

2. Indus Corporation

Indus was a diversified company operating in a number of niche markets that were largely independent of each other, that is, customer buying decisions in each of these markets were made independently. The company's primary basis for competitive advantage in each of these markets was to be the first mover (and leader) in product innovation. The company faced the following customer/production situations:

Case A: The customer was mainly performance sensitive rather than price sensitive. Also, there was little production synergy across the various product lines.

Case B: The customer was mainly performance sensitive rather than price sensitive. However, there was considerable production synergy across the various product lines.

Case C: The customer was equally sensitive regarding product performance and price. However, there was little production synergy across the various product lines.

Case D: The customer was equally sensitive regarding product performance and price. However, there was considerable production synergy across the various product lines.

Question

In each case, how should Indus be organized and controlled?

This case was prepared and copyrighted by Anil K. Gupta, University of Maryland.

CASE 4–2
NORTH COUNTRY AUTO, INC.

George G. Liddy, part owner of North Country Auto, Inc., was feeling pretty good about the new control systems recently put in place for his five department managers (new and used car sales, service, body, and parts departments). Exhibit 1 describes each department. Mr. Liddy strongly believed in the concept of evaluating each department individually as a profit center. But he also recognized the challenge of getting his managers to "buy in" to the system by working together for the good of the dealership.

Background

North Country Auto, Inc., was a franchised dealer and factory-authorized service center for Ford, Saab, and Volkswagen. Multiple franchises were becoming more common in the 1980s. But the value of multiple franchises did not come without costs. Each of the three manufacturers used a different computerized system for tracking inventory and placing new orders. They also required their dealerships to maintain an adequate service facility with a crew of trained technicians that, in turn, necessitated carrying an inventory of parts to be used in repairs. Exhibit 2 gives balance sheet data with a breakout of investment for each product line. North Country also operated a body shop, and in mid-1989 opened a "while-you-wait" oil change service for any make of vehicle.

The dealership was situated in an upstate New York town with a population of about 20,000. It served two nearby towns of about 4,000 people as well as rural areas covering a

20-mile radius. North Country began operations in 1968, and in 1983 moved one mile down the road to its current 6-acre lot, 25,000 square-foot facility. It was owned as a corporation by George Liddy and Andrew Jones, who were both equally active in day-to-day operations. Mr. Liddy purchased an interest in the dealership from a previous partner in 1988. Mr. Jones had been part owner since the start of the business. Whereas Mr. Liddy focused his energies on new and used car sales, Mr. Jones concentrated on managing the parts, service, and body shop departments—commonly referred to as the "back end" of a dealership.

The owners were determined to maintain a profitable back end as a hedge against depressed sales and lower margins in vehicles sales. In an industry characterized by aggressive discounting fueled by a combination of high inventories, a more educated consumer, and a proliferation of new entrants, alternative sources of cash flow were crucial. Industry analysts were estimating that fewer than 50 percent of the dealers in the US would make a profit on new car sales in 1990. Overall net profit margins were expected to fall below 1 percent of sales (*The Wall Street Journal,* December 11, 1989).

George Liddy's Challenge

Before George Liddy bought into the dealership, all the departments operated as part of one business. Department managers were paid salaries and a year-end bonus determined at the owners' discretion based on overall results for the year and a subjective appraisal of each manager.

George Liddy believed this system did not provide proper motivation for the managers. He believed in decentralized profit centers and performance-based compensation as superior models

---

This case was written by Mark C. Rooney (T'90) under the supervision of Professor Joseph Fisher. Copyright © by The Amos Tuck School of Business Administration, Dartmouth College.

EXHIBIT 1   North Country Auto, Inc.—The Departmental Structure

New Car Sales and Used Car Sales

The new and used car departments each had a sales manager. They shared six salespersons. In addition, these departments shared an office manager and clerks. The managers were paid a flat salary, plus a fixed sum per new or used vehicle sold, and a percentage of their department's gross profit (calculated as sales minus cost of vehicles sold). When the owners and the managers agreed on annual unit volume and margin goals, the dollar weights were set to make each portion approximately one-third of the manager's expected total compensation. The owners claimed that this type of dual incentive bonus structure allowed the managers flexibility in targeting margins and volume. George Liddy maintained, "If the margins are low, the sales manager can try to make it up in volume." The sales force was paid strictly a commission on gross profit. Many dealerships in the area were changing sales compensation to a flat salary plus a partial commission on gross profits generated.

The new car sales manager was responsible for recommending to Liddy new model orders and inventory mix among the three product lines. He also had the authority to approve selling prices and trade-in allowances on customer transactions. Typically, the new car manager was allowed to transfer the trade-in at blue book. However, if the car was obviously of below average quality, the used car department was asked for their estimate of value. The used car manager was responsible for controlling the mix of used car inventory through buying and selling used vehicles at wholesale auto auctions.

Service

The service department occupied over half of the building's usable square footage and was the most labor intensive operation. Service comprised 11 bays with hydraulic lifts, one of which was used for the oil change operation. The department employed a manager, 10 technicians, 3 semiskilled mechanics, 2 counter clerks, and 3 office clerks. The manager was paid a flat salary plus a bonus on the department's gross profit on labor hours billed (computed as labor dollars billed minus total wages of billable technicians and mechanics). Service revenue consisted of labor only. No markup for parts was realized by service department. The bonus portion was planned to be approximately 50 percent of his salary. The technicians, mechanics, and clerks were all paid a flat salary, regardless of actual hours billed. The technicians required specialty training to perform factory-authorized work on each of the specific lines. Sending a technician to school cost about $4,000 over a two-year period. The owners estimated that a new hire could cost as much as $10,000 in nonbillable overruns on warranty jobs, where reimbursement was limited to standard allowable labor hours. Of the 10 techs, 4 were certified for Ford, 3 for Saab, and 3 for Volkswagen. George Liddy and Andrew Jones contemplated reducing the cost of idle time by cross-training, but were averse to risks of turnover among highly skilled labor. Retraining costs could triple when one person quit.

The primary sources of service department revenue were warranty maintenance and repair work, nonwarranty maintenance and repair work, used car reconditioning, and the oil change operation. Warranty work was reimbursed by

of control. He instructed each of his departmental managers (new, used, service, body, and parts) to run his/her department as if it were an independent business. He knew that the success of the profit center control system was dependent upon the support of his managers. They must understand the rationale for allocating costs to their departments and believe that they had reasonable control over profitability. The managers' bonuses in 1989 were calculated on the basis of departmental *gross* profits. Expenses below the gross profit line were not considered in the bonus calculation. They were only told, in a statement outlining their responsibilities, to exercise "judicious control over discretionary expenses." Implementing a more comprehensive control system tied to actual departmental net profits would require that Liddy break down costs traditionally regarded as general overhead into separate activities associated with specific departments. His strategy with the managers involved a gradual phasing

EXHIBIT 1   *(continued)*

the factories at their prescribed labor rates, which were typically as much as 20 percent lower than the rates charged directly for nonwarranty work. Lower margins on warranty work were a potential problem for the dealership if they dissuaded the service manager from delivering prompt service to recent buyers. During times of near capacity utilization, the manager would be motivated to schedule higher margin nonwarranty jobs in the place of warranty work.

Parts

The parts department consisted of a manager, three stock keepers, and two clerks. The parts manager was paid a flat salary plus a bonus on department gross profits (computed as total parts sold less cost of parts). The parts manager was responsible for tracking parts inventory for the three lines and minimizing both carrying costs and "obsolescence." The owners defined obsolescence as a part in stock that was not sold in over a year. Mr. Liddy estimated that as many as 25 percent of the parts-on-hand fell into this category. Days supply of parts (inventory turnover) averaged 100 days for the industry. The manager had to be an expert on the return policies, stock requirements, and secondary market of three distinct and unrelated lines of merchandise. It was the parts manager's job to use factory return credits most effectively and identify outside wholesale opportunities so as to minimize large write-downs. Local wholesalers would pay as much as 80 percent of dealer cost for old parts.

Demand for parts was derived almost completely from other departments. Dollar sales volume in parts broke down as follows: 50 percent through service, 30 percent through the body shop, 10 percent wholesale, and 10 percent over-the-counter retail. Similar to service work, parts needed in warranty work were reimbursed at rates as much as 20 percent less than prices charged for nonwarranty work.

Body Shop

The body shop consisted of a manager, three technicians, and a clerk. The manager, like the others, was paid a flat salary plus a bonus on departmental profitability. To keep the shop in business in the long run, North Country Auto needed to invest an additional $50,000 in new spray-painting equipment. As it was, the body shop was showing a loss after allocation of fixed overhead. Gross margins as high as 60 percent could be attained, but rework and hidden damage beyond estimates tended to drive them down to closer to 40 percent.

Oil Change Operation

The dealership's oil change business operated under the nationally franchised "Qwik Change" logo, using one bay in the service department and one of the semiskilled mechanics. Volume averaged 68 changes per week. The operation was not evaluated as an independent profit center but as a means of filling unused capacity in the service department. The oil change franchise paid for all equipment, reducing the dealership's out-of-pocket investment to $500. After direct labor, direct parts, and the franchise fee, the dealership made about $10.00 on each oil change priced at $21.95. The owners were willing to devote an extra bay to this operation if volume warranted.

---

in over the next few years of an "almost" full-cost allocation system, where each department manager would eventually have responsibility for all controllable costs incurred in the department. Fixed expenses, such as interest expense, would be allocated by Liddy for his own decisions, but would not be used in the managers' bonus calculations.

The gradual changeover would allow Liddy, who was new to the dealership, time to become more knowledgeable about the intricacies of North Country Auto's accounting records. He did not want to lose credibility because of perceived arbitrary cost allocations. Exhibit 3 gives a breakdown of department profitability on an "almost" full-cost basis.

In addition to finding a way to effectively track departmental performance, George Liddy had to devise a sensible system for transfer pricing. Though Mr. Liddy believed that each department at North Country theoretically could operate as an independent business, he

Exhibit 2   Balance Sheet

NORTH COUNTRY AUTO, INC.
Balance Sheet
October 31, 1989
(In thousands)

Assets			Liabilities and Equity		
Cash	$	32	Accounts payable	$	73
Accounts			Notes payable—		
receivable		228	vehicles		1,294
Saab inventory		253	Long-term debt		344
VW inventory		243			
Ford inventory		773	Total liabilities		1,711
Used cars		231			
Saab parts		75			
VW parts		75			
Ford parts		226			
Body shop materials		6	Stockholders' equity		
Other current assets		89	Common stock	$	400
			Retained earnings		205
Property &					
equipment—Net*		85			
($377M gross)					
Total		$2,316	Total		$ 2,316

*North Country leases both the land and the building.

acknowledged that a complex interrelationship existed among the profit centers in the course of normal business transactions. A recent new vehicle purchase illustrates the potential problems that could arise.

Alex Walker, manager of the new car sales department, sold a new car for $14,150. This purchase was financed by a cash down payment of $2,000, a trade-in allowance of $4,800, and a bank loan of $7,350. The dealer's cost was $11,420, which included factory price plus sales commission.

The manager of the used car sales department, Amy Robbins, examined the trade-in vehicle. The trade-in had a wholesale guidebook value of $3,500. The guidebook, published monthly, was, at best, a near estimate of liquidation value. Actual values varied daily with the supply-demand balance at auto auctions. These variances could be as much as 25 percent of the book value.

Ms. Robbins believed that she could sell the trade-in quickly at $5,000 and earn a good margin, so she chose to carry it in inventory instead of wholesaling it for a value estimated to be $3,500. Mr. Walker, in turn, used the $3,500 value in calculating his actual profit on the new car sale.

In performing the routine maintenance check on the trade-in, the service department reported that the front wheels would need new brake pads and rotors and that the rear door lock assembly was jammed. The retail estimates for repair would be $300 for the brakes ($125 in parts, $175 in labor) and $75 to fix the lock assembly ($30 in parts, $45 in labor). Cleaning and touch-up (performed by service department as a part of the service order for lock and brake) would cost $75. The service department also recommended that a full tune-up be performed for a retail price of $255 ($80 in parts, $175 in labor).

The repair and tune-up work was completed and capitalized at retail cost into used car inventory at $705. These mechanical repairs would not necessarily increase wholesale value if the car subsequently were sold at the auction. The transfer price for internal work recently had changed from cost to full retail equivalent. The retail markup for labor was 3.5 times the direct hourly rate and about 1.4 times for parts.

George Liddy was concerned that the retail transfer price of the repairs in conjunction with his plan to eventually allocate full costs to each department (as illustrated in Exhibit 3) might encourage the used car sales manager to avoid the possibility of losses in her department by wholesaling trade-in cars that could be resold at a profit for the dealership. This might also hurt the dealership by making its deals less attractive for new car customers.

EXHIBIT 3   **Financial Statement**

NORTH COUNTRY AUTO, INC.
October 31, 1989 (10 months)
(Dollar figures in thousands)

	New	Used	Service	Body	Parts
Sales	$ 6,558	$1,557	$ 672	$ 231	$ 1,417
Gross profit	502	189	421	145	361
Number of units (vehicles, repairs, or parts)	474	390	9,795	406	40,139
Direct selling (commission & delivery)	$ 96	$ 25	n/a	n/a	n/a
Indirect labor	162	74	237	64	156
Department advertising	91	30	19	2	3
Policy work— parts & service (giveaways & rework)	29	12	14	12	1
Supplies & utilities	22	18	19	28	12
Depreciation	3	1	15	5	2
Rent	89	22	67	13	9
Profit before common expenses	$ 10	$ 7	$ 50	$ 21	$ 178
Other expenses:					
Interest (on new inventory)	$ 110				
Other interest	21				
Owners' salary	65				
Insurance	35				
Net operating profit	$ 35				

Notes to Financial Statement

1. New car sales and gross margins (000s) break down as:

	Sales	Gross profit	# Units
Ford	$3,114	$193	243
Saab	1,502	90	73
VW	1,794	117	158
Financing fees*	148	102	n/a
	$6,558	$502	474

2. Used car sales and margins break down as:

	Sales	Gross profit	# Units
Retail	$1,045	$212	177
Wholesale	423	(59)	213
Financing fees*	89	36	n/a
	$1,557	$189	390

Continued

EXHIBIT 3   *(continued)*

---

3. Notes payable for vehicles is a revolving line of credit secured by new car inventory. Payments to the bank are due upon sale of each vehicle financed in inventory. This liability has been reduced over the past 10 months by approximately $1.5 million.

4. Indirect labor consists of department managers, clerks, bookkeepers, and work involving tasks directly related to the activities in a specific department. It does not include sales commissions or billable employees in the back end.

5. Departmental advertising is assigned to departments based on actual ads placed.

6. Policy work consists of dealer concessions made to customers arising from disputes over dealer-installed options on new vehicles, warranty coverage, or cost of repairs. These costs are allocated to the departments in which they occur.

7. Depreciation is allocated by historical cost of leasehold improvements or equipment in each department.

8. Rent is allocated by square footage used by each department, adjusted for the value of the space.

9. Interest expense is treated as a common expense for the purpose of keeping investing and financing costs separate.

10. Insurance consists of both umbrella liability and property damage for the dealership as a whole. Because of the multiple types of coverages included and the bundled pricing, it is not feasible to break out coverage costs by department.

11. Approximately 75 percent of the fixed costs in the used car department related closely to retail vehicle sales and approximately 25 percent to wholesale sales.

12. Total number of parts sold during the year = 40,139 parts; total number of service orders undertaken during the year = 9,795 orders.

13. Using Exhibit 3, North Country determined the following allocations for overhead expenses:

    New: $835/vehicle = $396,000/474 vehicles

    Used: $665/vehicle = $157,000 * 0.75/177 vehicles

    Parts: $32 = $183,000/40,139 parts = 4.55/part * 7 parts
            (2 brake kits, 1 lock assembly, 4 tune-up parts)

  Service: $114 = $371,000/9,795 orders * 3 orders
            (lock, brakes, tune-up)

---

*Finance fees consist of income that the dealer earns on dealer-sourced auto loans. It also includes the dealer's commission on service contracts and extended warranties sold through the dealership.

Knowing how important it was to maintain credibility with each of the departments, Liddy called a meeting with the three department managers. He decided to use the recently completed new car sale to illustrate the effect that transaction would have on departments' profits. In his presentation, Mr. Liddy laid out the transaction and allocation of profits and costs. After this presentation, Mr. Liddy asked for the reactions of his department managers.

Alex Walker was the first to chime in, "I understand that the allowance above book value on the trade-in cannot be accounted for as profit. However, the real issue is how to set the price between me and Amy when we transfer the trade-in. I refuse to be responsible for any loss that might arise if the trade-in vehicle is liquidated at auction for an amount less than the wholesale guidebook value. Her department should be accountable for its valuation errors."

Amy Robbins vehemently disagreed. "My department should not have to subsidize the profits of the new car sales division."

Liddy quickly jumped into this deteriorating argument, "Obviously, we need to carefully consider how to set the price between the new and used car departments and who should be responsible for unexpected losses."

"Another item that concerns me," Robbins went on, "is using full retail price for parts and labor used in the repairs of trade-ins. Given underutilized capacity in service, I do not understand why I am charged full price. It doesn't make sense for the service department to mark up on projects undertaken for new and used car departments within our own dealership. I can't see how we can make profits when one part of our company sells to another."

Robbins added, "When I am unsure of the actual retail value, I tend to wholesale rather than take a risk of a negative margin at retail. However, when I do this, we may be losing as an organization as a whole."

"I agree with Amy on this," stated Walker, "and I have the same problem with dealer-installed options. When I am charged full price for options, I have no incentive to try to sell these items."

"Hold on," said the service department manager. "I make my profit by selling service, and these are the prices I would charge for outside work. To sell service for a lower price inside defeats the purpose of this profit center idea. But I do have a problem with getting full price for parts. The demand for parts is derived almost completely from service, and we are dependent on parts for quick delivery for repairs."

Liddy jumped back in. "Obviously, we are dependent on each other for quality and prompt service. We need to make sure that, as each of you maximizes profits in your departments, you do not negatively affect other departments."

Liddy continued, "I am also concerned about the impact of capitalizing trade-in repairs rather than expensing immediately. We all know that wholesale values drop with each publication of the new guidebook. I am afraid that, when a car is slow to sell, we might be reluctant to sell the car at a loss, even though we should. Car inventory ties up cash, and a key measure of departmental success is our inventory turnover [average industry inventory turnover was 75 days for new cars and 45 days for used cars]. In conclusion, while I think the profit center concept makes good sense for this business, I am concerned about the frictions that are taking place between the departments."

Questions

1. Using the data in the transaction, compute the profitability of this one transaction to the new, used, parts, and service departments. Assume a sales commission of $250 for the trade-in on a selling price of $5,000. (Note: Use the following allocations [new, $835; used, $665; parts, $32; service, $114] for overhead expenses while computing the profitability of this one transaction. These overhead allocations are also shown as Note 13 in Exhibit 3.)

2. How should the transfer-pricing system operate for each department (market price, full retail, full cost, variable cost)?

3. If it were found one week later that the trade-in could be wholesaled for only $3,000, which manager should take the loss?

4. North Country incurred a year-to-date loss of about $59,000 *before* allocation of fixed costs on the wholesaling of used cars (see Note 2 in Exhibit 3). Wholesaling of used cars is theoretically supposed to be a break-even operation. Where do you think the problem lies?

5. Should profit centers be evaluated on gross profit or "full cost" profit?

6. What advice do you have for the owners?

CASE 4–3
BOISE CASCADE CORPORATION

In July 1991, the Corporate Data Processing Services (CDPS) area of Boise Cascade Corporation changed the way it charged user groups for the personal computers (PCs) employed at the corporate headquarters building. A new charge of $100 per month per PC was established to offset a portion of the CDPS's costs of supporting PC users. Boise Cascade had charged users for central computer services for many years, and over the years, CDPS managers had implemented many changes in their billing system. The additional PC charge was just the latest change in the system's continuing evolution.

CDPS managers thought the current billing system worked quite well, although they acknowledged that it could probably be refined further in some small ways. Some users, however, had a number of complaints about the system. A few even thought that Boise Cascade would be better served if users received no charges for the computer services.

The Company

Boise Cascade Corporation, headquartered in Boise, Idaho, was an integrated forest products company with operations located primarily in the United States and Canada. The company manufactured and distributed paper and paper products, office products, and building products, and it owned and managed timberland to support these operations. From 1988 to 1990, annual sales were slightly in excess of $4 billion. Annual profits, which had been nearly $300 million in 1988 and 1989, fell sharply in 1990 to only $75 million.

Corporate Data Processing Services

CDPS was a part of the corporate Information Services department, reporting to Rex Dorman, chief financial officer. CDPS was responsible for running and maintaining the IBM 3090-200S mainframe computer and all ancillary data processing equipment, such as tape drives, disk drives, and printers, located at the corporate headquarters. It provided mainframe and data processing support services for users only within Boise Cascade; it had no outside customers. On average, CDPS was growing at an annual rate of 40% in terms of use of machine resources. In 1991, CDPS's total annual operating and capital budgets were $8.3 million and $4.8 million, respectively.

CDPS had not been responsible for developing application software (e.g., order processing) since 1983. Each of Boise Cascade's business divisions employed its own applications programmers and had its own capital budget that could be used to purchase computer hardware. A couple of the divisions owned minicomputers and ran some of their own applications software. The Office Products and Timber and Wood Products Divisions were very limited users of CDPS services. At the other extreme, the corporate staff groups, including human resources, corporate finance, legal, corporate communications, and medical claims processing, had no capital budgets and relied almost exclusively on CDPS for their computer needs.

CDPS billed out its services to user groups in approximately the following proportions: Paper Group, 35%; Timber and Wood Division, 25%; Human Resources, 25%; Corporate Finance, 10%; and other users, 5%. The Paper Group charges were high primarily because of their relatively heavy use of DB2, a relational data base, which consumed large quantities of mainframe CPU time. The Timber and Wood Division also used DB2 for some applications, and it ran its order processing and some modeling programs on the mainframe. The largest Human Resources applications were the personnel and payroll systems. Corporate Finance ran its bookkeeping and financial reporting programs on the mainframe.

Over the years, Boise Cascade's mainframe computer usage had shifted from primarily batch processing to primarily online processing. In 1991, 80% of jobs were run online. This change was significant because the bulk of online processing was done during regular working hours. In batch processing mode, computer demands can be spread more evenly over a 24-hour period. In online mode, work can only be shifted in significant ways to off hours if people are willing to work evenings and nights, but even then, many of the systems (e.g., order processing) were designed to interface with customers who were seen only during normal business hours.

CDPS had not formally benchmarked its performance in many years. However, outside service bureaus had looked at CDPS's operations and costs and decided not to submit a bid for the business.

CDPS's Billing Philosophy

CDPS billed users monthly for the costs of actual usage of each resource (e.g., CPU, disk drive, printer) plus a markup designed to provide a return of 22% pretax on total capital (PROTC). The PROTC return was set at 22%, the average return target for the corporation, so that the CDPS assets would not dilute the return of the operating groups when the corporate financial statements were consolidated.

CDPS billed for use of its services for the following reasons:

- To establish and account for the costs of providing the services

- To provide an incentive for users to "thoughtfully manage" their use of the resources
- To aid CDPS in managing computer capacity
- To facilitate financial justification for capital and expense requests.

On each user's invoice, CDPS summarized the billing data into six major service categories: batch processing, customer batch processing, remote job entry processing, CICS Processing, TP Processing, and TSO Processing. These categories were defined as follows:

Batch Processing. Defined as that service in which CDPS receives input data from the customer through the Data Control Department. This group provides data control and/or technical (i.e., job control language [JCL]) services and returns a completed report. No technical knowledge is required on the part of the user.

Customer Batch. This service allows the customer to submit the job directly to the computer for processing. All control, technical (JCL) services, and error conditions are the customer's responsibility.

Remote Job Entry. This service is similar to customer batch except that all work is submitted through the customer remote terminal.

CICS Processing. This is an online interactive system used primarily for shared databases.

TP Processing. This is an online interactive system similar to CICS.

Time Sharing Option (TSO). This service allows customers to process in an interactive mode and is similar to traditional services offered by other time sharing companies.

CDPS offered a 75% discount for "non-prime time" CPU usage. Non-prime time was defined as any time except between 8:00 AM and 5 PM,

EXHIBIT 1   Boise Cascade Corporation CDPS Revenue Category Definitions

Processing:	This was the charge for use of the mainframe computer's CPU. The charge was normalized to a 1 million instruction per second (mip) CPU.
Tape Hourly:	This was the clock time that a tape was mounted on a drive for a specific user.
Tape I/O:	The number of input/output instructions to tape.
Disk I/O:	The number of input/output instructions to disk.
Transaction Rate:	The number of times that a user presses the "enter" key on a terminal in online mode.
Execute (step):	The number of execution steps that a program has in batch mode.
Disk D.D.: (disk data definition)	The number of separate data files on disk that are accessed by a user.
Tape D.D.: (tape data definition)	The number of separate data files on tape that are accessed by a user.
Reader:	Use of the card reader.
Spool Charge:	Charge for volume of data that is read into and out of a disk to be printed later.
Local Print:	The charge for printing a job at corporate headquarters.
R/E Print:	The charge for printing a job in any city other than Boise. (Cheaper than local print because CDPS does not maintain printers.)
Class X/Night Discount:	The 75% discount for printing during non-prime hours.
Disk Storage:	The charge for storing data on disk.
Microfiche:	The charge for printing a job on microfiche rather than paper.

Boise time, Monday through Friday. This discount was set because, as Rex Dorman, chief financial officer, noted, "People are creatures of habit, and we want to encourage them to get in the habit of running their jobs at night."

The size of the discount was not based on cost considerations because the mainframe invariably had excess capacity at night, so the marginal cost of night processing was nearly zero. The 75% rate was based on its behavioral effects. When a non-prime time discount was first offered in 1979, the discount was set at 25%, and CDPS managers noted that users moved some work to night processing. They increased the discount to 50% and saw that a little extra work was moved to non-prime time. Finally they increased the discount to 75% and saw that only a tiny fraction of the work was moved to take advantage of the discount, so they became convinced that no price elasticity existed above this level of discount.

CDPS managers set charges for every type of resource usage they wanted their customers to worry about. In 1991, they had 15 defined "revenue categories," as is shown in Exhibit 1. Exhibit 2 shows the prices charged for each of the 15 revenue categories for each of the six major billing categories. Two of the 15 revenue categories, tape hourly and reader, were no longer active because CDPS managers found the costs in them to be insignificant. The charges varied across billing categories because the amount of support required was not constant.

As is shown in Exhibit 3, of the total CDPS charges for all user groups, 82% were for processing, 8% were for disk I/O (input/output), and 10% were for other services. The distributions of charges were, however, quite different for different users depending on the types of jobs they ran.

Users were billed monthly for CDPS services. The billing reports provided charges by

EXHIBIT 2   Boise Cascade Corporation CDPS Revenue Categories and Rates for 1991

Revenue Category	Units of Charge	Batch	Cust. Batch & RJE	TSO	TP	CICS	Misc.
Processing[1]	$/cpu second	.025	.025	.025	.106	.04	
Tape hourly	$/hour	0	0				
Tape I/O	$ per I/O	.0003	.0003				
Disk I/O	$ per I/O	.0002	.0002	.0002	.0002	.0002	
Transaction rate	$/enter	0	0	.0025	.0025	.0025	
Execute (step)	$/step	1.17	.07	0			
Disk D.D.	$/data set	0.07	0	0			
Tape D.D.	$/data set	0.75	.5	.5			
Reader	$/card	0	0	0			
Spool charge	$/line	.0001	.0001	.0001			
Local print	$/line	.0011	.0011	.0011			
RJE print	$/line	.0002	.0002	.0002			
Class X/Night discount			75%	75%	75%	75%	
Disk storage	$/Mega-byte/day						.06
Microfiche	$/line						.00031

[1]In 1972, CDPS designed a billing system for an IBM 370-158 mainframe computer which ran at 1 million instructions per second (mip). In 1991, CDPS operated with an IBM 3090-200S mainframe computer which ran at 42 mips. The billing system made adjustments over the years to normalize the CPU time used to a 1 mip environment.

major billing category but not by revenue category. CDPS managers had found that most users were not interested in the total revenue-category breakdown, although that information was available on request. The monthly bill did provide users with backup detail on costs by job. Most users looked at job costs by revenue category when they considered whether costs could be reduced. Exhibit 4 shows the cover sheet of the June 1991 bill for the Timber and Wood group.

CDPS had been decreasing its billing rates fairly steadily over the years. These decreases reflected improved economies of scale created by growth, and cost savings created by improved technologies, particularly increases in CPU speeds. CPU speeds per dollar of investment had been doubling approximately every five years. CDPS did not offer a rate reduction in 1988 or 1989 due to slow growth, but it did

reduce rates in both 1990 and 1991, and an overall reduction of 24% for processing rates was being planned for 1992.

New rate schedules were given to user groups in the summer so that they could be used in preparing the next year's budget. In addition, to highlight the savings provided by the lower rate schedule, CDPS provided users with a separate statement showing how an old bill would have been lower if the new rate schedule had been in place. In some cases, an overall rate decrease would decrease a group's bill, while in other cases it would increase the bill, depending on the mix of services used.

CDPS Financial Performance

CDPS had met its PROTC target in all but two years, even while decreasing its billing rates reasonably sharply. The two years in which the

EXHIBIT 3 Boise Cascade Corporation

1991 CDPS REVENUE CATEGORIES AND REVENUE BREAKDOWNS
CDPS 1991 Annualized Revenue Using Jan. 91 through Apr. 91

07/05/91

Item #	Revenue Category	Batch	C. Batch & RJE	C. Batch Discount	TSO	TSO Disc.	TP	TP Disc.	CICS	CICS Disc.	Misc	Total	% of Total
1	Processing	$ 50,905	$1,381,884	$1,473,672	$1,028,374	$85,460	$212,715	$5,976	$4,534,332	$183,304		$ 8,956,570	82%
2	Tape hourly	0	0	0								0	0
3	Tape I/O	8,676	24,342	80,536								113,553	1
4	Disk I/O	6,232	222,504	266,298	57,935	3,588	5,110	96	311,276	11,988		885,028	8
5	Transaction rate				167,916	7,584	10,157	278	139,123	12,270		337,329	3
6	Execute (step)	52,946	167,034	93,149	0	0						313,129	3
7	Disk D.D.	30,707	0	0	0	0						30,707	0
8	Tape D.D.	7,807	26,680	46,410								80,897	1
9	Reader	0	0	0	0							0	0
10	Spool charge	6,424	126,621	47,700	6,730	643						188,119	2
11	Local print	38,693	238,947	240,144	37,348	6,319						561,451	5
12	RJE print	3,081	15,338	21,697	758	62						40,936	0
13	Class X/Night disk		0	−1,695,728		−78,967						−1,774,695	−16
14	Disk storage										1,138,592	1,138,592	10
15	Microfiche										80,294	80,294	1
	Totals	$205,471	$2,203,351	$573,878	$1,299,011	$24,688	$227,982	$6,350	$4,984,731	$207,562	$1,218,886	$10,951,911	100%
	% of Total	2%	20%	5%	12%	0%	2%	0%	46%	2%	11%		100%

4	Months actual used to create 12 month total for 1991.	12
	Growth factor used for 1991 to achieve estimated revenue.	3.1%
	Resulting factor used to annualize 1991.	3.093

EXHIBIT 4

BOISE CASCADE CORPORATION
Cover Page of CDPS
Bill for services for
Timber and Wood Group,
June 1991

CDPS NO: 07-099 4-48

Boise Cascade Corporation

Corporate Data Processing Services   Date: 07/25/91

One Jefferson Square

Boise, Idaho 83728   Account Rep: Eileen Cirillo

Memo No. 118-07-099

Invoice Period

From: 06/22/91   To: 07/23/91

T&W Systems   P.O. No.

Attn: Dwight Kirscht

World Headquarters—3W   Customer No. 4-48 Dept #599

Terms

Services Description	Detail $ Amount	Total $ Amount

We Have Debited Our Cash Control Account

*********************Cash Control Memo*********************

Area	Dept.	Cost	Debit	Credit
			169,024.24	

Processing

	Detail	Total
Customer Batch	23,474.02	
Customer Batch (Discounted)	5,887.86	
Remote Job Entry	104.72	
TP Processing	10.00	
TP Processing (Discounted)	.32	
TSO Processing	9,037.20	
TSO Processing (Discounted)	23.16	
CICS Production	93,535.19	
CICS Production (Discounted)	6,289.93	
CICS Test	6,221.39	
CICS Test (Discounted)	209.77	
Data Storage	15,701.31	
COM (Microfiche) Processing	90.91	
Total		160,585.78
Data Processing Equipment		
Equipment Rental & Sales	8,176.14	
Total		8,176.14
Forms, Supplies, Services		
Items Billed at Cost	262.32	
Total		262.32
Total		169,024.24

PROTC target was missed were unusual in that a new computer had just been purchased and the full asset value was still on the books.

In 1991, CDPS had an embarrassment of riches. Its revenues exceeded budget by about $1 million, which translated into a 40.6% PROTC. This increase occurred because CDPS managers had budgeted conservatively to ensure that they met their PROTC target, and users consumed more mainframe resources than were planned for. The excess over budget was seen as undesirable because it indicated that users were actually being overcharged. The CDPS ideal was to be able to report exactly 22% PROTC.

Behavioral Effects of the Billing System

The billing system had both positive and negative behavioral effects. On the positive side, it caused users to consider CDPS costs in their decision-making. Jim Harder, the Director of Information Services, described an example. In early 1988, the medical claims processing department requested *real time* access to all claims entered in the last two years. Jim felt that the charges for disk space caused department personnel to think hard about the value of the benefit of having immediate access capability. By July 1991, the department had still not decided to convert its history files from disk to tape.

Rex Dorman also noted that the system made justifications of computer-related capital expenditures easier. Rex said, "The CEO thinks of us as a provider of services, and he lets my customer have as much service as they are willing to pay for."

On the other hand, Dwight Kirscht, the manager of data processing for the Timber and Wood Division and an informal spokesman for the critics of the CDPS billing system, thought that the system caused some significant problems. One of his concerns was that CDPS charged were unpredictable and uncontrollable.

Dwight had formerly managed a data processing (DP) center for Timber and Wood, and he knew that DP costs were basically all fixed costs. But, Dwight observed, the CDPS billing system caused user group to see all DP charges as variable costs. Dwight also saw wide swings in Timber and Wood's monthly charges from CDPS, and he found it difficult to trace down the causes of the differences. He noted that CPU times and therefore processing rates could fluctuate significantly based on the load placed on the mainframe, and he did not trust the accuracy of the billing algorithms which were designed in 1972 and were perhaps not accurate in the quite different 1991 environment.

Dwight did not charge individual users within Timber and Wood for their computer usage; he kept the CDPS billing detail in his organization. He used to have his experts try to figure out ways of cutting costs, but he found cost reductions elusive. He gave an example:

> We used to think that I/O (input/output) operations caused a significant cost and could be reduced. So we worked with our vendors to reduce the number of I/O operations. But we didn't see our costs change.

Dwight noted that his order processing volume had not changed in three years, and the CDPS rates had declined, but his order processing costs had actually increased. He had given up trying to understand the factors underlying the charges on his bills because he believed that the cost of investigations was greater than the benefits of the answers that could be derived. He said, "The charges are just a nuisance."

Dwight also explained that CDPS's billings had little or no influence on his decision to pursue a DP project. He noted that except in extreme cases no one could determine the production cost of a computer project before it was completely implemented, and at that point, after perhaps six months of development, it was too late to abandon the project. He said, "If you're concerned about runaway data processing costs, just limit the number of programmers

I have. If you limit them, your computer usage can't run away from you."

Dwight believed that if charges were necessary, CDPS managers should take their total operating costs and allocated them based on a simple, predetermined percentage of usage. He said, "I told them that if I use 33% of the machine, just charge me 33%. Then I'll always be on budget."

Dwight even thought that Boise Cascade would be better served if CDPS did not charge for its services at all. He gave a list of reasons. First, he explained that the charges cause people to stay away from the computer system. He was concerned that some people would try to do certain tasks by hand to save the computer charges when it was much more efficient for the company to have them do them using the computer. Dwight said that such computer avoidance is particularly harmful when the company is emphasizing a Total Quality Program because computer usage statistics and costs could cause people to limit the use of the computer in their processes, and these processes are key elements in a quality program. Second, Dwight noted that the billing system itself consumes considerable computer time; he guessed that it used about 10% of the capacity of the mainframe.[1] Third, he said that the charges consume manpower as people try to find out why their charges are higher than they expected, as explained above, and that this time often exceeds the benefit of the investigations. Fourth, he said that billing rates can sometimes encourage user groups to acquire their own computer resources rather than do their processing on the mainframe. Several Boise Cascade divisions

had made this choice some years ago. And finally, he was concerned that when some application functions were over budget, the normal reaction was to stop development activities. Over the long term this was harmful to the company.

The New Charges for Use of Personal Computers

In 1991, CDPS managers were considering making a fairly significant modification to their billing system—the addition of a charge for the use of personal computers. PCs comprised 18% of CDPS's capital budget and 8% of its operating budget. CDPS purchased the PCs used by the corporate staff groups and provided user support for all personal computers that were connected to the mainframe and the local area networks (LAN) used at corporate headquarters. CDPS also provided training and individual support for PC users.

To encourage PC use, CDPS had initially decided to undercharge PC users for the costs of PC support. PC staff users, whose PCs were carried on CDPS's asset list, were charged only depreciation (straight-line over a three-year life). After the PCs were fully depreciated, these users were charged 25% of the last year's depreciation annually for service and support. PC users in operating groups carried their PCs on their own balance sheets and were not assessed any charge. Lately, however, the PC support costs were becoming so significant that CDPS managers thought a PC-based charge was now warranted.

In 1991, CDPS managers estimated that the cost of providing PC support services was $122 per PC per month. (This analysis is shown in Exhibit 5.) But they decided to set the charge for each of the estimated 500 PCs connected to the mainframe conservatively, at $100 per month per PC. They believed users would have no dispute about the magnitude of this figure. Furthermore, they believed that with growth in

---

[1] Jim Harder noted that no statistics existed on the computer time used by the billing system because the billing system relied on the computer capacity measurement system for its inputs. Even if the billing system was not in place, Jim explained, the majority of the capacity the billing system used would still be needed to support capacity planning requirements.

EXHIBIT 5 Boise Cascade Corporation

ESTIMATION OF 1991 CDPS PERSONAL COMPUTER SUPPORT EXPENSES

User support expenses[1]	$349,062
Data center expenses[2]	175,615
Application development support expenses[3]	45,286
PC capital depreciation[4]	121,200
PROTC (33%[5] of $121,200)	40,000
Total annual expense for personal computer support	$731,163
Monthly support expense ($731,163/12)	$ 60,930
Monthly expense per PC ($60,930/500)[6]	$ 122/mo.

---

[1]Includes the costs of the people who provided direct user support and the equipment and software they used.

[2]Includes the costs of maintaining the PC bridge to the mainframe.

[3]Includes the costs of assisting the application development programmers in the operating units.

[4]This is 60% of the total CDPS PC capital depreciation, CDPS managers estimated that 60% of their PC base was used for direct support of PC users.

[5]33% of the depreciated value = 22% of the average investment over the asset's life.

[6]Current estimate = 500 billable customer PCs.

the number of PCs and basically fixed support costs, the $100 would be an accurate figure in 2–3 years. In addition to the support services charge, staff PC users would still be billed the same depreciation expense, but now a 22% PROTC markup would be added. This markup would add approximately one-third to the PC purchase price.

CDPS managers noted that this solution for charging for PC costs would require mainframe users to continue subsidizing PC support costs for a few years. But even so, this change accounted for 10% of the 24% reduction in billing rates planned for 1992.

The effect of this change on users was varied. The Timber and Wood Division would benefit from the change. It was an operating group and, therefore, owned all of its PCs. In addition, it used a lot of mainframe CPU time, and did most of its interfacing with the mainframe computer through dumb terminals. The Legal, Corporate Communications, and Planning departments would be hurt most by the billing change. Each had PC-LAN systems. Rex Dorman knew he would receive some complaints from these departments who originally based their decisions to use PCs on a cost comparison with mainframe use before the billing change. Rex said, "We know that some people will complain, but PCs have been subsidized up to this point and they [PC users] need to start carrying a portion of their costs."

Questions

1. Is Boise Cascade's CDPS a profit center?
2. Evaluate the CDPS billing system. Do Dwight Kirscht's criticisms have any merit?
3. Evaluate the new system for charging for the use of personal computers?

CASE 4–4
ABRAMS COMPANY

Abrams Company manufactured a wide variety of parts for use in automobiles, trucks, buses, and farm equipment. There were three major groups of parts: ignition parts, transmission parts, and engine parts. Abrams' parts were sold both to original equipment manufacturers (OEMs) and to wholesalers. The wholesalers, in turn, resold the parts to retailers who sold them as replacement parts to consumers. The latter market was called the "aftermarket" (AM).

Product and Marketing Divisions

As shown in the partial organization chart in Exhibit 1, Abrams had a "product division" for each of its three part groups. Each of these product divisions was managed by a vice president and general manager who was expected to earn a target return on investment (ROI). Each product division manufactured parts in several plants and sold a major portion of its manufactured parts to OEMs. Each product division had its separate OEM sales department (see Exhibit 1) that worked closely with OEMs to develop new products or change existing products. The remaining manufactured parts were sold by the product division to Abrams' fourth division, called the AM Marketing Division (see Exhibit 1) or "AM Division," as it was known to managers. This division was also managed by a vice president and general manager and was solely responsible for marketing Abrams' entire line of parts to AM wholesalers. The AM division operated several company-owned parts dis-

tribution warehouses in the US and foreign markets. The AM division was also expected to earn an annual return on investment target.

Inside and Outside Sales

In 1992, the four divisions' sales totaled $500 million, which included "inside" sales of $100 million from the three product divisions to the AM division. The $500 million sales were recorded as approximately $130 million for the ignition parts division, $100 million for the transmission parts division, $90 million for the engine parts division, and $180 million for the AM division. After elimination of inside sales, Abrams' outside sales totaled about $400 million. Because of anticipated growth in the parts' aftermarket due to the increase in the number of vehicles being driven and their ages, one of top management's goals for the AM Division was for its sales to reach 50 percent of Abrams' total outside sales.

ROI for the Manufacturing Plants

Continuing the company's ROI strategy, each manufacturing plant within the three product divisions had an annual ROI target to meet. Each product division's OEM sales were traced to the plants that made the parts. The plants maintained finished goods inventories and shipped parts directly to OEM customers. A plant's ROI target was based on budgeted profit (including allocations of division and corporate overhead expenses and an imputed income tax expense) divided by actual beginning-of-the-year net assets (defined as total assets less current liabilities). Exhibit 2 contains an example of the Rochester plant's actual 1992 ROI computation. Actual ROI was actual profit divided by actual beginning-of-the-year net assets.

This case was adapted (with permission) by Professor J. G. San Miguel from a case written by Professor J. S. Reece of the University of Michigan. Copyright © by Joe San Miguel and Jim Reece.

Exhibit 1
Partial organization chart

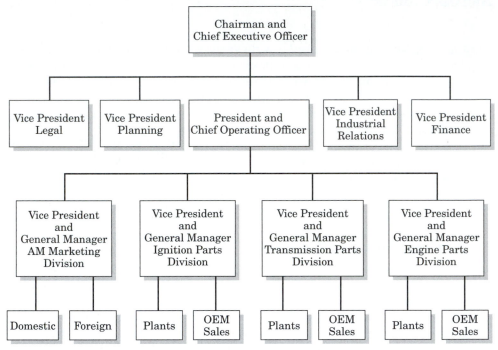

Top management's stated reason for including allocated overhead expenses and taxes in determining profit was to have the plant profit figure resemble the profit calculation for external financial reports to shareholders. The CEO felt this gave a plant manager a clearer perspective of the costs of doing business and the plant's contribution to the corporate bottom line, and added more realism to the plant's results.

The beginning-of-the-year net assets amount was used in the ROI measurement because, in management's view, investment added during a given year resulted in little, if any, incremental profit in that year. The investment would likely increase future profits. Top management felt that such investments might not be proposed if managers were penalized (in the form of higher net assets and lower ROI) in the first year of the new investment. Because the investment

base for the year was "frozen" at the beginning-of-the-year level, maximizing profit during the year was equivalent to maximizing ROI. For beginning-of-the-year net assets, cash and receivables were allocated to plants on the basis of sales revenue, while inventories, property, plant, equipment, and current liabilities were traced specifically to each plant. Historical cost less accumulated depreciation (book value) was used to value property, plant, and equipment. The AM division's ROI was measured in the same manner as the plants' ROIs.

Marketing Strategies

The OEM sales department within each of the three product divisions worked with the OEM's engineers to develop innovative and cost-effective new parts to meet the customers' requirements

EXHIBIT 2   Actual 1992 ROI Computation—Rochester Plant

Abrams Company—Transmission Parts Division
ROCHESTER PLANT
Profit and ROI Statement, December 31, 1992

Sales revenue	$124,866
Cost of goods sold	73,230
Gross margin	51,636
Operating expenses	20,792
Division expenses assigned	11,340
Corporate expenses assigned	3,420
Profit before taxes	16,084
Taxes imputed	4,825
Profit	$ 11,259

Net Assets Assigned as of January 1, 1992

Total Assets:	
Cash and receivables	$ 25,000
Inventories	12,875
Property, plant & equipment at book value	86,560
Total Assets	124,435
Less current liabilities	26,135
Net Assets	$ 98,300
Return on investment	11.5%

and serviced customer accounts for parts already being supplied to the OEMs. Each of these OEM sales departments was expected to meet an annual sales revenue target. Because the product divisions' customers (OEMs) were different from the AM division's customers, top management did not feel that the OEM and aftermarket sales organizations should be combined. Even the three product divisions' OEM marketing efforts were not consolidated in one sales organization because each division's OEM marketers tended to work with different people within a given OEM's organization (i.e., ignition, transmission, and engines). Moreover, two of the three product divisions were independent companies before being acquired by Abrams. Thus, there was a long tradition of doing their own OEM marketing.

According to Abrams' executives, the factors critical to success in the OEM market were: the ability to design innovative and dependable parts that met the customer's quality, performance, and weight specifications; meeting delivery schedule requirements so that the OEM could minimize its own parts inventories; and controlling costs. Cost control was important because the market was very price competitive. In the aftermarket business, availability of parts was by far the most important factor to the wholesaler, followed by quality and price.

Incentive Compensation Plan

Approximately 50 Abrams line and staff managers participated in an incentive bonus plan. The dollar amount of the corporatewide bonus pool was established by a fixed formula linked to corporate earnings per share. Each participant in the bonus plan received a number of standard bonus points. The higher the participant was in the organizational hierarchy, the more standard points he or she received. The total of these points for all participants was divided into the total bonus pool amount to arrive at a standard dollar award per point. Then, this standard rate was multiplied by the participant's number of standard points to arrive at the participant's standard bonus dollars. However, the actual bonus could vary (upward or downward) by as much as 25 percent at the discretion of the participant's superiors.

In the case of a plant manager, the standard award also was adjusted by a formula that related percent of standard award to the plant's profit variance (budget versus actual profit). For example, if the plant's actual profit for the year exceeded its budgeted profit by 4 percent, the plant manager's bonus was raised from 100 percent of standard to 110 percent of standard.

In making this bonus adjustment, the plant's actual profit was adjusted for any favorable or unfavorable gross margin variance caused by sales volume to the AM division being higher or lower than budgeted. For example, if a plant's favorable profit variance was attributable to a favorable gross margin volume variance on sales to the AM division, the plant manager's bonus would not be raised above 100 percent of standard. Similarly, the plant manager would not be penalized if the AM division actually purchased less from the plant than the amount that was agreed to by AM division when the plant's annual profit budget was approved by top management.

Management Comments

In general, top management was satisfied with the present management systems and performance measurement scheme. In discussions with the casewriter, however, they mentioned three areas of concern.

First, there always seemed to be a few disputes over transfer prices of parts sold by the product divisions to the AM division. Whenever possible, by corporate policy, internal sales of parts were made at outside OEM market prices. If a part had been sold as an OEM part several years earlier, the original OEM market price was adjusted upward for inflation to arrive at the sales price to the AM division. This procedure caused virtually no disputes. Problems occurred when the part being transferred was strictly an AM division part. That is, it was a part never sold by Abrams in the OEM market and for which there was neither a current OEM outside market price nor a former OEM market price that could be adjusted for inflation. Usually, such transfer price issues were resolved by the two divisions involved, but occa-

sionally the vice president of finance was asked to arbitrate a dispute.

Second, top management felt that the product divisions too often tended to treat the AM division as a captive customer. For example, when the AM division and an outside OEM customer were placing competing demands on a specific manufacturing plant, it appeared that the plant often favored the OEM customer because the OEM customer could take its business elsewhere, whereas the AM division could not purchase parts outside. Top management was not willing to let the AM division sell a competitor's product, feeling this would reflect adversely on the overall image of the company. The AM division was expected to convince the appropriate plant manager to undertake the manufacture of its part needs.

Third, top management felt that both the AM division and the three product divisions carried excessive inventories most of the year. The vice president of planning said, "Thank goodness we have a generous Christmas vacation policy here. At least the inventories get down to a reasonable level at year-end when our production volume is low because of a large number of employee holiday vacations."

Questions

1. Evaluate each of the concerns expressed by top management, and if necessary, make recommendations appropriate to the circumstances described in the case.

2. What is your overall evaluation of Abrams' management control system? Describe any strengths or weaknesses that you identified but did not include in answering the previous question. What changes, if any, would you recommend to top management?

TRANSFER PRICING

Today's organizational thinking is oriented toward decentralization. One of the principal challenges in operating a decentralized system is to devise a satisfactory method of accounting for the transfer of goods and services from one profit center to another in companies that have a significant number of these transactions. In this chapter we discuss various approaches to arriving at transfer prices for transactions between profit centers and the system of negotiation and arbitration that is essential when transfer prices are used. We also discuss the pricing of services that corporate staff units furnish to profit centers. We discuss international transfer pricing in Chapter 14.

Objectives of Transfer Prices

If two or more profit centers are jointly responsible for product development, manufacturing, and marketing, each should share in the revenue generated when the product is finally sold. The transfer price is the mechanism for distributing this revenue. The transfer price should be designed so that it accomplishes the following objectives:

- It should provide each business unit with the relevant information it needs to determine the optimum trade-off between *company* costs and revenues.
- It should induce *goal congruent* decisions—that is, the system should be designed so that decisions that improve business unit profits will also improve company profits.
- It should help measure the *economic performance* of the individual business units.
- The system should be *simple* to understand and *easy* to administer.

EXHIBIT 5–1   Transfer of Products between Profit Centers

	Govindarajan Survey
Number of usable responses	638
Companies with two or more profit centers	593 (93%)
Of the companies with two or more profit centers, companies that transfer products between profit centers	470 (79%)

Source: Vijay Govindarajan, "Profit Center Measurement: An Empirical Survey," The Amos Tuck School of Business Administration, Dartmouth College, 1994, p. 2.

Designing transfer pricing systems is a key management control topic for most corporations; the Govindarajan survey[1] (see Exhibit 5–1) found that 79 percent of companies transferred products between profit centers.

Transfer Pricing Methods

Some writers use the term "transfer price" to refer to the amount used in accounting for *any* transfer of goods and services between responsibility centers. We use a somewhat narrower definition and limit the term "transfer price" to the value placed on a transfer of goods or services in transactions in which at least one of the two parties involved is a *profit center*. Such a price typically includes a profit element because an independent company normally would not transfer goods or services to another independent company at cost or less. Therefore, we exclude the mechanics for allocating costs in a cost accounting system; such costs do not include a profit element. The term "price" as used here has the same meaning as it has when used in connection with transactions between independent companies.

Fundamental Principle

The transfer pricing issue is actually about pricing in general, modified slightly to take into account factors that are unique to internal transactions. *The fundamental principle is that the transfer price should be similar to the price that would be charged if the product were sold to outside customers or purchased from outside vendors.* Applying this principle is complicated by the fact that there is much disagreement in the literature as to how outside selling prices are established. Classical economics literature states that selling prices should be equal to marginal costs, and some authors advocate a trans-

---

[1]Vijay Govindarajan, "Profit Center Measurement: An Empirical Survey," The Amos Tuck School of Business Administration, Dartmouth College, 1994, p. 2.

fer price based on marginal cost.[2] This is unrealistic. Few companies follow such a policy in arriving at either selling prices or transfer prices.[3]

When profit centers of a company buy products from, and sell to, one another, two decisions must be made periodically for each product:

1. Should the company produce the product inside the company or purchase it from an outside vendor? This is the *sourcing decision.*
2. If produced inside, at what price should the product be transferred between profit centers? This is the *transfer price decision.*

Example.   CSX Corporation was the largest railroad holding company with both railroads and barge lines. CSX derived over two-thirds of its revenues from railroads. CSX divided its railroad operations into three profit centers—equipment (the freight-car fleet), rail transport (train operations, yard, track and locomotive maintenance), and distribution services (sales and marketing). The transfer price between profit centers was to be arm's-length negotiated market prices. The logic for the reorganization was to shift the power center from the operating department, which traditionally ran the railroad, to sales and marketing. If the most efficient way to move traffic from point X to point Y was by truck or barge, then the traffic would go by truck or barge, even though historically it would have gone by rail. In fact, since the profit center and transfer pricing systems were instituted, the bulk of the new traffic had gone to barge lines other than the ones owned by CSX.[4]

Transfer price systems can range from very simple to extremely complex, depending on the nature of the business. We start with the ideal situation and then describe increasingly complex situations.

The Ideal Situation

A *market price*–based transfer price will induce goal congruence if all the conditions listed below exist. Rarely, if ever, will all these conditions exist in practice. The list, therefore, does not set forth criteria that must be met to have a transfer price. Rather, it suggests a way of looking at a situation to see what changes should be made to improve the operation of the transfer price mechanism.

Competent People.   Ideally, managers should be interested in the long-run as well as the short-run performances of their responsibility centers. Staff people involved in negotiation and arbitration of transfer prices also must be competent.

---

[2]Jack Hirschleifer, "On the Economics of Transfer Pricing," *Journal of Business,* July 1956, pp. 172–84.

[3]A study by the authors of methods of arriving at market prices reported that only 17 percent of the 501 respondents from Fortune 1,000 companies followed such a policy. (Vijay Govindarajan and Robert N. Anthony, "How Firms Use Cost Data in Pricing Decisions," *Management Accounting,* July 1983, pp. 30–34.)

[4]"If It Isn't Profitable, Don't Do It," *Forbes,* November 30, 1987.

Good Atmosphere.   Managers must regard profitability, as measured in their income statements, as an important goal and a significant consideration in the judgment of their performance. They should perceive that the transfer prices are just.

A Market Price.   The ideal transfer price is based on a well-established, normal market price for the identical product being transferred—that is, a market price reflecting the same conditions (quantity, delivery time, and quality) as the product to which the transfer price applies. The market price may be adjusted downward to reflect savings accruing to the selling unit from dealing inside the company. For example, there would be no bad debt expense, and advertising and selling costs would be smaller when products are transferred from one business unit to another within the company. Although less than ideal, a market price for a similar, but not identical, product is better than no market price at all.

Freedom to Source.   Alternatives for sourcing should exist, and managers should be permitted to choose the alternative that is in their own best interests. The buying manager should be free to buy from the outside, and the selling manager should be free to sell outside. In these circumstances, the transfer price policy simply gives the manager of each profit center the right to deal with either insiders or outsiders at his or her discretion. The market thus establishes the transfer price. The decision as to whether to deal inside or outside also is made by the marketplace. If buyers cannot get a satisfactory price from the inside source, they are free to buy from the outside.

   This method is optimum if the selling profit center can sell all of its products to either insiders or outsiders and if the buying center can obtain all of its requirements from either outsiders or insiders. The market price represents the opportunity costs to the seller of selling the product inside. This is so because if the product were not sold inside, it would be sold outside. From a company point of view, therefore, the relevant cost of the product is the market price because that is the amount of cash that has been forgone by selling inside. The transfer price represents the opportunity cost to the company.

Full Information.   Managers must know about the available alternatives and the relevant costs and revenues of each.

Negotiation.   There must be a smoothly working mechanism for negotiating "contracts" between business units.

   If all of the above conditions are present, a transfer price system based on *market prices* would induce goal congruent decisions, with no need for central administration. In the next subsection, we consider situations in which not all of these conditions are present.

Constraints on Sourcing

Ideally, the buying manager should be free to make sourcing decisions. Similarly, the selling manager should be free to sell products in the most advantageous market. In real life, however, freedom to source might not be feasible or, if it is feasible, might be constrained by corporate policy. We now consider the situations in which profit center managers may not have the freedom to make sourcing decisions and the implications of constraints on sourcing on the appropriate transfer pricing policies.

Limited Markets.   In many companies, markets for the buying or selling profit centers may be limited. There are several reasons for this.

First, the existence of internal capacity might limit the development of external sales. If most of the large companies in an industry are highly integrated, as in the pulp and paper industry, there tends to be little independent production capacity for intermediate products. Thus, these producers can handle only a limited amount of demand from other producers. When internal capacity becomes tight, the market is quickly flooded with demands for the intermediate products. Even though outside capacity exists, it may not be available to the integrated company unless this capacity is used on a regular basis. If the integrated company does not purchase a product on a regular basis, it might have trouble obtaining it from the outside when capacity is limited.

Second, if a company is the sole producer of a differentiated product, no outside source exists.

Third, if a company has invested significantly in facilities, it is unlikely to use outside sources unless the outside selling price approaches the company's variable cost, which is not usual. For practical purposes, the products produced are captive. Integrated oil companies are good examples of this. The producing unit may be required to send the crude oil to the refining unit, even though the former could potentially sell the crude oil in the open market.

Even in the case of limited markets, the transfer price that best satisfies the requirements of a profit center system is the *competitive price*. Competitive prices measure the contribution of each profit center to the total company profits. In the case of an integrated oil company, use of crude oil market prices is the most effective way to evaluate the extracting and refining units as if they were stand-alone businesses. If internal capacity is not available, the company will buy outside at the competitive price. The difference between the competitive price and the inside cost is the money saved by producing rather than buying. Moreover, a competitive price measures how well a profit center may be performing against competitors.

How does a company find out what the competitive price is if it does not buy or sell the product in an outside market? Here are some ways:

1. If *published market prices* are available, they can be used to establish transfer prices. However, these should be prices actually paid in the marketplace, and the conditions that exist in the outside market should be consistent with those that exist within the company. For example, market prices that apply to relatively small purchases (e.g., a "spot" market) would not be valid for measuring what is essentially a long-term commitment.

2. Market prices may be set by *bids.* This generally can be done only if the low bidder stands a reasonable chance of obtaining the business. One company accomplishes this by buying about one-half of a particular group of products outside the company and one-half inside the company. The company puts *all* of the products out to bid but selects half to stay inside. It obtains valid bids because low bidders can expect to get some of the business. By contrast, if a company requests bids solely to obtain a competitive price and does not award contracts to the low bidder, it will soon find that either no one bids or that the bids are of questionable value.

3. If the *production profit center* sells similar products in *outside markets,* it is often possible to replicate a competitive price on the basis of the outside price. For example, if a manufacturing profit center normally earns a 10 percent profit over standard cost on the products that it sells to outside markets, it can replicate a competitive price by adding 10 percent to the standard cost of its proprietary products.

4. If the *buying profit center* purchases similar products from the *outside market,* it may be possible to replicate competitive prices for its proprietary products. This can be done by calculating the cost of the difference in design and other conditions of sale between the competitive products and the proprietary products.

Excess or Shortage of Industry Capacity.   Suppose the selling profit center cannot sell to the outside market all it can produce—that is, it has excess capacity. The company may not optimize profits if the buying profit center purchased from outside vendors while capacity is available on the inside.

Conversely, suppose the buying profit center cannot obtain the product it requires from the outside while the selling profit center is selling to the outside. This situation occurs when there is a shortage of capacity in the industry. In this case, the output of the buying profit center is constrained and, again, company profits may not be optimum.

If the number of intracompany transfers is small or if the situation is temporary, many companies let buyers and sellers work out their own relationships without central intervention. Even if the number of intracompany transfers is significant, some senior managements still do not intervene on the theory that the benefits of keeping the profit centers independent offset the loss from suboptimizing company profits.

Some companies allow either the buying or the selling profit center to appeal a sourcing decision to a central person or committee. For example, a selling profit center could appeal a buying profit center's decision to buy a product from outside when capacity was available inside. In the same way, a buying profit center could appeal a selling profit center's decision to sell outside. The person or group (called an *arbitration committee*) would then make the sourcing decision on the basis of the company's best interests. In every case, the transfer price would be the *competitive price.* In other words, the profit center is appealing only the sourcing decision. It must accept the product at the competitive price.

A word of caution is in order at this point: Given the option, buying profit centers in some companies prefer to deal with an outside source. One reason is the perception that outside sources provide better service. Another reason is the internal rivalry that sometimes exists in divisionalized companies. For whatever reason, management should be aware of the strong political overtones that sometimes occur in transfer price negotiations. There is no guarantee that a profit center will voluntarily buy from the inside source when excess capacity exists.

To conclude, even if there are constraints on sourcing, the market price is the best transfer price. *If the market price exists or can be approximated, use it.* However, if there is no way of approximating valid competitive prices, the other option is to develop *cost-based* transfer prices. These are discussed in the next section.

In arriving at the transfer price, companies typically eliminate advertising, financing, or other expenses that the seller does not incur in internal transactions. This is similar to the practice when two outside companies arrive at a price. The buyer ordinarily will not pay for cost components that do not apply to the contract.

Cost-Based Transfer Prices

If competitive prices are not available, transfer prices may be set on the basis of cost plus a profit, even though such transfer prices may be complex to calculate and the results less satisfactory than a market-based price. Two decisions must be made in a cost-based transfer price system: (1) how to define cost and (2) how to calculate the profit markup.

The Cost Basis.   *The usual basis is standard costs.* Actual costs should not be used because production inefficiencies will be passed on to the buying profit center. If standard costs are used, an incentive is needed to set tight standards and improve standards.

The Profit Markup.   In calculating the profit markup, there also are two decisions: (1) what the profit markup is based on and (2) the level of profit allowed.

The simplest and most widely used base is a *percentage of costs*. If this base is used, however, no account is taken of capital required. A conceptually better base is a *percentage of investment,* but calculating the investment applicable to a given product may pose a major practical problem. If the historical cost of the fixed assets is used, new facilities designed to reduce prices could actually increase costs because old assets are undervalued.

The second problem with the profit allowance is the amount of profit. Senior management's perception of the financial performance of a profit center will be affected by the profit it shows. Consequently, to the extent possible the profit allowance should approximate the rate of return that would be earned if the business unit were an independent company selling to outside customers. The conceptual solution is to base the profit allowance on the investment required to meet the volume needed by the buying profit centers. The investment would be calculated at a "standard" level, with fixed assets and inventories at current replacement costs.

Upstream Fixed Costs and Profits

Transfer pricing can create a significant problem in integrated companies. The profit center that finally sells to the outside customer may not even be aware of the amount of upstream fixed costs and profit included in its internal purchase price. Even if the final profit center were aware of these costs and profit, it might be reluctant to reduce its own profit to optimize company profit. Methods that companies use to mitigate this problem are described below.

Agreement among Business Units.   Some companies establish a formal mechanism whereby representatives from the buying and selling units meet periodically to decide on outside selling prices and the sharing of profits for products with significant upstream fixed costs and profit. This mechanism works only if the review process is limited to decisions involving a significant amount of business to at least one of the profit centers; otherwise, the value of these negotiations may not be worth the effort.

Two-Step Pricing.   Another way to handle this problem is to establish a transfer price that includes two charges. First, for each unit sold, a charge is made that is equal to the *standard variable cost* of production. Second, a periodic (usually monthly) charge is made that is equal to the *fixed costs* associated with the facilities reserved for the buying unit. One or both of these components should include a profit margin. For example, assume the conditions in Exhibit 5–2.

In this method, the transfer price of $11 per unit is a variable cost so far as Unit Y is concerned. However, the company's variable cost for product A is $5 per unit. Thus, Unit Y does not have the right information to make appropriate short-term marketing decisions. If Unit Y knew the company's variable costs, for example, it could safely take business at less than its normal price under certain conditions.

Two-step pricing corrects this problem by transferring variable cost on a per unit basis and transferring fixed cost and profit on a lump sum basis. Under this method, the transfer price for product A would be $5 for each unit that Unit Y purchases, plus $20,000 per month for fixed cost, plus $10,000 per month for profit:

$$\frac{\$1,200,000}{12} * 0.10$$

If transfers of product A in a certain month are at the expected amount of 5,000 units, under the two-step method Unit Y will pay the variable cost of $25,000 (5,000 units $*$ $5 per unit), plus $30,000 for fixed costs and profit—a

---

EXHIBIT 5–2   Two-Step Pricing: Assumed Situation

Business Unit X (manufacturer)	Product A
Expected monthly sales to Business Unit Y	5,000 units
Variable cost per unit	$ 5
Monthly fixed costs assigned to product	20,000
Investment in working capital and facilities	1,200,000
Competitive return on investment per year	10%

One way to transfer product A to Business Unit Y is at a price per unit, calculated as follows:

	Transfer Price for Product A
Variable cost per unit	$ 5
Plus fixed cost per unit	4
Plus profit per unit*	2
Transfer price per unit	$ 11

*10% of monthly investment per unit = $\dfrac{(\$1,200,000/12) * 0.10}{5,000}$

---

total of $55,000. This is the same amount it would pay Unit X if the transfer price were $11 per unit (5,000 * $11 = $55,000). If transfers in another month were less—say, 4,000 units—Unit Y would pay $50,000 ([4,000 * $5] + $30,000) under the two-step method, compared with the $44,000 it would pay if the transfer price were $11 per unit (4,000 * $11). The difference is its penalty for not using a portion of Unit X's capacity that it has reserved. Conversely, Unit Y would pay less under the two-step method if the transfer were more than 5,000 units in a given month. This represents the savings Unit X would have because it could produce the additional units without incurring additional fixed costs.

Note that under two-step pricing, the company's variable cost for product A is identical to Unit Y's variable cost for this product, and Unit Y will make the correct short-term marketing decisions. Unit Y also has information on upstream fixed costs and profit relating to product A, and it can use these data for long-term decisions.

The fixed-cost calculation in the two-step pricing method is based on the capacity reserved for the production of product A that is sold to Unit Y. The investment represented by this capacity is allocated to product A. The return on investment that Unit X earns on competitive (and, if possible, comparable) products is calculated and multiplied by the investment assigned to the product.

In the example, we calculated the profit allowance as a fixed monthly amount. It would be appropriate under some circumstances to divide the investment into variable (e.g., receivables and inventory) and fixed (e.g., plant) components. Then, a profit allowance based on a return on the variable assets would be added to the standard variable cost for each unit sold.

Following are some points to consider about the two-step pricing method:

- The monthly charge for fixed costs and profit should be negotiated periodically and will depend on the capacity reserved for the buying unit.
- Questions may be raised about the accuracy of the cost and investment allocation. In some situations, assigning costs and assets to individual products is not difficult. In any event, approximate accuracy is adequate. The principal problem usually is not the allocation technique; it's deciding how much capacity to reserve for the various products. Moreover, if capacity is reserved for a group of products sold to the same business unit, there is no need to allocate fixed costs and investments to individual products in the group.
- Under this pricing system, the manufacturing unit's profit performance is not affected by the sales volume of the final unit. This solves the problem that arises when marketing efforts by other business units affect the profit performance of a purely manufacturing unit.
- There could be a conflict between the interests of the manufacturing unit and those of the company. If capacity is limited, the manufacturing unit could increase its profit by using the capacity to produce parts for outside sale, if it is advantageous to do so. (This weakness is mitigated by stipulating that the marketing unit has first claim on the capacity for which it contracted.)
- This method is similar to the "take or pay" pricing that is used frequently by public utilities, pipelines, and coal mining companies, and in other long-term contracts.

Profit Sharing.   If the two-step pricing system just described is not feasible, a *profit sharing system* might be used to ensure congruence between business unit and company interests. This system operates as follows:

1. The product is transferred to the marketing unit at standard variable cost.
2. After the product is sold, the business units share the contribution earned, which is the selling price minus the variable manufacturing and marketing costs.

This method of pricing may be appropriate if demand for the manufactured product is not steady enough to warrant the permanent assignment of facilities, as in the two-step method. In general, this method does make the marketing unit's interest congruent with the company's.

Implementing such a *profit sharing system* produces several practical problems. First, there can be arguments over the way contribution is divided between the two profit centers, and senior management might have to intervene to settle these disputes. This is costly and time consuming and works against a basic reason for decentralization, namely, autonomy of business unit managers. Second, arbitrarily dividing up the profits between units does not give valid information on the profitability of each unit. Third, since the contribution is not allocated until after the sale has been made, the manufacturing unit's contribution depends on the marketing unit's ability to sell as well as the actual selling price. Manufacturing units may perceive this situation to be unfair.

Two Sets of Prices.   In this method, the manufacturing unit's revenue is credited at the outside sales price and the buying unit is charged the total standard costs. The difference is charged to a headquarters account and eliminated when the business unit statements are consolidated. This transfer pricing method is sometimes used when there are frequent conflicts between the buying and selling units that cannot be resolved by one of the other methods. Both the buying and selling units benefit under this method.

However, there are several disadvantages to the system of having two sets of transfer prices. First, the sum of the business unit profits is greater than overall company profits. Senior management must be aware of this situation when approving budgets for the business units and subsequently evaluating performance against these budgets. Second, this system creates an illusive feeling that business units are making money, while, in fact, the overall company might be losing money because of debits to headquarters. Third, this system might motivate business units to concentrate more on internal transfers where they are assured of a good markup at the expense of outside sales. Fourth, there is additional bookkeeping involved in first debiting the headquarters account every time a transfer is made and then eliminating this account when business unit statements are consolidated. Finally, the fact that conflicts between the business units would be lessened under this system could be viewed as a weakness. Sometimes, conflicts over transfer prices signal problems in either the organizational structure or other management systems. Under the two-sets-of-prices method these conflicts are smoothed over, thereby not alerting senior management to these problems.

Business Practice

Exhibit 5–3 summarizes the transfer pricing practices of US corporations and the methods practiced in selected countries outside the United States.

Pricing Corporate Services

In this section we describe some of the problems associated with charging business units for services furnished by corporate staff units. We exclude the cost of central service staff units over which business units have no control (e.g., central accounting, public relations, administration). As described in

Exhibit 5–3   Transfer Pricing Methods for Goods

	Percentage of Respondents Using the Transfer Pricing Method					
	United States[a]	*Australia*[b]	*Canada*[c]	*Japan*[d]	*India*[e]	*United Kingdom*[f]
Number of respondents	470	N/A	N/A	N/A	N/A	N/A
Cost-Based Methods						
Variable cost	11%	N/A	6%	2%	6%	10%
Full cost	25	N/A	37	44	47	38
Cost plus markup	17	N/A	N/A	N/A	N/A	N/A
Other	N/A	N/A	3	0	0	1
Total	53%	65%	46%	46%	53%	49%
Market price	31	13	34	34	47	26
Negotiated price	16	11	18	19	0	24
Other	N/A	11	2	1	0	1
	100%	100%	100%	100%	100%	100%

[a]Vijay Govindarjan, "Profit Center Measurement," p. 2.

[b]M. Joye and P. Blayney, "Cost and Management Accounting Practices in Australian Manufacturing Companies," Accounting Research Centre, The University of Sydney, 1991.

[c]R. Tang, "Canadian Transfer Pricing in the 1990s," *Management Accounting,* February 1992.

[d]R. Tang, C. Walter, and R. Raymond, "Transfer Pricing—Japanese vs. American Style," *Management Accounting,* January 1979.

[e]V. Govindarajan and B. Ramamurthy, "Transfer Pricing Policies in Indian Companies: A Survey," *The Chartered Accountant,* November 1983.

[f]C. Drury, S. Braund, P. Osborne, and M. Tayles, *A Survey of Management Accounting Practices in U.K. Manufacturing Companies,* London, UK: Chartered Association of Certified Accountants, 1993.

Chapter 4, if these costs are charged at all, they are allocated, and the allocations do not include a profit component. The allocations are not transfer prices.

There remain two types of transfers:

1. For central services that the receiving unit must accept but can at least partially control the amount used.
2. For central services that the business unit can decide whether or not to use.

Control over Amount of Service

Business units may be required to use company staffs for services such as information technology and research and development. In these situations, the business unit manager cannot control the *efficiency* with which these activities are performed but can control the *amount* of the service received. There are three schools of thought about such services.

One school holds that a business unit should pay the *standard variable cost* of the discretionary services. If it pays less than this, it will be motivated to use more of the service than is economically justified. On the other hand, if business unit managers are required to pay more than the variable cost, they might not elect to use certain services that senior management believes worthwhile from the company's viewpoint. This possibility is most likely when senior management introduces a new service, such as a new project analysis program. The low price is analogous to the introductory price that companies sometimes use for new products.

> **Example.** For many years, managers of the Corporate Data Processing Services (CDPS) department of the Boise Cascade Corporation did not allocate any of the costs of supporting personal computers (PC), such as purchasing, setup, and application assistance, to the PC users because they wanted to stimulate PC use. These costs were charged to all of the other CDPS users, primarily consumers of mainframe computer resources. Even when the PC support costs became so significant that a charge for them was deemed desirable, CDPS managers chose not to charge the full cost. They set the charge at around $100 per month per PC, rather than at their best current-year estimate of $121 per month.[5]

A second school of thought advocates a price equal to the standard variable cost plus a fair share of the standard fixed costs—that is, the *full cost.* Proponents argue that if the business units do not believe the services are worth at least this amount, something is wrong with either the quality or the efficiency of the service unit. Full cost represents the company's long-run costs, and this is the amount that should be paid.

A third school advocates a price that is equivalent to the *market price,* or to standard full cost plus a profit margin. The market price would be used if available (e.g., costs charged by a computer service bureau); if not, the price would be full cost plus a return on investment. The rationale for this position is that the capital employed by service units should earn a return just as the capital employed by manufacturing units does. Also, the business units would incur the investment if they provided their own service.

Optional Use of Services

In some cases, management may decide that business units can choose whether to use central service units. Business units may procure the service from outside, develop their own capability, or choose not to use the service at all. This type of arrangement is most often found for such activities as information technology, internal consulting groups, and maintenance work. These service centers are independent; they must stand on their own feet. If the internal services are not competitive with outside providers, the scope of their activity will be contracted or their services may be outsourced completely.

> **Example.** Commodore Business Machines outsourced one of its central service activities—customer service—to Federal Express. James Reeder, Commodore's

---

[5]Kenneth A. Merchant, "Boise Cascade Corporation," University of Southern California case A911-04.

vice president of customer satisfaction, said, "At that time we didn't have the greatest reputation for customer service and satisfaction." But this was FedEx's specialty, handling more than 300,000 calls for service each day. Commodore arranged for FedEx to handle the entire telephone customer service operation from FedEx's hub in Memphis.[6]

In this situation, business unit managers control both the *amount* and the *efficiency* of the central services. Under these conditions, these central groups are profit centers. Their transfer prices should be based on the same considerations as those governing other transfer prices.

Simplicity of the Price Mechanism

The prices charged for corporate services will not accomplish their intended result unless the methods of calculating them are straightforward enough for business unit managers to understand them. Computer experts are accustomed to dealing with complex equations, and the computer itself provides information on the use made of it on a second-by-second basis and at low cost. There sometimes is a tendency, therefore, to charge computer users on the basis of rules that are so complicated that a user cannot understand what the effect on costs would be if he or she decided to use the computer for a given application or, alternatively, to discontinue a current application. Such rules are counterproductive.

Administration of Transfer Prices

We have so far discussed how to formulate a sound transfer pricing policy. In this section we discuss how the selected policy should be implemented—specifically, the degree of negotiation allowed in setting transfer prices, methods of resolving transfer pricing conflicts, and classification of products according to the appropriate method.

Negotiation

In most companies, business units negotiate transfer prices with each other; that is, transfer prices are not set by a central staff group. Perhaps the most important reason for this is the belief that establishing selling prices and arriving at satisfactory purchase prices are among the primary functions of line management. If headquarters controls pricing, line management's ability to affect profitability is reduced. Also, many transfer prices require a degree of subjective judgment. Consequently, a negotiated transfer price often is the result of compromises made by both buyer and seller. If headquarters establishes transfer prices, business unit managers can argue that their low profits are due to the arbitrariness of the transfer prices. Another reason for having the business units negotiate their prices is that they usually have the

---

[6]James Brian Quinn, *Intelligent Enterprise* (New York: Free Press, 1992), p. 91.

best information on markets and costs and, consequently, are best able to arrive at reasonable prices.

> **Example.**   Business Unit A has an opportunity to supply a large quantity of a certain product to an outside company at a price of $100 per unit. The raw material for this product would be supplied by Business Unit B. Unit B's normal transfer price for this material is $35 per unit, of which $10 is variable cost. Unit A's process cost (excluding raw material) plus normal profit is $85, of which $50 is variable cost. Unit A's total cost plus normal profit, therefore, is $120; at this amount, the selling price of $100 is not attractive. Rejecting the contract would be dysfunctional for the company as a whole because both business units have available capacity. The two units, therefore, should negotiate a lower price for the raw material so that both units will make a contribution to their profit.
>
> If, instead of two business units within a single company, one company had an offer to sell raw material to another company that had a similar sales prospect, the two companies should negotiate in the same fashion. The fact that a transfer price was involved in the first example does not affect how reasonable managers should behave.[7]

Business units must know the ground rules within which these transfer price negotiations are to be conducted. In a few companies, headquarters informs business units that they are free to deal with each other or with outsiders as they see fit, subject only to the qualification that if there is a tie, the business must be kept inside. If this is done and there are outside sources and outside markets, no further administrative procedures are required. The price is set in the outside marketplace, and if business units cannot agree on a price, they simply buy from, or sell to, outsiders. In many companies, however, business units are required to deal with one another. If they do not have the threat of doing business with competitors as a bargaining point in the negotiation process, headquarters staff must develop a set of rules that govern both pricing and sourcing of intracompany products.

Line managers should not spend an undue amount of time on transfer price negotiations, so these rules should be specific enough to prevent negotiating skill from being a significant factor in determining the transfer price. Without such rules, the most stubborn manager will negotiate the most favorable prices.

Arbitration and Conflict Resolution

No matter how specific the pricing rules are, there may be instances in which business units will not be able to agree on a price. For this reason, a procedure should be in place for arbitrating transfer price disputes. There can be

---

[7]David Solomons, in *Divisional Performance: Measurement and Control* (Burr Ridge, IL: Richard D. Irwin, 1968, chapter VI), discussed a similar example. He concluded that the transfer pricing system would be dysfunctional because Division A would reject a contract that was in the best interest of the company. He did not mention the possibility of negotiation, and his conclusion was, therefore, incorrect.

widely different degrees of formality in transfer price arbitration. At one extreme, the responsibility for arbitrating disputes is assigned to a single executive—the financial vice president or executive vice president, for example—who talks to business unit managers involved and then orally announces the price. The other extreme is to set up a committee. Usually such a committee will have three responsibilities: (1) settling transfer price disputes, (2) reviewing sourcing changes, and (3) changing the transfer price rules when appropriate. The degree of formality employed depends on the extent and type of potential transfer price disputes. In any case, transfer price arbitration should be the responsibility of a high-level headquarters executive or group, since arbitration decisions can have an important effect on business unit profits.

Arbitration can be conducted in a number of ways. With a formal system, both parties submit a written case to the arbitrator. The arbitrator reviews their positions and decides on the price, sometimes with the assistance of other staff offices. For example, the purchasing department might review the validity of a proposed competitive price quotation, or the industrial engineering department might review the appropriateness of a disputed standard labor cost. As indicated above, in less formal systems the presentations may be largely oral.

It is important that relatively few disputes be submitted to arbitration. If a large number of disputes are arbitrated, this indicates the rules are not specific enough or are difficult to apply, or the business unit organization is illogical. In short, this is a symptom that something is wrong. Not only is arbitration time consuming to both line managers and headquarters executives, but arbitrated prices often satisfy neither the buyer nor the seller. In some companies, submitting a price dispute to arbitration is so cumbersome that very few are ever submitted. If, as a consequence, legitimate grievances do not surface, the results are undesirable. Preventing disputes from being submitted to arbitration will tend to hide the fact that there are problems with the transfer price system.

Irrespective of the degree of formality of the arbitration, the type of conflict resolution process that is used will also influence the effectiveness of a transfer pricing system. There are four ways to resolve conflicts: forcing, smoothing, bargaining, and problem solving.[8] The conflict resolution mechanisms range from conflict avoidance through forcing and smoothing to conflict resolution through bargaining and problem solving.

Product Classification

The extent and formality of the sourcing and transfer pricing rules depend to a large extent on the number of intracompany transfers and the availability

---

[8]Paul R. Lawrence and Jay W. Lorsch, *Organization and Environment* (Burr Ridge, IL.: Richard D. Irwin, 1967), pp. 73–78.

of markets and market prices. The greater are the number of intracompany transfers and the availability of market prices, the more formal and specific the rules must be. If market prices are readily available, sourcing can be controlled by having headquarters review make-or-buy decisions that exceed a specified amount.

Some companies divide products into two main classes:

Class I includes all products for which senior management wishes to control sourcing. These would normally be large-volume products; products for which no outside source exists; and products over whose manufacturing, for quality or secrecy reasons, senior management wishes to maintain control.

Class II is all other products. In general, these are products that can be produced outside the company without any significant disruption to present operations, products of relatively small volume, produced with general-purpose equipment. Class II products are transferred at market prices.

The sourcing of Class I products can be changed only by permission of central management. The sourcing of Class II products is determined by the business units involved. Both the buying and the selling units are free to deal either inside or outside the company.

Under this arrangement, management can concentrate on the sourcing and pricing of a relatively small number of high-volume products. Rules for transfer prices would be established using the various methods described in the preceding section, as appropriate.

Summary

Delegating authority depends on the ability to delegate responsibility for profits. Profit responsibility cannot be safely delegated unless two conditions exist:

1. The delegatee has all the relevant information needed to make optimum profit decisions.
2. The delegatee's performance is measured on how well he or she has made cost/revenue trade-offs.

Where segments of a company share responsibility for product development, manufacturing, and marketing, a transfer price system is required if these segments are to be delegated profit responsibility. This transfer price system must result in the two conditions described above. In complex organizations, devising a transfer price system that assures the necessary knowledge and motivation for optimum decision-making can be difficult.

Two decisions are involved in designing a transfer price system. First is the sourcing decision: Should the company produce the product inside the company or purchase it from an outside vendor? Second is the transfer price decision: At what price should the product be transferred between profit centers?

Ideally, the transfer price should approximate the normal outside market price, with adjustments for costs not incurred in intracompany transfers. Even when sourcing decisions are constrained, the market price is the best transfer price.

If competitive prices are not available, transfer prices may be set on the basis of cost plus a profit, even though such transfer prices may be complex to calculate and the results less satisfactory than a market-based price. Cost-based transfer prices can be made at standard cost plus profit margin, or by the use of the two-step pricing system.

A method of negotiating transfer prices should be in place and there should be an arbitration mechanism for settling transfer price disputes, but these arrangements should not be so complicated that management devotes an undue amount of time to transfer pricing.

There are probably few examples in complex organizations of completely satisfactory transfer price systems. As with many management control design choices, it is necessary to choose the best of several less-than-perfect courses of action. The important thing is to be aware of the areas of imperfection and to be sure that administrative procedures are employed to avoid suboptimum decisions.

Appendix
Some Theoretical Considerations

There is a considerable body of literature on theoretical transfer pricing models. Few, if any, of these models are used in actual business situations, however, and for reasons explained below, it is unlikely that they ever will be widely used. Consequently, we have not referred to these models in the body of this chapter. Although they are not directly applicable to real business situations, they are useful in conceptualizing transfer price systems. These models may be divided into three types: (1) models based on classical economic theory, (2) models based on linear programming, and (3) models based on the Shapley value.

Economic Models

The classic economic model was first described by Jack Hirschleifer in the 1956 article referred to in footnote 2 of this chapter. Professor Hirschleifer developed a series of marginal revenue, marginal cost, and demand curves for the transfer of an intermediate product from one business unit to another. He used these curves to establish transfer prices, under various sets of economic assumptions, that would optimize the total profit of the two business units. Using the transfer prices thus developed, the two units would produce the maximum total profit by optimizing their unit profits.

The difficulty with the Hirschleifer model is that it can be used only when a specified set of conditions exist: It must be possible to estimate the demand curve for the intermediate product; the assumed conditions must remain stable; and there can be no alternative uses for facilities used to make the intermediate product. Finally, the model is applicable only to the situation in which the selling unit makes a single intermediate product, which it transfers to a single buying unit, which uses that intermediate product in a single final product. Such conditions exist rarely, if at all, in the real world.

This model (and also the other models) assumes that transfer prices will be imposed by the central staff, and it denies the importance of negotiation among business units. Business unit managers usually have better information than is available to the central staff. *Indeed, if the central staff could determine the optimum production pattern, the question arises: Why is this pattern not imposed directly, rather than attempting to arrive at it indirectly via the transfer price mechanism?*

Linear Programming Model

The linear programming model is based on an opportunity cost approach. This model also incorporates capacity constraints. The model calculates an optimum company-wide production pattern, and using this pattern, it calculates a set of values that impute the profit contributions of each of the scarce resources. These are termed *shadow prices,* and one process of calculating them is called "obtaining the dual solution" to the linear program. If the variable costs of the intermediate products are added to their shadow prices, a set of transfer prices results that should motivate business units to produce according to the optimum production pattern for the entire company. This is so because, if these transfer prices are used, each business unit will optimize its profits only by producing in accordance with the patterns developed through the linear program.

If reliable shadow prices could be calculated, this model would be useful in arriving at transfer prices. However, to make the model manageable, even on a computer, many simplifying assumptions must be incorporated in it. It is assumed that the demand curve is known, that it is static, that the cost function is linear, and that alternative uses of production facilities and their profitability can be estimated in advance. As is the case with the economic model, these conditions rarely exist in the real world.

Shapley Value

The theoretical literature has a few articles advocating the use of a number termed the *Shapley value* as the transfer price. The Shapley value was developed in 1953 by L. S. Shapley as a method of dividing the profits of a coalition of companies or individuals among its individual members in proportion to the contribution that each of them made. This a problem that arises in the theory of games, and the Shapley value generally is considered to provide an equitable solution to that problem.

Whether the same technique is applicable to the transfer price problem is a highly debatable issue. Although the method has been described in the literature for a number of years, few practical applications have been reported. A partial reason for its lack of acceptance is that the computation is lengthy unless there are only a few products involved in the transfer. Another reason is that many of those who have studied the Shapley method do not believe that its underlying assumptions are valid for the transfer pricing problem.

Suggested Additonal Readings

Adler, Ralph W. "Transfer Pricing for World-Class Manufacturing." *Long Range Planning* 29, no. 1 (February 1996), pp. 69–75.

Anctil, R. M., and Sunil Dutta. "Negotiated Transfer Pricing and Divisional vs. Firm-wide Performance Evaluation." *The Accounting Review* 74, no. 1 (January 1999), pp. 87–104.

Cole, Robert T. *Practical Guide to U.S. Transfer Pricing.* New York: Aspen Publishers, 1999.

Crow, Stephen, and Eugene Sauls. "Setting the Right Transfer Price." *Management Accounting* 76, no. 6 (December 1994), pp. 41–47.

Emmanuel, Clive. *Transfer Pricing.* New York: Academic Press, 1994.

Feinschreiber, Robert. *Transfer Pricing Handbook.* New York: John Wiley & Sons, 1998.

Govindarajan, Vijay, and Robert N. Anthony. "How Firms Use Cost Data in Pricing Decisions." *Management Accounting,* July 1983, pp. 30–34.

Gupta, Anil K., and Vijay Govindarajan. "Resource Sharing among SBUs: Strategic Antecedents and Administrative Implications." *Academy of Management Journal* 29, no. 4 (1986), pp. 695–714.

Kovac, Edward J., and Henry P. Troy. "Getting Transfer Prices Right: What Bellcore Did." *Harvard Business Review,* September–October 1989, pp. 148–54.

Maher, Michael W., and Edward Deakin. *Cost Accounting.* Burr Ridge, IL: Richard D. Irwin, 1995.

Solomons, David. *Divisional Performance: Measurement and Control.* Burr Ridge, IL: Richard D. Irwin, 1968, chapter VI.

Venkatesan, Ravi. "Strategic Outsourcing: To Make or Not to Make." *Harvard Business Review,* November–December 1992, pp. 98–107.

CASE 5–1
TRANSFER PRICING PROBLEMS

1. Division A of Lambda Company manufactures Product X, which is sold to Division B as a component of Product Y. Product Y is sold to Division C, which uses it as a component in Product Z. Product Z is sold to customers outside of the company. The intracompany pricing rule is that products are transferred between divisions at standard cost plus a 10 percent return on inventories and fixed assets. From the information provided below, calculate the transfer price for Products X and Y and the standard cost of Product Z.

Standard Cost per Unit	Product X	Product Y	Product Z
Material purchased outside	$ 2.00	$ 3.00	$ 1.00
Direct labor	1.00	1.00	2.00
Variable overhead	1.00	1.00	2.00
Fixed overhead per unit ...	3.00	4.00	1.00
Standard volume	10,000	10,000	10,000
Inventories (average)	$70,000	$15,000	$30,000
Fixed assets (net)	30,000	45,000	16,000

2. Assume the same facts as stated in Problem 1, except that the transfer price rule is as follows: Goods are transferred among divisions at the standard variable cost per unit transferred plus a monthly charge. This charge is equal to the fixed costs assigned to the product plus a 10 percent return on the average inventories and fixed assets assignable to the product. Calculate the transfer price for Products X and Y and calculate the unit standard cost for Products Y and Z.

3. The present selling price for Product Z is $28.00. Listed below is a series of possible price

reductions by competition and the probable impact of these reductions on the volume of sales if Division C does not also reduce its price.

- Possible competitive price: $27.00; $26.00; $25.00; $23.00; $22.00.
- Sales volume if price of Product Z is maintained at $28.00: 9,000; 7,000; 5,000; 2,000; 0.
- Sales volume if price of Product Z is reduced to competitive levels: 10,000; 10,000; 10,000; 10,000; 10,000.

Questions

(a) With transfer price calculated in Problem 1, is Division C better advised to maintain its price at $28.00 or to follow competition in each of the instances above?

(b) With the transfer prices calculated in Problem 2, is Division C better advised to maintain its present price $28.00 or to follow competition in each of the instances above?

(c) Which decisions are to the best economic interests of the company, other things being equal?

(d) Using the transfer prices calculated in Problem 1, is the manager of Division C making a decision contrary to the overall interests of the company? If so, what is the opportunity loss to the company in each of the competitive pricing actions described above?

4. Division C is interested in increasing the sales of Product Z. The present selling price of Product Z is $28.00. A survey is made and sales increases resulting from increases in television

This case was prepared by Professors John Dearden and Robert N. Anthony.

advertising are estimated. The results of this survey are provided below. (Note that this particular type of advertising can be purchased only in units of $100,000.)

	(in thousands)				
Advertising expenditures	$100	$200	$300	$400	$500
Additional volume resulting from additional advertising	10	19	27	34	40

Questions

(a) As manager of Division C, how much television advertising would you use if you purchased Product Y at the transfer price calculated in Problem 1?

(b) How much television advertising would you use if you purchased Product Y for the transfer price calculated in Problem 2?

(c) Which is correct from the overall company viewpoint?

(d) How much would the company lose in suboptimum profits from using the first transfer price?

5. Two of the divisions of the Chambers Corporation are the Intermediate Division and the Final Division. The Intermediate Division produces three products: A, B, and C. Normally these products are sold both to outside customers and to the Final Division. The Final Division uses Products A, B, and C in manufacturing Products X, Y, and Z, respectively. In recent weeks, the supply of Products A, B, and C has tightened to such an extent that the Final Division has been operating considerably below capacity because of the lack of these products. Consequently, the Intermediate Division has been told to sell all its products to the Final Division. The financial facts about these products are as follows:

Intermediate Division

	Product A	Product B	Product C
Transfer price	$ 10.00	$ 10.00	$ 15.00
Variable manufacturing cost	3.00	6.00	5.00
Contribution per unit	$ 7.00	$ 4.00	$ 10.00
Fixed costs (total)	$50,000	$100,000	$75,000

The Intermediate Division has a monthly capacity of 50,000 units. The processing constraints are such that capacity production can be obtained only by producing at least 10,000 units of each product. The remaining capacity can be used to produce 20,000 units of any combination of the three products. The Intermediate Division cannot exceed the capacity of 50,000 units.

The Final Division has sufficient capacity to produce about 40 percent more than it is now producing because the availability of Products A, B, and C is limiting production. Also, the Final Division can sell all the products that it can produce at the prices indicated above.

Final Division

	Product X	Product Y	Product Z
Selling price	$ 28.00	$ 30.00	$ 30.00
Variable cost:			
Inside purchases	10.00	10.00	15.00
Other variable costs	5.00	5.00	8.00
Total variable cost	$ 15.00	$ 15.00	$ 23.00
Contribution per unit	$ 13.00	$ 15.00	$ 7.00
Fixed costs (total)	$100,000	$100,000	$200,000

Questions

(a) If you were the manager of the Intermediate Division, what products would you sell to the Final Division? What is the amount of profit that you would earn on these sales?

(b) If you were the manager of the Final Division, what products would you order from the Intermediate Division, assuming that the Intermediate Division must sell all its production to you? What profits would you earn?

(c) What production pattern optimizes total company profit? How does this affect the profits of the Intermediate Division? If you were the executive vice president of Chambers and prescribed this optimum pattern, what, if anything, would you do about the distribution of profits between the two divisions?

6. How, if at all, would your answers to Problem 5 change if there were no outside markets for Products A, B, or C?

7. The Chambers Company has determined that capacity can be increased in excess of 50,000 units, but these increases require an out-of-pocket cost penalty. These penalties are as follows:

Volume in Excess of Present Capacity (unit)	Product A	Product B	Product C
	Cost Penalty		
1,000	$10,000	$12,000	$10,000
2,000	25,000	24,000	20,000
3,000	50,000	50,000	35,000
4,000	80,000	80,000	50,000

Each of these increases is independent— that is, increases in the production of Product A do not affect the costs of increasing the produc-

tion of Product B. Changes can be made only in quantities of 100 units, with a maximum increase of 4,000 units for each product. All other conditions are as stated in Problem 5.

Questions

(a) What would be the Intermediate Division's production pattern, assuming that it can charge all penalty costs to the Final Division?

(b) The Final Division's optimum production pattern, assuming that it is required to accept the penalty costs?

(c) The optimum Company production pattern?

8. How would your answer to Problem 7 differ if the Intermediate Division had no outside markets for Products A, B, and C?

9.[1] Division A of Kappa Company is the only source of supply for an intermediate product that is converted by Division B into a salable final product. A substantial part of A's costs are fixed. For any output up to 1,000 units a day, its total costs are $500 a day. Total costs increase by $100 a day for every additional thousand units made. Division A judges that its own results will be optimized if it sets its price at $0.40 a unit, and it acts accordingly.

Division B incurs additional costs in converting the intermediate product supplied by A into a finished product. These costs are $1,250 for any output up to 1,000 units, and $250 per thousand for outputs in excess of 1,000. On the revenue side, B can increase its revenue only by spending more on sales promotion and by reducing selling prices. Its sales forecast is shown in the following table.

[1]Reproduced with permission from David Solomons, *Divisional Performance: Measurement and Control* (Burr Ridge, IL: Richard D. Irwin, 1968).

Sales Forecast

Sales (units)	Revenue Net of Selling Costs (per thousand units)
1,000	$ 1,750
2,000	1,325
3,000	1,100
4,000	925
5,000	800
6,000	666

Looking at the situation from B's point of view, we can compare its costs and revenues at various levels of output while considering both its own processing costs and what it is charged by A for the intermediates that A will supply. The relevant information is set out in Exhibit 1.

Exhibit 1 makes it clear that the most profitable policy for Division B, in the circumstances, is to set its output at either 2,000 or 3,000 units a day and to accept a profit of $350 a day. If its output is more than 3,000 or less than 2,000, it will make even less profit.

With Division B taking 3,000 units a day from it, Division A's revenue, at $0.40 a unit, is $1,200, and its total costs are $700. Therefore, A's separate profit is $500 a day. Adding this to B's profit of $350 a day, we get an aggregate profit for the corporation of $850 a day.

Assume now that the company abandons its divisionalized structure, and instead of having two profit centers, A and B, it combines them into a single profit center, with responsibility for both production of the intermediate and processing it to completion. Let us further suppose that, apart from this change of structure, all the other conditions previously present continue to apply. Then the market conditions that formerly faced Division B now confront the single profit center. Its costs are equal to the combined costs of A and B, eliminating, of course, the charge previously made by A to B for the

supply of intermediates. The schedule of costs and revenues for the single profit center will then appear as shown in Exhibit 2.

Exhibit 2 shows that the single profit center will operate more profitably than the two divisions together formerly did. By making and selling 4,000 units a day, it can earn a profit of $900 or $50 a day in excess of the best result achieved by the combined activities of Divisions A and B.

The company is seen to have been paying a price for the luxury of divisionalization. By suboptimizing (i.e., by seeking maximum profits for themselves as separate entities), the divisions have caused the corporation to less than optimize its profits as a whole. The reason was, of course, that Division B reacted to the transfer price of $0.40 a unit by restricting both its demand for the intermediate and its own output of the finished product. By making for itself the best of a bad job, it created an unsatisfactory situation for the company. But who can blame it? Assuming that the instructions to its general manager were to maximize the division's separate profit, the manager did just that, given the conditions confronting him or her. The responsibility for the final result really lay with Division A. Yet it is not fair to blame that division, either, for it, too, was only carrying out instructions in seeking to maximize its own profit; and a transfer price of $0.40, while it leads to a less than optimal result for the corporation, does maximize A's own profit.

One further feature of this illustration is worth noting. So far as its own profit was concerned, it was a matter of indifference to Division B whether it sold 2,000 or 3,000 units. We assumed that it decided to sell 3,000. If it had chosen to sell only 2,000, its own profit would have been unaffected, while A's profit would have been diminished by $300. In a situation like this, negotiations about the price between A and B would probably have prevented this further damage to the corporation resulting from suboptimization. But it is unlikely that

EXHIBIT 1

Division B's Output (units) (1)	B's Own Processing Costs (2)	A's Charge to B for Intermediates @ $0.40 a Unit (3)	B's Total Costs (4) = (2) + (3)	B's Revenue (net of selling costs) per 1,000 Units (5)	B's Total Revenue (6) = (1) * (5)	B's Profit (loss) (7) = (6) − (4)
1,000	$ 1,250	$ 400	$ 1,650	$ 1,750	$ 1,750	$ 100
2,000	1,500	800	2,300	1,325	2,650	350
3,000	1,750	1,200	2,950	1,100	3,300	350
4,000	2,000	1,600	3,600	925	3,700	100
5,000	2,250	2,000	4,250	800	4,000	(250)
6,000	2,500	2,400	4,900	666	4,000	(900)

EXHIBIT 2

Output (units) (1)	Cost of Producing Intermediates (2)	Cost of Processing to Completion (3)	Total Cost (4) = (2) + (3)	Total Revenue* (5)	Profit (6) = (5) − (4)
1,000	$ 500	$1,250	$1,750	$1,750	—
2,000	600	1,500	2,100	2,650	$ 550
3,000	700	1,750	2,450	3,330	850
4,000	800	2,000	2,800	3,700	900
5,000	900	2,250	3,150	4,000	850
6,000	1,000	2,500	3,500	4,000	500

*Taken from column (6) of Exhibit 1.

the divisions, left to themselves, would arrive at an optimal solution from the corporate point of view.

Questions

(a) What is the lowest price that Division A should be willing to accept from Division B for 4,000 units?

(b) What is the highest price at which Division B should be willing to buy 4,000 units from Division A?

(c) If Division A does sell 4,000 units to Division B, what should the transfer price be?

(d) Under what circumstances, if any, would the transfer price be dysfunctional?

CASE 5–2
BIRCH PAPER COMPANY

"If I were to price these boxes any lower than $480 a thousand," said James Brunner, manager of Birch Paper Company's Thompson Division, "I'd be countermanding my order of last month for our salesmen to stop shaving their bids and to bid full-cost quotations. I've been trying for weeks to improve the quality of our business, and if I turn around now and accept this job at $430 or $450 or something less than $480, I'll be tearing down this program I've been working so hard to build up. The division can't very well show a profit by putting in bids that don't even cover a fair share of overhead costs, let alone give us a profit."

Birch Paper Company was a medium-sized, partly integrated paper company, producing white and kraft papers and paperboard. A portion of its paperboard output was converted into corrugated boxes by the Thompson Division, which also printed and colored the outside surface of the boxes. Including Thompson, the company had four producing divisions and a timberland division, which supplied part of the company's pulp requirements.

For several years, each division had been judged independently on the basis of its profit and return on investment. Top management had been working to gain effective results from a policy of decentralizing responsibility and authority for all decisions except those relating to overall company policy. The company's top officials believed that in the past few years the concept of decentralization had been applied successfully and that the company's profits and competitive position definitely had improved.

This case was prepared by William Rotch under the supervision of Neil Harlan, Harvard Business School. Copyright by the President and Fellows of Harvard College. Harvard Business School case 158-001.

The Northern Division had designed a special display box for one of its papers in conjunction with the Thompson Division, which was equipped to make the box. Thompson's staff for package design and development spent several months perfecting the design, production methods, and materials to be used. Because of the unusual color and shape, these were far from standard. According to an agreement between the two divisions, the Thompson Division was reimbursed by the Northern Division for the cost of its design and development work.

When all the specifications were prepared, the Northern Division asked for bids on the box from the Thompson Division and from two outside companies. Each division manager was normally free to buy from whatever supplier he wished, and even on sales within the company, divisions were expected to meet the going market price if they wanted the business.

During this period, the profit margins of such converters as the Thompson Division were being squeezed. Thompson, as did many other similar converters, bought its paperboard, and its function was to print, cut, and shape it into boxes. Though it bought most of its materials from other Birch divisions, most of Thompson's sales were made to outside customers. If Thompson got the order from Northern, it probably would buy its linerboard and corrugating medium from the Southern Division of Birch. The walls of a corrugated box consist of outside and inside sheets of linerboard sandwiching the fluted corrugating medium. About 70 percent of Thompson's out-of-pocket cost of $400 for the order represented the cost of linerboard and corrugating medium. Though Southern had been running below capacity and had excess inventory, it quoted the market price, which had not noticeably weakened as a result of the oversupply. Its out-of-pocket costs on both liner and corrugating medium were about 60 percent of the selling price.

The Northern Division received bids on the boxes of $480 a thousand from the Thompson Division, $430 a thousand from West Paper Company, and $432 a thousand from Eire Papers, Ltd. Eire Papers offered to buy from Birch the outside linerboard with the special printing already on it, but would supply its own inside liner and corrugating medium. The outside liner would be supplied by the Southern Division at a price equivalent of $90 a thousand boxes, and it would be printed for $30 a thousand by the Thompson Division. Of the $30, about $25 would be out-of-pocket costs.

Since this situation appeared to be a little unusual, William Kenton, manager of the Northern Division, discussed the wide discrepancy of bids with Birch's commercial vice president. He told the vice president: "We sell in a very competitive market, where higher costs cannot be passed on. How can we be expected to show a decent profit and return on investment if we have to buy our supplies at more than 10 percent over the going market?"

Knowing that Mr. Brunner on occasion in the past few months had been unable to operate the Thompson Division at capacity, it seemed odd to the vice president that Mr. Brunner would add the full 20 percent overhead and profit charge to his out-of-pocket costs. When he was asked about this, Mr. Brunner's answer was the statement that appears at the beginning of the case. He went on to say that having done the developmental work on the box, and having

received no profit on that, he felt entitled to a good markup on the production of the box itself.

The vice president explored further the cost structures of the various divisions. He remembered a comment that the controller had made at a meeting the week before to the effect that costs which were variable for one division could be largely fixed for the company as a whole. He knew that in the absence of specific orders from top management Mr. Kenton would accept the lowest bid, which was that of the West Paper Company for $430. However, it would be possible for top management to order the acceptance of another bid if the situation warranted such action. And though the volume represented by the transactions in question was less than 5 percent of the volume of any of the divisions involved, other transactions would conceivably raise similar problems later.

Questions

1. Which bid should Northern Division accept that is in the best interests of Birch Paper Company?

2. Should Mr. Kenton accept this bid? Why or why not?

3. Should the vice president of Birch Paper Company take any action?

4. In the controversy described, how, if at all, is the transfer price system dysfunctional? Does this problem call for some change, or changes, in the transfer pricing policy of the overall firm? If so, what *specific* changes do you suggest?

CASE 5–3
GENERAL APPLIANCE CORPORATION

Organization

The General Appliance Corporation was an integrated manufacturer of all types of home appliances. As shown in Exhibit 1, the company had a decentralized, divisional organization consisting of four product divisions, four manufacturing divisions, and six staff offices. Each division and staff office was headed by a vice president. The staff offices had functional authority over their counterparts in the divisions, but they had no direct line authority over the divisional general managers. The company's organization manual stated: "All divisional personnel are responsible to the division manager. Except in functional areas specifically delegated, staff personnel have no line authority in a division."

The product divisions designed, engineered, assembled, and sold various home appliances. They manufactured very few component parts; rather, they assembled the appliances from parts purchased either from the manufacturing divisions or from outside vendors. The manufacturing divisions made approximately 75 percent of their sales to the product divisions. Parts made by the manufacturing divisions were generally designed by the product divisions; the manufacturing divisions merely produced the parts to specifications provided to them. Although all the manufacturing divisions had engineering departments, these departments did only about 20 percent of the total company engineering.

Transfer Prices

The divisions were expected to deal with one another as though they were independent compa-

nies. Parts were to be transferred at prices arrived at by negotiation between the divisions. These prices generally were based on the actual prices paid to outside suppliers for the same or comparable parts. These outside prices were adjusted to reflect differences in design of the outside part from that of the inside part. Also, if the outside price was based on purchases made at an earlier date, it was adjusted for changes in the general price level since that date. In general, the divisions established prices by negotiation among themselves, but if the divisions could not agree on a price, they could submit the dispute to the finance staff for arbitration.

Source Determination

Although the divisions were instructed to deal with one another as independent companies, in practice this was not always feasible because a product division did not have the power to decide whether to buy from within the company or from outside. Once a manufacturing division began to produce a part, the only way the product division buying this part could change to an outside supplier was to obtain permission of the manufacturing division or, in case of disagreement, appeal to the purchasing staff. The purchasing staff had the authority to settle disputes between the product and manufacturing divisions with respect to whether a manufacturing division should continue to produce a part or whether the product division could buy outside. In nearly every case of dispute, the purchasing staff had decided that the part would continue to be manufactured within the company. When the manufacturing divisions were instructed to continue producing a part, they had to hold the price of the part at the level at which the product division could purchase it from the outside vendor.

This case was prepared by John Dearden and Robert N. Anthony, Harvard Business School. Copyright by the President and Fellows of Harvard College. Harvard Business School case 160-003.

Exhibit 1
Organization chart

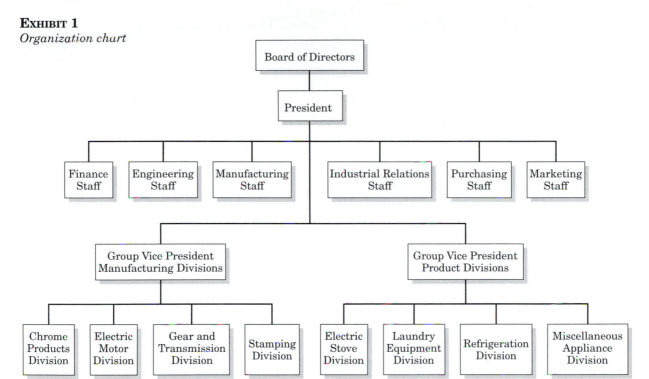

In the case of new parts, a product division had the authority to decide on the source of supply.

Even for new parts, however, a manufacturing division could appeal to the purchasing staff to reverse the decision if a product division planned to purchase a part from an outside vendor.

Stove Top Problem

The Chrome Products Division sold to the Electric Stove Division a chrome-plated unit that fitted on top of the stove; the unit had to be resistant to corrosion and stain from spilled food. It was also essential that the unit remain bright and new-looking. The Chrome Products Division had been producing this unit since January 1, 1986; prior to that time, it had been produced by an outside vendor.

The unit in question was produced from a steel stamping. Until June 1987, the stamping was processed as follows:

Operations	Processes
1	Machine buffing
2	Nickel plating
3	Machine buffing
4	Chrome plating
5	Machine buffing

About the middle of 1986, the president of General Appliance Corporation became concerned over complaints from customers and dealers about the quality of the company's products. A customer survey appeared to indicate quite definitely that, in the previous year, the company's reputation as a producer of quality products had deteriorated. Although this deterioration was believed to have been caused principally by the poor performance of a new electric motor, which was soon corrected, the president had come to the conclusion that the overall quality of the company's products had been decreasing for the past several years. Furthermore, he believed that it was essential for the company to reestablish itself as a leader in the production of quality products. Accordingly, early in 1987, he called in the manufacturing vice president (i.e., the director of the manufacturing staff office) and told him that for the next six months his most important job was to bring the quality of all products up to a satisfactory level.

In the course of carrying out this assignment, the manufacturing vice president decided that the appearance of the chrome-plated stove top was unsatisfactory. Until then, the bases for rejection or acceptance of this part by the quality control section of the Chrome Products Division were a corrosion test and an appearance test; appearance was largely subjective and, in the final analysis, dependent on the judgment of the quality control person. In order to make the test more objective, three tops were selected and set up as standards for the minimum acceptable quality. Because better than average units were selected, rejects increased to over 80 percent. Personnel from the Chrome Products Division and the manufacturing staff jointly studied the manufacturing process to find a way of making the stove tops conform to the new quality standards. They added copper plating and buffing operations at the beginning of the process and a hand-buffing operation at the end of the manufacturing cycle. The total cost of these added operations was 80 cents a unit. As soon as the new operations were put into effect in June 1987, the rejection rate for poor quality declined to less than 1 percent.

In July 1987, the Chrome Products Division proposed to increase the price of the stove top by 90 cents; 80 cents represented the cost of the

added operations, and 10 cents was the profit markup on the added costs. The current price, before the proposed increase, was $10 a unit. This price had been developed as shown in the following:

Development of Price

Price charged by an outside producer (12/31/85)	$ 9.00
Design changes since 12/31/85	0.50
Changes in raw materials and labor prices since 12/31/85	0.50
Price as of 6/30/87	$10.00

The Electric Stove Division objected to the proposed price increase, and after three weeks of fruitless negotiations, it was decided that the dispute should be submitted to the finance staff for arbitration. The positions of the parties to the dispute are summarized in the following sections.

Chrome Products Division.   In a letter to the vice president for finance, the general manager of the Chrome Products Division stated that he believed that he was entitled to the increased price because:

1. He had been required by the manufacturing staff to add operations at a cost of 80 cents a unit.

2. These operations resulted in improved quality that could benefit only the Electric Stove Division.

3. The present price of $10.00 was based on old quality standards. Had the outside supplier been required to meet these new standards, the price would have been 90 cents higher.

Electric Stove Division.   The general manager of the Electric Stove Division, in appealing the price increase, based his position on the following arguments:

1. There had been no change in engineering specifications. The only change that had taken place was in what was purported to be "acceptable appearance." This was a subjective matter that could not be measured with any degree of precision. Further, both the particular case and the possible effects of establishing a precedent were objectionable. "If we were to pay for any change in quality standards, not accompanied by a change in engineering specification, we would be opening up a Pandora's box. Every division would request higher prices based on giving us better quality based on some subjective standard. Every request by this division to a manufacturing division to improve quality would be accompanied by a price increase, even though we were requesting only that the quality be brought up to competitive levels."

2. The Electric Stove Division had not requested that quality be improved. In fact, the division had not even been consulted on the change. Thus, the division should not be responsible for paying for a so-called improvement that it had neither requested nor approved.

3. Whether there was any improvement in quality from the customer's viewpoint was doubtful, although to the highly trained eye of the quality control personnel there may have been an improvement. The customer would not notice a significant difference between the appearance of the part before and after the change in quality standards.

4. Even if there were an improvement in quality perceptible to the consumer, it was not worth 90 cents. By adding 90 cents to the cost of the stove, features could be added that would be far more marketable than the quality improvement.

5. Any improvement in quality brought the part up only to the quality level that the former outside producer had provided. The cost of the improved quality, therefore, was included in the $10.00 price.

Finance Staff Review. The finance staff reviewed the dispute. In the course of this review, the engineering department of the manufacturing staff was asked to review the added operations and comment on the acceptability of the proposed cost increases. The quality control department of the manufacturing staff was asked to verify whether quality was actually better as the result of the added operations and whether the new units were of higher quality than the units purchased from the outside vendor 18 months ago. The engineering department stated that the proposed costs were reasonable and represented efficient processing. The quality control department stated that the quality was improved and that the new parts were of superior quality to the parts previously purchased from outside sources.

Thermostatic Control Problem

One of the plants of the Electric Motor Division produced thermostatic control units. The Laundry Equipment Division bought all its requirements for thermostatic control units (about 100,000 a year) from the Electric Motor Division. The Refrigeration Division used a similar unit, and until 1985 it had purchased all its requirements (20,000 a year) from an outside supplier, the Monson Controls Corporation. In 1985, at the request of the Electric Motor Division, the Refrigeration Division purchased 25 percent of its requirements from the Electric Motor Division. In 1986, this percentage was increased to 50 percent, and in 1987 to 75 percent. In July 1987, the Refrigeration Division informed the Monson Controls Corporation that beginning January 1, 1988, it would buy all its thermostatic control units from the Electric Motor Division. The Refrigeration Division made these source changes as a result of Electric Motor Division requests, which were, it said, "in the best interest of the company." The units made outside and inside were comparable in quality, and the price paid to the Electric Motor Division was the same as the price paid to the Monson Controls Corporation. The Laundry Division also paid this same price to the Electric Motor Division.

In 1984, the demand for this kind of thermostatic control unit was high in relation to the industry's production capacity. Between 1985 and 1987, several appliance companies, including the General Appliance Corporation, built or expanded their own facilities to produce this unit so that, by the middle of 1987, the production capacity of the independent companies considerably exceeded the demand. One of the results of this situation was a declining price level. Prices of the Monson Controls Corporation had been as follows:

1984	$3.00
1985	2.70
1986	2.50
1987 (January–June)	2.40

As a result of these price reductions, which the Electric Motor Division had met, the profits of the Electric Motor Division on this product had dropped from a before-tax profit of 15 percent on its investment in 1984 to nearly zero in 1987.

In August 1987, after being told it could no longer supply the Refrigeration Division, the Monson Controls Corporation reduced its price to the Refrigeration Division by 25 cents, retroactive to July 1. The price reduction was not reflected immediately in the intracompany price because the three divisions involved had agreed to use $2.40 for the entire year.

In October 1987, the Electric Motor Division and the Refrigeration Division were negotiating 1988 prices. The Refrigeration Division proposed a price of $2.15, the price paid to the

Monson Controls Corporation. The Electric Motor Division, however, refused to reduce its prices below $2.40 to either the Refrigeration Division or the Laundry Equipment Division. After several weeks of negotiations, the disagreement was submitted to the finance staff for settlement.

Electric Motor Division.   The Electric Motor Division based its refusal to accept the last price reduction of the Monson Controls Corporation on the premise that it was made as a last, desperate effort to continue supplying General Appliance Corporation with this part. (Monson Controls Corporation continued to supply General Appliance Corporation with other products, although this control unit had been a major item.) As support for this premise, the Electric Motor Division indicated that at the lower price it would lose money. Since it was as efficient as the Monson Controls Corporation, it concluded that Monson must also be losing money. The price was, therefore, a distress price and not a valid basis for determining an internal price. To support its case further, the Electric Motor Division pointed out the downward trend in the price of this part as evidence of distress pricing practices growing out of the excess capacity in the industry.

The general manager of Electric Motor Division stated that it was going to take all his ability and ingenuity to make a profit even at the $2.40 price. At $2.15, he could never be in a profit position, and if forced to accept a price of $2.15, he would immediately make plans to close the plant and let outside suppliers furnish all the thermostatic control units.

Laundry Equipment Division.   The Laundry Equipment Division based its case for a $2.15 price on the intracompany pricing rules that required products to be transferred between divisions at competitive prices. The general manager pointed out that his annual volume was 100,000 units a year, compared to a total of only 20,000 for the Refrigeration Division. He believed that with his higher volume he could probably obtain an even more favorable price if he were to procure his requirements from outside the corporation.

Refrigeration Division.   The Refrigeration Division based its case on the fact that the division not only could, but did, buy the thermostatic control unit from a reliable outside supplier for $2.15. The division was sure that the Monson Controls Corporation had capacity to produce all its requirements and would be happy to do so for $2.15 a unit. Since patronage had been transferred to the Electric Motor Division only as a favor and to benefit the company as a whole, the Refrigeration Division believed it was unjust to make it pay a higher price than it would have paid if the division had not allowed the business to be taken inside the company.

As further evidence to support its case, the Refrigeration Division pointed to an agreement made with the Electric Motor Division at the time it had agreed to purchase all its requirements of the thermostatic control unit from that division. This agreement read, in part: "In the event of a major pricing disparity, it is agreed that further model requirements will be competitively sourced [i.e., sourced to the lowest bidder]."

The Refrigeration Division stated that in light of the major pricing disparity it should be allowed to request quotations from outside suppliers and place the business outside should such a supplier bid lower than the Electric Motor Division.

Finance Staff Review.   In the course of arbitrating this transfer price dispute, the finance staff asked the purchasing staff to review the outside market situation for the thermostatic control unit. The purchasing staff replied that there was excess capacity and that, as a result of this, prices were very soft. Eventually, the prices would rise—either when the demand for comparable units increased or when some of the suppliers went out of business. The purchasing staff had no doubt that the Refrigeration Division could purchase all its requirements for the next year or two at $2.15 a unit, or even less. The purchasing staff, however, believed that if all the corporation's requirements for this unit were placed with outside suppliers, the price would rise to at least $2.40 because this action would dry up the excess capacity.

Transmission Problem

The Laundry Equipment Division produced automatic washers. Initially, it had purchased its transmissions from two sources—the Gear and Transmission Division and the Thorndike Machining Corporation. The transmission had been developed and engineered by the Thorndike Machining Corporation. In consideration of an agreement to buy one-half of its transmissions from the Thorndike Machining Corporation, the General Appliance Corporation had been licensed to produce the transmission. The current agreement ran from 1977 to 1987; at the expiration of the 10 years, General Appliance would have the right to use the design without restrictions.

In early 1985, nearly two years before the end of the agreement, the management of the General Appliance Corporation decided that it would not extend the agreement when it expired, but that it would expand the facilities of the Gear and Transmission Division enough to produce all the company's requirements. Accordingly, in March 1985, the Thorndike Machining Corporation was notified that beginning January 1, 1987, the General Appliance Corporation would manufacture all its own transmissions and, consequently, would not renew the current agreement.

This notification came as a surprise to the Thorndike Machining Corporation. Furthermore, its implications were very unpleasant because the General Appliance Corporation took a major share of the output of an entire plant, and there was little likelihood that the lost business could be replaced. The Thorndike Machining Corporation consequently faced the prospect of an idle plant and a permanent reduction in the level of profits.

In April 1985, the president of the Thorndike Machining Corporation wrote to the president of the General Appliance Corporation, asking that the decision not to extend the current agreement be reconsidered. He submitted a proposed schedule of price reductions that would be made if the current agreement was extended. He stated that these reductions would be possible because (*a*) Thorndike would be better off obtaining a lower price than abandoning the special-purpose machinery used for transmissions; and (*b*) Thorndike expected increases in productivity. The proposed price reductions were as follows:

Present price	$14.00
Price effective 7/1/85	13.50
Price effective 7/1/86	13.00
Price effective 7/1/87	12.50
Price effective 7/1/88	12.00

The letter further stated that the corporation had developed a low-cost transmission suitable for economy washers. This transmission was designed to cost $2 less than the present models and could be made available by January 1, 1988.

On receiving a copy of the letter, the general manager of the Laundry Equipment Division reopened the issue of continuing to buy from the Thorndike Machining Corporation. He had been interested in adding a low-cost automatic washer to the line, and the possibility of a $10 transmission appealed to him. The general manager of the Gear and Transmission Division, however, was interested in expanding his production of transmissions. To satisfy the Laundry Equipment Division he offered to de-

velop a unit that would be comparable in price and performance to the proposed Thorndike Machining Corporation's economy unit. The offer was set forth in a letter signed by the general manager of the Gear and Transmission Division, dated April 22, 1985. The general manager of the Laundry Equipment Division accepted this offer, and no further question was raised about continuing to buy from the Thorndike Machining Corporation.

During the next two months, the engineering department of the Gear and Transmission and the Laundry Equipment Division jointly determined the exact performance features needed for the economy transmission; some of these features were different from those of the proposed Thorndike transmission. In June 1985, the general manager of the Gear and Transmission Division wrote a letter to the general manager of the Laundry Equipment Division, outlining the agreed-on engineering features and including the following price proposal:

Proposed selling price of Thorndike model		$10.00
Probable cost (assuming 11% profit)		9.00
Add:		
Cost of added design features	$0.85	
Increased cost of material and labor since date of quotation	0.75	1.60
Total cost		10.60
Profit		1.06
Adjusted price of G&T Unit		$11.66

The letter went on to say: "Because a price of $11.66 will not give us our objective profit, we propose to sell you this unit for $12. We believe that this is a fair and equitable price, and decidedly to your benefit."

This letter was never acknowledged by the Laundry Equipment Division.

In October 1985, the Gear and Transmission Division submitted a project proposal to the top management of the corporation, requesting money to build facilities to produce the new economy transmission. The project proposal included a profit projection based on a $12 price. The Laundry Equipment Division was quoted in the project proposal as agreeing to the price. There was no objection to this statement from the Laundry Equipment Division personnel who were asked to comment on the proposed project. The project was approved, and the Gear and Transmission Division proceeded to buy and install the equipment to produce the new transmission.

In the latter part of 1985, the Gear and Transmission Division opened negotiations with the Laundry Equipment Division on the price of the new transmission, proposing $12 plus some minor adjustments for changes in cost levels since the previous year. The Laundry Equipment Division refused to accept the proposed price and countered with an offer of $11.21, developed as shown below.

Development of $11.21 Price

Proposed selling price of Thorndike model	$10.00
Adjustments:	
Cost of added design features $0.85	
Cost of eliminated design features . . . (0.50)	
Increased cost of material and labor since date of quotation 0.75	
Net cost change 1.10	
Profit on added cost 0.11	
Total price increase	1.21
Proposed price	$11.21

The Gear and Transmission Division refused even to consider this proposal, and after several days of acrimonious debate, both divisions decided to submit the dispute to the finance staff for arbitration.

Laundry Equipment Division. The Laundry Equipment Division based its case on the following arguments:

1. The division could have purchased a transmission, comparable in performance characteristics to the Gear and Transmission Division's unit, from the Thorndike Machining Corporation for $11.21.
2. The Gear and Transmission Division had agreed to this price in consideration of being allowed to produce all the transmissions.
3. The intracompany pricing policy was that the supplying divisions should sell at competitive prices.

The general manager of the Laundry Equipment Division stated that it would be unfair to penalize him for keeping the transmission business inside the corporation as a benefit to the Gear and Transmission Division, particularly in the light of the promise made by the general manager of the Gear and Transmission Division.

The general manager also stated that he had not protested the price proposal included in the June 1985 letter because he believed that it was then too early to open negotiations. His cost analysts had not evaluated the proposal, but he assumed that the Gear and Transmission Division was approximately correct in its evaluation of the cost differences from the Thorndike unit. His position was that the difference of 34 cents between the adjusted Thorndike price and the quoted Gear and Transmission price was not worth negotiating until nearer the production date. The Laundry Equipment Division naturally had assumed that the Gear and Transmission Division would live up to its agreement and, therefore, regarded the request for $12 as just a negotiating gimmick.

Gear and Transmission Division. The Gear and Transmission Division based its case on two arguments:

1. The $10 quotation of the Thorndike Machining Corporation was invalid

because it represented a final desperate effort to keep a share of the transmission business. A price of this nature should not form a long-term intracompany pricing base. If the Thorndike Machining Corporation had received the business, it would have eventually raised its price.

2. The Laundry Equipment Division did not object to the Gear and Transmission Division's price proposal until after the facilities to build the transmission were already in place. The $12 price was used in the calculations that showed the profitability of the project, and on which the project approval was based. If the Laundry Equipment Division wished to object, it should have done so when the project was presented to top management. Because facilities were purchased on the assumption of a $12 price, the Laundry Equipment Division should not be allowed to object after the money had been spent.

Finance Staff Review

A review by the finance staff disclosed the following:

1. If the Thorndike Machining quotation of $10 were adjusted for the cost effect of changes in performance characteristics and the increase in general cost levels since the original quotation, the price would be $11.25, or approximately the same as that proposed by the Laundry Equipment Division. The price of $11.66 developed by the Gear and Transmission

Division was in error because it failed to allow for a design elimination that would reduce the cost of the Thorndike unit by 50 cents.

2. At $12, the Gear and Transmission Division could expect to earn an aftertax profit of 15 percent on its investment; this was equal to its profit objective. At the $11.25 price, the division would earn about 6 percent after taxes.

3. The purchasing staff stated that, in its opinion, the transmission could be obtained from the Thorndike Machining Corporation at the quoted price level for the foreseeable future.

Questions

1. Be prepared in each of the disputes to play all three of the following roles: general manager of the supplying division, general manager of the buying division, member of the financial staff responsible for arbitrating the dispute. In the case of the general managers, you should not simply repeat the arguments presented in the case; you should also be prepared to give ground where your position is weak, to introduce new (but realistic) arguments to buttress your case, and to deal rationally with your adversary's arguments.

2. What, if any, changes in the company's transfer price policies and procedures would you recommend?

CASE 5–4
STRIDER CHEMICAL COMPANY

On December 9, 1986, the president of Strider Chemical Company, which had sales of around $175 million, announced that on January 1, 1987, the company would be reorganized into separate divisions. Until that time, the company had been organized on a functional basis, with the manufacturing, sales, finance, and research departments each under one person's responsibility. Six divisions were to be set up—four by product group and two by geographical area. Each division was to have its own production, sales, and accounting staff, and a general manager who would be responsible for its operation. The division's operating performance was to be judged by the profit it produced in relation to the investment assigned to it. It was anticipated that the procedure for computing the investment base and the return thereon would have to be carefully worked out if the resultant ratio was to be acceptable to the new division managers as a reasonable measure of their performance.

One of the biggest obstacles to the establishment of the desired monthly profit and loss statement for each division was the pricing of products for transfer from one to another of the various divisions. At the time the divisions were established, the company's president issued a policy statement upon which a pricing procedure was to be used. The president's statement follows.

President's Statement of Policy

The *maximum,* and usual, price for transfers between profit units is that price which enables the producing unit to earn a return on the investment required, consis-

tent with what it can earn doing business with the *average* of its customers for the product group concerned.

Established prices will be reviewed each six months or when a general change in market prices occurs.

Discussion

Pricing policy between operating units is particularly important because, to the extent that the price is wrong, the return on one segment of the business is understated and the return on another is overstated. This not only gives a false measure of how well individuals are performing but also may make for bad decisions on the business as a whole, which will affect everyone.

Certain elements of expense that may not be found in intracompany relations are:

1. Deductions for cash discounts, freight, royalties, sales taxes, customer allowances, etc.
2. Usual selling expenses and, in many cases, order and billing services.
3. Certain customer services by the research laboratories, such as sales service where this applies.

The producing division that acts as a supplier will establish a price by discounting its *regular* price structure for the elements listed above which apply.

In case the buying division disagrees with the price as computed above, it will explain the basis of its disagreement to the president, who will decide what is to be done.

We are hopeful that this policy will work out equitably, giving each division a fair basis for the business they do. If, in practice, it is found that the policy is not working properly, is complicated in its application or calculation, or is working a hardship, the policy will have to be changed.

Williams Division

The largest of the newly formed divisions, the Williams Division, was strongly affected by the problem of transfer prices since about 23 percent of its sales would be to other divisions.

With only three weeks before the separation into divisions, it was important that a schedule of prices be established quickly for the transfer of products between divisions. The Williams Division's task was complicated by its large number of products. There were several hundred different compounds and materials for which a price had to be fixed. It was, therefore, partly for the sake of expediency that the Williams Division chose to set the prices on the basis of direct manufacturing cost. The figures used in this method were more readily available than those used in setting a price based on the current market price.

A week after the president's policy statement on transfer pricing had been distributed, the Williams Division issued an interpretation of the policy which stated its proposed method for setting prices for the sale of products by the Williams Division to other divisions. The key paragraphs from this statement were as follows:

> The Williams Division will charge the same price to another division as it charges to the average of its existing customers, less an allowance for those expenses incurred with average customers but not with interdivisional customers. These noncomparable expenses to be deducted include Sales Deductions and a part of Selling Expenses. The prices will be calculated in terms of a markup or multiplier factor on Direct Manufacturing Cost. A markup will be recalculated each six months, based on the prior 12 months' experience with regular customers.
>
> The markup for the first six months of 1987 will be 1.41 times Direct Manufacturing Cost as shown in Exhibit 1 which uses actual data for the 12-month period ended October 31, 1986.

By the end of March 1987, the president had received a number of letters from division managers, raising questions about transfer prices. Three of these are summarized as follows:

EXHIBIT 1   Markup Calculation

	Dollars	Percent
Gross sales to outside customers	$5,126,328	
Less: Amounts not applicable to internal sales:		
Freight, royalties, sales taxes	$ 58,625	
Selling expenses	260,123	
Total deductions	318,748	
Adjusted sales	4,807,580	100%
Direct manufacturing cost	3,404,923	71
Margin	1,402,657	29%
Computation 100 ÷ 71 = 1.41 times		

1. The Williams Division questioned the price which the Johnson Division had established for compound A, a raw material for the Williams Division. The Johnson Division had initially calculated a markup of 1.33, computed in the same way the Williams Division computed its markup of 1.41. At a markup of 1.33, however, the Johnson Division would show a net loss since the division had not operated at a profit in the preceding 12 months. It, therefore, raised its markup to 1.41, the same as that used by the Williams Division. At this markup, it would show about the same profit as that of the Williams Division. The Williams Division argued that this markup violated company policy.

2. The International Division questioned the transfer price of several products it purchased from the Williams Division for sale abroad. It said that at these prices the International Division could not meet competitive prices in European markets and still make a profit.

3. The Western Division purchased Chemical B from the Williams Division for resale to its own customers. It submitted data to show that at

the computed transfer price the Western Division would be better off to manufacture Chemical B in one of its own plants. Rather than do this, it proposed that the transfer price be cut by 15 percent, which would still leave a margin over direct manufacturing cost for the Williams Division.

As of the end of March, the president had not acted on any of these letters, other than to reply that existing relationships between divisions should be continued until further notice and that after the questions had been decided, adjustments in transfer prices would be made retroactive to January 1.

In view of the numerous questions that had arisen already about the markup, the president was considering the possibility of transferring all products at cost, without any markup.

Questions

1. How should the president respond to the three letters he had received from division managers raising questions about transfer prices?
2. What change, if any, should be made in the transfer price practices of Strider Chemical Company?

CASE 5–5
MEDOC COMPANY

The Milling Division of the Medoc Company milled flour and manufactured a variety of consumer products from it. Its output was distributed as follows:

1. Approximately 70 percent (by weight) was transferred to the Consumer Products Division and marketed by this division through retail stores. The Consumer Products Division was responsible for these items from the time of packaging; that is, it handled warehousing, shipping, billing, and collections as well as advertising and other sales promotion efforts.

2. Approximately 20 percent was sold by the Milling Division as flour to large industrial users.

3. Approximately 10 percent was flour transferred to the Consumer Products Division and sold by that division to industrial users, but in different industries than those serviced directly by the Milling Division.

Counting each size and pack as one unit, there were several hundred products in the line marketed by the Consumer Products Division. The gross margin percentage on these products was considerably higher than that on flour sold to industrial users.

Wheat was purchased by the Grain Department, which was separate from the Milling Di-vision. The price of wheat fluctuated widely and frequently. Other ingredients and supplies were purchased by the Milling Division.

The Milling Division and Consumer Products Division were 2 of 15 investment centers in the Medoc Company.

Products were transferred from the Milling Division to the Consumer Products Division at a unit price that corresponded to actual cost. There was a variation among products, but on the average, this cost included elements in the following approximate proportions:

Flour	30%
Other ingredients and packaging material	25
Labor and variable overhead	20
Nonvariable overhead	25
Total	100%

Also, 75 percent of the Milling Division's investment was charged to the Consumer Products Division in computing the latter's return on investment. This investment consisted of property, plant, equipment, and inventory, all of which was "owned and operated" by the Milling Division.

This transfer price resulted in friction between the Milling Division and the Consumer Products Division, primarily for three reasons.

1. As in many process industries, unit costs were significantly lower when the plant operated at capacity. Indeed, the principal reason for accepting the low-margin industrial busi-

This case was prepared by Robert N. Anthony, Harvard Business School. Copyright by the President and Fellows of Harvard College. Harvard Business School case 171-284.

ness was to permit capacity operations. There was general agreement that acceptance of such business at a low margin, or even at something less than full-cost, was preferable to operating at less than capacity. In recent years, the Milling Division had operated at no less than 98 percent of capacity.

The Milling Division alleged that the Consumer Products Division was not aggressive enough in seeking this capacity-filling volume. The Milling Division believed that the Consumer Products Division could increase the volume of consumer sales by increasing its marketing efforts and by offering more attractive special deals and that it could do more to obtain industrial business at a price which, although not profitable, nevertheless would result in a smaller loss than what the Milling Division incurred from sales made to the industry it served. This additional volume would benefit the company, even though it reduced the average profit margin of the Consumer Products Division. The Consumer Products Division admitted that there was some validity in this argument, but pointed out that it had little incentive to seek such business when it was charged full cost for every unit it sold.

2. The Consumer Products Division complained that although it was charged for 75 percent of the investment in the Milling Division, it did not participate in any of the decisions regarding the acquisition of new equipment, inventory levels, etc. It admitted, however, that the people in the Milling Division were technically more competent to make these decisions.

3. The Consumer Products Division complained that since products were charged to it at actual cost, it must automatically pay for production inefficiencies that were the responsibility of the Milling Division.

A careful study had been made of the possibility of relating the transfer price either to a market price or to the price charged by the Milling Division to its industrial customers. Because of differences in product composition, however, this possibility definitely had been ruled out.

The Consumer Products Division currently earned about 20 percent pretax return on investment, and the Milling Division earned about 6 percent.

Top management of the Medoc Company was convinced that, some way or other, the profit performance of the Milling Division and the Consumer Products Division should be measured separately; that is, it ruled out the simple solution of combining the two divisions for profit-reporting purposes.

One proposal for solving the problem was that the transfer price should consist of two elements: (*a*) a standard monthly charge representing the Consumer Products Division's fair share of the nonvariable overhead, plus (*b*) a per-unit charge equivalent to the actual material, labor, and variable overhead costs applied to each unit billed. Investment would no longer be allocated to the Consumer Products Division. Instead, a standard profit would be included in computing the fixed monthly charge.

The monthly nonvariable overhead charge would be set annually. It would consist of two parts:

1. A fraction of the budgeted nonvariable overhead cost of the Milling Division, corresponding to the fraction of products that was estimated would be transferred to the Consumer Products Division (about 80 percent). This amount would be changed only if there were changes in

wage rates or other significant noncontrollable items during the year.

2. A return of 10 percent on the same fraction of the Milling Division's investment. This was higher than the return that the Milling Division earned on sales to industrial users. The selection of 10 percent was arbitrary because there was no way of determining a "true" return on products sold by the Consumer Products Division.

Questions

1. What would you recommend given the organizational structure constraints in the case?

2. What would you recommend if there were *no* organizational structure constraints on your options?

6

Measuring and Controlling Assets Employed

In some business units, the focus is on profit as measured by the difference between revenues and expenses. This is described in Chapter 4. In other business units, profit is compared with the assets employed in earning it. We refer to the latter group of responsibility centers as *investment centers* and, in this chapter, discuss the measurement problems involved in such responsibility centers. In the real world, companies use the term "profit center," rather than investment center, to refer to both the responsibility centers discussed in Chapter 4 and those in this chapter. We agree that an investment center is a special type of profit center, rather than a separate, parallel category. However, there are so many problems involved in measuring the assets employed in a profit center that the topic warrants a separate chapter.

In this chapter we first discuss each of the principal types of assets that may be employed in an investment center. The sum of these assets is called the investment base. We then discuss two methods of relating profit to the investment base: (1) the percentage *return on investment,* referred to as ROI, and (2) *economic value added,* called EVA. We describe the advantages and qualifications of using each to measure performance. Finally, we discuss the somewhat different problem of measuring the economic value of an investment center, as compared to evaluating the manager in charge of the investment center.

Until recently, authors used the term "residual income" instead of economic value added. These two concepts are effectively the same. EVA is a trademark of Stern Stewart & Co. It illustrates how a firm can take a concept that has been described in this and other texts for many years, slap a new name on it, and then register this name as a trademark.

Structure of the Analysis

The purposes of measuring assets employed are analogous to the purposes we discussed for profit centers in Chapter 4, namely:

- To provide information that is useful in making sound decisions about assets employed and to motivate managers to make these sound decisions that are in the best interests of the company.
- To measure the performance of the business unit as an economic entity.

In our examination of the alternative treatments of assets and the comparison of ROI and EVA—the two ways of relating profit to assets employed—we are primarily interested in how well the alternatives serve these two purposes of providing information for sound decision-making and measuring business unit economic performance.

Focusing on profits without considering the assets employed to generate those profits is an inadequate basis for control. Except in certain types of service organizations, in which the amount of capital is insignificant, an important objective of a profit-oriented company is to earn a satisfactory return on the capital that the company uses. A profit of $1 million in a company that has $10 million of capital does not represent as good a performance as a profit of $1 million in a company that has only $5 million of capital, assuming both companies have a similar risk profile.

Unless the amount of assets employed is taken into account, it is difficult for senior management to compare the profit performance of one business unit with that of other units or to similar outside companies. Comparing absolute differences in profits is not meaningful if business units use different amounts of resources; clearly, the more resources used, the greater the profits should be. Such comparisons are used to judge how well business unit managers are performing and to decide how to allocate resources.

> **Example.**   Golden Grain, a business unit of Quaker Oats, had very high profitability and appeared to be one of Quaker Oats' best divisions. It was, however, acquired by Quaker Oats at a premium above its book value. Based on the assets employed as measured by this premium, Golden Grain actually was underperforming.[1]

In general, business unit managers have two performance objectives. First, they should generate adequate profits from the resources at their disposal. Second, they should invest in additional resources only when the investment will produce an adequate return. (Conversely, they should disinvest if the expected annual profits of any resource, discounted at the company's required earnings rate, are less than the cash that could be realized from its sale.) The purpose of relating profits to investments is to motivate business unit managers to accomplish these objectives. As we shall see, there are significant practical difficulties involved in creating a system that focuses on assets employed in addition to the focus on profits.

Exhibit 6–1 is a hypothetical, simplified set of business unit financial statements that will be used throughout this analysis. (In the interest of

---

[1]Brian McWilliams, "Creating Value," an interview with William Smithburg, chairman, Quaker Oats, in *Enterprise,* April 1993.

EXHIBIT 6–1   Business Unit Financial Statements

Balance Sheet
($000s)

Current assets:			Current liabilities:		
Cash		$ 50	Accounts payable		$ 90
Receivables		150	Other current		110
Inventory		200			
Total current assets		400	Total current liabilities		200
Fixed assets:					
Cost	$ 600		Corporate equity		500
Depreciation.	−300				
Book value		300			
Total assets		$700	**Total equities**		$700

Income Statement

Revenue		$1,000
Expenses, except depreciation	$850	
Depreciation.	50	900
Income before taxes		100
Capital charge ($500 ∗ 10%)		50
Economic value added (EVA)		50

$$\text{Return on investment} = \frac{\$100}{\$500} = 20\%$$

---

simplicity, income taxes have been omitted from this exhibit and generally will be omitted from discussion in this chapter. Including income taxes would change the magnitudes in the calculations that follow, but it would not change the conclusions.) The exhibit shows the two ways of relating profits to assets employed—namely, through return on investment and economic value added.

Return on investment (ROI) is a ratio. The numerator is income, as reported on the income statement. The denominator is assets employed. In Exhibit 6–1, the denominator is taken as the corporation's equity in the business unit. This amount corresponds to the sum of noncurrent liabilities plus shareholders' equity in the balance sheet of a separate company. It is mathematically equivalent to total assets less current liabilities, and to noncurrent assets plus working capital. (This statement can easily be checked against the numbers in Exhibit 6–1.)

Economic value added (EVA) is a dollar amount, rather than a ratio. It is found by subtracting a capital charge from the net operating profit. This capital charge is found by multiplying the amount of assets employed by a rate,

EXHIBIT 6–2   Methods Used to Evaluate Investment Centers

	United States[1]	*Holland[2]*	*India[3]*
Number of usable responses	638	72	39
Companies with 2 or more investment centers	500 (78%)	59 (82%)	27 (70%)
Percentage of companies using Residual Income or EVA (with 2 or more investment centers)	36%	19%	8%

[1]Vijay Govindarajan, "Profit Center Measurement: An Empirical Survey," The Amos Tuck School of Business Administration, Dartmouth College, 1994, p. 2.

[2]Elbert De With, "Performance Measurement and Evaluation in Dutch Companies," Paper presented at the 19th Annual Congress of the European Accounting Association, Bergen, 1996.

[3]V. Govindarajan and B. Ramamurthy, "Financial Measurement of Investment Centers: A Descriptive Study," Working paper, Indian Institute of Management, Ahbedabad, India, August 1980.

which is 10 percent in Exhibit 6–1. We shall discuss the derivation of this rate in a later section.

> **Example.**   AT&T used the economic value added measure to evaluate business unit managers. For instance, the Long-Distance Group consisted of 40 business units which sold services such as 800 numbers, telemarketing, and public telephone calls. All the capital costs, from switching equipment to new product development, were allocated to these 40 business units. Each business unit manager was expected to generate operating earnings that substantially exceeded the cost of capital.[2, 3]

In a Govindarajan survey, 78 percent of the respondents used investment centers (Exhibit 6–2).[4] Of the US companies using investment centers, 36 percent evaluated them on economic value added. Practices in other countries seem to be similar to those in the United States (See Exhibit 6–2).

For reasons to be explained later, EVA is conceptually superior to ROI, and, therefore, we shall generally use EVA in our examples. Nevertheless, it is clear from the surveys that ROI is more widely used in business than EVA.

Measuring Assets Employed

In deciding what investment base to use to evaluate investment center managers, headquarters asks two questions: First, what practices will induce business unit managers to use their assets most efficiently and to acquire the proper amount and kind of new assets? Presumably, when their profits are related to assets employed, business unit managers will try to improve their

[2]Shawn Tully, "The Real Key to Creating Wealth," *Fortune,* September 20, 1993, pp. 38–50.

[3]Joel M. Stern, "The Mathematics of Corporate Finance—or EVA = $NA[RONA–C]," pp. 26–33.

[4]Vijay Govindarajan, "Profit Center Measurement: An Empirical Survey," The Amos Tuck School of Business Administration, Dartmouth College, 1994, p. 2.

performance as measured in this way. Senior management wants the actions that they take toward this end to be in the best interest of the whole corporation. Second, what practices best measure the performance of the unit as an economic entity?

Cash

Most companies control cash centrally because central control permits use of a smaller cash balance than would be the case if each business unit held the cash balances it needed to weather the unevenness of its cash inflows and outflows. Business unit cash balances may well be only the "float" between daily receipts and daily disbursements. Consequently, the actual cash balances at the business unit level tend to be much smaller than would be required if the business unit were an independent company. Many companies, therefore, use a formula to calculate the cash to be included in the investment base. For example, General Motors was reported to use 4.5 percent of annual sales; Du Pont was reported to use two months' costs of sales minus depreciation.

One reason to include cash at a higher amount than the balance normally carried by a business unit is that the higher amount is necessary to allow comparisons to outside companies. If only the actual cash were shown, the return by internal units would appear abnormally high and might mislead senior management.

Some companies omit cash from the investment base. These companies reason that the amount of cash approximates the current liabilities. If this is so, the sum of accounts receivable and inventories will approximate the amount of working capital.

Receivables

Business unit managers can influence the level of receivables indirectly, by their ability to generate sales; and directly, by establishing credit terms and approving individual credit accounts and credit limits, and by their vigor in collecting overdue amounts. In the interest of simplicity, receivables often are included at the actual end-of-period balances, although the average of intraperiod balances is conceptually a better measure of the amount that should be related to profits.

Whether to include accounts receivable at selling prices or at cost of goods sold is debatable. One could argue that the business unit's real investment in accounts receivable is only the cost of goods sold and that a satisfactory return on this investment is probably enough. On the other hand, it is possible to argue that the business unit could reinvest the money collected from accounts receivable, and, therefore, accounts receivable should be included at selling prices. The usual practice is to take the simpler alternative—that is, to include receivables at the book amount, which is the selling price less an allowance for bad debts.

If the business unit does not control credits and collections, receivables may be calculated on a formula basis. This formula should be consistent with the normal payment period—for example, 30 days' sales where payment normally is made 30 days after the shipment of goods.

Inventories

Inventories ordinarily are treated in a manner similar to receivables—that is, they are often recorded at end-of-period amounts even though intraperiod averages would be preferable conceptually. If the company uses LIFO (last in, first out) for financial accounting purposes, a different valuation method usually is used for business unit profit reporting because LIFO inventory balances tend to be unrealistically low in periods of inflation. In these circumstances, inventories should be valued at standard or average costs, and these same costs should be used to measure cost of sales on the business unit income statement.

If work-in-process inventory is financed by *advance payments* or by *progress payments* from the customer, as is typically the case with goods that require a long manufacturing period, these payments either are subtracted from the gross inventory amounts or reported as liabilities.

> **Example.** With manufacturing periods a year or greater, Boeing received progress payments for its airplanes and recorded them as liabilities.[5]

Some companies subtract *accounts payable* from inventory on the grounds that accounts payable represent financing of part of the inventory by vendors, at zero cost to the business unit. The corporate capital required for inventories is only the difference between the gross inventory amount and accounts payable. If the business unit can influence the payment period allowed by vendors, then including accounts payable in the calculation encourages the manager to seek the most favorable terms. In times of high interest rates or credit stringency, managers might be encouraged to consider forgoing the cash discount to have, in effect, additional financing provided by vendors. On the other hand, delaying payments unduly to reduce net current assets may not be in the company's best interest since this may hurt its credit rating.

Working Capital in General

As can be seen, treatment of working capital items varies greatly. At one extreme, companies include all current assets in the investment base with no offset for any current liabilities. This method is sound from a motivational standpoint if the business units cannot influence accounts payable or other current liabilities. It does overstate the amount of corporate capital required

---

[5]The Boeing Company, *1993 Report.*

to finance the business unit, however, because the current liabilities are a source of capital, often at zero interest cost. At the other extreme, all current liabilities may be deducted from current assets, as was done in calculating the investment base in Exhibit 6–1. This method provides a good measure of the capital provided by the corporation, on which it expects the business unit to earn a return. However, it may imply that business unit managers are responsible for certain current liabilities over which they have no control.

Property, Plant, and Equipment

In financial accounting, fixed assets are initially recorded at their acquisition cost, and this cost is written off over the asset's useful life through depreciation. Most companies use a similar approach in measuring profitability of the business unit's asset base. This causes some serious problems in using the system for its intended purposes. We examine these problems in the following sections.

Acquisition of New Equipment.   Suppose a business unit could buy a new machine for $100,000. This machine is estimated to produce cash savings of $27,000 a year for five years. If the company has a required return of 10 percent, the investment is attractive, as the calculations in section A of Exhibit 6–3 illustrate. The proposed investment has a net present value of $2,400 and, therefore, should be undertaken. However, if the machine is purchased and the business unit measures its asset base as shown in Exhibit 6–1, the unit's reported economic value added will decrease, rather than increase, in the first year. Section B of Exhibit 6–3 shows the income statement without the machine (as in Exhibit 6–1) and the income statement if the machine is acquired (and in its first year of use). Note that acquiring the machine increases income before taxes, but this increase is more than offset by the increase in the capital charge. Thus, the EVA calculation signals that profitability has decreased, whereas the economic facts are that profits have increased. Under the circumstances, the business unit manager may be reluctant to purchase this machine. (In Exhibit 6–3, depreciation was calculated on a straight-line basis. Had it been calculated on an accelerated basis, which is not uncommon, the discrepancy between the economic facts and the reported results would have been even greater.)

Exhibit 6–4 shows how, in later years, the amount of economic value added will increase as the book value of the machine declines, going from –$3,000 in year one to +$5,000 in year five. The increase in economic value added each year does not represent real economic change. Although there appears to be constantly improving profitability, in fact there is no real change in profitability after the year the machine was acquired. Generalizing from this example, it is evident that business units that have old, almost fully depreciated assets will tend to report larger economic value added than units that have newer assets.

EXHIBIT 6–3   Incorrect Motivation for Asset Acquisition ($000)

A. Economic calculation

Investment in machine $100

    Life, 5 years

    Cash inflow, $27,000 per year

Present value of cash inflow ($27,000 * 3.791)*......   102.4

Net present value............................   2.4

Decision: Acquire the machine.

B. As reflected on business unit income statement

	As in Exhibit 6–1		First Year with Machine	
Revenue		$1,000		$1,000
Expenses, except depreciation	$850		$823	
Depreciation.....................	50	900	70	893
Income before taxes		100		107
Less capital charge at 10%†		50		60
EVA..		50		47

Note: Income taxes are not shown separately for simplicity. Assume they are included in the calculation of the cash flow.

*3.791 is the present value of $1 per year for five years at 10 percent.

†Capital charge on the new machine is calculated at its beginning book value, which for the first year is $100 * 10% = 10. We have used the beginning-of-the-year book value for simplicity. Many companies use the average book value—(100 + 80) ÷ 2 = 90. The results will be similar.

EXHIBIT 6–4   Effect of Acquisition on Reported Annual Profits ($000)

Year	Book Value at Beginning of Year (a)	Incremental Income* (b)	Capital Charge† (c)	EVA (b – c)	ROI b ÷ a
1	100	7	10	–3	7%
2	80	7	8	–1	9
3	60	7	6	1	12
4	40	7	4	3	18
5	20	7	2	5	35

Note: True return = approximately 11 percent.

*$27,000 cash inflow – $20,000 depreciation = $7,000.

†10 percent of beginning book value.

If profitability is measured by return on investment, the same inconsistency exists, as the last column of Exhibit 6–4 shows. Although we know from the present value calculation that the true return is about 11 percent, the business unit financial statement reports that it is less than 10 percent in the first year and increases thereafter. Furthermore, the average of the five annual percentages shown is 16 percent, which far exceeds what we know to be the true annual return.

It is evident that if depreciable assets are included in the investment base at net book value, business unit profitability is misstated, and business unit managers may not be motivated to make correct acquisition decisions.

> **Example.**   Quaker Oats discovered it was underinvesting because of the low book value of its 100-year-old plants. As one executive observed, "We've been in the business for over 100 years. As a result, we have a lot of plants and equipment with a small book value relative to our newer brands. And just because we're lucky enough to inherit a 100-year-old business doesn't mean we are exempt from substantially improving the controllable earnings of that business from year to year."[6]

Gross Book Value.   The fluctuation in economic value added and return on investment from year to year in Exhibit 6–4 can be avoided by including depreciable assets in the investment base at gross book value rather than at net book value. Some companies do this. If this were done in this case, the investment each year would be $100,000 (original cost), and the additional income would be $7,000 ($27,000 cash inflow – $20,000 depreciation). The economic value added, however, would decrease by $3,000 ($7,000 – $10,000 interest), and return on investment would be 7 percent ($7,000 ÷ $100,000). Both of these numbers indicate that the business unit's profitability has decreased, which, in fact, is not true. Return on investment calculated on gross book value always understates the true return.

Disposition of Assets.   If a new machine is being considered to replace an existing machine that has some undepreciated book value, we know that this undepreciated book value is irrelevant in the economic analysis of the proposed purchase (except indirectly as it may affect income taxes). Nevertheless, removing the book value of the old machine can substantially affect the calculation of business unit profitability. Gross book value will increase only by the difference between the net book value after year one of the new machine and the net book value of the old machine. In either case, the relevant amount of additional investment is understated, and the economic value added is correspondingly overstated. This encourages managers to replace old equipment with new equipment, even when replacement is not economically justified. Furthermore, business units that are able to make the most replacements will show the greatest improvement in profitability.

---

[6]McWilliams, "Creating Value."

**EXHIBIT 6–5   Profitability Using Annuity Depreciation—
Smoothing EVA ($000)**

Year	Beginning Book Value	Cash Inflow	EVA*	Capital Charge[†]	Depreciation[‡]
1	$100.0	$ 27.0	$0.6	$10.0	$ 16.4
2	83.6	27.0	0.6	8.4	18.0
3	65.6	27.0	0.6	6.6	19.8
4	45.8	27.0	0.6	4.6	21.8
5	24.0	27.0	0.6	2.4	24.0
Total		$135.0	$3.0	$32.0	$100.0

*Annuity depreciation makes the EVA the same each year by changing the amount of depreciation charged. Consequently, we must estimate the total EVA earned over the five years. A 10 percent return on $100,000 would require five annual cash inflows of $26,378. The actual cash inflows are $27,000. Therefore, the EVA (the amount in excess of $26,378) is $622 per year.

[†]This is 10 percent of the balance at the beginning of the year.

[‡]Depreciation is the amount required to make the EVA (profits after the capital charge and depreciation) equal $622 per year (rounded here to $600). This is calculated as follows:

$$\$27.0 - \text{Capital charge} - \text{Depreciation} = \$0.6$$

therefore,

$$\text{Depreciation} = \$26.4 - \text{Capital charge}$$

In sum, if assets are included in the investment base at their original cost, then the business unit manager is motivated to get rid of them—even if they have some usefulness—because the business unit's investment base is reduced by the full cost of the asset.

Annuity Depreciation.   If depreciation is determined by the annuity, rather than the straight-line, method, the business unit profitability calculation will show the correct economic value added and return on investment, as Exhibits 6–5 and 6–6 demonstrate. This is because the annuity depreciation method actually matches the recovery of investment that is implicit in the present value calculation. Annuity depreciation is the opposite of accelerated depreciation in that the annual amount of depreciation is low in the early years when the investment values are high and increases each year as the investment decreases; the rate of return remains constant.

Exhibits 6–5 and 6–6 show the calculations when the cash inflows are level in each year. Equations are available that derive the depreciation for other cash flow patterns, such as a decreasing cash flow as repair costs increase, or an increasing cash flow as a new product gains market acceptance.

Very few managers accept the idea of a depreciation allowance that increases as the asset ages, however. They visualize accounting depreciation as representing physical deterioration or loss in economic value. Therefore, they believe that accelerated, or straight-line, depreciation is a valid representation of what is taking place. As a result, it is difficult to convince them to accept the annuity method to measure business unit profit.

**EXHIBIT 6–6   Profitability Using Annuity Depreciation—
Smoothing Return on Investment ($000)**

Year	Beginning Book Balance	Cash Inflow	Net Profit*	Depreciation†	Return on Beginning Investment
1	$100.0	$ 27.0	$11.0	$ 16.0	11%
2	84.0	27.0	9.2	17.8	11
3	66.2	27.0	7.3	19.7	11
4	46.5	27.0	5.1	21.9	11
5	24.6	27.0	2.4	24.6	10‡
Total		$135.0	$35.0	$100.0	10%

*A return of $27,000 a year for five years on an investment of $100,000 provides a return of approximately 11 percent on the beginning of the year investment. Consequently, in order to have a constant 11 percent return each year, the net profit must equal 11 percent of the beginning-of-the-year investment.

†Depreciation is the difference between the cash flow and the net profit.

‡The difference results because the return is not exactly 11 percent.

EXHIBIT 6–7   Valuation of Plant and Equipment

	Percentage of Respondents Using the Method		
	United States[1]	Holland[2]	India[3]
Gross book value	6%	9%	17%
Net book value	93	73	79
Replacement cost	1	18	4
	100%	100%	100%

[1]Govindarajan, "Profit Center Measurement," 1994, p. 2.
[2]De With, "Performance Measurement and Evaluation in Dutch Companies."
[3]Govindarajan and Ramamurthy, "Financial Measurement of Investment Centers."

Annuity depreciation also presents some practical problems. For example, the depreciation schedule in Exhibits 6–5 and 6–6 was based on an estimated cash flow pattern. If the actual cash flow pattern differed from that assumed, even though the total cash flow might result in the same rate of return, expected profits would be higher in some years and lower in others. Should the depreciation schedule change each year to conform to the actual pattern of cash flow? This probably is not practical. Annuity depreciation would not be desirable for income tax purposes, of course, and although as a "systematic and rational" method it clearly is acceptable for financial accounting purposes, companies do not use it in their financial reporting. Indeed, surveys of how companies measure business unit profitability show practically no use of the annuity method (see Exhibit 6–7).

Other Valuation Methods.   Some companies use net book value but set a lower limit, usually 50 percent, as the amount of original cost that can be written off. This lessens the distortions that occur in business units with relatively old assets. A difficulty with this method is that a business unit with fixed assets that have a net book value of less than 50 percent of gross book value can decrease its investment base by scrapping perfectly good assets. Other companies depart entirely from the accounting records and use the asset's approximate current value. They arrive at this amount by periodically appraising assets (say, every five years or when a new business unit manager takes over), by adjusting original cost using an index of changes in equipment prices, or by applying insurance values.

A major problem with using nonaccounting values is that they tend to be subjective, as contrasted with accounting values, which appear to be objective and generally not subject to argument. Consequently, accounting data have an aura of reality for operating management. Although the intensity of this sentiment varies among managers, the further one departs from accounting numbers in measuring financial performance, the more likely that both business unit managers and senior managers will regard the system as playing a game of numbers.

A related problem with using nonaccounting amounts in internal systems is that business unit profitability will not be consistent with the corporate profitability reported to shareholders. Although the management control system does not have to be consistent with the external financial reporting, as a practical matter some managers regard net income, as reported on the financial statements, as constituting the "name of the game." Consequently, they do not favor an internal system that uses a different method of keeping score, regardless of its theoretical merits. Another problem with using current market values is deciding how to determine the economic values. Conceptually, the economic value of a group of assets equals the present value of the cash flows that these assets will generate in the future. As a practical matter, this amount cannot be determined. Although published indexes of replacement costs of plant and equipment can be used, most price indexes are not entirely relevant because they make no allowance for the impact of technology changes.

In any case, including the investment base of fixed assets at amounts other than those derived from the accounting records happens so rarely that it is of little more than academic interest (Exhibit 6–7).

Leased Assets

Suppose the business unit whose financial statements are shown in Exhibit 6–1 sold its fixed assets for their book value of $300,000, returned the proceeds of the sale to corporate headquarters, and then leased back the assets at a rental rate of $60,000 per year. As Exhibit 6–8 shows, the business unit's

EXHIBIT 6–8   Effect of Leasing Assets—Income Statement ($000)

	As in Exhibit 6–1		*If Assets Are Leased*	
Revenue		$1000		$1,000
Expenses other than below	$850		$850	
Depreciation	50	900		
Rental expense			60	910
Income before taxes		100		90
Capital charge $500 * 10%		50		
$200 * 10%				20
EVA		50		70

income before taxes would decrease because the new rental expense would be higher than the depreciation charge that was eliminated. Nevertheless, economic valued added would increase because the higher cost would be more than offset by the decrease in the capital charge. Because of this, business unit managers are induced to lease, rather than own, assets whenever the interest charge that is built into the rental cost is less than the capital charge that is applied to the business unit's investment base. (Here, as elsewhere, this generalization oversimplifies because, in the real world, the impact of income taxes must also be taken into account.)

Many leases are financing arrangements—that is, they provide an alternative way of getting to use assets that otherwise would be acquired by funds obtained from debt and equity financing. Financial leases (i.e., long-term leases equivalent to the present value of the stream of lease charges) are similar to debt and are so reported on the balance sheet. Financing decisions usually are made by corporate headquarters. For these reasons, restrictions usually are placed on the business unit manager's freedom to lease assets.

Idle Assets

If a business unit has idle assets that can be used by other units, it may be permitted to exclude them from the investment base if it classifies them as available. The purpose of this permission is to encourage business unit managers to release underutilized assets to units that may have better use for them. However, if the fixed assets cannot be used by other units, permitting the business unit manager to remove them from the investment base could result in dysfunctional actions. For example, it could encourage the business unit manager to idle partially utilized assets that are not earning a return equal to the business unit's profit objective. If there is no alternative use for the equipment, *any* contribution from this equipment will improve company profits.

Intangible Assets

Some companies tend to be R&D intensive (e.g., pharmaceutical firms such as Novartis spend huge amounts on developing new products); others tend to be marketing intensive (e.g., consumer products firms such as Unilever spend huge amounts on advertising). There are advantages to capitalizing intangible assets such as R&D and marketing and then amortizing them over a selected life.[7] This method should change how the business unit manager views these expenditures.[8] By accounting for these assets as long-term investments, the business unit manager will gain less short-term benefit from reducing outlays on such items. For instance, if R&D expenditures are expensed immediately, each dollar of R&D cut would be a dollar more in pretax profits. On the other hand, if R&D costs are capitalized, each dollar cut will reduce the assets employed by a dollar; the capital charge is thus reduced only by one dollar times the cost of capital, which has a much smaller positive impact on economic valued added.

Noncurrent Liabilities

Ordinarily, a business unit receives its permanent capital from the corporate pool of funds. The corporation obtained these funds from debt providers, equity investors, and retained earnings. To the business unit, the total amount of these funds is relevant but not the sources from which they were obtained. In unusual situations, however, a business unit's financing may be peculiar to its own situation. For example, a business unit that builds or operates residential housing or office buildings uses a much larger proportion of debt capital than would a typical manufacturing or marketing unit. Since this capital is obtained through mortgage loans on the business unit's assets, it may be appropriate to account for the borrowed funds separately and to compute an economic value added based on the assets obtained from general corporate sources rather than on total assets.

The Capital Charge

Corporate headquarters sets the rate used to calculate the capital charge. It should be higher than the corporation's rate for debt financing because the funds involved are a mixture of debt and higher-cost equity. Usually, the rate is set somewhat below the company's estimated cost of capital so that the economic value added of an average business unit will be above zero.

Some companies use a lower rate for working capital than for fixed assets. This may represent a judgment that working capital is less risky than fixed assets because the funds are committed for a shorter time period. In

---

[7]Stern, "The Mathematics of Corporate Finance", pp. 26–33.
[8]Tully, "The Real Key to Creating Wealth, pp. 38–50.

EXHIBIT 6–9   Assets Included in Investment Base

	Percentage of Respondents Including the Asset in the Investment Base	
	United States[1]	*Holland*[2]
Current assets		
Cash	47%	59%
Accounts receivable	90	94
Inventory	95	93
Other current assets	83	79
Fixed assets		
Land and buildings used solely by this profit center	97	82
Allocated land and buildings used by two or more profit centers	49	47
Equipment used solely by this profit center	96	88
Allocated equipment used by two or more profit centers	48	46
An allocation of assets of headquarters central research	19	16
Other		
Investments	53	N/A
Goodwill	55	N/A

[1]Govindarajan, "Profit Center Measurement," p. 2.
[2]De With, "Performance Measurement and Evaluation in Dutch Companies."

other cases, the lower rate is a way to compensate for the fact that the company included inventory and receivables in the investment base at their gross amount (i.e., without a deduction for accounts payable). It recognizes the fact that funds obtained from accounts payable have zero interest cost.

Surveys of Practice

Practices in investment center management are summarized in Exhibits 6–7, 6–9, and 6–10. Most companies include fixed assets in their investment base at their net book value. They do this because this is the amount at which the assets are carried in the financial statements and therefore, according to these statements, represents the amount of capital that the corporation has employed in the division. Senior managers recognize that this method gives misleading signals, but they believe individuals should make allowances for these errors when interpreting business unit profit reports and that alternative methods of calculating the investment base are not to be trusted because they are so subjective. They reject the annuity depreciation approach on the grounds that it is inconsistent with the way in which depreciation is calculated for financial statement purposes.

Exhibit 6–10   Liabilities Deducted in Calculating Investment Base

	Percentage of Respondents Deducting the Liability from the Investment Base	
	United States[1]	*Holland[2]*
Accounts payable	73%	91%
Intracompany payables	46	57
Other current liabilities	68	69
Deferred taxes	28	N/A
Other noncurrent liabilities	47	48

[1]Govindarajan, "Profit Center Measurement," p. 2.
[2]De With, "Performance Measurement and Evaluation in Dutch Companies."

EVA versus ROI

As shown in Exhibit 6–2, most companies employing investment centers evaluate business units on the basis of ROI rather than EVA. There are three apparent benefits of an ROI measure. First, it is a comprehensive measure in that anything that affects financial statements is reflected in this ratio. Second, ROI is simple to calculate, easy to understand, and meaningful in an absolute sense. For example, an ROI of less than 5 percent is considered low on an absolute scale, and an ROI of over 25 percent is considered high. Finally, it is a common denominator that may be applied to any organizational unit responsible for profitability, regardless of size or type of business. The performance of different units may be compared directly to one another. Also, ROI data are available for competitors and can be used as a basis for comparison.

The dollar amount of EVA does not provide such a basis for comparison. Nevertheless, the EVA approach has some inherent advantages. There are four compelling reasons to use EVA over ROI.

First, with EVA all business units have the same profit objective for comparable investments. The ROI approach, on the other hand, provides different incentives for investments across business units. For example, a business unit that currently is achieving an ROI of 30 percent would be reluctant to expand unless it is able to earn an ROI of 30 percent or more on additional assets; a lesser return would decrease its overall ROI below its current 30 percent level. Thus, this business unit might forgo investment opportunities whose ROI is *above* the cost of capital but *below* 30 percent.

> **Example.**   Based on ROI, Wal-Mart would have chosen to stop expanding since the late 1980s because its ROI on new stores slipped from 25 percent to 20 percent—even though both rates were substantially above its cost of capital.[9]

[9]G. Bennett Stewart III, "Reform Your Governance from Within," *Directors and Boards,* Spring 1993, pp. 48–54.

Similarly, a business unit that currently is achieving a low ROI—say, 5 percent—would benefit from anything over 5 percent on additional assets. As a consequence, ROI creates a bias toward little or no expansion in high-profit business units while, at the same time, low-profit units are making investments at rates of return well below those rejected by the high-profit units.

Second, decisions that *increase* a center's ROI may *decrease* its overall profits. For instance, in an investment center whose current ROI is 30 percent, the manager can increase its overall ROI by disposing of an asset whose ROI is 25 percent. However, if the cost of capital tied up in the investment center is less than 25 percent, the absolute dollar profit after deducting capital costs will decrease for the center.

The use of EVA as a measure deals with both these problems. They relate to asset investments whose ROI falls between the cost of capital and the center's current ROI. If an investment center's performance is measured by EVA, investments that produce a profit in excess of the cost of capital will increase EVA and therefore be economically attractive to the manager.

A *third* advantage of EVA is that different interest rates may be used for different types of assets. For example, a low rate may be used for inventories while a relatively higher rate may be used for investments in fixed assets. Furthermore, different rates may be used for different types of fixed assets to take into account different degrees of risk. In short, management control systems can be made consistent with the framework used for decisions about capital investments and resource allocation. It follows that the same type of asset may be required to earn the same return throughout the company, regardless of the particular business unit's profitability. Thus, business unit managers should act consistently when deciding to invest in new assets.

A *fourth* advantage is that EVA, in contrast to ROI, has a stronger positive correlation with changes in a company's market value.[10] Shareholders are important stakeholders in a company. There are several reasons why shareholder value creation is critical for the firm: It (*a*) reduces the risk of takeover, (*b*) creates currency for aggressiveness in mergers and acquisitions, and (*c*) reduces cost of capital, which allows faster investment for future growth. Thus, optimizing shareholder value is an important goal of an enterprise. However, since shareholder value measures the worth of the consolidated enterprise as whole, it is nearly impossible to use it as a performance criterion for an organization's individual responsibility centers. *The best proxy for shareholder value at the business unit level is to ask business unit managers to create and grow EVA.* Indeed, *Fortune*'s annual ranking of 1,000 companies according to their ability to create shareholder wealth indicates that companies with high EVA tend to show high market value added (MVA)

---

[10]Joel M. Stern, *EVA and Strategic Performance Measurement.* (New York: The Conference Board, 1996).

EXHIBIT 6–11   *Fortune's* **Annual List of Top Wealth Creators**
($ in millions)

1998 Rank	Top 5 in the List	Market Value Added[a]	EVA[b]
1	General Electric	$195,830	$1,917
2	Coca-Cola	158,247	2,615
3	Microsoft	143,740	2,781
4	Merck	107,418	1,921
	Bottom 5 in the List		
996	Hartford Financial Services Group	$ (1,524)	$ (435)
997	Kmart	(2,257)	(167)
998	RJR Nabisco	(9,530)	(1,140)
999	Loews	(10,081)	(1,350)
1000	General Motors	(13,876)	(4,120)

Source: "America's Greatest Wealth Creators," *Fortune,* November 9, 1998.

[a]"Market value added" shows the difference between what the capital investors have put into a company and the money they can take out.

[b]EVA is aftertax net operating profit minus cost of capital.

or high gains for shareholders (see Exhibit 6–11). When used as a perform-ance metric, EVA motivates managers to increase EVA by taking actions consistent with increasing stockholder value. This can be understood by considering how EVA is calculated. EVA is measured as follows:

$$\text{EVA} = \text{Net profit} - \text{Capital charge}$$

where

$$\text{Capital charge} = \text{Cost of capital} * \text{Capital employed} \tag{1}$$

Another way to state equation (1) would be:

$$\text{EVA} = \text{Capital employed (ROI} - \text{Cost of capital)} \tag{2}$$

The following actions can increase EVA as shown in equation (2): (*i*) increase in ROI through business process reengineering and productivity gains, without increasing the asset base; (*ii*) divest assets, products, and/or businesses whose ROI is less than the cost of capital; (*iii*) aggressive new investments in assets, products, and/or businesses whose ROI exceeds the cost of capital; and (*iv*) increase in sales, profit margins, or capital efficiency (ratio of sales to capital employed), or decrease cost of capital percentage, *without affecting the other variables in equation (2).* These actions clearly are in the best interests of shareholders.

Example.   In January 1996, John Bystone, a former General Electric manager, took over as CEO of SPX, a $1.1 billion maker of automobile parts, such as filters

EXHIBIT 6–12   Difference between ROI and EVA ($000)

ROI Method

Business Unit	*(1)* Cash	*(2)* Receivables	*(3)* Inventories	*(4)* Fixed Assets	*(5)* Total Investment	*(6)* Budgeted Profit	*(7)* ROI Objective *(6) ÷ (5)*
A	$10	$20	$30	$60	$120	$24.0	20%
B	20	20	30	50	120	14.4	12
C	15	40	40	10	105	10.5	10
D	5	10	20	40	75	3.8	5
E	10	5	10	10	35	(1.8)	(5)

EVA Method

Business Unit	*(1)* Profit Potential	Current Assets			Fixed Assets			Budgeted EVA *(1) – [(4) + (7)]*
		(2) Amount	*(3)* Rate	*(4)* Required Earnings	*(5)* Amount	*(6)* Rate	*(7)* Required Earnings	
A	24.0	$60	4%	$2.4	$60	10%	$6.0	$15.6
B	14.4	70	4	2.8	50	10	5.0	6.6
C	10.5	95	4	3.8	10	10	1.0	5.7
D	3.8	35	4	1.4	40	10	4.0	(1.6)
E	(1.8)	25	4	1.0	10	10	1.0	(3.8)

needed to service various models of engines. The sales revenues of SPX were declining and the company's stock price was on a downward spiral by 1995. As part of the turnaround, John Bystone implemented EVA as the basis for evaluating and rewarding business units, sending a strong signal that managers should build, hold, harvest, or divest their businesses if the returns exceeded the cost of capital. During the first two years of his tenure, SPX's sales revenues grew and so did its EVA. Between January 1996 and December 1997, the company's stock rose from $15.62 to $66.[11]

Differences between ROI and EVA are shown in Exhibit 6–12. Assume that the company's required rate of return for investing in fixed assets is 10 percent after taxes, and that the companywide cost of money tied up in inventories and receivables is 4 percent after taxes. The top section of Exhibit 6–12 shows the ROI calculation. Columns one through five show the amount of investment in assets that each business unit budgeted for the coming year. Column six is the amount of budgeted profit. Column seven is the

---

[11]"Another GE Veteran Rides to the Rescue," *Fortune,* December 29, 1997.

budgeted profit divided by the budgeted investment; this column, therefore, shows the ROI objectives for the coming year for each of the business units.

Only in Business Unit C is the ROI objective consistent with the companywide cutoff rate, and in no unit is the objective consistent with the companywide 4 percent cost of carrying current assets. Business Unit A would decrease its chances of meeting its profit objective if it did not earn at least 20 percent on added investments in either current or fixed assets, whereas Units D and E would benefit from investments with a much lower return.

EVA corrects these inconsistencies. The investments, multiplied by the appropriate rates (representing the companywide rates), are subtracted from the budgeted profit. The resulting amount is the budgeted EVA. Periodically, the actual EVA is calculated by subtracting from the actual profits the actual investment multiplied by the appropriate rates. The lower section of Exhibit 6–12 shows how the budgeted EVA would be calculated. For example, if Business Unit A earned $28,000 and employed average current assets of $65,000 and average fixed assets of $65,000, its actual EVA would be calculated as follows:

$$EVA = 28,000 - 0.04(65,000) - 0.10(65,000)$$

$$= 28,000 - 2,600 - 6,500$$

$$= 18,900$$

This is $3,300 ($18,900 – $15,600) better than its objective.

Note that if any business unit earns more than 10 percent on added fixed assets, it will increase its EVA. (In the cases of C and D, the additional profit will decrease the amount of negative EVA, which amounts to the same thing.) A similar result occurs for current assets. Inventory decision rules will be based on a cost of 4 percent for financial carrying charges. (Of course, there will be additional costs for physically storing the inventory.) In this way the financial decision rules of the business units will be consistent with those of the company.

EVA solves the problem of differing profit objectives for the same asset in different business units and the same profit objective for different assets in the same unit. The method makes it possible to incorporate in the measurement system the same decision rules used in the planning process: The more sophisticated the planning process, the more complex the EVA calculation can be. For example, assume the capital investment decision rules call for a 10 percent return on general-purpose assets and a 15 percent return on special-purpose assets. Business unit fixed assets can be classified accordingly, and different rates applied when measuring performance. Managers may be reluctant to invest in improved working conditions, pollution-control measures, or other social goals if they perceive them to be unprofitable. Such investments will be much more acceptable to business unit managers if they are expected to earn a reduced return on them.

EXHIBIT 6–13   Use of EVA in Planning and Control

Strategic Direction. IBM applied economic value added to evaluate the strategic plans for key Latin American markets such as Mexico, Brazil, and Argentina.

Acquisitions. In one of the largest acquisitions, AT&T used EVA in deciding on its $12.6 billion purchase of McCaw Cellular.

Operational Improvements. Briggs & Stratton recognized that its return on capital was poor and trending lower. Operations were restructured and economic value added was adopted as a way of focusing managers' attention on how they were employing capital. EVA became the firm's benchmark for product introductions, equipment purchases, supplier arrangements, quality initiatives, and process improvements.

Product Line Discontinuation. Economic value added helped Coca-Cola identify and sell businesses that failed to recoup their cost of capital.

Working Capital Focus. Quaker Oats used economic value added to account for the large dollar amount tied up in finished goods and packaging material inventories.

Cost of Capital Focus. Dow Chemical used economic value added to shed light on what it cost to run its businesses and return a profit.

Incentive Compensation. At Transamerica, 100 percent of the annual bonuses for the CEO and the CFO were based on economic value added.

Source: Excerpted from I. Shaked, A. Michel, and Pierre Leroy, "Creating Value through EVA—Myth or Reality," *Strategy & Business,* Fourth Quarter, 1997, p. 44.

Example.   In 1996 Mitsubishi Corporation, the Japanese multinational with sales revenues of $176 billion, employed investment centers as a management control tool. It divided the company into seven groups and set different targets across the groups. For instance, the Information Technology Group, which was working in the fast-growing field of multimedia, had a low target. The Food Group had a very high target.[12]

Exhibit 6–13 offers examples of how different companies use EVA in planning and control.

Additional Considerations in Evaluating Managers

In view of the disadvantages of ROI, it seems surprising that it is so widely used. We know from personal experience that the conceptual flaws of ROI for performance evaluation are real and contribute to dysfunctional conduct by business unit managers. We are unable to determine the extent of this dysfunctional conduct, however, because few managers are likely to admit its existence and many are unaware of it when it *does* exist.

We strongly advocate the use of EVA as a performance measurement tool. EVA, however, does not solve all the problems of measuring profitability in an investment center. In particular, it does not solve the problem of accounting

---

[12]Joel Kurtzman, "An Interview with Minoru Makihara," *Strategy & Business,* Issue 2, Winter 1996, pp. 86–93.

for fixed assets discussed above unless annuity depreciation is also used, and this is rarely done in practice. If gross book value is used, a business unit can increase its EVA by taking actions contrary to the interests of the company. If net book value is used, EVA will increase simply because of the passage of time. Furthermore, EVA will be temporarily depressed by new investments because of the high net book value in the early years. EVA does solve the problem created by differing profit potentials. All business units, regardless of profitability, will be motivated to increase investments if the rate of return from a potential investment exceeds the required rate prescribed by the measurement system.

Moreover, some assets may be undervalued when they are capitalized, and others when they are expensed. Although the purchase cost of fixed assets is ordinarily capitalized, a substantial amount of investment in start-up costs, new product development, dealer organization, and so forth may be written off as expenses and, therefore, will not appear in the investment base. This situation applies especially to marketing units. In these units the investment amount may be limited to inventories, receivables, and office furniture and equipment. When a group of units with varying degrees of marketing responsibility are ranked, the unit with the relatively larger marketing operations will tend to have the highest EVA.

Considering these problems, some companies have decided to exclude fixed assets from the investment base. These companies make an interest charge for *controllable assets* only, and they control fixed assets by separate devices. Controllable assets are essentially working capital items. Business unit managers can make day-to-day decisions that affect the level of these assets. If these decisions are wrong, serious consequences can occur quickly: For example, if inventories are too high, unnecessary capital is tied up and the risk of obsolescence is increased; if inventories are too low, production interruptions or lost customer business can result from the stock-outs.

Investments in fixed assets are controlled by the capital budgeting process before the fact and by postcompletion audits to determine whether the anticipated cash flows in fact materialized. This is far from completely satisfactory because actual savings or revenues from a fixed asset acquisition may not be identifiable. For example, if a new machine produces a variety of products, the cost accounting system usually will not identify the savings attributable to each product.

Evaluating the Economic Performance of the Entity

Discussion to this point has focused on measuring the performance of business unit managers. As pointed out in Chapter 4, reports on the economic performance of business units are quite different. Management reports are prepared monthly or quarterly, whereas economic performance reports are prepared at irregular intervals, usually once every several years. For reasons stated earlier, management reports tend to use historical information on actual costs incurred, whereas economic reports use quite different information. In this section we discuss the purpose and nature of the economic information.

Economic reports are a diagnostic instrument. They indicate whether the current strategies of the business unit are satisfactory and, if not, whether a decision should be made to do something about the business unit—expand it, shrink it, change its direction, or sell it. The economic analysis of an individual business unit may reveal that current plans for new products, new plant and equipment, or other new strategies, when considered as a whole, will not produce a satisfactory future profit, even though separately each decision seemed sound when it was made.

Economic reports are also made as a basis for arriving at the value of the company as a whole. Such a value is called the *breakup value*—that is, the estimated amount that shareholders would receive if individual business units were sold separately. The breakup value is useful to an outside organization that is considering making a takeover bid for the company, and, of course, it is equally useful to company management in appraising the attractiveness of such a bid. The report indicates the relative attractiveness of the business units and may suggest that senior management is misallocating its scarce time—that is, spending an undue amount of time on business units that are unlikely to contribute much to the company's total profitability. A gap between current profitability and breakup value indicates changes may need to be made. (Alternatively, current profitability may be depressed by costs that will enhance future profitability, such as new product development and advertising, as mentioned earlier.)

The most important difference between the two types of reports is that economic reports focus on future profitability rather than current or past profitability. The book value of assets and depreciation based on the historical cost of these assets is used in the performance reports of managers, despite their known limitations. This information is irrelevant in reports that estimate the future; in these reports, the emphasis is on replacement costs.

Conceptually, the value of a business unit is the present value of its future earnings stream. This is calculated by estimating cash flows for each future year and discounting each of these annual flows at a required earnings rate. The analysis covers five, or perhaps ten, future years. Assets on hand at the end of the period covered are assumed to have a certain value—the *terminal value*—which is discounted and added to the value of the annual cash flows. Although these estimates are necessarily rough, they provide a quite different way of looking at the business units from that conveyed in performance reports.

Summary

Investment centers have all of the measurement problems involved in defining expenses and revenues that were discussed in Chapters 3, 4, and 5. Investment centers raise additional problems regarding how to measure the assets employed, specifically which assets to include, how to value fixed assets and current assets, which depreciation method to use for fixed assets, which corporate assets to allocate, and which liabilities to subtract.

An important goal of a business organization is to optimize return on shareholder equity (i.e., the net present value of future cash flows). It is not practical to use such a measure to evaluate the performance of business unit managers on a monthly or quarterly basis. Accounting rate of return is the best surrogate measure of business unit managers' performance. Economic value added (EVA) is conceptually superior to return on investment (ROI) in evaluating business unit managers.

When setting annual profit objectives, in addition to the usual income statement items, there should be an explicit interest charge against the projected balance of controllable working capital items, principally receivables and inventories. There is considerable debate about the right approach to management control over fixed assets. Reporting on the economic performance of an investment center is quite different from reporting on the performance of the manager in charge of that center.

Suggested Additional Readings

Len, Kenneth, and Anil K. Makhija. "EVA & MVA: As Performance Measures and Signals for Strategic Change." *Strategy & Business* 24, no. 3 (May–June 1996), pp. 34–38.

Merchant, K. A. *Modern Management Control.* Englewood Cliffs, NJ: Prentice Hall, 1998.

Shaked, I., A. Michel, and Pierre Leroy. "Creating Value through EVA—Myth or Reality." *Strategy & Business* 9, Fourth Quarter, 1997, pp. 41–52.

Solomons, David. *Divisional Performance: Measurement and Control.* Burr Ridge, IL: Richard D. Irwin, 1965.

Stern, Joel M. *EVA and Strategic Performance Measurement.* New York: The Conference Board, 1996.

Stewart, G. Bennett, III. "EVA: Fact and Fantasy." *Journal of Applied Corporate Finance,* Summer 1994.

Walsh, Francis J. *Measuring Business-Unit Performance.* Research Bulletin No. 206. New York: The Conference Board, 1987.

CASE 6–1
INVESTMENT CENTER PROBLEMS (A)

1. The ABC Company has three divisions—A, B, and C. Division A is exclusively a marketing division, Division B is exclusively a manufacturing division, and Division C is both a manufacturing and marketing division. The following are the financial facts for each of these divisions:

	Division A	Division B	Division C
Current assets	$100,000	$ 100,000	$100,000
Fixed assets	—	1,000,000	500,000
Total assets	$100,000	$1,100,000	$600,000
Profits before depreciation and market development costs	$200,000	$200,000	$ 200,000

Question

Assume that the ABC Company depreciates fixed assets on a straight-line basis over 10 years. To maintain its markets and productive facilities, it has to invest $100,000 per year in market development in Division A and $50,000 per year in Division C. This is written off as an expense. It also has to replace 10 percent of its productive facilities each year. Under these equilibrium conditions, what are the annual rates of return earned by each of the divisions?

2. The D Division of the DEF Corporation has budgeted aftertax profits of $1 million for

1987. It has budgeted assets as of January 1, 1987, of $10 million, consisting of $4 million in current assets and $6 million in fixed assets. Fixed assets are included in the asset base at gross book value. The net book value of these fixed assets is $3 million. All fixed assets are depreciated over a 10-year period on a straight-line basis.

The manager of the D Division has submitted a capital investment project to replace a major group of machines. The financial details of this project are as follows:

New equipment:	
Estimated cost	$2,000,000
Estimated aftertax annual saving*	300,000
Estimated life	10 years
Old equipment to be replaced:	
Original cost	$1,500,000
Original estimate of life	10 years
Present age	7 years
Present book value ($1,500,000 – $1,050,000)	$ 450,000
Salvage value	0

*These are cash inflows, disregarding depreciation and capital gains or losses (except for their tax impact).

Questions

The capital investment project was approved, and the new machinery was installed on January 1, 1987. Calculate the rate of return that is earned on the new investment, using the divisional accounting rules, and calculate the revised 1987 and 1988 budgeted rate of return:

(a) Assuming that the investment and savings are exactly as stated in the project.

This case was prepared and copyrighted by Professor John Dearden. Suggestions by Jim Reece are incorporated.

Note: In solving these problems, ignore taxes. Most of the problems state that savings or earnings are "after taxes." Assume that the amount of income taxes will not be affected by alternative accounting treatment.

(b) Assuming that the investment is overrun by $500,000 and the annual savings are only $200,000.

Notes to Problem 2:

A. In answering Problem 2, ignore the time value of money in your calculations. Use composite straight-line depreciation over the 10-year period. The essential differences between "composite" and "unit" depreciation are these: (1) Under "unit" depreciation, each asset is accounted for as an individual entity. One result of this is that assets disposed of for more (or less) than their net book value give rise to an accounting gain (or loss), which is included in the profit calculation. (2) Under "group" or "composite" depreciation, a pool of assets is accounted for by applying an annual depreciation rate to the gross book value (i.e., original cost) of the entire pool. When an individual asset is retired, the gross book value of the pool of assets is reduced by the original cost of the asset, and the accumulated depreciation account for the pool is reduced by the difference between the asset's original cost and scrap value, if any (i.e., a retired asset is assumed to be fully depreciated). Thus, any gains or losses from the disposal of assets are "buried" in the accumulated depreciation account and do not flow through the income statement.

B. Assume everything is as stated in Problem 2—*except* that the company used *unit* depreciation. Answer the questions in Problem 2 for the years 1987 and 1988.

3. Assume everything is as stated in Problem 2—except that the fixed assets are included in the divisional assets base at their net book value at the end of the year. Answer the questions in Problem 2 for 1987 and 1988.

Questions

(a) Do Problem 3 using *unit* depreciation.

(b) Do Problem 3 using *composite* depreciation.

(c) Do Problem 3 on the basis that DEF Corporation depreciates the pool of assets on the basis of the sum-of-the-years'-digits method, using composite depreciation. Calculate the rate of return on the new investment for 1987 and 1988 using the divisional accounting rules, assuming that:

  (1) The investment and savings were exactly as stated in the project proposal.

  (2) The investment was overrun by $500,000, and the annual savings were only $200,000.

Incorporate the following numbers to do your calculations:

$$\text{Sum of digits } 1 - 10 = 55$$
$$\$2,000 * 10/55 = \$364$$
$$\$2,000 * 9/55 = \$327$$
$$\$2,500 * 10/55 = \$455$$
$$\$2,500 * 9/55 = \$409$$
$$\$1,500 * 3/55 = \$82$$
$$\$1,500 * 2/55 = \$55$$

4. The G Division of the GHI Corporation proposes the following investment in a new product line:

Investment in fixed assets	$100,000
Annual profits before depreciation but after taxes (i.e., annual cash flow)	25,000
Life	5 years

The GHI Corporation used the time-adjusted rate of return, with a cutoff rate of 8 percent in evaluating its capital investment proposals. A $25,000 cash inflow for five years on an investment of $100,000 has a time-adjusted return of 8 percent. Consequently, the proposed investment is acceptable under the company's criterion. Assume that the project is approved and that the investment and profit were the same as estimated. Assets are included in the divisional investment base at the average of the beginning and end of the year's net book value.

Questions

(a) Calculate the rate of return that is earned by the G Division on the new investment for each year and the average rate for the five years, using straight-line depreciation.

(b) Calculate the rate of return that is earned by the G Division on the new investment for each year, and the average for the five years using the sum-of-the-years'-digits depreciation.

5. A proposed investment of $100,000 in fixed assets is expected to yield aftertax cash flows of $16,275 a year for 10 years. Calculate a depreciation schedule, based on annuity-type depreciation, that provides an equal rate of return each year on the investment at the beginning of the year, assuming that the investment and earnings are the same as estimated.

6. The JKL Company used the economic value added method for measuring divisional profit performance. The company charges each division a 5 percent return on its average current assets and a 10 percent return on its average fixed assets. Listed below are some financial statistics for three divisions of the JKL Company.

	Division		
	J	K	L
Budget-data ($000s):			
1987 budgeted profit	$ 90	$ 55	$ 50
1987 budgeted current assets	100	200	300
1987 budgeted fixed assets	400	400	500

	Division		
	J	K	L
Actual data ($000s):			
1987 profits	$ 80	$ 60	$ 50
1987 current assets	90	190	350
1987 fixed assets	400	450	550

Questions

(a) Calculate the ROI objective and actual ROI for each division for 1987.

(b) Calculate the EVA objective for each division for 1987.

(c) Calculate the actual EVA for each division for 1987 and calculate the extent that it is above or below objective.

7. Refer to the budgeted profits and assets of the three divisions of the JKL Company provided in Problem 6. Listed below are four management actions, together with the financial impact of these actions. For each of these situations, calculate the impact on the budgeted ROI and EVA for each division. (Another way of looking at this problem is to calculate the extent to which these actions help or hurt the divisional managers in attaining their profit goals.)

Situation 1. An investment in fixed assets is made. This action increases the average fixed assets by $100,000 and profits by $10,000.

Situation 2. An investment in fixed assets is made. This action increases the average assets by $100,000 and profits by $7,000.

Situation 3. A program to reduce inventories is instituted. As a result, inventories are reduced by $50,000. Increased costs and reduced sales resulting from the lower inventory levels reduce profits by $5,000.

Situation 4. A plant is closed down and sold. Fixed assets are reduced by $75,000, and profits (from reduced sales) are decreased by $7,500.

CASE 6–2
INVESTMENT CENTER PROBLEMS (B)

1. The Complete Office Company has three divisions: Layout and Marketing, Office Furniture, and Office Supplies. Layout and Marketing is primarily a consulting and sales group with no fixed assets and minimal current assets. Office Furniture is a manufacturing division with machinery for the production and assembly of desks, chairs, and modular dividers. The Office Supplies Division has light machinery for the packaging and distribution of paper and other office supplies. It has current assets in the form of inventory and receivables, and it has some fixed assets in the form of machinery.

The Complete Office Company depreciates all of its fixed assets over 10 years on a straight-line basis, and it calculates ROA on beginning-of-year gross book value of assets. The operating expenses for each division (besides depreciation on fixed assets) are $200,000 for Layout and Marketing, $100,000 for Office Furniture, and $150,000 for Office Supplies. The company's assets and gross profits for 1997 are as follows:

	Layout and Marketing	Office Furniture	Office Supplies
Current assets	$ 200,000	$ 200,000	$200,000
Fixed assets	—	1,000,000	500,000
Total assets	200,000	1,200,000	700,000
Gross profit from sales	400,000	400,000	400,000

This case was prepared by Professor Ed Barrett, Thunderbird Graduate School of Management, Phoenix, AZ. Copyright by Ed Barrett.

Question

Please compute an ROA figure for each division for 1997.

2. The manager of the Big Spender Division of Growing Industries has received formal approval to buy a specific new machine for his division. Given the following assumed data excerpted from his capital expenditure request, what ROAs (based on gross book value) will his division earn for 1996 and 1997?

Data Excerpted from Capital Expenditure Request:

(1) Budgeted aftertax profits of $3,000,000 per year.

(2) January 1, 1996, budgeted assets of $30,000,000, consisting of $12,000,000 in current assets and $18,000,000 in fixed assets, at gross book value.

(3) Net book value of the existing fixed assets was $9,000,000.

(4) All fixed assets are depreciated over 10 years on a straight-line depreciation method. There are no noncash expenses or revenues other than depreciation, and the same depreciation method is used for tax and books.

(5) Data relevant to the new equipment:

Budgeted cost	$6,000,000
Estimated annual aftertax saving*	900,000
Estimated depreciable life	10 years
Date of expected purchase	1/1/96

*These are cash inflows net of all tax impacts. That is, they are computed so as to disregard depreciation and book gains or losses except for their tax impact.

(6) Data relative to the old equipment to be replaced:

Gross book value	$4,500,000
Depreciable life	10 years
Present age	7 years
Depreciation taken to date	3,150,000
Salvage value	—

3. The manager of the Big Spender Division did install his new machine. What ROA was really earned in 1996 and 1997 if his machine had installation cost overruns of $1,500,000 and produced cost savings of only $600,000 per year? (All other facts are the same as in Problem 2.)

4. Assume that instead of calculating ROA on gross book value, all divisions of Growing Industries calculated ROA using end-of-year net book values. How would that change the projected results for the Big Spender Division? (Use the same projections as in Problem 2.)

5. Again, assume that Growing Industries calculates ROA on net book values at end of year. The manager of the Big Spender Division finds that he has a $1,500,000 installation cost overrun and only $600,000 savings per year. How will his actual ROA look for 1996 and 1997?

6. Ace Corporation allows the managers of its divisions a good deal of freedom in choosing their method of computing ROA, as long as the method chosen is consistent from year to year so that performance in each of the years can be compared.

The new manager of the Diamond Division of Ace Corporation wanted the books to show him managing a relatively large amount of assets and showing improved year-to-year results, so for calculating ROA he used *beginning*-of-year book values and straight-line depreciation so that the assets would show the highest net book value. The Diamond Division had just been formed to run a new machine which cost $10,000,000, was expected to have a five-year life, and it was hoped to produce after-tax cash inflows of $2,500,000 per year.

Questions

(a) What will the new manager's ROA on this machine be for the five years of its expected life?

(b) What will be the average ROA?

(c) If the new manager's bonus was calculated as $100 for each percent of ROA, what would his bonus be in each year?

(d) What is the IRR on this project?

7. The more experienced manager of the Spade Division of Ace Corporation also wants to look good. He's also interested, however, in demonstrating that the bonus plan is not well conceived. He chooses to employ *end*-of-year net book values for calculating his ROA.

Questions

If the Spade Division were to buy the same machine with the same life, depreciation, and expected aftertax cash inflows as shown in Problem 6:

(a) Calculate the manager's ROA for the five years of expected life of the machine.

(b) What would be the average ROA?

(c) What would be *his* bonuses if they were also calculated on the basis of $100 for each percent of ROA each year?

(d) What is the IRR on this project?

8. The far older and wiser manager of the Heart Division of Ace Corporation decided to depreciate the $10,000,000 in new assets in his division over five years using the sum-of-the-years' digits method. He also decides to use beginning-of-the-year net book values. His ma-

chines also are expected to produce aftertax cash inflows of $2,500,000 per year.

Questions

(a) What would be the manager's ROA each year?

(b) What would be the average ROA?

(c) What would his bonuses be over the five-year period?

(d) What is the IRR?

9. The corporate management of Ace Corporation later decided to try a different type of machine investment. The machine involved in this decision would last 10 years, although it would have aftertax cash inflows of only $1,627,500 per year. The machine cost $10,000,000. The financial staff chose to use an annuity method of depreciation. (In this method, the depreciation *increases* each year as the machine grows older. In concept, the net book value and the return—after depreciation—on the machine *decrease* commensurately, so as to help create a consistent ROA over the life of the machine.)

Questions

(a) Please construct an annuity depreciation schedule that provides an equal ROA (using net book value of assets at the beginning of the year) for each of the expected 10 years' life of the project.

(b) What advantages or disadvantages do you see with this methodology?

10. The Ultima Company employs a return-on-investment (ROI) methodology to measure divisional performance. "Investment" in their calculations consists of a figure representing average annual current assets plus average annual fixed assets. Following are both the budgeted and then the actual data for five divisions of Ultima Company for the year 1997 (in thousands of dollars).

Divisions	Budgeted Profits	Budgeted Average Current Assets	Budgeted Average Fixed Assets
A	90	100	400
B	55	200	400
C	50	300	500
D	100	200	800
E	150	400	800

Divisions	Actual Profits	Actual Average Current Assets	Actual Average Fixed Assets
A	80	90	400
B	60	190	450
C	50	350	550
D	105	200	800
E	155	200	800

Questions

(a) Please compute budgeted ROI for each division.

(b) Please compute actual ROI for each division.

(c) Comment on the comparison of the two sets of results.

11. Some new managers at Ultima Company feel that there should be a way to measure divisional performance, taking into account the basic cost of capital. They suggest running the same numbers for Ultima as in Problem 10, based on the concept of economic value added, charging 5 percent for the usage of current assets and 10 percent for the usage of fixed assets.

Questions

Using the budgeted and actual figures for Ultima Company from Problem 10, and using the charges for capital given above:

(a) Please compute budgeted EVA for each division.

(b) Please compute actual EVA for each division.

(c) Comment on the comparison of the two sets of results, and a comparison with the results of Problem 10.

12. The Ultima Company decides to make an investment in fixed assets costing $100,000. This investment is expected to produce profits of $10,000 per year. How would this investment help the managers of each division attain their budgeted ROI and EVA goals if this project were added to their divisions?

Questions

Using the budgeted figures for Ultima Company in Problem 10, please find the impact of this project on:

(a) Budgeted ROI goals of each division.

(b) Budgeted EVA goals of each division.

(c) Please analyze the resulting data.

13. If, instead of making an investment in fixed assets, the Ultima Company decides to make an investment in current assets of $100,000 with an expected profit of $7,000 per year, how would that affect its budgets?

Questions

Using the figures given in Problem 10, please compute:

(a) Budgeted ROI for 1997.

(b) Budgeted EVA for 1997.

(c) Please analyze the resulting data.

14. If, instead of expanding operations, Ultima Company decides to retrench in a declining market, what would be the effect on budgeted ROI and EVA of reducing inventories by $50,000? It is expected that slightly increased delivery costs and definitely reduced sales will result in profits lowered by $5,000 per year.

Questions

Starting with the figures for Ultima Company given in Problem 10, please calculate the effect these changes would have on:

(a) Budgeted ROI in 1997.

(b) Budgeted EVA in 1997.

(c) Your analysis of the resultant data.

15. If, instead of reducing inventories, Ultima Company prefers to handle its retrenchment by selling a plant, it will reduce fixed assets by $75,000. It is expected that this move will also decrease sales by $5,000 per year.

Questions

What will be the effect of this move on the data about Ultima Company given in Problem 10?

(a) Please compute the effect this sale will have on ROI in 1997.

(b) Please compute the effect this sale will have on EVA in 1997.

(c) Please analyze and comment upon the resultant data.

CASE 6–3
QUALITY METAL SERVICE CENTER

In early March 1982, the casewriter met with Edward Brown, president and chief executive officer of Quality Metal Service Center (Quality). Following is an excerpt of their conversation:

> *Brown:* It has been quite a while since we took a hard look at our planning and control systems. Since you have a special interest in this area, I thought you might want to spend some time examining our systems.
>
> *Casewriter:* Do you perceive any weaknesses in your current systems?
>
> *Brown:* I'm not sure. Though I am satisfied with our past performance, I believe that we are capable of achieving even higher levels of sales and profits. Considering the market expansion and the state of competition, I feel we might have missed out on some growth opportunities. I don't know if our controls have inhibited managers from pursuing our goals of aggressive growth and above-average return on assets, as compared to the industry, but you might keep that in mind while evaluating our systems.

The Metal Distribution Industry[†]

Service centers bought metals from many of the mills including USS, Bethlehem, Alcoa, Reynolds, and such smaller firms as Crucible, Northwestern, and Youngstown. These suppliers sold their products in large lots, thereby op-

timizing the efficiencies associated with large production runs. Service centers sold their products to metal users in smaller lots and on a short lead-time basis.

The metal distribution industry was generally regarded as a mature, highly competitive, and fragmented industry. All the same, the percentage of industrial steel products shipped through service centers had increased dramatically during 1974–82. In 1982, about 22 million tons were shipped through service centers, accounting for approximately 33 percent of all steel shipments in the United States, up from 18 percent in 1974. There were a number of key trends in the metal industry that were enhancing service centers' growth potential.

Steel Mill's Retrenchment. In their efforts to become more competitive through increased productivity, most of the major domestic metals producers had been scaling back product lines by dropping low-volume specialty products. Further, they had cut back on service to customers by reducing sales force size and technical support. Full-line service centers, recognizing that many customers preferred to deal with only a few primary suppliers, had profited from this trend by maintaining wide product lines and increasing customer service.

Just-in-Time Inventory Management. Given the high cost of ownership and maintenance of inventory, most metal users attempted to reduce their costs by lowering their levels of raw materials inventories ("just-in-time" inventory management). This resulted in smaller order quantities and more frequent deliveries. Metal service centers had a natural advantage over the mills here because inventory was the service center's stock-in-trade.

This case was prepared and copyrighted by Vijay Govindarajan.

[†]The sections marked with a dagger are taken from Michael Simpson, "Opportunities for Innovation in the Metals Industry," *Journal of Business Strategy,* Summer 1986, pp. 84–87.

While the service center's price was always higher than buying from the mills, customers were increasingly willing to pay the extra charge. They recognized that the savings they generated from lower inventories and handling costs, plus reduced scrap and risk of obsolescence, would lower the total cost of getting the metal into their production system.

Productivity Improvement and Quality Enhancement.   Quality and productivity had become overriding issues with metal users. They had implemented major quality and productivity improvement programs aimed at increasing both the reputation of their products and the overall profitability of operations. In their attempt to focus on quality, end users were reducing the number of suppliers with whom they did business and were concentrating their purchases with those that were best able to meet their specific quality, availability, and service requirements. End users found that closer relationships with fewer suppliers resulted in better quality conformance and stronger ties between supplier and customer as each sought to maximize the long-term benefits of the relationship.

Quality Metal's Strategy†

Quality Metals had been established a century ago as a local metals distributor. Since then, it had grown into a firm with national distribution, and its sales in 1981 were well over $300 million. Quality's business strategy provided the framework for the development of specific goals and objectives. According to Mr. Brown, three fundamental objectives guided Quality.

Objective 1: To Focus Sales Efforts on Targeted Markets of Specialty Metal Users. During the 1970s, Quality recognized that it could compete much more effectively in specialty product lines of its own selection than in the broader commodity carbon steel markets where price was the primary determining fac-

tor. Consequently, Quality decided to diminish its participation in commodity product lines and redeploy those resources into higher-technology metals, such as carbon alloy bars, stainless steel, aluminum, nickel alloys, titanium, copper, and brass, which offered higher returns and had less-effective competition. More than 60 percent of its revenues were derived from higher-technology metals in 1982, compared with 29 percent in 1972.

Quality had made a long-term commitment to high-technology metal users. The company's recent introduction of titanium, a natural adjunct to the existing product line, was indicative of the company's strategy of bringing new products to the market to meet the needs of existing customers. Previously, titanium was not readily available on the distributor market. Quality planned to continue to diversify into complementary higher-technology products as new customer requirements arose.

Objective 2: To Identify Those Industries and Geographic Markets Where These Metals Were Consumed.   To identify more accurately the major industries and geographies for these products, Quality developed the industry's first metal usage data base in the early 1980s. Mr. Brown believed that this data base, which was continually refined and updated, was the most accurate in the country. Its use enabled Quality to profile product consumption by industry and by geography. It also enabled the company to analyze total market demand on a nationwide basis and to project potential sales on a market-by-market basis. As a result, Quality had a competitive edge in determining where customers were located and what products they were buying. It used this information in selecting locations for opening new service centers.

Objective 3: To Develop Techniques and Marketing Programs That Would Increase Market Share.   To build market share, Quality offered programs that assisted its customers in implementing just-in-time inventory management systems coordinated with their materials requirement planning programs. The company worked with customer representatives in purchasing, manufacturing, and quality assurance to determine their precise requirements for product specifications, quantities, and delivery schedules.

Similarly, Quality emphasized value-added business by offering a wide range of processing services for its customers, such as saw cutting to specific sizes, flame cutting into both pattern and nonpattern shapes, flattening, surface grinding, shearing, bending, edge conditioning, polishing, and thermal treatment. Because of Quality's volume, the sophisticated equipment required for these production steps was operated at a lower cost per unit than most customer-owned equipment.

Organizational Structure

Since the Great Depression, Quality had experienced rapid sales growth and geographical expansion. In 1982, Quality operated in 27 locations, situated in markets representing about 75 percent of metal consumption in the United States. Consistent with this growth was the necessity to decentralize line functions. The firm currently had 4 regions, each of which had about 6 districts for a total of 23 districts. There were staff departments in finance, marketing, operations, and human resources. A partial organizational structure is given in Exhibit 1.

Typically, a district manager had under him a warehouse superintendent, a sales manager, a credit manager, a purchasing manager, and an administration manager (Exhibit 1). The decision-making authorities of these managers are described below:

The Warehouse Superintendent oversees transportation, loading and unloading, storage, and reproduction processing.

The Sales Manager coordinates a staff that includes "inside" salespersons who establish contacts and take orders over the phone, and an "outside" team who make direct customer contacts and close large deals. Sales price and discount terms are generally established by the District Manager; freight adjustments are also made at the district level.

The Credit Manager assesses the risk of new customer accounts, approves customer credit periods within a range established by corporate headquarters, and enforces customer collections.

The Purchasing Manager acquires inventory from the regional warehouse, other districts, and outside companies. Districts have freedom to purchase from outside suppliers. However, senior management has established Economic Order Quantity guidelines for the purchase of inventory, and metals are stocked in a district warehouse only if local demand is sufficient to justify it. Within this overall constraint, the Purchasing Manager has authority to choose suppliers and negotiate credit terms, although payments to suppliers are handled centrally at the home office.

Capital expenditures in excess of $5,000 and all capital leasing decisions require corporate approval.

Responsibility Allocation and Performance Measurement

District managers were responsible for attaining predetermined return on asset (ROA) levels, which were agreed to at the beginning of the year. The following items were included in the asset base for ROA calculations.

1. Land, warehouse buildings, and equipment were included in the asset base at gross book value.
2. Leased buildings and equipment (except for leased trucks) were included in the asset base at the capitalized lease value. (Leased trucks were not capitalized; rather, lease expenses on trucks were reported as an operating expense.)
3. Average inventory, in units, was calculated. The replacement costs, based on current mill price schedules, were determined for these units and included in the asset base.
4. Average accounts receivable balance for the period was included in the asset base. (Cash was excluded from district's assets; the amounts were trivial.)

EXHIBIT 1
Partial organizational chart

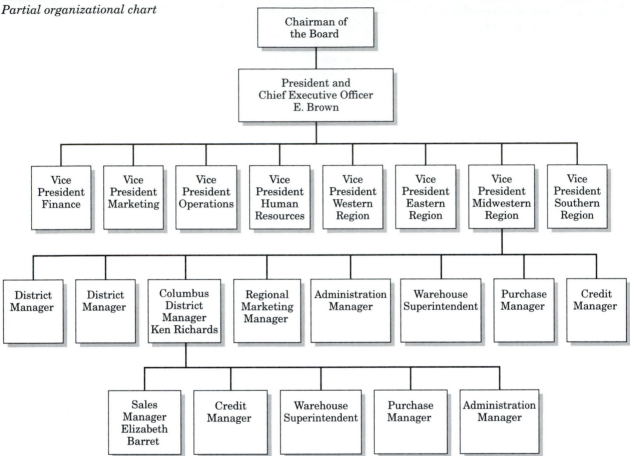

5. As a general rule, accounts payable was not deducted from the asset base. However, an adjustment was made if the negotiated credit period was greater than the company standard of 30 days. If this occurred, "deferred inventory," a contra-asset account, was deducted from the amount of the inventory value for the period in excess of the 30-day standard. This was equivalent to a reduction of inventory asset corresponding to the excess credit period. For example, if a district negotiated a credit period of 50 days, then the inventory expenditure was removed from the asset base for 20 days. However, a penalty was not assessed if the negotiated credit period was less than the 30-day company standard.

Income before taxes, for each district, was calculated in accordance with generally accepted accounting principles, except for cost of sales, which was calculated based on current inventory replacement values. Expenses were separated into controllable and noncontrollable categories. Controllable expenses included such items as warehouse labor and sales commis-

---

EXHIBIT 2   Incentive Calculation Procedure

Step 1: Measure actual asset base and compare it with targeted asset base.
   If actual assets exceed targeted assets, multiply excess by the targeted ROA for the district and charge this amount to profits.

$$\text{Assets overemployed} * \text{District ROA target} = \text{Charge to profits}$$

   If actual assets are less than targeted assets, multiply difference by the district's ROA target and credit this to profits.

$$\text{Assets underemployed} * \text{District ROA target} = \text{Credit to profits}$$

Step 2: Adjusted profits, are compared with 90% of the original profit objective.

$$\text{Adjusted profits} - (90\% \text{ of objective}) = \text{Incentive profits}$$

Step 3: Incentive profit ÷ 90% of objective = Payout rate
Step 4: Payout rate * Manager's base salary = Bonus payable
Step 5: Bonuses are awarded on the basis of incentive profits. If incentive profits are less than zero, no bonus is awarded. The bonus increases in proportion to incentive profit, with a maximum bonus of 75 percent of manager's base salary.

---

sions; noncontrollable expenses included rent, utilities, and property taxes.

No corporate overhead expenses were allocated to the districts. A few years earlier, the company had considered a proposal to allocate corporate overheads to the districts. However, the proposal had been rejected on the grounds that the "allocation bases" were arbitrary and that such expenses could not be controlled at the district level.

Performance Evaluation and Incentives

ROA was the sole performance criterion for evaluation of district managers. The incentive bonus for district managers was based on a formula that rigidly tied the bonus to meeting and exceeding 90 percent of their ROA targets. Exhibit 2 contains the detailed procedure used to calculate the incentive bonus. The calculations determine an applicable payout rate, which was then multiplied by the district manager's base salary to yield the amount of the bonus award. Thus, the size of the bonus depended on (1) the amount of the manager's base salary and (2) how far 90 percent of the ROA target was exceeded; there was a maximum bonus amount.

The bonus of a district manager was also affected by his or her region's performance. In 1982, 75 percent of a district manager's bonus was based on district performance, and 25 percent was based on his or her region's performance. The bonus of the district manager's staff was based solely on the performance of that district.

Meeting with the Columbus District Manager

A few days after speaking with Mr. Brown, the casewriter visited Ken Richards, the district manager for the Columbus Service Center. Mr. Brown recommended him as one of the company's brightest and most successful district managers. The district had been highly successful in recent years, consistently earning well above 30 percent ROA (pretax).

Exhibit 3   Memorandum

To: Kenneth Richards, District Manager

From: Elizabeth Barret, Sales Manager

Subject: Purchase of Processing Equipment

This district, at present, sells no inventory that has been altered through preproduction processing. Such alterations can be made at other districts with processing capabilities, but many customers in this area complain that because of transportation time, the lead times are too great to satisfy their needs in acquiring such inventory.

Market research has established that a reasonable demand for processed inventory exists within this district. Therefore, our district should consider obtaining the processing equipment necessary to satisfy this demand.

The economics of this project is summarized in the attached sheet [Exhibit 4]. Let me provide some information as background for these calculations.

We can acquire the equipment for $600,000. Since its expected life is 10 years (negligible salvage value), Quality would benefit from a 10% Investment Tax Credit, making the net investment equal to $540,000.

Sales projections were made by the district's sales department, and costs were based upon the experiences of districts with processing capabilities. Growth in sales and costs include a 7% inflation factor and projected increases in production.

Annual cash flows are calculated by adjusting Earnings after Taxes to account for depreciation, which is expensed by the sum-of-the-years'-digit method, and growth in Working Capital investment, which is calculated using our standard 20% of sales on incremental growth. The resultant end-of-year cash flows, discounted at the cost of capital of 15% (which is the rate head office requires on projects in similar risk classes), yield a positive net present value of $286,000. The payback period for this project is 4.5 years, which is well within the company's criterion of 10 years.

This investment is worth your careful consideration, Ken. This district has the opportunity to expand into a new market and to benefit from favorable earnings and positive sales growth.

I hope you will submit this proposal to the home office for consideration. Please let me know if you have any questions.

Sd/-
Elizabeth Barret

For 1982, Ken Richards's targeted figure for operating profit was $3.8 million; targeted assets were set at $10 million. He felt that an ROA of 38 percent was reachable, considering historical performance and market opportunities.

As of March 1982, Ken was reviewing a capital investment proposal (for the purchase of new processing equipment), which he had received from his sales manager (Exhibits 3 and 4). Before submitting the proposal to corporate headquarters for approval, Ken wanted to make sure that the new investment would have a favorable effect on his incentive bonus for 1982. Using 1982 profit and asset targets as the benchmark, he compared his incentive bonus for 1982 with and without the new investment. These calculations are shown in Exhibit 5.

EXHIBIT 4   **Columbus District Processing Equipment Proposal**

	1982	1983	1984	1985	1986	1987	1988	1989	1990	1991
I. Cash flows (000s)										
Sales *(1)*	$ 600	1,375	1,510	1,665	1,830	2,010	2,215	2,435	2,680	2,945
Cost of sales	$(560)	(1,145)	(1,236)	(1,355)	(1,490)	(1,660)	(1,845)	(2,051)	(2,290)	(2,545)
Earnings before taxes	40	230	274	310	340	350	370	384	390	400
Tax at 50%	$ (20)	(115)	(137)	(155)	(170)	(175)	(185)	(192)	(195)	(200)
Earnings after taxes	20	115	137	155	170	175	185	192	195	200
Depreciation	110	100	85	75	65	55	45	35	20	10
Working capital investment *(2)*	$(120)	(155)	(25)	(35)	(30)	(35)	(45)	(40)	(50)	535
Cash flow	$10	60	197	195	205	195	185	187	165	745
(1) Revenue for 1982 reflects 3-month start-up period										
(2) Working capital investment										
20% of sales	$ 120	275	300	335	365	400	445	485	535	590
Old level	0	120	275	300	335	365	400	445	485	535
Increase in working capital	$(120)	(155)	(25)	(35)	(30)	(35)	(45)	(40)	(50)	(55)
Recovery of working capital										590
Net incremental investment in working capital	$(120)	(155)	(25)	(35)	(30)	(35)	(45)	(40)	(50)	535

II. Project evaluation

  A. Payback period: 4.5 years

  B. Internal rate of return: 21.8%

  C. Net present value (at 15% cost of capital): $286,000

Questions

1. Is the capital investment proposal described in Exhibit 3 an attractive one for Quality Metal Service Center?

2. Should Ken Richards send that proposal to home office for approval?

3. Comment on the general usefulness of ROA as the basis of evaluating district managers' performance. Could this performance measure be made more effective?

4. In deciding the investment base for evaluating managers of investment centers, the general question is: What practices will motivate the district managers to use their assets most efficiently and to acquire the proper amount and kind of new assets? Presumably, when his return on assets is being measured, the district manager will try to increase his ROA, and we desire that the actions he takes toward this end be actions that are in the best interest of

EXHIBIT 5   Incentive Bonus for Columbus District Manager for 1982

A. Incentive Bonus for 1982 without the New Project

	Target for 1982	Projected Actual for 1982*
Profit	$ 3,800,000	$ 3,800,000
Asset	$10,000,000	$10,000,000

Incentive profit = Actual profit – (90% of targeted profit)

= $3,800,000 – $3,420,000 = $380,000

$$\text{Payout rate} = \frac{\text{Incentive profit}}{90\% \text{ of targeted profit}}$$

$380,000/$3,420,000 = 11.1%

Therefore, incentive bonus without the new project = 11.1% of base salary.

*Assumes that actual results exactly meet the targets in 1982.

B. Incentive Bonus for 1982 with the New Project

	Target for 1982	Projected Actual for 1982†
Profit	$ 3,800,000	$ 3,840,000
Asset	$ 10,000,000	$10,720,000

Step 1: Actual assets – Target assets = Asset overemployed

$10,720,000 – $10,000,000 = $720,000

Step 2: Asset overemployed * District ROA target

= Change to profits

$720,000 * 0.38 = $273,600

Actual profits – Charge to profits = Adjusted profits

$3,840,000 – $273,600 = $3,566,400

Step 3: Adjusted profits – 90% of targeted profit

= Incentive profit

$3,566,400 – $3,420,000 = $146,400

Step 4: $\dfrac{\text{Incentive profit}}{90\% \text{ of targeted profit}}$ = Payout rate

$$\frac{\$146,400}{\$3,420,000} = 4.28\%$$

Therefore, incentive bonus with the new project = 4.28% of base salary.

†Reflects marginal effects of project implementation *only*—that is, an addition of earnings before taxes of $40,000 and an addition to assets of $720,000 (equipment $600,000 plus working capital $120,000). Otherwise, assumes that other district operations meet targets exactly in 1982.

the whole corporation. Given this general line of reasoning, evaluate the way Quality computes the "investment base" for its districts. For each asset category, discuss whether the basis of measurement used by the company is the best for the purpose of measuring districts' return on assets. What are the likely motivational problems that could arise in such a system? What can you recommend to overcome such dysfunctional effects?

5. While computing district profits for performance evaluation purposes, should there be a charge for income taxes? Should corporate overheads be allocated to districts? Should profits be computed on the basis of historical costs or on the basis of replacement costs? Evaluate these issues from the standpoint of their motivational impact on the district managers.

6. Evaluate Quality's incentive compensation system. Does the present system motivate district managers to make decisions which are consistent with the strategy of the firm? If not, make specific recommendations to improve the system.

CASE 6–4
ALOHA PRODUCTS

"I'm completely fed up. How am I supposed to run a profitable plant when I don't have any control over the price of my inputs and none over the volume, price, or mix of my outputs? I'm held hostage by the whims of the purchasing and marketing departments. I didn't go to business school so I could be evaluated on the basis of someone else's performance."

> Lisa Anderson
> Aloha Products Plant Manager, Dayton, Ohio
> October 1994

Aloha Products, founded in 1910 and headquartered in Columbus, Ohio, sold its own brands of coffee throughout the Midwestern and Middle Atlantic states. In 1994, the sales revenues of the company were $150 million. The company's stock was closely held by members of the founder's family. The president and the secretary-treasurer were part of the family and the only members of the management team to have equity stakes.

The Coffee Industry

Coffee in its raw state is referred to by buyers and sellers as "green coffee." This refers to the green beans that are picked from the coffee trees. There are two types of coffee beans: arabica and robusta. Arabica, a favorite of American consumers, is grown primarily in South America. Robusta coffee's major grower is the Ivory Coast. It has a stronger flavor than arabica and is favored by processors who make instant coffee. Thus, as demand for instant coffee has increased, so has demand for robusta beans.

This case was written by Ruthard C. Murphy (T'93) and Anil R. Chitkara (T'94) under the supervision of Professors Vijay Govindarajan and Robert N. Anthony. The case is based on an earlier Note on Coffee prepared by Scott Barrett (T'89) and an earlier case prepared by Russell H. Hassler, Harvard University.

Suppliers.   Coffee generally is grown in tropical regions. Brazil, the largest producer, supplies 20 to 30 percent of the world's green coffee. Other large exporting countries include Colombia, Indonesia, the Ivory Coast, and Mexico. Coffee is harvested somewhere in the world almost every month of the year. For example, Brazil harvests coffee April through September, Colombia from October into March, and the Ivory Coast from November into April.

Buyers.   The United States is the world's largest single importer of coffee. It buys most of its coffee from Brazil and Colombia. Europe is second, purchasing a little less than half of all coffee exported.

Buyers fall into two categories: roasters and brokers. Roasters include large food processing companies such as Philip Morris (which acquired General Foods, including its Maxwell House brand), P&G, and Nestlé, as well as regional and local coffee companies. Large players purchase their coffee supplies directly from the growers. Their financial strength generally allows them to negotiate favorable terms with the growers and to inventory coffee stock as protection against future price increases.

Smaller coffee processors normally buy their coffee from brokers—either a "pure" broker or a trade firm. Pure brokers don't actually purchase the coffee; they merely match buyer and seller in the marketplace. Trade firms do purchase coffee from its country of origin and then sell it to a food processor. Generally, they finance their transactions through secured loans from commercial banks. These banks usually allow a creditworthy company to borrow 80 to 90 percent of the market value (based on the spot price) of the coffee purchased. The bank holds the title to the coffee until the trade firm sells the product to end users. Once the loan is repaid, the trade firm takes the remaining proceeds of the sale as profit.

For large and small buyers, the coffee business is a relationship business. Developing strong relationships with the growers is important to maintain a steady supply of coffee. Although coffee is a commodity product and, as such, its supply and demand depend on price, one cannot fly down to Colombia and expect to buy a million bags of coffee easily. Growers want to deal with buyers they trust and vice versa.

A strong relationship provides two things: information about the coffee market and an inside track on a grower's crop. This is especially important if a roaster needs a certain type of coffee (e.g., Colombian mild) to maintain a standard blend of ground coffee that will keep consumers drinking "to the last drop."

Factors Affecting Price.   Weather, specifically frost and drought, is the most important factor affecting production and hence price for Western Hemisphere coffees. The commodity sections in most major newspapers often carry stories concerning the effect of weather on harvests. Coffee crops from Eastern Hemisphere countries most often are damaged by insects. The level of coffee inventories in major producing and consuming countries is another important market consideration. Actual or threatened dock strikes may cause a buildup of coffee stocks at a port of exit. Marketing policies of various exporting countries also affect prices. On the consumer side, high retail prices or concerns about health can reduce consumption, which, in turn, may exert downward pressure on prices.

The Futures Market.   Futures markets for coffee exist in New York, London, and Paris. In New York coffee futures are traded on the Coffee, Sugar, and Cocoa Exchange. Predicting prices and availability of green coffee beans entails considerable uncertainty. Thus, the normal use of the coffee futures market is to set up a hedge to protect one's inventory position against price fluctuations. A hedge is commonly defined as the establishment of a position in the futures market approximately equal to, but in the opposite direction of, a commitment in the cash market (also known as the physical, or actual, commodity). Only 2 percent of all futures contracts result in actual delivery of coffee beans. The majority of contracts are closed out by purchasing a contract in the opposite direction or by selling one's own contract.

For example, a company that owns an inventory of coffee establishes a short position in the futures market. This position offsets a drop in the value of the firm's inventory in case coffee prices decline. The short position obligates the holder to sell coffee at a predetermined price at some future date. If, in the future, coffee prices drop, the short position increases in value because the holder locked in at a higher sales price. This offsets the decline in value of the actual coffee inventory. It is virtually impossible to set up a perfect hedge position because of imperfections between the physical and futures markets, but the markets do protect the value of one's inventory.

Hedging also allows coffee merchants to get bank credit. Banks seldom lend money to commodity holders who do not attempt to hedge their positions properly.

Coffee Consumption Trends.   Per capita coffee consumption has declined precipitously since 1965. Exhibit 1 shows US liquid consumption in several drink categories. While overall coffee consumption declined, specialty premium and gourmet coffees bucked this trend and sold well. Gourmet coffee sales alone climbed from approximately $500 million in 1987 to $780 million in 1992. During this period, total coffee sales moved only from $6.3 billion to $6.8 billion. Specialty brands attracted new coffee consumers who were younger and more affluent than the coffee drinkers of 30 years earlier.

EXHIBIT 1   A Generation of Evolving Tastes—US Liquid Consumption Trends (gallons per capita)

	1965	1975	1985	1990
Soft drinks	17.8	26.3	40.8	47.5
Coffee[1]	**37.8**	**33.0**	**25.8**	**25.2**
Beer	15.9	21.6	23.8	23.4
Milk	24.0	21.8	19.8	19.0
Tea[1]	3.8	7.3	7.3	7.2
Bottled water	—	1.2	5.2	8.8
Juices	6.3	6.8	7.4	6.9
Powdered drinks	—	4.8	6.2	5.3
Wine[2]	1.0	1.7	2.4	2.0
Distilled spirits	1.5	2.0	1.8	1.4
Subtotal	108.1	126.5	140.5	146.7
Imputed water consumption	74.4	56.0	42.0	35.8
Total	182.5	182.5	182.5	182.5

[1]Data are based on 3-year moving averages to counterbalance inventory swings, and to show consumption more realistically.
[2]1985 and 1990 figures include wine coolers.
Source: Beverage Industry—*Annual Manual 1992.*

Gourmet and premium coffees accounted for 19 percent of total consumption in 1992, and this percentage was expected to increase in the future.

Many small firms stepped in to both create and take advantage of this shift in consumer preference. One of them was Seattle-based Starbucks Coffee Company. Starbucks purchased and roasted high-quality whole bean coffees and sold them, along with fresh-brewed coffee, a variety of pastries and confections, and coffee-related accessories and equipment, primarily through its company-operated retail stores. To ensure compliance with its rigorous coffee standards, Starbucks purchased green coffee beans for its many blends from coffee-producing regions throughout the world and custom roasted them to its exacting standards. It also controlled the packing and distribution of coffee to its retail stores. For the year ended October 1994, Starbucks generated $284 million of sales from 400 company-operated retail outlets.

Green Mountain Coffee Roasters (GMCR), based in Shelburne, Vermont, enjoyed $11 million in sales for 1991. This company had seven retail outlets and more than 1,000 restaurant and gourmet food store accounts. GMCR kept its prices high and was decidedly high tech, using a computerized roaster and a data base to help customers manage their coffee inventories.

While the specialty coffee industry had high hopes for consumer demand in the early 90s, some trends in consumer products pointed to opportunities in the nonspecialty segments. In the wake of an economic recession, consumers were cost conscious. Accordingly, demand for lower-priced store brands (private labels) increased. It was not yet clear how this trend would manifest itself in the coffee retail market in the years ahead.

Competitors. Nestlé was the largest coffee company in the world. In the United States, the largest coffee producers were Philip Morris (Maxwell House) and P&G (Folgers). These companies had considerable resources: infrastructure, distribution networks, brand equity, production resources, and marketing expertise. They had competed largely through heavy advertising[1] and aggressive pricing. Sensitive to shifts in coffee consumption, all three had introduced many new coffee products. (Selected financial data on the major competitors are provided in Exhibit 2.) In addition to these coffee giants, there were several niche players such as Starbucks.

[1]In 1990 Philip Morris and P&G each spent roughly $100 million on coffee advertising.

<table>
<tr><td colspan="2">EXHIBIT 2   Selected 1992 Segment
Sales and Expense Data[1]
($ in millions)</td></tr>
</table>

	Nestlé[3]	Procter & Gamble	Philip Morris
Sales	$9,658	$3,709	$29,048
Cost of sales	4,369	2,373	19,685
Marketing and administration[2]	3,564	1,157	6,594

[1]Since these companies participate in multiple industries, only the segment data for the food or beverage segment (that included the company's coffee business) are provided.

[2]Marketing and administration expenses include research and development costs.

[3]Financial information for Nestlé was converted from Swiss francs into dollars using the average exchange rate for 1992—SF1.40/$.

Source: 1992 Annual Reports.

EXHIBIT 3   Profit & Loss Statement for Plant No. 1

Net sales (shipment at billing prices)			100%
Less: Cost of sales:*			
Green coffee at contract cost		50%	
Roasting and grinding			
Labor	5%		
Fuel	3		
Manufacturing expense	5	13%	
Packaging			
Container	11%		
Packing carton	1		
Labor	2		
Manufacturing expense	4	18%	
Total manufacturing cost			81%
Gross margin			19%

*Cost of sales is expressed as percent of net sales revenue. Dollar amounts have been omitted.

Aloha Products

The vice president of sales for Aloha Products and his two assistants centrally managed the sales policies. The company president and the vice president of sales jointly assumed responsibility for advertising and promotion. The vice president of manufacturing oversaw the roasting, grinding, and packaging of Aloha's coffees.

The company operated three roasting plants in the Midwest, each plant with its own profit and loss responsibility. A plant manager's bonus was a percentage of his or her plant's gross margin. Headquarters prepared monthly gross margin statements for each plant, as illustrated in Exhibit 3.

At the start of each month, headquarters presented plant managers with production schedules for the current month and a projected schedule for the succeeding month.

Each plant had a small accounting office that recorded all manufacturing costs and prepared payrolls. The home office managed billing, credit, and collection, and prepared all of the company's financial statements.

Plant managers had no control over buying the green (unprocessed) coffee beans. A special purchasing unit within the company handled these purchases. The unit was located in New York City, the heart of the green coffee business, because this allowed constant contact with coffee brokers. The purchasing group was largely autonomous. It kept all of its own records and handled all of the financial transactions related to purchasing, sales to outsiders, and transfers to the three company-operated roasting plants. The unit's manager reported directly to the company's secretary-treasurer.

The purchasing unit's primary function was to obtain the necessary varieties and quantities of green coffee for the roasting plants to blend, roast, pack, and deliver to customers. The purchasing group dealt with more than 50 types and grades of coffee beans grown in tropical countries all over the world.

Using projected sales budgets, the purchasing group entered into forward green coffee bean contracts with exporters. Forward contracts required green coffee delivery 3 to 12 months out at specific prices. The group also had the option of purchasing on the spot market—that is, purchase for immediate delivery. Spot purchases were kept to a minimum. A purchasing agent's knowledge of the market was critical; the agent had to judge market trends and make commitments accordingly.

The result of this process was that the green coffee purchasing unit bought a range of coffees in advance for delivery at various dates. At the actual delivery date, the company's sales were not always at the level expected when the original green coffee contract was signed. The difference between actual deliveries and current requirements was handled through either sales or purchases on the spot market. The company would sell to, or buy from, coffee brokers and sometimes from other roasters.

As an example, commitments for Kona No. 2 (a grade of Hawaiian coffee) might specify delivery in May of 22,000 bags (a bag contains 132 lbs. of green coffee). These deliveries would be made under 50 contracts executed at varying prices, 3 to 12 months before the month of delivery. If for some reason demand for the company's products fell in May, the plant's raw material needs could correspondingly fall to 17,000 bags. In this case, the purchasing unit would have to decide between paying to store 5,000 surplus bags in noncompany facilities or selling the coffee on the open market. This example had been typical of the company's normal operation.

Generally, the company's big volume purchases permitted it to buy on favorable terms and to realize a normal brokerage and trading profit when it sold smaller lots to small roasting companies. Hence, the usual policy was to make purchase commitments based on maximum potential plant requirements and sell the surplus on the spot market.

The company accounted for coffee purchases by maintaining a separate cost record for each contract. This record was charged with payments for coffee purchased as well as shipping charges, import expenses, and similar items. For each contract, the purchasing group computed a net cost per bag. Thus, the 50 deliveries of Kona No. 2 cited in the example would come into inventory at 50 different costs. The established policy was to treat each contract individually. When green coffee was shipped to a plant, a charge was made for the cost represented by the contracts that covered that particular shipment of coffee. There was no element of profit or loss associated with this transfer. When the company sold green coffee on the open market, the sales were likewise costed on a specific contract basis with a resulting profit or loss on the transaction.

The operating cost of running the purchasing unit was charged directly to the central office. The cost was recorded as an element in the general corporate overhead.

For the past several years, the plant managers had been dissatisfied with the method of computing gross margin (as evident from the quote at the beginning of this case). Their complaints finally motivated the president to request that the controller study the whole method of reporting the results of plant operations, sales and marketing, and the purchasing groups.

Questions

1. Evaluate the current control systems for the manufacturing, marketing, and purchasing departments of Aloha Products.

2. Considering the company's competitive strategy, what changes, if any, would you make to the control systems for the three departments?

CASE 6–5
INDUSTRIAL PRODUCTS CORPORATION

In 1996 the Industrial Products Corporation (IPC) manufactured a variety of industrial products in more than a dozen divisions. Plants were located throughout the country, one or more to a division, and company headquarters was in a large Eastern city. Each division was run by a division manager and had its own balance sheet and income statement. The company made extensive use of long- and short-run planning programs, which included budgets for sales, costs, expenditures, and rate of return on investment. Monthly reports on operating results were sent in by each division and were reviewed by headquarters executives. For many years the principal performance measure for divisions had been their rate of return on investment.

The Baker Division of IPC manufactured and assembled large industrial pumps, most of which sold for more than $5,000. A great variety of models were made to order from the standard parts which the division either bought or manufactured for stock. In addition, components were individually designed and fabricated when pumps were made for special applications. A variety of metalworking machines were used, some large and heavy, and a few designed especially for the division's kind of business.

The division operated three plants, two of which were much smaller than the third and were located in distant parts of the country. Headquarters offices were located in the main plant where more than 1,000 people were employed. They performed design and manufacturing operations and the usual staff and clerical work. Marketing activities were carried out by sales engineers in the field, who worked closely with customers on design and installation. Reporting to Mr. Brandt, the division manager, were managers in charge of design, sales, manufacturing, purchasing, and budgets.

The division's product line was broken down into five product groups so that the profitability of each could be studied separately. Evaluation was based on the margin above factory cost as a percentage of sales. No attempt was made to allocate investment to the product lines. The budget director said that not only would this be difficult in view of the common facilities, but that such a mathematical computation would not provide any new information since the products had approximately the same turnover of assets. Furthermore, he said, it was difficult enough to allocate common factory costs between products, and that even margin on sales was a disputable figure. "If we were larger," he said, "and had separate facilities for each product line, we might be able to do it. But it wouldn't mean much in this division right now."

Only half a dozen people monitored the division's rate of return; other measures were used in the division's internal control system. The division manager watched volume and timeliness of shipments per week, several measures of quality, and certain cost areas such as overtime payments.

The Division Manager's Control of Assets

During 1996 the total assets of the Baker Division were turned over approximately 1.7 times, and late that year they were made up as follows:

This case was prepared by Professor William Rotch, University of Virginia. Copyright © by the University of Virginia Darden School Foundation, Charlottesville, VA. To order copies send an e-mail to Dardencases@virginia.edu.

Cash	8%
Accounts receivable	21
Inventory	
Raw material	7
About 3% metal stock	
About 4% purchased parts	
Work in process	9
About 6% manufactured parts	
About 3% floor stocks	
Finished goods	2
Machinery (original cost)	29
Land and buildings (original cost)	24
	100%

Cash (8 percent of total assets)

The Baker Division, like all divisions in IPC, maintained a cash account in a local bank, to which company headquarters transferred funds as they were needed. This local account was used primarily for the plant payroll and for payment of other local bills. Payment of suppliers' invoices as well as collection of accounts receivable was handled by headquarters for Baker as well as for most of the other divisions.

The division's cash account at headquarters was shown on the division's balance sheet as cash and marketable securities. The amount shown as cash had been established by agreement between top management and the division manager, and was considered by both to be about the minimum amount necessary to operate the division. The excess above this amount was shown on the division's balance sheet as marketable securities; it earned interest from headquarters at the rate of 5 percent a year. This account varied with receipts and disbursements, leaving the cash account fixed as long as there was a balance in the securities account. It was possible for the securities account to be wiped out and for cash to decline below the

minimum agreed upon, but if this continued for more than a month or two, corrective action was taken. For Baker Division the minimum level was equal to about two weeks' sales, and in recent years cash had seldom gone below this amount.

Whether or not the company as a whole actually owned cash and marketable securities equal to the sum of all the respective divisions' cash and security accounts was the concern of headquarters management. It probably was not necessary to hold this amount of cash and securities since the division accounts had to cover division peak needs and not all the peak needs occurred at the same time.

The size of a division's combined cash and marketable securities accounts was directly affected by all phases of the division's operations which used or produced cash. It also was affected in three other ways. One was the automatic deduction of 40 percent of income for tax purposes. Another was the payment of "dividends" by the division to headquarters. All earnings that the division manager did not wish to keep for future use were transferred to the company's cash account by payment of a dividend. Since a division was expected to retain a sufficient balance to provide for capital expenditures, dividends were generally paid only by the profitable divisions which were not expanding rapidly.

The third action affecting the cash account occurred if cash declined below the minimum, or if extensive capital expenditures had been approved. A division might then "borrow" from headquarters, paying interest as if it were a separate company. At the end of 1996 the Baker Division had no loan and had been able to operate since about 1990 without borrowing from headquarters. Borrowing was not, in fact, currently being considered by the Baker Division.

Except for its part in the establishment of a minimum cash level, top management was not involved in the determination of the division's investment in cash and marketable securities. Mr. Brandt could control the level of this investment by deciding how much was to be paid in dividends. Since only a 5 percent return was received on the marketable securities and since the division earned more than that on its total investment, it was to the division manager's advantage to pay out as much as possible in dividends. When asked how he determined the size of the dividends, Mr. Brandt said that he simply kept what he thought he would need to cover peak demands, capital expenditures, and contingencies. Improving the division's rate of return may have been part of the decision, but he did not mention it.

Accounts Receivable
(21 percent of total assets)

All accounts receivable for the Baker Division were collected at company headquarters. Around the 20th of each month a report of balances was prepared and forwarded to the division.

Although in theory Mr. Brandt was allowed to set his own terms for divisional sales, in practice it would have been difficult to change the company's usual terms. Since Baker Division sold to important customers of other divisions, any change from the net 30 terms could disturb a large segment of the corporation's business. Furthermore, industry practice was well established, and the division would hardly try to change it.

The possibility of cash sales in situations in which credit was poor was virtually nonexistent. Credit was investigated for all customers by the headquarters credit department and no sales were made without a prior credit check. For the Baker Division this policy presented no problem, for it sold primarily to well-established customers.

In late 1996 accounts receivable made up 21 percent of total assets. The fact that this corresponded to 45 average days of sales and not to 30 was the result of a higher than average level of shipments the month before, coupled with the normal delay caused by the billing and collection process.

There was almost nothing Mr. Brandt could do directly to control the level of accounts receivable. This asset account varied with sales, lagged behind shipments by a little more than a month, and departed from this relationship only if customers happened to pay early or late.

Inventory: Raw Material Metal Stock
(about 3 percent of total investment)

In late 1996 inventory as a whole made up 18 percent of Baker Division's total assets. A subdivision of the various kinds of inventory showed that raw material accounted for 7 percent, work in process 9 percent, and finished goods and miscellaneous supplies 2 percent. Since the Baker Division produced to order, finished goods inventory was normally small, leaving raw material and work in process as the only significant classes of inventory.

The raw material inventory could be further subdivided to separate the raw material inventory from a variety of purchased parts. The raw material inventory was then composed primarily of metals and metal shapes, such as steel sheets or copper tubes. Most of the steel was bought according to a schedule arranged with the steel companies several months ahead of the delivery date. About a month before the steel company was to ship the order, Baker Division would send the rolling instructions by shapes and weights. If the weight on any particular shape was below a minimum set by the steel company, Baker Division would pay an extra charge for processing. Although this method of purchasing accounted for the bulk of steel purchases, smaller amounts were also bought as needed from warehouse stocks and specialty producers.

Copper was bought by headquarters and processed by the company's own mill. The divisions could buy the quantities they needed, but the price paid depended on corporate buying practices and processing costs. The price paid by Baker Division had generally been competitive with outside sources, though it often lagged behind the market both in increases and in reductions in price.

The amounts of copper and steel bought were usually determined by the purchasing agent without recourse to any formal calculations of an economic ordering quantity. The reason for this was that since there was such a large number of uncertain factors that had continually to be estimated, a formal computation would not improve the process of determining how much to buy. Purchases depended on the amounts on hand, expected consumption, and current delivery time and price expectations. If delivery was fast, smaller amounts were usually bought. If a price increase was anticipated, somewhat larger orders often were placed at the current price. Larger amounts of steel had been bought several years earlier, for example, just before expected labor action on the railroads threatened to disrupt deliveries.

The level of investment in raw material varied with the rates of purchase and use. There was a fairly wide range within which Mr. Brandt could control this class of asset, and there were no top management directives governing the size of his raw material inventory.

Inventory: Purchased Parts and Manufactured Parts (about 10 percent of total assets—4 percent in raw material, 6 percent in work in process)

The Baker Division purchased and manufactured parts for stock to be used later in the assembly of pumps. The method used to determine the purchase quantity was the same as that used to determine the length of production run on parts made for work-in-process stocks.

The number of parts bought or manufactured was, with the exception of special adjustments made in two places, based on a series of calculations which led to an economic order quantity (EOQ). Since there were several thousand different items bought and manufactured, these calculations had been made routine. A computer program had been developed which received data from existing files such as parts usage and price over the past six months, and contained some constants which could be manually changed. The program periodically went through the following steps:

1. Using data on past usage, the program computed a forecast of future usage, using a preset forecasting algorithm.

2. The forecast could then be adjusted by a factor entered to reflect known trends for a specific part or as a constant for all parts. Currently, Mr. Brandt had entered a .9 factor to be used for all parts, in an effort to push inventories down.

3. The program then computed the Economic Order Quantity in dollars and in units, using the following information:

    a. Adjusted forecasted usage rate in dollars from step 2.

    b. For purchased parts the order handling cost, covering paperwork and receiving cost, which Able division's controller had developed using activity-based costing. Currently this was $28.50 per order and was reviewed annually.

    For parts manufactured by the Baker Division, a batch setup cost was used. Again activity-based costing had been used to compute this batch cost which included costs of machine setup, materials handling, first piece inspection, and data reporting. The actual amount used in the EOQ computation depended on the complexity of the setup and currently ranged from $15 to $75.

    c. Inventory carrying cost, which consisted of two components: one was the cost of capital (currently computed to be an annual rate of 12 percent) and the other was a charge for storage, insurance, taxes, and obsolescence. The current annual rate of 8 percent for those items could be adjusted, if, for example, special storage conditions were required.

The formula used to compute EOQ was as follows:

$$EOQ = \sqrt{\frac{2AS}{I}}$$

where

A = annual usage in dollars

S = either the order handling cost for purchased parts or the setup cost for manufactured parts

I = the inventory carrying cost, expressed as a percent or decimal to be applied to average inventory

For purchased parts, another analysis tested whether supplier quantity discount for purchases above the EOQ would be worthwhile. This adjustment worked as follows:

1. EOQ times unit price times expected orders per year = material cost (A).

2. Order quantity required for discount times price times orders per year = discounted material cost (B).

3. Annual savings on material cost (A – B) or (S).

4. Decreased ordering cost per year because of fewer orders (C).

5. Increase in carrying cost other than cost of capital: Discount quantity times discount price minus EOQ quantity times EOQ price, all divided by 2 (D). This was the increase in average inventory. Then D times the carrying cost other than capital cost gave the annual increased cost due to higher average inventory (E).

6. Computation of return on investment:

$$\frac{S + C - E}{D} = \text{Return on investment}$$

Though IPC's cost of capital was computed to be 12 percent, Baker Division usually required a higher return before volume discounts would be taken. The judgment was entirely up to the Baker Division. The inventory control supervisor who made the decision considered general business conditions, the time required to use up the larger order, the specialization of the particular part, and any general directives made by the division manager concerning inventory levels. A return below 15 percent was probably never acceptable—more than 20 percent was required in most instances—and any quantity discount yielding 25–30 percent or more usually was taken, though each case was judged individually.

The final step of the computer program was developing an order review point. With an estimate of expected delivery time, the program signaled when an order should be placed.

The level of purchased and manufactured parts inventory in the Baker Division varied with changes in rate of consumption and purchase. If the rules for calculating economic order quantity were adhered to, inventory levels increased with usage faster than the rate of usage increased up to a certain level (determined by order or setup cost, and carrying cost), and thereafter increased usage resulted in an inventory increase rate that was lower than the usage increase rate. Most parts purchased and made by Baker Division were above that breakpoint, which meant that growth in sales generally resulted in increased return on investment. Of course, since there were several opportunities for Baker Division's management to intervene in the purchase quantity computation, the relationship would not necessarily hold true in practice. By setting the forecasting adjustment, for example, Mr. Brandt had tilted the process toward inventory reduction. Furthermore, continued efforts to reduce setup cost and order handling cost had pushed toward the reduction in inventories.

Inventory: Floor Stocks (about 3 percent of total investment)

Floor stock inventory consisted of parts and components which were being worked on and assembled. Items became part of the floor stock inventory when they were requisitioned from the storage areas or when delivered directly to the production floor.

Pumps were worked on individually so that lot size was not a factor to be considered. There was little Mr. Brandt could do to control the level of floor stock inventory except to see that there was not an excess of parts piled around the production area.

Inventory: Finished Goods (2 percent of total investment)

As a rule, pumps were made to order and for immediate shipment. Finished goods inventory consisted of those few pumps on which shipment was delayed. Control of this investment was a matter of keeping it low by shipping the pumps as fast as possible.

Land, Buildings, and Machinery (53 percent of total investment)

Since the Baker Division's fixed assets, stated at gross, comprised 53 percent of total assets at the end of 1996, the control of this particular group of assets was extremely important. Changes in the level of these investments depended on retirements and additions, the latter being entirely covered by the capital budgeting program.

Industrial Products Corporation's capital budgeting procedures were described in a planning manual. The planning sequence was as follows:

1. Headquarters forecasts economic conditions. (March)

2. The divisions plan long-term objectives. (June)

3. Supporting programs are submitted. (September) These are plans for specific actions, such as sales plans, advertising programs, and cost reduction programs, and include the facilities program which is the capital expenditure request. The planning manual stated under the heading "General Approach in the Development of a Coordinated Supporting Program" this advice:

Formulation and evaluation of a Supporting Program for each product line can generally be improved if projects are classified by purpose. The key objective of all planning is Return-on-Assets, a function of Margin and Turnover. These ratios are in turn determined by the three factors in the business equation—Volume, Costs, and Assets. All projects therefore should be directed primarily at one of the following:

- To increase volume;
- To reduce costs and expenses; and
- To minimize assets.

4. Annual objective submitted (November 11 by 8:00 AM!)

The annual objective states projected sales, costs, expenses, profits, cash expenditures, and receipts, and shows pro forma balance sheets and income statements.

Mr. Brandt was "responsible for the division's assets and for provision for the growth and expansion of the division." Growth referred to the internal refinements of product design and production methods and to the cost reduction programs. Expansion involved a 5- to 10-year program including about two years for construction.

In the actual capital expenditure request there were four kinds of facilities proposals:

1. Cost reduction projects, which were self-liquidating investments. Reduction in labor costs was usually the largest source of the savings, which were stated in terms of the payback period and the rate of return.

2. Necessity projects. These included replacement of worn-out machinery, quality improvement and technical changes to meet competition, environmental compliance projects, and facilities for the safety and comfort of the workers.

3. Product redesign projects.

4. Expansion projects.

Justification of the cost reduction proposals was based on a comparison of the estimated rate of return (estimated return before taxes divided by gross investment) with the 20 percent standard as specified by headquarters. If the project was considered desirable, and yet showed a return of less than 20 percent, it had to be justified on other grounds and was included in the necessities category. Cost reduction proposals made up about 60 percent of the 1997 capital expenditure budget, and in earlier years these proposals had accounted for at least 50 percent. Very little of Baker Division's 1997 capital budget had been allocated specifically for product redesign and none for expansion, so that most of the remaining 40 percent was to be used for necessity projects. Thus a little over half of Baker Division's capital expenditures were justified primarily on the estimated rate of return on the investment. The remainder, having advantages which could not be stated in terms of the rate of return, were justified on other grounds.

Mr. Brandt was free to include what he wanted in his capital budgeting request, and for the three years that he had been division manager his requests had always been granted. However, no large expansion projects had been included in the capital budget requests of the last three years. As in the 1997 budget, most of the capital expenditure had been for cost-reduction projects, and the remainder was for necessities. Annual additions had approximately equaled annual retirements.

Since Mr. Brandt could authorize expenditures of up to $250,000 per project for purposes approved by the board, there was in fact some flexibility in his choice of projects after the budget had been approved by higher management. Not only could he schedule the order of expenditure, but under some circumstances he could substitute unforeseen projects of a similar nature. If top management approved $100,000 for miscellaneous cost reduction projects, Mr. Brandt could spend this on the projects he considered most important, whether or not they were specifically described in his original budget request.

For the corporation as a whole, about one-quarter of the capital expenditure was for projects of under $250,000, which could be authorized for expenditure by the division managers. This proportion was considered by top management to be about right; if, however, it rose much above a quarter, the $250,000 dividing line would probably be lowered.

Questions

1. To what extent did Mr. Brandt influence the level of investment in each asset category?

2. Comment on the general usefulness of return on investment as a measure of divisional performance. Could it be made a more effective device?

CASE 6–6
MARDEN COMPANY

A typical division of Marden Company had financial statements as shown in Exhibit 1. Accounts receivable were billed by the division, but customers made payments to bank accounts (i.e., lockboxes) maintained in the name of Marden Company and located throughout the country. The debt item on the balance sheet is a proportionate part of the corporate 9 percent bond issue. Interest on this debt was not charged to the division.

Question

Recommend the best way of measuring the performance of the division manager. If you need additional information, make the assumption you believe to be most reasonable.

This case was prepared and copyrighted by Professor Robert N. Anthony.

EXHIBIT 1   Typical Division Financial Statements

**Balance Sheet
End of Year (condensed; $000)**

Assets		Equities	
Cash	$ 100	Accounts payable	$ 400
Accounts receivable	800	Total current liabilities	400
Inventory	900		
Total current assets	1,800	Debt	700
Plant and equipment, cost	1,000	Equity	1,300
Depreciation (straight line)	400		2,000
Plant and equipment, net	600		
Total assets	$2,400	Total equities	$2,400

Divisional Income Statement

Sales	$4,000
Costs, other than those listed below	3,200
Depreciation	100
Allocated share of corporate expenses	100
Income before income tax	600

CASE 6–7
LEMFERT COMPANY

Lemfert Company was a large manufacturing company organized into divisions, each with responsibility for earning a satisfactory return on its investment. Division managers had considerable autonomy in carrying out this responsibility. Some divisions fabricated parts; others—here called "end-item divisions"—assembled these parts, together with purchased parts, into finished products and marketed the finished products. Transfer prices were used in connection with the transfer of parts among the various fabricating divisions and from the fabricating divisions to the end-item divisions. Wherever possible, these transfer prices were the lowest prices charged by outside manufacturers for the same or comparable items, with appropriate adjustments for inbound freight, volume, and similar factors.

Parts that were not similar to those manufactured by outside companies were called "type K items." In most fabricating divisions, these items constituted only 5 to 10 percent of total volume. In Division F, however, approximately 75 percent of total volume was accounted for by type K items. Division F manufactured 10 such items for various end-item divisions; they were less than 5 percent of the total cost of any one of these end-item divisions. The procedure for arriving at the transfer price for type K items is described below.

First, a tentative transfer price was calculated by the value analysis staff of the corporate purchasing department and was submitted to the two divisions involved for their consideration. This price was supposed to be based on the estimated costs of an "efficient producer"

plus a profit margin. An efficient producer was considered to be one conducting its purchasing and using modern equipment in a manner that could reasonably be expected of the company's principal competitors.

The material cost portion of the total cost was based on current competitive price levels. Direct labor cost was supposed to reflect efficient processing on modern equipment. Overhead cost represented an amount that could be expected of an efficient producer using modern equipment. Depreciation expense, expenditures on special tooling, and a standard allowance for administrative expense were included in the overhead figure.

The profit margin was equal to the divisional profit objective applied to the cost of the assets employed to produce the product in question. Assets employed was the sum of the following items.

> Cash and receivables—18 percent of the total manufacturing cost.
>
> Inventories—the value of the optimum inventory size required at standard volume.
>
> Fixed assets—the depreciated book value (but not less than one-half original cost) of assets used to fabricate the part, including a fair share of buildings and other general assets, but excluding standby and obsolete facilities.

The percentage used for cash and receivables was based on studies of the cash and receivables balances of the principal outside manufacturers of parts similar to those manufactured in the fabricating divisions. The standard volume was an estimate of the volume that the plants should *normally* be expected to produce, which was not necessarily the same as current volume or projected volume for the next year.

This case was prepared by Professor Robert N. Anthony, Harvard Business School. Copyright by the President and Fellows of Harvard College. Harvard Business School case 113-116.

For an average division, the budgeted profit objective was 20 percent of assets employed; but there were variations among divisions. The divisional budgeted profit objective multiplied by the assets employed, as calculated above, gave the profit margin for the item. This profit was added to the cost to arrive at the suggested transfer price, which then was submitted to the two divisions. If either the buying or the selling division believed that the price thus determined was unfair, it first attempted to negotiate a mutually satisfactory price. If the parties were unable to agree, they submitted the dispute to the controller for arbitration. Either party might appeal the results of this arbitration to the executive vice president.

Questions

1. Are these the best transfer price practices for the Lemfert Company? If not, how should they be revised?

2. For what types of companies would the revised policy not be best? Why?

3. Do you think the attempt to measure profitability in Division F is worthwhile? If not, how would you measure performance in this division?

THE MANAGEMENT CONTROL PROCESS

In practice, the *managment control process* is behavioral, manifesting itself in interactions among managers and between managers and their subordinates. Because managers differ from one another in technical ability, leadership style, interpersonal skills, experience, approach to decision-making, affinity for numbers, and in many other ways, the details of the management control process vary from company to company and among the responsibility centers within a company. The differences relate mainly to the way the control system is used. To function effectively, nevertheless, the *formal management control system* must be basically the same throughout an organization.

In Part II, we discuss the sequential steps in the management control process as they occur in practice: strategic planning in Chapter 7; budget preparation in Chapter 8; analyzing financial performance in Chapter 9; and the development of the balanced scorecard, which incorporates both financial and nonfinancial measures, in Chapter 10. In Chapter 11 we consider management compensation as it relates to the management control process.

STRATEGIC PLANNING

This is the first of five chapters that describe the management control process. Chapter 7 describes strategic planning, which is the first activity, sequentially, in the process. The first section of Chapter 7 describes the nature of strategic planning. The second part discusses techniques for analyzing and deciding on proposed new programs. The third part describes techniques that are useful in analyzing ongoing programs. The final part describes the several steps in the strategic planning process.

The discussion implicitly assumes a moderately large organization, typically consisting of a headquarters and several decentralized business units. In such an organization, strategic planning takes place both at headquarters and in the business units. If the organization is small, and especially if it does not have business units, the process involves only senior executives and a planning staff. In a very small organization, the process may involve only the chief executive officer.

Nature of Strategic Planning

Most competent managers spend considerable time thinking about the future. The result may be an informal understanding of the future direction the entity is going to take, or it may be a formal statement of specific plans about how to get there. Such a formal statement of plans is here called a *strategic plan,* and the process of preparing and revising this statement is called *strategic planning* (elsewhere called *long-range planning* and *programming*). *Strategic planning is the process of deciding on the programs that the organization will undertake and on the approximate amount of resources that will be allocated to each program over the next several years.*

Relation to Strategy Formulation

We draw a distinction between two management processes—strategy formulation and strategic planning. Because "strategy" or "strategic" is used in both terms, there is a possibility of confusion. The distinction is that *strategy formulation is the process of deciding on new strategies, whereas strategic planning is the process of deciding how to implement the strategies.* In the strategy formulation process, management arrives at the goals of the organization and creates the main strategies for achieving those goals. The strategic planning process then takes the goals and strategies as given and develops programs that will carry out the strategies and achieve the goals efficiently and effectively. The decision by an industrial goods manufacturer to diversify into consumer goods is a strategy formulation, a *strategic decision,* after which a number of *implementation issues* have to be resolved: whether to diversify through acquisition or through organic growth, what product lines to emphasize, whether to make or to buy, which marketing channels to use. The document that describes how the strategic decision is to be *implemented* is the *strategic plan.*

In practice, there is a considerable amount of overlap between strategy formulation and strategic planning. Studies made during the strategic planning process may indicate the desirability of changing goals or strategies. Conversely, strategy formulation usually includes a preliminary consideration of the programs that will be adopted as a means of achieving the goals. Nevertheless, it is important to keep a conceptual distinction between strategy formulation and strategic planning, one reason being that the planning process tends to become institutionalized, putting a damper on purely creative activities. Segregating strategy formulation as a separate activity, at least in the thinking of top management, can offset this tendency. Strategy formulation should be an activity in which creative, innovative thinking is strongly encouraged.

Strategic planning is systematic; there is an annual strategic planning process, with prescribed procedures and timetables. Strategy formulation is unsystematic. Strategies are reexamined in response to perceived opportunities or threats. Thus, ideally, a possible strategic initiative may surface at any time from anyone in the organization. If judged to be worth pursuing, it should be analyzed immediately, without waiting upon a prescribed timetable. Once a strategy is accepted, the planning for it follows in a systematic way.

In many companies, unfortunately, goals and strategies are not stated explicitly enough or communicated clearly to the managers who need to use them as a framework for their program decisions. Thus, in a formal strategic planning process an important first step often has to be to write descriptions of the organization's goals and strategies. This may be a daunting task, for although top management presumably has an intuitive feel for what the goals and strategies are, they may not be able to verbalize them with the specificity necessary for making good program decisions. Planners may have to interpret or elicit management thinking as a first step.

Evolution of Strategic Planning

Fifty years ago the strategic planning process in most organizations was unsystematic. If management gave thought to long-range planning, it was not in a coordinated way. A few companies started formal strategic planning systems in the late 1950s, but most early efforts were failures; they were minor adaptations of existing budget preparation systems. The required data were much more detailed than was appropriate; staff people rather than line management did most of the work; participants spent more time filling in forms than thinking deeply about alternatives and selecting the best ones. As time went on, management learned their lessons—the objective should be to make difficult choices among alternative programs, not to extrapolate numbers in budgetary detail; time and effort should go into analysis and informal discussion, relatively less on paperwork; the focus should be on the program itself rather than on the responsibility centers that carried it out.

Currently, many organizations appreciate the advantages of making a plan for the next three to five years. The practice of stating this plan in a formal document, or model, is widely, but by no means universally, accepted. The amount of detail is usually much less than in the strategic plans of the 1950s.

Benefits and Limitations of Strategic Planning

A formal strategic planning process can give to the organization: (1) a framework for developing the annual budget; (2) a management development tool; (3) a mechanism to force managers to think long term; and (4) a means of aligning managers with the long-term strategies of the company.

Framework for Developing the Budget.   An operating budget calls for resource commitments over the coming year; it is essential that management make such resource commitments with a clear idea of where the organization is heading over the next several years. A strategic plan provides that broader framework. Thus, *an important benefit of preparing a strategic plan is that it facilitates the formulation of an effective operating budget.*

As Exhibit 7–1 suggests, a company without a strategic planning process considers too many strategic issues in the budgeting stage, potentially leading to information overload, inadequate consideration of some strategic alternatives, or neglect of some choices altogether—a dysfunctional environment that can seriously affect the quality of resource allocation decisions. *An important benefit of strategic planning is to facilitate optimal resource allocation*

EXHIBIT 7–1

*A company without
a strategic planning
process*

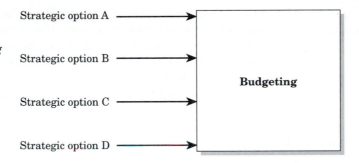

EXHIBIT 7–2

*A company with a
strategic planning
process*

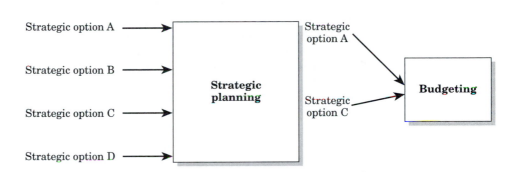

decisions in support of key strategic options. Exhibit 7–2 shows how the strategic planning process narrows the range of options such that planners can make intelligent resource allocation decisions during the budgeting process. Thus, the strategic plan helps the organization understand the implications of strategic decisions for action plans in the short term.

Management Development Tool.   *Formal strategic planning is an excellent management education and training tool that provides managers with a process for thinking about strategies and their implementation.* It is not an overstatement to say that in formal strategic planning, the *process* itself is a lot more important than the *output* of the process, which is the plan document.

Mechanism for Forcing Management to Think Long Term.   Managers tend to worry more about tactical issues and managing the present, day-to-day affairs of the business than about creating the future. *Formal strategic planning forces managers to make time for thinking through important long-term issues.*

Means of Aligning Managers with Corporate Strategies.   *The debates, discussions, and negotiations that take place during the planning process clarify corporate strategies, unify and align managers with such strategies, and reveal the implications of corporate strategies for individual managers.*

As we will show, program decisions are made one at a time, and the strategic plan brings them all together. Preparing the strategic plan may reveal that individual decisions do not add up to a satisfactory whole. Planned new investments may require more funds in certain years than the company can obtain in those years; planned changes in direct programs may require changes in the size of support programs (e.g., research and development, administrative) that were not taken into account when these changes were considered separately. The profit anticipated from individual programs may not add up to satisfactory profit for the whole organization.

> **Example.**   In 1996, Texaco, a large, complex oil and gas producer, had a capital spending and exploration budget of $3.6 billion. Some of its 1996 projects included " . . . Developing offshore projects in the North Sea, Nigeria, Angola, Australia, and Southeast Asia. Continuing to increase production in the neutral zone between Saudi Arabia and Kuwait." With the level of risk associated with the different projects and the amount of resources available, strategic planning was a necessity for Texaco in choosing among projects.[1]

Limitations.   There are several potential pitfalls or limitations to formal strategic planning. First, there is always a danger that *planning can end up becoming a "form-filling," bureaucratic exercise, devoid of strategic thinking.* In order to minimize this risk of bureaucratization, organizations should periodically ask, "Are we getting fresh ideas as a result of the strategic planning process?"

A second danger is that *an organization may create a large strategic planning department and delegate the preparation of the strategic plan to that staff department,* thus forfeiting the input of line management as well the educational benefits of the process. Strategic planning is a line management function. The staff in strategic planning departments should be kept to a minimum and their role should be as a catalyst, an educator, and a facilitator of the planning process.

Finally, *strategic planning is time consuming and expensive.* The most significant expense is the time devoted to it by senior management and managers at other levels in the organization. A formal strategic plan is desirable in organizations that have the following characteristics:

1. Top management is convinced that strategic planning is important. Otherwise, strategic planning is likely to be a staff exercise that has little impact on actual decision-making.

2. The organization is relatively large and complex. In small, simple organizations, an informal understanding of the organization's future directions is adequate for making decisions about resource allocations, the principal purpose of preparing a strategic plan.

3. Considerable uncertainty about the future exists, but the organization has the flexibility to adjust to changed circumstances. In a relatively stable

---

[1]"More U.S. Companies Map 1996 Spending Plans," *Oil & Gas Journal,* January 29, 1996. p. 39.

organization, a strategic plan is unnecessary; the future is sufficiently like the past, so the strategic plan would be only an exercise in extrapolation. (If a stable organization foresees the need for a change in direction, such as a decline in its markets or drastic changes in the cost of materials, it prepares a contingency plan showing the actions to be taken to meet these new conditions.) On the other hand, if the future is so uncertain that reasonably reliable estimates cannot be made, preparation of a formal strategic plan is a waste of time.

In summary, a formal strategic planning process is not needed in small, relatively stable organizations, and it is not worthwhile in organizations that cannot make reliable estimates about the future or in organizations whose senior management prefers not to manage in this fashion.

Program Structure and Content

In most industrial organizations, programs are products or product families, plus research and development, general and administrative activities, planned acquisitions, or other important activities that do not fit into existing product lines. At Procter & Gamble, for example, each product line is a program. By contrast, General Electric structures its programs by profit centers—that is, business units; each business unit is responsible for a specified number of product lines.

In service organizations, programs tend to correspond to the types of services rendered by the entity. The federal government divides its activities into 10 main programs. In a multi-unit service organization, such as a hotel chain, each unit or each geographical region may constitute a program.

The typical strategic plan covers a period of five future years. Five years is a long enough period to estimate the consequences of program decisions made currently. The consequences of a decision to develop and market a new product or to acquire a major new capital asset may not be fully felt within a shorter period. The horizon beyond five years may be so murky that attempts to make a program for a longer period are not worthwhile. Many organizations prepare very rough plans that extend beyond five years. In some organizations the strategic plan covers only the next three years.

The dollar amounts for each program show the approximate magnitude of its revenues, expenses, and capital expenditures. Because of the relatively long time horizon, only rough estimates are feasible. Such estimates are satisfactory as a basis for indicating the organization's general direction. If the strategic plan is structured by business units, the "charter," which specifies the boundaries within which the business unit is expected to operate, is also stated.

Organizational Relationships

The strategic planning process involves senior management and the managers of business units or other principal responsibility centers, assisted by their staffs. A primary purpose is to improve the communication between corporate and business unit executives by providing a sequence of scheduled activities through which they can arrive at a mutually agreeable set of objectives and plans. Managers of individual departments usually do not participate in the strategic planning process.

In some organizations, the controller organization prepares the strategic plan; in others, there is a separate planning staff. Strategic planning requires analytical skills and a broad outlook that may not exist in the controller organization; the controller organization may be skilled primarily in the detailed analytical techniques that are required in fine-tuning the annual budget and analyzing variances between actual and budgeted amounts.

Even if there is a separate planning staff, the controller organization usually does the work of disseminating guidelines and assembling the proposed numbers, as we describe in a later section. The numbers in the strategic plan, in the annual budget, and in the accounting system must be consistent with one another, and the best way of assuring this consistency is to assign responsibility for all three to the same staff. Moreover, some companies include the numbers for all three systems in a single computer model.

Headquarters staff members facilitate the strategic planning process, but they should not intervene too strongly. The best role of staff members is as a catalyst; they ensure that the process is properly carried out, but they do not make the program decisions. In particular, if business unit managers perceive that the headquarters staff is overly influential in the decision-making process, these managers will be reluctant to have the frank discussions with staff that are essential in developing sound plans. (Business unit managers, of course, have their own staffs who presumably are loyal to them.)

Top Management Style.   Strategic planning is a management process, and the way in which it is conducted in a given company is heavily dependent on the style of the chief executive officer. Some chief executives prefer to make decisions without the benefit of a formal planning apparatus. If the controller of such a company attempts to introduce a formal system, he or she is likely to be unsuccessful. No system will function effectively unless the chief executive actually uses it; if other managers perceive that the system is not a vital part of the management process, they will give only lip service to it.

In some companies, the chief executive wants some overall plan for the reasons given earlier but by temperament has an aversion to paperwork. In such companies, the system can contain all the elements we describe in a later section, but with minimum detail in the written documents and relatively greater emphasis on informal discussion. In other companies, senior management prefers extensive analysis and documentation of plans, and in these companies the formal part of the system is relatively elaborate.

Designers of the system must correctly diagnose the style of senior management and see to it that the system is appropriate for that style. This is a difficult task because formal strategic planning has become something of a fad, and some managers think they may be viewed as old-fashioned if they do not embrace all its trappings. Thus, they may instruct the staff to install an elaborate system, or permit staff to install one, that they later feel uncomfortable using.

Analyzing Proposed New Programs

Ideas for new programs can originate anywhere in the organization: with the chief executive, with a headquarters planning staff, or in various parts of the operating organization. For example, in 3M Corporation, the idea for "Post-It" notepads originated down in the organization, not at the initiative of the CEO. Some units are a more likely source of new ideas than others, for obvious reasons. The R&D organization is expected to generate ideas for novel products or processes, the marketing organization for marketing innovations, and the production engineering organization for better equipment and manufacturing methods.

Proposals for programs are essentially either *reactive* or *proactive*—they arise either as a reaction to a perceived threat such as rumors of the introduction of a new product by a competitor, or as an initiative to capitalize on an opportunity. Because a company's success depends in part on its ability to find and implement new programs and because ideas for these can come from a wide variety of sources, the atmosphere needs to be such that ideas come to light and receive appropriate management attention. A highly structured, formal system may create the wrong atmosphere for this purpose. The system should be flexible enough and receptive enough so that good new ideas do not get killed off before they come to the attention of the proper decision-maker.

Planners should view the adoption of a new program not as a single all-or-nothing decision but rather as a series of decisions, each one a relatively small step in testing and developing the proposed program. They should decide to carry through full implementation and its consequent significant investment only if the tests indicate that the proposal has a good chance of success. Most new programs are not like the Edsel automobile, which committed several hundred million dollars in a single decision; rather, they involve many successive decisions: agreement that the initial idea for a product is worth pursuing, examining its technical feasibility in a laboratory, examining production problems and cost characteristics in a pilot plant, testing consumer acceptance in test markets, and only then making a major commitment to full production and marketing. The system must provide for these successive steps, and for a thorough evaluation of the results of each step as a basis for making the decision on the next step.

Capital Investment Analysis

Most proposals require significant new capital. Techniques for analyzing capital investment proposals attempt to find either (*a*) the net present value of the project—the excess of the present value of the estimated cash inflows over the amount of investment required; or (*b*) the internal rate of return implicit in the relationship between inflows and outflows. An important point is that these techniques are used in only about half the situations in which, conceptually, they are applicable.[2] There are at least four reasons for not using present value techniques in analyzing all proposals.

1. The proposal may be so obviously attractive that a calculation of its net present value is unnecessary. A newly developed machine that reduces costs so substantially that it will pay for itself in a year is an example.

2. The estimates involved in the proposal are so uncertain that making present value calculations is believed to be not worth the effort—one can't draw a reliable conclusion from unreliable data. This situation is common when the results are heavily dependent on estimates of sales volume of new products for which no good market data exist. In these situations, the "payback period" criterion is used frequently.

3. The rationale for the proposal is something other than increased profitability. The present value approach assumes that the "objective function" is to increase profits, but many proposed investments win approval on the grounds that they improve employee morale, the company's image, or safety.

4. There is no feasible alternative to adoption. Environmental laws may require investment in a new program, as an example.

The management control system should provide an orderly way of deciding on proposals that cannot be analyzed by quantitative techniques. Systems that attempt to rank nonquantifiable projects in order of profitability won't work; many projects do not fit into a mechanical ranking scheme.

We describe briefly some considerations that are useful in implementing capital expenditure evaluation systems.

Rules.   Companies usually publish rules and procedures for the approval of capital expenditure proposals of various magnitudes. Proposed small expenditures may be approved by the plant manager, subject to a total specified amount in one year, and larger proposals go successively to business unit managers, to the chief executive officer, and, in the case of very important proposals, to the board of directors.

The rules also contain guidelines for preparing proposals and the general criteria for approving proposals. For example, small cost-saving proposals may require a maximum payback period of two (sometimes three) years. For larger proposals, there is usually a minimum required earnings rate, to be used either in net present value or internal rate of return analysis. The required earnings rate may be the same for all proposals, or there may be different rates for projects with different risk characteristics; also, proposals for additional working capital may use a lower rate than proposals for fixed assets.

---

[2]For information on the prevalence of various techniques in practice, see Thomas Klammer, Bruce Koch, and Neil Wilmer, *Capital Budgeting Practice: A Survey of Corporate Use* (Denton, TX: University of North Texas Press, 1990).

Avoiding Manipulation.   Sponsors who know that their project with a negative net present value is not likely to be approved may nevertheless have a "gut feeling" that the project should be undertaken. In some cases, they may make a proposal attractive by adjusting the original estimates so that the project meets the numerical criteria—perhaps by making optimistic estimates of sales revenues or by reducing allowances for contingencies in some of the cost elements. One of the most difficult tasks of the project analyst is to detect such manipulations. The reputation of project sponsors can provide a safeguard; the analyst may place more reliance on numbers from a sponsor who has an excellent track record. In any event, although all proposals that come up for approval are likely to satisfy the formal criteria for this reason, not all of them are truly attractive.

Models.   In addition to the basic capital budgeting model, there are specialized techniques, such as risk analysis, sensitivity analysis, simulation, scenario planning, game theory, option pricing models, contingent claims analysis, and decision tree analysis. Some of them have been oversold, but others are of practical value. The planning staff should be acquainted with them and require their use in situations in which the necessary data are available.

Organization for Analysis

A team may evaluate extremely large and important proposals, and the process may require a year or more. Even for small proposals, considerable discussion usually occurs between the sponsor of the proposal and the headquarters staff. As many as a dozen functional and line executives may sign off on an important proposal before it is submitted to the chief executive officer. The CEO may return the proposals for further analysis several times before making the final decision to go ahead with or reject the project. And as noted earlier, the decision to proceed may require a succession of development and testing hurdles be crossed before full implementation.

Recent work in the rapidly developing field of *expert systems* uses computer software in the analysis of proposed programs. The new software permits each participant in the team that is considering a proposal to vote on, and to explicitly rank, each of the criteria used to judge the project. The computer tabulates the results and uncovers inconsistencies or misunderstandings and raises questions about them. A succession of votes on criteria can lead to a conclusion that expresses the consensus of the group.

There is no set timetable for analyzing investment proposals. As soon as people are available they may start analysis. Planners collect approved projects during the year for inclusion in the capital budget. There is a deadline in the sense that the capital budget for next year has a deadline (usually just prior to the beginning of the budget year). If a proposal doesn't make that deadline, its formal approval may wait until the following year, unless there are unusual circumstances. The capital budget contains the authorized capital expenditures for the budget year, and, if additional amounts are approved, cash plans must be revised; there may be problems in financing the additional amount.

**Analyzing
Ongoing
Programs**

In addition to developing new programs, many companies have systematic ways of analyzing ongoing programs. Several analytical techniques can aid in this process. This section describes value chain analysis and activity-based costing.

Value Chain Analysis

The value chain for any firm is the linked set of value-creating activities of which it is a part, from acquiring the basic raw materials for component suppliers to making the ultimate end-use product and delivering it to the final consumers. Each firm must be understood in this context of its place in some overall chain of value-creating activities.

From the strategic planning perspective, the value chain concept highlights three potentially useful areas:

1. Linkages with suppliers.
2. Linkages with customers.
3. Process linkages within the value chain of the firm.

Linkages with Suppliers. As Exhibit 7–3 on the next page indicates, the linkage with suppliers should be managed so that both the firm and its suppliers can benefit. Taking advantage of such opportunities can dramatically lower costs, increase value, or both.

> **Example.** When delivery of bulk chocolate began in liquid form in tank cars instead of in 10-pound molded bars, an industrial chocolate firm (i.e., the supplier) eliminated the cost of molding and packing bars, and a confectionery producer (i.e., the firm) saved the cost of unpacking and melting.[3]

Linkages with Customers. As Exhibit 7–4 on the next page indicates, customer linkages can be just as important as supplier linkages. There are many examples of mutually beneficial linkages between a firm and its customers.

> **Example.** Some container producers (i.e., the firms) have constructed manufacturing facilities next to beer breweries (i.e., the customers) and deliver the containers through overhead conveyors directly onto the customers' assembly lines. This results in significant cost reductions for both the container producers and their customers by expediting the transport of empty containers, which are bulky and heavy.[4]

---

[3]M. Hergert and D. Morris, "Accounting Data for Value Analysis," *Strategic Management Journal* 10 (1989), pp. 175–88.
[4]Ibid.

EXHIBIT 7–3

Profit improvement opportunities through linkages with suppliers

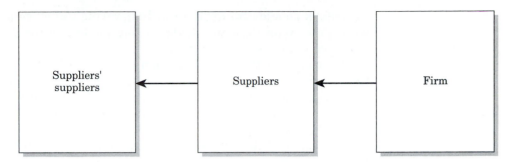

EXHIBIT 7–4

Profit improvement opportunities through linkages with customers

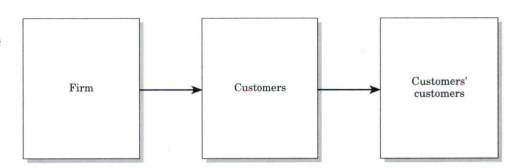

Process Linkages with the Value Chain of the Firm.   Value chain analysis explicitly recognizes the fact that the individual value activities within a firm are not independent but rather are interdependent.

Example.   At McDonald's, the timing of promotional campaigns (one value activity) significantly influences capacity utilization in production (another value activity). These linked activities must be coordinated if the full effect of the promotion is to be realized.

A company might want to analyze the process linkages within the value chain, seeking to improve their efficiency. The overall objective of this analysis is to move materials from vendors, through production, and to the customer at the lowest cost, in the shortest time, and of acceptable quality.

Efficiency of the design portion of the value chain might be increased by reducing the number of separate parts and increasing their ease of manufacture.

Example.   Japanese VCR producers were able to reduce prices from $1,300 in 1977 to $295 in 1984 by emphasizing the impact of an early step in the chain (product design) on a later step (production) by drastically reducing the number of parts in VCRs.[5]

---

[5]Ibid., p. 320.

A firm should also work toward improving the efficiency of every activity within the chain through a better understanding of the drivers that regulate costs and value for each activity.

Efficiency of the *inward* portion (i.e., the portion that precedes production) might be improved by reducing the number of vendors; by having a computer system place orders automatically; by limiting deliveries to "just-in-time" amounts (which reduces inventories); and by holding vendors responsible for quality, which reduces or eliminates inspection costs.

Efficiency of the *production* portion might be improved by increased automation, perhaps by using robots; by rearranging machines into "cells," each of which performs a series of related production steps; and by better production control systems.

Efficiency of the *outward* portion (i.e., from the factory door to the customer) might be improved by having customers place orders electronically (which is now common in hospital supply companies and in certain types of retailing); by changing the locations of warehouses; by changing channels of distribution and placing more or less emphasis on distributors and wholesalers; by improving the efficiency of warehouse operations; and by changing the mix between company-operated trucks and transportation furnished by outside agencies.

> **Examples.**   Procter & Gamble places order-entry computers in Wal-Mart stores, eliminating errors that used to occur when Wal-Mart buyers transmitted orders to P&G order-entry clerks, reducing the cost of operation in both firms, and reducing the time between initiation of an order and shipment of the goods. Levi Strauss has a similar system with its own retail stores.

These efficiency-oriented initiatives usually involve trade-offs. For example, direct orders from customer computers may speed delivery and reduce paperwork but lead to an increase in order-filling costs because of the smaller quantities ordered. Thus, it is important that all related parts of the value chain be analyzed together; otherwise, improvements in one link may be offset by additional costs in another.

Activity-Based Costing

Increased computerization and automation in factories have led to important changes in systems for collecting and using cost information. Sixty years ago, most companies allocated overhead costs to products by means of a plantwide overhead rate based on direct labor hours or dollars. Today, an increasing number of companies collect costs for material-related costs (e.g., transportation, storage) separately from other manufacturing costs; and they collect manufacturing costs for individual departments, individual machines, or individual "cells," which consist of groups of machines that perform a series of related operations on a product. In these cost centers, direct labor costs may be combined with other costs, giving *conversion cost*—that is, the labor and factory overhead cost of converting raw materials and parts into finished products. In addition to conversion costs, the newer systems also assign R&D, general and administrative, and marketing costs to products. The newer systems also use multiple allocation bases. In these newer systems, the word *activity* is often used instead of *cost center,* and *cost driver* used instead of *basis of allocation;* and the cost system is called an *activity-based cost system* (ABC).[6]

The basis of allocation, or cost driver, for each of the cost centers reflects the *cause* of cost incurrence—that is, the element that explains why the amount of cost incurred in the cost center, or activity, varies. For example, in procurement, the cost driver may be the number of orders placed; for internal transportation, the number of parts moved; for product design, the number of different parts in the product; and for production control, the number of set-ups. Note that "cause" here refers to the factor causing the costs in the individual cost center.

> **Examples.**   General Motors used ABC analysis to formulate a component make-or-buy strategy. In a single plant, its ABC system had over 5,000 activity cost pools and over 100 different cost drivers (i.e., drivers that traced activity cost pools to products).[7]
>
> Schrader Bellows, a division of Scovill, Inc., used ABC analysis to reevaluate marketing and product line strategies. Its ABC analysis had 28 activity cost pools and 16 cost drivers. Its previous system had one cost pool for each of the five production departments and used one cost driver (direct labor) to allocate the cost pools to products.[8]

The ABC concept is not particularly subtle or counterintuitive. In fact, it is very much in line with common sense. But in earlier days factories tended to produce fewer different products, cost was labor dominated (high labor cost relative to overhead), and products tended to differ less in the amount of support services they consumed. Thus, the activity basis for overhead allocation was not likely to result in product costs much different from a simple volume-driven basis tied to labor cost.

Today, labor cost in many companies is not only dramatically less important, it is also viewed less and less as a cost to be varied when production volume varies. Indirect cost is now the dominant part of cost in many companies. In the prototypical "flexible factory," raw material is the only production volume–dependent cost and the only cost directly relatable to individual

---

[6]We use the term *traditional* to refer to systems used by many, but by no means all, companies. As Shank points out, many of the essentials of ABC go back to J. M. Clark's 1923 book, *Studies in the Economics of Overhead Costs.* John K. Shank, "Strategic Cost Management: New Wine or Just New Bottles," *Journal of Management Accounting Research,* Fall 1989, p. 48.

[7]George Beaujon and Vinod Singhal, "Understanding the Activity Costs in an Activity-Based Cost System," *Journal of Cost Management for the Manufacturing Industry,* Spring 1990, pp. 51–72.

[8]Robin Cooper, "Schrader Bellows," Harvard Business School case 186-272.

products. Advocates of ABC maintain that a meaningful assessment of full cost today *must* involve assigning overhead in proportion to the activities that generate it in the long run.

Use of ABC Information

ABC, when used as part of the strategic planning process, may provide useful insights. For example, it may show that complex products with many separate parts have higher design and production costs than simpler products; that products with low volume have higher unit costs than high-volume products; that products with many setups or many engineering change orders have higher unit costs than other products; and that products with a short life cycle have higher unit costs than other products. Information on the magnitude of these differences may lead to changes in policies relating to full line versus focused product line, product pricing, make-or-buy decisions, product mix decisions, adding or deleting products, elimination of non value added activities, and to an emphasis on better factory layouts and simplicity in product design.

> **Examples.** In 1992, Chrysler benefited from ABC analysis in a pilot project that examined the designs for wiring harnesses for the company's popular minivans. The harnesses yoke together bundles of wires. Nine departments, from design to assembly to finance, set out to reckon the optimum number of wiring harnesses. The assembly people favored using just one kind of harness, the design group wanted nine, and so on. When ABC was used to cost out activities across the entire production of the vehicles, everyone saw the optimum number was two.
>
> Hewlett-Packard's successful products, new models of HP 3000 and HP 9000 midrange computers, benefited from better cost information. When ABC showed that testing new designs and parts was extremely expensive, engineers changed their plans to favor components that required less testing, thus lowering costs.[9]

Other companies have realized significant cost savings as a result of reducing complexity.

> **Examples.**   Procter & Gamble had standardized product formulas and packages. P&G used just two basic packages for shampoo in the United States, saving $25 million a year.[10]
>
> General Motors had reduced the number of US car models from 53 to 44 and combined its Pontiac and GMC division to simplify marketing.[11]

Strategic Planning Process

In a company that operates on a calendar-year basis, the strategic planning process starts in the spring and is completed in the fall, just prior to the preparation of the annual budget. The process involves the following steps:

---

[9]Ibid.

[10]Zachary Schiller, "Making It Simple," *Business Week,* Setember 9, 1996, pp. 96–104.

[11]Ibid.

1. Reviewing and updating the strategic plan from last year.
2. Deciding on assumptions and guidelines.
3. First iteration of the new strategic plan.
4. Analysis.
5. Second iteration of the new strategic plan.
6. Review and approval.

Reviewing and Updating the Strategic Plan

During the course of a year, decisions are made that change the strategic plan; management makes decisions whenever there is a need to do so, not in response to a set timetable. Conceptually, the implications of each decision for the next five years should be incorporated in the strategic plan as soon as the decision is made. Otherwise, the formal plan no longer represents the path that the company plans to follow. In particular, the plan may not represent a valid base for testing proposed strategies and programs, which is one of the plan's principal values. As a practical matter, however, very few organizations continuously update their strategic plans. Updating involves more paperwork and computer time than management believes is worthwhile.

The first step in the annual strategic planning process, therefore, is to review and update the strategic plan that was agreed to last year. Actual experience for the first few months of the current year is already reflected in the accounting reports, and these are extrapolated for the current best estimate of the year as a whole. If the computer program is sufficiently flexible, it can extend the impact of current forces to the "out years"—that is, the years beyond the current year; if not, rough estimates are made manually. The implications of new program decisions on revenues, expenses, capital expenditures, and cash flow are incorporated. The planning staff usually makes this update. Management may be involved if there are uncertainties or ambiguities in the program decisions that must be resolved.

Deciding on Assumptions and Guidelines

The updated strategic plan incorporates such broad assumptions as the growth in Gross Domestic Product, cyclical movements, labor rates, prices of important raw materials, interest rates, selling prices, market conditions such as the actions of competitors, and the impact of government legislation in each of the countries in which the company operates. These assumptions are reexamined and, if necessary, are changed to incorporate the latest information.

The updated strategic plan contains the implications on revenues, expenses, and cash flows of the existing operating facilities and changes in these facilities from opening new plants, expanding existing plants, closing plants, and relocating facilities. It shows the amount of new capital likely to be available from retained earnings and new financing. These conditions are examined to ensure that they are currently valid, and the amounts are extended for another year.

The resulting update is not done in great detail. A rough approximation is adequate as a basis for senior management decisions about objectives that are to be attained in the plan years and about the key guidelines that are to be observed in planning how to attain these objectives. The objectives usually are stated separately for each product line and are expressed as sales revenue, as a profit percentage, or a return on capital employed. The principal guidelines are assumptions about wage and salary increases (including new benefits programs that may affect compensation), new or discontinued product lines, and selling prices. For overhead units, personnel ceilings may be specified. At this stage, they represent senior management's tentative views. In the next stage, business unit managers have an opportunity to present their views.

Management Meetings.   Many companies hold an annual meeting of corporate and business unit managers (often called a "summit conference") to discuss the proposed objectives and guidelines. Such a meeting typically lasts several days and is held away from company facilities to minimize distractions. In addition to the formal agenda, such a meeting provides an opportunity for managers throughout the corporation to get to know one another.

First Iteration of the Strategic Plan

Using the assumptions, objectives, and guidelines, the business units and other operating units prepare their "first cut" of the strategic plan, which may include different operating plans than those included in the current plan, such as a change in marketing tactics; these are supported by reasons. Business unit staffs do much of the analytical work, but business unit managers make the final judgments. Depending on the personal relationships, business unit personnel may seek the advice of the headquarters staff in the development of these plans. Members of the headquarters staff often visit the business units during this process for the purpose of clarifying the guidelines, assumptions, and instructions and, in general, to assist in the planning process.

The completed strategic plan consists of income statements; of inventory, accounts receivable, and other key balance sheet items; of number of employees; of quantitative information about sales and production; of expenditures for plant and other capital acquisitions; of any other unusual cash flows; and of a narrative explanation and justification. The numbers are in considerable detail (although in much less detail than in the annual budget) for the next year and the following year, with only summary information for the later years.

Analysis

When headquarters receives the business unit plans, they aggregate them into an overall corporate strategic plan. Planning staff and the marketing, production, and other functional executives at headquarters analyze this plan in depth. Business Unit X plans a new marketing tactic; is it likely that the resulting sales will be as large as the plan indicates? Business Unit Y plans an increase in general and administrative personnel; are the additional people really needed? Business Unit Z assumes a large increase in productivity; is the supporting justification realistic? Research and development promises important new products; are the business units prepared to manufacture and sell these products? Some business unit managers tend to build *slack* into their estimates, so their objectives are more easily accomplished; can some of this slack be detected and eliminated?

The headquarters people examine the business unit plans for consistency also. If one business unit manufactures for another unit, are the planned shipments from the manufacturing unit equal to the planned sales of the sales unit? In particular, are planned shipments to overseas subsidiaries consistent with the planned sales volume of these subsidiaries?

Headquarters staff and their counterparts in the business units resolve some of these questions by discussion and report others to corporate management, at which point they are the basis for discussions between corporate managers and business unit managers. These discussions are the heart of the formal planning process, usually requiring several hours and often going on for a day or more in each business unit.

In many cases, the sum of the business unit plans reveals a *planning gap*—that is, the sum of the individual plans does not add up to attainment of the corporate objectives. There are only three ways to close a planning gap: (1) find opportunities for improvements in the business unit plans, (2) make acquisitions, or (3) review the corporate objectives. Senior management usually focuses on the first.

From the planning numbers, the headquarters staff can develop planned cash requirements for the whole organization. These may indicate the need for additional financing or, alternatively, the possibility of increasing dividends.[12]

Second Iteration of the Strategic Plan

Analysis of the first submission may require a revision of the plans of only certain business units, but it may lead to a change in the assumptions and guidelines that affect all business units. For example, the aggregation of all plans may indicate that the cash drain from increasing inventories and capital expenditures is more than the company can safely tolerate; if so, there may be a requirement for postponing expenditures throughout the organization. These decisions lead to a revision of the plan. Technically, the revision is much simpler to prepare than the original submission, because it requires

---

[12]For a discussion of this point, see V. Govindarajan and John K. Shank, "Cash Sufficiency: The Missing Link in Strategy Planning," *Journal of Business Strategy,* Summer 1986, pp. 88–95.

changes in only a few numbers; but organizationally, it is the most painful part of the process because it calls for difficult decisions.

Some companies do not require a formal revision from the business units. They negotiate the changes informally and enter the results into the plan at headquarters.

Final Review and Approval

A meeting of senior corporate officials usually discusses the revised plan at length. The plan also may be presented at a meeting of the board of directors. The chief executive officer gives final approval. The approval should come prior to the beginning of the budget preparation process, because the strategic plan is an important input to that process.

Summary

A strategic plan shows the implications, over the next several years, of implementing the company's strategies.

In the period since the current strategic plan was prepared, the organization has made capital investment decisions. The process of approving proposed capital investments does not follow a set timetable; senior managers make the decisions as soon as the need for them is identified. Planners incorporate in the strategic plan the implications of these decisions, as well as assumptions and guidelines about external forces such as inflation, internal policies, and product pricing.

Using on this information, the business units and support units propose new strategic plans, and these are discussed in depth with senior management. If the resulting corporate plan does not indicate that profitability will be adequate, there is a planning gap, which is dealt with by a second iteration of the strategic plan, sometimes entailing painful curtailments of business unit plans.

Several analytical techniques, such as value chain analysis and activity-based costing, can aid in the strategic planning process.

APPENDIX
MERCK'S RESEARCH PLANNING MODEL

Research is the life blood of the pharmaceutical industry; but research by its nature is risky, because management must invest without knowing if that investment is ever going to yield a new drug. Exacerbating this is the trend of increasing R&D costs, which means companies are putting more of their shareholders' money at risk to find that next new drug. To discover one drug, companies must evaluate thousands of compounds, and, even after identifying that one promising drug, there is still only a one in eight chance that it will complete the seven-year-development phase and be approved for sale. Of those drugs that are eventually commercialized, only three in ten ever recover their full cost of discovery and development. A recent study estimated that the cost to discover and develop a new chemical entity was approximately $230 million, including the cost of failures and the time value of money. Consequently, management must actively monitor its research investments to increase the likelihood of returning the company's cost of capital.

To facilitate the R&D management process at Merck & Co., Inc., a comprehensive quantitative planning model, which combines discounted cash flow analysis with probabilistic risk analysis, was developed. This model incorporates monetary and nonmonetary factors affecting an R&D project, and then it applies state-of-the-art financial evaluation techniques to quantify the expected returns and to measure the risks associated with a project or a portfolio of projects.

The Merck model covers a twenty-year time horizon and includes drivers of commercial performance, such as unit volume forecasts, pricing projections, manufacturing costs, manufacturing capital, and exchange and inflation rate projections. To capture the variability and uncertainty that is inherent in projecting these variables, the model uses inputs in the form of frequency distributions, rather than just single point estimates.

As an example of how the inputs are derived, the sales forecast for a product is made by the product manager who takes into consideration the factors that affect the product's performance over the forecast period. These factors include such things as patent life, other competitive products, size of market, and therapeutic or diagnostic profile. For each year, the product manager provides estimates of the optimistic, most likely, and pessimistic forecast levels. These forecasts are then submitted to senior marketing management for approval.

In addition to the financial variables, the model also requires assumptions for key nonmonetary variables, such as dosage, launch date, and, most important, the probability of technical success.

The Merck model runs several hundred iterations for each product development candidate, and then statistically describes several critical output variables, including annual nominal and constant dollar sales projections, cash flows, return on investment, and net present value (NPV). Frequency distributions for key variables are created in order to quantify riskiness in terms of dispersion of results, as well as the expected value of the project.

This appendix was written by Judy C. Lewent, Vice President, Finance, and Chief Financial Officer of Merck & Co., Inc.

Exhibit 1

*Probability
of exceeding
cost of capital*

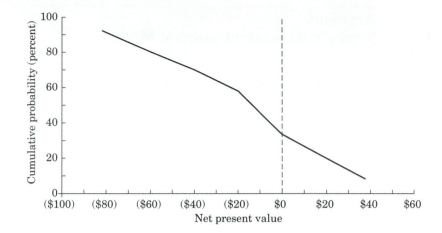

An example of a frequency table for one of the output statistics, net present value, is shown in Exhibit 1. In this case, the project has a 30 percent chance that the NPV will exceed the cost of capital. By selecting points along the x- and y-axis, the probability of a certain NPV being achieved can be determined.

Periodically, forecasts from the Merck model are compared with the actual results for that same period. This process helps test the accuracy and reliability of the model's projections, and highlights areas where assumptions in future forecasts may need to be more closely examined. It also helps to identify areas for future methodological improvements.

This model is used extensively within Merck in three ways: to evaluate business opportunities; to help manage R&D; and to assist in long-range planning. Concerning business opportunities, the model is used in evaluating proposed product licensing candidates, capital expenditures, existing businesses, and acquisition candidates. Regarding management of R&D, it is employed in: making the go/no go investment decisions for product development candidates at various stages of the development process; quantifying the value of back-up compounds; optimizing the portfolio of development projects undertaken; and providing a measure for judging productivity of the R&D organization. Last, the Merck model is used to extend the time horizon of the company's five-year long-range operating plan to ten- and fifteen-year projections. Such projections can be used to identify strategic issues that face the company, as well as to assess the impact of proposed business alliances on the company's longer-term growth prospects.

Suggested Additional Readings

Banker, Rajiv D., and Holly H. Johnston. "An Empirical Study of Cost Drivers in the
    U.S. Airline Industry." *The Accounting Review* 68, no. 3 (July 1993), pp. 576–601.
Brethauer. *The Power of Strategic Costing: Uncover Your Competitors' and Suppliers'
    Costs.* AMACOM, 1999.
Cooper, R., and R. Slagmulder. *Supply Chain Development for the Lean Enterprise:
    Interorganizational Cost Management.* Productivity Press, September 1999.

Govindarajan, Vijay, and John K. Shank. "Strategic Cost Management: The Value Chain Perspective." *Journal of Management Accounting Research* 4 (Fall 1992), pp. 179–97.

Haka, S. F., L. A. Gordan, and G. E. Pinches. "Sophisticated Capital Budgeting Selection Techniques and Firm Performance." *The Accounting Review,* October 1985, pp. 651–69.

Hicks, D. T. *Activity-Based Costing: Making It Work for Small and Mid-Sized Companies.* 2nd ed. New York: John Wiley & Sons, 1999.

Porter, Michael E. *Competitive Advantage.* New York: Free Press, 1985.

Shank, John K., and Vijay Govindarajan. *Strategic Cost Management.* New York: Free Press, 1993.

Tucker, K. *Scenario Planning.* Association Management, April 1999.

Ulwick, A. W. *Business Strategy Formulation: Theory Process, and the Intellectual Revolution.* Westport, CT: Quorum Books, 1999.

CASE 7–1
ALLIED OFFICE PRODUCTS

The TFC Business

In 1992, Allied Office Products was a corporation with annual sales of $900 million in business forms and specialty paper products, such as writing paper, envelopes, note cards, and greeting cards. In 1988 the company had expanded into business forms inventory management services. This was an area where Allied believed it could offer value-added services to differentiate it from other business forms manufacturers. The forms manufacturing business was mature by 1988, and all competitors were seeking ways to generate sales growth. Allied embarked on a campaign to enroll its corporate clients in a program which it called "Total Forms Control" (TFC).

By 1992, sales from TFC were about $60 million and Allied had established a separate company within the business forms division to handle these accounts. The services provided under TFC included warehousing and distribution of forms (including inventory financing) as well as inventory control and forms usage reporting. Allied used a sophisticated computer systems network to monitor a client's forms inventory, forms usage, and ordering activities. They provided this information to their clients via comprehensive yet simple-to-read management reports.

As part of its distribution services, Allied also offered "pick pack" service where trained workers actually opened full cartons to pick the exact number of forms requested by the clients. Allied's philosophy was that a well-run warehousing and distribution network is vital to any forms management program—"we know what you need . . . the *right* product at the *right* place at the *right* time."

For a small number of clients Allied also offered "desk top delivery," where Allied personnel would distribute the forms to individual offices (forms were usually delivered only to the loading dock). As a comprehensive forms management provider, Allied's product line also had to be comprehensive. Their product line included everything from standard computer printout paper and fax paper to custom-designed forms tailored to meet the exact business needs of the client.

Current Cost Accounting System

Allied operated its forms manufacturing and TFC activities as separate profit centers. The transfer of product to TFC was at arm's length with the transfer price set at fair market value.

Allied manufactured business forms in 13 locations. Although the company encouraged internal sourcing for customer orders, TFC salespeople had the option of outsourcing product if necessary. The industry value chain for TFC is shown in Exhibit 1.

Clients who participated in the forms management program kept an inventory of forms at one of Allied's 10 distribution centers. The forms were distributed to the client as needed. The client was charged a service fee to cover the cost of warehousing and distribution based on a percentage of the cost of sales of the product for that month, regardless of the specific level of service provided to that client.

If a TFC client made use of any of the distribution services, they were supposed to be charged a price for the forms which was high enough to allow for an additional 32.2 percent of product cost to cover warehousing and distribution expenses, the cost of capital tied up in

This case was adapted by Professor John Shank of the Amos Tuck School, by permission, from earlier versions prepared by Professor Vijay Govindarajan and Jay Weiss (T'93) of the Amos Tuck School, Dartmouth College.

Exhibit 1

The value chain concept—TFC

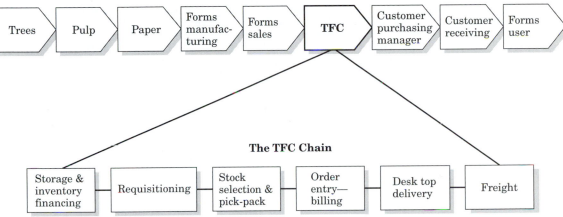

EXHIBIT 2   Calculation of Service Fee Charges (000s)

1990 Product sales at cost	$24,059
1990 Warehousing/distribution expense	$ 4,932
% of product cost	20.5%
1990 Average inventory balance	$10,873
1990 Average cost of capital	10.4%
Total cost of inventory financing	$ 1,131
% of product cost	4.7%
1990 Total freight charges	$ 1,684
% of product cost	7.0%
Total services costs	32.2%
Standard price = (Product cost * 1.32) * 1.2	

inventory and freight expense. This percentage was determined based on actual 1990 financial data so that on an aggregate basis, in total, all expenses were covered (see Exhibit 2). The sales force then marked up the cost of product and services by 20 percent, on average. As shown in Exhibits 3 and 4, prices for individual accounts could vary from the standard formula.

Understanding Customer Profitability

With TFC profitability suffering in October 1992, General Manager John Malone began to question the appropriateness of the distribution charges.

"The Business Forms Division in 1988 earned a 20 percent Return on Investment (ROI). But returns have been dropping for several years. TFC is projected to earn an ROI of only 6 percent for 1992. Something tells me that we are not managing this business very well! It seems to me that the charge for services needs closer scrutiny. I believe we should charge our clients for the services they use. It doesn't seem fair that if two clients buy the same amount of product from us, but one keeps a lot of inventory at our distribution center and is constantly requesting small shipments and the other hardly bothers us at all, both should pay the same service fees."

John looked through his records and found two accounts of similar size, accounts A and B, which were handled by different sales people. Accounts A and B both had annual sales of $79,320 with the cost of the product being $50,000. Under the current system, these accounts carried the

EXHIBIT 3   **Top 20 TFC Accounts for August 1992**
             (ranked by contribution $)

Account	Actual Net Sales	Product Cost	ABC-Based Service Costs	Revised Contribution
1	$ 76,904	$ 49,620	$ 2,862	$ 24,422
2	130,582	74,396	34,578	21,608
3	72,956	48,216	3,456	21,284
4	64,903	37,981	6,574	20,348
5	45,088	26,098	1,309	17,681
6	104,689	62,340	25,356	16,993
•	•	•	•	•
•	•	•	•	•
•	•	•	•	•
18	45,893	29,570	6,904	9,419
19	62,954	41,034	13,746	8,174
20	26,699	16,830	2,236	7,633
Total	$1,279,133	$779,003	$209,852	$290,278

EXHIBIT 4   **Bottom 20 TFC Accounts for August 1992**
             (ranked by contribution $)

Account	Actual Net Sales	Product Cost	ABC-Based Service Costs	Revised Contribution
1081	$ 3,657	$ 2,356	$ 2,325	$ −1,024
1082	38,467	26,301	13,740	−1,574
1083	5,926	3,840	4,214	−2,128
1084	163	89	2,390	−2,316
1085	3,256	2,006	3,590	−2,340
1086	82,086	61,224	23,756	−2,894
•	•	•	•	•
•	•	•	•	•
•	•	•	•	•
1098	74,569	50,745	45,698	−21,874
1099	88,345	64,930	53,867	−30,452
1100	113,976	82,987	72,589	−41,600
Total	$717,142	$486,035	$417,472	$−186,365

Distribution Center: Activity Analysis

same service charges, but John noticed that these accounts were similar only in the value of the product being sold; they were very different on the level of service they required from Allied.

In the past year, customer A had submitted 364 requisitions for product with a total of 910 lines[1] (all of them "pick-pack") while customer B had submitted 790 requisitions with a total of 2500 lines (all "pick-pack"). Customer A kept an average of 350 cartons of inventory at the distribution center while customer B kept 700 on average. Customer B's average monthly inventory balance was $50,000 ($7,000 of which had been sitting around for a whole year) while that of customer A was only $15,000. Because of the greater activity on customer B's account, a shipment went out three times a week at an annual freight cost of $7,500 while Customer A required only one shipment a week at an annual freight cost of $2,250. In addition, customer B had requested desk top delivery 26 times during the past year, while customer A did not request desk top delivery at all. John Malone turned to TFC Controller Melissa Dunhill and Director of Operations Tim Cunningham for help.

John said, "How can I better understand customer profitability?" "Well," Tim said, "if we can figure out, without going overboard of course, what exactly goes on in the distribution centers, maybe we can have a much better idea of what it costs to serve our various clients." Tim knew that two primary activities took place in the distribution centers—the warehousing of forms and the distribution of those forms in response to a customer requisition. He and John decided to talk to some people in the field to get more specific information.

John and Tim visited Allied's Kansas City, Missouri, distribution facility. Site manager Wilbur Smith confirmed, "All we do is store the cartons and process the requisitions. The amount of warehouse space we need just depends on the number of cartons. It seems like we've got a lot of cartons that just sit here forever. If we created some flexible lease programs and changed aisle configurations, we could probably adjust our space requirements if the number of cartons we stored were to change. The other thing that really bothers me is that we've got some inventory that's been sitting here forever. What's it to the client? They don't pay for it until they requisition it. Isn't there a way we can make them get this stuff out of here?

"As far as the administration of the operation goes, everything depends on the number of requisitions. And, on a given requisition, the customer can request as many different items as they like."

The team then interviewed warehouse supervisor Rick Fosmire, who said, "I don't care if I get a hundred requisitions with one line each or one requisition with a hundred lines on it, my guys still have to go pick a hundred items off the shelves. And those damn "pick-pack" requests. Almost everything is "pick-pack" nowadays. No one seems to order a whole carton of 500 items anymore. Do you know how much more labor it requires to pick through those cartons? And on top of that, this desk top delivery is a real pain for my guys. Sure, we offer the service, but the clients who use it should have to pay something extra. It's not like my guys don't have enough to do."

John and Tim were starting to get a pretty good idea of what goes on in the distribution centers, but there was still one person to talk to. They knew that a lot of money was spent on data processing, mostly labor. They needed to know how those people spent their time.

Hazel Nutley had been a data entry operator at Allied for 17 years. "All I do is key in those

[1]Whenever a customer requires forms, they submit a requisition for all the different products they need. Each separate product request is a "line." If the request is for whole cartons, it is considered a "carton line." For quantities less than a whole carton, it is considered a "pick-pack line."

requisitions, line by line by line. I've gotten to the point where I know the customers so well that all the order information is easy. The only thing that really matters is how many lines I have to enter."

Using the interviews and observations, Tim and John broke distribution down into six primary value-added activities—storage, requisition handling, basic warehouse stock selection, "pick-pack" activity, data entry, and desk top delivery. With Melissa's help, they assigned costs to these activities as follows for a sample of five of the distribution centers (see Exhibit 5 for calculations):

Storage	$1,550
Requisition handling	1,801
Basic warehouse stock selection	761
"Pick-pack" activity	734
Data entry	612
Desk top delivery	250
Total	$5,708

Tim then estimated the following for 1992 based upon historical information and current trends for the sample of five warehouses:

EXHIBIT 5   Breakdown of Expenses by Activity (000s)

	Total Expense	Activity Costs*
Rent	$ 1,424 × 85%	$ 1,211
Depreciation	$ 208 × 85%	177
Utilities	$ 187 × 85%	159
Security	$ 3	3
Total storage expense		$ 1,550
Rent	$ 1,424 × 15%	$ 214
Depreciation	$ 208 × 15%	31
Utilities	$ 187 × 15%	28
Salaries + fringes	$ 909	909
Telephone	$ 96	96
Taxes/insurance	$ 104	104
Travel/entertainment	$ 40 × 75%	30
Postage	$ 56	56
Hourly payroll + fringes	$ 316	316
Temp help	$ 17	17
Total requisition handling expense		$ 1,801
Variable warehouse pay + fringes	$ 1,735	$ 1,735
Travel and entertainment (25%)	$ 40 × 25%	10
Total warehouse activity		$ 1,745
Basic warehouse stock selection (44%)		$ 761
"Pick-pack" activity (42%)		734
Desk top delivery (14%)		250
Data processing expense	$ 612	612
Total	$ 5,708	$ 5,708

*Some expense items were allocated between activities.

- On average, these five distribution centers scattered across the country will have combined inventories of approximately 350,000 cartons (most cartons are of fairly standard size).
- They will process about 310,000 requisitions for 1992.
- Each requisition will average 2.5 lines.
- About 90 percent of the lines will require "pick-pack" activity (as opposed to shipping an entire carton).
- Cost of capital in 1992 was probably about 13 percent.

"Our new computer system is coming on line soon, which will track individual freight charges," said Tim, "so, we can just charge the client for what it actually costs us." John and Melissa agreed that this sounded fair.

Some things that were said at the distribution center still stuck in Tim's mind. "Don't you think we should do something to get that old inventory moving? What about charging something extra, say 1.5 percent per month, for anything that's been there over nine months."

"Great idea," Melissa said. "This will also help protect us against the loss we often take on old inventory when the clients end up changing their forms. You know we just eat that and never charge them for it."

They were almost finished. "What about desk top delivery?" Tim said. "I think we should charge extra for it, but I don't want this to get too complicated."

John said, "How much extra time does it take your guys on average to run around the client company?"

"I'd say about an hour and a half to two hours at $15 per hour, that's about $30 each time. Sound fair?"

"Sounds OK to me. Also, that ties pretty well to the $250,000 overall assignment, since we will process somewhere around 8,500 'desk top' requests this year."

Services Based Pricing (SBP)

The entire management team, including Doug Kingsley, Chief Financial Officer of the Business Forms Division, felt that there had to be a better way of charging out distribution services to help TFC become more profitable. They now had a much better understanding of the drivers of costs involved in distribution services.

"It wouldn't be easy getting the sales force to accept an activity-based pricing program," John said. "Some of them get pretty stuck in their ways and don't like change. Some accounts would see increases because of the additional distribution charges under a Services Based Pricing (SBP) scheme. These salespeople wouldn't be very happy. On the other hand, some salespeople may see their margins increase." Overcoming these organizational problems would be only the tip of the iceberg.

The accounting department maintained a data base which showed all activity against individual accounts and calculated a contribution from that account. However, they had not yet been able to use this information effectively. TFC management took their data and began to analyze it.

Although TFC maintained 1100 separate accounts, a large portion of the business came from very few accounts. The top 40 accounts represented 48 percent of the company's net sales (see Exhibit 6).

Exhibit 6   TFC Net Sales, 1991

Annual Sales/Account	Number of Accounts	% of TFC Net Sales
>$ 300,000	40	48%
>$ 150,000	53	19
>$ 75,000	86	15
>$ 30,000	143	11
>$ 0	778	7
Total	1100	100%

As a way of understanding customer profitability, TFC management reworked the information in the data base as if the accounts had been charged service fees based on actual usage, leaving net sales and product cost the same as before. They recalculated contribution based on these figures. They ranked the accounts according to profit contribution. Exhibit 3 shows the top 20 accounts for the month of August and Exhibit 4 shows the bottom 20.

Since such a large part of the profit opportunity rested with so few accounts, management felt that it might be possible to significantly improve profitability by concentrating on individual account management. The team felt they were on the right track for improving account profitability and wondered what should be the next step. They also wondered what other issues might be important for improving the overall profitability of TFC.

Questions

1. Using the information in the text and in Exhibit 5, calculate "ABC"-based services costs for the TFC business.

2. Using your new costing system, calculate distribution services costs for "Customer A" and "Customer B."

3. What inference do you draw about the profitability of these two customers?

4. Should TFC implement the SBP pricing system?

5. What managerial advice do you have for Allied about the Total Forms Control (TFC) business? How does Exhibit 1 relate to this question?

CASE 7–2
COPLEY MANUFACTURING COMPANY

Copley Manufacturing Company had begun formal corporatewide planning in 1981. Its planning system was modified in 1982 and modified again in 1983. Company executives reviewed the experiences of these three years to see what lessons could be learned that would lead to an improved planning system.

Copley had grown fairly steadily in size and profitability since its founding in 1919; its growth was particularly rapid in the late 1960s and the 1970s. For most of its history, it was primarily a manufacturer of a wide line of cutting tools and related parts and supplies, and the Cutting Tool Division in 1983 was the largest division. In 1983, there were eight other operating divisions, each making and selling a line of industrial products. Some of these divisions were the outgrowth of acquisitions; others had their origin in products developed by the corporate research department. Divisions had considerable autonomy. Sales volume in 1983 was $700 million, net income was $42 million, and there were 17,000 employees.

Introduction to Formal Planning

The formal planning effort at the corporate level was an outgrowth of work initiated by Russell A. Wilde, in mid-1977. Mr. Wilde had been head of the Precipitator Division's commercial development department and, as such, had been deeply involved in the division's efforts beginning early in 1977 to "plan ahead." Mr. Wilde's effort at the corporate level actually began as a search for companies to acquire, since Copley's top management saw the key question to be: "How should we diversify?"

This case was prepared by Robert N. Anthony, Harvard Business School. Copyright © by the President and Fellows of Harvard College. Harvard Business School case 176-189.

Within six months, Mr. Wilde was arguing that the crucial questions to be asked really were: "What are our objectives?" and "What is our potential?"

One result of the dialogue that followed was a request by Stanley Burton, president of Copley, for the divisions to look 10 years ahead and to predict sales, profit, cash flow, and return on investment. Mr. Wilde composed the actual questions asked of the divisions and coordinated collection of the data. The resulting consolidated growth projection was not ideal in the eyes of top management, but no imminent crisis was seen.

The 10-year look indicated that many of Copley's markets were mature, that its profits were indeed sensitive to cyclical swings, and that a large cash flow could be expected in the coming years. Before the end of 1978, Charles N. Sagan was appointed director of corporate development, reporting to Mr. Burton. Mr. Sagan was to be mainly concerned with growth through acquisition and merger.

Late in 1980, Mr. Sagan began reporting to Mr. Albert, executive vice president. The two easily agreed that regular formal planning should become part of management's way of life at Copley. They were encouraged to work toward this end when Samuel K. Savage, chairman of the board, suggested that Copley should do some five-year sales forecasting.

The 1981 Effort

A corporate planning committee was set up in February 1981 by Mr. Albert to guide the move toward a regular formal planning process. The planning committee comprised the vice president for research, the controller, the corporate economist, Mr. Albert, and Mr. Sagan. The latter was named chief coordinator of the committee.

The planning committee met almost weekly for the next few months and attacked two major questions.

1. By what process should formalized planning be ingrained into life at Copley?
2. What are appropriate corporate goals for Copley?

A year later, in early 1982, no answer had yet been given to the second question, but decisions were made concerning the first.

A March 21, 1981, memorandum from Mr. Albert to division general managers cited a need for regular formal planning and outlined a plan and schedule for starting such an effort. The basic idea was to survey divisional planning history and attitudes and, after discussions, to issue guidelines for the preparation of divisional "provisional plans."

Visits by Corporate Groups

The concept of formal planning activities was introduced by the organization through a series of visits to the divisions by corporate groups beginning June 6. The composition of the groups varied somewhat but always included Mr. Albert and Mr. Sagan. In these introductory meetings, Mr. Albert explained the importance of the planning effort, and Mr. Sagan explained the details. Divisions were asked to produce a five-year plan by October 1, 1981. It was left to the divisions to decide exactly who would do what in the process and in what format the final plans would be presented. Corporate staff groups were also instructed to submit plans.

The controller described the financial data to be submitted in the five-year plan in a memorandum dated July 19, 1981, as follows:

Sales—Please state past and future sales at 1981 prices and also in actual dollars, in total, by major product group, and by market group (e.g., domestic customers, export customers, intercompany).

Profit before Taxes—Analyze projected dollar profit in terms of variance from projected 1981 dollar profit. The significant areas of variance should be:

Price Realization—The change in profit due to prices being higher or lower than 1981.

Volume and Product Mix—The change in profit contribution due to changes in physical volume and product mix. This is calculated by applying 1981 contribution ratios to the change in physical volume, by product line.

Cost Variances—Changes in unit variable costs or aggregate fixed costs should be stated. These aggregated changes should be separated into *price* (wage and material rates) variances and *efficiency* (all other) variances.

Profit after Taxes—Translate pretax to aftertax profit dollars for future years at the 1981 tax rate. Show income taxes and investment credit separately.

Cash Flow—The following should be drawn by years in total and by product line where a determination can be made. *Full* product line data is not required, but some indication of cash flow, say, inventories and capital expenditures, by product line will be helpful.

Profit after taxes.
Depreciation.
Accounts receivable.
Inventories.
Capital expenditures.
Other working capital items:
    Cash (working balance only).
    Prepaid expense.
    Accounts payable and accruals.
    Etc.
All other.
Total Cash Flow.

Planning Review Meetings

Meetings to review divisional plans were held in November and December. As was expected, the format of the divisional plans and presentations varied widely. Attendance at the planning reviews varied, also. The planning committee always attended, as did the head of the division being reviewed. In addition, members of the executive committee attended on occasion. Divisions were free to bring whomever they wished to their planning review. Representatives of divisions other than the one being reviewed on a given day were not invited to attend.

Planning Response Meetings

A second series of meetings was started December 28, 1981. In these meetings, the planning committee commented on the divisional presentation to the division general managers. The divisions had been expecting some reaction by corporate management ever since the planning reviews, and these planning responses were designed to meet this expectation. Typical of these meetings was that of the Cutting Tool Division, whose general manager, Mr. Tyler, had recently become a member of the planning committee. The Cutting Tool Division discussion lasted three hours, with Mr. Tyler and the rest of the committee openly evaluating the Cutting Tool Division's plans and its planning review.

Mr. Albert sent a memorandum to the general manager of each division after its "planning response" meeting. Each memorandum summarized the major points agreed upon in the meeting, thanked the participants for their effort in 1981, and expressed the desire for continued progress in making planning a way of life for the Copley manager.

The results of the first planning cycle were judged as mixed by Mr. Sagan and by members of top management. It was generally felt that the divisions had made a good beginning, but that they had only begun to dent the planning task. Divisional plans were seen generally to be optimistic extrapolations of past operating trends. Some members of management criticized the effort as having been a numbers game. Others countered that these results were a necessary first step. Most agreed that the plans had been helpful in providing information that would aid top management in understanding better the various business activities of the corporation.

1982 Organizational Changes

In 1982 a number of organizational changes affected planning in major ways. Chief among these was the elevation of Mr. Albert to president in March. The corporate planning function moved up with Mr. Albert, continuing to report directly to him.

Several other important organizational changes followed shortly after. Two corporate staff functions were created, one for marketing and the other for research/development. Operating responsibility was further delegated: the International Division was to report to the new executive vice president, John A. Tyler, the former general manager of the Cutting Tool Division. The Cutting Tool Division was divided along product lines to become two separate divisions.

Two group vice presidents were named, each responsible for three divisions, with the remaining four divisions reporting directly to Mr. Tyler.

Beginning of the 1982 Planning Activities

In contrast with the "numbers" orientation of the 1981 planning efforts, Mr. Sagan recommended an increased emphasis on strategic concepts in 1982. After some discussion, the planning committee decided to separate the formal planning cycle into three phases. The first phase, to be held in the spring, was termed the *Strategy Development* phase. The second, or *Quantitative,* phase would summarize, during the fall, the financial and manpower implications of the strategies selected in the first phase. The final, or *Action,* phase would aim to translate the results of planning into specific programs for action.

In mid-March, the new president, Mr. Albert, sent a letter to each division manager outlining the planning cycle for 1982 and the objectives for the planning efforts that had been agreed to by the planning committee.

The division's strategic plans were presented to corporate management by each division in a review meeting and subsequently evaluated in a response meeting. Unlike 1981, when they were held a month apart, these meetings in 1982 followed each other on the same day.

Further Developments in 1982

Several developments were to impede progress of the planning efforts in 1982. As already mentioned, there was a new president, who introduced seven persons into new corporate executive positions. These changes in top management were temporarily disruptive to the planning effort.

Also, considerable management effort was required in assimilating a recently acquired large company and in working out the split-up of the old Cutting Tool Division into the two new divisions.

In 1981, the company had reported its highest sales and earnings ever. The annual report stated that prospects were for a strong 1982. But the machine tool industry was to suffer from depressed market conditions. Sales were down 1.6 percent from 1981; earnings per share declined 35.8 percent. Efforts to counter the unfavorable business conditions became a dominant preoccupation for key line executives.

On July 11, after completion of the strategy development phase of the beginning cycle, the planning committee met to consider the planning efforts for the remainder of 1982. In view of the developments noted above, it decided against proceeding with the quantitative phase originally scheduled for the fall. It did, however, recommend that staff departments begin the planning process by analyzing past results and identifying resources, strengths, weaknesses, major problems, and major opportunities of their divisions. Mr. Albert approved the recommendations. The Corporate Goals Committee also lessened its efforts to prepare a statement of corporate goals.

In view of the disruption of formal planning at Copley, top management made special efforts to declare that long-range planning was there to stay. In a letter to division managers dated October 24, Mr. Albert explained the decision to curtail formal planning and emphasized that nothing would be allowed to stand in the way of doing the complete planning job in 1983. He reaffirmed his intention to emphasize planning at Copley in his president's statement in the 1982 annual report: "Long-range planning will become a way of life at our Company. By this medium we will set specific goals, allocate resources of talent and money, and measure our progress. There will be increased emphasis on the delegation of responsibility and in the measurement of performance against predetermined goals."

Situation in 1983

The Copley Company recovered financially in 1983 with a 6.2 percent improvement in net sales and a 58 cent gain in earnings per share.

The corporate goals committee held several informal dinner meetings during the first half of 1982 to discuss a framework developed by Mr. Sagan for arriving at corporate goals. Although a definite statement of corporate goals was not drawn up, the members generally felt that much progress had been made and that it had been a useful and educational experience for all who had participated. The committee as originally constituted was inactive in late 1982 and early 1983, but Mr. Sagan continued to work independently with Mr. Albert on that task. In line with these activities, Mr. Albert was quoted in the business press as stating corporate expectations to include a minimum annual profit growth of 10 percent and a return on equity of 12.5 percent.

In 1983, the planning process in large part came to be influenced and administered by Mr. Tyler, executive vice president. Mr. Tyler, who had moved up from head of the Cutting Tool Division when Mr. Albert assumed the presidency of Copley, enjoyed the reputation among his colleagues as a hard-driving, no-nonsense line manager who had little patience for elaborate staff support.

In Mr. Tyler's opinion, division managers had been planning in previous years largely to satisfy the requirements set by the planning staff and had failed to become committed to the plans. He saw voluminous documentation required in 1982 to present a divisional strategy and financial plan as one reason for this failure to identify with the planning output. Thus, in 1983, division managers were asked to present each product group strategy in a statement of two pages or less and the related financial five-year plan on only one page.

The divisional strategy statements were to cover information on such items as industry trends, market size, competition, and major opportunities or threats, as well as a description of the proposed strategic response. For the financial plan, divisions were required to submit figures for only the first, second, and fifth years of the five-year plan. The purpose of this abbreviation was to reduce the time spent on the numbers, thereby allowing divisional management more time for strategic considerations.

The management review process was also altered. Divisional presentations before the planning committee were replaced by two other meetings. The first of these was a one-hour "premeeting" attended by Mr. Albert, Mr. Tyler, the division general manager, and the responsible group vice president. In this premeeting, Albert and Tyler explained Copley's strategy and acquisition policy and reviewed the findings and conclusions of the Product Line Study. During the remainder of the hour, the division manager had to explain and to defend the division's strategy for the coming year. At the end of the one-hour meeting the president gave his decision on the division's plans. This review was immediately followed by a three-hour meeting in which the division manager and his staff presented their plans for the first time to the remaining members of the Executive Committee and to selected members of the corporate staff.

Mr. Sagan, director of corporate development, became visibly disturbed by the recent turn of events in planning. He felt himself increasingly limited to corporate merger and acquisition studies. He was fearful that the company would revert to a short-term orientation if it continued along the present path. In voicing these objectives to Mr. Albert, he realized that the formal planning system that he had worked so hard to develop was at stake. As a result of these discussions, he felt that he still had the full confidence and support of the chief executive. At the same time, Mr. Albert publicly acknowledged the benefits of getting increased line involvement in planning.

Recent Developments

In an interview in late 1984, Mr. Tyler described recent developments:

> As was John Albert's desire, we believe planning is now a way of life at Copley. There just does not appear to be as much need today for a structured management of the process with a planning department per se at the corporate level. This is not to say that all line managers develop plans and strategies to the same degree of effectiveness. But the actual responsibility for planning has been placed directly on the line—that is, the executive vice president, the group vice presidents, and, in turn, their various division managers.
>
> For various reasons, Charlie Sagan left the company earlier this year. Fred Fisher has been appointed director of corporate development, but his job description was rewritten to put the emphasis on the planning and execution of growth through acquisition.
>
> The planning process in 1983 followed pretty well the steps we had laid out.
>
> In January 1984, we changed the format for the divisional planning presentations. My letter of January 30 [Exhibit 1] describes our current system of informing all key managers within the company of each division's long-range plans and broad strategies.
>
> This technique of communicating divisional plans was preceded in December of 1983 by a two-day conference in Bermuda, with essentially the same group in attendance. At that conference, we reviewed all of the divisional plans up until that point and announced the broad corporate goals and strategies.

In the same interview Mr. Tyler furnished a copy of a recent talk in which he stated his personal belief about management.

> I believe that corporate planning is *the* major responsibility of top management. It involves the direction of the whole company (not the parts) in deciding specifically what businesses the company wants to be in, in determining what rate of growth is desirable, in determining what method of growth is intended (research, acquisition, merger). I am a believer in decentralization; in delegating a great deal of authority; giving people their head; permitting some experiments and some mistakes; but sink or swim is the theory.
>
> I do not believe in too many specialized staff functions to clutter up an organization. I avoid "assistant

EXHIBIT 1   Letter Announcing a Series of Executive Meetings (excerpts)

January 30, 1984

It is always difficult to draw lines across an organization, but those to whom this letter is addressed are either managing profit centers or are directing broad staff functions vital to Copley's operations and to its future growth.

We believe it is important to provide the means for keeping each person in this group better informed of the plans and progress of each division and each staff function as well as the total corporate programs.

The method selected to provide better communications will be tested over the next 12 months and will involve a series of 9 meetings; the time and place of each are listed on the attached schedule. Each meeting will start at 1:30 PM on the first Monday of the month. They will end at 5:00 PM. A different division will host each meeting on a rotating basis.

An agenda is planned as follows. From 1:30 to 2:00 PM five or six prepared talks of five minutes' duration will be given on subjects of current and general interest selected by the chairman in consultation with others. The following half hour (2:00–2:30) will be devoted to announcements from both the floor and the chairman.

At 2:30, the division manager serving as host will take charge of the meeting. He will have a total of two and one-half hours, during which he is asked to present his long-range plans, allow time for questions and comments, and complete a plant tour of some portion of his facilities.

The group of key executives in attendance does not make up a decision-making committee or a review board in the general sense. They are, however, encouraged to ask questions for interpretation and better understanding. The long-range plans presented by the division manager will previously have been approved by the president, executive and group vice presidents. The division managers are asked to present their plans in simply written reports using an expanded outline technique. Copies will be reproduced by the division manager following the meeting on a request basis.

This test period will last through the February 1985 meeting. If it is felt these meetings cannot be made to serve their original intention, they will be discontinued.

/s/John A. Tyler

Executive Vice President

---

to's" and "administrative assistants" except for short-term projects or as training spots in someone's career.

I believe a good manager by definition must put out the daily fires, improve the current quarter's earnings, and at the same time be a long-range planner. If a manager cannot do both, I do not believe the solution lies in shoring him up via a corporate planning department. I *do* believe it lies in using the talent of both line and specific staff personnel who surround him.

I believe in using the talents already present in marketing, finance, research, and manufacturing—and the head of each of these areas must be a planner himself or *he* will fail. I am opposed to separating the division managers from the top management by allowing any staff group to represent or speak for them—or to take their cues from them.

I believe that America's greatest companies succeeded because one man or group of individuals with strong convictions made things happen. They had vision and used intuition in varying degrees but they did their own planning and monitoring of results. I may be overgeneralizing, but normally a company has its best all-around talent in top line positions. They are there because they have a good balance of talents and experience.

For that reason, their judgment should have the greatest influence in strategy formation as well as final decision making. By this, I do not mean to imply that line personnel think more strategically than staff personnel. The opposite may, in fact, be true. There are often individuals way down the organization in both line and staff who are thinking persons.

Finally, I strongly believe there is a great tendency in American business to overmanage, overplan, overstaff, and overorganize, which is contributing in a major way to our declining ability to compete in world markets. Our fixed costs in staff and management are often a larger factor than factory labor in making us noncompetitive.

Questions

1. How do you appraise formal planning efforts at the Copley Company?

2. What do you predict will occur with respect to formal planning at Copley?

3. How would *you* handle formal planning at Copley?

Case 7–3
DairyPak

Earle Bensing had some very tough decisions to make in the summer of 1988. As Vice President for the DairyPak Division of Champion International he faced:

- Declining market share in the growing "branded juice" segment of the domestic paperboard carton market.
- A technologically outmoded manufacturing system in terms of the expanding markets.
- A very limited output capability which had not grown in 10 years.
- A dramatically expanding international market which the corporation had seen as fraught with more problems than opportunities.

The capital spending and strategic positioning decisions he needed to make in 1988 would shape the future of the DairyPak division for many years to come.

I. Liquid Packaging and the Pure-Pak Carton

Millions of Americans, Europeans, Asians and South Americans started their day with milk or juice poured from a paperboard carton. Worldwide, paperboard was still the dominant form of milk and juice packaging in 1988. But the industry had changed dramatically since the "gabled top" Pure-Pak carton rose to prominence in the 1950s.

The Plastic Substitute.   Polyethylene replaced paraffin to coat paperboard in 1961. It didn't take long after that before someone in the oil industry thought of making plastic *car-*

This case was written by Professor John Shank of the Amos Tuck School with the assistance of Mr. David Anthony, T '89. Copyright © by John K. Shank.

tons instead of plastic *coating* for paper cartons. Shell Chemical and Hoover International (now Johnson Controls) changed the liquid packaging industry overnight in 1965 when they combined to introduce the plastic resin pellet and the "blow molding" machine to manufacture plastic jugs. The blow molding machine was so easy to use that paper packaging dropped from 82 percent of the milk market in 1971 to 37 percent in 1985.

But the interesting story here was that although plastic captured 100 percent of the *gallon* size carton market, it had not eliminated the other sizes of paper carton as many had predicted it would. Plastic was more economical when resin prices were low. When the price rises, paper looks good. Guessing future levels of ethylene gas prices (the basic driver of polyethylene price) was a notoriously difficult task.

And the dairy owner also had important nonfinancial reasons for staying with the paper carton. First, the dairy did not want to be at the mercy of oil companies. By using dual suppliers—paper and plastic—the dairy created a hedge against volatile input prices. Also, as new uses of the plastic resin were created (industrial and consumer uses of plastic containers), the input price would not go lower since the plastic was just a by-product of ethylene gas. Second, the dairy believed that paper was the best product nutritionally. University studies had shown that paper protected milk vitamins and flavor much better than translucent plastic. Also, recent legislation prohibiting the dumping of plastic in Suffolk County on Long Island had created doubt about the long run viability of plastic.

The Competitors.   Exhibit 1 is a global overview of the paperboard packaging business in 1988. There were five players in the domestic

EXHIBIT 1

*The paperboard
packaging industry
in 1988*

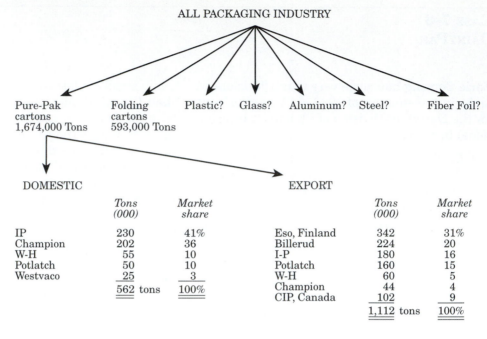

ALL PACKAGING INDUSTRY

Pure-Pak cartons 1,674,000 Tons | Folding cartons 593,000 Tons | Plastic? | Glass? | Aluminum? | Steel? | Fiber Foil?

DOMESTIC

	Tons (000)	Market share
IP	230	41%
Champion	202	36
W-H	55	10
Potlatch	50	10
Westvaco	25	3
	562 tons	100%

EXPORT

	Tons (000)	Market share
Eso, Finland	342	31%
Billerud	224	20
I-P	180	16
Potlatch	160	15
W-H	60	5
Champion	44	4
CIP, Canada	102	9
	1,112 tons	100%

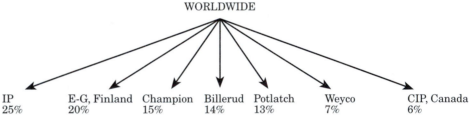

WORLDWIDE

IP	E-G, Finland	Champion	Billerud	Potlatch	Weyco	CIP, Canada
25%	20%	15%	14%	13%	7%	6%

Pure-Pak industry—International Paper, Champion, Potlatch, Westvaco, and Weyerhaeuser. All of these companies were vertically integrated producers of the carton all the way back to the wood chip. Also, because of the scale and integration economies of these firms, new vertically integrated entrants were effectively shut out. In fact, because of the scale economies in producing a Pure-Pak carton, it was more likely that a small current player would drop out of the industry—as Georgia Pacific did in 1981 or as Weyco did in the Eastern United States in 1982.

International Paper was the industry leader. IP was considered to be the low cost producer, having achieved significant economies with a large and diverse extruding and converting capacity. IP was also the technological leader, with significant investment in aseptic (germ free) packaging and rotogravure printing (state-of-the-art technology). IP continued to expand capacity, aggressively growing in the nondairy segments by emphasizing their aseptic, hot fill, and other extended life packages, and aggressively pursuing their own off-shore converting operations (e.g., Korea and Japan). Along with these strategies, IP continued to price aggressively. But often IP was considered an unreliable supplier *domestically* because of their willingness to leave a customer when necessary to grow their offshore converting operations.

EXHIBIT 2   Domestic Competitor Review—1986

Company	Extruders	Folding Carton Capacity (000 annual tons) (Liquid Packaging was one use for folding carton stock.)	Liquid Packaging		Pure-Pak Converting Locations	
			Domestic	Export		
International Paper	4—Pine Bluff, AR 1—Raleigh, NC 2—Mobile, AL 1—Texarkana, TX	709	230	180	Atlanta, GA Bastrop, LA Framingham, MA Kalamazoo, MI	Kansas City, KA Philadelphia, PA Turlock, CA
Champion	2—Waynesville, NC	250	202	44	Athens, GA Clinton, IA Ft. Worth, TX	Morristown, NJ Olmsted Falls, OH
Potlatch	2—Lewiston, ID	300	50	160	Ft. Wayne, IN Pomona, CA Sikeston, MO	
Weyerhaeuser	2—Longview, WA	193	55	60	Los Angeles, CA Vancouver, WA	
Westvaco	1—Covington, VA 2—Laurel, MD	147	25	—	Richmond, VA	

Champion was currently a strong number 2, with more domestic volume than the other three players combined (see Exhibit 1).

Potlatch, Westvaco, and Weyerhaeuser all ranked in a third tier of competition. All three faced difficulties related to quality and inefficient scale. Weyerhaeuser and Potlatch responded by looking increasingly to export markets while trying to maintain selected domestic niches. Westvaco was holding on to its domestic niche. Exhibits 1 and 2 summarize the estimated competitive situation for 1988.

Outside of the United States there were three major manufacturers supplying Pure-Pak cartons:

Enso-Gutzeit–Finland—They professed to be the world's top exporter and the world's second-largest producer of liquid packaging board—342,000 tons of liquid packaging and fast-food board was supplied during 1987.

Billerud–Sweden—Paperboard production of 224,000 tons in 1988. This corresponded to a world market share of 14 percent. Most of the production was exported. TetraPak was the largest single customer.

CIP–Montreal, Canada—Three plants (Quebec, Ontario, and Alberta) converted CIP's polycoated stock into cartons for milk and juice. Its plants had a capacity of only 34,000 tons per year.

The Pure-Pak Customers. There were four groups of customers who formed, filled, and sealed Pure-Pak cartons. Champion's position in these four segments is summarized in Exhibit 3.

Domestic Dairies. In 1976 there were approximately 10,000 dairies across the United States processing and distributing milk and juice. Fewer than 1,000 dairies survived in 1988, but dairies were still the largest purchaser of paperboard cartons in the United States. In 1988, a typical dairy was a large

Exhibit 3   Market Segments for Pure-Pak 1987

US Dairies	Branded Juicers		Export
(Milk and OJ)	*Minute Maid and Citrus Hill*	*Tropicana*	
Historically, Champion has emphasized this segment (about 150,000 tons in 1988).	Relatively Minor Volume (about 2,000 tons)	Zero Volume	32,000 tons (Coated) 12,000 tons (uncoated)
Our tons have been shrinking 3% per year since 1980.	Flat since 1980	Lost this business for quality reasons in 1981.	Champion's "swing" market
Overall market has been shrinking about 3% per year since 1980.	Overall market growing at 10%; potential to grow faster (growth in ready-to-serve; greater market penetration in Midwest		Overall market growing at more than 10% per year
We have maintained market share (40%) in this declining segment.	Are we the "backup" supplier in this segment?		Champion has not been willing to commit here for the long run.

regional packager of many private brands of milk and juice. The dairy's product was usually considered a commodity—no ability to achieve a price premium for the brand name. Industry-wide, dairy profit margins were quite slim. Overall, the profits came from the very high turnover rates from being the sole supplier in a region. Overall, this segment had declined 3 percent per year over the previous five years, but, by 1988, it had stabilized.

Differentiated Juicers. The second-largest segment was the high quality, *differentiated* juice packager—basically Seagrams (Tropicana), Coca-Cola (Minute Maid), and Procter & Gamble (Citrus Hill). This segment was created in the 50s by Tropicana. Coca-Cola entered in the 1960s using its Minute Maid brand name. Procter & Gamble entered in the 1980s with a new brand name (Citrus Hill). In the five years prior to 1988, chilled juice sales increased more than 82 percent, compared with 17 percent for the whole juice industry. In 1988 it was estimated that *chilled* would outsell *concentrate* for

the first time, buoyed by America's craving for convenience. This was the fastest-growing segment in liquid packaging in 1988 (approximately 10 percent a year). The segment was extremely competitive as one would guess from the three key players, giants in consumer products: "An orange juice war is intensifying as major players try to squeeze bigger shares" (*Wall Street Journal,* 4/27/88). The big three juice processors represented over 50 percent of the ready-to-serve orange juice market—clearly, a great opportunity for the paperboard industry (see Table 1).

The big three customers wanted high impact graphics to market the juice, a technologically advanced carton that retained essential oils, and a carton that would hold the juice over 50 days (versus 14 days for milk). These customers were willing to pay for the differentiated carton.

"Special Uses." The third segment for polyethylene coated board included "ovenable board" (frozen food dishes or microwave dishes) and Pure-Pak cartons used to hold such nonliq-

TABLE 1   Differentiated Juice Segment

	Domestic Share of Market for Ready to Serve Orange Juice	Orange Juice Manufacturers' Use of Paperboard Cartons (tons)	
	1988	1980	1987
Tropicana	27.3%	11,000	15,000
Minute Maid	17.7	7,000	10,000
Citrus Hill	9.1	0	7,000
Dairies	45.9	18,000	15,000
Total	100%	36,000	47,000

TABLE 2   The International Market

US Folding Carton Stock Export for Liquid Packaging by Destination (000 tons)

	1985	1986	1987
Far East	214	233	248
Europe	50	56	59
Australia	30	35	36
Africa	30	28	35
Canada	9	17	33
South America	30	29	29
Central America	13	8	14
Caribbean	3	5	7
Middle East	2	10	6
Other	14	11	14
Total	395	432	481
Uncoated rolls	94	103	116
Coated rolls	272	313	336
Converted cartons	29	16	29

uid items as nails or mothballs. This market had grown slowly. Overall volume and volume per customer were still low. Overall this was only 4 percent of Champion's volume.

Export. The fourth group of customers for the Pure-Pak carton was the export market. Worldwide production of Pure-Pak cartons was estimated to be slightly over 1,600,000 tons in 1987 with only one-third (562,000) of that used in the United States. The international market had grown by over 16 percent from 1985 to 1988, with consumption increasing by over 100 percent in some countries as shown in Table 2.

II. Champion DairyPak—The Evolution of a "Harvest" Strategy

DairyPak began operation in Cleveland, Ohio, with 12 employees in December 1947 as one of the original licensees of the Pure-Pak technology. By 1950 DairyPak shipped 540 million cartons— over $5 million worth—and the company needed another plant to meet the growing demand. Expansion included converting plants built in Athens, Georgia, in 1951; Clinton, Iowa, in 1952; Fort Worth, Texas, in 1954; and Morristown, New Jersey, in 1958. These five similar converting plants remained intact in 1988 as Champion's milk and juice carton converters.

Since the early 60s through 1988, Champion had produced about 250,000 tons of polyethylene coated board annually. Until 1980, virtually all these tons were converted by the five DairyPak plants and sold to dairies. The primary goal of Champion was to be the low cost producer in a commodity market.

The intrusion of plastic containers in the 1960s dramatically affected the paperboard carton industry and Champion's perspective on DairyPak. Champion watched to see what the dairy industry would do. A consulting study by Booz, Allen Hamilton in 1968 which circulated throughout the industry suggested that by the mid-80s not a single paperboard carton would be sold. Champion's reaction was to watch and wait. While Champion watched and waited, the paper carton did not die, but the Champion infrastructure began to get old and technologically outdated. In fact, since a new machine to

TABLE 3   Champion's Market Position

| | Domestic Consumption of Pure-Pak Cartons (000) | | | Champion's Domestic Pure-Pak Cartons | | | |
| | 1980 | 1987 | | 1980 | | 1987 | |
	Tons	*Tons*	*% Change*	*Tons*	*% Share*	*Tons*	*% Share*
Dairy	506	374	−26%	200	39%	150	40%
Nondairy*	66	120	+82	30	46	30	25
Total	572	494	−14%	230	40%	180	36%

| Champion's Paperboard Production | | |
	1980 Tons	*1987 Tons*
Dairy	200	150
Nondairy*	30	30
Ovenable	0	10
Domestic coated	9	2
Domestic uncoated	10	10
Export coated	11	32
Export uncoated	0	12
Total	260	246

*Represents juice processors and special end uses of paperboard.

produce the raw paperboard had been built in 1965, very few capital improvements had been implemented or considered until the summer of 1988. Of Champion's 33 converting machines, 29 were installed before 1963.

The Situation in 1988.   In the early 80s, the explosion of the juice market created new opportunities for the Pure-Pak Carton—opportunities for which Champion was unprepared.

Table 3 shows the changing markets for Champion. These data clearly indicate that Champion had successfully retained share in the declining market segment while losing almost half its share in the fastest-growing segment.

The Cost Structure—A Process Flow Perspective.   One way to understand Champion's

DairyPak position in 1980 is to study the process flow from wood chips all the way to Pure-Pak cartons.

The trees which become chips were a combination of southern pine and hardwood species. The two chip inputs were mixed with cooking and bleaching chemicals to produce pulp. The Canton Mill had paper processing capacity of 1550 tons per day, but only 1400 tons of pulping capacity. Therefore 150 tons of processed pulp were purchased on the open market at $700/ton (the in-house pulp cost $278/ton). The paper processing capacity of the mill was divided into 850 tons of envelope paper and 700 tons of paperboard.

The purchased pulp and slush pulp (in-house) were mixed in the paper machine where the pulp was dried to make uncoated paper-

Exhibit 4   Champion DairyPak System-Selected Segments

| | Paper Mill | | Waynesville Extruding Plant | | | | Converting Plants | |
| | Uncoated Board Sales | | Coated Sales to DairyPak | | Coated Sales to Export | | DairyPak Sales | |
	1980	*1987*	*1980*	*1987*	*1980*	*1987*	*1980*	*1987*
Net revenue/ton	$448	$530	$497	$663	$517	$577	$697	$994
Cost/ton	$365	$471[1]	$444	$540	$444	$540[2]	$671	$992
Profit before tax/ton	$ 83	$ 59	$ 53	$123	$ 67	$ 37	$ 26	$ 2
Tons (000)	10	22	230	180	11	32	230	180

(1) Pulp cost	$319	424	(2) Mill cost	$424
Machine cost	105		Freight to extruder	3
Freight to customer	47		Extruder cost	94
	$471		Freight to customer	19
				$540

board. The paper machine stage added approximately $105 per ton of cost to the pulp.

The uncoated rolls (weighing about one ton each) were then shuttled to the nearby Waynesville, North Carolina, extruding plant at a cost of $3 per ton. Polyethylene was applied to both sides of the board at a cost of $94 per ton. From Waynesville, the rolls of coated board traveled either to Champion's five converting plants at an average freight cost of $35 per ton, or were sold to export. Canton also sold some uncoated board each year to other converters for other carton applications (see Exhibit 4).

The five DairyPak locations paid a fixed transfer price of $680 per ton for the coated board, which included freight. In the first stage of the converting operation, rolls of coated board were spliced together to form a long, continuous web. Next, each particular dairy's name, logo, and design were printed on one side using flexographic printing which was essentially a 1960s technology. The total cost of the conversion operation was $231 per ton, plus $10 per ton for freight to the end customers. Industry averages showed that one ton of board

equals 14,400 one-half gallon cartons and the individual carton price was between $.06 and .08 depending on the volume. Average price to a customer for half-gallon cartons was $936 per ton. The half-gallon size was not the most profitable item, but represented over 50 percent of sales. This process flow was the same for both milk and juice cartons since Champion did not distinguish between the two.

At the juice processor or dairy, the rolls of flat cartons moved along the sealing machines where their polyethylene coating was heated by a gas flame. Each carton was folded and conveyed through "ironing" rolls where it emerged joined together, or "side seamed." Filler machines then formed and sealed the bottom, filled the carton with liquid, and sealed the gabled top. The cycle was complete when dairies and juice processors delivered their product to stores and supermarkets where consumers chose the paper carton over the plastic jug.

A small dairy would usually pay $.08 per half-gallon carton since it could not achieve volume discounts. The milk purchased from dairy farmers would cost $.75 per half gallon.

The pasteurizing process would cost $.06 per half gallon, and the distribution and shrinkage would add another $.06. The small dairy could sell a half gallon of unbranded milk for an average of $1.04. When a small dairy produced orange juice, the costs were similar except that oranges cost $.80 per half gallon. The price to supermarkets was $1.20 per half gallon, delivered.

Minute Maid, a large branded juice processor had very different economics. The half-gallon carton would usually cost only $.06 because of volume discounts. The oranges themselves would be only $.64 per half gallon, again because of the tremendous volume. Converting, distribution, and shrinkage would total $.11. One major cost a branded juice processor added was national selling and advertising, which averaged 25 percent of the $1.42 wholesale price to supermarkets.

A large New Hampshire supermarket serving a population base of 50,000 sold regional dairy milk for $1.16, Tropicana orange juice for $2.26 (cost of $1.79), Minute Maid for $1.89, and local dairy orange juice for $1.50. This large supermarket sold 1,700 paper half gallons of milk and 7,000 plastic gallons of milk per week. On the orange juice side, 170 half gallons of Tropicana, 170 half gallons of Minute Maid and Citrus Hill together, and 280 half gallons of dairy orange juice were sold each week.

If Champion's accounting system were to separate a half-gallon milk carton from a half-gallon orange juice carton, there would certainly be differences in costs. Table 4 identifies the process differences between the two segments. Costing these process differences is beyond the scope of this case.

Champion Strategy Today. Given the cost structure and changing environment already outlined, Champion still believed that the domestic dairy market would continue to be the principal area of profits, even with the contraction due to plastic. Champion would attempt to defend its dominant position, but could not expect improvement in current volume unless one of the major competitors (IP, Westvaco, Weyerhaeuser, or Potlatch) left the business. For example, in 1982 Weyerhaeuser exited the paperboard carton industry in the East when their paper mill in North Carolina was converted from board to disposable diapers. It was estimated that Champion picked up 30,000 to 40,000 tons a year of Weyerhaeuser's old business through 1988.

Overall, Champion recognized its strengths as:

- Large and efficient board machine.
- Efficient and geographically well located extrusion facility.
- Five competitive and strategically located carton converting plants.
- Successful ovenable board converting plant (in the Midwest).
- Very successful position in the dairy market east of the Rockies.
- Excellent service reputation among domestic dairies.
- Knowledgeable operating people throughout the system.

But Champion also recognized its weaknesses:

- Limited extrusion capacity.
- Lack of rotogravure printing.
- Champion had been unable to respond efficiently to the diverse needs of the nondairy segment.
- Although tremendous progress had been made, there were still nagging problems with the quality of the board (see the complaint letter that is quoted in Exhibit 5).
- Lack of competitors role-wrapping and labeling capability at the extruding plant.
- Reputation of uncertain commitment in export markets.

TABLE 4 Differences between Milk and Orange Juice Cartons

	Champion Milk Board	*Ideal Orange Juice Board*
Converting Plant	Faster speeds Shorter runs Lower print quality Higher services costs	Slower speeds Longer runs (lower setup/ton) Higher print quality and cost More customer support More sales time per ton sold
Extruding Plant	Lighter coat, "profile" coating Standard approach for most customers	Heavier coat, "flat" coating Differing requirements for different customers—no "standard" approach
The Paperboard Machine	Production focus "Get out the tons" Faster speeds (lower printability) Not as strong as OJ (shorter shelf life)	Higher "Z" strength board Twice as much wet strength resins (vs. milk) Slower speeds (higher printability) Stronger than milk (longer shelf life)
Pulping	The envelope paper machine receives pulp requirements first; milk board last. Result is more variation for milk board.	Standard pulp mixture that would never change

EXHIBIT 5 Example of Quality Complaint

Champion International Corporation

To: Canton Mill, Manufacturing Office

From: DairyPak Customer Services

Date: May 19, 1988

Subject: Board Surface Quality

In our constant effort to improve the print quality of our finished product, one fact is obvious: no matter how good the quality of our inks, plates, artwork, machines, and people, we cannot accomplish the high degree of printing excellence we are striving for when our board surface is covered with dimples and potholes.

The finer the settings on our presses, the more these surface imperfections show up. Please note the enclosed samples. What you see here is the rule, not the exception.

We would greatly appreciate your help in working with whomever necessary to find a way to supply us with a smooth printing surface with which to work. If we may be of assistance, please don't hesitate to call.

As always, your comments and/or suggestions are welcome.

cc: Joe Deal, Jr.
    Robert Ray
    Charlie Ward
    Ed Fritch

The Champion strategy was to be the low cost producer in the commodity dairy segment, trying to make inroads in the differentiated juice segment, to cautiously upgrade its infrastructure but not to invest in latest printing and roll-wrapping equipment, and to view export and special end-use segments as ancillary (no need for major commitments).

III. The Summer of 1988

Where to compete and how much to invest were the two difficult questions Earle Bensing faced in 1988.

The first proposal he was considering was to renovate the paperboard machine at a total cost of $43,000,000. Phase I of this proposal would cost $16,000,000 to rebuild the "wet end" of the machine and would result in improved internal strength of the board (stronger cartons and improved printability). Phase II would cost another $27,000,000 at the "dry end" of the machine (improved smoothness for better print quality).

A second proposal was to add a third extruder at the Waynesville, North Carolina, plant. A state-of-the-art extruder cost approximately $17,000,000 and would allow Champion to compete in multilayered polymer coating applications. The newly emerging packages in the juice industry required multiple plastic resins and foils to extend shelf life and to hold difficult liquids. The new extruder would be dedicated to expanding Champion's product line to serve customers with complex co-extrusion needs.

A third proposal Bensing was considering was to add roll wrapping equipment at the Waynesville location. In 1988 coated rolls were shipped overseas unsealed, exposed while they were handled in transit and while in a cargo hold. This led to both sanitary and aesthetic problems, since moisture and bacteria could attack the board. State-of-the-art roll wrapping equipment would cost $1,750,000 for the initial capital outlay, one operator for the machine at $30,000 a year, and $2.50 per one-ton roll in material expense. Champion could not charge customers more for wrapped rolls.

The fourth potential area for investment was adding rotogravure printing. Currently Dairy-Pak used flexography which printed from plates made of rubber. This method was very popular because it was inexpensive. After the initial capital expense of $1.5 million, the plates were about $150 apiece and six were needed for a six-color process. The quality was not as good as with offset or rotogravure printing, but high-quality printing was never required in the dairy segment of the business.

In rotogravure (or intaglio) printing, the plate cylinder itself was machined and coated to receive the printing image photographically. The portions of the cylinder's surface which would print were etched as microscopic, cuplike cells while the nonprinting areas remained untouched. Rotogravure gave an extremely accurate and high-quality finish—but it was expensive. The initial capital expense was similar to flexography (approximately $1.5 million) but one cylinder cost $2,500. With a six-color process, only *one* run would cost $15,000. And once that run was complete, those cylinders would probably never be used again. Table 5 summarizes these investment opportunities.

Not only did Bensing face investment decisions, he also had to decide who would get the limited amount of board that Champion produced each year. Would it be the dairies, whose total market had been declining 3 percent a year but who had always been the main customer of DairyPak? Would it be the big juice manufacturers (Coca-Cola or Procter & Gamble)—whose market was growing at 10 percent and who would pay top dollar for board but who demanded a consistent quality that Champion had been unable to produce? Or would it be the export market—which was growing rapidly each year, and where a top price was possible because of a favorable currency situation, but where Champion had never tried to compete

TABLE 5   Resource Allocation Options 1988

1. Rebuild the paperboard machine:

Phase I—Rebuild "wet end"	$16 million
Phase II—Rebuild "dry end"	$27 million

2. Add a third extruder at Waynesville, $17 million.

3. Add roll wrapping equipment:

Capital cost		$1.75 million
Operating costs:	Labor	$30,000/year
	Materials	$2.50/one-ton roll

4. Add rotogravure printing as an option for customers:

Capital cost	$1.5 million
Operating costs	$15,000 per run

aggressively, either as a board supplier or a converter?

The marketing of paperboard cartons to the juice industry offered tremendous potential. Although the New York area made up only 7 percent of the US population, New Yorkers consumed 14 percent of the orange juice sold. If the big three's expansion was successful outside New York and New England, quality carton volume could explode. This was a great opportunity for Champion, if it was ready to compete in that market.

The opportunity was definitely there for DairyPak. But did Earle Bensing have the right information to make his decisions? Was there an accurate picture of the costs and value created at the paper machine, the extruding plant, and the converting plants? Was there enough information concerning the competitors and the marketplace? Overall, did Mr. Bensing have the financial tools to evaluate the investment and marketing options open to him?

Questions

1. Can you construct a "value chain" of costs and profits from the pulp mill all the way through to the supermarket for milk, for dairy orange juice, and for Minute Maid orange juice? Present all the calculations on the basis of one ton of board.

2. What insights for the business does the "value chain" provide? For example, of the total profit earned per ton of board, how much would be earned by the supermarket, by the processor, and by Champion?

3. When asset data (as shown below) are included, what inferences do you draw about resource option allocation for Champion, the dairy, the juice processor, and the retailer?

Assets in the Process Flow

Assets	1988 Market Value	Per Ton of Board
Pulp mill	$400,000,000	$1,600
Paper machine	300,000,000	1,200
Extruder	42,000,000	190
Converting plants	141,000,000	830
Juice processor	55,000,000	2,890
Small dairy	2,100,000	5,400
Supermarket—space and display cases (dairy section)	103,500	1,800

4. Note that unless a major expansion was undertaken, Champion's output was limited to about 250,000 tons per year of coated board. Which segment(s) do you believe should be targeted?

Case 7–4
Emerson Electric Company

Emerson Electric Company was founded in 1890 as a manufacturer of motors and fans. In 1993, Emerson marked its thirty-sixth consecutive year of improved earnings per share. On $8.2 billion sales, the diversified St. Louis-based company reported a 1993 profit of $708 million. In addition, the company had $2 billion in unconsolidated sales in international joint ventures. Since 1956, Emerson's annual return to shareholders has averaged 18 percent. Sales, earnings per share, and dividends per share grew at a compound rate of 9 percent, 8 percent, and 7 percent, respectively, over the 1983–93 period. International sales have grown to 40 percent of total sales and present a growth area for the company.

Emerson is a major domestic electrical manufacturer. It manufactures a broad range of electric, electromechanical, and electronic products for industry and consumers. Brand names include Fisher Control Valves, Skil, Dremel, and Craftsman power tools, In-Sink-Erator waste disposals, Copeland compressors, Rosemount instruments, Automatic Switch valves, and US Electric Motors in the power transmission market. Its US-based competitors include companies such as General Electric, Westinghouse, and Honeywell. Its foreign competitors include companies such as Siemens and Hitachi. Emerson has had the narrowest focus as a broadly diversified manufacturing company among its primary competitors. Other manufacturers, such as GE and Westinghouse, are diversified into financial services, broadcasting, aircraft engines, plastics, furniture, etc. Emerson follows a growth-through-acquisition strategy, but no one acquisition has been very large. There are periodic divestitures as management

seeks the appropriate or complementary mix of products.

In 1973, Charles F. Knight was elected Chief Executive Officer, after joining the company the prior year. Under Knight's leadership, Emerson analyzed historical records as well as data on a set of "peer companies" the investment community valued highly over time. From this analysis, top management concluded that Emerson needed to achieve growth and strong financial results on a consistent basis reflecting constant improvements. The company set growth rate targets based on revenue growth above and beyond economy-driven expectations.

During the 1980s, the company maintained a very conservative balance sheet rather than using leverage. Top management felt that this was a competitive weapon because it permitted flexibility to borrow when an attractive business investment became available. In the economic downturn of the 1990s, Emerson, unlike a number of companies, was not burdened by heavy debt and interest payments.

Organization

Historically, Emerson was organized into 40 decentralized divisions consisting of separate product lines. Each division was run by a president. The goal was to be number one or two in the market for each product line. The company resisted forming groups, sectors, or other combinations of divisions as found in other large companies until 1990, when Emerson organized its divisions into eight business segments: fractional horsepower electric motors; industrial motors; tools; industrial machinery and components; components for heating and air conditioning; process control equipment; appliance components; and electronics and computer support products and systems. This new structure exploits common distribution channels, organizational capabilities, and technologies.

Management of the company is directed by the Office of the Chief Executive (OCE), which consists of the Chief Executive Officer, the President, two Vice Chairmen, seven business leaders, and three other corporate officers. The OCE meets 10 to 12 times a year to review division performance and discuss issues facing individual divisions or the corporation as a whole.

Each division also has a board of directors, which consists of a member of the OCE who serves as chairman, the division president, and the division's key managers. The division boards meet monthly to review and monitor performance.

Corporate staff in 1993 consisted of 311 people, the same number as in 1975, when the company was one-sixth its current size in terms of sales. Staff is kept to a minimum because top management believes that a large staff creates more work for the divisions. To encourage open communication and interaction among all levels of employees, Emerson does not publish an organization chart.

Best Cost Producer Strategy

In the early 1980s, the company was not globally competitive in all of its major product lines, and recognized that its quality levels in some product areas did not match levels available from some non-US competitors, particularly the Japanese. Therefore, top management changed its 20-year strategy of being the "low cost producer" to being the "best cost producer." There were six elements to this strategy:

1. Commitment to total quality and customer satisfaction.
2. Knowledge of the competition and the basis on which they compete.
3. Focused manufacturing strategy, competing on process as well as product design.
4. Effective employee communications and involvement.
5. Formalized cost-reduction programs, in good times and bad.
6. Commitment to support the strategy through capital expenditures.

Since the 1950s, the low cost producer strategy had required the divisions to set cost-reduction goals at every level and required plant personnel to identify specific actions to achieve those goals. Improvements of 6 percent to 7 percent a year, in terms of cost of goods sold, were targeted. With the best cost producer strategy, Emerson now aimed for higher levels of cost reduction through its planning process. For example, machine tools were used to streamline a process to save labor costs, and design changes saved five ounces of aluminum per unit. Sometimes a competitor's products were disassembled and studied for cost improvements. Products and cost structures of competitors were used to assess Emerson's performance. Factors such as regional labor rates and freight costs were also included in the analyses. For example, before investing millions of dollars in a new plant to make circular saws, top management wanted to know what competitors, domestic and global, were planning.

In the period 1983 to 1993, capital investments of $1.8 billion were made to improve process technology, increase productivity, gain product leadership, and achieve critical mass in support of the best cost producer strategy. Division and plant management reported every quarter on progress against detailed cost reduction targets.

Quality was an important factor in Emerson's best cost producer strategy. Improvements were such that Emerson was counting defects in parts per million. For example, in one electric motor line, employees consistently reached less than 100 rejects per one million motors.

Planning Process

The following comments on Emerson's planning process were made by CEO Knight:

> Once we fix our goals, we do not consider it acceptable to miss them. These targets drive our strategy and determine what we have to do: the kinds of businesses we're in, how we organize and manage them, and how we pay management. At Emerson this means planning. In the process of planning, we focus on specific opportunities that will meet our criteria for growth and returns and create value for our stockholders. In other words, we "identify business investment opportunities."[1]

Emerson's fiscal year starts October 1. To initiate the planning process, top management sets sales growth and return on total capital targets for the divisions. Each fiscal year, from November to July, the CEO and several corporate officers meet with the management of each division at a one or two day division planning conference. Knight spends 60 percent of his time at these division planning conferences. The meetings are designed to be confrontational in order to challenge assumptions and conventional thinking. Top management wants the division to stretch to reach its goals. It also wants to review the detailed actions that division management believes will lead to improved results.

Prior to its division planning conference, the division president submits four standard exhibits to top management. Developing these four exhibits requires months of teamwork and discipline among each division's operating managers.

The "Value Measurement Chart" compares the division's actual performance five years ago (1989), the current year's expected results (1994), and the long-range forecast for the fifth year (1999). See Exhibit 1. (Note: the numbers in all exhibits are disguised.) The Value Measurement Chart contains the type, amount, and

[1]C. F. Knight, "Emerson Electric: Consistent Profits, Consistently," *Harvard Business Review,* January–February 1992, p. 59.

growth rates of capital investment, net operating profit after tax (NOPAT), return on average operating capital, and "economic profit" (NOPAT less a capital charge based on the cost of capital). To create shareholder value, the goal is to determine the extent to which a division's return on total capital (ROTC) exceeds Emerson's cost of capital. Use of the cost of capital rate (Line 3000 on Exhibit 1) is required in all division plans.

The next two exhibits contain sales data. The "Sales Gap Chart" and "Sales Gap Line Chart" show the current year's expected sales (1994) and five-year sales projections (1995–1999). See Exhibits 2 and 3. These are based on an analysis of sources of growth, the market's natural growth rate, market penetration, price changes, new products, product line extensions, and international growth. The "gap" represents the difference between the division's long-range sales forecast and top management's target rate for sales growth (Line 19 in Exhibit 2). Exhibit 2 shows the five-year sources of sales growth in Column H. These are illustrated in the Sales Gap Line Chart in Exhibit 3 for one of the divisions for the 1995–99 period. The division president must explain what specific steps are being taken to close the gap.

The "5-Back by 5-Forward P&L" Chart in Exhibit 4 contrasts detailed division data for the current year (1994) with five prior years of historical data and five years of forecast data (1995–99). This comprises 11 years of profit statements including sales; cost of sales; selling, general and administrative expenses; interest; taxes; and return on total capital (ROTC). This statement is used to detect trends. Division management must be prepared with actions to reverse unfavorable movements or trends.

Beyond the review and discussion of the four required exhibits, the division planning conference belongs to the division president. Top management listens to division management's view of customers, markets, plans for new products,

EXHIBIT 1 The Value Measurement Chart Assesses Value Creation at a Glance*

	Line No.	5th Prior Year Actual FY 1989		Current Year Expected FY 1994		5th Year Forecast FY 1999		5-Year Increment Historical CY vs. 5th PY		5-Year Increment Forecast 5th Yr. vs. CY		10-Year Increment 5th Yr. vs. 5th PY	
		Amt.	% Sales	Amt.	% Sales	Amt.	% Sales	Amt.	% Sales	Amt.	% Sales	Amt.	% Sales
		A	B	C	D	E	F	G	H	I	J	K	L
Growth Rate and Capital Requirements													
Working capital operating-Y/E	1127	117.1	29.8%	120.2	21.8%	153.3	18.5%	3.1	1.9%	33.1	12.0%	36.2	8.3%
Net noncurrent assets-Y/E	1128	92.9	23.6%	150.0	27.2%	221.6	26.8%	57.1	35.9%	71.6	26.0%	128.7	29.6%
Total operating capital-Y/E	1129	210.0	53.4%	270.2	48.9%	374.9	45.3%	60.2	37.9%	104.7	38.0%	164.9	37.9%
Average operating capital	1130	201.1	51.1%	267.1	48.4%	370.4	44.7%						
Incremental investment	1584							66.0		103.3		169.3	
Net oper. prof. aft. tax (NOPAT)	1119	33.4		49.5		79.0		16.1		29.5		45.6	
Return on incremental investment								24.4%		28.6%		26.9%	
NOPAT growth rate								8.2%		9.8%		9.0%	
Capital growth rate								5.8%		6.8%		6.3%	
Rate of Return													
Return on total capital = NOPAT / Avg. oper. cap.		16.6%		18.5%		21.3%							
Net sales	0001	393.2		552.2		827.9		159.0		275.7		434.7	
Sales growth rate								7.0%		8.4%		7.7%	
NOPAT margin		8.5%		9.0%		9.5%		10.1%		10.7%		10.5%	
Operating capital turnover (T/O)		1.96		2.07		2.24		2.41		2.67		2.57	
Cost of capital	3000	12.0%		12.0%		12.0%							
Capital charge (L1130 X L3000)	3001	24.1		32.1		44.4		8.0		12.3		20.3	
Economic profit (L1119-L3001)		9.3		17.4		34.6		8.1		17.2		25.3	

*In millions of dollars (all numbers in the exhibit are disguised).

Source: Charles F. Knight, "Emerson Electric: Consistent Profits, Consistently," *Harvard Business Review*, January–February 1992, p. 63. Used with permission of the Emerson Electric Company. All numbers are disguised.

349

EXHIBIT 2 The Sales Gap Chart Forecasts Five-Year Plans*

	Line No.	Prior Year Actual FY 93 (A)	Current Year Expected FY 94 (B)	Forecast FY 95 (C)	FY 96 (D)	FY 97 (E)	FY 98 (F)	FY 99 (G)	5-Year Source of Growth (%) (H)	5-Year Company Annual Growth (%) (I)
Domestic Excluding Exports										
Current year domestic sales base @ 10/1 prices	1		305.7	305.7	305.7	305.7	305.7	305.7		
Served industry-growth/(decline)	2			3.0	24.6	39.0	49.6	58.3	21.1%	3.6%
Penetration-increase/(decrease) (Including-new line extension/ buyouts)	3			6.3	14.1	21.0	29.8	37.6	13.6	2.0
Price increases-current year through 5th year	4		3.3	7.6	14.7	21.6	29.5	38.0	12.6	1.7
Incremental new products:										
Prior 5 year introduction	5		16.1	16.4	17.7	17.4	17.5	19.0	1.1	
Current year through 5th year	6		1.4	5.6	11.6	18.5	25.9	34.2	11.9	
Other	7		3.1	1.4	1.6	2.3	2.5	2.8	-0.1	
Total domestic	8	363.7	329.6	346.0	390.0	425.5	460.5	495.6		8.5
International Excluding Sales to United States										
Current year international sales base @ 10/1 prices	9		202.9	202.9	202.9	202.9	202.9	202.9		
Served industry-growth/(decline)	10			(0.1)	8.8	17.0	24.8	35.4	12.9	3.3
Penetration-increase(decrease) (Including-new line extensions/buyouts)	11			(0.5)	18.8	27.2	36.2	45.1	16.4	3.6

Price increases-current year through 5th year	12	2.0	4.9	8.5	12.5	16.9	21.7	7.1	1.4
Incremental new products:									
Prior 5 year introduction	13		6.9	7.1	6.7	7.1	8.0	9.2	0.8
Current year through 5th year	14		1.1	4.5	6.3	10.1	14.3	16.9	5.7
Currency	15		9.3						-3.4
Other	16		0.4	0.8	0.7	0.9	1.0	1.1	0.3
Total international	17	204.3	222.6	219.6	252.7	277.7	304.1	332.3	8.3
Total consolidated	18	568.0	552.2	565.6	642.7	703.2	764.6	827.9	8.4
Annual growth %—nominal			-2.8%	2.4%	13.6%	9.4%	8.7%	8.3%	
Gap:									
15% Target—nominal	19			635.0	730.2	839.8	965.7	1,110.6	15.0
Sales gap—over(under)	20			(69.4)	(87.5)	(136.6)	(201.1)	(282.7)	
US exports (excluding to foreign subsidiaries)	21	35.3	31.3	33.7	35.9	39.9	43.9	47.6	8.7
Foreign subsidiaries (excluding sales to United States.)	22	169.1	191.4	185.8	216.8	237.8	260.3	284.7	8.3

*In millions of dollars (all numbers in the exhibit are disguised).

Source: Charles F. Knight, "Emerson Electric: Consistent Profits, Consistently," *Harvard Business Review*, January–February 1992, p.64. Used with permission of the Emerson Electric Company.

EXHIBIT 3

The sales gap line chart projects sales growth against other targets

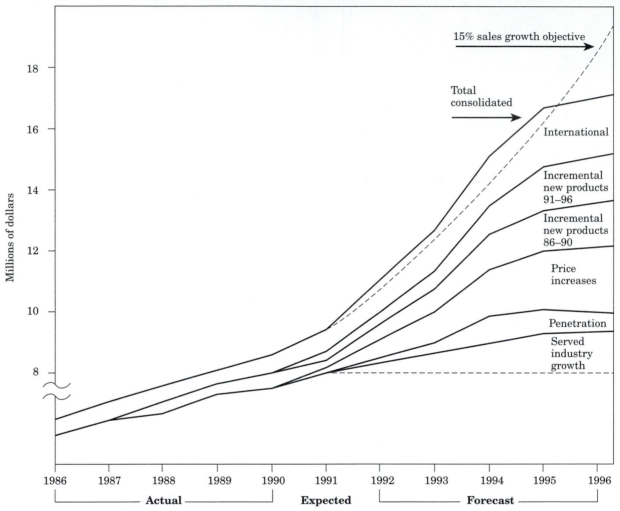

Note: All numbers in the exhibit are disguised.

Source: Charles F. Knight, "Emerson Electric: Consistent Profits, Consistently," *Harvard Business Review,* January–February 1992 p. 65. Used with permission of the Emerson Electric Company.

analyses of competition, and reviews of cost reductions, quality, capacity, productivity, inventory levels, and compensation. Any resulting changes in the division plan must be submitted for approval by top management. The logic and underlying assumptions of the plan are challenged so that managers who are confident of their strategies can defend their proposals. CEO Knight views the test of a good planning conference as whether it results in manager actions that significantly impact the business. According to Knight:

Since operating managers carry out the planning, we effectively establish ownership and eliminate the artificial distinction between strategic and operating decisions. Managers on the line do not—and must never—delegate the understanding of the business. To develop a plan, operating managers work together for months. They often tell me that the greatest value of the planning cycle lies in the teamwork and discipline that the preparation phase requires.[2]

Late in the fiscal year, the division president and appropriate division staff meet with top management to present a detailed forecast for the coming year and conduct a financial review of the current year's actual performance versus forecast. The forecast is expected to match the data in the plan resulting from the division planning conference, but top management also requests contingency plans for several lower levels of activity. A thorough set of actions to protect profitability at lower sales levels is presented. These are known as contingency plans. Changes to the division's forecast are not likely unless significant changes occurred in the environment or in the underlying assumptions. Changes in the forecast must be approved by top management. It is not Emerson's practice to aggregate financial reports for planning and controlling profits between the division and corporation as a whole.

In August, the information generated for and during the division planning conferences and financial reviews is consolidated and reviewed at corporate headquarters by top management. The objective is to examine the total data and prepare for a corporatewide planning conference.

In September, before the start of the next fiscal year, an annual corporate planning conference is attended by top management and top officers of each division. At this meeting, top management presents the corporate and division forecasts for the next year as well as the strategic plan for the next five years. The conference is viewed as a vehicle for communication. There is open and frank discussion of success stories, missed opportunities, and future challenges.

Reporting

At its meetings the OCE uses the President's Operating Report (POR) to review division performance. Each division president submits the POR (see Exhibit 5), on a monthly basis. This reporting system is different from budget reports found in other companies.

First, the POR contains three columns of data for the "current year." The third column of data (Forecast) reflects the plan agreed to by the division president and top corporate management at the beginning of the fiscal year. The forecast data are not changed during the fiscal year and the division president's performance is measured using the fiscal year's forecast. The first column reports the actual results for completed quarters or expected amounts for the current and future quarters. The division president may update expected quarterly results each month. The second column reports the "prior expected" results so that each month's updated expectations can be compared with data submitted in the prior month's POR. Updated expectations are also compared with the forecast data.

Second, in addition to current year data, the POR lists the prior year's actual results. This permits a comparison with the current year's actual results for completed quarters (or expected results for subsequent quarters), and over (O) or under (U) percentages are reported. Midway through the fiscal year, expected data for the first quarter of the next fiscal year are added to the POR.

Corporate top management meets quarterly with each division president and his or her chief financial officer to review the most recent POR and monitor overall division performance. The meetings are taken very seriously by all concerned, and any deviations from forecast get close attention. When a division's reported

[2]Ibid., p. 63.

EXHIBIT 4 The 5-Back-by-5-Forward Chart Provides 11 Years of P&L Measures*

		Actual/Restated					Current Year	Forecast				
	Line No.	5th PY FY 89 A	4th PY FY 90 B	3rd PY FY 91 C	2nd PY FY 92 D	Prior Year FY 93 E	Expected FY 94 F	Next Yr. FY 95 G	2nd Yr. FY 96 H	3rd Yr. FY 97 I	4th Yr. FY 98 J	5th Yr. FY 99 K
Order entries	1143	71,363	77,057	92,716	100,164	126,591	128,247	142,612	157,972	173,743	189,856	207,133
Sales backlog (year end)	1144	13,310	14,051	17,098	16,534	29,334	29,842	31,509	33,082	34,805	36,591	38,363
Net sales	0001	71,163	76,316	89,669	100,728	113,791	127,739	140,945	156,399	172,020	188,070	205,361
Annual growth												
%-nominal			7.2%	17.5%	12.3%	13.0%	12.3%	10.3%	11.0%	10.0%	9.3%	9.2%
%-real							11.3%	7.8%	8.4%	6.7%	6.8%	6.1%
Cost of sales	0009	36,802	39,382	46,487	51,593	60,003	67,651	74,432	82,109	89,966	98,173	106,997
% to sales		51.7%	51.6%	51.8%	51.2%	52.7%	53.0%	52.8%	52.5%	52.3%	52.2%	52.1%
Gross profit	0010	34,361	36,934	43,182	49,135	53,788	60,088	66,513	74,290	82,054	89,897	98,364
% to sales		48.3%	48.4%	48.2%	48.8%	47.3%	47.0%	47.2%	47.5%	47.7%	47.8%	47.9%
SG&A expenses	0011	21,773	22,558	26,246	29,941	32,163	36,150	40,169	44,887	49,714	54,366	59,555
% to sales		30.6%	29.6%	29.3%	29.7%	28.3%	28.3%	28.5%	28.7%	28.9%	28.9%	29.0%
Operating profit	0012	12,588	14,376	16,936	19,194	21,625	23,938	26,344	29,403	32,340	35,531	38,809
% to sales		17.7%	18.8%	18.9%	19.1%	19.0%	18.7%	18.7%	18.8%	18.8%	18.9%	18.9%

Line item	Code											
Other (inc.)/ded. (excl. int.)	0235	423	1,090	1,395	1,232	1,488	1,764	1,766	1,794	1,530	1,438	1,423
Earnings before interest & taxes	0240	12,165	13,286	15,541	17,962	20,137	22,174	24,578	27,609	30,810	34,093	37,386
% to sales		17.1%	17.4%	17.3%	17.8%	17.7%	17.4%	17.4%	17.7%	17.9%	18.1%	18.2%
Interest (income)/ expense, net	0230	(771)	(1,041)	(1,127)	(1,326)	(1,781)	(2,224)	(2,330)	(2,576)	(2,734)	(2,903)	(3,070)
Pretax earnings	0015	12,936	14,327	16,668	19,288	21,918	24,398	26,908	30,185	33,544	36,996	40,456
% to sales		18.2%	18.8%	18.6%	19.1%	19.3%	19.1%	19.1%	19.3%	19.5%	19.7%	19.7%
Income taxes	0016	5,445	6,785	7,788	8,447	9,668	10,551	11,753	13,101	14,497	15,948	17,387
Effective tax rate		42.1%	47.4%	46.7%	43.8%	44.1%	43.2%	43.7%	43.4%	43.2%	43.1%	43.0%
Net earnings	0017	7,491	7,542	8,880	10,841	12,250	13,847	15,155	17,084	19,047	21,048	23,069
% to sales		10.5%	9.9%	9.9%	10.8%	10.8%	10.8%	10.8%	10.9%	11.1%	11.2%	11.2%
Return on total capital	1324	20.4%	19.7%	20.3%	23.6%	23.8%	25.1%	26.1%	28.0%	30.1%	32.0%	33.9%
ROTC excluding goodwill	1323	27.3%	28.0%	27.2%	30.6%	31.5%	32.5%	32.9%	34.7%	36.6%	38.3%	40.2%

*In thousands of dollars (all numbers in the exhibit are disguised).

Source: Charles F. Knight, "Emerson Electric: Consistent Profits, Consistently," *Harvard Business Review*, January–February 1992, p. 66. Used with permission of the Emerson Electric Company.

Exhibit 5 President's Operating Report Division—Fiscal Year by Quarters/Actual and Expected

(Thousands of Dollars)

Line No.	Current Year						Prior Year		% Act/Exp O/(U) PY
	Actual/Expected	% Sales	Prior Expected	% Sales	Forecast	% Sales	Actual	% Sales	
1st Quarter Ending December 31									
1 Intercompany sales	36		36		34		37		−2.7%
2 Net sales	29,613		29,613		29,463		25,932		14.2
3 Gross profit	14,065	47.5%	14,065	47.5%	13,790	46.8%	12,384	47.8%	13.6
4 SG&A expenses	8,312	28.1	8,312	28.1	8,281	28.1	7,650	29.5	8.7
5 Operating profit	5,753	19.4	5,753	19.4	5,509	18.7	4,734	18.3	21.5
6 Earnings before interest & tax	5,280	17.8	5,280	17.8	5,048	17.1	4,343	16.7	21.6
2nd Quarter Ending March 31									
7 Intercompany sales	5		5		9		56		−91.1%
8 Net sales	33,324		33,324		31,765		22,661		25.0
9 Gross profit	15,283	45.9%	15,283	45.9%	14,812	46.6%	12,518	47.0%	22.1
10 SG&A expenses	9,301	27.9	9,301	27.9	8,937	28.1	7,395	27.8	25.8
11 Operating profit	5,982	18.0	5,982	18.0	5,875	18.5	5,123	19.2	16.8
12 Earnings before interest & tax	5,785	17.4	5,785	17.4	5,612	17.7	4,918	18.4	17.6
3rd Quarter Ending June 30									
13 Intercompany sales	25		25		39		146		−82.9%
14 Net sales	32,845		32,845		33,424		30,678		7.1
15 Gross profit	15,353	46.7%	15,353	46.7%	15,664	46.9%	14,310	46.6%	7.3
16 SG&A expenses	8,916	27.1	8,916	27.1	9,399	28.2	8,424	27.4	5.8
17 Operating profit	6,437	19.6	6,437	19.6	6,265	18.7	5,886	19.2	9.4
18 Earnings before interest & tax	6,126	18.7	6,126	18.7	5,645	16.9	5,378	17.5	13.9

4th Quarter Ending September 30

19 Intercompany sales	94		94		94		25		276.0%
20 Net sales	36,611		36,611		35,722		30,521		20.0
21 Gross profit	17,109	46.7%	17,109	46.7%	16,832	47.1%	14,576	47.8%	17.4
22 SG&A expenses	10,537	28.7	10,537	28.7%	10,029	28.1%	8,695	28.5%	21.2%
23 Operating profit	6,572	18.0	6,572	18.0	6,803	19.0	5,881	19.3	11.7
24 Earnings before interest & tax	6,122	16.7	6,122	16.7	8,146	22.8	5,498	18.0	11.3

Fiscal Year Ending September 30

25 Intercompany sales	160		160		176		264		−39.4%
26 Net sales	132,393		132,393		130,374		113,792		16.3
27 Gross profit	61,810	46.7%	61,810	46.7%	61,098	46.9%	53,788	47.3%	14.9
28 SG&A expenses	37,066	28.0	37,066	28.0	36,646	28.1	32,164	28.3	15.2
29 Operating profit	24,744	18.7	24,744	18.7	24,452	18.8	21,624	19.0	14.4
30 Earnings before interest & tax	23,313	17.6	23,313	17.6	24,451	18.8	20,137	17.7	15.8
31 Pretax earnings	25,154	19.0	25,154	19.0	24,771	19.0	21,918	19.3	14.8
32 Net earnings	14,361	10.8	14,361	10.8	14,024	10.8	12,250	10.8	17.2

Expected First Quarter Next Fiscal Year

33 Intercompany sales	67		65				36		86.1%
34 Net sales	32,830		32,311				29,613		10.9
35 Gross profit	15,142	46.1%	15,143	46.9%			14,065	47.5%	7.7
36 SG&A expenses	9,179	27.9	9,217	28.6			8,312	28.1	10.4
37 Operating profit	5,963	18.2	5,925	18.3			5,753	19.4	3.7
38 Earnings before interest & tax	5,628	17.1	5,619	17.4			5,280	17.8	6.6

Used with permission of the Emerson Electric Company. All numbers are disguised.

results and expectations are weak, a shift to contingency plans is sometimes ordered by top management. Emerson does not allocate corporate overhead to the divisions but does allocate interest and taxes to divisions at the end of the fiscal year.

Compensation

During the year, each division assesses all department heads and higher level managers against specific performance criteria. Those with high potential are offered a series of assignments to develop their skills. Human resources are identified as part of the strategy implementation. In addition, personnel charts on every management team are kept at corporate headquarters. The charts include each manager's photo, function, experience, and career path. About 85 percent of promotions involve internal managers.

Each executive in a division earns a base salary and is eligible for "extra salary," based on division performance according to measurable objectives (primarily sales, profits, and return on capital). An extra salary amount, established at the beginning of the year, is multiplied by "1" if the division hits targeted performance. The multiplier ranges from .35 to 2.0. Doing better than target increases the multiplier. In recent years, sales and profit margin, as identified in the POR forecast column, have had a 50 percent weighting in computing compensation targets. Other factors include inventory turnover, international sales, new product introductions, and an accounts receivable factor. In addition, stock options and a five-year performance share plan are available to top executives.

Communication

Top management strongly encourages open communication. Division presidents and plant managers meet regularly with all employees to discuss the specifics of the business and the competition. As a measure of communication,

top management feels that each employee should be able to answer four essential questions about his or her job:

1. What cost reduction are you currently working on?
2. Who is the competition?
3. Have you met with your management in the past six months?
4. Do you understand the economics of your job?

The company also conducts opinion surveys of every employee. The analysis uncovers trends. Some plants have survey data for the prior twenty years. The CEO receives a summary of every opinion survey from every plant.

Recent Events

As a result of a $2 billion investment in technology during the past 10 years, new products as a percent of sales increased from 13 percent in 1983 to 24 percent in 1993. A new product is defined as a product introduced within the past five years. About 87 percent of total US sales are generated from products that are either first or second in domestic position. Still, some in the investment community do not view Emerson as a technology leader, but as a very efficient world-class manufacturer. Although internally generated new products are part of the planning process, Emerson is sometimes a late entrant in the marketplace. For example, in 1989, a competitor introduced a low-cost, hand-held ultra-sonic gauge. Within 72 days, Emerson introduced its own version at 20 percent less cost than its competitor's gauge. Emerson's gauge was also easier to use and more reliable. It was a bestseller within a year.

To some Wall Street observers, it seems that Emerson is attempting to reduce its dependence on supplying commodity-type products, such as motors and valves, to US-based appliance and other consumer-durables manufacturers by moving into faster growing global markets, such as process controls. As the economy recovers, Emerson is likely to continue its acquisition strategy, with an emphasis on foreign acquisitions, and international joint ventures.

The impact of the recent business segment organization structure on the planning and control process is not clear. The added layer of management between the division managers and top management might change the previous relationship between them.

Questions

1. Evaluate Chief Executive Officer Knight's strategy for the Emerson Electric Company. In view of the strategy, evaluate the planning and control system described in the case. What are its strong and weak points?

2. What changes, if any, would you recommend to the CEO?

3. What role should the eight business segment managers have in Emerson's planning and control system?

BUDGET PREPARATION

This and the following two chapters focus on management control of operations in the current year. Chapter 8 describes the process of budget preparation that takes place *before* the year begins. Chapter 9 describes the appraisal of financial performance *after* its occurrence. Chapter 10 focuses on performance measurement using evaluation of both financial and nonfinancial information.

Chapter 8 starts by describing the purposes of a budget and distinguishing a budget from a strategic plan and from a forecast. The discussion then moves to several types of budgets and some of the details given in a typical operating budget. The following section describes the steps in preparing an operating budget. Finally, there is a discussion of the behavioral implications of the budget preparation process.

Nature of a Budget

Budgets are an important tool for effective short-term planning and control in organizations. *An operating budget usually covers one year and states the revenues and expenses planned for that year.* It has these characteristics:

- A budget estimates the profit potential of the business unit.
- It is stated in monetary terms, although the monetary amounts may be backed up by nonmonetary amounts (e.g., units sold or produced).
- It generally covers a period of one year.[1]
- It is a management commitment; managers agree to accept responsibility for attaining the budgeted objectives.
- The budget proposal is reviewed and approved by an authority higher than the budgetee.

---

[1]In businesses that are strongly influenced by seasonal factors, there may be two budgets per year—for example, apparel companies typically have a fall budget and a spring budget.

- Once approved, the budget can be changed only under specified conditions.
- Periodically, actual financial performance is compared to budget, and variances are analyzed and explained.

The process of preparing a budget should be distinguished from (a) strategic planning and (b) forecasting.

Relation to Strategic Planning

Strategic planning, as we discussed in Chapter 7, is the process of deciding on the nature and size of the several programs that are to be undertaken in implementing an organization's strategies. Both strategic planning and budget preparation involve planning, but the types of planning activities are different in the two processes. The budgeting process focuses on a single year, whereas strategic planning focuses on activities that extend over a period of several years. Strategic planning precedes budgeting and provides the framework within which the annual budget is developed. A budget is, in a sense, a one-year slice of the organization's strategic plan, although for reasons discussed later in this chapter the budgeting process involves more than simply carving out a slice.

Another difference between a strategic plan and a budget is that the former is essentially structured by product lines or other programs, while the latter is structured by responsibility centers. This rearrangement of the program—so it corresponds to the responsibility centers charged with executing it—is necessary, because the budget will be used to influence a manager's performance before the fact and to appraise performance after the fact.

Contrast with Forecasting

A budget differs in several respects from a forecast. A *budget* is a management plan, with the implicit assumption that positive steps will be taken by the budgetee—the manager who prepares the budget—to make actual events correspond to the plan; a *forecast* is merely a prediction of what will most likely happen, carrying no implication that the forecaster will attempt to so shape events that the forecast will be realized. As contrasted with a budget, a forecast has the following characteristics:

- A forecast may or may not be stated in monetary terms.
- It can be for any time period.
- The forecaster does not accept responsibility for meeting the forecasted results.
- Forecasts are not usually approved by higher authority.
- A forecast is updated as soon as new information indicates there is a change in conditions.
- Variances from forecast are not analyzed formally or periodically.

An example of a forecast is one that is made by the treasurer's office to help in cash planning. Such a forecast includes estimates of revenues, expenses, and other items that affect cash flows. The treasurer, however, has no responsibility for making the actual sales, expenses, or other items conform to the forecast. The cash forecast is not cleared with top management; it may change weekly or even daily, without approval from higher authority; and usually the variances between actual and forecast are not systematically analyzed.

From management's point of view, a financial forecast is exclusively a planning tool, whereas a budget is both a planning tool and a control tool. All budgets include elements of forecasting, in that budgetees cannot be held responsible for certain events that affect their ability to meet budgeted objectives. If, however, a budgetee can change a so-called budget each quarter without formal approval, such a document is essentially a forecast, rather than a true budget. It cannot be used for evaluation and control because, by the end of the year, actual results will always equal the revised budget.

Use of a Budget

Preparation of an operating budget has four principal purposes: (1) to fine-tune the strategic plan; (2) to help coordinate the activities of the several parts of the organization; (3) to assign responsibility to managers, to authorize the amounts they are permitted to spend, and to inform them of the performance that is expected of them; and (4) to obtain a commitment that is a basis for evaluating a manager's actual performance.

Fine-Tuning the Strategic Plan.   As discussed in Chapter 7, the strategic plan has the following characteristics: it is prepared early in the year, it is developed on the basis of the best information available at that time, its preparation involves relatively few managers, and it is stated in fairly broad terms. The budget, which is completed just prior to the beginning of the budget year, provides an opportunity to use the latest available information and is based on the judgment of managers at all levels throughout the organization. The "first cut" at the budget may reveal that the overall performance of the organization, or of a business unit within the organization, would not be satisfactory. If so, budget preparation provides an opportunity to make decisions that will improve performance before a commitment is made to a specific way of operating during the year.

Coordination.   Every responsibility center manager in the organization participates in the preparation of the budget. Then, when the staff assembles the pieces into an overall plan, inconsistencies may show up. The most common is the possibility that the plans of the production organization are not consistent with the planned sales volume, in total or in certain product lines. Within the production organization, plans for shipments of finished products may be inconsistent with the plans of plants or departments within plants to provide components for these products. As another example, line organizations may be assuming a higher level of service from support organizations than those organizations plan to provide. During the budget preparation process, these inconsistencies are identified and resolved.

Assigning Responsibility.   The approved budget should make clear what each manager is responsible for. The budget also authorizes responsibility center managers to spend specified amounts of money for certain designated purposes without seeking the approval of higher authority.

Basis for Performance Evaluation.   The budget represents a commitment by the budgetee to his or her superior. It is therefore a benchmark against which actual performance can be judged. The commitment is subject to change if the assumptions on which it is based change, but the budget nevertheless is an excellent starting point for performance appraisal. The budget assigns responsibility to each responsibility center in the organization. At the top level, the budget summary assigns responsibility to individual profit centers. Within profit centers, the budget assigns responsibility to functional areas (such as marketing). Within functional areas, the budget assigns responsibility to individual responsibility centers (such as regional sales offices in the marketing organization).

> **Examples.**   Nicolas G. Hayek, the chief executive officer of SMH (makers of Swatch and Omega watches), has been credited with both a dramatic turnaround of SMH as well as the revitalization of the Swiss watch industry itself. Nicolas Hayek uses the budgets as part of his broader set of tools in this revitalization process. Hayek has remarked: "We are big believers in decentralization. This company has 211 profit centers. We set tough, demanding budgets for them. I personally participate in detailed budget reviews for our major profit centers. Then we track performance closely. We get monthly sales figures for all profit centers on the sixth day of the following month. We get profit and loss statements about 10 or 15 days later. The moment anything looks strange, we react very quickly, very decisively, very directly."[2]

Content of an Operating Budget

Exhibit 8–1 shows the content of a typical operating budget and contrasts the operating budget with other types of planning documents: the strategic plan; and the capital budget, the cash budget, and the budgeted balance sheet (which will be described in a later subsection). The amounts are the planned dollar amounts for the year, together with quantitative amounts, such as head counts (i.e., number of employees) and sales in units.

---

[2]William Taylor, "Message and Muscle: An Interview with Swatch Titan Nicolas Hayek," *Harvard Business Review,* March–April 1993, p. 110.

Exhibit 8–1

Types of plans and their contents

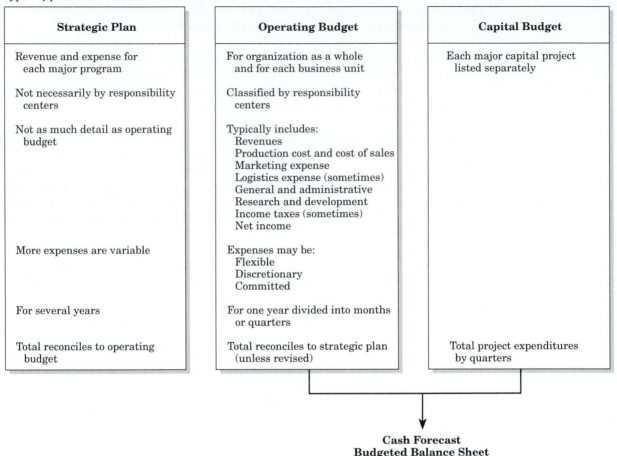

Strategic Plan	Operating Budget	Capital Budget
Revenue and expense for each major program	For organization as a whole and for each business unit	Each major capital project listed separately
Not necessarily by responsibility centers	Classified by responsibility centers	

Not as much detail as operating budget	Typically includes:
	  Revenues
	  Production cost and cost of sales
	  Marketing expense
	  Logistics expense (sometimes)
	  General and administrative
	  Research and development
	  Income taxes (sometimes)
	  Net income	

More expenses are variable	Expenses may be:
	  Flexible
	  Discretionary
	  Committed	

For several years	For one year divided into months or quarters	
Total reconciles to operating budget	Total reconciles to strategic plan (unless revised)	Total project expenditures by quarters

Cash Forecast
Budgeted Balance Sheet

Operating Budget Categories

In a relatively small organization, especially one that has no business units, the whole budget may fit on one page. In larger organizations, there is a summary page, and other pages contain the details for individual business units, plus research and development, and general administrative expenses. The revenue item is listed first, both because it is the first item on an income statement and also because the amount of budgeted revenues influences the amount of many of the other items.

Revenue Budgets.   A revenue budget consists of unit sales projection multiplied by expected selling prices. Of all the elements of a profit budget, the revenue budget is the most critical, but it is also the element that is subject to the greatest uncertainty. The degree of uncertainty differs among companies, and within the same company the degree of uncertainty is different at different times. Companies with large backlogs or companies whose sales volumes are constrained by production capacity will have more certainty in sales projections than companies whose sales volumes are subject to the uncertainties of the marketplace. The revenue budget usually is based on forecasts of some conditions for which the sales manager cannot be held responsible. For example, the state of the economy must be anticipated in preparing a revenue budget, but the marketing manager obviously has no control over it. Nevertheless, effective advertising, good service, good quality, and well-trained salespeople influence the sales volume, and the marketing manager does control these factors.

Budgeted Production Cost and Cost of Sales.   Although textbook illustrations typically show that direct material cost and direct labor cost are developed from the product volumes contained in the sales budget, this often is not feasible in practice because these details depend on the actual mix of products that are to be manufactured. Instead, the standard material and labor costs of the planned volume level of a *standard mix of products* are shown in the budget. Production managers make plans for obtaining quantities of material and labor, and they may prepare procurement budgets for long lead-time items. They also develop production schedules to ensure that resources needed to produce the budgeted quantities will be available.

The budgeted cost developed by the production managers may not be for the same quantities of products as those shown in the sales budget; the difference represents additions to or subtractions from finished goods inventory. Nevertheless, the cost of sales reported in the summary budget is the standard cost of the products budgeted to be sold. Similarly, the budgeted cost of sales in wholesale and retail establishments is not necessarily the cost of the goods that will be purchased in the budget year. Control over the amounts that may be purchased is obtained by detailed "open to buy" authorizations made during the year, rather than by the amounts shown in the budget. As is the case with manufacturing companies, the difference between purchases and sales represents additions to or decreases in inventory.

Marketing Expenses.   Marketing expenses are expenses incurred to obtain sales. A considerable fraction of the amounts included in the budget may have been committed before the year begins. If the budget contemplates a selling organization of a specified number of sales offices with specified personnel, then plans for opening or closing offices and for hiring and training new personnel (or for laying off personnel) must be well under way before the year begins. Advertising must be prepared months in advance of its release, and contracts with media also are placed months in advance.

Logistics expenses usually are reported separately from order in getting expenses. They include order entry, warehousing and order picking, transportation to the customer, and collection of accounts receivable. Conceptually, these expenses behave more like production costs than marketing costs; that is, many of them are engineered costs. Nevertheless, many companies include them in the marketing budget, because they tend to be the responsibility of the marketing organization.

General and Administrative Expenses.   These are G&A expenses of staff units, both at headquarters and at business units. Overall, they are discretionary expenses, although some components (such as bookkeeping costs in the accounting department) are engineered expenses. In budget preparation, much attention is given to these categories; because they are discretionary, the appropriate amount to authorize is subject to much debate.

Research and Development Expenses.   The R&D budget uses either of two approaches, or a combination of them. In one approach, total amount is the focus. This may be the current level of spending, adjusted for inflation; or it may be a larger amount, in the belief that more can be spent in good times, if the company expects an increase in sales revenue or if there is a good chance of developing a significantly new product or process. The alternative approach is aggregating the planned spending on each approved project, plus an allowance for work that is likely to be undertaken even though it is not currently identified.

Many companies decide to spend a specified percentage of sales revenue on R&D, but this percentage is based on a long-run average—that is, R&D spending is not geared to short-run changes in sales volume. To permit R&D spending to reflect the short run could have undesirable effects on the R&D organization; hiring and organizing researchers is a difficult task, and, if spending fluctuates in the short run, inefficiencies are likely.

Income Taxes.   Although the bottom line is income after income taxes, some companies do not take income taxes into account in preparing the budgets for business units. This is because income tax policies are determined at corporate headquarters.

Other Budgets

Although we focus primarily on the preparation of the operating budget, the complete budget also consists of a capital budget, a budgeted balance sheet, and a budgeted cash flow statement. Some companies also prepare a statement of nonfinancial objectives.

Capital Budget

The capital budget states the approved capital projects, plus a lump-sum amount for small projects that do not require high-level approval. It usually is prepared separately from the operating budget and by different people.

During the year, proposals for capital expenditures are considered at various levels within the organization, and some are finally approved. This is part of the strategic planning process.

At budget time, the approved projects are assembled into an overall package and examined in total. It may turn out that this total exceeds the amount that the company is willing to spend on capital projects; if so, some projects are deleted, others are reduced in size, and others are deferred. For the projects that remain, an estimate of the cash that will be spent each quarter is prepared. This is necessary in order to prepare the cash flow statement.

Budgeted Balance Sheet

The budgeted balance sheet shows the balance sheet implications of decisions included in the operating budget and the capital budget. Overall, it is not a management control device, but some parts of it are useful for control. Operating managers who can influence the level of inventories, accounts receivable, or accounts payable often are held responsible for the level of those items.

Budgeted Cash Flow Statement

The budgeted cash flow statement shows how much of the cash needs during the year will be supplied by retained earnings and how much, if any, must be obtained by borrowing or from other outside sources. It is, of course, important for financial planning. As its title indicates, the cash flow statement shows the inflows and outflows of cash during the year, usually by quarters. In addition, the treasurer needs an estimate of cash requirements for monthly (or even shorter) intervals as a basis for planning lines of credit and short-term borrowing.

Management by Objectives

The financial objectives that managers are responsible for attaining during the budget year are set forth in the budgets described above. Implicit in the budget amounts are also certain specific objectives: open new sales offices, introduce a new product line, retrain employees, install a new computer system, and so on. Some companies make these objectives explicit. The process of doing so is called *management by objectives* in the literature. The objectives of each responsibility center are set forth in quantitative terms wherever possible, and, as in the case with the budgeted amounts, are accepted by the responsible manager. If nonfinancial objectives can be stated as numbers, they may serve a useful purpose in motivating managers and in appraising their performance.

Unfortunately, some management by objectives (MBO) systems are separated from the budget preparation process. In part, this is because MBO was initially advocated by authors of personnel texts and articles, whereas the financial budget is the province of management accounting texts. MBO and budgeting should be two parts of the same planning process.

> **Example.**   Lee Iacocca used MBO at Ford Motor company and later at Chrysler Corporation. To quote Iacocca: "Over the years, I've regularly asked my key people—and I've had them ask their key people, and so on down the line—a few basic questions: "What are your objectives for the next 90 days? What are your plans, your priorities, your hopes? And how do you go about achieving them? [This] quarterly review system makes employees accountable to *themselves*. Not only does it force each manager to consider his [or her] own goals, but it's also an effective way to remind people not to lose sight of their dreams.[3]

Budget Preparation Process

Organization

Budget Department.   The budget department, which normally (but not always) reports to the corporate controller, administers the information flow of the budgetary control system. The budget department performs the following functions:

- Publishes procedures and forms for the preparation of the budget.
- Coordinates and publishes each year the basic corporatewide assumptions that are to be the basis for the budgets (e.g., assumptions about the economy).
- Makes sure that information is properly communicated between interrelated organization units (e.g., sales and production).
- Provides assistance to budgetees in the preparation of their budgets.
- Analyzes proposed budgets and makes recommendations, first to the budgetee and subsequently to senior management.
- Administers the process of making budget revisions during the year.
- Coordinates the work of budget departments in lower echelons (e.g., business unit budget departments).
- Analyzes reported performance against budget, interprets the result, and prepares summary reports for senior management.

With the computer, and especially the Internet, these functions can be performed more accurately, with fewer copying and arithmetic errors, and much more quickly. However, the need for decisions and for interactions between the individuals involved is unchanged.

The Budget Committee.   The budget committee consists of members of senior management, such as the chief executive officer, chief operating officer, and the chief financial officer. In some companies, the chief executive officer decides without a committee. The budget committee performs a vital role. It reviews and either approves or adjusts each of the budgets. In a large

---

[3]Lee Iacocca, *Iaccoca, An Autobiography* (New York: Bantam Books, 1984), p. 47.

diversified company, the budget committee might meet only with the senior operating executives to review the budgets for a business unit or group of business units. In some companies, however, each business unit manager meets with the budget committee and presents his or her budget proposals. Usually, the budget committee must approve major budget revisions made during the year.

Issuance of Guidelines

If a company has a strategic planning process, the first year of the strategic plan (which is usually approved in the summer) is the beginning of the budget preparation process. If the company has no strategic plan, management needs to think about the future in the manner suggested in Chapter 7 as a basis for budget preparation.

Unlike budget preparation, development of the strategic plan usually does not involve lower-level responsibility center managers. Thus, whether or not there is a strategic plan, the first step in the budget preparation process is to develop guidelines that govern the preparation of the budget, for dissemination to all managers. These guidelines are those that are implicit in the strategic plan, modified by developments that have occurred since its approval, especially the company's performance for the year to date and its current outlook. All responsibility centers must follow some of these guidelines, such as assumed inflation in general and inflation for specific items such as wages; corporate policies on how many persons can be promoted; compensation at each wage and salary level, including employee benefits; and a possible hiring freeze. Other guidelines are specific to certain responsibility centers.

The budget staff develops the guidelines and senior management approves them. In some cases lower-level managers may discuss the guidelines before approval. Staff also develops a timetable for the steps in the budget preparation process. The budget department then disseminates this material throughout the organization.

Initial Budget Proposal

Using the guidelines, responsibility center managers, assisted by their staffs, develop a budget request. Because most responsibility centers will start the budget year with the same facilities, personnel, and other resources that they have currently, this budget is based on the existing levels, which are then modified in accordance with the guidelines.[4] Changes from the current level of performance can be classified as (*a*) changes in external forces and

---

[4]In the 1970s, there was a proposal for "zero-base budgeting," which involved analyzing each responsibility center's expenses from scratch. Some economists also criticize starting with the current spending levels; they disparage this as "incremental budgeting." Experience has shown that starting from zero is not practical in the time available for budget formulation, nor is it necessary in view of the ongoing nature of most activities.

(*b*) changes in internal policies and practices. They include, but are not limited to, the following.

Changes in External Forces
- Changes in the general level of economic activity as it affects the volume of sales (e.g., expected growth in the demand for a product line).
- Expected changes in the price of purchased materials and services.
- Expected changes in labor rates.
- Expected changes in the cost of discretionary activities (e.g., marketing, R&D, and administration).
- Changes in selling prices. These often are equal to the sum of the changes in the related costs, which assumes that changes in costs can be recovered in selling prices because similar changes will be experienced by competitors.

Changes in Internal Policies and Practices
- Changes in production costs, reflecting new equipment and methods.
- Changes in discretionary costs, based on anticipated changes in workload.
- Changes in market share and product mix.

Some companies require that specific changes from the current level of spending be classified by such causes as the above. Although this involves extra work, it provides a useful tool for analyzing the validity of proposed changes.

Negotiation

The budgetee discusses the proposed budget with his or her superior. This is the heart of the process. The superior attempts to judge the validity of each of the adjustments. Ordinarily, a governing consideration is that performance in the budget year should be an improvement over performance in the current year. The superior recognizes that he or she will become the budgetee at the next level of the budget process and, therefore, must be prepared to defend the budget that is finally agreed to.

Slack.   Many budgetees tend to budget revenues somewhat lower, and expenses somewhat higher, than their best estimates of these amounts. The resulting budget, therefore, is an easier target for them to achieve. *The difference between the budget amount and the best estimate is called slack.* In examining the budget, superiors attempt to discover and eliminate slack, but this is a difficult task.

Review and Approval

The proposed budgets go up through successive levels in the organization. When they reach the top of a business unit, analysts put the pieces together and examine the total. In part, the analyst studies consistency—for example, is the production budget consistent with planned sales volume? Are service and support centers planning for the services that are being requested of them? In part, the examination asks whether the budget will produce a satisfactory profit. If not, it is often sent back for reworking. The same type of analysis takes place at corporate headquarters.

Final approval is recommended by the budget committee to the chief executive officer. The CEO also submits the approved budget to the board of directors for ratification. This happens in December, just prior to the beginning of the budget year.

Budget Revisions

One of the principal considerations in budget administration is the procedure for revising a budget after it has been approved. Clearly, if it could be revised at will by the budgetee, there would be no point in reviewing and approving the budget in the first instance. On the other hand, if the budget assumptions turn out to be so unrealistic that the comparisons of actual against budget are meaningless, budget revisions may be desirable.

There are two general types of budget revisions:

1. Procedures that provide for a systematic (say, quarterly) updating of the budgets.
2. Procedures that allow revisions under special circumstances.

Systematic updating obviously requires extra work. Nevertheless, large Japanese companies believe this is worthwhile. They prepare a budget for the whole year, but only the first six months of this budget is formally approved by senior management. The budget for the second six months is revised and approved shortly before the period begins.[5]

If budget revisions are limited only to unusual circumstances, such revisions should be adequately reviewed. In general, permission to make revisions should be difficult to obtain. Budget revisions should be limited to those circumstances in which the approved budget is so unrealistic that it no longer provides a useful control device. That is to say, *budget revisions must be justified on the basis of significantly changed conditions from those existing when the original budget was approved.*

---

[5]John F. Rechfield, "What Working for a Japanese Company Taught Me," *Harvard Business Review,* November–December 1990, pp. 168–69.

Example.   In 1995, postal rates increased, apparel demand dropped, and paper prices doubled. Lands' End, a $1 billion catalog sales company, chose to cut back mailings to lower costs instead of continuing with the budgeted number of mailings. The dramatic changes in business conditions required Lands' End to change its plans.[6]

An important consideration is that managers should not be required to adhere to plans that subsequent events prove to be suboptimum. This can be a serious problem in budgeting. Because of the time required for budget preparation and review, budgets must provide for actions that are planned months ahead of the time they take place. It is important, therefore, that management actions be based on the latest information available. Consequently, managers should act according to the most recent information. Performance continues to be measured against the original budget, but explanations for reasonable variances are acceptable.

Contingency Budgets

Some companies routinely prepare contingency budgets that identify management actions to be taken if there is a significant decrease in the sales volume from what was anticipated at the time of developing the budget (e.g., actions to be taken based on a decrease of 20 percent from the best estimate of sales volume). The contingency budget provides a way of quickly adjusting to changed conditions if the situation arises. If sales volume declines by 20 percent, business unit managers can determine for themselves, according to the predetermined contingency budget, actions to be taken.

Examples.   A large diversified firm required contingency budgets from its business units. The budget for business units closed with a series of comparative financial statements, which depicted the estimated item-by-item effect if sales fell to 60 percent or 80 percent of forecast or increased to 120 percent of forecast. For each of these levels of possible sales, costs were divided into three categories: fixed costs, unavoidable variable costs, and management discretionary costs. Business unit managers described the specific actions they would take to control employment, total assets, and capital expenditures in cases of a reduction in sales, and when these actions would be put into effect.

Behavioral Aspects

One of the purposes of a management control system is to encourage the manager to be effective and efficient in attaining the goals of the organization. Some motivational considerations in the preparation of operating budgets are described below.[7]

---

[6]Susan Chandler, "Lands' End Looks For Terra Firma," *Business Week,* July 8, 1996, pp. 130–31.

[7]For a description of the behavioral problems associated with budget systems, see G. H. Hofstede, *The Game of Budget Control* (New York: Barnes & Noble, 1968).

Participation in the Budgetary Process

A budget process is either "top down" or "bottom up." With top down budgeting, senior management sets the budget for the lower levels. With bottom up budgeting, lower-level managers participate in setting the budget amounts. The top down approach rarely works, however. It leads to a lack of commitment on the part of budgetees; this endangers the plan's success. Bottom up budgeting is most likely to generate commitment to meeting the budgeted objectives; however, unless carefully controlled, it may result in amounts that are too easy or that may not match the company's overall objectives.

Actually, an effective budget preparation process blends the two approaches. Budgetees prepare the first draft of the budget for their area of responsibility, which is "bottom up"; but they do so within guidelines established at higher levels, which is "top down." Senior managers review and critique these proposed budgets. A hardheaded approval process helps to ensure that budgetees do not "play games" with the budgeting system. The review process, nevertheless, should be perceived as being fair; if a superior changes the budgeted amounts, he or she should try to convince the budgetee that such a change is reasonable.

Research has shown that budget participation (i.e., a process in which the budgetee is both *involved* in and has *influence* over the setting of budget amounts) has positive effects on managerial motivation for two reasons:

1. There is likely to be greater acceptance of budget goals if they are perceived as being under managers' personal control, rather than being imposed externally. This leads to higher personal commitment to achieve the goals.

2. Participative budgeting results in effective information exchanges. The approved budget amounts benefit from the expertise and personal knowledge of the budgetees, who are closest to the product/market environment. Further, budgetees have a clearer understanding of their jobs through interactions with superiors during the review and approval phase.

Participative budgeting is especially beneficial for responsibility centers that operate in dynamic and uncertain environments because managers in charge of such responsibility centers are likely to have the best information regarding the variables that affect their revenues and expenses.

Degree of Budget Target Difficulty

The ideal budget is one that is challenging but attainable. In statistical terms, this may be interpreted as meaning that a manager who performs reasonably well has at least a 50 percent chance of achieving the budget amount. Merchant and Manzoni, in a field study of business unit managers, concluded that business unit budget achievability in practice is usually considerably higher than 50 percent.[8] There are several reasons why senior management approves achievable budgets for business units:

- If the budgeted target is too difficult, managers are motivated to take short-term actions that may not be in the long-term interests of the company. Attainable profit targets are a way of minimizing these dysfunctional actions.
- Achievable budget targets reduce the motivation for managers to engage in data manipulation (e.g., inadequate provision for warranty claims, bad debts, inventory obsolescence, and the like) to meet the budget.
- If business unit profit budgets represent achievable targets, senior management can, in turn, divulge a profit target to security analysts, shareholders, and other external constituencies with a reasonable expectation of being correct.
- A profit budget that is very difficult to attain usually implies an overly optimistic sales target. This may lead to an overcommitment of resources to gear up for the higher sales activity. It is administratively and politically awkward to downsize operations if the actual sales levels do not reach the optimistic targets.
- When business unit managers are able to meet and exceed their targets, there is a "winning" atmosphere and positive attitude within the company.

One limitation of an achievable target is the possibility that business unit managers will not put forth satisfactory effort once the budget is met. This limitation can be overcome by providing bonus payments for actual performance that exceeds the budget.

If a business unit manager achieves more than the budgeted profit, senior management should not automatically increase the profit budget for the following year. If this happens, business unit managers may not perform up to their maximum capacity in order to avoid showing too large a favorable variance.

Senior Management Involvement

Senior management involvement is necessary for any budget system to be effective in motivating budgetees. Management must participate in the review and approval of the budgets, and the approval should not be a rubber stamp. Without their active participation in the approval process, there will be a great temptation for the budgetee to "play games" with the system—that is, some managers will submit easily attained budgets or budgets that contain excessive allowances for possible contingencies.

---

[8]K. A. Merchant and J. Manzoni, "The Achievability of Budget Targets in Profit Centers: A Field Study," *The Accounting Review* LXIV, no. 3 (July 1989), pp. 539–58.

Management also must follow up on budget results. If there is no top management feedback, with respect to budget results, the budget system will not be effective in motivating the budgetee.

The Budget Department

The budget department has a particularly difficult behavioral problem. It must analyze the budgets in detail, and it must be certain that budgets are prepared properly and that the information is accurate. To accomplish these tasks, the budget department sometimes must act in ways that line managers perceive as threatening or hostile. For example, the budget department tries to ensure that the budget does not contain excessive allowances (i.e., "water"). In other cases, the explanation of budget variances provided by the budgetee may hide or minimize a potentially serious situation; and when the budget department discloses the facts, the line manager is placed in an uncomfortable position. The budget department must walk a fine line between helping the line manager and ensuring the integrity of the system.

To perform their function effectively, the members of the budget department must have a reputation for impartiality and fairness. If they do not have this reputation, it becomes difficult, if not impossible, for them to perform the tasks necessary to maintaining an effective budgetary control system. The members of the budget department should, of course, also have the personal skills required to deal effectively with people.

Quantitative Techniques

Although mathematical techniques and computers improve the budgetary process, they do not solve the critical problems of budgetary control. The critical problems in budgeting tend to be in the behavioral area.

Simulation

Simulation is a method that constructs a model of a real situation and then manipulates this model in such a way as to draw some conclusions about the real situation. The preparation and review of a budget is a simulation process. With a computer simulation, senior management can ask what the effect of different types of changes would be and receive almost instantaneous answers. This gives senior management a chance to participate more fully in the budgetary process.

Several computer software packages are available. Some are specific to certain industries, others are general purpose. Most require adaptation to the company's own way of doing things; and this process may require a year, or several years, of intensive effort on the part of company employees or consultants. In some cases, the resulting program has proved to be more complicated than managers will tolerate. If the needs of managers, both budgetees and senior management, are properly taken into account, however, the resulting program can have great benefits.

Probability Estimates

Each number in a budget is a point estimate—that is, it is the single "most likely" amount. For example, sales estimates are stated in terms of the specific number of units of each type of product to be sold. Point estimates are necessary for control purposes. For planning purposes, however, a range of probable outcomes may be more helpful. After a budget has been tentatively approved, it may be possible with a computer model to substitute a probability distribution for each major point estimate. The model then is run a number of times, and a probability distribution of the expected profits can be calculated and used for planning purposes. This is called a *Monte Carlo* process.

Some authors have proposed that budgets be prepared initially using probability distributions instead of point estimates; that is, the budget committee would approve a number of probability distributions, rather than specific amounts. Subsequent variance analysis would be based on these probability distributions. The work involved in making these estimates is considerable, however. Also, if the procedure is to ask for three numbers—pessimistic, most likely, and optimistic—the result is likely to be a normal curve, with an expected value equal to the most likely number. This is no better than estimating the most likely number in the first instance, except that, theoretically, a measure of dispersion is reported. In any event, probabilistic budgets are rarely found in practice.

Summary

A budget is in a sense a one-year slice of the strategic plan. However, it is prepared in more detail than the strategic plan, and its preparation involves managers at all levels in the organization. An operating budget shows the details of revenues and expenses for the budget year for each responsibility center and for the organization as a whole. It is so structured that amounts are identified with specific responsibility centers. The process starts with the dissemination of guidelines approved by senior management. Using these guidelines, each responsibility center manager prepares a proposed budget, which is reviewed with his or her superior, and an agreed position is negotiated. When these individual pieces reach the top of the business unit or of the whole organization, analysts review them for consistency and adherence to overall corporate goals. The whole process is primarily behavioral. Responsibility center managers must participate in the process, but they do so within constraints decided on by senior management. Participative budgeting, in which managers feel they have influence on the process, has benefits generally for the organization.

Suggested Additional Readings

Dunk, Alan S. "The Effect of Budget Emphasis and Information Asymmetry on the Relation between Budgetary Participation and Slack." *The Accounting Review* LXVIII, no. 2 (April 1993), pp. 400–410.

Frucot, Veronique, and Winston T. Shearon. "Budgetary Participation, Locus of Control, and Mexican Managerial Performance and Job Satisfaction." *The Accounting Review* LXVI (January 1991), pp. 80–99.

Govindarajan, Vijay. "Impact of Participation in the Budgetary Process on Managerial Attitudes and Performance; Universalistic and Contingency Perspectives." *Decision Sciences* 17, no. 4 (Fall 1986), pp. 496–516.

Moose, C. J. *Budgeting.* Rourke, 1997.

Penne, Mark. "Accounting Systems, Participation in Budgeting, and Performance Evaluation." *The Accounting Review* LXV, no. 2 (April 1990), pp. 303–14.

Rachlin, R. (ed). *Handbook of Budgeting.* 4th ed. New York: John Wiley & Sons, 1998.

———. *Total Business Budgeting.* New York: John Wiley & Sons, 1997.

Schick, A. *Modern Budgeting.* 1998.

Seitz, N. E. *Capital Budget and Long Term Finances.* New York: Harcourt, 1997.

CASE 8–1
SOUND DYNAMICS, INC.

In April 1990, the manufacturing director of the Reichard subsidiary of Sound Dynamics, Inc., submitted a memorandum (Appendix A to this case) to the managing director of the subsidiary that asked for a supplemental budget for the production control department and explained why increased personnel and funds were needed. In accordance with the company's standard procedure, the request was passed to the subsidiary's financial controller, Ms. Martha Larson, for review. Ms. Larson, after studying the matter, decided the supplemental budget was not justified and wrote a memorandum (Appendix B) to the manufacturing office explaining her position. The manufacturing office, in the latter part of July, sent a memorandum (Appendix C) to Ms. Larson outlining its disagreement with her conclusions and supporting analysis. Now, early in August, Ms. Larson was considering what action she should take on this matter.

Sound Dynamics was a US-based international manufacturer of audio recording equipment, including consumer and commercial lines. Annual sales volume was approximately $1 billion (US) and total employment had passed the 10,000 mark. Sound Dynamics was organized in three sectors, commercial, consumer, and international. In the commercial sector, based out of Atlanta, there were two divisions. One division designed, produced, and sold custom components for recording studios in the United States. The other division provided services and supplies for those systems. The consumer sector, based in Charlotte, had three divisions, which manufactured audio components and supplies (tapes, cleaners, etc.). The international sector was composed of subsidiaries in 20 countries that distributed Sound Dynamics products throughout the world. Several of the larger subsidiaries also manufactured some parts of the product line under license agreements with the parent company.

Reichard Produkten, GmbH, located in Munich, was one of the larger subsidiaries in the sector. It produced commercial components and supplies for distribution throughout Western Europe.

During the last quarter of 1989, the Reichard subsidiary had absorbed the commercial products manufacturing and related activities of the company's Italian affiliate, San Remo, which was located in the German-speaking region of Northern Italy, near the Austrian border. The San Remo factory was converted from commercial component manufacturing to consumer components for all of the EC market. Overall responsibility for product planning and marketing of San Remo and Reichard components, however, remained with the international sector sales vice president.

A major reason for the consolidation of manufacturing activities was to achieve scale economies wherever possible. There had been an anticipated annual saving in Reichard's production control department, for example, of $184,000 from a reduction in the number of salaried personnel by 12 through eliminating duplicate jobs. There also had been an expected saving from computerization of production scheduling and control.

Prior to consolidation, the San Remo subsidiary had been using a computerized scheduling and control system, whereas Reichard had been using a manual system. In December 1989, a study was made to determine which system of control would best serve the consolidated commercial manufacturing operation. This study indicated that annual savings of about $138,000 in salary and related expenses, associated with the anticipated elimination of

---

This case was adapted by Professor John Shank from an earlier case written by Professor Robert Anthony. The industry described in the case is disguised.

11 positions, could be realized from computerization. The manufacturing office of Reichard had concurred with the findings of this study, and the decision was made to computerize production control for the consolidated manufacturing operation.

Strong budgetary control was exercised throughout the Sound Dynamics organization. In the fall of each year, every department manager throughout the worldwide organization developed a proposed budget for the next year. The first step in this annual budget review was the establishment of a realistic timetable and the development of budget assumptions by the budget section of the corporate controller's office. Individual business units tended to base their budget proposals on different assumptions unless instructed otherwise. Within these assumptions, the next step was to establish realistic budget objectives (forecasts) for next year's administrative expenditures based on known assumptions. To develop objectives, the budget section of the corporate controller's office normally began with the current budget, including all supplemental budgets that are of a continuing nature, and then adjusted for any known changes, such as projected cost reductions, or increases based on new programs. The objectives were then reviewed and approved by corporate and sector management, who in turn informed the subsidiaries and divisions that this was to be the basis for their budget planning. These objectives became the primary benchmark against which business units' proposals were reviewed. Each proposed budget then entered an extensive process of analysis, revision, consolidation, review, and approval by higher levels of management, first within a division or subsidiary and then at sector and corporate levels. At each management level, budgets for subordinate units were consolidated prior to submission to the next higher management level. Financial controllers at each level participated closely in this process. In each business unit a budget analyst reviewed all budgets personally with top management to make certain that they

were understood. The budget review process does not save money, but it does apply a "back pressure" on line and staff managers to make sure they are "cost conscious." Therefore, a close working relationship with division or subsidiary management and a good selling job by the personnel of the budget section are essential.

Once formal approval had been given to a budget, it became a firm commitment for the responsible manager. To exceed this budget required submitting and obtaining approval of a supplemental budget. A supplemental budget was prepared and processed in essentially the same way as the original budget. Policy prescribed that a *supplemental budget could only be justified on the basis of changes in conditions after the original budget was approved.*

Although administrative expense budgets were treated as "fixed" budgets without automatic volume adjustments, years of reviewing these budgets had shown that workload standards, quite similar to those employed in "variable" budgets, could be established for many functions. For instance, in the general manufacturing office, workload in the plant management staff can be measured in part by the number of component lines and subassemblies, and in the production scheduling department, workload can be measured by the number of unique parts and the number of separate production runs.

Since the 1990 budgets had been approved prior to the consolidation of commercial manufacturing for Reichard and San Remo, there was a separate budget for each subsidiary, including the production control departments. The approved budgets for 1990 for these two production control departments are summarized in Exhibit 1, together with the estimated savings resulting from consolidation and computerization. The supplemental budget requested by the manufacturing office is also shown for purposes of comparison.

As Ms. Larson reviewed the situation, she saw three possible courses of action: (1) to concur with the manufacturing director's position, in which case the request would very likely receive the necessary approval of the managing director; (2) to continue her opposition, in which case her views and those of the manufacturing office would be placed before the managing director, who would then decide all matters at issue; and (3) to reply with a further analysis, in the hope that the manufacturing office would become convinced of the soundness of her position.

Questions

1. Try to reconcile the numbers in the various positions reflected in the memos in Appendixes A, B, and C. Prepare a *brief* summary that reconciles the differences. Of the disputed differences, how many people and how much money are attributable to alleged workload increase? To salary mix change? To unanticipated one-time computerization implementation costs?[1]

---

[1]The basic question here is, What should the controller do next? The contest is one of a "tight" control system, where budgets have teeth in them and cost control is not just a nice phrase—it is a way of life.

2. Having struggled with Question 1 for a while, what do you think is really going on in the memos?
3. Based on your analysis of the situation, what is a "reasonable" budget for the department for 1990?
4. What should Ms. Larson do now?
5. What lessons for effective controllership should we draw from this case?

You should first try to reconcile the difference that is floating around. What factors account for the difference, in managerial terms, and what is the dollar impact of each factor you identify? Push this idea far enough so you get a handle on the real "agendas" here. This is an involved case, and you will find it difficult to make much progress without doing some analysis of the conflicting presentations.

Based on this analysis, what seems to be a "reasonable" budget allowance for the production control department for 1990? Why is the number you propose for dollars and people the most "reasonable" one?

Once you have developed a viewpoint on what constitutes a "reasonable" solution, how do you propose that the controller respond to the manufacturing office?

Finally, take a few steps backward from the problems and ask yourself what approach to management is at work here and what you see as the strengths and weaknesses of this approach.

EXHIBIT 1   Budgets and Approved Changes for 1990 Production Control Department— Consolidated Operations in Germany

	Reichard		San Remo		Total	
	Number of Salaried Personnel	*Dollars (000)*	*Number of Salaried Personnel*	*Dollars (000)*	*Number of Salaried Personnel*	*Dollars (000)*
Approved budget (before consolidation)	38	$722	27	$668	65	$1,390
Savings from consolidation			(12)	(184)	(12)	(184)
Savings from computerization*	(11)	(138)			(11)	(138)
Budget for the consolidated operations as of 1st January 1990	27	$584	15	$484	42	$1,068
Proposed increase to budget (supplemental budget request)					12	390
Total					54	$1,458

*Based on the study completed in December 1989, concurred in by the manufacturing director of the Reichard Subsidiary.

APPENDIX A
MEMORANDUM

To: Managing Director—Reichard GmbH.
From: Manufacturing Office
Date: April 6, 1990
Subject: Supplemental Budget for 1990

An increase of 12 in the personnel ceiling for our production control department is requested for the fiscal year 1990. This increase is necessitated by the increased workload of the newly consolidated department.

The proposed personnel ceilings for the consolidated department, broken down by section, are summarized in Table A–1. The approved San Remo personnel ceiling as of December 31, 1989, is shown first, followed by the expected savings in personnel from the consolidation. The reduced personnel requirements for San Remo, plus the Reichard requirements, equal the total personnel requirements for the department.

The consolidated system of production control will have about the same operating characteristics as the computerized system employed earlier by San Remo. Therefore, the workload relationships used to develop the proposed personnel requirements for the consolidated department were derived from last year's workload and authorized personnel levels for San Remo.

Our justification for the proposed personnel ceiling for each of our sections is outlined in the remainder of this memorandum.

Parts Design Control Section (12 people)

Last year, 7 employees were approved in the parts design section at San Remo: 5 processed design change orders, and 2 were clerical and supervisory.

Workload for the design changes activity is determined by the number of product or component changes that have to be processed. Last year, the 5 analysts in the San Remo section processed 2,964 change orders, for an average of 592 change orders per person. In Reichard, 3,680 design change orders were processed.

Design change orders, in turn, are influenced by the number of unique parts. An analysis of both San Remo and Reichard data indicate that there is a definite relationship between the number of design changes processed and the number of unique parts. The nature of this relationship is summarized in Table A–2.

For 1990, the number of unique model parts required for Reichard and San Remo components is estimated at 11,600 and 4,800, respectively. The reason for these large changes from 1990 is that Reichard had added a new line of control boards, and San Remo had dropped a line of components. On the basis of these estimates, we have calculated that 10 design change order personnel are required to handle the workload for 1990, as shown in Table A–3.

TABLE A–1   Proposed Personnel Ceilings—Production Control Department, 1990

San Remo Commitment Section	Consolidation 12/31/89	Proposed Levels			
		Savings	San Remo	Reichard	Total
Parts design control	7	3	4	8	12
Production control	15	6	9	24	33
Production planning	3	1	2	5	7
Manager's office	2	2	—	2	2
Total	27	12	15	39	54

TABLE A–2   **Relationship of Number of Unique New Parts to Design Change Orders**

Division	Unique Parts for 1989	Number of Design Change Orders	Design Change Orders per Unique Part
Reichard*	8,810	3,680	0.42
San Remo*	6,584	2,964	0.45
Total	15,394	6,644	0.43

*Although Reichard and Sam Remo have been consolidated, they are shown separately in this memorandum for calculating purposes.

TABLE A–3   **Estimated Personnel Requirements for Parts Design Control Section**

A. Equivalent Personnel

Business Unit	Estimated Number of Unique Parts	*	Design Change Orders per Unique Part	÷	Actual Output per Worker	=	Equivalent Personnel
Reichard	11,600		0.42		592		8.2
San Remo	4,800		0.45		592		3.6
Total	16,400						11.8

B. Personnel

Business Unit	Equivalent Personnel	–	Planned Effeciency† (Approx. 10%)	–	Planned Overtime (Approx. 5%)	=	Personnel Ceiling Required
Reichard	8.2		0.8		0.4		7
San Remo	3.6		0.4		0.2		3
Total	11.8		1.2		0.6		10

C. Support Positions

Unit Supervisor	1
Clerk Typist	1
Total	2

D. Total Request

10 + 2 = 12 personnel

†"Planned Efficiency" reduces the calculated personnel requirements to a level approximately consistent with the lowest workload level anticipated during the coming year. In order to handle periodic workload increases during a year, the department is forced to improve its efficiency and, if necessary, to use overtime or temporary clerical help from outside agencies.

Production Control Section (33 people)

In this section, the number of unique parts to be processed is the key determinant of the workload. In 1989, 13 production controllers were required at San Remo to handle 6,584 unique parts, for an average of 506 parts per coordinator. On the basis of 11,600 unique parts for the Reichard division and 4,800 for the San Remo subsidiary, 29 production controllers are required for 1990, as shown in Table A–4.

TABLE A–4   Estimated Number of Production Controllers Required, 1990

A. Business Unit	Estimated Number of Unique Parts	+	Actual Output Per Person	=	Equivalent Personnel	–	Planned Efficiency (Approx. 5%)	–	Planned Overtime (Approx. 5%)	=	Personnel Ceiling Required
Reichard	11,600		506		22.9		1.2		1.2		20.5
San Remo	4,800		506		9.5		0.5		0.5		8.5
Total	16,400				32.4		1.7		1.7		29.0

B. Position	Total
Section Supervisor	1
Unit Supervisor	2
Clerk Typist	1
Total	4

C. Total Request

29 + 4 = 33 personnel

TABLE A–5   Relationship of Number of Unique Parts to Personnel Production Planning Section

Position	San Remo Personnel	Number of Unique Parts for San Remo	Output per Worker (Unique Parts)
Computer Programming	1.75	6,584	3,762
Programming Timing and Coordination	1.25	6,584	5,267
	3.00		

Production Planning Section (7 people)

In this section, the principal indicator of overall workload is the number of unique parts handled. The relationship between the number of unique parts handled and the number of people fulfilling the functions of this section are summarized in Table A–5. All figures are actual data from the San Remo system for 1989.

On the basis of these relationships and the number of unique parts estimated for 1990, we have estimated that 6 programming personnel are required. The supporting calculations are summarized in Table A–6.

In addition to these 6 people, a section supervisor is required for the planning section. Therefore, the total requirement for operating this section is 7 people.

Manager's Office (2 people)

Two people are required, the manager of the Production Control Department and a secretary.

Estimated Dollar Requirements.   We estimate that a total of $1,458,000 will be needed to operate the consolidated Production Control Department for 1990. This figure is broken down as follows:

Personnel	$1,160,000
Material and supplies	45,000
Computer services	245,000
Miscellaneous	8,000
Total	$1,458,000

Personnel Expenses. This estimate was arrived at by applying to each position in the requested personnel ceiling the actual salary for that position, plus approved fringe benefits.

Materials and Supplies Expenses. This estimate is about $10,000 greater than the 1989 San Remo actual; this represents an increase of only about 30 percent. However, the job to be accomplished by the consolidated operation in 1990 is about 2 1/2 times as great as the job accomplished by San Remo in 1989. The small increase in the materials and supplies expense is thus the result of efficiencies in programming and reporting which, in turn, will mean savings in materials and supplies.

Computer Services. In 1989 the San Remo subsidiary spent $190,000 for computer services. For 1990, we have proposed $245,000; included in this amount is $34,000 for start-up costs associated with the conversion of the manual Reichard system to a computerized system. Therefore, the real cost for computer services in the consolidated division is $211,000 or only about 10 percent more than the 1989 San Remo actual. Yet the job to be done in the consolidated operation in 1990 is 2½ times as great as the job performed by San Remo in 1989. This great increase in output for a nominal increase in expense is the result of efficiencies in programming and reporting.

**TABLE A–6   Estimated Number of Programming Personnel Required—
Planning and Control Section, 1990**

Position	Number of Unique Parts, 1990 — Reichard	San Remo	+	Output per Worker	=	Estimated Equivalent Personnel	−	Efficiency Savings (10%)	−	Overtime Allowance (10%)	=	Ceiling Requested
Programming Computer	11,600	4,800		3,762		4.4		.45		.45		3.5
Programming Timing and Coordination	11,600	4,800		5,267		3.1		.30		.30		2.5
Total						7.5		.75		.75		6.0

APPENDIX B
MEMORANDUM

To: Manufacturing Office—Reichard GmbH.
From: Financial Controller
Date: May 16, 1990
Subject: Supplemental Budget Request dated
              6 April, 1990
cc: Managing Director

The manufacturing office has proposed a personnel ceiling of 54 people and a budget of $1,458,000 for the consolidated production control department for 1990. This proposed budget should include both the savings from computerization of the Reichard system and the savings from consolidation of the two separate operations.

The approved 1990 budgets for the separate production control departments are summarized in Table B–1, together with the proposed budget for the consolidated department submitted by the manufacturing office.

Although the proposed budget for 1990 shows a decrease of 11 personnel, total expenses show an increase of $68,000, despite the planned savings from computerization and consolidation. Further analysis of the Reichard and San Remo requirements shows the following:

Reichard Requirements. According to Table B–1, the apparent effect of computerization on the approved 1990 Reichard budget, which was based on a manual system, is to *increase* personnel requirements by one person and expenses by $252,000. We are at a loss to understand why these increases should result from computerization. In fact, the manufacturing office committed itself to a *savings* of 11 people and $138,000 in the Reichard department when its proposal for a computerized system was approved. Thus, the proposed budget is actually 12 people and $390,000 *over* the committed levels. For this reason, we feel that the proposed levels are completely inappropriate.

San Remo Requirements. The proposed San Remo requirements reflect savings of 12 people and $184,000. This reduction is the result of (*a*) a reduction of supervisory and clerical personnel, which is directly due to the consolidation, and (*b*) a reduction in the 1990 unique parts count. This savings of 12 people and $184,000, therefore, had nothing to do with computerization and would have occurred in the San Remo budget either under a computerized or a manual system.

TABLE B–1   **Budget Comparison for Production Control Department**
                (000 omitted for $ figures)

	Reichard		San Remo		Total	
Budget Status	*Number*	*Dollars*	*Number*	*Dollars*	*Number*	*Dollars*
Budget before consolidation	38	$ 722	27	$ 668	65	$1,390
Proposed	39	974	15	484	54	1,458
Net change	1	$ 252	(12)	$(184)	11	$ 68
Explanation of Changes						
Savings from computerization of Reichard system	(11)*	$(138)*	—	—	(11)	$ (138)
Savings from consolidation	—	—	(12)	$(184)	(12)	(184)
Proposed increase to Reichard budget	12	390	—	—	12	390
Net change	1	$ 252	(12)	$(184)	(11)	$ 68

*Based on study of December 1989; concurred in by manufacturing office.

Consequently, we believe that the revised budget under a *combined,* computerized system should be as summarized in Table B–2 below.

In this calculation the Reichard personnel ceiling of 27 is based on the precomputerization figure (38) minus the savings agreed to by the manufacturing office as a result of computerization (11). Reichard's budget dollars are based on the same sort of analy-sis: $722,000 minus $138,000. Similarly, the San Remo personnel ceiling of 15 is based on the preconsolidation figure (27) minus the savings from consolidation and reduced parts count (12), and the budget dollars are the result of $668,000 minus $184,000. Thus, the total budget figures for the consolidated department should be 42 people and $1,068,000.

The main reason for computerizing Reichard's system of production control was financial savings. In view of this analysis, we feel that the manufacturing office should hold to its 1990 consolidated budget for the production control department. If the manufacturing office wishes to continue with their computerized system, reductions in personnel and related expenses in the nature of those summarized in Table B–3 will be required in order to contain the 1990 budget within these recommended levels, based on what a combined manual system would have cost at current workloads.

TABLE B–2 Proposed 1990 Budget (000 omitted for $ figures)

	Reichard	San Remo	Total
Number of personnel	27	15	42
Budget dollars	$584	$484	$1,068

TABLE B–3 Reductions Required to Meet Recommended Maximum 1990 Budget (000 omitted for $ figures)

Proposals	Personnel	Reichard Dollars	Personnel	San Remo Dollars	Personnel	Combined Dollars
Manufacturing office's request	39	$ 974	15	$484	54	$1,458
Controller's recommended reductions:						
Salary mix	—	(85)	—	—	—	(85)
Overtime	—	(27)	—	(21)	—	(48)
Required personnel (to meet financial objective)	(12)	(197)	—	—	(12)	(197)
Total recommended reductions	(12)	$(309)	—	$ (21)	(12)	$ (330)
Total recommended level	27	$ 665	15	$463	42	$1,128

APPENDIX C
MEMORANDUM

To: Financial Controller—Reichard GmbH.
From: Manufacturing Office
Date: July 29, 1990
Subject: Supplemental Budget Request dated
                   6 April, 1990

In our supplemental budget request of April 6, we requested that the personnel ceiling for our production control department be set at 54, and that the department's budget be revised upward to $1,458,000 for 1990. In your memorandum of May 16, you have recommended that we reduce these proposed 1990 levels by 12 people and $330,000. We cannot agree to these recommended reductions.

We do agree that, generally speaking, a computerized production control system should not be any more costly than a manual system. However, we disagree with your recommendations, since your analysis did not take into account a number of important factors. We feel that the following elements, omitted from your analysis, must be considered:

A. Workload content and volume adjustments.

B. Unavoidable increases in salary mix.

C. Association with integrated data processing plan.

D. Nonrecurring cost penalties.

E. Functional improvements and advantages.

A. Workload Content and Volume Adjustments

Our proposed budget includes additional people to handle an increased workload over the estimated levels that were used in developing the original 1990 Reichard budget for a manual system. There has been an increase of 1,400 new parts for Reichard over the original estimates. In addition, the entire workload for San Remo has been taken on. The parts counts estimates used in developing the original 1990 budget for Reichard (manual system) and the proposed budget for the consolidated department (computerized system) are summarized in Table C–1.

This increased parts count would have resulted in a requirement for at least 5 more people under the manual system, at a cost of about $90,000, plus an estimated $4,000 for operating expenses.

B. Unavoidable Increases in Salary Mix

As a result of the consolidation, and the resulting personnel changes, the average salary per employee retained in the production control department has increased significantly. This increase has resulted from the retention of employees on the basis of seniority. The approved budget for 1990 provided for an average annual salary of $14,218. Our proposed consolidated budget, based on actual salaries, provides for an average annual salary in excess of $15,900. Therefore, if average salaries had remained unchanged after the consolidation, our budget proposal would have been $91,560 less, as shown in Table C–2.

TABLE C–1   **Estimates of Number of Unique Parts**

Business Unit	1990 Original Budget Estimates	Current Known Conditions
Reichard	10,200	11,600
San Remo	—	4,800
Total	10,200	16,400

TABLE C–2   Budget Increase Due to Salary Mix

Salary Base	Proposed Personnel Ceiling	*	Average Annual Salary	=	Total Annual Salaries
At approved budget rates	54		$14,218		$ 767,796
At proposed budget rates	54		$15,914		859,356
Difference					$ (91,560)

C. Association with Integrated Data Processing Plan

By implementing the computerized production control system, we have taken an important step forward in the company's integrated data processing plan, which provides for eventual establishment of a completely computerized master manufacturing system. This step will make it possible to reduce significantly the original expense estimates associated with setting up this master system.

The original proposal for providing a master manufacturing control system, which was submitted prior to the consolidation of the two production control departments, included cost estimates of $94,887 for 1990, and $104,672 for each year thereafter. Had we gone to an all-manual system in the consolidated production control department, the cost estimates for installing the integrated data processing plan would have increased to $111,872 and $159,241, respectively. As a direct result of implementing the computerized production control system, however, we should be able to reduce these costs by $103,000 during 1990, and $98,000 for each year thereafter. The figures supporting these savings estimates are summarized in Table C–3.

D. Nonrecurring Cost Penalties

Our proposed budget includes a first-year cost penalty of $112,305. This one-time penalty results from changes in our organization and procedures, and is composed of $72,305 in salaries and wages, and $40,000 in computer expenses. If the volume of work in future years remained unchanged from that in 1990, we would expect our budgets for these years to be lower by this $112,305. The bases for this estimate are summarized in Table C–4.

TABLE C–3   Effective Cost Decrease of Master Manufacturing Control System Due to Computerization

Revised Cost Factors	1990	1991 Ongoing Level
Original cost estimates based on manual system	$ 94,887	$104,672
Additional cost of consolidation and revised assumptions, based on manual system	16,985	54,569
Total cost estimates to include effect of consolidation based on a manual system	$111,872	$159,241
Revised cost estimates to include effect of consolidation, based on computerized system	(8,700)	(61,010)
Savings directly associated with computerized versus manual system	$103,172	$ 98,231

TABLE C–4   Estimate of Nonrecurring Costs

Budget Items	1990	Future Years	Reductions
Average personnel ceiling	58	54	4
Personnel costs	$1,158,876	$1,086,571	$72,305
Computer expense	245,000	205,000	40,000
Other operating costs	54,136	54,136	—
Total	$1,458,012	$1,345,707	$112,305

TABLE C–5   Summary of Adjustments to Cost Estimates

Costs	1990 Cost Comparison (000)	
Unadjusted Costs	*Manual System*	*Computerized System*
Reichard GmbH	$ 722	$ 974
San Remo	406	484
Total unadjusted costs	$1,128*	$1,458†
Increases due to:		
Parts count	94	—
Average salaries	92	—
Cost of implementing computerized operations control system in accordance with company's integrated data processing plan	112	9
Total adjusted costs	$1,426	$1,467

*Estimated by controller's office.
†Proposed by manufacturing office.

E. Functional Improvements and Advantages

In addition to the savings outlined above, a computerized production control system offers certain other advantages over a manual system, as follows:

1. It provides a single and better integrated program progress report that reflects the status of engineering, manufacturing, and purchasing actions against schedules on a more timely basis than does a manual system.

2. It provides a master file that, once stored in the computer, can be used to produce other useful information.

3. It is compatible with the objective to computerize the issuance of sales confirmation notices which will result in a more efficient method of handling this activity.

While we cannot put a dollar value on these advantages, it is reasonable to expect that they will yield significant cost savings in the future.

Summary

The foregoing adjustments, which we feel are essential to a proper comparison of the costs for a computerized production control system with a manual system, are summarized in Table C–5. On the basis of this analysis, the cost of the computerized system is only $41,000 a year more than that of a manual system, which is more than compensated by the substantial systemwide benefits we will earn. Therefore, our requested budget of $1,458,000 for the combined operations control department is not unreasonable.

CASE 8–2
BOSTON CREAMERY, INC.

Frank Roberts, Vice President for Sales and Marketing of the Ice Cream Division of Boston Creamery, was pleased when he saw the final earnings statement for the division for 1973 (see Exhibits 1 and 3). He knew that it had been a good year for ice cream, but he hadn't expected the results to be quite this good.

Only the year before, the company had installed a new financial planning and control system. This was the first year that figures comparing budgeted and actual results were available. Jim Peterson, president of the division, had asked Frank to make a short presentation at the next management meeting commenting on the major reasons for the favorable operating income variance of $71,700. Peterson asked him to draft his presentation in the next few days so that the two of them could go over it before the meeting. Peterson said he wanted to illustrate to the management group how an analysis of the profit variance could highlight those areas needing corrective attention as well as those deserving a pat on the back.

The Profit Plan for 1973

Following the four-step approach (see Appendix to this case), the management group of the Ice Cream Division prepared a profit plan for 1973 (Table 1).

Based on an anticipated overall ice cream market of about 11,440,000 gallons in their marketing area and a market share of 50 percent, forecasted overall gallon sales were 5,720,329 for 1973. Actually, this forecast was the same as the latest estimate of 1972 actual gallon sales. Since the 1973 budget was being

done in October of 1972, final figures for 1972 were not yet available. The latest revised estimate of actual gallon volume for 1972 was thus used. Rather than trying to get too sophisticated on the first attempt at budgeting, Mr. Peterson had decided just to go with 1972's estimated volume as 1973's goal or forecast. He felt that there was plenty of time in later years to refine the system by bringing in more formal sales forecasting techniques and concepts.

This same general approach was also followed for variable product standard costs and for fixed costs. Budgeted costs for 1973 were just expected 1972 results, adjusted for a few items which were clearly out of line in 1972.

Actual Results for 1973

By the spring of 1973 it had become clear that sales volume for 1973 was going to be higher than forecasted. In fact, actual sales for the year totaled over 5,968,000 gallons, an increase of about 248,000 gallons over budget. Market research data indicated that the total ice cream market in their marketing area was 12,180,000 gallons for the year as opposed to the budgeted figure of about 11,440,000 gallons.

A revised profit plan for the year at the actual volume level is given in Table 2.

The fixed costs in the revised profit plan are the same as in the original plan, $1,945,900. The variable costs, however, have been adjusted to reflect the actual volume level of 5,968,000 gallons instead of the forecasted volume of 5,720,000 gallons, thereby eliminating all cost variances due strictly to the difference between planned volume and actual volume.

For costs which are highly volume dependent, variances should be based on a budget which reflects the volume of operation actually

This case was prepared by Professor John Shank of the Amos Tuck School from an earlier version he wrote at Harvard Business School with the assistance of William J. Rauwerdink, Research Assistant.

TABLE 1   Original Profit Plan for 1973

	Standard Contribution Margin / Gallon	Forecasted Gallon Sales	Forecasted Standard Contribution Margin
Vanilla	$.4329	2,409,854	$1,043,200
Chocolate	.4535	2,009,061	911,100
Walnut	.5713	48,883	28,000
Buttercrunch	.4771	262,185	125,000
Cherry Swirl	.5153	204,774	105,500
Strawberry	.4683	628,560	294,400
Pecan Chip	.5359	157,012	84,100
Total	$.4530	5,720,329	$2,591,300

Breakdown of Budgeted Total Expenses

	Variable Costs	Fixed Costs	Total
Manufacturing	$5,888,100	$ 612,800	$6,500,900
Delivery	187,300	516,300	703,600
Advertising	553,200	—	553,200
Selling	—	368,800	368,800
Administrative	—	448,000	448,000
Total	$6,628,600	$1,945,900	$8,574,500

Recap

Sales	$9,219,900
Variable Cost of Sales	6,628,600
Contribution Margin	2,591,300
Fixed Costs	1,945,900
Income from Operations	$ 645,400

attained. Since the level of fixed costs is independent of volume anyway, it is not necessary to adjust the budget for these items for volume differences. The original budget for fixed-cost items is still appropriate.

Assume, for example, that cartons are budgeted at $.04 per gallon. If we forecast volume of 10,000 gallons, the budget allowance for cartons is $400. If we actually sell only 8,000 gallons but use $350 worth of cartons, it is misleading to say that there is a favorable variance of $50 ($350 − $400). The variance is clearly unfavorable by $30 ($350 − $320). This only shows

up if we adjust the budget to the actual volume level:

Carton allowance	=	$.04 per gallon
Forecast volume	=	10,000 gallons
Carton budget	=	$400
Actual volume	=	8,000 gallons
Actual carton expense	=	$350
Variance (based on forecast volume)	=	$400 − $350 = $50F
Variance (based on actual volume)	=	$320 − $350 = $30U

TABLE 2   Revised Profit Plan for 1973

	Standard Contribution Margin / Gallon	Actual Gallon Sales	Standard Contribution Margin
Vanilla	$.4329	2,458,212	$1,064,200
Chocolate	.4535	2,018,525	915,400
Walnut	.5713	50,124	28,600
Buttercrunch	.4771	268,839	128,300
Cherry Swirl	.5153	261,240	134,600
Strawberry	.4683	747,049	349,800
Pecan Chip	.5359	164,377	88,100
Total	$.4539	5,968,366	$2,709,000

Breakdown of Budgeted Total Expenses

	Variable Costs	Fixed Costs	Total
Manufacturing	$6,113,100	$ 612,800	$6,725,900
Delivery	244,500	516,300	760,800
Advertising	578,700	—	578,700
Selling	—	368,800	368,800
Administrative	—	448,000	448,000
Total	$6,936,300	$1,945,900	$8,882,200

Recap

Sales	$9,645,300
Variable Cost of Sales	6,936,300
Contribution Margin	2,709,000
Fixed Costs	1,945,900
Income from Operations	$ 763,100

Analysis of the 1973 Profit Variance

Exhibit 1 is the earnings statement for the division for the year. The figures for the month of December have been excluded for purposes of this case. Exhibit 2 is the detailed expense breakdown for the manufacturing department. The detailed expense breakdowns for the other departments have been excluded for purposes of this case.

Three days after Jim Peterson asked Frank Roberts to pull together a presentation for the management committee analyzing the profit variance for 1973, Frank came into Jim's office to review his first draft. He showed Jim the schedule shown in Table 3 on page 395.

Frank said that he planned to give each member of the management committee a copy of this schedule and then to comment briefly on each of the items. Jim Peterson said he thought the schedule was okay as far as it went, but that it just didn't highlight things in a manner which indicated what corrective actions should be taken in 1974 or indicated the real causes for the favorable overall variance. Which elements were uncontrollable, for example? He suggested

---

EXHIBIT 1   Earnings Statement

ICE CREAM DIVISION
Earnings Statement
December 31, 1973

	Month		Year-to-Date	
Actual	*Flexible Budget*		*Actual*	*Flexible Budget*
		Sales—net	$9,657,300	$9,645,300
		Manufacturing cost (Schedule A-2)[a]	6,824,900[b]	6,725,900
		Delivery (Schedule A-3)	706,800	760,800
		Advertising (Schedule A-4)[c]	607,700	578,700
		Selling (Schedule A-5)	362,800	368,800
		Administrative (Schedule A-6)	438,000	448,000
		Total Expenses	$8,940,200	$8,882,200
		Income from Operations	$ 717,100	$ 763,100
		(Variance Analysis in Exhibit 3.)		

---

[a]Schedules A-3 through A-6 have not been included in this case. Schedule A-2 is reproduced as Exhibit 2.
[b]See Exhibit 3.
[c]In 1973 the company changed from an advertising "budget" of $.06 per gallon sold to a "budget" of 6% of sales.

---

that Frank try to break down the sales volume variance into the part attributable to sales mix, the part attributable to market share shifts, and the part actually attributable to overall volume changes. He also suggested breaking down the unfavorable manufacturing variance to indicate what main corrective actions are called for in 1974. For example, he said, how much of the total was due to price differences versus quantity differences? Since the division was a pure "price taker" for commodities like milk and sugar, he wondered how to best treat the price variances. Finally, he suggested that Frank call on John Vance, the corporate controller, if he needed some help in the mechanics of breaking out these different variances.

As Frank Roberts returned to his office, he considered Jim Peterson's suggestion of getting John Vance involved in revising the variance report. Frank did not want to consult John Vance unless it was absolutely necessary because he thought Vance always went overboard on the technical aspects of any accounting problem. Frank couldn't imagine a quicker way to put people to sleep than to throw one of Vance's number-filled six-page memos at them. Jim Peterson specifically wants a nontechnical presentation, Frank thought to himself, and that rules out John Vance. Besides, he thought, you don't have to be a CPA to focus on the key variance areas from a general management viewpoint.

A telephone call to John Vance asking about any written materials dealing with mix variances and volume variances produced, in the following day's mail, the document shown here as the Appendix. Vance said to see Exhibit A (in Appendix) for the variance analysis breakdown. Armed with this document and his common sense, Frank Roberts dug in again to the task of preparing a nontechnical breakdown of the profit variance for the year.

EXHIBIT 2   **Expense Breakdown**

ICE CREAM DIVISION
Schedule A-2
Manufacturing Cost of Goods Sold
December 31, 1973

Month			Year-to-Date	
Actual	*Flexible Budget*		*Actual*	*Flexible Budget*
		Variable Costs:		
		Dairy ingredients	$3,679,900	$3,648,500
		Milk price variance	57,300	—
		Sugar	599,900	596,800
		Sugar price variance	23,400	—
		Flavoring (Including fruits and nuts)	946,800	982,100
		Cartons	567,200	566,900
		Plastic wrap	28,700	29,800
		Additives	235,000	251,000
		Supplies	31,000	35,000
		Miscellaneous	3,000	3,000
		Subtotal	$6,172,200	$6,113,100
		Fixed Costs:		
		Labor—cartonizing and freezing*	$ 425,200	$ 390,800
		Labor—other	41,800	46,000
		Repairs	32,200	25,000
		Depreciation	81,000	81,000
		Electricity and water	41,500	40,000
		Spoilage	31,000	30,000
		Subtotal	$ 652,700	$ 612,800
		Total	$6,824,900	$6,725,900

*The primary reason for the increase in labor for cartonizing and freezing and decrease in delivery cost was a change during the year to a new daily truck loading system.

Before: Every morning, each route sales delivery driver loads the truck from inventory, based on today's sales orders, before leaving the plant. Drivers spend up to 2 hours each day loading the truck before they can begin their sales route.

After: Carton handling workers sort daily production each day onto pallets grouped by delivery truck, based on tomorrow's sales orders. This substitutes lower cost factory labor for higher cost driver labor for loading the trucks and also frees up some driver time each day for more customer contact and point of sale merchandising.

The next day Frank Roberts learned that his counterpart, John Parker, Vice President for Manufacturing and Operations, had seen the draft variance report and was very unhappy about it. Roberts and Parker were the only two vice presidents in the division. Parker had apparently told Jim Peterson that he felt Roberts was "playing games" with the numbers to make himself look good at Parker's expense. Organizationally, Sales, Marketing and Advertising reported to Roberts, and Manufacturing, Delivery and Administration to Parker.

TABLE 3   Variance Analysis

Favorable variance due
to sales:

Volume	$117,700F	
Price[a]	12,000F	$129,700F

Unfavorable variance due
to operations:

Manufacturing	$ 99,000U	
Delivery	54,000F	
Advertising	29,000U	
Selling	6,000F	
Administration	10,000F	58,000U
Net variance—favorable		$ 71,700F

[a]This price variance is the difference between the actual sales value of the gallons actually sold and the standard sales value ($9,657,300 − $9,645,300).

EXHIBIT 3   Analysis of Variance from Forecasted Operating Income

	Month	*Year-to-Date*
(1) Actual income from operations		$717,100
(2) Budgeted income at forecasted volume		645,400
(3) Budgeted income at actual volume		763,100
Variance due to sales volume and mix [(3) minus (2)]		117,700F
Variance due to operations [(1) minus (3)]		46,000U
Total variance [(1) minus (2)]		$ 71,700F

Questions

1. What changes, if any, would you make in the variance analysis schedule proposed by Frank Roberts? Can the suggestions offered by Jim Peterson be incorporated without making the schedule "too technical"?

2. Can you speculate about how John Parker might structure the variance analysis report? For example, Parker felt it was Marketing's responsibility to set prices so as to recover all commodity cost increases.

3. Indicate the corrective actions you would recommend for 1974, based on the profit variance analysis. Also indicate those areas which deserve commendation for 1973 performance.

4. The approach to "profit planning and control" described in the case is still very common in the 1990s. Many people still consider this approach to be "bread and butter" management theory. What do you see as the main weakness in this approach to management? What is your overall assessment of this "management tool," from a contemporary perspective?

APPENDIX
BOSTON CREAMERY, INC.[1]

The Financial Planning and Control System for the Ice Cream Division

The beginning point in making a profit plan is separating cost into fixed and variable categories. Pure variable costs require an additional amount with

[1]This description of the financial planning and control system is taken from a company operating manual.

each increase in volume. The manager has little control over this type of cost other than to avoid waste. The accountant can easily determine the variable manufacturing cost per unit for any given product or package by using current prices and yields. Variable marketing cost per unit is based on the allowable rate (for example, $.06 per gallon for advertising). Costs that are not pure variable are classified as fixed, but they, too, will vary if significant changes in volume occur. There will be varying degrees of sensitivity to volume changes among these costs, ranging from a point just short of pure variable to an extremely fixed type of expense which has no relationship to volume.

The reason for differentiating between fixed and variable so emphatically is that variable cost spending requires no decision; it is dictated by volume. Fixed costs, on the other hand, require a management judgment and decision to increase or decrease the spending. Sugar is an example of a pure variable cost. Each change in volume will automatically bring a change in the sugar cost; only the yield can be controlled. Route salesmen's salaries would be an example of a fixed cost that is fairly sensitive to volume, but not pure variable. As volume changes, pressure will be felt to increase or decrease this expense, but management must make the decision; the change in cost level is not automatic. Depreciation charges for plant would be an example of a relatively extreme fixed cost. Very large increases in volume can usually be realized before this type of cost is pressured to change.

In both cases of fixed cost, a decision from management is required to increase or decrease the cost. It is this dilemma that management is constantly facing: to withstand the pressure to increase or be ready to decrease when the situation demands it. It would be a mistake to set a standard variable cost for items like route salesmen's salaries or depreciation, based on past performance, because they must constantly be evaluated for better and more efficient methods of doing the task.

Advertising is the only cost element not fitting the explanation of a variable cost given in the first paragraph. Advertising costs are set by management decision rather than being an "automatic" cost item like sugar or packaging. In this sense, advertising is like route salesmen's expense. For our company, however, management has decided that the allowance for advertising expense is equal to $.06 per gallon for the actual number of gallons sold. This management decision, therefore, has transformed advertising into an expense which is treated as variable for profit planning purposes.

Following is an example of the four-step approach to one-year profit planning.

The *first step* in planning is to develop a unit standard cost for each element of variable cost, by product and package size. Examples of two different packages for one product are shown below. As already pointed out, the accountant can do this by using current prices and yields for material costs and current allowance rates for marketing costs. After the total unit variable cost has been developed, this amount is subtracted from the selling price to arrive at a standard marginal contribution per unit, by product and package type.

Step 2 is perhaps the most critical in making a profit plan, because all plans derive from the anticipated level of sales activity. Much thought should be given in forecasting a realistic sales level and product mix. Consideration should be given to the number of days in a given period, as well as to the number of Fridays and Mondays, as these are two of the heaviest days and will make a difference in the sales forecast. Other factors that should be considered are:

1. General economic condition of the marketing area
2. Weather
3. Anticipated promotions
4. Competition

Step 3 involves setting fixed-cost budgets based on management's judgment as to the need, in light of the sales forecast. It is here that good planning makes for a profitable operation. The number of routes needed for both winter and summer volume is planned. The level of manufacturing payroll is set. Because this system is based on a one-year time frame, manufacturing labor is considered to be a fixed cost. The level of the manufacturing work force is not really variable until a time frame longer than one year is adopted. Insurance and taxes are budgeted, and so on. After Step 4 has been performed, it may be necessary to return to Step 3 and make adjustments to some of the costs that are discretionary in nature.

Step 4 is the profit plan itself. By combining our marginal contribution developed in Step 1 with our sales forecast from Step 2, we arrive at a total marginal contribution by month. Subtracting the fixed cost budgeted in Step 3, we have an operating profit by month. If this profit figure is not sufficient, a new evaluation should be made for Steps 1, 2 and/or 3.

Once the plan is completed and the year begins, profit variance is calculated monthly as a "manage-

STEP 1
VANILLA ICE CREAM

Item	Regular 1-Gallon Paper Container	Premium 1-Gallon Plastic Container
Dairy ingredients	$ .53	$ .79
Sugar	.15	.15
Flavor	.10	.12
Production	.10	.16
Warehouse	.06	.08
Transportation	.02	.025
Total manufacturing	.96	1.325
Advertising	.06	.06
Delivery	.04	.04
Total marketing	.10	.10
Packaging	.10	.25
Total variable	1.16	1.675
Selling price	1.50	2.40
Marginal contribution per gallon	.34	.725

STEP 2
VANILLA ICE CREAM SALES FORECAST IN GALLONS

	January	. . .	December	Total
1 gallon, paper	100,000		100,000	1,200,000
1 gallon, plastic	50,000		50,000	600,000
2 gallons, paper	225,000		225,000	2,700,000
1 gallon, premium	120,000		120,000	1,440,000
Total	495,000	. . .	495,000	5,940,000

ment control" tool. To illustrate the control system, we will take the month of January and assume the level of sales activity for the month to be 520,000 gallons, as shown below. Looking back to our sales forecast (Step 2), we see that 495,000 gallons had been forecasted. When we apply our marginal contribution per unit for each product and package, we find that the 520,000 gallons have produced $6,125 less standard contribution than the 495,000 gallons would have produced at the forecasted mix. So even though there has been a nice increase in sales volume, the mix has

been unfavorable. The $6,125 represents the difference between standard profit contribution at forecasted volume and standard profit contribution at actual volume. It is thus due to differences in volume and to differences in average mix. The impact of each of these two factors is also shown in Exhibit A.

Exhibit B shows a typical departmental budget sheet for the month of January comparing actual costs with budget. A sheet is issued for each department, so the person responsible for a particular area of the business can see the items that are in line and

STEP 3
BUDGET FOR FIXED EXPENSES

	January	*. . .*	*December*	*Total*
Manufacturing expense				
Labor	$ 7,280	. . .	$ 7,920	$ 88,000
Equipment repair	3,332	. . .	3,348	40,000
Depreciation	6,668	. . .	6,652	80,000
Taxes	3,332	. . .	3,348	40,000
Total	$20,612	. . .	$21,268	$248,000
Delivery expense				
Salaries—general	$10,000	. . .	$10,000	$120,000
Salaries—drivers	10,668	. . .	10,652	128,000
Helpers	10,668	. . .	10,652	128,000
Supplies	668	. . .	652	8,000
Total	$32,004	. . .	$31,956	$384,000
Administrative expense				
Salaries	$ 5,167	. . .	$ 5,163	$ 62,000
Insurance	1,667	. . .	1,663	20,000
Taxes	1,667	. . .	1,663	20,000
Depreciation	833	. . .	837	10,000
Total	$ 9,334	. . .	$ 9,326	$112,000
Selling expense				
Repairs	$ 2,667	. . .	$ 2,663	$ 32,000
Gasoline	5,000	. . .	5,000	60,000
Salaries	5,000	. . .	5,000	60,000
Total	$12,667	. . .	$12,663	$152,000

those that need attention. In our example, there is an unfavorable operating variance of $22,750 ($570,537 − $593,287). You should note that the budget for variable cost items has been adjusted to reflect actual volume, thereby eliminating cost variances due strictly to the difference between planned and actual volume.

Since the level of fixed costs is independent of volume anyway, it is not necessary to adjust the budget for these items for volume differences. The original budget for fixed-cost items is still appropriate. The totals for each department are carried forward to an earnings statement, Exhibit C. We have assumed all other departments' actual and budget are in line, so the only operating variance is the one for manufacturing. This variance, added to the sales volume and mix variance of $6,125U, results in an overall variance from the original plan of $28,875U.

STEP 4
THE PROFIT PLAN

	Standard Marginal Contribution	January Gallons	Dollars	. . .	Total Year
1 gallon, paper	$.340	100,000	$ 34,000		$ 408,000
1 gallon, plastic	.305	50,000	15,250		183,000
2 gallons, paper	.265	225,000	59,625		715,500
1 gallon, premium	.725	120,000	87,000		1,044,000
Total Marginal Contribution	$.3957	495,000	$195,875		$2,350,500
Fixed cost (see Step 3)					
Manufacturing expense			$ 20,612		$ 248,000
Delivery expense			32,004		384,000
Administrative expense			9,334		112,000
Selling expense			12,667		152,000
Total fixed			$ 74,617		$ 896,000
Operating profit			$121,258		$1,454,500

EXHIBIT A
JANUARY

	Actual Gallon Sales	Standard Contribution per Gallon	Total Standard Contribution
1 gallon, paper	90,000	$.340	$ 30,600
1 gallon, plastic	95,000	.305	28,975
2 gallons, paper	245,000	.265	64,925
1 gallon, premium	90,000	.725	65,250
Total	520,000	$.3649	$189,750
Forecasted standard contribution (at 495,000 gallons)			195,875
Variance			6,125U

	Planned	Actual	Difference
Gallons	495,000	520,000	25,000F
Contribution	$195,875	$189,750	$6,125U
Average std. contribution	$ .3957	$ .3649	$.0308U

F, favorable; U, unfavorable.

Variance due to volume
25,000 gallonsF * $.3957 = $9,892F

Total variance = $6,125U

Variance due to mix
$.0308U * 520,000 gallons = $16,017U

EXHIBIT B
MANUFACTURING COST
January

Month			Year-to-Date	
Actual	Flexible Budget		Actual	Flexible Budget
$312,744	$299,000	Dairy ingredients		
82,304	78,000	Sugar		
56,290	55,025	Flavorings		
38,770	37,350	Warehouse		
70,300	69,225	Production		
11,514	11,325	Transportation		
$571,922	$549,925	Subtotal—variable		
7,300	7,280	Labor		
4,065	3,332	Equipment repair		
6,668	6,668	Depreciation		
3,332	3,332	Taxes		
$ 21,365	$ 20,612	Subtotal—fixed		
$593,287	$570,537	Total		

EXHIBIT C
EARNINGS STATEMENT
January

Month			Year-to-Date	
Actual	Flexible Budget		Actual	Flexible Budget
$867,750	$867,750	Total ice cream sales		
$593,287	$570,537	Manufacturing cost of goods sold		
52,804	52,804	Delivery expense		
31,200	31,200	Advertising expense		
76,075	76,075	Packaging expense		
12,667	12,667	Selling expense		
9,334	9,334	Administrative expense		
$775,367	$752,617	Total expense		
$ 92,383	$115,133	Operating profit		

Variance Recap

Actual profit before taxes	92,383	(1)
Original profit plan	121,258	(2)
Revised profit plan, based on actual volume	115,133	(3)
Variance due to volume and mix (3 – 2)	= 115,133 – 121,258 =	6,125U
Variance due to operations (1 – 3)	= 92,383 – 155,133 =	22,750U
Total variance (2 – 1)	= 121,258 – 92,383 =	28,875U

CASE 8–3
RIVERVIEW

In April 1994, Jerry Johnson, financial vice president of Montvale Corporation, made a three-day visit to Riverview, its newest retirement community. From time to time thereafter, he pondered how he should respond to a suggestion for a new approach to financial planning that had been discussed at one of the meetings there. Was it worth serious exploration? Or was it a well-intentioned but impractical idea from a novice in the retirement home industry?

Montvale Corporation and Riverview

Montvale Corporation was a nonprofit corporation, organized and controlled by the headquarters office of a religious denomination. It supervised the operation of several continuing care retirement communities (CCRC) located throughout the United States. The first was established in 1970. All had operated consistently "in the black." Riverview was the newest. Plans for another retirement community were being discussed.

Construction of Riverview began in 1990, the first residents entered in July 1992, and the first full year of operation was fiscal year 1993 (ended September 30, 1993). Riverview consisted of 199 apartments, ranging in size from a studio to two bedrooms plus a den. Most were located in four connected frame buildings, each three stories high. A few of the larger apartments were in single story, separate buildings. The total population at capacity would be 356 persons, some of whom would be couples and the remainder single persons. In addition, there was a separate, but connected, health center with 70 beds.

Riverview had a dining room for apartment residents; another dining room for health center residents; a coffee shop; a general room for concerts, lectures, and social events, seating 200; several rooms for arts and crafts; a library; a small gift shop; a branch bank; a hair-styling shop; an exercise room; and an indoor swimming pool. The buildings were set on 40 acres of land.

In January 1994, occupancy reached 95 percent of capacity, which was a criterion for accreditation by the CCRC accrediting association. By April 1994, occupancy was 99 percent. Several hundred persons and couples were on a waiting list that extended to 2004; each had made a deposit of $1,100, $1,000 of which was refundable.

Pricing Policy

As was the case with many retirement communities, Riverview charged an entrance fee. Each resident also was charged a monthly fee, covering meals, health care costs, electricity, cable TV, heating and air conditioning, and housekeeping—that is, almost everything except telephone. In 1994 the entrance fee averaged $186,000 per apartment, and the monthly fee averaged $2,100 for one person, plus $770 for a second person. Both the entrance fee and the monthly fee varied, depending primarily on the size of the apartment. The monthly fee was reduced if the resident had only one or two meals a day, and also if the resident was away for at least one month at a time. Part of the entrance fee was refunded if the occupant died or moved out; the refund decreased by 2 percent a month for each month of occupancy. As of April 1994, only one person had moved out and obtained a refund.

Montvale's policy was that the fees should be fair, both to the residents and to the organization.

This case was written by Professor Robert N. Anthony with the assistance of Peter T. Magee (T'94) and is copyrighted by Robert N. Anthony.

This meant that fees for a year should cover the costs relevant to occupancy in that year, plus a modest allowance that was to provide for working capital and for contingencies. It was planned that this amount would eventually equal several months' cash costs. (The amount had not yet been decided.)

Johnson, the financial vice president, said that he did not know of a logical way of dividing the total amount of revenue needed in a year between the entrance fee and the monthly fee. Practice varied widely in the industry. At one extreme, some retirement communities charged only a small entrance fee (or charged a fee that, although large, permitted the occupant's estate to sell the apartment to another party after the occupant's death) and charged correspondingly higher fees for apartment rental, meals, and various services. Montvale's policy of a large entrance fee and a correspondingly lower monthly fee was near the other extreme.

In the accounting system, entrance fees were recognized as annual revenues on a straight-line basis, spread over the years of expected life of each resident, obtained from standard mortality tables.

The April Meeting

One long meeting during Johnson's April visit dealt with financial matters. At that meeting, he met with Walter Heaney, Riverview administrator, and Jeanne Mills, Riverview controller.

Heaney, age 40, had been the Riverview administrator from the beginning of construction. He had 15 years of experience in the retirement home industry before coming to Riverview.

Mills, age 30, joined the organization as controller in 1990. She had worked in the controller's department of a medium-sized city for nine years and had been controller for the last three years. She left that job because there was no likelihood of further promotion in her municipality.

The first topic of the April meeting was a review of financial performance of the current year. Since actuals were close to budgeted amounts, this review went quickly.

The discussion then focused on the strategic financial plan, which was part of a larger project to decide on the goals and objectives of the Montvale organization. Development of such a plan had just been started at all Montvale communities. It was to cover operating activities for the fiscal years 1995 through 1999 and capital requirements for 1995 through 2014.

Heaney and Mills presented a first draft of this plan at the April meeting. Mills had prepared this draft based primarily on data obtained from Montvale. As was the case in each of its retirement communities, Montvale prepared an estimate, covering 20 future years, as a basis for judging the feasibility of a proposed community, for estimating the financing required, and for demonstrating credit worthiness to prospective lenders. Mills used the general format of this plan, which was similar to that in the annual budget, and also used many of the assumptions in the Riverview 20-year plan. The most important Riverview assumptions were:

For inflation:	
Monthly fee	4.5% (1995 and 1996)
	5.0% (other years)
Entrance fee	4.0%
Wages	4.0%
Benefits	5.0%
Utilities	8.0%
New entrants per year:	11 in 1985, increasing to 33 in 1999
Health care residents:	38 in 1995, increasing to 70 in 1999
Employees:	124 in 1995, increasing to 150 in 1999

The Proposal

Following this discussion, Heaney turned the meeting over to Jeanne Mills, who described a new approach to strategic planning that Mills had developed and that Heaney supported.

Mills made two main proposals: (1) a different format and (2) a different treatment of fixed assets. A summary of Mills's explanation of each point follows.

Format.   The Montvale format focuses on a bottom line that results from certain assumed revenue increases. My suggestion is that we should focus on the amount of monthly fees needed to cover our estimated expenses (including a contingency allowance). The monthly fee revenue, therefore, becomes the bottom line; it shows how much revenue needs to be increased, if at all, in order to obtain the desired financial result.

This is the way many municipalities budget. The governing concept is called *interperiod equity,* which means that in a given year taxpayers should provide the revenues that would be needed to meet the expenses associated with the services that the municipality provides in that year. This amount, divided by the assessed valuation, determines the tax rate for the year. A higher tax rate than this amount means that taxpayers will be paying more than the municipality needs for that period, and a lower rate means that the resulting deficit will burden taxpayers in future periods.

Fixed Assets.   My approach eliminates the depreciation number. Depreciation is a useless number for planning purposes. It is determined by past decisions, and no current or future decisions can change it. It has no cash flow implications.

I suggest that instead of depreciation, we use three other numbers in our strategic plan: (1) debt-service principal, (2) minor capital expenditures, and (3) a provision for renewal. Each of these numbers affects future cash flows, and, except for debt-service principal, each can be changed by management decision.

Debt-service principal is easily calculated.

We currently capitalize and depreciate all fixed asset acquisitions costing more than $1,000 each. Excluding a few major items, our planned asset acquisitions total approximately $125,000 a year. I suggest that we count the planned amount of these minor capital acquisitions, as shown in the capital budget, as an expense in each of the years 1995–1999.

I suggest that we establish a fund to provide for major renewals planned over the next 20 years. We now list six such projects, as shown on Exhibit 3. For some of them, actual expenditures will be made over three years, and I have used the middle year of the three in the calculation. Annual charges to this fund, plus interest earned on the fund, will pay for the renewals in the year in which expenditures for them are made. For the next several years, this charge

would be $70,000 annually, calculated as the present value of these expenditures, using a 4 percent interest rate.

In addition to these renewals, we plan to expand the health-care unit in the year 2000 at a cost of $840,000 (in 1994 dollars). This is not a renewal, and I assume that it will be paid for by new borrowing made at that time.

Construction costs at Riverview were $900,000 for land, $1,900,000 for land improvements, and $40,200,000 for other depreciable assets—a total of $43,000,000. These costs were financed by a 30-year, 8 percent bond issue in the amount of $43,000,000. Level semiannual payments, consisting of principal payments and interest, were required for these bonds. Mills explained that the principal component of these payments added up to the cost of the borrowing—$43,000,000. The $43,000,000 exceeded the cost of depreciable assets because land is not depreciated.

To illustrate her proposal, Mills passed out two exhibits. Both were based on the current draft of Riverview's five-year strategic plan. In both exhibits, the bottom line was the amount of fee revenue needed to meet the annual expenses. They therefore differed from the current format in which fee revenue, calculated at the assumed annual rate of interest, was one of the revenue items at the top of the exhibit.

Exhibit 1 was based on the current method of planning, and the numbers for 1995–1999 were taken from that plan. The numbers for the later years used the same assumptions as those used to develop the current strategic plan.

Exhibit 2 eliminated depreciation, included the new amounts described in her proposal, and also included a small contingency fund. In all other respects, the numbers in Exhibit 2 were the same as those in Exhibit 1.

Discussion of the Proposal

Johnson first pointed out that the proposal to eliminate depreciation would not be consistent

EXHIBIT 1   Riverview Current Strategic Plan ($000s)

	Budget FY 1994	Plan FY 1995	Plan FY 1996	Plan FY 1997	Plan FY 1998
Revenues					
Medicare & other insurance	461	477	493	511	529
Entrance fees earned	3,160	3,287	3,418	1,490	1,981
Interest income	1,269	897	940	952	999
Other program services	168	166	174	183	192
Other revenue	18	19	19	20	21
Total revenues (except residential fees)	5,076	4,846	5,044	3,156	3,722
Expenses					
Administration					
Personnel	440	464	486	511	540
Insurance & other	375	392	409	428	447
Management fee	492	500	513	541	572
Housekeeping					
Personnel	509	572	621	649	693
Other	57	78	87	96	103
Maintenance					
Personnel	427	483	506	558	586
Other	192	219	232	246	263
Food service					
Personnel	958	991	1,099	1,160	1,266
Raw food	305	328	359	398	423
Other	164	176	193	215	311
Health services					
Personnel	1,303	1,428	1,635	1,822	2,047
Other	345	380	413	446	478
Utilities	601	650	701	758	818
Real estate taxes	547	674	603	633	665
Amortization (start-up costs)	115	115	115	115	115
Other expenses	87	91	95	98	102
Interest expense	4,036	3,998	3,956	3,911	3,862
Depreciation	1,155	1,167	1,182	1,199	1,211
Total expenses	12,108	12,706	13,205	13,784	14,502
Income (before fees)	(7,032)	(7,860)	(8,161)	(10,628)	(10,780)
Residential fees	7,069	9,100	9,700	12,500	13,000

EXHIBIT 2   Riverview Current Strategic Plan ($000s)

	Budget FY 1994	Plan FY 1995	Plan FY 1996	Plan FY 1997	Plan FY 1998
Revenues					
Medicare & other insurance	461	477	493	511	529
Entrance fees earned	3,160	3,287	3,418	1,490	1,981
Interest income	1,269	897	940	952	999
Other program services	168	166	174	183	192
Other revenue	18	19	19	20	21
Total revenues (except residential fees)	5,076	4,846	5,044	3,156	3,722
Expenses					
Administration					
Personnel	440	464	486	511	540
Insurance & other	375	392	409	428	447
Management fee	492	500	513	541	572
Housekeeping					
Personnel	509	572	621	649	693
Other	57	78	87	96	103
Maintenance					
Personnel	427	483	506	558	586
Other	192	219	232	246	263
Food service					
Personnel	958	991	1,099	1,160	1,266
Raw food	305	328	359	398	423
Other	164	176	193	215	311
Health services					
Personnel	1,303	1,428	1,635	1,822	2,047
Other	345	380	413	446	478
Utilities	601	650	701	758	818
Real estate taxes	547	674	603	633	665
Amortization (start-up costs)	115	115	115	115	115
Other expenses	87	91	95	98	102
Interest expense	4,036	3,998	3,956	3,911	3,862
Debt-service principal	473	512	554	599	648
Minor capital expenditures	419	116	151	169	123
Provision for renewal	70	70	70	70	70
Contingency fund	152	145	151	95	112
Total expenses	12,067	12,382	12,949	13,563	14,244
Income (before fees)	(6,991)	(7,536)	(7,905)	(10,407)	(10,522)
Residential fees	7,069	8,800	9,200	11,700	11,800

Exhibit 3   Major Item, 1995 Provision

	Amount	First Year of Contribution	Year of Expenditure*	Years of Contribution	Annual Charge†
Paving	$113,000	1995	2006	12	$ 7,520
Fire alarm system	200,000	1995	2009	15	9,988
Lighting fixtures	258,000	1995	2005	11	19,130
Emergency generator	90,000	1995	2012	18	3,509
Roofing	200,000	1995	2013	19	7,228
Elevators	495,000	1995	2011	17	20,888

*Middle year of expenditure.
†Annual charge at 4% needed to cumulate to amount needed in future year.

with generally accepted accounting principles. Mills replied that these numbers would be used only for internal purposes, and the published financial statements would continue to include depreciation. Johnson said that Montvale's audit committee usually did not look favorably on internal accounting practices that were inconsistent with those in the published statements.

There was considerable discussion of how the policy of fairness applied to this situation. With conventional depreciation, residents would pay their share of the actual cost of the fixed assets they used each year. Under the proposal, they would not pay for depreciation as such, but they would help pay for the cost of future renewals that would not benefit them. Mills argued that their current usage of the assets was the ultimate cause of the need for renewal, and that having current residents pay for this cost was fair. Johnson wondered how this argument would apply to technological improvements that were unknown but likely, especially in the case of medical equipment in the health care facility.

Johnson asked why the discount rate on the proposed fund for renewals was the low rate of 4

percent. Mills replied that with this rate, inflation need not be taken into account because the renewal fund should earn 4 percent plus inflation and the excess over 4 percent would offset the error of including renewal costs at 1994 prices.

In the course of the discussion, the issue of a possible tennis court was raised. A recent survey showed that about 40 couples wanted to play tennis on the premises. (The nearest tennis courts were about a five-minute drive.) If two tennis courts were built (at a total cost of approximately $50,000), should all residents, in effect, pay for them via their monthly fees? Or should they be financed by a levy on users and/or a fee for using the facility, as was the case when residents used a nearby golf course?

Next Steps

Jerry Johnson knew that if he decided to back the proposal, he would need the support of Montvale's president. He would also need the consent of the audit committee and the budget committee of the board of trustees. If he decided not to proceed, he was obligated to explain his reasons.

Questions

1. What should Johnson do?

2. What are the implications of your conclusion for the concept of "fairness" in arriving at prices and fees in nonprofit organizations?

3. Suggest a way of deciding how the proportion of total revenue from residents should be divided between entrance fees and monthly fees.

4. Who should pay for the tennis court if it is built?

ANALYZING FINANCIAL PERFORMANCE REPORTS

This chapter focuses on analyzing financial performance measures. The first part describes how variances between actual and budgeted data are calculated for business units. Since expense and revenue budgets are part of the budgets for business units, the discussion can be extended to cover expense and revenue centers as well. The second part describes how reports of these variances are used by senior management to evaluate business unit performance. In the next chapter, we describe how nonfinancial performance measures can be incorporated into the management control process.

Calculating Variances

Although the focus of this section is on comparing actual performance with the budget, competent operating managers nevertheless adopt a continuous improvement or *Kaizen* mentality; they do not assume that optimal performance is being "on budget." Most companies make a monthly analysis of the differences between actual and budgeted revenues and expenses for each business unit and for the whole organization (some do this quarterly). Some companies merely report the amount of these variances, as in Exhibit 9–1. This statement shows that the actual profit was $52,000 higher than budget, and that the principal reason for this was that revenues were higher than budget. It doesn't illustrate why the revenues were higher or whether there were significant offsetting differences in the variances of the expense items that were netted out in the overall numbers.

A more thorough analysis identifies the causes of the variances and the organization unit responsible. Effective systems identify variances down to the lowest level of management. Variances are hierarchical. As shown in Exhibit 9–2, they begin with the total business unit performance, which is divided into revenue variances and expense variances. Revenue variances are further divided into volume and price variances for the total business unit

---

EXHIBIT 9–1   Performance Report, January (000s)

	Actual	Budget	Actual Better (Worse) than Budget
Sales	$875	$600	$275
Variable costs of sales	583	370	(213)
Contribution	292	230	62
Fixed overhead	75	75	—
Gross profit	217	155	62
Selling expense	55	50	(5)
Administration expense	30	25	(5)
Profit before taxes	$132	$ 80	$ 52

---

and for each marketing responsibility center within the unit. They can be further divided by sales area and sales district. Expense variances can be divided between manufacturing expenses and other expenses. Manufacturing expenses can be further subdivided by factories and departments within factories. Therefore, it is possible to identify each variance with the individual manager who is responsible for it. This type of analysis is a powerful tool, without which the efficacy of profit budgets would be limited.

The profit budget has embedded in it certain expectations about the state of the total industry and about the company's market share, its selling prices, and its cost structure. Results from variance computations are more "actionable" if changes in actual results are analyzed against each of these expectations. The analytical framework we use to conduct variance analysis incorporates the following ideas:

- Identify the key causal factors that affect profits.
- Break down the overall profit variances by these key causal factors.
- Focus on the profit impact of variation in each causal factor.
- Try to calculate the specific, separable impact of each causal factor by varying only that factor while holding all other factors constant ("spinning only one dial at a time").
- Add complexity sequentially, one layer at a time, beginning at a very basic "commonsense" level ("peel the onion").
- Stop the process when the added complexity at a newly created level is not justified by added useful insights into the causal factors underlying the overall profit variance.

Exhibit 9–3 provides details of the budget of the business unit whose performance is reported in Exhibit 9–1.

EXHIBIT 9–2

Variance analysis disaggregation

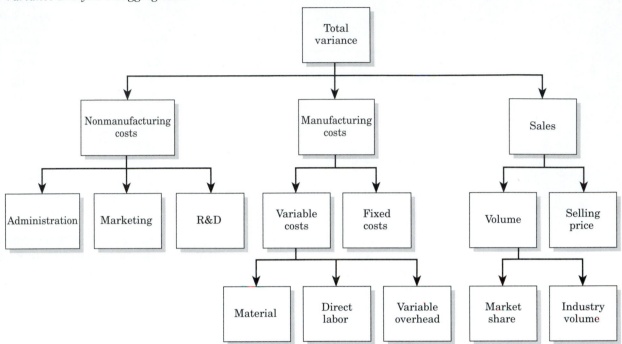

Revenue Variances

In this section, we describe how to calculate selling price, volume, and mix variances. The calculation is made for each product line, and the product line results are then aggregated to calculate the total variance. A positive variance is favorable, because it indicates that actual profit exceeded budgeted profit, and a negative variance is unfavorable.

Selling Price Variance.   The selling price variance is calculated by multiplying the difference between the actual price and the standard price by the actual volume. The calculation is shown in Exhibit 9–4. It shows that the price variance is $75,000, unfavorable.

Mix and Volume Variance.   Often the mix and volume variances are not separated. The equation for the combined mix and volume variance is:

$$\text{Mix and volume variance} = (\text{Actual volume} - \text{Budgeted volume})$$
$$* \text{Budgeted unit contribution}$$

EXHIBIT 9–3   Budget for January ($000s)

	Product A 100*		Product B 100*		Product C 100*		Total Budget
	Unit	*Total*	*Unit*	*Total*	*Unit*	*Total*	
Sales	$1.00	$100	$2.00	$200	$3.00	$300	$600
Standard variable cost:							
Material	0.50	50	0.70	70	1.50	150	270
Labor	0.10	10	0.15	15	0.10	10	35
Variable overhead	0.20	20	0.25	25	0.20	20	65
Total variable cost	0.80	80	1.10	110	1.80	180	370
Contribution	$0.20	20	$0.90	90	$1.20	120	230
Fixed costs:							
Fixed overhead		25		25		25	75
Selling expense		17		17		17	50
Administrative expense		8		8		8	25
Total fixed costs		50		50		50	150
Profit before taxes		$ (30)		$ 40		$ 70	$ 80

*Standard volume (units).

EXHIBIT 9–4   Selling Price Variances, January (000s)

	Product			
	A	*B*	*C*	*Total*
Actual volume (units)	100	200	150	
Actual price per unit	$ 0.90	$ 2.05	$ 2.50	
Budget price per unit	1.00	2.00	3.00	
Actual over/(under) budget per unit	(0.10)	0.05	(0.50)	
Favorable/(unfavorable) price variance	(10)	10	(75)	(75)

The calculation of mix and volume variance is shown in Exhibit 9–5; it is $150,000 favorable.

The volume variance results from selling more units than budgeted. The mix variance results from selling a different proportion of products from that assumed in the budget. Because products earn different *contributions* per unit, the sale of different proportions of products from those budgeted will result in a variance. If the business unit has a "richer" mix (i.e., a higher proportion of products with a high contribution margin), the actual profit will be

EXHIBIT 9–5   Sales Mix and Volume Variance, January ($000s)

(1) Product	(2) Actual Volume	(3) Budgeted Volume	(4) Difference (2) – (3)	(5) Unit Contribution	(6) Variance (4) * (5)
A	100	100	—	—	—
B	200	100	100	$0.90	$ 90
C	150	100	50	1.20	60
Total	450	300			$150

EXHIBIT 9–6   Mix Variance, January ($000s)

(1) Product	(2) Budgeted Proportion	(3) Budgeted Mix at Actual Volume	(4) Actual Sales	(5) Difference (3) – (4)	(6) Unit Contribution	(7) Variance (5) * (6)
A	⅓	150[†]	100	(50)	$0.20	$(10)
B	⅓	150	200	50	$0.90	45
C	⅓	150	150	—	—	—
Total		450	450			$35

[†]⅓ * 450 = 150.

higher than budgeted; and if it has a "leaner" mix, the profit will be lower. Since the volume and mix variances are joint, techniques for separating them are somewhat arbitrary. One such technique is described below.

Mix Variance.   The mix variance for each product is found from the following equation:

Mix variance = [(Total actual volume of sales * Budgeted proportion) – (Actual volume of sales)] * Budgeted unit contribution

The calculation of the mix variance is shown in Exhibit 9–6. It shows that a higher proportion of product B and a lower proportion of product A were sold. Since product B has a higher unit contribution than product A, the mix variance is favorable, by $35,000.

Volume Variance.   The volume variance can be calculated by subtracting the mix variance from the combined mix and volume variance. This is $150,000 minus $35,000, or $115,000. It can also be calculated for each product as follows:

EXHIBIT 9–7   Sales Volume Variance, January ($000s)

(1) Product	(2) Budgeted Mix at Actual Volume	(3) Budgeted Volume	(4) Difference (2) – (3)	(5) Unit Contribution	(6) Volume Variance
A	150	100	50	$0.20	$ 10
B	150	100	50	0.90	45
C	150	100	50	1.20	60
Total	450	300	150		$115

EXHIBIT 9–8   Revenue Variances by Product, January ($000s)

	Product			
	A	B	C	Total
Price variance	$(10)	$ 10	$(75)	$(75)
Mix variance	(10)	45	—	35
Volume variance	10	45	60	115
Total	$(10)	$100	$(15)	$ 75

Volume variance = [(Total actual volume of sales) * (Budgeted percentage)]
 – [(Budgeted sales) * (Budgeted unit contribution)]

The calculation of the volume variance is shown in Exhibit 9–7.

Other Revenue Analyses.   Revenue variances may be further subdivided. In our example, Exhibits 9–4, 9–6, and 9–7 provide the information needed to classify them by product. Such a classification is shown in Exhibit 9–8.

Market Penetration and Industry Volume.   One extension of revenue analysis is to separate the mix and volume variance into the amount caused by differences in market share and the amount caused by differences in industry volume. The principle is that the business unit managers are responsible for market share, but they are not responsible for the industry volume because that is largely influenced by the state of the economy. To make this calculation, industry sales data must be available. This calculation is given in Exhibit 9–9.

EXHIBIT 9–9   Industry Volume and Market Share Variances, January ($000s)

A. Budgeted Sales Volume

	Product			
	A	*B*	*C*	*Total*
Estimated industry volume (units)	833	500	1,667	3,000
Budgeted market share	12%	20%	6%	10%
Budgeted volume (units)	100	100	100	300

B. Actual Market Share

	Product			
	A	*B*	*C*	*Total*
Actual industry volume, units	1,000	1,000	1,000	3,000
Actual sales (units)	100	200	150	450
Actual market share	10%	20%	15%	15%

C. Variance Due to Market Share

	Product			
	A	*B*	*C*	*Total*
(1) Actual sales (units)	100	200	150	450
(2) Budgeted shares at actual industry volume	120	200	60	380
(3) Difference (1 – 2)	(20)	—	90	70
(4) Budgeted unit contribution	$0.20	$0.90	$1.20	
(5) Variance due to market share (3 * 4)	(4.00)	—	108	$104

D. Variance Due to Industry Volume

	Product			
	A	*B*	*C*	*Total*
(1) Actual industry volume	1,000	1,000	1,000	3,000
(2) Budgeted industry volume	833	500	1,667	3,000
(3) Difference (1 – 2)	167	500	(667)	—
(4) Budgeted market share	12%	20%	6%	
(5) (3 * 4)	20	100	(40)	
(6) Unit contribution (budget)	$0.20	$0.90	$1.20	
(7) Total (5 * 6)	4.00	90.00	(48.00)	$46

Section A of Exhibit 9–9 provides the assumptions that were made in the original budget shown in Exhibit 9–1, and Section B provides details on actual industry volume and market share for the month of January.

The following equation is used to separate the effect of market penetration from industry volume on the mix and volume variance:

Market share variance = [(Actual sales) – (Industry volume)]
* Budgeted market penetration
* Budgeted unit contribution

The market share variance is found for each product separately, and the total variance is the algebraic sum. The calculation is shown in Section C. It shows that $104,000 of the favorable mix and volume variance of $150,000 resulted from the fact that market penetration was better than budget. The remaining $46,000 resulted from the fact that actual industry dollar volume was higher than the amount assumed in the budget.

The $46,000 industry volume variance can also be calculated for each product as follows:

Industry volume variance = (Actual industry volume – Budgeted industry
volume) * Budgeted market penetration
* Budgeted unit contribution

This calculation of variance due to industry volume is shown in Section D.

Expense Variances

Fixed Costs.   Variances between actual and budgeted fixed costs are obtained simply by subtraction, since these costs are not affected by either the volume of sales or the volume of production. This is shown in Exhibit 9–10.

Variable Costs.   Variable costs are costs that vary directly and proportionately with volume. The budgeted variable manufacturing costs must be adjusted to the actual volume of production. Assume that the January production was as follows: product A, 150,000 units; product B, 120,000 units;

EXHIBIT 9–10   Fixed-Cost Variances, January ($000s)

	Actual	Budget	Favorable or Unfavorable Variances
Fixed overhead	$ 75	$ 75	$ —
Selling expense	55	50	(5)
Administrative expense	30	25	(5)
Total	$160	$150	$(10)

Exhibit 9–11   Variable Manufacturing Expense Variances, January ($000s)

| | Product | | | | | Favorable/ (Unfavorable) Variances |
	A	B	C	Total	Actual	
Material	$ 75	$ 84	$300	$459	$470	$(11)
Labor	15	18	20	53	65	(12)
Overhead (variable)	30	30	40	100	90	10
Total	$120	$132	$360	$612	$625	$(13)

---

product C, 200,000 units. Assume also that the variable manufacturing costs incurred in January were as follows: material, $470,000; labor $65,000; variable manufacturing overhead, $90,000. Exhibit 9–3 shows the standard unit variable costs.

The budgeted manufacturing expense is adjusted to the amount that should have been spent at the actual level of production by multiplying each element of standard cost for each product by the volume of production for that product. This calculation is shown in Exhibit 9–11.

This exhibit shows that there was an unfavorable variance of $13,000 in January. This is called a *spending* variance because it results from spending $13,000 in excess of the adjusted budget. It consists of unfavorable material and labor variances of $11,000 and $12,000, respectively. These are partially offset by a favorable overhead spending variance of $10,000.

The volume that is used to adjust the budgeted variable manufacturing expenses is the *manufacturing* volume, not the *sales* volume, which was used in finding the revenue variances. In the simple example given here, we assumed that the two volumes were the same—namely, that the quantity of each product manufactured in January was the same as the quantity sold in January. If production volume differed from sales volume, the cost difference would show up in changes in inventory. Depending on the company's inventory costing method, this might or might not result in a production volume variance. Calculation of such a variance is explained in the next section.

In this example, we assumed that all the nonmanufacturing expenses were fixed. If some of them had variable components, the variances should be calculated in the same way as was used for the calculation of manufacturing cost variances.

Summary of Variances

There are several ways in which the variances can be summarized in a report for management. One possibility is shown in Exhibit 9–12. It was used pri-

---

EXHIBIT 9–12   Summary Performance Report, January ($000s)

Actual profit (Exhibit 9–1)	$132
Budgeted profit (Exhibit 9–l)	80
Variance	$ 52
Analysis of Variance—Favorable/(Unfavorable)	
Revenue variances:	
Price (Exhibit 9–4)	$ (75)
Mix (Exhibit 9–6)	35
Volume (Exhibit 9–7)	115
Net revenue variances	$ 75
Variable-cost variances (Exhibit 9–11):	
Material	$ (11)
Labor	(12)
Variable overhead	10
Net variable-cost variances	$ (13)
Fixed-cost variances (Exhibit 9–10):	
Selling expense	$ (5)
Administrative expense	(5)
Net fixed-cost variances	$ (10)
Variance	$ (52)

---

marily because the amounts can be traced easily to the earlier exhibits. Another form of presentation is to show the actual amounts, as well as the variances. This gives an indication of the relative importance of each variance as a fraction of the total revenue or expense item to which it relates.

Variations in Practice

The example given above, although complicated, is a relatively straightforward way of identifying the variances that caused actual profit in a business unit to be different from the budgeted profitability. Some variations from this approach are described in this section.

Time Period of the Comparison

The example compared January's budget with January's actuals. Some companies use performance for the year to date as the basis for comparison; for the period ended June 30, they would use budgeted and actual amounts for the six months ending on June 30, rather than the amounts for June. Other companies compare the budget for the whole year with the current estimate of actual performance for the year. The *actual* amounts for the report prepared as of June 30 would consist of actual numbers for the first six months plus the best current estimate of revenues and expenses for the second six months.

A comparison for the year to date is not as much influenced by temporary aberrations that may be peculiar to the current month and, therefore, that need not be of as much concern to management. On the other hand, it may mask the emergence of an important factor that is not temporary.

A comparison of the annual budget with current expectation of actual performance for the whole year shows how closely the business unit manager expects to meet the annual profit target. If performance for the year to date is worse than the budget for the year to date, it is possible that the deficit will be overcome in the remaining months. On the other hand, forces that caused actual performance to be below budget for the year to date may be expected to continue for the remainder of the year, which will make the final numbers significantly different from the budgeted amounts. Senior management needs a realistic estimate of the profit for the whole year, both because it may suggest the need to change the dividend policy, to obtain additional cash, or to change levels of discretionary spending, and also because a current estimate of the year's performance is often provided to financial analysts and other outside parties.

Obtaining a realistic estimate is difficult. Business unit managers tend to be optimistic about their ability to perform in the remaining months because, if they are pessimistic, this casts doubt on their ability to manage. To some extent, this tendency can be overcome by placing the burden of proof on business unit managers to show that the current trends in volume, margins, and costs are not going to continue. Nevertheless, an estimate of the whole year is *soft,* whereas actual performance is a matter of record. An alternative that lessens this problem is to report performance both for the year to date and for the year as a whole.

Focus on Gross Margin

In the example, we assumed that selling prices were budgeted to remain constant throughout the year. In many companies, changes in costs or other factors are expected to lead to changes in selling prices, and the task of the marketing manager is to obtain a budgeted gross margin—that is, a constant spread between costs and selling prices. Such a policy is especially important in periods of inflation. A variance analysis in such a system would not have a selling price variance. Instead, there would be a gross margin variance. *Unit gross margin is the difference between selling prices and manufacturing costs.*

The variance analysis is done by substituting "gross margin" for "selling price" in the revenue equations. Gross margin is the difference between actual selling prices and the *standard* manufacturing cost. The current standard manufacturing cost should take into account changes in manufacturing costs that are caused by changes in wage rates and in material prices (and, in some companies, significant changes in other input factors, such as electricity in aluminum manufacturing). The standard, rather than the actual, cost is used so that manufacturing inefficiencies do not affect the performance of the marketing organization.

Evaluation Standards

In management control systems, the formal standards used in the evaluation of reports on actual activities are of three types: (1) predetermined standards or budgets, (2) historical standards, or (3) external standards.

Predetermined Standards or Budgets.   If carefully prepared and coordinated, these are excellent standards. They are the basis against which actual performance is compared in many companies. If the budget numbers are collected in a haphazard manner, they obviously will not provide a reliable basis for comparison.

Historical Standards.   These are records of past actual performance. Results for the current month may be compared with the results for last month, or with results for the same month a year ago. This type of standard has two serious weaknesses: (1) conditions may have changed between the two periods in a way that invalidates the comparison, and (2) the prior period's performance may not have been acceptable. A supervisor whose spoilage cost is $500 a month, month after month, is consistent; but we do not know, without other evidence, whether the performance was consistently good or consistently poor. Despite these inherent weaknesses, historical standards are used in some companies, often because valid predetermined standards are not available.

External Standards.   These are standards derived from the performance of other responsibility centers or of other companies in the same industry. The performance of one branch sales office may be compared with the performance of other branch sales offices. If conditions in these responsibility centers are similar, such a comparison may provide an acceptable basis for evaluating performance.

Some companies identify the company that they believe to be the best managed in the industry and use numbers from that company—either with the cooperation of that company or from published material—as a basis of comparison. This process is called *benchmarking.*

Data for individual companies are available in annual and quarterly reports and in Form 10K. (Form 10K data are available from the Securities and Exchange Commission and are published on the Internet for about 13,000 companies.) Data for industries are published in Dun & Bradstreet, Inc., Key Business Ratios; Standard & Poor's Compustat Services, Inc.; Robert Morris Associates Annual Statement Studies; and annual surveys published in *Fortune, Business Week,* and *Forbes.* Trade associations publish data for the companies in their industries.

Many companies publish their financial statements on the Internet. A problem with using this information as a basis for comparison with competitors' performance is that the names for account titles are not the same. The American Institute of CPAs has a project that seeks to establish a standard set of account titles used in Internet reports. This is named the XBRL project. When these titles become accepted, it should be easy to obtain averages and other data for competitors by a simple computer program. Current information about this project can be obtained from the AICPA Web site: www.oasis.open.org/cover/siteindex.html. The Financial Executives Institute provides information about performance of member companies, but most is available only to subscribers of its project. Tidbits are published in its journal, *Financial Executive*.

Limitations on Standards.   A variance between actual and standard performance is meaningful only if it is derived from a valid standard. Although it is convenient to refer to *favorable* and *unfavorable* variances, these words imply that the standard is a reliable measure of what performance should have been. Even a standard cost may not be an accurate estimate of what costs should have been under the circumstances. This situation can arise for either or both of two reasons: (1) the standard was not set properly; or (2) although it was set properly in light of conditions existing at the time, changed conditions have made the standard obsolete. An essential first step in the analysis of a variance is an examination of the validity of the standard.

Full-Cost Systems

If the company has a full-cost system, both variable and fixed overhead costs are included in the inventory at the standard cost per unit. If the ending inventory is higher than the beginning inventory, some of the fixed overhead costs incurred in the period remain in inventory rather than flowing through to cost of sales. Conversely, if the inventory balance decreased during the period, more fixed overhead costs were released to cost of sales than the amount actually incurred in the period. Our example assumed that the inventory level did not change. Thus, the problem of treating the variance associated with fixed overhead costs did not arise.

If inventory levels change, and if actual production volume is different from budgeted sales volume, part of the production volume variance is included in inventory. Nevertheless, the full amount of the production volume variance should be calculated and reported. This variance is the difference between budgeted fixed production costs at the actual volume (as stated in the flexible budget) and standard fixed production costs at that volume.

If the company has a variable-cost system, fixed production costs are not included in inventory, so there is no production volume variance. The fixed production expense variance is simply the difference between the budgeted amount and the actual amount.

The important point is that production variances should be associated with *production* volume, not sales volume.

Amount of Detail

In the example, we analyzed revenue variances at several levels: first, in total; then by volume, mix, and price; then by analyzing the volume and mix variance by industry volume and market share. At each of these levels, we analyzed the variances by individual products. The process of going from one level to another is often referred to as "peeling the onion"—that is, successive layers are peeled off, and the process continues as long as the additional detail is judged to be worthwhile. Some companies do not develop as many layers as shown in our example; others develop more. It is possible, and in some cases worthwhile, to develop additional sales and marketing variances, such as the following: by sales territories, and even by individual salesperson; by sales to individual countries or regions; by sales to key customers, principal types of customers, or customers in certain industries; by sales originating from direct mail, from customer calls, or from other sources. Additional detail for manufacturing costs can be developed by calculating variances for lower-level responsibility centers and by identifying variances with specific input factors, such as wage rates and material prices.

These layers correspond to the hierarchy of responsibility centers. Taking action based on the reported variances is not possible unless they can be associated with the managers responsible for them.

With modern information technology, about any level of detail can be supplied quickly and at reasonable cost. The problem is to decide how much is worthwhile. In part, the answer depends on the information requested by individual managers—some are numbers-oriented, others are not. In the ideal situation, the basic data exist to make any conceivable type of analysis, but only a small fraction of these data are reported routinely.

Engineered and Discretionary Costs

As we pointed out in Chapter 3, variances in engineered costs are viewed in a fundamentally different way from variances in discretionary costs.

A "favorable" variance in engineered costs is usually an indication of good performance; that is, the lower the cost the better the performance. This is subject to the qualification that quality and on-time delivery are judged to be satisfactory.

By contrast, the performance of a discretionary expense center is usually judged to be satisfactory if actual expenses are about equal to the budgeted amount, neither higher nor lower. This is because a favorable variance may indicate that the responsibility center did not perform adequately the functions that it had agreed to perform. Because some elements in a discretionary expense center are in fact engineered (e.g., the bookkeeping functions in the controller organization), a favorable variance is usually truly favorable for these elements.

Limitations of Variance Analysis

Although variance analysis is a powerful tool, it does have limitations. The most important limitation is that although it identifies where a variance occurs, it does not tell *why* the variance occurred or what is being done about it. For example, the report may show there was a significant unfavorable variance in marketing expenses, and it may identify this variance with high sales promotion expenses. It does not, however, explain why the sales promotion expenses were high and what, if any, actions were being taken. A narrative explanation, accompanying the performance report, should provide such an explanation.

A second problem in variance analysis is to decide whether a variance is significant. Statistical techniques can be used to determine whether there is a significant difference between actual and standard performance for certain processes; these techniques are usually referred to as *statistical quality control.* However, they are applicable only when the process is repeated at frequent intervals, such as the operation of a machine tool on a production line. The literature contains a few articles suggesting that statistical quality control be used to determine whether a budget variance is significant; but this suggestion has little practical relevance at the business unit level because the necessary number of repetitive actions is not present. Conceptually, a variance should be investigated only when the benefit expected from correcting the problem exceeds the cost of the investigation; but a model based on this premise has so many uncertainties that it is only of academic interest. Managers, therefore, rely on judgment in deciding what variances are significant. Moreover, if a variance is significant but is uncontrollable (such as unexpected inflation), there may be no point in investigating it.

A third limitation of variance analysis is that as the performance reports become more highly aggregated, offsetting variances might mislead the reader. For example, a manager looking at business unit manufacturing cost performance might notice that it was on budget. However, this might have resulted from good performance at one plant being offset by poor performance at another. Similarly, when different product lines at different stages of development are combined, the combination may obscure the actual results of each product line.

Also, as variances become more highly aggregated, managers become more dependent on the accompanying explanations and forecasts. Plant managers know what is happening in their plant and can easily explain causes of variances. Business unit managers and everyone above them, however, usually must depend on the explanations that accompany the variance report of the plant.

Finally, the reports show only what has happened. They do not show the future effects of actions that the manager has taken. For example, reducing the amount spent for employee training increases current profitability, but it may have adverse consequences in the future. Also, the report shows only those events that are recorded in the accounts, and many important events are not reflected in current accounting transactions. The accounts don't show the state of morale, for instance.

Management Action

There is one cardinal principle in analyzing formal financial reports: *The monthly profit report should contain no major surprises.* Significant information should be communicated quickly by telephone, fax, electronic mail, or personal meetings as soon as it becomes known. The formal report confirms the general impression that the senior manager has learned from these sources. Based on this information, he or she may have acted prior to the receipt of the formal report.

The formal report is nevertheless important. *One of the most important benefits of formal reporting is that it provides the desirable pressure on subordinate managers to take corrective actions on their own initiative.* Further, the information from informal sources may be incomplete or misunderstood; the numbers in the formal report provide more accurate information, and the report may confirm or cast doubts on the information received from informal sources. Also, the formal report provides a basis for analysis because information from the informal sources often is general and imprecise.

Usually, there is a discussion between the business unit manager and his or her superior, in which the business unit manager explains the reasons for significant variances, the action being taken to correct unfavorable situations, and the expected timing of each corrective action. These explanations are necessarily subjective, and they may be biased. Operating managers, like most people, don't like to admit that unfavorable variances were caused by their errors. A senior manager has an opinion, based on experience, as to the likelihood that a business unit manager will be frank and forthcoming, and he or she judges the report accordingly.

Profit reports are worthless unless they lead to action. The action may consist of praise for a job well done, suggestions for doing things differently, "chewing out," or more drastic personnel actions. However, these actions are by no means taken for every business unit every month. As long as business is going well, praise is the most that may be necessary, and most people don't even expect praise routinely.

Summary

Business unit managers report their financial performance to senior management regularly, usually monthly. The formal report consists of a comparison of actual revenues and costs with budgeted amounts. The differences, or variances, between these two amounts can be analyzed at several levels of detail. This analysis identifies the causes of the variance from budgeted profit and the amount attributable to each cause.

Suggested Additional Readings

Brownell, Peter, and Mark Hirst. "Reliance on Accounting Information, Budgetary Participation, and Task Uncertainty: Tests of a Three-Way Interaction." *Journal of Accounting Research* XXIV, no. 2 (Autumn 1986), pp. 241–49.

Brownell, Peter, and Morris McInnes. "Budgetary Participation, Motivation, and Management Performance." *The Accounting Review,* October 1986, pp. 587–600.

Chenhall, R. H., and D. Morris. "The Impact of Structure, Environment, and Interdependence on the Perceived Usefulness of Management Accounting Systems." *The Accounting Review* LXI, no. I (January 1986), pp. 16–35.

Dearden, John. "Measuring Profit Center Managers." *Harvard Business Review,* September–October 1987, pp. 84–86.

Dunk, Alan S. "Reliance on Budgetary Control for Manufacturing Process Automation and Production Subunit Performance." *Accounting, Organizations and Society* XVII, no. 4 (April–May 1992), pp. 195–204.

Govindarajan, Vijay. "Appropriateness of Accounting Data in Performance Evaluation: An Empirical Examination of Environment Uncertainty as an Intervening Variable." *Accounting, Organizations and Society* IX, no. 2 (1984), pp. 125–35.

Govindarajan, Vijay, and John K. Shank. "Profit Variance Analysis: A Strategic Focus." *Issues in Accounting Education* 4, no. 2 (Fall 1989), pp. 396–410.

Horngren, Charles T., George Foster, and Srikant Datar. *Cost Accounting: A Managerial Emphasis.* Englewood Cliffs, NJ: Prentice Hall, 2000, chapter 17.

Institute of Management Accountants. "Fundamentals of Reporting Information to Managers." *Statement on Management Accounting.* Supplement 5–6. Montvale, NJ, 1992.

Umpathy, Srinivasan. *Current Budgeting Practices in U.S. Industry: The State of the Art.* Westport, CT.: Quorum Books, 1987.

CASE 9–1
VARIANCE ANALYSIS PROBLEMS

I. In this case you are asked to analyze the February and March financial performance of the Temple Division of the ABC Company as compared with its budget, which is shown in Exhibit 9–3 of the text.

Part A—February 1988

Below are the data describing the actual financial results of the Temple Division for the month of February 1988.

Sales	$781
Variable cost of sales	552
Contribution	229
Fixed manufacturing costs	80
Gross profit	149
Selling expense	57
Administrative expense	33
Net profit	$ 59

Sales

Product	Unit Sales	Price	Dollar Sales
A	120	$0.95	$114
B	130	1.90	247
C	150	2.80	420
Total	400		781

Production

		Manufacturing Cost			
Product	Units Produced	Material	Labor	Variable Overhead	Total
A	150	$ 80	$20	$ 40	$140
B	130	91	21	35	147
C	120	190	15	30	235
Total	400	361	56	105	522

This case was prepared by John Dearden. Copyright Osceola Institute.

Questions

1. Prepare an analysis of variance from profit budget assuming that the Temple Division employed a variable standard cost accounting system.

2. Prepare an analysis of variance from profit budget assuming that the Temple Division used a full standard cost accounting system. Under this assumption, the actual cost of sales amount would be $632,000. (Can you derive this figure?)

3. Industry volume figures are presented below. Separate the mix and volume variance into the variance resulting from differences in market penetration and variance resulting from differences in industry volume. Make the calculation for the variable cost system only. Industry volume, February 1988:

	Units (000)
Product A	600
Product B	650
Product C	1,500

Part B—March 1988

Below are the data describing the actual financial results for the Temple Division for the month of March 1988.

Income Statement	
Sales	$498
Variable cost of sales	278
Contribution	220
Fixed manufacturing costs	70
Gross profit	150
Selling expense	45
Administrative expense	20
Net profit	$ 85

Sales

Product	Unit Sales	Price	Dollar Sales
A	90	$1.10	$ 99
B	70	2.10	147
C	80	3.15	252
Total	240		498

Production

	Units	Manufacturing Cost			
Product	Produced	Material	Labor	Variable Overhead	Total
A	90	$ 40	$ 8	$17	$ 65
B	80	55	10	18	83
C	100	150	8	19	177
Total	270	245	26	54	325

Question

Answer the same questions posed at the end of Part A. The actual cost of sales using full standard costing would be $340,500 in March. Industry volume for March was:

	Units (000)
Product A	500
Product B	600
Product C	1,000

II. The profit budget for the Crocker Company for January 1988 was as follows:

	($000)
Sales	$2,500
Standard cost of sales	1,620
Gross profit	880
Selling expense	$250
Research and development expense	300
Administrative expense	120
Total expense	670
Net profit before taxes	$ 210

The product information used in developing the budget was as follows:

	E	F	G	H
Sales—units (000)	1,000	2,000	3,000	4,000
Price per unit	$0.15	$0.20	$0.25	$0.30
Standard cost per unit:				
Material	0.04	0.05	0.06	0.08
Direct labor	0.02	0.02	0.03	0.04
Variable overhead	0.02	0.03	0.03	0.05
Total variable cost	0.08	0.10	0.12	0.17
Fixed overhead ($000)	20	60	60	160
Total standard cost per unit	0.10	0.13	0.14	0.21

The actual revenues and costs for January 1988 were as follows:

	($000)
Sales	$2,160
Standard cost of sales	1,420
Net standard cost of variances	160
Actual cost of sales	1,580
Gross profit	580
Selling expense	$290
Research and development expense	250
Administrative expenses	110
Total expense	650
Net loss	$ (70)

Operating statistics for January 1988 were as follows:

	E	F	G	H
Sales (units)	1,000	1,000	4,000	3,000
Sales price	$0.13	$0.22	$0.22	$0.31
Production	1,000	1,000	2,000	2,000
Actual manufacturing costs (000):				
Material	$360			
Labor	200			
Overhead	530			

Question

Prepare an analysis of variance between actual profits and budgeted profits for January 1988.

CASE 9–2
SOLARTRONICS, INC.

John Holden, president and general manager of Solartronics, Inc., was confused. Lisa Blocker, the firm's recently hired controller and financial manager, had instituted the preparation of a new, summarized income statement. This statement was to be issued on a monthly basis. Mr. Holden had just received a copy of the statement for January 1984 (see Exhibit 1).

Solartronics, Inc., a small, Texas-based manufacturer of solar energy panels, had been in business since mid-1977. By the end of 1983, it had survived some bad years and positioned itself as a reasonably good-sized firm within the industry. As part of a conscious effort to "professionalize" the firm, Mr. Holden had added Ms. Blocker to the staff in the autumn of 1983. Previous to that time, Solartronics had em-

ployed the services of a full-time, full-charge bookkeeper.

Mr. Holden's confusion arose from the fact that he had not expected the firm to report a loss for the month of January. While he knew that sales had been down, primarily due to the normal seasonal downturn, and that production had been scaled back to help reduce the level of inventory, he was still surprised. He wondered if this first month's results were a bad omen in terms of the likelihood of meeting the budgeted results for the year (see Exhibit 2). Even though the 1984 budget represented only a 10 percent increase in sales volume over 1983, he was concerned that such a poor start to the year might make it difficult to get "back on stream."

EXHIBIT 1

SOLARTRONICS, INC. (B)
Summarized Income Statement
January 1984

Sales			$165,000
Less: Cost of goods sold (at standard)			108,900
Gross margin			$ 56,100
Less: Selling expenses		$26,500	
General corporate overhead		18,000	
Operating variances:			
Direct labor	$ (3,500)		
Direct material	500		
Variable factory overhead	(1,500)		
Fixed factory overhead—spending	2,000		
Fixed factory overhead—volume	(17,500)	20,000	64,500
Profit before tax			$ (8,400)

EXHIBIT 2

SOLARTRONICS, INC. (B)
Budgeted Income Statement
Calendar Year 1984

Sales		$3,000,000[3]
Less: Cost of goods sold (at standard)[1]		1,980,000
Gross margin		$1,020,000
Less: Selling expenses[2]	$420,000	
General corporate overhead	240,000	660,000
Profit before tax		$ 360,000

---

[1]The standard cost of goods sold consisted of: $420,000 direct labor; $780,000 direct material; $360,000 variable factory overhead; and $420,000 fixed factory overhead. Ms. Blocker treated direct labor and direct materials as variable costs.

[2]Of this amount, $120,000 was considered to be fixed. The remaining $300,000 represented the 10 percent commission paid on sales.

[3]The expected sales volume for the year was 5,000 equivalent units. An "equivalent unit" represented the most popular model sold by Solartronics.

Questions

1. Why are the reported results for January so poor, particularly in light of the expected, average monthly profit of $30,000?

2. What additional data would be useful in analyzing the firm's January performance? Why?

CASE 9–3
GALVOR COMPANY

When M. Barsac replaced M. Chambertin as Galvor's controller in April of 1974, at the age of 31, he became the first of a new group of senior managers resulting from the acquisition by Universal Electric. It was an accepted fact that, in the large and sprawling Universal organization, the controller's department represented a key function. M. Barsac, who was a skilled accountant, had had 10 years' experience in a large French subsidiary of Universal.

He recalled his early days with Galvor vividly and admitted they were, to say the least, hectic.

> I arrived at Galvor in early April 1974, a few days after M. Chambertin had left. I was the first Universal man here in Bordeaux and I became quickly immersed in all the problems surrounding the change of ownership. For example, there were no really workable financial statements for the previous two years. This made preparation of the Business Plan, which Mr. Hennessy and I began in June, extremely difficult. This plan covers every aspect of the business, but the great secrecy which had always been maintained at Galvor about the company's financial affairs made it almost impossible for anyone to help us.

M. Barsac's duties could be roughly divided into two major areas: first, the preparation of numerous reports required by Universal, and, second, supervision of Galvor's internal accounting function. While these two areas were closely related, it is useful to separate them in describing the accounting and control function as it developed after Universal's acquisition of Galvor.

To control its operating units, Universal relied primarily on an extensive system of financial reporting. Universal attributed much of its success in recent years to this system. The system was viewed by Universal's European con-

troller, M. Boudry, as much more than a device to "check up" on the operating units. According to M. Boundry:

> In addition to measuring our progress in the conventional sense of sales, earnings, and return on investment, we believe the reporting system causes our operating people to focus their attention on critical areas which might not otherwise receive their major attention. An example would be the level of investment in inventory. The system also forces people to think about the future and to commit themselves to specific future goals. Most operating people are understandably involved in today's problems. We believe some device is required to force them to look beyond the problems at hand and to consider longer-range objectives and strategy. You could say we view the reporting system as an effective training and educational device.

Background

The Galvor Company had been founded in 1946 by M. Georges Latour, who continued as its owner and president until 1974. Throughout its history, the company had acted as a fabricator, buying parts and assembling them into high-quality, moderate-cost electric and electronic measuring and test equipment. In its own sector of the electronics industry—measuring instruments—Galvor was one of the major French firms; however, there were many electronics firms in the more sophisticated sectors of the industry that were vastly larger than Galvor.

Galvor's period of greatest growth began around 1960. Between 1960 and 1971, sales grew from 2.2 million 1971 new francs to 12 million, and aftertax profits from 120,000 1971 new francs to 1,062,000. Assets as of December 31, 1971, totaled 8.8 million new francs. (One 1971 new franc = $0.20.) The firm's prosperity resulted in a number of offers to purchase equity in the firm, but M. Latour had remained steadfast in his belief that only if he had complete ownership of Galvor could he direct its affairs

This case was prepared by Professor L. E. Morrissey and is copyrighted by International Institute for Management, Lausanne, Switzerland.

with a free hand. As owner/president, Latour had continued over the years to be personally involved in every detail of the firm's operations, including signing of all of the company's important checks.

As of early 1972, M. Latour was concerned about the development of adequate successor management for Galvor. In January 1972 Latour hired a "technical director" as his special assistant, but this person resigned in November 1972. Following the 1973 unionization of Galvor's work force, which Latour had opposed, Latour (then 54 years old) began to entertain seriously the idea of selling the firm and devoting himself "to family, philanthropic, and general social interests." On April 1, 1974, Galvor was sold to Universal Electric Company for $4.5 million worth of UE's stock. M. Latour became chairman of the board of Galvor, and David Hennessy was appointed as Galvor's managing director. Hennessy at that time was 38 years old and had been with Universal Electric for nine years.

The Business Plan

The heart of Universal's reporting and control system was an extremely comprehensive document—the Business Plan—which was prepared annually by each of the operating units. The Business Plan was the primary standard for evaluating the performance of unit managers, and everything possible was done by Universal's top management to give authority to the plan.

Each January, the Geneva headquarters of Universal set tentative objectives for the following two years for each of its European operating units. This was a "first look"—an attempt to provide a broad statement of objectives that would permit the operating units to develop their detailed Business Plans. For operating units that produced more than a single product line, objectives were established for both the unit as a whole and for each product line. Pri-

mary responsibility for establishing these tentative objectives rested with eight product-line managers located in Geneva, each of whom was responsible for a group of product lines. On the basis of his knowledge of the product lines and his best judgment of their market potential, each product-line manager set the tentative objectives for his lines.

For reporting purposes, Universal considered that Galvor represented a single product line, even though Galvor's own executives viewed the company's products as falling into three distinct lines—multimeters, panel meters, and electronic instruments.

For each of over 300 Universal product lines in Europe, objectives were established for five key measures.

1. Sales.
2. Net income.
3. Total assets.
4. Total employees.
5. Capital expenditures.

From January to April, these tentative objectives were "negotiated" between Geneva headquarters and the operating managements. Formal meetings were held in Geneva to resolve differences between the operating unit managers and product-line managers or other headquarters personnel.

Negotiations also took place at the same time on products to be discontinued. Mr. Hennessy described this process as a "sophisticated exercise which includes a careful analysis of the effect on overhead costs of discontinuing a product and also recognizes the cost of holding an item in stock. It is a good analysis and one method Universal uses to keep the squeeze on us."

During May, the negotiated objectives were reviewed and approved by Universal's European headquarters in Geneva and by corporate headquarters in the United States. These final reviews focused primarily on the five key measures noted above. In 1976, the objectives for total capital expenditures and for the total number of employees received particularly close surveillance. The approved objectives provided the foundation for preparation of Business Plans.

In June and July, Galvor prepared its Business Plan. The plan, containing up to 100 pages, described in detail how Galvor intended to achieve its objectives for the following two years. The plan also contained a forecast, in less detail, for the fifth year hence (e.g., for 1981 in the case of the plan prepared in 1976).

Summary Reports

The broad scope of the Business Plan can best be understood by a description of the type of information it contained. It began with a brief one-page financial and operating summary containing comparative data for:

Preceding year (actual data).

Current year (budget).

Next year (forecast).

Two years hence (forecast).

Five years hence (forecast).

This one-page summary contained condensed data dealing with the following measures for each of the five years:

Net income.

Sales.

Total assets.

Total capital employed (sum of long-term debt and net worth).

Receivables.

Inventories.

Plant, property, and equipment.

Capital expenditures.

Provision for depreciation.

Percent return on sales.

Percent return on total assets.

Percent return on total capital employed.

Percent total assets to sales.

Percent receivables to sales.

Percent inventories to sales.

Orders received.

Orders on hand.

Average number of full-time employees.

Total cost of employee compensation.

Sales per employee.

Net income per employee.

Sales per $1,000 of employee compensation.

Net income per $1,000 of employee compensation.

Sales per thousand square feet of floor space.

Net income per thousand square feet of floor space.

Anticipated changes in net income for the current year and for each of the next two years were summarized according to their cause, as follows:

Volume of sales.

Product mix.

Sales prices.

Raw material purchase prices.

Cost reduction programs.

Accounting changes and all other causes.

This analysis of the causes of changes in net income forced operating managements to appraise carefully the profit implications of all management actions affecting prices, costs, volume, or product mix.

Financial Statements

These condensed summary reports were followed by a complete set of projected financial statements—income statement, balance sheet, and a statement of cash flow—for the current year and for each of the next two years. Each major item on these financial statements was then analyzed in detail in separate reports, which covered such matters as transactions with headquarters, proposed outside financing, investment in receivables and inventory, number of employees and employee compensation, capital expenditures, and nonrecurring write-offs of assets.

Management Actions

The Business Plan contained a description of the major management actions planned for the next two years, with an estimate of the favorable or unfavorable effect each action would have on total sales, net income, and total assets. Among some of the major management actions described in Galvor's 1976 Business Plan (prepared in mid-1975) were the following:

Implement standard cost system.

Revise prices.

Cut oldest low-margin items from line.

Standardize and simplify product design.

Create forward research and development plan.

Implement product planning.

Separate plans were presented for each of the functional areas—marketing, manufacturing, research and development, financial control, and personnel and employee relations. These functional plans began with a statement of the function's mission, an analysis of its present problems and opportunities, and a statement of the specific actions it intended to take in the next two years. Among the objectives set for the control area in the 1976 Business Plan, M. Barsac stated that he hoped to:

Better distribute tasks.

Make more intensive use of IBM equipment.

Replace nonqualified employees with better-trained and more dynamic people.

The Business Plan closed with a series of comparative financial statements which depicted the estimated item-by-item effect if sales fell to 60 percent or to 80 percent of forecast or increased to 120 percent of forecast. For each of these levels of possible sales, costs were divided into three categories: fixed costs, unavoidable variable costs, and management discretionary costs. Management described the specific actions it would take to control employment, total assets, and capital expenditures in case of a reduction in sales, and when these actions would be put into effect. In its 1976 Business Plan, Galvor indicated that its program for contraction would be put into effect if incoming orders dropped below 60 percent of budget for two weeks, 75 percent for four weeks, or 85 percent for eight weeks. It noted that assets would be cut only 80 percent in a 60 percent year and to 90 percent in an 80 percent year, "because remodernization of our business is too essential for survival to slow down much more."

Approval of Plan

By midsummer, the completed Business Plan was submitted to Universal headquarters; and beginning in the early fall, meetings were held in Geneva to review each company's Business Plan. Each plan had to be justified and defended at these meetings, which were attended by senior executives from both Universal's European and American headquarters and by the general managers and functional managers of many of the operating units. Universal viewed these meetings as an important element in its constant effort to encourage operating managements to share their experiences in resolving common problems.

Before final approval of a company's Business Plan at the Geneva review meeting, changes were often proposed by Universal's top management. For example, in September 1976, the 1977 forecasts of sales and net income in Galvor's Business Plan were accepted; but the year-end forecasts of total employees and total assets were reduced about 9 percent and 1 percent, respectively. Galvor's proposed capital expenditures for the year were cut 34 percent, a reduction primarily attributable to limitations imposed by Universal on all operating units throughout the corporation.

The approved Business Plan became the foundation of the budget for the following year, which was due in Geneva by mid-November. The general design of the budget resembled that of the Business Plan, except that the various dollar amounts, which were presented in the Business Plan on an annual basis, were broken down by months. Minor changes between the overall key results forecast in the Business Plan and those reflected in greater detail in the budget were not permitted. Requests for major changes had to be submitted to Geneva no later than mid-October.

Reporting to Universal

Every Universal unit in Europe had to submit periodic reports to Geneva according to a fixed schedule of dates. All units in Universal, whether based in the United States or elsewhere, adhered to essentially the same reporting system. Identical forms and account numbers were used throughout the Universal organization. Since the reporting system made no distinction between units of different size, Galvor submitted the same reports as a unit with many times its sales. Computer processing of these reports facilitated combining the results of Universal's European operations for prompt review in Geneva and transmission to corporate headquarters in the United States.

The main focus in most of the reports submitted to Universal was on the variance between actual results and budgeted results. Sales and expense data were presented for both the latest month and for the year to date. Differences between the current year and the prior year also were reported, because these were the figures submitted quarterly to Universal's shareholders and to newspapers and other financial reporting services.

Description of Reports

Thirteen different reports were submitted by the controller on a monthly basis, ranging from a statement of preliminary net income, which was due during the first week following the close of each month, to a report on the status of capital projects due on the last day of each month. The monthly reports included:

Statement of preliminary net income.

Statement of income.

Balance sheet.

Statement of changes in retained earnings.

Statement of cash flow.

Employment statistics.

Status of orders received, canceled, and outstanding.

Statement of intercompany transactions.

Statement of transactions with headquarters.

Analysis of inventories.

Analysis of receivables.

Status of capital projects.

Controller's monthly operating and financial review.

The final item, the controller's monthly operating and financial review, often ran to 20 pages or more. It contained an explanation of the significant variances from budget, as well as a general commentary on the financial affairs of the unit.

In addition to the reports submitted on a monthly basis, approximately 12 other reports were required less often, either quarterly, semiannually, or annually.

Cost of the System

The control and reporting system, including preparation of the annual Business Plan, imposed a heavy burden in both time and money on the management of an operating unit. M. Barsac commented on this aspect of the system in the section of Galvor's 1976 Business Plan dealing with the control functional area.

Galvor's previous administrative manager [controller], who was a tax specialist above all, had to prepare a balance sheet and statement of income once a year. Cost accounting, perpetual inventory valuation, inventory control, production control, customer accounts receivable control, budgeting, et cetera did not exist. No information was given to other department heads concerning sales results, costs, and expenses. The change to a formal monthly reporting system has been very difficult to realize. Due to the low level of employee training, many tasks, such as consolidation, monthly and quarterly reports, budgets, the Business Plan, implementation of the new cost system, various analyses, restatement of prior years' accounts, et cetera must be fully performed by the controller and chief accountant, thus spending 80 percent of their full time in spite of working 55–60 hours per week. The number of employees in the controller's department in subsequent years will not depend on Galvor's volume of activity, but rather on Universal's requirements.

Implementation of the complete Universal Cost and Production Control System in a company where nothing existed before is an enormous task, which involves establishing 8,000 machining and 3,000 assembly standard times and codifying 15,000 piece parts.

When interviewed early in 1977, M. Barsac stated:

Getting the data to Universal on time continues to be a problem. We simply don't have the necessary people who understand the reporting system and its purpose. The reports are all in English and few of my people are conversant in English. Also, American accounting methods are different from procedures used in France. Another less serious problem concerns the need to convert all of our internal records, which are kept in francs, to dollars when reporting to Universal.

I am especially concerned that few of the reports we prepare for Universal are useful to our operating people here in Bordeaux. Mr. Hennessy, of course, uses the reports, as do one or two others. I am doing all that I can to encourage greater use of these reports. My job is not only to provide facts but to help the managers understand and utilize the figures available. We have recently started issuing monthly cost and expense reports for each department showing the variances from budget. These have been well received.

Mr. Hennessy also commented on meeting the demands imposed by Universal's reporting system.

Without the need to report to Universal, we would do some things in a less formal way or at different times. Universal decides that the entire organization must move to a certain basis by a specified date. There are extra costs involved in meeting these deadlines. It should be noted, also, that demands made on the controller's department are passed on to other areas, such as marketing, engineering, and production.

M. Boudry, Universal's European controller, acknowledged that the cost of the planning and reporting system was high, especially for smaller units.

The system is designed for a large business. We think that the absolute minimum annual sales volume for an individual unit to support the system is about $15 million; however, we would prefer at least $30 million. By this standard, Galvor is barely acceptable. We really don't know if the cost of the system is unnecessarily burdensome in the sense that it requires information which is not worth its cost. A reasonable estimate might be that about 50 percent of the information would be required in any smartly managed independent business of comparable size, another 25 percent is required for Universal's particular needs, and 25 percent is probably "dead underbrush" which should be cleaned out. Ideally, every five years we should throw the system out the window and start again with the essentials.

As an indication of some of his department's routine activity, M. Barsac noted that at the end of 1976 Galvor was preparing about 200 invoices each working day. At that time the company had approximately 12,000 active customers.

Early in 1977, 42 people were employed in the controller's department. The organization of the department is described in Exhibit 1.

Headquarters Performance Review

Galvor's periodic financial reports were forwarded to M. Boudry in Geneva. The reports were first reviewed by an assistant to M. Boudry, one of four financial analysts who together reviewed all reports received from Universal's operating units in Europe.

In early 1977, M. Boudry described the purpose of these reviews:

The reviews focus on a comparison of performance against budget for the key measures—sales, net income,

Exhibit 1

Organization of controller's department (January 1977)*

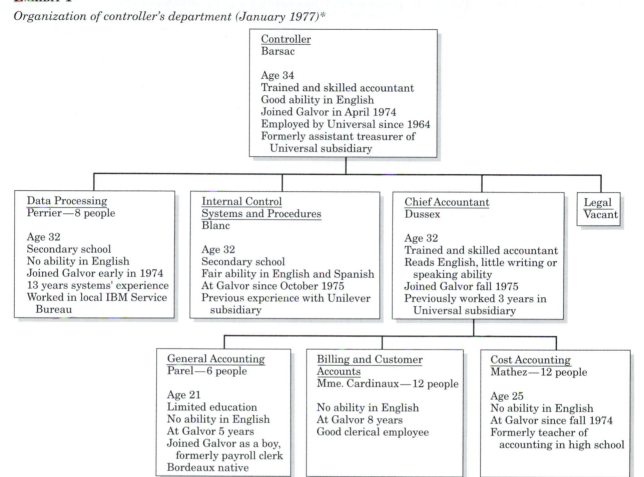

*Immediately prior to Galvor's takeover by Universal Electric, there had been fewer than 20 people in the controller's department.

total assets, total employees, and capital expenditures. These are stated as unambiguous numbers. We try to detect any trouble spots or trends which seem to be developing. Of course, the written portions of the reports are also carefully reviewed, particularly the explanations of variances from budget. If everything is moving as planned, we do nothing.

The reports may contain a month-by-month revision of forecasts to year end; but if the planning objectives for the year are not to be met, we consider the situation serious.

If a unit manager has a problem and calls for help, then it becomes a matter of common concern. He can probably expect a bad day in explaining how it happened, but he can expect help, too. Depending on the nature of the problem, either Mr. Forrester, Galvor's product-line manager, or one of our staff specialists would go down to Bordeaux. In addition to the financial analysts, one of whom closely follows Galvor's reports, we have specialists on cost systems and analysis, inventory control, credit, and industrial engineering.

We have not given Galvor the help it needs and deserves in data processing, but we have a limited staff here in Geneva and we cannot meet all needs. We hope to increase this staff during 1977.

Exhibit 2   Telex from Poulet to Hennessy, Concerning Level of Inventory

TO: HENNESSY—GALVOR
FROM: POULET—UE
DATE: SEPTEMBER 26, 1976

FOLLOWING ARE THE JULY AND AUGUST INVENTORY AND SALES FIGURES WITH THEIR RESPECTIVE VARIANCES FROM BUDGET ($000s).

	ACTUAL	JULY BUDGET	VARIANCE	ACTUAL	AUGUST BUDGET	VARIANCE
INVENTORY	2,010	1,580	(430)	2,060	1,600	(460)
SALES TO DATE	3,850	3,900	(50)	4,090	4,150	(60)

LATEST AUGUST SALES FORECAST REFLECTS DECREASE IN YEAR-END SALES OF 227 VERSUS INCREASE OF 168 IN YEAR-END INVENTORIES OVER BUDGET.

REQUEST TELEX LATEST MONTH-BY-MONTH INVENTORY AND SALES FORECAST FROM SEPTEMBER TO DECEMBER, EXPLANATION OF VARIANCE IN INVENTORY FROM BUDGET AND CORRECTIVE ACTION YOU PLAN IN ORDER TO ACHIEVE YEAR-END GOAL. INCLUDE PERSONNEL REDUCTIONS, PURCHASE MATERIAL CANCELLATIONS, ETC.

POULET

With reference to Galvor's recent performance, M. Boudry states:

Galvor is small and we don't give it much time or help unless its variances appear to be off. This happened in the second half of 1976, when we became increasingly concerned about the level of Galvor's inventories. A series of telexes on this matter between Mr. Hennessy and M. Poulet, our director of manufacturing here in Geneva, illustrate how the reports are used. [See Exhibits 2 through 5.]

We feel the situation is under control and the outlook for Galvor is OK despite the flat performance between 1973–75 and the downturn in 1976. The company has been turned about and 1977 looks promising.

Although the comprehensive reporting and control system made it appear that Universal was a highly centralized organization, the managements of the various operating units had considerable autonomy. For example, Mr. Hennessy, who was judged only on Galvor's performance, was free to purchase components from other Universal units or from outside sources. There were no preferred "in-house"

prices. A slight incentive was offered by Universal to encourage such transactions by not levying certain headquarters fees, amounting to about 2 percent of sales, against the selling unit.

Similarly, Universal made no attempt to shift its taxable income to low-tax countries. Each unit was viewed as though it were an independent company subject to local taxation and regulation. Universal believed that this goal of maximizing profits for the individual units would in turn maximize Universal's profits. Forcing every unit to maximize its profits precluded the use of arbitrary transfer prices for "in-house" transactions.

Recent Developments at Galvor

A standard cost system, which included development and tooling costs as well as manufacturing and assembly, had been in effect since March 1976.

According to Mr. Hennessy:

Exhibit 3   Telex from Hennessy to Poulet Concerning Level of Inventory

TO: POULET—UE
FROM: HENNESSY—GALVOR
DATE: SEPTEMBER 27, 1976
YOUR 26.9.76
MONTHLY INVENTORY FORECAST SEPTEMBER TO DECEMBER BY CATEGORY AS FOLLOWS ($000s):

	SEPT. 30	*OCT. 31*	*NOV. 30*	*DEC. 31*
RAW MATERIALS	53	51	50	50
PURCHASED PARTS	180	185	190	195
MANUFACTURED PARTS	95	93	93	91
WORK-IN-PROCESS	838	725	709	599
FINISHED GOODS	632	694	683	705
OTHER INVENTORIES	84	84	82	80
ENGINEERING IN PROCESS	55	58	48	44
RESERVE	(14)	(14)	(14)	(20)
INDICA	50	52	55	55
TOTAL	1,973	1,928	1,896	1,799

THE MAIN EXPLANATIONS OF PRESENT VARIANCE ARE THREE POLICIES ADOPTED END OF 1975 AND DISCUSSED IN MONTHLY LETTERS BUT WHICH LEFT DECEMBER 1976 BUDGET OPTIMISTICALLY LOW. FIRST WAS TO HAVE REASONABLE AMOUNTS OF SELLING MODELS IN STOCK WITHOUT WHICH WE COULD NOT HAVE ACHIEVED 19 PERCENT INCREASE IN SALES WE ARE MAKING WITH OUTMODED PRODUCT.

SECOND POLICY WAS TO MANUFACTURE LONGER SERIES OF EACH MODEL BY DOUBLE WHEREVER SALES WOULD ABSORB IT, OTHERWISE MANY OF OUR COST REDUCTIONS WERE NEARLY ZERO. THIS MEANS OUR MANUFACTURING PROGRAM ANY MONTH MAY CONTAIN FIVE MONTHS' WORTH OF 15 MODELS INSTEAD OF 10 WEEKS' WORTH OF 30 MODELS (OUT OF 70). THIRD WAS NEW POLICY OF REDUCING NUMBER OF PURCHASE ORDERS BY MAINTAINING A MINIMUM STOCK OF MANY THOUSANDS OF LOW-VALUE ITEMS WHICH YOU AGREED WOULD AND DID INCREASE STOCK UPON FIRST PROCUREMENT BUT WE ARE ALREADY GETTING SLIGHT REDUCTION. CORRECTIVE ACTIONS NUMEROUS INCLUDING RUNNING 55 PEOPLE UNDER BUDGET AND ABOUT 63 BY YEAR END PLUS REVIEWING ALL PURCHASE ORDERS MYSELF PLUS SLIDING A FEW SERIES OF MODELS WHICH WOULD HAVE GIVEN SMALL BILLING IN 1976 INTO 1977 PLUS THOSE POSTPONED BY CUSTOMERS. THIS WILL NOT HAVE DRAMATIC EFFECT AS NEARLY ALL THESE SERIES ARE PROCURED AND HAVE TO BE MADE FOR RELATIVELY SURE MARKETS BUT SOME CAN BE HELD IN PIECEPARTS UNTIL JANUARY. WE ARE WATCHING CAREFULLY STOCKS OF SLOW MOVING MODELS AND HAVE MUCH CLEANER FINISHED STOCK THAN END 1975.

FINAL AND GRAVE CONCERN IS ACCURACY OF PARTS, WORK-IN-PROCESS, AND FINISHED GOODS-VALUATION SINCE WE BEGAN STANDARD COST SYSTEM. INTERIM INVENTORY COUNT PLUS VARIANCES VALUED ON PUNCH CARDS STILL DOESN'T CHECK WITH MONTHLY BALANCE USING CONSERVATIVE GROSS MARGINS, BUT NEARLY ALL GAPS OCCURRED FIRST FOUR MONTHS OF SYSTEM WHEN ERRORS NUMEROUS AND LAST 4 MONTHS NEARLY CHECK AS WE CONTINUE REFINING. EXTENSIVE RECHECKS UNDERWAY IN PARTS, WORK-IN-PROCESS, AND FINISHED GOODS AND CORRECTIONS BEING FOUND DAILY.

YOUR INVENTORY STAFF SPECIALISTS ARE AWARE OF PROBLEM AND PROMISED TO HELP WHEN OTHER PRIORITIES PERMIT. WILL KEEP THEM INFORMED OF EXPOSURE WHICH STARTED WITH RECORDING ALL PARTS AND BEGINNING NEW BALANCES WITH NEW STANDARDS AND APPEARS CLOSELY RELATED TO ERRORS IN THESE OPERATIONS. WE CAN ONLY PURGE PROGRESSIVELY WITHOUT HIRING SUBSTANTIAL INDIRECT WORKERS.

HENNESSY

Exhibit 4   Telex from Poulet to Hennessy Concerning Level of Inventory
---

TO   HENNESSY—GALVOR

FROM: POULET—UE

DATE: NOV. 10, 1976

SEPTEMBER INVENTORY INCREASED AGAIN BY 64,000 COMPARED TO AUGUST WHILE SEPTEMBER SALES WERE 145,000 UNDER BUDGET REFERRING TO YOUR LATEST TELEX OF SEPTEMBER 27 IN WHICH YOU HAVE A BREAKDOWN OF THE SEPTEMBER FORECAST. REQUEST DETAILED EXPLANATION FOR NOT MEETING THIS FORECAST IN SPITE OF YOUR CURRENT CORRECTIVE ACTIONS.

SEPTEMBER	*YOUR FORECAST*	*ACTUAL*	*VARIANCE*
RAW MATERIALS	53	96	(43)
PURCHASED PARTS	180	155	25
MANUFACTURED PARTS	95	108	(13)
WORK-IN-PROCESS	838	917	(79)
FINISHED GOODS	632	723	(91)
OTHER INVENTORIES	84	87	(3)
ENGINEERING IN PROCESS	55	52	3
RESERVE	(14)	(14)	—
INDICA	50	51	(1)
TOTAL NET	1,973	2,175	(202)

IN ORDER TO MEET YOUR DECEMBER FORECAST OF 1,799 YOUR WORK-IN-PROCESS HAS TO BE REDUCED BY 318. THIS MEANS A REDUCTION OF ABOUT 100 PER MONTH FROM SEPTEMBER 30 TO DECEMBER 31. THEREFORE, I ALSO WOULD LIKE ACTUAL ACHIEVEMENTS AND FURTHER REDUCTION PLANS DURING OCTOBER, NOVEMBER, AND DECEMBER CONCERNING THE POINTS MENTIONED IN YOUR SAME TELEX OF SEPTEMBER 27. CONSIDER AGGRESSIVE ACTIONS IN THE FOLLOWING SPECIFIC AREAS:

1. REALISTIC MASTER PRODUCTION SCHEDULES.
2. SHORT-TERM PHYSICAL SHORTAGE CONTROL TO ENSURE SHIPMENTS.
3. WORK-IN-PROCESS ANALYSIS OF ALL ORDERS TO ACHIEVE MAXIMUM SALABLE OUTPUT.
4. MANPOWER REDUCTION.
5. ELIMINATION OF ALL UNSCHEDULED VENDOR RECEIPTS. HAVE YOU ADVISED OTHER UNIVERSAL HOUSES NOT TO SHIP IN ADVANCE OF YOUR SCHEDULE UNLESS AUTHORIZED?
6. ADVISE FULL DETAILS ON ALL CURRENT SHORTAGES FROM OTHER UNIVERSAL HOUSES WHICH ARE RESPONSIBLE FOR INVENTORY BUILD-UP.

POULET

EXHIBIT 5   Telex from Hennessy to Poulet Concerning Level of Inventory

```
TO:      POULET—UE
FROM:    HENNESSY—GALVOR
DATE:    NOV. 15, 1976
         YOUR 10.11.76
```

WE NOW HAVE OCTOBER 31 FIGURES. OUR ACTUAL ACHIEVEMENTS FOLLOW: RAW MATERIALS 54 VARIANCE PLUS 3, PURCHASED PARTS 173 VARIANCE MINUS 12, MANUFACTURED PARTS 110 VARIANCE PLUS 17, WORK-IN-PROCESS 949 VARIANCE PLUS 224, FINISHED GOODS 712 VARIANCE PLUS 18, OTHER 82 VARIANCE MINUS 2, ENGINEERING 54 VARIANCE MINUS 4, RESERVE MINUS 14 VARIANCE NIL, INDICA 55 VARIANCE PLUS 3, TOTAL 2,175 VARIANCE PLUS 247. EACH ITEM BEING CONTROLLED AND THE ONLY SIGNIFICANT VARIANCES 224 WORK-IN-PROCESS AND 18 FINISHED GOODS ARE MY DECISION UPON SALES DECLINE OF SEPTEMBER AND OCTOBER OF 311 TO DELAY COMPLETION OF SEVERAL SERIES IN MANUFACTURE IN FAVOR OF ANOTHER GROUP OF SERIES, MOSTLY GOVERNMENT, WHICH ARE LARGELY BILLABLE IN 1976 IN ORDER TO PARTLY REGAIN SALES. LAST EIGHT DAYS' ORDERS AND THEREFORE SALES ARE SHARPLY UP AND NONE OF THIS WORK-IN-PROCESS WILL BE ON HAND MORE THAN 3 TO 6 WEEKS LONGER THAN WE PLANNED.

NEVERTHELESS YOU SHOULD BE AWARE WE MANUFACTURE 4 TO 8 MONTHS WORTH OF MANY LOW-VOLUME MODELS. AN EXAMPLE OF HOW WE DETERMINE ECONOMIC SERIES WAS FURNISHED YOUR STAFF SPECIALIST THIS WEEK. WE CANNOT MAKE SIGNIFICANT COST REDUCTIONS IN A BUSINESS WHERE AT LEAST 70 OF 200 MODELS HAVE TO BE ON SHELF TO SELL AND TYPICAL MODEL SELLS 15 UNITS MONTHLY. REGARDING YOUR 5 SUGGESTIONS AND TWO QUESTIONS ARE CARRYING OUT ALL 5 POINTS AGGRESSIVELY AND HAVE NO INTERHOUSE SHORTAGES OR OVERSHIPMENTS.

HENNESSY

We had hoped to start in January, but we were delayed. On the basis of our experience in 1976, all standards were reviewed and, where necessary, they were revised in December. We now have a history of development and tooling experience, which we have been accumulating since 1975. This has proved extremely useful in setting cost standards. Simultaneously, we have integrated market and sales forecasts more effectively into our pricing decisions.

Before Universal acquired Galvor, a single companywide rate was used to allocate factory overhead to the costs of products. For many years this rate was 310 percent of direct labor. In a discussion of his pricing policies in 1972, Mr. Latour said: "I have been using this 310 percent for many years and it seems to work out pretty well, so I see no reason to change it."

M. Chambertin had long argued that the less-complex products were being unfairly burdened by the use of a single overhead rate, while electronic products should bear more.

Mr. Latour's response to this argument was:

I have suspected that our electric products are too high priced, and our electronic products are too low priced. So what does this mean? Why should we lower our prices for multimeters and galvanos? At our current prices, we can easily sell our entire production of electric products.

M. Chambertin remained convinced that eventually Galvor would be forced by competitive pressures to allocate its costs more realistically.

In 1976, as part of the new standard cost system, Galvor did indeed refine the procedure for allocating overhead costs to products. Fifteen different cost centers were established, each with a separate burden rate. These rates, which combined direct labor cost and overhead, ranged from 13.19 francs to 38.62 francs per direct labor hour.

Concluding his comments about recent developments, Mr. Hennessy said:

> A formal inventory control system went into effect in January 1977. This, together with the standard cost system, allows us for the first time to really determine the relative profitability of various products, and to place a proper valuation on our inventory.
>
> We are installing a new computer in February, which we will use initially for customer billing and for marketing analysis. We hope this will reduce the number of people required in our customer billing and accounts receivable operations from 12 to 6 or 7.

Questions

1. What is your overall assessment of the effectiveness of Universal Electric's (UE's) planning system as it is applied to Galvor?

2. Identify, in as much detail as possible, all of the new management systems and techniques that UE has required Galvor to establish. In particular, trace the various steps Galvor goes through in preparing its long-range as well as annual plans.

3. What is your evaluation of the effectiveness of the working relationships between Hennessy and the UE executives in Geneva? What do you infer from the telexes about Hennessy's autonomy as a managing director? (Note: You might want to give the telexes a careful and critical reading.)

4. Look at the system from Galvor's viewpoint. Suppose Galvor were an independent company (i.e., not part of Universal Electric). If you were a consultant to Galvor, how would the management planning and control practices you would recommend for the company differ from those that have been imposed by UE? (Please answer this as completely and specifically as you can, going beyond the response "they would be less detailed and less formal," for example.)

5. Look at the system from UE's viewpoint. How (if at all) can UE's imposing planning and control practices different from those required by an independent Galvor be justified? (Again, please try to be specific.)

6. To what extent should a large international organization, such as UE, rely on a comprehensive system of financial reporting and control to achieve its strategic objectives?

7. What specific changes, if any, would you make in UE's planning systems? In its other management systems? If the management processes need improving, how would you change them?

PERFORMANCE MEASUREMENT

In Chapter 9 we described a report that measures actual financial performance compared with budgeted financial performance. This is one type of performance measurement. But financial performance, although important, is only one aspect of an organization's performance. In this chapter we describe other aspects.

In the first part of the chapter, we discuss *performance measurement systems,* which blend financial information with nonfinancial information. The objective of performance measurement systems is to help implement strategy. In the next part of the chapter we discuss *interactive control*—the use of a subset of management control information in developing new strategies.

Performance Measurement Systems

The goal of performance measurement systems is to implement strategy. In setting up such systems, senior management selects measures that best represent the company's strategy. These measures can be seen as current and future critical success factors; if they are improved, the company has implemented its strategy. The strategy's success depends on its soundness. A performance measurement system is simply a mechanism that improves the likelihood the organization will implement its strategy successfully.

Exhibit 10–1 gives the framework for designing a performance measurement system. Strategy defines the critical success factors; if those factors are measured and rewarded, people are motivated to achieve them.

Limitations of Financial Control Systems

An important goal of a business enterprise is to optimize shareholder returns. However, optimizing short-term profitability does not necessarily ensure optimum shareholder returns since shareholder value represents the net present value of expected future earnings. At the same time, the need for ongoing

Exhibit 10–1

Framework for designing performance measurement systems

Source: This chart was suggested by Craig Schneir.

feedback and management control requires companies to measure and evaluate business unit performance at least once a year. In Chapters 3 to 6, we discussed management considerations involved in measuring *financial responsibility* (costs, revenues, profits, EVA) to organizational subunits. However, relying *solely* on financial measures is inadequate and can, in fact, be dysfunctional for several reasons.

First, it may encourage short-term actions that are not in the company's long-term interests. The more pressure that is applied to meet current profit levels, the more likely the business unit manager will be to take short-term actions that may be wrong in the long run. To illustrate, the manager may deliver inferior-quality products to customers to meet sales targets, and this will adversely affect customer goodwill and future sales. These are errors of *commission.*

> **Example.**   Some divisional presidents in Bausch & Lomb, under pressure to produce bottom-line results, began using tactics that were costly for the company in the long term but which maximized their short-term bonuses. One favorite tactic was extending unusually long credit terms to customers in exchange for big orders.[1]

Second, business unit managers may not undertake useful long-term actions, in order to obtain short-term profits. For instance, managers may not make investments that promise long-term benefits because they hurt short-term financial results. A common example is managers' investing inadequate dollars in research and development; R&D investments must be expensed in the year in which they are incurred but their benefits show up only in the future. Again, managers may not propose risky investments—investments

---

[1]Joyce Barnathan, "Blind Ambition," *Business Week,* October 23, 1995, pp. 78–92.

about whose future cash flows there is a great deal of uncertainty—because cash flow uncertainty reduces the probability of meeting short-term financial targets. In other words, managers may propose "safe" investments (which are quite likely to produce adequate future cash flows) instead of high-risk projects that may produce high returns. These are errors of *omission*.

Third, using short-term profit as the sole objective can distort communication between a business unit manager and senior management. If business unit managers are evaluated based on their profit budget, they may try to set profit targets they can easily meet, leading to erroneous planning data for the whole company because the budgeted profit may be lower than the amount that could really be achieved. Also, business unit managers may be reluctant to admit during the year that they are likely to miss their profit budget until it is evident that they cannot possibly attain it. This delays corrective action.

Fourth, tight financial control may motivate managers to manipulate data. This can take several forms. At one level, managers may choose accounting methods that borrow from future earnings to meet current period targets (e.g., by making inadequate provision for bad debts, inventory shrinkage, and warranty claims). At another level, managers may falsify data—that is, deliberately provide inaccurate information.

> **Example.**   Tight financial controls led to data manipulation at Bausch & Lomb, according to *Business Week:* "Under pressure to beat sales targets in 1993, contact lens managers shipped products that doctors never ordered and forced distributors to take up to two years of unwanted inventories . . . , while assuring many [distributors] they wouldn't have to pay until they sold the lenses."[2]

In sum, relying on financial measures alone is insufficient to ensure strategy will be executed successfully. The solution is to measure and evaluate business unit managers using multiple measures, nonfinancial as well as financial. We refer to nonfinancial measures that support strategy implementation as *key success factors* or *key performance indicators*.

Companies used financial and nonfinancial measures in the past. However, they tended to use nonfinancial measures at lower levels in the organization for task control and financial measures at higher organizational levels for management control. A blend of financial and nonfinancial measurements is, in fact, needed at all levels in the organization. It is important for senior executives to track not only financial measures, which indicate the results of past decisions, but also nonfinancial measures, which are leading indicators of future performance. Similarly, employees at lower levels need to understand the financial impact of their operating decisions.

General Considerations

Comparing performance measurement systems to an instrument panel on a dashboard provides important insights about the mix of financial and

---

[2]Ibid.

nonfinancial measures needed in a management control system: A single measure cannot control a complex system; and too many critical measures make the system uncontrollably complex. Expanding the analogy will clarify this.

A performance measurement system—like a dashboard—has a series of measures that provide information about the operation of many different processes. Some of these measures tell the driver (or the manager) what *has* happened—the odometer that registers the passage of 40,000 miles (or a report that shareholder equity is currently $1 billion), for instance. Other measures tell the driver (or the manager) what *is* happening, such as the tachometer at 6,000 RPM (or an on-time-delivery percentage of 70). All these measures have implicit interactions, and changes in one often reflect changes in another: reducing RPMs will increase miles per gallon (or improving on-time delivery will increase customer satisfaction).

Usually, there are multiple ways to change one measure, let us say RPM, that may or may not improve the other measure, in this case miles per gallon. Being aware of the series of measures on a dashboard allows a driver to make the necessary trade-offs, such as running the car at 6,500 RPM in second gear instead of shifting to fifth gear (at the cost of gas consumption) because shifting would take extra time—with some other consequences, perhaps, that may or may not be ignored. By making trade-offs, a manager too can choose between behavior that benefits the short- or long-term success of the organization.

The Balanced Scorecard

The balanced scorecard is an example of a performance measurement system. According to proponents of this approach, business units should be assigned goals and then measured from the following four perspectives:[3]

- Financial (e.g., profit margins, return on assets, cash flow).
- Customer (e.g., market share, customer satisfaction index).
- Internal business (e.g., employee retention, cycle time reduction).
- Innovation and learning (e.g., percentage of sales from new products).

The balanced scorecard fosters a balance among different strategic measures in an effort to achieve goal congruence, thus encouraging employees to act in the organization's best interest. It is a tool that helps the company's focus, improves communication, sets organizational objectives, and provides feedback on strategy.

Every measure on a balanced scorecard addresses an aspect of a company's strategy. In creating the balanced scorecard, executives must choose a mix of measurements that (1) accurately reflect the critical factors that will

---

[3]Robert S. Kaplan and David P. Norton, *Balanced Scorecard* (Boston: Harvard Business School Press, 1996).

determine the success of the company's strategy; (2) show the relationships among the individual measures in a cause-and-effect manner, indicating how nonfinancial measures affect long-term financial results; and (3) provide a broad-based view of the current status of the company.

Performance measurement systems have been discussed in this and other texts for many years. The balanced scorecard is an example of "old wine in a new bottle." The ideas are essentially the same as performance measurement systems but are repackaged under a new label.

Performance Measurement Systems: Additional Considerations

A performance measurement system attempts to address the needs of the different stakeholders of the organization by creating a blend of strategic measures: outcome and driver measures, financial and nonfinancial measures, and internal and external measures.

Outcome and Driver Measures.   *Outcome* measurements indicate the result of a strategy (e.g., increased revenue). These measures typically are "lagging indicators"; they tell management what has happened. By contrast, *driver* measures are "leading indicators"; they show the progress of key areas in implementing a strategy. Cycle time is an example of a driver. Whereas outcome measures indicate only the final result, driver measures can be used at a lower level and indicate incremental changes that will ultimately affect the outcome.

By focusing management attention on key aspects of the business, driver measures affect behavior in the organization. If a business unit's desire is to improve time-to-market, focusing on cycle time allows management to track how well this goal is being achieved, which, in turn, encourages employees to improve this particular measure.

Outcome and driver measures are inextricably linked. If outcome measures indicate there is a problem but the driver measures indicate the strategy is being implemented well, there is a high chance that the strategy needs to be changed.

Financial and Nonfinancial Measures.   Organizations have developed very sophisticated systems to measure financial performance. Unfortunately, as many US firms discovered, during the 1980s industries were being driven by changes in nonfinancial areas, such as quality and customer satisfaction, that eventually impacted companies' financial performance.

> **Example.**   By every financial measure during the 1970s, Pan Am Airlines, US Steel, Xerox, and IBM dominated their markets. Yet, by the mid-1980s, their positions were under serious attack by competitors who achieved higher quality, higher customer satisfaction, higher levels of innovation, and better business models. These could not be measured by financial means until it was too late.

Even though they recognize the importance of nonfinancial measures, many organizations have failed to incorporate them into their executive-level performance reviews because these measures tend to be much less sophisticated than financial measures and senior management is less adept at using them.

Internal and External Measures.   Companies must strike a balance between external measures, such as customer satisfaction, and measures of internal business processes, such as manufacturing yields. Too often companies sacrifice internal development for external results or ignore external results altogether, mistakenly believing that good internal measures are sufficient.

> **Example.**   One of the early adopters of the corporate scorecard discovered that although all of the internal measures indicated the company's performance had dramatically improved (defects were reduced by tenfold and on-time delivery had jumped from the 50 percent range into the 90 percent range), its financial performance and stock prices were stagnant. Rather than acting on both signals, the company chose to continue to act on the internal measures alone for almost four years. During this entire time, the firm's external measures were indicating the strategy was not working, yet they continued it. The company's financial results finally turned around after it changed strategies in response to the prolonged poor external measures.

Measurements Drive Change.   The most important aspect of the performance measurement system is its ability to measure outcomes and drivers in a way that causes the organization to act in accordance with its strategies. The organization achieves goal congruence by linking overall financial and strategic objectives with lower-level objectives that can be observed and affected at different organizational levels. With these measures, all employees can understand how their actions impact the company's strategies.

Because these measures are explicitly tied to an organization's strategies, the measures in the scorecard must be strategy-specific and therefore organization-specific. While a generic performance measurement framework exists, there is no such thing as a generic scorecard.

The scorecard measures are linked from top to bottom and tied to specific targets throughout the entire organization. Objectives can further clarify a strategy so that the organization knows both what it needs to do and how much must be done.

Finally, the scorecard emphasizes the idea of cause-and-effect relationships among measures. By explicitly presenting the cause-and-effect relationship, an organization will understand how nonfinancial measures (e.g., product quality) drive financial measures (e.g., revenue). Exhibit 10–2 presents an example of how the measures link to each other in a cause-and-effect relationship. Better selection, training, and development of manufacturing employees (measured in terms of "manufacturing skills") lead to better product quality (measured in terms of "first-pass yields") and better on-time delivery

EXHIBIT 10–2

Cause–effect relationships among measures

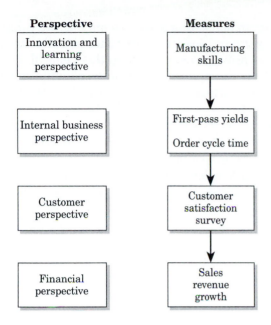

Perspective	Measures
Innovation and learning perspective	Manufacturing skills
Internal business perspective	First-pass yields / Order cycle time
Customer perspective	Customer satisfaction survey
Financial perspective	Sales revenue growth

(measured in terms of "order cycle time"). These improvements, in turn, lead to improved customer loyalty (measured through "customer satisfaction surveys") which leads to enhanced sales (measured in terms of "sales growth").

The scorecard must not simply be a laundry list of measures. Rather, the individual measures in the scorecard must be linked together explicitly in a cause–effect way, as a tool to translate strategy into action.

The better these relationships are understood, the more readily each individual in the organization will be able to contribute directly and clearly to the success of the organization's strategies.

Key Success Factors

In Chapters 3, 4, 5, and 6, we described several financial measures. Here we discuss several nonfinancial measures, also referred to as *key success factors*. We emphasize that fewer key variables are selected for a given business unit than the number of items discussed below.

Customer-Focused Key Variables.   The following key variables focus on the customer:

- *Bookings.* In most business units, some aspect of sales volume is a key variable. Ideally, this is sales orders booked, since unexpected changes in this variable can have future repercussions throughout the business. Because bookings precede sales revenue, this is a better indicator than sales revenue itself. A decrease in this variable signals that adjustments to marketing activities may be warranted—in the hope of increasing sales or production activities or both—to change operating levels. There are many variations in this general idea. In magazine publishing, for example, the percentage of expiring subscriptions that renew is a key variable; a decrease indicates something is wrong with promotional efforts or the contents of the magazine. In restaurants, it is the number of meals served adjusted for the day of the week, season of the year, the weather, and possibly other factors.

- *Back orders.* An indication of an imbalance between sales and production, back orders can suggest customer dissatisfaction.
- *Market share.* Unless the market share is watched closely, a deterioration in the unit's competitive position can be obscured by reported increases in sales volume that result from overall industry growth.
- *Key account orders.* In business units that sell to retailers, the orders received from certain important accounts—large department stores, discount chains, supermarkets, mail-order houses—may indicate early the entire marketing strategy's success.
- *Customer satisfaction.* This can be measured by customer surveys, "mystery shopper" approaches, and number of complaint letters.
- *Customer retention.* This can be measured by the lengths of customer relationships.
- *Customer loyalty.* This can be measured in terms of repeat purchases, customer referrals, and sales to the customer as a percentage of the customer's total requirements for the same product or service.

Key Variables Related to Internal Business Processes.   The following key variables relate to internal business processes:

- *Capacity utilization.* Capacity utilization rates are especially important in businesses in which fixed costs are high (e.g., paper, steel, aluminum manufacture). Similarly, in a professional organization, the percentage of the total available professional hours that is billed to clients—*sold time*—is a measure of fixed-resource utilization. In a hotel, the percentage of rooms occupied each day—*occupancy rate*—is the capacity utilization measure.
- *On-time delivery.*
- *Inventory turnover.*
- *Quality.* Indicators of quality include the number of defective units delivered by each supplier, number and frequency of late deliveries, number of parts in a product, percentage of common versus unique parts in a product, percentage yields, first-pass yields (i.e., percentage of units furnished without rework), scrap, rework, machine

breakdowns, number and frequency of times production and delivery schedules were not met, number of employee suggestions, number of customer complaints, level of customer satisfaction, warranty claims, field service expenses, number and frequency of product returns, and so on.

- *Cycle time.* This equation for cycle time is a tool used to analyze inventory requirements:

$$\text{Cycle time} = \text{Processing time} + \text{Storage time} + \text{Movement time} + \text{Inspection time}$$

Only the first element, processing time, adds value to the product. The other three elements do nothing to make the product more valuable. The analysis, therefore, attempts to identify all activities that do not directly add value to the product and to eliminate, or reduce the cost of, these activities. For example, transporting in-process work from one workstation to another does not add value, so an effort is made to rearrange the location of workstations to minimize transportation costs.

A just-in-time system focuses management attention on *time* in addition to the traditional focus on *cost*. Reducing cycle time can lead to a reduction in cost. One of the effective ways to monitor progress on just-in-time is to compute the following ratio:

$$\frac{\text{Process time}}{\text{Cycle time}}$$

Ideally, the goal for this ratio should be equal to 1, but it cannot be achieved overnight. The just-in-time system is not a turnkey installation; rather, it is an evolutionary system that seeks to continually improve the manufacturing process. The firm can establish targets for this ratio, monitoring progress against the targets. Best results can be obtained by emphasizing continuous improvements in this ratio toward the ideal number of 1.

The Appendix to this chapter contains descriptions of the performance measurement systems at Dell Computer and Sears.

Implementing a Performance Measurement System

Implementation of a performance measurement system involves four general steps:

1. Define strategy.
2. Define measures of strategy.
3. Integrate measures into the management system.
4. Review measures and results frequently.

Each of these steps is iterative, requiring the participation of senior executives and employees throughout the organization. Though the controller may be responsible for overseeing its development, it is a task for the entire management team.

Define Strategy.   The scorecard builds a link between strategy and operational action. Therefore, the process of defining a scorecard begins by defining the organization's strategy. In this phase, it is important that the organization's goals are explicit and that targets have been developed.

For a single industry firm (e.g., Analog Devices, Maytag, Wrigley), the scorecard should be developed at the corporate level and then cascaded down to functional levels and below. However, for a multibusiness firm (e.g., General Electric, Du Pont, Corning Glass Works), the scorecard should be developed at the business unit level. It is important that functional departments within a business unit have their own scorecards, and that the business-unit scorecard and the scorecards below that level be aligned. As a final step, for a multibusiness-unit organization, a corporatewide scorecard should be developed to address, among other things, synergies across business units.

Define Measures of Strategy.   The next step is to develop measures to support the articulated strategy. The organization must focus on a few critical measures at this point or management will be overloaded with measures (too many gauges on the "dashboard," to recall our analogy). Also, it is important that the individual measures be linked with each other in a cause–effect manner, as we discussed and as Exhibit 10–2 illustrated.

Integrate Measures into the Management System.   The scorecard must be integrated with the organization's formal and informal structures, culture, and human resource practices. For instance, the effectiveness of the scorecard will be compromised if managers' compensation is based only on financial performance.

Review Measures and Results Frequently.   Once the scorecard is up and running, it must be consistently and continually reviewed by senior management. The organization should look for the following:

- How is the organization doing according to the outcome measures?
- How is the organization doing according to the driver measures?
- How has the organization's strategy changed since the last review?
- How have the scorecard measures changed?

The most important aspects of these reviews are as follows:

- They tell management whether the strategy is being implemented correctly and how successfully it is working.

- They show that management is serious about the importance of these measures.
- They keep measures aligned to ever-changing strategies.
- They improve measurement.

These review sessions complete the four steps and provide the impetus to start the cycle again.

Difficulties in Implementing Performance Measurement Systems

Unless the following problems are suitably dealt with, they could limit the usefulness of the performance measurement system.

Poor Correlation between Nonfinancial Measures and Results.   Simply put, there is no guarantee that future profitability will follow target achievements in any nonfinancial area. This is a serious problem since there is an inherent assumption that future profitability does follow from achieving individual measures. Identifying the cause–effect relationships among the different measures (as illustrated in Exhibit 10–2) is easier said than done.

This is a problem when we try to develop proxy measures for future performance. While it does not mean that systems with several measures should be abandoned, it is important for companies to understand that the links between nonfinancial measures and financial performance are not well understood.

> **Example.**   In its 1991 annual report, Whirlpool announced that it had established objectives and measures to track progress toward performance goals in four areas in which it felt it must perform well in order to create an ROE of 18 percent a year. Between 1991 and 1995, Whirlpool did not achieve an ROE above 13.9 percent, averaging only 11.9 percent. This was less than their average ROE of 12.1 percent for the previous five years, from 1986 to 1990.

Fixation on Financial Results.   As previously discussed, not only are most senior managers well trained and adept with financial measures, they also keenly feel pressure regarding the financial performance of their companies. Shareholders are vocal, and boards of directors frequently apply pressure on the shareholders' behalf. This pressure may overwhelm the long-term, uncertain payback of the nonfinancial measures.

Poorly designed incentive programs create additional pressure. Senior managers most often are compensated for financial performance. This can disrupt goal congruence, causing managers to be more concerned about financial measures than any other measure. Even companies that have tied rewards to multiple measures may have a disproportionate bias toward financial performance.

Example. Cigna Insurance Company's Property and Casualty Division tied its scorecard to bonuses. Of the four categories in the scorecard, financials had the largest impact, counting for a full one-half of the bonus.[4]

Measures Are Not Updated. Many companies do not have a formal mechanism for updating the measures to align with changes in strategy. As a result, the companies continue to use measures based on yesterday's strategy. Additionally, measures often build up inertia, particularly as people get comfortable using them.

Measurement Overload. How many critical measures can one manager track at one time without losing focus? There is no right answer to this question, except to say that it is more than one and less than fifty! If the number is too few, the manager is ignoring measures that are critical to monitoring strategy execution. If there are too many measures, the manager may risk losing focus in trying to do too many things at once.

Difficulty in Establishing Trade-Offs. Some companies combine financial and nonfinancial measures into a single report and give weights to the individual measures. But most scorecards do not assign explicit weights across measures. Without such weights, it becomes difficult to establish trade-offs between financial and nonfinancial measures.

Measurement Practices

The results of the Lingle and Schiemann study (see Exhibit 10–3) provide insights into what companies are actually measuring, the perceived quality of these measures, and which measures are being linked to compensation.

Types of Measures. The Lingle and Schiemann study found that 76 percent of the responding companies included financial, operating, and customer satisfaction measures in regular management reviews, but only 33 percent indicated they included innovation and change measures in regular management reviews.

Quality of Measures. Exhibit 10–3 shows that the financial performance measures were the only measures that were considered to be high quality, current, and tied to compensation. Most responding companies had operating and customer satisfaction measures, and over 79 percent of the companies considered this information to be highly valuable. Unfortunately, there was often a large difference between the perceived value of these measures and the quality of information they produced.

---

[4]Brian McWilliams, "The Measure of Success," *Across the Board,* February 1996, pp. 16–20.

EXHIBIT 10-3 **Companies' Use of/Opinion about Measurement Practices**

	Percentage of Respondents Practices Using/Favorable				
Measure of	*Highly Valued Information*	*Quality of Information*	*Clear Measures*	*Measures Regularly Updated*	*Linked to Compensation*
Financial performance	82%	61%	92%	88%	94%
Operating efficiency	79	41	68	69	54
Customer satisfaction	85	29	48	48	37
Employee performance	67	16	17	27	20
Innovation/change	52	16	13	23	12

Source: Adapted from John H. Lingle and William A. Scheimann, "From Balanced Scorecard to Strategic Gauges: Is Measurement Worth It?" *Management Review,* American Management Association, March 1996, pp. 56–61.

The study results shown in Exhibit 10–3 leave no doubt that measures of employee performance and innovation and change have generally been considered poorly defined and of poor quality. Ironically, most companies in this study considered information about the company's performance in these areas to be highly valuable.

Relationship of Measures to Compensation. Most management systems link financial measures to compensation. As Exhibit 10–3 points out, of the companies surveyed, about one-third used customer satisfaction and less than one-quarter used innovation and change measures to drive compensation decisions.

Interactive Control[5]

The primary role of management controls is to help execute strategies. Under this view, as indicated in Exhibit 10–4, the chosen strategy defines the critical success factors which become the focal point for the design and operation of control systems. The end result is the strategy's successful implementation. In industries that are subject to very rapid environmental changes, management control information can also provide the basis for thinking about new strategies. This is illustrated in Exhibit 10–5. It is called *interactive control.*[6]

In a rapidly changing and dynamic environment, creating a learning organization is essential to corporate survival. *Learning organization* refers to the ability of an organization's employees to learn to cope with environmental changes on an ongoing basis. An effective learning organization is one in

[5]This section is based on the research of Robert Simons, *Levers of Control* (Boston: Harvard Business School Press, 1995).
[6]Ibid., pp. 91–124.

EXHIBIT 10–4

*Control system
as a strategy
implementation tool*

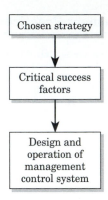

EXHIBIT 10–5

Interactive control

which employees at all levels continuously scan the environment, identify potential problems and opportunities, exchange environmental information candidly and openly, and experiment with alternate business models in order to successfully adapt to the emerging environment. *The main objective of interactive control is to facilitate the creation of a learning organization.*

While *critical success factors* are important in control system design to implement the chosen strategy, strategic uncertainties guide the use of a subset of management control information interactively in developing new strategies. *Strategic uncertainties* are fundamental environmental shifts (changes in customer preferences, technologies, competitors, lifestyles, substitute products, etc.) that could potentially disrupt the rules by which an organization is playing today.

There is a fundamental difference between *critical success factors* and *strategic uncertainties.* Critical success factors are derived from chosen strategies; as such, they support the implementation of strategies for current products and markets (Exhibit 10–4). Strategic uncertainties, on the other hand, are the basis for the firm to search for new strategies; as such, they help in developing new businesses. Strategic uncertainties result in questions, not answers: What has changed? Why has it changed? What new business models can we develop to exploit this discontinuity?

Interactive controls alert management to strategic uncertainties, either troubles (e.g., loss of market share, customer complaints) or opportunities

EXHIBIT 10–6

Control system as a strategy formation tool

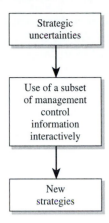

(e.g., opening a new market because certain governmental regulations have been removed). These become the basis for managers to adapt to a rapidly changing environment by thinking about new strategies (Exhibit 10–6).

Interactive control has the following characteristics:

1. A subset of the management control information that has a bearing on the strategic uncertainties facing the business becomes the focal point.
2. Senior executives take such information seriously.
3. Managers at all levels of the organization focus attention on the information produced by the system.
4. Superiors, subordinates, and peers meet face-to-face to interpret and discuss the implications of the information for future strategic initiatives.
5. The face-to-face meetings take the form of debate and challenge of the underlying data, assumptions, and appropriate actions.

Strategic uncertainties relate to fundamental, nonlinear shifts in the environment that potentially can create new business models. Firms should monitor the following technological discontinuities:

1. Internet and e-commerce growth have potential implications for many firms. Some of the particular items to monitor include:
   • Growth in the number of Internet users.
   • Roll-out of broadband communications.
   • Emergence of ubiquitous point-and-click interfaces that are based on open standards, cheap to set up and run, and global.
   • Increasing power of computing and communication technologies.
   • Growth in mobile communications for both voice telephony and Internet access.

- Development and deployment of speech recognition and machine-based language translation technologies that may make it possible for people speaking or writing different languages to communicate with each other in real time.

2. Converging technologies will have the following effects:
   - Convergence of voice, data, and image has implications for firms operating in consumer electronics (Phillips), telecommunications (British Telecom), and computer (IBM) industries.
   - Integration of chemical and digital technologies has impact on firms such as Eastman Kodak.
   - Blending of hardware and software has impact on firms such as Sony.
   - Merging of plant engineering and biotechnology opens up opportunities for firms in life sciences (Monsanto, Hoechst).

3. Miniaturization can provide opportunities for firms in consumer electronics (Sony) as well as appliances (Whirlpool, Electrolux).

4. Shift from physical goods to services is rapidly transforming the automobile industry (Ford) and consumer durable goods business (General Electric).

The following discontinuities created by globalization have the potential to create new opportunity:

1. Liberalization, deregulation, and privatization have the potential to create huge new customer segments in emerging markets such as China, India, and Brazil.

2. New competitors from emerging markets may become global players in the future. For instance, the list of emerging global competitors from India includes Infosys (software), Ranbaxy (pharmaceuticals), Reliance Industries (petrochemicals), and the diversified Tata Group (varied manufacturing and service industries).

Interactive controls are not a *separate* system; they are an integral part of the management control system. Some management control information helps managers think about new strategies. Interactive control information usually, but not exclusively, tends to be nonfinancial. Since strategic uncertainties differ from business to business, senior executives in different companies might choose different parts of their management control system to use interactively, as the following examples illustrate:

Examples.   A business in the hospital supply industry competed as the low-cost producer of intravenous drug delivery products. This business manufactured and sold large quantities of standardized, disposable products such as syringes, wipes, tubing, and plasma containers. Critical performance variables for this low-cost, high-volume strategy related to product quality and manufacturing and distribution efficiencies. These factors were not the strategic uncertainties perceived by senior managers. Strategic uncertainties related to fundamental changes in drug delivery technology which could undermine business's ability to deliver products valued by the market. What if advances in technology led to ways of delivering drugs orally, or through skin patches, or through some other, as yet uncontemplated, technology? What if the nature of drug technology changed? Could the business adapt?[7] Senior management used a project management system (one element of the management control system) interactively to focus organizational attention on a dozen or so emerging technological issues. Senior managers met several days each month to debate the impact of technologies—introduced by competitors, or in related industries, or developed in-house—on their business. New strategies emerged from these discussions.[8]

Pepsi used the market share data released by Nielsen every week as an interactive control system.[9] Some of the key strategic uncertainties confronting Pepsi included replacement of soft drinks by other drinks; customer response to pricing, promotion, and advertising moves of Coke; and customer preference for diet drinks. These strategic uncertainties affected market share. Hence, Pepsi used market share information to debate future strategic actions. According to John Sculley, Pepsi's former CEO, "Pepsi's top managers would carry in their wallets little charts with the latest Nielsen figures. . . . We would pore over the data, using it to search for Coke's vulnerable points where an assault could successfully be launched, or to explore why Pepsi slipped a fraction of a percentage point in the game. . . . The Nielsens defined the ground rules of competition for everyone at Pepsi."[10]

A subsystem should satisfy the following conditions before it can be used as an interactive control system:

1. *The data contained in the subsystem should be unambiguous and simple to understand and interpret.* Pepsi's use of market share data released by Nielsen is an example.

2. *The subsystem must contain data on strategic uncertainties.* For the hospital supply company mentioned above, the key strategic uncertainty revolved around drug delivery technology. The company's project management system contained data on emerging technologies in drug delivery and thus was useful as an interactive control.

3. *The data in the subsystem should help the firm develop new strategies.* If Amazon.com intends to expand its physical distribution logistics in India, the company needs to carefully monitor the following variables as they pertain to the Indian market: the number of personal computers sold, telephone penetration, and the number of Internet connections. Dramatic shifts in these variables enable Amazon.com to formulate new action plans.

---

[7]Ibid., pp. 94–95.

[8]Robert Simons, "Control in an Age of Empowerment." *Harvard Business Review,* March–April 1995, p. 87.

[9]Ibid., p. 86.

[10]J. Sculley, *Odyssey: Pepsi to Apple . . . A Journey of Adventure, Ideas, and the Future* (New York: Harper & Row, 1987).

Summary

A performance measurement system provides a mechanism for linking strategy to action. It operates on the assumption that financial measures alone are not sufficient to operate an organization and that special attention must be placed on developing sophisticated, nonfinancial measures. The scorecard uses a variety of different types of measures, including outcome and driver, financial and nonfinancial, and internal and external. The key belief behind the scorecard is that measurement will drive change as the organization conforms to what is being measured. There are many pitfalls that a company may encounter when trying to implement a scorecard: poor correlation between driver and outcome measures, fixation on financial results, no mechanism for making improvements, failure to update the measures, too many measures, and difficulty making trade-offs.

The primary role of management controls is to help execute chosen strategies. In industries that are subject to very rapid environmental changes, management control information can also provide managers with a tool for thinking about new strategies; this is called interactive control. Interactive controls are not a separate system but an integral part of the management control system; interactive control information tends to be nonfinancial.

APPENDIX
DELL COMPUTER CORPORATION AND SEARS

Performance Management Systems at Dell Computer[11]

As of 1999, Dell Computer Corporation was the world's largest direct-selling computer company, with 16,000 employees in 33 countries and customers in 170 countries. The company was headquartered in Round Rock, Texas, near Austin. Michael Dell founded it in 1984 when he pioneered the process of selling custom-built computers directly to customers. Within the short space of 15 years, Dell became the number-one retailer of personal computers, outselling IBM, Hewlett-Packard, and Compaq. Businesses of all sizes, government agencies, educational institutions, and individual customers ordered Dell's desktop and notebook computers, workstations, and network servers by phone or via the Internet. In 1996 Dell embraced the Web; by late 1999, over 40 percent of the company's sales emanated from this channel. Dell computer systems were assembled one at a time, as ordered, at factories in Austin; Limerick, Ireland; and Penang, Malaysia.

Dell outpaced its competitors in both growth and profitability. The company's market capitalization was about $700 million at its June 1988 initial public offering. By

---

[11]This Appendix is based on Vijay Govindarajan and Anil K. Gupta, *World Wise: Building the Global Corporation of Tomorrow* (Boston: Harvard Business School Press, 2000), chap. 8.

1999 it had exploded to well above $100 billion, an increase of more than 140 times over an 11-year period—a gain dramatically above that of Standard & Poor's 500. At age 34, Michael Dell was the richest man in the world under 40.

Sources of Dell's Competitive Advantage.   Traditional PC manufacturers, such as IBM, H-P, and Compaq, designed and built their products with preconfigured options based on market forecasts. Products were first stored in company warehouses and later dispatched to resellers, retailers, and other intermediaries who typically added 20 to 30 percent markup before selling to their customers. Dell Computer, on the other hand, used a "direct" model. It (a) outsourced all components but performed assembly, (b) eliminated retailers and shipped directly from its factories to end customers, and (c) took customized orders for hardware and software over the phone or via the Internet.

Dell custom-built its machines *after* receiving an order, instead of making machines for inventory in anticipation of orders. Thus, the firm had dramatically low levels of components as well as finished-goods inventory (on average, 7–11 days for Dell versus 70–100 days combined for other PC manufacturers and their resellers). Radical inventory reductions translated into major savings in the cost of capital tied up in inventory investments. More important, low inventory gave Dell a huge technology advantage. Microprocessor and other component technologies kept advancing at a relentless pace. Dell's PC components were 60 days newer than those in IBM or Compaq PCs.

Performance Management Systems at Dell.   Dell's performance management systems supported the company's direct model. The company's scorecard included financial measures (selling price, margins, overhead costs, and profits) as well as nonfinancial measures (inventory turns, accounts receivable days, accounts payable days, and cash-conversion cycle). Kevin Rollins, vice chairman of Dell Computer Corporation, noted, "At Dell, we use the balance sheet and the fundamentals of the P&L on a monthly basis as tools to manage operations. From the balance sheet, we track three cash-flow measures very closely. We look at weekly updates of how many days of inventory we have, broken out by product component. We can then work closely with our suppliers so we end up with the right inventory. When it's not quite right, we can use our direct-sales model to steer customers toward comparable products that we do have. So we use inventory information to work both the front and back ends at the same time.

"We also track and manage receivables and payables very tightly. This is basic blocking and tackling, but we give it a high priority. The payoff is that we have a negative cash-conversion cycle of five days—that is, we get paid before we have to pay our suppliers. Since our competitors usually have to support their resellers by offering them credit, the direct model gives us an inherent cost advantage. And the more we can shorten our cash-collection cycle, the greater our advantage.

"The real-time performance measures in the P&L that we regard as the best indicators of the company's health are our margins, our average selling price, and the overhead associated with selling. We split the P&L into these core elements by customer segment, by product, and by country. These metrics can alert us instantly to problems, for example, with the mix of products being sold in any particular country."[12]

----

[12]Joan Magretta, "The Power of Virtual Integration: An Interview with Dell Computer's Michael Dell," *Harvard Business Review*, March–April 1998, p. 81.

Performance Management Systems at Sears[13]

Strategy of Sears.   In 1992 Sears faced a bleak future and was dubbed a "dinosaur" by the media. But by January 1998, Sears had posted several years of strong growth and profitability under the leadership of Arthur Martinez, the company's chairman and CEO. During 1992–97, Sears even surpassed companies like Coca-Cola and Disney in terms of the total return to stockholders. In 1996 Martinez was recognized by *Financial World* as CEO of the Year.

Martinez's strategy for Sears consisted of several elements: (1) Historically, Sears had targeted the male shopper. However, when Martinez looked closely at his customers, he found that women did most of the shopping at Sears for their families. Martinez refocused the stores to market to this audience. (2) Recognizing that the stores were starting to look dated, he authorized a massive $4 billion renovation of full-line stores. (3) Revitalizing Sears's mall-based stores was not enough. Shoppers were migrating away from malls and toward "category killers," such as Home Depot and outlet malls. To head off this exodus, Martinez accelerated plans to expand into off-mall stores. (4) Over 60 percent of merchandise—more for hard lines—was purchased with the Sears card. Among retail establishments, Sears was the number-one credit card provider. Martinez decided to improve the company's marketing effectiveness by making use of the enormous data library that it had collected on customer purchasing patterns.

He also created a new vision statement: "Sears: A compelling place to work, shop, and invest." He then turned to developing a series of objectives and measures for the key constituencies: employees (compelling place to work), customers (compelling place to shop), and stockholders (compelling place to invest).

Performance Management Systems at Sears.   The framework for performance measurement at Sears was the employee-customer-profit chain. The logic for this framework was simple: Good employee attitudes result in strong customer satisfaction, customer loyalty, and customer retention which, in turn, lead to profits. The company developed a series of measures to track performance on employee behavior (broken down into employee attitudes about the job and the company), customer impressions (broken down into service, helpfulness, merchandise, and value), and financial performance (Figure A).

The company had figured out precisely how the behavior of the front-line employees affected customers and thus sales revenues and, ultimately, the return to shareholders. "We have also calculated a lag time between a change in any of [the] metrics and a corresponding change in financial performance, so that when we see a shift in, say, employee attitudes, we know not only *how* but also *when* it will affect results.[14]

The firm developed an integrated performance scorecard: Sears total performance indicators (TPI). This performance management system showed the cause–effect linkages between employee attitudes, customer satisfaction, and profits. TPI was how Sears made the employee-customer-profit chain operational. Figure A indicates TPI, placing employees, customers, and stockholders into a single integrated business model. Within Sears, the model for corporate success was viewed as *Work * Shop = Invest.*

---

[13]This Appendix is based on "Sears," a case prepared by Vijay Govindarajan, 1998; and Anthony J. Rucci, Steven P. Kirn, and Richard T. Quinn, "The Employee-Customer-Profit Chain at Sears," *Harvard Business Review,* January–February 1998.

[14]Rucci et al., "The Employee-Customer-Profit Chain at Sears," p. 84.

FIGURE A

Sears total performance indicators (TPI)[15]

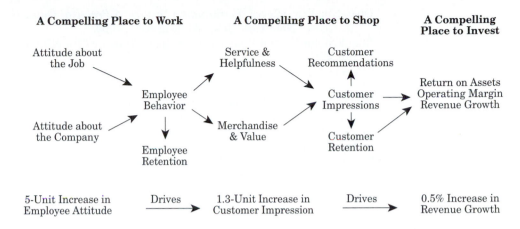

Econometrically, Sears took the employees' answers regarding their attitudes about their jobs and the company and used them to predict customer impressions and, in turn, financial performance (see Figure A, bottom line).

TPI was adopted into the compensation of employees at every level. All long-term senior management compensation was tied to financial as well as nonfinancial performance indicators; customer, employee, and financial measures each were the focus of one-third of the evaluation. Other managers found a percentage of their pay tied to improvements in customer satisfaction.

---

[15]Ibid.

Suggested Additional Readings

Dixon, J. R., A. J. Nanni, and T. E. Vollmann. *The New Performance Challenge: Measuring Operations for World-Class Competition.* Burr Ridge, IL: Dow Jones-Irwin, 1990.

Eccles, Robert G., and Philip J. Pyburn. "Creating a Comprehensive System to Measure Performance." *Management Accounting,* October 1992, pp. 41–44.

Harbour, Jerry L. *The Basics of Performance Measurement.* Portland, OR: Productivity Inc., 1997.

Holloway, Jacky, et al., eds. London and Thousand Oaks, CA: *Performance Measurement and Evaluation.* Sage, 1995.

Kaplan, Robert S., and David P. Norton. *The Balanced Scorecard: Translating Strategy into Action.* Boston: Harvard Business School Press, 1996.

Kawada, Makoto, and Daniel F. Johnson. "Strategic Management Accounting—Why and How." *Management Accounting,* August 1993, pp. 32–38.

Keating, Patrick J., and Stephen F. Jablonsky. *Changing Roles of Financial Management.* Morristown, NJ: Financial Executives Research Foundation, 1990.

Lingle, John H., and William A. Schiemann. "From Balanced Scorecard to Strategic Gauges: Is Measurement Worth It?" *Management Review,* March 1996, pp. 56–61.

McKinnon, Sharon, and William Bruns. *The Information Mosaic.* Boston: Harvard Business School Press, 1992.

McWilliams, Brian. "The Measure of Success." *Across the Board,* February 1996, pp. 16–20.

Olve, Nils-Goran, et al. *Performance Drivers: A Practical Guide to Using the Balanced Scorecard.* New York: John Wiley & Sons, 1999.

Shank, John K., and Vijay Govindarajan. *Strategic Cost Management.* New York: Free Press, 1993.

Shapior, Carl, and Hal R. Varian. *Information Rules.* Boston: Harvard Business School Press, 1999.

Sieger, Joseph M. "Manage Your Numbers to Match Your Strategy." *Management Review,* February 1992, pp. 46–48.

Simons, Robert. "Control in an Age of Empowerment." *Harvard Business Review,* March–April 1995, pp. 80–88.

Tesoro, Ferdinand, and Jack Tootson. *Implementing Global Performance Measurement Systems.* San Francisco: Jossey-Bass, 1999.

Vitale, Mike R., and Sarah C. Mavrinac. "How Effective Is Your Performance Measurement System?" *Management Accounting,* August 1995, pp. 43–47.

Case 10–1
Analog Devices, Inc.

"Much remains to be done. We face unprecedented opportunities and we are poised for extraordinary growth. It is up to all of us to seize these opportunities and to create the future for Analog Devices."

Ray Stata
Chairman and CEO, Analog Devices, 1996

Analog Devices Inc. (ADI) was a leading manufacturer of integrated circuits that convert between analog and digital data. From 1981 through 1996, ADI experienced periods of growth and stagnation, both achieving record profits and sales and experiencing its first loss ever. To meet the needs of the changing market, management at ADI introduced a number of different management tools to implement change. One such tool was its *corporate scorecard.*

ADI's corporate scorecard was recognized as a management best practice in a survey the Nolan-Norton Group conducted in 1991. Despite this accolade, ADI's management was wondering in 1996 how to change the scorecard to best fit the needs of management, specifically, how fast to change it and how best to use it to focus management attention in the future.

Background

Analog Devices was founded in 1965 in Cambridge, Massachusetts, by Ray Stata and Matthew Lorber. Stata had a B.S.E.E. and an M.S.E.E., both from MIT. In 1996 the company operated predominantly in one industry segment: the design, manufacture, and marketing of a broad line of high-performance linear, mixed-signal, and digital integrated circuits ("ICs") that addressed a wide range of real-

This case was prepared by Kirk Hendrickson (T '97) under the supervision of Professor Vijay Govindarajan. Copyright © V. Govindarajan.

world signal processing applications. The company's principal products were divided among four classifications: general-purpose, standard-function linear, and mixed-signal ICs ("SLICs"); special-purpose linear and mixed-signal ICs ("SPLICs"); digital signal processing ICs ("DSP ICs"); and assembled products. SLICS were the largest product segment for the company, accounting for 65 percent of total sales.

Nearly all the company products were components that typically were incorporated by original equipment manufacturers (OEMs) in a wide range of equipment and systems for use in communications, computer, industrial instrumentation, military/aerospace, and high-performance consumer electronics applications. The company sold products worldwide; in 1996 one-half the sales came from outside the US.

Industry Background.   Real-world phenomena—temperature, pressure, sound, images, speed, acceleration, position, and rotation angle—are inherently analog in nature, consisting of continuously varying information. Analog sensors can detect and measure this information. The signals are usually converted to digital form for input to a microprocessor, which is used to manipulate, store, or display the information. In many cases, the signals are further processed using a technology called *digital signal processing.* In addition, digital signals frequently are converted to analog form to provide signals for analog display, sound, or control functions. Collectively, these manipulations and transformations are known as *real-world signal processing.*

Significant advances in semiconductor technology have led to substantial increases in the performance and functionality of ICs used for signal processing applications. These advances include the ability to create very large scale integration (VLSI) mixed-signal ICs that contain both high-performance analog circuitry and large amounts of high-density digital circuitry. The analog circuitry portion of the IC is used to manipulate real-world signals while still in analog form and to convert analog signals into digital form (or vice versa). The digital portion is used to further process analog signals after they have been converted to digital form.

Company Strategy.   In 1996 Analog Devices' strategy was technological leadership. The company wanted to be first-to-market with new products that had superior performance features. Analog Devices was one of the world's largest suppliers of SLIC products.

During the period 1990–96, Analog sought to balance its traditionally stable SLIC business with growth opportunities for SPLICs and DSP ICs. The company built upon its expertise in linear IC technology, developing special-purpose linear and mixed-signal ICs tailored to specific high-volume applications in target markets. Analog also extended its expertise in analog signal processing and data conversion to develop DSP ICs. These DSP ICs and its SPLICs addressed the emerging demand for high-performance levels in many communications, computer, and other high-volume applications. These products had a high level of functionality (i.e., many functions on one chip) to satisfy OEMs' requirements for an integrated solution with low cost per function.

To build upon its position as a leader in real-world signal processing, Analog was pursuing the following strategies in 1996: (1) expand traditional SLIC business; (2) become a major supplier of general purpose DSP ICs; (3) pursue growth opportunities for system-level signal processing ICs; and (4) leverage core technologies to develop innovative products.

Total Quality at ADI, 1983–86

From the inception of the company in 1965 till the early 1980s, sales at Analog Devices grew at a rate of 27 percent a year. Yet in 1983, Ray Stata recognized that ADI was having problems with the quality of its production. Its on-time delivery record was under 60 percent. Its process yields, in some cases, were as low as 10 percent.[1] ADI's customers were complaining about quality, and its competitors had on-time delivery records and yields well above ADI's level. At this time, Stata attended Philip Crosby's Quality School. This was ADI's first introduction to the concept of total quality management (TQM).

Interested in implementing TQM but not wanting to add additional staff to create a quality improvement function, Stata charged the human resources division with establishing a TQM program at ADI. The first TQM effort never got beyond managers' trying to become TQM gurus on their own by reading books and going to seminars. As one general manager said, "I was focused on growing the business, not on TQM."[2]

By the end of 1984, ADI's sales had reached $313 million. During fiscal year 1984, revenue had grown by 46 percent, profits by 105 percent, and orders booked promised another record year in 1985. ADI management felt it was in the middle of some of the fastest-growing segments in the economy. Many in the company were starting to talk about ADI becoming a $1 billion firm by 1988.

Unfortunately, between the end of 1984 and the end of 1986, sales had grown only 6.7 percent, and profits had fallen by 38 percent. As Stata stated,

> [F]or the first time, between 1982 and 1987, we missed our five-year goals—and by a country mile. True enough,

---

[1]Howell, Shank, Soucy, Fisher, *Cost Management for Tomorrow,* Financial Executives Research Foundation, 1992, p. 128.

[2]Unless otherwise indicated, the statements in this case attributed to Analog Devices' Ray Stata (CEO and chairman) and Goodloe Suttler (vice president of strategic planning, quality improvement, and corporate marketing) were based on interviews.

like other semiconductor companies we were affected by the malaise in the US electronics industry and by the strong dollar. But the external environment was only part of the problem: something was also wrong internally, and it had to be fixed.[3]

The factory was missing over 40 percent of its committed delivery dates. When 20 executives with regular customer contacts were asked, "When the phone rings and it is an angry customer, what did he say?" the executives responded, "The customer said, 'Where's my order?!'"

The defect level of product that reached the customer was more than 20,000 parts per million (PPM). Competitors such as Motorola were achieving results under 1,000 PPM. Furthermore, the poor quality caused a substantial amount of waste at ADI, such as front-to-back IC yields of less than 15 percent, meaning that only 15 out of every 100 ICs that ADI started made it through the process. These were well below industry yields.

Although in 1985 ADI's analog IC sales declined by about 5 percent, 1986 industrywide analog IC sales grew by 25 percent. The analog circuits industry had returned to growth, yet ADI's revenues were stagnant and its profitability was declining.

The Quality Specialist

In 1986 ADI hired Art Schneiderman as vice president of quality and productivity improvement. Schneiderman had been a consultant with Bain & Co., where he had been directly involved in establishing many quality improvement programs. He was seen as someone who could link ADI to the "mainstream of experience and knowledge that is rapidly accumulating in [TQM]" and be a teacher who could "help [ADI's] managers become more expert practi-

tioners."[4] Stata wanted the quality improvement process (QIP), as ADI called its total quality program, to become a way of life at ADI.

Many of the general managers at ADI were skeptical of this new quality program, having undergone the earlier, unsuccessful quality program. Additionally, they believed the quality goals and the company's financial goals were in conflict. The financial basis of ADI's incentive and performance measurement systems reinforced this belief.

Half-Life. Schneiderman believed that "any defect level, subjected to legitimate QIP, decreases at a constant rate, so that when plotted on semi-log paper against time, it falls on a straight line."[5] The result is that every process can experience a 50 percent reduction in defects at a consistent time interval. Schneiderman called this the *half-life* of the improvement process. As Sterman et al. note, "The basis for the half-life dynamic is the interactive learning loop at the heart of TQM. Improvement teams identify the root causes of defects, rank them in order of importance, then propose, design, test, and implement solutions using the Plan-Do-Check-Act or 'PDCA' cycle. The team continues to cycle around the learning loop until the root causes of most of the defects are corrected, then moves to the next most important source of defects."[6]

Schneiderman had collected data on improvement activities. Exhibit 1 shows three examples of the data he collected. The examples are shown on log-linear graphs to capture the full effect of the half-life concept. By plotting improvements this way, it was easy for someone to see the line indicating the improvement rate. As Exhibit 1 illustrates, each process had

[3]Ray Stata, "Organizational Learning—The Key to Management Innovation," *Sloan Management Review,* Spring 1989, p. 63.

[4]Ibid., p. 63.
[5]Arthur M. Schneiderman, "Setting Quality Goals," *Quality Progress,* April 1988, p. 53.
[6]John D. Sterman, Nelson P. Repenning, and Fred Kofman, "Unanticipated Side Effects of Successful Quality Programs: Exploring a Paradox of Organizational Improvement," *Management Science* 43, no. 4 (April 1997), pp. 504–5.

EXHIBIT 1

Three examples of half-life

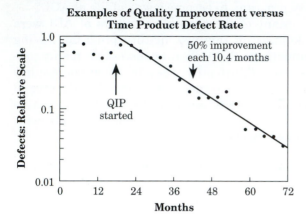

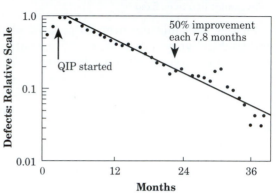

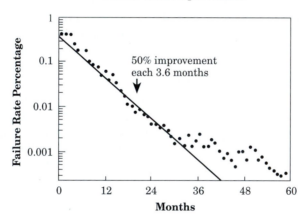

Source: Ray Stata, "Organizational Learning—The Key to Management Innovation," *Sloan Management Review,* Spring 1989, p. 69.

its own unique rate, determined by finding the slope of the line fit to the data. This unique rate was the process's half-life. (See Appendix 1, The Half-Life/Complexity Matrix, and Appendix 2, Relationship of Half-Life to the Experience Curve, for additional background on the half-life concept.)

Using the 1987 five-year plan as a tool, Schneiderman introduced goals for a series of quality measures (Exhibit 2) that corresponded to what he considered to be ADI's critical suc-

cess factors: having innovative, high-quality products and being a reliable, responsive supplier. The goals were determined by combining customer demands with realistic expectations of each measure's half-life.

He proposed reductions such as dropping process defect levels from 5,000 PPM in 1987 to fewer than 10 PPM by 1992. Many managers just laughed at him. Stata recalled,

The first reaction of our organization was to recoil from what looked like unrealistic objectives. But we reminded

EXHIBIT 2   **Analog Devices Quality Improvement Goals**

Measurement	1987	Half-Life (in months)	1992
External			
On-time delivery	85%	9	>99.8%
Outgoing defect level	500 PPM	9	<10 PPM
Lead time	10 weeks	9	<3 weeks
Internal			
Manufacturing cycle time	15 weeks	9	4–5 weeks
Process defect level	5,000 PPM	6	<10 PPM
Yield	20%	9	>50%
Time to market	36 months	24	6 months

Source: Stata, "Organizational Learning," p. 70.

our managers that if a company really gets its quality improvement act together, there is no fundamental reason why these goals cannot be achieved.[7]

ADI's Scorecard. Schneiderman put together a single-page scorecard that showed three categories of measures: financial, new products, and QIP (Exhibit 3). Measures within these categories indicated how well ADI was moving toward its goals. The scorecard was prepared once a quarter.

ADI considered the scorecard to be a breakthrough because it condensed pages of reports into a simple, single report. It measured each critical success factor as well as financial performance.

Schneiderman added to it the half-life and target for each of the measurements for the next few periods. He did this to provide a link between short-term results and ADI's long-term plans, such as improving on-time deliveries to 99.8 percent by 1992.

Making the Scorecard Work. Schneiderman developed the following rules about how to construct the scorecard:

[7]Stata, "Organizational Learning," p. 70.

EXHIBIT 3   **Example Corporate Scorecard for FY 1988**

	FY88	
	Target	Actual
Financial		
Revenue	$M	
Revenue growth	%	
Profit	$M	
ROA	%	
New Products		
NP introductions	#	
NP bookings	$M	
NP breakeven	#	
NP peak revenue	$M	
Time to market	Months	
QIP		
On-time delivery	%	
Cycle time	Weeks	
Yield	%	
Outgoing defects	PPM	
Cost	$M	
Employee productivity	%	
Turnover	%	

EXHIBIT 4

On-time customer service performance monthly data (August 1987– July 1988)

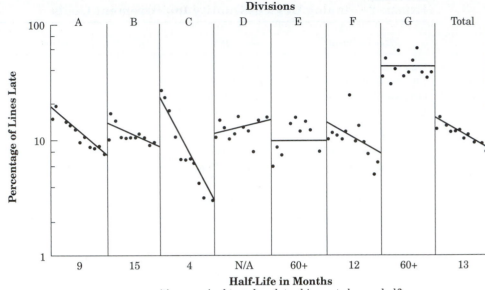

Source: Stata, "Organizational Learning," p. 72.

- The entire scorecard had to fit on one 8½″ by 11″ sheet of paper.
- The font size had to be 12 points or bigger.
- There were to be six times as many nonfinancial measures as financial measures.

In addition to the scorecard and TQM, Schneiderman helped change ADI from doing five-year planning every five years to doing five-year planning every year.

He also helped create divisional scorecards. The measures for most divisions overlapped; all could be tied directly to ADI's overall scorecard. The company allowed each division to use the same scorecard or a unique one. By tailoring scorecards to each division, Schneiderman gave all divisions the means to negotiate their goals and determine the appropriate half-lives of their measures.

In 1988 Schneiderman began to roll out the balanced scorecard to the entire company. Each

division gradually developed its own scorecard and had successive levels develop theirs. They also were not required to have unique scorecards. Lower-level management scorecards typically placed less emphasis on financial measures than on nonfinancial measures on which managers could have an impact. Each division was required to share the quarterly scorecard results with all its employees.

Division results for each scorecard measure were compared. Exhibit 4 shows how different divisions compare in on-time customer service performance results. Each division was shown together, and the slope, or half-life, of the improvement was shown. In addition to distributing reports like Exhibit 4, Schneiderman compared the scorecard performance results with the target results during executive council meetings. He pointed out large favorable variations (which he circled in green) and large unfavorable variations (circled in red), and asked divisional general managers to explain the causes.

EXHIBIT 5   **Consolidated Statement of Income, 1986–95**
(dollars in millions except per share data)

	1995	1994	1993	1992	1991	1990	1989	1988	1987	1986
Net sales	$ 941	$773	$663	$567	$538	$485	$453	$439	$370	$334
Cost of sales	464	394	351	302	272	244	215	201	172	151
Gross margin	476	379	315	266	265	241	238	238	199	183
Research and development expense	134	107	94	88	89	80	69	60	56	45
Selling, marketing, general, and administrative expense	184	170	159	151	152	136	126	122	108	97
Total operating expenses	319	277	253	239	248	235	194	183	164	143
Operating income	157	102	63	26	17	6	44	55	34	40
Total nonoperating expenses (income)	(2)	5	7	7	8	20	7	4	9	8
Income before income taxes	159	97	56	19	9	(14)	36	52	26	32
Net income	119	74	44	15	8	(13)	28	38	19	23
Net income per share	$1.00	$ .64	$ .39	$ .14	$ .08	($.28)	$ .58	$ .80	$ .40	$ .51

According to Goodloe Suttler, a graduate of the Tuck School at Dartmouth College and a vice president and general manager of ADI's semiconductor division, the company used the corporate scorecard as a communication tool. To the employees, it said,

- Measurement is the key to determining success.
- You cannot know how well you are doing unless you have measures.
- Here is what is happening in your division/plant.

To management, it said,

- These scorecard items are the metrics of success.
- Focus on the items critical to success.
- You must meet objectives measured in the scorecard.

By 1991 the corporate scorecard was being used aggressively on a daily basis throughout the organization.

Performance.[8]   Analog Devices showed dramatic improvements in its quality measures by 1990. Between July 1987 and July 1990, on-time delivery increased from 70 percent to 96 percent, cycle time decreased from 15 weeks to 8 weeks, average yields improved from 26 percent to 51 percent, and defects in products shipped declined from 500 PPM to 50 PPM. Other variables did not improve during the 1987–91 period. Product development time did not decline. The stock price dropped from $25 in 1987 to $9 by 1991, a much larger decline than performance by the market as a whole or the semiconductor industry in particular. In 1990 Analog Devices experienced its first loss (Exhibits 5 and 6). It missed its profitability goal for 1991 by 50 percent and suffered its first-ever layoff of 600 employees (12 percent of its workforce). In response to the financial crisis, Analog decided to shift its strategy of focusing predominantly on

---

[8]Sterman, Repenning, and Kofman, "Unanticipated Side Effects of Successful Quality Programs," pp. 503–21.

the SLIC business to emphasizing the growth areas of SPLICs and DSP ICs.

Changing Roles.   During this time, ADI's management directly under Stata changed considerably. The company promoted Jerry Fishman to president and named eight new vice presidents, including five from outside ADI. A number of longtime vice presidents retired. The changes reflected ADI's efforts to infuse a different culture. As one of the new vice presidents from the outside said, "Analog had a product orientation, not a customer orientation. The financial dip helped bring dramatic changes."

Following Stata's lead, the entire senior management team stepped up to the role of quality leaders to demonstrate that improvement is everyone's responsibility. Schneiderman had been ADI's torchbearer during the era of the quality specialist; now it was time to begin the era of senior management. In mid-1992, Art Schneiderman resigned from ADI and passed the torch to the new management team.

TQM Off-Track.   TQM's primary focus on cost reduction left many managers feeling most cost reduction was done by the early 1990s. Many also believed the investment necessary to stay with, and constantly improve, the TQM program outweighed the many advantages of continuing it. Some at the company simply had no faith in the program. "There is some closeted cynicism about quality [programs] in the company," noted Stata. "Among the engineers, it isn't even closeted. They think it's crap."[9] The end result was increased pressure to abandon TQM.

By the mid-1990s, ADI was bouncing back financially. Management believed that QIP had improved the firm's profitability by reducing waste but, because it was primarily a cost reduction tool, did not credit it with ADI's growth.

In fact, although ADI was experiencing high growth and profitability, many of the measures of quality were declining. The program appeared to be at a standstill. Management still recognized TQM's value but felt that it was insufficient to address the new problems facing the company.

Changing Systems.   After Schneiderman left, many of the systems he had put in place changed or withered away. In Goodloe Suttler's opinion, there was a "performance paradox." Borrowing ideas from Professor Marshall Meyer at University of Pennsylvania's Wharton School of Management, Suttler believed that all performance measures would eventually degrade. Performance would improve. Variability would be reduced to the point where further improvements were of little value. People would game the system. As a result, new performance measures would need to be constantly introduced. According to Meyer, with new performance measures driving faster change, "Accelerated learning rates suggest we will cycle through measures with greater rapidity." Simply put, the better your measure helps you to improve, the sooner it will lose its value. As Stata observed, "We are now recognizing as we get more sophisticated, it is harder to get numbers that are meaningful."

ADI began to look for new tools that could make the numbers more meaningful, particularly numbers that were leading indicators of value growth. As Suttler said, "The big problem with TQM is that it has little to say about business strategy. TQM works well at stopping wealth-reducing activities, but wealth creation doesn't naturally come from TQM."

Suttler pointed to evidence that TQM had been successful at ADI, such as the reduction of outgoing electrical defectives from more than 20,000 PPM in 1987 to fewer than 50 PPM in 1994, and the improvement of front-to-back IC yields from fewer than 15 percent to more than 60 percent in the same period. On the other

---

[9]Rahul Jacob, "TQM, More than a Dying Fad?" *Fortune,* October 18, 1993, pp. 66–72.

EXHIBIT 6   Consolidated Balance Sheet, 1986–95

(dollars in millions)

	1995	1994	1993	1992	1991	1990	1989	1988	1987	1986
Assets										
Current assets:										
Cash, cash equivalents, short-term investments	$151	$182	$ 81	$ 18	$ 17	$ 8	$ 30	$ 23	$ 6	$ 6
Accounts receivable, net	181	162	146	112	95	98	82	88	76	66
Inventories	144	131	150	142	117	108	98	97	84	79
Total current assets	526	505	403	297	249	232	223	221	176	162
Property, plant and equipment, net	432	282	248	237	224	224	209	201	186	173
Intangible assets, deferred charges, and other assets	44	29	27	27	30	31	21	27	35	34
	1,002	816	678	562	503	487	453	449	397	369
Liabilities and Stockholders' Equity										
Current liabilities:										
Short-term borrowings, current portion of long-term debt, and capital lease obligations	2	23	2	3	6	11	9	7	7	10
Accounts payable and accrued liabilities	174	135	99	82	77	93	51	55	46	37
Deferred income on shipments to domestic distributors	28	19	16	13	9	0	0	0	0	0
Income taxes payable	50	29	15	2	5	2	4	11	5	14
Total current liabilities	254	206	133	100	97	106	63	73	58	60
Long-term debt & capital lease obligations	80	80	100	71	37	24	12	23	30	29
Other noncurrent liabilities	11	8	13	17	15	14	14	13	12	10
Stockholders' equity	656	522	432	375	354	343	363	341	298	270
	1,002	816	678	562	503	487	453	449	397	369

hand, he noted that ADI started TQM at a point where the cost of waste was 25–35 percent of sales and reduced that to under 15 percent in seven years. ADI believed that reducing the cost caused by waste to 3 percent would take another seven years. Although management considered cost reduction important, it was considered less critical than finding ways to grow revenues. Using a model of dynamic complexity (see Exhibit 7), ADI's management concluded that growing revenue was a more difficult process than reducing cost and would take longer to implement.

Hoshin. ADI began searching for new methodologies to create wealth. Ray Stata learned about a technique called *Hoshin kanri* as part of his participation in the Center for

EXHIBIT 7

*Dynamic complexity
of processes*

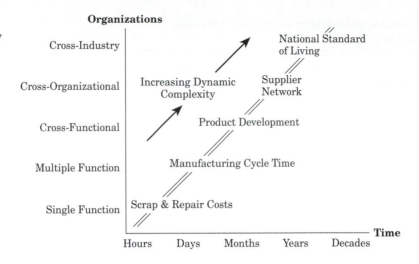

Quality Management. For Stata, Hoshin was an extension of the QIP effort at ADI and a realistic approach to center the company's energies on wealth creation. Its main idea was to focus improvement on one or two breakthrough objectives for the company.

Hoshin, as described by Suttler,

> literally means "policy deployment and control." Hoshin tells us to focus on the most important objectives. Analog Devices has two: on-time delivery and new products. Everything you do in Hoshin is based on data collection and PDCA [Plan-Do-Check-Act cycle].

Hoshin also leveraged many of the techniques that ADI learned from its QIP program. Nevertheless, the company found that implementing Hoshin required more effort than expected.

Hoshin was believed to provide a mechanism for growth, so it assumed a prominent place on the ADI scorecard. The computer products division placed its Hoshin measures at the top of its 1996 division scorecard; the measures took a key position on scorecards throughout the firm. Hoshin goals for ADI in 1996 were (1) 98 percent on-time delivery to platinum accounts and (2) 25 percent sales from new products (products introduced within the last six quarters).

Key Success Factors. Complementing ADI's scorecard were measurements called key suc-

cess factors that measured milestones related to the firm's business plan. These factors were monitor points for the tactical plans of ADI's strategy. They derived from the company's five-year plan, which was updated yearly or, in some cases, quarterly because of the speed at which ADI's market was changing. The company believed its key success factors were more closely related to wealth creation than was the scorecard.

One difference between the two measures was that the key success factors were discrete events. As Suttler stated, "The key success factors do not lend themselves to quarterly monitoring. On the other hand, the measures on the scorecard are intrinsically limited, failing to capture key milestones in each business strategy that also need periodic review." The key success factors either were met or they were not. They did not continue from quarter to quarter. The scorecard measures, such as on-time delivery, continued to be tracked every quarter.

In 1994 Stata charged Suttler with integrating TQM and planning. Suttler introduced several new tools, such as the 10-step planning methodology adapted from Hewlett-Packard, to try to understand wealth creation in a way TQM had not addressed. These techniques were used during the five-year planning exercise and in developing tactical plans for ADI. The key success factors were developed with these tools.

One aspect of the new planning system was that teams, rather than a centralized planning group, did the planning. These teams included individual contributors, line managers, and mid-level managers—the very people responsible for implementing the plans they developed.

Sixty teams were set up in 1997 to work on topics such as business plans and competitor analysis. ADI management believed the teams would be highly committed to the business plans because they had developed them. For Suttler, the most difficult part of this process was letting go of the strategic strings, an adjustment echoed in a *Harvard Business Review* article by Gary Hamel:

> Despite years of imploring people to bring their brains to work, to get involved in quality circles, process reengineering, and the like, senior managers have seldom urged them to participate in the process of strategy creation. But if senior managers can't address the challenges of operational improvements by themselves . . . why would they be able to take on the challenge of industry revolution?[10]

In Suttler's opinion, because they resulted from employee involvement, these business plans became far more important to ADI than the scorecard.

Compensation System.   Analog Devices did not link incentive compensation to performance on the scorecard measures. Compensation for corporate officers (senior management) was based on appreciation in stock prices. Compensation for all other employees was based on an equally weighted combination of two factors: growth in company revenues and operating profits for the company before taxes. Noted Suttler, "We do not tightly link managers' compensation to scorecard performance. We are in an industry that is moving like the wind. We've

got to change our scorecard every year to respond to that environment. Our compensation philosophy is based on cross-functional coordination and the highest degree of teamwork."

Vision 2000

> Now is the time to set a new vision for the future that builds on the accomplishments of the past; fully exploits our leadership in signal processing; captures new opportunities in rapidly emerging markets; and catapults ADI to a multibillion dollar enterprise.[11]

As part of its 1995 planning process, ADI developed what it called Vision 2000, which set forth three major objectives:

- Build leadership positions in seven critical areas of signal processing.
- Increase the growth rate for sales and profits to greater than 20 percent.
- Grow the organization and develop the skills and competencies of all employees.[12]

Through the Hoshin process, these goals had been translated into specific and measurable objectives for every function of ADI. Vision 2000 also included a plan for 1996 that divided the critical measures into four business drivers (see Exhibit 8).

Each business driver was supported by underlying objectives. For example, the objective of 95 percent on-time delivery by year-end supported the customer satisfaction business driver. The objectives for the four business drivers for 1996 were clear and measurable. Some of these objectives, such as on-time delivery, were also part of the scorecard. Others objectives, such as achieving $175 million in net research and development spending, appeared as key success factors.

ADI was using Hoshin, QIP, the corporate scorecard, and critical success factors to create, deploy, and implement strategy. While the

---

[10]Gary Hamel, "Strategy as Revolution," *Harvard Business Review,* July–August 1996, pp. 75–76.

[11]*Vision 2000: Leadership for the 21st Century,* Analog Devices, Inc., 1996.
[12]Ibid.

EXHIBIT 8

The four business drivers for 1996

Customer Satisfaction	New Product Development
95% on-time delivery by year-end	$300 million in new product sales at 45% gross margin
107,000 6-inch CMOS wafers from external foundries	90% success rate from first silicon with customer
13,000 6-inch CMOS wafers from Limerick	6 months to first silicon
3,500 6-inch wafers from Wilmington Mod D	15 months' time to market
2,000 6-inch wafers from Sunnyvale	1.5 tapeouts per new product
Organizational Capabilities	**Financial Expectations**
1,000 new employees	$1.2 billion in revenue for 25% growth
150 new college graduates	50% gross margin, including new fabs
Employee turnover less than 7%	$175 million in net research and development spending
90% of new employees on board within less than 90 days of requisitions	$200 million in sales, marketing, general, and administrative (SMG&A) spending or 16% of sales
Voice-of-the-Employee baseline score established	$225 million in operating profit

Source: *Vision 2000: Leadership for the 21st Century,* Analog Devices, Inc., 1996.

systems were in place, the questions still remained: How should Stata and ADI implement needed change? How important was ADI's corporate scorecard in creating change? How must these systems evolve for ADI to achieve its objectives for Vision 2000?

APPENDIX 1
THE HALF-LIFE/COMPLEXITY MATRIX

Arthur M. Schneiderman, 1999

If you are using a state-of-the-art improvement process, you should be able to close the gap between your current performance and the ultimate process capability at a constant rate given by the process *half-life*. The half-life is not the same for all processes. Instead, it depends on the complexity of the process. There are two dimensions to complexity: technical and organizational.

As an example of technical complexity, a numerically controlled machine tool is more complex than a lathe. Technical complexity is high for new technologies, where part of the learning process is related to understanding and refining that technology. Over time, as the technology matures and its use becomes more routine and familiar, technical complexity declines.

Organizational complexity arises when a process has linkages (intermediate inputs and/or outputs) to processes outside of its boundaries. These processes may be internal or external (outside suppliers or cus-

Months

Organizational Complexity		Low	Medium	High
	High	14	18	22
	Medium	7	9	11
	Low	1	3	5

Technical Complexity

rived at the matrix of average half-life shown in Figure A.

For processes of low organizational and technical complexity, I observed a rate of improvement of 50% per month, while for processes at the other extreme, the rate of improvement slowed by more than a factor of 20 to 50% improvement every 22 months. Note also that organizational complexity had 2 to 3 times the effect of technical complexity in slowing improvement.

Note that flattening organizational structure or organizing around processes rather than functions does much to reduce organizational complexity and thereby increase the potential rate of improvement (that is, reduce the process half-life).

This half-life/complexity matrix can be used in several ways. As a *goal-setting* tool it allows rational determination of future performance based on the use of state-of-the-art incremental improvement tools and methods. As a *diagnostic* tool, it allows a team to benchmark its improvement efforts against best practice for processes of similar complexity. As a *measure of organizational learning,* it is easily consolidated from the level of the team, through the business unit, to an overall organizationwide metric. As a *specification* for an improvement process, it allows potential users the ability to make comparisons with alternative methodologies.

tomers) to the organization. The linkages may be one-way or two-way, one-time or interactive, routine or requiring real-time negotiation. So processes can run the full organizational gambit, from completely self-contained (uni-functional) to cross-functional or cross-organizational. We would expect the rate of improvement to slow as the cultures, goals, and objectives of the various players come into potential conflict.

By sorting the improvement efforts that I studied into the nine bins formed by classifying each in terms of the process's apparent organizational and technical complexity (low, medium, or high), I ar-

APPENDIX 2
RELATIONSHIP OF HALF-LIFE TO THE EXPERIENCE CURVE

Arthur M. Schneiderman, 1999

In the 1970s, Bruce Henderson, founder of The Boston Consulting Group, promoted, under a new name, the *Learning Curve* that was discovered by T. P. Wright and published by him in 1936. The learning curve, developed in the aircraft industry, was based on the observation that unit direct labor usage, expressed in total man-months, declined with increasing experience. Henderson noted that the same was true for unit cost. Based on this observation, he went on to develop a strategy model with the experience curve at its foundation.

The experience curve, like the half-life, is also an empirical observation. It states that for each dou-

bling of cumulative experience (total units produced from the very beginning, not just this year), real unit cost drops by a constant percent, for example, 20%. If your first million units cost $10 each, then your next million units should cost $8 each. The next two million units, $6.40, the next four million units, $5.12, etc. Because cost is driven by cumulative units produced (1 + 1 + 2 + 4 million in our example), the rate of decline of cost drops over time unless unit volume grows at a sufficiently high exponential rate.

The half-life method, on the other hand, predicts that the rate of decline of defect level is constant over time. Why the difference? We can't say for sure, since the experience curve is a purely empirical observation and is not based on any underlying theory. We can list the things that probably affect the slope of the experience curve, but we can't write an equation in which they are the independent variables. On the other hand, there is a theoretical basis for the half-life model.

The Pareto chart is a graphical tool (bar chart) for displaying the rank-ordered causes for a particular defect. With very rare exceptions, these charts follow the 80/20 rule: 20% of the causes account for 80% of the defects. This leads to exponentially declining Pareto diagrams. In fact, the biggest cause, that is the "root cause," usually accounts for 20% to 40% of the total defects. Let's take 30% as a typical number. For a process of average complexity, an experienced improvement team takes about four months for each cycle of improvement; 30% improvement in four months corresponds to a half-life of 8 months, consistent with the *half-life/complexity matrix.* For less complex processes, the root cause is often larger and the improvement cycle time shorter, accounting for the shorter half-lives. For more complex processes, there tend to be many more causes so that the root cause is smaller while the improvement cycle time is longer.

Note that I said an "experienced" improvement team. Proficiency in using the improvement process takes several improvement cycles, so that initially, half-lives can be significantly longer. For this reason, I encourage organizations to attack less complex processes at the beginning as the organization masters their new improvement paradigm.

Also keep in mind that the half-life deals with defects, not cost. Of course defects, defined as any gap between current and potential performance, are the principal driver of unit costs, so the two are clearly related. Twenty years ago, experience curve practitioners were baffled by the unexplainable leapfrogging done by Japanese industry. How could they possibly achieve experience curve slopes two or more times steeper than their Western counterparts? Initial reaction was that they were using predatory pricing, selling below cost. The furor even made its way to the US Congress. But careful study showed that their hyper-fast cost reduction was real and the result of a new approach to process improvement.

The experience curve became the very basis of competitive strategy after its discovery, leading to a focus on the positive feedback loop between market share, cumulative experience, and unit cost. I believe that the half-life model can provide a similar strategic nucleus.

Questions

Time Frame: 1986–90

1. What was Analog Devices' strategy in the second half of the 1980s?
2. Critically evaluate the "half-life" concept, in light of Analog Devices' strategy. What are the potential benefits and the limitations of the half-life concept? How would a company develop the half-life for different processes? How is the half-life concept different from the experience curve concept?
3. Identify the conflicts that exist between the QIP measures and the measures reported by the financial system. Which numbers should we believe? Can they be reconciled?
4. Critically assess the usefulness of the information contained in the corporate scorecard in Exhibit 3 as a way to implement Analog Devices' strategy. What role does each set of measures play in strategy execution? What should be the relative importance of financial versus nonfinancial measures? What additional information would you like to see included in the scorecard?

Time Frame: 1990–96

5. Evaluate the evolution of the corporate scorecard and related management planning and control systems at Analog Devices during the period 1990–95 in light of Analog Devices' strategy in the first half of the 1990s.
6. Do you agree with the compensation philosophy of Analog Devices?
7. Describe Analog Devices' strategy as of 1996. How should the corporate scorecard and other management systems change in 1996 to best fit the strategic needs of the company?

CASE 10–2
CUP CORPORATION

The CUP Vorstand (Board of Directors) decided to create a Customer Care Center (CCC) to stem the increasing defection of customers resulting in part from dissatisfaction with the firm's services. The central idea was to provide private customers with one telephone number to be used for all their questions and problems and for all types of insurance offered by CUP. The CCC would be staffed 24 hours a day, 7 days a week to make sure someone was always available for the customer. The CUP personnel would be able to address all inquires and handle customer problems 90 percent of the time on the first call. The remaining 10 percent of the problems would be resolved in one day with a follow-up call.

Derrick Westmuller was assigned as the project manager responsible for the creation and development of the CCC. In developing this center he was tasked to display the kind of entrepreneurial behavior the chairman of CUP was seeking to develop. Mr. Kirk, the energetic and dynamic chairman, was seeking to change the CUP insurance company from a stiff bureaucracy to a nimble entrepreneurial-driven firm. The design was to have the center function as a central services profit center supporting the separate insurance business units of CUP.

Derrick, a seasoned manager, saw this assignment as a real career opportunity. He began to think about meaningful indicators and measures for success of the center. He was politically savvy and wanted the performance of this center to stand on its true accomplishments.

This case was prepared by Professor Lawrence Carr, Babson College. Copyright by Lawrence Carr.

Background: Product Lines Responding to Declining Growth Rates

CUP was one of the largest insurance firms based in Europe. It had a worldwide operation and was recently acquired by another major insurance company. CUP had enjoyed remarkable growth of more than 25 percent each year over the past 10 years. The firm had used a series of acquisitions to broaden the type of insurance offerings and had also grown internally to meet the expanding needs of its served market. It sold various forms of insurance in the health, life, casualty, property, and automotive areas.

Over the last couple of years the growth of premium income in the German insurance industry had leveled off. In 1993 and 1994, the industry still enjoyed high growth rates and grew at 10.3 percent and 9.5 percent, respectively. By 1995, however, the growth rate had decreased to only 4.8 percent. By 1996 and 1997, growth was flat instead of the planned 3 percent and the expectation was that "growth will only be moderate, if any growth is recorded at all."

The declining growth rates resulted from a set of reinforcing trends:

1. Worsening economic climate with increasing economic downsizing, increasing unemployment, and stagnating real income.
2. Higher taxes and social welfare levies, in part due to the reunification of Germany.
3. Increasing competition resulting from the deregulation of the European market, which was "fully noticeable for the first time" in 1995.
4. Extensive satisfaction of the basic demand for insurance in Germany, an area of sustained growth up to 1994.

Despite these worsening market conditions, the operating divisions of CUP were often able to gain market share. However, the squeeze of increasing competition and increasing client price sensitivity led in the private insurance market to shorter contracts and more cancellation of existing contracts. This effect varied in intensity by product line.

In response, product lines and the branch offices began to pay more attention to providing a better service as a way to keep agents, brokers, and existing clients satisfied. There was a range of ideas and responses to the problem, varying from remaking newsletters for customers to creating "a Calling Center." The latter was in response to the complaints of many customers, agents, and brokers about the difficulties of reaching clerks and about the level of service they received if and when they could reach them.

Within the decentralized structure of CUP, in which product lines operated rather independently, a number of "calling centers" were created. Those more concentrated product lines, such as Life and Health, created their own central telephone centers. Some branch offices also created "telephone centers" for those product lines that had decentralized much of their clerical work to the branches.

Reforming the "Lapse Rate" Problem as a Customer Loyalty Problem

Traditionally the firm, through its two brand names, CUP and Southern, had focused on the lower middle segment of the market that was not very price sensitive. Exclusive agents handled 70 percent of this business. The increasing defection rate began to draw the attention of some senior executives. They ordered a study by an international management consultant.

In March 1996, this firm reported that the "lapse rate"—the number of customers canceling contracts compared to the total amount of contracts—had reached DM 800M in 1995 (DM 900M in 1996), which is around 10 percent of total premium revenue. The lapse rate percentage was comparable to other German insurance firms. In some products, such as car insurance, the figures were much higher (20 percent) and had passed a pain threshold.

The firm also reported that the commissions of the agents were almost exclusively tied to generating new contracts. The agents were spending 70 percent of their time just generating enough new business to keep up with cancellations. If this trend were to continue, they would have to spend 100 percent of their time by the year 2000 on just finding new business to keep up with cancellations.

In-depth interviews with defected customers, or "root cause interviews," indicated that 58.7 percent of the defections could be influenced by CUP (without changes in the contracts), indicating that 5.8 percent of the customer base of the firm was lost through the firm's own fault. Dissatisfied customers mentioned (apart from price, 33.3 percent): problems with agents (34.7 percent), bad claims processing (13.3 percent), slow and bureaucratic responses (9.3 percent), and too little information (4.0 percent). When customers mentioned high price, it would often not be an issue as such but in combination with other problems such as dissatisfaction about the agent.

Finally, the firm found the following:

- Customers who had more than one insurance contract were less likely to defect.
- Trigger events (e.g., exasperation about being passed from one clerk to another without getting any help) seemed to precipitate cancellation.
- If a customer with several policies canceled one, it was likely that the customer would not continue when other contracts came up for renewal.

The traditional market research techniques used by CUP, the consultant maintained, were not able to detect these kinds of problems because they were geared more toward customer satisfaction with a (new) product and not event/action related.

The "lapse rate" problem for CUP was summarized by the image of a leaking bucket; new customers would flow into the bucket while at the same time many leaked out through big holes. The focus of product lines was on increasing the inflow rather than intelligently addressing the outflow. This was not only the case within CUP but also the case throughout the German insurance industry.

Instead of focusing on the "lapse rate" or "customer defection rate" of individual product lines, the problem was restated as a customer loyalty problem that cut across product lines and was considered a corporate problem.

A Corporate Problem: From Vicious to Virtual Cycles

Customers looked at the firm as a whole, not as a product line with whom they had one contract. It turned out that the more contracts customers had, the longer they remained loyal to CUP. The longer they remained with the firm, the lower the commissions for new products and the lower the damage rate. If this virtual cycle were to lead to small improvements in customer retention, profitability would be significantly improved.

Conversely, if customers had only one contract, they canceled much more frequently. Replacement then led to a commission for the agent. And when this process gained enough momentum—as it did—all insurance firms suffered from high lapse rates and paid high commissions. Hence a vicious cycle.

To induce a virtual cycle, customer retention would have to become a strategic target. There were many positive ideas and responses in CUP's product lines and branch offices at the time. There were also managers who thought quite differently. They felt the responses were often geared to symptoms, and would have little positive effect on the business. With regard to the telephone centers, a senior manager from one of the product lines mentioned that they lacked critical mass. There would be insufficient sophisticated technology and training of personnel, and not enough would be learned from the customer.

The customer needed to be viewed as a person, a family, or even an extended family, going through a life-cycle with critical events (like getting a driver's license, getting married, having kids, buying a house, setting up a retirement fund, etc.) each creating new insurance needs. The firm was a collection of product lines. In anticipation of future business, CUP should try to satisfy the customer needs in all of these stages.

Moreover, rather than the risk of each customer being treated as part of a large pool with certain statistical averages, customers could and should be segmented into highly profitable groups, not-profitable groups, and loss-generating groups. The firm as a whole should proactively pick and target the most profitable group, and learn more about the customers. At the same time, it should defend its existing customer base through (i) becoming sensitive to early signals of defection, (ii) monitoring carefully trigger events, and (iii) trying to recover "lost" contracts/customers.

While the efforts of individual product lines would be important, clearly, some executives at the corporate level felt that there was a need for a comprehensive and integrated approach. However, such an approach should be taken in incremental steps.

The First Step: "Quick Hits" and New Discoveries

The data suggested that CUP could benefit from using a number of ideas for customer retention derived from the practices of leading US insurance firms and banks as well as new internal intentions. The CUP Vorstand (Board of Directors) ordered a specific study of customer loyalty for CUP between May 1996 and October

1996. It was anticipated that this would create ideas for "quick hits" and begin to close "the holes in the bucket."

But the project also led to new discoveries about the prevailing thinking in the firm concerning the customers. According to one of the consultants:

1. A customer typically called because his or her agent was either unreachable (either a part-timer, or trying to generate new business) or could not effectively address a question. When a customer called one product line, say, Health, and then had a question about life insurance, the Health clerk would say, "I don't know." On average, it would take a client four contacts to get to the right person, and even then, in 30 percent of the cases, the questions were not resolved. Customers tended to cancel when a specific question or problem was dealt with in the wrong way.

2. A clerk working in one product line had only one screen (related to the contract that line had with the client) and had little access to information about other contracts the customer may have had. However, if a customer with multiple policies canceled one policy because the customer was dissatisfied with the service in one product line, this person was likely to cancel the other policies as well. The clerks often did not sense the business was at risk because, quite literally, it was "not on their screen," and therefore the pattern of defections remained hidden.

3. Car insurance played a critical role in binding clients because it was often the first contract. It appeared that most people bought a car on the weekend when insurance firms were closed. In addition, it was difficult to create a team to help clients because, in general, customers could not reach a clerk after 5:00 and trade unions did not allow work after 6:00. Therefore, the response to the idea was often "yes, but it can't be done."

4. Most CUP people talked about the customer but didn't do anything about improving the customer service. The firm had a strong ana-lytical culture. When confronted with the figures, they would say, "this is true for health but not for life" or "it is worse with other insurance firms."

5. When customer focus groups were organized in June 1997, the Vorstand (Board of Directors) members were invited to attend. Only one showed up apart from the manager of the study. The others maintained that "we know the customer."

The Customer Care Center

By October 1996 when the results of the customer loyalty studies were in, the CUP Vorstand ordered a feasibility study for a CCC reaching far beyond specific product lines. The key idea was to provide customers with one telephone number and professionally trained people who could effectively answer a variety of questions, and thereby increase the service dramatically. In addition, a center would be able to eliminate process steps in the future and eliminate sources of errors. Finally, it was believed that the center would be a cheaper and more efficient way of processing information.

By January 1997, an outline for the center design was ready and specified the following goals:

1. CUP's private customers would have one and only one telephone number for all their questions and problems. This service would be available to them in addition to the agents.

2. The center would be open 24 hours per day and 7 days per week. It would be able to finalize 90 percent of all customer inquiries in one telephone call. It would lead to a significant increase in service quality and efficiency.

3. CUP would benefit from a reduction in the lapse rate, specifically, in cases where, in the past, the client's inquiry was not addressed or the service was unsatisfactory.

4. Additional goals of CUP were (*a*) becoming a service leader in the insurance industry, (*b*) increasing the number of customers with multiple policies.

Concerns and Inventing Solutions

The proposal generated a number of concerns. For instance, the agents saw the center as a threat to their relationship with the client. In response, it was decided that agents would be informed of any communication between the center and his or her clients. Moreover the center could act as a backup for the agent in case the agent was inaccessible to the client (e.g., at night and on the weekend). Finally, the center could help agents by contacting prospective clients. Typically, an agent might get one out of ten potential insurance contracts. The center could provide a first screen by telephone and improve this ratio.

The product lines had a different concern. They thought that it was impossible that a "generalist" could address questions related to their specialized business and that it would take "at least ten years" of experience to learn to do this. However, it was discovered that product line clerks got caught in a vicious cycle. Typically, the clerks intended to provide the highest possible quality when talking to customers but in doing so tended to become too technical. Their response was "over-engineered" and they tended to waste their time while the client became exasperated.

In addition, many customers had the same kinds of questions. An expert might become annoyed when having to repeat the answers or might forget to mention part of the answers. Less specialized persons with additional skills, however, might quite easily answer questions based on scripts that provide "good answers."

Finally, it turned out that at least 70 to 80 percent of the questions (depending on the product lines) were rather mundane and did not need a specialist to answer them because the question was merely about the status of a claim or the customer gave a change of address, etc. Again, an expert might become exasperated with such questions. A special team with extended product knowledge could still address the remaining 20 to 30 percent.

A final set of concerns had to do with the fact that calling centers were already established in some product lines and branch offices. For instance, if somebody changed an address, a product line would argue that this couldn't be dealt with by a center because a change of address might have implications for insurance related to the house. Or some product lines would say, "We are learning from the market through our own calling center, and now we lose our ear," or "Why break up a winning team?"

At the time that a central center was discussed, some of the branch offices had just installed their own telephone centers as a way to screen calls to the back office. Branch office managers had received employee acceptance by claiming that "this was their future." Dismantling their unit would undermine trustworthiness. The first two concerns could be dealt with through agreements about making information in the center readily accessible to the product lines. The latter concern might be dealt with, in part, by a promise that the center would be in or around the two branch offices with telephone centers. This would make it easy for employees to apply for jobs in the central center.

By April 1997, the Vorstand had agreed on the following critical aspects for the center's design.

1. The CCC would be a "greenfield" solution and it would be the only center within the CUP. Other newly established calling centers in branches and some product lines would be closed down.

2. It would centralize all customer inquiries and be available 100 percent of the time, and able to address effectively 90 percent of all questions and problems.

3. The center would be established outside the existing organizational structure of CUP, i.e., it would not be part of any of the product lines or operating divisions. This would also make it possible to sign more flexible employment contracts (flexible working hours and compensation).

4. The center would be a profit center and be paid on a telephone call basis by the product lines rather than a cost center supported by corporate or the operating divisions' overhead.

5. The center would be a stand-alone central service business unit with a mission to support the product lines.

6. The product lines would supply insurance technical know-how and competent personnel, and interface with the product lines would be clearly organized.

During the first year, the center would focus on "inquiry" initiated by the client. In addition, it would also initiate inquiries on behalf of product lines in case a customer canceled a contract. This initial set-up would require an EDP system with the least integration into the rest of the IT infrastructure of the CUP, allowing for an autonomous EDP center for the CCC with only a relatively small link to the Central EDP.

However, as soon as the center operated effectively (expected within half a year of its opening), new tasks could be added. For instance, the center could become involved in the claims processing, in correcting errors, or changing information such as addresses, etc. It could also carry out marketing research at the request of the product lines. And finally, it might become the care center for agents and brokers as well.

The customers (depending on the product line) would expect the center to address 70 to 80 percent of the inquiries through its generalists. The remaining 20 to 30 percent of questions would be passed on to specialized teams with extended product knowledge in the center. Not only would the processing within the center be "transparent and traceable," thereby reducing errors, the links to the product lines would be transparent and traceable as well.

Indicators and Measurement of Success

The center would have to be up and running within one year, in May 1998. The effort would be widely watched within the firm and within the German insurance industry. If successful, CUP would have a first-mover advantage and be instrumental in reshaping the industry.

But what were meaningful indicators of success of the CCC and how to measure that success? Should Derrick, the project manager for the new center, focus on one indicator, or on a set of indicators reflecting a wider sense of performance? How many should he focus on, and which are really critical? Which indicators can he really influence and how?

When asked how he would measure success with the clients, Derrick initially mentioned: "a decreasing lapse rate—that part of the lapse rate, connected to the service quality of the CUP, should decrease." However, other executives differed about what constitute a "Balanced Score Card." For instance, a senior executive suggested: "speed of processing, efficiency in terms of cutting out process steps, quality in terms of fewer errors, accessible all the time, and friendliness of the telephone operators."

Another senior executive, responsible for sales through the agent channel, said the critical question was "whether we lose fewer clients." At the moment, the firm lost and added 12 percent per year of its customer base. If the center could stem losses to 11 percent, that would be success. However, "50 percent of the agents grow more than the market." If the agents' sales force was trimmed, then larger, more professional and entrepreneurial agents could be created. If the commission structure was adjusted, agents would remain a formidable sales force.

One consultant drew a more complex picture for measuring success with clients: "How to measure defection if you have two channels to the customer: the center and the agents?" Some customers would call; others not. The first group would call because the agent channel did not work for them. But as for the second group of customers: Are they satisfied with the agent, are they indifferent? One measure could be: if an existing customer had recommended CUP to a new customer who complained about having to work through an agent (of a competitor), did the existing customer mention the center? Also, the picture of what led people to defect should change. The percentages for "bad claim processing," "slow and bureaucratic responses," and "too little information" should significantly decrease.

For shareholder value, this consultant suggested a look at a decreasing defection rate and selling more contracts. Finally, for innovation and learning, he thought that the center would generate information that was at present with the agents and inaccessible to the firm, for instance, if the total number of calls was 20,000 per week and 1,500 were about a new topic, and increasing, this factor could be a trend to be monitored. Finally, he was surprised that the product lines did not realize the opportunity created for them. Rather than thinking about the drawbacks, what could the center do for them?

During a final meeting with Derrick, he repeated that "the hard figure" for success was the following rate: the number of cancellations (attributable to poor service) after the center had made an effort to "recover" them versus the total amount of cancellation. If customers blamed the product lines or the agents, the question remained, "Can we get them back?"

Derrick, politically astute and considered a competent manager, wanted to ensure the success of the CCC. The key in his mind was getting the measures right. These measures had to work for all the stakeholders: the CCC workers, the product lines, corporate managers, the customers, and finally himself.

Questions

1. As an advisor to the project manager, Derrick Westmuller, what set of measures would you advise they adopt?

2. Develop a balanced measurement system showing how the measures and measurements link to what you believe are the key success factors of the CCC.

CASE 10–3
ENAGER INDUSTRIES, INC.

I don't get it. I've got a nifty new product proposal that can't help but make money, and top management turns thumbs down. No matter how we price this new item, we expect to make $390,000 on it pretax. That would contribute over 15 cents per share to our earnings after taxes, which is more than the 10 cent earnings-per-share increase in 1993 that the president made such a big thing about in the shareholders' annual report. It just doesn't make sense for the president to be touting e.p.s. while his subordinates are rejecting profitable projects like this one.

The frustrated speaker was Sarah McNeil, product development manager of the Consumer Products Division of Enager Industries, Inc. Enager was a relatively young company, which had grown rapidly to its 1993 sales level of over $222 million. (See Exhibits 1 and 2 for financial data for 1992 and 1993.)

Enager had three divisions—Consumer Products, Industrial Products, and Professional Services—each of which accounted for about one-third of Enager's total sales. Consumer Products, the oldest of the three divisions, designed, manufactured, and marketed a line of houseware items, primarily for use in the kitchen. The Industrial Products Division built one-of-a-kind machine tools to customer specifications (i.e., it was a large "job shop"), with a typical job taking several months to complete. The Professional Services Division, the newest of the three, had been added to Enager by acquiring a large firm that provided land planning, landscape architecture, structural architecture, and consulting engineering services. This division has grown rapidly, in part because of its capability to perform "environmental impact" studies, as required by law on many new land development projects.

This case was updated by Professor Vijay Govindarajan and Anil Chitkara (T '94) based on an earlier case prepared by James S. Reece, University of Michigan. Copyrighted by the University of Michigan.

EXHIBIT 1

INCOME STATEMENTS
For 1992 and 1993
($000s, except earnings-per-share figures)

| | Year Ended December 31 | |
	1992	*1993*
Sales	$212,193	$222,675
Cost of goods sold	162,327	168,771
Gross margin	49,866	53,904
Other expenses:		
Development	12,096	12,024
Selling and general	19,521	20,538
Interest	1,728	2,928
Total	33,345	35,490
Income before taxes	16,521	18,414
Income tax expense	5,617	6,261
Net income	$ 10,904	$ 12,153
Earnings-per-share (1,500,000 and 1,650,000 shares outstanding in 1992 and 1993, respectively)	$ 7.27	$ 7.37

Because of the differing nature of their activities, each division was treated as an essentially independent company. There were only a few corporate-level managers and staff people, whose job was to coordinate the activities of the three divisions. One aspect of this coordination was that all new project proposals requiring investment in excess of $1,500,000 had to be reviewed by the chief financial officer, Henry Hubbard. It was Hubbard who had recently rejected McNeil's new product proposal, the essentials of which are shown in Exhibit 3.

EXHIBIT 2

BALANCE SHEETS
For 1992 and 1993
($000s)

	As of December 31	
	1992	*1993*
Assets		
Cash and temporary investments .	$ 4,212	$ 4,407
Accounts receivable	41,064	46,821
Inventories	66,486	76,401
Total current assets	111,762	127,629
Plant and equipment:		
Original cost	111,978	137,208
Accumulated depreciation	38,073	47,937
Net	73,905	89,271
Investments and other assets	6,429	9,357
Total assets	$192,096	$226,257
Liabilities and Owners' Equity		
Accounts payable	$ 29,160	$ 36,858
Taxes payable	3,630	3,135
Current portion of long-term debt .	0	4,902
Total current liabilities	32,790	44,895
Deferred income taxes	1,677	2,955
Long-term debt	37,866	46,344
Total liabilities	72,333	94,194
Common stock.	52,104	58,536
Retained earnings	67,659	73,527
Total owners' equity	119,763	132,063
Total liabilities and owners' equity	$192,096	$226,257

Performance Evaluation

Prior to 1992, each division had been treated as a profit center, with annual division profit budgets negotiated between the president and the respective division general managers. At the urging of Henry Hubbard, Enager's president, Carl Randall, had decided to begin treating each division as an investment center, so as

EXHIBIT 3 **Financial Data from New Product Proposal**

1. Projected asset investment*

Cash	$ 150,000
Accounts receivable	450,000
Inventories	900,000
Plant and equipment†	1,500,000
Total	$3,000,000

2. Cost data:

Variable cost per unit	$ 9
Differential fixed costs (per year)‡	$ 510,000

3. Price/market estimates (per year):

Unit Price	Unit Sales	Break-Even Volume
$18	100,000 units	56,667 units
21	75,000	42,500
24	60,000	34,000

*Assumes 100,000 units sales.

†Annual capacity of 120,000 units.

‡Includes straight-line depreciation on new plant and equipment.

to be able to relate each division's profit to the assets the division used to generate its profits.

Starting in 1992, each division was measured as based on its return on assets, which was defined to be the division's net income divided by its total assets. Net income for a division was calculated by taking the division's "direct income before taxes," then subtracting the division's share of corporate administrative expenses (allocated on the basis of divisional revenues) and its share of income tax expense (the tax rate applied to the division's "direct income before taxes" after subtraction of the allocated corporate administrative expenses). Although Hubbard realized there were other ways to define a division's income, he and the president preferred this method since "it made the sum of the [divisional] parts equal to the [corporate] whole."

Similarly, Enager's total assets were subdivided among three divisions. Since each division operated in physically separate facilities, it was easy to attribute most assets, including receivables, to specific divisions. The corporate-office assets, including the centrally controlled cash account, were allocated to the divisions on the basis of divisional revenues. All fixed assets were recorded at their balance sheet values—that is, original cost less accumulated straight-line depreciation. Thus, the sum of the divisional assets was equal to the amount shown on the corporate balance sheet ($226,257 as of December 31, 1993).

In 1991, Enager had as its return on year-end assets (net income divided by total assets) a rate of 5.2 percent. According to Hubbard, this corresponded to a "gross return" of 9.3 percent; he defined gross return as equal to earnings *before* interest and taxes ("EBIT") divided by assets. Hubbard felt that a company like Enager should have a gross (EBIT) return on assets of at least 12 percent, especially given the interest rates the corporation had had to pay on its recent borrowing. He, therefore, instructed each division manager that the division was to try to earn a gross return of 12 percent in 1992 and 1993. In order to help pull the return up to this level, Hubbard decided that new investment proposals would have to show a return of at least 15 percent in order to be approved.

1992–93 Results

Hubbard and Randall were moderately pleased with 1992 results. The year was a particularly difficult one for some of Enager's competitors, yet Enager had managed to increase its return on assets from 5.2 percent to 5.7 percent, and its gross return from 9.3 percent to 9.5 percent.

At the end of 1992, the president put pressure on the general manager of the Industrial Products Division to improve its return on investment, suggesting that this division was not "carrying its share of the load." The divi-

sion manager had bristled at this comment, saying the division could get a higher return "if we had a lot of old machines the way Consumer Products does." The president had responded that he did not understand the relevance of the division manager's remark, adding, "I don't see why the return on an old asset should be higher than that on a new asset, just because the old one cost less."

The 1993 results both disappointed and puzzled Carl Randall. Return on assets fell from 5.7 percent to 5.4 percent, and gross return dropped from 9.5 percent to 9.4 percent. At the same time, return on sales (net income divided by sales) rose from 5.1 percent to 5.5 percent, and return on owners' equity also increased, from 9.1 percent to 9.2 percent. The Professional Services Division easily exceeded the 12 percent gross return target; Consumer Products' gross return on assets was 10.8 percent; but Industrial Products' return was only 6.9 percent (see Exhibit 4). These results prompted Randall to say to Hubbard:

> You know, Henry, I've been a marketer most of my career, but, until recently, I thought I understood the notion of return on investment. Now I see in 1993 our profit margin was up and our earnings-per-share were up; yet two of your return on investment figures were down; return on invested capital went down, and return

EXHIBIT 4   Calculation of Gross Return on Assets, 1993

| | | | Specific Assets | | | | |
Division	Sales	EBIT	W/C	Fxd.	Alloc.	Total	Gross ROA
Consumer	74.3	10.8	60.8	34.6	4.6	100.0	10.8
Industrial	74.2	7.2	44.4	54.6	4.6	103.6	6.9
Professional services	74.2	3.3	18.0	0.0	4.6	22.6	14.6
Total		21.3	123.2	89.2	13.8	226.2	9.4

on owners' equity went up. I just don't understand these discrepancies.

Moreover, there seems to be a lot more tension among our managers the last two years. The general manager of Professional Services seems to be doing a good job, and she's happy as a lark about the praise I've given her. But the general manager of Industrial Products looks daggers at me every time we meet. And last week, when I was eating lunch with the division manager at Consumer Products, the product development manager came over to our table and really burned my ears over a new product proposal of hers you rejected the other day.

I'm wondering if I should follow up on the idea that Karen Kraus in Personnel brought back from the two-day organization development workshop she attended over at the university. She thinks we ought to have a one-day off-site retreat of all the corporate and divisional managers to talk over this entire return on investment matter.

Questions

1. Why was McNeil's new product proposal rejected? Should it have been? Explain.

2. What inferences do you draw from a cash flow statement for 1993? Is a breakdown by divisions useful?

3. What inferences do you draw from the comparative balance sheets and income statements for 1992 and 1993?

4. Evaluate the manner in which Randall and Hubbard have implemented their investment center concept. What pitfalls did they apparently not anticipate?

5. What, if anything, should Randall do now about his investment center approach?

6. Design a balanced scorecard for Consumer, Industrial, and Professional Products Divisions of Enager Industries. Be *specific* for *each* division.

7. What other advice do you have for Randall and Hubbard?

Case 10–4
Warren Insurance Company

Joseph Allen was assistant to the controller of Warren Insurance, a large insurance company. Emily Scott, the controller, handed him an article, "Your Company's Most Valuable Asset: Intellectual Capital,"[1] and asked Allen to look into the topic discussed therein and recommend what, if any action, Scott should take. The article contained a number of examples of companies that were making efforts to measure and manage intellectual capital. They are summarized in Exhibit 1.

Skandia Navigator

Allen was intrigued by the practices of Skandia, an international insurance and financial services corporation based in Sweden, referred to in the article. Allen wrote to the company, and received its 1994 and 1995 annual reports together with "supplements" to these reports describing Skandia's views on intellectual capital. Excerpts from these supplements are given in Exhibit 2.

According to its annual reports, Skandia is a dominant provider of life and nonlife insurance and financial services in Sweden, with a marketshare of over 40 percent in life insurance.

Skandia also has strong operations in other Nordic countries and competitive operations worldwide. In addition, Skandia is the world leader in a few specialized areas of insurance, such as aviation insurance. Eighty-five percent of Skandia's premiums are generated outside of Sweden.

In 1995 Skandia's premiums were 52,521 million Swedish Kronor (8,097 million USD).[2] Fifty percent of Skandia's premium revenue came from its worldwide life reassurance business. Since 1991 Skandia had seen its profitability vary from a loss of 2,369 MSEK (365 MUSD) in 1992 to a gain of 1,384 MSEK (213 MUSD) in 1993.

With the article and the Skandia supplements, Allen needed to decide if measuring intellectual capital was worth further investigation and consideration by Warren Insurance.

Questions

1. What is your evaluation of Skandia's approach to measuring intellectual capital? How about other companies included in Exhibit 1?
2. What advice do you have for Allen in terms of measuring intellectual capital for Warren Insurance?

This case was prepared by Kirk Hendrickson (T '97) under the supervision of Professor Vijay Govindarajan. The case is mostly based on materials furnished by Skandia.

[1] Thomas A. Stewart, *Fortune*, July 8, 1994, pp. 68–74.

---

[2] The exchange rate is an estimate computed on the basis of 6.49 Swedish Kronor (SEK) to 1.00 U.S. dollar (USD).

Exhibit 1 **Examples of Measuring and Managing Intellectual Capital**

Canadian Imperial Bank of Commerce

CIBC has changed its lending strategy to lend on the basis of intellectual, "soft" assets instead of tangible, "hard" assets. CIBC believes that hard assets can devalue more rapidly than soft assets, so companies based on intellectual assets are at a lower risk of default than those based on tangible assets.

CIBC defines intellectual capital in three ways: human capital, structural capital, and customer capital. Human capital comes from each employee's ability to provide value to the customer. Structural capital is assets such as brands, databases, and work methodologies that leverage employee skills to satisfy customers' demands. Customer capital is the base of customers that interact with the company and their attitudes and actions towards the company.

CIBC has a goal of being able to compare all investment opportunities in a direct fashion so that managers can trade off between investments in hard and soft assets. To do this, CIBC uses a series of measures for the different types of intellectual capital. For example, human capital is measured by such measurements as the speed of learning in a department, weaknesses in competencies within a department, and the number of new ideas implemented. Customer capital is measured by the level of customer satisfaction, the speed of solving customer complaints, the length of a customer relationship, and the level of price sensitivity.

One major area of change as a result of its intellectual capital perspective is that CIBC established a set of competencies that each employee needs to develop. The level to which all employees have developed these competencies measures the level of human capital at CIBC. Different positions require different competencies at varying levels. Each employee is responsible for developing the skills necessary for his/her current job. As a result, CIBC has eliminated its formal training program, which was costing the company $30 million per year, replacing it with a variety of self-paced learning tools and learning centers.

Dow Chemical

Gordon Petrash, Dow Chemical's Director of Intellectual Asset Management, wants to make managing patents as easy as managing tangible assets. Petrash is responsible for actively managing Dow's portfolio of patents, of which Dow has about 29,000 in force.*

The Intellectual Asset Management group builds and prunes Dow's patent portfolio by managing patents that were frequently ignored. These patents were not being commercialized or licensed and no one was responsible for doing this, even though each patent could cost up to $250,000 per year to keep in force. Additionally, the group seeks out new opportunities for applying and enhancing the patents.

(continued)

---

*Petrash believes that patents are the best of the intellectual assets to start managing.

EXHIBIT 1   *Continued*

Petrash developed a six-step approach to managing intellectual assets that assesses, analyzes, and evaluates, or applies value to, various assets; the result of his approach is the formation of a new intellectual assets portfolio.

Dow Chemical credits this six-step process with a number of successes in reducing costs, increasing patent enforceability, and discovering new products.

Hughes Space & Communications Division

A division of Hughes Aircraft and a designer of communication satellites, Hughes Space & Communications Division is involved in trying to create what it calls its "knowledge highway." The "knowledge highway" is an attempt to turn contextual knowledge into usable tools for its engineers.

Arian Ward, head of business engineering at HSCD, believes that there are two types of knowledge, rules based and contextual.[†] Rules-based knowledge relies on following a set of rules to get a correct answer. Contextual knowledge uses wisdom, stories, and experience that change meaning depending on the context in which they are applied. Ward feels that HSCD is losing contextual knowledge created when it develops a satellite. The result is that knowledge is often reinvented, consuming many other resources to recreate the intellectual assets.

Ward is implementing "lessons-learned" databases and "knowledge maps" to prevent the loss of intellectual capital. The lessons-learned databases are for improving access to past decisions, designs, and problems, by recording design decisions and how they were made in a format that is more accessible to current engineers. The knowledge maps are for locating where the knowledge is in the company, in what systems and in whose heads. Rather than just being an index of experts, these maps provide paths to the knowledge, leading through the different individuals who possess the intellectual assets. Both systems will improve the contextual knowledge because Ward feels that "people think in terms of stories, not facts." He believes these systems will preserve the stories, not just the facts.

From Thomas Stewart, "Your Company's Most Valuable Asset: Intellectual Capital," *Fortune,* July 8, 1994, pp. 68–74. © 1994 Time Inc. All rights reserved.

[†]While Ward did not directly use the word *contextual,* it summarizes the variety of terms with which he described this second type of knowledge.

EXHIBIT 2   Excerpts from Skandia Annual Reports

A: Visualizing Intellectual Capital in Skandia*

Auditors, analysts, and accounting people have long lacked instruments and generally accepted norms for accurately evaluating service companies and their "intellectual capital." . . . At Skandia we have always maintained that our intellectual capital is at least as important as our financial capital in providing truly sustainable earnings. . . . Back in 1991 we instituted a function in our AFS unit to develop a method for describing Skandia's human capital, structural capital, and customer capital. Leif Edvinsson was appointed the world's first director of intellectual capital (according to Tom Stewart, *Fortune,* October 1994). The intention was to try to devise adequate valuation indicators that could at the same time serve as management tools for a service company. . . . As we now extend this information to cover additional Skandia units, we do so under the name *Skandia Navigator,* to underscore the fact that it is an instrument to help us navigate into the future . . .

Hidden Assets in the Company

The aggregate sum of these intangible values [in knowledge-intensive operations] can be called Intellectual Capital, which comprises both human capital and structural capital.

Human capital represents the knowledge, skill, and capability of the individual employees to provide solutions to the customer. Structural capital consists of everything that remains when the employees go home: databases, customer files, software, manuals, trademarks, organizational structures, and so on—in other words, organizational capability. Customer capital, i.e., the relationships built up with the customers, is a significant part of structural capital. Structural capital can be owned, which is not the case with human capital.

Human capital and structural capital are an indication of a company's future value and ability to generate financial results.

Early Indicators

Although substantial investments are made today in intellectual capital, the payoff and value will not be visible in the financial accounting until some time later on. Through systematic accounting of developments in various areas—such as customer base, staff competence, and processes—an earlier indication of the company's future performance can be obtained.

Skandia Navigator

Skandia's new reporting model, the Skandia Navigator [see Figure 1] is designed to provide a balanced picture of the financial and intellectual capital. The focus on financial results, capital, and monetary flows is complemented by a description of intellectual capital and its development. . . . At Skandia the intellectual capital ratios are grouped into major focus areas: the Customer focus, the Process focus, the Human focus, and the Renewal & Development focus.

(continued)

*Supplement to Skandia's 1994 Annual Report.

EXHIBIT 2 *Continued*

FIGURE 1

The Skandia Navigator

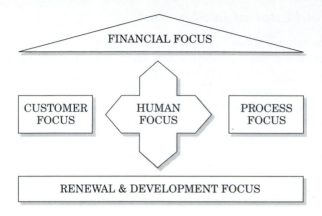

This broadened, balanced type of accounting and reporting results in a more systematic description of the company's ability and potential to transform intellectual capital into financial capital. The specific ratios compiled from the measurements will then become leading indicators.

B: Intellectual Capital: Value-Creating Processes[†]

The Supplement to Skandia's 1995 Annual Report includes Skandia Navigator results for nine selected divisions throughout Skandia's worldwide operations. Each division selected different measures within the five focus areas that they felt best reflected their business situation. The measures and results for three of these divisions are shown below.

Skandia International, Mexico (Table 1)

Twenty-five people work in Mexico with nonlife reinsurance, mainly of fire risks. . . . Due to the risk exposure, it is crucial that Skandia sets the right rate level and keeps its total risk exposure controlled.

TABLE 1 Skandia International, Mexico

Financial Focus	1995	1994	1993
Insurance result, net (MSEK)	66	56	35
Claims ratio, net	48%	37%	63%
Premium income, net (MSEK)	222	185	121
Customer Focus			
Number of visits/underwriter & year	65	65	65
Number of alliances	130	130	130

[†]Supplement to Skandia's 1995 Annual Report.

Table 1   (*continued*)

Human Focus			
Number of employees	25	24	24
Insurance result/employee (MSEK)	2.6	2.3	1.5
Process Focus			
Number of offers and endorsements handled	6,550	n.a.	4,320
Adm. costs/premium income, net	3%	n.a.	9%
Renewal & Development Focus			
Repeat ratio (# of renewed contracts in relation to total number of contracts)	98%	98%	98%
Increase in net premium	20%	53%	38%

One way of measuring the value of regular contacts with customers is to analyse the number of contracts renewed by the office. Coupled with information on profitability, it is possible to calculate the value of the customer portfolio. The renewal rate also affects internal efficiency, since a customer who returns year after year requires less work from the second year onwards.

Customer loyalty and the quality of customer relationships are shown in the contract renewal rate. During the past five years this has been very high, amounting to approximately 90 percent, with average duration of customers at 4.5 years.

SkandiaLink (Table 2)

. . . SkandiaLink provides unit linked assurance with a focus on the Swedish market.

TABLE 2   SkandiaLink

Financial Focus	*1995*	*1994*	*1993*
Premium income, gross (MSEK)	2,087	1,874	1,145
Management operating result (MSEK)	176	132	136.5
Funds managed (MSEK)	6,641	4,257	n.a.
Customer Focus			
Number of contracts	153,104	114,919	74,253
Surrender rate	1.1%	1.0%	n.a.
Human Focus			
Number of employees	48	51	52
Empowerment index (max. value = 1,000)	464	534	n.a.
Process Focus			
Admin. expense/premium income, gross	5.0%	4.5%	5.7%
IT expense/administrative expense	29.7%	28.0%	26.0%
Renewal & Development Focus			
Number of contracts/employee	3,180	2,253	1,439
Fund switches through Telelink	40%	22%	n.a.

(*continued*)

EXHIBIT 2 *Continued*

To establish a "continuous improvement" culture, a control model has been introduced which uses operational indicators that are coupled to the daily work performed by the customer service organization. These indicators measure the parameters that customers—according to surveys—consider to be essential for meeting their quality standards. In addition, through changed work methods, customers should also be able to directly impact these indicators. The responsible departmental heads regularly monitor changes in the indicators through an information system. This enables the company to take corrective measures at an early stage.

Skandia Life UK Group (Table 3)

Skandia Life provides a range of unit linked assurance products, from strictly savings-oriented products, to contracts with varying degrees of insurance protection. The group's products are sold primarily to customers in the UK . . .

TABLE 3   **Skandia Life UK Group**

Financial Focus	*1995*	*1994*	*1993*
Return on net asset value	22.5%	33.2%	21.8%
Management operating result (MGBP)	36.8	41.5	22.5
Funds managed (MGBP)	3,675	2,942	2,249
Customer Focus			
Number of contracts	250,807	228,397	189,076
Savings/contract (GBP 000s)	15.0	12.8	11.9
Service Awards (max. value = 5)	5	5	5
Human Focus			
Number of employees (full-time)	797	720	566
Process Focus			
Number of contracts/employee	315	317	334
Renewal & Development Focus			
Increase in net premium, new sales	–34%	95%	92%
Pension products, share of new sales	23%	13%	24%
Increase in funds managed	25%	31%	58%

. . . Skandia Life started a companywide programme in 1993, entitled "Clearly First." This programme continues to yield superb results by focusing the minds of all staff on the prime objective in order to meet the needs of their customers, internal as well as external. The company is striving to be "clearly the first choice provider for the IFA [Independent Financial Advisors] market."

C: Organizational Capital Summary‡

In addition to the Skandia Navigator, Skandia has also included a summary of each division's value-creating processes. Each division focuses on the value-creating processes, developing methods for capturing the intellectual capital. These methods are described in the organization capital column, as they are what creates organizational capital. The third column contains Skandia's description of the effect that these value-creating processes and the ability to create organizational capital have on the division's business performance.

Creating Organizational Capital (Table 4)

Systematic management of intellectual capital creates growth in shareholder value. This is accomplished, among other things, through the continuous recycling and creative utilization of shared knowledge and experience. This, in turn, requires the structuring and packaging of competencies with the help of technology, process descriptions, manuals, networks, and so on, to ensure that the competence will remain with the company when the employees go home.

Based on Skandia's model for development of indicators, critical value-creating work processes can be identified. Once packaged, these become a part of the company's structural capital—or more precisely, its organizational capital.

TABLE 4   Value-Creating Work Processes by Business Unit

Business Unit	Value-Creating Processes	Organizational Capital	Business Effects
Vesta Processes for profitable customer relationships	• Systematized risk assessment and selection • Development of distribution channels to extend the duration • Development of IT-based support systems	• Database with overview of customer categories, so-called observation risks, no-risk, authorization system • Routine manuals & for sales, customer care, customer renewal, operations, claims handling • Offer handling & analysis system	• Risk level (claims ratio) better than average • Improved distribution effectiveness • Growing market share • Increasing customer loyalty • Decreasing overhead ratio • Growing sales via alliances
Mexico Process for risk management	• Risk assessment, management and selection • Relationship development, customer care • Competence cooperation	• Guidelines, manuals for risk management • Work procedures for relationship development and customer care • Packaged, communicated strategy	• Greater customer loyalty • Higher contract renewal rate • Greater number of offers handled • Falling administrative expense ratio

(continued)

‡Supplement to Skandia's 1995 Annual Report.

EXHIBIT 2   *Continued*

Table 4   (*continued*)

SkandiaLink Learning processes	• Automated fund switching • Transaction processing & telephone accessibility • Staff reward system • Augmentation of customer care	• SkandiaLink Investment Analysis (SIA) • Value development process • Automatic fund-switching service, Telelink • FLINK Index (administrative routines for business handling) • Routine handbook for transaction processing • Customer Centres • Customer Care groups	• Shorter processing times • Decreasing expense ratio • Growing volume of assignments/ representatives • Increased number of automatic fund switches • Greater staff commitment
Skandia Life UK Group Commitment to service—"Clearly First"	• Market referencing • Weekly measurement of administrative processes • Staff programme—"Clearly First"	• Quality processes • Fund management concept • "Investment Department" with 6,000 specialists	• Service Awards • Investment Performance Awards • Growth in market share
American Skandian From process focus to core competence	• Streamlined processes and work routines • Model for identifying value-creating processes—process knowledge • Knowledge from fund managers and IT department	• Process inventory and imaging system/workflow system • Process measurement system • On-line product and rule library (Lotus SmarText) • Sales support & electronic package (ASSESS)	• Streamlining of paperwork flows through image-processing techniques • Structured processes in customer service unit • Assessment of company's IT literacy • Process Hierarchy inventory

Source: Intellectual Capital Value-Creating Processes: Supplement to Skandia's 1995 Annual Report.

Glossary[§]

Contract:	Insurance contract (policy) between Skandia and a policyholder.
Empowerment index:	From a recurring SIFO (the Swedish Institute of Public Opinion Research) survey, an index is created to measure employee motivation, support in the organization, sensitivity to quality demands, matching of responsibility and authority, and competence. The scale is from 0 to 1,000.
Intellectual capital:	The gap between stock market value and book value, also called Tobin's Q, as well as the sum of human capital plus structural capital.
Managed assets:	The amount at a given point in time that is managed on behalf of investors in funds.

[§]Supplement to Skandia's 1995 Annual Report.

Organizational capital: Systematized and packaged competence, plus systems for leveraging the company's innovative strength and value-creating organizational capability.

Surrender ratio: Surrenders (during the year) in relation to the average mathematical reserve (net).

Unit linked assurance: A form of life assurance in which the policyholder can choose from a number of investment alternatives offered by the insurance company for the savings portion of paid-in-premiums.

Value-creating processes: Term describing various related activities that create value which customers are cognizant of and are willing to pay for.

Case 10–5
General Electric Company

The General Electric Company is a large multi-location corporation engaged in the manufacture and marketing of a wide variety of electrical and allied products. In 1964, there were almost 400 separate product lines and over three million catalog items. Sales volume in that year totaled $4,941 million, and net income was $237 million. Total employment was about 262,000.

Early in the 1950s, General Electric initiated an extensive decentralization of authority and responsibility for the operations of the company. The basic unit of organization became the product department. As of 1964, there were over 100 of these departments.

The company recognized that if this decentralization was to be fully effective it would need an improved system of management control. It also recognized that any improved system of control would require better measures of performance. To meet this need, the company established a measurements project and created a special organizational unit to carry out this project. This case summarizes the main features of this project, with particular emphasis on measuring performance of the operating (i.e., product) departments.

The Measurements Project

The measurements project was established in 1952. Responsibility for the project was assigned to accounting services, one of the corporate functional services divisions. A permanent organizational unit, initially called measurement service, was set up to carry out this project.

This case was prepared by R. H. Caplan/R. N. Anthony, Harvard Business School. Copyright © by the President and Fellows of Harvard College Harvard Business School case 113-121.

An early step in the measurements project was the development of a set of principles by which the project was to be governed. Five such principles were formulated:

1. Measurements were to be designed to measure the performance of *organizational components,* rather than of *managers.*
2. Measurements were to involve common *indexes* of performance, but not common *standards* of performance. (For example, rate of return on investment might be the index of performance common to all product departments, but the standard in terms of this index might be 12 percent for one department and 25 percent for another.)
3. Measurements were to be designed as aids to judgment in appraisal of performance, and not to supplant judgment.
4. Measurements were to give proper weight to future performance as well as current performance, in order to facilitate the maintenance of a balance between the long run and the near term.
5. Measurements were to be selected so as to facilitate constructive action, not to restrict such action.

The overall measurements project was divided into three major subprojects:

1. Operational measurements of the results of a product department.
2. Functional measurements of the work of engineering, manufacturing, marketing and finance, employee and plant community relations, and legal components of the organization.
3. Measurements of the work of managing as such—planning, organizing, integrating, and measuring itself.

The first step in the subproject on operational measurements was to develop an answer to the following question:

What are the specific areas for which measurements should be designed, bearing in mind that sound measurements of overall performance require a proper balance among the various functions and among the aspects (planning, organizing, for example) of managing?[1]

In seeking an answer to this question, the organization made a careful analysis of the nature and purposes of the basic kinds of work performed by each functional unit with the purpose of singling out those functional objectives that were of sufficient importance to the welfare of the business[2] as a whole, to be termed "key result areas."

The Key Result Areas

In order to determine whether an area tentatively identified according to the preceding analytical framework was sufficiently basic to qualify as a key result area, the organization established a criterion in the form of the following test question.

> Will continued failure in this area prevent the attainment of management's responsibility for advancing General Electric as a leader in a strong, competitive economy, even though results in all other key areas are good?[3]

As an outcome of analysis and application of this test, eight key result areas were decided on. These were as follows:

1. Profitability.
2. Market position.
3. Productivity.
4. Product leadership.
5. Personnel development.
6. Employee attitudes.
7. Public responsibility.
8. Balance between short-range and long-range goals.

Each of these key result areas is described below.

Profitability.   The key index used by General Electric to measure profitability was "dollars of residual income." Residual income was defined as net profit after taxes, less a capital charge. The capital charge was a certain percentage (say, 6 percent) of the net assets assigned to the department; it corresponded to an imputed interest charge. The criteria formulated to guide the development of a satisfactory measure of profitability were expressed as follows:

1. An index that recognized the contribution of capital investment to profits.
2. An index that recognized what human work and effort contribute to profits.
3. An index that recognized the "corporate facts of life" (e.g., one consistent with General Electric's needs and organizational objectives).
4. An index that served to make the operating decisions of individual managers in the company's best interests.

In the process of selecting and developing a measure of profitability, the measurements organization considered several more conventional indexes, including rate of return on investment, ratio of profit to sales, and ratio of profit to value added. A weakness of these ratios or indices was stated in this way:

> . . . the acid test of an index should be its effectiveness in guiding decentralized management to make decisions in the best interests of the company overall, since operating managers' efforts naturally will be to improve the performance of their businesses in terms of the index used for evaluation. This test points up the particular weakness of rate of return and of other ratio indexes, such as percent profit to sales. This weakness is the tendency to encourage concentration on improvement of the *ratios* rather than on improvement in *dollar* profits. Specifically, the business with the better results in terms of the ratios will tend to make decisions based on the effect the decisions will have on the particular business's current *ratio* without consideration of the *dollar*

---

[1]Lewis, "Measuring, Reporting and Appraising Results of Operations," p. 30.

[2]The word *business* is used here to refer to a product department, not to the whole company.

[3]Lewis, "Measuring, Reporting and Appraising Results of Operations," p. 30.

profits involved. This tends to retard incentive to growth and expansion because it dampens the incentive of the more profitable businesses to grow.[4]

Market Position.

Performance in this key result area was measured in terms of the share of the market obtained during a given measurement period. The measurement was expressed as a percentage of available business in the market. Market, as used in this sense, was expressed in dollars or units, kilowatt-amperes, or other meaningful terms.

The first major consideration in designing market position measurements is a determination of what constitutes a product line and what constitutes the market for each product line of a business. A product line may be defined as a grouping of products in accordance with the purposes they serve or the essential wants they satisfy. The definition is somewhat misleading in that a product line may be a broad classification, such as clocks, or it may be a narrow classification, such as alarm clocks, kitchen clocks, or mantel clocks. In addition, product lines may overlap so that a particular product could be included in several product lines. Hence, the actual grouping of products by product lines must be accurately identified.

There may be wide variations in the interpretation of what constitutes the market for a given product line. Therefore, it is important that for each of their lines, our product departments identify such things as:

1. Whether the market includes not only directly competing products but also indirectly competing products (electric ranges versus electric ranges; electric ranges versus all types of ranges— electric, gas, oil, and others).

2. Whether the market includes sales by all domestic competitors or only those reporting to trade associations.

3. Whether the market includes imports, if foreign sellers are competing in the domestic market.

4. Whether the market includes export sales.

5. Whether the market includes captive sales.

6. Whether the market is considered to be represented by sales to distributors, or to retailers, or to ultimate users.

In other words, in establishing measurements of market position there should be a clear understanding of precisely what comprises the product line and what comprises the market. The purpose of having sharp definitions of these two items is, of course, to avoid being misled into thinking we are doing better than we actually are simply because of failure to identify the nature and extent of our competition.[5]

Productivity.

Although the concept of productivity is a relatively simple one—a relationship of output of goods and services to the resources consumed in their production—this concept proved a difficult one to make operational as a measure of performance. For the national economy as a whole, it has been the practice to look at productivity simply in terms of the amount of output per unit of labor input. In any given firm, however, labor is only one of the factors contributing to output. Therefore, the company sought to develop an index that would accomplish two things: (1) broaden the input base so as to recognize that capital as well as labor contributed to improvements in productivity, and (2) eliminate from the measure those improvements contributed by suppliers of materials.

On the output side of the productivity ratio, the company considered several refinements of sales billed. One such refinement was the use of value added (e.g., sales billed less the cost of goods or services acquired outside the company). On the input side, the company considered payroll dollars plus depreciation dollars. Payroll dollars were included in the variable, rather than labor hours, so as to give effect to differences in the labor skills employed. The inclusion of depreciation charges constituted an attempt to include the consumption of capital resources. All factors were to be readjusted for changes in the price level, so that changes in the resulting ratio would more nearly reflect real changes in productivity.

[4]Ibid., p. 32.

[5]Ibid., p. 33.

Product Leadership. Product leadership was defined as "the ability of a business to lead its industry in originating or applying the most advanced scientific and technical knowledge in the engineering, manufacturing and marketing fields to the development of new products and to improvements in the quality or value of existing products."[6] To make this definition operational, procedures were established for appraising periodically the products of each department. These appraisals were directed at providing answers to the following questions.

1. How did each product compare with competition and with company standards?
2. Where within the company was the research conducted upon which the product was based?
3. Who first introduced the basic product and subsequent improvements, General Electric or a competitor?

The appraisal procedures were based largely on qualitative rather than quantitative considerations. Appraisals were made by appropriate experts from the areas of engineering, marketing, accounting, and manufacturing. In general, these experts were located within the product department for which the appraisal was to be made. Standard forms were employed so as to facilitate as high a degree of consistency as possible. The trends revealed by these appraisals over a period of time were considered to be as significant as the specific information revealed by an appraisal for a particular period.

Personnel Development. For the purposes of measurement, personnel development was defined as "the systematic training of managers and specialists to fill present and future needs of the company, to provide for further individual growth and retirements and to facilitate corporate growth and expansion."[7] Management of General Electric defined personnel development as including "programs in each field of functional endeavor, such as engineering, manufacturing, marketing and finance, and broad programs aimed at developing an understanding of the principles of managing. Such programs must be designed to provide a continuous flow of potentially promotable employees in sufficient numbers to permit proper selection and development of individuals for each position. And, at the same time, these programs must encourage competition and initiative for further individual growth."[8]

Three steps were involved in the measurement of performance in this key result area. (1) The basic soundness of the various programs or techniques being sponsored by a product department for the development of its employees was appraised. (2) An inventory was taken of the available supply of trained men, as well as their qualifications, for the key positions that must eventually be filled within the department. (3) The effectiveness with which the department executed its personnel development programs was evaluated.

The first step consisted of judgments regarding the adequacy of the following elements in the development process:

Recruitment. How good a job was being done in the selection of candidates for the development process?

On-the-job training. What programs were available for training candidates, for providing information and knowledge about both general company matters and job particulars, and for advanced training for those who had been on the job for a while?

Review and counsel. Was there any provision for periodically reviewing the performance of the men, for discussing with an individual the caliber of his work, for providing help and consultation, and for identifying especially promising talent?

Placement. What was being done to see that recruits were placed in jobs commensurate with their interests and abilities, that the more promising were rotated, and that promotions came to those who merited them?

The second step was accomplished with the aid of manning tables and related inventorying procedures. These procedures were directed

---

[6]Ibid., pp. 35–36.
[7]Ibid., p. 37.

---

[8]Ibid.

primarily at determining the training background of each employee in the inventory, that is, graduates of company-sponsored programs, those hired from outside the company, and those who attained their positions without the benefit of a company-sponsored program.

The investigating group used two statistical measures in carrying out the third step. The first of these was the ratio of the number of employees promoted (both within department and through transfer to another department) in a given period (usually a year) to the total number of employees regarded as "promotable" during the same period. The second measure was tied in with the personnel rating procedure employed throughout the company. At the conclusion of each performance review cycle, the rating forms for a particular department were analyzed to determine the proportions of employees whose performance was considered to be (a) improving, (b) unchanged, and (c) deteriorating.

Employee Attitudes. For purposes of developing measurements of performance in this key area, the group defined an attitude as "a generalized point of view toward objects, events, or persons which might serve to influence future behavior." It used two basic approaches to the measurement of attitudes. The first involved the use of statistical indicators, such as turnover rate, absenteeism, number of grievances, lateness, and accident experience. The second approach involved a periodic survey of employees through questionnaires.

Several shortcomings were recognized in the first approach. (1) The statistical indicators provided little or no information about underlying causes. (2) In general, the indicators told of trouble only after the harm had been done. (3) Because these indicators were traditionally associated with the personnel functions, managers tended to minimize their importance or else place responsibility for improvement on the personnel function. (4) Unfavorable trends in certain of these indicators might be due to ex-

ternal factors (e.g., short labor supply) rather than to some shortcomings of management.

The attitude survey made use of a standardized questionnaire designed to reveal the attitudes of employees in a number of broad areas. The survey was administered at intervals of about 18 months. Results for each attitude area were tabulated in terms of proportion of responses that were favorable. Tabulations were made by work groups and not by individual employees; this practice helped protect the anonymity of responses, and thus the validity of the surveys.

Public Responsibility. This key result area evolved from General Electric's recognition of its obligation to conduct itself as a good citizen within society, complying faithfully with the laws and ethics governing business conduct. The company believed its progress required not only an active recognition of the broad public interest, but also a responsiveness to certain special publics who had a stake in the success of the business—namely, shareowners, customers, employees, vendors, dealers and distributors, the plant community, educational institutions, and government.

While the responsibility to certain publics such as shareowners, educational institutions, and the federal government could best be measured from an overall company viewpoint rather than departmentally, nevertheless, the actions taken by a product department (including the individual acts of employees of that department) could have an important impact on the whole company's reputation as a good corporate citizen. Accordingly, the company attempted to assure wholehearted observance of the legal and ethical standards of business by insisting that all managerial and professional employees at least once a year conducted periodical surveys of the activities of those who reported to them with respect to antitrust compliance, conflict of interest, and other areas of business practice. These matters were discussed with each individual, who then signed a statement affirming his understanding and compliance.

Other measurements related to the effectiveness of department action in strengthening the company's reputation and business relationships. With respect to fulfilling obligations to customers, it was determined that the previously mentioned product leadership and market position areas were the best indicators. For the remaining publics, the following measures were recommended.

Shareowners.   The total shares of General Electric Company stock were to be "allocated" to the various operating components that were assigned responsibility for preserving and enhancing "their portion" of the shareowners' investment in the company.

Vendors, Dealers, and Distributors.   Suppliers of raw materials and parts were to be surveyed periodically to determine their appraisal of the department's practices in conducting its business as compared with the practices of others who bought from them. Dealers and distributors were likewise to be interviewed from time to time to measure whether these important relationships were being responsibly maintained.

Plant Community.   Again, comprehensive reaction surveys were to be used, aimed at identifying the impact of the actions of a product department on the individuals who made up the community. These reactions disclosed by the opinion surveys were to be supplemented by use of trends developed from various types of data such as community wage rates, number of employment applications received, volume of purchases made locally, contributions to local charities, and participation in civic, church, and business organizations.

Balance between Short-Range and Long-Range Goals.   This factor was set out separately as a key result area in order to emphasize the importance of the long-term survival and growth of the company. Short-range goals

and performance had to be balanced against the need for satisfactory performance 5, 10, 15 years in the future, since undue pressure for current profits could, in effect, borrow from the future.

Various means were employed to experiment with suggested measures in this key result area. However, it is important to note that when the eight key result areas were established, each of the first seven had both short-range and long-range dimensions. The eighth area, balance between short-range and long-range goals, had been specifically identified to make sure that the long-range health of the company would not be sacrificed for short-term gains. The plans, goals, and actions in each of the other areas were, therefore, to be appraised in terms of both their short-term and their long-term implications.

Initial Implementation

During the period after the measurements project was established in 1952, deep research work was carried on to establish the specific measurements in each of the eight key result areas. Before communicating these measures to the product departments, the investigators reviewed the recommendations in each area with operating personnel and with officers, for their comments, suggestions, and final approval.

The company's business planning, budgeting, and forecasting program incorporated the use of selected key result areas in (1) reviewing the recent history and current status, (2) setting standards for each department, (3) planning to achieve the standards, and (4) periodic reporting and measurement of accomplishment. Since the first four key result areas lent themselves readily to numerical evaluations, they were a part of the planning, budgeting, forecasting, reporting, and measuring system. Building on this experience in using the key result areas to plan and measure performance, management at the General Electric Company made the search for effective business measurements a continuing, evolutionary process.

Questions

1. For the purpose described, how should profitability be defined? The definition should be specific enough so that a quantitative measure can be constructed from it.

2. What, if anything, do the factors other than profitability add to the proposed measurement system? Isn't the impact of the other factors reflected in the profitability measure if it is properly constructed?

MANAGEMENT COMPENSATION

Incentive compensation is an important mechanism that encourages and motivates managers to achieve organizational objectives. Managers typically put forth a great deal of effort on activities that are rewarded and less on activities that are not rewarded. There are many examples of compensation systems that do not reward behavior leading to organizational goals or that reward behavior countering these goals. In this chapter, we discuss the design of incentive compensation plans for general managers in order to avoid the "folly of rewarding A while hoping for B."

We first discuss research findings on organizational incentives. We then describe the nature of incentive compensation plans and distinguish between short-term and long-term plans. These plans must be approved by the shareholders. Next, we describe how the compensation of individual managers is decided at both the corporate and business-unit levels. These decisions typically are made by the board of directors on the basis of the chief executive officer's recommendations. Finally, we describe agency theory—an approach for deciding on the best type of incentive compensation plan.

Research Findings on Organizational Incentives

The key to motivating people to behave in a manner that furthers an organization's goals lies in the way the organization's incentives relate to the individuals' goals. People are influenced by both positive and negative incentives. A positive incentive, or "reward," is an outcome that increases satisfaction of individual needs. Conversely, a negative incentive, or "punishment," is an outcome that decreases satisfaction of those needs. Reward incentives are inducements to satisfy their needs that individuals cannot obtain without joining the organization. Organizations reward participants who perform in agreed-upon ways. Research on incentives tends to support the following:

- Individuals tend to be more strongly motivated by the potential of earning rewards than by the fear of punishment, which suggests that management control systems should be reward-oriented.

- A personal reward is relative or situational. Monetary compensation is an important means of satisfying needs. Beyond a certain satisfaction level, however, the amount of compensation is not necessarily as important as nonmonetary rewards.

- If senior management signals by its actions that it regards the management control system as important, operating managers will also regard it as important. If senior management pays little attention to the system, operating managers will follow suit.

- Individuals are highly motivated when they receive reports, or feedback, about their performance. Without such feedback, people are unlikely to feel a sense of achievement or self-realization or to figure out how they can change their behavior to meet their objectives.

- Incentives become less effective as the period between an action and feedback on it increases. At lower levels in the organization, the optimal frequency may be only hours; for senior management, it may be months.

- Motivation is weakest when the person believes an incentive is either unattainable or too easily attainable. Motivation is strong when it takes some effort to attain the objective and when the individual regards this attainment as important in relation to his or her needs.

- The incentive that a budget or other statement of objective provides is strongest when managers work with their superiors to arrive at the budgeted amounts. Objectives, goals, or standards are likely to provide strong incentives only if the manager perceives them as fair and is committed to attaining them. The commitment is strongest when it is a matter of public record—that is, when the manager has explicitly agreed that the budgeted amounts are attainable.

Characteristics of Incentive Compensation Plans

A manager's total compensation package consists of three components: (1) salary, (2) benefits (principally retirement and health care, but also perquisites of various types), and (3) incentive compensation. Managers typically receive higher compensation in large companies than in small firms, and companies in the same industry tend to compete with each other on compensation. Otherwise, few other generalizations can be made about the level of management compensation.

The three components are interdependent, but the third is related specifically to the management control function; this chapter, therefore, discusses primarily the incentive compensation component.

A study of the pay and bonuses received by 14,000 managers over the period 1981–85 (70,284 observations from 219 organizations) found that, on average, bonuses were 20 percent of base pay, but that there were substantial differences among organizations, even those in the same industry. There were greater differences in the proportion of bonus payments than in base pay. Organizations with higher ratios of bonuses tended to have better subsequent financial performance than other organizations.[1]

Most corporate bylaws and securities regulations require incentive compensation plans and revisions of existing plans to be approved by the shareholders. (By contrast, shareholders do *not* approve salaries, nor does the annual proxy statement give information about compensation, except for each of the five highest paid officers and the total for all officers and directors.) It follows that the plan must be approved by the board of directors before it is voted on at the annual meeting. Before submitting a plan to the board, senior management works to ensure it is the best one for the organization, often hiring outside consultants to assist in this effort. The compensation committee of the board of directors usually participates extensively in discussions of the proposed plan.

Incentive compensation plans can be divided into short-term and long-term plans. Short-term incentive plans are based on performance in the current year. Long-term plans tie compensation to longer-term accomplishments and are related to the price of the company's common stock. A manager may earn a bonus under both plans. The bonus in a short-term plan usually is paid in cash, and the bonus in a long-term plan usually is an option to buy the company's common stock.

Short-Term Incentive Plans

The Total Bonus Pool.   The total amount of bonus that can be paid to a qualified group of employees in a given year is called the "bonus pool." In a short-term incentive plan, shareholders vote on the formula that will be used to arrive at it. This formula usually is related to the overall company profitability in the current year. In deciding on the size of this pool, the overriding issue is to make sure the total compensation paid to executives is competitive.

There are several ways to establish the bonus pool.

The simplest method is to make the bonus equal to a set percentage of the profits. For example, if profits of $50 million represent an average profitable year, and if a $1 million bonus fund is required to make the executive compensation package competitive, the bonus formula then could be set up to pay 2 percent of net income in bonuses.

Many companies don't like using this method because it means paying a bonus even when profitability is low. Moreover, it fails to reflect additional investments; thus, profits and, consequently, bonuses can increase simply as

---

[1]Barry Gerhart and George T. Milkovich, "Organizational Differences in Managerial Compensation and Financial Performance," *Academy of Management Journal,* December 1990, pp. 663–91.

a result of new investments, even though the company's performance may be static or even deteriorating. Many firms, therefore, use formulas that pay bonuses only after a specified return has been earned on capital. There are several ways to do this.

One method is to base the bonus on a percentage of earnings per share after a predetermined level of earnings per share has been attained. Using our earlier example, assume the following situation:

1. Estimated level of satisfactory profitability: $50 million.
2. Desired amount of bonus at the above level of profitability: $1 million.
3. Number of shares outstanding: 10 million.
4. Minimum earnings per share before bonus payments: $2.50.
5. Bonus formula: 4 percent of profits after subtracting $2.50 per share.

This method, however, does not take into account increases in investment from reinvested earnings. The solution is to increase the minimum earnings per share each year by a percentage of the annual increase in retained earnings. In the example above, assume that the estimated profits for the year are $50 million before bonuses and that dividends are $30 million. The plan might stipulate that a 6 percent return must be earned on additional investments before any additional bonuses are paid. The $2.50 minimum earnings per share thus would be adjusted for the coming year in the following manner:

Increase in retained earnings:

$$\$50,000,000 \text{ (profit)} - \$500,000 \text{ (bonus after taxes)}$$
$$- \$30,000,000 \text{ (dividends)} = \$19,500,000$$

Increase in required earnings before bonus:

$$\text{Total} = \$19,500,000 * 0.06 = \$1,170,000$$

$$\text{Per share} = \$1,170,000 \div 10,000,000 = \$0.117$$

Adjusted minimum earnings per share:

$$\$2.50 + \$0.12 = \$2.62$$

No reductions in the required earnings per share are normally made when the company experiences a loss; however, the required earnings would not be increased until retained earnings exceeded the preloss level.

Another method of relating profits to capital employed is to define capital as shareholder equity plus long-term liabilities. The bonus is equal to a percent of the profits before taxes and interest on long-term debt, minus a capital charge on the total of shareholder equity plus long-term debt. (This is similar to the economic value added concept discussed in Chapter 6.) Companies using this method reason that managerial performance should be based on employing corporate net assets profitably, and because financial policy—not operating managers—determines the proportion of long-term debt to total capital, this proportion should not influence the judgment about operating performance.

Yet another option is to define capital as equal to shareholder equity. A difficulty with both this and the preceding method is that a loss year reduces shareholder equity and thereby increases the amount of bonus to be paid in profitable years. This might tempt management to take a "big bath" in a year with otherwise low profits to make earning future bonuses easier.

A few companies base the bonus on increases in profitability over the preceding year. This not only rewards a mediocre year that follows a poor one but also fails to reward a good year that follows an excellent one. This problem can be partially corrected by basing the bonus on an improvement in the current year that is above a moving average of the profits in a number of past years.

Some companies base bonuses on their profitability relative to that of their industry. Obtaining comparable industry data may be difficult, however, because few companies have the same product mix or employ identical accounting systems. This method also could result in a high bonus in a mediocre year, because one or more competitors had a poor year.

In calculating both the profit and the capital components of these formulas, adjustments may be made in the reported amount of net income and in the reported amount of shareholder equity. Certain types of extraordinary gains and losses, and gains and losses from discontinued operations, may be excluded. Additionally, goodwill that results from acquiring other companies may be excluded even though it is included in the published financial statements.

Carryovers.   Instead of paying the total amount in the bonus pool, the plan may provide for an annual carryover of a part of the amount determined by the bonus formula. Each year a committee of the board of directors decides how much to add to the carryover, or how much of the accumulated carryover to use if the bonuses would otherwise be too low. This method offers two advantages: (1) It is more flexible, since payment is not determined automatically by a formula and the board of directors can exercise their judgment. (2) It can reduce the magnitude of the swings that occur when the bonus payment is based strictly on the formula amount calculated each year. Thus, in an exceptionally good year, the committee may decide to pay out only a portion of the bonus. Conversely, in a relatively poor year, the committee may decide to pay out more than the amount justified by the current year's performance by drawing from the carryover amount. The disadvantage of this method is that bonuses relate less directly to current performance.

Deferred Compensation.   Although the amount of the bonus is calculated annually, payments to recipients may be spread out over a period of years, usually five. Under this system, executives receive only one-fifth of their bonus in the year in which it was earned. The remaining four-fifths are paid out equally over the next four years. Thus, after the manager has been working under the plan for five years, the bonus consists of one-fifth of the bonus for the current year plus one-fifth of each of the bonuses for the preceding four years. In some companies, the deferred period is three years. This deferred payment method offers the following advantages:

- Managers can estimate, with reasonable accuracy, their cash income for the coming year.
- Deferred payments smooth the manager's receipt of cash, because the effects of cyclical swings in profits are averaged in the cash payments.
- A manager who retires will continue to receive payments for a number of years; this not only augments retirement income but also usually provides a tax advantage, because income tax rates after retirement may be lower than rates during working life.
- The deferred time frame encourages decision makers to think long term.

A disadvantage of deferred bonus plans is that they do not make the deferred amount available to the executive in the year earned. Because bonus payments in a year are not related to performance in that year, they may act as less of an incentive.

When bonus payments are deferred, the deferred amount may or may not vest. In some instances, a manager will not receive the deferred bonus if he or she leaves the company before it is paid. This arrangement is called a *golden handcuff* because it acts as a disincentive for managers to leave an organization.

Long-Term Incentive Plans

A basic premise of many long-term incentive plans is that growth in the value of the company's common stock reflects the company's long-run performance. There are several types of such plans. Their popularity is affected by changes in the income tax law, changes in accounting treatment, the state of the stock market, and various other factors. Consequently, different plans are popular at different times.

Stock Options.   A stock option is a right to buy a number of shares of stock at, or after, a given date in the future (the *exercise date*), at a price agreed upon at the time the option is granted (usually the current market price or 95 percent of the current market price). The major motivational benefit of stock option plans is that they direct managers' energies toward the long-term, as well as the short-term, performance of the company.

> **Example.**   Wendy's was having trouble with high turnover—300 percent per year among crew members. After introducing a stock option plan for crew managers, Wendy's reduced turnover in this group, which, in turn, reduced turnover among assistant managers from 60 percent to 38 percent. This contributed to a reduction in turnover among crew members to about 150 percent per year.[2]

---

[2]Kerry Cappell, "Options for Everyone," *Business Week,* July 22, 1996, pp. 80–84.

The manager gains if he or she later sells the stock at a price that exceeds the price paid for it. Unlike some of the alternatives mentioned below, the outright purchase of stock under a stock option plan gives managers equity that they can retain, even if they leave the company, and a gain that they can obtain whenever they decide to sell the stock. However, many stock options are for *restricted stock*. Managers are not permitted to sell this stock for a specified period after it was acquired.

> **Examples.** Stock options are a popular form of rewarding employees in Internet and information technology companies such as Microsoft, Amazon.com, eBay, Yahoo!, PSINet, and Cisco. There are several reasons for this. First, stock options and their upside potential tend to attract highly talented employees to these companies. Internet companies depend on the high caliber of their human capital to succeed. Second, innovation is the key to success in technology companies. Innovative ideas reside inside human beings. Employees will volunteer their ideas only if they can profit from them. Stock options, therefore, provide the right motivation for employees to freely share their creative ideas to enhance the company's market share and competitive positioning, which, in turn, bolsters the company's stock price, thus benefiting the employees. Third, companies can pay employees lower salaries and bonuses because of the stock option program. Internet start-ups are strapped for cash, and stock option plans help conserve cash. Fourth, the value of stock options does not reduce the bottom line; salaries and bonuses do. Finally, stock options encourage employees to focus on the long term.

Phantom Shares. A phantom stock plan awards managers a number of shares for bookkeeping purposes only. At the end of a specified period (say, five years) the executive is entitled to receive an award equal to the *appreciation* in the market value of the stock since the date of award. This award may be in cash, in shares of stock, or in both. Unlike a stock option, a phantom stock plan has no transaction costs. Some stock option plans require the manager to hold the stock for a certain period after it was purchased. This involves a risk of a decrease in the market price as well as interest costs associated with holding the stock. This risk and these costs are not involved in a phantom stock plan.

Stock Appreciation Rights. A stock appreciation right is a right to receive cash payments based on the increase in the stock's value from the time of the award until a specified future date. Stock appreciation rights and phantom shares are types of deferred cash bonuses in which the bonus amount is a function of the market price of the company's stock. Both plans have the advantages of a stock option plan. Compared to a cash bonus paid currently, they involve uncertainty—in both directions—about the ultimate amount paid.

> **Example.** Avis Inc., the rental car company that "tries harder," agreed to be purchased by hotel franchiser HFS Inc. for $763 million, including $85 million in phantom stock and stock appreciation rights for Avis Inc.'s management.[3]

---

[3]Aaron Bernstein, "Should Avis Try Harder—For Its Employees?" *Business Week,* August 12, 1996, pp. 68–69.

Performance Shares.   A performance share plan awards a specified number of shares of stock to a manager when specific long-term goals have been met. Usually, the goals are to achieve a certain percentage growth in earnings per share over a three-to-five-year period; therefore, they are not influenced by the price of the stock. The advantage of this plan over the stock option and phantom stock plans is that the award is based on performance that the executive can control, at least partially. Also, the award does not depend on an increase in stock prices, although the increase in earnings is likely to result in an increase in stock prices. This plan suffers from the limitation of basing the bonus on accounting measures of performance. Under some conditions, actions that corporate executives take to improve earnings per share might not contribute to the economic worth of the firm.

Performance Units.   In a performance unit plan, a cash bonus is paid when specific long-term targets are attained. This plan thus combines aspects of stock appreciation rights and performance shares. It is especially useful in companies with little or no publicly traded stock. Long-term targets must be carefully established in order for this plan to succeed.

Incentives for Corporate Officers

In the preceding section, we described how the total bonus pool is calculated. In this section and the next, we describe how the total is divided among the corporate officers and among the business unit managers, respectively.

Each corporate officer, except the chief executive officer, is responsible *in part* for the company's overall performance. These corporate officers are motivated by, and entitled to, a bonus for good performance. However, the part of performance that each of them generated cannot be measured. For example, how can one measure the contribution to profits made by the chief financial officer or the human resources vice president or the chief counsel?

To stimulate motivation, the chief executive officer (who recommends awards to the compensation committee of the board of directors) usually bases awards on an assessment of each person's performance. These assessments are necessarily subjective. Some companies use a management by objectives system (MBO) in which specific objectives are agreed upon at the beginning of the year and their attainment is assessed by the chief executive officer.

CEO Compensation

The chief executive officer's compensation usually is discussed by the board of directors compensation committee *after* the CEO has presented recommendations for subordinates' compensation. The CEO's general attitude toward the appropriate percentage of incentive compensation in a given year is fairly obvious from this presentation. In ordinary circumstances, the committee may simply apply the same percentage to the CEO's compensation. However, the committee may signal a different appraisal of the CEO's performance by deciding on a higher or lower percentage. This, perhaps more than any other expression of the board's opinion, is a critical sign of how the board regards the CEO's performance. It should be accompanied by a frank explanation of the reasons for the decision.

Some people believe that the compensation of chief executives in the United States (and also of some professional athletes and performing artists) is too high and does not relate to company performance.[4] They cite instances of what they regard as excess compensation: *golden parachutes* (i.e., incentive packages for an incumbent CEO as insurance against takeovers), extraordinary bonuses, lavish perquisites, and bonuses unrelated to profits. Directors who make decisions about compensation respond that excellent CEOs receive only a tiny fraction of the profits that result from their actions, and that boards must set CEO compensation to be comparable with that in competing companies.

Each year *Forbes* magazine publishes a list of the compensation of hundreds of CEOs, compared with the profits for which they presumably are responsible. Although the details of its analysis are subject to criticism, the general message is that compensation is indeed high relative to performance in some situations, but this is not the general pattern. Moreover, compensation within different industries varies considerably. In any event, given CEOs' unique skills and capabilities, assessing true "market prices" for chief executives is nearly impossible. The following example highlights the difficulty in ascertaining the right compensation for CEOs.[5]

> **Example.**   In 1998 Stephen M. Wolf, US Airways chairman, received $34 million in pay, bonuses, and stock options plus $56 million in unexercised stock options. One could argue that this compensation is excessive by comparing it with the base pay and bonus for the chairmen of United Airlines ($1.5 million), Delta Airlines ($1.6 million), and American Airlines ($1.7 million) for the same year. On the other hand, one could justify Wolf's compensation by the remarkable turnaround of US Airways during his tenure. The company's stock price rose from $14 a share when Wolf took over in January 1996 to $80 by mid-1998, far outstripping the share price gains of other airlines during the same period.

Incentives for Business Unit Managers

A wide array of options exists in developing an incentive compensation package for business unit managers (see Exhibit 11–1).

Types of Incentives

Some incentives are financial, others are psychological and social. Financial incentives include salary increases, bonuses, benefits, and perquisites (automobiles, vacation trips, club memberships, and so on). Psychological and

---

[4]The literature has many discussions about the allegedly excessive pay of executives. See especially the books by Graef S. Crystal and Derek Bok listed under suggested readings.

[5]Frank Swoboda, "A Sky-High Incentive to Stay Put: US Airways Shareholders to Vote on Compensation Plan for Chairman," *The Washington Post,* May 18, 1999, p. E1.

EXHIBIT 11–1   **Incentive Compensation Design Options for Business Unit Managers**

A. Types of Incentives
1. Financial Rewards
   a. Salary increase
   b. Bonuses
   c. Benefits
   d. Perquisites
2. Psychological and Social Rewards
   a. Promotion possibilities
   b. Increased responsibilities
   c. Increased autonomy
   d. Better geographical location
   e. Recognition

B. Size of Bonus Relative to Salary
1. Upper Cutoffs
2. Lower Cutoffs

C. Bonus Based on
1. Business Unit Profits
2. Company Profits
3. Combination of the Two

D. Performance Criteria
1. Financial Criteria
   a. Contribution margin
   b. Direct business unit profit
   c. Controllable business unit profit
   d. Income before taxes
   e. Net income
   f. Return on investment
   g. Economic value added

2. Time Period
   a. Annual financial performance
   b. Multiyear financial performance
3. Nonfinancial Criteria
   a. Sales growth
   b. Market share
   c. Customer satisfaction
   d. Quality
   e. New product development
   f. Personnel development
   g. Public responsibility
4. Relative Weights Assigned to Financial and Nonfinancial Criteria
5. Benchmarks for Comparison
   a. Profit budget
   b. Past performance
   c. Competitor's performance

E. Bonus Determination Approach
1. Formula-Based
2. Subjective
3. Combination of the Two

F. Form of Bonus Payment
1. Cash
2. Stock
3. Stock Options
4. Phantom Shares
5. Performance Shares

social incentives include promotion possibilities, increased responsibilities, more autonomy, a better geographical location, and recognition (trophy, participation in executive development programs, and the like). In this part of the chapter, we discuss the *financial* incentives for business unit managers, while recognizing that managers' motivation is influenced by both financial and nonfinancial incentives.

Example.   In addition to commissions based on the sales revenue generated by the sales force they supervised, directors (i.e., supervisors) of Mary Kay Cosmetics received a dozen pink roses, a plaque, and a custom-designed suit at an award ceremony. If they maintained a certain level of performance, they were given the use of a pink Buick or Cadillac for two years.[6]

---

[6]From "Mary Kay Cosmetics," Case 12–5, *Management Control Systems,* 9th ed., 1997.

EXHIBIT 11–2

Two philosophies on incentive compensation

Size of Bonus Relative to Salary

There are two schools of thought about how to mix fixed (salary and fringe benefits) and variable (incentive bonus) rewards in managers' total compensation. One school states that we recruit good people, pay them well, and then expect good performance (see Exhibit 11–2). Companies subscribing to this school emphasize salary, not incentive bonus. This is called a *fixed pay* system. Compensation is not linked to performance and therefore is not at risk. This raises the question, What happens if the person does not perform well? A fixed pay system, however, has merit under certain circumstances, as the following example illustrates:

> **Example.**   The Charles Schwab Corporation pioneered the discount brokerage concept. Unlike traditional brokerage houses, Schwab brokers earned fixed salaries, not sales commissions. Brokers who work under the commission system are motivated to maximize transactions in order to earn more commissions. Thus, commissioned sales personnel do not necessarily act in their customers' best interests. Schwab's brokers, working for salary rather than commission, tended to be less pushy and acted in customers' long-term best interests. Customer service was one of the reasons behind Schwab's superior performance vis-à-vis its industry.[7]

---

[7]"The Charles Schwab Corporation," case by Vijay Govindarajan, 1999.

Another school states that we recruit good people, expect them to perform well, and pay them well *if* performance is actually good (Exhibit 11–2). Companies subscribing to this philosophy practice *performance-based pay;* they emphasize incentive bonus, not salary.

In general, performance-based pay systems have been gaining favor among companies. An American Compensation Association Survey of 2,800 major companies revealed the percentage of companies offering variable pay was 63 percent in 1999, up from less than 15 percent in 1990.[8]

The fundamental difference between the two philosophies arises from the fact that compensation comes first and performance comes later under fixed pay. Conversely, performance comes first and compensation comes later under performance-based pay. The two philosophies have different motivational implications for managers. Since salary is an assured income, emphasizing salary may encourage conservatism and complacency. Emphasizing incentive bonus, on the other hand, tends to motivate managers to put forth maximum effort. For this reason, many companies employ incentive bonuses for business unit managers.

> **Examples.** From 1993 to 1999, Yoichi Morishita, president of Matsushita, embarked on a strategic overhaul of the company. He shifted the firm's focus from low-margin consumer electronics business to high-tech products, such as digital cellular phones, digital TVs, and digital video discs, and into new industries, such as software engineering and network-communications technology. Japanese companies (including Matsushita) traditionally awarded bonus almost entirely on seniority. Breaking with tradition, Matsushita switched to a compensation system based on performance rather than seniority, plus stock options for key executives. Performance-based pay was seen as critical to implementing Matsushita's strategic shift since 1993. Many of the best ideas in the emerging digital technologies come from young engineers who would not be adequately rewarded for their ideas in the traditional seniority-based system.[9]
>
> The ultimate performance-based pay is manifested in the wide popularity of stock options among Internet companies. Infosys, the applications software provider for the Internet, is an Indian company with practically 100 percent of its sales revenues derived from global customers. During the 1990s, the firm registered over 100 percent annual growth. Infosys attributed its phenomenal success to its employee stock ownership program (ESOP) because the program aligned employees' interests with those of the corporation. As of February 2000, 200 of the firm's 5,000 employees were multimillionaires in US dollars and 1,800 were multimillionaires in Indian rupees.[10]

Cutoff Levels. A bonus plan may have upper and lower cutoff levels. An upper cutoff is the level of performance at which a maximum bonus is reached. A lower cutoff is the level below which no bonus awards will be

---

[8]"Workers Thinking, Investing Like Entrepreneurs," *The Valley News,* January 9, 2000, p. E1.

[9]"Putting the Bounce Back into Matsushita," *The Economist,* May 22, 1999, pp. 67–68.

[10]Discussions with Infosys executives at Bangalore, India, February 2, 2000.

made. Both cutoffs may produce undesirable side effects. When business unit managers recognize that either the maximum bonus has been attained or that there will be no bonus at all, the bonus system may work against corporate goals. Instead of attempting to optimize profits in the current period, managers may be motivated to decrease profitability in one year (by overspending on discretionary expenses, such as advertising or research and development) to create an opportunity for a high bonus the following year. Although this would affect only the timing of expenses, such action usually is undesirable.

One way to mitigate such dysfunctional actions is to carry over the excess or deficiency into the following year—that is, the bonus available for distribution in a given year would be the amount of bonus earned during the year plus an excess, or minus any deficiency, from the previous year.

Bonus Basis

A business unit manager's incentive bonus could be based solely on total corporate profits or on business unit profits or some mix of the two. One argument for linking bonus to unit performance is that the manager's decisions and actions more directly impact the performance of his or her own unit than that of other business units. However, such an approach could severely impair interunit cooperation.

> **Example.**   Quantum Corporation created a team called "Lethal" to design, make, and deliver a 2.5-inch disk drive (the company made 3.5-inch disk drives at that time) in 14 months. (In the past, the company had taken 24 months for such new products.) Lethal was a cross-functional team consisting of members from engineering, manufacturing, marketing, finance, and human resources. Instead of setting up performance measures for each function, Lethal set up team-based performance measures which helped the team introduce its new product on time.[11]

In a single industry firm whose business units are highly interdependent, the manager's bonus is tied primarily to corporate performance because cooperation between units is critical. In a conglomerate, on the other hand, the business units usually are autonomous. In such a context, it would be counterproductive to base business unit managers' bonuses primarily on company profits; this would weaken the link between performance and rewards. Such a system creates *free-rider* problems. Some managers might relax and still get a bonus based on the efforts of other, more diligent managers. Alternatively, in a poor profit year for the company, a unit that turns in an outstanding performance will not be rewarded adequately. In a conglomerate, therefore, it is desirable to reward business unit managers primarily based on business unit performance and so foster the entrepreneurial spirit.

---

[11]Christopher Meyer, "How the Right Measures Help the Team Excel," *Harvard Business Review,* May–June 1994, pp. 98–99.

For related diversified firms, it might be desirable to base part of business unit managers' bonuses on unit profits and part on company profits to provide the right mixture of incentives—namely, to optimize unit results while, at the same time, cooperating with other units to optimize company performance.

> **Example.**   Motorola is a related diversified firm with business units such as pagers, cellular telephones, and two-way radios. These businesses share a common wireless radio-frequency design technology. In order to encourage business units to cooperate, the compensation of business unit general managers was based on companywide performance.[12]

Performance Criteria

A difficult problem in the incentive bonus plan for business unit managers is to decide which criteria shall be used to determine the bonus.

Financial Criteria.   If the business unit is a profit center, choosing financial criteria could include contribution margin, direct business unit profit, controllable business unit profit, income before taxes, and net income. If the unit is an investment center, decisions need to be made in three areas: (1) definition of profit, (2) definition of investment, and (3) choice between return on investment and EVA. We discussed the considerations involved in choosing performance criteria for profit centers and investment centers in Chapters 4 and 6, respectively. If the responsibility center is a revenue center, the financial criteria would be sales volume or sales dollars.

> **Example.**   Avon, a global cosmetics company, had about 445,000 sales representatives in the United States who called on customers to make sales and who were rewarded on the basis of sales volume. This reward system for its sales force will be even more critical as Avon enters developing countries like India. In developing countries, retailing outlets are not sophisticated, so direct sales to the end-use customer becomes very important. Also, women in most developing countries want to work a flexible, part-time schedule as a way to supplement family income.[13]

Adjustments for Uncontrollable Factors.   In addition to selecting the financial criteria, companies must determine what adjustments they will make for uncontrollable factors. Typically, they adjust to two kinds of influences. One adjustment removes expenses that result from decisions made by executives above the business-unit level.

> **Example.**   A major consumer products company reported, "A few years ago we decided to close a factory in Germany that was working at 30 percent of capacity. The expenses were deducted at the corporate level. It was not the decision of the manager in Germany, so we couldn't penalize him."[14]

---

[12]"Motorola," *Business Week,* May 4, 1998, p. 142.

[13]"Scents and Sensibility," *The Economist,* July 13, 1996, pp. 57–58.

[14]Kenneth A. Merchant, *Rewarding Results: Motivating Profit Center Managers* (Boston: Harvard Business School Press, 1989), p. 121.

Another adjustment eliminates the effects of losses caused by "acts of nature" (fires, earthquakes, floods) and accidents not caused by the manager's negligence.

> **Example.** The following comment by an executive in a distribution company, who was asked if he would make an adjustment if a fire occurred in a warehouse, is typical: "I would start with the assumption that this couldn't be foreseen. Then I would look at the causes. Was the fire caused by a breach of security or a lackadaisical attitude toward safety? If the fire was outside the manager's control, I would make the adjustment."[15]

Benefits and Shortcomings of Short-Term Financial Targets. It is a good idea to link business unit managers' bonus to achieving annual financial targets (after making allowances for uncontrollable events). It induces managers to search for different ways to perform existing operations and initiate new activities to meet the financial targets.

However, relying only on financial criteria could cause several dysfunctional effects.[16] First, it could encourage short-term actions that are not in the company's long-term interests (e.g., undermaintenance of equipment). Second, managers might not undertake promising long-term investments that hurt short-term financial results. Third, managers may be motivated to manipulate data to meet current period targets.

> **Example.** Sunrise Medical, Inc., a medical products company, decentralized its operations and linked division managers' bonuses to their own divisions' bottom lines. If a division did not make suitable profits, its general manager did not receive a bonus, even if the company as a whole was profitable. On January 4, 1996, Sunrise's directors disclosed that one of its divisions, Sunrise Bio Clinic, had falsified its accounting records to show higher-than-actual profits. Some argued that the bonus system was partly to blame for Bio Clinic's falsified accounts.[17]

Mechanisms to Overcome Short-Term Bias. *Supplementing* financial criteria with additional incentive mechanisms may overcome the short-term orientation of annual financial goals. For example, a firm might base part of its managers' bonus on *multiyear performance* (i.e., performance over a three-to-five-year period). Although this has the obvious advantage of extending the time horizon of managers, there are certain weaknesses. First, managers have difficulty seeing the connection between their efforts and rewards in a multiyear award scheme, which lessens the motivational effect of such awards. Second, if a manager retires or is transferred during the multiyear period, implementing such a plan becomes more complex. Third, it is more likely that factors beyond the manager's control will influence the achievement of long-range targets.

---

[15]Ibid., pp. 125–26.
[16]J. J. Curran, "Companies That Rob the Future," *Fortune,* July 4, 1988, pp. 84–89; "More than Ever, It's Management for the Short Term," *Business Week,* November 24, 1986, pp. 92–93.
[17]Tom Petruno, "Bonuses Can Have a Darker Side," *Valley News,* February 4, 1996, p. E3.

Example.   In investment banking and brokerage houses, it is not uncommon to give bonuses to traders based on profits on each deal they make. This creates incentives for the traders to take big risks in the hope of big paychecks. However, it could potentially lead to serious financial problems for the organization. The collapse of Barings, an investment bank in the United Kingdom, is a case in point. In order to mitigate this problem, Salomon Brothers altered its bonus scheme. Employees at Salomon were entitled to a bonus on a deal only if the company achieved predetermined return on equity. Further, a portion of the bonus was decided based on multiyear performance to be sure that Salomon's future profits were not sacrificed by short-term actions.[18]

Another method to correct for the inherent inadequacies of financial criteria is to develop a scorecard that includes one or more nonfinancial criteria, such as sales growth, market share, customer satisfaction, product quality, new product development, personnel development, and public responsibility. Each of these factors will affect long-run profits. Senior management can create the desired long-term versus short-term profit orientation on the part of business unit managers and allow for factors that are not reflected in the financial measure by selectively choosing financial and nonfinancial criteria and appropriate weights among these criteria.

Examples.   When John Martin, CEO of PepsiCo's fast-food restaurant chain Taco Bell, embarked on his transformation program in 1988, he shifted decision-making from the company's headquarters to restaurant managers and increased each manager's responsibility from 5 to 20 restaurants. This empowerment was supported by a fundamental change in the reward system. A bonus scheme, linked to customer service levels, profit targets, and sales, significantly increased both managerial and hourly compensation. If Taco Bell managers performed, they earned more than three times the fast-food industry average. This, coupled with bonuses based on length of service, reduced the appeal of hopping from one fast-food chain to the next in search of higher pay, a practice thought to be endemic among fast-food restaurant managers. As a result, Taco Bell reduced restaurant manager turnover by more than 50 percent and hourly employee turnover to 30 percent. These changes in the roles and rewards of restaurant managers contributed significantly to Taco Bell's dramatic improvement since 1988. Between 1988 and 1993, the company opened more than 2,000 new restaurants, increased worldwide sales from $1.5 billion to nearly $4 billion, and more than tripled net income to over $250 million. Over the same period, there was a sharp improvement in customer satisfaction—measured by value-for-money perceptions—while that of competitors declined.[19]

PA Consulting, a management and technology consulting firm based in Britain, was organized by business units. The company tied the bonus of consultants to the profits from their own units. This system had the potential to create an uncooperative environment. In order to prevent that, employees' bonuses were also based on the clients they brought in and those they served, and on subjective reviews by peers, subordinates, superiors, and clients. If a consultant referred a

---

[18]"Pay and Performance: Bonus Points," *The Economist,* April 15, 1995, pp. 71–72.
[19]"Renewal at Taco Bell," *Transformation,* Gemini Consulting 6, Spring 1995, p. 8.

client to another unit, he or she received a bonus. Similarly, a consultant who felt that a client could be served better by taking the help of staff from another unit was motivated to do so since it led to better reviews by clients and colleagues.[20]

Another mechanism to correct for the short-term bias is to base part of the business-unit managers' bonus on *long-term incentive plans,* such as stock options, phantom shares, and performance shares. These plans focus business unit managers on (1) companywide performance and (2) long-term performance. Advantages and limitations of these plans were discussed earlier.

> **Example.**   Interpublic, which runs four advertising agencies (McCann-Erickson, Lintas, Dailey & Associates, and the Lowe Group), designed incentive systems for its business units to make sure they focused on profitability and growth. The compensation for managers was based on long-term performance: four years' performance but awarded every two years. This helped keep managers from jumping ship, an ever-present agency business threat. Employees were rewarded with stock and bonuses for exceeding their numbers and for qualitative results, such as setting up succession plans and servicing clients.[21]

Benchmarks for Comparison.   A business unit manager's performance can be appraised by comparing actual results to the profit budget, past performance, or competitors' performance. The typical practice is to evaluate a business unit manager against the profit budget. As discussed in Chapter 8, the following considerations are important when using the profit budget as a motivational tool: (1) The business unit manager participates in the development of the profit budget and (2) the budget is challenging but attainable.

Bonus Determination Approach

A bonus award for a business unit manager can be determined by using a strict formula, such as a percentage of the business unit's operating profit, or by a purely subjective assessment by the manager's superior, or by some combination of the two.

> **Example.**   In 1992 employees of FormPac did not receive bonuses, even though they worked hard, because the company was not making profits. The employees did not know why they had not received bonuses because the bonuses were strictly based on the discretion of an uncommunicative CEO. This demotivated employees and generated distrust. In order to regain credibility in the bonus system, FormPac's CEO, William Duff, published the monthly and year-to-date sales and profit figures on a display board and linked employees' bonuses to published sales growth and profit figures. By 1996 FormPac's employees seemed to have more faith in the bonus system.[22]

---

[20]"Pay Purview," *The Economist,* August 29, 1998, pp. 59–60.
[21]"Sibling Rivalry," *Forbes,* February 15, 1993, pp. 119–20.
[22]Donna Fenn, "Bonuses That Make Sense," Inc., March 1996, p. 95.

Relying exclusively on objective formulas has some clear merits: Reward systems can be specified with precision; there is little uncertainty or ambiguity about performance standards; and superiors cannot exercise any bias or favoritism in assessing the performance of subordinate managers. However, one major drawback is that objective formulas are likely to induce managers to pay less attention to the performance of their business units along dimensions that are important but difficult to quantify (e.g., research and development, and human resource management). Some subjectivity in determining bonuses, therefore, is desirable in most units, especially when a manager's personal control over a unit's performance is low. In such situations, numerical indicators of the unit's performance are less valid measures of the manager's performance. This type of situation is likely to happen under the following circumstances:

- When the business unit manager inherits problems created by a predecessor.
- When the business unit is highly interdependent with other units and therefore its performance is influenced by the decisions and actions of outside individuals.
- When the strategy requires much greater attention to longer-term concerns (as is the case in a business unit aggressively building market share or business units in rapidly evolving industries).

Example.   Lucent Technologies used subjective performance reviews and loose controls over new ventures in fields ranging from digital radio and Internet telephony to electroplating and public safety—new ventures where innovation was critical.[23]

Agency Theory

Agency theory explores how contracts and incentives can be written to motivate individuals to achieve goal congruence.[24] It attempts to describe the major factors that should be considered in designing incentive contracts. An incentive contract, as used in agency theory, is the same as the incentive compensation arrangements discussed in this chapter. Agency theory attempts to state these relationships in mathematical models. This introduction describes the general ideas of agency theory without giving actual models.

---

[23]"A Survey of Innovation in Industry," *The Economist,* February 20, 1999, pp. 5–28.

[24]The term *agency* suggests that the topic is related to agency law, but this is not the case. Agency law defines the obligations for an agent to a principal and the obligations of a principal to the agent, but these legal obligations do not govern or adequately explain the behaviors of superior managers and subordinate managers to one another. "Commitments" and "understandings" between superiors and subordinates are not legal contracts; subordinates rarely are sued for breach of contract.

Concepts

An agency relationship exists whenever one party (the principal) hires another party (the agent) to perform some service and, in so doing, delegates decision-making authority to the agent. In a corporation, shareholders are principals and the chief executive officer is their agent. The shareholders hire the CEO and expect that he or she will act in their interest. At a lower level, the CEO is the principal and the business unit managers are the agents. The challenge becomes how to motivate agents so that they will be as productive as they would be if they were the owners.

One of the key elements of agency theory is that principals and agents have divergent preferences or objectives. Incentive contracts can reduce these divergent preferences.

Divergent Objectives of Principals and Agents.   Agency theory assumes that all individuals act in their own self-interest. Agents are assumed to receive satisfaction not only from financial compensation but also from the perquisites involved in an agency relationship, such as generous amounts of leisure time, attractive working conditions, country club memberships, and flexible working hours. For example, some agents may prefer leisure to hard work or effort. Leisure is assumed to be the opposite of effort. Managers' efforts increase the value of the firm, while leisure does not. An agent's preference for leisure over effort is called *work aversion*. Deliberately withholding effort is called *shirking*.

Principals (i.e., shareholders), on the other hand, are assumed to be interested only in the financial returns that accrue from their investment in the firm.

Agents and principals also diverge with respect to *risk preferences*. Agency theory assumes that managers prefer more wealth to less, but that marginal utility, or satisfaction, decreases as more wealth is accumulated. Agents typically have much of their wealth tied up in the fortunes of the firm. This wealth consists of both their financial wealth and their human capital. Human capital—the manager's value as perceived by the market—is influenced by the firm's performance. Because of the decreasing utility for wealth and the large amount of agent capital that depends on the company, agents are assumed to be *risk averse:* They value increases from a risky investment at less than the expected (actuarial) value of the investment.

On the other hand, company stock is held by many owners, who reduce their risk by diversifying their wealth and owning shares in many companies. Therefore, owners are interested in the expected value of their investment and are *risk neutral*. Managers cannot as easily diversify away this risk, which is why they are risk averse.

Nonobservability of Agents' Actions.   Divergent preferences associated with compensation and perquisites arise whenever the principal cannot easily monitor the agent's actions. Shareholders are not in a position to monitor the CEO's activities daily to ensure that he or she is working in their best interest. Likewise, the CEO is not in a position to monitor daily the activities of business unit managers.

Because the principal has inadequate information about the agent's performance, the principal can never be certain how the agent's effort contributed to actual company results. This situation is referred to as *information asymmetry*. These asymmetries can take on several forms. Without monitoring, only the agent knows whether he or she is working in the principal's best interest. Moreover, the agent may know more about the task than the principal. This additional information that an agent may have is called *private information*.

The divergence of preferences between the principal and agent, and the agent's private information, may lead the agent to misrepresent information to the principal. This misrepresentation is of such a general nature that the name *moral hazard* has been given to the situation in which an agent being controlled is motivated to misrepresent private information by the nature of the control system.

Control Mechanisms

Agency theorists state that there are two major ways of dealing with the problems of divergent objectives and information asymmetry: monitoring and incentives.

Monitoring.   The principal can design control systems that monitor the agent's actions, limiting actions that increase the agent's welfare at the expense of principal's interest. An example of a monitoring system is the audited financial statement. Financial reports are generated about company performance, audited by a third party, and then sent to the owners.

Agency theory has attempted to explain why different agency relationships involve different levels of monitoring. For example, monitoring is more effective if the agent's task is well defined and the information, or "signal," used in monitoring is accurate. If the task is not well defined or easily monitored, then incentive contracting becomes more appealing as a control device. Monitoring and incentives are not mutually exclusive alternatives. In most firms, the CEO has an incentive contract along with audited financial statements that act as a monitoring device.

Incentive Contracting.   A principal may attempt to limit divergent preferences by establishing appropriate incentive contracts. The more an agent's reward depends on a performance measure, the more incentive there is for the agent to improve the measure. Therefore, the principal should define the performance measure so that it furthers his or her interest. The ability to accomplish this is referred to as *goal congruence*. When the contract given to the agent motivates the agent to work in the principal's best interest, the contract is considered goal congruent.

A compensation scheme that does not incorporate an incentive contract poses a serious agency problem. For example, if CEOs were paid a straight salary, they might not be motivated to work as diligently as when compensation consisted of a salary plus bonus. The latter case motivates CEOs to work harder to increase profits, increasing their compensation and, at the same time, benefiting the principal. Therefore, contracts are written that align the interests between the two parties by incorporating an incentive feature—that is, the principal writes a contract permitting management to share in the wealth when firm value is increased.

> **Example.** To protect against its CEO's possible risk aversion, CBS included a protection clause in CEO Les Moonves's contract that would pay him $5 million in the event CBS was sold to another company. A few months after Moonves arrived at CBS, Westinghouse purchased CBS and the clause was activated.[25]

Principals face the challenge of identifying signals that are correlated with both agent effort and firm value. The agent's effort, along with outside factors (e.g., the general economy, natural disasters), combine to determine performance. The more closely an outcome measure reflects the manager's effort, the more valuable the measure is in an incentive contract. If the performance measure is not closely correlated with the agent's effort, there is little incentive for the agent to increase his or her effort.

None of the incentive arrangements can ensure complete goal congruence. This is because of the difference in risk preferences between the two parties, the asymmetry of information, and the costs of monitoring. These differences cause additional costs. Even an efficient system of incentive alignments will still result in some divergence of preferences; this is called the *residual loss*. The addition of the incentive compensation costs, the monitoring costs, and the residual loss are formally titled *agency costs*.

CEO Compensation and Stock Ownership Plans. A company that pays its CEO a bonus in the form of stock options offers an example of the agency costs inherent in incentive compensation. One cost is the risk-preference differences between the owners and the CEO. The agent, already risk averse, incurs additional risks when his or her pay is based on stock price performance. To compensate the CEO for taking on this risk, the contract will have to increase the amount of expected pay. In addition, to minimize the possible downside potential, the agent may not take on high risk/high return projects that the principal may find desirable.

A second problem with a stock ownership bonus plan is the lack of direct causal relationship between the agent's effort and the change in stock price. Stock prices are affected by factors outside the agent's control (e.g., general economic conditions, government intervention). If these factors cause the stock price to rise, then the agent receives increased pay at the owners' expense without any increased effort. On the other hand, the stock price may decrease even if the agent works hard.

---

[25]Marc Gunther, "Turnaround Time for CBS," *Fortune,* August 19, 1996, pp. 65–68.

In spite of these two problems, the stock ownership incentive contract is preferred to a contract that does not have an incentive feature. As pointed out earlier, a flat salary has larger agency costs associated with it.

Business Unit Managers and Accounting-Based Incentives.   The relationship between a business unit manager's effort and the stock price is more remote than that between the CEO's effort and the stock price. It is difficult to isolate the contributions that individual business units make to increases in the firm's stock price. For this reason, a company might base the business unit manager's bonus on business unit net income. However, this incentive contract still has agency costs similar to those discussed in the CEO stock ownership plan. For example, market demand for a product may fall because of a new substitute product, but the manager may still perform well within the new smaller market. If the bonus is based strictly on net income, however, the agent's compensation will decrease. In addition, the agent may inflate net income through accounting manipulations that do not affect firm value. One instance of this is the sale of fixed assets that have a market value in excess of book value. While a contract based on business unit net income may have lower agency costs than straight salary, these costs do not go to zero.

A Critique

Agency theory was invented in the 1960s and since then has been written about extensively in academic journals. But the theory has had no discernible practical influence on the management control process. There has been no real-world payoff. By "payoff" we mean that a manager used the results of agency theory to make a better compensation decision. Many managers are not even aware of agency theory.

Agency theory implies that managers in nonprofit and governmental organizations, who cannot receive incentive compensation, inherently lack the motivation necessary for goal congruence; many people do not accept this implication.

Some who have studied agency theory aver that the models are no more than statements of obvious facts expressed in mathematical symbols. Others state that the elements in the models can't be quantified (what is the "cost of information asymmetry"?), and that the model vastly oversimplifies the real-world relationship between superiors and subordinates. The models incorporate only a few elements. They disregard other factors that affect this relationship, such as the personalities of the participants, agents who are not risk averse, nonfinancial motives, the principal's trust in the agent, the agent's ability on the present assignment and potential for future assignments, and so on.

We describe the theory in the hope that students will find it useful in thinking about how incentive compensation influences the motivation of managers, but we caution about using it to solve actual compensation problems.

Summary

The incentive compensation system is a key management control device. Incentive compensation plans can be divided roughly into two types: those that relate compensation to profits currently earned by the company, called "short-term incentive plans"; and those that relate compensation to longer-term performance, called "long-term incentive plans." Several factors should be considered when allocating the total bonus pool to corporate executives and business unit managers. An incentive system that explicitly incorporates the following has a much better chance of success:

- The needs, values, and beliefs of the general managers who are rewarded.
- The culture of the organization.
- External factors, such as industry characteristics, competitors' compensation practices, managerial labor markets, and tax and legal issues.
- The organization's strategies.

Suggested Additional Readings

Betcher, John G. *How to Design & Implement a Results-Oriented Variable Pay System*. New York: AMACOM, 1996.

Bok, Derek. *The Cost of Talent*. New York: Free Press, 1993.

Bruns, William J., Jr. *Performance Measurement, Evaluation and Incentives*. Boston: Harvard Business School Press, 1991.

Chingos, Peter T., and Peat Marwick, eds. *Paying for Performance: A Guide to Compensation Management*. New York: John Wiley & Sons, 1997.

Crystal, Graef S. *In Search of Excess: The Overcompensation of the American Executive*. New York: W. W. Norton, 1992.

Finkelstein, Sydney, and Donald C. Hambrick. *Strategic Leadership: Top Executives and Their Effects on Organizations*. St. Paul, MN: West, 1996.

Fisher, Joseph, and Vijay Govindarajan. "Profit Center Manager Compensation: Impact of Market, Political, and Human Capital Factors." *Strategic Management Journal,* March 1992, pp. 25–27.

Griner, Emmett H. "Stock Option Compensation, CEO Pay, and Corporate Performance: A Board-Level Perspective." *Journal of Managerial Issues* 8, no. 2 (Summer 1996), pp. 143–53.

Henderson, Andrew D., and James W. Fredrickson. "Information-Processing Demands as a Determinant of CEO Compensation." *Academy of Management Journal* 39, no. 3 (June 1996), pp. 575–606.

Henderson, Richard I., and Richard J. Henderson. *Compensation Management in a Knowledge-Based World*. Upper Saddle River, NJ: Prentice Hall, 1996.

Hills, Frederick S., et al. *Compensation Decision Making*. Harcourt Brace Jovanovich College and School Division, 1997.

Lederer, Jack L., and Carl R. Weinberg. "Are CEOs Paid Too Much?" *Chief Executive,* May 1996, pp. 26–31.

Martocchio, Joseph J. *Strategic Compensation: A Human Resource Management Approach.* Upper Saddle River, NJ: Prentice Hall, 1997.

Milkovich, George T., and Jerry M. Newman. *Compensation.* 3rd ed. Burr Ridge, IL: BPI/Irwin, 1990.

———. *Compensation.* New York: McGraw-Hill College Division, 1999.

Rodrick, Scott S., ed. *Incentive Compensation and Employee Ownership.* Oakland, CA: National Center for Employee Ownership, 1999.

Stern, Joel M. "EVA and Strategic Performance Management." *Global Finance 2000.* New York: The Conference Board, 1996.

Weisenfeld, Leslie W., and Larry N. Killough. "A Review and Extension of Using Performance Reports: A Field Study Based on Path-Goal Theory." *Journal of Management Accounting Research* (Fall 1992), pp. 209–25. (Has an extensive bibliography.)

CASE 11–1
LINCOLN ELECTRIC COMPANY (A)

People are our most valuable asset. They must feel secure, important, challenged, in control of their destiny, confident in their leadership, be responsive to common goals, believe they are being treated fairly, have easy access to authority and open lines of communication in all possible directions. Perhaps the most important task Lincoln employees face today is that of establishing an example for others in the Lincoln organization in other parts of the world. We need to maximize the benefits of cooperation and teamwork, fusing high technology with human talent, so that we here in the USA and all of our subsidiary and joint venture operations will be in a position to realize our full potential.

George Willis, CEO, The Lincoln Electric Company

The Lincoln Electric Company was the world's largest manufacturer of arc-welding products and a leading producer of industrial electric motors. The firm employed 2400 workers in two US factories near Cleveland and an equal number in eleven factories located in other countries. This did not include the field sales force of more than 200. The company's US market share (for arc-welding products) was estimated at more than 40 percent.

The Lincoln incentive management plan had been well known for many years. Many college management texts referred to the Lincoln plan as a model for achieving higher worker productivity. Certainly, the firm was successful according to the usual measures.

When James F. Lincoln died in 1965, there had been some concern, even among employees, that the management system would fall into disarray, that profits would decline, and that year-end bonuses might be discontinued. Quite the contrary, 24 years after Lincoln's death, the company appeared to be as strong as ever. Each year, except the recession years 1982 and 1983, saw high profits and bonuses. Employee morale and productivity remained very good. Employee turnover was almost nonexistent except for retirements. Lincoln's market share was stable. The historically high stock dividends continued.

A Historical Sketch

In 1895, after being "frozen out" of the depression-ravaged Elliott-Lincoln Company, a maker of Lincoln-designed electric motors, John C. Lincoln, took out his second patent and began to manufacture his improved motor. He opened his new business, unincorporated, with $200 he had earned redesigning a motor for young Herbert Henry Dow, who later founded the Dow Chemical Company.

Started during an economic depression and cursed by a major fire after only one year in business, the company grew, but hardly prospered, through its first quarter-century. In 1906, John C. Lincoln incorporated the business and moved from his one-room, fourth-floor factory to a new three-story building he erected in east Cleveland. He expanded his work force to 30 and sales grew to over $50,000 a year. John preferred being an engineer and inventor rather than a manager, though, and it was to be left to another Lincoln to manage the company through its years of success.

In 1907, after a bout with typhoid fever forced him to leave Ohio State University in his senior year, James F. Lincoln, John's younger brother, joined the fledgling company. In 1914 he became active head of the firm, with the titles General Manager and Vice President. John remained President of the company for some years but became more involved in other business ventures and in his work as an inventor.

This case was prepared by Arthur D. Sharplin, McNeese State University. Copyright © by the *Case Research Journal* and Arthur D. Sharplin.

One of James Lincoln's early actions was to ask the employees to elect representatives to a committee (called the "Advisory Board") which would advise him on company operations. The Advisory Board met with the Chief Executive Officer every two weeks. This was only the first of a series of innovative personnel policies which, over the years, distinguished Lincoln Electric from its contemporaries.

The first year the Advisory Board was in existence, working hours were reduced from 55 per week, then standard, to 50 hours a week. In 1915, the company gave each employee a paid-up life insurance policy. A welding school, which continues today, was begun in 1917. In 1918, an employee bonus plan was attempted. It was not continued, but the idea was to resurface later.

The Lincoln Electric Employees' Association was formed in 1919 to provide health benefits and social activities. Over the years, it assumed several additional functions. In 1923, a piece-work pay system was in effect, employees got two weeks paid vacation each year, and wages were adjusted for changes in the Consumer Price Index. Approximately 30 percent of the common stock was set aside for key employees in 1914. A stock purchase plan for all employees was begun in 1925.

The Board of Directors voted to start a suggestion system in 1929. Cash awards, a part of the early program, were discontinued in the mid-1980s. Suggestions were rewarded by additional "points," which affected year-end bonuses.

The legendary Lincoln bonus plan was proposed by the Advisory Board and accepted on a trial basis in 1934. The first annual bonus amounted to about 25 percent of wages. There was a bonus every year after that. The bonus plan became a cornerstone of the Lincoln management system, and recent bonuses approximated annual wages.

By 1944, Lincoln employees enjoyed a pension plan, a policy of promotion from within, and continuous employment. Base pay rates were determined by formal job evaluation, and a merit rating system was in effect.

In the prologue of James F. Lincoln's last book, Charles G. Herbruck wrote regarding the foregoing personnel innovations:

> They were not to buy good behavior. They were not efforts to increase profits. They were not antidotes to labor difficulties. They did not constitute a "do-gooder" program. They were expressions of mutual respect for each person's importance to the job to be done. All of them reflect the leadership of James Lincoln, under whom they were nurtured and propagated.

During World War II, Lincoln prospered as never before. By the start of the war, the company was the world's largest manufacturer of arc-welding products. Sales of about $4 million in 1934 grew to $24 million by 1941. Productivity per employee more than doubled during the same period. The Navy's Price Review Board challenged the high profits. The Internal Revenue Service questioned the tax deductibility of employee bonuses, arguing they were not "ordinary and necessary" costs of doing business, but the forceful and articulate James Lincoln was able to overcome the objections.

Certainly after 1935 and probably for several years before that, Lincoln productivity was well above the average for similar companies. The company claimed levels of productivity more than twice those for other manufacturers from 1945 onward. Information available from outside sources tended to support these claims.

Company Philosophy

James F. Lincoln was the son of a Congregational minister, and Christian principles were at the center of his business philosophy. The confidence that he had in the efficacy of Christ's teachings was illustrated by the following remark taken from one of his books:

> The Christian ethic should control our acts. If it did control our acts, the savings in cost of distribution would be tremendous. Advertising would be a contact of the expert consultant with the customer, in order to give the

customer the best product available when all of the customer's needs are considered. Competition then would be in improving the quality of products and increasing efficiency in producing and distributing them; not in deception, as is now too customary. Pricing would reflect efficiency of production; it would not be a selling dodge that the customer may well be sorry he accepted. It would be proper for all concerned and rewarding for the ability used in producing the product.

There was no indication that Lincoln attempted to evangelize his employees or customers—or the general public, for that matter. Neither the Chairman of the Board and Chief Executive, George Willis, nor the President, Donald F. Hastings, mentioned the Christian gospel in speeches and interviews. The company motto, "The actual is limited, the possible is immense," was prominently displayed, but there was no display of religious slogans and no company chapel.

Attitude toward the Customer. James Lincoln considered the customer's needs the raison d'être for every company. "When any company has achieved success so that it is attractive as an investment," he wrote, "all money usually needed for expansion is supplied by the customer in retained earnings. It is obvious that the customer's interests, not the stockholder's, should come first." In 1947 he said, "Care should be taken . . . not to rivet attention on profit. Between 'How much do I get?' and 'How do I make this better, cheaper, more useful?' the difference is fundamental and decisive." Willis, too, ranked the customer as management's most important constituency. This was reflected in Lincoln's policy to "at all times price on the basis of cost and at all times keep pressure on our cost." Lincoln's goal, often stated, was "to build a better and better product at a lower and lower price." "It is obvious," James Lincoln said, "that the customer's interests should be the first goal of industry."

Attitude toward Stockholders. Stockholders were given last priority at Lincoln. This was a continuation of James Lincoln's philosophy: "The last group to be considered is the stockholders who own stock because they think it will be more profitable than investing money in any other way." Concerning division of the largess produced by incentive management, he wrote, "The absentee stockholder also will get his share, even if undeserved, out of the greatly increased profit that the efficiency produces."

Attitude toward Unionism.   There was never a serious effort to organize Lincoln employees. While James Lincoln criticized the labor movement for "selfishly attempting to better its position at the expense of the people it must serve," he still had kind words for union members. He excused abuses of union power as "the natural reactions of human beings to the abuses to which management has subjected them." Lincoln's idea of the correct relationship between workers and managers was shown by this comment: "Labor and management are properly not warring camps; they are parts of one organization in which they must and should cooperate fully and happily."

Beliefs and Assumptions about Employees. If fulfilling customer needs was the desired goal of business, then employee performance and productivity were the means by which this goal could best be achieved. It was the Lincoln attitude toward employees, reflected in the following comments by James Lincoln, which was credited by many with creating the success the company experienced:

> The greatest fear of the worker, which is the same as the greatest fear of the industrialist in operating a company, is the lack of income. . . . The industrial manager is very conscious of his company's need for uninterrupted income. He is completely oblivious, evidently, of the fact that the worker has the same need.
>
> [The worker] is just as eager as any manager is to be part of a team that is properly organized and working for the advancement of our economy. . . . He has no desire to make profits for those who do not hold up their end in production, as is true of absentee stockholders and inactive people in the company.

If money is to be used as an incentive, the program must provide that what is paid to the worker is what he has earned. The earnings of each must be in accordance with accomplishment.

Status is of great importance in all human relationships. The greatest incentive that money has, usually, is that it is a symbol of success. . . . The resulting status is the real incentive. . . . Money alone can be an incentive to the miser only.

There must be complete honesty and understanding between the hourly worker and management if high efficiency is to be obtained.

Lincoln's Business

Arc welding had been the standing joining method in shipbuilding for decades. It was the predominant way of connecting steel in the construction industry. Most industrial plants had their own welding shops for maintenance and construction. Manufacturers of tractors and all kinds of heavy equipment used arc welding extensively in the manufacturing process. Many hobbyists had their own welding machines and used them for making metal items such as patio furniture and barbecue pits. The popularity of welded sculpture as an art form was growing.

While advances in welding technology were frequent, arc-welding products, in the main, hardly changed. Lincoln's Innershield process was a notable exception. This process, described later, lowered welding cost and improved quality and speed in many applications. The most widely used Lincoln electrode, the Fleetweld 5P, was virtually the same from the 1930s to 1989. For at least four decades, the most popular engine-driven welder in the world, the Lincoln SA-200, had been a gray-colored assembly, including a four-cylinder Continental "Red Seal" engine and a 200-ampere direct-current generator with two current-control knobs. A 1989 model SA-200 even weighed almost the same as the 1950 model, and it certainly was little changed in appearance.

The company's share of the US arc-welding products market appeared to have been about 40 percent for many years. The welding products market had grown somewhat faster than the level of industry in general. The market was highly price-competitive, with variations in prices of standard items normally amounting to only 1 or 2 percent. Lincoln's products were sold directly by its engineering-oriented sales force and indirectly through its distributor organization. Advertising expenditures amounted to less than 0.75 percent of sales. Research and development expenditures typically ranged from $10 million to $12 million, considerably more than competitors spent.

The other major welding process, flame welding, had not been competitive with arc welding since the 1930s. However, plasma arc welding, a relatively new process which used a conducting stream of superheated gas (plasma) to confine the welding current to a small area, had made some inroads, especially in metal tubing manufacturing, in recent years. Major advances in technology which would produce an alternative superior to arc welding within the next decade or so appeared unlikely. Also, it seemed likely that changes in the machines and techniques used in arc welding would be evolutionary rather than revolutionary.

Products.   The company was primarily engaged in the manufacture and sale of arc-welding products—electric welding machines and metal electrodes. Lincoln also produced electric motors ranging from 0.5 to 200 horsepower. Motors constituted about 8 to 10 percent of total sales. Several million dollars had recently been invested in automated equipment that would double Lincoln's manufacturing capacity for 0.5- to 20-horsepower electric motors.

The electric welding machines, some consisting of a transformer or motor and generator arrangement powered by commercial electricity and others consisting of an internal combustion engine and generator, were designed to produce 30 to 1500 amperes of electrical power. This electrical current was used to melt a consumable metal electrode, with the molten metal being transferred in superhot spray to the metal joint being welded. Very high temperatures and hot sparks were produced, and operators usually had to wear special eye and face protection and leather gloves, often along with leather aprons and sleeves.

Lincoln and its competitors marketed a wide range of general-purpose and specialty electrodes for welding mild steel, aluminum, cast iron, and stainless and special steels. Most of these electrodes were designed to meet the standards of the American Welding Society, a trade association. They were thus essentially the same as to size and composition from one manufacturer to another. Every electrode manufacturer had a limited number of unique products, but these typically constituted only a small percentage of total sales.

Welding electrodes were of two basic types:

1. Coated "stick" electrodes, usually 14 inches long and smaller than a pencil in diameter, were held in a special insulated holder by the operator, who had to manipulate the electrode in order to maintain a proper arc width and pattern of deposition of the metal being transferred. Stick electrodes were packaged in 6-to-50-pound boxes.

2. Coiled wire, ranging in diameter from 0.035 to 0.219 inch, was designed to be fed continuously to the welding arc through a "gun" held by the operator or positioned by automatic positioning equipment. The wire was packaged in coils, reels, and drums weighing from 14 to 1000 pounds and could be solid or flux-cored.

Manufacturing Processes. The main plant was in Euclid, Ohio, a suburb on Cleveland's east side. There were no warehouses. Materials flowed from the ½-mile-long dock on the north side of the plant through the production lines to a very limited storage and loading area on the south side. Materials used on each workstation were stored as close as possible to the workstation. The administrative offices, near the center of the factory, were entirely functional. A corridor below the main level provided access to the factory floor from the main entrance near the center of the plant. *Fortune* magazine declared the Euclid facility one of America's 10 best-managed factories,[1] and compared it with a General Electric plant also on the list:

> Stepping into GE's spanking new dishwasher plant, an awed supplier said, is like stepping "into the Hyatt Regency." By comparison, stepping into Lincoln Electric's 33-year-old, cavernous, dimly lit factory is like stumbling into a dingy big-city YMCA. It's only when one starts looking at how these factories do things that similarities become apparent. They have found ways to merge design with manufacturing, build in quality, make wise choices about automation, get close to customers, and handle their work forces.

A new Lincoln plant, in Mentor, Ohio, housed some of the electrode production operations, which had been moved from the main plant.

Electrode manufacturing was highly capital-intensive. Metal rods purchased from steel producers were drawn down to smaller diameters, cut to length, coated with pressed-powder "flux" for stick electrodes or plated with copper (for conductivity), and put into coils or spools for wire. Lincoln's Innershield wire was hollow and filled with a material similar to that used to coat stick electrodes. As mentioned earlier, this represented a major innovation in welding technology when it was introduced. The company was highly secretive about its electrode production processes, and outsiders were not given access to the details of those processes.

Lincoln welding machines and electric motors were made on a series of assembly lines. Gasoline and diesel engines were purchased partially assembled, but practically all other components were made from basic industrial

---

[1]Gene Bylinsky, "America's Best-Managed Factories," *Fortune,* May 28, 1984, p. 16.

products (e.g., steel bars and sheets and bar copper conductor wire).

Individual components, such as gasoline tanks for engine-driven welders and steel shafts for motors and generators, were made by numerous small "factories within a factory." The shaft for a certain generator, for example, was made from raw steel bar by one operator who used five large machines, all running continuously. A saw cut the bar to length, a digital lathe machined different sections to varying diameters, a special milling machine cut a slot for the keyway, and so forth, until a finished shaft was produced. The operator moved the shafts from machine to machine and made necessary adjustments.

Another operator punched, shaped, and painted sheet-metal cowling parts. One assembled steel laminations onto a rotor shaft, then wound, insulated, and tested the rotors. Finished components were moved by crane operators to the nearby assembly lines.

Worker Performance and Attitudes. Exceptional worker performance at Lincoln was a matter of record. The typical Lincoln employee earned about twice as much as other factory workers in the Cleveland area. Yet the company's labor cost per sales dollar in 1989, 26 cents, was well below the industry average. Worker turnover was practically nonexistent except for retirements and departures by new employees.

Sales per Lincoln factory employee exceeded $150,000. An observer at the factory quickly saw why this figure was so high. Each worker was proceeding busily and thoughtfully about the task at hand. There was no idle chatter. Most workers took no coffee breaks. Many operated several machines and made a substantial component unaided. The supervisors were busy with planning and record-keeping duties and hardly glanced at the people they "supervised." The manufacturing procedures appeared to be efficient—no unnecessary steps, no wasted mo-

tions, no wasted materials. Finished components moved smoothly to subsequent work stations.

The Appendix to this case gives summaries of interviews with employees.

Organizational Structure

Lincoln never allowed development of a formal organization chart. The objective of this policy was to ensure maximum flexibility. An open-door policy was practiced throughout the company, and personnel were encouraged to take problems to the persons most capable of resolving them. Once, Harvard Business School researchers prepared an organization chart reflecting the implied relationships at Lincoln. The chart became available within the company, and management felt that the chart had a disruptive effect. Therefore, no organization chart appears in this case.

Perhaps because of the quality and enthusiasm of the Lincoln work force, routine supervision was almost nonexistent. A typical production foreman, for example, supervised as many as 100 workers, a span of control which did not allow more than infrequent worker-supervisor interaction.

Position titles and traditional flows of authority did imply something of an organizational structure, however. For example, the Vice President, Sales, and the Vice President, Electrode Division, reported to the President, as did various staff assistants such as the Personnel Director and the Director of Purchasing. Using such implied relationships, it was determined that production workers had two or, at most, three levels of supervision between themselves and the President.

Personnel Policies

As mentioned earlier, Lincoln's remarkable personnel practices were credited by many with the company's success.

Recruitment and Selection.   Every job opening was advertised internally on company bulletin boards, and any employee could apply for any job so advertised. External hiring was permitted only for entry-level positions. Selection for these jobs was done on the basis of personal interviews; there was no aptitude or psychological testing. Not even a high school diploma was required—except for engineering and sales positions, which were filled by graduate engineers. A committee consisting of vice presidents and supervisors interviewed candidates initially cleared by the Personnel Department. Final selection was made by the supervisor who had a job opening. Out of over 3500 applicants interviewed by the Personnel Department during one period, fewer than 300 were hired.

Job Security.   In 1958 Lincoln formalized its guaranteed continuous employment policy, which had already been in effect for many years. There had been no layoffs since World War II. Since 1958, every worker with over two years' longevity had been guaranteed at least 30 hours per week, 49 weeks per year.

The policy was never so severely tested as during the 1981–1983 recession. As a manufacturer of capital goods, Lincoln had business that was highly cyclical. In previous recessions the company had been able to avoid major sales declines. However, sales plummeted 32 percent in 1982 and another 16 percent the next year. Few companies could withstand such a revenue collapse and remain profitable. Yet, not only did Lincoln earn profits, but no employee was laid off and year-end incentive bonuses continued. To weather the storm, management cut most of the nonsalaried workers back to 30 hours a week for varying periods of time. Many employees were reassigned, and the total work force was slightly reduced through normal attrition and restricted hiring. Many employees grumbled at their unexpected misfortune, probably to the surprise and dismay of some Lincoln managers. However, sales and profits—and employee bonuses—soon rebounded, and all was well again.

Performance Evaluations.   Each supervisor formally evaluated subordinates twice a year using the cards shown in Exhibit 1. The employee performance criteria—"quality," "dependability," "ideas and cooperation," and "output"—were considered to be independent of each other. Marks on the cards were converted to numerical scores which were forced to average 100 for each evaluating supervisor. Individual merit rating scores normally ranged from 80 to 110. Any score over 110 required a special letter to top management. These scores (over 110) were not considered in computing the required 100-point average for each evaluating supervisor. Suggestions for improvements often resulted in recommendations for exceptionally high performance scores. Supervisors discussed individual performance marks with the employees concerned. Each warranty claim was traced to the individual employee whose work caused the defect. When that happened, the employee's performance score might be reduced, or the worker might be required to repay the cost of servicing the warranty claim by working without pay.

Compensation.   Basic wage levels for jobs at Lincoln were determined by a wage survey of similar jobs in the Cleveland area. These rates were adjusted quarterly in accordance with changes in the Cleveland area wage index. Insofar as possible, base wage rates were translated into piece rates. Practically all production workers and many others—for example, some forklift operators—were paid by piece rate. Once established, piece rates were never changed unless a substantive change in the way a job was done resulted from a source other than the worker doing the job.

In December of each year, a portion of annual profits was distributed to employees as

EXHIBIT 1

Merit rating cards

———➤ **Increasing Quality** ———➤

This card rates the QUALITY of work you do.
It also reflects your success in eliminating errors and in reducing scrap and waste.

Quality

This rating has been done jointly by your department head and the inspection department in the shop and with other department heads in the office and engineering.

———➤ **Increasing Dependability** ———➤

This card rates how well your supervisors have been able to depend on you to do those things that have been expected of you without supervision.
It also reflects your ability to supervise yourself, including your work safety performance, your orderliness, care of equipment, and the effective use you make of your skills.

Dependability

This rating has been done by your department head.

———➤ **Increasing Ideas & Cooperation** ———➤

This card rates your Cooperation, Ideas, and Initiative.
New ideas and new methods are important to your company in our continuing effort to reduce costs, increase output, improve quality and work safety, and improve our relationship with our customers. This card credits you for your ideas and initiative used to help in this direction.
It also rates your cooperation—how you work with others as a team.
Such factors as your attitude toward supervision, coworkers, and the company, your efforts to share knowledge with others, and your cooperation in installing new methods smoothly are considered here.

Ideas & Cooperation

This rating has been done jointly by your department head and the Time study department in the shop and with other department heads in the office and engineering.

———➤ **Increasing Output** ———➤   **Days Absent**

This card rates HOW MUCH PRODUCTIVE WORK you actually turn out. It also reflects your willingness not to hold back and recognizes your attendance record.

Output

This rating has been done jointly by your department head and the production control department in the shop and with other department heads in the office and engineering.

bonuses. Incentive bonuses since 1934 had averaged about 90 percent of annual wages and somewhat more than aftertax profits. The average bonus for 1988 was $21,258. Even for the recession years 1982 and 1983, bonuses averaged $13,998 and $8,557, respectively. Individual bonuses were proportional to merit rating scores. For example, assume the amount set aside for bonuses was 80 percent of total wages paid to eligible employees. A person whose performance score was 95 would receive a bonus of 76 percent (0.80 $*$ 0.95) of annual wages.

Vacations.   The company was shut down for two weeks in August and two weeks during the Christmas season. Vacations were taken during these periods. For employees with over 25 years of service, a fifth week of vacation could be taken at a time acceptable to superiors.

Work Assignment.   Management had authority to transfer workers and to switch between overtime and short time as required. Supervisors had undisputed authority to assign specific parts to individual workers, who might have their own preferences due to variations in piece rates. During the 1982–1983 recession, fifty factory workers volunteered to join sales teams and fanned out across the country to sell a new welder designed for automobile body shops and small machine shops. The result— $10 million in sales and a hot new product.

Employee Participation in Decision Making.   Thinking of participative management usually evokes a vision of a relaxed, nonauthoritarian atmosphere. This was not the case at Lincoln. Formal authority was quite strong. "We're very authoritarian around here," said Willis. James F. Lincoln placed a good deal of stress on protecting management's authority. "Management in all successful departments of industry must have complete power," he said. "Management is the coach who must be obeyed. The workers, however, are the players who alone can win the game." Despite this attitude,

there were several ways in which employees participated in management at Lincoln.

Richard Sabo, Assistant to the Chief Executive Officer, related job enlargement/enrichment to participation. He said, "The most important participative technique that we use is giving more responsibility to employees. We give a high school graduate more responsibility than other companies give their foremen." Management put limits on the degree of participation which was allowed, however. In Sabo's words:

> When you use "participation," put quotes around it. Because we believe that each person should participate only in those decisions he is most knowledgeable about. I don't think production employees should control the decisions of the chairman. They don't know as much as he does about the decisions he is involved in.

The Advisory Board, elected by the workers, met with the Chairman and the President every two weeks to discuss ways of improving operations. As noted earlier, this board had been in existence since 1914 and had contributed to many innovations. The incentive bonuses, for example, were first recommended by this committee. Every employee had access to Advisory Board members, and answers to all Advisory Board suggestions were promised by the following meeting. Both Willis and Hastings were quick to point out, though, that the Advisory Board only recommended actions. "They do not have direct authority," Willis said, "and when they bring up something that management thinks is not to the benefit of the company, it will be rejected."

Under the early suggestion program, employees were awarded one-half of the first year's savings attributable to their suggestions. Later, however, the value of suggestions was reflected in performance evaluation scores, which determined individual incentive bonus amounts.

Training and Education.   Production workers were given a short period of on-the-job training and then placed on a piecework pay system. Lincoln did not pay for off-site education, unless very specific company needs were identified. The idea behind this policy, according to Sabo, was that not everyone could take advantage of such a program, and it was unfair to expend company funds for an advantage to which there was unequal access. Recruits for sales jobs, already college graduates, were given on-the-job training in the plant, followed by a period of work and training at one of the regional sales offices.

Fringe Benefits and Executive Perquisites.
A medical plan and a company-paid retirement program had been in effect for many years. A plant cafeteria, operated on a break-even basis, served meals at about 60 percent of usual costs. The Employee Association, to which the company did not contribute, provided disability insurance and social and athletic activities. The employee stock ownership program resulted in employee ownership of about 50 percent of the common stock. Under this program, each employee with more than two years of service could purchase stock in the corporation. The price of the shares was established at book value. Stock purchased through this plan could be held by employees only.

Dividends and voting rights were the same as for stock which was owned outside the plan. Approximately 75 percent of the employees owned Lincoln stock.

As to executive perquisites, there were none. Executives had crowded, austere offices; no executive washrooms or lunchrooms; and no reserved parking spaces. Even the top executives paid for their own meals and ate in the employee cafeteria. On one recent day, Willis arrived at work late because of a breakfast speaking engagement and had to park far away from the factory entrance.

Financial Policies.   James F. Lincoln felt strongly that financing for company growth should come from within the company—through initial cash investment by the founders, through retention of earnings, and through stock purchases by those who worked in the business. He saw the following advantages to this approach:

1. Ownership of stock by employees strengthened team spirit. "If they are mutually anxious to make it succeed, the future of the company is bright."

2. Ownership of stock provided individual incentive because employees felt that they would benefit from company profitability.

3. "Ownership is educational." Owner-employees "will know how profits are made and lost; how success is won and lost. . . . There are few socialists in the list of stockholders of the nation's industries."

4. "Capital available from within controls expansion." Unwarranted expansion would not occur, Lincoln believed, under his financing plan.

5. "The greatest advantage would be the development of the individual worker. Under the incentive of ownership, he would become a greater man."

6. "Stock ownership is one of the steps that can be taken that will make the worker feel that there is less of a gulf between him and the boss. . . . Stock ownership will help the worker to recognize his [or her] responsibility in the game and the importance of victory."

Until 1980, Lincoln Electric borrowed no money. The company's liabilities consisted mainly of accounts payable and short-term accruals.

The unusual pricing policy at Lincoln was succinctly stated by Willis: "At all times price on the basis of cost, and all times keep pressure on our cost." This policy resulted in the price for the most popular welding electrode going from 16 cents a pound in 1929 to 4.7 cents in 1938.

EXHIBIT 2   Lincoln Electric's Financial History

	1974	1979	1980	1981	1982	1983	1987	1988	1989
Sales (in millions of dollars)	$233	$385	$401	$469	$329	$277	$377	$478	$582
Return on equity*	25%	19%	16%	19%	9%	9%	15%	16%	12%
Debt to equity ratio†	0%	0%	0%	0%	0%	0%	2%	7%	11%
Segment data:									
Arc-welding products (% of total sales)						91%	91%	91%	91%
Other products (% of total sales)						9%	9%	9%	9%

*Return on equity = $\dfrac{\text{Profit after tax}}{\text{Stockholders' equity}}$

†Debt to equity ratio = $\dfrac{\text{Long-term debt}}{\text{Long-Term debt + Stockholders' equity}}$

More recently, the SA-200 welder, Lincoln's largest-selling portable machine, had decreased in price from 1958 through 1965. According to Dr. C. Jackson Grayson of the American Productivity Center in Houston, Texas, Lincoln's prices had increased only one-fifth as fast as the Consumer Price Index from 1934 to about 1970. This resulted in a welding products market in which Lincoln became the undisputed price leader for the products it manufactured. Not even the major Japanese manufacturers, such as Nippon Steel for welding electrodes and Osaka Transformer for welding machines, were able to penetrate this market.

Substantial cash balances were accumulated each year preparatory to paying the year-end bonuses. The bonuses totaled $54 million for 1988. The money was invested in short-term US government securities and certificates of deposit (CDs) until needed. The company's financial history is shown in Exhibit 2.

How Well Did Lincoln Serve Its Stakeholders?

Lincoln Electric differed from most other companies in the importance it assigned to each of the groups it served. Willis identified these groups, in the order of priority ascribed to them, as (1) customers, (2) employees, and (3) stockholders.

Certainly the firm's customers had fared well over the years. Lincoln prices for welding machines and welding electrodes were acknowledged to be the lowest in the marketplace. Quality was consistently high. The cost of field failures for Lincoln products had recently been determined to be a remarkable 0.04 percent of revenues. The "Fleetweld" electrodes and SA-200 welders had been the standard in the pipeline and refinery construction industry, where price was hardly a criterion, for decades. A Lincoln distributor in Monroe, Louisiana, said that he had sold several hundred of the popular AC-225 welders, which were warranted for one year, but never handled a warranty claim.

Perhaps best-served of all management constituencies were the employees. Not the least of their benefits, of course, were the year-end bonuses, which effectively doubled an already average compensation level. The foregoing description of the personnel program and the comments in the Appendix further illustrate the desirability of a Lincoln job.

While stockholders were relegated to an inferior status by James F. Lincoln, they did very well indeed. Recent dividends had exceeded

$11 a share, and earnings per share approached $30. In January 1980, the price of restricted stock, committed to employees, had been $117 a share. By 1989, the stated value at which the company would repurchase the stock if tendered was $201. A check with the New York office of Merrill Lynch, Pierce, Fenner and Smith at that time revealed an estimated price on Lincoln stock of $270 a share, with none being offered for sale. Technically, this price applied only to the unrestricted stock owned by the Lincoln family, a few other major holders, and employees who purchased it on the open market. Risk associated with Lincoln stock, a major determinant of stock value, was minimal because of the small amount of debt in the capital structure, because of an extremely stable earnings record, and because of Lincoln's practice of purchasing the restricted stock whenever employees offered it for sale.

A Concluding Comment

It was easy to believe that the reason for Lincoln's success was the excellent attitude of the employees and their willingness to work harder, faster, and more intelligently than other industrial workers. However, Sabo suggested that appropriate recognition be given to Lincoln executives, whom he credited with carrying out the following policies:

1. Management limited research, development, and manufacturing to a standard product line designed to meet the major needs of the welding industry.
2. New products had to be reviewed by manufacturing and all producing costs verified before the products were approved by management.

3. Purchasing was challenged not only to procure materials at the lowest cost but also to work closely with engineering and manufacturing to ensure that the latest innovations were implemented.
4. Manufacturing supervision and all personnel were held accountable for reduction of scrap, energy conservation, and maintenance of product quality.
5. Production control, material handling, and methods engineering were closely supervised by top management.
6. Management made cost reduction a way of life at Lincoln, and definite programs were established in many areas, including traffic and shipping, where tremendous savings could result.
7. Management established a sales department that was technically trained to reduce customer welding costs. This sales approach and other real customer services eliminated nonessential frills and resulted in long-term benefits to all concerned.
8. Management encouraged education, technical publishing, and long-range programs that resulted in industry growth, thereby assuring market potential for the Lincoln Electric Company.

Sabo wrote, "It is in a very real sense a personal and group experience in faith—a belief that together we can achieve results which alone would not be possible. It is not a perfect system, and it is not easy. It requires tremendous dedication and hard work. However, it does work, and the results are worth the effort."

APPENDIX
EMPLOYEE INTERVIEWS

Typical questions and answers from employee interviews are presented below. The employees' names have been changed to protect their privacy.

Interview 1

Ed Sanderson, a 23-year-old high school graduate who had been with Lincoln four years and who was a machine operator in the Electrode Division at the time of the interview.

Q: How did you happen to get this job?
A: My wife was pregnant, and I was making three bucks an hour and one day I came here and applied. That was it. I kept calling to let them know I was still interested.
Q: Roughly what were your earnings last year including your bonus?
A: $45,000.
Q: What have you done with your money since you have been here?
A: Well, we've lived pretty well, and we bought a condominium.
Q: Have you paid for the condominium?
A: No, but I could.
Q: Have you bought your Lincoln stock this year?
A: No, I haven't bought any Lincoln stock yet.
Q: Do you get the feeling that the executives here are pretty well thought of?
A: I think they are. To get where they are today, they had to really work.
Q: Wouldn't that be true anywhere?
A: I think more so here because seniority really doesn't mean anything. If you work with a guy who has 20 years here, and you have 2 months and you're doing a better job, you will get advanced before he will.
Q: Are you paid on a piece-rate basis?
A: My gang does. There are nine of us who make the bare electrode, and the whole group gets paid based on how many electrodes we make.
Q: Do you think you work harder than workers in other factories in the Cleveland area?

A: Yes, I would say I probably work harder.
Q: Do you think it hurts anybody?
A: No, a little hard work never hurts anybody.
Q: If you could choose, do you think you would be as happy earning a little less money and being able to slow down a little?
A: No, it doesn't bother me. If it bothered me, I wouldn't do it.
Q: Why do you think Lincoln employees produce more than workers in other plants?
A: That's the way the company is set up. The more you put out, the more you're going to make.
Q: Do you think it's the piece rate and bonus together?
A: I don't think people would work here if they didn't know that they would be rewarded at the end of the year.
Q: Do you think Lincoln employees will ever join a union?
A: No.
Q: What are the major advantages of working for Lincoln?
A: Money.
Q: Are there any other advantages?
A: Yes, we don't have a union shop. I don't think I could work in a union shop.
Q: Do you think you are a career man with Lincoln at this time?
A: Yes.

Interview 2

Roger Lewis, a 23-year-old Purdue graduate in mechanical engineering who had been in the Lincoln sales program for 15 months and who was working in the Cleveland sales office at the time of the interview.

Q: How did you get your job at Lincoln?
A: I saw that Lincoln was interviewing on campus at Purdue, and I went by. I later came to Cleveland for a plant tour and was offered a job.
Q: Do you know any of the senior executives? Would they know you by name?

A: Yes, I know all of them—Mr. Hastings, Mr. Willis, Mr. Sabo.

Q: Do you think Lincoln salespeople work harder than those in other companies?

A: Yes. I don't think there are many salespeople for other companies who are putting in 50-to-60-hour weeks. Everybody here works harder. You can go out in the plant, or you can go upstairs, and there's nobody sitting around.

Q: Do you see any real disadvantage to working at Lincoln?

A: I don't know if it's a disadvantage, but Lincoln is a spartan company, a very thrifty company. I like that. The sales offices are functional, not fancy.

Q: Why do you think Lincoln employees have such high productivity?

A: Piecework has a lot to do with it. Lincoln is smaller than many plants, too; you can stand in one place and see the materials come in one side and the product go out the other. You feel a part of the company. The chance to get ahead is important, too. They have a strict policy of promoting from within, so you know you have a chance. I think in a lot of other places you may not get as fair a shake as you do here. The sales offices are on a smaller scale, too. I like that. I tell someone that we have two people in the Baltimore office, and they say, "You've got to be kidding." It's smaller and more personal. Pay is the most important thing. I have heard that this is the highest-paying factory in the world.

Interview 3

Joe Trahan, a 58-year-old high school graduate who had been with Lincoln 39 years and who was employed as a working supervisor in the tool room at the time of the interview.

Q: Roughly what was your pay last year?

A: Over $56,000; salary, bonus, stock dividends.

Q: How much was your bonus?

A: About $26,000.

Q: Have you ever gotten a special award of any kind?

A: Not really.

Q: What have you done with your money?

A: My house is paid for—and my two cars. I also have some bonds and the Lincoln stock.

Q: What do you think of the executives at Lincoln?

A: They're really top-notch.

Q: What is the major disadvantage of working at Lincoln Electric?

A: I don't know of any disadvantage at all.

Q: Do you think you produce more than most people in similar jobs with other companies?

A: I do believe that.

Q: Why is that? Why do you believe that?

A: We are on the incentive system. Everything we do, we try to improve to make a better product with a minimum of outlay. We try to improve the bonus.

Q: Would you be just as happy making a little less money and not working quite so hard?

A: I don't think so.

Q: Do you think Lincoln employees would ever join a union?

A: I don't think they would ever consider it.

Q: What is the most important advantage of working at Lincoln?

A: Compensation.

Q: Tell me something about Mr. James Lincoln, who died in 1965.

A: You are talking about Jimmy, Sr. He always strolled through the shop in his shirt sleeves. Big fellow. Always looked distinguished. Gray hair. Friendly sort of guy. I was a member of the Advisory Board one year. He was there each time.

Q: Did he strike you as really caring?

A: I think he always cared for people.

Q: Did you get any sensation of a religious nature from him?

A: No, not really.

Q: And religion is not part of the program now?

A: No.

Q: Do you think Mr. Lincoln was a very intelligent man, or was he just a nice guy?

A: I would say he was pretty well educated. A great talker—always right off the top of his head. He knew what he was talking about all the time.

Q: When were bonuses for beneficial suggestions done away with?

A: About 18 years ago.

Q: Did that hurt very much?

A: I don't think so, because suggestions are still rewarded through the merit rating system.

Q: Is there anything you would like to add?

A: It's a good place to work. The union kind of ties other places down. At other places, electricians only do electrical work, carpenters only do carpenter work. At Lincoln Electric we all pitch in and do whatever needs to be done.

Q: So a major advantage is not having a union?

A: That's right.

Questions

1. How would you characterize Lincoln Electric's strategy? In this context, what is the nature of Lincoln's business and upon what bases does this company compete?

2. What are the most important elements of Lincoln's overall approach to organization and control that help explain why this company is so successful? How well do Lincoln's organization and control mechanisms fit the company's strategic requirements?

3. What is the corporate culture like at Lincoln Electric? What type of employees would be happy working at Lincoln Electric?

4. What is the applicability of Lincoln's approach to organization and control to other companies? Why don't more companies operate like Lincoln?

5. What could cause Lincoln's strategy implementation approach to break down? What are the threats to Lincoln's continued success?

6. Would you like to work in an environment like that at Lincoln Electric?

CASE 11–2
WORTHINGTON INDUSTRIES

In 1999 Worthington Industries enjoyed sales revenues of $1.8 billion in steel processing and metals-related businesses. The company, head-quartered in Columbus, Ohio, operated 53 plants in 11 countries and boasted 7,500 employees. John H. McConnell founded the company in 1955. His son John P. McConnell became chairman and CEO in 1996. The financial performance of the company for the past five years is given in Exhibit 1. The company consistently outperformed its industry. *Fortune* magazine selected Worthington as one of the "100 Best Places to Work" in 1998 and 1999.

The company was organized into three business units: Worthington Steel, Worthington Cylinders, and Dietrich Industries.

Worthington Steel.   The Worthington Steel Company, founded in 1955, essentially invented the steel processing industry as it exists today. An established leader with more than 1,000 customers, Worthington Steel served a broad range of markets, including automotive, lawn and garden, construction, hardware, furniture and office equipment, electrical controls, leisure and recreation, appliances, and farm implements. The company offered the widest range of services in the industry, from slitting and blanking to hydrogen annealing, hot-dipped galvanizing, and nickel plating.

Worthington earned its leadership position as a custom processor of flat-rolled steel by providing superior quality and service. It provided value-added services that bridged the capabilities of major steel producers and the specialized expectations of steel end-users.

Worthington Cylinders.   Worthington Cylinders offered the most complete line of pressure cylinder vessels in its industry:

- LPG (liquefied petroleum gas) cylinders were used to hold fuel for everything from gas barbecue grills and camping equipment to residential heating systems and industrial forklift trucks. Outside North America, LPG cylinders were used to hold fuel for commercial and residential cooking needs, such as gas burners and stoves.
- Refrigerant cylinders were used to service commercial and residential air-conditioning and refrigeration systems as well as automotive air-conditioning systems.

EXHIBIT 1   Financial Performance: 1995–99
(dollars in millions)

	1995	*1996*	*1997*	*1998*	*1999*
Net sales	$1,126	$1,127	$1,428	$1,624	$1,763
Gross margin	$ 183	$ 178	$ 207	$ 253	$ 294
Gross margin as percentage of net sales	16%	16%	15%	16%	17%
Operating income	$ 115	$ 99	$ 111	$ 136	$ 146
Operating income as percentage of stockholders' equity	19%	15%	16%	18%	21%

This case was prepared by Vijay Govindarajan.

- Industrial and specialty high-pressure, acetylene, and composite cylinders were used to hold gases for various applications, such as cutting and welding metals, breathing (medical, diving, firefighting), semiconductor production and beverage delivery, and compressed natural gas.

Dietrich Industries.   America's largest manufacturer of steel framing materials, Dietrich Industries was an important segment of the Worthington Industries family of value-added, metals-related businesses. Acquired in 1996, the Pittsburgh-based subsidiary produced steel studs, floor joists, roof trusses, and other metal accessories for wholesale distributors and commercial and residential building contractors.

Dietrich unveiled an interactive CD to make it easier than ever to choose steel framing. This design tool allowed developers, architects, contractors, and builders to develop building specifications by accessing the industry's broadest line of metal framing products. It could be used by a novice to finish a basement or by an expert designing a major office building.

Administrative Systems[1]

The administrative systems of Worthington are considered under the following sections: values, organization structure, human resource policies, and reward systems.

Values.   John H. McConnell developed the company's values and, over the years, they remained constant (see Box 1). At their core was the golden rule: to treat others the way one wanted to be treated. While the values clearly stated that the firm's first duty was to shareholders, they also underwrote a culture in which customers, suppliers, and especially employees were treasured assets. In fact, all employees were encouraged to become shareholders by participating in the profit-sharing plan.

Worthington expected employees to work hard and help it succeed, but it treated them well, believing people would be fair and honest if they were treated fairly and honestly. Employees were praised for good work and urged to develop their skills. The company offered a tuition reimbursement program to help them continue their education. Managers kept their office doors open to signal their accessibility. They encouraged open communication and tried to keep company discussions free of politics. These and other measures enabled Worthington to enjoy a high level of trust between its workers and managers.

This climate of mutual respect ultimately benefited Worthington's customers. Employees knew their work was valued and took pride in doing their jobs well. The profit-sharing plan acted as an additional incentive for them to help the company succeed. As a result, Worthington was very customer focused. Workers produced high-quality products and gave attentive service. Worthington's salespeople worked not just to meet, but to exceed, customers' needs.

The company treated its suppliers equally well and prized their loyalty as well as that of its customers.

Organization Structure.   Worthington considered its organization structure to be flat. Its profit-sharing plan, for example, recognized only four basic levels: production, administrative, professional, and executive. This and the fact that the company favored smaller plants—fewer than 150 employees—made it easier for employees to communicate with each other. It also helped them to identify with, and commit to, Worthington.

Plant managers enjoyed considerable autonomy, operating their facilities as individual profit centers. Some functions, such as purchasing, were centralized because it was more economical for the company to do so. Similarly, human resource services were shared because this allowed Worthington to provide the same

---

[1]This section is based on work by Joseph A. Maciariello in *Lasting Value* (New York: John Wiley & Sons, 2000), chap. 11.

Box 1
Worthington Industries' Philosophy

Earnings: The first corporate goal for Worthington Industries is to earn money for its shareholders and increase the value of their investment. We believe that the best measurement of the accomplishment of our goal is consistent growth in earnings per share.

Our Golden Rule: We treat our customers, employees, investors, and suppliers, as we would like to be treated.

People: We are dedicated to the belief that people are our most important asset. We believe people respond to recognition, opportunity to grow, and fair compensation. We believe that compensation should be directly related to job performance and therefore use incentives, profit sharing or otherwise, in every possible situation. From employees we expect an honest day's work for an honest day's pay. We believe in the philosophy of continued employment for all Worthington people. In filling job openings, every effort is expended to find candidates within Worthington, its divisions or subsidiaries. When employees are requested to relocate from one operation to another, it is accomplished without financial loss to the individual.

Customer: Without the customer and his need for our products and services we have nothing. We will exert every effort to see that the customer's quality and service requirements are met. Once a commitment is made to a customer, every effort is made to fulfill that obligation.

Suppliers: We cannot operate profitably without those who supply the quality raw materials we need for our products. From a pricing standpoint, we ask only that suppliers be competitive in the marketplace and treat us as they do their other customers. We are loyal to suppliers who meet our quality and service requirements through all market situations.

Organization: We believe in a divisionalized organizational structure with responsibility for performance resting with the head of each operation. All managers are given the operating latitude and authority to accomplish their responsibilities within our corporate goals and objectives. In keeping with this philosophy, we do not create corporate procedures. If procedures are necessary within a particular company operation, that manager creates them. We believe in a small corporate staff and support group to service the needs of our shareholders and operating units as requested.

Communication: We communicate through every possible channel with our customers, employees, shareholders and operating units as requested.

Citizenship: Worthington Industries practices good citizenship at all levels. We conduct our business in a professional and ethical manner when dealing with customers, neighbors, and the general public worldwide. We encourage all our people to actively participate in community affairs. We support worthwhile community causes.

Source: Joseph A. Maciariello, *Lasting Value* (New York: John Wiley & Sons, 2000), p. 182.

services companywide—a move that especially benefited new acquisitions. Otherwise, Worthington essentially was decentralized.

Human Resource Policies.   At Worthington, managers weren't the only key decision-makers. Production workers on the employee councils also participated in various managerial decisions. Workers were appointed to the councils at most plants. They met at least once a month to talk about critical issues, such as plant safety, and conveyed this information to their fellow employees every quarter.

One of their primary responsibilities was to decide whether new employees should become permanent. New workers were required to complete a 90-day probationary period before they were eligible for permanent status. During this time, council members discussed the individual's job performance with his or her co-workers. If the comments were favorable, the council approved a permanent hire by majority vote. Once approved, the new employee drew a salary, rather than an hourly wage, and became eligible for the profit-sharing plan. Managers could make recommendations or, if circumstances warranted it, fire the employee. But, generally, they acknowledged that workers on the production floor were better positioned to evaluate how well other employees performed.

Relationships between councils and managers were cordial. Managers appreciated the unique perspective that production workers brought to problems. They enjoyed working with them as team members. Employees, in turn, responded with trust and openness.

Workers who wanted to move up the ladder had plenty of opportunity at Worthington. The company filled 95 percent of its job openings with internal candidates. Getting promoted depended largely upon merit. Promotion-minded employees were encouraged to further their personal and professional development by taking courses and assuming other jobs throughout the company. People with common sense, who could lead and work well with people, were considered manage-

ment material; these skills outweighed product knowledge. The company offered numerous success stories, among them that of Donald Malenick. He started out on the production floor and retired, in 1999, as president of the company.

Reward Systems.   Employees were rewarded for good performance through competitive salaries and Worthington's profit-sharing plan. Salaries were in the top quartile for comparable jobs in each plant's location.

Profit sharing, distributed quarterly, was equally generous. Employees were vested in the plan according to their status as production workers, administrators, professionals, or executives. As an individual rose through the ranks, shares made up a greater portion of his or her compensation. Executives' shares, for example, were calculated according to a set formula and made up as much as 60 percent of their total compensation. By comparison, profit shares made up 20 to 25 percent of production workers' total compensation. The size of the pool they shared with administrators and professionals hinged on both the company's performance and that of individual plants. Employees recognized that the better Worthington and its plants did, the more money they made.

This point was reinforced by Worthington's sales force training program. It was designed to increase profitability through increased customer satisfaction. Every salesperson spent six months working in a plant that made the products they sold, filling orders alongside production workers, learning plant capability, and gaining expertise in technical areas. They also acquired a greater understanding of order profitability. At Worthington, if an order was not profitable, it was not taken. Employees understood that neither they nor the company could afford it.

Question

Evaluate the management systems at Worthington Industries from the standpoint of how they help the company to outperform its competitors.

Case 11–3
Anita's Apparel

For 88 years Nordstrom has been guided by its founder's philosophy: offer the customer the best service, selection, quality and value.

Nordstrom Philosophy

Anita Lamont, founder and CEO of Anita's Apparel, a retailer of high-end women's business apparel, had just opened her fourth retail store in the Midwest. While Lamont was pleased with the company's progress, she was concerned by the growing number of customer complaints and the low sales per square foot compared to some of her better-known competitors.

When it was just one store that she individually owned and operated, she was able to control most of the details of the business. While she worked with a few employees, she always knew what they were doing. As the number of stores and the size of the stores increased, the number of employees grew more than proportionately. When she was running the single store, she rarely heard a customer complaint, her pilferage costs were very low, and her sales per square foot were $250, compared with $220 today. This concerned Lamont greatly as her expansion plans for Anita's Apparel had slowed down because the stores were not producing the returns that she expected.

When she opened the second store, she added a store manager at each location. While both managers seemed to be doing well, the number of customer complaints increased. Lamont assumed that this would happen when she had more stores and more customers. By the time that she had opened the fourth store, the number of customer complaints had grown by eightfold from when there was only one store.

The store managers were also complaining to Lamont because of the high training costs of bringing on new employees. The turnover rate seemed to be very high and Lamont could not understand why. She was paying one of the highest wages in the area to the sales clerks and store managers, yet they were leaving to go work elsewhere. The customers were also complaining about the lack of helpfulness of the sales clerks. Even after extensive employee retraining, Lamont was still hearing many complaints.

Lamont knew that there had to be a better way. Many of her competitors were well known for customer service and high sales per square foot. One of her best-known competitors that had appeared to have solved these problems was Nordstrom, Inc. In a visit to Seattle, Lamont had the opportunity to shop at a Nordstrom and she was impressed by the level of service provided by the cheerful and helpful sales clerks. Lamont could tell that there was a large difference between the level of service that she had received at Nordstrom and the level of service that sales clerks were providing at Anita's Apparel stores.

A few days later, Lamont received in the mail a handwritten thank-you letter from the Nordstrom sales clerk who had helped her in Seattle. Lamont decided right then that she had to find out more about what Nordstrom was doing that was so different from Anita's Apparel. She began by getting a copy of Nordstrom's 1995 Annual Report. Next she read *The Nordstrom Way* by Robert Spector and Patrick McCarthy. Then she found a few magazine articles that discussed Nordstrom and its success. The following is some of what she discovered about Nordstrom and the secrets of its success.

This case was prepared by Kirk Hendrickson (T '97) under the supervision of Professor Vijay Govindarajan. Many of the examples and statistics in this case are from *The Nordstrom Way* by Robert Spector and Patrick D. McCarthy, 1995.

EXHIBIT 1 Selected Financial Statements 1992 to 1996
(dollars in thousands except square footage and per share amounts; year ended January 31)

	1996	1995	1994	1993	1992
Financial Position					
Customer accounts receivable, net	$ 874,103	$ 655,715	$ 565,151	$ 584,379	$ 585,490
Merchandise inventories	626,303	627,930	585,602	536,739	506,632
Current assets	1,612,776	1,397,713	1,314,914	1,219,844	1,177,638
Current liabilities	832,313	690,454	627,485	511,196	553,903
Working capital	780,463	707,259	687,429	708,648	623,735
Property, buildings and equipment, net	1,103,298	984,195	845,596	824,142	856,404
Long-term debt	439,943	373,910	438,574	481,945	511,000
Shareholders' equity	1,422,972	1,343,800	1,166,504	1,052,031	939,231
Total assets	2,732,619	2,396,783	2,177,481	2,053,170	2,041,875
Operations					
Net sales	4,113,517	3,894,478	3,589,938	3,421,979	3,179,820
Cost and expenses:					
Cost of sales and related buying and occupancy	2,806,250	2,599,553	2,469,304	2,339,107	2,169,437
Selling, general and administrative	1,120,790	1,023,347	940,579	902,083	831,505
Interest, net	39,295	30,664	37,646	44,810	49,106
Service charge income and other	(125,130)	(94,644)	(88,509)	(81,140)	(87,443)
Total costs and expenses	3,841,205	3,588,920	3,359,020	3,199,860	2,962,605
Earnings before income taxes	272,312	335,558	230,918	222,119	217,215
Income taxes	107,200	132,600	90,500	85,500	81,400
Net earnings	165,112	202,958	140,418	136,619	135,815
Dividends per share	.50	.385	.34	.32	.31
Sales per square foot for company-operated stores	382	395	383	381	388

Source: Robert Spector and Patrick D. McCarthy, *The Nordstrom Way* (New York: John Wiley and Sons, 1995), p. 98.

History

Nordstrom was founded in 1901 as Wallin & Nordstrom shoe store by Carl F. Wallin and John W. Nordstrom. On their opening day, their total sales were $12.50. In fiscal year 1995, Nordstrom had sales of $4.1 billion (see Exhibit 1 for financial information going back five years). During the intervening 94 years, Nordstrom had become the largest independently owned fashion specialty retailer in the United States, offering a wide variety of fine quality apparel, shoes, and accessories for men, women, and children.

In 1995 the third generation of the Nordstrom family stepped down from the day-to-day management of Nordstrom. Six members of the fourth generation were promoted to co-presidents. The fourth generation has inherited one of the 50 largest retailing chains in the United States and one of the seven largest department stores.

Nordstrom operates 93 stores in 15 states, and is expanding into other states. Its 1996 plans called for new stores in Philadelphia and Dallas. Beyond 1996 Nordstrom planned to open stores in Detroit, Denver, Cleveland, and Atlanta.

Nordstrom stores have consistently performed well, often at the expense of its competitors. Nordstrom captured one-third of the southern California market in 10 years. The Tyson Corner, Virginia, Nordstrom is credited with driving Garfinckels into bankruptcy.[1] Nordstrom stores average sales of $382 per square foot compared with Federated's $190 and May Department's $183.[2] Nordstrom has one of the lowest shrinkage costs in the industry at 1.5 percent versus the 3.0 percent average.

Creating a Customer Service Environment

Nordstrom has developed a number of specific systems that are designed to create the Nordstrom customer service environment:

- Inverted pyramid management
- Commissions
- Unconditional returns
- Rewards
- Recognition
- Heroics

Inverted Pyramid Management. Nordstrom draws its organizational chart as an inverted pyramid. The inverted pyramid shows the customers on top and the salespeople as the top level of the company. Each level below is responsible for supporting the salespeople and the customers. As co-chairman Raymond Johnson stated, "The only thing we have going for us is the way we take care of our customers and the people who take care of the customers are on the floor."[3]

As part of the pyramid, Nordstrom promotes strictly from within. Every manager and buyer

started as a salesperson, including the current six co-presidents who are all Nordstrom family members. As James F. Nordstrom, former co-chairman, stated, "One of the reasons our system has continued to work is that all of us, including the family, have served at every level from stock person to buyer. We've all been salespeople for a long time."[4]

Commissions. Since the 1950s, Nordstrom salespeople have been paid on commission. Standard commission rates in 1995 ranged from 6.75 percent for apparel to 13 percent for children's shoes.[5] Each salesperson receives a draw against his or her commissions up to $11 per hour. Nordstrom monitors sales per hour: If an employee's draw rate is $10 per hour and the employee is selling women's shoes at a 10 percent commission, then the employee would need to sell $100 per hour to cover his or her draw. Before computing sales per hour, any returns are subtracted from an employee's total sales.

At Nordstrom each department has a minimum hourly sales target. Salespeople who consistently fail to meet the sales per hour quotas receive coaching from their department managers. Salespeople are let go if they miss quota for three consecutive months.[6]

The commission system enables Nordstrom sales associates to earn almost twice what they would be able to make at a competitor's store. As a result, Nordstrom's selling expense is one of the highest in the industry.

Unconditional Returns. At Nordstrom a customer can return any item for any reason and receive his or her money back. Former co-chairman Bruce Nordstrom explains the return policy to sales people as follows: "If a customer came into the store with a pair of five-year-old

[1]Dori Jones Yang and Laura Zinn, "Will 'The Nordstrom Way' Travel Well?" *Business Week,* September 3, 1990, pp. 82–83.
[2]Seth Lubove, "Don't Listen to the Boss, Listen to the Customer," *Forbes,* December 4, 1995, pp. 45–46.
[3]Robert Spector and Patrick D. McCarthy, *The Nordstrom Way* (New York: John Wiley and Sons, 1995), p. 99.

[4]Ibid.
[5]Ibid., pp. 113–14.
[6]"Nordstrom: Respond to Unreasonable Customer Requests!" *Planning Review,* May/June 1994, pp. 17–18.

shoes and complained that the shoes were worn out and wanted her money back, you have the right to use your best judgment to give my money away. As a matter of fact, I order you to give my money away."[7] Nordstrom returns are legendary: shoplifted items and a set of tires (Nordstrom does not even sell tires) have been taken back, no questions asked.

Rewards.   Nordstrom's general manager of its Southern California region, Jammie Baugh, states that at Nordstrom, "We tend to manage by contest. When we have something we want to improve on, then we have a contest."[8] These contests include monthly "Make Nordstrom Special" contests, which reward good suggestions; daily sales contests, which reward top sellers for the day; and fourth quarter 1993's "$250,000 Super Service Challenge," which awarded individual and team prizes for the best customer service.

Recognition.   Nordstrom uses a number of different methods to recognize the accomplishments of its employees. Nordstrom management acknowledges employee "Pacesetters" and "Customer Service All-Stars"; morning announcements and monthly meetings are opportunities for managers to praise the sales and customer service efforts of the salespeople. The Pacesetter program recognizes the top 8 to 12 percent of each division's sales force based on exceeding a yearly sales target goal (targets which now top $350,000). Pacesetters receive certificates, increased store discounts, events, and trips. The Customer Service All-Stars are selected according to sales volume, customer service, and service to co-workers. The Customer Service All-Stars are selected monthly by store managers. The winners are given increased Nordstrom discounts and priority for selecting work shifts. Every morning, the store manager also praises

departments and individuals during the pre-opening announcements for customer service and sales. At the monthly meetings, managers read letters from customers and employees celebrate sales achievements.

Heroics.   An additional piece of employee recognition is the stories of customer service "heroics." Salespeople who consistently perform customer service heroics are recognized by their department and store. They are often selected "Employee of the Month" and have their deeds printed up in a weekly collection of heroics by the sales associates. The following is one example of a heroic deed:

> A Nordstrom's sales associate discovered that a customer had left her airline tickets at the counter. After calling the service representative for the airline, who refused to help, the sales associate took a cab out to the airport, found the customer, and gave her the tickets.[9]

Union Dispute

In November of 1989, Locals 1001 and 367 of the United Food and Commercial Workers Union (UFCW), which represented about 1600 Nordstrom sales associates in the Seattle-Tacoma area, filed a complaint with the Washington State Department of Labor and Industries Employment Standards Section (ESAC). The complaint charged that Nordstrom required or encouraged employees to attend meetings, perform stock work, and attend to customer service activities, such as hand-carrying items to customers or writing thank-you notes, outside of normal business hours without compensation. UFCW felt that the policy of ranking employees and managers on sales per selling hour caused managers to encourage or coerce employees into underreporting their hours worked.

On February 15, 1990, ESAC concluded that Nordstrom's work practices violated the state's Minimum Wage Act and that Nordstrom had to

---

[7]Spector and McCarthy, *The Nordstrom Way,* p. 100.
[8]Ibid., p. 119.

[9]Ibid., p. 125.

change these policies and retroactively compensate employees for time worked. Joe Peterson, the president of Local 1001, suggested that claims could be as high as $40 million in Washington State and $300 million in California. Based on this news, poor revenue projections, and the threat of a class-action lawsuit being filed by Peterson covering Nordstrom employees nationwide, Nordstrom's stock price fell by almost 10 percent in one day.

On February 20, 1990, *The Wall Street Journal* printed a front-page article describing horrendous working conditions.[10] The story opened with a discussion of a former Nordstrom employee alleging that he was unlawfully discharged when Nordstrom discovered that he had AIDS. It followed with employment counselor Alice Synder describing how she regularly received visits from Nordstrom employees, "suffering from ulcers, colitis, hives and hand tremors," because of the stress of working at Nordstrom. A series of former employees were interviewed for the article. Patty Bemis, former Nordstrom employee, said, "The managers were these little tin gods, always grilling you about your sales. You felt like your job was constantly in jeopardy."

Over the next week, Nordstrom announced that it would change its time-keeping procedures and established a $15 million reserve for back-pay claims. Joe Peterson called the reserve "Wholly inadequate. It won't even cover claims of employees in Washington state."[11] After that the union filed more unfair labor practice lawsuits. The AIDS Coalition to Unleash Power (ACT UP) protested at Nordstrom's downtown San Francisco store. A class action lawsuit was also filed on behalf of shareholders.

As the dispute grew, *60 Minutes* did a segment on Nordstrom which changed some minds. As Marti Galovic Palmer, producer for *60 Minutes,* stated, "A lot of what I was looking for in terms of hard complaints turned out to be from people who just wanted a job that didn't demand a whole lot."[12]

Bruce Nordstrom gave Nordstrom's perspective on the conflict:

> Freedom is the issue, not just freedom to belong or not belong to a union, but freedom to wait on customers in the best way, freedom to go the extra mile, freedom to pursue a career in sales or in management, freedom to make customer service decisions right there on the sales floor without a lot of silly rules and interference, and freedom from being called "clock-punchers" as they have been by this union's management.[13]

In his comment about the freedom not to belong to the union, Bruce Nordstrom was referring to a request that had been made to Nordstrom by employees to have the union become an open shop where employees could choose to belong to the union or not. Nordstrom had a closed shop in the Seattle area stores where all employees had to be members of the union.

Nordstrom made this request in the 1987 contract negotiation and again in the 1989 contract negotiations. In 1989 Nordstrom would not remove it from the proposed contract. In addition to the contract negotiations, a group called Nordstrom Employees Opposed to Union Representation (NEOUR) began a campaign to have local 1001 decertified. The NLRB disallowed NEOUR's first petition for decertification because of the outstanding charges of labor practice violations by the union. In July of 1990, however, the union was decertified by over a five-to-two margin.

In the end, the class-action lawsuit by the union was settled out of court. Employee claims from the settlement totaled about $5 million, far less than the $300 million that Peterson

---

[10]Susan Faludi. "Sales Job: At Nordstrom Stores, Service Comes First—But at What Price," *The Wall Street Journal,* February 20, 1990, pp. A1, A16.

[11]George Tibbits, "Earnings Fall 34 Percent in 4th Quarter; $15 Million Charge for Back Pay," Seattle Priority: Rush, February 26, 1990, Associated Press.

[12]Spector and McCarthy, *The Nordstrom Way,* p. 175.
[13]Ibid., p. 176.

predicted for California. The union reportedly received $6.6 million in the settlement.

Anita's Decision

As Anita Lamont considered what she had learned about Nordstrom, she focused on the fact that while she paid her employees good wages, they were still paid by the hour. Anita's Apparel had few incentive plans for the sales clerks and a very strict return policy. Also, about the only heroics that she had ever heard come out of Anita's Apparel were from her own days when she had started. Many of these heroics had become the basis for some of the current policies.

While she recognized the many merits to the Nordstrom approach of commission compensa-tion and incentive pay, Lamont was concerned that the costs and risks associated with Nordstrom's commission-based compensation system would be greater than any benefits that Anita's Apparel might derive. In addition, if she did decide to change her compensation system, what else would need to be changed at Anita's Apparel in order to really improve the level of customer satisfaction and the sales per square foot?

Questions

1. How do you evaluate Nordstrom's compensation and other systems in support of its strategy?
2. How would you advise Anita Lamont about compensating her employees?

CASE 11–4
WAYSIDE INNS, INC.

It was May 11, 1992, and Kevin Gray was conducting a routine quarterly inspection of the Memphis Airport Wayside Inn. The property was one of those that fell under his jurisdiction as regional general manager for Wayside Inns, Inc. During his inspection tour Gray was called aside by the Inn's manager, Layne Rembert, who indicated some concern about a proposed expansion of his motel.

"I'm a little worried, Kevin, about that plan to bring 40 more rooms on stream by the end of the next fiscal year."

"Why all the concern, Layne? You're turning away a significant number of customers and, by all indications, the market will be growing considerably."

"Well, I've just spoken with Ed Keider. He's certain that the 80-room expansion at the central Toledo property has lowered his return on investment. I'd really like to chat with you about what effects the planned expansion will have on my incentive compensation and how my income for the year would be affected."

The Company

Wayside Inns, Inc., located in Kansas City, Missouri, was formed in 1980 as the successor corporation to United Motel Enterprises, a company that operated several franchised motels under licensing agreements from two national motel chains. Because of the complicated and restrictive contract covenants, United was unable to expand the scope of either of their two motel operations through geographical dispersion.

The successor corporation was formed to own, operate, and license a chain of motels

under the name Wayside Inns, as well as to continue to operate the present franchises held by United. Management felt that the strategy of developing their own motel chain would afford them greater flexibility and would allow them to more easily attain the long-term growth strategies. Another major reason for the move was that the new corporate strategy would allow management to pursue the implementation of a comprehensive marketing plan which they had been slowly developing over the last seven years.

The company's fundamental strategy was to cater to those business travelers who were generally not interested in elaborate settings. There were no common areas such as lobbies, convention rooms, bars, or restaurants. The chain emphasized instead clean rooms, dependable service, and rates that generally were 15 to 20 percent lower than other national motel chains. A free-standing restaurant was always located on the motel's property—in some cases it was operated by Wayside. In general, however, concessionary leases were granted to regional restaurant chains.

Wayside's management made it a point to locate their properties near interstate highways or major arteries convenient to commercial districts, airports, and industrial or shopping facilities. In a given city, one would often find Wayside Inns at various strategic locations. This strategy was founded on the belief that it was preferable to have a total of 600 rooms in five or six locations within one city rather than have one large hotel with 600 rooms. The strategy resulted in the clustering of hotels in those cities that could support the market. Once several hotels had been built in a particular city, management would seek new properties in regions commercially linked to that city.

This case was prepared by Charles T. Sharpless, research assistant, under the supervision of Professor M. Edgar Barrett. Copyright © by M. Edgar Barrett.

Wayside was well aware that their aggressive strategy was successful only to the extent that unit managers followed corporate policies to the letter. In order to ensure an aggressive spirit among the unit managers a multifaceted compensation plan was developed. The plan was composed of four elements, but was basically tied to profitability. A base salary was calculated which was loosely tied to years of service, dollar volume of sales, and adherence to corporate goals. An incentive bonus was calculated on sales volume increases. An additional incentive bonus was calculated using the Inn's return on investment. Fringe benefits were the final element and were a significant factor in the package. (See Exhibit 1.) Generally, base salaries ranged from $16,000 to $21,000 and total compensation was in the neighborhood of $24,000 to $30,000. The unit manager always lived on the premises and his wife usually played a role in managing the Inn. As a result, the average couple were in their late 40s or beyond. Many did not have previous motel experience.

The firm had grown substantially since its inception, and the prospects for future growth were favorable. The company's expansion strategy had evolved into a three-tiered attack. Most importantly, management actively pursued the construction of new motels seeking an ever-widening geographical distribution. Second, 76- and 116-room properties were expanded if analysis demonstrated that they were operating near or at full capacity. Third, old properties that became a financial burden or did not contribute the required rate of return were sold. Wayside Inns were usually constructed in one of three sizes— 76 rooms, 116 rooms, or 156 rooms.

Wayside Inns was a public corporation listed on the American Stock Exchange. It had 1,542,850 shares outstanding, with an average float of 400,000 shares. The common stock price had appreciated considerably, and analysts felt that investor interest was due to a number of factors but was primarily linked to their innovative marketing strategy. Wayside's average occupancy rate on established properties was 10 to 20 percent higher than competitive motels. Their specifically targeted market segment (the business traveler) was generally unaffected by seasonal or environmental factors. Additional company strengths, considered significant by service industry analysts, were an aggressive management, reduction of construction costs and completion times due to standardization, and efficient quality control of present properties.

The Memphis Airport Wayside Inn

The Wayside Inn at Memphis Airport was one of the mid-sized units in the chain—one of the original 116-room properties. It was located at the intersection of Brooks Road and Airways Road, approximately five miles from the center of the city. The motel had opened on February 9, 1984, and had developed a very good following in the succeeding years. While the occupancy rate had averaged near 43 percent for the first year, it had increased steadily over the years. By 1991, it operated at near full capacity for five nights a week. The Inn depended on salesmen and commercial travelers for approximately 80 percent of its revenue.

The property had been originally purchased in 1982 for $225,675. Construction costs for the motel had amounted to approximately $923,020, and furnishings, hardware, software, and office equipment had been purchased for $265,500.

Wayside Inns had contributed an initial equity capitalization of $75,000. The parent had also loaned $275,000 to the subsidiary which was secured by promissory notes. A national insurance company granted a mortgage of $950,000 on the land and physical plant. Finally, $405,000 had been received from Memphis Interstate Bank to finance equipment and supply purchases and to provide the necessary working capital. (See Exhibits 2 and 3 for operating data and Exhibits 4 and 5 for financial statements.)

Exhibit 1   Unit Managers' Compensation Package

Base Salary

Base salary ranges are calculated on the basis of years of service and relative sales volume for a particular inn. Salaries are subject to annual review, and the amount of adjustment will largely depend upon the recommendation of the regional general manager. Every attempt will be made to keep salary levels consistent with competitive chains.

Sales Volume Incentive

Every unit manager, having earned a profit before taxes, will receive a bonus equal to 1 percent of any revenue increase over the previous year's level. In the event of a revenue decrease, there will be no bonus and the following year's bonus will be calculated using the revenue of the year preceding the decline as a base figure.

Return on Investment Bonus

Investment will be defined as current assets, fixed assets, other assets, and any deferred expenses. Return is defined as profit before interest expense and taxes.

The formula for the bonus calculation will be:

$$ROI * PF = ROI \text{ bonus}$$

where:

$$ROI = \frac{EBIT}{Investment} \text{ and PF = Performance factor}$$

The performance factor is used to differentiate between the larger and smaller investments and to offset the inherent complexities of managing the larger properties.

Size of Investment ($)	Value of Performance Factor ($)*
0 – 600,000.	$15,000
600,000 – 1,200,000.	$25,000
1,200,000 – 1,800,000.	$36,000
1,800,000 – 2,500,000.	$45,000
2,500,000 – up	$50,000

*The regional general manager has the discretion to reduce or increase the value of the performance factor for a particular property upon central headquarters' approval.

Fringe Benefits

Each unit manager shall receive an apartment (two bedrooms, full kitchen, and den) on the premises, a company car for sales calls, laundry service, and local phone service at no expense.

EXHIBIT 2   Selected Operating Statistics (*for the Periods January 1 to December 31*)

	1991	1990	1989	1988	1987
Occupancy report					
Room nights available	41,975	41,975	41,975	41,975	41,975
Occupied room nights........................	36,634	35,595	33,454	32,613	31,522
Occupancy rate (%)..........................	87.3	84.8	79.7	77.7	75.1
Room revenue ($)	998,277	857,839	680,789	577,250	510,656
Average room rate ($).......................	27.25	24.10	20.35	17.70	16.20
Weekly occupancy (%)					
Monday	99	89	95	94	92
Tuesday...................................	99	99	94	92	91
Wednesday	99	98	96	94	89
Thursday..................................	99	97	92	87	86
Friday	91	87	72	70	65
Saturday	61	55	51	50	48
Sunday....................................	63	59	58	57	55
*Turnaway tally**					
Monday	26.1	22.8	15.1	10.1	11.5
Tuesday...................................	27.7	21.0	19.3	16.0	12.1
Wednesday	38.2	33.2	26.9	19.5	13.3
Thursday..................................	43.9	36.3	31.4	20.4	16.6
Friday	22.6	15.8	10.9	5.2	2.4
Saturday	9.6	5.7	2.8	0.2	0.6
Sunday....................................	8.5	6.4	3.0	1.3	0.5

*A turnaway is considered a customer who either calls the motel, requests a room in person, or calls central reservation service and is told there are no vacancies. See Exhibit 3 for further data.

EXHIBIT 3   Daily "Turnaway" Statistics for 1991

Week	Sun.	Mon.	Tues.	Wed.	Thurs.	Fri.	Sat.
1	0	25	26	36	45	0	0
2	0	23	21	24	25	0	0
3	0	10	11	17	23	3	0
4	0	20	21	16	46	5	0
5	0	16	17	25	38	0	0
6	0	20	15	38	43	7	0
7	0	25	32	45	25	0	0
8	0	10	12	42	46	10	0
9	0	21	14	40	71	12	0
10	0	23	28	39	23	15	0
11	0	19	25	41	45	16	0
12	0	25	30	43	39	20	0

(continued)

EXHIBIT 3   Daily "Turnaway" Statistics for 1991—*Continued*

Week	Sun.	Mon.	Tues.	Wed.	Thurs.	Fri.	Sat.
13	0	46	42	24	45	21	0
14	0	28	25	58	40	30	0
15	0	35	14	61	63	32	0
16	0	24	22	25	45	43	4
17	0	13	46	26	49	15	11
18	0	25	29	13	45	12	2
19	0	43	40	61	71	10	15
20	0	22	55	62	68	45	23
21	20	42	36	67	55	46	36
22	22	39	35	50	47	39	33
23	23	22	33	38	35	38	32
24	24	28	25	25	41	17	0
25	10	29	24	15	41	25	10
26	0	24	20	39	35	18	6
27	0	30	18	25	24	42	38
28	25	29	15	35	35	45	27
29	29	26	66	41	82	11	12
30	15	25	50	62	65	18	9
31	13	42	43	47	48	16	5
32	17	31	25	35	50	17	15
33	18	32	16	28	32	18	12
34	12	15	22	23	28	20	14
35	10	14	25	27	26	21	23
36	6	17	24	61	67	15	12
37	19	56	27	43	40	15	16
38	18	55	71	39	42	20	18
39	14	16	35	46	41	23	17
40	5	12	20	48	47	27	6
41	16	23	15	45	53	29	5
42	7	25	18	42	43	31	4
43	0	18	20	41	39	43	4
44	0	19	21	48	53	46	11
45	0	29	23	19	47	47	4
46	0	31	24	25	29	41	16
47	0	20	26	31	33	52	12
48	10	22	16	49	52	26	10
49	15	24	18	40	38	20	8
50	16	21	19	31	41	10	4
51	43	37	45	47	37	15	2
52	35	31	40	38	42	6	20
Total	442	1,357	1,440	1,986	2,283	1,175	498

EXHIBIT 4   Memphis Airport Wayside Inn

**INCOME STATEMENT
FOR THE YEARS ENDED DECEMBER 31**

	1990	*1991*
Revenues:		
Room revenue	$857,839	$ 998,277
Restaurant rental	29,148	32,304
Other	15,798	19,148
Total revenues	902,785	$1,049,729
Operating costs and expenses:		
Room	194,620	229,520
Selling and administrative	204,767	217,020
Depreciation and amortization	48,118	58,320
Utilities	41,610	45,473
Maintenance and repairs	46,672	48,498
Management and reservations fees	46,372	53,394
Operating income:	320,626	397,504
Interest expense	159,617	168,610
Profit before taxes:	161,009	228,894
Federal taxes	55,746	83,406
Net earnings	$105,263	$ 145,488

There were approximately 10 competitive motels, which were franchises of the major national chains, within a two-mile radius of the Memphis Airport Inn. There also existed a number of independent motels within the area. However, they were generally of the budget type and did not offer the quality on which Wayside based their reputation. Recent surveys conducted by the Memphis Chamber of Commerce indicated that average occupancy rates hovered near 72 percent and that the average room sold for $29.00. Expansion plans by the major chains were expected to account for an additional 800 rooms across the whole city in the following 18 months.

The Proposed Expansion. Wayside's Project Development staff had arrived at a projected schedule of costs that would be associated with the completion of a 40-room expansion. Cost adjustments would be necessary depending on the particular city and conditions. However, variances were not expected to be significant.

Engineering and legal fees were expected to be somewhere in the neighborhood of $18,000. Environmental Impact Studies to comply with federal regulations and the local building permits were estimated to cost $12,000. Construction costs for the expansion and adjoining parking facility were expected to be near $1,050,000. Such an expansion was expected to generate additional annual, nondirect operating costs of $46,000 (largely for personnel, utilities, and maintenance). Direct room expenses were expected to remain at an average of 23 percent of room revenue. Management and reservation fees paid to the parent were based on a formula of 5 percent of room revenue plus $30 per room per year.

EXHIBIT 5   Memphis Airport Wayside Inn

BALANCE SHEET

	1990	1991
Assets		
Current assets:		
Cash.	$ 19,050	$ 18,800
Trade receivables	86,825	101,620
Merchandise	22,817	25,312
Prepaid expenses:		
Insurance	4,622	4,110
Mortgage interest	8,524	8,022
Linens	2,320	2,480
Total current assets.	144,158	160,344
Fixed assets:		
Land.	225,675	225,675
Building, equipment, furniture, and fixtures	1,327,740	1,370,515
Less: Accumulated depreciation.	(268,375)	(326,695)
Total fixed assets	1,285,040	1,269,495
Other assets:		
Franchise.	12,000	10,500
Supplies	28,540	28,450
Total other assets.	40,540	38,950
Total assets	$1,469,738	$1,468,789
Liabilities		
Current liabilities:		
Accounts payable	$ 68,671	$ 53,066
Taxes payable	23,240	27,212
Accrued expenses	59,915	52,611
Total current liabilities	151,826	132,889
Long-term liabilities:		
Mortgage payable	684,000	646,000
Notes payable	302,500	248,000
Notes payable to parent	140,000	105,000
Total long-term liabilities	1,126,500	999,000
Net worth:		
Capital stock	75,000	75,000
Retained earnings.	116,412	261,900
Total net worth	191,412	336,900
Total liabilities	$1,469,738	$1,468,789

EXHIBIT 6   Effect of Proposed Expansion on Rembert's Income

Total Compensation for 1991		*Projected Compensation after Expansion*	
Base salary..............................	$18,500	Base salary......................................	$18,500
Sales volume incentive		Sales volume incentive	
(1,049,729 – 902,785) * .01		(1,485,859 – 1,049,729) * .01	
146,944 * .01 =........................	1,469	436,130 * .01 =...............................	4,361
Return on investment bonus		Return on investment bonus	
$\dfrac{397,504}{1,468,789} * 36,000$		$\dfrac{624,235}{2,573,789} * 45,000$	
.2706 * 36,000 =........................	9,743	.2425 * 45,000 =..............................	10,914
Total compensation....................	$29,712	Total compensation...........................	$33,775

Projected income statement (as calculated by Gray):

Revenue:		
Room revenue...		$1,420,238
Restaurant rental......................................		40,571
Other...		25,050
Total revenues......................................		1,485,859
Operating costs and expenses:		
Room...		326,700
Operating expenses		376,832
Depreciation and amortization		82,400
Management and reservation fees		75,692
Operating income......................................		$ 624,235

Remarks: Room revenue projected as 47,184 occupied room nights at an average price of $30.10. This figure is attributed slightly to annual growth but largely to turnaways accommodated.

Investment is figured loosely and may vary in actuality, but variance will not significantly affect ROI.

Performance Evaluation

After dinner that evening, Kevin Gray decided to review his file on Layne Rembert's compensation package and on his related performance evaluation. He checked his records to determine what the Rembert's total compensation had been for 1991. He then performed a rough calculation of what it would be for 1992 if the additional 40 rooms were to have been available during all of this time period (see Exhibit 6).

Over the past few years, Gray had also developed a 20-point performance evaluation report which he used to base his decisions on salary increases (see Exhibit 7). This system was derived from one he had witnessed when he had been previously employed by a national food service organization. While the report had been developed primarily for his own use in helping to determine who should receive merit increases in salary, Gray placed a great deal of weight on his report. In fact, he was entertaining the notion of recommending that it be instituted companywide. He made no bones about letting unit managers know that he looked for other things than pure return on investment.

EXHIBIT 7   Performance Evaluation Report

	Ranking				
	(1) Poor	*(2)* Average	*(3)* Good	*(4)* Superior	
Motel environment					
Exterior appearance	_____	_____	_____	_____	* .2 = _____
Interior appearance	_____	_____	_____	_____	* .5 = _____
Maintenance work	_____	_____	_____	_____	* .3 = _____
Room spot check	_____	_____	_____	_____	* .5 = _____
Personnel attitude	_____	_____	_____	_____	* .3 = _____
Managerial factors					
Accurate reports	_____	_____	_____	_____	* .3 = _____
Reservation control	_____	_____	_____	_____	* .2 = _____
Accounts receivable	_____	_____	_____	_____	* .2 = _____
Payroll	_____	_____	_____	_____	* .3 = _____
Controllable costs	_____	_____	_____	_____	* .5 = _____
Occupancy rate	_____	_____	_____	_____	* .5 = _____
Other factors					
Cooperation with RGM	_____	_____	_____	_____	* .3 = _____
Sales calls	_____	_____	_____	_____	* .3 = _____
Personnel turnover	_____	_____	_____	_____	* .3 = _____
Complaints	_____	_____	_____	_____	* .3 = _____
Total	_____	_____	_____	_____	_____

Ranking

20.0–17.8	Excellent
17.7–15.0	Good
14.9–11.0	Must improve
10.0–5.0	Very poor

He felt that there were a number of variables that could seriously affect profitability over which the unit manager had no control. In addition, he believed an efficient operation was to a large extent contingent on customer satisfaction.

Questions

1. Is the proposed investment likely to be a good one for Wayside Inns, Inc.?
2. Is Layne Rembert's concern justified?
3. Is the current compensation package for inn managers an appropriate one? If not, what would be?
4. Should the performance measurement system for a regional general manager be focused upon the same factors that are used by Kevin Gray and Wayside Inns to evaluate and compensate an inn manager? (An RGM has responsibility for a geographical area containing anywhere from 10 to 15 motels.)

VARIATIONS IN MANAGEMENT CONTROL

Chapters 7 through 11 described the management control process in what we believe to be fairly typical situations. In this part of the book, we describe factors that lead to modifications of these typical practices and suggest the nature of these modifications. The essentials of the control system are similar, but the environment results in differences in the details. In Chapter 12 we discuss how to differentiate controls in accordance with differentiated corporate and business unit strategies. In Chapters 13 and 14, we discuss the modifications that are needed in management control practices as applied to certain types of organizations. These types are service organizations (Chapter 13) and multinational organizations (Chapter 14). Characteristics of these organizations and their implications for management control are considered in these chapters. In Chapter 15, we discuss the management control of projects, which is somewhat different from the management control of ongoing operations that has been the focus hitherto.

12

CONTROLS
FOR DIFFERENTIATED
STRATEGIES

Many factors jointly influence the organization structure and the management control process in a company. Researchers have attempted to examine these factors by applying what is called *contingency theory;* the name simply means that structure and process depend, or are contingent, upon various external and internal factors. Research studies have identified important factors that influence control system design, among them size, environment, technology, interdependence, and strategies.

Given the overall framework of this book—namely, that the purpose of a management control system is primarily to help to implement strategies—we suggest in this chapter how different strategies influence the management control process. Two general observations are important. First, the suggestions made in this chapter are tendencies, not hard-and-fast principles. Second, system designers need to consider the influence of other external and internal factors (environment, technology, size, culture, geographical location, management style) when designing control systems.

In the first part of the chapter, we discuss the implications of different corporate strategies—single industry, related diversification, and unrelated diversification—for control system design. Next we discuss the relationship between different business-level strategies—various missions (build, hold, harvest) and competitive advantages (low cost, differentiation)—and the form and structure of control systems. Finally, we discuss the implications of management style for control system design and operation.

Corporate Strategy

The logic for linking controls to strategy is based on the following line of thinking:

- Different organizations generally operate in different strategic contexts.
- Different strategies require different task priorities, key success factors, skills, perspectives, and behaviors for effective execution.

- Control systems are measurement systems that influence the behavior of the people whose activities are being measured.
- Thus, a continuing concern in the design of control systems should be whether the behavior induced by the system is consistent with the strategy.

Concept of Corporate Strategy

Corporate strategy is about being in the right mix of businesses. Thus, corporate strategy is concerned more with the question of *where* to compete than with *how* to compete in a particular industry. "How" is the domain of business unit strategy. At the corporate level, the issues are (1) the definition of businesses in which the firm will participate and (2) the deployment of resources among those businesses.

In terms of their corporate-level strategy, companies can be classified into one of three categories. A *single industry* firm operates in one line of business. Exxon, which is in the petroleum industry, is an example. A *related diversified* firm operates in several industries, and the business units benefit from a common set of core competencies. Procter & Gamble is an example of a related diversified firm. It has business units in diapers (Pampers), detergent (Tide), soap (Ivory), toothpaste (Crest), shampoo (Head & Shoulders), and other branded consumer products. P&G has two core competencies that benefit all of its business units: *(a)* core skills in several chemical technologies and *(b)* marketing and distribution expertise in low-ticket branded consumer products. An *unrelated business* firm operates in businesses that are not related to one another; the connection between business units is purely financial. Textron is an example. This corporation operates in businesses as diverse as writing instruments, helicopters, chain saws, aircraft engine components, forklifts, machine tools, specialty fasteners, and gas turbine engines.

Implications for Organization Structure

Corporate strategy is a continuum with "single industry" strategy at one end and "unrelated diversification" at the other end. A firm's location on the continuum depends on the extent and type of its diversification. Different corporate strategies imply different organization structures and, in turn, different controls. The organization structure implications of different corporate strategies are given in Exhibit 12–1.

At the single industry end, the company tends to be functionally organized. Senior managers are responsible for developing the company's overall strategy to compete in its chosen industry as well as its functional strategies in such areas as research and development, manufacturing, and marketing. However, not all single industry firms are functionally organized. For instance, chains of fast-food restaurants, hotels, supermarkets, and drugstores are "single industry" firms, but they are organized by business units; they have both production and marketing functions at many locations. In contrast,

EXHIBIT 12–1

Different corporate strategies: organizational structure implications

	Single Industry	Related Diversified	Unrelated Diversified
Organizational structure	Functional	Business units	Holding company
Industry familiarity of corporate management	High	⟶	Low
Functional background of corporate management	Relevant operating experience (mfg, mktg, R&D)	⟶	Mainly finance
Decision-making authority	More centralized	⟶	More decentralized
Size of corporate staff	High	⟶	Low
Reliance on internal promotions	High	⟶	Low
Use of lateral transfers	High	⟶	Low
Corporate culture	Strong	⟶	Weak

every unrelated diversified company (conglomerate) is organized into relatively autonomous business units. Given the large and diverse set of businesses, senior managers in such firms tend to focus on portfolio management (i.e., selection of businesses in which to engage and allocation of financial resources to the various business units), and they delegate the development of product/market strategy to the business unit managers. Thus, at the single industry end of corporate strategy, senior managers are likely to be extremely familiar with the industry in which the firm competes and many of them tend to have expertise in research and development, manufacturing, and marketing. In contrast, at the unrelated diversified end, many senior managers tend to be experts in finance.

As a firm moves from the single industry end to the unrelated diversified end, the autonomy of the business unit manager tends to increase for two reasons. First, unlike in a single industry firm, senior managers of unrelated diversified firms may not have the knowledge and expertise to make strategic and operating decisions for a group of disparate business units. Second, there is very little interdependence across business units in a conglomerate, whereas there may be a great deal of interdependence among business units in single industry and related diversified firms; greater interdependence calls for more intervention by top managers.

Because corporate-level managers are less involved in business unit operations, the size of a conglomerate's corporate staff, compared to that of a same-sized single industry firm, tends to be low. Given the unrelated nature of its varied business units, promoting from within or by laterally transferring executives from one business unit to another is less likely to benefit a conglomerate. Also, a conglomerate may not have the single, cohesive, strong corporate culture that a single industry firm often has.

Implications for Management Control

Any organization, however well aligned its structure is to the chosen strategy, cannot effectively implement its strategy without a consistent management control system. While organization structure defines the reporting relationships and the responsibilities and authorities of different managers, it needs an appropriately designed control system to function effectively. In this part of the chapter, we discuss the planning and control requirements of different corporate strategies.

Different corporate strategies imply the following differences in the context in which control systems need to be designed:

- As firms become more diversified, corporate-level managers may not have significant knowledge of, or experience in, the activities of the company's various business units. If so, corporate-level managers for highly diversified firms cannot expect to control the different businesses on the basis of intimate knowledge of their activities, and performance evaluation tends to be carried out at arm's length.

- Single industry and related diversified firms possess *corporatewide core competencies* (wireless technology in the case of Motorola) on which the strategies of most of the business units are based. Communication channels and transfer of competencies across business units, therefore, are critical in such firms. In contrast, there are low levels of interdependence among the business units of unrelated diversified firms. This implies that as firms become more diversified, it may be desirable to change the balance in control systems from an emphasis on fostering cooperation to an emphasis on encouraging entrepreneurial spirit.

Specific tendencies in the design of control systems corresponding to variations in corporate strategies are given in Exhibit 12–2.

Strategic Planning.   Given the low level of interdependencies, conglomerates tend to use vertical strategic planning systems—that is, business units prepare strategic plans and submit them to senior management to review and approve. Because of the high level of interdependencies, strategic planning systems for related diversified and single industry firms tend to be both vertical and horizontal. The horizontal dimension might be incorporated into the strategic planning process in a number of different ways. First, a group

Exhibit 12–2

Different corporate strategies: management control implications

	Single Industry	Related Diversified	Unrelated Diversified
Strategic planning	Vertical-cum-horizontal	⟶	Vertical only
Budgeting: Relative control of business unit manager over budget formulation	Low	⟶	High
Importance attached to meeting the budget	Low	⟶	High
Transfer pricing: Importance of transfer pricing	High	⟶	Low
Sourcing flexibility	Constrained	⟶	Arm's-length market pricing
Incentive compensation: Bonus criteria	Financial and nonfinancial criteria	⟶	Primarily financial criteria
Bonus determination approach	Primarily subjective	⟶	Primarily formula-based
Bonus basis	Based both on business unit and corporate performance	⟶	Based primarily on business unit performance

executive might be given the responsibility to develop a strategic plan for the group as a whole that explicitly identifies synergies across individual business units within the group. Second, strategic plans of individual business units could have an interdependence section, in which the general manager of the business unit identifies the focal linkages with other business units and how those linkages will be exploited. Third, the corporate office could require joint strategic plans for interdependent business units. Finally, strategic plans of individual business units could be circulated to managers of similar business units to critique and review.

These methods are not mutually exclusive. In fact, several of them could be pursued fruitfully at the same time.

Example. NEC Corporation, a related diversified firm, adopted two planning systems: a normal business unit planning system and a corporate business plan (CBP) system. Strategic plans in the CBP system were prepared for important programs that cut across business units. It forced interdependent business unit managers to agree on a strategic plan for exploiting such linkages. In effect, the system required a special plan for important horizontal issues.[1]

Budgeting.   In a single industry firm, the chief executive officer may know the firm's operations intimately and corporate and business unit managers tend to have more frequent contact. Thus, chief executives of single industry firms may be able to control the operations of subordinates through informal and personally oriented mechanisms, such as frequent personal interactions. If so, this lessens the need to rely as heavily on the budgeting system as the tool of control.

On the other hand, in a conglomerate it is nearly impossible for the chief executive to rely on informal interpersonal interactions as a control tool; much of the communication and control has to be achieved through the formal budgeting system. This implies the following budgeting system characteristics in a conglomerate:

- Business unit managers have somewhat greater influence in developing their budgets since they, not the corporate office, possess most of the information about their respective product/market environments.
- Greater emphasis is often placed on meeting the budget since the chief executive has no other informal controls available.

Transfer Pricing.   Transfers of goods and services between business units are more frequent in single industry and related diversified firms than in conglomerates. The usual transfer pricing policy in a conglomerate is to give sourcing flexibility to business units and use arm's-length market prices. However, in a single industry or a related diversified firm, synergies may be important, and business units may not be given the freedom to make sourcing decisions. In Chapter 5 we discussed how constraints on sourcing affect the appropriate transfer pricing policies.

Incentive Compensation.   The incentive compensation policy tends to differ across corporate strategies in the following ways:

Use of formulas. Conglomerates, in general, are more likely to use formulas to determine business unit managers' bonuses; that is, they may base a larger portion of the bonus on quantitative, financial measures, such as X percent bonus on actual economic value added (EVA) in excess of budgeted EVA. These formula-based bonus plans are employed because senior management typically is not familiar with what goes on in a variety of disparate businesses.

Senior managers of single industry and related diversified firms tend to base a larger fraction of the business unit managers' bonus on subjective

---

[1]Michael E. Porter, *Competitive Advantage* (New York: Free Press, 1985), p. 403.

factors. In many related diversified firms, greater degrees of interrelationships imply that one unit's performance can be affected by the decisions and actions of other units. Therefore, for companies with highly interdependent business units, formula-based plans that are tied strictly to financial performance criteria could be counterproductive.

Profitability measures. In the case of unrelated diversified firms, the incentive bonus of the business unit managers tends to be determined primarily by the profitability of that unit, rather than the profitability of the firm. Its purpose is to motivate managers to act as though the business unit were their own company.

In contrast, single industry and related diversified firms tend to base the incentive bonus of a business unit manager on both the performance of that unit and the performance of a larger organizational unit (such as the product group to which the business unit belongs or perhaps even the overall corporation). When business units are interdependent, the more the incentive bonus of general managers emphasizes the separate performance of each unit, the greater the possibility of interunit conflict. On the other hand, basing the bonus of general managers more on the overall corporate performance is likely to encourage greater interunit cooperation, thereby increasing managers' motivation to exploit interdependencies rather than their individual results.

> **Example.**   In Textron, a conglomerate, the most important measure of performance in allocating bonus awards to business unit managers was return on investment of their respective business units. Thus, the incentive bonus system was formula-based tied to a financial criterion, and the bonus depended on the performance of the business unit.[2]

Business Unit Strategy

So far we have discussed variations in control systems across firms, taking the whole firm as our unit of observation. In this section, we consider *intrafirm* differences in control systems. Diversified corporations segment themselves into business units and typically assign different strategies to the individual business units. Many chief executive officers of multibusiness organizations do not adopt a standardized, uniform approach to controlling their business units; instead, they tailor the approach to each business unit's strategy.

Concept of Business Unit Strategy

The strategy of a business unit depends on two interrelated aspects: (1) its mission ("what are its overall objectives?") and (2) its competitive advantage ("how should the business unit compete in its industry to accomplish its mis-

---

[2]Malcom S. Salter, "Tailor Incentive Compensation to Strategy," *Harvard Business Review,* March–April 1973, pp. 94–102.

sion?"). Typically, business units choose from four missions: build, hold, harvest, and divest.

Build. This mission implies an objective of increased market share, even at the expense of short-term earnings and cash flow. Examples are America On Line's Internet media business, IBM's e.solutions, Monsanto's biotechnology, Corning Glass's optical fibers, and Black and Decker's handheld electric tools.

Hold. This strategic mission is geared to the protection of the business unit's market share and competitive position—for example, IBM's mainframe computers.

Harvest. The objective of this mission is to maximize short-term earnings and cash flow, even at the expense of market share. American Brands' tobacco products and General Electric's and Sylvania's light bulbs are examples.

Divest. This mission indicates a decision to withdraw from the business either through slow liquidation or outright sale.

The business unit has two generic ways to compete and develop a sustainable competitive advantage: low cost and differentiation.

Low cost. Cost leadership can be achieved through such approaches as economies of scale in production, experience curve effects, tight cost control, and cost minimization (in such areas as research and development, service, sales force, and advertising). Some firms following this strategy include Charles Schwab in discount brokerage, Wal-Mart in discount retailing, Texas Instruments in consumer electronics, Emerson Electric in electric motors, Hyundai in automobiles, Dell in computers, Black and Decker in machine tools, NuCor in steel, Lincoln Electric in arc-welding equipment, and BIC in pens.

*Differentiation.*The primary focus of this strategy is to differentiate the product offering of the business unit, creating something that customers perceive as unique. Approaches to product differentiation include brand loyalty (Coca-Cola and Pepsi Cola in soft drinks), superior customer service (Nordstrom in retailing), dealer network (Caterpillar Tractors in construction equipment), product design and product features (Hewlett-Packard in electronics), and technology (Motorola in communications). Other examples of differentiation strategy include Mercedes in automobiles, eBay in auctions, Stouffer's in frozen foods, Neiman-Marcus in retailing, Mont Blanc in pens, and Rolex in wristwatches.

Mission

The mission for existing business units could be either build, hold, or harvest. These missions constitute a continuum, with "pure build" at one end and "pure harvest" at the other end. To implement effectively, there should be congruence between the mission chosen and the types of controls used. We develop the control-mission "fit" using the following line of reasoning:[3]

---

[3]This section draws from an extensive body of research that has focused on strategy implementation issues at the business-unit level. Some of the key references are Govindarajan (1988), Govindarajan and Fisher (1990, 1993), Govindarajan and Gupta (1985). See the "Suggested Additional Readings" for this chapter.

- The mission of the business unit influences the uncertainties that general managers face and the short-term versus long-term trade-offs they make.
- Management control systems can be systematically varied to help motivate the manager to cope effectively with uncertainty and make appropriate short-term versus long-term trade-offs.
- Thus, different missions often require systematically different management control systems.

Mission and Uncertainty.   "Build" units tend to face greater environmental uncertainty than "harvest" units for several reasons:

- Build strategies typically are undertaken in the growth stage of the product life cycle, whereas harvest strategies typically are undertaken in the mature/decline stage of the product life cycle. Such factors as manufacturing process; product technology; market demand; relations with suppliers, buyers, and distribution channels; number of competitors; and competitive structure change more rapidly and are more unpredictable in the growth stage than in the mature/decline stage.
- An objective of a build business unit is to increase market share. Since the total market share of all firms in an industry is 100 percent, the battle for market share is a zero-sum game; thus, a build strategy puts a business unit in greater conflict with its competitors than does a harvest strategy. Competitors' actions are likely to be unpredictable, and this contributes to the uncertainty that build business units face.
- On both the input side and the output side, build managers tend to experience greater dependencies on external individuals and organizations than do harvest managers. For instance, a build mission signifies additional capital investment (greater dependence on capital markets), expansion of capacity (greater dependence on the technological environment), increase in market share (greater dependence on customers and competitors), increase in production volume (greater dependence on raw material suppliers and labor markets), and so on. The greater the external dependencies a business unit faces, the greater the uncertainty it confronts.
- Since build business units are often in new and evolving industries, build managers are likely to have less experience in their industries. This also contributes to the greater uncertainty that managers of build units face in dealing with external constituencies.

Mission and Time Span.   The choice of build versus harvest strategies has implications for short-term versus long-term profit trade-offs. The share-building strategy includes *(a)* price cutting, *(b)* major R&D expenditures (to

EXHIBIT 12–3

Different strategic missions: implications for strategic planning process

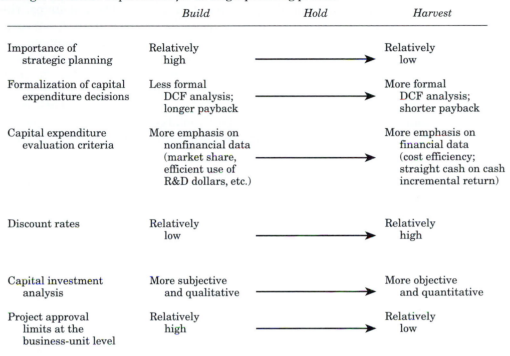

	Build	Hold	Harvest
Importance of strategic planning	Relatively high	$\longrightarrow$	Relatively low
Formalization of capital expenditure decisions	Less formal DCF analysis; longer payback	$\longrightarrow$	More formal DCF analysis; shorter payback
Capital expenditure evaluation criteria	More emphasis on nonfinancial data (market share, efficient use of R&D dollars, etc.)	$\longrightarrow$	More emphasis on financial data (cost efficiency; straight cash on cash incremental return)
Discount rates	Relatively low	$\longrightarrow$	Relatively high
Capital investment analysis	More subjective and qualitative	$\longrightarrow$	More objective and quantitative
Project approval limits at the business-unit level	Relatively high	$\longrightarrow$	Relatively low

introduce new products), and *(c)* major market development expenditures. These actions are aimed at establishing market leadership, but they depress short-term profits. Thus, many decisions that a build unit manager makes today may not result in profits until some future period. A harvest strategy, on the other hand, concentrates on maximizing short-term profits.

We now discuss how the form and structure of control systems might differ across business units with different missions.

Strategic Planning.   While designing a strategic planning process, several design issues need to be considered. A business unit's response to these issues tends to depend upon the mission it is pursuing (see Exhibit 12–3).

When the environment is uncertain, the strategic planning process is especially important. Management needs to think about how to cope with the uncertainties, and this usually requires a longer-range view of planning than is possible in the annual budget. If the environment is stable, there may be no strategic planning process at all or only a broad-brush strategic plan. Thus, the strategic planning process is more critical and more important for build, as compared with harvest, business units. Nevertheless, some strategic planning of the harvest business units may be necessary because the company's overall strategic plan must encompass all of its businesses to effectively balance cash flows.

In screening capital investments and allocating resources, the system may be more quantitative and financial for harvest units. A harvest business unit operates in a mature industry and does not offer tremendous new investment possibilities. Hence, the required earnings rate for such a business unit may be relatively high to motivate the manager to search for projects with truly exceptional returns. Since harvest units tend to experience stable environments (with predictable products, technologies, competitors, and customers), discounted cash flow (DCF) analysis often can be used more confidently. The required information used to evaluate investments from harvest units is primarily financial.

A build unit, however, is positioned on the growth stage of the product life cycle. Since the corporate office wants to take advantage of the opportunities in a growing market, senior management may set a relatively low discount rate, thereby motivating build managers to forward more investment ideas to corporate office. Given the product/market uncertainties, financial analysis of some projects from build units may be unreliable. For such projects, nonfinancial data are more important.

Budgeting.   Implications for designing budgeting systems to support varied missions are shown in Exhibit 12–4. The calculational aspects of variance analysis comparing actual results with the budget identify variances as either favorable or unfavorable. However, a favorable variance does not necessarily imply favorable performance, nor does an unfavorable variance imply unfavorable performance. The link between a favorable or unfavorable variance, on the one hand, and favorable or unfavorable performance, on the other hand, depends upon the strategic context of the business unit under evaluation.

> **Example.**   An industrial-measuring-instruments manufacturer disaggregated the overall profit variance by key causal factors for its two business units: Electric Meters, a "harvest" business, and Electronic Instruments, a "build" business. Senior management interpreted market share, selling price, and manufacturing cost variances very differently in the performance evaluations of the managers in charge of the harvest and build businesses.[4]

A related issue is how much importance should be attached to meeting the budget when evaluating a business unit manager's performance. We pointed out in Chapter 9 that the greater the uncertainty, the more difficult it is for superiors to regard subordinates' budget targets as firm commitments and to consider unfavorable budget variances as clear indicators of poor performance. For this reason budgets are relied on less in build units than in harvest units.

---

[4]John K. Shank and Vijay Govindarajan, *Strategic Cost Analysis* (Burr Ridge, IL: Richard D. Irwin, 1991), pp. 95–113.

Exhibit 12–4

Different strategic missions: implications for budgeting

	Build	Hold	Harvest
Role of the budget	More a short-term planning tool	───────►	More a control tool ("document of restraint")
Business unit manager's influence in preparing the budget	Relatively high	───────►	Relatively low
Revisions to the budget during the year	Relatively easy	───────►	Relatively difficult
Frequency of informal reporting and contacts with superiors	More frequent on policy issues; less frequent on operating issues	───────►	Less frequent on policy issues; more frequent on operating issues
Frequency of feedback from superiors on actual performance versus the budget	Less often	───────►	More often
"Control limit" used on periodic evaluation against the budget	Relatively high (i.e., more flexible)	───────►	Relatively low (i.e., less flexible)
Importance attached to meeting the budget	Relatively low	───────►	Relatively high
Output versus behavior control	Behavior control	───────►	Output control

Example. The SCM Corporation adopted a two-dimensional yardstick to evaluate business units: bottom-line performance against budget was one dimension, and performance against specific objectives was another. The ratios of the two were made to vary according to the mission of the business unit. For instance, "pure harvest" units were evaluated 100 percent on budget performance; "pure hold," 50 percent on budget and 50 percent on completion of objectives; "pure build," 100 percent on completion of objectives.[5]

The following additional differences in the budget process are likely to exist between build and harvest units:

---

[5]George E. Hall, "Reflections on Running a Diversified Company," *Harvard Business Review,* January–February 1987, pp. 88–89.

- In contrast to harvest units, budget revisions are likely to be more frequent for build units because their product/market environment changes more frequently.
- Build unit managers may have greater input and influence than harvest unit managers in formulating the budget. This is because "build" managers operate in rapidly changing environments and have better knowledge than senior management of these changes. For harvest units with stable environments, the manager's knowledge is less important.

Incentive Compensation System.   In designing an incentive compensation package for business unit managers, the following questions need to be resolved:

1. What should the size of incentive bonus payments be relative to the general manager's base salary? Should the incentive bonus payments have upper limits?
2. What measures of performance (e.g., profit, EVA, sales volume, market share, product development) should be used when deciding the general manager's incentive bonus awards? If multiple performance measures are employed, how should they be weighted?
3. How much reliance should be placed on subjective judgments in deciding on the bonus amount?
4. How frequently (semiannual, annual, biennial, and so on) should incentive awards be made?

The mission of the business unit influences decisions on these design variables (see Exhibit 12–5). With respect to the first question, many firms use the principle that the riskier the strategy, the greater the proportion of the general manager's compensation in bonus compared to salary (the "risk/return" principle). They maintain that since managers in charge of more uncertain task situations should be willing to take greater risks, they should have a higher percentage of their remuneration in the form of an incentive bonus. Thus, "build" managers are more likely than "harvest" managers to rely on bonuses.

As to the second question, when rewards are tied to certain performance criteria, behavior is influenced by the desire to optimize performance with respect to those criteria. Some performance criteria (cost control, operating profits, and cash flow from operations) focus more on short-term results, whereas other performance criteria (market share, new product development, market development, and people development) focus on long-term profitability. Thus, linking incentive bonus to short-term criteria tends to promote a short-term focus on the part of the general manager and, similarly, linking incentive bonus to long-term criteria is likely to promote long-term focus. Considering the relative differences in time horizons of build and harvest

Exhibit 12–5

Different strategic missions: implications for incentive compensation

	Build	Hold	Harvest
Percent compensation as bonus	Relatively high	——————————————➤	Relatively low
Bonus criteria	More emphasis on nonfinancial criteria	——————————————➤	More emphasis on financial criteria
Bonus determination approach	More subjective	——————————————➤	More formula-based
Frequency of bonus payment	Less frequent	——————————————➤	More frequent

managers, it may not be appropriate to use a single, uniform financial criterion, such as operating profits, to evaluate the performance of every business unit. A better idea would be to use multiple performance criteria, with differential weights for each criterion depending on the business unit's mission.

Examples.   Analog Devices and General Electric Company tailor compensation packages to the different missions of their individual businesses.

Analog Devices designed a bonus system for its business units (SBUs) based on each unit's potential for growth and profit. For instance, a business unit in the test-instrument market faced considerably different conditions and competition from those faced by a business unit in the microprocessor market. While some SBUs may not have much growth potential, they might have the ability to deliver high Return on Assets (ROA); other SBUs would be able to generate very high growth but deliver lower ROA. For SBUs pursuing a "harvest" strategy, greater weight was placed on ROA and lower weight on sales growth in determining the SBU manager's bonus. For "build" SBUs, on the other hand, bonuses were weighted more heavily on sales growth and less on ROA.[6]

GE had mature as well as young businesses. In the mature businesses, short-term incentives might dominate the compensation packages of managers who were charged with maximizing cash flow, achieving high profit margins, and retaining market share. In the younger businesses, where developing products and establishing marketing strategies were most important, nonfinancial measures geared to executing long-term performance might dictate the major portion of managers' remuneration.[7]

---

[6]Ray Stata and Modesto A. Maidique, "Bonus System for Balanced Strategy," *Harvard Business Review,* November–December 1980, pp. 156–63.

[7]"Executive Compensation: Looking to the Long Term Again," *Business Week,* May 9, 1983, p. 81.

The third question asks how much subjective judgment should affect bonus amounts. At one extreme, a manager's bonus might be a strict formula-based plan, with the bonus tied to performance on quantifiable criteria (e.g., X percent bonus on actual profits in excess of budgeted profits). At the other extreme, a manager's incentive bonus amounts might be based solely on the superior's subjective judgment or discretion. Alternatively, incentive bonus amounts might also be based on a combination of formula-based and subjective approaches. Performance on most long-term criteria (market development, new product development, and people development) is harder to measure objectively than is performance along most short-run criteria (operating profits, cash flow from operations, and return on investment). Since, as already noted, build managers, in contrast with harvest managers, should concentrate more on the long run, they typically are evaluated more subjectively than are harvest managers. The following examples from 3M and Xerox illustrate the need to have loose controls over business units that focus on innovation and growth.[8]

> **Examples:** At 3M, technical staff are encouraged to spend 15 percent of their time "bootlegging"—working on pet ideas that they hope will one day become new products for the company. Not only do they get time off to pursue these ideas, but they can also get money to buy equipment or even hire extra help.
>
> Xerox set up Xerox Technology Ventures (XTV) with less-vigorous financial controls to exploit ideas developed at the company's Palo Alto Research Center. By 1999, XTV had established more than a dozen units to pursue new product concepts.

As to the final question, the frequency of bonus awards does influence the time horizon of managers. More frequent bonus awards encourage managers to concentrate on short-term performance by motivating them to focus on those facets of the business that they can affect in the short run. Calculating and paying bonuses less frequently encourage managers to take a long-term perspective. Thus, build managers tend to receive bonus awards less frequently than harvest managers.

> **Example.** Premark International used a similar logic in designing the incentive bonus for the general manager of its Tupperware Division, whose mission was to build market share: "[If you award the bonus annually], Tupperware could reduce advertising and promotional activities and you can look good in profits that year. Then, the franchise starts to go to hell. If you're shooting for an award after three years, there's less tendency to do things short term."[9]

---

[8]These examples are excerpted from "A Survey of Innovation in Industry," *The Economist,* February 20, 1999, pp. 5–28.

[9]I. Reibstein, "Firms Trim Annual Pay Increase and Focus on Long Term: More Employers Link Incentives to Unit Results," *The Wall Street Journal,* April 10, 1987, p. 25.

Competitive Advantage

A business unit can choose to compete either as a differentiated player or as a low-cost player. Choosing a differentiation approach, rather than a low-cost approach, increases uncertainty in a business unit's task environment for three reasons.

First, product innovation is more critical for differentiation business units. This is partly because a differentiation business unit focuses primarily on uniqueness and exclusivity, which require greater product innovation, whereas a low-cost business unit, with its primary emphasis on reducing cost, typically prefers to keep its product offerings stable over time. A business unit with greater emphasis on new product activities tends to face greater uncertainty, since the business unit is betting on unproven products.

Second, low-cost business units typically tend to have narrow product lines to minimize inventory carry costs and benefit from scale economies. Differentiation business units, on the other hand, tend to have a broader set of products to create uniqueness. Product breadth creates high environmental complexity and, consequently, higher uncertainty.

Third, low-cost business units typically produce no-frill commodity products, and these products succeed primarily because they are priced lower than competing products. However, products of differentiation business units succeed if customers perceive that they offer advantages over competing products. Since customer perception is difficult to learn about and customer loyalty can change for a number of reasons, it's more difficult to predict the demand for differentiated products than the demand for commodities.

The specifics of the control systems for low-cost and differentiation business units are similar to those described earlier for harvest and build business units. This is because the uncertainty facing low-cost and differentiation business units is similar to the uncertainty facing harvest and build business units.

> **Example:** A broad-based chemicals manufacturer used differentiated management control, focusing on the different key success factors for its yellow dye unit, which followed a cost leadership strategy, and its red dye unit, which followed a differentiation strategy. The manager in charge of yellow dye was tightly held to *theoretical* standard costs rather than currently achievable standard costs. The results of these tight financial controls were remarkable. Within a period of two years, actual cost for yellow dye decreased from $5.72 per lb. to $3.84 per lb., giving the yellow dye unit a major cost advantage. The key strategic issue for red dye was product differentiation, not cost leadership. The management control reports for the red dye unit, therefore, focused on product leadership variables (e.g., milestone reporting on the development project for hot spray dyeing) rather than cost control variables.[10]

---

[10]Shank and Govindarajan, *Strategic Cost Analysis,* pp. 114–30.

Senior managers at one large, high-tech manufacturer took direct responsibility for adding customer satisfaction, quality, market share, and human resources to their formal measurement system. The impetus was their realization that the company's existing system, which was largely financial, undercut its strategy, which focused on differentiation through customer service.[11]

Top Management Style

The management control function in an organization is influenced by the style of senior management. The style of the chief executive officer affects the management control process in the entire organization. Jeff Bezos at Amazon.com, Steve Case at AOL, John Chambers at Cisco, Jack Welch at General Electric, Harold Geneen at ITT, and Percy Barnevik at ABB are well-publicized examples. Similarly, the style of the business unit manager affects the unit's management control process, and the style of functional department managers affects the management control process in their functional areas. If feasible, designers should consider management style in designing and operating control systems. (If chief executive officers actively participate in system design, as should be the case, the system will reflect their preferences.)

Differences in Management Styles

Managers manage differently. Some rely heavily on reports and certain formal documents, others prefer conversations and informal contacts. Some think in concrete terms, others think abstractly. Some are analytical, others use trial and error. Some are risk takers, others are risk averse. Some are process-oriented, others are results-oriented. Some are people-oriented, others are task-oriented. Some are friendly, others are aloof. Some are long-term-oriented, others are short-term-oriented. Some dominate decision-making ("Theory X"), others encourage organization participation in decision-making ("Theory Y"). Some emphasize monetary rewards, others emphasize a broader set of rewards.

Management style is influenced by the manager's background and personality. Background includes things like age, formal education, and experience in a given function, such as manufacturing, technology, marketing, or finance. Personality characteristics include such variables as the manager's willingness to take risks and his or her tolerance for ambiguity.

Implications for Management Control

The various dimensions of management style significantly influence the operation of the control systems. Even if the same reports with the same set of data go with the same frequency to the CEO, two CEOs with different styles

---

[11]Robert G. Eccles, "The Performance Measurement Manifesto," *Harvard Business Review,* January–February 1991, pp. 131–37.

would use these reports very differently to manage the business units. The dramatic shift in the control process within General Electric when Jack Welch succeeded Reginald Jones as the CEO, as described in Chapter 2, vividly illustrates this point.

Style affects the management control process—how the CEO prefers to use the information, conducts performance review meetings, and so on—which, in turn, affects how the control system actually operates, even if the formal structure does not change under a new CEO. In fact, when CEOs change, subordinates typically infer what the new CEO really wants based on how he or she interacts during the management control process (e.g., whether performance reports or speeches and directives take precedence).

Personal versus Impersonal Controls.   Presence of personal versus impersonal controls in organizations is an aspect of managerial style. Managers differ on how much importance they attach to formal budgets and reports as well as informal conversations and other personal contacts. Some managers are "numbers-oriented"; they want a large flow of quantitative information, and they spend much time analyzing this information and deriving tentative conclusions from it. Other managers are "people-oriented"; they look at a few numbers, but they usually arrive at their conclusions by talking with people, judging the relevance and importance of what they learn partly on their appraisal of the other person. They visit various locations and spend time talking with both supervisors and staff to get a sense of how well things are going.

Managers' attitudes toward formal reports affect the amount of detail they want, the frequency of these reports, and even their preference for graphs rather than tables of numbers, and whether they want numerical reports supplemented with written comments. Designers of management control systems need to identify these preferences and accommodate them.

Tight versus Loose Controls.   A manager's style affects the *degree* of tight versus loose control in any situation. The manager of a routine production responsibility center can be controlled relatively tightly or loosely, and the actual control reflects the style of the manager's superior. Thus, the degree of tightness or looseness often is not revealed by the content of the forms or aspects of the formal control documents, rules, or procedures. It is a factor of how these formal devices are used.

The degree of looseness tends to increase at successively higher levels in the organization hierarchy: higher-level managers typically tend to pay less attention to details and more to overall results (the bottom line, rather than the details of how the results are obtained). However, this generalization might not apply if a given CEO has a different style.

> **Example.**   The classic illustration of this point is ITT under Harold Geneen. One could argue that ITT, being a conglomerate, should be managed based on monitoring the business unit bottom line and not through a detailed evaluation of

every aspect of the business unit operations. This is so since, in a conglomerate, the CEO typically has "capacity limitations" in understanding the nuts and bolts of various business unit operations. In such a context, it was Harold Geneen's personal style that explains the detailed evaluations he made of the business unit managers.[12]

When Rand Araskog succeeded Harold Geneen at ITT, he altered the detailed and tight control system since, among other things, Araskog's personal style was not oriented toward exercising tight controls.[13]

The style of the CEO has a profound impact on management control. If a new senior manager with a different style takes over, the system tends to change correspondingly. It might happen that the manager's style is not a good fit with the organization's management control requirements. If the manager recognizes this incongruity and adapts his or her style accordingly, the problem disappears. If, however, the manager is unwilling or unable to change, the organization will experience performance problems. The solution in this case might be to change the manager.

Summary

Designers of management control systems should take explicit notice of the strategic context in which the controls are being applied. The strategies that a firm selects can be arrayed along a continuum, with single industry firms at one extreme and unrelated diversified firms (conglomerates) at the other. The management control process differs according to the firm's strategy in this dimension.

Business units have missions that can be classified as "build," "hold," or "harvest," and their managers can also decide to build competitive advantage based on low cost or differentiation. The appropriate management control process is influenced by which of these strategies is selected for a given business unit.

The discussion in this chapter on linking controls to strategies should not be used in a mechanistic manner; the suggestions made here are tendencies, not universal truths. In fact, control systems should be designed in the context of each organization's *unique* external environment, technology, strategy, organization structure, culture, and top management style.

---

[12]"The Case for Managing by the Numbers," *Fortune,* October 1, 1984, pp. 78–81.

[13]"ITT: Groping for a New Strategy," *Business Week,* December 15, 1980, pp. 66–80.

Suggested Additional Readings

Fisher, Joseph, and Vijay Govindarajan. "Incentive Compensation Design, Strategic Business Unit Mission, and Competitive Strategy." *Journal of Management Accounting Research* 5 (Fall 1993), pp. 129–44.

Galbraith, Jay. *Designing Organizations.* San Francisco: Jossey-Bass, 1995.

Govindarajan, Vijay. "A Contingency Approach to Strategy Implementation at the Business Unit Level: Integrating Administrative Mechanisms with Strategy." *Academy of Management Journal* 31, no. 4 (1988), pp. 828–53.

Govindarajan, Vijay, and Joseph Fisher. "Impact of Output versus Behavior Controls and Resource Sharing on Performance: Strategy as a Mediating Variable." *Academy of Management Journal,* June 1990, pp. 259–85.

Govindarajan, Vijay, and Anil K. Gupta. "Linking Control Systems to Business Unit Strategy: Impact on Performance." *Accounting, Organizations, and Society,* 1985, pp. 51–66.

Holloway, Jacky, et al., eds. *Performance Measurement and Evaluation.* London and Thousand Oaks, CA: Sage, 1995.

Hope, Tony, and Jeremy Hope. *Transforming the Bottom Line: Managing Performance with Real Numbers.* Boston: Harvard Business School Press, 1996.

Kotter, John. *Leadership.* Boston: Harvard Business School Press, 2000.

Omae, Kenichi. *The Borderless World: Power and Strategy in the Interlinked Economy.* New York: HarperBusiness, 1999.

Simons, Robert. *Performance Measurement and Control Systems for Implementing Strategy.* Upper Saddle River, NJ: Prentice Hall, 1999.

Tesoro, Ferdinand, and Jack Tootson. *Implementing Global Performance Measurement Systems.* San Francisco: Jossey-Bass, 1999.

Ulwick, Anthony W. *Business Strategy Formulation: Theory, Process, and the Intellectual Revolution.* Westport, CT: Quorum Books, 1999.

CASE 12–1
PELICAN INSTRUMENTS, INC.

Steve Park, president and principal stockholder of Pelican Instruments, Inc., sat at his desk reflecting on the 1997 results (Exhibit 1). For the second year in succession, the company had exceeded profit budget. Steve Park was obviously very happy with the 1997 results. All the same, he wanted to get a better feel for the relative contributions of the R&D, manufacturing, and marketing departments in this overall success. With this in mind, he called his assistant, a recent graduate of a well-known business school, into his office.

"Amy," he began, "as you can see from our recent financial results, we have exceeded our profit targets by $622,000. Can you prepare an analysis showing how much R&D, manufacturing, and marketing contributed to this overall favorable profit variance?"

Amy Shultz, with all the fervor of a recent convert to professional management, set to her task immediately. She collected the data (Exhibit 2) and was wondering what her next step should be.

Pelican Instrument's products can be grouped into two main lines of business: electric meters (EM) and electronic instruments (EI). Both EM and EI are industrial measuring instruments and perform similar functions. However, these products differ in their manufacturing technology and their end-use characteristics. EM is based on mechanical and electrical technology, whereas EI is based on microchip technology. EM and EI are substitute products in the same sense that a mechanical watch and a digital watch are substitutes.

Pelican Instruments uses a variable costing system for internal reporting purposes.

EXHIBIT 1   Income Statement for the Year 1997

		Budget (000s)		Actual (000s)
Sales		$16,872		$17,061
Cost of goods sold		9,668		9,865
Gross margin		$ 7,204		$ 7,196
Less: Other operating expenses:				
Marketing	$1,856		$1,440	
R&D	1,480		932	
Administration	1,340	4,676	1,674	4,046
Profit before taxes		$ 2,528		$ 3,150

This case was prepared by Vijay Govindarajan and John K. Shank, The Amos Tuck School of Business Administration, Dartmouth College. Copyright by Osceola Institute.

EXHIBIT 2 Additional Information

	Electric Meters (EM)	Electronic Instruments (EI)
Selling prices per unit:		
Average standard price	$40.00	$180.00
Average actual prices, 1997	30.00	206.00
Variable product costs per unit:		
Average standard manufacturing cost	20.00	50.00
Average actual manufacturing cost	21.00	54.00
Volume information:		
Units produced and sold—actual	141,770	62,172
Units produced and sold—planned	124,800	66,000
Total industry sales, 1997—actual	$44 million	$76 million
Total industry variable product costs, 1997—actual	$16 million	$32 million
United's share of the market (percent of physical units):		
Planned	10%	15%
Actual	16%	9%
	Planned	*Actual*
Firmwide fixed expenses (000s):		
Fixed manufacturing expenses	$3,872	$3,530
Fixed marketing expenses	1,856	1,440
Fixed administrative expenses	1,340	1,674
Fixed R&D expenses (exclusively for electronic instruments)	1,480	932

Questions

1. Prepare the report that you feel Amy Shultz should present to Mr. Park.

2. Put yourself in the position of the following six managers: general manager (EM); marketing manager (EM); manufacturing manager (EM); general manager (EI); marketing manager (EI); manufacturing manager (EI). These six managers compete for a share in the company's bonus pool. For each of the six, how would you make a case for your obtaining a share of the bonus pool?

3. As Mr. Park, how would you feel about the 1997 performance of each of the six managers who are competing for a share of the bonus pool? (*Note:* Consider the strategy of EM and EI business units in your performance assessment.)

CASE 12–2
PC&D, INC.

When we promoted you to the presidency five years ago, we expected that there would be changes, but we never expected you to diminish the importance of the old line businesses to the extent that you have. I think you have erred in doing so. . . .

The new entrepreneurial subs are certainly dynamic and have brought positive press to the company. But by investing all new resources in them, you are jeopardizing the health of the company as a whole. . . .

My division's reputation has been built over the past 50 years on the superior quality of its products and sales force. But as the leadership of our products begins to erode, my salesmen are beginning to leave. Without resources, I cannot stop this trend, and, as much as it saddens me to say so, I am losing my own motivation to stay with the company.

These were some excerpts from a letter that the senior vice president and head of the Machinery Division, George McElroy, 58, sent to John Martell, president of PC&D, Inc., in February 1976. McElroy was highly respected in both the company and the industry, a member of the board of directors, and a senior officer of the company for 20 years. Therefore, Martell knew that it was important to respond and to resolve the issues with McElroy successfully. At the same time Martell had no intention of giving up his own prerogatives to direct the company.

History of PC&D, Inc.

Payson and Clark Company. Payson & Clark, the forerunner of PC&D, was founded during the merger movement around the turn of the century. With the growth of industry across the country at the time, the demand for heavy machinery also grew rapidly. The new company benefited from economies of scale, both in production and distribution, and so it prospered.

This case is an abridged version of Harvard Business School case 380-072, prepared by Richard Hammermesh. Copyright © by the President and Fellows of Harvard College.

By 1965 Payson & Clark Company was an old, stable company still producing machinery. With revenues of $300 million and net aftertax profits of $6 million, it was still the largest firm in the industry. The company offered the most complete line of heavy industrial equipment in the industry, with its different configurations of standard and custom models filling a large, encyclopedic sales manual.

Although Payson & Clark was the leader in quality and breadth of its product line, it was not the leader in innovations. Rather, it left expensive R&D to others, copying products after they were widely accepted. It could afford to follow others primarily because the industry itself was slow-moving. In 1965 the business was essentially the same as when the company was founded.

In 1965 the company was still structured as it had been in the 1920s, with a standard functional organization and highly centralized chain of command. Its top executives were old-time managers, the average age being 55. Many had spent their entire careers with the firm and could remember the days when old Mr. Payson had kept tight reins on the company in the 1930s and 1940s. Harold C. Payson IV, age 53 in 1965, was president of the company from the late 1940s and the president and chairman since 1955. Although the company was publicly held, the Payson family still owned a considerable amount of its stock.

In the early 1960s, Mr. Payson began to consider succession. One way in which Mr. Payson sought to implement this suggestion was to use some of the excess capital thrown off by the machinery business to enter into joint ventures with young, new companies developing high-technology innovative products. Several such investments were made in the early 1960s, including one with the Datronics Company in 1962.

Datronics Company. In 1965, the Datronics Company was 10 years old with revenues of $50 million. The company had started as an engineering firm subsisting on government research grants and contracts. As a by-product of the government project, the company also developed several types of sophisticated electronic equipment with wide industrial applications. The company concentrated its efforts on R&D, however, subcontracted production, and bought marketing services for its commercial products. The lack of control over marketing and production and the lost profits passed to the marketers and subcontractors displeased the company's young president, John Martell. In his opinion, the company's growth was limited until the right product emerged to justify becoming a full manufacturing and marketing company.

Following Payson & Clark's investment in 1962, Datronic's engineers developed an existing new product toward the end of 1964 that promised to sell extremely well due to its increased capacity and lower cost. Martell saw the promise of the new product as the waited-for opportunity to expand the company. It was clear, however, that a major influx of capital was needed to bring the product to the market, build a sales force, and begin volume production. Therefore, Martell began a search for external capital that included a presentation to the joint venture partner, Payson & Clark, which already owned 20 percent of Datronics' stock.

Meanwhile, Mr. Payson had been following the activities at Datronics closely and was quite aware of the growth potential of the company before Martell's visit. Further, Mr. Payson recognized that Datronics, once its manufacturing operations started, would have a continual need for new capital. If Payson & Clark invested once, it would not be long until another request for resources came from Datronics. With these factors in mind, Mr. Payson decided that the most beneficial arrangement for both parties would be for his company to acquire Datronics.

Martell agreed to this offer and negotiations for a friendly takeover were consummated. Payson & Clark acquired Datronics for $42 million in November 1965, with Martell himself receiving $8.4 million in cash, notes, and securities. The acquisition provided an opportunity for Payson & Clark to update its image. Patterning itself after other successful growth companies of the time, it changed its name to PC&D, Inc., to denote the beginning of a new era in the company.

PC&D, 1965–1970

After the acquisition, Mr. Payson restructured the company with the help of consultants, setting up a divisional organization. The old Payson & Clark Company now became the Machinery Division headed by George McElroy, formerly vice president of manufacturing. The Datronics Company became the Electronics Division headed by Martell.

Electronics Division. At the time of the acquisition, the Datronics Company consisted of several scientific labs, some test equipment, 10 professional engineers, an administrative staff, and Martell. An electrical engineer by training, Martell was a man in his mid-30s. He was energetic and a risk taker by nature, and even as a child in Iowa could not imagine working for someone else all his life. After college at MIT, he worked for eight years at a large scientific equipment company in the Boston area. Initially, he was hired for the research group, but he was more attracted to the company's management positions. He transferred first to the corporate planning office and then became a division plant manager. With his technical competence and management experience, it was not surprising that he was approached by several of the more innovative of the company's research engineers to invest in and head up a new, independent R&D company. Martell bought in for 25 percent of the founding stock and thus began the Datronics Company.

During his term as president of Datronics, Martell was highly regarded by the small group of employees. Although he had a respectable command of the technology, he left the research to the engineers, devoting his time to developing sources of challenging and lucrative contracts.

After the acquisition by the Payson & Clark Company, Martell retained full control of the operations of his old organization, which became the Electronics Division. He hired an experienced industrial marketer from a large technical firm to set up the marketing operations and a friend from his old employer to head up the production operations. As expected, the demand for the division's new product was very high. Five years later, in 1970, the division was a successful growing enterprise, having expanded into other electronics fields. It had 700 employees, marketing offices established or opening throughout the United States, Europe, and Japan, plants at three different sites, and revenues of over $160 million. The business press reported these activities very favorably, giving much credit to Martell's leadership.

Machinery Division.   Meanwhile, the Machinery Division continued to be the stalwart of the industry it had always been, retaining its structure and activities of the earlier time. George McElroy, division manager and senior vice president, was considered the division's mainstay. He had joined the company in the early 1950s and was primarily responsible for the plastics innovations of that time. Advisor and confidant of Mr. Payson, McElroy was thought by his subordinates to be next in line for the presidency.

Mr. Payson limited his involvement in the company's internal affairs to reviewing budgets and year-end results, while spending most of his time with community activities and lobbying in Washington. He felt justified in this hands-off policy, because of the quality of both his division vice presidents, McElroy and Martell. PC&D's performance further supported Mr. Payson's approach. Revenues climbed to $530 million, and profits aftertax to

$14 million, by 1970. The solid 26 multiple of its stock price reflected the confidence in PC&D's prospects (see Exhibit 1).

The compensation schemes reflected the extent to which Mr. Payson allowed the division managers to be autonomous. McElroy's compensation was 90 percent salary, with a 10 percent bonus based on ROI. Martell received two-thirds of his pay as a bonus based on growth in revenues. Compensation policies within each division were entirely at the discretion of either Martell or McElroy. In general, Martell made much greater use of incentive compensation than McElroy.

Change at PC&D, 1970.   Toward the end of 1970, Mr. Payson decided that it was time to limit his involvement to that of chairman of the board and to name a new president of PC&D. He supported the appointment of McElroy as the next president. McElroy was the next senior officer in the company and, after years of working with Mr. Payson, held many of the same views on the traditional values of PC&D. Mr. Payson agreed with the school of thought, however, that chief executives should not choose their own successors. He, therefore, established a search committee, consisting of three outside members of the board of directors, and a thorough job was done. The result was the nomination of Martell. Although because of his relative youth this was a surprise to some, the search committee's report explained the thinking behind the choice: "During the past five years PC&D has experienced an exciting and profitable period of growth and diversification. But it is essential that the company not become complacent. One of our major criteria in choosing a new president was to find a person with the energy and vision to continue PC&D's growth and expansion." The board unanimously approved the selection of Martell as president and CEO.

Martell began his new position with the board's mandate in mind. He planned to con-

EXHIBIT 1   PC&D, Inc., Income Statement and Balance Sheet, 1966–1970 ($ millions, except per share data)

	1966	*1967*	*1968*	*1969*	*1970*
Sales:					
Machinery	$ 315.1	$ 327.5	$ 340.2	$ 354.1	$ 368.2
Electronics	66.1	84.7	106.7	132.3	161.4
Total sales	381.2	412.2	446.9	486.4	529.6
COGS:*					
Machinery	251.7	264.3	271.8	284.7	297.9
Electronics	49.6	63.0	79.6	96.8	118.5
Total COGS	301.3	327.3	351.4	381.5	416.4
Gross margin	79.9	84.9	95.5	104.9	113.2
Expenses:					
Marketing G&A expense	46.1	48.3	50.3	51.6	53.1
Product development—machinery	4.9	4.6	4.7	4.1	4.5
R&D—electronics	4.2	5.3	10.3	17.8	27.3
Total expense	55.2	58.2	65.3	73.5	84.9
Profit before interest and tax	24.7	26.7	30.2	31.4	28.3
Interest	3.0	3.0	0.2	0.2	0.2
Profit before tax	21.7	23.7	30.0	31.2	28.1
Income tax	10.8	11.8	15.0	15.6	14.0
Net profit	10.9	11.9	15.0	15.6	14.1
Earnings per share	$ 3.63	$ 3.97	$ 5.00	$ 5.20	$ 4.70
Average stock price	$ 94	$ 111	$ 145	$ 146	$ 103
Total assets	286	320	345	385	427
Total current assets	187	214	231	260	292
Total current liabilities	122	130	135	145	165
Total long-term debt	16	30	35	49	57

*COGS means cost of goods sold.

tinue the diversification of PC&D into high-growth industries. He expected to follow both an acquisition mode and a start-up mode, using the excess funds from the Machinery Division and PC&D's rising stock to finance the growth. For start-ups, Martell planned to use joint ventures supporting newer companies, much as the old Payson & Clark Company had supported his venture in its early days.

Martell brought to his position a very definite management style. He was a strong be-liever in the benefits deriving from an opportunistic, entrepreneurial spirit, and he wanted to inject PC&D with this kind of energy. He was concerned, however, that the people with this kind of spirit would not be attracted to work with PC&D because of the stigma, real or imagined, of working for a large company, Martell commented:

It was my experience that there are two worlds of people, some of whom are very secure and comfortable and satisfied in their career pursuits in large institutionalized companies, and others of whom are, I think, wild ducks, and who are interested in perhaps greater challenges that small companies present in terms of the necessity to succeed or die.

Martell himself credited the success of the Electronics Division to Mr. Payson's willingness to turn the reins completely over to him. The secret, Martell thought, was in spotting the right person with both ability and integrity. Corporate headquarters' role should be to provide resources in terms of both money and expertise as needed, to set timetables, to provide measurement points and incentive, and then to keep its hands off.

Although the board's directives were clear to Martell, the specifics for implementation were not. Not only were the larger questions of which way to diversify or how to encourage innovation unanswered, but questions of how to plan and who to involve were also left unclear. Martell was not given the luxury of time to resolve these issues. Within the first week in his new position, three professionals from the Electronics Division called on Martell. Bert Rogers and Elaine Patterson were the key engineers from the research department and Thomas Grennan was head of marketing, western region. They had been working on some ideas for a new product (not competing with any of PC&D's existing lines), and they were ready to leave the company to start their own business to develop and market it. Indeed, they had already had a prospectus prepared for their new venture with the hope that either Martell, personally, or PC&D might be able to provide some venture capital. The president particularly liked these three and admired their willingness to take such personal risks with a product as yet unresearched as to market or design. With his energy and can-do aggressive style, Grennan reminded Martell of himself just a few years ago when he left to start the Datronics Company.

Martell liked the product and saw the idea as a possible route for continuing PC&D's diversification and growth, but there was a prob-lem. It was clear from the presentation of the three, that much of their motivation came from the desire to start their own company and, through their equity interest, reap the high rewards of their efforts if successful. Martell did not fault this motivation, for it had been his route as well. He could not expect PC&D's managers to take large personal risks if there was no potential for a large payoff. Further, a fair offer to the group, if in salary, required more than PC&D could afford or could justify to the older divisions. Martell told Rogers, Patterson, and Grennan that he was very interested and asked if he could review the prospectus overnight and get back to them the next day. That night he devised a plan with a major feature called the Entrepreneurial Subsidiary. Martell presented this proposal to Grennan, Rogers, and Patterson the next day. They readily accepted it, and thus a pattern began for most PC&D's diversification over the next five years.

The Entrepreneurial Subsidiary

Martell's plan, of which he was particularly proud, worked as follows. When a proposal for a new product area was made to the PC&D corporate office, a new subsidiary would be incorporated—the entrepreneurial subsidiary. The initiators of the idea would leave their old division or company and become officers and employees of the new subsidiary. In the above example, the new subsidiary would be the Pro Instrument Corporation with Grennan as president and Rogers and Patterson as vice presidents.

The new subsidiary would issue stock in its name, $1 par value, 80 percent of which would be bought by PC&D and 20 percent by the entrepreneurs involved—engineers and other key officers. This initial capitalization, plus sizable direct loans from PC&D, provided the funds for the research and development of the new product up to its commercialization. In the case of Pro Instruments, Patterson and Rogers hired 10 other researchers, while Grennan hired a market researcher and a finance-accounting person. These 15 people invested $50,000 together and PC&D invested another $200,000.

Two kinds of agreements were signed between the two parties. The first was a research contract between the parent company and the subsidiary, setting time schedules for the research, defining requirements for a commercializable product, outlining budgets, and otherwise stipulating obligations on both sides. In general, the subsidiary was responsible for the R&D and production and testing of a set number of prototypes of a new product, while the parent company would market and produce the product on an international scale. Pro Instruments' agreement stipulated two phases, one lasting 18 months to produce a prototype and another lasting 6 months to test the product in the field and produce a marketing plan. Detailed budget and personnel needs were outlined, providing for a $900,000 working capital loan from PC&D during the first phase and $425,000 during the second.

Although PC&D had proprietary rights on the product and all revenues received from marketing it, the agreement often included an incentive kicker for the key engineers in the form of additional stock to be issued if the finished product produced certain specified amounts of revenue by given dates. This was the case for Pro Instruments: 5,000 shares in year 1, to be issued if net profits were over $250,000; 20,000 shares in year 2 if profits were over $1 million; and 10,000 in year 3 if profits were over $3 million.

The second agreement specified the financial obligations and terms for merger. Once the terms of the research contract were met, PC&D, with board approval, had the option for a stated time period (usually four years) to merge the subsidiary through a one-for-one exchange of PC&D stock for the stock of the subsidiary, which would then be dissolved. To protect the interests of entrepreneurs, PC&D was required to vote on merger of the subsidiary within 60 days if it met certain criteria. For Pro Instruments, the criteria were (1) the product earned cumulative profits of $500,000 and (2) if the earnings of PC&D and the subsidiary were consolidated, dilution of PC&D's earnings-per-share would not have occurred over three consecutive quarters. If PC&D did not choose to merge during the 60 days, then the subsidiary had a right to buy out PC&D's interest.

Since PC&D's stock was selling for $103 in 1970 and subsidiary stock was bought for $1/share, the exchange of stock represented a tremendous potential return. Depending on the value of PC&D's stock at the time of merger, the net worth of the entrepreneurs who originally invested in the subsidiary multiplied overnight. Indeed, as subsidiaries were merged in ensuing years, typical gains ranged from 100 to 200 times the original investments in the entrepreneurial subsidiary. For example, PC&D exercised its option to merge Pro Instruments when its product was brought to market in 1972. Grennan, who had bought 6,000 shares of Pro Instruments stock, found his 6,000 shares of PC&D valued at $936,000 (PC&D common selling for $156 on the New York Stock Exchange at the time). By the end of 1974, Pro Instruments' new product had earned $50 million in revenue and $4.8 million in profits, thus qualifying the original entrepreneurs for stock bonuses. Grennan received another 4,200 shares valued at $684,600. Thus, in four years, he had earned about $1.6 million on a $6,000 investment.

By setting up entrepreneurial subsidiaries, like Pro Instruments, Martell had several expectations. In the process of setting up a subsidiary with the dynamics of a small, independent group, Martell hoped to create the loyalty, cohesion, and informal structure conducive to successful R&D efforts. The subsidiary would have a separate location and its own officers who decided structure and operating policies. Further, it provided the opportunity to buy into and reap the benefits of ownership in the equity of a company.

PC&D, 1970–1975

During the first five years of Martell's presidency, PC&D's growth was quite impressive. With revenues topping the billion dollar mark in 1975, growth had averaged about 15 percent in revenues and 35 percent in profits after tax during the five years (see Exhibit 2 for financials). Such growth had been achieved, to a large extent, from new products developed in entrepreneurial subsidiaries. In 1975, sales of $179.2 million and profit before taxes and interest of $22.1 million came from these new products.[1] All together, 11 entrepreneurial subsidiaries had been organized during the 1970–1975 time frame. Of these, four had successfully developed products and had been merged into PC&D—one in 1972, one in 1973, and two in 1974. The other seven were younger and their work was still in process; to date, none had failed.

Most subsidiaries grew out of needs of the Electronics Division or Pro Instruments. Competitors in the electronics equipment industry were beginning to integrate backward, thus lowering costs by producing their own semiconductors. The need to remain cost competitive caused PC&D to establish entrepreneurial subsidiaries to develop specialized components, including semiconductors, assuming that these could be used both by PC&D and sold in outside markets. In the process of selling semiconductors to outside customers, ideas for new products using PC&D components were stimulated, and new subsidiaries were formed to develop these equipment products. The cost of merging the two types of subsidiaries—components or equipment—differed, however. Equipment subsidiaries were cheaper, because they could share the already existent sales force of the Electronics Division; many parts could be stan-

dard ones already utilized in other products; and the processes were similar to other Electronics products. But with semiconductors, new plant, new sales channels, new manufacturing processes, and new skills at all levels had to be built. Although Martell thought the move into semiconductors promised a large cash flow in the future in a booming industry, some in the company were concerned that the cash drain was not the best use of scarce cash resources.

When Martell first became president, he made few changes in PC&D's organization structure. McElroy continued as vice president of the Machinery Division and retained control over that division's structure and policies. Martell himself retained his responsibilities as manager of the Electronics Division. This he did reluctantly and with all intentions of finding a new executive for the job: however, the unexpected nature of his promotion left Martell without a ready candidate.

As the subsidiaries were merged, beginning with Pro Instruments in 1972, questions of organization began to rise. In typical fashion, Martell wanted to pass involvement in these decisions down to the appropriate managers. There was also no question that Pro Instruments' president, Grennan, had proven himself with the new subsidiary. Therefore, in 1972, Martell appointed Grennan to division vice president, Electronics, based on Grennan's superlative performance. Further, because the products were complementary, all of the subsidiaries merged during this period were placed in the Electronics Division. Moreover, in recognition of the increased number of products, Grennan reorganized the Electronics Division. He appointed his Pro Instruments colleague, Bert Rogers, to be director of research, which was organized by product area. Manufacturing, also organized by product, reflected the development by subsidiary as well. Marketing, on the other hand, was organized by region as it had been previously. Until they were merged, however, subsidiary presidents reported directly to Martell for resolution of problems that

[1]Of PC&D's total assets in 1975, approximately 40 percent were devoted to the Machinery Division, 35 percent to the traditional Electronics Division, and 25 percent to the entrepreneurial subsidiaries.

EXHIBIT 2   PC&D, Inc., Income Statements and Balance Sheets, 1971–1975 ($ millions, except per share data)

	1971	1972	1973	1974	1975
Sales:					
Machinery	$ 382.9	$ 397.8	$ 412.5	$ 426.9	$ 440.6
Electronics*	193.6	235.6	300.1	397.4	561.4
Total sales	576.5	633.4	712.6	824.3	1,002.0
COGS:†					
Machinery	311.3	322.6	338.2	350.9	359.1
Electronics	145.2	174.3	216.1	282.2	421.1
Total COGS	456.5	496.9	554.3	633.1	780.2
Gross margin	120.0	136.5	158.3	191.2	221.8
Expenses:					
Marketing G&A expense	54.7	56.3	59.1	63.3	67.7
Development—machinery	5.0	5.1	5.2	5.2	5.3
R&D—electronics	28.4	29.5	30.7	31.9	33.5
Total	88.1	90.9	95.0	100.4	106.5
Profit and taxes:					
Before interest	31.9	45.6	63.3	90.8	115.3
Interest	0.2	3.0	3.0	7.0	11.0
Profit before tax	31.7	42.6	60.3	83.8	104.3
Income tax	15.8	21.3	30.1	41.9	52.1
Net profit	15.9	21.3	30.2	41.9	52.2
EPS	$ 5.30	$ 6.45‡	$ 8.39	$ 10.47	$ 13.05
Average stock price	$ 106	$ 156	$ 158	$ 163	$ 238
Total assets	468	505	586	706	882
Total current assets	327	359	427	500	617
Total current liabilities	192	205	229	250	315
Total long-term debt	55	58	84	138	193

*Sales figures for Electronics included both sales by the original division and sales of new subsidiaries after they are merged. Thus, in 1975, the $561.4 million in sales for Electronics included $179.2 from products developed in subs. Profit before interest and taxes from new products was $22.1 million.

†COGS means cost of goods sold.

‡Number of shares increased in 1972 by 0.3 million from the merger of Pro Instruments. They increased in 1973 by 0.3 million from merger of Sub #2, and again by 0.4 million in 1974 from the merger of Subs #3 and #4. Thus, in 1974, there was a total of 4 million shares outstanding. In late 1973, there was a secondary offering of 1 million shares.

arose (see Exhibit 3 for a 1975 organization chart).

By 1975, the Electronics Division's enlarged marketing and production departments employed 4,000 people, with production plants in three different locations. Electronics then had sales of $561.4 million, compared to Machinery's $440.6 million.

Although successful development projects from subsidiaries had been largely responsible for the sales growth at PC&D, this result had not come without costs. First, the subsidiaries required funds—$60 million by the end of 1975. Some of these funds came from retained earnings, but much was new money raised in the form of long-term debt. Further, stock issued to

Exhibit 3

Organization chart

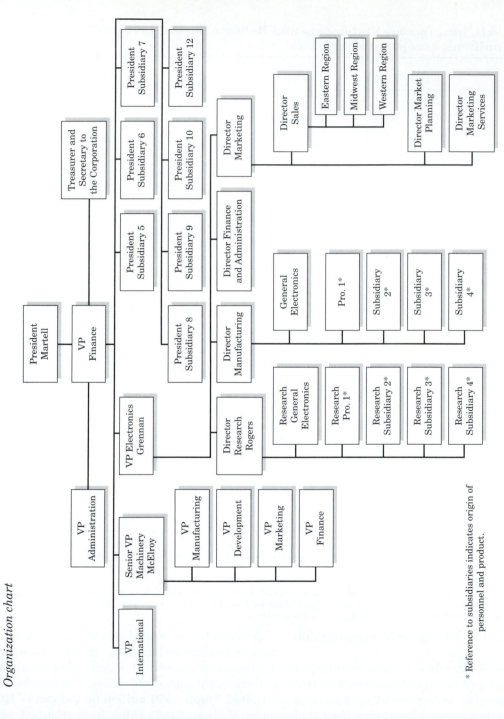

* Reference to subsidiaries indicates origin of personnel and product.

capitalize subsidiaries and pay bonuses to entrepreneurs had a diluting effect on PC&D's shares. If all subsidiaries were merged and successful, the number of new shares could be significant. Although raising such a sizable amount of new funds was not particularly difficult for a company as large as PC&D, the needs arising from the subsidiaries left little new money for the core businesses of PC&D. The Machinery Division, for example, had not had its development budget increased at all during the five years ending 1975.

Further Concerns.   Despite PC&D's successes, Martell was not without worries— several problems had appeared in both the Electronics and Machinery Divisions. In Electronics, personnel and products originating in subsidiaries now equaled or surpassed those from the original division. It had been part of the strategy of the entrepreneurial subsidiaries to use them as devices to attract talent from other firms. A key researcher hired from outside was encouraged to hire, in turn, the best of his or her former colleagues. Thus, the loyalty and friendships between key entrepreneurs and their staffs were often strong and long-standing. As the entrepreneurial subsidiaries were merged, their personnel tended to retain this loyalty to the president or key officers of the old subsidiary, rather than transferring it to PC&D. Thus, several warring spheres of influence were developing in the division, particularly in the research department and between research and other departments. Martell was concerned that such influences and warring would lead to poor decisions and much wasted energy in this division.

Turnover in Electronics was also increasing. This was of particular concern to Martell, for it was those talented engineers that the entrepreneurial subsidiaries were meant to attract who were beginning to leave. For example, Elaine Patterson, formerly of Pro Instruments, left during 1975 to start her own company, taking 20 research engineers with her. The source of the turnover was unclear, but possible factors included distaste for the kind of warring atmosphere mentioned above and the inability to be a part of a large corporate R&D department with its demand for budgets and reports.

For many employees, however, the sudden absence of monetary incentives changed the climate drastically. This lack of incentive, coupled with the discovery that the most challenging projects were taken on by newly formed subsidiaries, which favored hiring outside expertise, caused dissatisfaction. For Martell, such turnover was of greatest concern in the long run, for the inability to create a strong central R&D department in Electronics created a continuing need for more entrepreneurial subsidiaries. These subsidiaries were still too new an idea for Martell to want to risk his entire future R&D program on their successes. Further, most of the new products were in highly competitive areas. Without continuing upgrades, these products would soon become obsolete. A strong central R&D department was needed for follow-up development of products started by subsidiaries.

Finally, Martell was concerned by indications of serious operating problems in the Electronics Division. This was particularly disturbing, since Martell had placed complete faith in Grennan's managerial ability. The most recent cost report, for example, indicated that the division's marketing, G&A, and engineering expenses were way out of line. Further, the marketing and production departments reported problems in several products originating in the subsidiaries. One product, with expected obsolescence of four years, now showed a six-year breakeven just to cover the engineering and production costs. Another product, completing its first year on the market, had been forecasted by the subsidiary to achieve $20 million in sales in its first two years. During the first six months, however, losses had been incurred because of customer returns. A report on the causes of the returns showed a predominance of product failures. The chances for breakeven on this product looked bleak. While none of these problems had affected operating results to date, Martell was especially concerned that these operating problems would have a negative impact on 1976 first-quarter earnings.

Martell had not confronted Grennan with these operating problems. He wanted to see how the division itself was attacking these issues through its long-range plan. Martell had requested that Grennan prepare a long-range plan (five years) as well as the usual one-year operating plan. The product of this effort had just arrived (February 1976) and Martell had not had a chance to study it. Its 100-page bulk loomed on Martell's desk. Quick perusal had indicated four pages of prose scattered through the plan, and dozens of charts, graphs, and tables of numbers, every one of which manifested an upward trend.

In an attempt to get employee feedback on all of these problems, Martell contracted an outside consulting firm to carry out confidential interviews with personnel in the Electronics Division. The interviews found middle managers quite concerned over the confusion in the division which was causing a loss of morale there. The consultant's report cited concrete problems, including lost equipment, missed billings, and confusion in the plant. Typical comments from lower-level personnel included the following:

> Either upper management is not being informed of problems or they don't know how to solve them.
> Morale is very poor, job security is nil.
> There is little emphasis on production efficiencies.
> Scrap is unaccounted for.
> Market forecasts are grossly inaccurate.
> Production schedules have a definite saw-tooth pattern. There is very little good planning.
> There are no systematic controls.

These were not the sorts of comments Martell expected from the division responsible for the major portion of PC&D's future growth. His concern was not so much the problems themselves but what was being done about them. His preferred policy was to stay out of day-to-day operating problems. He wondered how long it was prudent to allow such problems to continue without some intervention on his part.

Meanwhile, the Machinery Division had its own problems. The last major construction of a new plant had been in the early 1950s. Since that time, McElroy had upgraded production methods, which succeeded in checking rising costs. Since 1965, however, resources for such improvements had not been increased, and, with inflation in the 1970s, less and less could be done on a marginal basis. McElroy believed that capacity was sufficient for the short term, but that it was impossible to remain state of the art.[2] Indeed, the Machinery Division's products were beginning to fall behind the new developments of competitors, and the costs of Machinery's products were beginning to inch up. As the production line aged, quality control reported an increasing percentage of defective goods. In contrast to the situation in Machinery, the rather extensive investment in new plant for the production of semiconductors did not sit too well with McElroy, who was concerned with the lack of flexibility that could result from backward integrating. He thought component needs should be farmed out to the cheapest bidder from the numerous small component firms. Martell was concerned with how long he could keep McElroy satisfied without a major investment in Machinery and how long he could count on the cash flow from Machinery for other users.

---

[2]McElroy suspected that the Machinery Division would require an investment of $100–$125 million over two or three years to revitalize the product line and plant and equipment. McElroy believed that in the long term the return on this investment would match the division's historic ROI.

Turnover, a problem never before experienced in the Machinery Division, had also appeared. Here, however, it was the salespeople who were leaving. Martell worried about this trend, for the sales force was the division's strength. According to the head of marketing, the salespeople considered themselves the best in the industry, and they did not wish to sell products that were not the best. They saw Machinery's products as no longer the best in quality or state of the art. Further, they did not wish to work for a company where they felt unimportant. Whether it was true or not, the sales force appeared less aggressive than in previous times.

Martell was not overly surprised, therefore, when he received McElroy's letter, nor was he certain that some of McElroy's anger concerning the Electronics Division was not justified. Martell know he had to do something about McElroy, as well as Grennan and the Electronics Division. He also had to decide whether entrepreneurial subsidiaries should continue to be part of PC&D's research and development strategy. Finally, all of Martell's decisions concerning the divisions and subsidiaries needed to be consistent with a strategy that would continue PC&D's growth.

Questions

1. Identify and evaluate the strategy of and controls over the Electronics Division and Machinery Division during 1965–70.

2. Evaluate the concept of the Entrepreneurial Subsidiary.

3. Identify and evaluate the strategy of and controls over the Electronics Division, Machinery Division, and Entrepreneurial Subsidiary since 1970.

CASE 12–3
3M CORPORATION

To further accelerate our growth, we're focusing on products that create a new basis of competition. We have about 30 Pacing Plus programs under way. These products serve high-growth industries and offer the potential to generate several billion dollars of new sales.

L. D. DeSimone
Chairman of the Board and Chief Executive Officer
3M Corporation

In 1999, the Minnesota Mining & Manufacturing Corporation (3M), with sales revenues in excess of $16 billion, was a diversified manufacturer of commercial, industrial, consumer, and health care products. Its business was divided into three major segments:

- Industrial and consumer markets.
- Transportation, safety, and specialty material markets.
- Health care markets.

Founded in 1902 as a corundum mining operation, 3M had to change directions quickly as the mine was completely unsuccessful, reportedly selling only one ton of ore.[1] Over the years, 3M has been regarded as one of the most innovative companies. Examples of new products and new markets created by 3M include:

- Waterproof sandpaper.
- Scotch™ Transparent and Masking Tapes.
- Scotchgard™ Protectors.
- Reflective sheeting for transportation and worker safety.
- Post-it® Notes.
- Hypoallergenic surgical tapes.

- Tape closures for disposable diapers.
- Maintenance-free respirators.

3M's vision was to be the most innovative enterprise and the preferred supplier by:

- Developing technologies and products that create a new basis of competition.
- Earning customers' loyalty by helping them grow their businesses.
- Expanding internationally, where 3M already generated more than half its sales.
- Improving productivity and competitiveness worldwide.

In 1999, 3M made more than 60,000 products; they produced 900 varieties of adhesive tapes alone, as diverse as for reflective material for highway safety and for home cleaning sponges. Additionally, in 1995 3M was awarded the National Medal of Technology®, the US government's top award for innovation. Financial data on 3M during the 1990–98 period are given in Exhibit 1.

Early on in 3M's history, William L. McKnight, former Chairman and CEO of 3M and long considered to be "spiritual founder" of 3M, introduced polices and philosophies that are considered to be responsible for 3M's ability to consistently innovate (see Exhibit 2). Current management still embraced these policies and philosophies, seeing innovation as the cornerstone of 3M's future success. In 1999, for instance, 30 percent of 3M's sales revenues came from products new to the market within the past four years.

This case was written by Kirk Hendrickson (T '97), under the supervision of Professor Vijay Govindarajan. Copyright © Osceola Institute.

[1]James C. Collins and Jerry I. Porras, *Built to Last: Successful Habits of Visionary Companies* (New York: HarperBusiness, 1995), p. 238.

Question

Evaluate the policies and philosophies of 3M from the standpoint of helping 3M implement its strategy rooted in innovation.

Exhibit 1 Selected Financial Data for 3M Corporation
(dollars in millions, except per-share amounts)

	1998*	1997†	1996	1995	1994	1993	1992	1991	1990
Operating Results									
Net sales	$15,021	$15,070	$14,236	$13,460	$12,148	$11,053	$10,817	$10,281	$9,931
Operating income	2,039	2,675	2,491	2,221	2,095	1,796	1,811	1,683	1,304
Income from continuing operations	1,213	2,121	1,516	1,306	1,207	1,133	1,116	984	1,070
Per share—basic	3.01	5.14	3.63	3.11	2.85	2.61	2.55	2.24	2.42
Per share—diluted	2.97	5.06	3.59	3.09	2.84	2.59	2.54	2.23	2.41
Net income	1,175	2,121	1,526	976	1,322	1,263	1,233	1,154	1,308
Per share—basic	2.91	5.14	3.65	2.32	3.13	2.91	2.81	2.63	2.95
Per share—diluted	2.88	5.06	3.62	2.31	3.11	2.89	2.80	2.62	2.94
Economic profit	307	720	629	502	530	429	404	270	NA
Financial Ratios									
Percent of sales									
Cost of goods sold	58.2%	57.0%	56.9%	57.3%	56.3%	57.4%	57.3%	57.3%	55.9%
Selling, general and administrative expenses	25.2	25.3	25.6	25.6	26.5	26.4	26.8	26.3	25.9
Operating income	13.6	17.7	17.5	16.5	17.2	16.2	16.7	16.4	18.2
Income from continuing operations	8.1	14.1	10.7	9.7	9.9	10.3	10.3	9.6	10.8
Return on invested capital	13.0%	18.0%	17.3%	16.3%	17.4%	16.0%	16.8%	16.1%	NA
Return on average stockholders' equity	19.7	34.1	24.4	19.2	18.2	17.3	17.3	15.9	18.6
Total debt to total capital	34	30	24	23	22	19	18	19	20
Current ratio	1.4	1.5	1.8	1.8	1.8	1.8	1.8	1.7	1.6

*1998 results include a restructuring charge of $493 million ($313 million after tax) or 77 cents per diluted share, and an extraordinary loss on early extinguishment of debt of $38 million (net of tax), or 9 cents per diluted share.

†1997 results include a gain of $803 million ($495 million after tax), or $1.18 per diluted share, on the sale of National Advertising Company.

Exhibit 2   Selected Policies and Philosophies of 3M†

15 percent option:	Many employees have the option to spend up to 15 percent of their work week pursuing individual projects of their own choice.
30 percent rule:	Thirty percent of business unit revenues must come from products introduced in the last four years. Business unit bonuses are based on how successfully each manager achieves this goal.
Dual-ladder career path:	There are two career ladders, a technical career ladder and a management career ladder. Both allow advancement while allowing employees to stay focused on their research and professional interests.
Genesis Grants:	Provides awards up to $50,000 to employees to conduct independent research, product development, and test marketing in areas of emerging technology. About 90 such awards are given each year.
Carlton Award:	This technical honor society honors 3M technical employees who have made large contributions to 3M through fundamental technical innovation.
Golden Step program:	Awards cross-functional teams within 3M who successfully launch new business ventures.
3 tiered research:	*Business Unit Laboratories:* Focuses on specific markets, with near-term products.
	Sector Laboratories: Focuses on applications with a 3-to-10-year time horizon for product viability.
	Corporate Laboratories: Focuses on basic research with a time horizon of as much as 20 years.
Knowledge Sharing:	3M supports formal and informal forums for sharing knowledge throughout the company. Includes extensive e-mail directories, sharing of new products introduced by a business unit, and awards for successful sharing of new technology between business units.
Customer contact:	Scientists are regularly sent into the field to meet with customers and see how the customers are using 3M's products. Also, customers are frequently invited to participate in generating product ideas with 3M scientists.
Intrapreneurs:	Product inventors recruit action teams to develop the product. The team is allowed to champion the product, grow its business, and develop line extensions. As the product achieves certain revenue goals, the team members receive raises and promotions. Those on the management track become project managers, department managers, and then division managers as the product line revenues grow.
Tolerance for Failure:	Company culture emphasizes that a failure can turn into a success. There is no punishment for a product failing in the market. 3M has developed a series of legends around famous failures that have made good, such as the weak adhesive that became the adhesive for Post-it Notes.
Small Business Units:	Business units are split up after they reach a size of approximately $200 to $300 million. It is required that the business unit managers know the names of everyone who works for them.
Profit Sharing:	Almost all of 3M employees are entitled to the profit sharing plan.
R&D Spending:	3M spends approximately 6.5 percent to 7 percent of sales on research and development, and has consistently increased R&D spending over the last two decades.

---

†These policies and philosophies are summarized in the following sources: James C. Collins and Jerry I. Porras, *Built to Last: Successful Habits of Visionary Companies* (New York: HarperBusiness, 1995), pp. 156–58, Ronald A. Mitsch, "Three Roads to Innovation," *The Journal of Business Strategy,* September/October 1990, pp. 18–21.

CASE 12–4
TEXAS INSTRUMENTS AND HEWLETT-PACKARD

Texas Instruments (TI) and Hewlett-Packard (HP) developed, manufactured, and sold high technology electric and electronic products. Texas Instruments had three main lines of business in 1984: *components,* which included semiconductor integrated circuits, semiconductor subassemblies, and electronic control devices; *digital products,* which included minicomputers, personal computers, scientific instruments, and calculators; and *government electronics,* which included radar systems, missile guidance and control systems, and infrared surveillance systems. The three businesses generated 46 percent, 19 percent, and 24 percent, respectively, of TI's sales in 1984. Hewlett-Packard operated in two main lines of business: *computer products,* which included factory automation computers, engineering workstations, data terminals, personal computers, and calculators; and *electronic test and measurement systems,* which included instruments that were used to evaluate the operation of electrical equipment against standards, instruments that would measure and display electronic signals, voltmeters, and oscilloscopes. These businesses generated 53 percent and 37 percent, respectively, of HP's 1984 sales. Summary financial information for each company is presented in Exhibit 1.

Although Texas Instruments and Hewlett-Packard competed in similar industries, the strategies chosen by these two firms were very different. Exhibit 2 summarizes five major concepts related to the content of strategy for both Texas Instruments and Hewlett-Packard. Per-

Reprinted by permission of Steven C. Wheelright, "Strategy, Management, and Strategic Planning Approaches," *Interfaces,* January–February 1984, pp. 19–33. Copyright 1984 by the Operations Research Society of America and The Institute of Management Sciences, 290 Westminster Street, Providence, Rhode Island 02903, USA.

EXHIBIT 1   Summary Financial Information
($ in millions)

Texas Instruments

	1980	1981	1982	1983	1984
Assets	$2,414	$2,311	$2,631	$2,713	$3,423
Equity	1,165	1,260	1,361	1,203	1,541
Sales	4,075	4,206	4,327	4,580	5,742
Operating profit	379	253	236	(288)	526
ROI	32.5%	20.1%	17.3%	n.a.	34.1%

Hewlett-Packard

	1980	1981	1982	1983	1984
Assets	$2,337	$2,782	$3,470	$4,161	$5,153
Equity	1,547	1,890	2,349	2,887	3,545
Sales	3,099	3,578	4,254	4,710	6,044
Operating profit	523	567	676	728	860
ROI	33.8%	30.1%	28.8%	25.2%	24.2%

haps the most significant distinction between TI and HP was their generic business and functional strategies (Exhibit 2). They pursued very different approaches. TI preferred to pursue competitive advantage based on larger, more standard markets and a long-term, low-cost position. HP, on the other hand, sought competitive advantage in selected smaller markets based on unique, high-value, high-feature products. The functional strategies used to support those desired competitive advantages also differed.

With regard to the product life cycle (Exhibit 3), TI favored early entry, followed by expansion and consolidation of its position, resulting in a dominant market share when the product matured. HP, on the other hand, tended to create new markets, but then exited (or introduced

EXHIBIT 2   Contrasting Strategies of TI and HP

	Texas Instruments	Hewlett-Packard
	Business Strategy	
	Competitive advantage for large, standard markets based on long-run cost position	Competitive advantage for selected small markets based on unique, high value/high features products
	Functional Strategy	
Marketing:	High volume/low price Rapid growth Standard products	High value/high price Controlled growth Custom features
Manufacturing:	Scale economies and learning curve Vertical integration Large, low-cost locations	Delivery and quality driven Limited vertical integration Small, attractive locations
R&D:	Process and product Cost driven Design to cost	Product only Features and quality driven Design to performance
Financial:	Aggressive Higher debt Tight ship	Conservative No debt Margin of safety (slack)

EXHIBIT 3   *Differences in strategy between Texas Instruments and Hewlett-Packard*

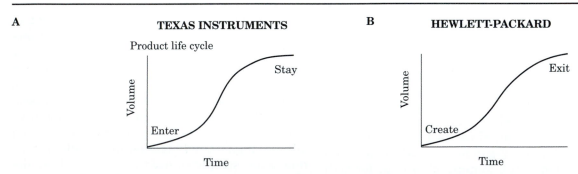

TI tended to enter early in a product's life cycle, and stayed through maturity. HP tended to create a new product and then replaced it when it matured.

C   **Costs and Prices (Learning Curve)**   **D**

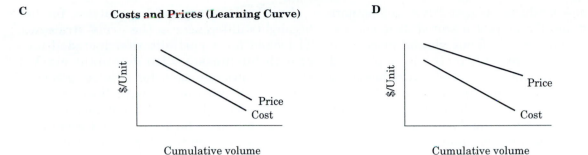

TI emphasized aggressive cost improvements, with equally aggressive price cuts. HP desired cost improvements, but sought higher margins and held prices longer.

E   **Product/Process Matrix**   **F**

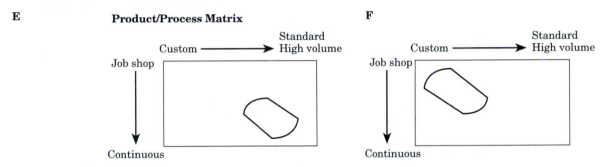

TI concentrated on more capital-intensive, cost-effective production processes to match high-volume, standard product needs. HP concentrated on flexible production processes to match low-volume, more custom product needs.

G   **Portfolio: Positioning and Resource Movement**   **H**

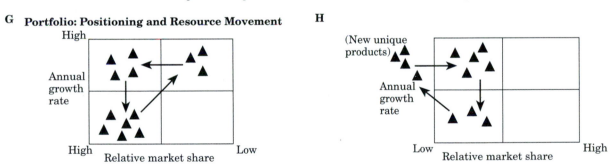

TI sought a balanced portfolio of businesses where mature, large businesses provide resources for young, high-growth businesses. HP sought all high-growth, high-margin businesses that met their own resource needs, largely on an individual basis.

other new products) as cost-driven competitors entered and the market matured. It is not surprising that the two firms viewed prices and costs, the third area, differently. TI emphasized continual price cuts to parallel cost reduction in order to build volume and take advantage of shared experience and learning. HP, on the other hand, put less emphasis on manufacturing cost reductions and held prices longer so that profit margins expanded during the initial periods. The early returns generated allowed early exit from the market with good returns on investment and provided funds for further product research and development.

A fourth concept that highlights their differences in strategy is the product process matrix, which matches the product life cycle with its production counterpart, the process life cycle. HP concentrated on more flexible production processes (such as job shop and batch operations) to meet the needs of its custom and low-volume markets, while TI concentrated on more capital-intensive and cost-effective production processes (assembly lines and continuous flow operations) to supply its more standard, high-volume markets.

A fifth concept, portfolio analysis, further highlights differences in the firms' strategies. TI looked for a portfolio that included low-growth businesses with dominant market shares to provide cash for a select group of high-growth businesses with lower market shares but with the prospect of becoming dominant, high-growth businesses, and eventually "cash cows." HP, on the other hand, wanted all high-growth businesses with dominant market shares, and to reallocate major resources only to fund new businesses. In fact, the traditional solution to any profit problem at HP had been new products and new businesses.

Question

Given the differences in strategy between the two firms, what would you expect would be the differences between TI and HP in their planning and control systems: strategic planning systems; budgeting systems; reporting systems; performance evaluation systems; and incentive compensation systems?

CASE 12–5
TEXAS INSTRUMENTS

Paul Elmer, vice president for corporate planning at Harvey-Hudson Electronics (HHE), pushed the papers away from him and leaned back in his chair. Mr. Elmer had been reviewing his files on Texas Instruments, Inc. (TI), and its complex and much-talked-about set of management systems. His hope was that he could learn enough about TI's systems to be able to assess whether a similar system should be considered for use at HHE.

Over the past several weeks, he and several of his immediate subordinates had been poring over various documents, articles, annual reports, and brochures dealing with TI and its management systems. Soon, they would need to pull their thoughts together and come to some conclusions about how well they understood the various systems and about the strengths and weaknesses associated with them.

TI—Some Overview Points

Texas Instruments was a multinational corporation producing a wide variety of products, virtually all of which had a tie of some kind to the electronics industry. In addition to its US plants, TI maintained facilities in Canada, Latin America, Europe, Australia, and the Far East. Around one-third of sales came from outside the United States.[1] Worldwide employment was 85,000.[2]

Since 1946, sales at TI had grown at an average annual rate of 24 percent. Profits had outpaced the sales figure, increasing between 1971 and 1980 at an average annual rate of 34 percent.

The electronics industry was expected to boom in the 1980s, reaching the $280 billion mark by the later part of the decade.[3] TI's sales were expected to increase significantly as a result of lower prices and, therefore, higher volume. The pattern of fast growth in the electronics industry, however, posed a challenge for each firm in the industry—how to balance the amount of relative priority accorded to innovation versus volume. A typical product/price life cycle pattern began with the introduction of a new product into the market at small volume and at high prices. In the presence of sufficient demand, volume quickly expanded, resulting in lower unit costs and a corresponding reduction in prices. Given the above situation, the value of inventories could drop dramatically in a matter of months. Such a scenario would require steady write-downs in inventory valuation. Equipment to deal with specialized products posed another problem. Because of rapid technological turnover, a machine had to pay out in a short time or else become unaffordable. Therefore, there was a basic conflict between production and innovation—in other words, expenditures for research versus production. TI's approach to this dilemma was quite succinct. "TI [was] determined to lead in both."[4]

This case was prepared from published sources by Donna Bergstedt, Research Assistant, and Professor M. Edgar Barrett. Copyright © by M. Edgar Barrett.

[1] L. M. Rice Jr., "Texas Instruments Management Philosophies and Growth Experience," remarks to Instituto Panamericano de Alta Direccion de Empresa, Mexico, Texas Instruments, Inc., May 1980, p. 1.
[2] Ibid.

[3] Floyd G. Lawrence, "Could This Be America's Best-Managed Company? Part II—Texas Instruments Is Determined to Grow and Never to Grow Old," *Today's Manager,* May–June 1977, p. 5.
[4] Ibid.

Company History[5]

Growth at Texas Instruments had been based on innovation as opposed to acquisitions. With the exception of the 1959 merger with Metals and Controls Corporation, TI's growth had come primarily from the sales revenues resulting from the internal development of new products and services. In 1980, sales at TI reached $4.1 billion, and net income was $212 million.

TI had been a technologically based company throughout its history. It originated in 1930 as Geophysical Services Inc. (GSI). The primary activities of GSI focused on the discovery of petroleum reserves throughout the world.

This was accomplished by means of reflection seismology, which had been invented by the organization's first president and founder, Dr. J. C. Karcher. The importance of petroleum as a resource helped maintain GSI's growth even during the Depression and eventually led the company into the international arena. By 1946, GSI had 16 geophysical crews operating in different countries throughout the world and billings of $2.25 million.[6] Nearly all of these billings related to the original innovation—seismology.

In 1946, Patrick E. Haggerty joined TI (still GSI). Under his influence the company began to formulate a new objective, the purpose of which was to move the organization beyond geophysical exploration into engineering and manufacturing.

The strategy which was most influential centered around the development of semiconductors. By 1956, work had progressed sufficiently so as to prompt management to begin to play with the idea of producing whole circuits processed on tiny wafers of pure silicon. In 1958, Jack Kilby of TI created the first practical integrated circuit.

Around 1959, management at TI began to believe that a pattern existed in the strategic development of its innovative successes. They further believed that innovation was necessary not only in the creation of improved products but also in the method of developing and marketing such products. This belief eventually led to the development of the "OST System."

By the early 1980s, TI was engaged in activities in four major areas: (1) electronics, (2) geophysical exploration, (3) government electronics, and (4) nonelectronic industry products. In the field of electronics, TI concentrated on three major growth areas which centered around (1) *Semi-Conductor Devices,* (2) *Distributed Computing,* and (3) *Consumer Electronics.* The first area was to be focused upon because it constituted the foundation of the electronics revolution. Distributed computing would place data processing systems within businesses and factories as need required. The last area was thought to offer the potential for lucrative markets in the 1980s.[7]

Corporate Culture

A strong internal culture had developed at Texas Instruments and was considered by top management to be a key factor in the company's success. This culture stressed hard work, loyalty to the corporation, and team spirit. It was sustained in part by its practice of hiring 80 percent of its professional workers directly out of school and socializing them according to the rather rigorous norms of the organization.[8] It was also supported by the company's emphasis on internal growth in contrast to acquisitions. Few executives were brought into the organization at the middle or top management levels. According to one TI vice president, "The TI culture is a religion . . . the climate

---

[5]Patrick E. Haggerty, "Three Lectures at the Salzburg Seminar on Multinational Enterprise," Texas Instruments, Inc., February 1977. This source has been used extensively as background for this section as well as for much of the remainder of the case.
[6]Haggerty, "Three Lectures," p. 9.

[7]"Texas Instruments Shows U.S. Business," p. 70.
[8]Bro Uttal, "Texas Instruments Wrestles with the Consumer Market," *Fortune,* December 3, 1979, p. 51.

polarizes people—either you are incorporated into the culture or rejected."[9]

TI's ability to make the firm's management systems work seemed to stem partly from the atmosphere created by this culture. TI had been compared by some to a Japanese company in terms of management style. This comparison was not viewed unfavorably by TI's senior managers. In the words of J. Fred Bucy, TI's president:

> Japan has a culture and society well suited to achieving increased productivity and the growth that results from it. They are hardworking, dedicated people . . . and are highly motivated, in part, because of a culture that assigns personal responsibility for the quality of work. . . . There is a strong tendency in the Japanese culture to align personal goals with goals set by their companies.[10]

Organizational Structure

Although technological in orientation, TI produced a wide variety of products. By 1980, the firm had divided its line management structure into six groups for the sake of operational flexibility. These groups are illustrated in Exhibit 1 and were arranged in the following manner: (1) Semiconductor Products; (2) Distributed Computing Products; (3) Consumer Electronic Products; (4) Materials and Electrical Products; (5) Government Electronic Products; and (6) Geophysical Exploration Services. In charge of each group was a senior manager who reported directly to the president. These top-level managers were responsible for the worldwide strategic direction of their businesses, as well as for the regular, daily management functions.

Each group was further subdivided into divisions, which were, in turn, broken down into product customer centers (PCCs). A PCC was considered to be a complete business unit responsible for a particular family of products or services targeted at a specific market segment. The PCC manager assumed a profit and loss

responsibility. As of 1980, there were more than 80[11] PCCs within TI. These PCCs were said to be designed in such a way as to allow the firm to have a close relationship with customers. They were also designed to provide entrepreneurial experience for the firm's middle managers.

Objectives, Strategies, and Tactics[12]

The OST System evolved at TI as a system for managing change and innovation. The system, known as the OST System (for objectives, strategies, and tactics) was employed to define the strategies the company intended to follow for further growth and development and to identify the tactics required to successfully implement such strategies. These tactics were set forth in a quantitative manner so that performance could be measured against agreed-upon quantitative goals. The system allowed for a clear separation of strategic and operational activities.

The OST System can be more easily understood if viewed in three stages. The first stage is a presentation of the hierarchy of goals. The second explains the dual responsibility of line management. The third stage discusses the impact of a matrix organization composed of strategic and operating modes.

Hierarchy of Goals.   The Hierarchy of Goals requires that a single statement of quantitative goals be made at the top of the organization and that that statement be supported in a hierarchical or pyramidal fashion by strategies and tactics. This hierarchy is illustrated in Exhibits 2 and 3.

At the top of the structure is the corporate objective. This is an overall statement of what

[9]"Texas Instruments Shows U.S. Business," p. 68.
[10]Ibid.

[11]Rice, "Texas Instruments Management Philosophies," p. 11.
[12]Speeches by Mr. Grant A. Dove of TI at the London School of Business Studies, May 22, 1970, and Haggerty, "Three Lectures," were used extensively in the preparation of this section.

EXHIBIT 1

Organizational structure

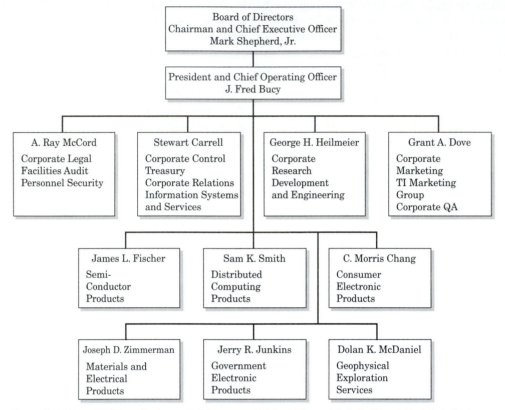

Source: L. M. Rice, Jr., "Texas Instruments Management Philosophies and Growth Experience," remarks to Instituto Panamericano de Alta Direccion de Empresa, Mexico, Texas Instruments Inc., May 1980, p. 2.

the company hopes to achieve considering its products, markets, and its perception of the expectations of society. It claims to define the financial goals desired by the company in the context of its responsibilities to shareholders, employees, and society as a whole.

At the next level in the hierarchy are business objectives which describe long-range opportunities in different business areas. Each business objective expresses: (1) the goal of the individual business; (2) the boundaries of that business; (3) an appraisal of potential opportunities; (4) a study of the technical and market trends relating to that business; and (5) an overview of the industry structure and foreseeable trends within the industry.

Performance measures are also established at the business objective level which include such indicators as sales goals, expected profits, return on assets, and market penetration in terms of percentage of served available market. Business objectives relate to 5- and 10-year periods extending into the future. Expectations for the first two years are broken down into quarters; the others remain in annual terms.

Each business objective is reviewed at least once a year in order to adjust the objective for successes or failures of TI or competitors and

EXHIBIT 2

A hierarchy of goals

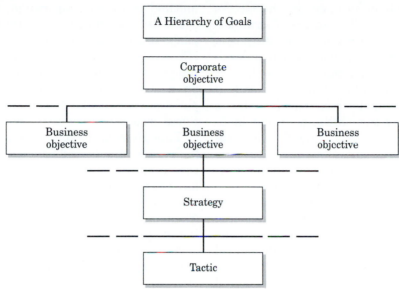

Source: E. W. Helms, "Texas Instruments Objectives, Strategies and Tactics System," remarks to Instituto Panamericano de Alta Direccion de Empresa, Mexico, Texas Instruments, Inc., May 1980, p. 3.

EXHIBIT 3

The hierarchy of goals within the OST structure

Source: E. W. Helms, "Texas Instruments Objectives, Strategies and Tactics System," remarks to Instituto Panamericano de Alta Direccion de Empresa, Mexico, Texas Instruments, Inc., May 1980, p. 3.

for changes in the economic environment. Business objectives are also adjusted if they are perceived as being not ambitious enough. In a speech, Mr. Grant A. Dove expressed this in the following manner.

> We expect the objective to be challenging enough, even shocking enough to force a radical rethinking of the strategies and tactics. For example, any time we have enough well-defined strategies to give us a high confidence level in exceeding the goals stated in a business objective, then that business objective probably is not ambitious enough, and the probability of truly innovative strategic thinking is likely to be low.[13]

The third level in the hierarchy is composed of strategies which support the business objectives.

---

[13]Grant A. Dove, speech presented at the London School of Business Studies, May 22, 1970.

The strategies focus on the economic and opportunity environment and ask one question—What action is necessary in order to ensure the success of the firm's objectives? The process of formulating strategies involves a competitive analysis, a thorough study of market opportunity in order to estimate the potential for market growth, contingency planning for unforeseen events, and an overall review of company resources in order to determine whether the skills, business techniques, and current markets of the firm are sufficient to support the strategy and ensure its success. If not, the innovations and commitments required to do so must be determined.

Major, long-run financial checkpoints are established at the strategy level to help determine if the company is progressing on schedule. The lifetime of a strategy statement extends several years into the future, usually 5 to 10 years.

Tactical Action Programs (TAPs) are found at the bottom level of the hierarchy. Several TAPs support each strategy, and each TAP is under the direction of a program manager. A TAP usually has a relatively short lifetime, from 6 to 18 months.

The TAP document is a detailed description of the quantitative goals set by the program and the resources necessary in terms of manpower and capital. It also delineates responsibility for different parts of the program and establishes a schedule of completion dates to which managers are committed. Overall, a TAP defines the contribution of the program to the strategy.

The level of detail becomes increasingly complex as one moves down the hierarchy. The TAP, which lies at the bottom of the hierarchy, is composed of individual work packages which serve as a base for planning and resource allocation within the OST System.

As of 1980, TI had 9 business objectives, over 60 strategies, and more than 250 TAPs.[14]

[14]E. W. Helms, "Texas Instruments Objectives, Strategies and Tactics System," remarks to Instituto Panamericano de Alta Direccion de Empresa, Mexico, Texas Instruments, May 1980, p. 6.

Dual Responsibility of Management.   The purpose of the OST System was to provide a method whereby long-range, strategic goals could become the prime motivator of the company, while still allowing the company to deal effectively with day-to-day operations. TI's attempt to combine this long-run and short-run orientation is reflected by their method of superimposing the OST System onto the traditional corporate structure. (See Exhibit 4.)

This gives management a responsibility for both a "strategic" and an "operating" mode. In this manner, a manager of a PCC may also have responsibility for a TAP; a division manager may also be a strategy manager; and a group manager may also be in charge of managing the progress of a business objective.

About 75 percent of the managers at TI are responsible for both a strategic mode and an operating mode.[15] TI feels that this gives balance to long-term growth and short-term profitability, which often are in conflict. (See Exhibit 5.)

TI's apparent philosophy is that by assigning dual responsibility to managers they will force these managers to apportion their time in such a manner so as not to overlook the long-term innovative needs of the firm. These managers will be "wearing two hats," with goals of both growth and profitability.

In the operating mode, a manager is first concerned with the current operating results within the unit. In other words, the manager is primarily concerned with short-term profitability. Performance is measured according to planned operating profits. In the strategic mode, the manager is concerned with the success of his or her specific strategy. This specific strategy, in turn, is a part of the long-range plan set forth under the OST System. As such, the manager will be measured according to the speed and effectiveness of the utilization of the OST budgeted expenses.

One of the responsibilities of a strategy manager is the identification of the different

[15]Dove, speech at London School of Business Studies.

EXHIBIT 4

Dual responsibility of management

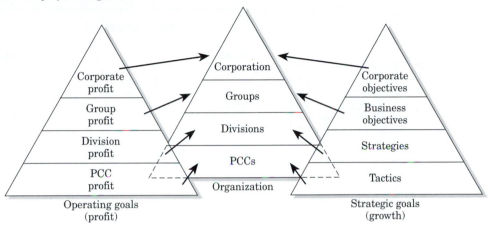

Operating goals
(profit)

Strategic goals
(growth)

Source: E. W. Helms, "Texas Instruments Objectives, Strategies and Tactics System," remarks to Instituto Panamericano de Alta Direccion de Empresa, Mexico, Texas Instruments, Inc., May 1980, p. 7

EXHIBIT 5

Conflict between strategic and operating mode

Strategic mode	Operating mode
Long-range-oriented	Short-range-oriented
Stable	Flexible
Aligned with corporate objectives	Aligned with operating necessities
Responsible for progress on strategic activities	Responsible for operating profit
Articulates growth viewpoint	Articulates profit viewpoint

←——— Conflict ———→

Competition for critical resources
Marketing pricing policies
Distribution of operating/strategic cost

Source: E. W. Helms, "Texas Instruments Objectives, Strategies and Tactics System," remarks to Instituto Panamericano de Alta Direccion de Empresa, Mexico, Texas Instruments, Inc., May 1980, p. 10.

TAPs necessary for the achievement of the strategy. The manager must pull together from across the company the TAPs necessary in the structuring of a coordinated strategic plan. In such a case, the "strategic" responsibility of the manager may exceed his or her "operating" authority. The manager may well be required to gain the cooperation of other operating units in order to fully execute the strategic role.

Exhibit 6

Matrix composed of the operating and strategic mode

	OBJ	STRAT	TAP	OPERATING MODE						
				GROUP 1					GROUP 2	
				Division A			Division B		Division C	
				PCC1	PCC2	PCC3	PCC4	PCC5	PCC6	PCC7
STRATEGIC MODE			1			X				
			2					X		
		A	3						X	
	1		4		X					
			5					X		
		B	6				X			
			7	X						
			8	X						
	2	C	9							X

Source: E. W. Helms, "Texas Instruments Objectives, Strategies and Tactics System," remarks to Instituto Panamericano de Alta Direccion de Empresa, Mexico, Texas Instruments, Inc., May 1980, p. 7.

Impact of Dual Mode Structure. An easy way to visualize the functioning of this dual system is by comparison to a matrix organization. A traditional matrix organization is arranged so that the project organization overlaps the functional operating structure. Any one project may involve one task in a single operating unit or require the completion of many tasks which cut across several different operating units. The system at TI differs in that the overlap shows the relationship between the strategic and the operating mode. (See Exhibit 6.)

Any one strategy may require TAPs to be completed across several PCCs but within one division and one group, or it may require resources from across several divisions, groups, and the corresponding PCCs. For example, Strategy A requires four TAPs. TAP 1 is to be completed in Group One, Division A, and PCC 3. TAP 3 will find the necessary resources in Group 2, Division C, and PCC 6. The other two TAPs will be channeled to the appropriate operating unit in the same manner. In this way, a strategic program can be implemented without creating a new organizational structure. This is done by identifying the resources necessary for the completion of the strategy and locating the appropriate TAPs in those PCCs that can supply the necessary resources and skills.

Resource Allocation System

The distinction between the operating and strategic mode was also apparent in the resource allocation system at TI. Funding for each of the two functions responded to the profitability of the firm but was in large part a top-level decision concerning the desired trade-off between long-term and short-term goals. The result of this distinction was the preparation of two budgets—one for operating expenses and the other for OST funds. In addition, the internal operating statements showed operating and strategic expense as two separate line items.

EXHIBIT 7

Planning cycle

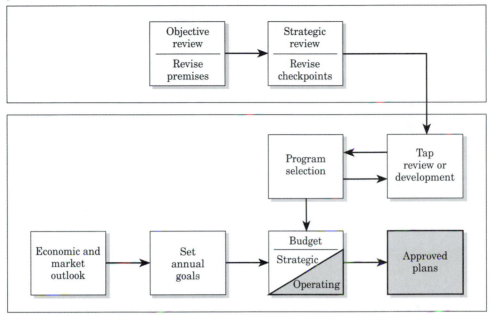

Source: E. W. Helms, "Texas Instruments Objectives, Strategies and Tactics System," remarks to Instituto Panamericano de Alta Direccion de Empresa, Mexico, Texas Instruments, Inc., May 1980, p. 13.

Planning Cycle. In the third quarter of the year, a corporate development committee reached a decision on the amount of OST funding necessary for the forthcoming year. (See Exhibit 7.)

This decision was based on an analysis of the economic and market outlook which was translated into annual goals. Funds assigned to the strategic mode were allocated by a method called "decision package ranking." Funds assigned to the operating mode were distributed according to a technique called zero-based budgeting.

Strategic Funds. The OST funds were allocated among the business objectives using each objective's long-term opportunities, momentum, and priorities as decision criteria. TI felt that the continual review of objectives, strategies,

and tactics kept the OST System up-to-date as a strategic map of the firm's long-term goals and expectations.

Decision package ranking involved several steps. Tactics, as did objectives and strategies, had to be adjusted for any environmental change or directional change in the company's long-term focus. New TAPs had to be generated to fill in any gaps that may have been discovered leading to the desired long-term goals. These TAPs then were ordered into decision packages. "A decision package is so called because it contains all the resources necessary to implement the innovation."[16] The strategy manager then rank ordered these packages by importance. A cutoff line was drawn based on

---

[16]Haggerty, "Three Lectures," p. 33.

EXHIBIT 8

Decision package ranking

```
          DECISION PACKAGE RANKING
    RANK   PROGRAM    COST
     1        A       $XXX     CUMULATIVE
                               COST CUTOFF
     2        Q        XXX     AT DISCRETIONARY
     3        K        XXX     FUNDING LEVEL
     •                  •
     •                  •
     ▼       etc.      ▼        ▼
  ─────────────────────────────
    447       X       $XXX  ⎤
                           ⎥  CREATIVE
    448       Y        XXX  ⎥
                           ⎥  BACKLOG
    449       Z        XXX  ⎦
             etc.
```

Source: Patrick E. Haggerty, "Three Lectures at the Salzburg Seminar on Multinational Enterprise," Texas Instruments Inc., February 1977, p. 34

the amount of funds made available to the business objectives and individual strategies. Those packages falling above the line received funding while those falling below were put into a "creative backlog." (See Exhibit 8.)

The creative backlog was composed of decision packages which could be funded when additional funds became available or through a direct decision package funding from the corporate level. A small percentage of the OST funds (once cited as being 10 percent) were retained at the corporate level for this purpose and for new opportunities which might arise over time.

The entire procedure was repeated at the objective level in order to adjust the allocation of funds among the objective's strategies. In the same manner as with tactical decision packages, the managers responsible for strategic decision packages had the opportunity to request another review in order to receive special funding in one case that they fell below one cutoff line and were of special potential. TI felt that

this allowed them to undertake new ventures which could normally not have been considered.

Operating Funds.   Funds allocated to the operating budget were distributed among projects and departments by means of a technique called zero-based budgeting (ZBB). A company using ZBB requires of each division or section an annual report which justifies their budgeting requirements for the year. ZBB can be compared to the traditional budgeting approach, which is incremental in nature. The traditional approach seeks to identify planned changes from the previous year's expenditure level and then simply adds the additional funds necessary to the previous year's budget. In contrast, managers using ZBB must start from scratch each year in identifying the funds necessary for the smooth operation of the business unit and then must justify this need. TI believed that, while the process required a great deal of effort to implement, it fulfilled the purpose of an increased managerial involvement in the budgeting process. They also felt that it gave visibility to the use and need of funds in an operating unit and, therefore, resulted in increased efficiency in the resource allocation process.

Timing of Planning Cycle.   TI followed what they called a "four-loop planning system" in order to explain the time base of the planning cycle and for organizing activities within the corporation. (See Exhibit 9.)[17] Mr. L. M. Rice, group vice president at TI, offered an explanation of this system:

> The first loop is *long-range planning*. Its focal point is our annual Strategic Planning Conference, where we concentrate on where we are going over the next 10 years. In addition to setting measurable quantitative goals, this planning emphasizes projections of markets and products and the technology advances required to impact those areas.

---

[17]Rice, "Texas Instruments Management Philosophies," p. 13.

EXHIBIT 9

Four-loop planning system

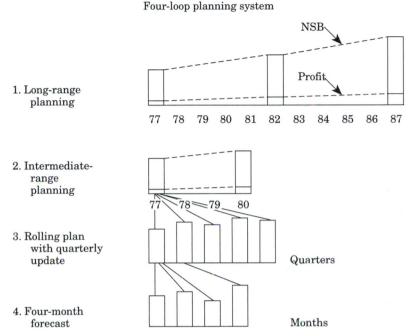

Four-loop planning system

1. Long-range
   planning

2. Intermediate-
   range
   planning

3. Rolling plan
   with quarterly
   update

4. Four-month
   forecast

Source: L. M. Rice, Jr., "Texas Instruments Management Philosophies and Growth
Experience," remarks to Instituto Panamericano de Alta Direccion de Empresa, Mexico, Texas
Instruments Inc., May 1980, p. 13.

The second loop is *intermediate-range planning*. In planning facilities, manufacturing equipment, products, and cost reduction, one year is too short, and 10 years is too long. The intermediate loop fills the gap by concentrating on the current year plus three years ahead. Authorizations for new products, personnel additions, and capital expenditures are based on the intermediate-loop plan. In this second loop, the current year plus one is critical because it ties strategic, intermediate, and rolling planning together.

The third loop is the *"rolling plan,"* a quarterly update of the current year and the coming year. Rolling plans are our prime mechanism for operating in near real time, with quick response to changing business conditions.

The fourth loop is the *four-month forecast* cycle. This is a monthly operational planning effort that originates at the profit center level and consolidates to the corporate level. It constitutes TI's real-time error detection and control mechanism for near-term profitability.

For each of these loops, financial models and plans are used to forecast and measure performance. The models and plans are supported by computerized management systems to handle the data in as close to real time as possible. With these computerized systems, both the immediate and long-term impact of changes may be quickly evaluated and actions taken as required.[18]

The Reporting System

The Reporting System at TI separated operating expenses from strategic expenses on the income statement as illustrated in Exhibit 10.

Managers assumed responsibility for these differing expenses depending on their role in

_____
[18]Ibid.

EXHIBIT 10

Separation of strategic and operating expenses on the profit and loss statement

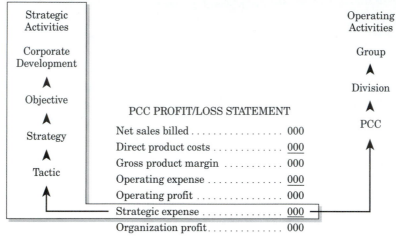

Source: Patrick E. Haggerty, "Three Lectures at the Salzburg Seminar on Multinational Enterprise," Texas Instruments Inc., February 1977, p. 33.

the organization, that is, on whether they were strategy managers, operating managers (e.g., PCC manager), or both.

Progress was reviewed at successively higher levels in the organization in both modes. Accountability passed from the TAP to strategy to objective level in the strategic mode and from the PCC to division to group level in the operating mode. Monthly status reports of each TAP were distributed at all levels of the OST System, which allowed for a quick appraisal of a TAP's progress relative to several criteria (i.e., budget, scheduling, personnel, facilities).

Managers increasingly tended to assume both responsibilities as they moved up in the organization. It should also be noted that, in contrast to the operating expense, it was most often considered desirable to have spent the full amount of the budgeted strategic expense. To TI, this indicated expenditures in terms of innovative programs.

A difficulty in implementing such a system arose in one definition of what constituted an OST expense. TI attempted to resolve this prob-

lem by asking group managers to list those expenses which they viewed as "discretionary." Although the group managers were not in general agreement concerning the matter, TI felt that the approach was valid as long as there was some general consistency in terms of the definition used.

Incentive Compensation System

The two formal aspects of the overall incentive compensation system at TI were (1) the Key Personnel Analysis (KPA) system and (2) a stock-option plan.

KPA.[19]   The KPA System, by means of an annual comparative assessment of individual TIers, seeks to identify those managers who have, by their performance, contributed most to the company. The process of identifying those in-

---

[19]This section is paraphrased from a speech given by Grant A. Dove at the London School of Business Studies, May 22, 1970.

dividuals begins at the bottom level of management with the immediate supervisor. Individuals at this level are rank ordered on the basis of their relative contribution to the firm. The ranks are then combined across the department.

This procedure is repeated at successive levels of the organization until the department level is reached. At this point, the department manager identifies those people whom he judges as having made equal contributions to the firm regardless of their specific function and job level. These "equal" people are called "benchmark" people. The purpose of benchmarking is to allow the various sets of rankings to be merged into a single departmental ranking. From here, each individual is categorized into one of five comparative rating groups. Those in the top 20 percent group are then paired-compared in order to produce a new rank-ordering. These "benchmarking" and "pair-compare" procedures are then repeated at the division and group levels.

Bonuses are awarded to individual TIers in response to their contribution to the firm as reflected by the rankings. Up to 20 percent of the employees receive a bonus in addition to the regular adjustment to their base salary. Even though the majority of bonuses are given to managers at the upper management levels, the KPA System forces an examination of all levels.

Stock-Option Plan.   TI's second form of incentive compensation is its stock-option plan. Participants in the plan are required to remain with the firm a certain number of years in order to be eligible. The award of a certain number of shares of the firm's stock is further tied to the attainment of a target EPS figure per year.

Several other programs have been installed in an attempt to increase productivity at all levels in the organization.

IDEA.   TI attempts to recognize the fact that good ideas often come from those employees directly engaged in the production of its products.

A program dubbed "IDEA" has been introduced in an attempt to draw out as many innovative ideas as possible. Grants up to $25,000[20] are distributed to employees with promising ideas involving a product or process improvement. A well-known result of this program is TI's "Speak and Spell," a talking, learning device for teaching spelling.

Executive Retirement.   Executives at TI are urged to retire at an early age, 55 years. The purpose of this policy is the assurance of competent management succession. The retired officers have the opportunity to use their skill and expertise in an advisory role, that of "Officer of the Board." The early retirement allows younger management more upward mobility, in that top positions are vacated earlier.

Operating Committee.   The Operating Committee dealt with operational as well as strategic issues and defined the OST budget for the forthcoming year. Two corporate-level committees allocated the OST funds. The two committees were: (1) the Corporate Development Committee and (2) the People and Asset Effectiveness Committee. (See Exhibit 11.)

The Corporate Development Committee was responsible for external business analysis and the initiation of new ventures which lay outside the current scope of business. In addition, it was in charge of a continual review of strategic activities.

The People and Asset Effectiveness Committee was responsible for reviewing potential productivity improvements of the firm based on leveraging the effective utilization of the firm's people and assets. On the "people effectiveness" side, TI had policies, such as educational and training programs, promotion from within, electronic aids for the office, reward based on merit and the posting of new job openings, the purpose of which was to motivate and involve the employees to give their utmost to the firm.

---

[20]"Texas Instruments Shows U.S. Business," p. 82.

EXHIBIT 11

Corporate committees

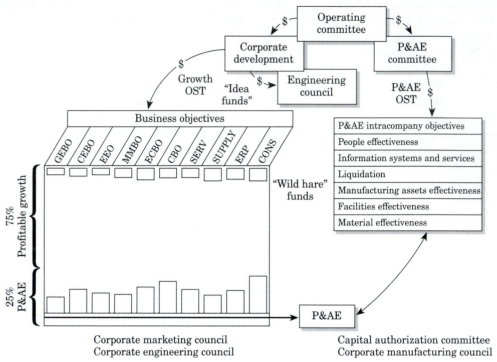

Corporate marketing council
Corporate engineering council

Capital authorization committee
Corporate manufacturing council

Source: Charles H. Phipps, "The OST System," Texas Instruments Inc., 1979, p. 14.

Progress in this latter area was measured with an index of "net sales billed/payroll plus benefits." TI believed this program to be a success, and TI management had been quoted as saying:

> It is a whole bunch of things acting synergistically. It's the attitudes, team improvement programs, the campus involvement, the open-door management policy, the non-structural pecking order. It's the unified goal approach—with everyone looking at his own piece of that goal. . . . [T]he key is flexibility. Two things people want in life. They want to achieve, and they want to be loved. And if you provide an atmosphere where these things can occur with a minimum amount of structure in the work flow, you are going to get what you want.[21]

TI believed in the intensive use of assets and remaining at the forefront of asset productivity by an aggressive asset renewal cycle. "Asset Effectiveness" was the second aspect of the People and Asset Effectiveness Program. Progress in this area was measured by means of a ratio of "net income (after tax)/average assets."[22]

Conclusion

Mr. Elmer had already called a meeting of his immediate subordinates, those who had been involved in the review of the TI material, for later in that same week in order to reach some

[21]"How Texas Instruments Turns Its People On," *Business Week,* September 29, 1973, p. 88.

[22]Rice, "Texas Instruments Management Philosophies," p. 14.

resolution as to whether HHE should adopt a similar system. A decision would involve completing their analysis of the OST System and assessing how well the system worked at TI. In addition, an analysis of industry characteristics and/or corporate objectives and policies which would be conducive to the success of such a system would be an important consideration in reaching a decision.

Questions

1. Summarize the major features of Texas Instruments' management systems. To what extent, and how, are these systems mutually reinforcing?

2. How does Texas Instruments ensure that its operating managers appropriately allocate their time between short term and long term?

3. Why do you believe the OST System worked so effectively for TI in the 70s? Why was it not working effectively for the company in the mid-to-late 80s?

4. Would systems like these be appropriate in other organizations, such as Harvey-Hudson Electronics? What implementation problems would you foresee?

13

SERVICE ORGANIZATIONS

Much of the discussion in the previous chapters referred, at least implicitly, to manufacturing organizations—that is, to organizations that produce and market tangible goods. In this chapter, we describe the management control process in service organizations—organizations that produce and market intangible services. We first discuss the characteristics that distinguish service organizations in general from manufacturing organizations. We then discuss the special problems that arise in professional, financial service, health care, and nonprofit organizations.

Service Organizations in General

In the 18th and the early part of the 19th century, the work force in the United States was predominantly in agriculture. After that, it was predominantly in manufacturing. Early in the 20th century, employment in the service sector overtook employment in the manufacturing sector. By 2000, service sector employment had grown to more than twice that of manufacturing. In this chapter we provide insights into management control systems for service organizations.

Characteristics

For several reasons, management control in service industries is somewhat different from management control in manufacturing companies. Some factors that have an impact on most service industries are discussed in this section. (Others, which are characteristics of particular service industries, are discussed later.) These factors apply also to the management control of legal, research and development, and other service departments in companies generally.

Absence of Inventory Buffer.   Goods can be held in inventory, which is a buffer that dampens the impact on production activity of fluctuations in sales volume. Services cannot be stored. The airplane seat, hotel room, hospital operating room, or the hours of lawyers, physicians, scientists, and other professionals that are not used today are gone forever. Thus, although a manufacturing company can earn revenue in the future from products that are on hand today, a service company cannot do so. It must try to minimize its unused capacity.

Moreover, the costs of many service organizations are essentially fixed in the short run. In the short run, a hotel cannot reduce its costs substantially by closing off some of its rooms. Accounting firms, law firms, and other professional organizations are reluctant to lay off professional personnel in times of low sales volume because of the effect on morale and the costs of rehiring and training.

A key variable in most service organizations, therefore, is the extent to which current capacity is matched with demand. Service organizations attempt this matching in two ways. First, they try to stimulate demand in off-peak periods by marketing efforts and price concessions. Cruise lines and resort hotels offer low rates in off seasons; airlines and hotels offer low rates on weekends; public utilities offer low rates on slack periods during the day. Second, if feasible, service organizations adjust the size of the work force to the anticipated demand by such measures as scheduling training activities in slack periods and compensating for long hours in busy periods with time off later. The loss from unsold services is so important that occupancy rates, "sold hours," load factors, student enrollment, hospital admissions, and similar indications of success in selling available services are normally key variables in service organizations.

Difficulty in Controlling Quality.   A manufacturing company can inspect its products before they are shipped to the consumer, and their quality can be measured visually or with instruments (tolerances, purity, weight, color, and so on). A service company cannot judge product quality until the moment the service is rendered, and then the judgments are often subjective. Restaurant management can examine the food in the kitchen, but customer satisfaction depends to a considerable extent on the way it is served. The quality of education is so difficult to measure that few educational organizations have a formal quality control system.

Labor Intensive.   Manufacturing companies add equipment and automate production lines, thereby replacing labor and reducing costs. Most service companies are labor intensive and cannot do this. Hospitals do add expensive equipment, but mostly to provide better treatment, and this increases costs. A law firm expands by adding partners and new support personnel.

Multi-Unit Organizations.   Some service organizations operate many units in various locations, each unit relatively small. These organizations are fast-food restaurant chains, auto rental companies, gasoline service stations, and many others. Some of the units are owned; others operate under a franchise. The similarity of the separate units provides a common basis for analyzing budgets and evaluating performance not available to the manufacturing company. The information for each unit can be compared with systemwide or regional averages, and high performers and low performers can be identified. However, because units differ in the mix of services they provide, in the resources that they use, and in other ways, care must be taken in making such comparisons.

Historical Development

Cost accounting started in manufacturing companies because of the need to value work-in-process and finished goods inventories for financial statement purposes. These systems provided raw data that were easily adapted for use in setting selling prices and for other management purposes. Standard cost systems, separation of fixed and variable costs, and analysis of variances were built on the foundation of cost accounting systems. Until a few decades ago, most texts on cost accounting dealt only with practices in manufacturing companies.

Many service organizations (with the notable exception of railroads and other regulated industries) did not have a similar impetus to develop cost data. Their use of product cost and other management accounting data is fairly recent—mostly since World War II. Nowadays, their management control systems are rapidly becoming as well developed as those in manufacturing companies.

Professional Service Organizations

Research and development organizations, law firms, accounting firms, health care organizations, engineering firms, architectural firms, consulting firms, advertising agencies, symphony and other arts organizations, and sports organizations (such as baseball teams) are examples of organizations whose products are professional services.

Special Characteristics

Goals.   As explained in Chapter 2, a dominant goal of a manufacturing company is to earn a satisfactory profit, specifically a satisfactory return on assets employed. A professional organization has relatively few tangible assets; its principal asset is the skill of its professional staff, which doesn't appear on its balance sheet. Return on assets employed, therefore, is essentially meaningless in such organizations. Their financial goal is to provide adequate compensation to the professionals.

In many organizations, a related goal is to increase their size. In part, this reflects the natural tendency to associate success with large size. In part, it reflects economies of scale in using the efforts of a central personnel staff and units responsible for keeping the organization up to date. Large public accounting firms need to have enough local offices to enable them to audit clients who have facilities located throughout the world.

Professionals.   Professional organizations are labor intensive, and the labor is of a special type. Many professionals prefer to work independently, rather than as part of a team. Professionals who are also managers tend to work only part time on management activities; senior partners in an accounting firm participate actively in audit engagements; senior partners in law firms have clients. Education for most professions does not include education in management, but quite naturally stresses the skills of the profession, rather than management; for this and other reasons, professionals tend to look down on managers. Professionals tend to give inadequate weight to the financial implications of their decisions; they want to do the best job they can, regardless of its cost. This attitude affects the attitude of support staffs and nonprofessionals in the organization; it leads to inadequate cost control.

Output and Input Measurement.   The output of a professional organization cannot be measured in physical terms, such as units, tons, or gallons. We can measure the number of hours a lawyer spends on a case, but this is a measure of input, not output. Output is the effectiveness of the lawyer's work, and this is not measured by the number of pages in a brief or the number of hours in the courtroom. We can measure the number of patients a physician treats in a day, and even classify these visits by type of complaint; but this is by no means equivalent to measuring the amount or quality of service the physician has provided. At most, what is measured is the physician's efficiency in treating patients, which is of some use in identifying slackers and hard workers. Revenues earned is one measure of output in some professional organizations; but these monetary amounts, at most, relate to the quantity of services rendered, not to their quality (although poor quality is reflected in reduced revenues in the long run).

> **Example.**   There are more than 1,300 articles and books dealing with research on student ratings of teachers. They describe as many as 22 dimensions of teaching performance (e.g., "explains clearly," "uses class time well") and 20 variables that affect the ratings (e.g., size of course, time of day, gender, level of course). The best of these rating systems can identify very good teachers and very poor teachers, but none do a satisfactory job of ranking the 70 or 80 percent of teachers who are not at these extremes.[1]

---

[1]Based on William E. Cashin, "Reliability, Validity, and Generalizability of Student Ratings of Instruction," *IDEA Paper no. 20,* Center for Faculty Evaluation and Development, Kansas State University, September 1988.

Furthermore, the work done by many professionals is nonrepetitive. No two consulting jobs or research and development projects are quite the same. This makes it difficult to plan the time required for a task, to set reasonable standards for task performance, and to judge how satisfactory the performance was. Some tasks are essentially repetitive: the drafting of simple wills, deeds, sales contracts, and similar documents; the taking of a physical inventory by an auditor; and certain medical and surgical procedures. The development of standards for such tasks may be worthwhile, although in using these standards, unusual circumstances that affect a specific job must be taken into account.

Some professionals, notably scientists, engineers, and professors, are reluctant to keep track of how they spend their time, and this complicates the task of measuring performance. This reluctance seems to have its roots in tradition; usually, it can be overcome if senior management is willing to put appropriate emphasis on the necessity of accurate time reporting. Nevertheless, difficult problems arise in deciding how time should be charged to clients. If the normal work week is 40 hours, should a job be charged for 1/40th of a week's compensation for each hour spent on it? If so, how should work done on evenings and weekends be counted? (Professionals are "exempt" employees—that is, they are not subject to government requirements for overtime payments.) How to account for time spent reading literature, going to meetings, and otherwise keeping up to date?

Small Size.   With a few exceptions, such as some law firms and accounting firms, professional organizations are relatively small and operate at a single location. Senior management in such organizations can personally observe what is going on and personally motivate employees. Thus, there is less need for a sophisticated management control system, with profit centers and formal performance reports. Nevertheless, even a small organization needs a budget, a regular comparison of performance against budget, and a way of relating compensation to performance.

Marketing.   In a manufacturing company there is a clear dividing line between marketing activities and production activities; only senior management is concerned with both. Such a clean separation does not exist in most professional organizations. In some, such as law, medicine, and accounting, the profession's ethical code limits the amount and character of overt marketing efforts by professionals (although these restrictions have been relaxed in recent years). Marketing is an essential activity in almost all organizations, however. If it can't be conducted openly, it takes the form of personal contacts, speeches, articles, conversations on the golf course, and so on. These marketing activities are conducted by professionals, usually by professionals who spend much of their time in production work—that is, working for clients.

In this situation, it is difficult to assign appropriate credit to the person responsible for "selling" a new customer. In a consulting firm, for example, a new engagement may result from a conversation between a member of the firm and an acquaintance in a company, or from the reputation of one of the firm's professionals as an outgrowth of speeches or articles. Moreover, the professional who is responsible for obtaining the engagement may not be personally involved in carrying it out. Until fairly recently, these marketing contributions were rewarded subjectively—that is, they were taken into account in promotion and compensation decisions. Some organizations now give explicit credit, perhaps as a percentage of the project's revenue, if the person who "sold" the project can be identified.

Management Control Systems

Pricing.   The selling price of work is set in a traditional way in many professional firms. If the profession is one in which members are accustomed to keeping track of their time, fees generally are related to professional time spent on the engagement. The hourly billing rate typically is based on the compensation of the grade of the professional (rather than the compensation of the specific person), plus a loading for overhead costs and profit. In other professions, such as investment banking, the fee typically is based on the monetary size of the security issue. In still others, there is a fixed price for the project. Prices vary widely among professions; they are relatively low for research scientists and relatively high for accountants and physicians.

In manufacturing companies, the profit component of the selling price is normally set so as to obtain, on average, a satisfactory return on assets employed. As noted above, the principal "asset" of a professional organization is the skill of its professionals, which is not measurable. Actually, the total value of the whole organization is greater than the sum of what the value of the individuals would be if they worked separately. This is because the firm already has incurred the cost of acquiring and training these individuals, has organized them according to their personality "fit" and other considerations, and has developed policies and procedures for assuring that the work is done efficiently and effectively. In this manner, the firm accepts responsibility for producing a satisfactory product, including the risk of loss if the work is not well done, and it absorbs the cost of personnel who are not working on revenue-producing work. These considerations implicitly affect the size of the "profit" component that is included in the fee.

Profit Centers and Transfer Pricing.   Support units, such as maintenance, information processing, transportation, telecommunication, printing, and procurement of material and services, charge consuming units for their services. The principles for transfer pricing are those described in Chapter 5.

Strategic Planning and Budgeting.   In general, formal strategic planning systems are not as well developed in professional organizations as in manufacturing companies of similar size. Part of the explanation is that professional organizations have no great need for such systems. In manufacturing companies, many program decisions involve commitments to procure plant and equipment; they have a predictable effect on both capacity and on costs for several future years, and, once made, they are essentially irreversible. In a professional organization, the principal assets are people; although the organization tries to avoid short-run fluctuations in personnel levels, changes in the size and composition of the staff are easier to make and are more easily reversed than changes in the capacity of a physical plant. The strategic plan of a professional organization typically consists primarily of a long-range staffing plan, rather than a full-blown plan for all aspects of the firm's operation.

The budgeting process in professional organizations is similar to that described in Chapter 8.

Control of Operations.   Much attention is, or should be, given to scheduling the time of professionals. The *billed time ratio,* which is the ratio of hours billed to total professional hours available, is watched closely. If, to use otherwise idle time or for marketing or public service reasons, some engagements are billed at lower than normal rates, the resulting price variance warrants close attention.

The inability to set standards for task performance, the desirability of carrying out work by teams, the consequent problems of managing a matrix organization, and the behavioral characteristics of professionals all complicate the planning and control of the day-to-day operations in a professional organization. When the work is done by project teams, control is focused on projects. A written plan for each project is needed, and timely reports should be prepared that compare actual performance with planned performance in terms of cost, schedule, and quality, as described in Chapter 15.

Performance Measurement and Appraisal.   As noted above in regard to teachers, at the extremes the performance of professionals is easy to judge. Appraisal of the large percentage of professionals who are within the extremes is much more difficult. For some professions, objective measures of performance are sometimes available: The recommendations of an investment analyst can be compared with actual market behavior of the securities; the accuracy of a surgeon's diagnosis can be verified by an examination of the tissue that was removed; and the doctors' skill can be measured by the success ratio of operations. These measures are, of course, subject to appropriate qualifications, and in most circumstances the assessment of performance is finally a matter of human judgment by superiors, peers, self, subordinates, clients.

Judgments made by superiors are the most common. For these, professional organizations increasingly use formal systems to collect performance appraisals as a basis for personnel decisions and for discussion with the professional. Some systems require numerical ratings of specified attributes of performance and provide for a weighted average of these ratings. Compensation may be tied, in part, to these numerical ratings. In a matrix organization, both the project leader and the head of the functional unit that is the professional's organizational "home" judge performance.

Appraisals by a professional's peers, or by subordinates, are sometimes part of a formal control system. In some organizations, individuals may be asked to make a self-appraisal. Expressions of satisfaction or dissatisfaction from clients are also an important basis for judging performance, although such expressions may not always be readily forthcoming.

> **Example.** One firm that sells investment advice to institutional clients keeps a record of letters of commendation and criticism received from its clients, classifies these according to the analysts who made the relevant criticisms or recommendations, and uses this information as part of its performance evaluation system.

The budget can be used as the basis for measuring cost performance, and the actual time taken can be compared with the planned time. Budgeting and control of discretionary expenses is as important in a professional firm as in a manufacturing company. Such financial measures are relatively unimportant in assessing a professional's contribution to the firm's profitability, however. The professional's major contribution is related to quantity and above all quality of work, and its appraisal must be largely subjective. Furthermore, the appraisal must be made currently; it cannot wait until one learns whether a new building is well designed, a new control system actually works well, or a bond indenture has a flaw.

In some professions, internal audit procedures are used to control quality. In many accounting firms, the report of an audit is reviewed by a partner other than the one who is responsible for it, and the work of the whole firm is "peer reviewed" by another firm. The proposed design of a building may be reviewed by architects who are not actively involved in the project.

Financial Service Organizations

Financial service organizations include commercial bank and thrift institutions; insurance companies; and securities firms. These companies are in business primarily to manage money. Some act as intermediaries; that is, they obtain money from depositors and lend it to individuals or companies. Others act as risk shifters; they obtain money in the form of premiums, invest these premiums, and accept the risk of the occurrence of specific events, such as death or damages to property. Still others are traders; they buy and sell securities, either for their own account or for customers.

The Financial Services Sector

Several general observations can be made about the financial services sector. First, in 1999, financial services firms accounted for over $300 billion, or about 5 percent, of the gross domestic product, but their importance in the overall performance of the economy is considerably greater than this percentage indicates. The financial services sector constitutes an important backbone to the US and world economies. The Dow Jones Industrial Average (composite of 30 stocks) was approximately 4,000 on December 31, 1995, and grew by 300 percent over a four-year period to 11,750 as we entered the new millennium.

Second, 30 years ago, commercial banking, investment banking, retail brokerage, and insurance existed as distinct and separate industries; firms specialized in a single industry and tended to compete in a single country. Nothing could be further from the truth today. Deregulation (e.g., the weakening of the Glass-Steagall Act) has blurred industry and geographic boundaries. Financial services firms not only operate in multiple segments (investment banking, brokerage, etc.) but also are global in scope. In the 1990s several megamergers led to the consolidation of the financial services industry (examples: merger of Citicorp and Travellers; Morgan Stanley's acquisition of Dean Witter; Deutsche Bank's acquisition of Bankers Trust). Blurring of industry boundaries, globalization, and consolidation of financial services firms will accelerate in the 21st century.

Third, financial services firms have used the information technology revolution to innovate new products and discover new methods of trading. For instance, the Charles Schwab Corporation introduced TeleBroker (an automated telephone touchpad order entry system), VoiceBroker (an automated voice recognition quote system), and e.Schwab (Internet-based brokerage service). New entrants such as E*Trade and Ameritrade were able to dramatically lower brokerage commissions through Web-based trading. In 1999, over 30 percent of all stock trades by individuals were done via the Internet; yet, four years earlier, this segment did not exist.[2]

Fourth, the need for controls in the financial services sector has become paramount. The Asian financial crisis during the second half of the 1990s was, in part, the result of inadequate controls in banks in Thailand, Indonesia, Japan, and other Asian countries which, in turn, allowed the banks to make highly risky and bad loans. Most notable failure among financial services firms was the collapse of Barings, Britain's oldest merchant bank, in 1995. Deficient control partly contributed to Barings' debacle.[3]

Finally, during the 1990s, new forms of financial instruments (such as derivatives) designed by financial service firms sometimes resulted in millions of dollars of losses for their clients. In December 1994 Orange County in California lost $1.7 billion in leveraged interest-rate products. In April 1994 Procter & Gamble sued Bankers Trust because of its loss of over $100 million on interest-rate swaps designed by Bankers Trust. In July 1994 Glaxo incurred losses of $180 million on derivatives and asset-based bonds.[4]

---

[2]Bruce Judson, *HyperWars* (New York: Scribner, 1999), p. 24.

[3]Thomas Sheridan, "The Barings Debacle," *Management Accounting,* May 1995, pp. 6–7.

[4]"Corporate Risk Management: A New Nightmare in the Boardroom," *The Economist,* February 10, 1996, pp. 3–22.

Special Characteristics

While the general principles and concepts of management control systems apply, they need to be adapted to the following special characteristics of the financial services industry.

Monetary Assets.   Most of the assets of financial service firms are monetary. The current value of monetary assets is much more easily measured than the value of plant and other physical assets, or patents and other intangible assets. Currency is the extreme example of a fungible commodity. At any time, dollars held by all companies have the same value; each dollar is worth a dollar, valued at both its face amount and its purchasing power. Its purchasing power changes with time, but at any given future time, all dollars have equal value. This means that everyone's dollar has the same quality at any given moment. In the financial services industry, quality refers to the quality of services rendered and to the quality of financial instruments other than money; there is no need for quality control safeguards for money.

Financial assets also can be transferred from one owner to another easily and quickly. In an electronic funds transfer, money moves almost instantaneously. In other transactions, it moves in a few days at most. Its portability is tempting to thieves and forgers. For this reason, firms that handle financial assets, especially money, must take strong measures to protect them. These involve not only physical measures to safeguard currency and documents, but also measures designed to maintain the integrity of the system for transferring money from one party to another.

Time Period for Transactions.   The ultimate financial success or failure of a bond issue, a mortgage loan to an individual, or a life insurance policy may not be known for 30 years or more. During this period, the soundness of the loan or policy may change, and the purchasing power of money will certainly change. This means that the ultimate performance of those involved in authorizing and structuring the loan, or in selling and pricing the insurance policy, cannot be measured at the time the initial decision is made. It also means that control requires that there be a means of continued surveillance of the soundness of the transaction during its life, including periodic audits of all outstanding loans. (Failure to identify "troubled loans" at an early stage is one important reason for the rash of failures of banks and thrift institutions.)

At the other extreme, some transactions are completed quickly. Many trades are made on the basis of information that the trader has acquired in the previous few minutes, or even seconds. For currency transactions and for listed securities, new information may become available almost instantaneously in markets throughout the world. Traders either buy or sell securities on the basis of the information they have. If they buy securities, future changes in prices will change the value of the securities held. Therefore, there is a need for a system to report securities held and to assess the risk to the organization if prices move against the trader's securities. This means that the firm must have an accurate, prompt system for obtaining this information, for summarizing it, for estimating the risk of the securities held (if applicable), and for making this information available to traders; a computer model ("expert system") evaluates the information and in some cases acts without human intervention.

Risk and Reward.   Many financial services firms are in the business of accepting risks in return for rewards. Most business decisions involve a trade-off between risks and rewards. The greater the risk, the greater should be the anticipated reward. In financial services firms, this trade-off is more explicit than in business investments such as those involving the purchase of a machine or the introduction of a new product. Interest rates on loans and premiums on insurance policies are based on assumptions about risk that may, or may not, turn out to be accurate.

Technology.   Technology has revolutionized the financial services industry. Financial service firms have used information technology as a way to offer innovative services. Automated teller machines of banks are just one example. Insurance and mutual funds have developed electronic marketplaces. Financial service firms, via their Web site on the Internet, market their products electronically to consumers. Investment banks, using concepts from quantum physics and high-level mathematics formulas, have designed new forms of financial instruments. Banks have become "virtual" by offering cyber-payment systems. Online brokerage services are a fast-growing segment.[5]

Health Care Organizations

Health care organizations consist of hospitals, clinics, and similar physicians' organizations; health maintenance organizations; retirement and nursing homes; home care organizations; and medical laboratories, among others. They constitute the largest industry in the United States: 14 percent of the gross national product, which is about the same percentage as the *total* of all durable goods manufacturers.[6] Although they have most of the characteristics of nonprofit organizations, which are discussed in the next section, many of them are profit-oriented companies.

Special Characteristics

Difficult Social Problem.   Society is gradually coming to grips with the fact that the present health care delivery system is unworkable. Although physicians are bound by the Hippocratic oath to provide adequate health care

---

[5]"Technology in Finance," *The Economist,* October 26, 1996, pp. 3–22.

[6]Data in this section are taken from the following tables in the *Statistical Abstract of the United States,* 1999: No. 136 (overall expenditures); No. 166 (hospitals); and No. 629 (employment). For more detailed data, see the following annual publications: US National Center for Health Statistics, *Health, United States;* US Health Care Financing Administration, *Health Care Financing Review;* American Hospital Association, *Hospital Statistics.*

to their patients, the system cannot do this. On the one hand, the cost per treatment is inevitably increasing with the development of new equipment and new drugs; hospital expenses increased from $28 billion in 1970 to over $360 billion by 1999. (Contrast this trend with the typical experience of manufacturing companies, in which new equipment usually reduces unit costs.) On the other hand, the number of ill persons is increasing because medical advances prolong the lives of elderly people, who are the most likely to require treatment. Society cannot pay for the predictable increases if the present rate of increase in cost continues much longer. Health care providers are aware of this problem; but they don't know how society, especially the Congress, will deal with it. It is clear, however, that health care delivery will change drastically. Health care organizations must be alert to these changes.

Change in Mix of Providers.   Within the overall increase in health care cost, significant changes have occurred in the way in which health care is delivered and, hence, in the viability of certain types of providers. Many services that traditionally were provided in hospitals on an inpatient basis are now provided in outpatient clinics or in patients' homes. Entrepreneurs have entered the industry to provide these new services. There also has been a shift from small local hospitals to larger regional or medical center hospitals. The number of hospital beds decreased by more than 30 percent from 1970 to 1999. To remain viable, hospitals must have the flexibility to adapt to these changes, either by providing more outpatient services themselves or by eliminating inpatient services that are no longer profitable.

Third-Party Payers.   Of the more than $900 billion total expenditures for health care in 1999, 43 percent were financed by the government, 35 percent by insurance companies, and only 22 percent by individual patients. The largest government program is Medicare, a federal program that provides support for persons age 65 and up and for younger persons with certain disabilities. The Medicaid program pays for services provided to low-income people; it is financed by the states within general guidelines set by the federal government.

Until 1983, Medicare reimbursed on the basis of "reasonable" costs incurred, which gave health care providers little incentive to control costs. Currently, Medicare reimburses hospitals on the basis of Diagnostic Related Groups (DRGs). Medical and surgical procedures are classified into one of about 500 DRGs, each DRG is priced annually at a set dollar amount, and hospitals are reimbursed for these amounts, regardless of the actual length of stay or the actual costs incurred for individual patients. Other third-party payers have moved toward a similar system of reimbursement.

The DRG system, and the increase in hospital costs per patient, has motivated hospitals to install sophisticated cost accounting systems, usually systems that they purchase from an outside computer software organization and then adapt to their own needs. Some hospitals provide information processing services to other hospitals on a contract basis. These systems provide information on individual patients (similar to job-cost systems in automobile repair shops), and they report actual costs compared with standard costs for each DRG; costs are classified by departments and even by attending physicians within departments.

This information is in addition to information traditionally collected in hospitals; it focuses on outputs (patient care), as well as on inputs (cost per laboratory test).

Increasingly, health maintenance organizations (HMOs) reimburse physicians, hospitals, and other providers. They contract with companies to provide medical services to employees at a fixed cost per person covered. In turn, the HMO contracts with hospitals and other providers, in some cases at a specified amount per DRG. The HMO therefore has the difficult task of controlling its payments so that they do not exceed the fees earned, but nevertheless seeing to it that adequate health care is provided.

Professionals.   In 1999, the health care industry employed over 3 million professionals (physicians, dentists, registered nurses, and therapists), which was more than any other industry except education. The management control implications of professionals are the same as those discussed in the preceding section. Their primary loyalty is to the profession, rather than to the organization. Departmental managers typically are professionals whose management function is only part-time; the chief of surgery does surgery. Historically, physicians have tended to give relatively little emphasis to cost control. In particular, there has been an impression that they prescribe more than the optimum number of tests, partly because of the danger of malpractice suits if they don't detect all the patient's symptoms.

Importance of Quality Control.   The health care industry deals with human lives, so the quality of the service it provides is of paramount importance. There are tissue reviews of surgical procedures, peer review of individual physicians, and outside review agencies mandated by the federal government.

Management Control Process

Subject to the characteristics described above, the management control process in the health care industry is similar to that described in Chapters 7 through 11. Because of the shift in the product mix and because of the increase in the quantity and cost of new equipment, the strategic planning process in hospitals is important. The annual budget preparation process is conventional. Huge quantities of information are available quickly for the control of operating activities. Financial performance is analyzed by comparing actual revenues and expenses with budgets, identifying important variances, and taking appropriate actions on them.

Nonprofit Organizations

A nonprofit organization, as defined in law, is an organization that cannot distribute assets or income to, or for the benefit of, its members, officers, or directors. The organization can, of course, compensate its employees, including officers and members, for services rendered and for goods supplied. This definition does not prohibit an organization from *earning* a profit; it prohibits only the *distribution* of profits. A nonprofit organization needs to earn a modest profit, on average, to provide funds for working capital and for possible "rainy days."

Nonprofit organizations that meet the criteria of Section 501(c) of the Internal Revenue Code are exempt from income taxes (except for their "unrelated business income"); over 1.2 million organizations satisfy these criteria in the United States. If they are religious, charitable, or educational organizations as defined in Section 501(c)(3) of the code, contributions made to them are tax deductible by the contributor; they are called "501(c)(3) organizations." Many such organizations are exempt from property taxes and from certain types of sales taxes.

In many industry groups, there are both nonprofit and profit-oriented (i.e., business) organizations. There are nonprofit and for-profit hospitals, nonprofit and for-profit ("proprietary") schools and colleges, and even for-profit religious organizations. SRI International is a nonprofit research organization that competes with Arthur D. Little, Inc., a for-profit research organization.

Special Characteristics

Absence of the Profit Measure.   A dominant goal of most businesses is to earn a satisfactory profit; net income measures performance toward this goal. No such measure of performance exists in nonprofit organizations. Many of them have several goals, and an organization's effectiveness in attaining its goals rarely can be measured by quantitative amounts. The absence of a satisfactory, quantitative, overall measure of performance is the most serious management control problem in a nonprofit organization.

The income statement is the most useful financial statement in a nonprofit organization, just as it is in a business. The net income number is interpreted differently in the two types of organizations, however. In a business, as a general rule, the larger the income, the better the performance. In a nonprofit organization, net income should average only a small amount above zero. A large net income signals that the organization is not providing the services that those who supplied resources had a right to expect; a string of net losses will lead to bankruptcy, just as in a business. Although financial performance is not the dominant goal in a nonprofit organization, it is a necessary goal because the organization cannot survive if its revenues on average are less than its expenses.

Contributed Capital.   There is only one major difference between the accounting transactions in a business and those in a nonprofit organization; it relates to the equity section of the balance sheet. A business corporation has transactions with its shareholders—issuance of stock and the payment of dividends—that a nonprofit organization doesn't have. A nonprofit organization receives contributed capital, which few businesses have. (In both businesses and nonprofit organizations, equity is increased by earning income.)

There are two principal categories of contributed capital: plant and endowment. Plant includes contributions of buildings and equipment, or contributions of funds to acquire these assets; works of art; and other museum objects. Endowment consists of gifts whose donors intend that the principal amount will remain intact indefinitely (or at least for many years); only the income on this principal will be used to finance current operations.

The receipt (or pledge) of a contributed capital asset is not revenue—that is, neither contributions of plant nor of endowment are available to finance the operating activities of the period in which the contribution is received. Endowment assets must be kept separate from operating assets. This is a legal requirement for a "true" endowment, and it is sound policy for a "board-designated" endowment—that is, funds that the trustees have decided to treat as endowment, even though there is no legal requirement that they do so. It follows that capital contributions should be reported separately from operating contributions, that is, from revenues from annual fund drives, grants, and other gifts intended to finance current operations.

Thus, a nonprofit organization has two sets of financial statements. One set relates to operating activities; it includes an operating statement, a balance sheet, and a statement of cash flows that are the same as those found in business. The second set relates to contributed capital; it has a statement of inflows and outflows of contributed capital during a period and a balance sheet that reports contributed capital assets and the related liabilities and equity. Inflows of contributed capital are capital contributions received in the period and gains on the endowment portfolio; outflows are the endowment income that is reported as operating revenue, losses on the endowment portfolio, and write-offs of plant.

Fund Accounting.   Many nonprofit organizations use an accounting system that is called "fund accounting." Accounts are kept separately for several funds, each of which is self-balancing (i.e., the sum of the debit balances equals the sum of the credit balances). Most organizations have (1) a *general fund or operating fund,* which corresponds closely to the set of operating accounts mentioned above; (2) a *plant fund* and an *endowment fund,* which account for the contributed capital assets and equities mentioned above; and (3) a variety of other funds for special purposes. Some of these other funds, such as the pension fund, are also found in business, although in business they are reported in the notes to the financial statements, rather than in the financial statements themselves. Others are useful for internal control purposes. For management control purposes, the primary focus is on the general fund.

Governance.   Nonprofit organizations are governed by boards of trustees. Trustees usually are not paid, and many of them are unfamiliar with business management. Therefore, they generally exercise less control than the directors of a business corporation. Moreover, because performance is more difficult to measure in a nonprofit organization than in a business, the board is less able to identify actual or incipient problems.

The need for a strong governing board in a nonprofit organization is greater than in a business because the vigilance of the governing board may be the only effective way of detecting when the nonprofit is in difficulty. In a profit-oriented organization, a decrease in profits signals this danger automatically.

Management Control Systems

Product Pricing.   Many nonprofit organizations give inadequate attention to their pricing policies. Pricing of services at their full cost is desirable.

A "full-cost" price is the sum of direct costs, indirect costs, and, perhaps, a small allowance for increasing the organization's equity. This principle applies to services that are directly related to the organization's objectives. Pricing for peripheral activities should be market-based. Thus, a nonprofit hospital should price its health care services at full cost, but prices in its gift shop should be market-based.

In general, the smaller and more specific the unit of service that is priced, the better the basis for decisions about the allocation of resources. For example, a comprehensive daily rate for hospital care, which was common practice a few decades ago, masks the revenues for the mix of services actually provided. Beyond a certain point, of course, the cost of the paperwork associated with pricing units of service outweighs the benefits.

As a general rule, management control is facilitated when prices are established prior to the performance of the service. If an organization is able to recover its incurred costs, management is not motivated to worry about cost control.

Strategic Planning and Budget Preparation.   In nonprofit organizations that must decide how best to allocate limited resources to worthwhile activities, strategic planning is a more important and more time-consuming process than in the typical business. The process is similar to that described in Chapter 7, except that the absence of a profit measure makes program decisions more subjective.

The budget preparation process is similar to that described in Chapter 8. Colleges and universities, welfare organizations, and organizations in certain other nonprofit industries know, before the budget year begins, the approximate amount of their revenues. They do not have the option of increasing revenues during the year by increasing their marketing efforts. They budget expenses so the organization will at least break even at the estimated amount of revenue. They require that managers of responsibility centers limit spending close to the budget amounts. The budget is, therefore, the most important management control tool, at least with respect to financial activities.

Operation and Evaluation.   In most nonprofit organizations, there is no way of knowing what the optimum operating costs are. Responsibility center managers, therefore, tend to spend whatever is allowed in the budget, even though the budgeted amount may be higher than is necessary. Conversely, they may refrain from making expenditures that have an excellent payoff simply because the expenditure was not included in the budget.

Although nonprofit organizations have had a reputation for operating inefficiently, this perception has been changing for good reasons. Many organizations have had increasing difficulty in raising funds, especially from government resources. This has led to belt-tightening and to increased attention to management control. As mentioned above, the most dramatic change has been in hospital costs, with the introduction of reimbursement on the basis of standard prices for diagnostic-related groups.

Summary

Management control in service organizations is different from that in manufacturing organizations, primarily because of the absence of an inventory buffer between production and sales, because of the difficulty of measuring quality, and because service organizations are labor intensive. Professional organizations do not have the dominant goal of return on assets employed; professionals' behavioral characteristics do not include attention to costs, output measurements are subjective, and there is no clear line between marketing and production activities. Performance appraisal may be achieved by peer reviews; in any case it tends to be subjective. Financial services organizations differ in two fundamental respects from industrial companies. First, their "raw material" is money. At any given time, the value of each unit of money in inventory is the same for all organizations, negating any need for control in this area; however, the cost of using money obtained from various sources varies considerably. Second, the profitability of many transactions cannot be measured until years after the commitment has been made, necessitating continual periodic audits. In particular, the financial services company is profitable only if the future revenues obtained from current loans, investments, and insurance premiums exceed the cost of the funds associated with these revenues (which is analogous to cost of sales in a manufacturing company) by an amount that is sufficient to cover operating expenses and losses. Health care organizations have tried to use the DRG system to standardize costs; they, and society, must face the fact that the current control and delivery system is unworkable. Nonprofit organizations lack the advantages for control that the profit measure provides; they must account for contributed capital, a category that rarely occurs in a business. Expenditure decisions are subjective for nonprofits; nevertheless, they have succeeded in becoming more efficient in response to shrinking sources of funds.

In spite of these differences, the essentials of the management control systems in service organizations are the same as those described in the earlier chapters of this text.

Suggested Additional Readings

Anthony, Robert N., and David W. Young. *Management Control in Nonprofit Organizations.* 6th ed. Burr Ridge, IL.: Richard D. Irwin, 1999.

Botten, Neil, and John McManus. *Competitive Strategies for Service Organizations.* Purdue, IN: Purdue University Press, 1999.

Crawford, Richard D., and William W. Sihler. *Financial Service Organizations: Cases in Strategic Management.* New York: HarperCollins College Division, 1994.

Douglas, Patricia P. *Governmental and Nonprofit Accounting.* Orlando, FL.: Harcourt Brace Jovanovich, 1991.

Hayes, Samuel L., ed. *Financial Services: Perspectives and Challenges,* Boston: Harvard Business School Press, 1993.

McFarlan, Warren F. "Working on Nonprofit Boards: Don't Assume the Shoe Fits." *Harvard Business Review,* November–December 1999, pp. 64–80.

McLean, Daniel. *Managing Financial Resources in Sport and Leisure Service Organizations.* Champaign, IL: Sagamore, 1999.

Prince, Thomas R. *Financial Reporting and Cost Control for Health Care Entities.* Chicago: Health Administration Press, 1992.

Quinn, J. B. *Innovation Explosion.* New York: Free Press, 1999.

Sandretto, Michael J. "Controlling Financial Instruments." *Management Accounting,* May 1993, pp. 55–61.

CASE 13–1
O'REILLEY ASSOCIATES

In 1990 O'Reilley Associates was one of the largest advertising agencies in the United States. Billings for the ad industry were over $260 billion on a worldwide basis that year, compared to $125 billion in 1984. The 20 largest firms accounted for nearly 35 percent of worldwide billings in 1990. Fourteen of these were independent agency networks and six were advertising groups (firms with more than one agency network). Most of the firms were based in the United States or United Kingdom. The proliferation of extensive advertising groups grew out of increased demand for services around the world as clients entered global markets.

Companies of all sizes retained advertising agencies to create and execute marketing plans, advertising strategies, and campaigns. The agencies ranged from those that provided only traditional advertising services to others with extensive market research and consulting capabilities. To best serve clients, an agency had to be extremely knowledgeable about its clients' products and strategies. The most successful partnerships between advertisers and agencies lasted for years. O'Reilley Associates had worked with many of its clients for more than 20 years.

Advertising agencies were compensated by their clients in one of two ways. Traditionally, an ad agency received a 15 percent commission on advertising placed in television, radio, or print. The client would be billed the full amount, and 15 percent would be "kicked back" to the agency from the medium. Creative work and campaign development were

not charged to the client (except out-of-pocket expenditures).

With the increased use of nonadvertising services, a fee-based system was introduced. These services included design, graphics, market research, sales promotion, direct mail campaigns, merchandising, event planning, and public relations. For these nontraditional services, clients were charged billable hours plus expenditures (similar to the compensation arrangement used by law firms). For production of the campaign (actually producing material or copy), the client was billed cost plus 15 percent. This fee structure was necessary because the kickback scheme no longer was feasible with the new services and different media.

O'Reilley Associates was organized into six divisions, as indicated below:

Account management: The account executive and her staff were responsible for overall client contact. This group developed the marketing plan, handled strategy, and coordinated other divisions within the advertising firm.

Creative management: The creative division conceived, created, and developed advertising copy and artwork for the advertisements.

Information management: The information division primarily planned and conducted market research. It also recommended promotion strategies and merchandising programs. A library and training group was maintained for client sales training.

Media management: The media division developed the media strategy and purchased space and time in various media.

Administrative management: This division managed the advertising agency itself, including the human resource, finance, and support functions.

This case was adapted by Anil Chitkara (T'94) (with permission) from an earlier case by J. M. McInnes and J. R. Yeager.

Production management: In the past, agencies hired producers, booked studios, and produced television and radio copy externally. As O'Reilley Associates grew, it established a production department that employed a staff of producers, directors, and production personnel. The department owned some production and editing equipment. This group worked closely with the creative and account management teams.

The account executive ultimately was responsible for managing the client account, including coordinating the creative, marketing, and media strategies within the agency. A new account executive typically was given one account. As her career progressed, additional accounts would be transferred to her. The frequent turnover required these managers to learn new businesses each time an account was transferred to them. The learning was an expensive undertaking, but O'Reilley Associates believed it brought fresh thinking to their clients' products.

New Client Decisions

One of senior management's most critical roles was deciding which new clients to accept. Potential clients whose products competed with an existing client's products were not even considered. Aside from this, O'Reilley Associates considered any new client that (1) had a solid business reputation, (2) was in good standing in the community, and (3) whose product met a consumer need.

O'Reilley Associates applied its past experience to assess the profit potential of new accounts. The agency served approximately 50 clients and over 250 products, covering a wide range of product categories. It used cost data from these current accounts to estimate the cost of servicing new accounts. Additionally, it estimated the spending necessary to build up a product to desired market share. Typically, a product's cost included an allowance for advertising costs. If the advertising allowance could cover the expected cost of building market share and maintaining the product, that was sufficient evidence for accepting the assignment.

New Product Introduction

A host of issues needed to be studied before launching new products. The information management division began by conducting marketing studies and using focus groups to determine if there was a consumer need. If a need existed, the consumer benefit was identified. This test marketing stage was intended to gauge consumer acceptance. O'Reilley Associates maintained a research panel of several thousand consumers around the country to conduct test marketing.

Once a consumer need was identified, a creative strategy, based primarily on the consumer benefit, was developed. Test marketing continued to determine the effectiveness of executing this strategy. If this part of the test marketing was unsuccessful, it was assumed that the selling message was not conveyed effectively and the execution was changed.

When the agency finished test marketing, it gave recommendations to the client about the probable outcome of a full-scale product launch. Only after the client decided to proceed would the agency generate any significant revenue from the assignment. This revenue was a function of the advertising budget needed to support the full-scale product launch and had to cover all expenses up to that time. Management's early assessment of the product's chances of succeeding was critical to the profitability of O'Reilley Associates.

Existing Product Support

Advertising strategy for existing products was quite different from that for new products. Market acceptance of existing products was better known, although product obsolescence was a constant concern. Existing products needed advertising to maintain consumer awareness of their attributes. The client's marketing group worked closely with the agency to develop new plans to increase these products' market share.

A new campaign for an existing product began when the previous campaign's run period ended. The decision to develop a new campaign required both the client's and the agency's judgment. A drop in a product's market share was a definite sign that a new campaign should be considered. Additionally, meeting competitive threats was a critical part of maintaining a product.

Account executives managed new campaigns within the agency. First, the creative department developed a strategy. The account executive and her staff reviewed the strategy with the client's sales team. The parties would agree on an advertising strategy and marketing plan, and the necessary advertisements, commercials, and other promotional material were prepared. Then the media department arranged to execute the plan through various media.

Account Profitability

Another critical responsibility of the agency's top management was to assess the profitability of various accounts. The most profitable accounts were those that advertised frequently with the same copy. The agency incurred its major expenses up to, and including, the preparation of advertising copy. After that, the agency simply executed the advertising plan by purchasing media time and space. A client who required a constant stream of new copy was far less profitable than one who used the same copy repeatedly. Constant development meant additional creative strategy and copywriting, which were expensive undertakings.

A client's size frequently affected its profitability. In large client organizations, the advertising plan had to be cleared at numerous levels, which involved a great deal of time and effort on the agency's part. Additional revisions to the plan and numerous conferences sometimes made a large client's account unprofitable.

There were more compelling reasons than profitability to keep a client account. An unprofitable product account might be retained if the agency held accounts for a client's other products that were profitable. Additionally, the client might choose to continue a marginally profitable product line for competitive reasons. In this case, little advertising was in order. The agency continued to handle such an account, albeit minimally.

Personnel Costs

Personnel constituted much of the cost associated with servicing an account. Payroll accounted for 60 to 65 percent of O'Reilley Associates' gross revenues. In a typical agency, other expenses accounted for 20 to 25 percent of revenues, and the remaining 10 to 20 percent was pretax profit.

All employees except administrative staff filed time sheets that recorded the number of hours they worked, broken down by client account. Administrative personnel who could allocate their time to a specific client did so. Approximately 85 percent of the payroll was accountable to individual clients. Since 65 percent of revenues covered payroll and 85 percent of payroll was accountable, 55 percent of revenues were direct personnel expenses. At O'Reilley Associates, if direct payroll associated with an account was less than 55 percent of revenues, the account was considered profitable.

Approximately 20 percent (4 to 5 percent of revenues) of the nonpayroll expenses could be allocated to a client. This included travel, entertainment, rough copy costs, research, and copy pretests. Indirect expenses included rent, telephone, and utilities. These expenses were allocated based on direct payroll.

O'Reilley Associates was extremely secretive about the profitability of its accounts. Only three people knew its account profitability: the company's chairman, president, and treasurer. This policy was created to encourage teams to provide the highest level of service to their clients without regard to the accounts' profitability. The agency's management believed employees would be less enthusiastic about working on unprofitable accounts and their work would suffer. It was top management's job to decide on account retention. The rest of the firm was responsible for serving the clients.

T&D Corporation Account

T&D Corporation was a large manufacturer of tools and dies that were sold to industrial customers. The corporation had many divisions, each of which conducted its own business except when the overall corporate image was involved. This included advertising. The corporation's divisions used O'Reilley Associates as well as other advertising agencies.

Until a recent review, each of the T&D divisions that used O'Reilley Associates was thought to be profitable to the agency. However, a recent review of T&D's International Division account raised questions about its profitability. A profit and loss worksheet for the T&D International Division account is provided in Exhibit 1.

The International Division did not advertise in the mass media. It did its own artwork in-house. O'Reilley Associates' main responsibilities were to provide advertising copy and buy media space. The O'Reilley Associates account executive on T&D International had spent considerable time and energy learning the client's business and understanding T&D Corporation's objectives. This was done to create an advertising plan that would be supported by the client's corporate management. The account executive also spent considerable time familiarizing copywriters with the company to ensure that the copy was in line with T&D's corporate policies.

Anil Chitkara, a member of O'Reilley Associates' staff at headquarters, was told to prepare a report for the agency's top management review of the T&D International account. The report was to cover all relevant issues, set forth alternative courses of action, estimate the consequences of each, and articulate Chitkara's recommendations.

EXHIBIT 1   Income Statement for T&D International Division

Customer = T&D International Division
Product = Professional Prod.
Period = Year to 12/31/89

Billing	$870,000
Commission and fees	$154,500
Direct payroll:	
Account management	45,000
Copy	55,000
Art	25,000
Media	7,500
Administrative	3,750
	136,250
Other direct expenses:	
Unbillable costs	1,500
Travel	500
Entertainment	1,500
	3,500
Indirect expenses:	
Occupancy	20,000
Employee benefits	8,000
Telephone	5,250
Indirect service departments	36,500
Other indirect	17,000
	86,750
Total expense	226,500
Profit (loss) before taxes	($ 72,000)

Questions

1. What management control system would you recommend for O'Reilley Associates?

2. What would you include in Anil Chitkara's report described at the end of the case?

Case 13–2
Williamson and Oliver

In early 1984, the policy board of Williamson and Oliver approved the suggestion of Ted Johnson, national managing partner, to institute an incentive compensation plan applicable to all the partners in the firm. (The plan is described in Exhibit 1.) One senior partner in the firm observed:

> In my opinion, this incentive plan is a step in the right direction. We want our partners to improve current profits; but, at the same time, we cannot lose sight of the longer-term development of our firm. I think the incentive plan explicitly considers the multidimensional nature of the partner's tasks. I am sure, though, that the plan needs to be fine-tuned as we gain more experience.

In 1984 Williamson and Oliver was one of the largest and fastest-growing public accounting firms in the United States. It had offices in more than 50 major cities and had over 500 partners. A major part of the firm's growth came from bases established through acquisition of local and regional CPA practices. Each office engaged in auditing, management advisory services, and taxation services. The practice offices were grouped into five areas, each headed by an area director. Reporting to the area directors were partners-in-charge (PIC), who managed the individual offices. Each area director was also the partner-in-charge for one of the offices in the area. About 15 partners and the related supporting staff constituted the executive office of the firm. The executive partners, including the national managing partner, reported to the policy board, which was a rotating group elected by the partners.

The Public Accounting Profession

Although there are literally thousands of CPA firms in this country, the profession is domi-

nated by a small set of about 10 international firms. These firms account for perhaps 90 percent of the annual audits of publicly traded companies. For each of these 10 firms, auditing accounts for somewhere between 60 and 75 percent of gross billings. Taxation advisory services and management consulting services make up the remainder of the billings. The percentage of total billings from auditing has been falling for all the firms over the past 15 years. Each of the major firms maintains offices in most major cities across the country and offers a full range of client services in each office. No one firm is dominant in any region. In fact, it is extremely rare for any one firm to have even a 20 percent share of market in any one city or state.

The canons of professional ethics prohibit the corporate legal form, but the major firms all operate much like closely held professional service corporations, anyway, in terms of governance, management succession, and distribution of profits. The accounting business has been an excellent one over the past 40 years in terms of growth and profitability. In the 10 top firms, compound growth rates over the years have been in excess of 10 percent per year, and partner income averaged more than $100,000 per year in 1984.

Auditing has been the traditional "major profit machine" for all the firms. In recent years, however, the auditing business has shown many signs of maturity, such as slowed growth, declining margins, fierce price competition, and declining client loyalty. Although many people believe the annual audit is becoming a "commodity," this business was still highly profitable, on average, in 1984.

Different firms are responding to the changes in the auditing environment in different ways, including ignoring it while hoping it

This case was prepared by Vijay Govindarajan and John K. Shank, The Amos Tuck School of Business Administration, Dartmouth College.

Exhibit 1   Office Evaluation System

The Policy Board has approved 15 percent of distributable earnings as variable compensation for fiscal year 1984, 10 percent to be distributed based on partner performance against goals set forth in accountability statements, and 5 percent to be allocated to offices based upon an office evaluation system.*

The system is designed to produce improvement in critical areas of office practice management and to reward offices that improve or maintain existing high standards. The measurement criteria can be changed to emphasize areas where management feels the partners' attention should be focused. Thus, emphasis can be varied from net income to chargeable hours, or from performance versus last year to performance versus standard, simply by changing the allocation percentages. It also will provide peer pressure to achieve improvement since each office will be rated and the listing will be circulated.

The system will measure the four key responsibility areas: Practice Management, Practice Development, Human Resources, and Client Service.

Within these key responsibility areas, six specific factors on which to evaluate the office will be considered. They are:

- Net income.
- Collections (outstanding days).
- Chargeable-hours growth.
- Client service.
- Human resources development.
- One-firm commitment.

The system will be fully implemented over the next few years. In fiscal 1984, evaluation would be based on performance in net income, collections, and chargeable hours. The remaining three factors will be added as soon as possible.

Weighting

As can be seen from the attached **Schedule A,** each of the three factors has been assigned a percentage, under the column heading *"Weight,"* namely, 60 percent, 15 percent, and 25 percent for all practice offices in fiscal 1984.

Schedule A also shows the three criteria used to measure each factor.

Performance versus budget.

Performance versus last year.

Performance versus "ideal" or standard.

These, too, have been assigned a percentage, under the column heading *"Composite Weight,"* which places emphasis where management considers it most appropriate, namely, 50 percent, 20 percent, and 30 percent, respectively.

Grading

The "basic score" shown on **Schedule A** is the level at which a practice office is rated, as follows:

5 Excellent.

4 Above average.

3 Average.

2 Below average.

1 Unsatisfactory.

To determine where an office is to be rated, the following criteria were developed:

Net Income

1. Percent of net income versus budget.
2. Percent of net income versus last year.
3. Percent of net income versus deal target of 20 percent.

(continued)

Exhibit 1   *Continued*

Outstanding Days (Collections)

4. Percent of outstanding days versus budget.

5. Percent of outstanding days versus last year.

6. Percent of outstanding days versus standard (105 days).

Chargeable-Hours Growth

7. Percent of chargeable hours growth versus budget.

8. Percent of chargeable hours growth versus last year.

—(Percent of chargeable hours growth versus standard, which is 5 percent, is not used because it would duplicate performance versus last year, since the firm achieved the 5 percent goal last year.)

Offices are then separated into two groups based on their budgeted net billings.

—Over $2.2 million.

—Under $2.2 million.

Offices are ranked within their group in each of the eight criteria and given a rate (5 to 1) using the bell curve theory as follows:

Top   10%—5
        20%—4
        40%—3
        20%—2
Bottom 10%—1

In measuring performance against budget for 1984, budget will be the amount agreed upon by the Area Director, Deputy Director, and PIC as a reasonable level of attainment by that office. This will enable us to continue to improve our budgeting procedures in 1984. *This plan contemplates that budgets are at reasonable levels of attainment for each office.*

Exceptions

• Offices with an operating loss at year end are excluded from bonus pool allocation, unless a development loss is budgeted and approved by the National Director-Operations. Their grade will show as zero in all eight criteria, disregarding what results could have been obtained in collections and chargeable hours.

• Offices with net income as a percent of net fees under 10 percent for last year are adjusted to 10 percent for grading purposes. This is done to prevent offices with a loss or low net income the year before from getting a high grade when compared to this year's results, illustrated as follows:

	Actual 1983	*Actual 1984*	*Percent of '84 over '83*
Office A:			
Net fees	1,000	1,050	
Net income	20	40	100%
Office B:			
Net fees	1,000	1,200	
Net income	300	400	33%

Without the rule, Office A would rank considerably higher than Office B, which is not logical. After adjusting Office A net income to 10 percent of its net fees in 1983, the result would be:

	1983	*1984*	*Percent '84 / '83*
Net income	100	40	(60%)

- Mergers in current year or last year or both will be deducted from actual results in both years to make the comparison valid.
- New offices (which do not have "last year" results) will be weighted as follows:

  Performance versus budget 70%
  Performance versus standard 30%

After all of the foregoing is applied, the mathematical result will be determined (**Schedule B**) and offices listed in decreasing order according to their final weighted score. Then a final grade is given, using the bell curve theory. The bonus pool is allocated based on the following table:

Percent Applied to Base Compensation

Rank	*Average*	*Highest*	*Lowest*
5	10.0%	11.25%	8.80%
4	7.5	8.75	6.30
3	5.0	6.25	3.80
2	2.5	3.75	1.25
1	0.0	—	—

Distribution of the 5 percent incentive pool will be based on the grading shown and will be the percentage of base compensation in each office as shown above.

The incentive pool award will be allocated to the individual partners in an office based on performance relative to accountability statement goals. This allocation is subject to the approval of both Area and Deputy Directors.

Final Comments

It is very important to realize the only component of the office evaluation system that does not change from year to year is its philosophy. The others might and likely will change according to the firm's needs.

Office Evaluation Summary FY 1984 Office _____   **Schedule A**

	Composite Weight	*Basic Score*	*Adjusted Score*	*Weight*	*Total*
Net Income					
Percent of income versus budget	50%				
Percent of net income versus last year	20%		—		
Performance versus standard	30%				
Total	100%			60%	—

(continued)

EXHIBIT 1   *Continued*

	Composite Weight	Basic Score	Adjusted Score	Weight	Total
Outstanding Days (collections)					
Percent of outstanding days versus budget	50%				
Percent of outstanding days versus last year	20%		—		
Performance versus standard	30%				
Total	100%			15%	—
Chargeable-Hours Growth					
Percent growth in chargeable hours versus budget	50%				
Percent growth in chargeable hours versus last year	50%				
Total	100%		—	25%	—
Total				100%	—

Office Evaluation Summary FY 1984 Office Hypothetical _____   **Schedule B**

	Composite Weight	Basic Score	Adjusted Score	Weight	Total
Net Income					
Percent of income versus budget	50%	3	1.5		
Percent of net income versus last year	20%	5	1.0		
Performance versus standard	30%	4	1.2		
Total	100%		3.7	60%	2.22
Outstanding Days (collections)					
Percent of outstanding days versus budget	50%	4	2.0		
Percent of outstanding days versus last year	20%	5	1.0		
Performance versus standard	30%	3	0.9		
Total	100%		3.9	15%	0.59
Chargeable-Hours Growth					
Percent growth in chargeable hours versus budget	50%	3	1.5		
Percent growth in chargeable hours versus last year	50%	4	2.0		
Total	100%		3.5	25%	0.89
Total				100%	3.70

Case note: The pool of funds to be distributed through the office evaluation system, 5 percent of partner earnings, could be about $2 million in a normal year. Individual awards could range from $15,000 to zero.

EXHIBIT 2   **An Accounting Practice**

	Mix of Services			
			Consulting	
Size of Clients	*Opinion Audits*	*Taxation Advisory Services*	*Project Consulting*	*General Advisory Services*
Large (Fortune 1,000 companies)	(1)	(4)	(7)	(10)
Medium (publicly traded, but not huge)	(2)	(5)	(8)	(11)
Small (privately held, not large enough to have professional financial management)	(3)	(6)	(9)	(12)

The following comments relate to these individual practice niches:

(1) This is a very-low-growth business. There is erosion from expansion of corporate internal auditing. There is rising price sensitivity among clients, resulting in efforts to "manage the audit fee," and growing price competition among accounting firms. Many people believe that the basic legally mandated opinion audit is very much a "commodity" now. A "Big Eight" image is critical to be a participant in this niche.

(2) Almost all real growth in the audit business is here. Accounting firms can use nonaudit work as a way to gain audit clients here. This niche is also price sensitive; but there is still much room to push differentiation, based on high-quality personal service to the client. As client companies grow, they usually reach a point where they switch to a major auditing firm, even if they did not start out with a major firm.

(3) This is a very minor niche, because small firms typically do not have annual audits unless required by a bank or other lender.

(4) This is a limited niche, because major companies tend to have their own tax planning and tax advisory personnel.

(5), (6) These are large, growing, and very profitable niches. They represent an excellent example of a niche that represents very low price sensitivity coupled with very high perceived product differentiation.

(7), (8), (9) These are all profitable niches with relatively low price sensitivity and relatively high differentiation. The clear competitive advantage and the perceived areas of expertise for CPA firms lie in projects related to financial controls, computer-based financial systems, and financial planning. The major accounting firms differ substantially in the breadth of projects they are willing to undertake, ranging all the way to virtually a full-range management consulting practice.

(10), (11) These are very small niches, because the relevant expertise is as likely to exist in the company as in the accounting firm.

(12) This is a significant and profitable niche that is exploited very aggressively by some of the accounting firms but not by all.

---

will go away, emphasizing product differentiation to justify a price premium, trying to develop low-cost leadership to make possible aggressive pricing, and trying to shift the product mix toward nonaudit services, which are still highly differentiated and, thus, less price sensitive.

Competitive position for an accounting firm or an individual office within a firm can be looked at in terms of a two-dimensional grid with service mix on one dimension and mix of client size on the other dimension (see Exhibit 2).

Although each of the major firms probably generates some billings each year from each of the 12 niches, no two firms are comparable in terms of aggregate positioning within the grid.

Since all the firms are constrained by their ability to attract and retain first-class professional staff, careful delineation of where, within the grid, to place particular emphasis is a major element in strategic planning for a firm.

Because the only productive resource for a CPA firm is people, successful management of the people resource is critically important to the continued prosperity of all such firms. High turnover (both voluntary and forced) has always been part of the structure of the business—of every 10 staff accountants hired, no more than 4 will stay beyond four years and no more than 1 or 2 will become partners. There are no career professionals below the partner level. The rule is "up or out." Admission to the partnership typically comes somewhere between 8 and 15 years. In the major firms, the ratio of partners to staff accountants ranges from a low of 1 to 5 to a high of 1 to 12. Apparently, the partner/staff ratio is a strategic variable.

Traditionally, 40 percent of billings go to pay the professional staff (each staff member should generate billings of 2.5 times salary), 40 percent go to pay overhead (much of which is salary for support personnel), and 20 percent go to the partners as profit. This 40-40-20 economic model has been amazingly durable across firms and over the years.

The Firm of Williamson and Oliver

The name Williamson and Oliver (WO) is an amalgam of parts of the names of predecessor firms dating back more than 50 years. Through a long series of more than 40 mergers of local and regional CPA practices, the current firm gradually emerged. In fact, although the current name was less than 10 years old, Messrs. Williamson and Oliver had both been dead for more than 20 years.

The current firm comprised more than 2,500 professionals in addition to the more than 500 partners. Billings in 1983 were more than $200 million, with 20 offices doing more than $5 million. In about half of the top 50 market areas, the firm is one of the top six in size. It is the largest firm in about 10 of those 50 markets. Counting its international affiliates around the world, Williamson and Oliver is one of the top few firms in terms of billable hours. Its major client strength is in "medium-sized" companies. The firm's situation is comparable to the other major firms in terms of history, size, services mix, and management challenge. One distinguishing characteristic of WO is that, for about two-thirds of its offices, it is not one of the six largest firms in town. It, thus, has a particularly severe marketing challenge in a great many of its offices.

The Job of an Office PIC

Essentially, the PIC for an office is the general manager of a moderately autonomous profit center. Each office is part of the WO network and, thus, does part of its work for local affiliates of WO clients from other offices. Also, each office farms out some work on its clients to other WO offices. But a major share of the work in each office is done for clients of that office. The PICs are responsible for managing businesses ranging in size from about $1 million in annual billings to over $30 million and serving markets as diverse as Manhattan or Muncie, Indiana.

The career path for virtually every PIC is the same—college graduate in accounting, entry-level staff accountant (technical professional in a work team), senior-level accountant (supervising the work team on individual jobs), managing accountant (supervising several work teams while also maintaining a heavy client load), client service partner (managing the overall relationship for several clients while still carrying a heavy load of chargeable hours), then promotion to running an office. The person may have come from audit, tax, or consulting and may or may not have had a staff assignment somewhere along the line; but the overall theme is the same—progression up the technical ladder of the firm.

This career path raises some important issues in considering the job of the PIC and the role of an incentive compensation system in that job context. First, virtually no PICs have had any general management experience until they arrive at the PIC job—their experience is as technical professionals. Second, the set of skills associated with success up the career ladder to the PIC job is not necessarily highly correlated with the set of skills required of a successful general manager—"managing" is different from "doing." Third, while it is the dream of every newly hired staff accountant to someday become a PIC, having *become* one, many persons don't seem to like *being* one. The things they enjoyed while becoming a PIC included task-oriented project work, providing technical service to clients, the status associated with having your expertise valued by clients, heavy involvement with work teams, and success in managing a work schedule paced by defined projects with deadlines. These things have very little to do with the job of *being* a successful PIC. In fact, although many PICs try to maintain some involvement in the work of the office (because they enjoy it), the policy of the firm is that a PIC should not have any chargeable hours at all—100 percent of each PIC's time should be devoted to managing the business. It is not necessarily surprising that the kind of person who enters the accounting profession and then is successful in a large CPA firm may not really want to be a general manager and may not be very good at it. What is surprising is that the dramatic change from being a client service partner to being a PIC comes as such an unpleasant surprise to so many of the newly minted PICs.

Ted Johnson's View of the Incentive Program

Ted Johnson was in the middle of his first five-year term as national managing partner of WO. He could serve additional terms if he were willing and if the policy board reelected him. He had come up through the ranks in one of the predecessor firms that merged into WO. He had run one of the largest WO offices for 10 years and been an area director before becoming national managing partner. He saw his task as helping to improve the profitability of the firm while also ensuring that the right strategic decisions were made to keep the firm prosperous over the longer term. The concept of strategic planning was embryonic at WO, and at the other large CPA firms as well. Johnson was grasping for a way to identify the critical strategic issues and to coalesce the management of the firm around an appropriate strate-

gic thrust. But, at the same time, on the day-to-day front he was "hip deep in alligators."

One major problem was inexperience. One third of the PICs had less than four years' tenure in the job. About 10 had less than two years' tenure. Thus, in a substantial number of offices, a critical issue was just getting the PIC to "think like a general manager," rather than like a client service professional. Also, in many offices, profits were not as good as the partnership felt they should be. This was not only true for offices with an inexperienced PIC. Tough-minded, day-to-day business management skills seemed to be lacking too often. This was particularly troublesome to Ted Johnson, because his election to the top job had been based in large part on a consensus view that he could lead the firm to a better realization of its profit potential. His predecessor's retirement had been somewhat "early" because of widespread concern that the firm was not being managed aggressively enough.

Another problem for Ted Johnson was that many of the PICs just wanted to be left alone by senior management. They were content running a self-contained business. They were willing to pay an "overhead assessment" to the executive office in exchange for use of the national name and for access to national technical expertise. However, they had not made the psychological transition from a local firm to a local office of a national firm. They had to be convinced, somehow, that their local prosperity was significantly related to the prosperity of the national firm.

Finally, Johnson was convinced that managing primarily for short-run profits would hurt the business in the long run. Thus, in addition to getting the PICs oriented to profit and committed to profit growth, he had to try to make them think longer term and beyond their local offices. To top off this challenge, Johnson was not totally sure that the growth theme being pushed in the firm ("We must prove that WO is a firm of comparable stature to the other major firms") was appropriate to bring about the profit growth upon which his future and that of the firm depended. Overall, Ted Johnson believed that the new incentive system would help "calibrate" the partners' actions appropriately for the success of the firm.

The casewriters obtained the following comments from partners in the firm about the new incentive plan.

The Partner-in-Charge of a Large Office in a Fast-Growing Urban Area.

The real focus of this plan is on short-term profits. Net income, collections, and chargeable hours all relate directly to the bottom line. But it is just as important for me to build new clients in this high-growth area. That depends on my efforts to project a favorable image with prospective clients. That means I have to give speeches, be seen and liked around the country club, participate in community activities, and participate in business leadership activities like Rotary and Chamber of Commerce. In addition, I have to develop people internally to manage the future growth in our business. That means paying high salaries, allowing heavy training time, and programming in heavy supervision and "mentoring" time. All these activities are negative in terms of their impact on current billings and short-run profit. In fact, all of these activities take my time away from billable work and from collection efforts. Also, if I am successful in developing talented young people in this office, the chances are very good that those people will get "exported" to other offices because of the firmwide need for good managers. So, I wind up with a thank you and the chance to start all over again spending extra people-related dollars, which hurts current profits. As I see it, I am not personally rewarded for developing the firm, just for being profitable.

An Area Director.

Profit is the name of the game in this firm. It ought to be, because that is what matters most in ultimate analysis. This is a business and the way businesses keep score is the bottom line. Sure it's tough to balance growth goals and intangible factors as well as profitability, but we pay our partners very well to do exactly that. Profit without growth or growth without profit is pretty easy—

the trick is getting both. Outstanding partners are the ones who can give you both. I think the incentive plan's focus on short-run profits, with some attention to longer-run issues, is right on track.

The Partner-in-Charge of a Major Office.

The system says that by 1985 we will include "client service," "human resource development," and "one firm commitment" as additional factors on which a partner's compensation will depend. Let me raise a few issues. What do we mean by "client service"? by "human resource development"? by "one firm commitment"? How do we measure performance on these factors on a monthly or even annual basis? When there are six factors in the equation, what weights are we going to assign to them? Would these weights be the same or different across the practice offices? Who would decide the weights? I think we have to resolve some fundamental questions before we can be sure that our incentive plan would motivate our partners to do the things that senior management wants them to do.

Questions

1. Is Williamson and Oliver committing the "fallacy of hoping for A while rewarding B"?

2. Can you expect PICs to worry a lot about factors not in the formal reward system?

3. Can the "soft," future-oriented performance areas be sufficiently quantified to permit inclusion in the reward system?

4. Given the management task at hand, how would you structure the set of measurements for an office of WO? (What measures and what weights across the set of measures?) Would your answer vary across offices?

5. Given your understanding of the industry situation, WO's position within the industry, and Ted Johnson's sense of mission for WO, is the new incentive plan a positive or a negative factor in the management of the firm?

Case 13–3
Harlan Foundation

Harlan Foundation was created in 1953 under the terms of the will of Martin Harlan, a wealthy Minneapolis benefactor. His bequest was approximately $3 million and its purpose was broadly stated: Income from the funds was to be used for the benefit of the people of Minneapolis and nearby communities.

In the next 35 years, the trustees developed a wide variety of services. These included three infant clinics, a center for the education of special needs children, three family counseling centers, a drug abuse program, a visiting nurses program, and a large rehabilitation facility. These services were provided from nine facilities, located in Minneapolis and surrounding cities. Harlan Foundation was affiliated with several national associations whose members provided similar services.

The foundation operated essentially on a break-even basis. A relatively small fraction of its revenue came from income earned on the principal of the Harlan bequest. Major sources of revenue were fees from clients, contributions, and grants from city, state, and federal governments.

Exhibit 1 is the most recent operating statement. Program expenses included all the expenses associated with individual programs. Administration expenses included the costs of the central office, except for fund-raising expenses. Seventy percent of administration costs were for personnel costs. The staff members (excluding two senior officers) earned an average of $18,000 per year in salaries and fringe benefits.

In 1987, the foundation decided to undertake two additional activities. One was a summer camp, whose clients would be children with

This case was prepared and is copyrighted by Robert N. Anthony, Harvard Business School.

Exhibit 1   Operating Statement for the Year Ended June 30, 1986

Revenues:	
Fees from clients	$ 917,862
Grants from government agencies	1,792,968
Contributions	683,702
Investment income	426,300
Other	24,553
Total revenues	3,845,385
Expenses:	
Program expenses:	
Rehabilitation	1,556,242
Counseling	157,621
Infant clinics	312,007
Education	426,234
Drug abuse	345,821
Visiting nurses	267,910
Other	23,280
Total program expenses	3,089,115
Support:	
Administration	480,326
Dues to national associations	24,603
Fund-raising	182,523
Other	47,862
Total support	735,314
Total expenses	3,824,429
Net income	$ 20,956

physical disabilities. The other was a seminar intended for managers in social service organizations. For both of these ventures, it was necessary to establish the fee that should be charged.

Camp Harlan

The camp, which was renamed Camp Harlan, was donated to the foundation in 1986 by the person who had owned it for many years and who decided to retire. The property consisted of 30 acres, with considerable frontage on a lake, and buildings that would house and feed some 60 campers at a time. The plan was to operate the camp for eight weeks in the summer and to enroll campers for either one or two weeks. The policy was to charge each camper a fee sufficient to cover the cost of operating the camp. Many campers would be unable to pay this fee, and financial aid would be provided for them. The financial aid would cover a part, or in some cases all, of the fee and would come from the general funds of the foundation or, it was hoped, from a government grant.

As a basis for arriving at the fee, Henry Coolidge, financial vice president of the foundation, obtained information on costs from the American Camping Association and from two camps in the vicinity. Although the camp could accommodate at least 60 children, he decided to plan on only 50 at a time in the first year, a total of 400 camper-weeks for the season. With assured financial aid, he believed there would be no difficulty in enrolling this number. His budget prepared on this basis is shown in Exhibit 2.

Coolidge discussed this budget with Sally Harris, president of the foundation. Harris agreed that it was appropriate to plan for 400 camper-weeks and also agreed that the budget estimates were reasonable. During this discussion, questions were raised about several items that were not in the budget.

Exhibit 2   Budget for Camp Harlan

Staff salaries and benefits	$ 90,000
Food	19,000
Operating supplies	4,000
Telephone and utilities	9,000
Insurance	15,100
Rental of equipment	7,000
Contingency and miscellaneous (5%)	7,200
Total	$151,300

The central office of the foundation would continue to plan the camp, do the necessary publicity, screen applications and make decisions on financial aid, pay bills, and do other bookkeeping and accounting work. There was no good way of estimating how many resources this work would require. Ten staff members worked in administration, and as a rough guess about half a person-year might be involved in these activities.

There were no plans to hire an additional employee in the central office. The work load associated with other activities usually tapered off somewhat during the summer, and it was believed that the staff could absorb the extra work.

At the camp itself, approximately four volunteers per week would help the paid staff. They would receive meals and lodging, but no pay. No allowance for the value of their services was included in the budget.

The budget did not include an amount for depreciation of the plant facilities. Lakefront property was valuable, and, if the camp and its buildings were sold to a developer, perhaps as much as $500,000 could be realized.

The Seminar

The foundation planned to hold a one-day seminar in the fall of 1987 to discuss the effect on social service organizations of the income tax act passed in 1986 and other recent regulatory developments. (Although these organizations were exempt from income taxes, except on unrelated business income, recent legislation and regulations were expected to have an impact on contributions, investment policy, and personnel policies, among other things.) The purposes of the seminar were partly to generate income and partly to provide a service for smaller welfare organizations.

In the spring of 1987, Harris approved the plans for this seminar. The following information is extracted from a memorandum prepared by Coolidge at that time.

It is estimated that there will be 30 participants in the seminar.

The seminar will be held at a local hotel, and the hotel will charge $200 for rental of the room and $20 per person for meals and refreshments.

Audiovisual equipment will be rented at a cost of $100.

There will be two instructors, and each will be paid a fee of $500.

Printing and mailing of promotional material will cost $900.

Each participant will be given a notebook containing relevant material. Each notebook will cost $10 to prepare, and 60 copies of the notebook will be printed.

Coolidge will preside, and one Harlan staff member will be present at the seminar. The hotel will charge for their meals and for the meals of the two instructors.

Other incidental out-of-pocket expenses are estimated to be $200.

Fees charged for one-day seminars in the area range from $50 to $495. The $50 fee ex-cluded meals and was charged by a brokerage firm that probably viewed the seminar as generating customer goodwill. The $495 fee was charged by several national organizations that run hundreds of seminars annually throughout the United States. A number of one-day seminars are offered in the Minneapolis area at a fee in the range of $150 to $250, including a meal.

Except for the number of participants, the above estimates were based on reliable information and were accepted by Harris.

Questions

1. What weekly fee should be charged for campers?

2. Assuming a fee of $100, what is the break-even point of the seminar?

3. What fee should be charged for the seminar?

CASE 13–4
PIEDMONT UNIVERSITY

When Hugh Scott was inaugurated as the 12th President of Piedmont University in 1984, the university was experiencing a financial crisis. For several years enrollments had been declining and costs had been increasing. The resulting deficit has been made up by using the principal of "quasi-endowment" funds. (For true endowment funds, only the income could be used for operating purposes; the principal legally could not be used. Quasi-endowment funds had been accumulated out of earlier years' surpluses with the intention that only the income on these funds would be used for operating purposes; however, there was no legal prohibition on the use of the principal.) The quasi-endowment funds were nearly exhausted.

Scott immediately instituted measures to turn the financial situation around. He raised tuition, froze faculty and staff hirings, and curtailed operating costs. Although he had come from another university and, therefore, was viewed with some skepticism by the Piedmont faculty, Scott was a persuasive person, and the faculty and trustees generally agreed with his actions. In the year ended June 30, 1986, there was a small operating surplus.

In 1986, Scott was approached by Neil Malcolm, a Piedmont alumnus and partner of a local management consulting firm, who volunteered to examine the situation and make recommendations for permanent measures to maintain the university's financial health. Scott accepted this offer.

Malcolm spent about half time at Piedmont for the next several months and had many conversations with Scott, other administrative officers, and trustees. Early in 1987, he submitted his report. It recommended increased recruiting

and fund-raising activities, but its most important and controversial recommendation was that the university be reorganized into a set of profit centers.

At that time the principal means of financial control was an annual expenditure budget submitted by the deans of each of the schools and the administrative heads of support departments. After discussion with the president and financial vice president, and usually with minor modifications, these budgets were approved. There was a general understanding that each school would live within the faculty size and salary numbers in its approved budget, but not much stress was placed on adhering to the other items.

Malcolm proposed that in future the deans and other administrators would submit budgets covering both the revenues and the expenditures for their activities. The proposal also involved some shift in responsibilities and new procedures for crediting revenues to the profit centers that earned them and charging expenditures to the profit centers responsible for them. He made rough estimates of the resulting revenues and expenditures of each profit center using 1986 numbers; these are given in Exhibit 1.

A series of discussions about the proposal were held in the University Council, which consisted of the president, academic deans, provost, and financial vice president. Although there was support for the general ideas, there was disagreement on some of the specifics, as described below.

Central Administrative Costs

Currently, no universitywide administrative costs were charged to academic departments. The proposal was that these costs would be allocated to profit centers in proportion to the rel-

---

This case was prepared and is copyrighted by Robert N. Anthony, Harvard Business School.

Exhibit 1   Piedmont University: Rough Estimates of 1986 Impact of the Proposals ($ millions)

Profit Center	Revenue	Expenditures
Undergraduate liberal arts school	$30.0	$29.2
Graduate liberal arts school	5.6	11.5
Business school	15.3	12.3
Engineering school	17.0	17.3
Law school	6.7	6.5
Theological school	1.2	3.4
Unallocated revenue*	5.0	
Total, academic	80.8	80.2
Other:		
Central administration	10.1	10.1
Athletic	2.6	2.6
Computer	3.4	3.4
Central maintenance	5.7	5.7
Library	3.4	3.4

*Unrestricted gifts and endowment revenue, to be allocated by the president.

ative costs of each. The graduate school deans regarded this as unfair. Many costs incurred by the administration were in fact closely related to the undergraduate school. Furthermore, they did not like the idea of being held responsible for an allocated cost that they could not control.

Gifts and Endowment

The revenue from annual gifts would be reduced by the cost of fund-raising activities. The net amount of annual gifts plus endowment income (except gifts and income from endowment designated for a specific school) would be allocated by the president, according to his decision on the needs of each school, subject to the approval of the board of trustees. The deans thought this was giving the president too much authority. They did not have a specific alternative but thought that some way of reducing the president's discretionary powers should be developed.

Athletics

Piedmont's athletic teams did not generate enough revenue to cover the cost of operating the athletic department. The proposal was to make this department self-sufficient by charging fees to students who participated in intramural sports or who used the swimming pool, tennis courts, gymnasium, and other facilities as individuals. Although there was no strong opposition, some felt that this would involve student dissatisfaction, as well as much new paperwork.

Maintenance

Each school had a maintenance department that was responsible for housekeeping in its section of the campus and for minor maintenance jobs. Sizable jobs were performed at the school's request by a central maintenance department. The proposal was that in future the central maintenance department would charge schools and other profit centers for the work they did at the actual cost of this work, including both direct and overhead costs. The dean of the business school said that this would be acceptable provided that profit centers were authorized to have maintenance work done by an outside contractor if its price was lower than that charged by the maintenance department. Malcolm explained that he had discussed this possibility with the head of maintenance, who opposed it on the grounds that outside contractors could not be held accountable for the high-quality standards that Piedmont required.

Computer

Currently, the principal mainframe computers and related equipment were located in and supervised by the engineering school. Students and faculty members could use them as they wished, subject to an informal check on overuse by people in the computer rooms. About one quarter of the capacity of these computers was used for administrative work. A few departmental mainframe computers and hundreds of microcomputers and word processors were located throughout the university, but there was no central record of how many there were.

The proposal was that each user of the engineering school computers would be charged a fee based on usage. The fee would recover the full cost of the equipment, including overhead. Each school would be responsible for regulating the amount of cost that could be incurred by its faculty and students so the total cost did not exceed the approved item in the school's budget. (The computers had software that easily attributed the cost to each user.) Several deans objected to this plan. They pointed out that neither students nor faculty understood the potential value of computers, and they wanted to encourage computer usage as a significant part of the educational and research experience. A charge would have the opposite effect, they maintained.

Library

The university library was the main repository of books and other material, and there were small libraries in each of the schools. The proposal was that each student and faculty member who used the university library would be charged a fee, either on an annual basis or on some basis related to the time spent in the library or the number of books withdrawn. (The library had a secure entrance at which a guard was stationed, so a record of who used it could be obtained without too much difficulty.) There was some dissatisfaction with the amount of paperwork that such a plan would require, but it was not regarded as being as important as some of the other items.

Cross Registration

Currently, students enrolled at one school could take courses at another school without charge. The proposal was that the school at which a course was taken would reimburse the school in which the student was enrolled. The amount charged would be the total semester tuition of the school at which the course was taken, divided by the number of courses that a student normally would take in a semester, with adjustments for variations in credit hours.

Questions

1. How should each of the issues described above be resolved?
2. Do you see other problems with the introduction of profit centers? If so, how would you deal with them?
3. What are the alternatives of a profit center approach?
4. Assuming that most of the issues could be resolved to your satisfaction, would you recommend that the profit center idea be adopted, rather than an alternative?

CASE 13–5
CHEMICAL BANK

Chemical Bank, with deposits averaging well over $1 billion, was one of the largest banks in the United States in 1960. Its banking operations were conducted in a main office and in several dozen branch offices located throughout the New York metropolitan area. A partial organization chart is shown in Exhibit 1.

Branch offices operated as if they were independent banks. They served individual, commercial, and industrial customers by accepting demand, savings, and time deposits, by extending various types of loans, and by performing other services normally expected of a bank. The sizes and operating characteristics of the branches varied over a wide range. Average deposits outstanding ranged from $1 million to over $100 million; average loans outstanding, from no loans to over $100 million. Moreover, the ratio of deposits to loans varied considerably from one branch to another; most branches had more deposits than loans, but a few had more loans than deposits. In brief, both the magnitude and composition of assets and liabilities were significantly different among the different branches. Inasmuch as these differences were related to the geographical location of the branches, the difficulty of evaluating and comparing the performance of branches for the purpose of overall planning and control was inherent in the situation. The design and operation of a planning and control system for this purpose was the responsibility of the control division.

Among various reports reaching top management, the quarterly comparative earnings statement (see Exhibits 2 and 3) played a central role in the evaluation of branch performance. The report was designed to show the ex-

tent to which branches attained three important goals: (1) branches should operate within their budgets, (2) branches should grow in deposits and loans, and (3) branches should earn satisfactory profits. Accordingly, the statement showed for each branch the budgeted and actual amounts of deposits and loans outstanding, and income, expenses, and earnings for the current quarter, the year to date, and the year to date for the preceding year.

Budget

In early November, each branch prepared a budget for the following year for submission to headquarters of the banking division and to top management. The branches were furnished a booklet containing sample forms, 24 pages of detailed instructions, and a brief set of policy guides from top management to facilitate the preparation of their budgets. The instructions gave the procedures to be followed in arriving at the budget amounts for specific items. It was, for instance, specified that the starting point for forecasting was to be the prior year's figures on the quarterly basis, that the income item of interest on loans was to be derived from the projected volume of loans and loan rates, that painting cost should not be included in the item for building maintenance expense, and so on.

Since salaries were the biggest single expense item, and the hiring and releasing of employees involved considerable cost, utmost care was required in budgeting this item. Branches were instructed to arrive at staffing requirements for the next year after a thorough examination of anticipated increases in productivity arising from computerization or otherwise improved operating procedures, of anticipated changes in the volume of activity, and of advantages and disadvantages of using overtime or temporary

---

This case was prepared by R. N. Anthony, Harvard Business School. Copyright by the President and Fellows of Harvard College. Harvard Business School case 172–228.

EXHIBIT 1

Partial organization chart

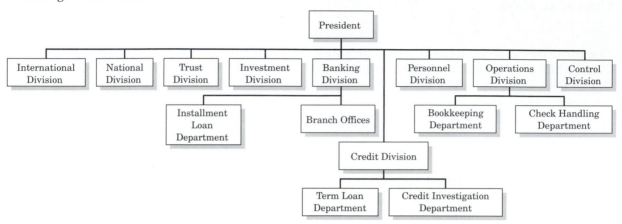

or part-time help. If the number of the required staff of a branch thus determined exceeded the number previously authorized by top management, the reason for the difference had to be thoroughly documented and substantiated to banking division headquarters and the budget committee. Top management was extremely critical of subsequent requests by the branches for staff increases that had not been reflected in the budgets.

In general, there were two types of income and expense items—those directly identifiable with a particular branch, and those not directly identifiable with a particular branch. Branches were instructed to budget only those direct expenses under their control. Indirect expenses were allocated to branches by the control division. In addition, the budgeting of certain direct expenses, such as depreciation of fixtures, employee benefits, and deferred compensation, was done by the control division because the branches had only secondary control over these expenses.

Earnings Statement

The control division had encountered a number of serious problems in trying to produce an earnings statement that would be most useful for the branches and for the management of the banking division. The control division resolved some of these problems in the following ways.

Installment Loans.   Recordkeeping, issuance of coupon books, and part of collection work for installment loans generated by all branches were handled centrally by the installment loan department; and income earned from installment loans, therefore, was credited initially to this department. This income was in large part attributable to the branches that generated the loans and, therefore, was redistributed to them. The current procedure was to distribute gross operating income less the direct cost of "borrowed" funds and operating expenses of the department on the basis of the total indirect installment loans generated by the branch during a revolving annual cycle.

An alternative basis that had been considered was to apportion the net income of the installment department according to the number of payments received by branches, since this measure of activity reflected the clerical time spent for coupon handling. This alternative was not adopted, on the grounds that it did not give branches enough motivation to seek more new

EXHIBIT 2   Comparative Statement of Earnings, 1960 (Branch A)

3rd Quarter			January 1 through September 30	
Actual	*Budget*		*Actual*	*Budget*
		Income:		
$ 13,177	$ 12,600	Interest on loans	$ 33,748	$ 35,200
6,373	4,800	Service chgs.—regular A/Cs	14,572	14,100
3,816	3,600	Service chgs.—special ck	11,114	10,700
1,168	1,300	Safe deposit rentals	4,317	4,500
2,237	2,154	Installment loans (net)	5,126	5,406
—	—	Special loans (net)	—	—
1,010	1,200	Fees, comm., other income	3,321	3,300
27,781	25,654	Total direct income	72,198	73,206
104,260	102,128	Interest on excess (borr.) funds	324,434	306,166
$ 132,041	$ 127,802	Gross income	$ 396,632	$ 379,372
		Expenses:		
$ 32,363	$ 32,617	Salaries	$ 96,151	$ 97,164
2,995	2,995	Deferred compensation	8,865	8,865
5,232	4,689	Employee benefits	14,925	14,067
11,485	11,489	Rent and occupancy	34,398	33,947
6,824	7,560	Interest on deposits	20,455	21,780
9,458	8,090	Other direct	25,688	23,930
3,128	3,097	Office administration	9,676	9,725
19,183	17,642	Service departments	57,059	52,399
6,415	5,061	Indirect and overhead	14,964	14,273
97,043	93,200	Gross expenses	282,181	276,150
34,998	34,602	Net earnings before taxes	114,451	103,222
18,955	18,741	Income tax prov. (credit)	61,978	55,906
$ 16,043	$ 15,861	Net earnings after taxes	$ 52,464	$ 47,316
$12,655,000	$12,550,000	Average deposits—Demand	$13,134,000	$12,650,000
979,000	1,100,000	Savings	986,000	1,057,000
55,000	55,000	Time	40,000	43,000
233,000	190,000	US	213,000	183,000
$13,922,000	$13,895,000	Total	$14,373,000	$ 33,000
900,000	870,000	Average loans	775,000	827,000
5.82	5.76	Average loan rate	5.82	5.69
		Earnings rate on:		
4.08	3.95	Excess (borr.) funds	4.05	3.95
6.50	6.40	Savings deposits	6.46	6.40
26.5%	27.1%	Net earnings ratio (before taxes)	28.9%	27.2%
		Memo:		
—	—	Losses—before taxes	—	—
—	—	Recoveries—before taxes	—	—

Exhibit 3   Comparative Statement of Earnings, 1960 (Branch B)

| 3rd Quarter | | | January 1 through September 30 | |
Actual	Budget		1960 Actual	1960 Budget
		Income:		
$ 951,617	$ 833,300	Interest on loans	$ 2,646,813	$ 2,202,750
7,015	7,400	Service chgs.—regular A/Cs	24,020	21,900
8,211	7,600	Service chgs.—special ck	23,284	22,600
2,049	2,100	Safe deposit rentals	6,712	7,100
9,202	9,478	Installment loans (net)	21,402	23,790
—	212	Special loans (net)	85	556
8,081	3,100	Fees, comm., other income	22,517	12,800
986,175	863,190	Total direct income	2,744,933	2,291,496
(191,650)	(121,960)	Interest on excess (borr.) funds	(430,444)	(121,493)
$ 794,525	$ 741,230	Gross income	$ 2,314,489	$ 2,170,003
		Expenses:		
$ 69,308	$ 62,633	Salaries	$ 197,572	$ 185,634
5,646	5,646	Deferred compensation	16,938	16,938
9,180	7,989	Employee benefits	25,833	23,967
27,674	27,775	Rent and occupancy	82,726	83,375
15,878	18,230	Interest on deposits	47,589	52,650
25,637	23,660	Other direct	86,112	71,400
17,232	17,072	Office administration	53,321	53,606
89,724	95,719	Service departments	290,082	283,531
22,406	18,001	Indirect and overhead	53,643	51,166
282,685	276,725	Gross expenses	853,816	822,267
511,840	464,505	Net earnings before taxes	1,460,673	1,347,736
277,212	251,576	Income tax prov. (credit)	791,100	729,934
$ 234,628	$ 212,929	Net earnings after taxes	$ 669,573	$ 617,802
$67,901,000	$70,000,000	Average deposits—Demand	$69,425,000	$72,667,000
2,354,000	2,700,000	Savings	2,328,000	2,600,000
74,000	90,000	Time	52,000	66,000
5,194,000	1,900,000	US	4,086,000	1,733,000
$75,523,000	$74,690,000	Total	$75,891,000	$77,066,000
72,129,000	65,500,000	Average loans	67,446,000	57,666,000
5.25	5.10	Average loan rate	5.24	5.10
		Earnings rate on:		
4.08	3.95	Excess (borr.) funds	4.05	3.95
6.50	6.40	Savings deposits	6.46	6.40
64.4%	62.7%	Net earnings ratio (before taxes)	63.1%	62.1%
		Memo:		
—	—	Losses—before taxes	5,559	—
—	66	Recoveries—before taxes	798	—

EXHIBIT 4   Calculation of Interest Income on Excess Funds, Branch A (first three quarters of 1960)

Calculation of Excess Funds	(000s)		
Total demand deposits	$13,134		
Less: reciprocal bank balances; float	(727)		
Plus: treasury tax and loan a/c	221		
Adjusted demand deposits	12,628		
Less: reserve at 18%	(2,273)		
Net demand deposits		$10,355	
Savings deposits	1,026		
Less: reserve at 5%	$ (51)		
Net savings deposits		975	
Net deposits available for investment		11,330	
Less: loans, cash, other assets		(1,229)	
Net excess funds		$10,101	

Calculation of Interest Income on Excess Funds	Principal	Annual Rate	Three Quarters	Interest
In special investment pool (63%)	$ 614,000	* 7.88%	* 3/4 =	$ 36,270
In regular investment pool (37%)	361,000	* 4.05%	* 3/4 =	10,962
Savings deposits (100%)	975,000	* 6.46%	* 3/4 =	47,232
In regular investment pool—demand deposits	9,126,000	* 4.05%	* 3/4 =	277,202
Net excess funds	$10,101,000			
Interest on excess funds				$324,434

installment loans, particularly since customers could make their installment payments at any branch they chose. An alternative basis considered was the amount of average loans outstanding. The controller thought this might be more equitable than the currently used basis, but he was of the opinion that the gain to be obtained from the adoption of the new basis was not large enough to offset the additional necessary record keeping.

Interest on Excess (or Borrowed) Funds. Branches and other operating units, with funds available for investment in excess of their own requirements for loans, cash, and other assets, shared in the net earnings of the investment di-

vision; branches and other operating units whose asset requirements exceeded their available funds were charged for funds "borrowed." There was a wide variation in the ratio of deposits to loans among branches, and some branches were credited with the interest on excess funds in an amount higher than their direct income. An example of the calculation of this important income or charge item is shown in Exhibit 4.

As shown in the top section of Exhibit 4, the first step was to compute the amount of excess (or borrowed) funds for the branch. Funds were divided into two pools: (1) special pool—earnings from special long-term, high-yield municipal securities, which were considered as an investment of part of the savings and time deposits; and (2) regular pool-earnings from other portfolio securities investments, interest on certain loans, and sundry earnings. As a result, the special-pool investments yielded a higher rate of return than the regular-pool investments.

Third, branches with savings deposits were credited at the interest rate of the special pool on the basis of their pro rata share of savings deposits. Net savings deposits in excess of the principal of investment in the special pool, together with excess funds other than savings deposits, received pro rata credit from the earnings of the regular investment pool. Branches that borrowed funds were charged at the regular-pool rate. In summary, the two rates from the two pools were as follows:

Special-pool rate: Net earnings of special pool/ special pool securities principal (part of total savings deposits)

Regular-pool rate: Net earnings from regular pool ÷ excess funds less borrowed funds less special securities principal.

For the first three quarters of 1960, the budgeted regular pool rate and special pool rate were 3.95 percent and 7.81 percent; the actual rates were 4.05 percent and 7.88 percent, respectively. Thus, for Branch A the interest on excess funds for the first three quarters was calculated as shown in the lower section of Exhibit 4.

Rent and Occupancy Cost.   Some branches operated in leased space, whereas others operated in bank-owned buildings. The first group was charged with the actual rent paid; but the second was charged with the "fair rental value," which was determined by outside real estate appraisers. The practice was thought to put the two groups on the same footing. The fair rental value charges were internal bookkeeping entries offset by credits to real estate accounts and, therefore, indicated the profitability of each building. The determination of the fair rental value was not difficult, and there had been no significant controversies involving its calculation.

Advertising.   General or institutional advertising was charged to other indirect expenses. (See below for the allocation of other indirect expenses.) Advertising related to a specific branch was charged directly to that branch, except that, when advertising was placed in mass media, such as radio, television, and newspapers with general circulation, 33 percent of the expense was allocated to other indirect expenses and 67 percent was allocated to the specific branches involved. The theory of the exception was that when mass media were used, the whole bank benefited to a certain extent.

Banking Division Headquarters and General Administration.   All expenses of the banking division headquarters, including the salaries of officers in the division headquarters, were allocated to branches on the basis of their prior year's average gross deposits. The figure for average gross deposits was considered as the best single measure of branch activity.

The salaries of general administrative officers of the bank were first allocated among divisions on the basis of the time spent on problems of each division as estimated by each officer. The amount of general administrative salaries thus allocated to the banking division was, in turn, allocated among branches on the basis of gross deposits in the prior year. All other general administrative expenses were charged on the same basis.

Bookkeeping Department.   Much of the bookkeeping work was centralized for the whole bank. However, since the central department had been established only in 1959, several offices continued to do their own bookkeeping in 1960. The expenses of the central bookkeeping department, therefore, were allocated only to the branches it serviced. There were eight functional cost centers in the bookkeeping department, and each cost center had its own basis of allocation. The bases of four of the cost centers are given below.

1. *Regular Bookkeeping Cost Center.* In the bookkeeping department, a permanent clerical staff was assigned to process the accounts of each branch. Allocations to branches were based on the salaries of this assigned staff, plus fringe benefits and related overhead cost.

2. *Bank Ledgers Cost Center.* Allocation was on the basis of debit and credit activity as determined by an analysis made from time to time. Inasmuch as the main activity of this cost center was the posting of transactions to ledger sheets, the number of debit and credit entries was preferred to any other basis (e.g., number of accounts). A new survey of debit and credit statistics was made by the analysis department whenever it was believed that there had been a material change from the prior survey period and, in any event, at least once a year.

3. *Special Checking Cost Center.* Same as 2.

4. *Special Statement Section.* Allocation was on the basis of a number of accounts handled. The activity of the section was to send out special statements on customers' special requests.

Before adoption of the current method based on the cost center concept, weight of statements mailed out had been the basis of allocation for the expenses of the entire department. The current practice was regarded as more accurate, because there were very few temporary movements of staff and machine services from one cost center to another and because there was a significant variation in the activity measures of the cost centers.

According to the controller, the main controversy involving the expenses of the bookkeeping department was not with respect to the basis of allocation but, rather, with respect to the absolute level of expenses of the department. Complaints were heard from those branches serviced by the department to the effect that they were handicapped relative to branches that did their own bookkeeping, because the cost charged by the central bookkeeping department was considerably higher than the cost that would be incurred if the branch did its own bookkeeping. The controller thought branches that had this opinion failed to recognize that the bookkeeping expenses shown in the earnings statements of the branches with their own bookkeeping were only part of the true bookkeeping cost, because an appropriate portion of supervisory salaries, occupancy costs, supplies, etc., was not included in the item. When the bookkeeping was centralized for a branch, the benefit gained from relieving the supervisors of supervising bookkeeping activity usually appeared as increased loans and deposits, and better management generally.

Check Clearance Department.   The total cost of this department was divided among 12 functional cost centers, based on the number of employees assigned to each and the volume of its work. The cost of each cost center was, in turn, charged to branches. Examples of the basis of allocation are given below.

1. *IBM proof machine operation—exchanges:* allocated on the basis of number of checks handled.

2. *IBM proof machine operation—deposits:* allocated on the basis of the number of deposit items.

3. *Check desk:* allocated on the basis of the number of checks handled.

4. *Transit clerical:* allocated on the basis of number of deposit items.

5. *Supervision:* allocated to the various check clearance department cost centers in ratio to labor costs.

As was the case with the bookkeeping centers, the measures of activity (checks handled and number of deposit items) were based on periodic surveys and remained unchanged until significant changes in the relative activity of branches indicated the need for a new survey. Every cost center's activity was reviewed at least once a year for this purpose.

There were two important sources of trouble in allocation of the expenses of the check clearance department. One was that branches cashed checks issued by other branches; the other was that branches received deposits for customers whose accounts were in other branches. In the periodic activity analyses made to determine the basis of allocating cost, the "number of checks cashed" was the number of checks actually cashed in the branch, whether or not the account was located in the branch. Similarly, the "number of deposit items" was the number of deposits made in the branch. Although it had been believed that the effect of these interbranch services largely offset one another, a recent study by the control division indicated that they, in fact, resulted in distortions with respect to certain branches. The control division was currently working on a method of allocation by which the charge would be made to the branch that benefited most—that is, the branch in which the account was located.

Credit Investigation Department. Although most branches had their own credit analysis staffs, they often asked the central credit department to make investigations. The expenses of the central credit investigation department, therefore, were allocated to the branches that requested its service. The basis of allocation was the number of requests for credit investigation weighted by the typical time required for the analyses performed. The weight for the various types of investigation was determined by the analysis department on the basis of an actual time study.

Term Loan Department. Income from term loans was credited to the branches that generated the loans. Officers of the term loan department actively counseled the branches in negotiating terms with customers, in drawing up loan contracts, and in reviewing existing loans. It was necessary, therefore, that the expenses of the term loan department be allocated to the branches that used its service. The basis of allo-

cation was the number of loans considered, the number of loans outstanding, and the number of amendments to existing loans, weighted by the unit handling time of each of three classes. To determine the weight, the analysis department asked the staff of the term loan department to estimate the time spent on each class.

Personnel Division. The expenses of this division were allocated to all operating units in the ratio of the number of employees in each operating unit to the total.

Other Indirect Expenses. Items of a general overhead nature, such as expenses of the operations division (except the direct cost of examining a branch, which was charged directly), cost of the senior training program, general institutional advertising, contributions, etc., were included under this heading. The basis of allocation of these expenses among branches was the ratio of annual operating expenses (excluding other indirect expenses and interest on deposits) of each branch to the total operating expenses of all branches.

Deposits and Loans. In the lower part of the comparative statement were shown the budgeted and actual loans and deposits outstanding. Both top management and branch managers exercised a close watch over these primary indicators of the level of the branch's operation. The controller, however, believed that the ultimate test of the office performance should not rest with these items but, rather, with earnings. He maintained that the effect of changes in deposits and loans should and would be reflected in the earnings statement.

Controller's Views on Allocations

The controller believed that some arbitrariness was inevitable in the allocation of the income and expense items described above. With dozens of branches, each with its own operating characteristics, it was impossible to have a "perfect" or "right" system for all of them. What was more important, according to the controller, was agreement on the part of the branch managers that the system was generally equitable. If managers agreed on the fairness of the system, he believed, it was likely to be a success. The controller, therefore, let it be known to branch managers that the system was always open for revision, and he encouraged them to make known any criticisms they had. After the control division had done its best to find a workable system, the initiative for suggesting changes was with the branch managers. The controller said that several changes had been made as a result of branch managers' suggestions.

He warned them, however, against a blind and apathetic acceptance; the acceptance should be positive and constructive. On acceptance of the system, branch managers should be concerned with the reported result and make necessary efforts to improve it. Thus, he said, branch managers were told clearly that the earnings statement was used to evaluate their performance. This, he thought, attached sufficient importance to the matter to prevent any possible indifference.

Attitudes of Branch Managers on Allocations.   The managers of two offices, A and B, held different opinions about the system. The operating characteristics of these branches were different, as indicated by their comparative statements of earnings for the third quarter of 1960, reproduced in Exhibits 2 and 3. Branch A was relatively small and deposit-heavy, did its own bookkeeping, and operated in a leased space, whereas Branch B was larger, loan-heavy, used the centralized bookkeeping department, and operated in a bank-owned building.

> **Comment by Manager of Branch A.**   The statement is useful because I like to see, at least quickly, whether I am within the budget and what caused the deviations from it, if any.
>
> The earnings of our branch are relatively low, because the volume of business is limited by the location.

We have more deposits than our loan requirements; consequently, we get credit for the excess funds. In fact, as you see, for the first three quarters of 1960, interest on excess funds was more than four times the total direct income. The 4.05 percent rate on the excess funds seems fair enough, but we try always to increase our loans in order to increase our earnings. However, the location of our office is a limiting factor.

Since rent and occupancy is the actual rent paid to the owner of the building, we can't have any quarrel about that, but the service department charges are certainly too high. We don't have any control over these costs; yet we are charged for them. I am not complaining that this is unfair; on the contrary, I believe branches should share the burden. My only misgiving is whether those service departments are doing enough to cut down on their costs.

About one-half of the service department expenses charged to our branch is for check clearing service. Although I don't know the basis of allocation, I don't doubt that it is fair. Besides, even if I should have some questions about the basis, probably it wouldn't reach up there; the communication channel from here to the top is long and tedious.

At present, we do our own bookkeeping, but soon this will be centralized. I have heard some managers complain that the cost charged to them for the centralized bookkeeping is higher than the cost when they did their own bookkeeping. However, such intangible gains as prestige and customer relations may justify a little higher cost. At any rate, we wouldn't have any choice if top management decides to centralize our bookkeeping. It may be better in the long run.

Although I don't know exactly what items are included in other direct and indirect and overhead expenses, I don't think they are excessive. The control division is trying to be fair.

In summary, I think the statement is useful, but there are many factors you should consider in interpreting it.

> **Comment by Manager of Branch B.**   The statement is a fair measure of how branches are doing. It is true that the location of a branch has a lot to do with its operation; in evaluating a particular branch, the location is an important element to be taken into account. To take the extreme case, you don't need a branch in a desert. If a branch can't show earnings after being charged with its fair share of all costs, perhaps the purpose of its existence is lost.
>
> High volume and efficient operation have contributed to our high level of earnings. Our branch has more loans than can be sustained by our own deposits; thus, we are charged with interest on borrowed funds on the theory that we would have to pay the interest if we borrowed

from outside. Of course, by increasing deposits we could meet the loan requirements and add to our earnings a good part of the interest on borrowed funds; indeed, we have been trying to lure more deposits to our branch. Quite apart from this special effort, however, we do not neglect to seek more loan opportunities, for loans increase earnings even after the interest charge.

Our office is in a bank-owned building; but, instead of controversial depreciation and maintenance charges, we are charged with the fair rental value. We are satisfied with this practice.

The bookkeeping of our branch is centralized. I believe we could do it for less money if we did our own bookkeeping; but competing banks have centralized bookkeeping departments, and we have to go along. I suspect there are some intangible benefits being gained, too.

If I really sat down and thoroughly examined all the allocation bases, I might find some things that could be improved. But the fact of life is that we must draw a line somewhere; some arbitrariness will always be there. Furthermore, why should our branch raise questions? We are content with the way things are.

Comments by Banking Division Headquarters. We call this report [Exhibits 2 and 3] our Bible, and, like the actual Bible, it must be interpreted carefully. Many factors affect the performance of a branch that do not show up on the report. For example, in an area that is going downhill the manager of a branch has to work terribly hard just to keep his deposits from declining, whereas in a growing area, the manager can read the *New York Times* all day and still show an impressive increase in deposits. The location of the branch in the neighborhood, its outward appearance, its decor, the lay-out of its facilities—all can affect its volume of business. Changes in the level of interest rates, which are noncontrollable, also have a significant effect on income. At headquarters, we are aware of these factors and take them into account when we read the reports. The unfortunate fact is that some managers—for example, those in declining areas—may not believe that we take them into account. Such a manager may worry about his apparently poor performance as shown on the report, and this has a bad psychological effect on him.

One other difficulty with the report is that it may encourage the manager to be interested too much in his own branch at the expense of the bank as a whole. When a customer moves to another part of town, the manager may try to persuade him to leave his account at the same branch, even though the customer can be served better by a branch near his new location. We even hear of two branches competing for the same customer, which certainly doesn't add to the reputation of the bank. Or, to take another kind of problem, a manager may be reluctant to add another teller because of the increased expense, even though he actually needs one to give proper service to his customers.

Of course, the earnings report is just one factor in judging the performance of a bank manager. Among the others are the growth of deposits compared with the potential for the area; the number of calls he makes soliciting new business (we get a monthly report on this); the loans that get into difficulty; complaint letters from customers; the annual audit of operations made by the control division; and, most important, personnel turnover, or any other indications of how well he is developing his personnel. Some of these factors are indicated in these statistics [see Exhibit 5], which are prepared at banking division headquarters.

EXHIBIT 5 Branch Office Report

Line	All Dollar Amounts in Thousands Unless Otherwise Stated	JAN.	FEB.	MAR.	APRIL	MAY	JUNE	JULY	AUG.	SEPT.	OCT.	NOV.	DEC.	YEAR AVERAGE
	DEPOSITS—AVERAGE													
1	Demand—(Ind., Part., Corp.) $	14 038	13 473	12 330	12 919	13 108	12 911	12 596	11 907	12 746	12 202			
2	Demand—Banks $	50	50	—	—	—	—	—	—	—	—			
3	Special Checking $	221	218	220	251	235	216	237	244	236	219			
4	Treas. Tax & Loan Account $	118	149	238	124	270	321	232	202	265	196			
5	Savings $	987	974	1 001	990	976	1 012	972	978	986	1 013			
6	Christmas Club $	15	23	30	35	41	46	51	55	60	63			
7	Time $	—	—	—	—	—	—	—	—	—	—			
8	Total $	15 429	14 887	13 819	14 319	14 630	14 506	14 088	13 386	14 293	13 693			
	NUMBER OF ACCOUNTS													
9	Demand—(Ind., Part., Corp.)	1 515	1 513	1 507	1 503	1 516	1 511	1 514	1 497	1 478	1 473			
10	Demand—Banks	1	—	—	—	—	—	—	—	—	—			
11	Special Checking	868	865	884	892	894	900	903	911	939	948			
12	Savings	585	587	593	589	587	591	593	587	621	645			
13	Christmas Club	540	536	534	538	533	530	526	519	516	511			
14	Time	—	—	—	—	—	—	—	—	—	—			
15	Total	3 509	3 501	3 518	3 522	3 530	3 532	3 536	3 514	3 554	3 577			
	LOANS													
16	Total Loans—Average $	723	755	720	627	672	773	841	889	971	961			
17	Installment Loan—Volume $	20	24	36	31	35	22	25	34	27	39			
18	Spec. Loan Dept.—Month End $	—	—	—	—	—	—	—	—	—	—			
	NUMBER OF BORROWERS													
19	Total Loans	48	58	50	49	51	54	55	60	62	63			
20	Installment Loan—Made	24	37	46	50	32	30	28	45	44	39			
21	Special Loan Dept.	—	—	—	—	—	—	—	—	—	—			
22	Staff—Number of Officers	4	4	4	4	4	4	4	4	3	3			
23	No. of Employees—Auth Budget	25	25	25	25	25	25	25	25	25	25			
24	Total	29	29	29	29	29	29	29	29	28	28			
25	Overtime & Supper Money Payments (To nearest dollar) $	276	135	273	93	496	123	536	370	350	220			*YEAR—TOTALS*
	SERVICE CHARGES (To nearest dollar)													
26	Regular Checking Accounts $	1 543	1 578	1 445	2 225	2 550	2 858	2 378	1 998	1 997	1 833			
27	Special Checking Accounts $	1 017	1 119	1 220	1 397	1 223	1 322	1 313	1 237	1 266	1 340			
28	Total $	2 560	2 697	2 665	1 622	3 773	2 180	3 691	3 235	3 263	3 173			

Income and Expense By Quarters and Cumulative

To Nearest Dollar	1st Quarter	2nd Quarter	Jan. thru June	3rd Quarter	Jan. thru Sept.	4th Quarter	Jan. thru Dec.
Gross Income $	133 060	131 531	264 591	132 041	396 632		
Gross Expenses $	92 050	93 088	185 138	97 043	282 181		
Net Before Taxes $	41 010	38 443	79 453	34 998	114 451		
Net After Taxes $	18 799	17 622	36 421	16 043	52 464		

	1st Quarter	2nd Quarter	Jan. thru June	3rd Quarter	Jan. thru Sept.	4th Quarter	Jan. thru Dec.
Average Loan Rate	5.80	5.83	5.81	5.82	5.82		
Earn. Rate—Excess Funds	4.02	4.06	4.04	4.08	4.05		
Earn. Rate—Savings Deposits	6.52	6.55	6.54	6.59	6.55		

(continued)

EXHIBIT 5 Continued

1960

Location and Office No. A

All Dollar Amounts in Thousands	JAN.	FEB.	MAR.	APRIL	MAY	JUNE	JULY	AUG.	SEPT.	OCT.	NOV.	DEC.	YEAR TOTALS	
Regular Checking Accounts—Number														
Opened—New	26	17	7	15	16	17	10	9	14	11				1
Opened—A/C Trans. within Office	—	1	1	1	4	—	1	—	—	—				2
Opened—A/C Trans. from other Off.	—	1	1	—	3	—	2	—	1	—				3
Total Number Opened	26	19	9	16	23	17	13	9	15	11				4
Close	24	17	12	17	6	19	9	17	24	14				5
Closed –A/C Trans. within Office	—	2	1	2	2	—	—	8	6	1				6
Closed –A/C Trans. to other Offices	4	3	2	1	2	3	1	1	4	1				7
Total Number Closed	28	22	15	20	10	22	10	26	34	16				8
Net Opened or Closed	-2	-3	-6	-4	+13	-5	+3	-17	-19	-5				9
Regular Checking Accounts Average Deposits Closed—Monthly														
Closed $	16	7	8	15	7	14	4	11	18	7				10
Closed—Trans. within Office $	—	19	2	4	2	—	—	6	4	1				11
Closed—Trans. to other Offices $	5	6	2	—	1	3	1	1	2	2				12
Total Average—Closed Accts. $	21	32	7	19	10	17	5	18	24	10				13
Accounts Since Jan. 1st—Cumulated*														
*No. Opened (Line 1)	26	43	50	65	81	98	108	117	131	142				14
No. Closed (Line 5)	24	41	53	70	76	95	104	121	145	159				15
*Opened—Current Mo. Avg. (Line 14) $	83	191	162	143	120	102	120	109	114	127				16
Closed—Total Avg. Bal. (Line 10) $	16	23	26	41	48	62	66	77	95	102				17
													YEAR TOTALS	
Business Development														
No. of calls—Customers	3	8	7	4	10	8	6	9	5	5				18
No. of calls—Prospects	3	4	4	4	1	4	2	6	5	5				19
Total	6	12	11	8	11	12	8	15	10	10				20
Spec. Checking Accts.—Opened	26	21	31	21	19	22	15	33	37	29				21
Spec. Checking Accts.—Closed	13	24	12	13	17	16	12	25	9	20				22
Spec Checking Accts.—Net	+13	-3	+19	+8	+2	+6	+3	+8	+28	+9				23
Savings Accounts—Opened	17	9	22	9	15	24	15	9	52	39				24
Savings Accounts—Closed	21	7	16	13	17	20	13	15	18	15				25
Savings Accounts—Net	-4	+2	+6	-4	-2	+4	+2	-6	+34	+24				26
S. D. Boxes—New Rentals	9	6	3	9	3	6	5	6	4	—				27
S. D. Boxes—Surrendered	9	4	9	11	12	10	6	7	7	3				28
S. D. Boxes—Net	—	+2	-6	-2	-9	-4	-1	-1	-3	-3				29
No. of Personal Money Orders Sold	523	543	583	643	421	467	447	419	452	367				30

Questions

This case deals with the use of the profit center concept as a management control device for branch offices in a service industry. A particular problem in banking is how to set the transfer price for money.

Discuss the adequacy of the following structural components' of Chemical's control systems.

1. **Cost allocation** of headquarters' expense. Should these costs be allocated? Are these methods of allocation appropriate?

2. **Noncontrollable costs** included in performance reports. Should noncontrollable costs be omitted from the earnings statement? If so, what items would be affected?

3. **Performance evaluation** of dissimilar branches. Does this reporting system provide enough information? Too much? Should Exhibit 5 be discontinued?

4. **Profit center** organization of branches. Do you believe branches should be evaluated as "profit centers"? What factors are critical to the success of a branch bank? To what extent are these factors controllable by a branch manager?

5. **Transfer pricing** system used. If you believe the profit center system should be continued as a control device, discuss the appropriateness of the data developed in Exhibit 4 for transfer pricing purposes. Can you suggest better ways to price the transfer of funds between branches? Bank of America, one of the largest banks in the United States, charges its profit centers for the use of money at current interest rates for obtaining funds of like maturities and risk. For example, if a branch makes a 90-day loan, it would be charged at the current rate that the bank pays on 90-day certificates of deposit. Should Chemical Bank adopt this practice?

CASE 13–6
METROPOLITAN BANK

Fred Marple, senior vice president of Metropolitan Bank, studied the Chemical Bank case as a participant in a senior management development program during August 1993. The instructor informed the class that this case was originally written in the early 1960s. Mr. Marple told the case writer how and why Metropolitan's system differed from the system described in that case.

Background

With deregulation of consumer banking in the early 1970s, commercial banking became a highly profitable business. Banks earned an interest rate spread (the difference between the rate generated on loans and the rate paid out to depositors) that provided a profitable margin over expenses. Loan growth and expense control increased profitability. The 1980s brought unprofitable times to the banking industry as ill-fated loans to less developed countries went into default and huge loan losses drained earnings. Also in the late 1980s and early 1990s, losses on real estate loans and leveraged transactions were large. Banking became intensely competitive with nonbank competitors such as brokerage houses entering the business with money market accounts. Consequently, commercial banks examined individual areas to identify profitable lines of business and look for downsizing opportunities.

The bank was divided into two operating units: Global Bank and Regional Bank. Global Bank provided sophisticated lending, corporate finance, and treasury services to Fortune 1000 companies, foreign multinationals, and public sector clients. Regional Bank was responsible for retail banking, middle-market commercial banking, and private banking for high net-worth individuals.

This case describes the Retail Banking Group that was a component of Regional Bank. In 1992, Regional Bank generated approximately 32 percent of the revenues and net income of Metropolitan Bank and constituted 28 percent of Metropolitan's assets.

In 1991, in order to analyze its retail banking business, Metropolitan Bank decided that it needed a better assessment of the profitability of its customers and products. A team was assembled for this purpose. The team developed a new organization structure and management control system.

The team recognized that the entire organization had to be mobilized in a coherent and focused direction. To that end they developed the following mission, strategy, and business synergies/linkages.

Retail Bank Mission

"Our mission is to achieve superior customer focus and responsiveness. We view our customers as our most important corporate asset. We believe that the best way to create value for the corporation is to create value for our customers. Value is the experience of conducting business with Metropolitan. It is the combination of product, price, convenience, and service. By providing the best value for our customers, Metropolitan will be recognized as the leader in retail financial services within our chosen markets."

Retail Bank Strategy

The Retail Bank strategy is to grow its franchise by creating superior customer value.

This case was prepared by Anil R. Chitkara (T'94) under the supervision of Professor Robert N. Anthony. Copyright by Osceola Institute.

1. Creating superior customer value engenders the following four principles:
   a. Understanding and anticipating customer needs.
   b. Developing products and services to meet important needs.
   c. Delivering conveniently with high quality service.
   d. Pricing competitively.
2. Continuation of this strategy will drive revenue growth and strengthen the franchise by:
   a. Acquiring new customers through aggressive pursuit of new value propositions.
   b. Expanding and strengthening relationships with existing and new customers.

The Retail Bank is moving aggressively to implement a strategic platform to grow the franchise by generating superior customer value. Execution of this platform involves a broad range of business unit and cross organization initiatives.

Business Synergies and Linkages

Understand the Market.   Identify performance opportunities where significant market segments are currently under- or overserved and *we* could more appropriately meet their needs—set the benefit and pricing parameters for the value proposition.

Develop and Communicate the Value Proposition.   Translate our improved market understanding into a profitable, unique service proposition and communicate this proposition to our target audience—define the cost, capability, and service-level objectives for the delivery system.

Adapt the Delivery System.   Ensure that the value proposition is being delivered to max-
imize profitability and build required capabilities—finalize the quantitative business models (e.g., market and supply) to support rigorous performance management.

Upgrade the Performance Management Systems.   Ensure that the goal-setting, planning, performance measurement, and reward systems stimulate behavior at all organization levels which optimizes operating performance—identify requirements to upgrade the business models or develop market understanding, value proposition or delivery system. See Exhibit 1.

Retail Banking Group

The Retail Banking Group (RBG) served three classes of customers: regional consumers, commercial and professional businesses, and consumers on a national basis. The RBG previously had been organized around the branch banking network. Under the new organizational structure, RBG was organized around three major business lines: Local Markets, Retail Card Services, and National Consumer Business Group. Local Markets Group works with branch dependent customers for deposits, insurance, investments, and small business lending; Retail Card Services Group handles payment systems and revolving credit on a nationwide basis; and National Consumer Business Group consists of nonpayment system related lending, including mortgages, home equity, education, recreational vehicles, and automobiles (see Exhibit 2).

Organization of the Local Market Group

Local Market Development.   The Market Development Group was responsible for understanding the market. The objective of the Market Development Group was to identify significant performance opportunities where current value propositions poorly or unprofitably serve significant segments. Key steps in this process

EXHIBIT 1

The performance improvement wheel is a systematic discipline to identify and prioritize all significant performance opportunities and embed a continuous improvement system.

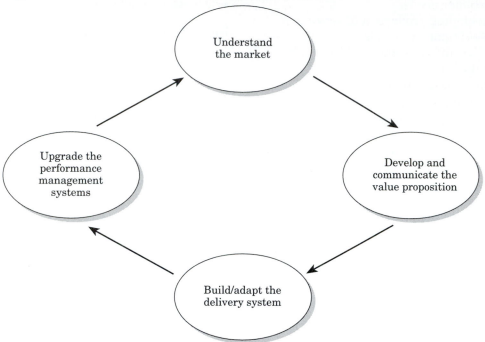

included understanding needs segmentation and the value of current service offerings, estimating economic opportunity from redesigned offerings, evaluating current competitive position, and conducting environmental scans (i.e., regulation, technology, economy, demographics). Major groups of customers were separated into various segments, each indicating similar characteristics such as demographic, behavioral, and psychographic profile. The segments were tracked based on use of products, services, and distribution channels. The objective of monitoring customer segments was to assess profitability dynamics, value propositions, and examine processes whereby nonvalue processes would be eliminated via reengineering. The performance of the Market Development Group was measured on major market segment profitability, its progress in developing new market

segment programs, and effective management of the overall Local Markets marketing budget.

This group also served as the catalyst to develop new business lines. As competition intensified, the need to expand business offerings was essential; therefore major business line strategies surrounding insurance, investments, and electronic banking (i.e., Debit Cards, Home Banking) were employed.

Product Management.   The Product Management Group was responsible for working with the Market Development Group to ensure product offerings were aligned with customer needs, included the appropriate value functions, and were priced profitably. The overall objective was to develop a service offering which uniquely meets segment needs/values at profitable prices and communicates the value

EXHIBIT 2

Partial organization chart

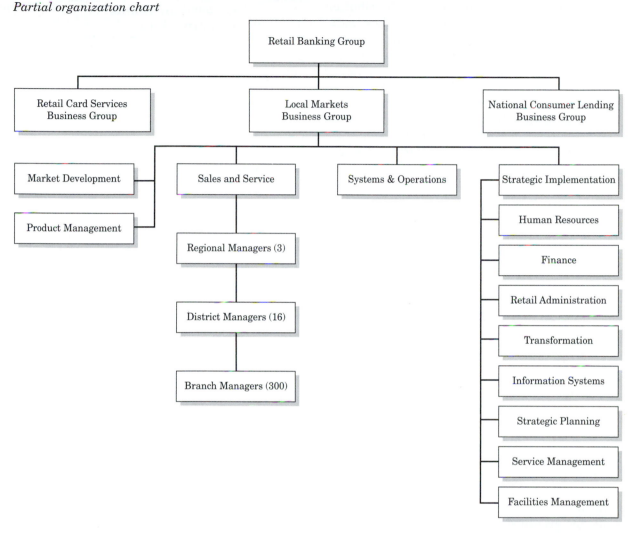

proposition to target segments. The key steps included designing the new value proposition by adding/eliminating features on the basis of willingness to pay and establishing pricing levels/structure, functionality, service levels, and access. Communicating the new value proposition included message development, channel selection, and brand management. Every week the Product Management Group prepared a report detailing the changes in volume for the products and listed Metropolitan's prices and its competitor's prices (obtained both internally and from an outside data-gathering organization). These findings, together with recommendations for product feature enhancements, new products, and pricing, were presented at a pricing committee meeting that included members of each group within Local Markets. The performance of the Product Management Group was measured on major product grouping's profitability.

Sales & Service. The Sales and Service Group (S&S) supervised the local distribution channel of the bank, including branches, automated teller machines (ATMs), and customer telephone service lines. This group was responsible for executing the product management and market development strategies. The overall objective of S&S was to build/adapt the delivery system to ensure that the value proposition is delivered to maximize profitability and build required capabilities. Key steps in the process included assessing the gap between actual and target activity performance measures (i.e., cost, customer satisfaction, service levels, revenue, product delivered), assuring value created by all activities, and performing internal and external surveys via benchmarking and best practice comparisons (i.e., scale, service levels, technology). The performance of S&S was measured against key performance measures designed to reflect the goals of the strategies and growth targets.

Branch managers were within the S&S group, and their performance was measured by the Bonus Incentive Plan (BIP) linked directly to the strategies and growth targets of the market segments and product groupings. The BIP set forth 11 specific criteria (see Exhibit 3). Each criterion had a point weighting and a band around which the point weighting fluctuated. Each branch was given specific goals for each of the 11 criteria. If the goal was met, the branch received the points assigned to it. If the goal was exceeded, additional points within the band were earned; if performance was below goal, fewer points were earned. Compensation of district managers, branch managers, and key personnel was affected by the Bonus Incentive Plan. These measures differed markedly from the profit center system described in the Chemical Bank case.

Support Functions. Centralized support groups such as Human Resources, Finance, Strategic Planning, Service Management, Sys-

Exhibit 3   Weighting of Evaluation Criteria for Bonus Incentive Plan

Deposit growth		
Personal transactions	12	
Personal investments	8	
Business investments and transactions	15	
Subtotal		35
Asset growth:		
Mortgage loans	3	
Home equity and quick loans	7	
Direct installment loans	3	
Revolving credit	5	
Business lending	6	
Subtotal		24
Revenue:		
Nonbank investments	12	
Fees	9	
Subtotal		21
Customer satisfaction		20
Total		100

tems, Back Office Operations, Retail Facilities and Transformation,[1] were treated as expense centers, and their financial performance was measured against their budgets, the group's financial performance including specific Key Performance Measures, and implementation of appropriate tactics to support the Market Product and Sales & Service groups.

Organization of the National Business Groups

The Retail Card Services and National Consumer Business Groups served Metropolitan's national consumer base. The groups were re-

---

[1]Transformation consists of reengineering the retail bank and includes productivity enhancements and operations and service workflow redesigning (i.e., balance retention programs, quality, and customer focus).

sponsible for asset originations, credit approval, customer service, quality control, and remittance processing of the national customer business base. The performance of the groups was measured on their own profitability.

Retail Card Services Business Group

Mission. Retail Card Services Business Group will take advantage of its national customer base and direct communications channel to help shape a competitively advantaged national purchase and payment system, based on fundamental, "real value" propositions to the customer. These propositions would be used to build durable, meaningful relationships with customers over the course of their lives, using the credit product as a "wedge."

Beyond repositioning its card products, Retail Card Services Business Group was defining a vision for the future that will allow Metropolitan to fully realize its potential in the new world as well as serve as a beacon for "Evolving Card Business Developments."

The strategic functions were redefined as follows:

1. Primary role is to provide strategic blueprints that will bring together and give direction to marketing, operations, product development, product management, etc.

2. Ensure that the organization does not get focused solely on deals and transactions, but creates a context and framework for these efforts. Dedicated attention to the big picture helps the entire organization develop the ability to adapt to change.

3. Expand to a broader view of Purchase/Payment System products and services in order to competitively position the Metropolitan franchise and grow the earnings base.

4. Provide increased project management and implementation support.

National Consumer Business Group

Mission. The mission was to establish a multichannel, broad-based, and cost-effective origination capability that generated assets with attractive risk-adjusted returns.

1. Leveraging risk-management capabilities to offer competitive products at competitive pricing to a broader customer base, while providing a level of service that resulted in high customer satisfaction.

2. Becoming a top-tier player in the home secured market. Home Equity products provided a strong base on which to build because of the size and depth of the market, the profitability of the product for lenders, and the attractive demographics of home-secured borrowers. Metropolitan Bank had an established expertise to take advantage of the existing fragmentation within the market.

3. Continuing to offer consumer loans where our leadership position in these products resulted in superior economic returns and/or opportunities to attract new customers.

The National Consumer Business Group was composed of four major business lines, each with strong competitive positions:

1. Metropolitan had created a Mortgage franchise with enormous value. The mortgage industry was undergoing rapid consolidation and Metropolitan had become a top-tier player in both originations and servicing. Scale economics, effective risk management, and technological enhancements in new origination, servicing, and secondary marketing systems were major challenges.

   Servicing represented the store of economic value to be harvested over the life of a mortgage loan. Efficiency was the key. The new systems and technology (automated workflow/imaging) being implemented will enhance our position.

2. Metropolitan had also become one of the largest Guaranteed Student Loan providers. In a consolidating industry, it was one of the few vertically integrated processors. The guaranteed nature of Student Loans produced a stable earnings stream with very low equity requirements. The challenge was to continue to achieve growth while reducing operating risk.

3. National Consumer Finance was a profitable consumer finance business operating through a national network of 12 regional offices. Their national distribution system will continue to be leveraged to expand the origination of home equity loans through correspondents.

4. Consumer Asset Group was a high margin, high ROE business focused in the local area. Metropolitan had a dominant market share of total consumer loan households, representing a strong second position.

Transfer Pricing

Metropolitan Bank used transfer prices for funds and services provided by one bank unit to another. The Retail Banking Group generated funds in the form of deposits, and these funds were used to finance loans and investment activities throughout the Bank. All funds received were transferred into Metropolitan's Treasury Group, a corporate function. The Treasury Group's primary responsibility was to remove interest rate risk in the business unit's results, thereby minimizing the impact of profits or losses associated with the mismatching of asset and liability terms.

The Treasury Group calculated interest rates, or "pool rates," for different products[2] with differing maturities. Pool rates were based on an average of a "core rate" and the current (or slightly lagged) LIBID[3] rate. The core rate was the historical average interest rate earned by the Bank. It was applied to a specified fraction of the total amount of money in the pool. For other products, the interest rate was based entirely on the LIBID, and for still others it was related to the interest on wholesale borrowings of the same maturity. Some rates were modified to take account of rates charged by competing banks, based on information obtained by the Product Management Group and supplied by an outside data-gathering organization.

Sales and Service (branches and telephone service) also provided a wide array of services to other major areas of the corporation that housed the large corporate, middle market, and private banking customers. Compensation (payment for services provided) was set for approximately 75 different services including deposits, checks cashed, account maintenance, automatic teller machine transactions, and payroll preparation. Individual charges were set at the beginning of the year by estimating the quantity of the services to be provided and the total expenses associated with each service. Transaction cost per unit of service was calculated by multiplying the rate agreed to by the actual volume.

Profit Planning Process

The Retail Bank Group budget preparation process had four phases. First, the Market

---

[2]Demand deposits, NOW accounts, savings accounts, 91-day certificates of deposit, and 6-month certificates of deposit are examples of products.

[3]LIBID is an acronym for "London Inter Bank Interest Rate on Deposits," a commonly used short-term interest rate.

Development Group set gross revenue targets for each major customer segment. Next, the Product Management Group developed specific product functions and pricing to support the marketing programs and gross revenue projections. Third, the Sales and Service and support groups developed the expense levels and appropriate compensation goals based on key performance measures needed to meet the market and product groups' plans. The final phase was consolidation of the three previous phases and development of a coherent plan for the entire Retail Banking Group. The planning process required five months, beginning in early July.

Questions

1. Compare the Retail Banking Group in Metropolitan Bank with the corresponding organization in Chemical Bank.

2. Do you think the organizational structure and control systems are consistent with the bank's strategies?

3. What changes to the organization structure and control systems would you recommend for Metropolitan Bank?

CASE 13–7
CITIBANK INDONESIA

In November 1983 Mehli Mistri, Citibank's country manager for Indonesia, was faced with a difficult situation. He had just received a memorandum from his immediate superior, David Gibson, the division head for Southeast Asia, informing him that during their just-completed review of the operating budgets, Citibank managers at corporate had raised the SE-Asia division's 1984 aftertax profit goal by $4 million. Mr. Gibson, in turn, had decided that Indonesia's share of this increased goal should be between $500,000 and $1,000,000. Mr. Mistri was concerned because he knew that the budget he had submitted was already very aggressive; it included some growth in revenues and only a slight drop in profits, even though the short-term outlook for the Indonesian economy, which was highly dependent on oil revenues, was pessimistic.

Mr. Mistri knew that to have any realistic expectation of producing profits for 1984 higher than those already included in the budget, he would probably have to take one or more actions that he had wanted to avoid. One possibility was to eliminate (or reduce) Citibank's participation in loans to prime government or private enterprises, as these loans provided much lower returns than were earned on the rest of the portfolio. However, Citibank was the largest foreign bank operating in Indonesia, and failing to participate in these loans could have significant costs in terms of relations with the government and prime customers in Indonesia and elsewhere. The other possibility was to increase the total amount of money lent in Indonesia, with all of the increase going to

commercial enterprises. But with the deteriorating conditions in the Indonesian economy, Mr. Mistri knew that it was probably not a good time for Citibank to increase its exposure. Also, the government did not want significant increases in offshore loans to the private sector at this time because of their adverse impact on the country's balance of payments and services account.

So, Mr. Mistri was contemplating what he should do at an upcoming meeting with Mr. Gibson. Should he agree to take one or both of the actions described above to increase 1984 profits? Should he accept the profit increase and hope that the economy turned around and/or that he was able to develop some new, hitherto unidentified sources of income? Or should he resist including any of the division's required profit increase in his budget?

Citibank

Citibank, the principal operating subsidiary of Citicorp, is one of the leading financial institutions in the world. The bank was founded in 1812 as a small commercial in New York City, and over the years it had grown to a large global financial services intermediary. In 1983, the bank had revenues of almost $5.9 billion and employed over 63,000 people in almost 2,600 locations in 95 countries.

Citibank's activities were organized into three principal business units: institutional banking, individual banking, and the capital markets group. The institutional banking units provided commercial loans and other financial services, such as electronic banking, asset-based financing, and foreign exchange, to corporations and governmental agencies around the world. The individual banking units, which operated in the United States and 18 other countries, provided transactional, savings, and lend-

This case was prepared by Associate Professor Kenneth A. Merchant, Harvard Business School. Copyright by the President and Fellows of Harvard College. Harvard Business School case 185-061.

EXHIBIT 1   Selected Citicorp Financial Data—1983 (dollars in millions)

	Citicorp Consolidated	*Institutional Bank*	*Individual Bank*	*Capital Markets Group*
Revenues	$5,883	$2,896	$2,380	$587
Net income	860	758	202	128
Return on shareholders' equity	16.5%	22.0%	17.7%	32.2%
Return on assets	0.64%	0.87%	0.69%	1.26%

Source: 1983 Citicorp *Annual Report.*

EXHIBIT 2

Citibank Indonesia partial organization chart

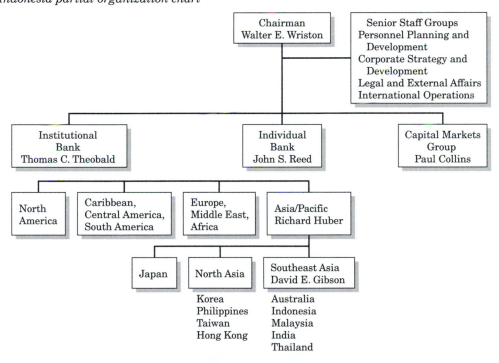

---

ing services to consumers. The capital markets group served as an intermediary in flows of funds from providers to users. With a staff of 3,500, this group was one of the largest investment banks in the world. (Exhibit 1 shows the relative size of these activities, and Exhibit 2 shows a summary corporate organization chart.)

Mehli Mistri

Mehli Mistri, Citibank's country corporate officer for Indonesia, joined Citibank as a management trainee in the Bombay office in 1960, just after finishing a B.A. degree in economics from the University of Bombay. Between 1960 and 1964, Mehli gained experience in a number of assignments in the Bombay office, and in 1965 he transferred to New York to work in the credit analysis division. He returned to Bombay in 1966, and then became manager of Citibank branches in Madras (1968), Calcutta (1969–71), New Delhi (1972), and Beirut (1973). In 1974, he was promoted to regional manager with responsibility for five countries in the Middle East (Turkey, Syria, Iraq, Jordan, Lebanon), and he held that position until 1979, when he was appointed the country head of Indonesia. He remained in that position up until the time of this case. In 1982, Mehli attended the Advanced Management Program at the Harvard Business School.

Control of International Branches

Citibank managers used two formal management processes to direct and control the activities of the corporation's international branches: reviews of sovereign risk limits for each location and reviews of operating budgets and accomplishments.

Sovereign Risk Limits.

Each year Citibank management set sovereign risk limits for its international branches based on country risk analyses. The term *sovereign risk* actually refers to a wide spectrum of concerns that would impair the bank's ability to recapture the capital it invested in foreign countries. These included macroeconomic risk—foreign exchange controls that the government of the host country might employ that would make it difficult for clients to pay their obligations, or, in the extreme, expropriation of assets. Once Citibank had opened a given branch, however, it intended to keep it open, so the reviews of sovereign risk were concerned only with setting limits of the amount of money a branch could lend in foreign currency.

The sovereign risk review process started in midyear with the country manager proposing a sovereign risk limit. This limit was discussed with division and group managers and was fi-

nally approved, on a staggered time schedule, by a senior international specialist on the corporate staff. The foreign currency lending limit for Indonesia had grown substantially as the branch had grown.

The sovereign risk limit set during these reviews was an upper guideline. When the economic conditions in a country changed in the period between sovereign risk reviews, country managers sometimes chose to operate their branches with self-imposed sovereign risk limits that were below the limits set by management in New York. Corporate managers encouraged this behavior because they knew that the managers on site often had a better appreciation of the risks in the local environment.

Budgeting.

Budgeting at Citibank was a bottom up process which started in July when headquarters sent out instructions to the operating units describing the timing and format of the submissions and the issues that needed to be addressed. The instructions did not include specific targets to be included in the budget, although it was widely recognized that the corporation's combined long-term goals were approximately as follows:

> Growth: 12–15% per annum.
> Return on assets: 1.25% (125 basis points).
> Return on equity: 20%.

The above norms were established for Citibank as a whole, but a number of international branches, including Indonesia, traditionally exceeded these norms, and these entities often established their own targets at higher levels.

At the time the operating managers received the budget instructions, they would have the results for half the year (through the end of June); and, in the period from July until the end of September, they would prepare a forecast for the remainder of the current year and a budget for the following year. The starting point for the preparation of the budget was projections about each of the major account rela-

---

EXHIBIT 3   Line Items on Budget Submission Form

Revenue/expense	*Profit center earnings*
Local currency NRFF	Equity adjustments—translations
Foreign currency NRFF	Placements (average)
Allocated equity NRFF	Total staff (EOP)
Bad debt reserve earnings	Total nonperforming loans—EOP
Net revenue from funds	Total nonperforming loans—EOP
Exchange	Rev./nonperforming loans
Translation gains/losses	Average total assets—local currency
Trading account profits	Average total assets—foreign currency
Trade financing fees	Allocated equity
Securities gains/losses	*Local currency—average volume*
Fees, commissions, and other revenue	Loans
Affiliate earnings	Sources—noninterest bearing
Gross write-offs	Sources—interest bearing
Gross recoveries	*Foreign currency—average volume*
Loan provision excess	Loans
Direct staff expenses	Sources—noninterest bearing
Direct charges	Sources—interest bearing
Other direct expenses	*End of period (EOP)*
Allocated processing costs	Past due obligations
Minority interest	Interest earned not collected
Other allocated costs	Loans
Matrix earnings	Assets
EBIT	
Foreign taxes	
US taxes	

---

tionships, and discussions continued until the summation of the account relationship projections could be reconciled with the desired profit center bottom line.

Then costs were considered. The budget submission form included all the line items shown in Exhibit 3. In some past years, the bank had prepared two- and five-year projections, but the numbers were seen to be very soft and not very useful.

Formal reviews of the annual budgets were held according to the following schedule:

Level of Review	Timing
Division	End of September
Group	Mid-October
Institutional bank	End of September

If the sovereign risk review for a particular entity had not yet been held, the budgets were submitted with the assumption that the risk limits would be approved as submitted. If this assumption proved to be incorrect, the budget had to be revised before it was incorporated in the corporate consolidated budget.

Performance was monitored and compared against budget each month during the year. Every quarter a new forecast for the remainder of the year was made. Whether these were reviewed formally by division managers varied widely, depending on the division manager's style. Some managers held relatively formal on-site reviews of performance and budget revisions, and others communicated only by mail or by telephone.

Mr. Mistri was very comfortable with the review processes:

> Every level of management has a role to play, and there is a lot of horse trading and give and take in the budget review processes. Usually there is more revision of the numbers at lower management levels, but revisions do not necessarily mean increased profit goals. I have seen cases where the division head thought the country level was being too aggressive and he asked for the budget to be lowered. The managers sitting further away are more objective, and the review processes are cosultative, collegial, and constructive.

Budgets were taken very seriously at Citibank, not only because they were thought to include the most important measures of success, but also because incentive compensation for managers at Citibank was linked to budget-related performance. For a country manager, incentive compensation could range up to approximately 70 percent of base salary, although awards of 30–35 percent were more typical. Assignment of bonuses was based approximately 30 percent on corporate performance and 70 percent on individual performance, primarily performance related to forecast. The key measures for assessing both corporate and international-branch performance were growth, profits, return on assets, and return on equity. However, in the analyses of individual performance for the purposes of assigning incentive compensation, considerable care was taken to differentiate base earnings from extraordinary earnings (or losses) for which the manager should not be held accountable.

Citibank in Indonesia

Indonesia was a relatively young country; it had achieved independence only in 1949 after being a Dutch colony for many years. Citibank had operated in Indonesia only since 1968, when President Suharto allowed eight foreign banks to set up operations in Jakarta. From the point of view of the Indonesian government, the role of the foreign banks was to help develop a young economy by transferring capital into the country, establishing a modern banking infrastructure, attracting foreign investment, and developing trained people.

The foreign banking community operated in Indonesia with some important restrictions. The most serious constraints were that foreign banks were not allowed to open branches outside the Jakarta city limits, and local currency loans could be made only to corporations with headquarters and principal operations within the Jakarta city limits. But on the other hand, the Indonesian government did not require any local ownership of equity, it set no lending quotas for the banks (e.g., requirements to lend certain amounts of money to certain types of businesses at favorable rates), and it valued and maintained a free foreign exchange system.

In explaining the goals of the government with respect to the foreign banks, Mr. Mistri commented:

> We consider ourselves privileged to be in Indonesia. We realize that the country wants to develop economically, and we know that the government sees us in the role of a development and change agent, attracting and developing not only capital but also new financial products, services, and techniques, and trained managers and professionals for the financial services industry. The government also expects us and other international banks to participate in extensions of credit to both the public and private sectors.

Citibank and the other foreign banks were interested in operating in Indonesia for several reasons: (1) to serve their international and local customers, (2) to assist in the economic development of the country, and (3) to share in

EXHIBIT 4   **Indonesia Gross Domestic Product (billions of rupiahs)**

Year	Gross Domestic Product	Gross Domestic Product (1980 prices)
1968	2,097	18,493
1969	2,718	20,188
1970	3,340	21,499
1971	3,672	22,561
1972	4,564	24,686
1973	6,753	27,479
1974	10,708	29,576
1975	12,643	31,049
1976	15,467	33,187
1977	19,011	36,094
1978	22,746	38,925
1979	32,025	41,359
1980	45,446	45,446
1981	54,027	49,048
1982	59,633	50,150
1983	72,111	52,674

Source: *International Statistics Yearbook,* 1984.

the potential for profits and growth the Indonesian economy offered. The Indonesian economy had tremendous potential: The country was the fifth-largest in the world in terms of population, and the economy had shown excellent growth for many years, as the figures shown in Exhibit 4 illustrate. The country was rich in raw materials, particularly oil and tin, and the Indonesian government was very interested in developing the country's industrial activities.

In 1983, Citibank's Indonesian operation included activities in each of the three major lines of business—institutional, individual, and capital markets. Mehli Mistri was the country corporate officer, and, as such, he was the primary spokesman for all of Citibank's activities in Indonesia. His prime line responsibility, however, was the institutional banking activity, which provided by far the greatest proportion of revenues and profits. Other individuals headed the individual banking and capital markets activi-

ties in Indonesia, and they reported through separate management channels (see Exhibit 5).

Since its inception, Citibank's Indonesian operation had been very successful. Its growth paralleled that of the Indonesian economy.

The Situation in 1983

In 1983, Mr. Mistri was concerned about the risk/return ratio in his branch. He felt comfortable with Indonesia's long-term prospects, but the country, which was highly dependent on oil revenues, had slipped into a recession when oil prices decreased significantly. His concern was whether the government would take strong enough steps to correct its balance-of-payments problem.

Inside the bank, Mr. Mistri was faced with a problem of high staff turnover. High turnover had been a problem for Citibank for many years, because the bank provided its people

Exhibit 5

Partial organization chart

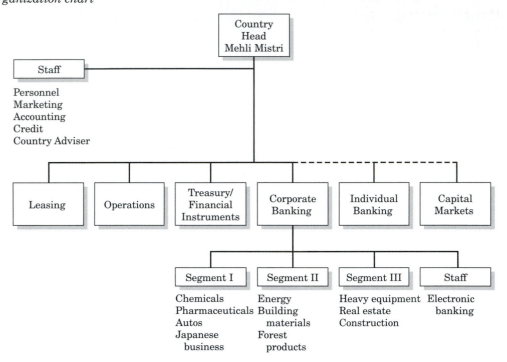

with training that was recognized as probably the best in Indonesia, and local financial institutions had lured many Citibank people away with generous offers. This had happened so often that Citibank had been given labels, such as "Citi-university" and "Harvard-on-wheels," and the government often held Citibank up as an example of how foreign banks could (and should) supply trained professionals to the country. To attempt to retain more of its trained people, Citibank had recently increased its compensation levels; but some people in the branch felt that the bank could not compete on the basis of salary because of its desire to be profitable, its limited domestic branch network, and significant career opportunities elsewhere.

The year 1983 was particularly difficult from a staff turnover standpoint, as the losses included Mr. Mistri's chief of staff and two senior officers. In mid-1983, the average account manager experience was under two years, and there were three unfilled slots at management levels. Mr. Mistri knew that the inexperience and people shortages in the branch were also serious constraints to growth.

Given these significant problems, Mr. Mistri thought that the budget he submitted, which projected modest growth, should be considered as aggressive. He wanted to submit an aggressive budget because "we are an aggressive organization. We like to stretch because we feel the culture of our corporation and the will and desire of our people to succeed and excel can make up the difference."

In reflection of the fast-changing uncertainties in the economy and the personnel problems, however, Mr. Mistri decided to operate with a self-imposed sovereign risk limit that was somewhat lower than what had been formally approved by management in New York. He knew that his responsibility was as much to manage risk as to generate profits.

In late October 1983, however, the budget for the whole Institutional Bank was reviewed at headquarters, and the consolidated set of numbers did not show the growth that top management desired. This led management to suggest some budget increases, and these increases presented Mr. Mistri with the dilemma described in the introduction to this case.

Questions

1. What should Mehli Mistri do about the budget issue described in the first three paragraphs of the case? (*Note:* You can assume that the amount by which Mehli is asked to increase his budget is about 10 percent of the original budget.)

2. Should Mehli Mistri be evaluated against a budget prepared in US dollars?

MULTINATIONAL ORGANIZATIONS

In this chapter we describe management control problems and practices in multinational (also called *transnational*) organizations. Most of the practices for controlling foreign operations are similar to those for controlling domestic operations. The planning and control processes that we described in Chapters 7 through 11—strategic planning, budget preparation, operating, variance analysis and reporting, performance evaluation, and management compensation—generally are applicable to multinational organizations, but they need to be tailored to the context of these organizations. As an example, foreign operations may be organized as expense centers, revenue centers, profit centers, or investment centers, and the considerations that govern the choice of a particular type of responsibility center are, in most respects, similar to those for domestic operations. One important difference, however, is that even if a foreign operation is an expense center or a revenue center for control purposes, it is often a profit center for accounting purposes. Many foreign operations are legal entities, incorporated in the host country, and, therefore, they must maintain a complete set of accounting records for legal and tax reasons.

There are three special problems of global organizations: cultural differences, transfer pricing, and exchange rates. This chapter is devoted to these three topics. Although our discussion is stated in terms of a US corporation and its foreign subsidiaries, the same general problems exist with respect to a parent company of any nationality and its foreign subsidiaries.

Cultural Differences

One of the important contextual variables that influence management control within a multinational enterprise is cultural differences across countries. By definition, a multinational organization operates in multiple countries and therefore has to contend with cultural differences as head office coordinates and controls its subsidiaries. Whether within an organization or a nationality, "culture" refers to shared values, assumptions, and norms of behavior. When an organization spans nationalities, cultural differences of a profound sort having to do with national and regional character abound and have an important bearing on management control. One way to understand cultures is proposed by Hofstede.[1] Hofstede made a systematic analysis of cultural differences, based on a questionnaire that was answered by approximately 80,000 employees of IBM located in 64 countries. According to Hofstede, cultures can differ across four dimensions.

1. *Power distance* refers to the extent to which power is unequally distributed and centralized. High power distance cultures include Philippines, Venezuela, and Mexico. Low power distance cultures include Israel, Denmark, and Austria.

2. *Individualism / collectivism* refers to the extent to which people define themselves as individuals or as part of a larger group. Highly individualistic cultures include United States, Australia, and Great Britain. Highly collectivistic cultures include Saudi Arabia, Venezuela, and Peru.

3. *Uncertainty avoidance* refers to the extent to which people feel threatened by ambiguous situations. Highest uncertainty avoidance cultures include Japan, Portugal, and Greece. Lowest uncertainty avoidance cultures include Singapore, Hong Kong, and Denmark.

4. *Masculinity / feminity* refers to the extent to which dominant values emphasize assertiveness and materialism ("masculine") versus concern for people and quality of life ("feminine"). Examples of highly "masculine" cultures include Austria, Switzerland, and Italy. Highly "feminine" cultures include Sweden, Norway, Netherlands, and Denmark.

Another classification scheme is proposed by Hall, according to whom cultures differ from each other on a spectrum from "low context cultures" at one end (Germany, Switzerland, Scandinavia, North America, Britain) where people get down to business quickly and negotiate as efficiently as possible to "high context cultures" at the other end (China, Korea, Japan, Saudi Arabia) where people attempt to establish personal relationships before getting down to business and where negotiations are slow and ritualistic.

Several inferences can be drawn regarding the type of planning and control systems that will be more effective in different cultures. In individualistic cultures, employees are likely to prefer rewards based on individual performance whereas group-based rewards are likely to be preferred by employees in collectivistic cultures. In cultures with low power distance, decentralization in decision-making and greater participation in budget preparation might be

---

[1]H. Hofstede, "Motivation, Leadership, and Organization: Do American Theories Apply Abroad?" *Organizational Dynamics,* Summer 1980, pp. 42–63.

preferred. The opposite might be true in high power distance cultures. Subjective performance evaluation will be more effective in low, rather than high, uncertainty avoidance cultures. Formal planning and control systems will be better received in low context cultures, whereas in high context cultures building interpersonal familiarity and trust is felt to be essential, and so informal controls are likely to be more effective.

Executives in multinational organizations must understand and respect cultural differences and adapt management controls across countries.

Transfer Pricing

Transfer pricing for goods, services, and technology represents one of the major differences between management control of domestic and of foreign operations. In domestic operations, the criteria for the transfer price system are almost exclusively those described in Chapter 5. In foreign operations, however, several other considerations are important in arriving at the transfer price. They include taxation, government regulations, tariffs, foreign exchange controls, funds accumulation, and joint ventures.

Taxation.   Effective income tax rates can differ considerably among foreign countries. A transfer price system that results in assigning profits to low-tax countries can reduce total worldwide income taxes.

Government Regulations.   In the absence of government regulations, the firm would set transfer prices to minimize taxable income in the countries with high income tax rates. However, government tax authorities are aware of such possibilities, and governments have passed regulations that affect the way in which transfer prices can be calculated.

Tariffs.   Tariffs are often levied as a percentage of the import value of a product. The lower the price, the lower the tariff. The incidence of tariffs is usually opposite to the incidence of income taxes in transfer pricing. Although tariffs for goods shipped to a given country will be low if the transfer price is low, the profit recorded in that country—and hence the local income tax on the profit—will be correspondingly high. Thus, the net effect of these factors must be calculated in deciding on the appropriate transfer price. Because income taxes are typically a larger amount than tariffs, international transfer pricing is usually driven more by income tax than by tariff considerations.

Foreign Exchange Controls.   Some countries limit the amount of foreign exchange available to import certain commodities. Under these conditions, a lower transfer price allows the subsidiary to bring in a greater quantity of these commodities.

Funds Accumulation. A company may wish to accumulate its funds in one country, rather than in another. Transfer prices are a way of shifting funds into or out of a particular country.

Joint Ventures. Joint ventures create additional complications in transfer pricing. Suppose a US firm has a joint venture operation in Japan with a local Japanese firm. If the US parent charges a higher price for a component transferred to Japan, the Japanese joint venture partner is likely to resist that price since it lowers the profits of the Japanese operation and, consequently, the share of the profits for the Japanese joint venture partner. Ford Motor Company, partly to avoid transfer pricing disputes, purchased the large British minority interest in Ford, Ltd., in 1961. For similar reasons, General Motors had not used joint ventures until its arrangement with Toyota in the late 1980s.

Use of Transfer Pricing Methods

Exhibit 14–1 shows the transfer pricing methods used by a sample of multinational companies headquartered in Canada, Japan, the United Kingdom, and the United States for their cross-border transfer of goods.

Legal Considerations

Almost all countries place some constraints on the flexibility of companies to set transfer prices for transactions with foreign subsidiaries. The reason is to prevent the multinational company from avoiding the host country's income taxes. An article in *The Wall Street Journal* highlights this point:[2]

> A House subcommittee investigation of 36 foreign-owned US companies has found that more than half paid little or no US income tax over a 10-year period.

Largely by inflating the prices they paid their foreign parents for goods, services, and technology, a number of the US subsidiaries were able to reduce their taxable income to almost nothing.
Among the cases the investigators cited were these:

- A foreign parent sold television sets to its US subsidiary at $250 each but charged only $150 to an unrelated distributor.
- A foreign auto manufacturer sold cars to its US subsidiary at an average of $800 more than it charged its Canadian subsidiary for identical cars.

---

[2]Hilary Stout, "Foreign Firms Pay Little US Tax, House Panel Says," *The Wall Street Journal,* July 11, 1994, p. 1.

EXHIBIT 14–1   **Transfer Pricing Methods Used by Multinational Companies**

Pricing Method	Canada[a]	Japan[b]	United Kingdom[c]	United States[d]
Cost-Based Methods:				
Variable cost—actual or standard	5%	3%	5%	1%
Full cost—actual	—	—	—	4
Full cost—standard	26	38	28	7
Variable cost plus markup	—	—	—	1
Full cost plus markup	2	—	5	28
Total cost-based	**33%**	**41%**	**38%**	**41%**
Market-Based Methods:				
Market price	—	—	—	26
Market price less selling expense	—	—	—	12
Other	—	—	—	8
Total market-based	**37%**	**37%**	**31%**	**46%**
Negotiated Price	**26%**	**22%**	**20%**	**13%**
Other	**4%**	—	**11%**	—
	100%	100%	100%	100%

Source: [a]R. Tang, "Canadian Transfer Pricing in the 1990s," *Management Accounting,* February 1992.
[b]R. Tang, C. Walter, and R. Raymond, "Transfer Pricing—Japanese vs. American Style," *Management Accounting,* January 1979, pp. 12–16.
[c]A. Mostafa, J. Sharp, and K. Howard, "Transfer Pricing—A Survey Using Discriminant Analysis," *Omega* 12, no. 5 (1984).
[d]Y. Roger, and W. Tang, "Transfer Pricing in the 1990s," *Management Accounting,* February 1992, pp. 22–26.

- A foreign company shipping trucks to a US subsidiary and an unrelated distributor in the United States charged almost $200 more per truck in shipping costs to the related company.

Regulations for the United States are basically set forth in Section 482 of the Internal Revenue Code. In general, Section 482 tries to ensure that financial transactions between the units of a *controlled taxpayer* (a company that can control transactions between domestic and foreign profit centers) are conducted as if the units were *uncontrolled taxpayers* (independent entities dealing with one another at arm's length). In case of a dispute, Section 482 permits the Internal Revenue Service to calculate what it believes to be the most appropriate transfer price, and the burden of proof is then on the company to show that this price is unreasonable. This is in contrast with most provisions of the Internal Revenue Code, which permit the company to select whatever permissible alternative it wishes and place the burden of proof on the Internal Revenue Service to show that the company's method is unacceptable.

Section 482 provides rules for determining the transfer price on sales between members of the controlled group. Acceptable intercompany pricing methods, listed in descending order of priority, are as follows:

1. *Comparable uncontrolled price method.* An arm's-length price is ascertained from comparable sales of goods or services between the multinational firm and unrelated customers, or between two unrelated firms.

Circumstances that may affect the price include the quality of the product, terms of sale, market level, and geographical area in which the item is sold; but quantity discounts, promotional allowances, and special losses due to currency exchange and credit differentials are excluded.

Lower prices, and even sales at a price below full cost, are permitted in certain instances, such as during the penetration of a new market or in maintaining an existing market in a particular area.

2. *Resale price method.* If comparable sales are not available, the next preferred method is the resale price method. Under this method, the taxpayer works back from the final selling price at which property purchased from an affiliate is resold in an uncontrolled sale. This *resale price* is reduced by an appropriate markup percentage based on uncontrolled sales by the same affiliate or by other resellers selling similar property in a comparable market. Markup percentages of competitors and industry averages are also helpful.

The regulations require that this method be used (1) if there are no comparable uncontrolled sales, (2) the resales are made within a reasonable time before or after the intercompany purchase, (3) the reseller has not added significant value to the property by physically altering it, other than packaging, labeling, and so forth, or by the use or application of intangible property.

3. *Cost-plus method.* Under this method, which is the lowest priority of the three prescribed methods, the starting point for determining an arm's-length price is the cost of producing the product, computed in accordance with sound accounting practices. To this is added an appropriate gross profit expressed as a percentage of cost and based on similar uncontrolled sales made by the seller, by other sellers, or the rate prevalent in the industry.

A schematic representation of these three methods is as follows:

1. *Comparable uncontrolled price method:*

$$\text{Transfer price} = \text{Price paid in comparable uncontrolled sales} \pm \text{Adjustments}$$

In a controlled sale, the transaction is between two members of a controlled group. In an uncontrolled sale, one of the two parties is not a member of the controlled group.

2. *Resale price method:*

$$\text{Transfer price} = \text{Applicable resale price} - \text{Appropriate markup} \pm \text{Adjustments}$$

Applicable resale price is the price at which property purchased in a controlled sale is resold by the buyer in an uncontrolled sale.

$$\textit{Appropriate markup} = \text{Applicable resale price} * \text{Appropriate markup percentage}$$

Appropriate markup percentage = Percent of gross profit (expressed as a percent of sales) earned by the buyer (reseller) or by another party in an uncontrolled purchase and resale similar to controlled resale.

3. *Cost-plus method:*

Transfer price = Costs + Appropriate markup ± Adjustments

Appropriate markup = Costs * Appropriate gross profit percent

Appropriate gross profit percent = Gross profit percent (expressed as a percent of cost) earned by seller or another party on uncontrolled sale similar to controlled sale.

Implications of Section 482

From a management control point of view, there are two important implications of Section 482, each of which is discussed below:

1. Although there are legal restrictions on a company's flexibility in transfer pricing, there is considerable latitude within these restrictions.
2. In some instances, the legal constraints may dictate the type of transfer prices that must be employed.

Latitude in Transfer Prices.   In many multinational companies there is a difference between the transfer prices that management would use purely for control purposes and the legally allowable transfer prices that minimize the sum of the tax and tariff impacts. Since a certain amount of subjectivity is involved in applying Section 482 to many goods and services, there may be a considerable range in the permissible transfer price for a particular item. Management can minimize the sum of income taxes and tariffs by maintaining transfer prices as far as possible at the appropriate end of the range. For example, if a US parent company sells a product to a subsidiary in a country with materially lower income tax rates than those in the United States, profits can be shifted to the foreign subsidiary by keeping the transfer price as low as is legally allowable. This practice, however, may cause a management control problem because profits in a foreign subsidiary would be reported as being higher, and profits in the American parent would be reported as being lower, than would be the case if the transaction took place between independent entities.

There are two extremes of policy in dealing with this problem. Some companies permit subsidiaries to deal with each other at arm's length and let the impact of taxes and tariffs fall where it may. With this policy, there is no question about the legality of transfer prices because the subsidiaries are trying to do exactly what the regulations say they should do—deal at arm's length. Under this policy, foreign transfer pricing policies will be essentially the same as domestic transfer pricing. Consequently, the transfer price system supports the management control system. On the other hand, this policy could result in higher total costs.

At the other extreme, foreign transfer prices may be controlled almost entirely by corporate headquarters, for the purpose of minimizing total corporate costs, maximizing dollar cash flow, or obtaining the optimum mix of currency positions. Such a policy can severely restrict the usefulness of the control system, however, because, in some instances, the transfer prices may bear little relationship to the prices that would prevail if the buying and selling units were independent. If this policy is followed, the question arises of what to do about the control system.

One possibility is to adjust profits for internal evaluation purposes to reflect competitive market prices. For example, the total differences between the prices actually charged and those that would have been in effect had taxation not been a consideration could be added to the selling subsidiary's revenue and the buying subsidiary's costs when profit budget reports are analyzed. This is a questionable practice, however, and few companies use it. If asked, a company would be required to disclose these adjustments to the Internal Revenue Service, and their existence could raise questions concerning the validity of the transfer prices being used for tax purposes.

Many companies that price to minimize taxes and tariffs use the same transfer prices for profit budget preparation and reporting as are used for accounting and tax purposes. The approved budget reflects any inequities arising from the transfer prices. To illustrate, a subsidiary that sells for lower than normal prices might have a budgeted loss. If reports of actual performance show that the subsidiary loses less than budget, its performance is considered to be satisfactory, other things being equal. In short, the transfer prices are considered both in preparing the budget and in analyzing results.

If profit budgets and reports reflect uneconomic transfer prices, care must be taken to make certain that subsidiary managers make decisions that are in the best interests of the company. For example, suppose that Subsidiary A purchases a line of products from Subsidiary B at a price that gives B most of the profit. In these circumstances, Subsidiary A can improve its reported profit performance by not selling B's products aggressively and by concentrating its marketing efforts on products that add more to its reported profits. Such a practice could be contrary to the best interests of the company as a whole. If uneconomic transfer prices are used in budgeting, therefore, it is important to guard against such situations. It may be necessary to use other measures of performance than profitability or, at least, other measures *in addition* to profitability, such as sales volume or market share.

Legal Constraints on Transfer Pricing Systems.   In some instances, legal constraints may require that a particular transfer pricing system be used, or that a preferred transfer system not be used. For example, the two-step transfer price system described in Chapter 5 might be questioned by the tax authorities simply because it is not mentioned in Section 482 and is not widely known abroad.

In other instances, the "full cost" approach implicit in Section 482 may limit a company's ability to transfer some products at less than full costs. For example, the marketing department may want to introduce a new product in a market at a price that is lower than its normal price, perhaps not even high enough to cover its full costs. This may be a sound marketing tactic, but the IRS may not recognize it as a valid basis for arriving at the transfer price.

If Section 482 requires the use of transfer prices different from the ones that would be used for control purposes, a company is in the same position as the company that used one set of transfer prices for taxation and another for control, except that such a company can safely adjust subsidiary revenues and costs for differences between the Section 482 transfer price and the preferred transfer price in most cases. Since the company presumably would have no objection to using the preferred transfer price for tax purposes, no harm comes from, in effect, keeping two sets of books.

Minority Interests

Whenever minority interests are involved, top management's flexibility in distributing profits between subsidiaries can be severely restricted because the minority parties have a legal right to a fair share of the corporation's profit. In this event, subsidiaries must deal with each other at arm's length, to the extent possible.

Exchange Rates

The cash flows of a domestic company are denominated in dollars, and at a given moment each dollar has the same value as every other dollar. By contrast, the cash flows of a multinational enterprise (MNE) are denominated in several currencies, and the value of each currency relative to the value of the dollar is different at different times. These variations complicate the problem of measuring the performance of subsidiaries and subsidiary managers. Specifically, MNEs face *translation, transaction,* and *economic* exposure to changes in exchange rates. We first discuss exchange rates briefly, and then we define the three types of exchange rate exposure and their implications for the design of management control systems.

Exchange Rates

An exchange rate is the price of one currency in terms of another currency. It can be expressed either as the number of units of the home currency that are needed to buy one unit of foreign currency (called the *direct quote),* or the

EXHIBIT 14–2   Exchange Rates for Various Foreign Currencies on January 19, 2000

Country	Monetary Unit	Dollar per Unit of Foreign Currency (direct quote)	Foreign Currency Units per Dollar (indirect quote)
Britain	Pound	.6128	1.6320
Germany	Mark	.5171	1.9337
Japan	Yen	.0095	104.85
Switzerland	Franc	.6265	1.5963
Europe	Euro	.9886	1.0115

number of units of the foreign currency that are needed to buy one unit of the home currency (called the *indirect quote)*. For example, if the US dollar ($) is the home currency and the French franc (FF) is the foreign currency, then to express the exchange rate as $0.20/FF is the direct quote, and to express it as FF5/$ is the indirect quote. In the markets for foreign exchange, both types of quotes are used, but traders usually use one or the other type for particular currencies. Exhibit 14–2 provides examples of both for exchange rates prevailing on January 19, 2000, for the most heavily traded currencies.

Exchange rates that are usually quoted (such as those above) are called *nominal* exchange rates. The *spot* exchange rate is the nominal exchange rate that prevails on a given day. The *real* exchange rate is the spot exchange rate *after* adjusting for inflation differentials between the two countries in question. There are also *forward* exchange rates, which are exchange rates known today at which transactions can be entered into for completion at some future point in time.

Using the direct quote, if the number of dollars required to buy a unit of foreign currency rises, then the dollar is said to have undergone a *depreciation* relative to the foreign currency; the reverse is true for an appreciation. Suppose, for example, that one year ago the spot US/UK exchange rate was $1/£, and today's spot rate is $1.20/£. These rates are "nominal" exchange rates that prevailed one year ago and are prevailing today, respectively. In nominal terms, we would then say that the US dollar depreciated 20 percent against the pound sterling, since it takes 20 percent more dollars to buy the same number of pounds sterling today, compared to a year ago.

However, suppose that the inflation during this period was 10 percent in the United States and 5 percent in the United Kingdom. Then, according to *purchasing power parity* (PPP), these inflation rates would predict that the US dollar should have depreciated against the UK pound sterling by about 5 percent, or to the approximate extent of the inflation differential between the two countries, and not by 20 percent. Thus, under PPP, we would have expected the exchange rate today to be $1.05/£. At the spot rate of $1.20/£, the nominal value of the US dollar depreciated by 14.3 percent *more* than PPP would predict. This additional depreciation of 14.3 percent in currency values in excess of the inflation differential between the two countries is the *real depreciation* of the US dollar; analogous arguments apply in the case of appreciation. The real exchange rate is the exchange rate after adjusting for inflation differentials between the United States and the United Kingdom and, in our example, it is $1.143/£.

Ever since the evolution of the floating exchange rate system in the early 1970s, there have been substantial swings in real exchange rates. In the broadest terms, real exchange rate changes create changes in the cost competitiveness of a domestic manufacturer against its foreign competitors: if all else remains equal and US real exchange rates depreciate by 10 percent against the Japanese yen, then US firms are likely to have become 10 percent more cost competitive, compared to their Japanese competitors. The explanation is as follows: A 10 percent real depreciation of the US dollar must mean that goods priced in US dollars have become 10 percent cheaper *over and above* the price adjustments that should have normally resulted from inflation in both the United States and Japan.

Different Types of Exchange Rate Exposure

Translation exposure to exchange rates is the income statement and balance sheet exposure on MNEs to changes in nominal exchange rates. It results from the fact that MNEs must consolidate their accounts in a single (usually home country) currency although their cash flows are denominated in multiple currencies. Understanding translation exposure in MNEs comes down to understanding the answer to the following question: Given that the cash flows of the firm are denominated in multiple currencies and given that there have been nominal changes in currency values during the year, how should revenues, expenses, assets, and liabilities be consolidated into one currency at a point in time?

Transaction exposure is the exchange rate exposure that the firm has in its cross-border transactions when such transactions are entered into today but payments to settle the transaction are made at some future time. During the period that payment or receipt commitments are outstanding, nominal exchange rates could change and put the value of transactions at risk. Examples of such transactions include receivables and payables and debt or interest payments outstanding in foreign currencies.

Economic exposure is the exchange rate exposure of the firm's cash flows to real exchange rate changes. Economic exposure is also referred to as *operating exposure* or *competitive exposure* to exchange rates.

Choice of Metric in Performance Evaluation

In a survey of MNEs, Choi and Czechowicz found almost all the respondents had performance evaluation systems that compared actuals against budgets

Exhibit 14–3

Choice of metric in performance evaluation

Tracking Budget

		Initial	Projected	Ending
	Initial	<u>1</u>	2	<u>3</u>
Setting Budget	Projected	4	<u>5</u>	<u>6</u>
	Ending	7	8	<u>9</u>

in assessing subsidiary performance.[3] There are basically three possibilities for choice of metric in setting and tracking budgets: the exchange rate prevailing at the time budgets are set (the *initial* exchange rate), the exchange rates projected at the time budgets are set (the *projected* exchange rate), or the actual exchange rates prevailing at the time budgets are tracked ("ending" exchange rate). There are, then, nine possible combinations of metrics in setting and tracking budgets, as shown in Exhibit 14–3.[4]

Not all nine cells are feasible, however; only the five underlined ones are. The obviously feasible ones consist of the three where the budget is set and tracked using the same metric (initial-initial, cell 1; projected-projected, cell 5; ending-ending, cell 9)[5]; similarly, it is feasible to set the budget using an "initial" rate and track it using an "ending" rate (cell 3), as well as to set at a "projected" rate and track at the "ending" exchange rate (cell 6). It is illogical, however, to set the budget at the "ending" exchange rate and then to track actuals using initial or projected exchange rates (thus ruling out 7 and 8). Similarly, to project an exchange rate in setting the budget and then to track it at the rate that initially prevailed also seems illogical (thus ruling out cell 4).

Control System Design Issues

From the point of view of performance evaluation, these are the important questions in control systems design:

---

[3]F. D. S. Choi and I. J. Czechowicz, "Assessing Foreign Subsidiary Performance: A Multinational Comparison," *Management International Review* 4 (1983), pp. 14–25.

[4]These possibilities were originally discussed in D. Lessard and P. Lorange, "Currency Changes and Management Control: Resolving the Centralization/Decentralization Dilemma," *Accounting Review,* July 1977, pp. 628–37.

[5]To set the budget at the "ending" rate means that at the time performance is being evaluated, the original budget is recast using the exchange rate prevailing at the end-of-period.

- Should subsidiary managers be held responsible for the impact of exchange rate fluctuations on their bottom line?
- Should the parent company use the home country currency, or should it use the local currency in performance evaluation? Further, should it use the initial exchange rate, the projected exchange rate, or the ending exchange rate in setting and tracking budgets?
- Should the parent company distinguish between the effects of different types of exchange rate exposure while evaluating the performance of the subsidiary manager? If yes, how?
- How should different types of exchange rate exposure affect the evaluation of the economic performance of the subsidiary, as distinct from the evaluation of the manager in charge of the subsidiary?

Translation Effects

Consider an example of a US company with a subsidiary in France. Exhibit 14-4 describes the budget and the actuals for the subsidiary. Suppose that the initial exchange rate was FF10/$ and the ending exchange rate was FF11/$ (that is, the French franc depreciated in both real and nominal terms by 10 percent relative to the dollar, so that the French inflation rate did not change). The subsidiary was given a volume target, based on which the budgeted profit at the initial exchange rate was $1, or FF10. Further, assume that the French subsidiary incurs all its costs in France and sells entirely in France; it does not engage in any *cross-border* transactions. Such a subsidiary is called a *balanced unit*. Assume that the subsidiary met all its volume targets, but the exchange rate changed to FF11/$. Under the new exchange rate, the dollar profits generated by the subsidiary would be only $0.91—or an unfavorable budget variance of about 10 percent in dollar terms—even though it met its volume objectives.

Should the manager of the French subsidiary be held accountable for exchange rate fluctuations even though the actual performance was exactly as budgeted? The French subsidiary is self-contained (i.e., it does not engage in

---

EXHIBIT 14–4   Budget and Actuals for Balanced Subsidiary (initial exchange rate: FF10/$; ending exchange rate: FF11/$)

	Budget		Actual	
	FF	*$*	*FF*	*$*
Revenue	100	10	100	9.09
Profit	10	1	10	0.91

cross-border transactions). Therefore, the manager of that subsidiary need not be concerned with strategic and operating decisions (such as pricing and sourcing) in response to exchange rate changes. In addition, changes in exchange rates are completely beyond the control of the subsidiary manager. It seems fair, therefore, that subsidiary managers not be held responsible for translation effects. The simplest way to achieve this objective is to set and track budgets using the same metric (cells 1, 5, or 9 in Exhibit 14–3).

In the example in Exhibit 14–4, if the budget was tracked using the same metric as that on which the budget was set (FF10/$), then the subsidiary would have been shown to have generated $1. Alternatively, if the budget at the end of the year was reset to the ending exchange rate of FF11/$, the subsidiary would have been only *expected* to generate $0.91 in profits. Thus, if the same metric is used to set and track the budget, then the choice of metric (whether local or foreign currency; whether initial, projected, or ending exchange rate) is not relevant; the resulting performance reflects the operating performance of the manager, independent of translation effects.

However, the parent company suffered a "translation" loss at the end of the year. Parent companies can do little to control such exchange rate shifts. If they use translation gains or losses in evaluating the subsidiary managers' performance, this could lead to several problems: (1) It would make the subsidiary managers responsible for factors that are beyond their control; (2) it does not get rid of the translation gain or loss; (3) it will not account for other types of exchange rate exposure that subsidiaries face (see next section); and (4) it will confound the performance of the manager and the subsidiary (see next section).

When companies report to stockholders, they have to consolidate the accounting numbers of foreign subsidiaries with the accounting numbers of the parent. Translation gains and losses arising out of converting the income statement and the balance sheet of the foreign subsidiary into the monetary unit of the parent company should *not* affect the performance evaluation of the subsidiary manager. The required method of calculating translation gains and losses for financial reporting purposes is described in the Appendix at the end of this chapter.

Economic Exposure

In the balanced unit that we considered above, exchange rates led only to translation effects. However, when subsidiaries have cross-border transactions, they also are subject to economic exposure. A control system that effectively deals with economic exposure differs in a fundamental way from the one that we have described for translation exposure. Under economic exposure, it would be appropriate for the control system to evaluate the subsidiary manager on decisions that would have enabled the subsidiary to respond to real exchange rate changes. We explain how this can be done by considering two generic types of subsidiaries in MNEs: "net importers" and "net exporters."

EXHIBIT 14–5   **Budgets for A, B, and C (initial exchange rate: 10FF/$)**

	A: Balanced		B: Net Importer		C: Net Exporter	
	FF	*US$*	*FF*	*US$*	*FF*	*US$*
Sales	100	10	100	10	100	10
Costs	90	9	90	9	90	9
Profit (value)	10	1	10	1	10	1
Profit (margin)	10%	10%	10%	10%	10%	10%

A *net importer* is a subsidiary that sells most of its products in its own country, but imports most of its inputs from outside that country (either from sister subsidiaries or from outside companies); a *net exporter* is a subsidiary that sells most of its products outside its own country (either to sister subsidiaries or to outside companies), but purchases most of its inputs within that country. As the following example shows, given an exchange rate shift, such subsidiaries will not only face translation effects but also "dependence" effects resulting from real exchange rate changes.

To keep the example simple, we will consider subsidiaries that have transactions only between the home country and the host country. The conclusions from this example can be generalized to any subsidiary that has cross-border transactions with sister subsidiaries or other companies outside the host country. Also, we will include the balanced unit in the analysis for purposes of comparison. Suppose a US MNE has three subsidiaries, A, B, and C, in France. Subsidiary A is the balanced unit, the one considered in the preceding section. B is a net importer; it obtains its inputs from its parent in the United States and sells all its output in France. C is a net exporter; it sources entirely in France and sells all of its outputs in the United States. The initial exchange rate is $1 = 10FF, and the budgets have been set as indicated in Exhibit 14–5.

Now, as before, suppose that the United States dollar appreciated against the French franc by 10 percent in *real* terms, with the new exchange rate being $1 = FF11 by the time the budget was tracked.[6] Suppose the parent company set the budget at the initial rate (FF10/$) and tracked it at the ending rated (FF11/$). Let us suppose that at the end of the year, the performance of the three subsidiaries looked like Exhibit 14–6 from the perspective of the parent company.

---

[6]We could have made the example somewhat more realistic by including nominal exchange rate changes as well—that is, we could assume that part of the exchange rate change was nominal and that we take out the purchasing power parity effect to include only real exchange rate changes. In this example, we simply assume that all of the exchange rate change is real. Conclusions are not altered by this assumption.

EXHIBIT 14–6   Performance of A, B, and C (current exchange rate: 11FF/$)

	A: Balanced		B: Net Importer		C: Net Exporter	
	FF	*US$*	*FF*	*US$*	*FF*	*US$*
Sales	100	9.09	103	9.36	109	9.91
Costs	90	8.18	95	8.63	95	8.63
Profit (value)	10	0.91	8	0.73	14	1.28
Profit (margin)	10%	10%	7.9%	7.9%	12.9%	12.9%

The net exporter outperformed the budget (in both $ and FF, both profit objective and margin), the balanced unit performed approximately at budgeted levels (met the profit objective in FF, but a bit below in $; met the margin objectives in both currencies), and the net importer underperformed the budget (in both $ and FF, profit value and margin).

Now let us examine the exchange rate effects a bit more closely. Note that, under the new real exchange rates scenario, the net exporter should have been able to achieve FF110, without any extra efforts. In fact, given the nature of its demand and cost structure, it may have been able to achieve much higher levels of sales than even FF110. Thus, its sales of FF109 represent *under*achievement relative to what should have been expected, given the real exchange rate shift. Further, its underperformance on the sales front was exacerbated by underperformance on the cost front (since it incurred local costs of FF95, although it was budgeted for FF90).

Now, consider the net importer. Under the new exchange rate scenario, Firm B became *less* cost competitive against its competitors that did not have similar exchange rate exposure in relation to inputs. Against B's cost of $8.63, competitors that were sourcing entirely locally (as, for example, the balanced subsidiary was doing) were incurring a cost of only $8.18. They could easily have (and perhaps did) undercut B in prices to gain both profits and market share. Yet, the net importer not only exceeded his FF sales target but, in the process, did so at a lower local input cost than originally budgeted.

This example not only underscores the point that setting and tracking budgets using different metrics can be unfair; it also highlights the problems of measuring management performance and subsidiary performance. In addition, such a situation confounds translation and dependence effects. If only the translation effect was considered, manager B would have been criticized and manager C rewarded. If the dependence effect was isolated from the translation effect, manager B would have been rewarded and manager C criticized. To illustrate, manager C would have been told that given the real appreciation of the US dollar, his or her sales performance of FF109 represents inadequate performance; if he or she expected to be rewarded for above-budget performance, the subsidiary should have done more.

For subsidiaries like B and C (which have cross-border transactions), real exchange rate changes require important strategic and operating decisions. For example, if the US$ depreciated against the foreign currencies, this implies that goods priced in US$ have become cheaper in real terms, compared to those priced in foreign currencies. For a subsidiary that imports from the United States, this provides major strategic opportunities—for example, it can now afford to costlessly pursue a market share strategy by dropping its local currency prices, thereby increasing demand and market share. Still, it would not suffer in terms of US$ profitability. Or the subsidiary could pursue a skimming strategy in which it retains local currency prices at predepreciation levels, and simply pockets the extra US$ profits without losing market share.[7]

While on the one hand we have shown that it is not fair to reward or penalize subsidiary managers for exchange rate changes per se, on the other hand it is important to evaluate the performance of the managers in terms of the quality of their decisions when changes in real exchange rates create strategic opportunities of the type described here. As in the case of the translation effect, the unfair reward or penalty can be avoided by setting and tracking the budget using the same metric.

Transaction Effects

The basic approach to dealing with transaction exposure is by appropriate foreign exchange hedging strategies. *Hedging* is any transaction by which risk associated with future cash flows is reduced. In the process, the company that buys the hedge shifts risk to the entity selling the hedge—typically a commercial bank in the case of foreign exchange markets. Naturally, such hedging services come at a price.

Hedging is commonly practiced by most firms—for example, whenever a company purchases insurance, it is, in effect, undertaking a hedge transaction. Hedging is particularly common among companies engaged in international transactions, and it is used as a means of counteracting the effects of transaction exposure.[8] There are many ways of hedging transaction exposure.

---

[7]The appropriate choice of pricing strategies, given a real currency movement, is dealt with in A. Sundaram and V. Mishara, "Currency Movements and Corporate Pricing Strategies," in *Recent Developments in International Banking and Finance,* vol. IV, North-Holland, 1990. Given the 35 percent real depreciation of the US$ between 1985 and 1987, many US firms pursued skimming, rather than market share, pricing strategies abroad. For example, articles in *The Wall Street Journal* (May 15, 1987) and *Business Week* (August 27, 1987) pointed out that the norm for US firms operating in Japan was to go for "profits rather than market share." There have been many reports of exactly the reverse pricing behavior on the part of Japanese firms operating in the United States, when the US$ appreciated between 1981 and 1984.

[8]One study suggests that 84 percent of treasurers at companies engaged in international trade hedge foreign transaction exposure; see Scott Flicker and Dennis Bline, "Managing Foreign Currency Exchange Risk," *Journal of Accountancy,* August 1990, pp. 128–30.

To illustrate the simplest: if an American company sells products to a French company at a price that is stated in French francs, it can simultaneously buy the right to purchase French francs at the same price as of the future date that the account receivable is due. If it has a transaction loss on the sale, it will have an equal gain on the hedge. Other hedging techniques include making use of the option market and matching assets/liabilities and revenues/ expenses in the same currency. The commonly used techniques of hedging use forward and future markets, as well as foreign currency options markets.[9] From the perspective of performance evaluation, the key question is whether to hold subsidiary managers responsible for hedging transaction exposure.

Hedging transactions are probably best done at the parent company level, rather than permitting individual subsidiaries to make them. There are a number of reasons for this. First, in most MNEs, there are payables and receivables in different parts of the overall firm that may naturally hedge each other if information on all such transactions is collected and dealt with at one central location. This reduces transaction costs associated with hedging. Second, the parent company probably has better access to a wider (and perhaps more sophisticated) range of hedging instruments, across a greater range of maturities, than a subsidiary typically has. Third, there is no reason to presume that the manager of a subsidiary can forecast exchange rates any better than the corporate treasurer; in fact, parent companies may not want managers of subsidiaries to hedge, since this runs the risk of making subsidiary managers exchange rate speculators.

Thus, from the perspective of performance evaluation, it is unnecessary to make subsidiary managers responsible for transaction effects.

Performance of the Subsidiary

We have thus far suggested that it is important to distinguish between the economic performance of the subsidiary and the performance of its manager, and the guidelines discussed above primarily have dealt with isolating the impact of exchange rates on the performance of the subsidiary manager. It is important to recognize that the economic performance of the subsidiary itself should reflect the negative or positive consequences of translation, transaction, and economic exposures.

If the long-term economic performance of the subsidiary (after incorporating exchange rate effects) continues to be poor, even though the performance of the manager is excellent, then the parent company should address a more basic question: Does it make continued economic sense for the MNE to carry on operations in that country, or should it take its business elsewhere? The answer to this question comes down to a business location decision, rather than a performance evaluation decision; these should be independent decisions.

[9]See, for example, D. Eiteman and A. Stonehill, *Multinational Business Finance* (Reading, MA: Addison-Wesley, 1989) or A. Shapiro, *Multinational Financial Management* (Boston: Allyn & Bacon, 1990).

Management Considerations

In designing performance evaluation systems of MNE subsidiaries, companies could use the following guidelines:

- Subsidiary managers should not be held responsible for translation effects. The simplest way to achieve this objective is to compare budgets and actual results using the same metric and isolate inflation-related effects through variance analysis. It is pointless for managers to worry about the appropriate metric. The MNE should choose whatever metric is more convenient.

- Transaction effects are best handled through centralized coordination of the MNE's overall hedging needs. This is likely to be cheaper and simpler, and it prevents the subsidiary manager from becoming a foreign exchange rate forecaster and speculator.

- The subsidiary manager should be held responsible for the dependence effects of exchange rates resulting from economic exposure.

- Evaluation of the subsidiary as a basis for a decision to locate operations in a country or to relocate operations from a country should reflect the consequences of translation, transaction, and economic exposures.

In a 1982 survey, Sapy-Mazella et al. found that in evaluating the subsidiary managers' performance, 79 percent of the respondents used different metrics to prepare budgets and report performance; 66 percent used some forecast of exchange rates to prepare the budget and used the actual end-of-period exchange rate to report the subsidiary's performance relative to the budget; and 13 percent used the initial exchange rate to prepare the budget and the end-of-period actual to report performance.[10] These findings are inconsistent with the guidelines we have developed above.

There are two possible explanations for this inconsistency. First, most of these control systems were developed in the 1950s and 60s, when exchange rates were fixed; given the recent vintage of flexible exchange rates, MNEs may not have tailored their performance evaluation system to the new reality. Second, many companies may not distinguish between the financial performance of the manager and the financial performance of the subsidiary.

Whatever the reason, it is important to recognize that an MNE that chooses to use different metrics to prepare subsidiary budgets and report actual performance runs the various types of risks we have discussed.

---

[10]Jean-Pierre Sapy-Mazella, R. Woo, and J. Czechowicz, "New Directions in Managing Currency Risk: Changing Corporate Strategies and Systems under FAS No. 52," *Business International Corporation,* New York, 1982.

Summary

From the standpoint of management control, three topics are unique to MNEs: cultural differences, transfer pricing, and exchange rates. In addition to goal congruence, other considerations are important in arriving at transfer prices in MNEs: taxation, government regulations, tariffs, foreign exchange controls, funds accumulation, and joint ventures.

An evaluation of the economic performance of the subsidiary should incorporate the negative or positive consequences of translation, transaction, and economic exposures. However, while evaluating the performance of the manager in charge of the subsidiary, effects of translation and transaction exposures should be removed; even so, the subsidiary manager should be held responsible for the dependence effects of exchange rates resulting from economic exposure.

APPENDIX
SFAS No. 52: FOREIGN CURRENCY TRANSLATION

Statement of Financial Accounting Standards No. 52 requires the all-current method for translating the balance sheet. Under this method all balance sheet items are translated at the rate of exchange in effect on the balance sheet date.[11] Conversion or translation gains and losses are reported as direct credits or charges to shareholders' equity; they do not affect net income for the year. This practice is similar to that used in the United Kingdom. Income statement items are translated at the exchange rate in effect on the date when the income or expense items are recognized, except that companies can use a weighted-average exchange rate if using the actual rates is too complicated.

An example of these exchange translations follows.

Assume that a United States corporation had a Swiss subsidiary with the following financial statements, expressed in Swiss francs (Sfr):

Beginning Balance Sheet
December 31, 1989

Assets	Sfr 100,000
Liabilities	Sfr 60,000
Capital stock	20,000
Retained earnings	20,000
	Sfr 100,000

---

[11]The name *all current* is used to contrast with the *current/noncurrent* method that the Financial Accounting Standards Board considered and rejected. Under the current/noncurrent method, only current assets and current liabilities are translated at current rates.

During 1990, the subsidiary had the following two transactions.
(1) Borrowed Sfr 10,000 from a local bank:

1990 Transactions

Assets	Sfr 10,000	
Liabilities		Sfr 10,000

(2) Earned Sfr 5,000 from operations:

Revenues	Sfr 15,000
Expenses	10,000
Profit	Sfr 5,000

The impact of (2) is to increase assets by Sfr 5,000 and retained earnings by Sfr 5,000.

Ending Balance Sheet
December 31, 1990

Assets	Sfr 115,000
Liabilities	Sfr 70,000
Capital stock	20,000
Retained earnings	25,000
	Sfr 115,000

Assume that the Swiss franc was worth $.60 on December 31, 1989, and $50 on December 31, 1990. The average value during 1990 was $.55.

Under *SFAS No. 52,* the subsidiary results would be consolidated with the parent company's financial statement as shown below.

Beginning Balance Sheet
December 31, 1989

Assets (Sfr 100,000 * .6)	$60,000
Liabilities (Sfr 60,000 * .6)	$36,000
Capital stock (Sfr 20,000 * .6)	12,000
Retained earning (Sfr 20,000 * .6)	12,000
	$60,000

Income Statement

Revenues (Sfr 15,000 * .55)	$8,250
Expenses (Sfr 10,000 * .55)	5,500
Profit	$2,750

Ending Balance Sheet
December 31, 1990

Assets (Sfr 115,000 * .5)	$57,500
Liabilities (Sfr 70,000 * .5)	$35,000
Capital stock (Sfr 20,000 * .5)	10,000
Retained earnings (Sfr 25,000 * .5)	12,500
	$57,500
Reconciliation of retained earnings in dollars:	
Beginning balance	$12,000
Profit	2,750
Indicate ending balance	14,750
Actual ending balance	12,500
Translation loss	$ 2,250

The United States corporation would include profit of $2,750 in its consolidated income statement and a reduction of $2,250 in a segregated part of retained earnings. This represents the financial effect of the fall in the Swiss franc; put another way, the rise in value of the dollar.

Suggested Additional Readings

Bartlett, Christopher A., and Sumantra Ghoshal. *Managing across Borders.* 2nd ed. Boston: Harvard Business School Press, 1999.

Eden, Lorraine. *Taxing Multinationals: Transfer Pricing and Corporate Income Taxation in North America.* Toronto: University of Toronto Press, 1998.

Glaister, Keith W. "Dimensions of Control in UK International Joint Ventures." *British Journal of Management* 6, no. 2 (June 1995), pp. 77–96.

Govindarajan, Vijay, and Anil Gupta. *World Wise: Building the Global Corporation of Tomorrow.* Boston: Harvard Business School Press, 2000.

Gupta, Anil, and Vijay Govindarajan. "Knowledge Flows within Multinational Corporations." *Strategic Management Journal,* March 2000.

Gupta, A. K., and V. Govindarajan. "Knowledge Flows and the Structure of Controls within Multinational Organizations." *Academy of Management Review,* October 1991, pp. 768–92.

Harzing, Anne-Wil Kathe. *Managing the Multinational: An International Study of Control.* Cheltenham, UK: Edward Elgar, 1999.

International Transfer Pricing. New York: Business International Corporation and Ernst & Young, Economist Intelligence Unit, 1993.

Millman, G. J. "The How of Dow: Managing Currency Risk." *Financial Executive,* November/December 1998, pp. 19–24.

OECD. *Transfer Pricing Guidelines for Multinational Enterprises and Tax Administration.* Organisation for Economic Co-operation & Development, 1998.

Pearce, Robert D. *Global Competition and Technology.* New York: Macmillan Press and St. Martin's Press, 1997.

CASE 14–1
AB THORSTEN

"You will see from my report that the XL-4 project shows an excellent rate of return on the Skr 700,000 investment and is also a logical extension of our product development and growth strategy here in Sweden. My management and I strongly recommend this project."

> Anders Ekstrom, Managing Director AB Thorsten,
> Stockholm (100 percent–owned subsidiary of Roget S.A.)

"Any extra XL-4 which Ekstrom might sell in Sweden can be produced in our existing plant in Gent for no additional investment. Ekstrom is not only very optimistic about the sales potential, he is also underestimating the manufacturing problems and costs he will face. I recommend that you inform Ekstrom that it is in Roget's best interest for him to import from Belgium any XL-4 he can sell in Sweden."

> Pierre Lambert, Vice President for Domestic and Export
> Sales and Manufacturing, Industrial Products Group,
> Roget S.A. Brussels

Roget S.A.

Roget S.A.[1] was one of the largest industrial companies in Belgium. The company was incorporated in 1928 by merging three smaller firms that all produced industrial chemicals for sale in Belgium. By 1981 Roget had expanded to produce 208 basic and specialty chemical products in 21 factories, for sale throughout Europe.

Until the mid-70s, Roger was organized with one large manufacturing division and one large sales division in Belgium. A department of the sales division was devoted to export sales. How-

ever, in the late 70s, exports grew so fast, and domestic markets became so complex, that the company created three main product divisions (Food, Industrial, and Textile), each with its own manufacturing plants and sales organization. In addition, the company created foreign subsidiaries to take over the businesses in certain areas. For example, in Industrial Chemicals the company had two subsidiaries—one in the United Kingdom and one in Sweden (Thorsten), which served all of Scandinavia. At the same time, the Domestic Department of the Industrial Chemicals Division exported to the rest of Europe. The United Kingdom and Sweden accounted for 9 percent and 5 percent, respectively, of sales in that Division.

Mr. Gillot (see Exhibit 1) was responsible for profits from all industrial chemicals; Mr. Lambert was responsible for profits from domestic operations (manufacturing and sales of industrial chemicals) and export sales to countries where the company did not have subsidiaries or factories; and Mr. Ekstrom was responsible for profits in Scandinavia. The company utilized a rather liberal bonus system to reward executives at each level, based on the profits of their divisions.

This, together with a policy of promotion from within, helped stimulate managers in Roget to a degree not enjoyed by some of its competitors. It also helped the company to retain key people in an industry where experience was of great importance. Many of the company's executives had been in the starch chemicals business all of their business lives. It was a complex business, and it took many years to learn it.

Certain policies—rules of the game—governed relationships with the subsidiary companies. These policies were intended to maintain the effi-

---

This case is adapted from AB Thorsten (A), (B), and (C) cases, which were prepared by Professors C. E. Summer and G. Shillinglaw and are copyrighted by the Institute for Management Development, Lausanne, Switzerland.

[1] "AB" and "S.A." are abbreviations used in Sweden and Belgium that are similar to "Corp." or "Inc." in the United States.

EXHIBIT 1

Roget S.A. organizational chart

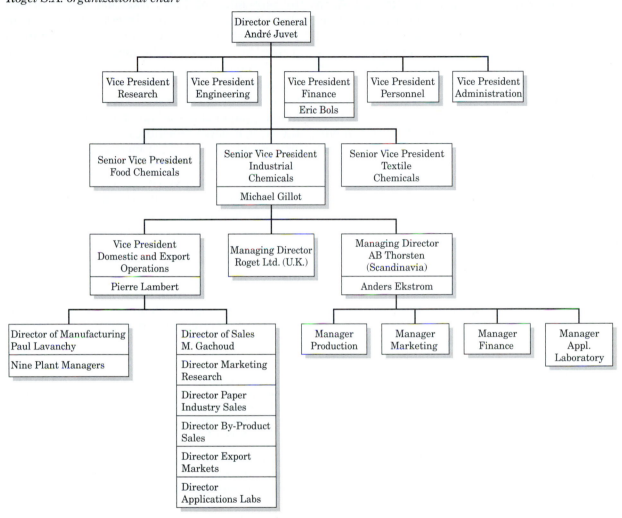

ciency of the whole Roget complex, while at the same time giving subsidiary managers autonomy to run their own businesses. For example, a subsidiary manager could determine what existing Roget products to sell in the local market. Export sales would quote the same price as they quote agents in all countries. Of course, all prices were subject to bargaining on both sides.

Second, subsidiaries were encouraged to propose to division management in Brussels the development of new products. If these were judged feasible, new products were manufactured in Belgium for supply to world markets. Third, the subsidiary managing director could build manufacturing plants if the investment in the local market were adequately justified.

AB Thorsten

AB Thorsten was purchased by Roget S.A. in 1972. Since that time, Thorsten's board of directors had consisted of four persons: Mr. Michel Gillot, senior vice president in charge of Roget's industrial chemicals division; Mr. Ingve Norgren, a Swedish banker; Mr. Ove Svensen, a Stockholm industrialist; and the managing director. Swedish law required any company incorporated in Sweden to have at least two outside directors, and the Roget management felt fortunate in finding two men as prominent as Norgren and Svensen to serve on the Thorsten board.

During the first four years of Roget's ownership, Thorsten's sales fluctuated between Skr. 5 and 7 million, but hit a low in 1976.[2] The Board decided at that time that the company was in serious trouble, and that the only alternative to selling the company was to hire a totally different management group to overhaul and streamline company operations.

On the advice of the Swedish directors, Mr. Anders Ekstrom, a 38-year-old graduate of the Royal Institute of Technology, was hired as managing director. He had 16 years of experience as a production engineer for a large paper machinery company and as division manager responsible for profits in a large paper company,

Ekstrom joined AB Thorsten in January of 1977. Since that time, sales had increased to Skr. 20 million and profits had reached levels that Roget's management found highly satisfactory.

Ekstrom said that at the time he joined Thorsten, he knew it was a risk:

> I liked the challenge of building a company. If I did a good job here I would have the confidence of Norgren and Svensen as well as of the Roget management in Brussels. I felt that succeeding in this situation would teach me things that would make me more competent as a top executive. So I chose this job even though I had at the time (and still have) offers from other companies.

---

[2]Most monetary amounts in this case are stated in Swedish kronor (Skr).

Initial Proposal for Manufacture of XL-4

In September of 1980, Ekstrom had informed the Thorsten board of directors that he proposed to study the feasibility of constructing a factory in Sweden for the manufacture of XL-4, a starch-based adhesive chemical used in drying paper. He explained that he and his customer engineers had discovered a new way of helping paper mills adapt the dryer sections of their huge paper machines at very low cost so that they could use XL-4 instead of competitors' products. Large paper mills would realize dramatic savings in material handling and storage costs and also shorten drying time substantially. Shortened drying time increases the effective capacity of a paper machine. It was Ekstrom's judgment that his innovation would allow him to develop a market in Sweden almost as big as Roget's present worldwide market for XL-4. This product was currently being produced in Roget's Domestic Department at the rate of 600 tons per year, with none going to Sweden. Ekstrom stated:

> At that meeting, Mr. Gillot and the other directors seemed enthusiastic. During the next six months, we did the analysis. My marketing director used modern market research techniques to estimate the total potential in Sweden at 800 tons of XL-4 per year, using the custom engineered approach we were proposing. We interviewed important customers and conducted trials in the mills of three big companies which proved that with the introduction of our machine designs, the large cost savings and capacity expansion would indeed materialize. We determined that if we could sell the product for Skr. 1,850 per ton, we could capture at least one-half of the market within a three-year period, or 400 tons a year. At the same time, I called the head of the corporate engineering division in Belgium and asked for his help in designing a plant to produce 400 tons of XL-4 per year and in estimating the cost of the investment. This is a routine thing. The central staff divisions are advisory and always comply with requests for help. He assigned a project manager and four other engineers to work on the design of factory and machinery and to estimate the cost. At the same time I assigned three men from my staff to work on the project. In three months this joint task group reported that the necessary plant could be built for about Skr 700,000. All of this we summarized in a pro forma calculation [Exhibit 2]. This calculation,

Exhibit 2   XL–4: The Swedish Proposal (in Skr.)

	1	2	3	4	5	6	7	8	9	10
End of Year	Plant	Working Capital	Sales Price/ Ton	Variable Cost/ Ton	Contribution/ Ton (col. 3 – 4)	Number of Tons	Total Contribution (col. 5 * 6)	Promotion Costs	Taxes†	Net Cash Flows (1 + 2 + 7 – 8 – 9)
0	–700,000	–56,000*								–756,000
1		–2,000*	2,000	1,000	1,000	200	200,000	130,000	(35,000)	103,000
2		–7,000*	1,850	1,000	850	300	255,000	75,000	20,000	153,000
3			1,850	1,000	850	400	340,000	50,000	75,000	215,000
4			1,850	1,000	850	400	340,000	50,000	75,000	215,000
5			1,850	1,000	850	400	340,000	50,000	75,000	215,000
6			1,850	1,000	850	400	340,000	50,000	145,000	145,000
7	+150,000‡	+65,000*	1,850	1,000	850	400	340,000	50,000	145,000	360,000

*These working capital investment amounts are net of tax credits.

†Taxes are calculated after depreciating Skr. 700,000 over a 5-year period on straight-line basis.

‡Sales value, net of appropriate taxes, assuming plant will be closed at end of seven years.

together with a complete written explanation, was mailed to Mr. Gillot in early April 1981. I felt rather excited, as did most of my staff. We all know that introduction of new products is one of the keys to our continued growth and profitability. The yield on this investment was well above the minimum 8 percent established as a guideline for new investment by the Roget vice president of finance. We also knew that it was a good analysis, using modern tools of management. In the cover letter, I asked that it be put on the agenda for the next Thorsten board meeting.

The minutes of the next board meeting held in Stockholm on April 28, 1981, quoted Ekstrom's remarks as he explained the proposal to other directors:

You will see from the summary table [Exhibit 2] that this project is profitable. Gentlemen, it seems clear from these figures that we can justify this investment in Sweden on the basis of sales to the Swedish market. The group vice president for finance has laid down the policy that any new investment should yield at least an 8 percent return. This particular proposal exceeds that substantially, using a very conservative seven-year life. My management and I strongly recommend this project.

Ekstrom later recalled Gillot's reactions in his role as chairman of the Thorsten board:

Gillot said that it seemed to him to be a clear case. He asked positive questions, mainly about the longer-term

likelihood that we could sell more than 400 tons a year, and about how we would finance any further expansion. I explained that we in Sweden were very firm in our judgment that we would reach 400 tons a year even before one year, but felt constrained to show a conservative estimate of a three-year transition period. We also showed him how we could finance any further expansion by borrowing in Sweden. That is, if Roget would furnish the initial capital, and if the 400 tons goal were reached quickly, any further expansion would easily be financed by local banks. The two Swedish directors confirmed this. The board voted unanimously to construct the plant.

Disagreement about the XL-4 Proposal

About a week later, Gillot telephoned Ekstrom:

I have been through some additional discussions with the production and marketing people here in the Domestic Department. They think the engineering design and plant cost is accurate, but that you are too optimistic on your sales forecast. It looks like you will have to justify this more.

Ekstrom said:

I pushed him to set up a meeting the following week. This was attended by myself and my marketing and production directors from Sweden, and four people from Belgium—Gillot, Lavanchy (director of manufacturing), Gachoud (director of sales), and Lambert (vice president for domestic and export). That was one of the worst meetings of my life. It lasted all day. Gachoud said that they had sales experience from other countries and that in his judgment the market potential and our share were too optimistic. I told him over and over how we arrived at this figure based on our custom engineered approach, but he just kept repeating the over-optimistic argument. Then Lavanchy said that the production of this product is complicated, and that he had difficulties producing it in Belgium, even with trained workers who had long experience. I told him I only needed five trained production workers and that he could send me two men for two months if he liked, to train Swedes to do the job. I impressed on him that they could oversee manufacturing for us in Sweden until we learn, if they did not have confidence in Swedish technology. He repeated that the difficulties in manufacturing were enormous.

Lavanchy then said that since the whole world market for Roget was only 600 tons a year, it was inconceivable that Sweden alone could make 400 tons. Gillot ended the meeting without a decision, and said that he hoped all concerned would do more investigation of this subject. He indicated that he would think about it himself and let us know when another meeting would be held.

Ekstrom returned to Stockholm and reported the meeting to his own staff, and to the two Swedish members of his board:

> They, like I, were really disgusted. Here we were, operating with initiative and with excellent financial techniques. Roget management had often made speeches in which they emphasized the necessity for decentralized profit responsibility, and for authority and initiative on the part of foreign subsidiaries. One of my men said that they seem to talk decentralization and act like tin gods at the same time. Mr. Norgren, the Swedish banker on Thorsten's board, expressed surprise. I considered this carefully. It is sound business for AB Thorsten, and XL-4 will help to build one more growth company in the Swedish economy. Somehow, the management in Brussels has failed to understand this. I dictated a letter to Mr. Gillot telling him that I didn't know why the project was rejected, that Roget has a right to its own reasons, but that I was prepared to resign as a director. It is not that I am angry, or that I have a right to dictate decisions for the whole worldwide Roget organization. It is simply that if I spend my time studying policy decisions, which are not appreciated by parent company management, then it is a waste of my time to continue.

Finally, Ekstrom stated:

> While I certainly wouldn't bring these matters out in a public meeting, I think those Belgian production and sales people simply want to build their empire and make

the money in Belgium. They don't care about Thorsten and Sweden. We have the ideas and initiative, and they take them and get the payoff.

Further Study

Mr. Gillot received Norgren's letter in late May 1981. He then contacted Messrs. Lavanchy, Gachoud, and Bols (V.P. finance, Roget) and told them that the Swedish XL-4 project had become a matter of key importance for the whole Roget Group, because of its implications for company profits, and for the morale and autonomy of subsidiary management. He asked them to study the matter very carefully and report their recommendations in one month. Meanwhile, he wrote Ekstrom, "Various members of the Corporate Headquarters are studying the proposal very seriously. You will hear from me within about six weeks regarding my final decision."

Lavanchy's Response

A month after he was asked to study the XL-4 project more closely, Lavanchy gave Gillot a memorandum explaining his reasons for opposing the proposal:

> At your request, I have reexamined thoroughly all of the cost figures that bear on the XL-4 proposal. I find that manufacture of this product in Sweden would be highly uneconomical, for two reasons: (1) overhead costs would be higher, and (2) variable costs would be greater.
>
> As to the first, we can produce XL-4 in Gent in our existing plant with less overhead cost. Suppose that Thorsten does sell 400 tons a year so that our total worldwide sales rise to 1,000 tons. We can produce the whole 1,000 tons in Belgium with essentially the same capital investment we have now. If we produce 1,000 tons, our fixed costs will decrease by Skr. 120 a ton.[3] That means Skr. 72,000 in savings on production for domestic and export to countries other than Sweden (600 tons a year), and Skr. 120,000 for worldwide production including Sweden (1,000 tons). Second we could also save on variable costs. If we were to produce the extra

---

[3]Total fixed cost in the Gent factory was the equivalent of Skr. 180,000 a year. Divided by 600, this equals Skr. 300 a ton. If it were spread over 1,000 tons, the average fixed cost would be Skr. 180.

EXHIBIT 3   XL–4: The Belgian Proposal (in Skr.)

	1	2	3	4	5	6	7	8	9	10
End of Year	Plant	Working Capital	Sales Price/ Ton	Variable Cost/ Ton[†]	Contribution/ Ton (col. 3 – 4)	Number of Tons	Total Contribution (col. 5 * 6)	Promotion Costs	Taxes	Net Cash Flows (1 + 2 + 7 – 8 – 9)
0	0	–54,000*								–54,000
1		–10,000*	2,000	1,380	620	200	124,000	130,000	(3,000)	–13,000
2		–10,000*	1,850	1,380	470	300	141,000	75,000	33,000	23,000
3			1,850	1,380	470	400	188,000	50,000	69,000	69,000
4			1,850	1,380	470	400	188,000	50,000	69,000	69,000
5			1,850	1,380	470	400	188,000	50,000	69,000	69,000
6			1,850	1,380	470	400	188,000	50,000	69,000	69,000
7		+74,000	1,850	1,380	470	400	188,000	50,000	69,000	143,000

*Working capital amounts are net of tax credits.

[†]Veriable cost per ton	= SKr.	1,380
Manufacturing	=	930
Shipping from Belgium to Sweden	=	50
Swedish import duty	=	400
Total variable cost	=	1,380

400 tons in Belgium, the total production of 1,000 tons a year would give us longer production runs, lower average setup costs, and larger raw material purchases, thus allowing mass purchasing and material handling and lower purchase prices. My accounting department has studied this and concludes that our average variable costs will decrease from Skr. 950 a ton to Skr. 930. This Skr. 20 per ton difference means a savings of Skr. 12,000 in Belgian domestic production and a saving of Skr. 20,000 for total worldwide production assuming that Sweden takes 400 tons a year. Taxes on these added profits are about the same in Belgium and Sweden—about 50 percent of taxable income. In conclusion, a new plant should not be built. Ekstrom is a bright young man, but he does not know the adhesives business. He would be caught up in costly production mistakes from the very beginning. I recommend that you inform the Thorsten management that it is in the Company's interest that they must buy from Belgium."

Bols's Response

The same week, Gillot received the following memorandum from Erik Bols, Roget's financial vice president:

I am sending you herewith estimates of the working capital requirements if Roget increases its production of XL-4 in our Belgian plant from 600 to 1,000 tons a year [Exhibit 3]. Initially, we will need Skr. 54,000, for additional inventories and accounts receivable. By the end of the second year, this will have increased to Skr. 74,000. The working capital amounts shown in this exhibit are based on the applicable law which permits businesses to deduct 60 percent of incremental inventory costs from taxable income. I have also looked at Lavanchy's calculations for the fixed and variable manufacturing costs, and am in full agreement with them. In conclusion, I see no reason to spend Skr 700,000 to build a factory in Sweden when we have excess capacity in our Belgian plant which can produce the incremental tons at lower cost and with lower manufacturing risk.

Gillot's Response

In early July 1981, Gillot sent a letter to Ekstrom indicating that the XL-4 proposal was turning out to be more of a problem than he had anticipated. He included copies of the memos from Lavanchy and Bols. He said he was not yet in a position to give final approval.

He said he would let Ekstrom know his decision as soon as possible.

Ekstrom's Thoughts

Ekstrom expressed some impatience with the way things were going:

> I have other projects that need developing for Thorsten, and this kind of long-range planning takes much time and energy. Also, just keeping on top of the normal operating problems of the business we already have takes up a lot of my time. Sometimes I feel like telling them to go and sell XL-4 themselves.

Questions

1. Using the numbers from Exhibit 2, what is your estimate of the NPV (at 8 percent) for the Swedish proposal. Also, what is the 6-year IRR?

2. What is the NPV (at 8 percent) and IRR of the Belgian proposal in Exhibit 3?

3. What are the key arguments for and against the alternatives presented by the contending parties from Belgium and Sweden?

4. Is everything that is being expressed by Ekstrom and the Belgium management above board? What are the respective hidden agendas that can be anticipated for each party, and in what way do they coincide? In what way can they be expected to diverge?

5. If you were in Gillot's shoes, would you support the Swedish or the Belgian proposal? Why?

6. Ignoring your answer to question 5, if the plant were not built and the products were shipped from Belgium to Sweden, what transfer price would be appropriate?

7. What are the competitive advantages of Roget S.A.? What is Roget's strategy in the industrial chemicals business? Are the management control systems designed to support this strategy?

8. What changes in the management control systems would you recommend to Gillot?

CASE 14–2
LINCOLN ELECTRIC COMPANY (B)

Mr. Willis took over the position of CEO in 1986 upon the death of Mr. Irrgang, who had ruled the company under its Lincoln-inspired conservatism since 1972. Don Hastings became the president. Since that time, the NIH (Not Invented Here) syndrome that Lincoln had labored under had begun to crack. As Mr. Hastings observed, "If we didn't develop it, we didn't want to make it. But today that feeling is gone."

Under the leadership of Willis and Hastings, the company broadened its geographical scope of operations. "Today we must be global, with worldwide manufacturing capabilities. We can't just produce in the US and export abroad," Mr. Hastings noted. Lincoln acquired capacity in Canada, Australia, Brazil, and Mexico, and built new plants in Venezuela and Japan. As the industry moved toward consolidation in Europe, Lincoln acquired companies in Germany, Italy, and Norway, to establish a manufacturing base to tap the potential of a unified Common Market.

In 1990 Lincoln acquired Harris Calorific, manufacturer and worldwide distributor of plasma and gas cutting and welding products with plants in the United States, Italy, and Ireland. Emerson Electric, Harris's former parent, also had a very strong corporate culture, placing a great deal of pressure on its divisions to perform and employing a low-cost strategy.

Exhibit 1 profiles Lincoln Electric's global expansion during 1986–98. Industry observers always wondered: Will Lincoln Electric be successful in exporting its unique culture and control systems to foreign locations? The results seem to be mixed. Lincoln Electric suffered financial losses in its foreign operations during 1990–1993 but the company appeared to have reversed this trend during the subsequent five years.

This case was prepared by Vijay Govindarajan.

How Lincoln Electric Successfully Transplanted Its DNA into Mexico[1]

Between 1988 and 1992, Lincoln Electric purchased three separate companies in Mexico and combined them to form Lincoln Electric Mexicana S.A. de C.V. Although all three plants were losing money at the time, their location promised Lincoln a thriving trade with customers in Central and South American countries—if it could turn them around. The Mexican workers knew about the acquisition and realized the US parent company would need to make changes to improve the business.

Lincoln set out to implement some of its basic systems, such as piece-work, merit ratings, and the bonus plan, at its Mexican subsidiary. James Delaney, an early manager of Lincoln Mexicana, introduced piece-work gradually by recruiting a few volunteers to try it out. When co-workers noticed how much more these volunteers were earning, they asked to participate too. The piece-work system was expanded in 1991 by David M. LeBlanc, then Lincoln Mexicana's operations manager. The expansion successfully tripled productivity over the next years.

LeBlanc made other changes as well. A great believer in Lincoln's principles, he was primarily responsible for incorporating the "Lincoln Way" into the Mexican subsidiary. However, LeBlanc understood that in order to succeed, Lincoln's ways had to adapt to Mexico's culture.

For example, the company's US plants were not unionized but its new Mexico City plant was. Mexico, in fact, was a highly unionized nation. Unscrupulous union organizers in that

[1] This section is based on work by Joseph A. Maciariello in *Lasting Value* (New York: John Wiley & Sons, 2000), chap. 8.

-**EXHIBIT 1   Lincoln Electric's Global Expansion**

1986   Acquired Airco with facilities in Montreal and Cleveland.

1987   Purchased L'Air Liquide with arc-welding operations in Australia.

1988   Purchased Brasoldas and Torsima, producers of welding equipment and consumables in Brazil.

1989   Built a greenfield plant for welding products in Japan.
        Constructed a plant for consumables in Venezuela.

1990   Completed purchase of the Harris Calorific business from Emerson Electric Company. Harris Calorific
        manufactured and distributed plasma and gas cutting products. Production facilities were located in Georgia,
        California, Italy, and Ireland.

1991   Purchased the German firm, Messer Griesheim GmbH, which produced arc-welding equipment in Volklingen,
        Germany.

1992   Purchased Lincoln Norweld of Oslo, Norway, with production facilities in Norway, the United Kingdom, and the
        Netherlands.
        Purchased two Mexican companies in 1988 and one more in 1992 and consolidated them into one operation.

1993   Purchased the outstanding minority interest in a Spanish company.

1996   Acquired Electronic Welding Systems, a designer and supplier of welding power supplies and plasma cutting
        equipment, based in Italy.

1998   Acquired 75% interest in Indalco Alloys, Inc., of Canada. Indalco was a premier supplier of aluminum welding
        wire.
        Purchased the German firm, Uhrhan & Schwill GmbH, a leader in the design and installation of welding systems
        for pipe mills.
        Acquired 50% equity interest in As Kaynak, a market-leading welding products manufacturing subsidiary of
        EcZacibasi Holdings, headquartered in Istanbul, Turkey.

Source: Annual Reports

country targeted nonunion companies, organizing workers in a manner that often crippled the firms' ability to function effectively.

Instead of trying to force the union out, LeBlanc chose to cultivate a positive relationship with it. He established an open-door policy and tried to get to know all of the plant's 420 employees. He worked to improve communications between these employees and union leaders. He negotiated an agreement with union leaders that exempted employees whose work did not involve piece-work, such as forktruck drivers and maintenance workers, from the union. This included 25–35 percent of Lincoln Mexicana's work force.

LeBlanc's efforts paid off. Union leadership converted to the Lincoln system and embraced the piece-work system, in part because they realized well-paid union workers were able to pay higher union dues.

In fact, Lincoln Mexicana's employees were very well paid. Lincoln typically paid its workers more than they would receive if they organized into a collective bargaining unit. Even though the Mexico City employees were represented by a union, Lincoln continued to apply this principle. Production workers earned between $5,000 and $7,000 a year—two to three times more than the going rate outside the firm. This practice enabled the company to be very selective in its hiring practices. And, although Lincoln could not promise to keep its workers fully employed in the wildly fluctuating South American markets, it did try to keep employees working whenever possible.

Employees who performed poorly were dismissed. Those who performed well were rewarded through the bonus system. In Mexico all companies were required to distribute 10 percent of pretax income to employees as bonuses. Lincoln Mexicana, in addition, distributed a second bonus to its workers, based on the company's merit rating system. This system had four ranking criteria: group goal achievement; self-improvement/initiative; discipline/quality; and teamwork/responsibility/leadership. These and the use of a more formal goal-setting process, which assigned goals to work groups as well as individuals, distinguished it from Cleveland's merit rating system. A comparison of the two systems appears below:

Lincoln Mexicana Merit Criteria	Original Lincoln Criteria
Group Goal Achievement	Output
Self Improvement/Initiative	Dependability
Discipline/Quality	Quality
Teamwork/Responsibility/ Leadership	Ideas and Cooperation

Although Lincoln Mexicana's system was more formal and more dependent on group performance than its Cleveland counterpart, its bonus fraction—the size of the bonus pool divided by the total wages of workers receiving the bonus—rose steadily. By 1998, the bonus fraction had increased to 60 percent from a base of zero. By contrast, Cleveland's bonus fraction was only 56 percent in 1998. The following chart illustrates the rise of Lincoln Mexicana's bonus fraction:

Year	Bonus Fraction
1994	0%
1995	19
1996	38
1997	55
1998	60

Lincoln Mexicana paid the government-mandated bonus in May and the merit bonus on December 12—the day on which Mexico honored its patron saint, the Virgin of Guadeloupe. Thus, the merit bonus was paid as a celebration bonus. Employees were not the only ones with cause to celebrate. The bonuses provided evidence of the growing productivity and increasing profitability of the Mexican subsidiary.

Difficulties in Implementing the Lincoln System in Some Foreign Operations[2]

Lincoln's efforts to transport its systems and principles were not as successful elsewhere around the world. In Germany, for instance, the company's plans hit a wall at the very beginning when it became clear that German workers were not as productive as Lincoln's US employees. As Hastings explained, "Even though German factory workers are highly skilled and, in general, solid workers, they do not work nearly as hard or as long as the people in our Cleveland factory. In Germany, the average factory workweek is 35 hours. In contrast, the average workweek in Lincoln's US plants is between 43 and 58 hours, and the company can ask people to work longer hours on short notice—a flexibility that is essential for the system to work. The lack of such flexibility was one reason why our approach would not work in Europe."[3]

Lincoln also had not adequately planned for government-mandated social welfare costs or labor laws that kept it from implementing systems that were the cornerstone of its operations. For example, German law did not permit piece rates. And it outlawed labor mobility and work force cross-training, making it difficult for Lincoln to create competitive incentive and management systems.

Brazilian law similarly crippled Lincoln's systems in that country. In Brazil bonuses paid to employees for two consecutive years become

---

[2]Ibid., chap. 1, pp. 17–19; chap. 8, pp. 116–18.
[3]Donald Hastings, "Lincoln Electric's Harsh Lessons from International Expansion," *Harvard Business Review,* May–June 1999, p. 174.

EXHIBIT 2   Financial Highlights 1990–98
(dollars in millions)

	1990	*1991*	*1992*	*1993*	*1994*	*1995*	*1996*	*1997*	*1998*
Net sales	$797	834	853	846	907	1,032	1,109	1,159	1,187
Net income	$ 11	14	(46)	(38)	48	61	74	85	94
Return on equity*	4%	6%	(20%)	(22%)	28%	24%	21%	21%	20%
Debt to equity ratio†	34%	40%	55%	62%	52%	26%	18%	17%	17%

Source: Annual Reports.

*Return on equity = $\dfrac{\text{Profit after tax}}{\text{Shareholder's equity}}$

†Debt to equity fatio = $\dfrac{\text{Long-term debt}}{\text{Long-term debt + Shareholders' equity}}$

EXHIBIT 3   Geographic Performance 1990–98
(dollars in thousands)

	1990	*1991*	*1992*	*1993*	*1994*	*1995*	*1996*	*1997*	*1998*
Sales:									
United States	$548,761	$507,518	$517,611	$572,535	$682,483	$765,287	$808,894	$865,254	$886,148
Europe	216,554	291,104	282,331	217,931	167,361	217,334	230,222	216,333	218,557
Other countries	100,439	101,146	95,286	96,079	115,254	127,878	145,975	162,800	173,365
Income before taxes:									
United States	39,946	45,742	24,860	42,570	81,091	87,044	101,236	112,565	125,693
Europe	(1,952)	(10,128)	(52,828)	(68,865)	5,843	11,350	10,264	10,014	14,935
Other countries	(4,444)	(1,346)	(7,183)	(22,903)	4,410	10,246	12,867	14,427	10,191
Identifiable assets:									
United States	283,998	289,682	294,730	389,247	350,012	404,972	416,911	489,431	542,462
Europe	209,315	284,341	246,457	172,136	161,691	188,906	183,938	163,519	186,666
Other countries	92,747	84,905	85,839	69,871	75,880	80,594	87,808	96,850	119,344

Source: Annual Reports.

part of their base wage. This undermined Lincoln's reward system. Eventually, these and other obstacles in Brazil, and in Venezuela, convinced Lincoln to restructure and divest itself of its German, Brazilian, Venezuelan, and Japanese operations.

The problem was that Lincoln tried to do too much, too fast. The company bought nine businesses and constructed two new plants within a five-year period between the late 1980s and early 1990s. In its haste, it neglected the very factor to which it attributes its success: people. It did not adequately plan for cultural differences and how they would affect its management systems, and it was stretched too thin to transfer the systems properly.

Furthermore, it paid premium prices for the properties in Europe despite the onset of a worldwide recession. It did so because multinational companies, who wanted to have a manufacturing presence in Europe before all internal European tariffs were eliminated under the European Union, had created a strong demand for these assets. After Lincoln purchased these properties, however, the recession caused massive redundancies in their production capability.

Management Changes[4]

Until 1993 Lincoln Electric's senior management primarily consisted of executives who rose through the ranks and who had little meaning-

ful international experience. To quote Hastings, "[In August 1992] I left for Europe. I had no choice, even though I lacked extensive international experience. None of the other senior managers had any either. The CFO, Ellis Smolik, who joined me on the trip, didn't even have a passport; we had to scramble to get him one at the last minute."[5]

Starting in 1993, Lincoln Electric deviated from its "promotion from within" policy and began recruiting senior executives from the outside. Executives from Goodyear, Westinghouse, and FMC, who had extensive international experience, joined the senior ranks of Lincoln Electric.

That same year, Lincoln appointed three new board members from the outside to replace three insiders. The company added another "outsider" to the board the following year. The new board members were CEOs or senior executives in General Electric, Westinghouse, American Spring Wire, and Key Bank. All had considerable global experience. See Exhibits 2 and 3 for company data for the 1990–98 period.

Question

On the basis of the experiences of Lincoln Electric, what lessons can be learned regarding exporting unique management systems into foreign operations?

---

[4]This section is based on the writings of Donald F. Hastings, chairman emeritus of Lincoln Electric Company. Donald Hastings, "Lincoln Electric's Harsh Lessons from International Expansion," *Harvard Business Review* May–June 1999, pp. 163–78.

[5]Ibid., pp. 170–71.

Case 14–3
Nestlé S.A.

In February 1980, Mr. G. Smith, a zone director in the Nestlé headquarters in Vevey was reviewing the status of the company's subsidiaries in Argentina. The political and economic situation in that country was unsettled, and these conditions impacted on the subsidiaries' performance. Mr. Smith was considering what, if any, actions he should take in view of this situation, the subsidiaries' recent performance, and their proposed budget for 1980, which had just arrived in Vevey.

The Company

Nestlé S.A. was the largest food company in the world. It was founded in 1867 in Vevey, Switzerland, and its headquarters, referred to as "Centre," was still in Vevey in 1980. It is the largest company in Switzerland, although only some 2.5 percent of its sales are made in Switzerland. In 1984, it had 138,000 employees, 292 factories located in 58 countries, and marketing organizations in almost every country in the world. In 1984, 44 percent of its employees were in Europe, 19 percent in North America, 22 percent in Latin America, 5 percent in Africa, 8 percent in Asia, and 2 percent in Australasia.

Nestlé's operating units were referred to as "markets." Each market was a profit center. Typically, a market consisted of all Nestlé activities, both production and marketing, in one country. Each profit center manager (referred to as "head of the market") reported to the managing director through a zone director whose office was in the Centre in Vevey. In 1980, there were five zone directors, each responsible for

Nestlé activities in one part of the world, and each assisted by a staff of around 20 persons.

At the Centre also were staff units for: production (called "technical"), including engineering, quality control, and purchasing; marketing, including advertising, market research, and recipes; finance and control, including treasury, internal control, audit, financial accounting, cost accounting, pensions, and planning; administration; legal; and personnel.

Argentina: Background

From 1966 through 1974, Argentina was governed by a military junta, most recently headed by General Juan Peron. Following Peron's death in 1974, there was a period of turbulence that left the economy in shambles. By early 1976, the economic growth rate was negative, the inflation rate was 650 percent, the trade balance was negative, capital was fleeing the country, and it appeared that Argentina might have to default on its international debts.

In March 1976, there was a coup, and a new military government took over. It immediately took measures to curb inflation, reduce imports, increase exports, reduce the budget deficit, and shift the economy away from state-owned entities to more private enterprise. These measures were successful in avoiding default on debt payments and they had some success in reducing the rate of inflation. However, inflation remained at a rate of 160 percent in 1977.

In 1978, the recovery drive had a sharp setback. After five successive quarters of growth, the gross domestic product decreased by 4.2 percent for the year as a whole. The decline resulted from the imposition of strict economic controls, a sharp reduction in the budget deficit, and an increase in interest rates. Inflation remained at 160 percent.

This case prepared by F. Voegtli. This condensed version was prepared by Professor Robert N. Anthony, Harvard Business School. Names of most persons are fictitious. Copyright Nestec S.A., Vevey, Switzerland.

In 1978 and 1979, the government took additional measures. Foreigners were encouraged to invest in all types of enterprises, import tariffs were reduced, and the program to shift from state-owned enterprises to private business was accelerated. The tariff reduction aimed at an average tariff of 15 percent in 1984, compared with an average of 60 percent in 1976. Restrictions of the flow of capital were eased, although there was a requirement that foreign loans had to have a maturity of at least one year, to discourage short-term capital movements for speculative purposes.

These changes in financial regulations had a rapid and significant impact. Since banks and companies could obtain one-year funds from foreign banks at a monthly cost of 5.5 percent, compared with 7.0 percent locally, they tended to switch to foreign funding. In 1979, Argentine liabilities to foreign banks grew by over 50 percent. The result was a pressure to reduce local interest rates; they became about 2 percent lower than the rates of inflation. This led to increased domestic investment and a growth of 13 percent in industrial production in the first nine months. A record harvest and an increase in the world price of export commodities (beef, wheat, and corn) also aided the economy. Nevertheless, inflation for the first three quarters of 1979 remained at an annual rate of 170 percent.

In the last quarter of 1979, there was an import boom of unprecedented proportions. Imports were up 53 percent, compared with the last quarter of 1978. Since exports increased by only 30 percent, there was a negative trade balance, which wiped out the positive impact of capital inflows. A consequence of the flood of imports was that many domestic plants were operating at low volumes.

Nestlé Argentina: Background

S.A. Nestlé de Productos Alimenticios (hereafter SANPA) opened an office in Buenos Aires in 1931 and built a large chocolate factory in a suburb of that city in the same year. In 1935, it built a milk factory and, as was its usual practice, devoted considerable resources to helping farmers improve their techniques to provide an adequate supply of milk. Between 1944 and 1959, three additional milk factories were built. In 1971, milk intake at all factories was 127 million kilograms (kg.); it reached a peak of 234 million kg. in 1976, was 196 million kg. in 1977, and 203 million kg. in 1978.

In the 1930s, regional distribution offices were established throughout the country, and the distribution network was gradually expanded thereafter. A large distribution center was established near Buenos Aires in 1968; in 1979, it handled almost half the domestic sales volume.

In 1978, Nestlé acquired Fruticon S.A., a manufacturer of canned tomato and fruit products with a staff of some 300 persons. Fruticon was operated as a separate company.

Although SANPA's sales volume grew rapidly, its profits did not keep pace. In addition to heavy start-up costs and marketing investments for new lines, such as ice cream, as well as strong competitive pressure, Nestlé suffered from the consequences of the government's economic programme.

Business was certainly not easy under the economic conditions prevailing in 1978, and SANPA's 1978 annual report stated:

> Interest rates remained at a high level, which forced us to intensify the controls over our working capital with a view to keeping the financing costs within an acceptable range. On the other hand, we had to maintain sufficient stocks of raw materials and finished products in line with the turnover (i.e., sales) growth objectives.

The Centre was satisfied that the end-1978 level of working capital was acceptable.

In June 1978, Mr. L. Gonzales, head of market, wrote to the zone director at the Centre that the government policy would eliminate much competition that had managed to maintain itself only because of the industrial protection of the last 20 years. Healthy companies would gain in strength. Under these circumstances, he said,

SANPA should "move away from the traditional policy of profitability maximization which had restrained volume growth" and during the next two years should "make up the lost ground with heavy marketing support." The Centre agreed with this strategy in a letter of September 1978.

Events of 1979

January to June.   SANPA's budget request for 1979 had been based on the new strategy and on a predicted gradual improvement in the economic situation; it forecasted a turnover increase of 150 percent, to pesos 303.7 billion. Considering the generally expected moderations of inflation in 1979, the budget appeared to be reasonably conservative and had been accepted by the Centre.

Actual sales of SANPA during the first six months of 1979 followed no regular patterns. Sales varied between 67 percent and 113 percent of the respective monthly budgets for the first five months and were approximately on budget in June.

SANPA sent a revised budget to the Centre in early April, showing considerably increased turnover forecasts; 1979 sales were now budgeted at pesos 410.8 billion, some 35 percent above the original budget and 239 percent above actual 1978 sales. This revision did not provoke any unusual reaction at the Centre.

SANPA's debt collection performance in the first half of the year was, similar to the one of sales, not always in line with expectations; but the monthly report of June was optimistic: "The debtors situation will improve in subsequent months; thanks to the planned reorganization of the sales force and a series of measures we shall try to reach the standard of 40 days."

July to September.   Inflation continued unabated in July (7.2 percent for the month) and August (11.5 percent), before coming down in September (6.8 percent), a month coinciding with the introductions of governmental wage increase limits.

Actual SANPA sales for this quarter fell short of revised budget figures by pesos 35.3 billion, or some 32 percent. For July, invoicing problems during the first 10 days of the month were cited as the main responsible factor. These were said to be due to changes in the marketing setup.

September saw another very poor performance of SANPA. Sales revenues for most product groups fell considerably behind budget. SANPA commented on the September sales results as follows:

> . . . continuous price increases of the products forming the household shopping basket and the rate of adjustments for services (electricity, etc.) had led to a marked reduction of consumer demand. The trade is faced with a slow stock rotation, high financing costs, as well as debt collection pressure by suppliers, which do not represent incentives to quickly replace stock sold; the trade works at minimum stock levels and tries to purchase only during special offers.

October.   On October 2, Mr. Smith, the zone director, sent a letter to Luis Gonzalez, the head of the Argentine market, reminding him "once more of the importance of maintaining working capital and especially the trade debtors at reasonable levels in view of the high financing costs and the increasing difficulties encountered in obtaining sufficient credit." The letter concluded: ". . . it would be a pity to jeopardize the achievements made with respect to product profitability by offering too generous selling conditions to the trade."

In October, SANPA reported record sales of close to pesos 70 billion, which was some 45 percent above the revised budget and nearly as much as total sales in the preceding three months. Some promotions, offering discounts of up to 20 percent, helped to smooth the impact of selling price increases. These increases ranged from 10 percent to 24 percent and were made to recover increases in production and operating costs. Collections reached only 61 percent of the forecasted amount, leaving SANPA debtors at 78 days and "causing our financial

EXHIBIT 1   **SANPA Excess Working Capital**

Month 1979	Month-End Stock Value Finished Goods (1)	Value of Stocks above Standard (3 months) (2)	Month-End Debtors Value (3)	Value of Debtors above Standard (40 days) (4)	Resulting Excess Working Capital (5) = (2) + (4)
January	24,678	4,577	24,440	12,665	17,242
February	28,339	5,931	23,960	9,971	15,902
March	30,660	5,326	32,775	7,779	13,105
April	32,786	3,498	34,707	13,002	16,500
May	32,753	354	37,734	12,850	13,204
June	31,270	—	45,240	14,333	14,333
July	29,769	—	59,953	28,471	28,471
August	33,372	1,096	58,986	21,281	22,377
September	39,201	177	62,334	29,447	29,624
October	32,829	1,145	107,303	16,811*	17,956
November	31,715	213	135,574	57,279	57,492
December	41,538	12,343	151,720	68,773	81,116

*Incorrect reporting: actual figures should have been some 11,000 higher.

position to continuously deteriorate, a situation which is not expected to change during the remainder of the year."

The technical section of the monthly report stated that the production programmes were exceeded by 20 percent for milk powders and by 11 percent for chocolates. Chocolate stocks still stood at four months, and the value of the total excess stock was indicated as pesos 1.1 billion (see Exhibit 1).

The end-September budget revision for SANPA contained the following forecasts of the 1979 results: total turnover pesos 368.86 billion, net operating loss pesos 6.00 billion, net loss pesos 3.00 billion. Debtors were expected to drop to 50 days by year end.

The revision reflected optimism for the whole of 1979, despite the dismal actual performance in the first nine months of the year. Given the high rate of inflation, the fact that the fourth quarter had often been buoyant in the past, and the possibility of cutting certain expenses, especially in the marketing area, the Centre did not

question this optimism. According to a letter from Mr. Gonzalez, the new estimate had been made with the knowledge of the actual results for the first eight months of 1979; a net operating loss of pesos 17 billion, equivalent to 10.3 percent of turnover for SANPA. He went on to say: "Higher prices will not only boost turnover but also help the net operating profit to reach its budgeted level." The letter of Mr. Gonzalez concluded: "You can be assured that we shall do the impossible to reach our budgeted sales for 1979." (Mr. Smith had urged this in a letter dated October 2.)

November. On November 28, the zone director wrote to Mr. Gonzalez, reminding him of the contents of the letter sent on October 2 and mentioning that "with a certain preoccupation I have taken note of the deterioration that has occurred in your trade debtors position. . . . While acknowledging the existence of considerable economical difficulties, with high inflation and a slow recovery pace, I insist once more on the crucial importance of paying special attention to this problem."

The monthly report for November, received at the Centre on December 21, again contained predominantly good news: Inflation was down to a monthly rate of 5.1 percent, the government published inflation estimates of 45 percent to 48 percent for 1980, interest rates had come down as a result of a more liquid financial market, and SANPA sales were pesos 66 billion, "exceeding the objectives of the month." Successful promotional activities, particularly in instant drinks and chocolates (20 percent discount for certain items), were given credit for the excellent performance, despite selling price increases of 11 percent to 16 percent for most products (none for chocolates). Ice cream sales were reportedly once more the victim of bad weather, remaining below budget and 10 percent below the November 1978 volume. "With view to making up for turnover shortfall due to lost volume," the Frigor Division modified its pricing policy, which had not planned for any adjustments before year end, and increased its selling prices by an average of 14.1 percent on November 26.

On the financial side, poor-debtors collection further increased SANPA's bank indebtedness, but it was hoped that this situation would improve by February 1980. There were no special comments concerning production.

December.   Ernst Keller, zone controller, paid a visit to the Argentine market from December 4 to 7. He summarized his impressions in a note to the vice president controlling, the finance director, and the zone director on December 20, as follows:

> Inflation estimated at 140 percent for 1979 and 70 percent for 1980; peso devaluation will be 60/70 percent in 1979 and 30 percent in 1980 according to optimistic forecasts. During my visit to our major distribution centre on December 5, I came across an anomaly in the delivery of ordered goods; there was a delivery on that day of an order invoiced on November 11. The manager of the distribution center admitted he had several such unde-

livered invoices; the goods had not been shipped because they were physically not available.

Ernst Keller went on to say that the invoices were for big customers, that the goods had been sold at the promotional discounts, and that exceptionally favorable payment terms of 90 days had been granted. If these goods could not be delivered by year end, Mr. Keller concluded, a reinvoicing would become necessary in January, at November 1979 prices and conditions. He also found that considerable quantities of goods were being stored on behalf of customers, even though they had already been recorded as sales.

The zone director immediately called the market head when he learned of this situation, asking him to take the necessary corrective actions at once.

On January 24, 1980, the monthly report of December reached the Centre. It stated that the government had reiterated its intention to stick to the planned devaluation scheme in 1980. It further stated that "positive real interest rates of up to 2 percent per month occurred in December despite a further reduction in nominal rates. In the capital goods sector, the softening of demand observed in November has continued, and there was a general increase in bankruptcies in the country."

Sales for December were disappointing. SANPA explained this by the "heavy sales of the preceding two months, which had not only reduced the demand due to oversaturation but also led to out-of-stock situations for several product lines." Unavailability of stocks was cited for important products, such as the instant drinks Nescafé and Nesquik. Selling prices had been increased for most products, ranging from 5 percent to 21 percent.

In the financial area, SANPA reported low debtors collections and an increase by US$5.5 million in its foreign currency loans.

Actual Results for 1979

The overall results for the whole year, reaching the Centre in early February 1980, showed a

EXHIBIT 2   SANPA Year-End Balance Sheets (in pesos millions)

	1977		1978		1979 Original Budget		1979 September Revision		1979 Actual		1980 Original Budget	
Assets												
Fixed assets	14,992	38.2	36,165	36.3	87,644	45.9	97,998	35.0	87,239	25.1	193,417	34.0
Raw and packaged materials	6,480	16.5	12,156	12.2	23,423	12.3	36,360	13.0	29,579	8.5	65,131	11.5
Finished products	4,553	11.6	10,761	10.8			35,477	12.7	31,120	9.0	85,155	15.0
Debtors	9,458	24.1	34,115	34.3	79,931	41.8	98,565	35.3	181,875	52.3	199,175	35.0
Sundry	3,741	9.6	6,357	6.4			11,117	4.0	17,771	5.1	25,718	4.5
Total	39,224	100%	99,554	100%	190,998	100%	279,517	100%	347,584	100%	568,596	100%
Liabilities												
Equity	13,038	33.2	37,339	37.5	80,483	42.2	100,287	35.9	91,243	26.3	202,237	36.5
Trade creditors	2,277	5.8	5,494	5.5	44,198	23.1	75,091	26.9	14,709	4.2	110,000	19.3
Accounts payable	15,026	38.3	22,042	22.2					65,497	18.8		
Bank credits	8,883	22.7	34,679	34.8	66,317	34.7	104,139	37.2	176,135	50.7	256,359	45.1
Total	39,224	100%	99,554	100%	190,998	100%	279,517	100%	374,584	100%	568,596	100%

combined net profit of around pesos 1 billion. SANPA net profit was pesos 4.15 billion on sales of pesos 363.00 billion. However, the net profit was primarily due to exceptional items of pesos 3.90 billion (mainly revaluation of fixed assets); the net operating profit (NOP) was only pesos 0.29 billion, or less than 0.1 percent of turnover. Of the nonproduct-related fixed expenses of pesos 101.2 billion incurred by SANPA in 1979, interest was the major cost item, reaching pesos 52.8 billion, or 14.5 percent of turnover, which was considerably more than in previous years.

Balance sheet data are given in Exhibit 2 and monthly sales in Exhibit 3.

Budget 1980

On January 10, 1980, the Argentine market sent a telex to the Centre, indicating the key figures of the budgets of SANPA and Fruticon S.A. for the year 1980 (figures in pesos billions):

	SANPA	*Fruticon*
Sales	880.35	38.78
Net operating profit/(loss)	32.32	(6.45)
Net profit/(loss)	36.57	(6.95)

On February 4, the hardcopy of the budget was received at the Centre, confirming the telexed key data. Under the economic heading, the report made reference to the government's free market policy and stated: "The increasing flow of imports, as a consequence of an overvalued peso, will probably lead to a negative trade balance, a fall in the gross domestic product (GDP), and to increasing difficulties for companies not able to obtain foreign financing, as well as for those confronted with improved competitive products." SANPA expected for 1980 an inflation of 69.4 percent p.a. (with monthly rates ranging from 7 percent in January to 3 percent in December), average local interest rates of

EXHIBIT 3   Sales SANPA 1979 (in pesos millions)

Month	Original Budget	Budget 1st Revision (March)	Actual Sales	Deviation from 1st Revision
1979:				
January	11,909	11,909	8,004	(3,905)
February	15,728	15,728	13,231	(2,497)
March	21,342	21,342	24,026	2,684
April	22,577	21,942	17,602	(4,340)
May	23,664	26,531	23,452	(3,079)
June	26,278	25,301	26,678	1,377
July	28,904	32,623	20,797	(11,826)
August	29,536	35,467	30,761	(4,706)
September	31,372	42,514	23,711	(18,803)
October	30,805	48,227	69,794	21,567
November	30,669	65,747	66,031	284
December	30,953	63,438	36,396*	(27,042)
Total 1979	303,737	410,769	360,483	(50,286)

*Result of canceled sales due to negative stock figures.

75 percent (reaching 50 percent by year end), and a devaluation of the peso of 31.6 percent. The optimism with respect to inflation was based on the government's budget with predicted deficit reduction to 2 percent of GDP and a limitation of public investments to 8 percent of GDP.

SANPA's objectives were to consolidate the market positions achieved in 1979 through constant and aggressive marketing activity and to increase selling prices in line with cost increases. A softening demand was expected for dietetic products and chocolates ("falling consumer purchasing power, strong competitive activity, and heavy pressure from cheap imports").

Regarding sales volumes, SANPA expected the following tonnage increases over 1979: milk products, 4 percent; dietetics, 15 percent; instant drinks, 7 percent; chocolates, 13 percent; catering products, 33 percent; culinary, 22 percent; Frigor ice cream, 4 percent; total SANPA, 7.6 percent.

SANPA planned to add 452 new persons to its payroll in 1980, bringing the total personnel at the end of 1980 to 4,556; the largest increases by function were for production (309 persons, or 12 percent), sales (63 persons, or 11 percent), and general management/administration at head office (53 persons, or 11 percent). Data on SANPA staffing are given in Exhibit 4.

Events of Early 1980

After receiving the (delayed) debtors and stocks report for December 1979, the zone controller wrote, for the signature of the zone director, a letter to Mr. Gonzalez on February 12, reminding him of the letters sent on October 2 and November 28, 1979, on the same subject and telling him that "the debtors situation has reached alarming proportions considering the 85 days outstanding at year end and the low collections in January." The zone director asked for immediate explanations and comments on corrective actions taken.

EXHIBIT 4   Selected Operating Data

	1976	1977	1978	1979
Sales (pesos millions)	15,160	45,523	121,237	363,001
Net operating profit (percent of sales)	19.3%	9.9%	5.9%	0.1%
Interest (pesos millions)	825	4,762	13,250	52,786
Employees:				
Head office	427	469	462	489
Marketing	514	646	616	695
Production	2,369	2,525	2,573	2,655
Total employees	3,310	3,640	3,650	3,839

On February 18, 1980, the monthly report for January arrived at the Centre. It stated that the inflation increase was 7.2 percent for the month of January; interest rates, however, continued to slide, reflecting a liquid situation of the local financial market. Demand for consumer goods had slowed further.

Sales were pesos 10.77 billion. SANPA debtors collections were only 60 percent of forecasts, which was said to be "due to holiday season," an explanation also used with respect to the poor sales, together with "the effects of our heavy efforts made in the last months of 1979 to achieve the budgeted volumes." Only dietetic products and chocolates exceeded budgeted sales, despite a selling price increase of 10 percent for the latter. The low debtors collections had an adverse impact on the financial situation.

In the production area, most programmes reportedly had been carried out at 87 percent to 110 percent of the planned tonnages, except for items with supply or technical problems.

The debtors and stocks report for end-January showed the following data: total accounts receivable, pesos 135.89 billion (104 days) representing an excess working capital of pesos 111.07 billion; total finished products stock, pesos 67.04 billion, with milk powders 1.5 months above the standard cover of 4.0 months ("due to advanced production"), resulting in an excess stock value of pesos 20.09 billion.

Upon receipt of this monthly report, the assistant to the zone manager immediately telephoned Mr. Gonzalez asking for clarification concerning the low level of January sales and the debtors situation. Mr. Gonzalez explained that the disappointing sales and collections were due rather to seasonal (holidays) and temporary factors than to fundamental changes in the business outlook. A letter was sent to Mr. Gonzalez on February 20, confirming the telephone conversation.

Questions

1. In a country with high inflation and unstable government actions, what should be Nestlé's policies? Consider such aspects as selling prices, accounts receivable terms, accounts payable, inventory levels, and billing in advance of shipment.

2. How can the Centre learn whether these policies have been adhered to?

3. What should Mr. Smith, the zone director, do on the basis of the information available as of the middle of February 1980?

CASE 14–4
XEROX CORPORATION (B)

"There is no real process difference between our international and domestic transfer pricing systems. The breadth of the issues, however, is far greater for the international. Transfer pricing and currency translation are not a problem for us. I manage the process and resolve potential conflicts very quickly as we operate under clear and simple guidelines."

Raghunandan "Sach" Sachdev, corporate controller

Sach was explaining the process by which Xerox takes the sting and frustration out of two very volatile topics for many global corporations—multinational transfer pricing and currency trading. He further illustrated the specifics of the system.

Transfer Pricing

As Sach described the transfer pricing policy, purely domestic transfers utilized a full standard cost price method while foreign transfers used an arm's-length market price method. This was the general rule, but the system was quite flexible, which enabled a quick response to changing market conditions. The document processing industry was extremely competitive, and Xerox management realized that they must respond to various global market pressures and competitive challenges. A manager from the Xerox Brazilian operation asserted the following: "The transfer pricing system is designed to attack the market place. We drive the products in the market place, and Xerox knows the source of the revenue is the customer."

The domestic transfer pricing was less complicated than the international situation. The controller for the US customer operations explained.

Prepared by Lawrence P. Carr, Associate Professor, Babson College. Copyright by Lawrence P. Carr.

We purchase copiers from one of the Webster, New York, factories, part of the Office Documents Products division. Normally, the transfer is made on a full standard cost basis, which includes a small percentage for administration. If we need to respond to a competitive pricing threat, we are unable to renegotiate. The manufacturing unit cannot sell below cost as they are structured to, at a minimum, cover their costs. In this case, the respective unit controllers would discuss possibilities of cost savings and the volume implications if pricing erodes unit sales. The corporate controller would step in, as appropriate, to help facilitate a solution. The aggressive business targets and the fierce competition made for some very heated and hard meetings. We were both under the same legal entity with the effects of transfer pricing balanced at consolidation. The primary concern was the influence of transfer pricing on achieving unit performance targets.

In the past, this (transfer pricing) would have been a big problem. We were totally focused on our individual business units given the tight unit performance targets. Today, we know the value of market share and the need to respond to competition. We learned that the performance comes from sales to external customers. Besides with TQL [total quality leadership] the factory has become very sensitive to their costs.

Transfer pricing between foreign units was a little more complicated due to a greater breadth of issues. There were different legal entities, two different sets of regulatory authorities (for tax, duty, etc.), and two different currencies. In this situation Xerox used a market-based transfer price (market price less a discount). This method conformed to the US tax laws and to the rules of most of the other taxing authorities. In addition, market price followed the OECD guidelines. The transfer price denomination (currency) varied based on the product value added (explained in the next section). The market-based transfer price provided a margin to the selling unit as well as sufficient margin to the buying unit. This enabled the buying unit to be competitive in their local market.

The buying unit was responsible for duty and regulatory compliance. The geographic sales offices cooperated with the factories and kept them well apprised of their country regulations and routinely communicated changing requirements to the factories. They also ensured that production facilities were aware of the competitive pressures. Xerox sales units constantly encouraged quality and price improvements (part of the TQL program).

The new Xerox culture enhanced the awareness of the customer. The selling unit knew that they must respond to their internal customer (the buying unit). At the same time, they understood that the source of successful business was the satisfaction of the outside customer.

The financial impact of transfer pricing on performance plans concerned managers from both the buying and selling units. External factors such as a change in duty rates or country regulations (i.e., quotas, etc.) may have an adverse effect on performance. The pressure eased somewhat with the recent incorporation of more operating statistics to evaluate unit and manager performance. Sach points out:

> We know what is going on and do not just manage by the financial numbers. Our regular controller conversations permit an open discussion of potential problems and offer a vehicle to explore alternative solutions. This is where the financial manager can help the line manager understand the full range of the business implications of their decisions. We also avoid surprises at corporate.

The arm's-length market price preserved the independence of the legal entity, but, at the same time, required managers to more closely consider the economic variables. A unit manager from South America said the following:

> The financial measures are fair. Sometimes, however, there are events beyond our control, like a devaluation or unanticipated local inflation or an uncertain regulatory environment, which can alter our performance. I feel it is unfair that management sometimes does not take this into account. We need financial measures which have a longer time horizon [greater than one year].

As with the domestic transfer pricing, multinational transfer prices were negotiated if there were changes in the current competitive situation or changes in the economic variables such as currency, tax, duty, and country regulations. In this case, they employed a market-based transfer price as a reference point for negotiation. The corporate controller resolved conflicts or impasses between entities.

Currency exposure can create major swings in the economics of transfer pricing and was critical in the consolidation of foreign operations. Sach explains the Xerox policy as follows:

> All units are responsible for their transaction currency exposure. There are no exceptions. The managers must manage. For product sourced through our manufacturing units the rule is simple. If manufacturing adds more than one-third of the product value, then the manufacturing unit is responsible for managing the currency hedging. Note that the transfer price uses the buyer's currency to calculate the price. If the manufacturing units add less than one-third of the product value, then the buying unit is responsible for the currency hedging. Note that the transfer price uses the seller's currency to calculate the price. In this case, the value passes through the marketing organization for recovery. In essence, we determine the denomination of the transfer price by the value added to the product based on the cost and the final selling price.

Xerox management used both local and US currencies for foreign unit performance measures. The foreign manager, however, realized that the consolidation currency was US dollars, and dollar reporting was the basis of the corporate plan. Foreign unit managers made their commitment in US dollars, and corporate managers expected them to meet that commitment. The pressure to manage local currency changes was clearly on the foreign manager.

Sach explains the translation exposure currency policy as follows:

> Normal changes in the foreign currency, from 3 to 5 percent, are the responsibility of the foreign unit management to cover. We consolidate and report the company's results in dollars, and we expect the managers to deliver

Exhibit 1

Venray plant reporting organization

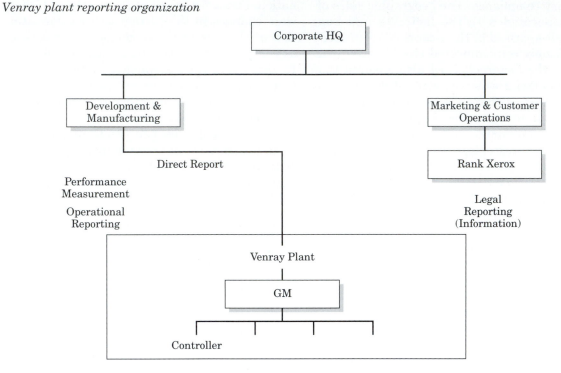

their plan. It is up to the local managers to oversee their translation currency exposure. If the currency swings vis-à-vis the dollar is greater than 3 to 5 percent, then the translation exposure becomes a corporate issue. We will peg off the standard (PDR) and coordinate and share the managing of the exposure with the foreign operation. We regularly discuss the currency topic during our weekly informal controller talks.

Sach indicated that if the currency goes in a favorable direction for the foreign operation, then corporate discounts the boosted financial results for unit performance measurement purposes. In this instance, corporate management may authorize the foreign operation to invest the currency-driven portion of their profits back into their unit, depending on the attractiveness of the proposals.

Sach said, "We regularly discuss the currency and transfer pricing topic at the FEC and on the telephone between controllers. We trust each other and are comfortable discussing the topics. This is how we prevent year-end surprises."

A subunit manager said the following:

In the Americas Customer Operations [Central and South America], the US dollar is our functional currency.[1] We make all our trades in dollars and our accounting based performance measures are in dollars. We work off a PDR (plan development rate), which is our reference point for all translations. We update the transfer prices on a quarterly basis.

---

[1]The local currency is the functional currency for all other parts of the world.

An example of the complexity of the transfer pricing, currency translation, and performance measurement system is the following.

The Venray, Netherlands, facility regularly sold or transferred copiers to the US marketing unit. The Venray plant was legally part of Rank Xerox, but for performance purposes the general manager reported to Manufacturing Support (MS), a central corporate function. Corporate management explained the following:

> The Venray site director currently reports to MS through the Rank Xerox Manufacturing Operations organization. We are currently working on recommendations on how to align and transition focus factories to report to the business teams/business divisions. The Venray product array does, however, support more than one business division. There will be areas that are not included in the focus factories and that will remain reporting to MS.

Note that within the Venray site (Exhibit 1) there were functions that reported to the Venray site director as well as to organizations outside Manufacturing Support.

Performance measures were driven by the Manufacturing Support organization with Supplies and the Materials and Supply functions being driven by the respective organizations managing them as indicated on the organization chart. This responsibility will transition to the divisions in line with the reporting structure referenced above with ongoing support from MS, Supplies, Integrated Supply Chain, and Customer Operations organization. In essence, central support organizations provided services for the business divisions and sustained the performance measures as appropriate.

Questions

1. You are the Western regional sales controller, and the sales manager has asked for your help. A major California bank with over 200 branches has chosen to cancel the Xerox copier contract (annual lease revenue of over $1 million per year) due to pricing. The competition with a West Coast assembly plant has made an offer 27 percent less than yours. You can make up 5–7 percent of the difference without materially affecting your budget. If the customer is to be preserved, you need pricing help from the factory. You call the US Customer Operations controller because the loss of sales revenue will significantly affect your budget. What are the options for Xerox, and how will Sach resolve the issue?

2. The Venray plant transfers copiers to the US Customer Operations for a FOB EC port price. If the US customer price is 100 percent and the Venray transfer price is 60 percent, answer the following:
   a. What currency is used to value the trade?
   b. Who is responsible for hedging?
   c. As the Venray controller, what is your currency exposure?
   d. How does this influence your performance measures?
   e. Does this system seem fair to you? What, if anything, would you change?

15

MANAGEMENT
CONTROL
OF PROJECTS

In earlier chapters we focused on management control in an organization that tends to carry on similar activities, day after day. Chapter 15 describes the somewhat different process that is used in the management control of projects. After a discussion of the nature of projects and how the management control process for projects differs from the control of ongoing operations, the main sections deal with (*a*) the environment in which project control takes place, and (*b*) the steps in the project control process—namely, project planning, project execution, and project evaluation.

Nature of Projects

A project is a set of activities intended to accomplish a specified end result of sufficient importance to be of interest to management. Projects include construction projects, the production of a sizable unique product (such as a turbine), rearranging a plant, developing and marketing a new product, consulting engagements, audits, acquisitions and divestitures, litigation, financial restructuring, research and development work, development and installation of information systems, and many others.

A project begins when management has approved the general nature of what is to be done and has authorized the approximate amount of resources that are to be spent in doing this work (or, in some cases, the amount to be spent in the first phase of the work). The project ends when its objective has been accomplished, or when it has been canceled. The construction of a building and the renovation of a building are projects; the routine maintenance of a building is not. The production of a television "special" is a project; the production of a nightly television news broadcast is an ongoing operation.

The completion of a project may lead to an ongoing operation, as in the case of a successful development project. The transition from the project organization to the operating organization involves complex management control issues, but these are not discussed here.[1]

Projects vary greatly. At one extreme, a project may involve one or a few persons working for a few days or weeks, performing work similar to that done many times previously—for example, an annual financial audit that is conducted by a public accounting firm. At the other extreme, a project may involve thousands of people working for several years, performing work unlike that ever done before, as was the case with the project to land the first men on the moon. The discussion here will not describe either of these extremes. Rather, it focuses on projects that have a formal control organization and that consume enough resources so that a formal management control system is necessary. Extremely complex first-of-a-kind projects have more complicated control problems than those described here, although the general nature of these problems and of the appropriate management control system are similar.

Contrast with Ongoing Operations

This section describes characteristics of projects that make the management control of projects different from the management control of ongoing activities.

Single Objective.   A project usually has a single objective; ongoing operations have multiple objectives. In addition to supervising day-to-day work, the manager of a responsibility center in an ongoing organization must both supervise today's work and also make decisions that affect future operations. Equipment that affects future operations is ordered; marketing campaigns are planned; new procedures are developed and implemented; and employees are trained for new positions. Although the project manager also makes decisions that affect the future, the time horizon is the end of the project. Project performance can be judged in terms of the desired end product; operating performance should be judged in terms of all the results that the manager achieves, some of which will not be known until a year or more later.

Organization Structure.   In many cases, the project organization is superimposed on an ongoing operating organization, and its management control system is superimposed on the management control system of that organization. These problems do not exist in an ongoing organization. Satisfactory relationships must be established between the project organization and the ongoing operating organization. Similarly, the management control system for

---

[1]For a discussion of this problem, see Paul R. Lawrence and Jay W. Lorsch, *Organization and Environment* (Burr Rdge, IL: Richard D. Irwin, 1969).

the project must mesh at certain points with the control system of the ongoing organization.

Focus on the Project.   Project control focuses on the project, whose objective is to produce a satisfactory product, within a specified time period, and at an optimum cost. In contrast, control in ongoing organizations focuses on the activities of a specified time period, such as a month, and on all the products worked on in that period. The primary focus of the management control of operating activities tends to be on cost, with quality and schedule being treated on an exception basis—that is, the formal system emphasizes cost performance, but special reports are prepared if quality and schedule are judged to be less than satisfactory.

Need for Trade-Offs.   Projects usually involve trade-offs between scope, schedule, and cost. Costs can be reduced by decreasing the scope of the project. The schedule can be shortened by incurring overtime costs. Similar trade-offs occur in ongoing organizations, but they are not typical of the day-to-day activities in such organizations.

Less-Reliable Standards.   Performance standards tend to be less reliable for projects than for ongoing organizations. Although the specifications of one project and the method of producing it may be similar to those for other projects, the project design literally is used only once.

Nevertheless, standards for repetitive project activities can be developed from past experience or from engineering analyses of the optimum time and costs. To the extent that the activities on a given project are similar to those on other projects, the experience on these projects can be used as a basis for estimating time and costs. If the project is the construction of a house, good historical information exists on the unit costs of building similar houses. (However, changes in materials, in the technology of house building, or in building codes may make this information unreliable as a guide to the cost of building the next house, and site-specific problems may also affect the actual cost of a given house.) Many projects are sufficiently different from prior projects, so that historical information is not of much help, and allowances must be made for their unique characteristics. The cost estimate for constructing a house usually contains a contingency allowance, whereas such an allowance is not customary in calculating the standard cost of producing a product in the factory.

Frequent Changes in Plans.   Plans for projects tend to be changed frequently and drastically. Unforeseen environmental conditions on a construction project or unexpected facts uncovered during a consulting engagement may lead to changes in plans. The results of one phase of the investigation in a research and development project may completely alter the work originally planned for subsequent phases.

Different Rhythm.   The rhythm of a project differs from that of ongoing operations. Most projects start small, build up to a peak activity, and then taper off as completion nears and only cleanup remains to be done. Ongoing activities tend to operate at the same activity level for a considerable time and then to change, in either direction, from that level to another.

Greater Environmental Influence.   Projects tend to be influenced more by the external environment than is the case with operations in a factory. The walls and roof of a factory protect production activities from the environment. Construction projects occur outdoors and are subject to climatic and other geographical conditions. If the project involves excavating, conditions beneath the earth's surface may cause unexpected problems, even for such a simple project as building a house. Consulting projects take place on the client's premises and involve "finding one's way around," both geographically and organizationally.

Resources for many projects are brought to the project site. Workers on a construction project go to the project, and a construction project has other logistical problems that do not ordinarily occur with production operations. Workers on a production line stay in one room.

Exceptions.   These distinctions are not clear-cut. A job shop, such as a printing company, produces dissimilar end products; however, the focus of management control in such an organization is on the totality of its activities during a month or other specified period, not on individual jobs. In some projects, team members are hired for the job; they are not associated with functional departments in an ongoing organization. Projects in a research laboratory are conducted on the premises rather than in outside facilities.

The Control Environment

Project Organization Structure

A project organization is a temporary organization. A team is assembled for conducting the project, and the team is disbanded when the project has been completed. Team members may be employees of the sponsoring organization, they may be hired for the purpose, or some or all of them may be engaged under a contract with an outside organization.

If the project is conducted entirely or partly by an outside contractor, the project sponsor should quickly establish satisfactory working arrangements with the contractor's personnel. These relationships are influenced by the terms of the contract, as will be discussed later. If the project is conducted by the sponsoring organization, some of the work may be assigned to support units within the organization, and similar relationships should be established with them. For example, a central drafting unit in an architectural firm may do drafting for all projects, and management control problems of such arrangements are similar to those involved in contracting with an outside drafting organization.

Matrix Organizations.   If members of the project team are employees of the sponsoring organization, they have two "bosses": the project manager and the manager of the functional department to which they are permanently assigned. Such an arrangement is called a *matrix organization.* In overhauling a ship, craftspeople (e.g., electricians, sheet metal workers, pipe fitters) are drawn from various functional departments in the shipyard, and they work on the project when their skills are needed. However, their basic loyalty is to their functional department. Whether they appear at the work site at the scheduled time depends in part on decisions made by the manager of their functional department, who considers the relative priorities of all projects requiring the resources he or she controls. The project manager, therefore, has less authority over personnel than the manager of a production department, whose employees have an undivided loyalty to that department.

Project managers want full attention given to their projects, while functional responsibility center managers must take into account all the projects on which the employees of that center work. This conflict of interest is inevitable; it creates tension. As Vancil writes, there is "an atmosphere of constructive conflict."[2]

Evolution of Organization Structure.   Different types of management personnel and management methods may be appropriate at different stages of the project. In the planning phase of a construction project, architects, engineers, schedulers, and cost analysts predominate. In the execution of the project, the managers are production managers. In the final stages, the work tapers off, and the principal task may be to obtain the sponsor's acceptance, with marketing skills being a principal requirement (especially in consulting projects).

Contractual Relationships

If the project is conducted by an outside contractor, an additional level of project control is created. In addition to the control exercised by the contractor who does the work, the sponsoring organization has its own control responsibilities. The contractor may bring its own control system to the project, and this system may need to be adapted to provide information that the sponsor needs. (This does not imply that there are duplicate systems; the sponsor's system should use data from the project system.)

The form of the contractual arrangement has an important impact on management control. Contracts are of two general types: fixed-price and cost reimbursement, with many variations within each type.

Fixed-Price Contracts.   In a fixed-price contract, the contractor agrees to complete the specified work by a specified date at a specified price. Usually,

---

[2]Richard F. Vancil, "What Kind of Management Control Do You Need?" *Harvard Business Review,* March–April 1973, p. 75.

there are penalties if the work is not completed to specifications or if the scheduled date is not met. It would appear, therefore, that the contractor assumes all the risks and consequently has all the responsibility for management control; however, this is by no means the case. If the sponsor decides to change the scope of the project, or if the contractor encounters conditions not contemplated by the contractual agreement, a *change order* is issued. The parties must agree on the scope, schedule, and cost implications of each change order. To the extent that change orders involve increased costs, these costs are borne by the sponsor. The construction of a conventional house may involve a dozen or so change orders; on some complex projects, there are thousands. In these circumstances, the final price of the work is actually not fixed in advance.

In a fixed-price contract, the sponsor is responsible for auditing the quality and quantity of the work to ensure that it is done as specified. This may be as comprehensive a task as auditing the cost of work under a cost-reimbursement contract.

Cost-Reimbursement Contracts.   In a cost-reimbursement contract, the sponsor agrees to pay reasonable costs plus a profit (often with a "not-to-exceed" upper limit). In such a contract, the sponsor has considerable responsibility for the control of costs and, therefore, needs a management control system and associated control personnel that are comparable to the system and personnel used by the contractor with a fixed-price contract. A cost-reimbursement contract is appropriate when the scope, schedule, and cost of the project cannot be estimated reliably in advance.

Contrasts in Contract Types.   The price for a fixed-price contract is bid by, or proposed by, the contractor. In arriving at this price, a competent contractor includes an allowance for contingencies, and the size of this allowance varies with the degree of uncertainty. Thus, for a project with considerable uncertainty and a correspondingly large contingency allowance, the sponsor may end up paying more under a fixed-price contract than under a cost-reimbursement contract in which there is no such contingency allowance. This extra payment is the contractor's reward for the assumption of additional risk.

Fixed-price contracts are appropriate when the scope of the project can be closely specified in advance and when uncertainties are low. In these circumstances, the contractor cannot significantly increase the price by negotiating change orders and, therefore, is motivated to control costs. If the contractor signs a contract that does not include adequate provisions for adjustments caused by changes in scope or by uncontrollable uncertainties, he will resist the sponsor's requests to make desirable changes, and, in the extreme case, he may be unwilling to complete the project. If the contractor walks away from the project, no one gains: The sponsor doesn't get the product, the contractor doesn't get paid, and both parties may incur legal fees.

In a cost-reimbursement contract, the profit component, or fee, usually should be a fixed monetary amount. If it is a percentage of costs, the contractor is motivated to make the costs high and thereby increase his profit. However, the fixed fee normally is adjusted if the scope or schedule of the project is significantly changed.

Variations.   Within these two general types of contracts are many variations. In an *incentive contract,* completion dates or cost targets, or both, are defined in advance, and the contractor is rewarded for completing the project earlier than the target date or for incurring less than the target cost. This reward is in the form of a completion bonus that is set at an amount per unit of time saved or a cost bonus that is set as a percentage of the costs saved, or both. Such a contract would appear to overcome the inherent weakness of a cost-reimbursement contract, which has no such rewards. However, if the targets are unrealistic, the incentive is ineffective. Thus, an incentive contract is a middle ground; it is appropriate when moderately reliable estimates of completion and cost can be made.

Different contract types may be used for different activities on the project. For example, direct costs may be reimbursed under a cost-reimbursement contract because of the high degree of uncertainty, while the contractor's overhead costs may be covered by a fixed-price contract, either as an amount for the total project or for each month. A fixed-price contract for overhead motivates the contractor to control these costs; avoids the necessity of checking on the reasonableness of individual salary rates, fringe benefits, bonuses, and other amenities; reduces the contractor's tendency to load the overhead payroll with less qualified personnel; and encourages the contractor to complete the work as soon as possible so supervisory personnel will be freed for other projects. However, such a contract may also motivate the contractor to skimp on supervisory personnel, on a good control system, or on other resources that help get the project completed in the most efficient manner.

If unit costs can be estimated reasonably well, but the quantity of work is uncertain, the contract may be for a fixed price per unit applied to the actual number of units provided—for example, in a catering activity, reimbursement is often a stated amount per meal served (plus, perhaps, a fixed monthly amount for overhead).

Information Structure

Work Packages.   In a project control system, information is structured by elements of the project. The smallest element is called a *work package,* and the way in which these work packages are aggregated is called the *work breakdown structure.*

A work package is a measurable increment of work, usually of fairly short duration (a month or so). It should have an unambiguous, identifiable completion point, which is called a *milestone.* Each work package should be the responsibility of a single manager.

If the project has similar work packages (e.g., a separate work package for the electrical work on each floor of an office building), each should be defined in the same way, so that cost and schedule information can be compared with similar work packages. Similarly, if an industry has developed cost or time standards for the performance of certain types of work packages (as is the case in many branches of the construction industry), or if the project organization has developed such standards on the basis of prior work, definitions used in these standards should be followed.

Indirect Cost Accounts.   In addition to work packages for direct project work, cost accounts are established for administrative and support activities. Unlike the work packages, these activities have no defined output. Their estimated costs usually are stated as per unit of time, such as a month, just as the overhead costs of ongoing responsibility centers are stated.

The chart of accounts, the rules for charging costs to projects, and the approval authorities and their specific signing powers also are developed in advance. Which cost items will be charged directly to work packages? What will be the lowest level of monetary cost aggregation? Should cost commitments be recorded, in addition to actual costs incurred? (For many types of projects, this is highly desirable.) How, if at all, will overhead costs and equipment usage be allocated to work packages?

If during the project it turns out that the work breakdown structure or the accounting system is not useful, it must be revised. This may require recasting much information, both information already collected and information describing future plans. Revising the information structure in midstream is a difficult, time-consuming, frustrating task. To avoid this work, the project planners should give considerable attention, before the project starts, to designing and installing a sound management control system.

Project Planning

In the planning phase, the project planning team takes as a starting point the rough estimates that were used as the basis for the decision to undertake the project. It refines these estimates into detailed specifications for the product, detailed schedules, and a cost budget. It also develops a management control system and underlying task control systems (or adapts these from systems used previously), and an organization chart. The boxes on this organization chart gradually are filled with the names of personnel who are to manage the work.

On a project of even moderate complexity, there is a *plan for planning,* that is, a description of each planning task, who is responsible for it, when it should be completed, and the interrelationships among tasks. The planning process is itself a subproject within the overall project. There is also a control system to ensure that the planning activities are properly carried out.

Nature of the Project Plan

The final plan consists of three related parts: scope, schedule, and cost.

The **scope** part states the specifications of each work package and the name of the person or organization unit responsible. If the project is one in which specifications are nebulous, as is the case with many consulting and research and development projects, this statement is necessarily brief and general.

The **schedule** part states the estimated time required to complete each work package and the interrelationships among work packages, that is, which work package(s) must be completed before another can be started. The set of these relationships is called a *network*. Networks are described in the next section.

Costs are stated in the project budget, usually called the *control budget*. Unless work packages are quite large, monetary costs are shown only for aggregates of several work packages. Resources to be used for individual work packages are stated as nonmonetary amounts, such as person-days or cubic yards of concrete.

Network Analysis

Several tools are available for constructing the time schedule for the project. They go by such acronyms as PERT (program evaluation and review technique) and CPM (critical path method). Each technique has three basic steps: (1) estimating the time required for each work package; (2) identifying the interdependencies among work packages (which work packages must be completed before a given work package can be started); and (3) calculating the critical path. Collectively, these are techniques for *network analysis*. A network diagram consists of (*a*) a number of *nodes* (i.e., *milestones*), each of which is a subgoal that must be completed to accomplish the project; and (*b*) lines joining these nodes to one another; these lines represent *activities*. The estimated time to carry out each activity is shown on the network diagram. An activity connecting two events, say, A and B, indicates that the activity leading to B cannot be started until event A has happened. These activities are work packages. Thus, a network diagram shows the chronological sequence in which events must be completed in order to complete the whole project.

Critical Path and Slack.   Computer programs are available for analyzing project networks. They identify the *critical path,* which is the sequence of events that has the shortest total time to complete the project. The nature of the critical path is shown in Exhibit 15–1. To complete event B, event A must first be completed; this requires two weeks. A–B requires an additional five weeks. Then B–C, requiring an additional three weeks, is done to complete the project. This is the critical path, and it is 10 weeks long. Note that to complete event B, activity X–B also must be undertaken, with an estimated time of four weeks. However, activity B–C cannot be started until both A–B and X–B have been completed. X–A and A–B require a total of seven weeks; and X–B, which requires only four weeks, can be performed at any time during this seven-week period. Activity X–B is said to have three weeks of *slack*.

Exhibit 15–1

Critical path (X–A, A–B, & B–C indicate critical path)

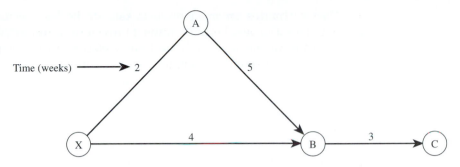

There are several management control implications in the concepts of critical path and slack. First, in the control process, special attention must be paid to those activities that are on the critical path, and less attention needs to be paid to slack activities (although time must not be allowed to slip by that eats up the amount of slack; the activity then automatically is on the critical path). Second, in the planning process, attention should be given to possibilities for reducing the time required for critical path activities; if such possibilities exist, the overall time required for the project can be reduced. Third, it may be desirable to reduce critical path times by increasing costs, such as incurring overtime; but additional money should not be spent to reduce the time of slack activities.

Probabilistic PERT.   As PERT was originally conceived, the estimated times required for each activity in the network were arrived at on a probabilistic basis. Three estimates were made for each activity; a most likely time, an optimistic time, and a pessimistic time. The optimistic and pessimistic times were supposed to represent probabilities of approximately 0.01 and 0.99 on a normal probability distribution. It was soon discovered that this approach had serious practical difficulties. Engineers, and others who were asked to make the three estimates, found this to be a most difficult task. It turned out not to be possible, in most cases, to convey what was intended by "optimistic" and "pessimistic" in a way that was interpreted similarly by all the estimators. Although probabilistic PERT is still referred to in the literature and in formal descriptions of the PERT technique, the probabilistic part is not widely used in practice.

Estimating Costs

For practical reasons, cost estimates are often made at a level of aggregation that incorporates several work packages. Resources used on individual work packages are controlled in terms of physical quantities, rather than costs, and costing out each work package would serve no useful purpose.

Cost estimates for most projects tend to be less accurate than those for manufactured goods, because projects are less standardized, and cost information that has been accumulated for similar work is therefore not as valid a basis for comparison. Nevertheless, if a contractor has performed similar work in the past, the costs incurred on these work packages provide a starting point in estimating the costs of the new project. For some work, industry norms, or rules of thumb, have been developed that are useful in estimating costs.

Obviously, no one knows what actually will happen in the future; therefore, no one knows for sure what future costs actually will be. In estimating what costs are likely to be, two types of unknowns must be taken into account. The first type is the *known unknowns*. These are estimates of the cost of activities that are known to be going to occur, such as digging the foundation for a house. The nature of the task is known; and the costs, although unknown, often can be estimated within reasonable limits on the basis of past experience. If unexpected rock or other conditions are encountered, however, these estimates may turn out to be far from the mark.

The other unknowns are the *unknown unknowns*. For these activities, the estimator does not know that they are going to occur, and obviously, therefore, has no way of estimating their cost. Work stoppages, destruction caused by storms or floods, delays in receiving materials, accidents, and failure of government inspectors to act in a timely manner are examples. A fixed-price contract usually states that costs caused by such events are added to the fixed price.

In using cost estimates in the evaluation phase, the impossibility of estimating the cost of unknown unknowns must be recognized. Their actual costs may range from zero up to any amount whatsoever. There is no definable upper limit. If the contract does not provide that all these costs are added to the fixed price, the estimator should include a contingency allowance for them.

Preparing the Control Budget

The control budget is prepared close to the inception of the work, allowing just enough time for approval by decision makers prior to the commitment of costs. For a lengthy project, the initial control budget may be prepared in detail only for the first phase of the project, with fairly rough cost estimates for later phases. Detailed budgets for later phases are prepared just prior to the beginning of work on these phases. Delaying preparation of the control budget until just prior to the start of work ensures that the control budget incorporates current information about scope and schedule, the results of cost analyses, and current data about wage rates, material prices, and other variables. It, therefore, avoids making budget estimates that are based on obsolete information; this is a waste of effort.

The control budget is an important link between planning and the control of performance. It represents both the sponsor's expectations about what the project will cost and also the project manager's commitment to carry out the project at that cost. If, as the project proceeds, it appears there will be a significant budget overrun, the project may no longer be economically justified. In these circumstances the sponsor may reexamine the scope and the schedule, and perhaps modify them.

Other Planning Activities

During the planning phase, other activities are performed: Material is ordered, permits are obtained, preliminary interviews are conducted, personnel are selected, and so on. All these activities must be controlled and integrated into the overall effort.

One set of activities involves the selection and organization of personnel. After personnel come on board, they get to know one another, they find out where they fit in the project organization, they learn what to expect and what not to expect from other parts of the organization, and they learn what is expected of them. Information learned and expectations developed during this stage are a part of the control *climate,* and they can have a profound effect on the successful completion of the project.

Project Execution

At the end of the planning process, there exists for most projects a specification of work packages, a schedule, and a budget; also, the manager who is responsible for each work package is identified. The schedule shows the estimated time for each activity, and the budget shows estimated costs of each principal part of the project. This information often is stated in a financial model. If resources to be used in detailed work packages are expressed in nonmonetary terms, such as the number of person-days required, the control budget states monetary costs only for a sizable aggregation of individual work packages. In the control process, data on actual cost, actual time, and actual accomplishment are compared with these estimates. The comparison may be made either when a designated milestone in the project is reached or at specified time intervals, such as weekly or monthly.

Basically, both the sponsor and the project manager are concerned with these questions: (1) Is the project going to be finished by the scheduled completion date? (2) Is the completed work going to meet the stated specifications? (3) Is the work going to be done within the estimated cost? If at any time during the course of the project the answer to one of these questions is "no," the sponsor and the project manager need to know why and they need to know the alternatives for corrective action.

These three questions are not considered separately from one another, for it is sometimes desirable to make trade-offs among time, specifications, and cost, using the financial model and other available information. For example, overtime might be authorized to assure completion on time, even though this would add to costs; or some of the specifications might be relaxed to reduce costs.

Nature of Reports

Managers need three somewhat different types of reports: trouble reports, progress reports, and financial reports.

Trouble reports report both on trouble that has already happened (such as a delay resulting from any of a number of possible causes) and also anticipated future trouble. Critical problems are flagged. It is essential that these reports get to the appropriate manager quickly, so corrective action can be initiated; they often are transmitted by face-to-face conversation, telephone, or facsimile. Precision is sacrificed in the interest of speed; rough numbers often are used—person-hours, rather than labor costs, or numbers of bricks, rather than material cost. If the matter reported on is significant, an oral report later is confirmed by a written document, so as to provide a record.

Progress reports compare actual schedule and costs with planned schedule and costs for the work done, and they contain similar comparisons for overhead activities not directly related to the work. Variances associated with price, schedule delays, and similar factors may be identified and measured quantitatively, using techniques for variance analysis that are similar to those used in the analysis of ongoing operations.

Financial reports are accurate reports of project costs that must be prepared as a basis for progress payments if there is a cost-reimbursement contract; and they usually are necessary as a basis for financial accounting entries for fixed-price contracts. However, these reports are less important for management control purposes than the cost information contained in progress reports. Because the financial reports must be accurate, they are carefully checked, and this process takes time. Approximate information that is available quickly is more important to project management.

Much of the information in management reports comes from detailed records collected in task control systems. These include such documents as work schedules, time sheets, inventory records, purchase orders, requisitions, and equipment records. In the design of these task control systems, their use as a source of management control information is one consideration.

Quantity of Reports.   To make certain that all needs for information are satisfied, management accountants sometimes create more than the optimum number of reports. An unnecessary report, or extraneous information in a report, incurs extra costs in assembling and transmitting the information. More important, users may spend unnecessary time reading the report, or they may overlook important information that is buried in the mass of detail. In the course of the project, therefore, a review of the set of reports often is desirable, and this may lead to the elimination of some reports and the simplification of others.

This *paperwork problem* (often referred to in the literature as *information overload*) is not necessarily serious. Competent managers learn which reports, or sections of a report, are likely to be useful to them, and they focus first on these. If, but only if, possible problems are identified from this inspection, they refer to more detailed information.

Percent Complete.   Some work packages will be only partially completed at the reporting date, and the percentage of completion of each such work package must be estimated as a basis for comparing actual time with scheduled time and actual costs with budgeted costs. If accomplishment is measured in physical terms, such as cubic yards of concrete poured, the percentage of completion for a given work package can be measured easily. If no quantitative measure is available, as in the case of many R&D and consulting projects, the percentage of completion is subjective. Some organizations compare actual labor-hours with budgeted labor-hours as a basis for estimating completion; but this assumes that the actual labor effort accomplished all that was planned, which may not have been the case. Narrative reports of progress may be of some help, but these often are difficult to interpret. If the percentage of completion is not ascertainable from quantitative data, the manager relies on personal observation, meetings, and other informal sources as a basis for judging progress.

Summarizing Progress.   In addition to determining the percentage of completion of individual work packages, a summary of progress on the whole project is useful. Progress payments often are made when specified milestones are reached. Thus, the system usually contains some method of aggregating individual work packages, which provides an overall measure of accomplishment. A simple approach is to use the ratio of actual person-hours on work packages completed to date to total person-hours for the project; but this is reliable only if the project is labor-intensive. If the system includes estimated costs for each work package, a weighting based on the planned cost of each work package may be informative.

Punch List.   Close to the end of a construction project, the sponsor prepares a list of items yet to be accomplished, including defects that need to be corrected. This punch list is negotiated with the project manager. Final payment is held up until the agreed-upon work has been done. Progress payments made during the course of the project are somewhat smaller than costs plus profits to date, thus providing a cushion for this purpose.

Use of Reports

Trouble Reports.   Managers spend much time dealing with reports of trouble. The typical project has many such reports, and one of the manager's tasks is to decide which ones have the highest priority. In the limited number of hours in a day, the manager of a large project cannot possibly deal with all the situations that have caused, or that may cause, the project to proceed less than smoothly. The manager, therefore, has to decide which problems will get his or her personal attention, which will be delegated to someone else, and which will be disregarded on the assumption that operating personnel will take the necessary corrective action.

Progress Reports.   Not only do managers try to limit the number of trouble spots to which they give personal attention, they also try to avoid spending so much time solving immediate problems that no time remains for careful analysis of the progress reports. Such an analysis may reveal potential problems that are not apparent in the reports of trouble, and the manager needs to identify these problems and plan how they are to be solved. The temptation is to spend too much time on current problems and not enough time identifying problems that are not yet apparent. Some managers deliberately set aside a block of time to reflect on what lies ahead.

The approach to analyzing progress reports is the familiar one of "management by exception." If progress in a particular area is satisfactory, no attention needs to be paid to the area (except to congratulate the persons responsible). Attention is focused on those areas in which progress is, or may become, unsatisfactory.

The analyses of reports that show actual time compared to the schedule, and actual cost compared to the budget, are relatively straightforward. In the interpretation of the time report, the usual presumption is that if a work package was completed in less than the estimated time, the responsible supervisor is to be congratulated; if more than the estimated time was spent, questions are raised. The interpretation of the cost report is somewhat different, for the possibility exists that if actual costs were less than budget, quality may have suffered. For this reason, unless there is some independent way of estimating what costs should have been, good cost performance often is interpreted to mean being on budget, neither higher nor lower.

It is important that actual costs be compared with the budgeted costs of the work done, which is not necessarily the same as the budgeted costs for the time period. The danger of misinterpretation is illustrated in Exhibit 15–2, which shows actual and budgeted costs for a project. As of the end of September, actual costs were $345,000, compared with budgeted costs of $300,000, which indicates a cost overrun of $45,000. However, the budgeted cost of the work actually completed through September was only $260,000, so the true overrun was $85,000.

Reports on indirect costs are prepared separately. These reports measure costs in a different dimension than do reports on the direct costs of project work. In the case of direct costs, actual costs are compared with budgeted costs for the work actually accomplished. In the case of indirect costs, the actual costs for a period, such as a month, are compared with the budgeted costs for that same period.

Cost to Complete.   In their progress reports, some organizations compare actual costs to date with budgeted costs for the work that has been done to

EXHIBIT 15–2

Interpretation of cost/schedule reports

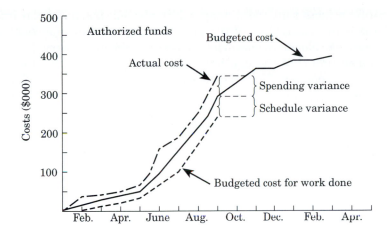

date. Others report the current estimate of total costs for the entire project, compared with the budgeted cost for the entire project. The current estimate is obtained by taking the actual cost to date and adding an estimated cost to complete—that is, the additional costs required to complete the project. The latter type of report is a useful way of showing how the project is expected to come out, provided that the estimated cost to complete is properly calculated.

In most circumstances, the current estimate of total cost should be at least equal to the actual cost incurred to date plus the *original* estimates made for the remaining work. If project managers are permitted to use lower amounts, they can hide overruns by making overly optimistic future estimates. In fact, if overruns to date are caused by factors that are likely to persist in the future, such as unanticipated inflation, the current estimates of future costs probably should be higher than the amounts estimated originally.

Informal Sources of Information

Because written reports are tangible, descriptions of management control systems tend to focus on them. In practice, these reports usually are less important than information that the project manager gathers from talking with people who actually do the work, from members of his or her staff, from regularly scheduled or ad hoc meetings, from informal memoranda, and from personal inspection of the status of the work. From these sources, the manager learns of potential problems and of circumstances that may cause actual progress to deviate from the plan. This information also helps the manager to understand the significance of the formal reports because these reports may not describe important events that affected actual performance.

In many cases, a problem may be uncovered and corrective action taken before a formal report is prepared, and the formal report does no more than confirm facts that the manager has already learned from informal sources. This is an illustration of the principle that *formal reports should contain no surprises.* Nevertheless, formal reports are necessary. They document the information that the manager has learned informally, and this documentation is important if questions about the project are raised subsequently, especially if there is a controversy about the results. Also, subordinate managers who read the formal reports may discover that these are not an accurate statement of what has happened, and they take steps to correct the misunderstanding.

Revisions

If a project is complex, or if it is lengthy, there is a good chance that the plan will not be adhered to in one or more of its three aspects: scope, schedule, or cost. A common occurrence is the discovery that there is likely to be a cost overrun—that is, actual costs will exceed budgeted costs. If this happens, the sponsor might decide to accept the overrun and proceed with the project as originally planned, decide to cut back on the scope of the project with the aim of producing an end product that is within the original cost limitation, or decide to replace the project manager if the sponsor concludes that the budget overrun was unwarranted. Whatever the decision, it usually leads to a revised plan. In some cases, the sponsor may judge that the current estimate of benefits is lower than the current cost-to-complete estimate and, therefore, decide to terminate the project. (Costs that have already been incurred are sunk and, therefore, should be disregarded in making this decision.)

If the plan is revised, the following question arises: Is it better to track future progress against the revised plan or to track against the original plan? The revised plan is presumably a better indication of the performance that is currently expected, but there is a danger that a persuasive project manager can negotiate unwarranted increases in budgeted costs or that the revised plan will incorporate, and thus hide, inefficiencies that have accumulated to date. In either case, the revised plan may be a *rubber baseline*—that is, instead of providing a firm benchmark against which performance is measured, it may be stretched to cover up inefficiencies.

This possibility can be minimized by taking a hardheaded attitude toward proposed revisions. Nevertheless, there is a tendency to overlook the fact that a revised plan, by definition, does not show what was expected when the project was initiated. On the other hand, if performance continues to be monitored by comparing it with the original plan, the comparison may not be taken seriously because the original plan is known to be obsolete.

A solution to this problem is to compare actual cost with *both* the original plan and the revised plan. The first section of such a summary report shows the original budget, the revisions that have been authorized to date, and the reasons for making them. Another section shows the current cost estimate and the factors that caused the variance between the revised budget and the current estimate of costs. Exhibit 15–3 is an example of such a report.

EXHIBIT 15–3   Project Cost Summary ($000s)

Original budget	$1,000
Authorized revisions to date:	
For inflation	50
For specification changes....................	200
For time delays............................	60
For cost savings	(30)
Revised budget............................	1,280
Current estimate to complete	1,400
Variance	120
Explanation of variance:	
Material cost increases	$ 20
Overtime..................................	60
Spending variances	40
	120

Project Auditing

In many projects, the audit of quality must take place as the work is being done. If it is delayed, defective work on individual work packages may be hidden; they are covered up by subsequent work. (For example, the quality of plumbing work on a construction project cannot be checked after walls and ceilings have been finished.) In some projects, the audit of costs also is done as the work progresses; in others, the cost audit is not made until the project has been completed. In general, auditing as the work progresses is preferable; it may uncover potential errors that can be corrected before they become serious. However, project auditors should not take an undue amount of the time of those who are responsible for doing the work.

In recent years internal auditors have expanded their function into what is called *operational auditing*. In addition to examining costs incurred, they call attention to management actions that they believe are substandard. Properly done, operational auditing can be useful. However, there is the great danger that the auditors, who, after all, are not managers, will second-guess the decisions that managers made in the light of all the circumstances—as the managers understood them—at the time that decisions were made.

Project Evaluation

The evaluation of projects has two separate aspects: (1) an evaluation of performance in executing the project, and (2) an evaluation of the results obtained from the project. The former is carried out shortly after the project has been completed; the latter may not be feasible until several years later.

Evaluation of Performance

The evaluation of performance in executing the project has two aspects: (1) an evaluation of project management, and (2) an evaluation of the process of managing the project. The purpose of the former is to assist in decisions regarding project managers, including rewards, promotions, constructive criticism, or reassignment. The purpose of the latter is to discover better ways of conducting future projects. In many cases these evaluations are informal. If the results of the project were unsatisfactory and if the project was important, a formal evaluation is worthwhile. Also, formal evaluation of a highly successful project may identify techniques that will improve performance on future projects.

Because work on a project tends to be less standardized and less susceptible to measurement than work in a factory, evaluation of a project is more subjective than evaluation of production activities. It resembles the evaluation of marketing activities, in that the effect of external factors on performance must be taken into acount. A judgment about whether actual accomplishment was satisfactory under the actual circumstances encountered is highly subjective.

Cost Overruns.   When actual costs exceed budgeted costs, there is said to be a cost overrun. To some, this implies that actual costs were too high. An equally plausible conclusion, however, is that the budgeted costs were too low. If the higher costs resulted from changes in the scope of the project or from noncontrollable factors, the explanation is that there was an underestimate of costs, rather than excessive actual costs. Interpretation of the cost reports is complicated by the need to analyze both the budget and the actual costs.

A common error in analyzing costs is to assume that the budget represents what the costs should have been. It does not. At best, the budget estimates what the cost should have been *based on the information that was available at the time it was prepared.* This information rarely is an accurate reflection of conditions that will be encountered on the project; to the extent that it is inaccurate, the budget does not reflect what the costs should be. Moreover, budget numbers are estimates made by human beings, and they are based, in part, on judgments and assumptions. Although reasonable people can differ in their judgments and assumptions, only one set of conclusions is incorporated in the budget.

Hindsight.   In looking back at how well the work on the project was managed, the natural temptation is to rely on information that was not available at the time. With hindsight, one can usually discover instances in which the "right" decision was not made. However, the decision made at the time may have been entirely reasonable. The manager may not have had all the information at that time, the manager may not have addressed a particular problem because other problems had a higher priority, or the manager may have based the decision on personality considerations, trade-offs, or other factors not recorded in written reports.

Nevertheless, some positive indications of poor management may be identified. Diversion of funds or other assets to the personal use of the project manager is one obvious example. If there were major specification changes or cost overruns, these changes should have been authorized, and cash flows should have been recalculated to determine whether the return on the project was still acceptable. Another example of poor management is a manager's failure to tighten a control system that permits others to steal, but this is more difficult to judge because overly tight controls may impede progress on the project. Evidence that the manager regards cost control as much less important than an excellent product that was completed on schedule is another indication of poor management, but it is not conclusive. The sponsor may overlook budget overruns if the product is outstanding and financially successful, as often happens for motion picture projects and investment banking deals.

The evaluation of the process may indicate that reviews conducted during the project were inadequate, or that timely action was not taken on the basis of these reviews. For example, the review may indicate that on the basis of information available at the time, the project should have been redirected or even discontinued, but this was not done. This may suggest that more frequent or more thorough analyses of progress should have been made; consequently, requirements for such reviews on future projects should be modified.

The evaluation also may lead to changes in rules or procedures. It may identify some rules that impeded efficient conduct of the project. Conversely, it may uncover inadequate controls. As part of the evaluation, suggestions for improving the process should be solicited from project personnel.

Evaluation of Results

The success of a project cannot be evaluated until enough time has elapsed to permit measurement of its actual benefits and costs. This may take years. Unless the impact can be specifically measured, such an evaluation may not be worthwhile. To take extreme examples, the benefits of the introduction of a new product line usually can be measured because the revenues and expenses associated with that line will be known, whereas the benefits of installing a laborsaving machine will not be identifiable if the resulting costs are buried in a variety of product costs and not separately traced to the new machine. Furthermore, there is no point in attempting to evaluate a project unless some action can be taken based on this analysis.

For many projects, evaluation of results is complicated by the fact that the expected benefits were not stated in objective, measurable terms, and the actual benefits also were not measurable. In these cases, a quantitative benefit/cost analysis is not feasible, and reliance must be placed on judgments by knowledgeable people about the project's accomplishments. This is the situation in the majority of projects undertaken by governments and nonprofit organizations, many research and development projects undertaken by staff units, and projects whose objective is to improve safety or eliminate environmental deficiencies.

Part of the evaluation should be a comparison of the actual results with the results that were anticipated when the project was approved. The anticipated results were based on certain assumptions (e.g., for a new product: size of the market, market share, competitor's reactions, inflation), and these assumptions should have been documented during the process of approving the project. Unless the need for such documentation was recognized, the record is likely to be incomplete or vague. The evaluator should foresee the possible future need for this documentation and ensure that the necessary information is collected and preserved. Because of these limitations, the results of relatively few projects are subjected to a formal evaluation (often called a *post-completion audit*).[3] The points made in the preceding paragraph suggest criteria for selecting those that are to be evaluated:

1. The project should be important enough to warrant the considerable expenditure of effort that is involved in a formal evaluation.

2. The results usually should be quantifiable. Specifically, if the project was intended to produce a specified amount of additional profit, the actual profit attributable to the project should be measurable.

3. The effects of unanticipated variables should be known, at least approximately, and they should not swamp the effect of changes in the assumptions on which the project was approved. If the results of a new product introduction were unsatisfactory because the market for the product evaporated, not much worthwhile information can be learned from an evaluation.

4. Results of the evaluation should have a good chance of leading to action. In particular, the analysis may lead to better ways of proposing and deciding on future projects.

Occasionally, projects that do not meet these criteria should be selected for analysis. Deficiencies in the system for controlling relatively unimportant projects may be overlooked if the appraisal is limited only to major projects.

---

[3]In a survey using responses from 282 large industrial companies, only 25 percent reported use of what the survey authors described as "adequate post audit procedures," and these were used only for selected projects, usually projects with long-run implications and major resource commitments. (Lawrence A. Gordon and Mary D. Myers, "Postauditing Capital Projects," *Management Accounting,* January 1991, pp. 39–42.)

Summary

The most important difference between the management control of ongoing operations and the management control of projects is that the ongoing operations continue indefinitely, whereas a project ends. Exhibit 15–4 illustrates this point. The elements in the management control of operations recur: One leads to the next in a prescribed way and at a prescribed time. Although some operating activities change from one month to the next, many of them continue relatively unchanged, month after month, or even year after year. By contrast, a project starts, moves forward from one milestone to the next, and then stops. During its life, plans are made, they are executed, and the results are evaluated. The evaluations are made at regular intervals, and these may lead to revision of the plan.

Exhibit 15–4

*Phases
of management
control*

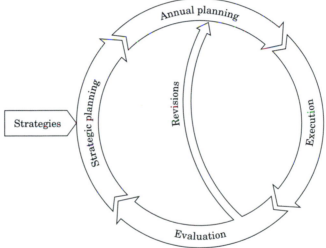

A. In an Operating Organization

Annual planning

Strategic planning

Revisions

Execution

Strategies

Evaluation

B. In a Project

Decision to undertake

Strategic planning | Detailed planning | Revision | Revision

Evaluation   Evaluation   Final evaluation

Phase 1 execution | Phase 2 execution   Phase *n* execution

Time ⟶   Start work ⟶   Complete

Suggested Additional Readings

Devaux, S. A. *Total Project Control*. New York: John Wiley & Sons, 1999.

Goldratt, E. M. *Critical Chain*. Great Barrington, MA: North River Press, 1997.

Lester, A. *Project Planning and Control*. Oxford: Butterworth-Heinemann, 1999.

Lewis, J. P. *Mastering Project Management: Applying Advanced Concepts of Systems Thinking, Control and Evaluation*. New York: McGraw-Hill, 1998.

Pillai, A. S., and K. Srinivasa Rao. "Performance Monitoring in R&D Projects." *R&D Management* 26, no. 1 (January 1996), pp. 57–60.

Sigurdsen, A. "Method for Verifying Project Cost Performance," *Project Management Journal* 24, no. 4 (December 1994), pp. 26–31.

Spinner, Manuel Pete. *Elements of Project Management: Plan, Schedule, and Control*. Upper Saddle River, NJ: Prentice-Hall, 1998.

CASE 15–1
NORTHEAST RESEARCH LABORATORY

On a Friday morning in late December 1973, Sam Lacy, head of the Physical Sciences Division of Northeast Research Laboratory (NRL), thought about two letters that lay on his desk. One, which he had received a few weeks before, was a progress report from Robert Kirk, recently assigned project leader of the Exco project, who reported that earlier frictions between the NRL team and the client had lessened considerably, that high-quality research was under way, and that the prospects for retaining the Exco project on a long-term basis appeared fairly good. The other letter, which had just arrived in the morning's mail, came from Gray Kenney, vice president of Exco, and stated that the company wished to terminate the Exco contract effective immediately.

Lacy was puzzled. He remembered how pleased Gray Kenney had been only a few months before when the Exco project produced its second patentable process. On the other hand, he also recalled some of the difficulties the project had encountered within NRL, which had ultimately led to the replacement of project leader Alan North to avoid losing the contract. Lacy decided to call in the participants in an effort to piece together an understanding of what had happened. Some of what he learned is described below. But the problem remained for him to decide what he should report to top management. What should he recommend to avoid the recurrence of such a situation in the future?

Company Background

Northeast Research Laboratory was a multidisciplinary research and development organization employing approximately 1,000 professionals. It was organized into two main sectors, one for economics and business administration, and the other for the physical and natural sciences. Within the physical and natural sciences sector, the organization was essentially by branches of science. The main units were called "divisions" and the subunits were called "laboratories." A partial organization chart is shown in Exhibit 1.

Most of the company's work was done on the basis of contracts with clients. Each contract was a project. Responsibility for the project was vested in a project leader, and through him up the organizational structure in which his laboratory was located. Typically, some members of the project team were drawn from laboratories other than that in which the project leader worked; it was the ability to put together a team with a variety of technical talents that was one of the principal strengths of a multidisciplinary laboratory. Team members worked under the direction of the project leader during the period in which they were assigned to the project. An individual might be working on more than one project concurrently. The project leader also could draw on the resources of central service organizations, such as model shops, computer services, editorial, and drafting. The project was billed for the services of these units at rates intended to cover their full costs.

Inception of the Exco Project

In October 1972, Gray Kenney, vice president of Exco, had telephoned Mac Davidson of NRL to outline a research project that would examine the effect of microwaves on various ores and minerals. Davidson was associate head of the Physical Sciences Division and had known Kenney for several years. During the conversation, Kenney asserted that NRL ought to be particularly intrigued by the research aspects of the

This case was prepared by Robert N. Anthony and Richard T. Johnson, Harvard Business School. Copyright by the President and Fellows of Harvard College, Harvard Business School case 175-184.

Exhibit 1

Organization chart (simplified)

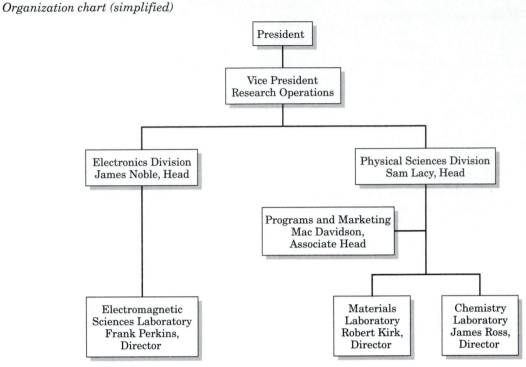

project, and Davidson readily agreed. Davidson also was pleased because the Physical Sciences Division was under pressure to generate more revenue, and this potentially long-term project from Exco would make good use of the available workforce. In addition, top management of NRL had recently circulated several memos indicating that more emphasis should be put on commercial, rather than government, work. Davidson was, however, a little concerned that the project did not fall neatly into one laboratory or even one division, but in fact required assistance from the Electronics Division to complement work that would be done in two different physical sciences laboratories (the Chemistry Laboratory and the Materials Laboratory).

A few days later, Davidson organized a joint client–NRL conference to determine what Exco wanted and to plan the proposal. Kenney sent his assistant, Tod Denby, who was to serve as the Exco liaison officer for the project. Representing NRL were Davidson; Sam Lacy; Dr. Robert Kirk, director of the Materials Laboratory (one of the two physical sciences laboratories involved in the project); Dr. Alan North, manager of Chemical Development and Engineering (and associate director of the Chemistry Laboratory); Dr. James Noble, executive director of the Electronics Division; and a few researchers chosen by Kirk and North. Davidson also would like to have invited Dr. James Ross, director of the Chemistry Laboratory, but Ross was out of town and couldn't attend the preproposal meeting.

Denby described the project as a study of the use of microwaves for the conversion of basic ores and minerals to more valuable commercial products. The study was to consist of two parts.

Task A—An experimental program to examine the effect of microwaves on 50 ores and minerals and to select those processes appearing to have the most promise.

Task B—A basic study to obtain an understanding of how and why microwaves interact with certain minerals.

It was agreed that the project would be a joint effort of three laboratories: (1) Materials, (2) Chemistry, and (3) Electromagnetic. The first two laboratories were in the Physical Sciences Division, and the last was in the Electronics Division.

Denby proposed that the contract be open-ended, with a level of effort of around $10,000–$12,000 per month. Agreement was quickly reached on the content of the proposal. Denby emphasized to the group that an early start was essential if Exco were to remain ahead of its competition.

After the meeting Lacy, who was to have overall responsibility for the project, discussed the choice of project leader with Davidson. Davidson proposed Alan North, a 37-year-old chemist who had had experience as a project leader on several projects. North had impressed Davidson at the preproposal meeting and seemed well suited to head the interdisciplinary team. Lacy agreed. Lacy regretted that Dr. Ross (head of the laboratory in which North worked) was unable to participate in the decision of who should head the joint project. In fact, because he was out of town, Ross was aware neither of the Exco project nor of his laboratory's involvement in it.

The following day, Alan North was told of his appointment as project leader. During the next few days, he conferred with Robert Kirk, head of the other physical sciences laboratory involved in the project. Toward the end of October, Denby began to exert pressure on North to finalize the proposal, stating that the substance had been agreed upon at the preproposal conference. North thereupon drafted a five-page letter as a substitute for a formal proposal, describing the nature of the project and outlining the procedures and equipment necessary. At Denby's request, North included a paragraph that authorized members of the client's staff to visit NRL frequently and observe progress of the research program. The proposal's cover sheet contained approval signatures from the laboratories and divisions involved. North signed for his own area and for laboratory director Ross. He telephoned Dr. Noble of the Electronics Division, relayed the client's sense of urgency, and Noble authorized North to sign for him. Davidson signed for the Physical Sciences Division as a whole.

At this stage, North relied principally on the advice of colleagues within his own division. As he did not know personally the individuals in the Electronics Division, they were not called upon at this point. Since North understood informally that the director of the Electromagnetic Sciences Laboratory, Dr. Perkins, was quite busy and often out of town, North did not attempt to discuss the project with Perkins.

After the proposal had been signed and mailed, Dr. Perkins was sent a copy. It listed the engineering equipment that the client wanted purchased for the project and described how it was to be used. Perkins worried that performance characteristics of the power supply (necessary for quantitative measurement) specified in the proposal were inadequate for the task. He asked North about it and North said that the client had made up his mind about the microwave equipment he wanted and how it was to be used. Denby had said he was paying for that equipment and intended to move it to Exco's laboratories after the completion of the NRL contract.

All these events had transpired rather quickly. By the time Dr. Ross, director of the Chemistry Laboratory, returned, the proposal for the Exco project had been signed and accepted. Ross went to see Lacy and said that he had dealt with Denby on a previous project and had serious misgivings about working with him. Lacy assuaged some of Ross's fears by observing that if anyone could succeed in working with Denby it would be North—a flexible man, professionally competent, who could move with the tide and get along with clients of all types.

Conduct of the Project

Thus, the project began. Periodically, when decisions arose, North would seek opinions from division management. However, he was somewhat unclear about whom he should talk to. Davidson had been the person who had actually appointed him project leader. Normally, however, North worked for Ross. Although Kirk's laboratory was heavily involved in the project, Kirk was very busy with other Materials Laboratory work. Adding to his uncertainty, North periodically received telephone calls from Perkins of the Electronics Division, whom he didn't know well. Perkins expected to be heavily involved in the project.

Difficulties and delays began to plague the project. The microwave equipment specified by the client was not delivered by the manufacturer on schedule, and there were problems in filtering the power supply of the radio-frequency source. Over the objection of NRL electromagnetic sciences engineers, but at the insistence of the client, one of the chemical engineers tried to improve the power supply filter. Eventually the equipment had to be sent back to the manufacturer for modification. This required several months.

In the spring of 1973, Denby, who had made his presence felt from the outset, began to apply strong pressure. "Listen," he said to North, "top management of Exco is starting to get on my back and we need results. Besides, I'm up for a review in four months and I can't afford to let this project affect my promotion." Denby was constantly at NRL during the next few months. He was often in the labs conferring individually with members of the NRL teams. Denby also visited North's office frequently.

A number of related problems began to surface. North had agreed to do both experimental and theoretical work for this project, but Denby's constant pushing for experimental results began to tilt the emphasis. Theoretical studies began to lapse, and experimental work became the focus of the Exco project. From time to time North argued that the theoretical work should precede or at least accompany the experimental program, but Denby's insistence on concrete results led North to temporarily deemphasize the theoretical work. Symptoms of this shifting emphasis were evident. One day a senior researcher from Kirk's laboratory came to North to complain that people were being "stolen" from his team. "How can we do a balanced project if the theoretical studies are not given enough workforce?" he asked. North explained the client's position and asked the researcher to bear with this temporary realignment of the project's resources.

As the six-month milestone approached, Denby expressed increasing dissatisfaction with the project's progress. To have concrete results to report to Exco management, he directed North a number of times to change the direction of the research. On several occasions, various members of the project team had vigorous discussions with Denby about the risks of changing results without laying a careful foundation. North himself spent a good deal of time talking with Denby on this subject, but Denby seemed to discount its importance. Denby began to avoid North and to spend most of his time with the other team members. Eventually the experimental program, initially dedicated to a careful screening of some 50 materials, deteriorated to a somewhat frantic and erratic pursuit of what appeared to be "promising leads." Lacy and Noble played little or no role in this shift of emphasis.

On June 21, 1973, Denby visited North in his office and severely criticized him for proposing a process (hydrochloric acid pickling) that was economically infeasible. In defense, North asked an NRL economist to check his figures. The economist reported back that North's numbers were sound and that, in fact, a source at U.S. Steel indicated that hydrochloric acid pickling was "generally more economic than the traditional process and was increasingly being adopted." Through this and subsequent encounters, the relationship between Denby and North became increasingly strained.

Denby continued to express concern about the Exco project's payoff. In an effort to save time, he discouraged the NRL team from repeating experiments, a practice that was designed to ensure accuracy. Data received from initial experiments were frequently taken as sufficiently accurate and, after hasty analysis, were adopted for the purposes of the moment. Not surprisingly, Denby periodically discovered errors in these data. He informed NRL of them.

Denby's visits to NRL became more frequent as the summer progressed. Some days he would visit all three laboratories, talking to the researchers involved and asking them about encouraging leads. North occasionally cautioned Denby against too much optimism. Nonetheless, North continued to oblige the client by restructuring the Exco project to allow for more "production line" scheduling of experiments and for less systematic research.

In August, North discovered that vertile could be obtained from iron ore. This discovery was a significant one, and the client applied for a patent. If the reaction could be proved commercially, its potential would be measured in millions of dollars. Soon thereafter, the NRL team discovered that the operation could, in fact, be handled commercially in a rotary kiln. The client was notified and soon began planning a pilot plant that would use the rotary kiln process.

Exco's engineering department, after reviewing the plans for the pilot plant, rejected them. It was argued that the rotary process was infeasible and that a fluid bed process would have to be used instead. Denby returned to NRL and insisted on an experiment to test the fluid bed

process. North warned Denby that agglomeration (a sticking together of the material) would probably take place. It did. Denby was highly upset, reported to Gray Kenney that he had not received "timely" warning of the probability of agglomeration taking place, and indicated that he had been misled about the feasibility of the rotary kiln process.[1]

Work continued, and two other "disclosures of invention" were turned over to the client by the end of September.

Personnel Changes

On September 30, Denby came to North's office to request that Charles Fenton be removed from the Exco project. Denby reported he had been watching Fenton in the Electromagnetic Laboratory, which he visited often, and had observed that Fenton spent relatively little time on the Exco project. North, who did not know Fenton well, agreed to look into it. But Denby insisted that Fenton be removed immediately and threatened to terminate the contract if he were allowed to remain.

North was unable to talk to Fenton before taking action because Fenton was on vacation. He did talk to Fenton as soon as he returned, and the researcher admitted that, due to the pressure of other work, he had not devoted as much time or effort to the Exco work as perhaps he should have.

Three weeks later, Denby called a meeting with Mac Davidson and Sam Lacy. It was their first meeting since the preproposal conference for the Exco project. Denby was brief and to the point.

Denby: I'm here because we have to replace North. He's becoming increasingly difficult to work with and is obstructing the progress of the project.

---

[1]Ten months later the client was experimenting with the rotary kiln process for producing vertile from iron ore in his own laboratory.

Lacy: But North is an awfully good man. . . .

Davidson: Look, he's come up with some good solid work thus far. What about the process of extracting vertile from iron ore he came up with. And . . . .

Denby: I'm sorry, but we have to have a new project leader. I don't mean to be abrupt, but it's either replace North or forget the contract.

Davidson reluctantly appointed Robert Kirk project leader and informed North of the decision. North went to see Davidson a few days later. Davidson told him that, although management did not agree with the client, North had been replaced to save the contract. Later Dr. Lacy told North the same thing. Neither Lacy nor Davidson made an effort to contact Exco senior management on the matter.

Following the change of project leadership, the record became more difficult to reconstruct. It appeared that Kirk made many efforts to get the team together, but morale remained low. Denby continued to make periodic visits to NRL but found that the NRL researchers were not talking as freely with him as they had in the past. Denby became skeptical about the project's value. Weeks slipped by. No further breakthroughs emerged.

Lacy's Problem

Dr. Lacy had received weekly status reports on the project, the latest of which is shown in Exhibit 2. He had had a few informal conversations about the project, principally with North and Kirk. He had not read the reports submitted to Exco. If the project had been placed on NRL's "problem list," which comprised about 10 percent of the projects that seemed to be experiencing the most difficulty, Lacy would have received a written report on its status weekly, but the Exco project was not on that list.

With the background given above, Lacy reread Kenney's letter terminating the Exco contract. It seemed likely that Kenney, too, had

not had full knowledge of what went on during the project's existence. In his letter, Kenney mentioned the "glowing reports" that reached his ears in the early stages of the work. These reports, which came to him only from Denby, were later significantly modified, and Denby apparently implied that NRL had been "leading him on." Kenney pointed to the complete lack of economic evaluation of alternative process in the experimentation. He seemed unaware of the fact that at Denby's insistence all economic analysis was supposed to be done by the client. Kenney was most dissatisfied that NRL had not complied with all the provisions of the proposal, particularly those that required full screening of all materials and the completion of the theoretical work.

Lacy wondered why Denby's changes of the proposal had not been documented by the NRL team. Why hadn't he heard more of the problems of the Exco project before? Lacy requested a technical evaluation of the project from Ronald M. Benton, director of the Process Economics Program. Dr. Benton's eight-page report concluded that the approach was technically sound, that the technical conduct of the project was good, that the patent on vertile was a significant accomplishment, and that three other developments, not mentioned in the above narrative, were also significant accomplishments. He pointed out the difficulties of the relationships with Denby. He did say that decisions on the project were not well documented, that the project leader did not convey the importance of some decisions to the client's management, and that there was inadequate coordination between Dr. North and personnel in the Electromagnetic Sciences Laboratory. He discussed each of the nine "claims" given by the client as reasons for terminating the contract made in the letter terminating the contract and found that some were "completely unfounded," others were a matter of interpretation, and still others could not be evaluated one way or the other because of a lack of documentation.

EXHIBIT 2

Weekly project status report

PROJECT/ACCOUNT STATUS REPORT

DIVISION: PHYSICAL SCI	ORG 325	PROJ/ACCT 3273
DEPARTMENT: CHEMISTRY LAB	SUB 000	W/O 000
	SUPERVISOR: ROBERT KIRK	LEADER: ROBERT KIRK

WEEK ENDING DATE 12-22-73

TYPE PROJ | REV TYPE INDUS | PRICE SCA | CLIENT YD | INT/COM DOMESTIC | NOTICES | PAGE 1

PROJECT TITLE: MICROWAVES IN CONVERSION OF BASIC ORES AND MINERALS

INST EXCO	READY DATE 11-06-72	STOP WORK DATE --	TEAM DATE 11-06-74	BURDEN'S % 28.00	OVERHEAD % 105.00	FEE % 15.00

Labor / Costs (DOLLARS and LABOR HOURS)

COST CATEGORIES	(OBJECT CODE)	DOLLARS PTD13WK1	DOLLARS TO DATE	LABOR HOURS ESTIMATE	LABOR HOURS TO DATE	BALANCE
SUPERVISOR						
SENIOR	(11, 12)	192	560		36	
PROFESSIONAL	(13)	150	17986		1348	
	(14)		16787		1678	
TECHNICAL	(15)	529	5299		1037	
CLER/SUPP	(16, 17, 18)		301		84	
OTHER	(10), (19)	72	72		12	
LABOR(S.T.)		943	41005		1644	
BURDEN		248	11481			
OVERHEAD		1227	55110			
OVERTIME PREM	(21)	160	1540			
OVS/OTH. PREM	(22-29)	242	476			
TOTAL PERSONNEL COSTS		2820	109612			
TRAVEL	(56-59)		776			
SUBCONTRACT	(36)					
MATERIAL	(41, 42)		3726			
EQUIPMENT	(43)					
COMPUTER	(37, 45)	2	507			
COMMUN	(62, 63, 70, 71)					
CONSULTANT	(74, 75)					
REPORT COST	(44, 47)					
OTHER M&S		54	99			
TOTAL M&S COST		56	5098			

LAST BILLING: DATE 11-30-73 AMOUNT 11350

ACCOUNT STATUS TO DATE: BILLED 154583 PAID 154583

TIME BALANCE % 39.4 | COST BALANCE % 43.5 | TIME BALANCE WKS. 41

Commitments

	DOLLARS PTD13WK1	DOLLARS TO DATE	ESTIMATED	BALANCE
COMMITMENTS		26847		
TOTAL LESS FEE	2876	141557	250435	108878
FEE (15.00)	158	24376	37565	13189
TOTAL	3031	165933	288000	122067

Commitment Status to Date

PO NO	OBJ	VENDOR/DESCRIPTION	TOTAL	CHARGES	BALANCE
A61289 11-21-73	41	MINNESOTA MINING	111	61	50
A61313 11-23-73	41	ALDRICH CHEMICAL	348		348
A95209 11-28-73	43	TENNECO CHEMICAL CO	5		5
A95093 11-15-73	41	UNION CARBIDE CORP	23194		23194
B95104 11-19-73	37	SCIENTIFIC PRODUCTS	600		600
B95232 11-25-73	41	VAN WATERS & ROGERS	2500		2500
O18046 12-15-73	57	ROGER MD	300	150	150
					T 26847

Transactions Recorded 12-15-73—12-22-73

LABOR

ORG	ID	W/E DATE	T/S NO	OBJ	NAME	HOURS WEEK	HOURS TO DATE
322	02345	12-22-73	363073	13	KIRK	6.0	150
322	02345	12-22-73	363073	22	KIRK	6.0	
322	03212	12-22-73	363082	13	DENSMORE	8.0	25
322	03260	12-22-73	236544	14	COOK	15.0	30
325	12110	12-08-73	C30093	15	HOWARD	15.0	82
325	12110	12-15-73	236548	15	HOWARD	36.0	
325	12110	12-22-73	376147	15	HOWARD	8.0	
325	12357	12-22-73	376149	15	SPELTZ	15.0	38
325	12369	12-22-73	376150	15	GYUIRE	15.0	17
325	12384	12-22-73	R08416	15	DILLON	40.0–	14
325	12397	12-22-73	336527	15	NAGY	31.0	31
325	12397	12-22-73	336527	21	NAGY	15.0	
652	12475	12-22-73	236548	15	KAIN	8.0	20
652	12475	12-22-73	236548	21	KAIN	15.0	

DOLLARS

	HOURS	DOLLARS
LABOR (STRAIGHT TIME)	117.0	943
PAYROLL BURDEN		248
OVERHEAD RECOVERY		1227
OVERTIME PREMIUM LABOR	30.0	160
OTHER PREMIUM LABOR	6.0	242
TOTAL PERSONNEL COSTS		2820 S

MATERIALS & SERVICES

PO NO	REF NO	OBJ		DESCRIPTION	REQUESTOR	DOLLARS
61289	54065	48	438	REA EXPRESS	KIRK	42
17234	87413	48	456	GED SUPPLY CO	COOK	10
	04461	71	FEE 448	P.T. & T. 326-6200	NAGY	2
				TOTAL M&S COSTS		56 S
				TRANSACTION TOTAL		158
						3034 T

EXHIBIT 3

MEMORANDUM

January 8, 1974

To: Sam Lacy

From: Mac Davidson

RE: The Exco Project—Conclusions

The decision to undertake this project was made without sufficient consideration of the fact that this was a "high-risk" project.

The proposal was technically sound and within the capabilities of the groups assigned to work on the project.

There was virtually no coordination between the working elements of Physical Sciences and Electronics in the preparation of the proposal.

The technical conduct of this project, with few exceptions, was, considering the handicaps under which the work was carried out, good and at times outstanding. The exceptions were primarily due to lack of attention to detail.

The NRL reports were not well prepared, even considering the circumstances under which they were written.

The client, acting under pressure from his own management, involved himself excessively in the details of experimental work and dictated frequent changes of direction and emphasis. The proposal opened the door to this kind of interference.

There was no documentation by NRL of the decisions made by the client which altered the character, direction, and emphasis of the work.

There was no serious attempt on the part of NRL to convey the nature or consequence of the above actions to the client.

Fewer than half of the major complaints made by the client concerning NRL's performance are valid.

The project team acquiesced too readily in the client's interference and management acquiesced too easily to the client's demands.

Management exercised insufficient supervision and gave inadequate support to the project leader in his relations with the client.

There were no "overruns" either in time or funds.

His final conclusion was that this was a high-risk project and that it should have been so identified and treated accordingly early in the project.

Lacy then asked Mac Davidson for his appraisal of the project. Davidson's reply is given in Exhibit 3.

Questions

1. What, if any, additional information did Lacy need to reach his own conclusion about the project?

2. Suggest steps that should be considered to lessen the likelihood that a similar situation would develop in the future.

Case 15–2
Modern Aircraft Company

Modern Aircraft Company (MAC) produced and marketed a very successful six-passenger, single-engine corporate jet (Model 69 C). Market research indicated that there was a need in friendly, less-developed countries for a relatively low-cost subsonic fighter/bomber aircraft for use in small, defensive air forces. The military version of the MAC corporate jet was designated as the F-69 fighter/bomber aircraft. It used "off-shelf" technology to provide a highly reliable and easily maintainable fighter/bomber.

MAC formed an F-69 project group with Nicky St. John as the project manager. The president made it crystal clear that the F-69 is MAC's project and that there should be no delays in the scheduled first flight test. That was crucial for the follow-on production contract of 100 F-69 aircraft at $5 million each.

The F-69 engine would be an existing jet engine model currently used on MAC's fighter/bomber. However, this engine was to be modified to include an afterburner section, which was part of the specifications for the F-69 fighter/bomber. Time estimates were: modification design (six months); engineering of the afterburner section to match the modified engine (four months); fabrication of modified engine and afterburner section (five months); prototype assembly and engine test-cell run (three months).

The airframe would be the MAC Model 69 C corporate jet, with the passenger compartment modified to a bomb bay and the nose baggage compartment modified for 7.62 mm machine-gun installation. Time estimates were: design airframe modification (seven months); engineering and wind tunnel testing (three

months); and prototype fabrication and assembly of airframe (six months).

Subsystems, such as the ultrahigh-frequency (UHF) radio, navigation units, autopilot, instruments, and so on would be off-the-shelf components—that is, subsystems in current use with high reliability and ease of maintenance. There would be no radar subsystem because of its complexity. The F-69 fighter/bomber would be a daytime fighter/bomber only. There would be a simple lead computing sight subsystem for gunnery and manual bombing purposes; this subsystem was also off-the-shelf hardware. Time estimates were: request for bids on subsystems (four months); selection of subsystems (two months); award of contracts (two months); delivery of subsystems (six months); and checkout and installation in prototype aircraft (three months).

Upon completion of the prototype F-69 fighter/bomber, there would be a series of powered checks, taxi tests, and the like for one month, followed immediately by the first test flight. If all tests were successful, the F-69 prototype design and the specifications would be used for the production phase.

Questions

1. Using the critical path method (CPM) technique, develop a network for the F-69 preproduction project.
2. What is the time in months for the prototype F-69 to the fully assembled?
3. What is the time in months for the first F-69 test flight?
4. What is the critical path (engine, airframe, subsystem)?
5. If there was a one-month delay in obtaining bomb bay racks for the F-69

This case was prepared by John E. Setnicky, Mobile College, Mobile, Alabama. Copyright by John E. Setnicky.

bomb bay, should Nicky St. John authorize the use of overtime to make up for this delay?

6. If there was a two-week delay in the receipt of an alignment jig for aligning the center axis of the engine with the center axis of the afterburner section, should Nicky St. John authorize the use of overtime to make up for this delay?

7. If there was a strike at one of the subsystem vendors that delayed delivery of the UHF radio by two months, should Nicky St. John authorize the formation of a second shift for the subsystem checkout and installation in the prototype aircraft activity?

COMPANY INDEX

A

AB Thorsten, case study, 708–714
Abrams Company, case study, 197–200
Acer, multiple stakeholder approach, 58
Aetna, restructuring, 118
Allied Office Products, case study, 322–328
Aloha products, case study, 283–287
AMAX Automobiles, profit center, 180
Amazon.com
    interactive controls, 457
    Internet sales, 13
    management, 580
    stock options, 511
America Online
    business unit strategy, 571
    management, 580
American Brands, business unit strategy, 571
Analog Devices
    case study, 463–476
    incentive compensation, 577
Anita's Apparel, case study, 548–553
Asea Brown Boveri
    management, 580
    profit centers, 167
    wholesale layoffs, 115
AT&T
    economic value added evaluation, 246
    profit centers, 173
    strategy formulation, 10

Avis, Inc., stock options, 511
Avon, incentives, 518

B

Barings, collapse, 520, 628
Barnes & Noble, revenues, 13
Bausch & Lomb, performance measures, 442, 443
BIC, business unit strategy, 571
Birch Paper Company, case study, 226–227
Black & Decker, business unit strategy, 571
Boeing
    business units, 70
    "design-build teams," 68
    progress payments, 248
Boise Cascade Corporation
    case study, 188–196
    support costs charges, 213
Borders, market value, 13
Boston Creamery, case study, 390–400

C

Canadian Imperial Bank of Commerce,
    intellectual capital, 489
Charles Schwab
    business unit strategy, 571

fixed salaries compensation, 515
TeleBroker, 628
Chemical Bank
    case study, 657–669
    profit center approach, 165
Chrysler, activity-based costing, 314
Cisco Systems
    management, 580
    stock options, 511
    Web site features, 14
Citibank Indonesia, case study, 678–685
Citicorp, strategy formulation, 10
Combustion Engineering, wholesale layoffs,
    115
Commodore Business Machines, outsourcing
    of services, 213–214
Copley Manufacturing Company, case study,
    329–334
Corning Glass, business unit strategy, 571
Cup Corporation, case study, 477–483

D

Daimler-Benz, differentiation strategy, 571
Dairy Pak, case study, 335–345
Deere & Co., functional structure adoption, 68
Dell Computer
    business unit strategy, 571
    performance measures, 458–460
Digital Equipment Corporation, case study,
    93–99
Disney, 55
    strategy formulation, 10
Dow Chemical, intellectual capital, 489–490
DuPont
    cash in investment base formula, 247
    divisionalization, 165

E

eBay
    differentiation strategy, 571
    stock options, 511
Emerson Electric Company
    business unit strategy, 571
    case study, 346–359
Enager Industries, Inc., case study, 484–487
Exxon, single industry firm, 565

F

Federal Express, outsourcing of services to,
    213–214
Ford, 55
    AutoXchange program, 13
    joint ventures, 689
    management by objectives, 368
    profitability, 57
FormPac, bonus plans, 521

G

Galvor Company, case study, 429–440
General Appliance Corporation, case study,
    228–236
General Electric
    business unit strategy, 571
    case study, 498–504
    centralization, 170
    dotted line relationship, 73
    incentive compensation, 577
    management style, 580, 581
    profitability strategy, 56
    structure and content, 305
General Motors, 55
    activity-based costing, 313, 314
    case study, 78–83
    cash in investment base formula, 247
    divisionalization, 165
    joint ventures, 689
Glaxo Wellcombe
    derivatives losses, 628
    "therapeutic strategy teams," 69
Golden Grain, assets employed analysis, 244
Grand Jean Company, case study, 160–163

H

Harland Foundation, case study, 651–653
Hewlett-Packard
    activity-based costing, 314
    case study, 601–604
Higashimaru Shoyu, profit centers, 167
Hughes Space & Communications Division,
    intellectual capital, 490
Hyundai, business unit strategy, 571

I

IBM
    business unit strategy, 571
    discretionary operations, 115
    multinational cultural differences, 687
    performance measures, 445
    research and development, 121–122
    strategy formulation, 9
Indus Corporation, profit center, 180
Industrial Products Corporation, case study, 288–294
Infosys, performance incentives, 516
ITT, management style, 580, 581

J

Johnson & Johnson, corporate culture, 60–61

K

Kinko's, centralization of operations, 170
Kodak, 55
Kyocera Corporation, profit centers, 167

L

Lands' End, lowered costs with reduced mailings, 372
Lemfert Company, case study, 296–297
Levi Strauss, order-entry computers in retail stores, 312
Lincoln Electric Company
    business unit strategy, 571
    case study, 529–544, 715–719
    multiple stakeholder approach, 59
Lodgian, Inc., revenue centers, 112
Lucent Technologies, performance reviews, 522

M

McDonald's, promotional campaigns, 311
Marden Company, case study, 295
Martex, controller organization, 86–92

Mary Kay Cosmetics, incentives, 514
Matsushita
    performance incentives, 516
    profit centers, 167
Medoc Company, case study, 240–242
Merck
    research planning model, 319–320
    strategy formulation, 10
Metropolitan Bank, case study, 670–677
Microsoft, stock options, 511
Mitsubishi, investment centers, 263
Modern Aircraft Company, case study, 763–764
Monsanto, business unit strategy, 571
Mont Blanc, differentiation strategy, 571
Motorola
    case study, 30–38
    performance incentives, 518

N

Nabisco, business units, 69
National Tractor and Equipment Company, case study, 100–107
NEC Corporation, strategic planning, 568
Neiman-Marcus, differentiation strategy, 571
Nestlé
    case study, 720–727
    centralization, 170
    chain of command, 74
New Jersey Insurance Company, case study, 133–139
North Country Auto, Inc., case study, 181–187
Northeast Research Laboratory, case study, 755–762
Novartis, research and development expenses, 256
Novell, profit center approach, 166
NuCor
    business unit strategy, 571
    case study, 20–29, 76–77
NYPRO, Inc., case study, 140–149

O

O'Reilley Associates, case study, 638–641

P

PA Consulting, business unit organization,
    520
Pan Am Airlines, performance measures, 445
PC&D, Inc., case study, 586–597
Pelican Instruments, case study, 584–585
Pepsi, interactive controls, 457
Piedmont University, case study, 654–656
Polaroid Corporation, research and
    development, 122
Premark International, incentive
    compensation, 578
Procter & Gamble
    activity-based costing, 314
    Bankers Trust lawsuit, 628
    order-entry computers in retail stores, 312
    related diversified firm, 565
    structure and content, 305
PSINet, stock options, 511

Q

Quaker Oats, undervaluation of equipment,
    251
Quality Metal Service Center, case study,
    275–282
Quantum Corporation, team-based
    performance measures, 517

R

Rendell Company, case study, 84–92
Riverview, case study, 401–407
Rolex, differentiation strategy, 571

S

Salomon Brothers, bonus scheme, 520
Schrader Bellows, activity-based cost system,
    313
SCM Corp., business units evaluation, 575
Scovill, Inc., activity-based cost system, 313
Sears, performance measures, 460–461
Shering-Plough, centralization efforts, 170
Singapore Airlines, profit centers, 172
Skandia, intellectual capital, 491–497
SMH, industry turnaround, 363
Solartronics, Inc., case study, 427–428
Sound Dynamics, Inc., case study, 378–389

SPX, economic value added process, 260–261
Stewart Box Company, case study, 39–45
Stouffer's, differentiation strategy, 571
Strider Chemical Company, case study,
    237–239
Sunrise Medical, bonus system, 519
Swissair, profit centers, 173
Sylvania, business unit strategy, 571

T

Taco Bell, transformation, 520
Texaco, strategic planning, 304
Texas Instruments
    business unit strategy, 571
    case study, 601–604, 605–619
Textron, incentive compensation, 570
3M
    case study, 598–600
    incentive compensation, 578
    research and development, 122, 307, 578

U

Unilever, advertising expenses, 256
US Airways, golden parachute, 513
US Steel, performance measures, 445

V

Vershire Company, case study, 127–132

W

Wal-Mart, 55
    business unit strategy, 571
    expansion, 258
    management control system, 7
    order-entry computers in retail stores, 312
Warren Insurance Company, case study, 488
Wayside Inns, case study, 554–562
Wendy's, stock option incentives, 510
Westport Electric Corporation, case study,
    155–159
Whirlpool, performance measurement, 451
Whiz Calculator Company, case study,
    150–154
Williamson and Oliver, case study, 642–650
Worthington Industries, case study, 544–547

X

Xerox
    case study, 46–52, 728–731
    copy machine introduction, 121
    incentive compensation, 578
    performance measures, 445
    research and development, 578

Y

Yahoo!, stock options, 511

Topical Index

A

ABC. *see* Activity–based cost system
Activity, 313
Activity-based cost system (ABC), 313. *see also*
    Costs
Administrative center. *see also* Responsibility
    center
    in general, 119–120
Administrative expenses, 366. *see also* Costs
Agency costs, 525
Agents, risk preferences, compared to
    principals, 523–524
Annuity depreciation, 252–253
Arbitration, in transfer price dispute, 215–216
Arbitration committee, 206
Asian financial crisis, 58, 628
Assets employed
    analysis structure, 243–246
    economic performance evaluation, 264–265
    EVA vs. ROI, 258–263
    in general, 243
    management evaluation considerations,
        263–264
    measurement
        annuity depreciation, 252–253
        capital charge, 256–257
        cash, 247
        disposition of assets, 251–252
        in general, 246–247
        gross book value, 251
        idle assets, 255
        intangible assets, 256
        inventories, 248
        leased assets, 254–255
        noncurrent liabilities, 256
        property, plant, equipment, 249–254
        receivables, 247–248
        surveys of practice, 257–258
        working capital, 248–249
    other valuation methods, 254

B

Balance sheet, budgeted, 367
Balanced scorecard, 444–445
Behavior in organizations. *see also*
    Organization
    controller functions
        business unit controller, 73–74
        in general, 71
        relation to line organization, 72
    formal control system, 63–65
    in general, 55
    goal congruence, 59
        factors affecting, 59–63
    goals
        in general, 55
        multiple stakeholder approach, 58–59
        profitability, 56–57
        risk, 58

shareholder value, 57–58
organization types
  business unit, 69–70
  functional organizations, 66–69
  in general, 65–66
  system design implications, 70–71
Benchmark. *see also* Milestone
  financial reports, 419
  management compensation, 521
Biological control, 2–3
Black box, 4
Bonus pool, management compensation, 507
Budget. *see also* Budget preparation; Costs
  budgeted balance sheet, 367
  budgeted cash flow statement, 367
  capital budget, 366–367
  compared to actual expense, 116
  contingency, 372
  contrasted to forecasting, 361
  corporate strategy for, 569
  in general, 360–361
  management by objectives, 367–368
  operating budget
    categories, 364–366
    content, 363–364
  relation to strategic planning, 361
  revenue budget, 364–365
  using, 362–363
Budget preparation. *see also* Budget
    preparation process
  administrative or support center, 120
  business unit strategy and, 574–576
  control budget preparation, 742–743
  in general, 16–17, 360
  incremental budgeting, 116–117
  management by objectives, 116, 367–368
  research and development, 123
  strategic planning for, 302–304
  "zero-base budgeting," 369n
  zero-based review, 117–118
Budget preparation process
  behavioral aspects
    budget department, 375
    budget target difficulty, 373–374
    in general, 372
    management involvement, 374–375
    participation in process, 373
  contingency budgets, 372
  guidelines, 369
  initial proposal, 369–370
  negotiation, slack, 370
  organization, 368–369
  quantitative techniques
    probability estimates, 376

simulation, 375
  review and approval, 371
  revisions, 371–372
Business unit. *see also* Business unit strategy;
    Subsidiary
  agreements among, 208
  "build" vs. "harvest" units, 572
  compared to profit center, 164
  controller, 73–74
  discussed, 69–70
  management objectives, 244–245
  as profit center, 169–170
Business unit strategy. *see also* Strategic
    planning
  competitive advantage, 579–580
  concept, 570–571
  mission, 571–578
    budgeting, 574–576
    incentive compensation, 576–578
    strategic planning and, 573–574

C

Capital budget. *see also* Budget
  discussed, 366–367
Capital investment analysis, strategic
    planning, 307–309
Cash. *see also* Assets employed
  measurement as asset, 247
  working capital, 248–249
Cash flow statement, budgeted, 367
CEO. *see* Chief executive officer
Chief executive officer (CEO). *see also*
    Management compensation
  compensation, 512–513, 525–526
Chief financial officer (CFO). *see* Controller
Chief information officer (CIO), duties, 72
Communication, perception and, 63
Competition, between profit
    centers, 168
Conflict resolution, among transfer price
    participants, 215–216
Contingency theory, 564
Contractual relationships
  cost-reimbursement contracts, 737
  fixed-price contracts, 736–737
  incentive contract, 738
  projects control and, 736–738
Control, interactive, 8–9
Control system. *see also* Management control
    system
  elements, 1–4

Controller
  dotted line relationship, 73
  functions
    business unit controller, 73–74
    in general, 71
    relation to line organization, 72
Controls for differentiated strategies. *see also*
  Management control
  business unit strategy, 570–580
  corporate strategy, 564–570
  top management style, 580–582
Corporate services. *see also* Transfer pricing
  pricing
    control over services amount, 212–213
    in general, 211–212
Corporate strategy. *see also* Strategic
  planning
  in general, 564–565
    related diversified firm, 565, 567
    single industry firm, 565, 567
    unrelated business firm, 565
  management control implications,
    567–570
    budgeting, 569
    corporatewide core competencies, 567
    incentive compensation, 569–570
    strategic planning, 567–569
    transfer pricing, 569
  organization structure implications,
    565–567
Cost driver, 313
Cost overruns, 750
Cost variability, budget preparation, 118
Costs. *see also* Budget; Transfer price
  activity-based costing, 312–314
  agency costs, 525
  budgeted production costs, 365
  conversion cost, 312–313
  cost of sales, 365
  determining, 110
  discretionary, 114, 421
  engineered, 114, 421
  estimation, 741–742
  fixed, 415
  marketing expenses, 365–366
  between profit centers, 168
  in transfer price, 207–208
    fixed, 208–211
    variable, 415–416
CPM. *see* Critical path method
Critical path method (CPM), 740
Culture, 8
  corporate, 60–62
  multinational cultural differences,
    686–688

D

Decision-making, in profit centers, 166–167,
  168
Depreciation, exchange rates, 695, 696, 700
Division. *see* Business unit, s
Divisionalization, profit centers, 164, 165
Dotted line relationship, 73
Downsizing, 118

E

Economic models, 218–219
Economic performance. *see also* Performance
  measurement
  measurement, 174
Economic reports, 265
Economic value added (EVA)
  assets employed, 243, 245–246
  compared to return on investment,
    258–263
Effectiveness, in responsibility centers,
  110–112
Efficiency
  in functional structure, 66–67
  in responsibility centers, 110–112
  in transfer pricing, 212
Equipment, valuing as asset, 249–254
Error of commission, 442
Error of omission, 443
EVA. *see* Economic value added
Excellence, 120
Exchange rates. *see also* Interest rates
  economic exposure, 696
  forward, 695
  in general, 694–698
  hedging, 702–703
  nominal, 695
  real, 695
  SFAS No. 52: Foreign Currency
    Translation, 705–707
  subsidiary performance, 703–704
  transaction effects, 702–703
  transaction exposure, 696, 699–702
  translation effects, 696, 698–699
Expense center
  characteristics, 15, 53
  discretionary, 15, 115–116
  engineered, 15, 114–115
Expense variances. *see also* Financial
  performance reports; Variances
  discussed, 415–416
Expert systems, 309

F

Financial control system. *see also*
  Performance measurement
  limitations, 441–443
Financial Executive, 420
Financial performance reports analysis. *see
  also* Financial reports
  detail considerations, 421
  engineered and discretionary costs, 421
  evaluation standards, 419–420
    benchmarking, 419
  full-cost systems, 420
  variances
    expense variances, 415–416
    in general, 408–410
    market penetration and industry
      volume, 413–415
    mix variance, 412
    revenue variance, 410–415
    summary, 416–417
    volume variance, 412–413
  variances analysis, limitations, 422–423
  variations in practice, 417–421
Financial reports. *see also* Progress reports
  benchmarking, 419
  benefits, 423
  in general, 744
Financial responsibility
  measurement, 442
  profit centers, 166
  responsibility centers, 54, 108
Financial service organizations. *see also*
  Service organizations
  discussed, 627–630
Financial services sector, 627–628
Financing, advance payments, 248
Forecast, contrasted with budget, 361
Functional organization. *see also*
  Organization
  defined, 164
  discussed, 66–69

G

General fund, 634
Globalization, 456, 628. *see also* Multinational
  organizations
Goal congruence. *see also* Goals
  factors affecting
    external factors, 60
    in general, 59–60, 121

internal factors, 60–62
  management style, 62–63
  organizational informality, 63
management compensation, 524–525
process, 59
transfer pricing, 201
Goals. *see also* Goal congruence; Objectives
  corporate, 55
  in general, 3, 9
Golden handcuff, 510
Golden parachute, 513
Gross margin. *see also* Profit
  discussed, 418

H

Half-life/complexity matrix, 474–476
Health care organizations. *see also* Service
  organizations
  discussed, 630–632
Hedging, exchange rates, 702–703
Human resources management, 8

I

Incentives. *see* Management compensation
Information asymmetry, 524
Inputs, relation to outputs, 109–110, 121
Interactive control, performance
  measurement, 453–457
Interest rates. *see also* Exchange rates
  relation to assets, 259
Internal Revenue Service (IRS)
  transfer pricing regulations, 690–691
    implications, 692–694
Internet, 124
  impact on management control, 12–15
Inventory, as asset, 248
Investment, defined, 56
Investment center, characteristics, 16, 54

J

Joint ventures, transfer pricing and, 689

K

Kaizen mentality, 408

L

Liabilities, noncurrent, 256
Linear programming model, 219
Logistics activities, 124
Logistics expenses, 365–366
Long-range planning. *see* Strategic planning

M

Management by objectives. *see also* Objectives
    budget preparation, 116, 367–368
    incentives, 512
Management by walking around, 16
Management compensation. *see also*
        Performance measurement
    agency theory
        concepts, 523–524
        control mechanisms, 524–526
        in general, 522
        residual loss, 525
    benchmarks, 521
    business unit managers incentives
        bonus basis, 517–518
        bonus determination approach,
            521–522
        bonus size relation to salary, 515–517
        in general, 513–514, 526
        performance criteria, 518–521
    corporate officers incentives, 512–513
    golden handcuff, 510
    incentive compensation plans
        for business unit managers, 576–578
        carryovers, 509
        deferred compensation, 509–510
        in general, 506–507
        long-term plans, 510–512, 521
        short-term plans, 507–510
    incentive contracting, 524–525
    incentives, 505–506
        corporate strategy for, 569–570
        free-rider problems, 517
    performance criteria
        financial, 518
        short-term bias, 519–520
        uncontrollable factors adjustments,
            518–519
Management control. *see also* Projects control
    activities, 6–7
    compared to strategy formulation, 5–6, 10
    compared to task control, 11–12
    financial/nonfinancial emphasis, 8
    goal congruence, 7

    implementation tools, 7–8
    Internet impact on, 12–15
    management style and, 62–63, 580–582
    process, 16–17
    strategy development, 8–9
    tight vs. loose, 581–582
    variations in, 17–18
Management control environment
    expense center, 15
    investment center, 16
    profit centers, 16
    responsibility center, 15
    revenue center, 15–16
Management control process, 299
Management control systems
    boundaries, 5–6
    concepts, 1–5
    formal
        in general, 63
        manuals, 64–65
        physical controls, 64
        rules, 64
    service organizations and, 625–627
    simpler control systems and, 4–5
Management performance. *see also*
        Performance measurement
    measurement, 174
Management style
    discussed, 62–63
    strategic planning and, 306–307
    top management style, 580–582
Managers reports, 17. *see also* Financial reports
Manuals, control system, 64–65
Manufacturing center, as profit center, 171–172
Manufacturing Resource Planning (MRP II)
        system, 11
Marketing center. *see also* Responsibility
        center
    foreign marketing activity, 171
    in general, 124–125
    as profit center, 171
Marketing expenses. *see also* Costs
    budgeting for, 365–366
Milestone, 738. *see also* Benchmark
Monte Carlo process, 376
Moral hazard, 524
MRP II. *see* Manufacturing Resource
        Planning system
Multinational organizations. *see also*
        Globalization
    cultural differences, 686–688
    exchange rates
        economic exposure, 699–702
        in general, 694–698

SFAS No. 52: Foreign Currency
Translation, 705–707
subsidiary performance, 703–704
transaction effects, 702–703
translation effects, 698–699
in general, 686
transfer pricing
criteria, 688–689
legal considerations, 689–692

N

Network analysis, planning and, 740–741
New programs
analyzing, 307–310
capital investment analysis, 307–309
Nonprofit organizations. *see also* Service
organizations
discussed, 633–636

O

Objectives. *see also* Goals; Management by
objectives
responsibility centers, 109
Organization. *see also* Behavior in
organizations
components, 3–4
informal, 63
learning organization, 453–454
types
business units, 69–70
functional, 66–69
system design implications, 70–71
Organizational structure, 8
Outputs, relation to inputs, 109–110

P

Paperwork, reports, 744–745
Parkinson's Second Law, 117
Percent of investment, in transfer price,
207–208
Performance measurement. *see also*
Management compensation
balanced scorecard, 444–445
financial control system limitations,
441–443
key performance indicators, 443
financial and nonfinancial, 8, 445–446
in general, 443–444

driver measures, 445
outcome measurement, 445
performance drives change, 446–447
implementation, 449–452
interactive control, 453–457
management, 178
measurement practices, 452–453, 626–627
research and development, 123
success factors
customer-focused variables, 447–448
internal business processes, 448–449
team-based, 517
PERT. *see* Program evaluation and review
technique
Physical plant, valuing as asset, 249–254
Planning. *see also* Strategic planning
project planning, 739–743
network analysis, 740–741
PPP. *see* Purchasing power parity
Private information, 524
Profit. *see also* Gross margin; Profit centers;
Profitability
compared to return on investment, 259
goals for, 57
role in responsibility center, 111–112
in transfer price, 207–208
fixed, 208–211
Profit centers. *see also* Transfer pricing
business unit as, 169–170
characteristics, 16, 53, 164
compared to business units, 164
functional units
manufacturing, 171–172
marketing, 171
service and support units, 172–173
general considerations, 164–168
advantages, 166–168
delegating responsibility, 164–165
difficulties with, 168
prevalence of, 165–166
profitability measurement, 174–178, 179
pseudo profit center, 172
sales and purchases to outside markets,
206
transfer price transactions, 202, 625
Profit sharing. *see also* Management
compensation
transfer pricing and, 210–211
Profitability
corporate strategy for, 570
defined, 56
goals for, 56–57, 164
measurement, 174–178, 179
contribution margin, 175–176

controllable profit, 176
direct profit, 176
income before taxes, 176–177
net income, 177
revenues, 177–178
between profit centers, 168
Program evaluation and review technique
(PERT), 740, 741
Progress reports. *see also* Financial reports
discussed, 744, 746–747
Project, defined, 732
Projects control. *see also* Management control
contrast with ongoing operations, 733–735
control environment
contractual relationships, 736–738
information structure, 738–739
project organization structure, 735–736
costs estimation, 741–742
nature of projects, 732–733
project evaluation, 749–757
cost overruns, 750
project execution, 743–749
informal information sources, 747–748
project auditing, 749
reports, 744–747
revisions, 748
project planning, 739–743
control budget preparation, 742–743
control climate, 743
Punch list, 745
Purchasing power parity (PPP), exchange
rates, 695–696

R

Receivables, as asset, 247–248
Reports. *see* Financial reports
Research and development (R&D) center. *see
also* Responsibility center
costs, 366
in general, 120–123
Residual income, 243
Residual loss, 525
Resources, inputs as, 110
Responsibility. *see* Financial responsibility
Responsibility center. *see also* Administrative
center; Expense center; Revenue center
administrative center, 119–120
budget preparation
cost variability, 118
incremental budgeting, 116–117
management by objectives, 116
performance measures, 118–119

characteristics, 15, 53, 108
efficiency and effectiveness, 110–112
financial responsibility, 54, 108
inputs and outputs relationship, 109–110
marketing center, 124–125
objectives, 109
profit, 111–112
research and development center, 120–123
revenues, 109
support center, 119–120
types, 112
Restructuring, 118
Return on investment (ROI)
assets employed, 243, 245
compared to economic value added,
258–263
Revenue
measurement, 177–178
responsibility center, 109
Revenue center
characteristics, 15–16, 53
discussed, 112–114
Rewards. *see* Incentives
Risk, profitability and, 58
Risk preferences, agents and principals,
523–524
ROI. *see* Return on investment

S

Satisficing, 57n
Scorecard, profitability, 166
Self-control, 5
Service organizations
financial service organizations, 627–630
characteristics, 629–630
in general, 620–622
health care organizations, 630–632
nonprofit organizations, 633–636
professional organizations
characteristics, 622–625
management control systems, 625–627
SFAS No. 52: Foreign Currency Translation,
705–707. *see also* Exchange rates
Shapley value, 219
Shareholder value, considerations for, 57–58
Shirking, 523
Slack
budget preparation and, 370
critical path and, 740–741
Sourcing. *see also* Transfer pricing
constraints on, 204–207
Sourcing decision, in transfer pricing, 203

Stakeholders, multiple stakeholder approach, 58–59

Stock options. *see also* Management compensation
    as incentive, 510–511, 516, 525–526
    performance shares, 512
    phantom shares, 511
    restricted stock, 511
    stock appreciation rights, 511

Strategic plan, 300

Strategic planning. *see also* Business unit strategy
    activity-based costing, 312–314
    benefits and limitations, 302–305
    business unit strategy and, 573–574
    corporate strategy and, 567–569
    described, 16
    formal control, 65
    in general, 72, 300
    implementation, 62
    new program analysis, 307–310
    nonprofit organizations, 635–636
    ongoing program analysis, 310–314
    organizational relationships, 305–307
    process
        analysis, 316–317
        assumptions and guidelines, 315–316
        in general, 314–315
    relation to budget, 361, 626
    relation to strategy formulation, 301–302
    structure and content, 305

Strategic uncertainties, 454

Strategy, 3–4
    implementation tools, 7–8
    relation to organizational structure, 65–66

Strategy formulation
    compared to management control, 5–6, 10
    in general, 9–10
    relation to strategic planning, 301–302

Subsidiary. *see also* Business unit
    balanced unit, 698
    net exporter, 700
    net importer, 700
    performance measurement, 703–704

Support center. *see also* Responsibility center
    in general, 119–120
    as profit center, 172–173

Surrogate numbers, output measurement, 110

T

Tariffs, transfer pricing and, 688, 693

Task control
    compared to management control, 5–6
    in general, 10–11

Taxes, income taxes, 366, 689–694

Taxpayer, controlled vs. uncontrolled, 690–691

Terminal value, 265

Thermostat, 2

Training, in profit centers, 167

Transfer price, 54, 201, 202, 625. *see also* Costs
    competitive-price based, 205, 206
    cost-based, 207–208, 213
    market-price based, 203, 204, 205–206, 207, 213
    sourcing decision, 203
    transfer price decision, 203
    two-step pricing based, 208–210, 211

Transfer pricing
    administration
        arbitration and conflict resolution, 215–216
        negotiation, 214–215
        product classification, 216–217
    corporate services pricing
        amount of service controls, 212–213
        in general, 211–212
        optional use of services, 213–214
    corporate strategy for, 569
    criteria, 688–689
    IRS regulations, 690–691
        implications, 692–694
    methods
        fundamental principle, 202–203
        in general, 202
        ideal situation, 203–204
    objectives, 201–202
    problems, 221–225
    sourcing constraints, 204–207
    upstream fixed costs and profits, 208–211
        profit sharing, 210–211
        two-step pricing, 208–210, 211

Transnational organizations. *see* Multinational organizations

Trouble reports, discussed, 744, 745–746

V

Value chain analysis, 310–312

Variance analysis, limitations, 422–423

Variances
    expense variances, 415–416
    in general, 408–410

revenue variances, 410–415
spending variance, 416
summary, 416–417

W

Wall Street Journal, 689
Work aversion, 523
Work breakdown structure, 738
Work ethic, 60
Work package, 738

Z

"Zero-base budgeting", 369n. *see also* Budget
    preparation
Zero-based review
    budget, 117–118
    compared to zero-based budget, 117n